How Revolutionary
Were the Bourgeois Revolutions?

Francisco Goya, *What Courage!* from *The Disasters of War* (1810–1815)

HOW REVOLUTIONARY
WERE THE BOURGEOIS REVOLUTIONS?

NEIL DAVIDSON

Haymarket Books
Chicago, Illinois

Published in 2012 by Haymarket Books
PO Box 180165
Chicago, IL 60618
www.haymarketbooks.org
773-583-7884

ISBN: 978-1-60846-067-0

Trade distribution:
In the US, Consortium Book Sales and Distribution, www.cbsd.com
In Canada, Publishers Group Canada, www.pgcbooks.ca
In the UK, Turnaround Publisher Services, www.turnaround-uk.com
In Australia, Palgrave Macmillan, www.palgravemacmillan.com.au
All other countries, Publishers Group Worldwide, www.pgw.com

Cover image of *La Liberté guidant le peuple*, 1830, by Eugène Delacroix.

Published with the generous support of Lannan Foundation and the Wallace Global Fund.

Printed in the United States by union labor on FSC certified stock.

Library of Congress cataloging-in-publication data is available.

10 9 8 7 6 5 4 3 2 1

SUSTAINABLE FORESTRY INITIATIVE

Certified Sourcing
www.sfiprogram.org
SFI-01234

CONTENTS

PART FOUR: THE SPECIFICITY OF THE BOURGEOIS REVOLUTIONS

In memory of Angus Calder (1942–2008),
Chris Harman (1942–2009),
and Charles Harrison (1942–2009): teachers

A NOTE ON THE REPRODUCTIONS

What image first comes to mind when we think about the bourgeois revolutions? Most commonly we think of France and the people in the act of insurgency; storming the Bastille perhaps, or mounting a barricade on the streets of Paris. The painting that captures the latter image more effectively than any other is Eugene Delacroix's *Liberty Guiding the People* (1830–31), a detail from which is featured on the front cover. Eric Hobsbawm has written of "the romantic vision of revolution and the romantic style of being a revolutionary" that it embodies: "Here saturnine young men in beards and top hats, shirtsleeved workers, tribunes of the people in flowing locks under sombrero-like hats, surrounded by tricolors and Phrygian bonnets, recreate the Revolution of 1793—not the moderate one of 1789, but the glory of the Year II—raising its barricades in every city of the continent."[1] The original title of the painting was *The 28th of July: Liberty Leading the People* and it refers to an actual event that took place on that date during the French revolution of 1830, namely the last attempt by insurgents to overcome the Swiss Guards at Pont d'Arcole. It is a mythical rendering: Liberty herself is shown both as a woman of the people she is guiding over the barricades and as the embodiment of a number of abstract revolutionary virtues: courage, audacity, leadership. Above all she is a representation of Marianne, since 1792 the symbol of the Great Revolution, the republic, and France itself. Could Liberty have been portrayed in any other way than as a half-mythical goddess? Certainly no other women are portrayed on the barricades, although we know that they participated in the revolution.[2] Of the four male figures Delacroix depicts in detail, only one is a bourgeois, identifiable by his top hat, waistcoat, and cravat—an armed participant to be sure, but a minority next to the sword- and musket-brandishing plebeians. Delacroix enshrined the heroic conception of the bourgeois revolution at precisely the moment when the process began to overlap with the formative stages of the working-class struggle. Are the revolutionary masses overspilling their barricade here also overstepping the boundaries of bourgeoisie order?[3] The people, after all, are charging toward the likely viewer of the

1830s; the bourgeois habitué of the gallery who would have contemplated the painting from the perspective of the forces of counterrevolution, which may explain its relative unpopularity when first exhibited. But this is not the only ambiguity. Liberty appears to be trampling on the people as much as leading them, which may be suggestive of Delacroix's own ambivalence toward the revolution.

If Delacroix's painting hints at one of the fracture lines of the bourgeois revolution, an earlier work, from the period of the first French Revolution of 1789–1815, portrays another, darker one. The illustration facing the title page is Francisco Goya's *What Courage!* The engraving was seventh in a sequence of eighty-five, collectively known as *The Disasters of War.* The artist produced these in the years leading up to 1820, but they were only published for the first time in 1863, thirty-five years after his death. Like Liberty, his subject fights on a pile of corpses, but this is virtually the only point of comparison with Delacroix's work. Goya certainly depicts a woman; she is not a mythical figure, however, but a historical one called Agustina Zaragoza Domenech, known as Agustina of Aragon for her part in the defense of the regional capital of Zaragoza in 1808. Goya emphasizes not glory but tragedy. Unlike the Scottish painter David Wilkie's saccharine version of the same episode, *The Defence of Saragoca* (1828), Goya does not show us Agustina's face, which is turned toward the enemy, but her back; a solitary figure lighting the fuse of a cannon in a landscape made desolate by war. And who is the enemy? The irony, of course, is that she is defending the city against the French. At home, the Napoleonic armies were the mainstay of an imperial dictatorship; abroad, they imposed the bourgeois revolution from above on the point of their bayonets. But in Spain at least, they were welcomed only by a relatively wealthy, politically liberal minority of the population; the majority rose against the invaders and their local supporters under the banner of church and king. *The Disasters of War* shows other aspects of the people than those celebrated by Delacroix: ignorant, bestial, in thrall to superstition—the best that can be said is that the French had provoked them with atrocities even more savage than those committed in response. But this is not all they show. No genuinely popular rising—as this one was—can ever be entirely reactionary. *What Courage!* is not alone among *The Disasters of War* in portraying the heroism of the Spanish resistance; and most of the others also feature women— Agustina's anonymous sisters. But even the titles convey the ambiguity of Goya's position: *The Women Inspire Courage* proclaims one, *And They Are Like Wild Beasts* shudders another.[4]

Despite the very different national contexts from which they sprang, both Delacroix's painting and Goya's engravings are recognizably part of a common bourgeois culture, which in these decades approached the summit of its greatness, and which can still speak to us today. The greatness of bourgeois art did not cease at this point, of course, but it did cease to be directly expressive or representative of the bourgeois worldview. The emergence of the modernist avant-garde in the second half of the nineteenth century may be an inescapable corollary of the consolidation of the bourgeoisie as an actual rather than a potential ruling class, in that its conditions of existence are no longer possible to directly express or represent.[5] *Liberty Guiding the People* shows a climactic moment of a successful bourgeois revolution from below, whose self-image a sympathetic if somewhat ambivalent artist was able to encapsulate successfully in the immediate aftermath of victory. *What Courage!* depicts a similarly heroic moment, but one that involved the defeat of an unwanted bourgeois revolution from above and outside, captured by an artist torn between his national pride and his Enlightenment principles in a period of reaction during which they appeared to be irreconcilable.[6] Yet despite what appears to be an almost polar opposition, the revolution of *Liberty Guiding the People* and the counterrevolution of *The Disasters of War* share one theme in common, which is suspicion of the bourgeoisie. In the case of the French, where a working class had begun to emerge as an independent social force, it is the beginning of a doubt about bourgeois intentions, the dawning realization that the rhetoric of national unity concealed irreconcilable class divisions. In the case of Spain, where the working class had barely begun the process of formation, it is an already firm conviction that the bourgeoisie not only had different economic interests from the popular majority—"a liberal is a man with a carriage," as the saying went—but was also prepared to advance them by betraying the nation to foreign invaders. In the former the bourgeoisie are regarded as being insufficiently opposed to the institution of monarchy; in the latter, of being insufficiently respectful of it. The ambivalence of the bourgeoisie toward the revolutions that bear its name and the contradictions of the bourgeoisie as a revolutionary class, which that relationship reveals, are themes that both these paintings explore in different ways: they are also the subject of this book.

PREFACE

I t should have come as no surprise that the years of neoliberal ascendancy saw Marxism attacked by the ideologues of a triumphalist bourgeoisie. What is surprising is that these attacks were often given theoretical support by Marxists themselves. Perhaps no other concept in historical materialism came under quite such sustained friendly fire as that of "bourgeois revolution," usually on the grounds that the version associated with Stalinism was the only one possible and that intellectual credibility therefore required it to be abandoned. Although the intention of these internal critics was to strengthen Marxism by discarding what they saw as an unnecessary and misleading foreign implantation, their arguments effectively converged with those of earlier anti-Marxists, who more accurately understood what was at stake: the integrity of historical materialism as a coherent intellectual tradition. The title of this book therefore reflects a widespread belief on the left that the bourgeois revolutions—or perhaps we should now describe them as the Events Formerly Known as the Bourgeois Revolutions—were far less significant than had previously been believed. To ask *how* revolutionary these revolutions were is therefore to ask *what type* of revolutions they were. In effect, the current consensus has downgraded them from social to political revolutions and it is precisely this reclassification that I want to challenge in what follows. Why? The relevance of this particular Marxist concept, which is concerned with historical events, may not be as immediately obvious as those dealing with, for example, economic crises, which, as we have recently been reminded, are still an inescapable feature of the contemporary world and will remain so as long as capitalism persists. Nevertheless, there are four major reasons why bourgeois revolutions should retain a claim to our attention.

First, this is not simply a question of history. Although it will no doubt astonish future generations, one of the persistent problems of the left for much of the twentieth century was an inability to distinguish between bourgeois and proletarian revolutions. The Third World revolutionary movements which followed the Second World War were rightly supported by most socialists on grounds of national self-determination. Doing so did not, however, have to involve claiming that the new regimes were socialist in any sense. How, for example, do we understand the social content of the Chinese Revolution of 1949? Was it as a proletarian revolution which—although not involving any actual proletarians—led to the creation of a workers' state transitional to socialism? Or was it, as will be argued here, a modern form of bourgeois revolution which led to the formation of a state capitalist regime, whose managers have—without any counterrevolution taking place—now adopted one of the most extreme versions of neoliberalism? In other words, how one defines bourgeois revolution and capitalism impacts in fundamental ways on how one defines proletarian revolution and socialism.

Second, if the theory of bourgeois revolution does illuminate the process by which capitalism in all its myriad forms came to dominate the world, certain political conclusions follow. Above all, the capitalist system, which its current beneficiaries present as having evolved peaceably by virtue of its congruence with human nature, was in fact imposed during centuries of revolutionary violence exercised by, or on behalf of, their predecessors. The political implications of this conclusion are twofold. On the one hand, it means that the claims that are regularly made about why revolutions should be avoided are clearly untrue. "If we ourselves are the product of a supremely successful revolution," writes Terry Eagleton, "then this in itself is an answer to the conservative charge that all revolutions end up failing, or reverting to how things were before, or making things a thousand times worse, or eating up their own children."[1] On the other hand, if the capitalist system did indeed come to dominate the world through revolution, this does rather raise the issue of why those who wish to see socialism replace it should not also avail themselves of the revolutionary option. The answer that supporters of capitalism usually give to this question is that it has created democracy, which renders any contemporary recourse to revolution illegitimate, except perhaps in regions where democracy is restricted or nonexistent. Neither point is defensible. If we take bourgeois democracy to involve, at a minimum, a representative government elected by the adult population, in which votes have equal weight and can be exercised without intimidation by the state, then it is a relatively recent development in the history of capitalism, long postdating the bourgeois revolutions in the West. Indeed, far from being intrinsic to bourgeois society, representative democracy has largely been introduced by pressure from the working class, often involving the threat of revolution, and extended by pressure from the oppressed.[2] Nor have capitalism and democracy been compatible since. As the author of one recent and by no means wholly critical study remarks, in unnecessarily tentative tones: "Capitalism's history suggests that democracy and capitalism might be decoupled because they generate values that are often in conflict."[3] If we review the counterreformist activities supported and in some cases initiated by the United States in the territories nearest it, and restrict our considerations to elected leaders whose names start with the first letter of the alphabet, then the fates of Allende in Chile, Árbenz in Guatemala, and Aristide in Haiti should dispel any notion that democratic choices will be respected where they are contrary to the interests of capitalist power.

Third, regardless of whether we call them bourgeois revolutions or not, the meaning of the events previously described in this way will remain contested until, as Gracchus Babeuf put it in the context of the French Revolution, they are overtaken by another revolution, which is greater, more solemn, and final. In other words, unless the socialist revolution is successfully achieved, neither the French nor any other bourgeois revolution will ever be truly "over," but will always be open to rediscovery, reinterpretation—and misappropriation. The most obvious example of this is not France in relation to the Revolution of 1789, but the United States in relation to the Revolution of 1776. "People want to know what Thomas Jefferson would think of affirmative action, or how George Washington would regard the invasion of Iraq," writes historian Gordon Wood: "Americans seem to have a special need for these authentic historical figures in the here and now."[4] In the case of the Tea Party, the right-wing populist movement that emerged in 2009 in the wake of Barack Obama's election as president, the issue is not so much what Jefferson or Washington would have thought of contemporary events—since Tea Party supporters claim to know precisely what they would have thought—but rather the way in which the Revolution is treated as an event outside of history, whose function is to provide the founding principles for an eternal struggle between "tyranny," understood as the activities of the state in relation to welfare and redistribution, and "liberty," understood as individual freedom from constraint, above all in relation to the accumulation of capital. In this respect, as Jill Lepore writes, "nothing trumps the Revolution." She continues, "From the start, the Tea Party's chief political asset was its name: the echo of the Revolution conferred upon a scattered, diffuse, and confused movement a degree of legitimacy and the appearance, almost, of coherence. Aside from the name and the costume, the Tea Party offered an analogy: rejecting the bailout is like dumping the tea; health care reform is like the Tea Act; our struggle is like theirs."[5]

The Tea Party attempt to claim the American Revolution is, in short, a perfect example of what Walter Benjamin warned against in 1940: "The only historian capable of fanning the spark of hope in the past is the one who is firmly convinced that *even the dead* will not be safe from the enemy if he is victorious. And this enemy has never ceased to be victorious."[6] This notoriously cryptic passage can be interpreted in several ways, but what Benjamin seems to mean is something close to the party slogan George Orwell has O'Brien make Winston Smith repeat in *Nineteen Eighty-Four*: "Who controls the past controls the future: who controls the present controls the past."[7] The past can be changed to suit the needs of the ruling class and only the victory of socialism will ensure that it remains safe. Benjamin could not perhaps have imagined how the fallen patriots of Lexington and Concord would be called from their graves to justify the goals of the Tea Party—nor, for that matter, could he have foreseen how the struggle to separate church and state in postrevolutionary France would today be turned into a justification for oppressing female Muslims by denying them the right to wear the hijab or burka. But the project of claiming particular figures or moments from the historical past for contemporary politics is neither new, nor confined to the United States, nor yet exclusive to the right. Indeed, right-wing appropriation of the American case is possible only because—as I argue in chapter 4—it was the least decisive and most ambiguous of all those generally thought to comprise the "classical" bourgeois revolutions. In relation to the Dutch, English, and French cases, it is the liberal and socialist left that has been the most active in identifying continuities between themselves and participants in these revolutions. The problem here is that the project of "fanning the spark of hope in the past" is not served by the left simply engaging in the same type of distortions as the right but from the opposite perspective. In most respects the revolutionaries of 1776 are as distant from modern socialists in their beliefs, aims, and values as they are from Sarah Palin and her supporters. The bourgeois revolutions are of historical importance regardless of whether individual episodes and participants constitute part of the socialist tradition or not.

Fourth, despite their opposition to Marxist conceptions of the bourgeois revolutions as historical phenomena, bourgeois commentators have recently begun to use their own interpretation of the term. In effect, the *only* type of social revolutions that bourgeois ideology recognized before 1989 were the so-called communist revolutions, since these supposedly involved a break with the evolutionary development of capitalism and the imposition of a different type of economy. Following the Eastern European revolutions of that year an additional type was identified: those which undid the original revolutions and allowed the economies to revert to capitalism. It was in the context of these events that the bourgeoisie reappropriated both the concept of bourgeois revolution and its link with capitalism, but in a way opposed to any Marxist conception. There were precursors to this semantic shift before 1989, notably in Britain among the supporters of Margaret Thatcher. One of her court historians, Norman Stone, wrote in 1988:

> Why were the English unique? According to Alan Macfarlane, the best writer on these matters, they were exceptional even in Anglo-Saxon times. . . . Other viewers disagree, claiming that the English difference really occurred in the mid-17th century when there was "a bourgeois revolution." If this is true, then most of continental Europe did not experience this until a century later, with events such as the French revolution. But I am tempted to ask: what English bourgeois revolution? In many respects we have never had one. . . . England's institutions still get in the way of successful capitalism and enterprise, though there are many signs that this is now changing.

Stone assessed the actions of the Thatcher regime as "a start towards that bourgeois revolution which, in my opinion, never really occurred in this country and if Margaret Thatcher goes down in history as the natural complement of Oliver Cromwell—good." Stone was of course less concerned with "bourgeois revolution" as an assault on a feudal aristocracy, but on the socialist working class, or more precisely, the organized labor movement and the postwar welfare state—"measures of socialism" welded to "this semi-modernized feudal structure."[8] The concept of "bourgeois revolution" has therefore been reincorporated into the discourse of bourgeois ideology, but only by reversing the original meaning. For in this version the bourgeois revolution was not conducted against precapitalist fetters on a system that they prevented from achieving full dominance, but against attempts to impose constraints on the capitalist system, whether these were effective trade unions, universal welfare provision, or state ownership in the West, the supposedly "postcapitalist" alternative represented by the Stalinist regimes in the East, or radical nationalist regimes insufficiently subservient to the dominant imperialist powers.

The eventual overthrow of the Stalinist regimes prompted more widespread use of the term "bourgeois revolution" and it has been used since to describe any movement for the removal of a regime to which Western powers are opposed, as in the cases of the so-called color revolutions in the former Soviet republics. One Ukrainian writer and intellectual, Olexander Invanets, was reported on the BBC as describing the demonstrations in Kiev during December 2004, which forced a rerun of the presidential elections, as "a Ukrainian bourgeois revolution."[9] And similar terminology has subsequently been applied in the Global South: the victory of the Indonesian People's Alliance for Democracy ("the yellow shirts") in forcing the resignation of Prime Minister Thaksin Shinawatra in 2006 was described as "the bourgeois revolution" of "the democracy-hating middle class."[10] However, bourgeois revolution has not only reentered the language of the bourgeois media as a description but also as a program. While cheerleading for the Gulf War of 2003, Christopher Hitchens claimed that the United States was waging a bourgeois revolution that would eventually encompass all of the Middle East. Whereas "in 1989 the communist world was convulsed by a revolution from below," the Iraqis would have to be rescued from their regime by a "revolution from above" delivered by "American intervention."[11] This is a theme to which Hitchens has repeatedly returned in his journalism: "What is happening in today's Iraq is something more like a social and political revolution than a military occupation. It's a revolution from above, but in some ways no less radical for that."[12] He takes the example of US involvement in Germany after the Second World War as his model, arguing that this, rather than the more limited changes imposed on Japan, "would be more like a revolution from above or what colonial idealists used to call 'the civilizing mission': everything from the education system to the roads."[13] Hitchens has the audacity to invoke heroes of the revolution that created the United States of America to justify contemporary American imperialism: "That old radical Thomas Paine was forever at Jefferson's elbow, urging that the United States become a superpower for democracy."[14] And if the motives of the leaders of the contemporary United States are not entirely free of self-interest, neither were those of their revolutionary predecessors: "The Union under Lincoln wasn't wholeheartedly against slavery."[15] Finally, in an unparalleled feat of insolence, Hitchens summons up one of the greatest fighters for black liberation to support his case for invasion of Iraq: "As Frederick Douglass once phrased it, those who want liberty without a fight are asking for the beauty of the ocean without the roar of the storm."[16] Douglass's remarks do of course have relevance for Afghanistan and Iraq, but not quite in the way Hitchens imagines. In his speech on West Indian emancipation Douglass recalled "the revolution—the wondrous transformation which took place in the British West Indies, twenty-three years ago," and quoted the Irish revolutionary Daniel O'Connell: "Who would be free, themselves must strike the blow." In other words, it is the context of anticolonial struggle in the Caribbean and Ireland that forms the context for the famous peroration that Hitchens so woefully abuses:

> If there is no struggle there is no progress. Those who profess to favor freedom and yet deprecate agitation are men who want crops without ploughing up the ground, they want rain without thunder and lightning. They want the ocean without the awful roar of its many waters. The struggle may be a moral one, or it may be a physical one, and it may be both moral and physical, but it must be a struggle. Power concedes nothing without a demand. It never did and it never will.[17]

We have recently heard the awful roaring of the waters again, in the demonstrations, risings, and strikes that began to sweep across North Africa and the Middle East in January 2011. The Arab Spring, the first great revolutionary movement of the twenty-first century, has disposed of liberal interventionist claims that the invasions of Afghanistan and Iraq, the so-called revolutions from above, were necessary because the Arab masses were incapable of liberating themselves. Attempts are of course under way to recuperate these revolutions even while they are still unfolding: the NATO intervention in Libya is one aspect of this, but another, more relevant to our subject, is the claim that they are essentially bourgeois, the work of respectable middle-class professionals organized through Facebook and Twitter. The new Arab revolution is still in motion: It has the potential to become a socialist revolution; it may end as a political revolution. What it is not, and will not become, is a bourgeois revolution. One of my aims in what follows is to demonstrate why this is so.

▣   ▣   ▣

This book grew out of another. In 2003, for the first time since it was established in 1969, the Isaac and Tamara Deutscher Memorial Prize Committee failed to agree on which contender for the prize should receive it. As a result it was jointly awarded to Benno Teschke for *The Myth of 1648* and to me for *Discovering the Scottish Revolution*. As my book was an attempt to establish the hitherto unidentified Scottish bourgeois revolution, it necessarily contained some general reflections on their nature. Nevertheless, these remarks were highly compressed and dispersed throughout the text to the sections where they seemed most relevant.[18] They lacked depth and focus compared with, for example, the extensive theoretical considerations that open two previous historical works to have been awarded the prize: Geoffrey de Ste. Croix's *The Class Struggle in the Ancient Greek World* (1981) and James Holstun's *Ehud's Dagger* (2000).[19] I would not necessarily have devoted further time to thinking about bourgeois revolutions except that the question of their existence was the one area where my book overlapped with Teschke's. Consequently, the subject provided us with a common theme for our presentations at the prize lecture—which was effectively a debate—on October 9, 2004. The editorial board of *Historical Materialism*, at whose conference the lecture took place, agreed to publish my contribution, even though its content ranged far wider than my remarks on the day and its excessive length required that it be spread over two issues.[20] Having begun to think in a more systematic way about the subject, I planned to develop the published lecture into a book, but competing priorities prevented me doing anything serious toward this goal for several years. When Anthony Arnove contacted me in 2008 on behalf of Haymarket Books, having heard that I was engaged in writing such a work and offering to publish it, I immediately accepted with the usual overoptimistic promises about when the text was likely to be delivered. Several missed deadlines later, this book is the result.

What follows is essentially an exercise in the history of ideas, in this case the idea of bourgeois revolution, although that history is of course inseparable from the events during which the idea emerged. Part 1 explores its complex prehistory in Reformation and Enlightenment thought. Part 2 follows its emergence during the formative period of Marxism then traces its transformation from an important instrument of historical materialist analysis into an aspect of Stalinist orthodoxy. Part 3 begins with the revisionist critique of that orthodoxy before surveying the subsequent attempts by Marxists to either reconstruct the concept or find a viable alternative to it. In part 4 I attempt, on the basis of the preceding discussion, to establish the structural relationship between revolution, class struggle, and the transition from one mode of production to another before situating bourgeois revolutions within this general framework, then conclude with an interpretive essay on the history of the bourgeois revolution, both as a series of national transformations and as a cumulative global process. In an epilogue, I take two monuments situated in Edinburgh and inspired by important moments in the overall history of the bourgeois revolution as the starting point for some concluding reflections on its meaning today.

Winning the Deutscher Memorial Prize set in train the process of writing the present work, but I also owe more substantive debts to Isaac Deutscher, not least to his personal example as a historian. Deutscher was not employed as an academic and, for at least part of his exile in Britain, had to earn his living providing instant Kremlinology for, among other publications, the *Observer* and the *Economist*. Even his most uncritical admirers would find it difficult to claim that the Memorial Prize would be the honor it is if these were his only writings. Nevertheless, his journalism enabled him to produce the great biographies of Stalin and Trotsky, and the several substantial essays of which his real legacy is composed. As someone like me, who for many years worked outside the university system, Deutscher was a model for how to produce historical work that combined political engagement with respect for scholarly standards. I did not always agree with the political conclusions that Deutscher reached, but the clarity of his style meant that, at the very least, it was always possible to say what these conclusions were. To put it mildly, this has not always been true of the theoretical idols of the left.[21] Of more direct relevance to our theme, Deutscher was one of the first people to properly consolidate and articulate the scattered insights on the subject of bourgeois revolution from the work of earlier Marxists. Some of the problems to which the concept gives rise, and to which he helped provide a solution, are suggested by the histories of our respective nations.

Scotland and Poland are obviously not comparable in terms of geographical location, territorial extent, population size, or political trajectory. In the early modern period, however, they were closely linked by both trade and one of the first great Scottish migrations; by the end of the seventeenth century, perhaps as many as 40,000 Scots lived and worked in Poland, mostly as merchants or soldiers.[22] Polish researchers have identified the names of 7,400 Scottish males in 420 areas of their country, most originating from my own birthplace in the Northeast of Scotland. Indeed, one Davidson—no relation, as far as I know—became wealthy through the possession of a monopoly granted by the Polish crown to import wine from Hungary into Poland.[23] The size of the Scottish presence in Poland is partly explicable by the features that the two kingdoms had in common. Although at opposite ends of the continent, they were the only two European states in which the ruling class had successfully resisted the growth of absolutism. If Scotland had escaped absolutism, it was not, like England, because the population had succeeded in overthrowing the state, but only because, like Poland, the feudal barons had proved too powerful for such a state to be constructed in the first place. Consequently, both retained the classical military-feudal socioeconomic organization of the estates monarchy into a period in which it had been overtaken everywhere else south of the Tweed and west of the Vistula. The similarities were widely recognized. The English republican James Harrington noted of Scotland in the late 1650s that "the nobility . . . governed that country much after the manner of Poland, except that the king was not elective."[24] Nor were the comparisons lost on the Scots themselves. "Factions rubb'd upon each other and with great severity," wrote John Clerk of Penicuik during the final years of the first Scottish Parliament, "so that we were often in the form of a Polish diet with our swords in our hands, or, at least, our hands at our swords."[25] The divergence of their subsequent fates is well known. Scotland was incorporated into the United Kingdom with neighboring England in 1707, shortly after Penicuik made this entry in his diary; but by the latter half of the eighteenth century, it had emerged as a contributor to Enlightenment thought, industrial development, and British imperial expansion of an importance quite disproportionate to its size. During the same period Poland also lost its sovereignty, but with totally the opposite effect. It suffered successive losses of territory and population at the hands of the surrounding absolutist states until, with the Third Partition in 1795, the nation vanished within the borders of Prussia, Austria, and Russia for over a hundred years. Despite these vastly different outcomes, the same question could be asked about both countries. Where, if anywhere, in their histories is the bourgeois revolution? Any serious concept has to be able to answer this question, either by identifying the periods in which they took place or by explaining why they were unnecessary.

▣   ▣   ▣

Apart from Deutscher, I also owe an intellectual debt to the other writers who helped to develop the approach I have taken here. In the course of the argument I have had occasion to cite authors in at least three different contexts: as examples of a particular intellectual tradition; as supporters of a theoretical position that I wish to support, modify, or oppose; and as a source of historical information. At certain points in the argument I have relied on particular writers—for example J. G. A. Pocock or Robert Brenner—as my authorities on historical events while disagreeing with them elsewhere about what these events mean. There is nothing paradoxical or inconsistent about this: in the debates over the bourgeois revolutions it is rarely the facts that are in question and almost always the interpretations that are put on them. It is also the case that some of the figures discussed here changed their views over time—in extreme cases, such as those of Georg Lukács and Christopher Hill, abandoning previous positions. It is only where such reversals have taken place that I draw attention to them, usually because they are indicative of a wider political and intellectual context. In other cases, writers have simply modified their earlier arguments without necessarily renouncing every aspect of them. Since any serious thinker can be expected to develop their positions in this way I have not drawn special attention to such shifts: it will be obvious from the discussion that, for example, Perry Anderson does not hold precisely the same views on the bourgeois revolution today as he did in 1964 or 1976 or 1987, to give the dates of three of the articles cited in what follows.

The work of those to whom I owe the most is acknowledged in the footnotes and bibliography, but it is only right to highlight here the names of David Blackbourn, Alex Callinicos, Geoff Eley, Paul Ginsburg, the late Christopher Hill, Gareth Stedman Jones, and Colin Mooers. I have disagreements with all of them (as indeed they have with each other), but the collective endeavor in which they have engaged, to which this is a contribution, may ultimately allow us to save the concept of bourgeois revolution for historical materialism. Knowledge is, however, not only acquired through the printed word and many individuals have contributed to my understanding of bourgeois revolutions over the years through more informal means of conversation, debate, and e-mail exchanges. They include: Jamie Allinson,

Alex Anievas, Anthony Arnove, Colin Barker, Paul Blackledge, Pepijn Brandon, Sebastian Budgen, Terry Byres, Joseph Choonara, Gareth Dale, Radhika Desai, Steve Edwards, Alan Freeman, John Game, the late Chris Harman, Mike Haynes, Henry Heller, James Holstun, Alex Law, Ken MacLeod, David McNally, China Miéville, Adam David Morton, Bertel Nygaard, Charlie Post, and Justin Rosenberg. (I trust that the presence to two leading sci-fi and fantasy authors on this list merely reflects the breadth of their interests rather than the character of my argument.) William Keach deserves a special mention for his supportive but critical editorial work on my ever-changing manuscript, as does Dao Tran for her editorial work on the epic that it eventually became. I would particularly like to thank all the participants in the very lively discussion that followed my presentation of this material at the Socialism 2009 event in the Wyndham O'Hare Hotel in Chicago on June 21, 2009. Several contributors to the discussion showed an understandable desire to claim Thomas Paine for the history of American radicalism; perhaps we can agree that one of the most important contributions by this great British-born figure was to transcend the national boundaries that the two bourgeois revolutions in which he participated did so much to establish.

Neil Davidson
West Calder
West Lothian
Scotland
March 2012

ONE

PREHISTORY:
INSIGHTS
AND LIMITATIONS

1

THE CONCEPT OF "REVOLUTION": FROM TRADITION TO MODERNITY

The concept of "bourgeois revolution" was first used by Karl Marx in 1847.[1] Generalizing from earlier events in the Netherlands, England, and especially France, he and Friedrich Engels then applied the concept both to these historical examples and to the contemporary situation in their native Germany, where revolution was expected in the near future.[2] Over the previous two hundred years less developed versions of the concept had been articulated with increasing frequency by bourgeois thinkers seeking to explain, either retrospectively or programmatically, why their class was entitled to take political power through revolutionary violence. There is nothing exceptional about this intellectual lineage. The concepts used by the founders of historical materialism tended to emerge from an engagement with the work of their bourgeois predecessors and socialist contemporaries—what Lenin would later call the "sources and component parts" of historical materialism: "German philosophy, English political economy and French socialism."[3]

The origin and nature of these concepts varied from case to case. The "labor theory of value" was not only a critique of the way in which the concept of value had been used by the classical political economists Adam Smith and David Ricardo, but also an attempt to consolidate and develop their insights on a more consistently scientific basis.[4] The "dictatorship of the proletariat," however, was an entirely new idea, formulated in the aftermath of the failed revolutions of 1848–49 to counterpose Marx's vision of socialism as collective self-rule by the entire working class to Auguste Blanqui's model of elite rule by a handful of revolutionary conspirators.[5] The origin of "bourgeois revolution" involved both types of response. Like the labor theory of value, it represented an extension and deepening of an existing concept that had only recently acquired a name. Like the dictatorship of the proletariat, it was a political intervention, from the same period, in a situation where distinguishing two different types of social revolution and then clarifying the relationship between them was of immediate practical relevance to the working-class movement. Unlike these two other concepts, however, that of bourgeois revolution remained relatively undeveloped by Marx and Engels themselves.

Revisionist historians, above all of the English Civil War and the French Revolution, reject the concept of bourgeois revolution on the grounds that Marx and Engels retrospectively treated as social revolutions events that their theoretical forebears regarded in quite different ways, at least before the French Revolution and perhaps even after it.[6] Contrary to these claims, Enlightenment thinkers did develop a materialist understanding of revolutionary social change long before the French Revolution. In this context, the advice offered by Antonio Gramsci in relation to the work of Benedetto Croce is also helpful in relation to the conception of bourgeois revolution inherited and developed by Marx and Engels:

> If one wishes to study the birth of a conception of the world which has never been systematically expounded by its founder (and one furthermore whose essential coherence is to be sought not in each individual writing or series of writings but in the whole development of the multiform intellectual work in which the elements of the conception are implicit) some preliminary detailed philological work has to be done. . . . It is necessary, first of all, to reconstruct the process of intellectual development of the thinker in question in order to identify those elements which were to become stable and "permanent"—in other words those which were taken up as the thinker's own thought, distinct from and superior to the "material" which he had studied earlier and which served as a stimulus to him. It is only the former elements which are essential aspects of the process of development.[7]

There are dangers in identifying the "stable and permanent elements" that were to enter Marx and Engels's own thought. One of the characteristics of what Perry Anderson calls the Western Marxist tradition was a tendency to supplement historical materialism with concepts drawn either from earlier thinkers, who were by no means all "sources and components" of Marxism, or from contemporaries of Marx and Engels who adhered to different traditions of thought.[8] Spinoza played this role for Althusser, Rousseau for Colletti, Pascal for Goldmann, and Leopardi for Timpanaro. But if we think of the role played by Darwin for Kautsky, Hegel for Lukács, and Machiavelli for Gramsci, it is evident that the classical Marxist tradition itself was not immune from the same tendency. In each case, the search for pre- or non-Marxist solutions to contemporary problems showed a reluctance to accept how completely Marxism had transcended previous positions. It is not my intention, therefore, to offer the work of, for example, James Harrington, Sir James Steuart, or Antoine Barnave as a new set of supplements required to complete the Marxist tradition: for, although I regard these three men as among the most important theorists of social revolution in general prior to Marx and Engels themselves, their achievement had already been subsumed into historical materialism. Nevertheless, given the way in which recent intellectual fashions have either striven to deny this, or affirm it only as a matter of regret, no study of this sort can avoid a discussion of their contribution. Clearly, there is a great deal more that could be said about the wider political thought of these and the other figures discussed below, both generally and in relation to the formation of Marxism; but my focus here is simply their contribution to the development of the concept that came to be called bourgeois revolution. The relative importance usually ascribed to authors in conventional histories of political thought has therefore no necessary bearing on their relevance to this discussion. For our purposes, Harrington is more important than Locke, Steuart than Ricardo, and Barnave than Rousseau.

EXPERIENCE, CONSCIOUSNESS, AND CONCEPTS

One of the central tenets of historical materialism is that some forms of consciousness arc not present throughout human history, but only become possible after new material conditions emerged of which people could then become conscious.[9] Consciousness eventually finds expression in words so, as Geoffrey de Ste. Croix points out, "If the Greeks did not 'have a word for' something we want to talk about, it may be a salutary warning to us that the phenomena we are looking for may not have existed in Greek times, or at any rate not in the same form as today."[10] The ancient Greeks or Romans would, for example, have found it impossible to understand what has been known since the late nineteenth century as "economics." Neither the title of the work that established this term as the replacement for "political economy," Alfred Marshall's *Principles of Economics* (1890), nor its basic categories like "labor" or "capital" can be translated into ancient Greek or Latin. Moses Finley writes that the ancients "lacked the concept of an 'economy,' and *a fortiori* . . . they lacked the conceptual elements which together constitute what we call 'the economy.'"[11] And the reverse is also true: some of the things for which the Greeks did have words are almost impossible to accurately convey in modern languages. According to Alasdair MacIntyre, the distance between the terms used in the Hellenistic world at the time of Homer and our own is not a question of translation but of "a difference between two forms of social life": "To understand a concept, to grasp the meaning of the words which express it, is always at least to learn what the rules are which govern the use of such words and so to grasp the role of the concept in language and social life. This in itself would suggest strongly that different forms of social life will provide different roles for concepts to play."[12] MacIntyre is primarily concerned with morality, arguing that we cannot now very easily comprehend what was meant by the Greek word *agathos*, which is usually and inadequately translated as "good"; but the argument is clearly capable of more general application. For, as the Greek example suggests, some social forms and the categories we use to discuss them are specific to capitalism. These may give us an insight into earlier forms: "Human anatomy contains a key to the anatomy of the ape," as Marx put it.[13] But identifying them with earlier forms, thus investing the categories with timeless relevance, is an obstacle to historical understanding.

I begin with this point because, ironically, the type of unhistorical approach I have just criticized is precisely what Marxists themselves are accused of adopting in relation to the bourgeois revolution. "Men cannot do what they have no means of saying they have done," writes Pocock, "and what they do must in part be what they can say and conceive that it is."[14] Pocock is not himself a revisionist, his interests lie elsewhere; but Jonathan Clark certainly is and he has set out the implications of this type of position in relation to the English Civil War: "We can safely leave it to social scientists to build models of institutions or processes (capitalism, class, party, revolution) and, if they wish, to carry their models back into the past in a search for phenomena which might seem to fit them. The historian should prefer to work more closely with his material and to be more responsive to the content of the categories employed in past time." According to Clark, neither rebellion nor revolution "carried their present meanings in the seventeenth or eighteenth centuries." In particular, the notion of revolution as "a fundamental challenge to the legitimacy of social structures, including patterns of hierarchy or stratification, and titles to economic ownership or control" is simply "anachronistic." His preferred category is "rebellion," which is "devoid of such implications" and his preferred explanation is in terms of religion, as he claims it was for the participants themselves.[15] It is true that the most popular contemporary explanation for events between 1640 and 1660 was that they arose from disputes over religion. Nevertheless, there are three problems with this argument.

First, Clark demands "attention to religion *as religion* and not as a sublimation of something else."[16] However, as James Holstun writes, "can one imagine any phrase more alien to William Laud, or William Prynne, or William Walwyn, or any seventeenth-century person, than 'religion *as religion*'?"[17] In a situation where virtually every issue, whether political, social, or economic, was discussed in religious terms, the pursuit of a historical method that took seventeenth-century people purely at their word would be forced to conclude that no one had any interests at all outside of religion—which might be regarded as an overly extreme position even at All Souls College. Indeed, long before the English Civil War the view had been expressed that religion was a disguise for the way in which the Roman Catholic Church supported earthly powers. "It is the opinion of the pope and all the cardinals, and even of Erasmus, that religion is all a fable, but that it should be preserved in order that the royal power and the papal monarchy may be maintained; these institutions, they think, would collapse without the fear of religion, and it would be impossible to hold the common people to their tasks."[18] The writer here is German, but he is Martin Luther, not Friedrick Engels. The delicate sensibilities of modern revisionists may of course be offended by the robustly functional, not to say conspiratorial terms in which Luther's views on the role of religion in maintaining social stability are expressed, but the views themselves can scarcely be regarded as the retrospective imposition of contemporary categories. Or, more directly relevant to our theme, consider two works published in England during 1651, both now considered classics of political thought, in which the authors gave diametrically opposite views of the relationship between religious and secular authority. One argues that they should be fused, or at least interlocked, "for it is not hard to reconcile our Obedience to God, with our Obedience to the Civil Sovereign, who is either Christian, or Infidel." And where the sovereign *is* a Christian, he continues: "There can be no contradiction between the Laws of God and the Laws of a Christian Commonwealth." The other argues that the sovereign or king by definition "denies the Scriptures and the true God of righteousness, though he pray and preach of the Scriptures, and keep fasts and thanksgiving days to God, to be a cloak to hide his oppression from the people, whereby he shows himself to be the great Antichrist and mystery of iniquity, that makes war with Christ and his saints under pretence of owning him." The first author is Thomas Hobbes, arguing that the civil war was caused by a popular failure to submit to the rightful form of ecclesiastical authority associated with the monarch.[19] The second is Gerrard Winstanley, claiming that the civil war was a necessary popular response to a monarch who justified his oppression by false scriptural authority and hypocritical religious observance.[20] It is interesting that, of the two men, it is the democrat Winstanley who takes religious doctrines most seriously, while the autocrat Hobbes devotes many pages to attacking the irrational aspects of religion—in this respect he is an Enlightenment figure in a way that Winstanley is not—but is mainly concerned with doctrine insofar as it encourages obedience to the state.[21] The point, however, is that both men consider religion to be inescapably political, whatever else it might have meant to them.

Second, what Marxists are concerned with is not simply consciousness, thought, and language, but the social experience that precedes and gives rise to them. As Christopher Hill writes, "people can experience things before they invent a name for them; one might perhaps say that they cannot name them until they have experienced them."[22] And, as Hill also notes, the process of naming can involve appropriating an existing word and investing it with new significance.[23] Take the term "state" as an example. States as public authorities superior to and distinct from the societies over which they ruled had existed for around five millennia before the concept finally emerged between the mid-thirteenth and early seventeenth centuries. The word (from the Latin *status*) was only used in this modern sense toward the end of that period, having originally referred to the current condition of a particular ruler or realm—a usage that still survives in the annual US presidential "State of the Union" address. Quentin Skinner argues that there were four preconditions for these conceptual and terminological developments. The most immediate was the separation of politics from moral philosophy as a distinct subject, although this was itself an expression of prior ideological shifts; the acceptance that political authority within a territory should be independent of external control; that such an authority should be unchallenged by internal rivals; and that the domain of politics should exclude other considerations, above all, those of religion.[24] What is missing from Skinner's account is any sense of why assumptions about the nature of public power began to change, the answer to which can only be found outside of the texts that he so comprehensively surveys, in the social world within which they were written.[25] The process by which "state" enters the modern vocabulary therefore began with the impact of social change that made people think about political institutions in new ways, then develop a new concept to express these thoughts and eventually change the meaning of an existing word to express that concept—a concept that then retrospectively revealed the existence of the state in historic periods prior to that of its discovery. As we shall see, there are similarities between the fate of the term "state" and that of the term "revolution": the modern use of the former was ultimately a response to the rise of what was subsequently called absolutism; the modern use of the latter is essentially a product of the struggle against it. In both cases, however, new conditions and new experiences not only made possible but also necessary the formation of new concepts and a redeployed vocabulary with which to express it. And in both cases the process was a prolonged one. Three hundred years lie between Brunetto Latini's *Book of Treasure* from the 1260s, where the notion of politics as a distinct subject is first raised, and Jean Bodin's *The Six Lives of a Commonweal* (1576), which is based on the premise that political institutions should be separate from both the rulers and the ruled. A similar length of time divides Benedetto Varchi's near contemporary references to the Florentine revolution of 1527 in his *Storia Fiorentina* from the 1530s, when the term was still novel, and François Guizot's *History of the English Revolution of 1640* (1826), when the author could expect his readership not only to know what he meant by revolution but also to agree that England had experienced one between 1640 and 1660.

Third, there were already writers at the time of the English Civil War who used the term "revolution" in what Clark calls the "socio-structural" sense. Clark's strategy in relation to this inconvenient fact is to consign these writers to a footnote: "Despite the writings of such pioneers as James Harrington ... and Gregory King ..., we should not exaggerate the willingness or ability of most seventeenth- and eighteenth-century Englishmen to think about their society in structural terms."[26] We should certainly avoid exaggeration, but since these writers presumably cannot be accused of complete invention, perhaps their explanation for what had happened was inspired by actual changes they had noticed taking place in the social structure? They may themselves have exaggerated the extent of social change, of course, but without some basis in reality it is difficult to see how they could have arrived at their views in the first place. Moreover, where a new and nonreligious concept appears in the historical record, at first as a minority position, but then with greater and greater frequency, in more and more countries under similar conditions with those in which it was first expressed, then we are surely entitled to treat it as more significant than the conventional or orthodox opinions from which it has broken. The concept of social revolution belongs in this category.

REVOLUTION AS TRADITION: THE CYCLE OF CONSTITUTIONS

Some concepts have existed since the origins of political thought. Beginning with "the categories employed by the ancient Greeks themselves," Ste. Croix was able to conclude that the ancient Greeks not only lived in a class society but were also highly conscious of it: "Far from being an anachronistic aberration confined to Marx and his followers, the concept of economic class as the basic factor in the differentiation of Greek society and the definition of its political divisions turns out to correspond remarkably well with the view taken by the Greeks themselves; and Aristotle, the great expert on the sociology and politics of the Greek city, always proceeded on the basis of a class analysis and takes it for granted that men will act, politically and otherwise, above all according to their economic position."[27] Greece and Rome were obviously not unique in the ancient world in being divided into social classes; but they were unique in the ancient world in the extent to which different social classes were able to publicly debate their opposing interests on the basis of common citizenship: this was the indispensable condition for the emergence of the distinct activity of politics, which first appears in these societies.[28] But if the ancient Greeks and Romans had the concept of "class," did they also have the concept of "revolution"?

Prior to the emergence of the Greek city-states, the concept of revolution was essentially indistinguishable from that of rebellion. In Egypt, for example, the monarchy embodied not only legitimacy, but also divine ordination; was the guarantor not only of social stability, but of the cosmic order itself against the chaos that would result from any successful attempt by a usurper to overthrow and replace it. Nevertheless, usurpation was successfully attempted on many occasions, particularly between the unification of the Northern and Southern kingdoms under Menes and the end of the New Empire. If the usurper was successful, of course, then the overthrow of the existing monarchy would be presented by the priestly bureaucracy, not as a disruption of the cosmic order, but as the necessary replacement of a weak by a strong ruler, the very success of the latter indicating the hostility of the gods toward the former. Although there are some indications that sections of the populace may have been involved in these acts of rebellion, their social impact seems to have been minimal, although a change of ruler often involved the worship of new or different gods—Set instead of Horus, or Aton instead of Amon.[29]

The assumption that society would remain essentially immobile beneath any changes of regime was retained in both Greek and Roman discussions. There are words in both Greek and Latin that, depending on the context, can be taken to mean an uprising (*neoterismos; res novae*) or a civil war (*stasis, bellum civilis*) leading to a change in regime or constitution; there were, however, a limited number of possible regimes or constitutions.[30] In classical accounts these either followed each other in cyclical succession or were simply available as alternatives, but in neither case were there more than six—or rather three, each of which had two aspects reflecting whether they were operated justly or unjustly: monarchy and tyranny, aristocracy and oligarchy, democracy and anarchy, or ochlocracy (mob rule).[31] But whether these types of regime were seen as endlessly recurring or as a set of options, at no point did the ancients see the possibility of a regime emerging on the basis of a reconstitution of their societies: changes were purely political and always revocable. For the modern concept of revolution to emerge there had to be the possibility of irreversible change to a new type of society. As Finley puts it, "there was no revolutionary transfer of power to a new class (or classes) because there were no new classes," and consequently: "At no time and in no place in classical antiquity . . . was there a genuine change in the class nature of the state."[32] The priority that Finley gives to class rather than the state seems, to me at any rate, to capture the essence of a social revolution far more than the claim, supported for example by Fred Halliday, that "no concept of revolution was possible before the modern state emerged," a position that would delay its emergence until the French Revolution.[33]

The Christian tradition opposed the cyclical theory of the classical world. In *The City of God*, written after the sack of Rome by Alaric in 410 AD, Saint Augustine accused Plato of believing that "the same city, the same school, the same disciples have appeared time after time, and are to reappear time after time in innumerable centuries in the future." Augustine was presumably aware that this was not what Plato or any of the other Greek thinkers actually believed: for them, cycles occurred in the sense that mankind was fated to repeat the same political processes, not the same actual events. It is nevertheless the latter position that Augustine dismisses as self-evidently absurd, in that it would involve the souls in Heaven and Hell being returned to the world from their eternal salvation or damnation.[34] Augustine may, however, have been the first person to use the term "revolution," to mean both the type of eternal recurrence in which he claimed the Greeks believed and bodily reincarnation.[35] Augustine could no more comprehend the possibility of fundamental social change than the thinkers he polemicized against. He did believe that there had been progress in the earthly city of the world, but its limits had been reached by the establishment of the Christian church; the only significant change that remained for mortals was to gain admission to the City of God, a fate for which they were either predestined or not.

Although the political concept of revolution did not emerge from Christian thought, that of reform may have. Between 1190 and 1195, the Cistercian abbot Joachin of Fiore reinterpreted the scriptures, and above all the Book of Revelation, in a way that revised Augustine's periodization. According to Joachim, the history of the world could be divided into three stages: the Age of the Father or the Law, from Adam to Abraham; the Age of the Son or the Gospel, from Elijah to Christ; and the Age of the Spirit, from Saint Benedict to the reign and overthrow of the Antichrist. This doctrine was by no means politically radical in intent; indeed, it was welcomed by several popes. It nevertheless inspired several millenarian movements in the German and Italian lands, adherents of which sought to play a more active role in bringing about the Age of the Spirit than the unworldly hermit Joachin had intended.[36] Eric Hobsbawm has argued that Joachim effectively proposed the first distinction between reform and revolution, in that his first two ages involved "the equitable regulation of social relations in an imperfect society," while the third involved "the reign of freedom, which is the perfect society."[37] The key point here, however, is that although reform of existing institutions was possible on earth, revolution was not, at least outside of the apocalypse that would signal the End of Days: human action could only hasten the coming of the next world, not the transformation of this one.

The origins of modern political thought in the Renaissance saw a reassertion of the pre-Christian position, as part of the rediscovery of classical thought. As Skinner notes, as early as 1379 scholars had already started to quote a passage from Ecclesiastes ("there is nothing new under the sun") explicitly rejected by Augustine, in support of this position. In contrast to him: "The humanists . . . revert to the claim originally advanced by Aristotle in Book V of the Politics, and reiterated by Polybius and Cicero, that the course of human events can be shown to proceed in a series of recurring cycles."[38] The extent of the way in which even the greatest political thinkers of the Renaissance remained enclosed within classical categories they had rediscovered can be seen from the work of Niccolo Machiavelli during the early 1500s:

> For *Principality* easily becomes *Tyranny*. From *Aristocracy* the transition to *Oligarchy* is an easy one. *Democracy* is without difficulty converted into *Anarchy*. So that if anyone who is organizing a commonwealth sets upon one of the three first forms of government, he sets up what will last but for a while, since there are no means whereby to prevent it passing into its contrary, on account of the likeness which in such a case virtue has to vice.

According to Machiavelli, this "is the cycle through which all commonwealths pass," unless the process is halted by conquest at the hands of a "neighboring and better organized state"; but on the basis of his own arguments, any successor state would be similarly liable to undergo these same changes in the nature of government.[39] His concept of revolution therefore remains traditional, as in this passage from *The Prince* addressed directly to his patron, Lorenzo il Magnifico: "It is not to be marveled at that none of the Italians . . . had succeeded in doing what, it is hoped, your illustrious House [of Medici] will do, or that in so many revolutions in Italy and so many martial campaigns it has always seemed that our military prowess has been extinguished."[40]

Several writers have presented Machiavelli as a more modern figure than these passages suggest. In his later writings Louis Althusser argued that Machiavelli was concerned with overcoming the feudal fragmentation of the Italian states.[41] The Bolshevik Lev Kamenev was more accurate when he wrote of the Florentine theorist: "His most famous work, 'The Prince,' is not a study of the changing social groups which have won power . . . it is concerned with the mechanism of the struggle for power within one narrow social group, in the period of the transition from feudalism to capitalism."[42] The last clause here is potentially misleading. Machiavelli certainly wrote at the beginning of the transition, but his work is unconcerned with social or economic aspects of the process and he was not a spokesman for the emergent bourgeoisie. Machiavelli was critical of feudalism solely because of its political effects, what he rightly saw as causing the weakness and disunity from which the peninsula suffered. His discussion of the reasons why some Italian princes were deposed stresses either technical failures such as "a common weakness in regard to their military organization" or an inability to attract or maintain support: "some of them incurred the hostility of the people or, if they had the people on their side, they did not know how to keep the allegiance of the nobles."[43] Nowhere does he suggest that the overthrow of the nobles—in other words a change in the class leadership of the Italian states—is required. Nor is he even an advocate for the absolutist form of the feudal state that was characteristic of the transition. Gramsci once wrote that Machiavelli "understood that only an absolute monarchy could resolve the problems of the time."[44] According to Gopal Balakrishnan, however, claims of this sort are "not plausible":

> For his conception of the state so emphatically accentuated the personality of the ruler or ruling body that it failed to capture or anticipate the dual nature of early modern absolutism, characterized at once by a hypostasization of the figure of the monarch, and an incipient depersonalization—"bureaucratization"—of the structure of feudal jurisdiction. Likewise, his strenuous attachment to a citizen militia stood in stark opposition to the whole pattern of absolutist state formation.

Indeed, it was apparent to at least one subsequent leading practitioner of absolutism that Machiavelli was concerned with a quite different form of state as Balakrishnan continues: "In his critique of *The Prince* written more than two centuries later, Frederick the Great of Prussia showed without difficulty how remote Machiavelli was from any understanding of the territorial scale, institutional architecture and aristocratic ethos of the dynastic world of absolutism, an order everywhere erected on the foundations on a quiescent and unarmed populace of peasants and burghers."[45] In fact, the reason for what Althusser calls "Machiavelli's solitude" lies in how he was alone in arguing for a state form, a "New Principality," at a time when the socioeconomic basis for it no longer existed in Italy and had not yet come into existence anywhere else.[46]

REVOLUTION AS MODERNITY: PROGRESS, RESISTANCE, AND PROPERTY

The actual term "revolution" had been used since the Middle Ages to indicate the cyclical movement of celestial bodies around the Earth and, from the work of Copernicus and Galileo onward, that of the Earth's orbit around the sun. It was in this sense of returning to a starting point that the term began to incorporate the traditional notion of the cycle of constitutions, inherited by the Renaissance from the ancient Greeks. Not coincidentally, this usage first appears in the Italian city-states, which not only saw the first revival of Arab astrological practices in Europe but also had a tradition of popular insurgency that led to the regular overthrow of communal governments. The insurrections against the oligarchy of Siena in 1355 and the risings for and against the Medici of Florence in 1494, 1512, and 1527 were all described by contemporaries as "revolutions" in this sense. But by the later sixteenth century the term enters more widespread use: the essayist Montaigne used it in relation to the French Wars of Religion in his 1595 essay "Of the Education and Institution of Children"; the political commentator Allesandro Giraffi applied it to the partly successful Neapolitan rising against Spanish rule of 1647, in a book written during the same year. Yet by the time of the last example, the term had taken on an additional meaning: no longer simply indicating return to a political point of origin, but an irreversible movement beyond it, propelled by underlying social changes. There were three intellectual preconditions for the emergence of a concept of social revolution in this sense identified above.

The first was a new way of looking at human history that recognized the existence of secular progress. Two developments were decisive here. One was the discovery, subjugation, and, in some cases, extermination of the indigenous peoples of the Americas, who seemed to offer a contemporary example of what European social organization might have been like in an earlier period. As John Locke wrote in the early 1680s, "In the beginning all the World was *America*."[47] The other was the scientific revolution, which in many respects was encouraged by the requirements of the explorers and the conquerors that followed them, notably for reliable means of navigation. In 1620 Sir Francis Bacon linked these two aspects in a biological metaphor drawn from the human life cycle that had a long future ahead of it. Age possesses more knowledge and judgment than youth, he wrote:

> And truly in the same way it is reasonable that greater things be expected from our age than from old times (if it only knew its strength and was willing to exert it); seeing that our age is the older age of the world enriched and studded with countless experiences and observations. We should also take into account that many things in nature have come to light and been discussed as a result of long voyages and travels (which have been more frequent in our time), and they are capable of shedding new light on philosophy.[48]

In the preface to a work of 1647 explaining one of these experiments (on the vacuum), Blaise Pascal contrasted humans and insects. A bee, he noted "forms that hexagon as exactly the first time as the last," but "it is different for man": "He is ignorant of life's first age, but he never ceases to learn as he goes forward, for he has the advantage not only of his own experience but of his predecessor's, because he always keeps in his memory the knowledge he has once acquired, and that of the ancients is always at hand in the books they have left." In this reading of history, the ancients "actually formed the childhood of man."[49]

As science began to change the perception of the world, the originally astronomical metaphor of "revolution" began to lose its cyclical associations: "The wheel of fortune no longer spins on a fixed course. Instead a revolution of the wheel means a leap onto a new plane, and an escape from its premeditated orbit. The wheel is transformed into a giant stone which once propelled to the summit of the hill, does not slip back, but rolls forward on the new level that has been attained."[50]

Jonathan Israel offers the case of René Descartes to demonstrate how "revolution" came to mean "not just linear, fundamental, and irreversible change, not just auto-emancipation from the intellectual and cultural shackles of the past, but also . . . something that changes everything." And in the same way as the old scientific meaning of revolution had been used in a more general sense, so too did the new meaning. Between 1670 and 1720 in particular:

> The idea of "revolution" as something that embraces, and stems from change in the basic concepts on which society is based, rapidly became central to European political and institutional, as well as intellectual and cultural life, since the intellectual supremacy of traditional categories, religious authority, precedent, and long-established patterns of learning, besides such traditional governmental and administrative forms as "divine right monarchy," the "ancient constitution," and customary law, were as much called into question by the conceptual revolution of the late seventeenth century, implicitly at least, as were the traditional astronomy, physics, alchemy, magic and medicine.[51]

The recognition that development had occurred in history was expressed in social terms by the discovery, or rather, the identification of feudalism. The term *feodalite* or "feudalism" seems to have been first used in 1515, but by the middle of the sixteenth century Renaissance legal historians (the "feudists") tended to refer to *jus feudale* or the "feudal law," by which they meant the series of legal arrangements established in Lombardy following the barbarian invasions, before spreading west to be adopted by the Normans. In other words, it was originally a legal, rather than political, social, or economic concept. In his book *Francogallia* (1573) François Hotman was the first to claim that the liberty of the French Estates in relation to the monarch was derived from the Germanic tribes. Whether these innovations originated in Roman law or were brought by the barbarians themselves remained a widely debated issue in the work of other French thinkers like Jacques Cujas or, by the early seventeenth century, their Scottish followers like Sir Thomas Craig.[52]

Craig was legal adviser to James VI of Scotland before his accession to the English throne in 1603, and the author of an important work on the feudal law, dedicated to James, which remained unpublished for nearly fifty years after his death in 1608. His book, *Jus Feudale*, as several authorities have noted, is not so much an analysis of Scottish law during the feudal period as a codification of the feudal law in general with special reference to Scotland. It is a codification that was only possible in retrospect, as the classic age of military feudalism gave way to that of absolutism. Yet precisely because Scotland had not made that transition, much of what Craig wrote about military feudalism was not a matter of historical retrospect but contemporary description, as events would confirm on several occasions over the next one hundred and fifty years. Craig attempts to play down the relevance of military tenures: "In Scotland, where military holdings are now old fashioned and feudal grants have become matters of commerce and profit, the feudal oath is entirely forgotten; but notwithstanding, we continue to hold our vassals bound by the obligations of fealty."[53] Yet he undermines his own argument in two respects. First, fealty requires the vassal to protect the "life or person ... honor and reputation" of his lord. If the lord requires vassals to participate in an 'armed endeavor,' then no special form of requisition is required: "For military service differs from all other kinds of feudal service in that it is (as every vassal knows) the radical condition of his tenure." Second, feudal superiors would sometimes grant a charter, known as a *feu*, conferring perpetual heritable possession to their tenants in return for a large initial down payment and payment thereafter of a fixed annual sum; but, as Craig points out, even where lands were feu-ed out "it is important to remember that a feu is presumed to be proper unless it is shown by the terms of its investiture to be that its proper or genuine character has been modified." "Proper," in this context, means "military."[54] As late as 1681, Sir James Dalrymple, first Viscount Stair, in a further codification of the existing feudal law much influenced by Craig, could write of wardholding that: "It is the most proper feudal right we have; and therefore wherever the holding appeareth not, or is unclear, there wardholding is understood [that is, assumed to be the prevailing form of tenure]."[55] What this meant in practice, outside these works of legal theory, was expressed with admirable clarity and concision in the early eighteenth century by Macdonell of Keppoch, who, when questioned about the size of his rent roll, simply replied: "I can call out and command 500 men."[56]

In England it took until the eve of the civil war for the subject to be discussed in comparable depth. The key figure here is Sir Henry Spelman, although his work was not published until the Restoration and only achieved its main impact later still. Independently of Craig, Spelman discuss the combination of tenancy and military service as constitutive of feudal law; his point, of course, was that Saxon England was not subject to it. He traces its origins to "the Germans and Northern nations," specifically to granting of lands to the French nobility by Hugh Capet in 988 to strengthen his dynastic faction, where it was adopted by the Normans and imposed on England following the Conquest of 1066.[57] As this reference to the Normans suggests, Spelman's argument was one of the first substantial discussions of the "the Norman yoke," the theory that existing feudal law was an alien imposition by a foreign ruling class.[58] In England, therefore, the concept of "the feudal law" had negative connotations and none of the neutral or even positive ones that it did in Scotland, a fact reflective of the vastly different levels of socioeconomic development achieved in these countries by the mid-seventeenth century.

The second and more directly political precondition for the concept of social revolution was the formation of a secular theory of the right to resistance. All patrician theories of resistance in the early modern world ultimately derived from the conciliar movement that arose within the Church after 1378, when the rival claimants to the Papacy had made the notion of obedience to one central authority within Christendom problematic, to say the least. Several general councils of the Church, most importantly in Constance (1414–18), proclaimed that the council was superior to the pope: he was simply a first minister; they represented Christ's authority on earth and the Church as a whole. Although the conciliar movement was defeated by the Papacy at the General Council of Basel (1431–49), the underlying theory remained alive in the universities of Northern and Western Europe. More importantly, the subordination of the pope to the council began to be applied, analogously, to the realm of politics, and to the relationship between monarchs and their subjects.[59] Consequently, as Quentin Skinner has emphasized, there was no distinct Calvinist theory of resistance, as both Lutherans and Calvinists essentially drew on the same Roman law and scholastic moral philosophy as their Catholic predecessors and opponents. Skinner draws attention, in the context of Scottish political theory, to the influence of the Catholic John Major on the Protestant George Buchanan; Calvinist theorists in turn attempted to win over Catholics by appealing to a tradition which the latter recognized as legitimate.[60]

Of the three Christian traditions, Calvinism was, however, the most prepared to put the theory into practice. Where the state was hostile to the Reformation, Calvinists drew two conclusions from it: The first was that the church had to be free of state control. The second was that where the present holders of state power were unwilling to allow this disassociation, particularly where they also oppressed Protestants, they must be overthrown—which suggested that permanent political change for the better, if only to ensure the purity of church organization, was both desirable and possible. By the 1570s, the theory of the right to resistance had become secularized, at the hands of French Huguenot thinkers, so that it was no longer based on the sinfulness of the ruler, but on natural rights and the sovereignty of the people.[61] For the first, but certainly not for the last time, a key question was the identity of "the people."

Hotman was a Huguenot and had written *Francogallia* before the Massacre of Saint Bartholomew in 1572, but that event seems to have both given him the impetus to publish the following year and given the work itself a heightened resonance; for he was not simply concerned with identifying the origins of the French liberties, but with justifying opposition to the monarch in order to protect them. As he was careful to clarify in later editions of his book, however, when he referred to "the people" (*populus*) he meant either the Estates or, more broadly, "the people in their assemblies," which immediately limited the applicability of the term.[62] Similarly, in *The Right of the Kingdom of Scotland* (1579), the Scottish political theorist George Buchanan provided the ideological justification for the 1567 deposition of Mary Queen of Scots, but was emphatic in distinguishing between the "naughty rabble" or the "vulgar," whose participation was not desired, and "right subjects" or "the better part" who could and should be relied upon. The latter turned out to be the feudal nobility—as generally tended to be the case in Scottish political theory before the 1640s.[63] But although the theory could be used to justify the resistance of feudal class forces to absolutist constraints on their power, it could just as easily be used by non- or post-feudal classes that opposed absolutism for quite different reasons. In 1643 William Prynne, a famous victim of the Star Chamber, but by no means the most radical of the English parliamentarians, could happily draw on the arguments of the conciliarists in his book *The Soveraigne Power of Parliaments and Kingdoms* to demonstrate that it was permissible to resist the king with force.[64] By 1649 Oliver Cromwell could cite "the principles of . . . Buchanan" in support of his decision to execute that Man of Blood, Charles Stuart.[65]

The discovery that human society had progressed and could potentially progress further and the claim that subjects had a right to resist absolutist monarchy on the basis of popular sovereignty—however ambiguously defined—were ultimately both mediated consequences of capitalist development. The third precondition for the emergence of a concept of social revolution was capitalist development itself—or rather, the recognition that the as-yet-unnamed system that would eventually be called capitalism was in the process of emergence.

The Dutch Revolt against the Spanish Empire, which is usually and rightly thought of as the first successful bourgeois revolution, was reaching the final stages of consolidation by the mid-1640s, indicating that the kind of irreversible movement suggested by the notion of social revolution had taken place. The United Netherlands and England were recognizably the same kind of societies, to the point where their respective regimes had seriously considered an "intrinsical union" during the 1650s.[66] But it was in the former that the first use of the word "capitalist" was recorded in the 1630s, and where by the 1690s it had become sufficiently accepted there for the States-General to identify capitalists as a distinct group liable to higher rates of taxation other citizens.[67] By the revolution of 1688, Lisa Jardine writes, "England and Holland were already so closely intertwined, culturally, intellectually, dynastically and politically, that the invasion was more like a merger."[68] And the two states continued in parallel into the next century. Anthony Ashley Cooper, Lord Shaftesbury, wrote to Jean Le Clerc in 1707: "There is a mighty light which spreads itself over the world, especially in those two free nations of England and Holland, on which the affairs of Europe now turn and, if Heaven sends soon a peace suitable to the great successes we have had, it is impossible but that letters and knowledge must advance in greater proportion than ever before."[69] Yet despite these similarities and connections, the new meaning of revolution did not emerge in the United Netherlands but only in England.[70]

The real difference between the two states was that, although in both cases capitalism preceded their respective revolutions, the Dutch Revolt was a war of liberation against the external power of Hapsburg Spain. "The resistance against Phillip II was essentially presented as a defence of liberty threatened by the lust for power and tyrannical ambitions of Phillip II's government."[71] The arguments of Dutch political thinkers were drawn from three main sources, all traditional: Aristotle, the classical Roman republicans, and the Old Testament. Unsurprisingly, therefore, their discussion still revolved around a choice of political alternatives: 'The Monarchy of the Romans would still be in full glory and power," claimed one anonymous pamphlet of 1582, "Athens would not have been brought down, no city would have fallen into desolation, had the subjects and government remained pious and faithful to each other."[72] The objective of the republic was understood as a revolution only in the existing sense of a return to an earlier state of political freedom. According to Israel, even Baruch Spinoza, in many respects the most radical thinker of the early Enlightenment, argued against drawing any general conclusions from the Dutch Revolt on the grounds that it merely restored the situation prior to Spanish lordship. For Spinoza, it "was a successful revolution and entirely justified, not owing to any general right, or advisability, of resistance to tyrants, but simply because Holland was not a monarchy and had never been subject to a sovereign monarch, sovereignty there having always been vested in the States."[73] Consequently, the political theories that emerged from the Dutch Revolt, notably those of Hugo Grotius, were less concerned with identifying the relationship between different social classes and forms of private property than with the rights of the state over its own citizens and with other states. Indeed, the writings of Grotius are still the legitimating basis for the theory of the "just war" today.[74]

Some writers did attempt to connect the economic nature of Dutch society with its opposition to absolutist or other forms of monarchical rule. During the 1660s the merchant capitalist and republican, Pieter de la Court, wrote of Holland that "the flourishing of manufactures, fishing, navigation, and traffic [i.e., trade], of which that province subsists . . . will infallibly produce great, strong, populous and wealthy cities, which by reason of their convenient situation, may be impregnably fortified: all of which to a monarch, or one supreme head, is altogether intolerable." And he went on to contrast the "mischief" involved in rule by "a monarch, or supreme lord" and the "temporal blessing" enjoyed by Holland as "a free commonwealth republic."[75] But this was a retrospective judgment: the external nature of Hapsburg rule meant that, while the revolution was under way, conceptualizations of the struggle could remain at the political level, as theories of resistance to an alien imposition. The nature of the revolution in England, an internal struggle of opposed but native social forces, provided the conditions for a more thoroughgoing analysis to emerge.

2
Interpreting the English Revolutions: Hobbes, Harrington, and Locke

L
ike the Dutch opponents of Phillip II, the English opponents of Charles
I also referred back to a preexisting age that required restoration—or
rather, they referred back to two different ages. One, to which I have already referred, was Anglo-Saxon society before the imposition of the Norman
yoke; but other than as mobilizing rhetoric, the political implications of this were
negligible, since no section of the parliamentarian side was seriously intent on re-
creating the world ruled by Harold Godwineson on the eve of the Battle of Hastings. The other was the Age of Elizabeth, before the innovations of the House of
Stuart, when a proper relationship of mutual respect supposedly existed between
Crown and Parliament, and when England was prepared to challenge the might
of Catholic Spain (and indirectly, of Rome) in battle. There was obviously a
greater prospect of re-creating a Golden Age set in the sixteenth century than the
eleventh, but to do so would still only involve a revolution that was political and
restorative rather than social and innovative. Nevertheless, it was the latter type of
revolution that was achieved.

Early in the seventeenth century, several English commentators, of whom Bacon
was the most important, had noted the emergence of and strengthening of new
social groups from the decomposition and fragmentation of lordly estates, a process
involving large-scale land transfers from the nobility to the gentry—an estate rather
than a single class—and the "yeomen," whom Bacon described as being "of a condition between gentlemen and cottagers or peasants."[1] These changes were usually
dated from the accession of Henry VII in 1485, and particularly from the passing
of enabling agrarian legislation that began to enter the statute book from 1489.
For Bacon at least, these and analogous if less dramatic changes elsewhere in Europe had the potential for causing a social crisis, in the form of "the civil wars which
seem to me about to spread through many countries—because of ways of life not
long since introduced." In the same passage Bacon identifies the two antipodal enemies of the Elizabethan compromise, external absolutist rivals ("the Spanish Empire") and internal puritan radicalism ("the malignity of sects"), whose combined

pressures on the English state threatened to produce a similar crisis.[2] Bacon would not live to see the civil war that would spread throughout England, but its significance was immediately recognized by two writers who were, in different ways, deeply in his intellectual debt. Hobbes was primarily influenced by Bacon's scientific methodology, from which he tried to construct a "social geometry" to explain what had occurred during the 1640s. Harrington followed Bacon's historiography, particularly his interpretation of English social development since 1485. Both men broke new theoretical ground but, as we shall see, Harrington was the first to develop a theory of social revolution.

HOBBES AND THE AUTONOMY OF THE STATE

Like his Machiavellian predecessors, Hobbes invoked the cycle of constitutions, which might indicate that he remained within the Renaissance frame of political reference. In this respect, however, as in most others, Hobbes subverts expectations by emphasizing not the distinctiveness of the constitutions but their similarity. In the book that brought him to notoriety, *Leviathan* (1651), he writes: "The difference between these three kinds of Commonwealth consists not in the difference of Power; but in the difference of Convenience, or Aptitude to produce the Peace and Security of the people; for which end they were constituted."[3] For Hobbes, the key issue is the construction of an effective "sovereign power" or state with which to constrain "that condition called war; and such a war, as is of every man, against every man."[4] The "war" to which Hobbes refers is not—or is not only—"the disorders of the present time," the literal state of war in the aftermath of which the book was written; but neither is it simply an eternal aspect of the human condition.[5] A passage dealing with the consequences of the war of all against all culminates in the phrase we most associate with his name:

> In such Condition, there is no place for Industry; because the fruit thereof is uncertain: and, consequently no Culture of the Earth; no Navigation, nor use of the commodities that may be imported by Sea; no commodious Building; no Instruments of moving, and removing such things as require much force; no Knowledge of the face of the Earth; no account of Time; no Arts; no Letters; no Society; and which is worst of all, continual fear, and danger of violent death; and the life of man, solitary, poor, nasty, brutish and short.[6]

Starting from the threat to economic activity, Hobbes foresees escalating chaos leading to the collapse of civilization itself; but the resulting "state of nature" is a possible outcome, not the existing state of affairs. Industry, cultivation, navigation, and so on—that these things *have* existed means there was a time before they were threatened. Hobbes is not therefore invoking the consequences of human nature, but of human nature under certain determinate conditions. What were they?

C. B. MacPherson has argued that Hobbes took the existence of "market society" as the context for his work. From this perspective, Hobbes thought the civil war was ultimately caused by the chaos attendant on the conflict of self-interested in-dividuals within a capitalist economy and their collective resistance to a state that not only failed to defend their interests but was also prepared to subjugate those interests to its own.[7] Insightful though this is as an explanation for the civil war, it is not an insight that Hobbes himself shared. If the breakdown of established po-litical authority, the coming of civil war and the resulting collapse of social cohesion had an immediate cause for Hobbes, then it lay in the religious divisions within England and the competing claims to authority to which they gave rise. It is this that lies behind his combination of extreme hostility to the irrational "darkness" exemplified by both Roman Catholicism and Puritanism—in this respect too he is Bacon's pupil—and his advocacy of an officially sanctioned religion that could act as a buttress to the state. The problem with Hobbes is that he does not explain how these religious divisions acquired their significance or why they led to civil war during the 1640s, rather than earlier or later. However, in his subsequent book *Behemoth*, written in 1668 but unpublished until after his death in 1679, he suggests an alternative or supplementary explanation to one based on the effects of religion. *Behemoth* is as concrete as *Leviathan* is abstract and they need to be treated as com-plementary works, together constituting the entirety of his argument.

There are several passages in *Behemoth* where he acknowledges the political im-portance of merchants and manufacturers on the parliamentary side of the conflict. Hobbes argued that the civil war had to be seen in the historical context of the Dutch Revolt, in that the same class was involved in resisting the monarchy in both cases: "the city of London and other great towns of trade, having in admiration the prosperity of the Low Countries after they had revolted from their monarch, the King of Spain, were inclined to think that the like change of government here, would to them produce the like prosperity."[8] Later, he goes into more detail about why "great capital cities" were at the forefront of these revolutions; for, "when re-bellion is upon pretence of grievances, [they] must needs be of the rebel party: be-cause the grievances are but taxes, to which citizens, that is, merchants, whose profession is their private gain, are naturally mortal enemies; their only glory being to grow excessively rich by the wisdom of buying and selling." *Behemoth* takes the form of a dialogue and, at this point, Hobbes makes his interlocutor defend the commercial classes: "But they are said to be of all callings the most beneficial to the commonwealth, by setting the poorer sort of people on work." His response is a kind of preemptive strike against the later fantasies of Political Economy, in which laborers are supposedly free to choose an employer: "That is to say, by making poor people sell their labour to them at their own prices; so that poor people, for the most part, might get a better living by working in Bridewell than by spinning, weaving, and other such labour as they can do; saving that by working slightly they may help themselves a little, to the disgrace of our manufacture."[9]

It is reasonably clear then, that Hobbes does not regard the purchasers of labor as representatives of "the people" in general. He also makes a connection between this class and the radical Presbyterians, although—as tends to be the case in his discussions of religion—he does so with the same cynicism he claims both groups display in their reciprocal interaction: "they did never in their sermons, or but lightly, inveigh against the lucrative vices of men of trade or handicraft; such as are feigning, lying, cozening, hypocrisy, or other uncharitableness, except want of charity to their pastors and to the faithful: which was a great ease to the generality of citizens and the inhabitants of market-towns, and no little profit to themselves."[10] Hobbes was suspicious and mistrustful of actual merchants, manufacturers, and financiers. In this respect he was the first, but—as our discussion of Adam Smith in chapter 3 will show—certainly not the last important theorist of emergent bourgeois society to regard its characteristic figures with deep ambivalence.

Hobbes was not, however, the first to discuss these tensions produced by capitalism in English culture. The dilemmas posed by the collapse of established authority occur in several of Shakespeare's later plays, above all in *King Lear*, written sometime between 1603 and 1606, when James VI became James I and acceded to the English throne. Here too we are presented with a (tactfully unspecified) period of social upheaval in which tradition and legitimacy are undermined by the transfer of property from its rightful owners to new upstarts. "Well then, Legitimate Edgar," says Gloucester's bastard son Edmund: "I must have your land."[11] Here too we have, against this background, the threatened collapse of all order. Later in the play, Albany guiltily remonstrates with Goneril:

> If that the heavens do not their visible spirits
> Send quickly down to tame these vile offences,
> It will come,
> Humanity will perforce prey on itself,
> Like monsters of the deep.[12]

Behemoth was, of course, a biblical monster of the deep and Hobbes the political theorist is in many ways as difficult to pin down as Shakespeare the playwright, from whom multiple interpretations might be expected. The level of abstraction at which *Leviathan* is written allowed Hobbes to cultivate a degree of ambiguity, but it is also the key to what he envisages. *Leviathan* is an abstract model, but it is not a model for a particular state *form*; it is rather a model for the *relationship* between the state, whose precise form Hobbes does not discuss, and its subjects—this is why, unlike previous thinkers, he pays so little attention to the issue of the constitution. His Leviathan did not therefore necessarily correspond to any of the state forms that actually existed in England during his lifetime, although, since he refers to "this man, or this Assembly of men," it might have corresponded to more than one of them.[13] Whether or not Hobbes assumed that English society was essentially organized along market principles, he believed that the state could not be safely based on the dominance of one competing interest. To do so would simply ensure the continuation of the "war of all against all" that he wished to avoid, as different social classes sought to seize the state to further their own interests. For Hobbes, the effectiveness of Leviathan in imposing stability and order depended instead on the degree of power and authority that it could exercise, which in turn required individual subjects to bestow upon Leviathan what Hobbes called their "authorization" to act for them and, in the case of some individuals, against them, if this was required for the public good. As one of Hobbes's modern conservative admirers has noted: "What . . . is excluded from Hobbes's *civitas* is not the freedom of the individual, but the independent rights of spurious 'authorities' and of collections of individuals such as churches, which he saw as the source of civil strife in his time."[14] Whatever actions Leviathan might take, these had effectively been endorsed in advance by the act of authorization. The only actions that were not permitted to the state, the only actions that could justify the withdrawal of authorization and outright rebellion were those that imperiled the fundamental task of maintaining safety and security; for as Hobbes put it, "the end of Obedience is Protection."[15]

The authoritarian aspect of Hobbes's thought has enabled him to be recuperated for the conservative tradition, but as the Restoration Cavaliers well knew, there is one implication of his thought that renders him unsuitable for inclusion in this pantheon. Some passages in *Leviathan* seem to imply that subjects were required to obey their existing earthly lord: "If a Monarch subdued by war, render himself Subject to the Victor; his subjects are delivered from their former obligation, and become obliged to the Victor. But if he be held prisoner, or have not the liberty of his own Body; he is not understood to have given away the Right of Sovereignty; and therefore his subjects are obliged to yield obedience to the Magistrates formerly placed, governing not in their own name, but in his."[16] Since Charles I never considered himself "subject to the victor," loyalty was presumably still owed to him and, following his execution, to Charles II, which is how the latter monarch certainly seems to have interpreted the argument—an interpretation that Hobbes found it politic not to challenge. Nevertheless, as many more astute royalists were perfectly aware, his arguments gave no more automatic support to their position than to that of their republican opponents: the Mortal God that Hobbes envisaged did not rely on the divine right of kings for its authority. Toward the end of *Leviathan*, Hobbes noted that, on evidence of political literature of the time, "the Civil wars have not yet sufficiently taught men, in what point of time it is, that a Subject becomes obliged to the conqueror." He set out to remedy this, referring back to the passage just quoted:

> I say, the point of time, wherein a man becomes subject to Conqueror, is that point, wherein having liberty to submit to him, he consents, either by express words, or by other sufficient sign, to be his Subject. When it is that a man hath the liberty to submit . . . namely, that for him that hath no obligation to his former Sovereign but that of an ordinary Subject, it is then, when the means of his life is within the Guards and Garrisons of his Enemy; for it is then, that he hath no longer Protection from

him, but is protected by the adverse party for his Contribution. Seeing therefore such contribution is everywhere, as a thing inevitable, (notwithstanding it be an assistance to the Enemy,) esteemed lawful; a total Submission, which is but an assistance to the Enemy, cannot be considered unlawful.[17]

This discussion of the question points in a quite different direction to the earlier one, namely to the switching of allegiances from the Stuarts to Cromwell and the Major-Generals. In short, if the authority of the state is derived from authorization rather than tradition, the beneficiary could just as easily be the radical military dictatorship of Cromwell as the reactionary absolutist monarchy of the Stuarts. Although Hobbes does not discuss revolution, his doctrines could be interpreted as justifying it, or at least as legitimating postrevolutionary regimes. In this respect he decisively broke, not only with the divine right of kings, but also with all former theories of resistance to absolutism that depended on the assertion of existing rights and privileges. In this respect at least, Hobbes was implicitly subversive of the existing order and one of the first truly modern thinkers. So too, although in a different way, was Harrington.

Harrington Discovers the Social Revolution

As a declared republican, Harrington's politics have none of the ambiguity characteristic of Hobbes; but in many respects, his attitude was one of admiration for him:

> It is true that I have opposed the politics of Mr. Hobbes, to show him what he taught me, with as much disdain as he opposed those of the greatest authors, in whose wholesome fame and doctrine the good of mankind being concerned, my conscience bears me witness that I have done my duty. Nevertheless in most other things I firmly believe that Mr. Hobbes is, and will in future ages be accounted, the best writer at this day in the world; and for his treatises of human nature, and of liberty and necessity, they are the greatest of new lights, and those which I have followed and shall follow.[18]

In what respects then did he differ from Hobbes in theoretical terms? To a greater extent, Harrington accepted the Machiavellian argument about the limited choice of possible constitutions, but he did not simply see these as endlessly succeeding each other without fundamental change occurring beneath them. In his fictionalized account of the English Civil War and its aftermath, *The Commonwealth of Oceana* (1656), Harrington argued that his own historical period had been preceded by two others, quite different in character:

> The one ending with the liberty of Rome, which was the course or empire, as I may call it, of ancient prudence, first discovered unto mankind by God himself in the fabric of the commonwealth of Israel, and afterwards picked out of his footsteps in nature, and unanimously followed by the Greeks and Romans. The other being with the arms of Caesar which, extinguishing liberty, were the transition of ancient into modern prudence, introduced by those innovations of Huns, Goths, Vandals, Lombards, Saxons which, breaking the Roman Empire, deformed the whole face of the world with those ill features of government, which at this time are becoming far worse

in these Western parts, except Venice which, escaping the hands of the barbarians by virtue of her impregnable situation, hath her eye fixed upon ancient prudence and is attained to a perfection beyond her copy.[19]

As this suggests, Harrington rejected the theory of the Norman yoke and argued instead that Anglo-Saxon England had been essentially the same kind of society before 1066 as Norman England afterward: both were equally based on the dominance of feudal landowners and therefore equally classifiable as examples of what he called the "Gothic balance" that emerged out of the fall of the Roman Empire. He accepted that there were important constitutional differences between Anglo-Saxon and Norman society, and the partial retention of the former led to conflicts of interest. Harrington describes as "a wrestling match" the three-cornered struggle among the the monarchy, nobility, and "the people" that characterized English history: "The nobility, as they have been stronger, have thrown the king, or the king, if he hath been stronger, hath thrown the nobility; or the king, where he hath had a nobility and could not bring them to his party, hath thrown the people, as in France or Spain; or the people, where they have had no nobility, or could not get them to be of their party, hath thrown the king, as in Holland and of latter times in Oceana."[20]

But, as a then-republican Henry Stubbe wrote during 1659, "It is necessary to know who the PEOPLE are."[21] For Harrington at least, membership of the people was determined by ownership of certain forms of property, above all in land. This is another aspect of his thought distinct from that of Hobbes: recognition of the decisive class changes that had taken place in the countryside. The overthrow of the king by the people in this sense was a new development in English history and one that had fundamentally changed the nature of the state. In this connection, Harrington argued that there were three types of states in Europe: "absolute monarchies," where the ruler was the sole or main landowner, as in Turkey; "mixed monarchies," where the power of the ruler is balanced by that of the nobility and clergy, as in Spain, Poland, or England until the late fifteenth century; and "commonwealths," where landownership, and consequently power, was widely distributed among a class of non-nobles, as in the Italian city-states, Switzerland, Holland, and England from the late fifteenth century.[22] How had England moved from the second to the third of these categories?

Harrington gave a more extended account of the changes in the nature of property ownership with which the predecessors were concerned: "By which means the houses were kept up, and of necessity enforce dwellers; and the proportion of land to be tilled being kept up, did of necessity enforce the dwellers not to be a beggar or cottager, but a man of some substance, that might keep friends and servants and set the plough on going." Harrington noted that these economic changes also weakened the social control of the existing ruling class, for by transferring "a great part of the lands into the freehold possession of the yeomanry, or middle people, who, not living in a servile or indigent fashion, were much unlinked from dependence upon their lords and, living in a free and plentiful manner, became a more excellent infantry, but such a one upon which the lords had so little power, that from henceforth they may be computed to have disarmed." The twin outcome was not only to disarm the lords, and also the monarch: "But a monarch divested of her nobility hath no refuge under heaven but an army."[23] The initial establishment of the republic was therefore based on a radical shift in the ownership of property with permanent social and political consequences, consolidated by revolution:

> Property comes to have a being before empire or government in two ways, either by natural or violent revolution. Natural revolution happeneth from within, or by commerce, as when a government is erected upon a balance, that for example of a nobility or a clergy, through the decay of their estates come to another balance; which alteration in the root of property leaves all into confusion, or produceth a new branch of government according to the kind or nature of the root. Violent revolution happeneth from without, or by arms, as when upon conquest there follows confiscation.[24]

Harrington's analysis constitutes the real founding moment of the concept of social revolution and like many of his writings the general argument is derived from very specific events. In this case, "natural revolution" refers to the process in England and "violent revolution" to the Cromwellian interventions in Scotland and Ireland, although he is not of course suggesting that violence was absent from the former. The aftermath of these revolutions required a constant struggle to maintain the "balance" that is a recurrent theme of Harrington's work, for "where the riches are, there will be power": "So, if a few be as rich as all the rest, a few will have as much power as all the rest; in which case the commonwealth will be unequal, and there can be no end of staving and tailing, till it be brought unto equality."[25]

Harrington can therefore be credited with being the first adherent of what the revisionists call the "social interpretation" of the English Civil War, as even Jonathan Clark has acknowledged. Yet the major commentators on Harrington have persistently downplayed this aspect of his work. Harrington occupies a central place in Pocock's reconstruction of the republican political tradition, second only to that of Machiavelli himself, but he fails to understand what distinguishes them from each other: "Harrington . . . had anchored politics in a history of property, but one consisting of a cyclical series of transformations rather than a mere tradition of inheritance."[26] Pocock shows a characteristic blindness here. In fact, Harrington had transcended the republican tradition precisely by recognizing that a break had taken place in the cycle of constitutions on the basis of new forms of property. Perry Anderson once observed that "the normal fate of original theorists" is "the necessity of working towards radically new concepts in an old vocabulary"; so that in the twentieth century, for example, "Gramsci often had to produce his concepts within the archaic and inadequate apparatus of Croce or Machiavelli."[27] In the seventeenth century, Harrington may have been the first thinker to advance beyond the positions Machiavelli had inherited from the ancient Greek world, while retaining Machiavelli's mode of discourse. Harrington described his intention as "to go his own way, and yet follow the ancients," and both clauses have to be respected.[28] As Perez

Zagorin pointed out long ago, his notion of the perfectibility of the Commonwealth "represented a complete departure from Machiavelli's view of life."[29]

But if Harrington had broken, as it were, vertically with the historical tradition from which he descended, he also made new horizontal connections with contemporaries who shared his perspectives. No one could accuse Pocock or Skinner of being fixated with a handful of recognized theorists: indeed, one of the most positive aspects of their joint endeavor has been the way they have shown how widely particular theories and concepts were used by authors beyond those of the canonical texts. However, there are definite limits to the views they are prepared to consider, and these limits exclude people who were not scholars and whose writings may have been confined to their personal correspondence or in reported speech: it was among them that Harrington found his followers. The identity of the people and the basis of its social weight in the contest with the king were, for example, raised by two Harringtonians in the House of Commons during the 1659 debates on the future of the House of Lords. Henry Neville claimed that the balance of property, and consequently of power, had shifted: "The gentry do not now depend upon the peerage. The balance is in the gentry. They have all the lands. Now Lords, old or new, must be supported by the people."[30] Captain Adam Baynes, Member of Parliament, speculator in confiscated Crown lands and supporter of the Yorkshire cloth manufacturing interest, later clarified who belonged, and who did not belong to "the people": "All Government is built on property, else the poor must rule it." Baynes went on, in terms that must have horrified Hobbes in its frank assertion of class interest as the basis of the state: "The people were too hard for the King in property; and then in arms too hard for him. We must either lay the foundation in property or it will not stand. Property, generally, is with the people, the government therefore must be there."[31]

Both Neville and Baynes were following what Harrington had written in *Oceana*; but Harrington himself was giving theoretical expression to widely held existing positions in that book. This is perhaps best shown in relation to "violent revolution from without" in Scotland. Pocock notes that several contributors to the New Model Army newspaper, *Mercurius Politicus* (subtitle: "In Defence of the Commonwealth, and for Information of the People"), argued for the necessity of destroying the power of the feudal lords in Scotland; he then discounts this as irrelevant, before concluding: "If there is little reason to believe that agitators and soldiers saw themselves as the emancipated heirs of vassals and retainers or that any other ideology stressing the end of feudal tenures was current and operative, it is probably better to think of Harrington as a scholar and speculative theorist, constructing his hypothesis by combing such works of learning as were, or may have, been known to him."[32] Yet the idea that Harrington might have learned anything from mere "agitators and soldiers" is perhaps less inconceivable than Pocock thinks. In a way, the anti-feudal radicalism of the English Revolution was demonstrated more clearly in Scotland than in England itself. In England, capitalist property relations had to a considerable extent already replaced those of feudalism before the civil war began.[33] In Scotland, feudal relations were still dominant and the extent of agreement among republicans on how to deal with them suggests that an "ideology stressing the end of feudal tenures" was widely "current and operative" and that Harrington was one of its adherents. As Pocock noted in an earlier and in some ways more perceptive discussion, "it does not seem likely that Harrington reached the conclusion that most of the land had passed to the gentry as a result of some train of thought peculiarly his own."[34]

In *Oceana* Harrington created a fictional Scotland called Marpesia, of which he wrote, "except the aristocracy in Marpesia be dissolved, neither can that people have their liberty there."[35] He was endorsing a position about the problems of Scottish society that had been expressed by English radicals in similar terms for more than a decade. In 1646 the first Leveller document described Scotland as a society where "the lords and great men overrule all, as they please; the people are scarce free in anything."[36] They nevertheless hoped that Scotland would follow the same path as England of its own accord. Thomas Margetts, while working for the Judge-Advocate of the New Model Army during its first incursion into Scotland during 1648, wrote a letter to the Leveller paper *The Moderate* explaining how England had experienced a "better learning" than Scotland, but held out the hope that "by degrees," the latter nation might "take out a new lesson and advance":

> When once the light breaks forth in this Kingdom (and I think the sun is near rising) it will warm and heal apace, but the clouds must be broken first, the foundation of the old fabric must be shaken; and when the poor, blind, dead people shall see the light and feel the warmth of the sun (sweet liberty) to redeem then out of their present slavery, then the strugglings of Scotland will be as great as those of England, which hath overcome a few of these, but not yet gotten to the top of its glory.[37]

An article in *Mercurius Politicus* from 1650 suggested that the classes below the great lords had begun to assert themselves: "The *Barons* and *Burghers* . . . know how to play their game now to best advantage for clipping the wings of the *Grandees*, who ride their poor Peasants and Clients à-la-mode, after the French Fashion, and make them bow like *Asses* under every burden. By this means they may learn to understand which is the way of true *Liberty*.[38]

But by 1651 it was apparent that no indigenous social forces of sufficient strength existed in Scotland that could accomplish the overthrow of the lords. It was therefore clear to military administrators and intellectual supporters of the Protectorate that they needed to take the measures that the Scottish people had been unable to take for themselves. In this they were at one with the Levellers who were crushed at Burford in 1648. On October 28, 1651, the English Parliament issued *A Declaration of the Parliament of the Commonwealth of England, Concerning the Settlement of Scotland*, which noted that "many of the people of *Scotland* who were vassals, or Tenants to, and had dependency upon the Noble-men and gentry (the chief Actors in these invasions and wars against *England*), were by their influence drawn into . . . the same Evils." These innocent victims were to be pardoned and, more importantly,

... cut free from their former dependencies and bondage-services, and shall be admitted as Tenants, Freeholders and Heritors, to form, hold, inherit, and enjoy from and under this Common-wealth, proportions of the said confiscated and forfeited Lands, sundry easy Rents, and reasonable conditions, as may enable them, their Heirs and Posterity, to live with a more comfortable subsistence than formerly, and like a free People, delivered (through God's goodness) from their former slaveries, vassalage and oppression.[39]

The following month, the Welsh regicide, Colonel John Jones, commented in a letter from Dublin on how the Parliament was liberating Scottish tenants on a principled basis, not merely for tactical advantage, as Charles Stuart had formerly done:

It is the interest of the Commonwealth of England to break the Interest of the great men in Scotland, and to settle the Interest of the common people upon a different foot from the Interests of their Lords and Masters. The late King seeing the interest of the Lords there to be then (when he attempted to invade them) against his interests, made a Proclamation that such as were Tenants to those great men that then opposed him should hold their lands of him, paying but one moiety, as I remember, of the Rents and Duties they were bound to pay their Landlords, but they were wise enough to keep this from the Tenants, and the issue was not tried. What he would have done upon Injurious grounds the Parliament may do upon honest and honorable grounds; the invasion in the year 1648, and the charge of the army in seeking Separation (which ought to have been given in an amiable way) amounts to a higher ace than all Scotland is worth. The great men will never be faithful to you, so long as you propound freedom to the people and Relief against their Tyranny.[40]

A further piece of legislation, the Ordinance of Union passed by the House of Commons on April 12, 1654, merged Scotland and England into one commonwealth, but also dissolved the Three Estates and abolished all feudal heritable jurisdictions and offices in the former nation.[41] The extent of Scottish aristocratic decline encouraged some of the republicans to believe that an irreversible shift in social relations had taken place. Cromwell himself imagined that this had been achieved by the end of his rule: "The meaner sort in Scotland live as well, and are as likely to come into a thriving condition under your Government," he told the House of Commons early in 1658, "as when they were under their own great Lords, who made them work for their living no better than the Peasants of France."[42] Harrington expressed a similar view the same year in *Oceana*, writing that the Scottish nobility "governed the country much in the manner of Poland ... till the people received their liberty, the yoke of the nobility being broken by the commonwealth of Oceana."[43] Unfortunately for the Scots, both Cromwell and Harrington were wrong to think this had happened on a permanent basis. Nevertheless, it should be clear that there was a widespread body of opinion, expressed in media as varied as personal letters and parliamentary legislation and shared by factions of the New Model Army otherwise at odds with each other, that power should be removed from the Scottish lords, for the sake of both the prosperity of their tenants and the security of the English Republic.[44] This body of opinion was not merely the context for the composition of *Oceana*; *Oceana* was one of its expressions. As R. H. Tawney once remarked: "To regard Harrington as an isolated doctrinaire is an error."[45]

What is true for "violent revolution" in Scotland was also true with regard to "natural revolution" in England itself. Harrington's work was both an analysis and a program, and his critics could accept the first while rejecting the second. According to Robert Ashton, Harrington was "an oddball figure" with "a very personal axe to grind." Yet even he admits that a similar analysis involving "material factors" was made by Edward Hyde, the Earl of Clarendon, "the greatest of all Civil War historians."[46] Several aspects of Clarendon's work have proved useful to revisionists like Ashton, notably his denial that there were any long-term causes of the civil war: "For I am not so sharp sighted as those, who have discerned this rebellion contrived from (if not before) the death of queen Elizabeth, and fomented by several princes and great ministers of state in Christendom, to the time it brake out." Also important for revisionists is his emphasis on contingency, on the "several accidents" that contributed to the course of events, to the absence of "familiarity and trust" between actors on the parliamentary side, which points away from any planned outcome, and above all to the sheer unpredictability of events when so many different social forces are involved, "like so many atoms contributing jointly to this mass of confusion before us."[47] Nevertheless, Clarendon does not ascribe events solely to chance. In the context of a discussion about the situation in Somersetshire during 1642 he notes that the attitude of the newly enriched became hostile to the king and established nobility partly because their acquisition of property in land had not necessarily increased their social power:

> For though the gentlemen of ancient families and estates in that country were, for the most part, well affected to the king, and easily discerned by what faction the parliament was governed; yet there were a people of an inferior degree, who, by good husbandry, clothing and other thriving arts, had gotten very great fortunes; and, by other degrees, getting themselves into the gentlemen's estates, were angry that they found not themselves in the same esteem and reputation with those whose estates they had; and therefore, with more industry than the other, studied all ways to make themselves considerable.[48]

Clarendon left a descriptive account of landowner behavior in one county rather than the grand theoretical interpretation offered by Harrington; but both men made essentially the same point: changes to political attitudes had followed changes in the nature of property ownership, and the conflict between representatives of different forms of property was the underlying cause of the civil war.

Clarendon was not alone on the Royalist side in arriving at this understanding. Harrington was a moderate republican, Clarendon a moderate Royalist; John Dryden moved from the first position to the second, before ending his as far-from-moderate Jacobite. En route toward his final political destination, however, he too affirmed the social basis of the revolution:

> *The Best, and of the Princes some were such,*
> *Who thought the power of Monarchy too much:*

Mistaken Men, and Patriots in their Hearts; Not wicked, but Seduc'd by Impious Arts.
By these the Springs of Property were bent,
And wound so high, they crack'd the Government.[49]

Revisionists are quite careful about which historical witnesses they call to give evidence, and the later Dryden, as a former supporter of revolution who subsequently reneged and, most importantly, also declared that the entire process had no positive consequences—indeed, had no discernible consequences at all—is regularly called upon to testify. Here, for example, is Blair Worden, ending a synoptic account of what he pointedly calls the English Civil Wars, by evoking Dryden's judgment:

> When the passions had subsided, what goals of the participants had they profited? Royalists at least regained the throne which the king had needlessly lost. But the parliamentarians who defeated him and demolished the nation's institutions, and whose exploits were swiftly and emphatically reversed in 1660, would have had no persuasive answer to a poem of 1700 by John Dryden, in which the writer's fancy delivered an address to the departing century and contemplated the conflict of its central decades. He had walked, with Milton and Marvell, in Cromwell's funeral procession. The years had made him a Tory and a Jacobite, but there is more wisdom than disdain in his assessment: "Thy wars brought nothing about."[50]

Dryden does indeed make this point repeatedly in *The Pilgrim*, from which the concluding line of this passage is taken. In the preceding stanzas, he has Momus repeat the same argument on several occasions, first to Mars:

Thy sword within the scabbard keep.
And let mankind agree;
Better the World were fast asleep,
Than kept awake by Thee.
The fools are only thinner.
With all our Cost and care;
But neither side a winner,
For things are as they were.

And later Momus addresses himself to Chronos in similar terms:

All, all, of a piece throughout;
Thy chase had a Beast in View;
Thy Wars brought nothing about;
Thy Lovers were all untrue.
'Tis well the Old Age is out,
And time to begin a New.[51]

But Worden is too anxious to press Dryden into service for the revisionist cause here. First, the immediate political context to which Dryden alludes here is less likely to be the civil war than the Nine Years War (1689–1697) and the debates about a standing army that followed it.[52] Second, Dryden's Jacobite politics, which nominally committed him to overthrowing the Williamite regime by force, scarcely suggests that he thought "things are as they were." The very existence of the Jacobite movement was an acknowledgement that, if not the revolution of 1640–60, then at least the sequel of 1688 had fundamentally changed the nature of the state and politics in Britain. Even before 1688, French state officials were aware of the difference between the state that they served and that of Restoration England. Le Comte de Cominges, French ambassador to the court of Charles II, wrote to Louis XIV about the British state early in the Restoration: "It has a monarchical appearance, as there is a king, but at bottom it is very far from being a Monarchy."[53] Nevertheless, the events of 1660 and 1688 suggested a problem in Harrington's analysis. John Aubrey reports him as saying, shortly before the Restoration of 1660: "Well, the King will come in. Let him come-in, and call a Parliament of the greatest Cavaliers in England, so they will be men of estates, and let them sit but 7 years, and they will all turn Commonwealth's men."[54]

Harrington's prediction telescoped the process, but ultimately proved to be accurate in 1688. Yet the search for a stable form of regime had not ended with "the people"—gentry, yeomanry, or however else conceived—in command of "the government," but with an imported constitutional monarchy presiding over a Parliament dominated by the great landed nobility. Hobbes had argued that intestine conflict could only be averted if the state overrode all competing group interests, reaching beneath these collectives to attain the authorization of individuals. The experience of England after the publication of *Leviathan* suggested that even where one group interest—that of mainly agrarian capital—had come to dominate society, its representatives were still incapable of directly ruling over their own political affairs. In this sense, a combination of Harrington's sensitivity to changes in class relations with Hobbes's awareness of what would later be called the autonomy of the state might have led to fruitful new directions in the theory of social revolution. Instead, the deeply conservative conclusion to the English Revolution in 1688–89 enshrined a partial retreat from the insights that had been gained during the course of the civil war. Harrington's work was buried almost as thoroughly as that of the Levellers and the other radicals to his left. Christopher Hill is right to say that "although the shift in meaning of 'revolution' had taken place well before 1688, the events of that year created new ambiguities."[55] These ambiguities are best demonstrated in the work of John Locke.

LOCKE AND THE RETREAT INTO IDEOLOGY

If Harrington had taken one step forward in relation to the concept of social revolution, Locke now took two steps back, not only in relation to revolution itself but also the conception of property that underlay it. Locke's major political work is the *Two Treatises of Government*, first published anonymously in 1690. Until the 1950s, it was assumed that the second treatise at least was written as a defence of the Glorious Revolution after the overthrow of James II and VII. Thanks to the work of Peter Laslett, however, we can be reasonably sure that the entire work was written between 1679 and 1683, with some references to contemporary events added prior to publication. (The order of composition of the two treatises within this overall timescale is still disputed, but this will not concern us here.) In other words, Locke was advocating a program of action rather than justifying one that had already been undertaken.[56]

Locke affirms the necessity for the right to resist, "whenever the *Legislators endeavor to take away, and destroy the Property of the People*, or to reduce them to Slavery Under an Arbitrary Power, they put themselves into a state of War with the People, who are therefore absolved from any farther Obedience, and are left to the common Refuge, which God hath provided for all Men, against Force and Violence."[57] Richard Ashcraft has argued that there is "no reason to suppose that when he speaks of the people as actors in resisting 'manifest acts of tyranny' he means some entity other than the majority of freemen." According to Ashcraft, Locke believed: "Resistance to tyranny is everyone's business."[58] Some of Locke's contemporaries certainly thought this was implied by his argument and the belief that he was for extending the right of resistance through the populace ensured that his remained a minority position among the majority of Williamite supporters at the time.[59] The enthusiasm for Locke and his *Two Treatises* during the eighteenth century, like that for Adam Smith and his *The Wealth of Nations* during the nineteenth century, did not manifest itself immediately on publication, nor did it necessarily reflect the views expressed by these authors. In the case of Smith his popularity involved a process of pretending he was less radical than he actually was; in the case of Locke, that he was more so.

In reality, Locke in many respects had reverted to the original, cyclical sense of revolution, to the idea of restoring what had been usurped, which in turn indicates the limits of his own political radicalism; for as we have seen, this doctrine explicitly denied the right of resistance to the vulgar mob or naughty rabble.[60] Locke emphasized the restorative aspects of his position in a letter to Edward Clarke, written during the Constitutional Convention of 1689, but before his book was published: "The settlement of the nation on the sure ground of peace and security . . . can no way so well be done as by restoring our ancient government; the best possible there ever was."[61] And in the second treatise itself he writes: "This slowness and aversion in the People to quit their old Constitutions, has, in the many Revolutions which have been seen in this Kingdom, in this and former Ages, still kept us to, or, after some interval of fruitless attempts, still brought us back again to our old Legislative of Kings, Lords and Commons: And whatever provocations have made the Crown be taken from some of our Prince's Heads, they have never carried the People so far, as to place it on another Line."[62] Locke obviously recognizes that there are distinct forms of government, one of which, absolute monarchy, he was concerned to oppose as "*inconsistent with Civil Society*."[63] Outside of the highly formal presentation of his case in the *Two Treatises*, Locke was also aware that the struggle against absolutism in England involved a geopolitical dimension.

As he wrote of James in another letter to Clarke: "If he ever return, under whatever pretences soever, Jesuits must govern and France be our master. He is too wedded to the one and relies too much on the other ever to part with either."[64]

On this point Locke was part of a wider consensus. Charles Davenant, for example, reflected in 1701: "The Late Revolution, and the war that happened upon it, were both carried on upon the same foot of opposing the French Monarchy."[65] But the class basis of both absolutism—potential in England, actual in France—and the forces ranged against it, their relationship to economic life, remain obscure in his work. The source of this obscurity lies in the area, unlike resistance theory, in which Locke made a genuine advance on previous thinkers: the theory of property.

Some Marxists have made strong claims for Locke as the preeminent theorist of agrarian capitalism. Neal Wood, for example, has claimed that "Locke was . . . a theorist of a special type of agricultural society emerging in England."[66] He and Ellen Meiksins Wood argue that "Locke is . . . a theorist of a 'rising' capitalism and . . . the argument of the *Two Treatises* was ideally suited to the class interests of a 'progressive' landed aristocracy engaged in capitalist agriculture and colonial trade."[67] To say that Locke's argument was "suited" to the interests of agrarian capitalists in England is demonstrably true in the sense that he provided the Whig wing of that class with their central political doctrines for the next century or more. Whether his views can be quite so completely identified with capitalist economy is another matter, and here too a comparison with Smith is relevant.

> *As much Land* as a Man Tills, Plants, Improves, Cultivates, and can use the product of, so much is his *Property*. He by his Labour does, as it were, inclose it from the Common. Nor will it invalidate his right to say, Every body else has an equal Title to it; and therefore he cannot appropriate, he cannot inclose, without the Consent of all his Fellow-Commoners, all Mankind. God, when he gave the World in common to all Mankind, commanded Man also to labour, and the penury of his condition required it of him.[68]

Locke does not, of course, mean that property accrues to a man only when he actually labors on it himself; on the contrary, the servants that he employs can also do the work for him. Locke then introduces the fundamental distinction: property originates in labour and labour is the basis of differences in value: "For 'tis *Labour* indeed that *puts the difference in value* on every thing; and let any one consider, what the difference is between an Acre of Land planted with Tobacco, or Sugar, sown with Wheat or Barley; and an Acre of the Same Land lying in common, without any Husbandry upon it, and he will find, that the improvement of *labour makes* the far greater part of *the value*."[69] This suggests that, for Locke, there is essentially society without property ("the original simplicity") and society with property; property itself has no particular distinctions other than its physical form. The fact that this hypothetical property-owner has servants is itself of great significance, but Locke does not suggest that this is a particularly new development:

Master and Servant are names as old as History, but given to those of far different condition [that is, the conditions of masters and servants are different]; for a Freeman makes himself a Servant to another, by selling him for a certain time, the Service he undertakes to do, in exchange for Wages he is to receive: And though this commonly puts him into the Family of his Master, and under the ordinary Discipline thereof; yet it gives the Master but a temporary Power over him, and no greater, than what is contained in the *Contract* between 'em.[70]

Leave aside for the moment the important question of whether a purely "agrarian" capitalism has ever existed, or could ever have existed; the claim that Locke was its theorist depends on the assumption that "improvement" is only possible on the basis of capitalist productive relations, so that this must be what Locke means when he discusses how the process of labor can add to the value of landed property. But this ignores the fact that improvements had already occurred in European history on a feudal basis, involving significant increases in agricultural productivity, between the tenth and thirteenth centuries.[71] The "servant" who labors in Locke's hypothetical field could just as easily be a feudal tenant farmer as a capitalist rural laborer. Indeed, in at least some areas Locke regarded the former as more desirable. A demonstration that he was not opposed in principle to feudalism as an economic system can be found in his draft constitution for the Carolinas, which includes provision for the classification of inhabitants as "leet-men"—effectively serfs tied to a particular manor, subject to the justice of the lord and whose children would inherit the same condition.[72] Locke was not proposing slavery for black Africans or Native Americans—that would have been unremarkable, but serfdom for white colonists of British descent, who had neither been defeated in war nor found guilty of any crime. What this suggests is that Locke was not exclusively supportive of capitalist productive relations, but simply accepted them on pragmatic grounds—in the same way as he defended the English constitution because it was tried and tested and seemed to benefit people like himself.

In this context it is important to understand the connection between his theory of property and his theory of resistance, and how both involved a major intellectual retreat. Harrington justified revolution in terms of historical development, as a means by which emergent social classes attained the political power denied them by the retrogressive immobility of the absolutist monarchy; Locke justified revolution in terms of historical preservation, as a means of restoring the ancient balance of the English constitution threatened from the destructive innovations of the same absolutist monarchy. Harrington, whatever the flaws in his analysis, was attempting to discern the social forces at work; Locke, for all the brilliance of his argumentation, is consciously disguising them behind a set of ahistorical abstractions.

THE DISADVANTAGES OF INTELLECTUAL PRIORITY

The aftermath of the English revolution of 1688 involved, in intellectual terms, the consolidation of a theory of revolution as defense of liberty, itself defined in terms of property, within a broader conceptual framework that conceived of hitherto unimaginable forms of human progress. The link between revolution and progress, namely prior changes in socioeconomic relations, had been briefly identified after the English Civil War (above all by Harrington), only to be consciously or unconsciously repressed during the Restoration by the theoreticians of a newly triumphant class (above all by Locke, for whom these insights had troubling implications). Consequently, as Hill once noted: "The historical insights of Marvell, Harrington, Hobbes, and Clarendon, significant though they were, remained undeveloped until the Scottish School picked them up in the eighteenth century."[73] Why did it fall to the Scots—or more precisely, the Scots and the French—to "pick up" these insights, rather than the English themselves?

Roy Porter once wrote that it was "anachronistic" to "draw rigid distinctions between the English and Scottish enlightened traditions."[74] In the context of the natural sciences, with which Porter is concerned at this point in his argument, this judgment can perhaps be sustained; but in the key discipline of political economy, and the associated ones that we now call history and sociology, the contrasts are stark indeed—not because of a retrospective imposition of nationalist categories. Despite Marx's later exasperation at what he called "the crude English method of discourse" the English did not suffer from any congenital deficiency in respect of theory.[75] The problem was rather that English Enlightenment thought emerged, in common and in parallel with English capitalism, over a period of several centuries, and the luxury of prolonged development brought with it the punishment of an empirical method resistant to systematic theorization, even among its greatest thinkers. In England, the bourgeois revolution was—as revisionists ceaselessly remind us—conducted largely under religious banners. Indeed, some of those who can be described as the standard-bearers of Enlightenment thought were, like Hobbes, at least as likely to support the absolutist regime as those who sought to overthrow it.[76] By the time Enlightenment thought became, with Locke, the province of those fully committed to commercial society and constitutional monarchy, at least in England itself: "England was too modern to need an Enlightenment and was already engaged upon a quarrel with modernity itself."[77] The new propertied classes had greater power and freedom to discuss how it should be exercised than any other national group in Europe. "In these circumstances," writes Porter, "enlightened ideologies were to assume a unique inflection in England: one less concerned to lambast the status quo than to vindicate it against adversaries left and right, high and low."[78] It was therefore left to thinkers from France and Scotland—countries where the transition from feudalism was still far from complete—to theorize questions of social development. In particular, their great achievement was to recognize, for the first time since Harrington, that history had involved a succession of fundamental social transformations and, in the case of the Scots at least, to claim that one leading to the dominance of "commercial society" still remained to be achieved.

3

STAGES OF DEVELOPMENT: FRENCH PHYSIOCRATS AND THE SCOTTISH HISTORICAL SCHOOL

Scotland was a most unexpected place for insights into social revolution to emerge. If the type of theoretical retreat characteristic of Locke had occurred in England, where capitalism was most developed, then it was unsurprising that the type of analysis developed by Harrington remained unknown in Scotland, in the absence of the social changes that informed his writings. Take, for example, the case of Andrew Fletcher of Saltoun, the most radical of the pre-Enlightenment Scottish political thinkers.

Fletcher had been one of the few Scots to declare himself in favor of a union with England during the revolutions of 1688; but, as his letters reveal, his support for a union was based on the assumption that Scotland would be conjoined with a truly radical England that could overcome feudal relations in the former country.[1] His politics were therefore comparable to those of the extreme Whigs or Commonwealth Men who were defeated in the English Convention Parliament. Consequently, as William Ferguson has shown, when it became clear that William of Orange intended to agree to the most conservative settlement possible, the very reason for seeking union disappeared and the possibility of achieving his goals within Scotland alone became his main project.[2] Fletcher did not thereafter simply become the chief opponent of the 1707 Treaty of Union, although this is the role for which he is now chiefly remembered. He was also committed to a program of radical reform that would have reduced the role of the Crown to a virtually ceremonial one and to the same degree strengthened the power of the Scottish Parliament. Fletcher was fully aware of the nature of absolutism, or what he called "the alteration in government which happened in most countries in Europe about the year 1500," and sketched a brilliant Harringtonian account of the rise of this state form as a continentwide phenomenon.[3] Scotland had never achieved a stable absolutism and Fletcher was concerned to ensure that it never would; but in the absence of extensive capitalist development, what could he offer as an alternative? His aim seems to have been a society that combined the independent peasant proprietors of the Swiss Cantons with the aristocratic republicanism of the Venetian city-state, or at least idealized versions of these models; but in the actual context of Scottish society this would have merely reinforced feudal property relations, as can be seen from his proposal to solve the great Scottish subsistence crisis of the 1690s.

Fletcher argued for extending the scope of serfdom from the occupations where it was still in force, among colliers and salters, to all members of the non-property-owning classes: a radical and systemic extension of the legal framework was required, which would not only enserf the unemployed or dispossessed, but also make provision for the continuing servitude of their descendants.[4] His proposal gained little support among other members of his class—not because of their revulsion at the extremity of his solution, but because it did not stop at enserfment. Linked to these measures against the poorest were others designed to break the tyranny of the landlords, the two most important of which were a ban on the charging of interest on money loans and the enforced sale of all land beyond that which a landowner could farm with his own servants—in other words, without subletting.[5] There was more, but these proposals alone were probably enough to persuade his contemporaries that, while Fletcher was undoubtedly principled, his views were dangerous to their interests; consequently, he had no social forces with which to accomplish his vision. Landlords greater than himself would scarcely abandon the income they accrued from interest and rent in pursuit of an abstract model of civic virtue, and the classes below him were unlikely to be won to a banner—even supposing he had been prepared to raise it—which promised them permanent servitude as a penalty for slipping further down the social order. In short, Fletcher, the most brilliant representative of the lairds who formed the lowest rung of the Scottish ruling class, was propounding a classic petty bourgeois utopia. Pocock has written that Fletcher's work "reveals to us a condition of thought about 1700 in which a bourgeois ideology, a civic morality for market man, was ardently desired but apparently not to be found."[6] In the absence of any economic mechanisms, all that Fletcher could offer as a means of inculcating civil virtue was military training and in this respect he remained far more of a classical Machiavellian than Harrington. Initially, therefore, it was the French who broke new ground.

THE AMBIGUITIES OF THE PHYSIOCRATS

Although superficial similarities between the French and English Enlightenment can be found, their context renders them quite different in implication: "*Cato's Letters* [by the Englishmen John Trenchard and Thomas Gordon] and *Letters Persanes* [by the Frenchman Montesquieu] alike denounce autocracy, priestcraft, and speculative corruption; but in lands where absolute monarchy and Tridentine Catholicism were realities and not bogeys, they could not be the rhetorical embellishments of the case against corruption that they were in England."[7] Radical though they were, however, the French thinkers concerned by no means represented the revolutionary bourgeoisie. Both Charles-Louis de Secondat Montesquieu and Anne-

Robert Turgot, for example, were members of the nobility and the latter was finance minister for the absolutist regime. In fact, those individuals who contributed most toward the stages theory belonged, like Turgot, to the Physiocratic school of economic thought. In essence, their theory saw agriculture as the only economic sector in which labor is productive and consequently the only one from which surplus value (as Marx would later call it) could be realized. As Marx himself wrote of the Physiocratic system, it had "the character of a bourgeois reproduction of the feudal system, of the domination of landed property; and the industrial spheres within which capital first develops independently are presented as 'unproductive' branches of labor, mere appendages of agriculture."[8] The thought of the Physiocrats and their contemporaries therefore has a transitional character.

In 1748, Montesquieu wrote that "if it be true that the temper of the mind and the passions of the heart are extremely different in different climates, the laws ought to be in relation both to the variety of those passions and to the variety of those tempers."[9] Montesquieu is here expressing a form of environmental determinism in which different meteorological and topographical conditions give rise to particular "modes of subsistence," which in turn gives rise to appropriate political forms. Two aspects of these modes are important here. First, they describe relations between human beings and nature at the point of either appropriation (as hunters and gatherers) or production (as pastoral or arable farmers), and although they assume that there must be cooperation for these activities to take place, other social relationships, particularly those involving exploitation, are absent. Second, the modes do not stand in successive relation to each other—indeed, the very emphasis that Montesquieu places on the physical environment ruled out such a relationship.

This second aspect was soon to change. It is implicit in the *Plan of Two Discourses on Universal History*, written by Turgot around 1750, that the three different modes—hunting, pasturage, and agriculture—were successive stages. In another essay from the early 1750s, "On Political Geography," he made this explicit: "The successive changes in the manner of life of men and the order in which they have followed one another: peoples who are shepherds, hunters, husbandmen."[10] It was obvious, however, that all societies were not undergoing these changes within the same historical time scale. Turgot noted that, at a global level, all the different stages of social development were simultaneously being played out: "Thus, the present state of the world, marked as it is by these infinite variations in inequality, spreads out before us at one and the same time all the gradations from barbarism to refinement, thereby revealing at a single glance, as it were, the records and remains of all the steps taken by the human mind, a reflection of all the stages through which it has passed, and the history of the ages." But these stages were all points on the road to the same ultimate destination: "Thus the human race, considered over the period since its origin, appears to the eye of a philosopher as one vast whole, which itself, like each individual, has its infancy and its advancement. . . . Finally, commercial and political ties unite all parts of the globe, and the whole human race, through alternate periods of weal and woe, goes on advancing, although at a slow pace, towards greater perfection."[11]

Turgot was actually more optimistic than many of his contemporaries in relation to these obstacles in the advance toward what he called "greater perfection." The constraints of the natural environment, highlighted by Montesquieu, continued to influence considerably more radical representatives of prerevolutionary French Enlightenment thought. Jean-Jacques Rousseau, for example, wrote in 1752: "Everything that facilitates communication among the various nations carries to some, not the virtues of the others but their crimes, and among all of them alters the morals that are proper to their climate and the constitution of their government."[12] The Physiocrats were forty years away from the revolution of 1789 that would bring down French absolutism and, in any event, this was not their goal. Turgot was one of the first writers to refer to "capitalists" and to distinguish between different varieties of the genus on the basis of whether they were landed proprietors, entrepreneurs, or moneylenders.[13] His attitude toward their activities, like that of his contemporaries, was supportive to an extent, but nevertheless envisaged commerce having a restricted role within the economy, compatible with growth but not so as not to threaten the structures of the state. From this perspective the emergence of a social group comparable to English agrarian capitalists was not desirable, although the feudal-absolutist state itself could introduce socioeconomic reforms necessary to stimulate a degree of subordinate and controlled commercial development. As Elizabeth Fox-Genovese and Eugene Genovese have pointed out, the Physiocrats learned from the experience of Britain, but they also had "a small disadvantage": "the theory of property aside, the reality of bourgeois property, so firmly established in Britain, existed precariously in France, where it was economically not powerful enough to command political resources but powerful enough to raise a host of dangerous enemies."[14] Turgot's own removal from office in 1776 was an indication of the extent to which even his very limited practical reforms were tolerable to the majority of the French ruling class.[15] Initially at least, French Enlightenment thinkers, including the most radical, could not see a stage of historical development beyond the one in which they were situated. Even before Rousseau rejected the *encyclopédistes* and embraced more moderate Enlightenment views, he still deployed the original sense of revolution as a cyclical change in constitutional regime, for example, in the second part of *A Discourse on Inequality* in 1755, where he writes of "new revolutions" that "dissolve the government altogether or bring it back to legitimacy."[16]

SCOTLAND: THEORIZING REVOLUTION FROM ABOVE

The Scots followed closely behind the French, but in a different social context that had implications for their version of the theory. By the 1750s, the Scottish revolution, unlike that of the French, lay in the past, not in the future. The context for this transformation was the global intersystemic conflict between England (from 1688) then Britain (from 1707) and France, in which Scotland was one of the main battlefields. The process had four key moments. First, a subsistence crisis at home and imperial failure abroad during the 1690s, the combined effects of which sent Scottish capitalist development into reverse. Second, and in response to the first, the Anglo-Scottish Union of 1707, which dissolved the Scottish Parliament and established the new British state, but left the feudal jurisdictions of the Scottish lords intact. Third, the failure of a French-backed attempt at counterrevolution, the last of which, the Jacobite revolt of 1745–46, led to the military suppression and juridical abolition of feudal social relations north of the border. Fourth, the imposition of capitalist social relations in the Scottish countryside by an alliance of former feudal landlords, "improving" tenant farmers and Enlightenment intellectuals, who then theorized the entire process in their discussion of "civil society."[17] Feudal political and military power was then systematically destroyed in Scotland, but not by the efforts of an indigenous bourgeoisie. The literati of the Scottish Enlightenment were thereafter deeply, painfully conscious of the extent to which their revolution had been secured by the power of the British state. As Sir John Dalrymple wrote, a decade after Culloden, "In the declension of almost every part of the feudal system, the English have gone before us: at the distance of one, and sometimes of many centuries, we follow."[18]

Scottish capitalism and the classes associated with it had grown from when Fletcher found himself at an impasse in 1698, but it still remained relatively weak and undeveloped at the middle of the eighteenth century. The uniqueness of the situation after 1746 was that political power was already in the hands of the bourgeoisie, while feudal social relations still prevailed, above all in the countryside. In one respect therefore the situation in Scotland was more typical of the aftermath of a proletarian than a bourgeois revolution, in the sense that the economy had to be consciously reconstructed after the conquest of political power, brought into line with the political superstructure that had already been created at the level of the British state—clearly the minority status of the forces that brought about this change make any other comparison invalid. After 1746 the nascent Scottish bourgeoisie were presented with an opportunity that would never again be available to any other: an opportunity to wage a revolution from above, safe in the knowledge that resistance would not be forthcoming from either the old feudal lords, who had already been defeated, or from the new working class, who had not yet been brought into existence. The theoretical basis for this transformation was provided by the intellectuals and theorists collectively known as the Scottish Historical School and whose individual social roles were generally those of university professors, Church of Scotland ministers, or lawyers. These were the theorists of capital; they were not, in most cases, its owners. The uniqueness of the Scottish situation meant that most members of the Scottish Historical School, however, were necessarily more concerned in their writings with the transformation of economic relations than the conquest of state power. As Roy Pascal pointed out in his pioneering Marxist analysis of their work: "Their revolution had already been won. When they attack the nobility it is not as an opposed class, but as land-monopolists, and they attack those agricultural monopolists as they do the monopolists in trade and industry. What they (in particular Adam Smith) demand is, not the victory of one class over another, but less interference by monopolists with the development of capitalism—politics they understand, in the main, as interference of this kind."[19]

Their situation had implications for their politics. Insofar as the Scottish Enlightenment was concerned with agrarian improvement, a relatively large component of its social base lay among those who were actual or potential beneficiaries; but as Andrew Noble comments: "The skepticism of Enlightenment thought was designed not for mass consumption so as to encourage the overthrow of established institutions but for a new urban elite who were to take over these institutions."[20] It also involved, and to a much greater extent, a new rural elite—but the central point is correct; social revolution as the act of a class or class fraction had been unnecessary for them. Roger Emerson has given an all-too-evocative picture of the political attitudes that tended to result:

> Radicalism in politics would be proscribed since it was likely to undercut their own positions as magistrates and beneficiaries of the system they were running. Not utopian dreams but an understanding of the historic rights and privileges of their region and or corporations would be most likely to come from their discussions or pens. They would not tend to view the extension of royal power as desirable but would advocate, when not defending the *status quo*, rational utilitarian changes which would benefit the professional, mercantile and landed classes. Few attacks on privilege would come from them, but some pleas for extension of liberties might be expected. Equality in their eyes would be for gentlemen if it were to exist at all. They would be for freedom—freedom from censorship, arbitrary arrest, standing armies and other devices of strong central governments. While believing in natural laws, they believed the social order specified by these laws to be hierarchical. Their sense of community implied their responsibility as a governing class and the conformity of others to their rational standards. They had, however, few illusions, as only men in power can have few illusions, about the willingness of men to conform.[21]

As this description suggests, Locke exercised a strong influence over the Scots.[22] There was, however, also an inevitable difference in their approach. Locke and the English writers who followed him were essentially justifying the outcome of a process that had taken hundreds of years to complete, while the Scots were concerned with producing a blueprint for how the process could be reproduced in their own country, over a period of decades. In doing so, they introduced two theoretical innovations.

INVENTING "COMMERCIAL SOCIETY"

The first innovation was to add a fourth and, as they saw it, final stage of subsistence to the French three-stage model of development: the commercial stage to which the Scots themselves aspired. Their role formulating the four-stage model has, how-ever, been disputed. Istvan Hont ascribes authorship, without references, to the sev-enteenth-century German writer, Samuel von Pufendorf.[23] Gareth Stedman Jones claims that the origins of the four-stage model lie even earlier in that century, in the work of Grotius.[24] Both Hont and Stedman Jones ignore the French contri-bution. In fact, neither Grotius nor Pufendorf adhered to a four-stage model. Ac-cording to Grotius, in a work of 1625 specifically referenced by Stedman Jones, "the Ancient Art of Agriculture, and of feeding Cattle, appeared early with two first brothers."[25] Since the Book of Genesis tells us that Cain and Abel were the third and fourth humans to have sought subsistence on earth, and Grotius believes that they simultaneously developed pasturage and husbandry, it is not entirely ob-vious how this corresponds to a succession of stages emerging over a prolonged period of historical time. Ronald Meek is therefore correct to write: "Grotius's main concern . . . is not with the question of the origin and development of society as such, but with the question of the origin and development of the right of private ownership in property." Meek sees certain suggestive hints that property might arise in successive forms, but no more than this: "We are still a very long way from the four stages theory in the form in which it was to dominate European social science in the latter half of the eighteenth century."[26] Fifty years after Grotius, Pufendorf wrote of the period "after mankind had departed from its primitive sim-plicity and various forms of profit-making had come in," which, if anything, implies a direct transition to the Age of Commerce.[27] It is true that these men influenced the Scottish Enlightenment: Gershom Carmichael, the first Chair of Moral Phi-losophy at Glasgow University, was enthusiastic about both thinkers and edited an edition of Pufendorf's *Of the Duty of Man and Citizen* in 1718; but their influence was precisely in relation to natural jurisprudence, not social development.[28] Inter-estingly, the Scottish thinker who follows them most closely, Adam Ferguson (1723–1816), is the only one who did not subscribe to the four-stage theory, but rather saw social development as taking place on a different, three-stage basis: no property, property uninshrined in law, and property as the basis of law.[29]

Adam Smith appears to have been the first person to make reference to the four-stage theory in his Edinburgh lectures on Moral Philosophy of 1750–51. But it was in Dalrymple's *Essay towards a General History of Feudal Property* (1757) that the term first appeared in print and signaled that the notion of four universal stages was now part of the general intellectual repertoire of the Enlightenment.[30] Smith wrote in 1762, for example, that "there are four distinct states which mankind passes through:—first, the Age of Hunters; second, the Age of Shepherds; third, the Age of Agriculture; and fourth, the Age of Commerce."[31] And Henry Home, Lord Kames, the legal theorist and agrarian reformer, had already observed in 1758 that "these progressive changes in the order now mentioned may be traced in all soci-eties."[32] It is true, as Christopher Berry has written, that "the Scots are not strong on explanation for the move from stage to stage."[33] In general, however, they believed that each successive stage is attained by cumulative increases in the numerical size of the population, the complexity of the division of labor, and the efficiency of productive techniques. The commercial stage is different from the preceding three in one important respect; since trade has taken place throughout human history, "commerce did not succeed the previous stages of subsistence, but rather developed in parallel throughout all the four stages."[34]

The attainment of the commercial stage was held to mean that humanity had reached the form of economic organization compatible with its nature. Consequently, it was both the last possible stage of human development and the one that had to be commended to those societies (which for Smith and Kames meant first of all their native Scotland) still mired in the Age of Agriculture. In 1776, the same year in which Smith's *The Wealth of Nations* was published, Kames asked whether it was too much to expect "that our progress may be rapid; and that agriculture will soon be familiar among us, and as skillfully conducted as in England."[35] In this perspective, development is characterized as the process in which the backward gradually attain the same level as the more advanced. In 1755, the first issue of the *Edinburgh Review* contained an editorial in which the extent of Scottish economic progress was considered in terms of the biological metaphor introduced by Bacon that was to become standard in future discussions of development: "If countries have their ages with respect to improvement, North Britain [that is, Scotland] may be considered as in a state of early youth, guided and supported by the more mature strength of her kindred country [England]."[36] Twenty years later, the metaphor had become fully established. As William Robertson wrote in his *History of America* (1777): "In order to complete the history of the human mind, and attain to a perfect knowledge of its nature and operations, we must contemplate man in all those various situations in which he has been placed. We must follow him in his progress through the different stages of society, as he gradually advances from the infant state of civil society towards his maturity and decline."[37]

We should note here that, unlike modern supporters of capitalism, Robertson takes the life-cycle metaphor seriously and assumes the inevitability of eventual social decline. Indeed, several of his contemporaries—Ferguson above all—thought that in moral terms there had *already* been a decline from the type of military heroism characteristic of the first three ages to the commercial calculation typical of their own. But the central point is stated by Robertson in two sentences that occur elsewhere in the same book: "In every inquiry concerning the operations of men when united together in society, the first object of attention should be their mode of subsistence. Accordingly as that varies, their laws and policy must be different."[38]

The position summarized in these few modest lines represents one of the greatest collective breakthroughs in the history of social thought, one foreshadowed only by Harrington. First, it gives priority ("the first object of attention"), not to politics, not to ideas, and not to morals, as had hitherto been the case, but to how human beings reproduce themselves ("their mode of subsistence"). Second, it suggests that politics, ideas, and morals are themselves variously shaped by these modes of subsistence. However, although the Scots had discerned four successive modes of subsistence, each with different "laws and policy," they did not argue that these necessarily had to be accompanied by particular forms of government. Their assumption seems to have been that the types of constitution inherited from the ancients via the Renaissance—monarchy, aristocracy, democracy, and their antinomies—could be adopted as required, either individually or, as in the case of the supposedly "matchless" British Constitution, in combination. As Robertson suggests, some types of regime would be more appropriate than others for a particular mode of subsistence, but modes of subsistence did not generate their own corresponding types of regime. The extent to which these views had penetrated Scottish intellectual life by the end of the eighteenth century is suggested by this type of comment, by another Church of Scotland minister, nominally committed to the doctrine of Original Sin, the Reverend John Mukersie, in his contribution to Sir John Sinclair's *Statistical Account of Scotland* during the 1790s: "In almost every instance, the local situations of men form their characters."[39]

Rethinking "Feudalism"

The second Scottish innovation was a refinement of the concept of "feudalism." Feudalism was a term in transition during the Enlightenment. As we have seen, by the first half of the eighteenth century, it had become the established term to describe the legal relationships increasingly dominant across Europe between the fall of the Roman Empire and c. 1000. Montesquieu used the term in this sense in *The Spirit of Laws* (1748):

> I should think my work imperfect were I to pass over in silence an event which never again, perhaps, will happen; were I not to speak of those laws which suddenly appeared over all Europe without being connected with any of the former institutions; of those laws which have done infinite good and infinite mischief; which have suffered rights to remain when the demesne has been ceded; which by vesting several with different kinds of seignory over the same things or persons have diminished the weight of the whole seignory; which have established different limits in empires of too great extent; which have been productive of rule with a bias to anarchy, and of anarchy with a tendency to order and harmony.

The admiring tone of these words, like those of Thomas Craig in the previous century, perhaps reflect the author's own social position: "The feudal laws," Montesquieu concluded, "form a very beautiful prospect."[40] It is this sympathy for feudalism that perhaps accounts for his hostility to Harrington: "Harrington, in his *Oceana*, has also inquired into the utmost degree of liberty to which the constitution of a state may be carried. But of him indeed it may be said that for want of knowing the nature of real liberty he busied himself in pursuit of an imaginary one; and that he built a Chalcedon, though he had a Byzantium before his eyes. . . . Harrington was full of the idea of his favorite republic of England, while a crowd of writers saw nothing but confusion where monarchy is abolished."[41]

The Scottish conception of feudalism represented a move away from that of the French. For the Scots, feudalism represented not a set of legal arrangements ("the feudal law"), nor a mode of subsistence, nor yet a type of society, but rather a type of decentralized social organization characterized by lordly territorial jurisdictions on the one hand, and by peasant military tenure and labor service on the other. Smith tended to follow Harrington in regarding feudalism in this sense as having been established in Scotland and England, as in the rest of Europe, shortly after the fall of the Roman Empire in the West:

> It would be a mistake to imagine that those territorial jurisdictions took their origin from the feudal law. Not only the highest jurisdictions both civil and criminal, but the power of levying troops, of coining money, and even that of making bye-laws for the government of their own people, were all rights possessed allodially [that is, not granted by a king or other superior] by the great proprietors of land several centuries before even the name of the feudal law was known in Europe. The authority and jurisdiction of the Saxon lords in England appear to have been as great before the conquest, as that of any Norman lords after it.... That the most extensive authority and jurisdictions were possessed by the great lords of France allodially, long before the feudal law was introduced into that country, is a matter of fact that admits no doubt.[42]

The term "feudalism" therefore sits uneasily in the Scottish discussions, as a kind of junction-concept, between the economic and political categories (modes of subsistence, types of constitution) that they otherwise used. For Smith, feudalism had no predecessors—he regarded slavery as compatible with all four modes of subsistence and any form of government—and no successor, since he did not refer to capitalism, but to capital, and he tended to assume that it had existed throughout history and under all modes of subsistence. There is no transition from feudalism to capitalism in Scottish Enlightenment thought: to treat the transition from the agricultural to the commercial stage as the equivalent of the transition from feudalism to capitalism is therefore either to commit a category mistake or to impose Marxist categories on a period before they were formulated.[43] The concept of feudalism, in other words, only emerged in its final, pre-Marxist, form when the notion of capitalism replaced that of commercial society, a shift that occurred in the early decades of the nineteenth century.

BETWEEN FEUDALISM AND COMMERCIAL SOCIETY

The Scottish Historical School therefore envisaged two separate processes: on the one hand, the emergence of a full-blown commercial society from agricultural society; on the other, the dismantling by political means of "unnatural" feudal social powers that would otherwise act to block the former process. The two processes were linked, in that feudalism was seen as an impediment that had to be cleared away to enable the proper functioning of commercial society. Smith outlined the social and political benefits that the resulting prosperity would bring in *The Wealth Of Nations*, claiming that "commerce and manufacturing introduce order and good government and with them, the liberty and security of individuals among the inhabitants of the country, who had lived almost in a continual state of war with their neighbors and of servile dependency on their superiors."[44] This passage suggests the vast change in attitude that had occurred since the beginning of the Enlightenment in the British Isles, 150 years before. The difference between Smith and Hobbes is particularly striking. "Hobbes needs state power to tame and control the violence of human nature and competition," writes Fredric Jameson, "in Adam Smith ... the competitive system, the market, does the taming and controlling all by itself, no longer needing the absolute state."[45] The difference is that between a writer who has experienced the trauma of revolution and civil wars and one who is experiencing—if indirectly—the benefits of their outcome. But how were the preexisting forms of power, that of the feudal nobles and the absolutist state, overthrown?

Kames discussed these issues in a book written, as the title page pointedly makes clear, during the last Jacobite attempt to reestablish absolutist rule across Britain in 1745–46. In response to "our late Troubles" Kames wrote, "he has at Heart to raise a Spirit in his Countrymen, of searching into their Antiquities ... being seriously convinced, that nothing will more contribute than this Study, to eradicate a Set of Opinions [the divine right of kings], which, by Intervals, have disquieted this Island for a Century and a Half."[46] The decaying feudal system that lay behind the Jacobite risings had long since been eroded by the infringements of commercialism:

> The Feudal Law was an institution adapted entirely to War, admirably conceived for that End. But it was an utter enemy to Labour and Industry, and even, among an Indolent People, scarce sufferable in peaceable times.... As land is one of the most desirable Objects, the Feudal law was most unnatural in this Respect, that the Property of Land was altogether withdrawn from Commerce, and scarce any Means to come at the Possession and Use of it; but by military service.... Superiors began to find, that they could make more of their Lands than by allotting them for military Service. They were willing to change this Service for Rent, and the Tenants turning themselves to Industry, or at least fond of Independency, were pleased with the Exchange. Other Superiors, to supply Means for Luxury, and tempted with a Price, were willing to give off detached Pieces of Land. And thus, by Degrees, Lands returned to their original Condition of being the principal Subject of Commerce.[47]

This passage clearly illustrates the extent to which the Scots regarded commerce as natural and feudalism as an aberration. The reversion to commerce, at a higher level, changed the nature of property and they were certainly conscious, like Harrington, that "power follows property." Dalrymple actually used the phrase during his 1757 comparison between feudal property in England and Scotland. His subsequent discussion is thoroughly Harringtonian: "The constitution of Scotland, till incorporated with that of England, was in fact a mixture of monarchy and oligarchy: the nation consisted of a commonality without the privilege of choosing their own representatives; of a gentry entitled indeed to represent by election, but unable to serve the nation; and of a nobility, who oppressed the one, and despised both." Dalrymple did not, however, restrict himself to this brutally accurate description, but also proposed a commendably materialist explanation for it, which penetrated beneath the level of political forms: "The similar constitutions of parliament in England and Scotland, by the introduction of the commons and of the new nobility, ought to have had, it would be thought, similar effects on both countries; yet they had not. In England, the commons rose immediately to vast power: in Scotland, they never attained any power in the legislature, and it is only since the revolution [of 1688] that they attained even common freedom." The difference with England was that in that country "the commons" (as Dalrymple calls the gentry and the mercantile classes) had acquired power through commerce, but: "In Scotland . . . we had little or no commerce; the land property was engrossed by the nobility, and it continued to remain so, as long as we had parliaments: the same cause then, which raised the commons in one country, depressed them in the other."[48] The centrality of the English experience as a normative model for development reappears throughout the Scottish discussions. Here is David Hume, giving a typically elegant demonstration in 1752 that the replacement of a class of subaltern feudal tenants by that of independent capitalist farmer was conducive to liberty:

> In rude unpolished nations, where the arts are neglected, all labour is bestowed on the cultivation of the ground; and the whole society is divided into two classes, proprietors of the land, and their vassals or tenants. The latter are necessarily dependent, and fitted for slavery and subjection; especially where they possesses no riches, and are not valued for their knowledge in agriculture; as must always be the case where the arts are neglected. The former naturally erect themselves into petty tyrants; and must either submit to an absolute master, for the sake of peace and order; or if they will preserve their independence, like the ancient barons, they must fall into feuds and contests among themselves, and throw themselves into such confusion, as is perhaps worse than the most despotic government. But where luxury nourishes commerce and industry, the peasants, by a proper cultivation of the land, become rich and independent; while the tradesmen and merchants acquire a share of the property, and draw authority and consideration to that middling rank of men, who are the best and firmest basis of public liberty. These submit not to slavery, like the peasants, from poverty and meanness of spirit; and having no hopes of tyrannizing over others, like the barons, they are not tempted, for the sake of that gratification, to submit to the tyranny of their sovereign. They covet equal laws, which may secure their property, and preserve them from monarchical, as well as aristocratic tyranny.[49]

The process Hume outlines here in general terms is based on the English experience, as the following passage from his *History of England* (1754–62) makes clear. Following Bacon and Harrington, Hume draws attention to the consequences of what he calls "the change in manners" in England following the accession of Henry VII:

The habits of luxury dissipated the immense fortunes of the ancient barons, and as the new methods of expense gave subsistence to mechanics and merchants, who lived in an independent manner on the fruits of their own industry, a nobleman, instead of that unlimited ascendant, which he was wont to assume over those who were maintained at his board, or subsisted by salaries conferred on them, retained only that moderate influence, which customers have over tradesmen, and which can never be dangerous to civil government. The landed proprietors also, having a greater demand for money than for men, endeavored to turn their lands to the best account with regard to profit, and either enclosing their fields, or joining many small farms into a few large ones, dismissed those useless hands, which formerly were always at their call in every attempt to subvert the government, or oppose a neighboring baron. By all these means the cities increased; the middle rank of men began to be rich and powerful; the prince, who, in effect, was the same [as] the law, was implicitly obeyed; and though the farther progress of the same causes begat a new plan of liberty, founded on the privileges of the commons. Yet in the interval between the fall of the nobles, and the rise of this order, the sovereign took advantage of the present situation, and assumed an authority almost absolute.[50]

Yet the Restoration of 1660 and the nature of the revolution of 1688 did raise questions about whether Harrington had been correct to assert that the earlier period between 1640 and 1660 had seen a process of irreversible change. Harrington had written: "Oceana, or any other nation of no extent, must have a competent nobility, or it is altogether incapable of monarchy. For where there is equality of estates, there must be equality of power; and where there is equality of power, there can be no monarchy."[51] Hume thought Harrington mistaken, writing of this passage: "Harrington thought himself so sure of his general principles, *that the balance of power depends on that of property*, that he ventured to pronounce it impossible ever to reestablish monarchy in England: but his book was scarcely published when the king was restored; and that monarchy has ever since subsisted on the same footing as before."[52] The point, however, is that the restored monarchy could not rule in the same manner as the Stuarts had previously done, or at least had aspired to do, because as Harrington correctly saw, the property relations on which it relied had fundamentally altered.

Other members of the Scottish Historical School were more sympathetic to Harrington's position. In *The Origins of the Distinction of Ranks* (1771) John Millar emphasized how the growth of commerce led to a reduction in the power of the hereditary nobility whose wealth was inherited and whose position depended on the possession of a retinue prepared to do his bidding. But it was possible even for members of this class to share in the benefits of commerce if they abandoned their formerly unproductive way of life:

A man of great fortune having dismissed his retainers, and spending a great part of his income in the purchase of commodities produced by tradesman and manufacturers, has no ground to expect that many persons will be willing either to fight for him, or to run any great hazard for promoting his interest. Whatever profit he means to obtain from the labour and assistance of others, he must give a full equivalent for it.

He must buy those personal services which are no longer to be performed either from attachment or from peculiar connections. Money, therefore, becomes more and more the only means of procuring honors and dignities; and the sordid pursuits of avarice are made subservient to the nobler pursuit of ambition.[53]

Smith took a similar view in *The Wealth of Nations* (1776), writing that "what all the violence of the feudal institutions could never have effected, the silent and insensible operation of foreign commerce and manufactures gradually brought about." In particular this was due to the unintended consequence of actions taken by two social groups, "who had not the least intention to serve the public," feudal landowners and those we would now call capitalists: "To gratify the most childish vanity was the sole motive of the great proprietors. The merchants and artificers, much less ridiculous, acted merely from a view to their own interest, and in pursuit of their own pedlar principle of turning a penny wherever a penny was to be got. Neither of them had either great knowledge or foresight of that great revolution which the folly of one, and the industry of the other, was gradually bringing about."[54]

Yet elsewhere Smith argued that the self-transformation of the noble proprietors could not be relied upon, and that the violent suppression their feudal power was essential for the rise of commercial society. As he explicitly stated in his lectures at Glasgow University delivered during the early 1760s: "The power of the nobles has always been brought to ruin before a system of liberty has been established, and this indeed must always be the case. For the nobility are the greatest opposers and oppressors of liberty that we can imagine. They hurt the liberty of the people even more than an absolute monarch." Absolute monarchy at least protected the people from the "petty lords" of their domains: "The people therefore never can have security in person or estate until the nobility have been greatly crushed."[55] In these remarks we can discern the voice Marx described as being "the *interpreter* of the frankly bourgeois upstart" who "speaks the language of the still revolutionary bourgeoisie, which has not yet subjected to itself society, the State, etc."[56] Smith diverges here from Hume, who argued that the decline of the nobility had been a spontaneous economic process that the monarchy had taken advantage of in order to establish an absolutist state. By contrast, Smith argued that at least part of the nobility had to be actively suppressed and that the preexisting absolutist state was the mechanism by which this had been achieved. Neither man discussed the relationship between the nobility and the absolutist state or how the latter was overthrown in its turn; in that sense both represented a retreat from the clarity that Harrington had achieved. Insofar as Smith does discuss this issue he implies that the dissolution of absolutism in England was rendered virtually inevitable by the commercial expansion it had itself encouraged. For, although the power of absolutism had continued to grow in France, Spain, and elsewhere in Europe: "In England alone a different government has been established from the *natural* course of things."[57] Millar was clearer than either Hume or Smith in tracing the political consequences of the supersession of landed by commercial wealth:

It cannot be doubted that these circumstances have a tendency to introduce a democratical government. As persons of inferior rank are placed in a situation which, in point of subsistence, renders them little dependent upon their superiors; as no one order of men continues in the exclusive possession of opulence; and as every man who is industrious may entertain the hope of gaining a fortune; it is to be expected that the prerogatives of the monarch and of the ancient nobility will be gradually undermined, that the privileges of the people will be extended in the same proportion, and that power, the usual attendant of wealth, will be in some measure diffused over the members of the community. . . . It may thence be expected that a conflict will arise between these two opposite parties, in which a variety of accidents may contribute to cast the balance upon either side. With respect to the issue of such a contest, it may be remarked that, in a small state, the people have been commonly successful in their attempts to establish a free constitution.[58]

Like Hume, Millar was to ground his discussion in the actual course of English history that he analyzed in a subsequent work, in his case, *An Historical View of English Government* (1787, published posthumously in 1803). Here, almost uniquely among the Scots, Millar makes direct reference to the causes and consequences of the civil war:

The adherents of the king were chiefly composed of the nobility and higher gentry, men who, by their wealth and station, had much to lose; and who, in the annihilation of the monarchy, and in the anarchy that was likely to follow, foresaw the ruin of their fortunes, and the extinction of their consideration and influence. The middling and inferior gentry, together with the inhabitants of the towns; those who entertained a jealousy of the nobles, and of the king, or who, by the changes in the state of society, had lately been raised to independence, became, on the other hand, the great supporters of parliament.[59]

Unlike most members of the Scottish Historical School, Millar was not a political economist but a protosociologist and perhaps for this reason had a greater awareness of the need for social revolution to complete a process of socioeconomic change. The greatest insights into this question came, however, from a man who was not associated with the Scottish Historical School in any way: Sir James Steuart.

Unlike Millar, Steuart certainly was a political economist. He was not the inventor of the term "political economy"—that honor goes to the French writer, Antoine de Montichretien, in his *Traicté de l'oeconomie politique* of 1615—but he did bring it into widespread usage. Nevertheless, although Hume was personally supportive toward him, most members of the Scottish Historical School and their later followers either ignored Steuart's theories or ridiculed them, in some cases simultaneously drawing on his ideas without acknowledgement. One reason for this was simply that, as Ronald Meek once put it, "Steuart was surely the unluckiest of men" in terms of timing: his magnum opus, *An Inquiry into the Principles of Political Economy* (1767), was overtaken in the public mind by Smith's *The Wealth of Nations* within a decade of its publication.[60] But this in turn was partly because of his former political career as a counterrevolutionary supporter of the Stuart dynasty who had been forced into European exile until 1763 for seventeen years after Culloden. Many of his contemporaries therefore regarded him, in the words of Donald Winch, as "a Jacobite traitor tainted with Continental notions."[61] In fact, the futility of the Jacobite enterprise after 1746 became apparent to him early in his exile (he began writing his book in 1749), but the experience of military defeat and his awareness of the conscious way in which Scottish agriculture began to be transformed after that date seems to have made him acutely sensitive to what Gramsci later called the "moment of force" in the establishment of any new economic system.[62] It was perhaps because of the distinctiveness of his personal situation among his contemporaries, that of being on the losing side in a great political and military conflict, that Steuart was able to make the greatest individual contribution to understanding the connection between socioeconomic change and social revolution since Harrington. Steuart's summary account of the emergence of the new system of political economy (the term he preferred to "commercial society") is one of those Enlightenment passages that read as if it had been directly incorporated by Marx and Engels into the opening pages of the *Manifesto of the Communist Party*:

> The great alteration in the affairs of Europe within these three centuries, by the discovery of America and the Indies, the springing up of industry and learning, the introduction of trade and the luxurious arts, the establishment of public credit, and a general system of taxation, have entirely altered the plan of government everywhere. From feudal and military, it is become free and commercial. I oppose freedom in government to the feudal system, to mark only that there is not found now that chain of subordination among subjects, which made the essential part of the feudal form.... Formerly the power of the barons swallowed up the independency of all inferior classes. I oppose commercial to military; because the military governments are now made to subsist from the consequences and effects of commerce only: that is, from the revenue of the state, proceeding from taxes. Formerly, every thing was brought about by numbers; now, numbers of men cannot be kept together without money. This is sufficient to point out the nature of the revolution in the political state, and of consequences in the manners of Europe.[63]

At this point, early in his book, Steuart expresses the themes common to all his Scottish contemporaries and to Harrington before them. Yet even here his emphasis on the impact of these changes on states and how they react in turn indicates his willingness to probe these issues more deeply than any previous thinker. He did this in two respects.

First, Steuart argued, like Smith, that the power of the feudal lords must certainly be broken if the new "system of political economy" was to become dominant. But if this were not to take place through a destructive revolution from below, politicians ("statesmen") must implement the changes themselves from above. Unlike Smith, he understands that this represents an inescapable moment of danger for the absolutist state. If these reforms were completed, they could not but involve the transformation of the state itself. If they were not completed, the politicians who left them unfinished would be swept aside by the very forces they had hoped to forestall:

In countries where the government is lodged in the hands of the great lords, as is the case in all aristocracies, as was the case under the feudal government, and as is still the case in many countries in Europe, where trade, however, and industry are gaining ground; the statesman who sets the new system of political economy on foot, may depend upon it, that either his attempt will fail, or the constitution of the government will change. If he destroys all arbitrary dependence between individuals, the wealth of the industrious will share, if not totally root out the power of the grandees. If he allows such a dependence to subsist, his project will fail. . . . Some kingdoms have been quit for a bloody rebellion or a long civil war. Other countries have likewise demonstrated the force of the principles here laid down: a wealthy populace has broken their chains to pieces, and overturned the very foundations of the feudal system. All these violent convulsions have been owing to the short-sightedness of statesman; who, inattentive to the consequences of growing wealth and industry, foolishly imagined that hereditary subordination was to subsist among classes, whose situation, with respect to each other, was entirely changed.[64]

In retrospect, these passages seem to predict the alternative paths to overturning "the very foundations of the feudal system," both of which led to the changes in "the constitution of the government": the French path, involving a series of partial reforms, which he had witnessed himself in exile, the consequences of which Steuart warned against; and the Prussian, which he commended to statesmen, but to which they would turn after 1848, partly as a result of the French experience.

Second, Steuart also recognizes that the role of force cannot be restricted only to breaking the social and political dominance of the lords—it must also be exercised against those over whom they had previously ruled: "That revolution must then mark the purging of the lands of superfluous mouths, and forcing those to quit their mother earth, in order to retire to towns and villages, where they may usefully swell the numbers of free hands and apply to industry."[65] In *The Wealth of Nations* Smith discussed the "original accumulation" of capital in terms of the capacity of capitalists to save, in passages notable for their uncharacteristic evasiveness and self-delusion. By contrast, Steuart presents a frank and unflinching vision of the same process as involving the forcing of the peasantry off the land, compelling them into wage labor, and freeing the land for productive investment. "Unlike Steuart," writes Michael Perelman, "Smith wrote what the reading public wanted to find." Specifically, Smith argued that "the market alone was capable of bringing about economic development." This was not an illusion that Steuart would ever have entertained, but the illusion was what his audience required. As Perelman writes, his "honesty . . . guaranteed his obscurity."[66]

Despite his relatively peripheral position in British intellectual life, there was one respect in which Steuart's work reflected a more general shift, or rather a recapitulation of the concept of revolution that had briefly crystallized in the work of Harrington. At many points in *An Inquiry into the Principles of Political Economy*, two from which I have already quoted, Steuart uses the term "revolution" in ways that indicate a sudden or dramatic change in socioeconomic conditions with epochal consequences.[67] And in this respect, if in no other, he was at one with his contemporaries. In 1776 Smith wrote in *The Wealth of Nations* that the respective fates of the Greek city-states, Carthage, and the Roman Empire in the West constituted the three "great revolution[s] in the affairs of mankind."[68] During the same year, Edward Gibbon began *The Decline and Fall of the Roman Empire* by explaining that his subject is the "memorable series of revolutions," lasting thirteen centuries that brought about the decline and fall; a process the cumulative effect of which was "a revolution which will ever be remembered, and is still felt by the nations of the earth."[69] The appropriate term now lay at hand, should a similarly momentous event occur.

4 THE AMERICAN THEORY OF POLITICAL REVOLUTION

The classic works by Smith and Gibbon were both published in 1776, as the tensions in Britain's American colonies finally exploded into open warfare. Thomas Paine, English-born, but perhaps the most compelling publicist of the American case, exalted to his new compatriots: "We have it in our power to begin the world over again."[1] After independence had been achieved, the leaders of the American Revolution, as the process was described by all sides, took the view that this was in fact what had occurred. James Madison explained that they had rejected "those forms which have crushed the liberties of the rest of mankind" and claimed: "They accomplished a revolution which has no parallel in the annals of human society."[2] Paine disagreed. On returning to America in 1802, after narrowly evading persecution in both Britain and France, he recalled his earlier optimism, now faded, in the last of a series of open letters. What, he asked, was the "independence of America" supposed to involve? "It was the opportunity of beginning the world anew, as it were and of bringing forward a new system of government in which the rights of all men should be preserved that gave value to independence."[3]

It is obvious then, that even before General Cornwallis surrendered at Yorktown, there were major disagreements about what the Revolution was intended to achieve. Afterward these intensified as participants, including revolutionary leaders, wondered what it had in fact achieved. These disputes have been reproduced in the subsequent historiography.[4] The dominant tendency has been a conservative one that emphasizes the purely political nature of the Revolution. Gordon Wood has observed, in a sophisticated version of this argument, the "social assault" the Americans waged on colonial society "was not the type we are used to today in describing revolutions":

> The great social antagonisms of the American Revolution were not poor versus rich, workers versus employers, or even democrats versus aristocrats. They were patriots versus courtiers—categories appropriated to the monarchical world in which the colonists had been reared. Courtiers were persons whose position or rank came artificially from above—from hereditary or personal connections that ultimately flowed

from the crown or court. . . . Patriots . . . were those who not only loved their country but were free of dependent connections and influence; their position or rank came naturally from their talent and from below, from recognition by the people.[5]

Views of this sort have been challenged by successive generations of radical, socialist, and Marxist critics who objected to the way in which these accounts downplayed or completely ignored both the role of supposed minority groups (Native Americans, blacks, women) and the social conflicts that occurred *within* the revolutionary side.[6] But valuable though alternative accounts are, they do not answer the question of whether or not events between 1776 and 1783 constituted a social revolution against precapitalist forms, since popular insurgencies during these years tended to be concerned either with the defense or extension of the franchise, or with resisting the inequalities resulting from existing *capitalist* relations of production. As Gary Nash writes of the merchants and planters who led the Revolution: "For these reluctant revolutionaries, 'freedom,' 'security,' and 'order' were the watchwords of *their* revolution. Challenging them from below were those who honored 'equality' and 'equity' as the watchwords of their revolution."[7] As Nash suggests, there were in effect two revolutions within the War of Independence and, in this respect at least, it fell into the same pattern as its predecessors. The Dutch Revolt and, to a far greater extent, the English Civil War involved two social revolutions that temporarily converged in opposition to foreign or native absolutism. One, which was successful, to consolidate the supremacy of capitalist relations of production; the other, which failed, to achieve equality of condition—a revolution that was, implicitly at least, directed as much against the new capitalism as the old feudalism. The American War of Independence was different, not in relation to the second type of revolution but to the *first*. Unlike the Dutch or the English, the Americans did not have to liberate themselves from a feudal absolutist state, but rather from a constitutional monarchy that emerged from the settlement of 1688, which they accused of betraying by behaving in an absolutist manner, which the Declaration of Independence variously describes as an "absolute despotism" and "absolute Tyranny."[8] The chief justice of South Carolina William Henry Drayton even argued that George III had committed acts against the American colonists that were more extreme than those committed by James II and VII against his British subjects. Pauline Maier summarizes his views:

> Drayton proceeded to compare, point by point, the charges against James II in the Declaration of Rights with the record of George III. King James "broke the original contract by not affording due protection to his subjects," but was not charged with seizing their towns, or laying them in ruins, or seizing their vessels, or with pursuing the people with "fire and sword" or declaring them rebels "for resisting his armies leveled to destroy their lives, liberties, and properties," all of which "George III had done . . . against America."[9]

Did this mean that the socioeconomic basis of the British imperial and American colonial states was the same?

THE ABSENCE OF FEUDALISM IN THE UNITED STATES

Thinkers in the classical Marxist tradition from Marx and Engels to Gramsci tended to assume that there had never been feudalism in the United States and that, even before the proclamation of the republic, society there was entirely bourgeois. This seemed to explain for them, as it did for the later school of Hartzian liberals, the failure of socialist ideas to achieve European levels of penetration in the working class.[10] Against this, some Marxists have emphasized how feudalism did exist, but was extinguished by the Revolution: "All of the Crown restrictions on the ready acquisition of western lands were ended. Primogeniture and entail, feudal remnants, were dealt their death blow by the revolution, and within 15 years after the Declaration of Independence were abolished in every state. These changes, together with the confiscation and breakup of the huge Tory estates constituted a virtual land revolution, opening the way for the population of the western lands on the basis of small free holding."[11]

Both positions contain serious distortions. It is true that capitalist development was uneven across the colonies. In some parts of North America, beginning in Massachusetts where the English Puritans first settled after 1630, it was from the beginning very far advanced indeed—perhaps in advance of England itself, since the structures of feudal absolutist power were far weaker. In others, such as the royal colony of Virginia after 1624 and particularly after 1642, the Cavaliers who ran it were intent on re-creating precisely the forms of social organization that was being destroyed across the Atlantic, first with white indentured servants, then black African slaves.[12] It is also true that there were three genuine attempts to install or "revive" systemic feudalism in a new colonial context, in New York, Maryland, and the Carolinas—as we have seen, in the case of the latter with a constitution involving hereditary serfdom drawn up by Mr. Agrarian Capitalism himself, John Locke. All were resisted; all failed. The main feudal mechanism that was consistently attempted was the charging of quit rents in lieu of certain kinds of labor service or other obligations. But since these obligations had not, in most cases, been performed by tenants in the first place, this represented less the introduction of feudalism and more a device by absentee capitalist landlords to supplement the rent paid by their tenants.[13] Feudal projects collapsed in the seventeenth century, not because America was too progressive to endure them, but because it was too primitive to sustain them. A feudal order necessarily implies a differentiation of function far beyond the capacity of new societies to create. In every colony the demographic base was too narrow.[14]

Some of the revolutionary radicals did polemicize against feudalism. William Gordon, the author of one the first histories of the Revolution, argued in 1776 that property qualifications for voting were "the most hurtful remnant of the Feudal Constitution."[15] The most detailed discussion of the question, however, was by John Adams, in a series of articles published in the *Boston Gazette* in 1765 and eventually published as "A Dissertation on the Canon and Feudal Law." Adams cites Kames and Rousseau as authorities to prove "the feudal system to be inconsistent with liberty and the rights of mankind."[16] His main point, however, is to demonstrate that the British monarchy was intent on imposing feudalism on the colonies:

> The first step that is intended, seems to be an entire subversion of the whole system of our fathers, by the introduction of the canon and feudal law into America. The canon and feudal systems, though greatly mutilated in England, are not yet destroyed. Like the temples and palaces in which the great contrivers of them once worshipped and inhabited, they exist in ruins; and much of the domineering spirit of them still remains. The designs and labors of a certain society, to introduce the former of them into America, have been well exposed to the public by a writer of great abilities; and the further attempts to the same purpose, that may be made by that society, or by the ministry or parliament, I leave to the conjectures of the thoughtful. But it seems very manifest from the Stamp Act itself, that a design is formed to strip us in a great measure of the means of knowledge, by loading the press, the colleges, and even an almanac and a newspaper, with restraints and duties; and to introduce the inequalities and dependencies of the feudal system, by taking from the poorer sort of people all their little subsistence, and conferring it on a set of stamp officers, distributors, and their deputies.[17]

Alas, restrictions on the franchise and interference with the freedom of the press are compatible with, or even characteristic of capitalist societies. In this context, it is significant that once independence had been achieved, discussion of the subject virtually ceased. The main subsequent consideration of feudalism among the writings of the Founding Fathers, by Alexander Hamilton, makes no reference to America but takes Scotland as a paradigmatic case and is in any case mainly (and typically) concerned with feudalism as a political system to show how confederacy can thwart or prevent the effective national government he wished to see the United States develop.[18]

Sons of 1688

Allen Kulikoff answers the question posed in the title of his article "Was the American Revolution a Bourgeois Revolution?" in the affirmative, "because its ideology meshed with bourgeois ideals, and the contingencies of war and state formation accelerated capitalist development. But the Revolution did not lead to a final or even partial victory for the bourgeoisie" (87). As I will argue later, bourgeois revolutions can be achieved without the guidance of bourgeois ideology or the bourgeoisie achieving direct power ("victory"); the really decisive issue is the extent to which the American Revolution contributed to capitalist development. On the latter point Kulikoff is on much stronger ground. Nevertheless two areas of doubt remain. One is whether the state itself was transformed into an institution geared to capital accumulation. The other, related issue, as Kulikoff himself recognizes, is that "slavery, supported by cotton production, became even more fully embedded in the South" (88).

The real obstacle to capitalist development in North America was not feudalism but slavery, the extension of which was enabled precisely by the success of the War of Independence. Slavery is not, of course, necessarily incompatible with capitalism, but in the South it became the basis of an entire society, and ultimately of a short-lived state (the Confederacy), the expansionist aims of which had they been successful, would have blocked or even rolled back the development of capitalism in the Americas, and perhaps even beyond. We might therefore agree with Kulikoff that the War of Independence constituted "an essential first step" (89), in the bourgeois revolution, but the decisive leap was still to come. But this is to anticipate events: for the purposes of this discussion, it is enough to note that the War of Independence involved a *political* revolution against British rule that neither achieved nor consolidated any change in social relations. Instead, it allowed all the social relations that existed in America—including small commodity production, capitalism, and slavery—to continue as before without the interference of the Crown in Parliament. But of all the different types of social relations it was capitalism that was initially the weakest. As Michael Merrill has pointed out, the principal difference between the Democratic Republicans and the Federalists following the achievement of independence was in their attitude to "commercial society." Smith could be invoked by both sides, of course, but insofar as he was in favor of a stable agrarian society in which the main economic actors were yeoman farmers and landowners (slave owners were a different matter), this could be done with greater credibility by the former. The latter, above all Hamilton, were interested in developing something closer to what we would now think of as capitalism—although as Merrill notes, this was largely as a means to an end, the end being the elevation of the monied commercial and industrial interest as a base to provide revenue through taxes and customs to construct a viable state power. In the short term it was the agrarians organized in the Democratic Republican Party who won out, following the victory of Thomas Jefferson in the presidential election of 1800.[19] As one of Hamilton's biographers observes, unlike the other founders of the Republic, who "were content merely to effect a political revolution," Hamilton saw the role of Lawgiver differently: "He set out to effect what amounted to a social revolution."[20] And he failed. The hostility of his opponents to the prospect of industrialization is suggested in a letter from Thomas Jefferson to John Jay in which he pondered what would become of "the cultivators" when the lands available to the republic were eventually full, resulting in agricultural overproduction and "a surplus of hands": "I should then perhaps turn them to the sea in preference to manufactures, because comparing the characters of the two classes I find the former to be the most valuable citizens. I consider the class of artificers as the panders of vice and the instruments by which the liberties of a country are generally overturned. However we are not free to decide this question on grounds of theory only."[21]

But whatever their other differences, the theoreticians of the American Revolution took as their historical reference point not 1649, but rather "the one major predecessor almost universally admired by contemporaries, however differently they interpreted it: England's Revolution of 1688."[22] In Madison's words, 1688 was "when a revolution took place in the government," rather than a social transformation—an interpretation that can be sustained only by treating the Glorious Revolution as a single episode rather than the culmination of a process stretching back fifty years, in which the most decisive moments had already occurred.[23] It is often assumed that, as a theoretical expression of this identification with 1688, their guiding political ideology was drawn from Locke's defense of the right to revolution, if not directly then filtered through the writings of later Whig radicals such as the authors of *Cato's Letters*, Trenchard and Gordon, who popularized the Lockean, Country Party ideology.[24] However, according to John Dunn's devastating assessment, few people in America had either read Locke or absorbed his views through more widespread dissemination before the Revolution. Locke was mainly known in the United States for his epistemological works. His political writings were not widely known outside of England; where they were known they were not considered particularly original, those aspects that were considered original were thought to be wrong, and insofar as they defended the revolution they were merely part of a far wider literature.[25] The most direct example of Locke's influence occurs in the wording of the Declaration of Independence itself, where Locke's claim that "political society" arose for the "mutual Preservation of . . . Lives, Liberties and Estates" finds an echo in the actually quite different assertion that "all men are endowed by their Creator with certain inalienable Rights," including "Life, Liberty, and the pursuit of happiness."[26] The former claims that, at some point in history, a contractual relationship was established between men to ensure their continued survival through constitutional protections for both their persons and their property: political rights exist to preserve economic relationships. The latter imagines that at the moment of creation, God conferred upon men not merely existence, but the freedom to pursue their own self-actualization. Locke is secular and materialist while the Declaration is religious and metaphysical; consequently, to discuss the latter as if it were a version of the former is to commit a category mistake. In effect, those modern Americans who think that capitalism is somehow enshrined in the Declaration can only do so by ignoring what the Founding Fathers actually wrote and pretending their views were identical with those of Locke, who was at any rate dealing with economic issues. In fact, as Garry Wills has confirmed, Jefferson, the main author, was far more influenced by the Scots, above all Kames and Dalrymple, than Locke.[27] But even here, in the absence of feudalism, what the Americans found important in the work of their Scottish contemporaries was not their theories of economic transition or social revolution, but in the realm of politics, above all in their hostility to participatory democracy, their concern with the unintended consequences of political action and their support for the rational construction of a balanced structure of government—all the most conservative aspects of the Scottish Enlightenment, in other words.[28]

It would seem unlikely that Locke's greater predecessor would have exercised more influence than he. Yet, as Judith Shklar once wrote, "If Harrington's ideas ever played any part in political life, it was in America." This claim may seem counterintuitive, but as Shklar continues, the reception of seventeenth-century English thought in the American colonies involved "de-radicalizing both Locke and Harrington": "The individualism of Locke was toned down and Harrington's demand for a harmony of interest was overlooked—probably because both had been realized to a sufficient degree not to be real challenges."[29] It was this that allowed Benjamin Rush, for example, to write in 1777: "Mr. Locke is an oracle as to the *principles*, Harrington and Montesquieu are oracles as to the *forms* of government."[30] In fact, the Americans did draw from Harrington his central understanding of the relationship between property and power. Madison, for example, wrote: "Government is instituted no less for protection of the property, than of the persons of individuals. This one as well as the other, therefore, may be considered as represented by those who are charged with the government. . . . The rights of property are committed into the same hands with the property rights. Some attention ought therefore to be paid to property in the choice of those hands."[31] Or as John Jay put it more simply: "The people who own the country ought to govern it."[32] But these admirably frank sentiments are not directed at both the monarchy *and* the "poor," as they were for example in the English Parliamentary debates of 1659, but simply at the latter. Madison was disturbed at the prospect of Republic being divided by what he called "factions," which he understood in essentially class terms: "The most common and durable source of factions, has been the various and unequal distribution of property. Those who hold, and those who are without property, have ever formed distinct interests in society. . . . A landed interest, a manufacturing interest, a mercantile interest, a monied interest, with many lesser interests, grow up of necessity in civilized nations, and divide them into different classes, actuated by different sentiments and views."[33] They nevertheless saw themselves as members of an international bourgeois class. In the aftermath of the War of Independence the victorious republic sent one of its ablest figures, Benjamin Franklin, to act as ambassador to the court of Absolutist France and in his post, Franklin deported himself as a member of his class, even at the relatively trivial level of dress and behavior:

> Franklin would never have dreamed of giving up his way of life, after moving to the extravagant neighbourhood of the French Royal household. He went about Paris and Versailles in a dress readily recognized by all as Third Estate garb. He wore his clothes with the same pride with which the marquises and dukes of France wore their silk coats. Deeply convinced that his middle-class country—and the republican form of government—represented the future, Franklin forced, by his appearance, the French nobility to honor his personality. . . . He daily defied his detested class enemy and put new heart into his French class-comrades.[34]

The American Revolution had divided opinion in Britain, but not in any fundamental way, since no one, including the rebellious colonists themselves, believed that it was intended to establish a new form of society. The alignment of supporters and opponents of the colonists naturally contained a class component and the issue acted as conductor for tensions within British society, with those excluded from political representation, notably Dissenters and the industrial classes, strongly supportive of the American case.[35] The secession of the colonies threatened the edifice of British imperial rule of course, but there was no agreement within Britain that maintaining an empire was in the long-term interest of national economic development: Smith for one thought that it was not.[36] "The American Revolution was a crucial inspiration for the French, Dutch, German and British democrats alike," writes Jonathan Israel: "But from the radical standpoint, it was also disturbingly defective, truncated revolution."[37] The French Revolution, which had far less immediate impact on Britain, was almost immediately seen as a different order of event, a different type of revolution, upon which no polite agreement to disagree was possible. "By the eighteenth century, everyone—finally even Louis XVI himself—knew what the events of 1789 should be called: not a revolt, sire, but a revolution."[38] The French revolutionaries, much as many of them admired the American experiment in republicanism, knew this. "The characteristic difference between your revolution and ours," wrote French radical aristocrat Sophie d'Houdetot to Jefferson in 1790 "is that having nothing to destroy, you had nothing to injure."[39] The Scottish Whig, Henry Cockburn, left a famous description of the atmosphere the French Revolution produced in Britain around 1800, but his comments are also true for the rest of Europe and the Americas: "Everything rung, and was connected with the Revolution in France; which for above 20 years, was, or was made, the all in all. Everything, nor this or that thing, but literally everything, was soaked in this one event."[40] An event of these cataclysmic proportions could not leave the theory of social revolution untouched, first of all, in the site of the revolution itself.

5

THE CONTRADICTIONS
OF THE FRENCH REVOLUTION (1):
BARNAVE AND HIS CONTEMPORARIES

French capitalism in 1789 was certainly much less developed than English capitalism in 1640, especially in the countryside, but it did exist, and often involved far more advanced forms of industrial wage labor than had existed in England during the previous century. In a speech to the National Assembly in September 1789, the Abbé Emmanuel Joseph Sieyès portrayed a world in which "political systems, today, are founded exclusively on labour: the productive faculties of man are all," and described "the largest number of men" as "nothing but laboring machines."[1] Such a world was far from being completely achieved even in Britain by that date; but it was the world that the French bourgeoisie wanted to achieve, that they saw emerging in England after 1688 and Scotland after 1746, and that was theorized by the thinkers of the Scottish Historical School. For Ellen Meiksins Wood, these aspirations had nothing to do with a desire to dispense with feudalism. She writes of the "bourgeois actors" of the French Enlightenment and Revolution that "their quarrel with the aristocracy has little to do with liberating capitalism from the fetters of feudalism." This, apparently, was because the Enlightenment itself was "rooted in noncapitalist social property relations" that represented "an alternative route out of feudalism."[2] Wood is referring, of course, to absolutism—or rather, her own special conception of absolutism as a mode of production, rather than the form taken by the late feudal state. However, the congruence between Scottish and French Enlightenment theory casts doubt on this thesis.

As Michel Malherbe notes, "Scottish philosophy exercised an ascendancy over Continental Europe from about 1760 to about 1840; mainly over Germany and France." One of the key moments in establishing this ascendancy was the virtually immediate translation of *The Wealth of Nations* into these languages (the academic distinction between "philosophy" and other forms of inquiry such as "economics" had not yet been established).[3] In 1790, a year into the revolution, Nicolas de Condorcet published a 220-page summary of Smith's work that he described as one of those "which does most honor to Great Britain."[4] Nor was French admiration for

the Scots restricted to works of theory: one semi-anonymous member of the National Assembly wrote an account in 1790 that enviously noted how far Scotland
had advanced in fifty years, how superior Scottish intellectual life now was to that
of England, and how much wealthier Scottish peasants were than those of France.[5]
Unsurprisingly then, we find very similar statements celebrating the overthrow of
feudalism in the Scottish and French countryside during the early 1790s. In 1792
the Reverend Mr. John Morrison, minister for the parish of Canisbay in Caithness,
could report to Sir John Sinclair: "Emancipation is everywhere prevailing, and the
monster Feudalism is hiding his head in shame."[6] The previous year, an address
from the Commune of Lourmarin to the Constituent Assembly of 1791 had declared: "We announce to you with peaceful joy that the destruction of the feudal
regime will bring death to aristocrats. It is in the hope of re-establishing it that
they emigrate, conspire and bestir themselves in all directions. . . . When you have
banished the monster feudalism, the aristocracy will be destroyed for ever and the
fields that are so desolate today will become the finest rampart of the Republic."[7]
Behind the similarities of language there are indeed differences in meaning, but
these are not because the benighted French peasants were dealing with absolutist
social property relations that they unaccountably mistook for feudalism. If the Scots
had been unable to accept the early eighteenth-century French support for the feudal system, the late eighteenth-century French were equally unable to accept the
Scottish unwillingness to address how the feudal system could be overthrown. It
was for this reason that the French were critical of aspects of Scottish doctrine, not
because the former were dealing with post-feudal, precapitalist social property relations unknown to the latter. The problem for the French was that, unlike the
Scots, they had no benevolent state that would intervene to remove feudal obstacles
to capitalism, since the state itself constituted the main obstacle to doing so. For
the Reverend Morrison then, the "monster feudalism" was a residual set of social
relationships that need to be abolished from above by improving landowners—
who in many cases were former feudal lords—supported by rank-and-file literati
like Morrison himself, while overall stability was guaranteed by the British state.
For the anonymous citizens of Lourmarin, who had themselves been victims of
the "monster feudalism," it remained embodied in the membership of a still-to-
be-defeated aristocracy whose final displacement required the consolidation of an
entirely new state.

These differences also took theoretical forms. Smith's *The Theory of Moral Sentiments* (1759), for example, had begun to attract attention in France during the
economic debates in the Assembly of Notables during 1788, mainly from readers
of *The Wealth of Nations* who wanted to explore his ideas further. During the Revolution, during the very Terror itself, the Jacobin Pierre-Louis Roederer undertook
a critique of the earlier work, apparently so distant from the central issues of power.
Although an admirer of Smith, Roederer was unhappy with the central argument
in *The Theory of Moral Sentiments*. Smith had claimed that human beings were mo-

tivated by impulses ("sentiments") that had their origin outside of self-interest: through the exercise of sympathy, men and women could empathize with others and vicariously enjoy or suffer their experiences. In lectures delivered in 1793, two months after the execution of Louis XVI, Roederer opposed Smith on two grounds. First, his was a dangerous doctrine, because it presented false arguments for both social inequality and admiring riches: not sympathy but the desire for emulation was the key, otherwise why should Frenchmen not admire the parasitic nobility who had contributed nothing toward their own wealth and who were now engaged in counterrevolution? Second, it had political implications, for if, as Smith suggested, the principle of sympathy inclined toward monarchy (albeit on the English model established in 1688), then what was to prevent a new or restored dynasty emerging even if, as in France, the king was executed and monarchy abolished?[8] For Roederer—incredible though this may seem in an age when Smith has been repackaged as the high priest of market fundamentalism—the author of *The Wealth of Nations* was insufficiently hostile to the nobility and insufficiently committed to the market.

Barnave Rediscovers the Social Revolution

In spite of these differences with the Scots, the formulations used by the French theorists to describe the origins of their revolution are still very similar to those used by the most acute of their British predecessors, Harrington, Steuart, and Millar. In particular, they similarly rejected explanations based on contingency and argued instead for an interpretation that was both social and based on general developments of an international character. These characteristics are best displayed in a manuscript by the greatest of all the French writers, Antoine Barnave, written in 1792, but only published after his death as "Introduction to the French Revolution." Barnave had read Ferguson's *History of Civil Society*, Hume's *History of England*, Smith's *The Wealth of Nations* and possibly also his *Theory of Moral Sentiments*, and Steuart's *Principles of Political Economy*; references suggest that he had also read Robertson's *History of America* and *History of Charles V* and that, if he was not familiar with Millar, then his thought was heading in the same direction.[9]

Typically, and unsurprisingly, revisionist attempts have been made to deny that Barnave's admirably self-explanatory text means what it says. Thus we learn from David Bates: "Despite efforts to place Barnave within a tradition of materialist interpretations of history . . . this fundamental text is not really an attempt to uncover economic or social structures that mechanically produce the events of the Revolution, 'beneath' the superstructural activities of the revolutionaries." Instead, "Barnave . . . wanted to understand how the inner nature of man, and the fundamental character of French society, were expressing themselves through externally visible historical forms, forms that could very well resist and pervert these foundational realities."[10] What does Barnave himself say?

We shall try in vain to form a correct idea of the great revolution which has just convulsed France if we consider it in isolation, detaching it from the history of the great states that surround us and the centuries that have preceded our own. . . . Certainly, revolutions of governments, like all natural phenomena which depend on the passions and will of man, cannot be subjected to those fixed, calculable laws which apply to the movements of inanimate matter. However, among the multitude of causes whose combined influence produces political events, there are some which are so intimately connected with the nature of things—whose regular and constant action dominates so clearly over accidental causes—that after a certain period of time that almost inevitably produce their effect. Almost always it is such elements that change the face of nations. All minor events are caught up in their general results. They prepare the great epochs of history, while the secondary causes to which [these epochs] are almost always attributed only serve to occasion them.[11]

Barnave argued that the French Revolution was an aspect of the transition to commercial society: "As the natural development of societies is to grow ceaselessly in population and industry until they have attained the highest degree of civilisation, the establishment of manufactures and of commerce should naturally succeed agriculture." But the process of "succession" had not occurred automatically in France, nor would it elsewhere in Europe: "Two powerful forces can considerably hasten or retard the progress of this last epoch: the geographical situation, which calls men to commerce or isolates them, opens or closes the sea to them; and political institutions, which make them esteem or despise commerce and direct their activity toward the arts of war, which diminish the population and inhibit wealth, or toward peaceful crafts which rapidly multiply men and goods."[12]

If the first "force" discussed by Barnave ("geographical situation") looks back to the environmental determinism of Montesquieu, the second ("political institutions") looks forward to the historical materialism of Marx. The former sees the determinations acting on human social development as lying prior to economic activity, in the geographical and topographical situations into which humans are born; the latter sees them as lying above it, in what Marx would call the superstructures that humans create for themselves, sometimes unintentionally, out of their economic activity. Much of this analysis could be found, for example, in Robertson; but the new focus on political institutions, and the implication that these might have to be overthrown in order to establish those appropriate to the latest stages of development, indicates that Barnave and the revolutionary French bourgeoisie to which he belonged had now overtaken the Scottish Historical School in the same way as its members had earlier overtaken the French Physiocrats. Here Barnave explains the movement from economic to social to political change:

Gradually the advances of the social state create new sources of power, weaken the old ones, and change the balance of forces. . . . So governments change form, sometimes by a slow imperceptible development and sometimes by violent shocks. . . . once the [mechanical] arts and commerce have succeeded in penetrating the people and creating a new means of wealth in support of the industrious classes (*classe laborieuse*), a revolution in political laws is prepared. Just as the possession of land gave rise to the aristocracy, industrial property increases the power of the people: they acquire their liberty, they multiply, they begin to influence affairs.[13]

France was not the first country to experience these developments, but in those which had experienced them earlier the revolution had been conducted on a different ideological basis: the English Revolution had occurred in the context of the Reformation, the French in that of the Enlightenment: "Because of the difference in the times the ferment of opinion that sustained democratic power in England was the passion of religious reform; in France the passion of philosophizing (*philosophisme*)—the former made the impetus more violent. The latter chiefly weakened the obstacles." Yet both events were examples of the "democratic explosion": "The democratic principle, almost stifled in all European governments as long as the feudal regime remained vigorous, has since that time increasingly gathered strength and moved towards its fulfillment."[14] But who would be exercising the "democratic principle"? Barnave did not, of course, specify who "the people" were, or how many of them would exercise the "democratic principle." As we have seen, this was a longstanding problem in bourgeois revolutions, extending at least as far back as the English Civil War; but democracy was certainly a more capacious notion for him than it was for Harrington or Locke: Albert Soboul was perhaps being unfair when he wrote, "Barnave writes *people* where we understand *bourgeoisie*."[15] Nevertheless, there were clear limits to how far Barnave was prepared to extend democracy. The French bourgeoisie had less economic power and a far stronger absolutist opponent than the English, and for this reason they had to rely to a greater extent on the intervention of a popular majority to overthrow the old regime; but they were also acutely aware that the masses upon whose strength they relied had other views about society, however unrealizable these might have been in the short term.

Here was the essence of Barnave's dilemma. The attentive reader will have noticed that Barnave wrote his "Introduction" in the year prior to his death, In fact, it was written in prison while he awaited trial and eventual execution for treason, specifically for plotting counterrevolution with the French royal family. This was not because Barnave was uncertain as to his own class position. "I hope," he wrote, "that the class to which I belong will be raised from the state of humiliation, to which a senseless government seems to condemn it more and more."[16] And *class* had by this time acquired its modern connotations. By the mid-eighteenth century: "Unlike the older language of orders, estates, degrees, and so forth, *classe* was part of a new language and a new way of thought which specifically isolated public functions from private (economic) interests and activities in ways which allowed the two to be cogently contrasted and opposed to one another."[17]

Barnave had been a member of the Jacobin Club before leading his followers out of it early in 1791 to take a position on the most moderate wing of the revolutionary movement. In effect, Barnave wanted France to have the equivalent of the English constitutional monarchy of 1688 before the equivalent of the English revolutionary dictatorship of 1649 had made it possible. This was not because he was opposed to violence as such: he famously dismissed the lynching of Jean-François

Foullon and Berthier de Sauvigny after the storming of the Bastille by saying that their blood was "not of the purest." It was rather because of the social implications of popular violence. He made his concerns explicit in a famous speech to the National Assembly on July 15, 1791: "Are we going to finish this revolution or start another? ... You have made all men equal in the eyes of the law; you have installed civil and political equality. One step further would be a fatal and unpardonable act. One step further along the path of equality would mean the destruction of private property."[18] As Ralph Miliband writes, this was "an explicit appeal for the repression of the radical movement" together with "a no less explicit appeal to the aristocracy for an acceptance of what had been achieved."[19] The very sensitivity that Barnave showed toward the changing nature of class power made him conscious of the need to bring the Revolution to an end, once what he regarded as the decisive victory had been achieved, with the ascendancy of a commercial "aristocracy" over the feudal nobility: "The aristocracy which today rules most of the republics of Europe has nothing in common with the equestrian and feudal nobility." Instead it is a "bourgeois aristocracy which ordinarily becomes the dominant element in commercial republics." The two sources of power are "military force and money" and it is the latter that is exercised in the commercial republics: "The rich capitalists, having nothing above them, become an aristocracy in relation to the people, while in the monarchies they remain [part of the] democracy, in opposition to the equestrian nobility and military power."[20] This brilliantly summarizes the position, not only of the "rich capitalists," but insofar as he represented their views, that of himself and his followers: they were ceasing to be part of "the people." In a speech to the National Assembly on November 25, 1790, Adam Philippe, Comte de Custine, asked: "Will this Assembly, which has destroyed all kinds of aristocracy, flinch before the aristocracy of capitalists, these cosmopolitans whose only fatherland is the one in which they can pile up their riches?"[21] Miliband's assessment of Barnave is valid, not only for its subject but for the majority of bourgeois politicians that would follow him in the nineteenth century: "In a sense, he was the victim of his own class consciousness; for that very class consciousness, which gave him so lucid a view of the causes of the Revolution, also fatally narrowed his field of political action."[22]

ROEDERER: INDUSTRIAL CAPITALIST AND REVOLUTIONARY BOURGEOIS

Barnave wrote "Introduction to the French Revolution" three years into the upheaval that would claim his life; Roederer, whom we have already met as a critic of Smith, also composed an analysis of events, but only after they had run their course. This remarkable figure was a lawyer, as his father had been before him, from a family that had been ennobled earlier in the eighteenth century; but his membership in the First Estate should alert us to the difficulties caused by accepting the classificatory criteria of the French absolutist state as a substitute for social analysis. Unusual among the leading political figures of the Revolution, Roederer was also an industrial capitalist with substantial interests, through marriage, in the glass industry in Lorraine. In 1786, he extended these interests by acquiring quarter shares of the Saint-Quirin glassworks in Metz as a result of his legal work on behalf of the company in breaking the state monopoly of its rival, Royal Saint Gobain. This gave Roederer a stake in a factory that used the most advanced technologies and employed between six hundred and seven hundred workers. Prior to the Revolution Roederer had possessed the venal office of Councilor to the Parliament of Metz. During the Revolution he became a deputy in the National Assembly, where he was a strong advocate of both representative democracy, in which suffrage would be on an individual basis rather than by Estate, and of free trade, by which the privileges of the monopolies would be abolished.[23] Like Barnave, Roederer was a member of the Jacobin Club, although he joined after the former had departed, under the Constitutional Monarchy of 1791–92; unlike Barnave, he survived the revolution to the end, seeing it conclude as a Bonapartist during the Hundred Days in 1815, but later reentering political life during the Restoration. Although his central work, "The Spirit of the Revolution of 1789" remained unpublished until 1831, it was written at the very end of the Revolution in 1815 and was therefore able to incorporate insights obtained from all stages of the process.

We should first note Roederer's exasperated dismissal of the argument that the French Revolution was simply a political squabble without social content: "And what a goal for a nation of twenty-five million men, what a deplorable goal for such a deployment of forces and wills—the overthrow of a king and his replacement by some upstart!"[24] Like Barnave, Roederer too noted the ideological change that had already taken place prior to 1789: "The revolution was made in men's minds and habits before it was made into law." And he thought he knew in whose minds these changes had occurred: "It was the opinion of the middle class that gave the signal to the lower classes."[25] The middle class, in his account are "the bourgeoisie," whom he describes as being "the first possessors of capital as the seigneurs had been the first possessors of the land."[26] But he did not believe that the revolution had been made for economic reasons: "The principal motive of the revolution was not to free lands and persons from all servitude, and industry from all restraint. It was not the interest of property nor that of liberty. It was impatience with the inequalities of right that existed at that time; it was the passion for equality." But just because the revolution was not directly made for economic reasons did not mean that it had no effect on economic development: "What the nation did for liberty and property was only the consequence and side effect of what it did to achieve equality of rights." Here Roederer was breaking new ground by suggesting that the release of new forms of property and production by the overthrow of absolutism might not have been the intention of the majority of actors, who may have had quite other objectives.[27] "Philosophy led to and prepared financial, military, and civil, moral and religious reform, but not a political revolution," Roederer continues, in a passage reminiscent of Steuart's warning about the dangers inherent in opening a process of reform without intending to complete it: "What made the revolution was public anger aroused by the most odious resistance to the most just reform, and enthusiasm aroused by the first victories of liberty over arbitrary power."[28]

As with Barnave, attempts have been made to incorporate Roederer as a support for revisionist accounts of the Revolution. According to Kenneth Margerison, "Roederer's career does not fit into the Marxist interpretation of the Revolution as a class struggle between the bourgeoisie and the aristocracy," because his manufacturing interests led him to see the "essential political contest" as taking place "within the Third Estate not, as Marxists think, between the Third and the Nobility."[29] It is always educative for Marxists to be told what they think, but insofar as Roederer is concerned, Margerison is simply wrong, since the former certainly *did* believe that at least one aspect of the French Revolution was a struggle between the Third Estate and the nobility. Here, for example, is his argument justifying class divisions based on the achievements of talent rather than the benefits of inheritance, in words very similar to those of Barnave:

> Since 1792 the nation has demonstrated that it was not motivated at that time by a total aversion for all aristocratic distinctions, titles, coats of arms and liveries, but by a hatred of the existing privileged nobility, because it was exclusive, offensive to merit, and because the common estate had been humiliated by it and wanted revenge. And if, since then, it has adopted a new nobility with the same honorary attributes, but which is not hereditary, this has signified not illogicality, repentance, or a return to the old order of things. It has been on the contrary a way of forgetting it more completely, of wreaking a surer revenge on it, of taking possession with all the éclat of the equality of rights that nation has won.[30]

If anything, this is a classical statement and defense of the distinction between feudal and capitalist wealth. Furthermore, Roederer actually believed that this "capitalist aristocracy" should directly constitute the governing class. One study of the debates over the Republican constitution notes Roederer's conclusion that "democracy was inappropriate in late eighteenth-century France"—"democracy" in this context meaning mass participation in the political process:

> The events of 1792 suggested to Roederer that this inappropriateness could rapidly become extremely dangerous. As he saw it, the modern republic needed to offer its citizens protection from a potentially over-extended unstable and destructive general will. The source of this perception was not the Terror, but the circumstances that led to it. A representative aristocracy, elected on grounds of merit and then permitted to govern without impediment, was his answer to the Revolution's quest for a viable form of government.[31]

Barnave and Roederer wrote their major contributions at opposite ends of the French Revolution, but argued essentially the same case. Their speeches and actions too were more or less consistent with texts written, initially at least, for their desk drawers. They were exceptional, not in what they believed, but in the extent to which they were prepared to state explicitly the contradiction that lies at the heart of all bourgeois revolutions, to one degree or another, namely that their effect is to secure the replacement of one ruling class with another. We can therefore reject the assertion by David Bell that "writers in this period [1789–1815] who described the French Revolution in terms of class conflict . . . were almost all British."[32] However, one of them certainly was British or, more precisely, Anglo-Irish; he was also the greatest intellectual opponent of the French Revolution and the man who identified its nature more accurately than those who have inherited his hostility without any of his insight: Edmund Burke.

6

THE CONTRADICTIONS
OF THE FRENCH REVOLUTION (2):
BURKE AND HIS CRITICS

There were many feudal reactionaries throughout the European mainland who railed against the French Revolution and blamed the usurping bourgeoisie for bringing it about, but who were able to console themselves with the thought that the bourgeoisie were themselves being usurped by those still lower down the social order. In 1798, for example, the exiled Royalist Abbé Augustin Barruel wrote of how "the irreligious sophists of all types despoil the clergy; the sophists of bourgeois jealousy despoil the nobility; the sophists of banditry despoil bourgeois merchants and all rich bourgeois; the atheistic sophists break the ultimate ties of society."[1] Burke's position was not only more sophisticated than this but also more complex. For one thing, he was not a feudal reactionary, although he shared many attitudes with them. According to Marx, Burke was himself "a vulgar bourgeois through and through," albeit one possessed of "talent."[2] The key to Burke's attitude toward the French Revolution can be found in his attitude to capitalism, the distinctions that he makes between different types of capitalists and bourgeois, and the political consequences that follow their rule. These positions were in many ways similar to those of Smith, whose earlier writings Burke admired, although he insisted that he had arrived at his economic views independently.[3] He also expressed them to very different effect.

FROM SMITH TO BURKE: AMBIVALENCE TO APOLOGETICS

To understand these differences we need to return to Smith's key work. His argument in *The Wealth of Nations* can be seen, in David McNally's words, as a defense of "agrarian-based capitalist development in a landed commonwealth ruled by prosperous and public-spirited country gentlemen" against the emergent "industrial and commercial capitalists" whose amorality Smith distrusted. In relation to his native Scotland, McNally notes: "Smith hoped that commercial forces could be used to hurry the development of an agrarian-based capitalism guarded by a state run by a natural aristocracy of landed gentlemen."[4] Yet as Richard Teichgraeber concludes from a study of the reception to *The Wealth of Nations* between 1776 and 1790: "A close inspection of the earliest responses to Smith's work shows that the arrival of *The Wealth of Nations* had no immediate impact on Britain or its colonies." The book was not completely ignored, of course, but as Teichgraeber notes, the concept of a stable agrarian order was not the aspect that drew the greatest attention:

> It is clear that Smith's contemporaries were not interested in all that he had to say. Instead, they focused almost entirely on his argument for free trade—especially as it applied to monopolies and the Corn Laws—because this was what they took to be the most interesting and useful aspect of the *Wealth of Nations*. As a result, when "free trade" emerged in the 1780s as a matter of practical politics, more people of different types gave the book greater attention and respect. This delayed recognition of Smith's achievement, however, also had a second and unintended result—namely, the reduction of the *Wealth of Nations* to a book whose single overarching concern was seen to be driving home the doctrine of free trade.[5]

Burke shared this vision and indeed may have been the first British writer to describe the agrarian class he and Smith admired as "landed capitalists," in a reference to the "surplus" produced beyond that required for "the immediate support of the producer" as "the income of the landed capitalist."[6] Burke was certainly not hostile to capitalism and, if anything, he shared with Roederer—whom he would otherwise have despised—a greater belief in the perfection of the market order than Smith ever held. In a tract written in the economic crisis year 1795 he gave perhaps the most extreme defense of what would later be called the "free" market to have appeared in print at that date:

> The balance between consumption and production makes price. The market settles, and alone can settle, that price. Market is the meeting and conference of the *consumer* and *producer*, when they mutually discover each other's wants. Nobody, I believe, has observed with any reflection what market is, without being astonished at the truth, the correctness, the celerity, the general equity, with which the balance of wants is settled. They who wish the destruction of that balance, and would fain by arbitrary regulation decree, that defective production should not be compensated by increased price, directly lay their *axe* to the root of production itself.[7]

Burke is here expressing a position very similar to that set out in what would become one of the most influential, if atypical chapters of *The Wealth of Nations*, "Digression Concerning the Corn Trade."[8]

Albert Hirschman has argued that the first supporters of commercial society, those who preceded Burke, believed it would tame the disastrous warlike passions inherent in feudalism, not because they held to an imbecilic faith in the ability of markets to resolve all human difficulties:

> The passions that needed bridling belong to the powerful, who are in a position to do harm on a huge scale and who were believed to be particularly well endowed with passions in comparison with the lesser orders. As a result the most interesting applications of the theory show how the willfulness, the disastrous lust for glory, and, in

general, the passionate excesses of the powerful are curbed by the interests—their own and those of their subjects.[9]

For Hirschman, it is Smith who first breaks this line of reasoning, upheld in Scotland by Steuart and Millar: "The main impact of *The Wealth of Nations* was to establish a powerful *economic* justification for the untrammeled pursuit of individual self-interest, whereas in the earlier literature . . . the stress was on the *political* effects of this pursuit."[10] Now, as John Dwyer has shown, the attempt to distinguish Smith from his contemporaries, "thereby transforming Smith into a much more revolutionary thinker than he really was," is by far the weakest part of Hirschman's argument. As Dwyer writes, Hirschman "reinforces the commonplace image of Smith as the prophet of individualism who makes the 'ordinary mortal' rather than the statesman or aristocrat, the model of social analysis." But this is to misunderstand his subject: "Smithian analysis cannot be applied to our notion of the average man. Instead, it referred to landed society, particularly the gentry and yeomanry, and included those middle-class men who served the public in a wide variety of bureaucratic functions. Most interestingly, it typically disparaged those individuals who lived by the profits of commerce and manufacturing, and whose unbridled self-interest could destroy national stability."[11]

Smith was aware that commercial society was not an unalloyed blessing. Long before capitalist industrialization began in earnest, he intuited that it would lead to massive deterioration in the condition of laborers and their reduction to mere "hands." It was uneasy anticipations such as these, which Smith shared with other thinkers of the Scottish Enlightenment, that later informed Hegel's conception of alienation and, through him, that of Marx.[12] Understood in the context of the Scottish Enlightenment conception of human potential, the description of pin manufacture in Book I of *The Wealth of Nations* not only celebrates the efficiency of the division of labor but also shows the soul-destroying repetition that awaited the new class of wage laborers.[13] In Book V, in contrast to the more frequently cited Book I, Smith explicitly considered the way in which the division of labor, while increasing the productivity of the laborers, did so by narrowing their intellectual horizons:

> The man whose whole life is spent in performing a few simple operations, of which the effects, too, are perhaps always the same, or very nearly the same, has no occasion to assert his understanding, or to exercise his invention, in finding out expedients for removing difficulties which never occur. He naturally loses, therefore, the habit of such exertion, and generally becomes as stupid and ignorant as it is possible for a human creature to become. The torpor of his mind renders him not only incapable of relishing or bearing a part in any rational conversation, but of conceiving any generous, noble, or tender sentiment, and consequently of forming any just judgment concerning many even of the ordinary duties of private life. Of the great and extensive interests of his country he is altogether incapable of judging; and unless very particular pains have been taken to render him otherwise, he is equally incapable of defending his country in war. . . . His dexterity at his own particular trade seems, in this manner, to be acquired at the expense of his intellectual, social, and martial virtues.[14]

Smith contrasts this unhappy state of affairs with that existing under earlier modes of subsistence—modes which, remember, he was committed to transcending:

> It is otherwise in the barbarous societies, as they are commonly called, of hunters, of shepherds, and even of husbandmen in that rude state of husbandry that precedes the improvement of manufactures, and the extension of foreign commerce. In such societies, the varied occupations of every man oblige every man to exert his capacity, and to invent expedients for removing difficulties which are continually occurring. Invention is kept alive, and the mind is not suffered to fall into that drowsy stupidity, which, in a civilized society, seems to benumb the understanding of the people. . . . Every man, too, is in some measure a statesman, and can form judgments concerning the interest of the society, and the conduct of those who govern it.[15]

In response he calls for the state to intervene to raise the educational level of the common people to that fitting of a "civilized and commercial society": "For a very small expense, the public can facilitate, can encourage, and can even impose upon almost the whole body of the people, the necessity of acquiring those most essential parts of education." Here he has before him the example of his own country, in one of the few occasions it features positively in *The Wealth of Nations*: "In Scotland, the establishment of such parish schools has taught almost the whole common people to read, and a very great proportion of them to write and account."[16]

By contrast, Burke refused to accept that the state might have a legitimate role in correcting the social consequences of the market. As Emma Rothschild notes, "Burke's view of government was very different from Smith's, with respect, for example, to the good commercial consequences of national expenditure on bridges, religion, and reverence" and his views in this respect hardened over time: "By 1795 Burke had become doubtful about what he now called government 'interference.'"[17] For Burke, the growth and dominance of the market in England had not broken the continuity of constitutional forms, religious observances, and even personal proprieties that maintained the stability of society. Clearly, England was uniquely blessed, but even those nations less favored by God could achieve comparable levels of wealth if they followed market principles and avoided the type of upheavals destructive of tradition. In effect, Burke synthesized Locke's interpretation of 1688 in England as a revolution in the original sense, restoring or preserving traditional rights endangered by a monarch who had exceeded the proper bounds of his social role, with the dominant Scottish interpretation of English economic development as an evolutionary process, unfolding in harmony with the dictates of nature, and untouched by the realm of politics. As C. B. MacPherson writes: "There is nothing surprising or inconsistent in Burke's championing at the same time the traditional English hierarchical society and the capitalist market economy. He believed in both, and believed that the latter needed the former."[18] Historically, his account of English development was both amnesiac in relation to the permanent constitutional changes established by the revolution of 1640 and blind to the destruction of peasant "traditions" by primitive accumulation in the countryside. Theoretically, it was a retreat from the attempts by Millar and Steuart to show the connections between socioeconomic and political change.

BURKE AND THE BOURGEOIS THREAT TO CAPITALIST STABILITY

Nevertheless, Burke also understood all too well the bourgeois nature of the French Revolution—indeed, that was precisely the basis of his opposition to it. Here he does echo Smith, who simultaneously insisted on the necessity for commercial society and market economy while disapproving of actual representatives of the commercial and mercantile interests. Smith specifically denied that they could represent society as a whole, writing of "the clamor and sophistry of merchants and manufacturers easily persuade [the public] that the private interest of a part, and of a subordinate part of the society, is the general interest of the whole" and concluding with his most famous comment on this subject: "People of the same trade seldom meet together, even for merriment and diversion, but the conversation ends in a conspiracy against the public, or in some contrivance to raise prices." For Smith, "merchants and master manufacturers" have a higher level of what we would now call class consciousness than landowners: "Their superiority to the country gentlemen is, not so much in their knowledge of the public interest, as their having a better knowledge of their own interest than he has of his." Any proposal emanating from these groups and claiming to be in the public interest should therefore be treated with the greatest suspicion: "It comes from an order of men, whose interest is never exactly the same with that of the public, who have generally an interest to deceive and even to oppress the public, and who accordingly have, upon many occasions, both deceived and oppressed it."[19]

It was this order of men, contained in England by its organic evolutionary traditions, that Burke believed was taking control in France. "After I had read over the list of the persons and descriptions elected to the *Tiers Etat*, nothing that they afterwards did could appear astonishing," he wrote in *Reflections on the Revolution in France* (1790). Burke was particularly concerned about the high proportion of lawyers elected to the National Assembly who were not "distinguished magistrates," nor "leading advocates," nor yet "renowned professors," but merely the "fomenters and conductors of the petty war of village vexation," a group collectively lacking "moderation" or "discretion" and solely committed to the pursuit of its own interests, not least "the lucrative jobs which follow in the train of all great convulsions and revolutions in the state, and particularly in all great and violent permutations of property."[20] Yet although lawyers were predominant within the revolutionary leadership, they would not be its sole or even main beneficiaries: "The whole of power obtained by this revolution will settle in the towns among the burghers, and the monied directors who lead them."[21] In a passage that bears comparison with Marx's subsequent discussion of the peasantry in *The Eighteenth Brumaire of Louis Bona-*

parte (1852), Burke points out that no groups from among the rural population were capable of performing this leadership role:

> The landed gentlemen, the yeoman, and the peasant have, none of them, habits or inclinations, or experience, which can lead them to share in this the sole source of power and influence now left in France. The very nature of a country life, the very nature of landed property, in all the occupations, and all the pleasures they afford, render combination and arrangement (the sole way of procuring and exerting influence) in a manner impossible among country-people. Combine them by all the art you can, and all the industry, they are always dissolving into individuality. Any thing in the nature of incorporation is almost impracticable among them.[22]

Burke then goes on to distinguish more closely between the different components of the "burgher" class that he expects to rule France if the Revolution continues: "All these considerations leave no doubt in my mind, that, if this monster of a constitution can continue, France will be wholly governed by the agitators in corporations, by societies in the towns formed of directors of assignats, and trustees for the sale of church lands, attorneys, agents, money-jobbers, speculators, and adventurers, composing an ignoble oligarchy founded on the destruction of the crown, the church, the mobility, and the people."[23] As Pocock writes, on this basis: "The Revolution was not the product of capitalist relations in France, but of its mismanagement."[24]

Before 1789 few writers had considered the spatial dimension of revolutionary movements, Millar's discussion of the advantages of restricted territoriality for republican movements being the main exception; but Burke's analysis of the emerging form of the new state recognized the decisive role, not only of the urban sector in general but of the capital Paris in particular:

> The power of the city of Paris is evidently one great spring of all their politics. It is through the power of Paris, now become the centre and focus of jobbing, that the leaders of this faction direct, or rather command the whole legislative and the whole executive government. Every thing must therefore be done which can confirm the authority of the other republics [i.e., the *departments*]. Paris is compact; she has an enormous strength, wholly disproportionate to the force of any of the square republics; and this strength is collected and condensed within a narrow compass. Paris has a natural and easy connection of its parts, which will not be affected by any scheme of geometrical constitution, nor does it much signify whether its proportion of representation be more or less, since it has whole draft of fishes in its dragnet.[25]

His emphasis on the central role of Paris, however, also contributed to the one area where his analysis is deficient; nationalism, the strength of which he completely failed to predict. Burke scorned the idea that "Gascons, Picards, Bretons, Normans" could ever become "Frenchmen, with one country, one heart, and one assembly": "But instead of being all Frenchmen, the greater likelihood is, that the inhabitants of that region will shortly have no country. No man ever was attached by a sense of pride, partiality, or real affection, to a description of square measurement. He never will glory in belonging to the Chequer, No. 71, or to any other badge ticket.... The power and pre-eminence of Paris does certainly press down and hold these republics to-gether, as long as it lasts. But . . . I think it cannot last very long."[26] In the short term the prediction was accurate, since the counterrevolutionary risings against the republic often took a regional form, most dramatically in the Vendee; but in the longer term the incorporation of geographical and social peripheries into the metropolitan idea of the French nation was a process that continued unabated even after the Revolution concluded. Burke had of course little with which to compare the process of nation-building in France: in Britain itself the construction of the nation-state and its at-tendant national consciousness was by no means complete even by the time of Burke's death in 1797, and was consciously undertaken partly in response to the combined pressures of the French Revolution and the internal radicalism it helped stimulate.

Burke famously began *Reflections* in response to the welcome extended to the French Revolution by English Whigs who saw in it a comparable event to the rev-olution of 1688. This has misled many commentators as to the real nature of his objection. Thus, Steven Blakemore writes: "Burke felt that if the French Revolution could be justified by comparing it favorably with the English Revolution, then the very legitimacy, the very principles of the English Revolution could be called into question."[27] But Burke was not so much concerned that the English Revolution would be discredited by association with the French as with the French becoming a model for further upheavals, including within Britain itself. "But I think I see many inconveniences only not to Europe at large," he wrote shortly before the pub-lication of *Reflections*, "but to this Country in particular from the total political ex-tinction of a great civilized nation situated in the heart of our Western system."[28] The extraordinarily modern-sounding notion of a "Western system" here indicates how Burke's concern with stability and continuity meant that he was prepared, as eventually the majority of the British ruling class would be prepared, to embrace as allies the European feudal absolutisms stretching as far east as Russia, if the al-ternative was the replication of the French experience: as this suggests, the ideo-logical and geographical flexibility of "the West" as a concept did not begin with the Cold War. There is a certain irony in the fact that Burke, even on the eve of publication of *Reflections*, was prepared to argue from the Whig position, which predated the revolution of 1688, of deep suspicion of the French absolutist regime, and the attraction that it posed for Charles II and James VII and II.[29] The contrast here with his later obsession with the persons of the French royal family is dramatic.

Burke's central concern was that what had begun as an attack on feudal property would not end there: "The leaders teach the people to abhor and reject all feodality as the barbarism of tyranny, and they tell them afterwards how much of that bar-barous tyranny they are to bear with patience." Burke imagines the peasants saying to their new governors:

> We know, without your teaching, that lands were given for the support of our feudal dignities, feudal titles, and feudal offices. . . . As there are now no hereditary honors, and no distinguished families, why are we taxed to maintain what you tell us ought

not to exist? . . . We see the burghers of Paris, through their clubs, their mobs, and their national guards, directing you at their pleasure, and giving that law to you, which, under your authority, is transmitted as law to us. Through you, these burghers dispose of the lives and fortunes of us all. Why should not you attend as much to the desires of the laborious husbandman with regard to our rent, by which we are affected in the most serious manner, as you do to the demands of these insolent burghers, relative to distinctions and titles of honor, by which neither they nor we are affected at all?

Finally, Burke claims that, insofar as the revolutionaries were themselves actual or aspirant property owners, they would ultimately be undone by their own attack on feudal property rights: "They have left nothing but their own arbitrary pleasure to determine what property is to be protected and what subverted." If, as Burke reported, the citizens of Lyons have refused to pay their taxes, what argument other than military force has the assembly to persuade them otherwise? "What lawful authority is there left to exact them?"[30]

Burke understood, from very early in the process, the logic of escalation that would come to dominate the revolution and drive it further than the bourgeoisie intended, and he understood this far earlier than either supporters or participants did. As we have seen, it took Barnave until the following year to fully appreciate the potential threat to bourgeois property rights and he was at the very heart of events. Yet Burke also had to explain how the revolution involved forces other than the bourgeoisie and aimed for goals incompatible with their material interests, in ways that rendered revolutions like the French not only unnecessary but also unpredictable, uncontrollable, and wholly destructive in their consequences. He tended to do this in two ways. On the one hand, he invoked the bestial appetites of the "swinish multitude," which had been unleashed by the breakdown of order: an age-old example of patrician contempt for the plebeians that, in relation to modern theories of revolution, can be found at least as far back as those of Buchanan in the sixteenth century. On the other, he emphasized the ideological convictions—including atheism, republicanism, and egalitarianism—of self-appointed revolutionary leaders: an enduring theme in subsequent conservative thought. Despite Burke's initial insights into the class dynamic of the French Revolution, this innovation represents the first major intellectual retreat in the analysis of social revolution, which had until this point, been advancing, albeit unevenly and irregularly. The argument was soon taken to phantasmagorical extremes in works like John Robison's *Proofs of a Conspiracy against All the Religions and Governments of Europe* (1798), in which the origins of the Revolution are to be found in schemes plotted by the international networks of the Illuminati, but it is Burke who provides the intellectually reputable version.[31]

Burke argued that the French Revolution was qualitatively different from any previous revolution, especially the English Revolution of 1688: "All circumstances taken together, the French Revolution is the most astonishing [crisis] that has hitherto happened in the world."[32] This was only partly a matter of the scale of the events; it was also, and more importantly, a matter of the motivation of the revolutionaries:

> There have been many internal revolutions in the government of countries, both as to persons and forms, in which the neighboring states have had no concern. . . . The present revolution in France seems to me to be of quite another character and description; and to bear little resemblance or analogy to any of those which have been brought about in Europe, with principles merely political. *It is a revolution of doctrine and theoretick dogma.* It has much greater resemblance to those changes which have been made upon religious grounds, in which a spirit of proselytism makes an essential part.

Burke sees the Reformation as the only moment in history comparable to the French Revolution, above all because of its internationalism, the drive "to introduce other interests into all countries than those which arose from the locality and natural circumstances."[33] In "Letters on a Regicide Peace" (1796), he acknowledged the "dreadful truth" of Jacobin superiority to the allies and argued that this lay precisely in how the former were unconstrained by mere national concerns:

> They saw the thing right from the start. Whatever were the first motives to the war among politicians, they saw that its spirit, and for its subjects, it was a *civil war*, and as such they pursued it. It is a war between the partisans of the ancient, civil, moral and political order of Europe against a set of fanatical and ambitious atheists which means to change them all. It is not France extending a foreign empire over other nations: it is a sect aiming at universal empire, and beginning with the conquest of France.[34]

Before Burke, classification of events that went beyond political revolution did not have a normative dimension: the fall of the Roman Empire or the rise of Islam could be described as "revolutions" in the sense that they involved vast, epochal changes in human civilization, but these were regarded as being almost too great, their impacts too diverse, to be ascribed either positive or negative values. The French Revolution was obviously one of these moments in history. Burke retained the category of purely political revolutions and argued that these might indeed upon occasion be necessary, as was the case in England during 1688. Yet although he understood that the French Revolution was something other, and in a way something greater, than a political revolution, he did not regard it as a social revolution, but attempted to remove it from the realm of social explanation altogether and relocate it to the domain of ideology: the catastrophic consequence of pursuing intellectual schemas unsanctified by tradition. For Burke they were "independent of any interest": "Nothing can be conceived more hard than the heart of a thoroughbred metaphysician. It comes nearer to the cold malignity of a wicked spirit than to the frailty and passion of a man. It is like that of the principle of evil himself, incorporeal, pure, unmixed, dephlegmated, defecated evil." Among these metaphysicians Burke included not only his contemporaries like the Abbé Sieyès, with his "nests of pigeonholes full of constitutions ready made, ticketed, sorted, and numbered; suited to every season and every fancy," but historical figures like—and by now the inclusion of this name should come as no surprise—Harrington, with his "seven different forms of republics."[35]

It was for supposed insights such as these that repentant former supporters of the Revolution like William Wordsworth were later to hail his departed spirit for forcing them to face reality: "Genius of Burke! Forgive the pen seduced/By specious wonders."[36] Following these apologetic lines from *The Prelude* (1805), the poet then imagines Burke declaiming against the doctrines that he held responsible for the Revolution:

> ... *he forewarns, denounces, launches forth,*
> *Against all systems built on abstract rights,*
> *Keen ridicule; the majesty proclaims*
> *Of Institutes and Laws, hallowed by time;*
> *Declares the vital power of social ties*
> *Endeared by Custom; and with high disdain,*
> *Exploding upstart Theory, insists*
> *Upon the allegiance to which men were born ...* [37]

Written over a period of fifty years and including passages reflective of Wordsworth's views from all points during that period, *The Prelude* is politically a more complex poem than this panegyric to the patron saint of counterrevolution, added late in the author's life, would suggest; but it nevertheless captures well one of the central aspects of Burke's thought. Joseph Priestley identified, in a tone of entirely justified sarcasm, the logical flaw with the argument advanced by Burke and many subsequent conservative thinkers for the acceptance of tradition and the rejection of dangerous innovations:

> You would, no doubt, have done the same with respect to any place, in which Peter, or Paul, was permitted to preach; the Christian religion being in their time, unfortunately, nothing more than a *sect*, taught in *conventicles*, and no where *authorized by law*. Had you lived at that time, you would, according to your general maxim, have "cherished the old" heathen "prejudices, because they were old," and have lived and died a humble worshipper of the Gods, and especially the *Goddesses*, of ancient Greece and Rome.[38]

Burke constructed the model of the new conservative ideology in its purest form: on the one hand, forms of mystified consciousness that the Enlightenment had at least begun to undermine, such as belief in supernatural beings or inherent national characteristics, were reasserted as the basis for the cohesion of the state; on the other, the universalist claims of the Enlightenment were reduced to a purely capitalist rationality, the calculation of profit and loss in the context of the market. In the master's own words: "We, the people, ought to be made sensible, that it is not in breaking the laws of commerce, which are the laws of nature, and consequently the laws of God, that we are to place our hope of softening the Divine displeasure to remove any calamity under which we suffer, or which hangs over us."[39] But since the political economy that venerated "market" (Burke tended to write the word without the definite article) was also an example of "upstart Theory" it too had to be removed from the realms of intellectual inquiry and treated as an expression of the Divine Will.

ANTI-BURKE

Burke's views did not immediately win majority support, even among his own class, and never achieved universal acceptance. In the brief interlude between the publication of *Reflections* and the suppression of voices supporting the French Revolution in Britain, his critics themselves made contributions to the theory of revolution in response to his denunciations.

The most obvious figure to introduce at this point in the discussion is Thomas Paine, whose *Rights of Man* (1791) was the most famous and influential reply to Burke's *Reflections*. Every modern socialist or radical will take Paine's side in this dispute, yet what becomes apparent from reading both works side by side is not only what divided them—the significance of tradition, the use of language itself—but the assumptions that they shared. In one sense this is unsurprising, as many of their ideas shared the same theoretical source. As Edward Thompson once noted: "In the 1790s the ambiguities of Locke seem to fall into two halves, one Burke, the other Paine. Where Burke assumes government and examines its operation in the light of experience and tradition, Paine speaks for the governed, and assumes that the authority of government derives from conquest and inherited power in a class-divided society."[40]

But as we have seen, Locke's own work involved a retreat from the social interpretation of revolution initiated by Harrington. Both Burke and Paine shared Locke's view of the English Revolution as an essentially conservative event and this formed the basis of their disagreement over its significance. For Paine, the essential difference between states was whether they were based on "hereditary" or "representative" systems of government, the former being mainly represented by monarchies and the latter by republics.[41]

Like many of his American compatriots, Paine believed that the British government had never fully made the transition from the first to the second. Consequently, he not only regarded the revolution of 1688 as being of limited significance but also the revolution of 1640: "In the case of Charles I and James II of England, the revolt was against the personal despotism of the men; whereas in France, it was against the hereditary despotism of the established government."[42] "Time, and change in circumstances and opinions, have the same progressive effect in rendering modes of Government obsolete, as they have upon customs and manners. Agriculture, commerce, manufactures, and the tranquil arts, by which the prosperity of Nations is best promoted, require a different system of Government, and a different species of knowledge to direct its operations, than what might have been required in the former condition of the world."[43] And in this respect the English revolutions were similar to most previous revolutions, which "had nothing in them that interested the bulk of mankind. They extended only to a change of persons and measures, but not of principles, and rose and fell among the common transactions of the moment."[44] The only two events to have involved more than "a change of persons, or an alteration of local circumstances" were "the Revolutions of America and

France," which involved "a renovation of the natural order of things, a system of principles as universal as truth and the existence of man, and combining moral with political happiness and national prosperity."[45] Burke would never have accepted that the American and French Revolutions were comparable, but otherwise Paine agreed with his analysis while reversing his value judgments.

If Burke articulated the views of the dominant fraction of the British ruling class, the agrarian capitalists whose power had been confirmed and consolidated in 1688, Paine spoke for a far more diverse constituency, which effectively included everyone (or at least every man) further down the class structure. Paine had a class analysis and situated himself within it; but as Thompson observes, his audience was not specifically workers, but rather "farmers, tradesmen and professional men," and the group to which he personally belonged: "men of the unrepresented and trading classes." In this sense Paine was as supportive of capitalism and as admiring of Smith as Burke: "In political society every man must have equal rights as a citizen: in economic society he must naturally remain employer or employed, and the State should not interfere with the capital of one or the wages of the other. The *Rights of Man* and *The Wealth of Nations* should supplement and nourish each other."[46] Despite the ferocity of the argument between Burke and Paine, at its heart lay a political division over the extent of the franchise, not a socioeconomic division over the nature of property. Paine saw the fundamental oppositions within society as occurring between what would later be called the "productive" and "unproductive" classes: between those who paid taxes and those who lived off taxation, between those who worked for their living and those who lived off the work of others, above all in the form of rent. In a sense then, he did not draw a distinction between the revolution that was occurring in France and the revolution that he wished would occur in Britain, since in both cases the enemy to be overthrown was an oppressive hereditary monarchy and its parasitic supporters, although he allowed that the changes he desired could be brought about in the latter country by a process of reform, without the necessity of repeating the entire French experience.[47]

Only in England, where the bourgeois revolution was an established fact and capitalism was more deeply embedded than anywhere else, could a debate have taken place that simultaneously so illuminated the arguments in relation to political democracy and so obscured them in relation to social revolution. In Scotland, where feudal social relations had survived longer than in England and were still in the process of being transformed during the early stages of the French Revolution, clarity was retained for slightly longer. One of Burke's Scottish interlocutors, James Mackintosh, explained in *Vindiciae Gallicae* (1792) why the leadership of the Third Estate did not fall directly to the commercial classes but to the lower reaches of the professions so despised by Burke:

> The representation of the third estate was, as he justly states, composed of Lawyers, Physicians, Merchants, Men of Letters, Tradesmen and Farmers. The choice was indeed limited by necessity, for except men of these ranks and professions, the *people* had no

objects of election, the Army and the Church being engrossed by the Nobility.—"No vestige of the landed interest of the country appeared in this representation."—For an obvious reason—Because the *Nobility* of France, like the Gentry of England, formed almost exclusively the landed interest of the kingdom.—These professions then could only furnish Representatives for the *Tiers Etat.*—They form the majority of that middle rank among whom almost all the sense and virtue of society reside. Their pretended incapacity for political affairs is an arrogant fiction of Statesmen which the history of Revolutions has ever belied. These emergencies have never failed to create politicians. The subtle counselors of Philip II were baffled by the Burgomasters of Amsterdam and Leyden. The oppression of England summoned into existence a race of Statesmen in her Colonies. The lawyers of Boston, and the planters of Virginia, were transformed into ministers and negotiators, who proved themselves inferior neither in wisdom neither as legislators, nor in dexterity as politicians. These facts evince that the powers of mankind have been unjustly depreciated, the difficulty of Political affairs artfully magnified, and that there exists a quantity of talent *latent* among men, which ever rises to the level of the great occasions that call it forth. . . . The majority of the Third Estate was indeed composed of lawyers. Their talents of public speaking, and their professional habits of examining questions analogous to those of politics, rendered them the most probable objects of popular choice, especially in a *despotic* country, where political speculation was no natural amusement for the leisure of opulence.[48]

Like Barnave, Mackintosh saw the French Revolution as the latest in a historical sequence that included those in the Netherlands and America, even though the leadership may have devolved onto different groups in each case. And, despite their absence from the revolutionary leadership, Mackintosh was prepared to defend "the commercial, or monied interest" against Burke's claims for the landed interest, writing that the former,

> . . . has in all nations of Europe (taken as a body) been less prejudiced, more liberal, and more intelligent, than the landed gentry. Their views are enlarged by a wider intercourse with mankind, and hence the important influence of commerce in liberalizing the modern world. We cannot wonder then that this enlightened class of men ever proves the most ardent in the cause of freedom, the most zealous for political reform. It is not wonderful that philosophy should find in them more docile pupils; and liberty more active friends, than in a haughty and prejudiced aristocracy. The Revolution in 1688 produced the same division in England.[49]

As the last sentence suggests, Mackintosh also rejected the attempt by both Burke and Paine to distinguish the events of 1688 in England from those of 1789 in France, but he was also aware that the subsequent hundred years had left the two countries with different economies and class structures: "France was catching up with Britain and so too would the rest of feudal Europe: unless historical analogy be altogether delusive, the *decease* of the *Gothic* Governments cannot be distant. Their maturity is long past, and symptoms of their decrepitude are rapidly accumulating."[50]

MacKintosh's response to Burke shows that, even at this stage British political thought, in Scotland at least, did not reject mass insurgency in all circumstances. Millar in particular had earlier looked favorably on how "the clamor and tumultuary proceedings of the populace in the great towns are capable of penetrating the inmost recesses of administration, of intimidating the boldest minister, and of displacing the most presumptuous favorite of the backstairs."[51] Indeed, as Hirschman notes, what is most "striking" about this passage is "the positive view Millar takes of the role of riots and other mass actions." This was not an attitude long sustained, even by radical members of the bourgeoisie like Millar. "A few decades later the climate had totally changed," Hirschman writes, the most significant change being that "the frequently 'contentious' working class had come into existence."[52] More worryingly for the ruling class, that working class was entering political life radicalized by the doctrines of the French Revolution. The new atmosphere of panic and repression infected theoretical work. Arguments, however esoteric, that implied the slightest support for mass action from below seemed deeply suspect to a ruling class who were in favor of Enlightenment when it increased their annual rentals, not when it encouraged the mob to demand the vote.

THE COUNTERREVOLUTION IN BRITISH POLITICAL THEORY

Alexander Carlyle wrote of Millar in 1800 that he "had even begun to distinguish himself by his democratical principles, and that skeptical philosophy which young noblemen and gentle men of legislative rank carried into the world with them from his law class and, many years afterwards, particularly at the period of the French Revolution, displayed with popular zeal, to the no small danger of perversion to all those under their influence."[53] Jonathan Israel is right to say that that the mainstream of Scottish Enlightenment thought was generally on the moderate, even conservative wing of the international movement.[54] One anonymous attack originally published in the *Glasgow Courier* during 1793 denounced the effects of "detestable, impracticable theories" on impressionable young minds and effectively called for a purge of all lecturers tainted with republican views: "Men of that description should either relinquish their tenets or their places; for, is there not a gross inconsistency in their eating the King's bread, and at the same time vilifying his Government?"[55] Millar characteristically saw the changed grounds of the counterrevolutionary argument, associated above all with Burke, as evidence of the success of liberal Enlightenment thought, writing that "so great has been the progress of opinion since [the Jacobite Rising of 1745–46], the more liberal part of the Tories have now caught universally the mode of reasoning employed by their adversaries, and are accustomed to justify the degree of monarchical power which they wish to establish, not by asserting that it is the inherent birthright of the sovereign, but by maintaining that it is necessary for the suppression of tumult and disorder."[56]

Few other thinkers active in the 1790s shared Millar's optimistic interpretation of events. Dugald Stewart came under closer scrutiny, even though he had never been so enamored of rioting crowds as Millar. He was appointed first professor of political economy at Glasgow—the first anywhere in the world—in 1793 and in his *Life and Writings of Adam Smith*, published during the same year, Stewart drew attention to parallels between and mutual influences on Smith and his French Enlightenment contemporaries like Condorcet. Here and in his other writings, Stewart attempted to maintain a balance between rejecting extreme interpretations of Enlightenment doctrine and urging the timely reform of the conditions that made such interpretations attractive to the unwary: "The danger, indeed, of sudden and rash innovations cannot be too strongly inculcated; and the views of those men who are forward to promote them cannot be reprobated with too great severity. But it is possible also to fall into the opposite extreme and bring upon society the very evils we are anxious to prevent, by an obstinate opposition to those gradual and necessary reformations which the genius of the times demands."[57]

Even these remarks, which would have passed unnoticed in enlightened publications fifty years earlier, or even during the American War of Independence, now bore the mark of the Jacobin beast. One of the Lords of Session, Lord Craig, wrote to Stewart on February 15, 1794, in terms that left no room for ambiguity:

> That even allowing the principles in that Chapter, however erroneous, to have been written with the most innocent intention at the time, that after the massacres in France, and the dreadful actings such principles had produced, and after the consequences of them had been expressed in such horrible and bloody characters, it could not only not be innocent to maintain those opinions, but that conduct could not be innocent which did not disown them; and to endeavor to correct their pernicious operation in the most explicit form.[58]

This was a demand for a recantation, which Stewart duly made, albeit with as much dignity as he could muster, on February 20: "As soon as I understood that the scope of my observations had been mistaken by a few whose characters I respect. I was anxious to guard against the possibility of such misapprehensions."[59] Cockburn wrote in his memoirs of the academic Whigs: "Stewart, in particular, though too spotless and too retired to be openly denounced, was an object of great secret alarm." But this indicated the extent of the terror: "If Dugald Stewart was for several years not cordially received in the city he adored, what must have been the position of an ordinary man who held liberal opinions in the country or in a small town, open to all the contumely and obstruction that local insolence could practice, and unsupported probably by any associate cherishing kindred thoughts[?][60]

The fate of Dugald Stewart is emblematic of the end of the Scottish Enlightenment, not in respect of his brush with repression, which was mild indeed compared, for example, to the sentence of transportation to Australia visited on his more outspoken pupil, Thomas Muir. It was emblematic rather in respect of the impact it had on his theoretical approach to political economy, for Stewart was primarily responsible for deradicalizing Smith: "It was Adam Smith the conservative theorist whom Stewart presented in his university lectures, and it happened that among the generations of students who listened to him were many who were to become important in British political life. . . . From Stewart they absorbed what was becoming the economic "commonsense" of middle-class Britain."[61] Teichgraeber has written of "the more dramatic impact *The Wealth of Nations* would make on readers after 1790," but of how obscure this process remains: "In 1793, Dugald Stewart talked of a hope that 'in due time' Smith's example would be followed by other students of political economy. Only ten years later, Francis Horner, a former pupil of Stewart and a founder of the *Edinburgh Review*, spoke of a 'superstitious worship' that had come to be attached to Smith's name."[62] In fact the conditions were optimal for a narrow, purely economic interpretation of Smith to become hegemonic. The generation of British Whig thinkers who rose to prominence after 1800, particularly those associated with the *Edinburgh Review*, illustrate the shift. They by no means completely abandoned scientific thought or even the desire for reform; but the issues over which these cadres were most deeply concerned were far narrower than those that had interested the Scottish Historical School. The new agenda was retrospectively listed by one leading figure, Sidney Smith, in 1839:

> The Catholics were not emancipated, the Corporation and Test Acts unrepealed— the Game Laws were horribly oppressive—Steel Traps and Spring Guns were set all over the country—Prisoners tried for their Lives could have no Council—Lord Eldon and the Court of Chancery pressed heavily upon mankind—Libel was punished by the most cruel and vindictive imprisonments—the principles of Political Economy were little understood—the Laws of Debt and of Conspiracy were upon the worst possible footing—the enormous wickedness of the Slave Trade was tolerated—a thousand evils were in existence.[63]

As John Saville has noted, what is most revealing here is what Smith omits from "his catalogue of social and political evils," which is anything related to questions of class or economic relations. Even before the emergence of the working class as an organized political force, the Whigs displayed "a marked decline in their reforming attitudes, above all through an unquestioned acceptance of the dogmas of political economy."[64] These changes were most marked in Britain, but were also indicative of a general intellectual trend, as Emma Rothschild explains: "The politics of economic reform, of individual rights, of rights to property, were linked, in the 1770s and 1780s, to the objective of constitutional change, in Paine's politics, or in Condorcet's. But the events of the [French] Revolution destroyed the possibility of political coalition between the supporters of market freedom and the supporters of Revolutionary freedom."[65]

Early in 1790 Paine wrote to Burke—whom he still regarded as an ally on the basis of his earlier support for the American colonists—describing what he saw as one of the main outcomes of the French Revolution: "The destruction of the Feudal System has deprived pride of its power and Aristocracy of its authority, and it is as probable, that those who pulled down the Bastille should build it up again and consent to be shut up in it, as that a Counter revolution should be worked."[66] For Paine, the changes that the Revolution had brought were irrevocable. Twenty-five years later, as the Congress of Vienna finalized the postrevolutionary settlement and the absolutist regimes reasserted their control over a continent they had divided between themselves and Britain, it was initially difficult to maintain this level of confidence. Two other leading figures of the American Revolution, Adams and Jefferson now contemplated the possibility that as they neared the end of their lives, the Bastille was indeed to be rebuilt and other instruments of feudal oppression they had opposed would also be reestablished, at least in Europe. Toward the end of 1815, Adams wrote to Jefferson in terms that expressed his fear that the age of the Enlightenment had not simply come to an end, but that its achievements might be reversed: "Is the Nineteenth Century to be a Contrast to the Eighteenth? Is it to extinguish all the Lights of its Predecessor? Are the Sorbonne, the Inquisition, the Index expurgatorius, and the Knights Errant of St Ignatius Loyola to be revived and restored?"[67] The Founding Fathers depressed both by what they saw as the excesses of the French Revolution and the restoration of absolutism across Europe, drew heart from the revolutions in Southern Europe and Latin America, which they saw—inaccurately, as it happens—as modeled on the American experience.[68] But even in Europe, their fears were exaggerated. In fact, although he never lived to see the Restoration, Paine's earlier assertion of irreversibility was nearer the truth. Whatever the wish-fulfillment fantasies of conservatives then and since, society post-1815 was not "a world restored."[69] One of the so-called doctrinaire liberals, Pierre Royer-Collard, made a speech in Parliament on the freedom of the press: "The revolution has left only individuals standing. . . . From an atomized society has emerged centralization. There is no need to look elsewhere for its origin. . . . where there are only individuals, all business which is not theirs is necessarily public business, the business of the state."[70] Royer-Collard here acknowledges that the social fragmentation that Ferguson and Smith feared would be the result of commercial society had come to pass. The eventual dominance of what was soon to be called "capitalism" beyond Britain and France was not in doubt to anyone but the most benighted reactionaries, whose leading representatives occupied or surrounded the throne of the Romanov dynasty in Russia. The only questions that remained were at what speed, under which conditions, and at whose hands would capitalism be introduced?

7

THE BOURGEOISIE AND THE CONCEPT OF SOCIAL REVOLUTION: FROM CONSOLIDATION TO ABDICATION

I t is only now, at the concluding stage in this prehistory of bourgeois revolution that we can introduce the figures that usually dominate most accounts. Sarah Maza refers to "attempts by a group of prominent liberal politicians during the Bourbon Restoration of 1815–30 to make a bourgeois class central to the history and politics of France."[1] The key figures to whom Maza refers were François Guizot, François Mignet, and Augustin Thierry. Guizot, the most conservative of the three and the only one to become a significant political figure in his own right, made particularly clear the limited nature of the political ideals that the Liberals were prepared to endorse. Needless to say, these were not the ideals characteristic of Year One of the French Republic. As Guizot wrote in 1837: "The world will no longer agitate for the sake of some abstract principle, some fanciful theory—some utopian government, which can exist only in the imagination of an enthusiast; nor will it put up with practical abuses and oppressions however favoured by prescription and expediency, where they are opposed to the just principles and the legitimate end of government."[2] In other words, he was in favor of constitutional limits on monarchical power and extending the franchise to members of the bourgeoisie. The very exclusionary nature of these goals led, as Anderson describes, to the "the repeated contrast between noble ideas and shabby actions" of the leading Liberals, with Guizot himself, "the frigid mechanic of exclusion and repression, chased from the country amid universal reprobation," in 1848.[3]

Yet in the thirty years before this *denouncement*, Guizot and his colleagues did recapitulate and consolidate the theoretical discussions that had been under way in Europe since Bacon first contemplated the changing agrarian structure of Tudor and Stuart England. "The Liberals must find a way to defend the Revolution," wrote Stanley Mellon of their dilemma after 1815, "while freeing themselves from the charge of *being* revolutionary." They found a way, as Mellon explains, in the writing of history, by treating the explosive events of the revolutionary period as matters that had found their resolution and therefore only needed to be understood.[4] They were not the first to adopt this attitude. Germaine de Staël, who unlike the French Liberals had been an active participant in these events, nevertheless wrote, in the immediate aftermath of the Bourbon Restoration: "My ambition shall be to speak of the age in which we have lived as if it were already remote."[5] In the first instance this meant situating "the age in which we have lived" with the entire history of civilization.

Guizot set out his basic assumptions early in his literary career, in terms that recall those of Robertson: "In order to understand political institutions, we must study the various strata existing in society and their mutual relationships. In order to understand these various strata, we must know the nature and the relations of landed property."[6]

The period covered by Guizot's *General History of Civilisation in Europe from the Fall of the Roman Empire to the French Revolution* (1828–30) is intended to represent the feudal era, in which feudalism is not merely a set of laws as it was for Montesquieu, nor a type of social organization as it was for Smith, but a society based on a distinct form of property relations that can be contrasted with what at the time were referred to as preceding tribal, oriental, and classical forms, all of which had previously been submerged into an undifferentiated agricultural mode of subsistence. Guizot describes "the feudal system" in this sense as a "combination of political, judicial, and military means" by which the mere possession of fiefs was converted into "laws and institutions." Guizot argued that, within this system, the bourgeoisie had been developing since the twelfth century. He did not claim, however, that the bourgeoisie remained unchanged and eternally "rising" throughout the subsequent period. He imagined a member of this class reborn at the end of the eighteenth century and being presented with a copy of Abbé Sieyès's *What Is the Third Estate?* "His eyes would fall upon this sentence which is the foundation of the pamphlet: 'The Third Estate is the French nation, less the nobility and the clergy.' I ask you, what would be the effect of such a phrase upon the minds of such a man? Do you suppose he would understand it? No, he would not understand the words, *the French nation*, because they would represent to him no fact with which he was acquainted, no fact of his age." In this respect Guizot held, against Burke and his followers, the modernist conception of the nation as a historical construction rather than a primordial essence. And, just as the bourgeoisie's consciousness had been subject to transformation over time, so too had its composition: "Whenever the bourgeoisie is spoken of, it seems to be supposed that at all epochs it was composed of the same elements. This is an absurd supposition. . . . So long as it did not include magistrates nor men of letters, so long as it was not what it became in the sixteenth century, it possessed neither the same importance nor the same character in the state."[7] Here, "the bourgeoisie" are not defined simply by geographical location in the Communes or even by their involvement in commerce, but as a much broader category, including state officials and intellectuals, linked by their antagonism to the feudal aristocracy, an antagonism that eventually erupted into what Guizot called "the class struggle [the contest of classes]": "Modern Europe was born of the struggle of the various classes of society. . . . In France, for example, in the seventeenth and eighteenth centuries, the social and moral separation of the classes was still very profound; yet the fusion was advancing; still, without doubt, at the time there was a veritable French nation, not an exclusive class, but which embraced them all, and in which all were animated by a certain sentiment in common, having a common social existence, strongly impressed, in a word, with nationality.[8] Guizot treats the triumph of the bourgeoisie as involving, on the one hand, the abolition of class conflicts and, on the other, the establishment of the nation-state, a historical interpretation by which the bourgeoisie comes to represent the people as a whole, which in turn embodies the nation as a collective. With these claims we have clearly passed from the realm of science into that of ideology.

BOURGEOIS METAPHYSICIANS VERSUS THE INDUSTRIAL CLASSES

A contrasting view of the bourgeoisie to that of Guizot and his cothinkers is provided by a writer who was older than any of them, but whose literary career overlaps with theirs. Henri Saint-Simon was linked to the Liberals through a relationship with Thierry, who acted as his secretary during the 1810s. He is usually regarded, along with Robert Owen, as the first of the utopian socialists, but this is undeserved. In fact, his doctrines have less to do with socialism than do those of the most radical figures of the French Revolution, above all, those of Gracchus Babeuf.[9] The attitude that places him in this company is his hatred of the bourgeoisie, although by this he meant a different social group than Guizot or his predecessors.

At the beginning of the Great French Revolution members of the group identified by the term "bourgeoisie" regarded themselves as a significant component of "the people" in a broader sense, if the most "active" in the sense in which the Convention recognized active citizenship. However, the relationship of the bourgeoisie to the people very quickly went through several iterations, the shifts being registered in a debate in the paper *Le Patriot Français* initiated by the then mayor of Paris, Jérôme Pétion de Villeneuve, and largely conducted on the right of the revolutionary movement. The most decisive intervention was by André Chénier, a moderate concerned about the direction of the Revolution on essentially the same grounds as Barnave. As Henry Heller notes, Chénier was concerned above all to distinguish the bourgeoisie from lesser sections of the former Third Estate. Indeed, he argued that the bourgeoisie represented the "true people": the virtuous and industrious majority as distinct from the twin minorities of the extravagantly wealthy and propertyless poor, respectively situated above and below it. What was particularly innovative in Chénier's position was that the bourgeoisie included both the capitalists in the economic sense (merchants, retailers, farmers) *and* professionals and rentiers.[10] By the revolution of 1830 it was no longer possible to credibly claim that even a broad definition of the bourgeoisie along these lines could mean anything more than a minority of the population. As Shirley Gruner points out, "the liberals of 1830 could have termed their revolution a 'bourgeois' revolution if the phrase had not been so completely turned against them."[11] Saint-Simon was more responsible for this reversal than any other political thinker.

In *Du système industriel* (1821), Saint-Simon wrote that "the industrial and scientific system was born and has developed under the domination of the feudal and theological system." Although the latter system had been mutated under the influence of the "lawyers and metaphysicians" and was badly weakened it still existed and consequently required to be overthrown: "When the French Revolution broke out it was no longer a question of modifying the feudal and theological system, which had already lost almost all of its real force. It was a question of organizing the industrial and scientific system, summoned by the level of civilisation to replace it."[12] Although feudalism is to be overthrown, it is not capitalism that is to replace it, but "industrialism," a system dominated by the productive classes that, as for Paine, include both workers and owners—as opposed to the parasites who had thrived under the "feudal and theological system." After 1789:

> The intermediate class then became the first class, and it is very curious to observe its conduct after it seized supreme power: it chose from among its ranks a bourgeois whom it made King. To those members who had played the chief role in the Revolution it gave the titles of prince, duke, count, baron, chevalier, etc. It created majorats [entailed estates] in favor of the new nobles. In short, it reconstituted feudalism to its advantage.... The bourgeoisie has no more social existence than the minor nobles; and the industrials are interested in ridding themselves simultaneously of the supremacy exercised over them by the descendants of the Franks and by the intermediate class which was created by the nobles, and which will consequently always be inclined to constitute feudalism in its own interests.[13]

According to Saint-Simon, the role or "natural function" of lawyers and metaphysicians should have ended "once the old system lost most of its power and the forces of the new system really became dominant in society," which in his view "was completely achieved by the middle of the last century." Because the "political career" of these groups carried on beyond this point, it has become "a complete hindrance." The coming of the French Revolution should have resulted in "industrials and scientists" coming to political power, but instead "the lawyers placed themselves at the head of the Revolution [and] directed it with the doctrines of the metaphysicians," leading to "strange wanderings" and "misfortunes."[14] This outcome could not be allowed to stand: "As long as the lawyers and metaphysicians direct public affairs, the revolution will not come to an end; the King and the nation will not escape from the precarious position in which they have lived for thirty years."[15]

Leaving aside the peculiarities of Saint-Simon's terminology, his fixation on the role of the lawyers and metaphysicians is similar to that of Burke and Mackintosh and, like them, he expresses the obvious truth that industrialists are not, by and large, likely to be at the forefront of physically destructive revolutionary movements, for obvious reasons connected with the nature of their property. All of which raises the obvious question of whether the Revolution would have succeeded at all if leadership had been left to the industrialists. Where Saint-Simon breaks with his French contemporaries is in treating the "lawyers and metaphysicians"—or the "bourgeoisie" in his special sense—as belonging to a different class from the "industrialists and scientists," and in this he is perhaps best seen as the precursor of the descent into mystification and obscurantism that was to increasingly characterize bourgeois thought as the nineteenth century unfolded: not a founder of socialism, in other words, but of sociology.

THE CLIMAX OF A THEORETICAL TRADITION

Maza sees the account of bourgeois revolution given by the French Liberals as merely a brief and passing episode: "The French bourgeoisie was briefly offered an inspiring story of this sort, the one written mostly in the 1820s," she notes. "That narrative did not, however, prove compelling for very long."[16] As we have seen, however, there had existed since before the English Civil War a theoretical position (or "narrative," in Maza's terminology), which certainly took on different inflections according to the precise times and places it was formulated, but which in every version held that the basis of political change lay in prior changes to the nature of property and in the individuals who owned that property. It appears in the work of Clarendon and Harrington, reappears in that of Millar and Steuart, recurs in that of Barnave and Roederer, and culminates in that of the historians to whom Maza refers. It is perhaps worth pausing for a moment to consider the significance of the intellectual consistency involved here, which suggests that it expressed, in however incomplete a form, real changes in society that were general, in varying degrees, throughout Europe. But even if we narrow our focus down to the narrative as it applied to France, it is evident that it had already been formulated before the Republic was proclaimed, by both opponents and supporters of the French Revolution. Neither Burke nor Barnave survived to see the Restoration that, in their different ways, both had desired; but neither needed the luxury of retrospect in order to understand and theorize the process under way in front of their eyes. In this respect, the postrestoration liberals did not innovate so much as recapitulate, consolidate. and systematize ideas that had been widely circulating both before and during the Revolution. The two most sophisticated previous discussions, by Roederer and Barnave, remained in manuscript form until 1831 and 1843, respectively, and therefore could not have directly influenced their work; but the fact that their analysis was broadly similar indicates how widely these arguments had already been disseminated and accepted. In short, if, as Maza says, the narrative of bourgeois ascendancy did not "remain compelling" for the bourgeoisie themselves, it was after a period of nearly two hundred years, not the two decades she imagines and the former is not a period that can be considered "brief" except in relation to geological time.

Nor did the French historians base their narrative exclusively on French history. Collectively, they did have one major advantage denied to all their forebears, with exception of Roederer: they were able to write the history of the French Revolution from a position of knowing how it ended. This overview of the whole process in turn enabled them to situate it more fully in the context of earlier revolutionary events and personalities, above all those of England. The ability to compare the military dictatorships of Cromwell and Napoleon or the restored monarchies of Charles II and Charles X allowed them to establish more completely than Barnave could have that the proper comparison with 1789 was 1640 and not 1688. De Staël was perhaps the first writer to identify the full chronological extent of the English Revolution as a whole:

> The revolutionary period of England may be said to have lasted nearly fifty years, if we reckon from the beginning of the civil wars under Charles I to the accession of William III in 1688; and the efforts of these fifty years had no other real and permanent object than the establishment of the existing constitution; that is, of the finest monument of justice and moral greatness existing in Europe. The same movement in the minds of men which brought about the revolution in England was the cause of that of France in 1789. Both belong to the third era in the progress of social order—the establishment of representative government—a point toward which the human mind is directing itself from all parts.[17]

With all his peculiarities, Saint-Simon was able to identify the similarities between the two revolutions (although this may be due to the influence of Thierry, with whom the following passage was coauthored in 1814): "All the enthusiasm, the madness, the horrors of the French Revolution are parallel in the English Revolution."[18] In the mid-1820s, Guizot dismissed as "superficial and frivolous" attempts to distinguish the English and French Revolutions: "Produced by the same causes, the decay of the feudal aristocracy, the church, and royalty, they both labored at the same work." His final judgment was that "though disappointed in premature hopes, it enabled English society to make a great stride out of the monstrous inequality of the feudal system. In a word, the analogy between the two revolutions is such, that the first would never have been thoroughly understood had not the second taken place."[19] There was, of course, an issue concerning whether the English or French Revolution was historically the more significant. The French tended to hail the superiority of their own revolution, at least in part displaying the nationalism that had been one of its characteristic features. As Mignet wrote, "the French Revolution . . . began the era of new societies in Europe, as the English revolution had begun the era of new governments"; unlike the English, the French "not only modified the political power, but it entirely changed the internal existence of the nation," it introduced a system "better suited to the times": "It substituted law in place of arbitrary will, equality in that of privilege; delivered men from the distinctions of classes, the land from the barriers of provinces, trade from the shackles of corporations and fellowships, agriculture from feudal subjection and the oppression of tithes, property from the impediment of entails, and brought everything to the condition of one state, one system of law, one people."[20] And despite his differences with the Liberals, Saint-Simon took a similar position on the respective merits of the English and French Revolutions:

> England was the First country to move towards the industrial regime. But in view of the imperfect state of civilisation when it undertook its political reform, it could obtain only a modification of the feudal regime. In reality it is the French nation which is summoned, by the nature of things, to commence the organisation of the industrial regime. . . . It was necessary to begin, before all else, by establishing a provisional and preparatory order: the parliamentary regime invented by the English, which experience had recognized as the best possible modification of the feudal system.[21]

These attitudes were not universally upheld in France. In particular, those authors whose sympathies lay with the defeated aristocracy rather than the bourgeoisie tended to compare the defeated French class unfavorably to their British equivalents, who had adapted and taken advantage of the new commercial world. Writing in the mid-1830s, Honoré de Balzac complained of the French aristocracy:

> Not only did the throne lack the kind of counselor capable of rising to circumstances, but the aristocracy lacked above all that comprehension of its general interests which might have made up for all the other deficiencies. . . . It might have done real service to the country by raising justices of the peace to gentle status, by interesting itself in agricultural improvement, by building roads and canals and playing its part as an active power in the land. But it sold its lands in order to speculate on the Stock Exchange. It might have filched from the bourgeoisie its men and women of action and talent whose ambition was undermining the government—by opening its ranks to them. It preferred to fight them—without weapons, for now it possessed only as a tradition what it had once possessed as a reality.[22]

But most importantly, acceptance of this "narrative" was not a purely French phenomenon. It is true that French intellectuals were far less likely to engage in the postrevolutionary self-censorship characteristic of their British rivals. The radical aspects of Smith's legacy, for example, were upheld far longer in Paris than in Edinburgh or London: Saint-Simon still spoke for many of his compatriots when in 1818 he described the "immortal Smith" as being responsible for "the most vigorous, most direct, and most complete critique ever made of the feudal regime."[23] But even in Britain, once the immediate crisis caused by the French Revolution had passed, the argument for the bourgeoisie as a revolutionary class continued to be put, at least until the majority of the bourgeoisie gained full political rights in 1832.

On March 2, 1831, Thomas Babington Macaulay made an incendiary speech in the House of Commons in support of the Great Reform Bill, in which he argued that political forms had to adapt to changed property relations. And his example is the more remarkable given the extent to which Macaulay shared Burke's adoration for tradition, his view of 1688 as a restorative revolution, and his hatred and contempt for Harrington. Nevertheless, he gave examples to the Honorable Members, including that of the French Revolution, to show how this had previously happened in history:

> But a great revolution took place. The character of the old corporations changed. New forms of property came into existence. New portions of society rose into importance. There were in our rural districts rich cultivators, who were not freeholders. There were in our capital rich traders, who were not liverymen. Towns shrank to villages. Villages swelled into cities larger than the London of the Plantagenets. Unhappily while the natural growth of society went on, the artificial polity continued unchanged. The ancient form of the representation remained; and precisely because the form remained, the spirit departed. Then came that pressure to bursting, the new wine in the old bottles, the new society under the old institutions. . . . All history is full of revolutions, produced by causes similar to those which are now operating in England. A portion of the Community which had been of no account expands and becomes strong. It demands a place in the system, suited, not to its former weakness, but to its present power. If this is granted, all is well. If this is refused, then comes the struggle between the young energy of one class and the ancient privileges of another. Such was the struggle between the plebeians and the patricians of Rome. Such was the struggle of the Italian allies for admission to the full rights of Roman citizens. Such was the struggle of our North American colonies against the mother country. Such was the struggle which the Third Estate of France maintained against the aristocracy of birth. Such was the struggle which the Roman Catholics of Ireland maintained against the aristocracy of creed. Such is the struggle which the free people of color in Jamaica are now maintaining against the aristocracy of skin. Such, finally, is the struggle which the middle classes in England are maintaining against an aristocracy of mere locality, against an aristocracy the principle of which is to invest a hundred drunken pot-wallopers in one place, or the owner of a ruined hovel in another, with powers which are withheld from cities renowned to the furthest ends of the earth, for the marvels of their wealth and of their industry.[24]

In one sense this is a weaker version of the argument than is present in the work of Barnave or, in a British context, of Millar. Macaulay has diluted the theory, so that the protagonists are not only social classes but social groups more generally, which although they can and do include classes ("the struggle between the young energy of one class and the ancient privileges of another"), also consist of those oppressed on account of their religious beliefs or "racial" identity. In this case, Macaulay was a participant in an interclass struggle within the bourgeoisie in which he was ranged with its industrial wing against an agrarian one that had for more than a hundred and fifty years largely consisted of Burke's "landed capitalists." But this process of dilution was also ongoing among French writers and for similar reasons. In 1837, for example, the French economist Jérôme-Adolphe Blanqui wrote: "In all the revolutions, there have always been but two parties opposing each other; that of the people who wish to live by their own labor, and that of those who would live by the labor of others . . . *Patricians and plebeians, slaves and freemen, guelphs and ghibellines, red roses and white roses, cavaliers and roundheads, liberals and serviles, are only varieties of the same species.*[25]

Macaulay was a Liberal, or more precisely, a Whig; Sir Walter Scott was a Conservative, or more precisely, a Tory. Scott's last political act was to drag his failing body to a meeting of freeholders in Jedburgh to express his opposition to the same reform bill that Macaulay had supported so passionately in the House of Commons nineteen days earlier. Interrupted by "riotous artisans" he informed his opponents, "I regard your gabble no more than the geese on the green," before withdrawing from the meeting uttering (in Latin) the words of the Roman gladiators, "we who are about to die salute you," which was true in his case, but melodramatic even by his exalted standards.[26] Yet despite his hysterical opposition to any extension of the vote, even to sections of the industrial bourgeoisie, Scott had expressed in his fiction an understanding of the historical class struggle at least as clearly as Macaulay. Indeed, if read in historical sequence, rather than order of composition, his key Scottish novels present the entire trajectory of that nation's bourgeois revolution from the first Bishops War of 1638 through to the last Jacobite Rising in 1745: *A Legend of Montrose, Old Mortality, The Black Dwarf, The Bride of Lammermoor, Rob Roy, The Heart of Midlothian, Waverley,* and *Redgauntlet.* In *Old Mortality* (1816) Scott was the first person to describe the English and Scottish revolutions of 1688 ("a new era") as jointly constituting "the British Revolution."[27] The plot of *Redgauntlet* (1823) concerns an imaginary second attempt by Charles Edward Stuart to regain the thrones of Britain for his dynasty, after the defeat of the Jacobite Rising of 1745–46. As with the real first attempt, Scott imagines French backing for an attempt to raise forces within Scotland with which to reimpose the absolutist regime. One of the Jacobites to attempt to mobilize his tenants for counterrevolution is the eponymous Sir Arthur Redgauntlet. In one dialogue between Redgauntlet's nephew Darsie Latimer, who opposes the rising, and Darsie's sister Lilias, who supports it, the siblings discuss whether any of the peasantry will rise on behalf of the Stuarts. Darsie thinks not, but Lilias disagrees:

> "Whatever these people may pretend, to evade your uncle's importunities, they cannot, at this time of day, think of subjecting their necks again to the feudal yoke, which was effectually broken by the act of 1748, abolishing vassalage and hereditary jurisdictions."
> "Aye, but that my uncle considers as the act of a usurping government," said Lilias.
> "Like enough he may think so," answered her brother, "for he is a superior, and loses his authority by the enactment. But the question is, what the vassals will think of it who have gained their freedom from feudal slavery, and have now enjoyed that freedom for many years?"[28]

Scott's views on feudalism were not restricted to Scotland: in this 1829 novel, *Anne of Geierstein,* Scott describes a "Secret Tribunal" (*Vehme*) organized to resist the threat to the Swiss Confederation from the Hapsburg Empire during the late fifteenth century: "Such an institution could only prevail at a time when ordinary means of justice were excluded by the hand of power, and when, in order to bring the guilty to punishment, it required all the influence and authority of such a confederacy. In no other country than one exposed to every species of feudal tyranny, and deprived of every ordinary mode of obtaining justice or redress, could such a system have taken root and flourished."[29]

Nevertheless, outside of Britain, it was more difficult to simultaneously support commercial society and oppose the revolutions necessary to achieve it. The problem was particularly acute for those who sympathized with the French Revolution and wished to see the measures associated with its early stages implemented in their own countries, but who feared the popular insurgencies it involved. The problems were identified early in the French Revolution by Maximilien Robespierre in a speech to the Jacobin Club on January 2, 1792. Robespierre famously opposed the war urged by the Girond on the grounds that the response of peoples to "armed missionaries" would be to "repel them as enemies." The most interesting aspect of this speech, however, is not his attitude to the war, which he was in any case soon to revise, but his insights into the likely response of the existing ruling classes, who had initiated the revolutionary process in France between 1787 and 1789. This, he argued, was unlikely to be repeated elsewhere in Europe:

> The parliaments, the noblemen, the clergy, the wealthy people were the ones that drove the Revolution forward; the people appeared only afterwards. They changed their minds or wanted, at least, to stop the Revolution when they realized that the people could recover their sovereignty; but they were the ones that started it. Without their resistance and their mistaken calculations, the nation would still be under the domination of the despotism. For that reason, in order to successfully "export" liberty (that is, the Revolution) it would be required to count on the support from the upper classes in the countries on which we intend to focus our action. But now those classes, well warned of how the situation in France evolved, will avoid repeating the "mistake" performed in France by their homologues! Even in Brabant, where the Revolution had been initiated before starting in France, but had been stopped afterwards, we will not find, not even there, the success and the reception imagined by those that put pressure so that freedom is exported.[30]

This was Robespierre at his most acute; but it was not simply the reformist nobility who would now be reluctant to challenge the absolutist regimes: so too would sections of the bourgeoisie. The German philosopher Johann Fichte captured some of the tension in their response to the French Revolution early on, albeit rather abstractly, in his "Contributions to the Correction of the Public's Judgment Concerning the French Revolution" (1793): "The dignity of Freedom must come from the bottom up: freedom without disorder can only come from the top down."[31] But this was only possible if there existed at the "top" social forces willing and able to introduce freedom from on high. One solution would be if the revolution could come, not only from above, but also "from without," as Harrington had described the English intervention in Scotland and Ireland during the 1640s and 1650s. In the context of the 1790s, the only realistic source of revolution from without was France itself.

Spain and Italy, or more specifically, the Kingdom of Naples, were the two areas where the contradictions of revolution from above were most dramatically played out. In the former country, the meaning of the term "revolution" varied depending on which group was using it at any time. As Ronald Fraser notes, following the French invasion of 1808: "For the absolutists, revolution retained its original sense, a complete turn of the celestial sphere to its starting point: as the heavens turned in their orbit, things changed so that everything might finally remain unchanged, with the sole exception of disbarring 'despotism' for ever. But to the progressives it signified a political (but not social) revolution: an institutional rupture with Bourbon centralism and its organs of power, and their replacement by new forms of government."[32]

But Naples also produced the main attempt to theorize the experience. A hundred years before the French Revolution, Scotland and Naples had shared similar problems of development, and consequently the objectives of Enlightenment thinkers in both kingdoms were very similar, enabling us to see them as part of a single movement; but they increasingly operated within very different economic and constitutional contexts. As John Robertson explains:

> By 1800 Scotland had been more or less comfortably integrated into the political system of the United Kingdom, and was making an increasingly important contribution to the economic transformation now known as the industrial revolution; Scotsmen, moreover, were disproportionately represented in the administration, military service, and commercial activities of the British Empire overseas. . . . By contrast, the formally independent kingdom of Naples ended the century locked into what was seemed an inescapable cycle of reform and reaction, revolution and renewed reaction. A monarchy which by 1790 seemed increasingly set on reform, determined at last to assert itself at the expense of the church and the feudal nobility, was transformed by the events of 1792–93 in France into a simple force of reaction, as the king and queen sought to ensure that they themselves did not suffer the fate of their French counterparts (and relatives).[33]

A revolution on the French model was impossible in Naples as the internal social basis was lacking. In January 1799 a republic was declared after a French invasion forced the Bourbon monarchy to flee. The French were supported by local Jacobins within the city, and, although the latter were the more radical in their ambitions to abolish feudalism, their regime could not survive the withdrawal of French troops in March and fell three months later amid scenes of counterrevolutionary carnage encouraged by the British under Lord Nelson. A state functionary under the short-lived Neapolitan or Parthenopean Republic, Vincenzo Cuoco, made the first attempt to deal with the predicament revealed by the debacle.[34] In "Historical Essay on the Neapolitan Republic of 1799" (1801), written in exile, Cuoco argued that the French model upon which the Neapolitan radicals relied "offered nothing to the entire nation, which in turn scorned a culture which was not useful and which it did not understand." He went on to describe the abortive revolution in these terms:

> Our revolution was passive, and the only way it could have been successful was if we had won over the opinion of the people. But the views of the patriots and those of the people were not the same: they had different ideas, different ways of doing things, and even two different languages. . . . The ideas of the Neapolitan revolution could

have been popular had they been drawn from the depths of the nation. Drawn from a foreign constitution, they were far from ours; founded on maxims too abstract . . . they sought to legislate all the customs, caprices, and at times all the defects of another people, who were far from our defects, caprices, and customs.[35]

In these passages Cuoco uses the concept of "passive revolution" as a criticism of the process in Naples, for not involving the people; yet later in his life, under the influence of Burke and other conservatives like Joseph de Maistre, he began to commend a strategy of passive revolution, precisely as a means of bypassing the involvement of the people. This strategy was to have a long and successful life ahead of it, but only after Cuoco's had come to an end and the passions aroused by the French Revolution had long subsided.

The Italian states were not the only site where these issues were discussed. In 1814, the year of the Restoration, Saint-Simon and Thierry predicted that the revolution would continue on a world scale, but the process could not now be the same in the countries that would follow Britain and France, as it had in these pioneers. In particular, they referred to the "conditions peculiar to Germany." These conditions, they wrote, "would increase the violence of her revolution: she has further to go than England or France. Not only must she unite her constitutions, she must also unite, and centralize in one government, a mass of separate governments."[36] Yet it would be here in relatively backward German conditions, which the great movements of the bourgeoisie had left behind, that its achievements would finally be theorized and be most fully understood. Germany was still a patchwork of thirty-nine German-speaking principalities still to be formed into a nation-state. Prussia, the main German state, had been at the forefront of opposition to the French Revolution, not, as in the case of Britain, because France represented a competitor in the emerging bourgeois world, but because the Revolution threatened to destroy the feudal world of which Prussia was a central part. Yet out of this unpromising background Georg Wilhelm Freidrich Hegel was able to distill from a distance the essence of the Great Revolution. Hegel was little interested in a theory of capital as such, despite writing: "Property is the first embodiment of Freedom."[37] And although he sees society developing through a succession of stages, these are not defined by the division of labor or the expansion of trade: "The History of the World is none other than the progress of the consciousness of Freedom; a process whose development according to the necessity of its nature, it is our business to investigate."[38] The progress from slavery to freedom is accompanied by the growing self-consciousness in Man that he exists as a vehicle for the unfolding of Spirit, or God: "The principle of *Development* involves also the existence of the latent germ of being—a capacity or potentiality striving to realize itself. This formal conception finds actual existence in Spirit; which has the History of the World for its theatre, its possession, and the sphere of its realization."[39] In what was perhaps an unwitting echo of Burke, Hegel claims the Reformation was the first step toward this awareness; the French Revolution the second and far more significant step: "It is not difficult to see that our epoch is a birth-time, and a period of transition. The spirit of the age has broken with the world as it has hitherto existed, and with the old ways of thinking, and as in the mind to let them all sink into the depths of the past and to set about its own transformation. It is indeed never at rest, but carried along the stream of progress ever onward."[40]

Hegel drew from the Scottish Historical School the idea that individuals pursuing their own interests produced end results that no one had consciously envisaged; the historical process in this way surmounting individual action or intention. For this reason alone, leaving aside all the others that could be cited, it is necessary to treat with extreme skepticism the claim that Hegel believed "the end of History" had been reached with the Restoration settlement in Prussia after 1815—or indeed that it would ever be reached.[41] More important for our purposes was the lesson he drew from the French Enlightenment—or more precisely, from the actual experience of the French Revolution—that the possibility of any stage in human development being transcended lay not in an evolutionary process of change but in the generation of a force internal to that stage that would resolve its contradictions. The two positions are linked. French absolutism nurtured a bourgeoisie for its own purposes, not imagining that it would seek power on its own behalf: an unintended consequence. The French bourgeoisie destroyed the absolutist state, thus transcending the feudal stage of social development. But this path was not open to every nation or polity:

> It is a false principle that the fetters which bind Right and Freedom can be broken without the emancipation of conscience—that there can be a Revolution without a Reformation.—These countries, therefore, sank back into their old condition—in Italy with some modifications of the outward political condition. Venice and Genoa, those ancient aristocracies, which could at least boast of legitimacy, vanished as rotten despotisms. Material superiority in power can achieve no enduring results: Napoleon could not coerce Spain into freedom any more than Phillip II could force Holland into slavery.[42]

Although expressed in typically idealist form, the parallels with Cuoco's conclusions in relation to Italy are unmistakable and indicate a dilemma that was not to find a solution until the torch of bourgeois revolution had long since passed from the hands of the bourgeoisie. Even while Hegel was alive, the solution had been advocated, or at least described, by a German writer as distant from Hegel as it is possible to imagine: the Romantic literary critic and philosopher Friedrich Schlegel, who observed in 1820 that the French Revolution "had been transformed into a great despotism and revolution from above" by Napoleon.[43]

"BAD CONSCIENCE AND EVIL INTENT": BOURGEOIS INTELLECTUALS IN RETREAT

Hegel and Roederer both died in 1831, Scott in 1832. By the opening of the 1830s then, the last thinkers to have theorized the bourgeois ascendancy while the French

Revolution was still taking place, and who in their different ways epitomized late Enlightenment thought, had departed the scene. A proto-theory of bourgeois revolution had been in development for more than two hundred years before their lives came to an end, yet its different economic, social, and political elements were never brought together in a coherent whole by any individual thinker, although some—notably Harrington in England, Steuart in Scotland, and Barnave in France—came closer than others. There is of course always a problem involved in forming an interpretation while events are ongoing and outcomes are uncertain; Hegel made the solution the subject of one of his most famous and beautiful aphorisms: "When philosophy paints its grey in grey, then has a form of life grown old. Philosophy cannot rejuvenate it, but only understand it. The owl of Minerva spreads its wings only with the coming of the dusk."[44] But even if a historical period can only be understood after it has come to an end, it would have been perfectly possible for bourgeois thinkers after 1815 to look back over the previous two centuries and draw the necessary conclusions: they did not. Indeed, the more securely embedded the capitalist system became, the more they retreated from even such clarity as had previously been achieved.

The terminological and conceptual transition from commercial society to capitalism was only completed at some point between the early 1830s and late 1840s.[45] By then the four-stage theory had therefore largely been abandoned. Henceforth, it was still invoked only in those European states attempting to catch up with Britain and France—or at least those that had a realistic chance of doing so and even there with diminishing frequency. "The industrial history of nations," wrote the German economist Frederick List in 1841,

> and of none more clearly than England, proves that the transition from the savage state to that pastoral one, from the pastoral to the agricultural, and from the agricultural to the first beginnings in manufacture and navigation, is effected most speedily and advantageously by means of free commerce with further advanced towns and countries, but that a perfectly developed manufacturing industry, an important mercantile marine, and foreign trade on a really large scale, can only be attained by means of the interposition of the power of the state.[46]

The concept of capitalism did, however, retain one characteristic of commercial society, namely the notion that it had existed throughout human history. "There was an increasing tendency," writes Ronald Meek, "for the economists to interpret development in the pre-commercial stages in terms of the economic categories appropriate to interpreting capitalism."[47] Such an ancient pedigree could surely mean only that capitalism was congruent with human nature itself, or as Smith put it, it represented "a certain propensity in human nature . . . to truck, barter, and exchange one thing for another."[48] So we find that in the work of the German historian Theodor Mommsen, his discussion of Rome during the fifth century BCE refers to "the disproportionate centralization of capital" and describes "great manufacturers" as "simultaneously traders and capitalists."[49] If the abandonment of the four-stage theory was potentially an advance in the scientific understanding of human development, retaining the notion that capitalism had existed throughout history involved an actual retreat from positions established by the French Liberals in the 1820s, a retreat in which they were complicit.

The necessarily unsavory aspects of the emergence and consolidation of capitalism were always difficult for bourgeois intellectuals to discuss, unless they were marginal figures like Steuart, less concerned with maintaining the polite fictions of the time. Smith, for example, failed to acknowledge the necessity of "primitive" accumulation for capital, referring instead to the "previous accumulation of stock"; a position that Marx later described as a form of "insipid childishness" that "is everyday preached to us in the defence of property."[50] But even those theories with which they had once boldly taunted the defenders of feudalism—above all the law of value—became more problematic once the imperative became less about demonstrating the unproductive nature of feudal retainers and more about denying that the working class was the only source of new value in production. One solution was to treat capitalism as a natural phenomenon, but there was nothing in the notion of capitalism existing throughout history that excludes the possibility of revolutions being required to ensure its dominance: such a reading could easily envisage these revolutions as necessary exceptions, one-off historical events required to unleash capitalist development. But none of the thinkers considered here, except the very earliest, were ever able to concede this: Harrington's new notion of social revolution confirming emergent property relations was ignored by Locke in favor of the traditional conception of political revolution restoring a preexisting constitution; Smith attributed the suppression of the nobility and the possibility of commercial society to the absolutist monarchy rather than any action by the bourgeoisie themselves; Burke hailed the "market" in England while denouncing attempts by the bourgeoisie to establish it in France; and even Barnave, who came closest in theory to overcoming the lacunae of his forerunners, retreated in practice from what was politically necessary for the safety and security of the revolution he had helped initiate, for fear of what it might unleash—a fear entirely justified by the type of declaration that was to appear within a few years of his execution. "The French Revolution is but the precursor of another revolution, far greater, far more solemn, which will be the last," wrote Gracchus Babeuf in 1796: "We aim at something more sublime and more just, the COMMON good or the COMMUNITY OF GOODS!"[51]

Babeuf was the figure who more than any other embodies the transition from Jacobinism to socialism. The concerns raised by his Conspiracy of Equals were serious enough: once the proletariat emerged as a wholly distinct class in society whose insurrectionary capabilities were displayed most dramatically in the French Revolution of 1830 and the agitation leading up to the 1832 Great Reform Bill in Britain, the bourgeoisie began to abandon its self-identity as a revolutionary class. Looking back from the 1860s, Marx was to identify what this meant for political economy:

In France and in England the bourgeoisie had conquered political power. Thenceforth, the class struggle, practically as well as theoretically, took on more and more outspoken and threatening forms. It sounded the knell of scientific bourgeois economy. It was thenceforth no longer a question, whether this theorem or that was true, but whether it was useful to capital or harmful, expedient or inexpedient, politically dangerous or not. In place of disinterested inquirers, there were hired prize fighters; in place of genuine scientific research, the bad conscience and the evil intent of apologetic.[52]

But the same point was more widely applicable. Under these new circumstances, which the bourgeoisie had itself brought about, any concession to the idea that class-based revolutions had been required for social transformation in the past were increasingly seen as giving dangerous encouragement to the idea that they were also necessary in the present. As this suggests, the bourgeoisie was becoming expert in covering its tracks and diverting attention onto false trails, at least where capitalism was already dominant, rewriting the history of their own revolutionary rise to power so that each individual moment appeared to be a political rather than social revolution. In other words, by the time Marx and Engels came to consider the issue, bourgeois thought had begun to reinterpret the great revolutions in terms that gave greater emphasis to "liberty," or the achievement of constitutional government, than to "property," or the unshackling of a new economic order. We can see the change, in a British context, in the work of Macaulay.

In his speeches on the Great Reform Bill during the crisis of 1831, his subject was the political representation of a new class, his class; when we turn to his great work, *The History of England from the Accession of James II* (1848–57), it is that of constitutional liberty. It is not too much to suggest that this change in attitude was produced, perhaps unconsciously, by the new fear of working-class revolution. Whatever the extent of Macaulay's hostility to the "aristocracy," with whom he wished his class to share political power, it was easily surpassed by his hostility to the working class, whom he wished to exclude from it. As he argued during the Chartist agitation later in 1830s, an ignorant and credulous crowd desperate for food, unable to understand that inequality was ultimately necessarily for the benefit of all classes, would be misled by "the professional agitators, the tempters" into the seizure of property, resulting in the collapse of the economy and "one vast spoliation" from which the only relief would be "strong military despotism"; but as for "the noble institutions" that had made Britain great: "We would not see them again." And if Parliament should be weak or foolish enough to give the vote to these "laborious mechanics": "We should not deserve to see them."[53] It is the continuity of English history—from which both James VII and II and his uncle Charles had temporarily broken—that is both celebrated and contrasted with that of France, where continuity was lost, leading to the horrors that he claimed the Chartists sought to reproduce. Macaulay is forced to downplay even the nature of the Cromwellian period. In his earliest work, written in 1830 but unpublished during his lifetime, he makes this comparison of the English Revolution of 1640 and the French Revolution of 1789:

The Royalists were overcome by the Presbyterians; but we had nothing like the massacres of September. The Presbyterians were overcome by the independents; but we had nothing like the vengeance inflicted by the Mountain on the Gironde. . . . [Cromwell] was less absolute than Napoleon because the English republicans had been less violent than the Jacobins, because the governments of the Stuarts had been milder than that of the Bourbons. The recoil was moderate, because the compression had been moderate.[54]

One explanation for the relative mildness of the English Revolution might have been the fact that capitalism was more advanced in England than in France, but Macaulay opts instead for a trivial conception of national character. For Macaulay, 1688 is "that revolution which terminated the long struggle between our sovereigns and their parliaments." In France: "The gulf of a great revolution completely separates the new from the old system. No such chasm divides the existence of the English nation into two distinct parts."[55] The comparison between the course of events in England and those on the European mainland, above all in France, is one to which he repeatedly returns:

When we compare [the English Revolution of 1688] with those revolutions which have, during the last sixty years, overthrown so many ancient governments, we cannot but be struck by its peculiar character. . . . It was revolution strictly defensive, and had prescription and legitimacy on its side. Here, and here only, a limited monarchy of the thirteenth century had come down unimpaired to the seventeenth century. . . . To those of us who have lived through the year 1848, it may seem almost an abuse of terms to call a proceeding, conducted with so much solemnity, and such minute attention to prescriptive etiquette, by the terrible name of revolution. . . . It was because we had a preserving revolution in the seventeenth century that we have not had a destroying revolution in the nineteenth.[56]

The French did not have a "preserving revolution" and consequently could not simply ignore or downplay the events of 1789 in the same way as the English did those of 1640.[57] Nevertheless, we are dealing here with a general ideological shift, in which the French failure to follow the English example could be presented as a deviation caused by the unwanted intervention of the plebeians.

The shift occurred everywhere in the wake of the bourgeois revolutions, inevitably involving unevenness. But when it occurred it touched all aspects of expression, art, and culture as much as politics and social theory. In Italy, for example, where national unification (the "Risorgimento") during the 1860s effectively comprised the bourgeois revolution, the difference between the composers Giuseppe Verdi (1813–1901) and Giacomo Puccini (1858–1924) indicates the extent of the change in attitude. Anthony Arblaster writes of Verdi's opera Don Carlo (1867): "Both Schiller's play and Verdi's adaptation of it testify to the symbolic importance which the Dutch struggle for independence had for a later liberalism. It was not accidental that Verdi's choruses of oppression were interpreted by Italian audiences as comments on their own situation under continuing Austrian rule." Compare this with the apolitical tone of Puccini's Tosca (1900), which actually deals with an early episode in the Italian bourgeois revolution, the aftermath of the destruction of the Roman Republic in 1800: "It is not hard to imagine what Verdi would have made of the theme of oppression, freedom and patriotism implicit in such a situation. With the dramatist Sardou, and following him, Puccini, the story becomes an ugly melodrama of sadism, lust and revenge. There is a significant contraction of scope: the public is reduced to the private."[58] In the former, Verdi takes the Dutch bourgeois revolution as a historical surrogate for contemporary events in Italy; in the latter, Puccini uses the Italian bourgeois revolution as a historical backdrop for a story that could have been set virtually anywhere at any time. The shift does not merely indicate a coarsening in the aesthetics of Italian opera but a decline in historical sensibility.

TOCQUEVILLE AS EXCEPTION

One liberal thinker did however retain the insights of his bourgeois predecessors: Alexis de Tocqueville. Tocqueville is as beloved by modern revisionists of the French Revolution as Clarendon is by revisionists of the English Revolution. In 1955, for example, Alfred Cobban quoted a famous passage from Tocqueville's memoirs in the founding statement of the revisionist position.[59] Writing in the aftermath of the French revolution of 1848–49, Tocqueville had criticized certain current interpretations of history: "I detest these absolute systems, which represent all the events of history as dependent upon great first causes linked to the chain of fatality, and which, as it were, suppress men from the history of the human race. They seem narrow, to my mind, under their pretence of broadness, and false beneath their air of mathematical exactness."[60] Here the echoes of Guizot's "abstract principle" and "fanciful theories" are strong: the "detested system" in both cases being socialism, whose red banner had first been raised in these years. As one of his biographers has noted, Tocqueville thought socialism involved "the worship of material goods, the abolition of private property, and the suppression of individual liberty"; in other words, the very opposite of what the revolution of 1789 had established: "The revolution of 1848 would deny the ideas of 1789 if it established socialism."[61] Later revisionist figures like François Furet have admired Tocqueville's supposed claim that, rather than transforming the French state, the French Revolution of 1789 expanded the apparatus of absolutism and left society untouched.[62] In the face of these endorsements, what Tocqueville actually wrote, both in his great work on the French Revolution and his autobiography, repays study. On the one hand it extended the work of his liberal predecessors: "In the late 1820s, Guizot's *History* [of *Civilization*] had helped persuade him of the futility of the ultra-royalist attempt to restore aristocratic privilege."[63] On the other, it is in many respects perfectly compatible with that of Marx and Engels, even though his political conclusions were the opposite of theirs.[64]

Tocqueville notes that there had been great revolutionary movements with the goal of equality prior to the French Revolution but that without the necessary socioeconomic context they could not have been permanently successful, with the result that "the firebrand that set all Europe ablaze in the eighteenth century was easily extinguished in fifteenth": "For doctrines of this kind to lead to revolutions, certain changes must already have taken place in the living conditions, customs, and manners of a nation and prepared men's minds for the reception of new ideas."[65] Nevertheless, for Tocqueville there was one country at least in which the legacy of the Middle Ages had been overcome before the French Revolution, and in this context one wishes he had been read as assiduously by revisionists of the English Revolution as by those of the French:

> at first sight one might think that the ancient European constitution still functioned [in England]. True, the old names and old offices were retained; but in the seventeenth century feudalism was to all intents and purposes a dead letter, classes intermingled, the nobility no longer had the upper hand, the aristocracy had ceased to be exclusive, wealth was a stepping-stone to power, all men were equal before the law and public offices open to all, freedom of speech and of the press was the order of the day. All this lay quite outwith the purview of the medieval mind, and it was precisely these innovations, gradually and adroitly introduced into the old order, that, without impairing its stability or demolishing ancient forms, gave it a new lease of life and a new energy. Seventeenth-century England was already a quite modern nation, which, however, venerated and enshrined within its heart some relics of the Middle Ages.[66]

It was the same task of overthrowing feudalism that the French Revolution was to accomplish, although in a far more thoroughgoing way than in England. To understand this, Tocqueville recommends that we ignore the superficial or contingent: "If we disregard various incidental developments which briefly modified its aspect at different periods and in different lands, and study it as it was essentially, we find that the chief permanent achievement of the French Revolution was the suppression of those political institutions, commonly described as feudal, which for many centuries had held unquestioned sway in most European countries." These institutions "still entered into the very texture of the religious and political institutions of almost the whole of Europe," but they had also produced a series of more intangible aspects— or what Marx would later call "superstructures,""a host of ideas, sentiments, manners, and customs, which, so to speak, adhered to them": "Thus nothing short of a major operation was needed to excise from the body politic these accretions and to destroy them utterly." The passage that follows was later to be one of the authorities for revisionism: "Radical though it may have been, the Revolution made far fewer changes than is generally supposed." Yet they do not appear to have read the sentences that follow, which suggest that this was not because it failed to transform French society, but because the transformation was already under way before the Revolution began:

> What in point of fact it destroyed, or is in the process of destroying—for the Revolution is still operative—may be summed up as everything that stemmed from aristocratic and feudal institutions, was in any way connected with them, or even bore, however faintly, their imprint. The only elements of the old order that it retained were those which had always been foreign to its institutions and could exist independently

of them. Chance played no part whatever in the outbreak of Revolution . . . it was the inevitable outcome of a process in which six generations had played an intermittent part. Even if it had not taken place, the old social structure would nonetheless have been shattered everywhere sooner or later. The only difference would have been that instead of collapsing with such brutal suddenness it would have crumbled bit by bit.[67]

Tocqueville did not, any more than Guizot, imagine that feudalism was unchanged since the Middle Ages, particularly in relation to political institutions. He nevertheless still regarded it as "basic to the economic structure of France" on the eve of the Revolution, and thought that it was precisely popular awareness that some aspects of feudalism had been dismantled that made the remainder harder to endure: "In this restricted form it was far more hated than in the heyday of feudalism, and we are fully justified in saying that the very destruction of some of the institutions of the Middle Ages made those which survived seem all the more detestable."[68] Tocqueville was of course to generalize this point in his famous "paradox" of revolution:

> It is not always when things are going from bad to worse that revolutions break out. On the contrary, it oftener happens that when a people which has put up with an oppressive rule over a long period without protest suddenly finds the government relaxing its pressure, it takes up arms against it. Thus the social order overthrown by a revolution is almost always better than the one immediately preceding it, and experience teaches us that, generally speaking, the most perilous moment for a bad government is one when it seeks to mend its ways.[69]

His overall assessment of the revolutionary movements in France since 1789, recorded in 1850 for his memoirs, is remarkable at the time for his insistence on their class basis:

> Our history from 1789 to 1830, viewed from a distance and as a whole, affords as it were the picture of a struggle to the death between the Ancien Regime, its traditions, memories, hopes and men, as represented by the aristocracy, and the New France led by the Middle Class. The year 1830 closed the first period of our revolutions, or rather our revolution: for there is but one. . . . In 1830 the triumph of the middle classes had been definite and so thorough that all political power, every franchise, every prerogative, and the whole government was confined and, as it were, heaped up within the narrow limits of this one class, to the statutory exclusion of all beneath them and the actual exclusion of all above.[70]

What enabled Tocqueville to retain these insights longer than his contemporaries? It may have been precisely because he was of aristocratic, rather than of bourgeois background, and consequently, with the zeal of the convert for ideas that were originally alien to his class, he was prepared to hold them with less circumspection. It is usual to see the period that climaxed in 1848 as one in which the bourgeoisie embraced the aristocracy as an ally against the working class; but in countries like France, where the bourgeois revolution lay in the past, the process of reconciliation went in both directions, as Sheldon Wolin explains:

The worker who embodied the contradiction between the new regime's professions of equality and its systematically induced inequalities unintentionally promoted a solidarity among the remnants of the old regime and representatives of the new regime. By arousing a common fear of equality, the worker united the two classes, which, as a result of the French Revolution, had experienced opposite reversals of fortune: the aristocracy, which had lost social and political preeminence, and the bourgeoisie, which had acquired economic power and was steadily increasing its social and political influence.[71]

Even if we treat Tocqueville as an exception, bourgeois thought scarcely came to a complete standstill during the 1830s: the giant figure of Charles Darwin was still in the early stages of his intellectual development, having recently absorbed the teachings of the Scottish Enlightenment directly at Edinburgh University.[72] But the type of education that the young Darwin would experience there had undergone a change from that which he would have received from Smith in Glasgow, fifty years earlier. The division of knowledge into discrete subjects was coincident with the postrevolutionary bourgeois attempt to prevent impressionable young minds from gaining a scientific overall worldview such as had been partially achieved during the Enlightenment. Academic specialization presents a world of fragments, something that would have been alien to Smith and his contemporaries, who still required scientific knowledge of the world as a whole. Insofar as specific subjects existed they were merely different ways of approaching human social development: their boundaries coexisted and often overlapped, to say the least, as examples show even if we restrict our examples to Scotland. In the late 1780s Dugald Stewart wrote in a letter that he was "now employed in premeditating two Lectures—the one on the Air-Pump, and the other on the Immortality of the Soul."[73] Sir John Dalrymple not only wrote "An Essay towards a History of Feudal Property in Great Britain," he was also a chemist who invented a process for manufacturing soap out of herrings.[74] The radical tenant farmer and theorist James Anderson wrote works ranging from the abolitionist *Observations on Slavery* (1789) to a *Practical Treatise on Drawing Bogs and Swampy Grounds* (1797).

But perhaps the unity of revolutionary bourgeois thought can best be seen in an example from south of the border, in the person of the industrial capitalist, dissenter, and abolitionist Josiah Wedgewood (1730–95). In 1766 Wedgewood wrote to his business partner, Thomas Bentley, in ecstatic terms about the electrical experiments then being conducted by the latter and Joseph Priestley: "But what daring mortals you are! to rob the Thunderer of his bolts,—and for what?— no doubt to blast the oppressors of the poor and needy, or to execute some public piece of justice in the most tremendous and conspicuous manner, that shall make the great ones of the earth tremble!"[75] As can be seen from these examples, there was no division between the social and natural sciences. As the name of Darwin suggests, however, insofar as it retained any radicalism this had moved from the former to the latter. The theory of social revolution would henceforth have to be developed elsewhere.

TWO

ORIGINS, DEVELOPMENTS, ORTHODOXY

8 MARX AND ENGELS (1) 1843–47: BETWEEN ENLIGHTENMENT AND HISTORICAL MATERIALISM

A s Ronald Meek writes, faced with the scale of the theoretical retreat undertaken by the bourgeoisie: "Marx saw the vital connections which had been forgotten and restored the unity that had been destroyed."[1] To have retained the original insights of the Enlightenment thinkers in relation to social revolution would in itself have been an important intellectual achievement; but did Marx and Engels do any more than this? One influential position, held by adherents of the school of "political Marxism," argues that they did not, at least in the field of political theory.[2] Rather than Marx and Engels imagining continuities between their work and that of their predecessors, as the revisionist historians claim, political Marxists regard these continuities as being only too real and think they involved the revolutionary duo in uncritically adopting bourgeois or, in some versions, "liberal" positions ultimately incompatible with historical materialism— or at least historical materialism as it is understood by the political Marxists.

According to this interpretation, Marx and Engels introduced a new terminology, but essentially continued to employ two existing theories to produce the concept of bourgeois revolution. On the one hand, they used the model of development associated with the Historical School of the Scottish Enlightenment to explain how capitalism emerged from within feudal society. On the other, they used the model of class-based revolution characteristic of the Liberal historians of the French Restoration to explain how the bourgeoisie were then able to overcome the absolutist obstacles to its ascendancy. As political Marxists correctly point out, the Scots did not in fact explain the origin of capitalism; instead, they merely identified how an already existing capitalism became dominant; or, in the terms the Scots themselves would have used, how the growth of commerce ultimately led to the establishment of "commercial society." However, the critique of political economy subsequently undertaken by Marx from the late 1850s led him to develop an alternative model of the origins of capitalism. He now rejected the assumption that capitalism had always existed, even in embryo, and identified instead the historical process by which what Robert Brenner calls "social property relations" changed from a feudal to a capitalist basis, the decisive aspect of which was not the *replacement* of the existing ruling class by another but the *transformation* of the existing ruling class into one that depended on a new and different mode of exploitation. The events that Marx and Engels called bourgeois revolutions were irrelevant to this process and the theory that they inherited was ideological in character, designed to highlight the undeserved reputation of the bourgeoisie as the vanguard of social progress against feudalism while obscuring the reality of how the subordinate classes were subjected to more intense forms of exploitation than ever before. One consequence of this argument is that the emergence of capitalism as an endogenous development (that is, not produced by external geopolitical or geoeconomic competitive pressures), far from being an uneven but essentially universal process, was one restricted to England and perhaps—although even this is controversial among political Marxists—to the United Netherlands. Opinion is divided about Marx's own subsequent position on bourgeois revolution. Some, including Brenner, seem to believe that Marx simply dropped the concept after the composition of his 1857–58 notebooks (the *Grundrisse*), during which any traces of Smithian influence are supposedly excised. Others, like George Comninel, regretfully conclude that although Marx completed his critique of political economy, he did not undertake a comparable critique of existing theories of class struggle. He therefore continued to employ the concept of bourgeois revolution, even though it retained the impress of its liberal materialist origins: it consequently remained an alien presence, a malignant tumor within the otherwise healthy body of Marx's mature work. In neither version, however, is Marx supposed to have consciously revised the concept.[3] It is certainly true that Marx and Engels were influenced by both Scottish and French writers, but not in the way suggested by the political Marxist account of their development. It was rather because they were the source of the two materialist theories of historical development (excluding Hegel's view of history as the unfolding of the World Spirit) available to Marx and Engels during the formation of their thought.

One, associated with the later French Physiocrats and the Scottish Historical School, was that society has developed through a succession of *modes of subsistence*, namely hunting and gathering, pasturage, agriculture, and commerce. As Smith had implied, the commercial mode was simultaneously the fourth and final mode of subsistence and one that had coexisted, in increasingly more developed forms, with all three previous modes: it appears last in the sequence, not by emerging out of the previous agricultural mode but by becoming dominant over it. Both the transitions from one mode to another and the gradual ascendancy of the overarching commercial mode were the result of the growth of population, the expansion of trade, and the evolution of the division of labor.[4] Marx and Engels were originally influenced by Smith's account of the emergence of commercial society, but, as we shall see, they had established their own alternative position, based on the development of the forces of production, a decade before Marx began to write the *Grundrisse*.

A far more enduring Scottish influence on them was the notion that history had proceeded through a succession of stages, although they differed from the Scots as to what these stages involved. Stedman Jones has claimed that "attempts to establish a direct link between the young Marx and the conjectural histories of the Scots have so far failed." He notes that, of the works with which Marx was familiar, Smith's *The Wealth of Nations* does not discuss stages of development, whereas Ferguson's *Essay on the History of Civil Society* does discuss them, but was only referenced by Marx for the first time in 1847, after he and Engels had formulated their own position.[5] Stedman Jones is wrong about Ferguson, since we now know that Marx read him in a French translation late in 1844 and early in 1845, during his first serious engagement with political economy.[6] We also know that Marx made a summary of Millar's *Origin of the Distinction of Ranks* during the same period, possibly after encountering references to it in the work of James Mill.[7] However, as Stedman Jones correctly argues, this is a "non-existent problem" anyway, since Marx would have encountered ideas "as different and disconnected strands of an inheritance dispersed in an array of social and political debates occasioned by the French Revolution and its aftermath."[8] They would certainly have absorbed Scottish ideas from the works of Hegel.[9] There were many aspects of political economy, and of Enlightenment thought more generally, where Marx and Engels differed from their predecessors not in theoretical but normative terms. Ferguson and Smith both recognized that the division of labor necessary for commercial society had certain detrimental effects on social life, leading to dehumanization and the decline of virtue, but regarded these as unavoidable if feudalism and absolutism were to be overcome. Marx and Engels did not dispute the assessment, but considered these effects were consequent on the capitalist mode of production and would cease with its overthrow. The real issue for them was whether there could be any form of society beyond what the Scots called commercial society.[10]

Two Scottish authors should be specifically mentioned here since in different ways their work left a great impress on historical materialism. Marx and Engels did not only absorb the stages theory of development from theoretical sources. Of the authors they admired, Balzac did more than more than any other to depict the established structures of bourgeois society, but it was Scott, the last literary representative of the Scottish Historical School, who did most to trace the process by which such a society came into being. As Eleanor Marx recalled, "Scott was an author to whom Marx again and again returned, whom he admired and knew as well as Balzac and Fielding."[11] And according to his son-in-law, Paul Lafargue, Marx considered at least one of Scott's novels, *Old Mortality* (1816), to be "a masterpiece."[12] Of the theoreticians, Marx's engagement with Steuart was more concentrated and occupied far less space in his collected works than that with Smith, but overall it was more wholeheartedly appreciative. In particular, the emphasis Marx places in *Capital* on the necessity of "primitive accumulation" is drawn directly from Steuart, as he acknowledged in this and similar passages: "He examines the process [of the genesis of capital] particularly in agriculture; and he rightly considers that manufacturing proper only came into being through this process of separation in agriculture. In Adam Smith's writings the process of separation is assumed to be already complete."[13] But Marx also recognized Steuart's broader achievement, describing him as "the first Briton to expound a general system of bourgeois economy": "He is particularly interested in the difference between bourgeois and feudal labour, having observed the latter in the stage of its decline both in Scotland and during his extensive journeys on the continent."[14]

The other materialist theory of historical development, first held by Harrington and his followers, and later revived by French revolutionary intellectuals like Barnave, was that there had been a succession of different types of *society*, based on distinct forms of property, namely ancient, feudal ("Gothic"), and commercial or bourgeois.[15] Marx and Engels do not seem to have been aware of the work of these two thinkers. Although they frequently referred to English materialists such as Hobbes, they never refer to Harrington. Similarly, although they were obviously aware of Barnave as a historical actor in the drama of the French Revolution, his "Introduction to the French Revolution" was only published in 1843 and there is no evidence that either man read it. It is likely then, that their sense of history as a succession of different social forms was derived from the French Liberal historians. But this has nothing to do with the function of revolution as means of consolidating the shift from feudal to bourgeois society.

Two quotations from Marx and Engels are often used to demonstrate their reliance on the French Liberals for the concept of bourgeois revolution.[16] The first is from a letter by Engels, written toward the end of his life in response to questions from one of his many correspondents: "While Marx discovered the materialist conception of history, Thierry, Mignet, Guizot, and all the English historians up to 1850 are the proof that it was being striven for, and the discovery of the same conception by Morgan proves that the time was ripe for it and that indeed it *had* to be discovered."[17] But this refers to historical materialism, not bourgeois revolution and, in any case, "striving for" a conception is not the same as actually achieving its realization. The second is another letter, in this case from Marx to the German socialist, Joseph Weydemeyer:

> Now as for myself, I do not claim to have discovered either the existence of classes in modern society or the struggle between them. Long before me, bourgeois historians had described the historical development of this struggle between the classes, as had bourgeois economists their economic anatomy. My own contribution was 1. to show that the *existence of classes* is merely bound up with *certain historical phases in the development of production*; 2. that the class struggle necessarily leads to the *dictatorship of the proletariat*; 3. that this dictatorship itself constitutes no more than a transition to the *abolition of all classes* and to a *classless society*.[18]

Before listing his own achievements, Marx acknowledged that two groups had identified class and class struggle before him. One, in relation to "historical development" was the work of "bourgeois historians," who certainly included, but were not restricted to, the French Liberals. Marx refers in this connection to Guizot and Thierry, but also to the English author John Wade.[19] Indeed, as late as 1854, Marx was still drawing on the recent work of Mignet, notably his *History of the Formation and Progress of the Third Estate* (1853), and described him to Engels as "the father [*le père*] of the 'class struggle.'"[20] The other group, in relation to "economic anatomy" was the work of the "bourgeois economists" who were mainly British. David Ricardo, for example, had a "distributionist" conception of class struggle, writing: "There can be no rise in the value of labour without a fall of profits"; and, in the same way, "the rate of profits can never be increased but by a fall in wages."[21] But a similar point applies here as in the letter by Engels: Marx is referring to the class struggle as a general category, not the bourgeois revolution as a specific example of it. Much later, Lenin wrote in a commentary on this passage: "To confine Marxism to the theory of the class struggle means curtailing Marxism, distorting it, reducing it to something acceptable to the bourgeoisie."[22] The bourgeoisie not only wage class war against the working class, the more honest of their representatives also acknowledge that they are doing so; the more tactless have even done so with reference to Marx himself.[23] What became intolerable to the bourgeoisie from the 1830s was not the existence of class struggle but the claim that the capitalist system came into being as a result, and that class struggle under capitalism might lead to a new and different form of society beyond it—to socialism, in other words. The key part of Marx's letter, in this context, is what he identifies as his first contribution, "that the *existence of classes* is merely bound up with *certain historical phases in the development of production*," because it suggests the ideological obstacles that prevented even the greatest bourgeois writers from producing an overall theory of bourgeois revolution was also that which prevented them from arriving at a completely materialist conception of history, even when their class was in its most revolutionary phase.

Guizot, for example, began to reconsider his previous positions when the French revolution of 1848 demonstrated that agitation for what he had earlier called "utopian" objectives had not disappeared. Marx then criticized him precisely because of the way in which, in his post-1848 pamphlet *Why Was the English Revolution So Successful?* (1850) he abandoned any social explanation for the English and French Revolutions: "Only political phrases have any meaning for him. . . . Consequently, as M. Guizot everywhere omits the most important factors, there is nothing left for him but to present a highly unsatisfactory and banal narration of merely political events.[24] Consequently, Guizot was now unable to show either the similarities or the differences between the English and the French Revolutions: "We can see from this pamphlet how even the most able figures of the ancien regime, even those whom in their way possess an unquestionable talent for history, have been so completely bewildered by the fateful events of February [1848] that they have lost all historical understanding, even of their own earlier actions. . . . It is not merely that *les rois s'en vont* [kings disappear] but also that *les capacités de la bourgeoisie s'en vont* [the leading authorities of the bourgeoisie disappear]."[25]

The Marxist theory of history *required* a concept of bourgeois revolution; but one did not lie readily at hand. The term was certainly in use by the time Marx and Engels entered political life, at least in relation to France, although not by thinkers belonging to the bourgeoisie. The French revolution of 1830 had been described by the followers of Saint-Simon as a revolution led by the bourgeoisie in their own interests.[26] Following this interpretation, the term seems to have been first employed by the very moderate socialist Louis Blanc, who proclaimed in 1839: "Behold the bourgeois revolution of '89!" Blanc then explained to his readers that in "this great laboratory of the ideas of the eighteenth century" the bourgeoisie had "taken material possession of a field which it had already conquered in moral terms."[27] Here the revolution is bourgeois by virtue of the fact that it is made, or at any rate led, by the bourgeoisie itself. But despite the availability of the term, Marx and Engels did not use it themselves until 1847, even in earlier writings concerned with the French Revolution. In fact, they arrived at the concept by an entirely separate route.

FROM POLITICAL TO SOCIAL REVOLUTION

The emergence of the concept of bourgeois revolution actually lay in the series of overlapping encounters with idealist German conceptions of the state, utopian French conceptions of communism, and speculative Scottish conceptions of development, which Marx and Engels successively undertook between 1843 and 1846. Each part of what would become the "sources and components" of Marxism contributed different elements toward the theory, their emphasis falling variously on economic transition, social revolution, or political representation depending on the historical periods and territorial places in which they were formulated. Peter Thomas has argued that "the philosophy of praxis emerged from a dynamic overdetermination of two elements (German philosophy and French politics) by a methodological element of the third (precisely, the immanentistic conception implicit in English political economy)."[28] Thomas ascribes this position to Gramsci, although it is not apparent that the relevant passage from the prison notebooks can bear this construal.[29] But regardless of whether this interpretation originates with Gramsci or Thomas himself, the point is a good one. The concept of bourgeois revolution emerged out of the specific overdetermination of the German theory of the state and the French theory of politics by the Scottish theory of staged development.

Several important works, complementary in their approach, have already reconstructed in detail the process through which Marx and Engels became first communists, then historical materialists.[30] I will not repeat the findings of their authors here, but since the concept of bourgeois revolution was formulated during the same period as the core principles of historical materialism and, indeed, is a specific application of those principles, some consideration of the relationship between them is necessary.

For Marx and Engels the era of the bourgeois revolutions preceded and to a certain extent overlapped with that of the proletarian revolutions in history. Consequently, the former concept is widely assumed to have also preceded the latter in the development of their thought, perhaps even acting as the inspiration for it. "Up to now, the 'proletarian revolution' has been modeled, more or less, on the 'bourgeois revolution,' claims Immanuel Wallerstein: "As the bourgeoisie overthrew the aristocracy, so the proletariat would overthrow the bourgeoisie."[31] But here the model of proletarian revolution is not derived from one of bourgeois revolution in general, but one of the French Revolution in particular. Perry Anderson, by contrast, has argued that the concept of bourgeois revolution "was essentially constructed through a retro-projection whose model was the proletarian revolution, implying the idea that the structure of the bourgeois revolution would be homologous with what was known—or thought to be known—of proletarian revolutions."[32] This is nearer to the truth, but where did the model of the proletarian revolution come from in the first place? The answer again is the French Revolution. In fact, Marx and Engels theorized *both* bourgeois *and* proletarian revolutions at the same time and in both cases drew heavily from the example of the French Revolution, but on different aspects in relation to each. If the *form* of the French Revolution (mass popular democratic upheavals) foreshadowed the *process* of proletarian revolution, the *consequences* (overthrow of feudal-absolutist restrictions on capitalist development) defined the *nature* of bourgeois revolutions.

Paine had hailed the French Revolution as an entirely new type of event in human history, fundamentally different from all earlier revolutions by virtue of not merely replacing one set of rulers with another, but establishing a new type of democratic politics. These claims for uniqueness, understandable as a response to conservative attacks, were nevertheless analytically untenable, as various bourgeois radicals from Mackintosh onward had demonstrated by drawing the inescapable historical parallels with the Dutch Revolt and the English Civil War.[33] From the 1830s, working-class radicals—at least those who saw themselves as socialists or communists—tended to follow the tradition of Babeuf rather than Paine and were consequently inclined to argue that even the French Revolution did not represent a qualitatively different type of event from earlier revolutions. In an article in the *London Mercury* of May 7, 1837, for example, the Irish Chartist leader Bronterre O'Brien asked:

> What means a social revolution? . . . Political revolutions seldom go beyond the surface of society. They seldom amount to more than a mere transfer of power from one set of political chiefs to another. . . . Even the establishment of our "commonwealth" after the death of Charles I was mere political revolution. It gave parliamentary privilege a temporary triumph over royal prerogative. It enabled a few thousand landowners to disenthrall themselves from the burden of feudal services, and to throw upon the people at large the expenses of maintaining the government.

O'Brien concluded by reviewing 1688, 1776, and 1789, which he describes as being "on a larger scale and of a more democratic character," but: "Nevertheless they were only political revolutions."[34] Similar views were also expressed during the 1830s by the Italian nationalist leader Giuseppe Mazzini, who wrote: "The French Revolution must be considered, not as a programme, but as a summary, not as the initiative of a new age, but as the last formula of an expiring age."[35] As late as 1864 the Russian socialist Alexander Herzen wrote of the necessity for "social revolution" across the "civilized world": "The political revolution which modifies the forms of the state without affecting the forms of life has gone as far as it possibly can."[36] Nor was this position confined to socialists or even radicals themselves: one of the first German commentators on the new movement, the conservative political economist Lorenz von Stein, wrote in 1842: "There is no longer any doubt that for the most part of Europe political reform and revolution are at an end; social revolution has taken their place and towers over all movements of the peoples with its terrible power and serious doubts."[37] From this perspective then, all revolutions to date, whatever the level of popular involvement, were merely political, because they involved the replacement of one ruling class by another rather than instituting rule by the people. Only a revolution that resulted in the latter could be described as a genuinely social in character; the only genuinely social revolution would be socialist.

The view that social revolutions had still to occur was initially held by both Marx and Engels, and the latter retained it for longer—another respect in which they did *not* begin with the position of the French Liberal historians, who ascribed far greater significance to the English and French Revolutions. In 1842, following the failure of the Chartist-led general strike, Engels wrote from England that in the ultimately successful English revolution that would surely follow, "it will be interests and not principles that will begin and carry through the revolution; principles can develop only from interests, that is to say, the revolution will be social, not political."[38] These are the opposed interests of the bourgeoisie and the proletariat: but did the bourgeoisie not also have "interests" in the civil war of the 1640s? Was it consequently not also a social revolution? Apparently not, but two years later, in his pathbreaking "Outline of a Critique of Political Economy," Engels clarified his position: "The eighteenth century, the century of revolution, also revolutionized economics," he wrote; but both revolutions were limited: "In politics no one dreamt of examining the premises of the state as such. It did not occur to economics to question the *validity of private property*."[39] As long as political life was dominated by the state and economic life was characterized by private property, which was certainly the case after both 1660 and 1815, no social revolution can be said to have occurred. What Engels did not allow for at this time was the existence of different types of states and different forms of private property. Engels did not regard the revolutions of 1640 and 1789 as being irrelevant, of course, but they were significant only to the extent that they made the forthcoming social revolution possible. The English Revolution was religious in form, the French irreligious, but for Engels their outcome "proves that a religious and irreligious revolution, as long as they remain political, will in the final analysis amount to the *same* thing.[40] Indeed, at times Engels conflates the preconditions for the social revolution, by which he means capitalist industrialization, with the social revolution itself: "The only true revolution is a social revolution, to which political and philosophical revolution must lead; and this social revolution has already been in progress in England for seventy or eighty years and is rapidly approaching its crisis at this very time."[41] Even as late as a series of speeches delivered in Elberfeld early in 1845, Engels still defines the coming revolution in Germany in these terms:

> A social revolution, gentlemen, is something quite different from the political revolutions which have taken place so far. It is not directed, as these have been, against the property of monopoly, but against the monopoly of property; a social revolution, gentlemen, *is the open war of the poor against the rich.* . . . Either the rebellious party only attacks the appearance, not the essence, only the form, not the thing itself, or it goes for the thing itself, grasps the evil by the root. In the first case private property will be allowed to continue and will only be distributed differently, so that the causes which have led to the present situation remain in operation and must sooner or later bring about a similar situation and another revolution.[42]

In a speech from 1845 Engels referred to the historical struggles of the English and French bourgeoisie as an inspiration and legitimation for the modern "poor" in their attempt to end the existence of private property: "The English revolution realised both the religious and the political principles whose suppression by Charles I caused it to break out; the French bourgeoisie in its fight against the aristocracy and the old monarchy achieved everything that it aimed for, made an end to all the abuses which drove it to insurrection. And should the insurrection of the poor cease before poverty and its causes have been eliminated?"[43]

Were all sections of the working class, or "the poor" more generally, capable of carrying through such a revolution? Engels was among the first commentators to see beyond the existential misery of the British working class—a subject that had already exercised such notably nonrevolutionary figures as Thomas Carlyle—to the potential power it possessed, and in this he was in advance of Marx himself. Nevertheless, in those sections of his first major work, *The Condition of the English Working Class* (1844), where his focus shifts away from the working class to a more general discussion of the industrialization process, Engels frequently repeats the ideological preconceptions of those bourgeois commentators whose analysis he had otherwise surpassed. In such passages we encounter him on the subject of the Scottish Highlands:

> In Scotland the Department of Public Works built since 1803 nearly 900 miles of roadway and more than 1,000 miles of bridges, by which the population of the Highlands was placed within reach of civilisation. The Highlanders had hitherto been chiefly poachers and smugglers, now they became farmers and hand-workers. And although Gaelic schools were organized for the purpose of maintaining the Gaelic language, yet Gaelic-Celtic customs and speech are rapidly vanishing before the approach of English civilisation.[44]

Such uncritical advocacy of "English civilization" in this context can only mean bourgeois civilization. Engels's references to the civilizing role of "Anglo-Saxon" industry in the Highlands are matched by similar effusions regarding its impact across the Irish Sea: "So, too, in Ireland; between the counties of Cork, Limerick, and Kerry lay hitherto a wilderness wholly without passable roads, and serving, by reason of its inaccessibility, as the refuge of criminals and the chief protection of the Celtic Irish nationality in the South of Ireland. It has now been cut through by public roads, and civilisation has thus gained admission even to this savage region." Not only was the region characterized by savagery, so too were the inhabitants: "The southern facile character of the Irishman, his crudity, which places him little above the savage, his contempt for human enjoyments, in which his very crudity makes him incapable of sharing, all favor drunkenness."[45] It is clear, therefore, that Engels does not place the blame for the misery of the native Irish entirely at the door of the British: "That poverty manifests itself in Ireland thus and not otherwise, is owing to the character of the people, *and* to their historical development."[46] That national character might itself be the product of historical development is another possibility that does not seem to have occurred to Engels at this stage.

Marx started from a similar position to Engels in relation to political and social revolutions. However, in his initial critique of Hegel from mid-1843, which is still largely conducted using the language and concepts of German idealist philosophy, Marx attempted to distinguish between different types of political revolution, which he terms "legislative" and "executive":

> The legislature made the French Revolution; in fact, wherever it has emerged as the dominant factor it has brought forth great, organic, universal revolutions. It has not attacked the constitution as such but only a particular antiquated constitution; this is because the legislature acted as the representative of the people, of the species-will [*Gattungswillen*]. In contrast to this, the executive has made all the petty revolutions, the retrograde revolutions, the reactions. Its revolutions were not made against an old institution and on behalf of a new one; they were fought against the constitution itself, simply because the executive was the representative of the particular will, subjective caprice, the magical aspect of the will.[47]

At this point in his development, "revolution" does not have a particularly positive connotation for Marx, since—in its executive aspect at least—in can include coups de état or even counterrevolutions. This was soon to change. In a letter to Marx written shortly after this engagement with Hegel, fellow-Young Hegelian Arnold Ruge asked of the Germans: "Shall we live long enough to see a political revolution?"[48] In his next substantial essay, "On the Jewish Question," Marx effectively took issue with this aspiration, highlighting the inadequacy of merely political revolutions, but now also attempting to define them in relation to how far they contributed to what he called "political emancipation." This, he argued, "may not be the last form of general human emancipation, but it is the last form of general human emancipation *within* the prevailing scheme of things."[49] In other words, the achievement of "political emancipation" does involve progress and to that extent Marx is using the modern (not cyclical) concept of revolution. Furthermore, his discussion shows a far greater sensitivity to the changing nature of the state than can be found in the work of Engels during this period, where it tends to remain an unchanging, undifferentiated source of oppression. For Marx, the key achievement of political revolution, the basis for "political emancipation," involved breaking the former unity of state ("politics") and civil society that had characterized feudalism:

> Political emancipation is at the same time the dissolution of the old society on which there rested the power of the sovereign, the political system as estranged from the people. The political revolution is the revolution of civil society. What was the character of the old society? It can be characterised in one word: *feudalism*. . . . The political revolution which overthrew this rule and turned the affairs of the state into the affairs of the people, which constituted the political state as a concern of the whole people, i.e., as a real state, inevitably destroyed all the estates, corporations, guilds and privileges which expressed the separation of the people from its community. The political revolution therefore *abolished* the *political character of civil society*. . . . Political emancipation was at the same time the emancipation of civil society from politics, from even the *appearance* of a universal content.[50]

Even in the still very abstract formulations typical of Marx's writings at this time, it is clear that he recognizes feudalism as a distinct form of society, as it had originally been for Guizot. Like Engels, however, he did not regard its supersession as a social revolution, since private property survived and consequently human liberation remained unachieved, even where this had been the intention of revolutionaries: "Of course, in periods when the political state as political state comes violently into being out of civil society and when human self-liberation attempts to realize itself in the form of human self-liberation, the state can and must proceed to the abolition of religion, to the destruction of religion; but only in the same way as it proceeds to the abolition of private property (by imposing a maximum, by confiscation, by progressive taxation) and abolition of life (by the guillotine)." The leadership of the French Revolution ("the state," in this context) was temporarily forced to suppress bourgeois private property: "But it only manages to do this in violent contradiction to the conditions of its own existence, by declaring the revolution permanent, and for that reason the political drama necessarily ends up with the restoration of religion, private property and all the elements of civil society, just as war ends with peace."[51]

Germany had not yet attained the level of France and, in 1843 and 1844 at least, Marx was skeptical about the capacity of the local bourgeoisie to achieve even this much, leading him to pronounce, in one of his earliest dialectical paradoxes: "It is not the *radical* revolution or *universal human* emancipation which is a utopian dream for Germany; it is the partial, *merely* political revolution, the revolution which leaves the pillars of the building standing." This led him to argue in more detail what the role of the French bourgeoisie had been in their revolution—a revolution that Marx still describes as political:

What is the basis of a partial and merely political revolution? Its basis is the fact that one *part of civil society* emancipates itself and attains *universal* domination, that one particular class undertakes from its *particular situation* the universal emancipation of society. This class liberates the whole of society, but only on condition that the whole of society finds itself in the same situation as this class, e.g., possesses or can easily acquire money and education. No class of civil society can play this role without awakening a moment of enthusiasm in itself and the masses. . . . If the *revolution of a people* and the *emancipation of a particular class* of civil society are to coincide, if one class is to stand for the whole of society, then all the deficiencies of society must be concentrated in another class, one particular class must be the class which gives universal offence, the embodiment of a general limitation; one particular sphere of society must appear as the *notorious crime* of the whole society, so that the liberation of this sphere appears as universal self-liberation. . . . The negative general significance of the French nobility and the French clergy determined the positive general significance of the class which stood nearest to and opposed to them—the *bourgeoisie*.[52]

But the embodiment of the general interest was illusionary in the case of the bourgeoisie, or at least real only to the extent that the pseudo-universal class was able to achieve formal equality before the law (although not yet democracy), leaving economic inequality untouched. Some other social force was therefore necessary in order to move beyond the mere bourgeois right established in France, but still to be established throughout most of Europe, a genuinely universal class. Already for Engels, and now for Marx, this was the working class: "A class with radical chains."[53]

What lay beyond bourgeois right was communism, a potential and desirable state of affairs familiar to young radicals like Marx and Engels through the projections of Utopian Socialists like Étienne Cabet or through the philosophical positions of Left Hegelians like Moses Hess. But for Marx at any rate, the proletariat still appears as a solution to the philosophical problem of agency: the proletariat is a universal class on the basis of its poverty and suffering, its lack of private property, but the proletarian "heart" remains on equal footing with the philosophical "head": "Philosophy cannot realize itself without the transcendence [*Aufhebung*] of the proletariat, and the proletariat cannot transcend itself without the realization [*Verwirklichung*] of philosophy."[54] Marx is, so to speak, still looking down the wrong end of the telescope and only changed his perspective as the result of his increasing knowledge of the working-class movement (the activities of the Chartists in Britain and, closer to home, the revolt of the Silesian weavers in June 1844) and cumulative encounters with actual workers (the secret societies and the League of the Just while in Paris during 1843–44).

The new conception of the working class that emerged was stated fully for the first time by both Marx and Engels in their first jointly written work, *The Holy Family* (1844), and developed in the collection of unfinished notes eventually published under the title of *The German Ideology* (1845–46):

> When socialist writers ascribe this world-historic role to the proletariat, it is not at all, as Critical Criticism pretends to believe, because they regard the proletarians as

gods. Rather the contrary.... [The proletariat] cannot emancipate itself without abolishing the conditions of its own life. It cannot abolish the conditions of its own life without abolishing all the inhuman conditions of society today which are summed up in its own situation.... It is not a question of what this or that proletarian, or even the whole proletariat, at the moment *regards* as his aim. It is a question of *what the proletariat is,* and what, in accordance with this *being,* it will historically be compelled to do. Its aim and historical action is visibly and irrevocably foreshadowed in its own life situation as well as the whole organisation of bourgeois society today. There is no need to explain here that a large part of the English and French proletariat is already conscious of its historic task and is constantly working to develop that consciousness into complete clarity.[55]

Marx and Engels make three claims here about the nature of the working class, which they would subsequently elaborate in much greater detail.

The first, which is really a concretization of Marx's earlier description of the working class as possessing "radical chains," is that it alone has the potential to become a universal class. One reason for this is that it has no property. "In order to become an 'unendurable' power, i.e., a power against which men make a revolution, it must necessarily have rendered the great mass of humanity 'propertyless,' and moreover in contradiction to an existing world of wealth and culture."[56] The process that characterized the origins of the system was the reduction of peasant farmers and urban artisans from people who had previously owned or controlled their means of production, and hence were able to provide for their own subsistence, to people who had nothing but their ability to labor and were therefore compelled to sell it in order to survive. Being propertyless does not, of course, mean that workers have no personal possessions, but these are simply commodities, not the means of accumulating capital.

The second claim is that the working class is forced to behave collectively. Factories, mines, and offices cannot be divided between their workers in the way that, for example, a landed estate can be divided up by peasants. As this suggests, it is not the case that the simple existence of the working class as an economic formation gives it the structural capacity for revolution. Wage labor is more than necessary to capital for, along with competitive accumulation, it is constitutive of the system, but wage laborers have not necessarily been capable of challenging for power at every stage in the development of capitalism. Rural laborers and domestic servants comprised the majority of workers in the eighteenth and nineteenth centuries respectively, but neither was in a position to overthrow the system. It is therefore not only the creation of a working class that we owe to capitalism but the particular way in which capitalism concentrates workers together into collective situations. The very fact of gathering workers together has a perverse if unavoidable outcome for employers: it created the possibility of the exercise of their collective strength in addition to the actuality of their collective exploitation.

The third claim is that that the working class must become aware of its position and role and act accordingly. In other words, it must attain class consciousness. But of what does this consciousness consist? Conflicts occur without the exploited class being fully, or at least uniformly aware, of why it is fighting. Most working-class people have some form of class consciousness, even if it remains at the pre-political level of "us and them," those who have absolutely internalized the worldview of the ruling class are almost as few—in normal circumstances—as those who have completely rejected it for revolutionary politics: "Both for the production on a mass scale of this consciousness, and for the success of the cause itself, the alteration of men on a mass scale is necessary, an alteration that can only take place in a practical movement, a *revolution*; the revolution is necessary, therefore, not only because the *ruling* class cannot be overthrown in any other way, but also because the class *overthrowing* it can only in a revolution succeed in ridding itself anew of all the muck of ages and become fitted to found society anew."[57] The emphasis here is on the working class, but it is also clear that Marx and Engels saw it as being the core of a much wider revolutionary agency. The social revolution would be carried out by the social movement. Again, the term was widespread throughout socialist and communist circles at the time. Toward the end of the notes published as *The German Ideology* there is an acerbic review by Engels of Karl Grün's 1845 book, *The Social Movement in France and Belgium*, but Engels uses the same term— that is, "the French social movement," indicating that he recognizes its existence and his quarrel is rather with Grün's discussion.[58]

One might have expected the discovery of the proletariat as a revolutionary class, and consequently the identification of the various ways in which it was distinct from the bourgeoisie, would merely have strengthened Marx and Engels in their existing conviction that only the proletarian revolution could be regarded as genuinely social. In fact, it is at precisely this moment that they extend the concept backward in history. Here we find some support for the claim that the concept of bourgeois revolution was a "retro-projection" of the concept of proletarian revolution; it is not the revolutions themselves that are being compared, however, but the classes associated with them as the bearers of a new form of society—which does not of course mean that the processes involved were similar. What Georg Lukács later called "the standpoint of the proletariat," allowed Marx and Engels to understand the role of the bourgeoisie in a way denied to the thinkers of the bourgeoisie themselves.[59]

The extension of the concept of social revolution was made explicit by Marx in linking political action with a social result:

> Every revolution dissolves the *old order of society*; to that extent it is *social*. Every revolution brings down the *old ruling power*; to that extent it is political. . . . All revolution—the overthrow of the existing ruling power and the dissolution of the old order—is a political act. But without revolution, socialism cannot be made possible. It stands in need of this political act just as it stands in need of destruction and dissolution. But as soon as its organizing functions begin and its goal, its soul emerges, socialism throws its political mask aside.[60]

By late in 1845, Engels too was declaring: "The French Revolution was a social movement from beginning to end, and after it a purely political democracy became a complete absurdity."[61]

If discovering the capacities of the working class as a revolutionary agent in relation to capitalism led Marx and Engels to perform the same investigation for the bourgeoisie and feudalism, it also led them to reconsider what was meant by feudalism. In this respect reconceptualizing the overthrow of feudalism as a social revolution also benefited from their engagement with British political economy, the most important aspect of which—in the context of this discussion, at least—was the Scottish tradition that emphasized the transition from one stage of development and from one mode of subsistence to another. Against this background, Marx and Engels returned to the original versions of the stages theories of subsistence and society, revising both and showing how the phenomena they describe related to each other in human history, as a transition from one mode to another—although as we shall see, these were no longer modes of subsistence—could lead to a corresponding transition from one type of society to another, providing a revolutionary agency existed to act as a bridge between them. Essentially, they exchanged positions with their bourgeois predecessors: where the latter increasingly denied that the revolutions against feudalism were social revolutions and now defined them in political terms, Marx and Engels affirmed the opposite but without accepting that these were the only such revolutions that had ever happened or would ever happen. "When the economists say that present-day relations—the relations of bourgeois production—are natural, they imply that these are the relations in which wealth is created and productive forces developed in conformity with the laws of nature. These relations are therefore themselves natural laws independent of the influence of time. They are eternal laws which must always govern society. Thus there has been history, but there is no longer any."[62] But revolutions had occurred earlier in history and would happen again in the form of the socialist revolution, which, by ending the existence of antagonistic social classes, would genuinely be the last social revolution.

From Social Revolution to the Forces and Relations of Production

The key statement in the development of their new position was in the drafts now known as *The German Ideology*, which as Marx later noted, were written for purposes of "self-clarification."[63] It is not in any sense a completed work, in the way that *The Holy Family* was overseen by the authors from composition to publication. Indeed, as Terrell Carver has shown, the published text involves a number of different projects and drafts "editorially constructed" into a finished book form by a team under David Ryazanov at the Marx-Engels Institute in Moscow during the 1920s, including the opening chapter, "I. Feuerbach," which is the only readable section and from which the majority of quotes below are taken.[64] None of this, however, is to suggest that the contents were altered to convey meanings unintended by the authors, or that their incomplete form invalidates their insights. Many commentators, including several who are far from being adherents of political Marxism, emphasize the extent to which *The German Ideology* is still influenced by the Scottish Historical School, above all through its reliance on the division of labor as an explanatory factor.[65] In fact, what is most significant about the work is the extent to which it decisively breaks with what is purely ideological in the work of Smith and his colleagues.

Marx and Engels continued to emphasize the points first identified by Robertson; the centrality of the means by which humans reproduce themselves and the relationship between these means and the other aspects of social life as the basis for any explanation of their history.

> ... the first premise of all human existence and, therefore, of all history, the premise, namely, that men must be in a position to live in order to be able to "make history." But life involves before everything else eating and drinking, a habitation, clothing and many other things. The first historical act is thus the production of the means to satisfy these needs, the production of material life itself. And indeed this is an historical act, a fundamental condition of all history, which today, as thousands of years ago, must daily and hourly be fulfilled merely in order to sustain human life.[66]

They go on to write that "in any conception of history one has first of all to observe this fundamental fact in all its significance and all its implications and to accord it due importance." It is to the extent that their predecessors have failed to do so that their accounts have been inadequate: "The French and English [*sic*], even if they have conceived the relation of this fact with so-called history only in an extremely one-sided fashion, especially since they remained within the toils of political ideology, have nevertheless made the first attempts to give the writing of history a materialistic basis by being the first to write histories of civil society, of commerce and industry."[67] What is new in their account is the claim that neither the economic category of "subsistence" nor the legal category of "property" can adequately explain the course of human development, which can only be done on the basis of a more fundamental, underlying social process—*production*:

> Men can be distinguished from animals by consciousness, by religion or anything else you like. They themselves begin to distinguish themselves from animals as soon as they begin to *produce* their means of subsistence, a step which is conditioned by their physical organisation. By producing their means of subsistence men are indirectly producing their actual material life. The way in which men produce their means of subsistence depends first of all on the nature of the actual means of subsistence they find in existence and have to reproduce. This mode of production must not be considered simply as being the production of the physical existence of the individuals. Rather it is a definite form of activity of these individuals, a definite form of expressing their life, a definite *mode of life* on their part. As individuals express their life, so they are. What they are, therefore, coincides with their production, both with what they produce and with how they produce. The nature of individuals thus depends on the material conditions determining their production.[68]

What is it that determines how "the production of material life itself" takes place? It is here for the first time that Marx and Engels introduce their version of the concept of the forces of production. This was already present in political economy but, as Goran Therborn notes, here it means not only "productivity or productive capacity"—as it had for, say, Ricardo—but also "the *different ways in which productivity is ensured*."[69] The forces of production have two aspects. One is the means of production, which include nature itself, the capacity to labor, the skills brought to the process, the tools used, and the techniques with which these tools are set to work. The other is the labor process, the way in which the different means of production are combined in the act of production itself. To say that forces of production have developed is to say that they have changed in such a way that the social productivity of labor has risen as a result; but it is also to say something else: "How far the productive forces of a nation are developed *is shown* most manifestly by the degree to which the division of labour has been carried. . . . The various stages of development in the division of labour are just so many different forms of property, i.e., the existing stage in the division of labour determines also the relations of individuals to one another with reference to the material, instrument, and product of labour."[70] In other words, both the increased complexity of the division of labor and the different forms of property through which this is expressed are a result of the prior development of the productive forces; they, not the growth of population or the expansion of trade, have primacy. In the outline of the different forms of property which follow, Marx and Engels repeatedly make the same connection, writing, for example, that "tribal property . . . corresponds to the undeveloped stage of production."[71] So too with feudalism:

> The feudal system was by no means brought complete from Germany, but had its origin, as far as the conquerors were concerned, in the martial organisation of the army during the actual conquest, and this only evolved after the conquest into the feudal system proper through the action of the productive forces found in the conquered countries. To what an extent this form was determined by the productive forces is shown by the abortive attempts to realize other forms derived from reminiscences of ancient Rome (Charlemagne, etc.).[72]

Critics of *The German Ideology* are correct that the terminology remains imprecise on a number of points, indicating that the process of "self-clarification" was not yet complete. In particular, the forces of production are twinned with "forms of intercourse," a vague and all-embracing category that includes such aspects of "social intercourse" as methods of transportation. Nevertheless, the nature and direction of the relationship is clear: "The form of this intercourse is again determined by production."[73]

The other key development in the context of this discussion is that, for the first time, Marx and Engels connect the possibility of revolution with prior changes to the material conditions of life: "These . . . determine also whether or not the revolutionary convulsion periodically recurring in history will be strong enough to overthrow everything that exists." For such an overthrow, "two material elements for a complete revolution" are required: on the one hand the existing productive forces, on the other the formation of a revolutionary mass, which revolts not only against separate conditions of the existing society, but against the existing "production of life" itself."[74] But between the forces of production and the masses stand the particular way in which they are organized within society, the "form of intercourse":

> The contradiction between the productive forces and the form of intercourse, which, as we saw, has occurred several times in past history, without, however, endangering its basis, necessarily on each occasion burst out in a revolution, taking on at the same time various subsidiary forms, such as all-embracing collisions, collisions of various classes, contradiction of consciousness, battle of ideas, political struggle, etc. From a narrow point of view one may isolate one of these subsidiary forms and consider it as the basis of these revolutions; and this is all the more easy as the individuals who started the revolutions had illusions about their own activity according to their degree of culture and the stage of historical development. Thus all collisions in history have their origin, according to our view, in the contradiction between the productive forces and the form of intercourse.[75]

The development of the productive forces has been both a cause and an effect of previous revolutions, but none of these have led to a sufficient level of development to overcome inequality. But "this development of productive forces . . . is an absolutely necessary practical premise, because without it privation, *want* is merely made general, and with *want* the struggle for necessities would begin again, and all the old filthy business would necessarily be restored."[76] Without this level of development, a revolution will, at best, lead to a new ruling class being established in power:

> All emancipation carried through hitherto has been based, however, on restricted productive forces. The production which these productive forces could provide was insufficient for the whole of society and made development possible only if some persons satisfied their needs at the expense of others, and therefore some—the minority—obtained the monopoly of development, while others—the majority—owing to the constant struggle to satisfy their most essential needs, were for the time being (i.e., until the creation of new revolutionary productive forces) excluded from any development. Thus, society has hitherto always developed within the framework of a contradiction—in antiquity the contradiction between free men and slaves, in the Middle Ages that between nobility and serfs, in modern times that between the bourgeoisie and the proletariat.[77]

The contradiction between the forces of production and the form of intercourse is expressed by the contradiction between the different opposing classes identified in the final sentence. In other words, the opposed classes represent different ways of organizing the form of intercourse, with one associated with the existing way, the other with an alternative.

Whatever problems there are with *The German Ideology*, it is clear that Marx and Engels's mature position on socioeconomic development was fully worked out by the following year at the latest, with the final elaboration of their new concepts in *The Poverty of Philosophy* (1847). Here, the concept of "form of intercourse" is replaced with that of "social relations," a specific form of which, namely the "social relations of production," combines with the forces to constitute a "mode of production."

Men make cloth, linen, or silk materials in definite relations of production.... These definite social relations are just as much produced by men as linen, flax, etc. Social relations are closely bound up with productive forces. In acquiring new productive forces men change their mode of production; and in changing their mode of production, in changing the way of earning their living they change all their social relations. The hand-mill gives you society with the feudal lord; the steam-mill, society with the industrial capitalist.[78]

The final sentence of this quotation is often treated as an example of irredeemable technological determinism; it seems to me to be rather a shorthand way of illustrating the connection between changes to the productive forces and subsequent changes to society, excluding all the actual intervening mediations. Although the forces of production change and develop, it is the specific relations of production, the means by which exploitation of the direct producers takes place—including the relationship of the latter to the means of subsistence and production—which distinguishes different modes of production from each other, determining whether a toiler in the fields is a slave, a serf, an independent producer, or a wage laborer: "There has been history, since there were the institutions of feudalism, and in these institutions of feudalism we find quite different relations of production from those of bourgeois society, which the economists try to pass off as natural and as such, eternal."[79] As a result, it is the social relations of production, not, as in *The German Ideology*, the forces of production, which determine the forms of property: "In each historical epoch, property has developed differently and under a set of entirely different social relations. Thus to define bourgeois property is nothing else than to give an exposition of all the social relations of bourgeois production. To try to give a definition of property as of an independent relation, a category apart, an abstract and eternal idea, can be nothing but an illusion of metaphysics or jurisprudence."[80] The central points distributed through *The Poverty of Philosophy* are made in a more focused and concentrated way in *Wage-Labour and Capital*, also written in 1847, but not published until 1849:

These social relations into which the producers enter with one another, the conditions under which they exchange their activities and participate in the whole act of production, will naturally vary according to the character of the means of production. With the discovery of a new instrument of warfare, firearms, the whole internal organization of the army necessarily changed, the relations within which individuals can constitute an army and act as an army were transformed, and the relations of different armies to one another also changed. *Thus*, the social relations within which individuals produce, *the social relations of production, change, are transformed, with the change and development of the material means of production, the productive forces. The relations of production in their totality constitute what* are called *the social relations, society*, and, specifically, a society at *a definite stage of historical development*, a society with a peculiar, distinctive character. Ancient society, feudal society, bourgeois society, are such totalities of productive relations, each of which denotes a special stage of development in the history of mankind.[81]

The reference to the army in this passage should remind us that social relations are not reducible to relations of production. Over the next five years Marx would introduce further refinements to clarify the distinction between different types of social relations, but in all essentials the key explanatory concepts of historical materialism had now been established. And it was at precisely this point, in *The Poverty of Philosophy*, that Marx introduced a concrete application of historical materialism in the form of the concept that is the subject of this book. "The revolution of the bourgeoisie destroyed the estates and their privileges," he wrote, describing the overthrow of the feudal ruling class.[82] Later in 1847, he introduced the term itself, in a discussion which reemphasizes the social nature of both the bourgeois and proletarian revolutions, and the development of the productive forces as a necessary condition for them to take place: "If therefore the proletariat overthrows the political rule of the bourgeoisie, its victory will only be temporary, only an element in the service of the *bourgeois revolution* itself, as in the year 1794, as long as in the course of history, in its 'movement,' the material conditions have not yet been created which make necessary the abolition of the bourgeois mode of production and therefore also the definitive overthrow of the political rule of the bourgeoisie."[83] In other words, Marx and Engels arrived at their mature theories of both economic transition and social revolution a decade before the composition of the *Grundrisse* and, as we shall see, it remained unchanged afterward. But no sooner had Marx introduced the concept of "bourgeois revolution," then he and Engels became participants in the very process it was intended to encapsulate.

A NOTE ON TERMINOLOGY

Throughout the period we have just discussed, and beyond the period covered in the next chapter, Marx and Engels used a wide range of terms to describe the successor to feudalism, including "modern bourgeois society" and "bourgeois civilization." The economy was similarly described as involving "bourgeois relations of production" and "the bourgeois mode of production." Although Marx and Engels also referred to capital and capitalists, the one term that neither man used until very much later was "capitalism." The honor of introducing the word into common use seems to go to Blanc, who as we saw earlier was also responsible for coining the actual term *bourgeois revolution*. Writing in 1850, in a revised edition of his *Organization of Labour*, he referred to a sophistry associated with his opponent, the economic liberal Frédéric Bastiat: "This sophism consists in perpetually confusing the utility of *capital* with what I will call *capitalism*, i.e., the appropriation of capital by some, to the exclusion of others."[84] By the 1850s, the term had entered popular use, to the point of appearing in the middle-class literature of the time, as in this passage by the British novelist, William Makepeace Thackeray, written in the mid-1850s, but referring to the previous decade: "The sense of capitalism sobered and dignified Paul de Florac: at the age of five-and-forty he was actually giving up being a young man, and was not ill pleased at having to enlarge his waistcoats, and to show a little grey in his moustache."[85] In *Capital* Marx still oscillates between referring to "the capitalist mode of production" in the opening sentence and "the bourgeois economic system" in a postface from 1873.[86] The earliest use of "capitalism" by Marx that I have been able to find dates from 1870, in a letter written on behalf of the First International: "If landlordism and capitalism are classical features in England, on the other hand, the *material conditions* for their *destruction* are the most mature here."[87]

The point, however, is that they did not tend to make the kind of pseudoscientific etymological distinctions between various terms in the way that so obsesses some of their followers. In particular, they did not distinguish between bourgeois and capitalist, writing at one point in the "Manifesto of the Communist Party": "the bourgeoisie, i.e., capital."[88] Marx later refers to "bourgeois capitalists" in *Capital*.[89] It should be fairly obvious, for example, that they did not take "bourgeois" to mean someone who lived in a town, whatever the original meaning of the term may have been. When they write, "bourgeois revolution," therefore, they do *not* mean—as the Saint-Simonists and Blanc would have meant—"a revolution carried out by the bourgeoisie, understood as a social group distinct from actual capitalists." This needs to be borne in mind during the discussions that follow.

9

MARX AND ENGELS (2) 1847–52: THE BOURGEOIS REVOLUTION IN THEORY AND PRACTICE

The vast majority of occasions on which Marx and Engels explicitly refer to the bourgeois revolution occurred between 1847 and 1852—in other words immediately before, during, and after the German Revolution of 1848–49 and the larger European revolutionary movement of which it was part. And with the exception of the Chartist mobilization in Britain and the Parisian insurrections of February and June 1848, *all* of these events, from Ireland in the West to Poland in the East, could be classified under the same heading. Everything written on the subject by Marx and Engels during this period, with the exception of a handful of more reflective pieces composed toward the end—above all, *The Eighteenth Brumaire of Louis Bonaparte*—was an intervention in the revolutionary process by active participants with the intention of affecting the outcome. Consequently, along with many insights, these works also involve polemical exaggerations uttered while debating courses of action, overoptimistic assessments to maintain the spirit of comrades in periods of reversal, and misunderstandings caused by confusion on the field of battle—literally, in some cases. In short, although all are more "finished" than *The German Ideology*, they cannot be treated as scholarly texts in which the order of presentation, choice of language, or selection of examples has been carefully considered over a period of years, as for example was the case in the drafting of *Capital*, volume 1.[1] In particular, references to the exemplary role historically played by the bourgeoisie in England and especially France have to be read in the knowledge of this context.

THE INESCAPABLE CONTEXT OF THE FRENCH REVOLUTION

When discussing the influence of the French Revolution it is important to recall that it was not transmitted solely from written texts. As Raya Dunayevskaya once put it, the French Revolution occurred in "life" as well as in "books."[2] For Marx and Engels, the French Revolution was not something only to be absorbed from works of history, whether they were written by French Liberals or anyone else, but a historical experience only recently past, whose effects and unfulfilled promises still defined the politics of the time—indeed, they directly influenced the material circumstances in which the Marx family lived. Marx was born and lived until young manhood in Trier on the Rhineland, a territory that bordered on France and that was the one part of the German Lands where the influence of the Revolution was most directly experienced, not least because of the intermittent French occupation from 1792. As Engels later recalled:

> Rhenish Prussia shares with Luxemburg, Rhenish Hesse and the Palatinate the advantage of having experienced since 1795 the French Revolution and the social, administrative and legislative consolidation of its results under Napoleon. When the revolutionary party in Paris succumbed the armies carried the revolution across the frontiers. Before these so recently liberated sons of peasants not only the armies of the Holy Roman Empire, but also the feudal rule of the nobility and the priests fell to pieces. For two generations the left bank of the Rhine has no longer known feudalism: the nobleman has been deprived of his privileges and the landed property has been passed from his hands and those of the church into the hands of the peasants, the land has been divided up and the peasant is a free landed proprietor as in France.[3]

It is important not to exaggerate the immediate benefits of French rule, as Engels tends to do in this passage. Feudal dues were abolished in the countryside and freedom of the press and constitutional government were introduced more generally, but the peasantry was burdened with new taxes and, by the end of the Napoleonic Wars, the area was being drained of resources to sustain the Grande Armée; nevertheless, these were no longer feudal exactions. Even after the Rhineland was awarded to Prussia by the Congress of Vienna, it retained the Code Napoleon and was not subject to the generalized reaction that otherwise swept that state after 1814, although Jews like Marx's father were still subject to discrimination. Later, and partly because of this history, the Rhineland was especially receptive to the ideas of Saint-Simon and Fourier in which these authors tried to develop the more radical aspects of French revolutionary thought. As late as 1830 workers and artisans in Cologne and Elberfeld rose for higher wages and lower taxes under the slogan: "Long Live Napoleon!" Yet despite these ineradicable imprints of the Great Revolution, the Rhineland still resembled in many respects the ancien régime that had been overthrown in France, dominated as it was by the feudal nobility in alliance with a conservative Prussian bureaucracy and a reactionary Catholic Church.[4] The tensions between the competing claims of archaism and modernity meant that there was going to be some sort of revolution in Germany, everybody but the dullest Prussian official knew that: but what kind of revolution? Would it—could it—simply be a repetition of the French Revolution? As Engels later recalled:

> When the February Revolution [of 1848] broke out, all of us, as far as our conceptions of the conditions and the course of revolutionary movements were concerned, were under the spell of previous historical experience, particularly that of France. It was,

indeed, the latter which had dominated the whole of European history since 1789, and from which now once again the signal had gone forth for general revolutionary change. It was, therefore, natural and unavoidable that our conceptions of the nature and the course of the "social" revolution proclaimed in Paris in February 1848, of the revolution of the proletariat, should be strongly colored by memories of the prototypes of 1789 and 1830.[5]

Henry Heller claims that "in Marx's eyes the revolution in France alongside the English Revolution was the classic form of a bourgeois revolution." This may be the case, but "classic" does not necessarily imply that it was typical or characteristic, still less that "it was a model against which the ascent of the bourgeoisie to power elsewhere could be judged."[6] At certain points Heller appears to recognize this, writing of Marx: "His view of the French Revolution as archetypical of bourgeois revolutions may . . . be questioned."[7] The problem was that, having arrived at a general theory of bourgeois evolution, Marx and Engels were then thrown into a situation where they had to constantly invoke a specific example, the Great French Revolution of 1789 and, to a lesser extent, its predecessors, first as inspiration, then as reproach to their own bourgeoisie. "The March revolution in Prussia should not be confused either with the English revolution of 1648 or with the French one of 1789," wrote Marx toward the end of 1848: "In both revolutions, the bourgeoisie was the class which was *genuinely* to be found at the head of the movement." By contrast: "Nothing of this is to be found in the *Prussian March revolution*."[8] "Reading these texts," comments Michael Löwy of this and similar passages, "one often gets the impression that Marx only extolled the virtues of the revolutionary bourgeoisie of 1789 the more effectively to stigmatize the 'misbegotten' German version of 1848."[9]

Elsewhere in their writings of the time Marx and Engels took a more realistic attitude to both the French Revolution and the revolutionary bourgeoisie more generally. Surprisingly, perhaps, this comes across most clearly in the *Manifesto of the Communist Party* (1847) itself. George Comninel writes: "That Marx's definitive statement of the concept of bourgeois revolution comes in the *Manifesto*—when he was rendering credit due to the bourgeoisie for their accomplishments, while proclaiming the time for their passing—is precisely indicative of the role the [French] Revolution played in Marx's thought."[10] Yet one interesting fact revealed by actually reading this immortal work is that it mentions the French Revolution precisely twice. Once in passing, as an example of changes in property relations: "The French Revolution, for example, abolished feudal property in favor of bourgeois property."[11] The other is on the final page in the context of a discussion on the nature of the forthcoming German revolution: "The Communists turn their attention chiefly to Germany, because that country is on the eve of a bourgeois revolution that is bound to be carried out under more advanced conditions of European civilisation, and with a much more developed proletariat, than that of England was in the seventeenth century, and of France in the eighteenth century, and because the bourgeois revolution in Germany will be but the prelude to an immediately following proletarian revolution."[12] The passage just quoted contains the only reference to the bourgeois revolution in the entire pamphlet, so it can scarcely be said to represent a "definitive statement of the concept of bourgeois revolution." Bearing these caveats in mind, several important generalizations about the nature of bourgeois revolutions until 1848 can be found in their writings across the period 1847–52 as a whole.

AN INTERNATIONAL PROCESS OF BOURGEOIS CONSOLIDATION

For Marx and Engels, the bourgeois revolutions were not merely a series of episodes from the history of individual countries but a cumulative international process, in which each successive moment until 1848 had recapitulated and extended the work of its predecessor. They never doubted that there were differences between the English and French cases, not least in the prior development of capitalist relations of production in the former country:

> The great puzzle of the conservative character of the English revolution, to which M. Guizot can solve only by attributing it to the superior intelligence of the English, is in fact explained by the lasting alliance of the bourgeoisie with the great landowners, an alliance which fundamentally distinguishes the English from the French revolution, the latter having destroyed large landed property by dividing it up into smallholdings. This class of large landowners allied with the bourgeoisie, which, it may be added, had already arisen under Henry VIII, was not, as were the French feudal landowners of 1789, in conflict with the vital interests of the bourgeoisie but rather in complete harmony with them. Their estates were indeed not feudal but bourgeois property. On the one hand, they provided the industrial bourgeoisie with the population necessary to operate the manufacturing system, and, on the other hand, they were in a position to raise agricultural development to the level corresponding to that of industry and commerce. Hence their common interests with the bourgeoisie; hence their alliance.[13]

Nevertheless, the patterns of development were similar enough for these revolutions to be categorized under the same heading, starting with the nature of the enemy that had to be overthrown: "Against these forces [of the bourgeoisie] stood the absolutist state, whose old social foundation had been conjured away from beneath its feet by the course of historical development; it had become a fetter and a hindrance for the new bourgeois society, with its changed mode of production and its changed needs. The bourgeoisie had to lay claim to a share in political power, if only to assert its purely material interests."[14] The course of the struggle against the absolutist state tended to produce a similar process in each country. Engels had already noted the parallels between the English and French Revolutions at a time when he still regarded them as essentially political, both in terms of their internal development and the role played by individual figures:

> The English revolution of the seventeenth century provides the exact model for the French one of 1789. In the "Long Parliament" the three stages which in France took the form of constituent and legislative Assembly and National Convention are easy

to distinguish: the transition from constitutional monarchy to democracy, military despotism, restoration and *juste-milieu* revolution [of 1830] is sharply delineated in the English Revolution. Cromwell is Robespierre and Napoleon rolled into one; the Presbyterians, Independents and Levellers correspond to the Gironde, the Montagnards and the Hebertists and Bavouvists.[15]

Above all, the outcomes were similar. This is, of course, a matter of major dispute, particularly for political Marxists who maintain that France remained precapitalist even after 1815. Comninel, for example, informs us that "while the French Revolution did so much to define the politics of the nineteenth century, it did very little in the way of transforming the essential social relations of production. The Revolution was not fought by capitalists, and it did not produce capitalist society."[16] He then quotes the passages from *The Eighteenth Brumaire of Louis Bonaparte* in which Marx describes the "frightful parasitic body" of the French state as late as 1852. From these descriptions Comninel naturally deduces that "it is far from absolutely clear that the 'bourgeois society' of which he is writing is capitalist." What is it then? According to Comninel, "the state-centered surplus extraction which he describes, the centralized rent extracted directly from the peasantry, seems to be a clear example of the 'extra-economic' modes of surplus extraction that Marx associated with non-capitalist societies in Volume 3 of *Capital*."[17] As is all too often the case with Comninel, rather than take his word for what Marx says, it is best to consult the latter directly. As we have already seen, Marx was aware that capitalism was much more highly developed in England than in France, prior to their respective revolutions. His views on the economic aftermath of the latter are conveyed in his discussion of the fate of the French peasantry:

> In the course of the nineteenth century [before this passage was written in 1852] the urban usurer replaced the feudal lord; the mortgage on the land replaced feudal obligations; bourgeois capital replaced aristocratic landed property. The peasant's smallholding is now only the pretext that allows the capitalist to draw profits, interest and rent from the soil, while leaving the tiller himself to work out how to extract the wage for his labour.... Owing to this enslavement by capital, inevitably brought on by its own development, small peasant property has transformed the mass of the French nation into troglodytes.[18]

This is unambiguous, but to reinforce the point, here is Marx twenty years later describing the imperial order established by Louis Bonaparte as being, "at the same time, the most prostitute and the ultimate form of the state power which nascent middle-class society had commenced to elaborate as a means of its own emancipation from feudalism, and which full-grown bourgeois society had finally transformed into a means for the enslavement of labour by capital."[19] Marx believes that French capitalism has heightened the oppressive nature of the state to level hitherto unseen, which is precisely why he welcomed its—alas temporary—destruction and replacement by the Paris Commune.[20] The divisions within the bourgeoisie, which are real enough, embody the separation of the capitalist class into two separate interests: "We refer to the two interests of the bourgeoisie because big landed property has in fact been completely bourgeoisified by the development of modern society, despite its feudal coquetry and racial pride."[21]

Were there any bourgeois revolutions prior to the English? Engels wrote in 1847, for example, that by liberating themselves from the Austrian Habsburg Empire in the fourteenth century, the Swiss had actually broken from what was progressive in absolutism and consequently "won their victory over the civilization of the time, and as punishment they were excluded from all further civilization."[22] Whatever one thinks of this judgment—and, as we shall see, the Swiss were not the only people disliked by Engels on the basis of irrational notions of an eternally deficient "national character"—there is no doubt that, on any serious criteria, the Swiss Confederation was not dominated by the capitalist mode of production until several centuries later. There were other contenders, however; Marx and Engels had observed in *The German Ideology* that, of the political philosophers of the English Revolution, "Hobbes and Locke had before their eyes . . . the earlier development of the Dutch bourgeoisie," which suggested an earlier bourgeois revolution in the United Netherlands.[23] Now that the concept was available, Marx extended it back in time to include the events leading to the emergence of the Dutch Republic:

> In 1648 the bourgeoisie was in alliance with the modern nobility against the monarchy, the feudal nobility and the established church. In 1789 the bourgeoisie was in alliance with the people against the monarchy, the nobility and the established church. The revolution of 1789 was (at least in Europe) only prefigured by the revolution of 1648, which in turn was only prefigured by the rising of the Netherlands against Spain. Both revolutions were approximately a century in advance of their predecessors, not only in time, but also in content.[24]

Marx accused Guizot of failing to notice that "around the same time [as the Cromwellian Commonwealth] in Lisbon, Naples and Messina attempts were also made to establish republics, and that, as in England, this was under the influence of the Dutch example."[25] Nevertheless their views on the Netherlands remained embryonic and, as Marcel van der Linden writes, "It seems likely that Marx and Engels did not see the Revolt as an important bourgeois revolution."[26]

THE TRANSFORMATION OF SOCIETY

The bourgeois revolution did not merely allow for the replacement of one ruling class or one form of private property with another but concluded the substitution of an entirely different system that involved new forms of behavior and social attitudes. Marx had highlighted the extent of the changes involved as early as his Paris manuscripts of 1844:

> The *real* course of development . . . results in the necessary victory of the *capitalist* over the *landowner*—that is to say, of developed over undeveloped, immature private

property—just as in general, movement must triumph over immobility; open, self-conscious baseness over hidden, unconscious baseness; *cupidity* over *self-indulgence*; the avowedly restless, adroit self-interest of *enlightenment* over the parochial, worldly-wise, respectable, idle and fantastic *self-interest of superstition*; and *money* over the other forms of private property.[27]

He now made a similar point in more concrete terms that focused on the role of the revolutionary process in achieving these transformations:

> The revolutions of 1648 and 1789 were not *English* and *French* revolutions; they were revolutions of a *European* pattern. They were not the victory of a *particular* class of society over the *old political order*; they were the *proclamation of the political order for the new European society*. In these revolutions the bourgeoisie gained the victory; but the *victory of the bourgeoisie* was at that time the *victory of a new social order*, the victory of bourgeois property over feudal property, of nationality over provincialism, of competition over the guild, of the partition of estates over primogeniture, of the owner's mastery of the land over the land's mastery of its owner, of enlightenment over superstition, of the family over the family name, of industry over heroic idleness, of civil law over privileges of medieval origin. The revolution of 1648 was the victory of the seventeenth century over the sixteenth century; the revolution of 1789 was the victory of the eighteenth century over the seventeenth century. Still more than expressing the needs of the parts of the world in which they took place, England and France, these revolutions expressed the needs of the whole world, as it existed then.[28]

This was a general theme of all their public pronouncements during the revolutionary period. Marx was arrested during late 1848 as one of the three members of the Rhineland District Committee of Democrats who had signed a proclamation urging nonpayment of taxes. At his trial, Marx gave a speech in his own defense during which he explained the meaning of the ongoing social revolution according to the principles of historical materialism to a suitably impressed panel of jurors—or so one assumes, since all three defendants were acquitted:

> The new bourgeois society, which rests on entirely different foundations and on a changed mode of production, had to seize political power for itself; it had to snatch this power from the hands of those who represented the interests of the foundering society, and whose political power, in its entire organisation, had proceeded from entirely different material relations of society. *Hence the revolution*. . . . What took place here was not a political conflict between two parties within the framework of *one* society, but a *conflict between two societies*, a social conflict, which had assumed a political form; *it was the struggle of the old feudal bureaucratic society with modern bourgeois society*, a struggle between the society of *free competition* and the *society of the guild system*, between the society of landownership and the industrial society, between the society of faith and the society of knowledge.[29]

But although the bourgeoisie are the bearers of this new society, this does not necessarily mean that as revolutionary actors they are consciously seeking to bring it about.

IDEOLOGY AND CONSCIOUSNESS
OF THE REVOLUTIONARY BOURGEOISIE

Marx and Engels have been accused of quite contradictory positions in relation to the bourgeoisie. On the one hand, they are said to have inherited an aristocratic intellectual disdain for the bourgeoisie from the feudal nobility and that this is the reason their language contains such a rich vocabulary of deprecation, derision, and condescension.[30] On the other hand, they—or at least the concept of bourgeois revolution—are also said to have endorsed the positive self-image of the bourgeoisie. Ellen Meiksins Wood has written of the "the idea of 'bourgeois revolution'" that "no matter how much it is dressed up in Marxist trappings, it is not fundamentally different from Euro-centric bourgeois accounts that treat the bourgeoisie as agents of progress and credit them with throwing off the feudal shackles that impeded it."[31]

In fact, their attitude was more dialectical than either of these complaints would suggest. If we turn to the pages of the *Manifesto* in which Marx and Engels discuss the achievements of the bourgeoisie, the revolutions to which it refers are "in the modes of production and exchange": "The bourgeoisie cannot exist without constantly revolutionizing the instruments of production, and thereby the relations of production, and with them the whole relations of society."[32] The hymns of praise to the bourgeoisie with which the *Manifesto* itself opens refer to its economic and social achievements, not to its political capacity for seizing power. Insofar as elements of the bourgeoisie do engage in revolutionary struggle, they cannot act with full clarity over their intentions: they are forced to deceive themselves. "For Marx," writes Patrice Higonnet, "the point about 1789 was not that the Jacobins of 1791–92 *did not* know what they wanted, but rather that they *could not* know what they truly wanted (bourgeois class rule) until both sans-culottes on the left and property owners on the right pressed them to present a clearer and more modern answer."[33] Marx and Engels first raised the issue in *The Holy Family*:

> Robespierre, Saint-Just and their party fell because they confused the *ancient, realistic-democratic commonweal* based on *real slavery* with the modern, spiritualistic-democratic representative state, which is based on *emancipated slavery, bourgeois society*. What a terrible illusion it is to have to recognize and sanction in the *rights of man* modern bourgeois society, the society of industry, of universal competition, of private interest, freely pursuing its aims, of anarchy, of self-estranged natural and spiritual individuality, and at the same time want to annul the *manifestations of the life* of this society in particular individuals and simultaneously to want to model the *political head* of that society in the manner of *antiquity*! [34]

The most substantial discussion, however, takes place in the opening passages of *The Eighteenth Brumaire of Louis Bonaparte*, possibly the most bravura literary performance in Marx's entire oeuvre: "Hegel remarks somewhere that all great events and characters of world history occur, so to speak, twice. He forgot to add:

the first time as tragedy, the second as farce."[35] The most plausible contender for the passage in Hegel to which Marx refers is at the end of his discussion of the Roman world, where he argues that the meaning of historical repetition is the same throughout history in that it confers *legitimacy* on the event and the actors, including particular episodes in the French Revolution and figures involved in them: "In all periods of the world a political revolution is sanctioned in men's opinions when it repeats itself. Thus Napoleon was twice defeated, and the Bourbons twice expelled. By repetition that which at first appeared merely a matter of chance and contingency, becomes a real and ratified existence."[36] Marx had already rehearsed the notion of shift from tragedy to comedy involved in historical repetition in 1843–44 in relation to the Prussian state so admired by Hegel:

> The modern *ancien régime* is merely the *clown* of a world order whose real heroes are dead. History is thorough and passes through many stages while bearing an ancient form to its grave. The last stage of a world-historical form is its comedy. The Greek gods, who already died once of their wounds in Aeschylus's tragedy *Prometheus Bound*, were forced to die a second death—this time a comic one—in Lucian's dialogues. Why does history take this course? So that mankind may part *happily* from its past.[37]

In *The Eighteenth Brumaire* Marx combines both conceptions. From Hegel he derives the notion of legitimacy, not in the eyes of the audience for the historical drama but rather in those of the actors themselves. From his own earlier writings he derives the passage from tragic to comedic modes, not in relation to the absolutist state but rather to its opponents:

> Men make their own history, but not of their own free will; not under circumstances they themselves have chosen, but under the given and inherited circumstances with which they are directly confronted. The tradition of the dead generations weighs like a nightmare on the minds of the living. And, just as they appear to be engaged in the revolutionary transformation of themselves and their material surroundings, in the creation of something that does not yet exist, precisely in such epochs of revolutionary crisis they timidly conjure up the spirits of the past to help them; they borrow their names, slogans, and costumes so as to stage the new world-historic scene in this venerable disguise and borrowed language. Luther put on the mask of the Apostle Paul, the Revolution of 1789–1814 draped itself alternately as the Roman republic and the Roman empire; and the Revolution of 1848 knew no better to do than to parody at some points 1789 and at others the revolutionary traditions of 1793–95.... If we reflect on this process of world-historical necromancy, we see at once a salient distinction. Camille Desmoulins, Danton, Robespierre, Saint Just and Napoleon, the heroes of the old French Revolution, as well as its parties and the masses, accomplished the task of their epoch, which was the emancipation and establishment of modern *bourgeois* society, in Roman costume and with Roman slogans.

The modern figures listed here, from Luther to Napoleon, are still playing a role as tragic as that of the ancients upon whom they modeled themselves; their lack of self-awareness was both a necessity for them to act and what constituted their tragedy—although even those who were most fully conscious of contradictions involved, like Barnave, were no more able to escape them. The turn to comedy is both a consequence of and testament to the triumph of the revolution:

> Once the new social formation had been established, the antediluvian colossi disappeared along with the resurrected imitations of Rome—imitations of Brutus, Gracchus, Publicola, the tribunes, the senators, and Caesar himself. Bourgeois society in its sober reality had created its true interpreters and spokesmen in such as Say, Cousins, Royer-Collard, Benjamin Constant and Guizot. The real leaders of the bourgeois army sat behind office desks while the fathead Louis XVIII served as the bourgeoisie's political head. Bourgeois society was no longer aware that the ghosts of Rome had watched over its cradle, since it was entirely absorbed in the production of wealth and the peaceful struggle of economic competitive. But unheroic as the bourgeois society is, it still required heroism, self-sacrifice, terror, civil war, and battles in which whole nations were engaged to bring it into being. And its gladiators found in the stern classical traditions of the Roman republic the ideals, art forms and self-deceptions they needed to hide from themselves the limited bourgeois content of their struggles and to maintain their enthusiasm at the high level appropriate to great historical tragedy. A century earlier, in the same way but at a different stage of development, Cromwell and the English people had borrowed for their bourgeois revolution the language, passions and illusions of the Old Testament. When the real goal had been reached, when the bourgeois transformation of English society had been accomplished, Locke supplanted Habakkuk.[38]

This analysis suggested two issues. The first is the nature of ideology among the triumphant French bourgeoisie, the "unheroic" successors to those who imagined they were reproducing the conflicts of ancient Rome. As we saw earlier, Marx believed that the French bourgeoisie by 1848 had divided into two antagonistic camps.

> It was not therefore so-called principles that kept these factions divided, but rather their material conditions of existence, two distinct forms of property; it was the old opposition between town and country, the old rivalry between capital and landed property. Who would deny that at the same time old memories, personal enmities, fears and hopes, prejudices and illusions, sympathies and antipathies, convictions, articles of faith and principles bound them to one or the other royal house? A whole superstructure of different and specifically formed sentiments, illusions, modes of thought, and views of life arises on the basis of the different forms of property, of the social conditions of existence. The entire class creates and forms them out of the material foundations and the corresponding social relations. The single individual, who derives these feelings, etc. through tradition and upbringing, may well imagine that they form the real motives and the starting-point of his activity. While Orleanist and Legitimist fractions each tried to make out to their opponents and themselves that that they were divided by their adherence to the two royal houses; facts later proved that it was rather the division between their interests which forbade the unification of the royal houses. A distinction is made in private life between what a man thinks and says of himself and what he really is and does. In historical struggles one must make a still sharper distinction between the phrases and fantasies of the parties and their real organization and real interests, between their conception of themselves and what they really are.[39]

The other, of more immediate pressing importance at the time, was what the necessity for revolutionary self-deception implied for those bourgeoisies, like the

German, which increasingly held the values of a postrevolutionary "unheroic" world, but lived in a society that still required heroism for the conquest of political power. During the entire period of the formation of historical materialism, Marx and Engels remained deeply skeptical about the capacity of the German bourgeoisie to play a revolutionary role comparable to that of the French: no one would confuse the average Bremen cotton manufacturer with Robespierre, let alone Brutus. However, as the hour of revolution approached, the pair were grudgingly prepared to give it the benefit of the doubt. As Engels wrote in the spring of 1847:

> The nobility is too much in decline, the petty bourgeoisie and peasants are, by their whole position in life, too weak, the workers are still far from sufficiently mature to be able to come forward as the ruling class in Germany. There remains only the bourgeoisie ... the only class in Germany which at least gives a great part of the industrial laborers, petty bourgeoisie, peasants, workers and even a minority among the nobles a share in its interests, and has united them under its banner. . . . The only question for us then is: Is the bourgeoisie compelled by necessity to conquer political rule for itself through the overthrow of the status quo, and is it strong enough, given its own power and the weakness of its opponents, to overthrow the status quo? We shall see.[40]

They did see. As the revolutions of 1848 ran their various courses to differing degrees of defeat, even the minimum expectations that Marx and Engels held about the revolutionary role of the German bourgeoisie were disappointed. Even they were shocked by the way in which the bourgeoisie opposed popular intervention virtually from the beginning of the revolutionary process, to the point of allying with absolutist reaction. Marx wrote toward the end of 1848: "[The workers] know that their own struggle against the bourgeoisie can only dawn with the day when the bourgeoisie is victorious. . . . They can and must accept the bourgeois *revolution* as a precondition for the workers' *revolution*. However, they cannot for a moment regard it as their ultimate goal."[41] The problem was that the bourgeoisie was not willing to wait until its own victory before beginning its struggle with the proletariat. What could explain this behavior?

> In this country, where the wretchedness of the absolute monarchy still persists with its whole appendage of run-down, semi-feudal estates and relationships, there also already partially exist, on the other hand, as a consequence of industrial development and Germany's dependence on the world market, the modern contradictions between bourgeoisie and working class and the struggle that results from them. . . . The German bourgeoisie therefore already finds itself in conflict with the proletariat even before being politically constituted as a class.[42]

The cowardice of the bourgeoisie is therefore a consequence of its historical belatedness: a social and historical attribute, rather than a personal and moral one. Unfortunately, although the bourgeoisie may have abandoned a revolutionary role, the absolutist state had not abandoned a reactionary one:

> The bourgeoisie would have liked so much to transform the *feudal monarchy* into a *bourgeois monarchy* in an *amicable* way. After depriving the feudal party of armorial

bearings and titles, which are offensive to its civil pride, and of dues appertaining to feudal property, which violate the bourgeois mode of appropriation, the bourgeoisie would have liked so much to unite with the feudal party and together with it enslave the people. But the old bureaucracy does not want to be reduced to the status of a servant of a bourgeoisie for whom, until now, it has been a despotic tutor. The feudal party does not want to see its marks of distinction and interests burnt at the altar of the bourgeoisie. Finally, the Crown sees the elements of the old feudal society—a society of which it is the crowning excrescence—its true, native social background, whereas it regards the bourgeoisie as a an alien, artificial soil which it bears only under the condition that it withers away.[43]

On the one hand: "The bourgeois gentlemen therefore seek as far as possible to make the change from *absolute* to *bourgeois* monarchy without a revolution, in an amicable fashion." On the other, "the absolute monarchy in Prussia, as earlier in England and France, will not let itself be amicably changed into a bourgeois monarchy."[44]

What Marx and Engels do not discuss at this point is the general implication of the preceding analysis. In a world where most states have not yet experienced bourgeois revolutions, where most are even more economically underdeveloped than Germany, they too will give rise to "belated" bourgeoisies, the implication being that it is Germany rather than France that represents the likely pattern of bourgeois development. At one point Marx speculated that on the basis of their behavior during the French revolution of 1848, *even in that country* the bourgeoisie did not want to assume direct political control of the state:

> People may ask, why did the [French] bourgeoisie fall back into royalism, if the February revolution brought bourgeois rule to its completion? The explanation is quite simple. The bourgeoisie would have liked to return to the period when it ruled without being responsible for its rule; when a puppet authority standing between the bourgeoisie and the people had to act for it and serve it as a cloak. . . . The bourgeoisie could use the King as a kind of lightning-conductor protecting it from the people, and the people as a kind of lightning-conductor protecting it from the King.[45]

If this was so, then revolutions, including those in which Marx and Engels were involved, faced a situation that might be summarized as follows: the absolutist states refused to concede ground but the bourgeoisies were, to varying degrees, unwilling to play a revolutionary role and might even play a counterrevolutionary one out of fear of the working class, meaning that the working class, and the popular masses more generally, constituted the only social force that could consistently be relied upon to seek the overthrow of absolutism.

THE ORIGINS OF PERMANENT REVOLUTION

The necessity for popular intervention was not entirely new in the history of bourgeois revolutions. The very fact that they involved such a comprehensive reordering of society meant that, even before 1848, the bourgeoisie could not be the only or even necessarily the major social force involved in the revolutionary process, since it remained a minority class, if a larger one than that of the existing rulers. Its leaders, consciously or unconsciously, had to mobilize the masses under ultimately deceptive slogans of universal right, necessary for a minority class to lead the coalitions that overthrew the old regimes, but disguising or simply avoiding the fact that exploitation would continue, albeit in new forms. But Marx was also aware that more than deception was involved here. The people whom Marx refers to as the "plebeians" had an interest in overthrowing absolutism, and their methods were required to achieve and defend both the English and French Revolutions, methods from which the bourgeoisie themselves shrank: "Therefore, where they stood in opposition to the bourgeoisie, as for example in 1793 and 1794 in France, [the plebeians] were fighting for the implementation of the interests of the bourgeoisie, although not *in the manner* of the bourgeoisie. The *whole of the French terror* was nothing other than a *plebeian manner* of dealing with the *enemies of the bourgeoisie*, with absolutism, feudalism and parochialism.[46] Yet again this raises questions about the capacity of the bourgeoisie even at its most revolutionary, which Marx and Engels left unanswered except by implication. For the issue here is not simply the lack of social weight possessed by the bourgeoisie and its consequent need for allies; the majority of its members would not *in any case* have demanded the necessary action without being pushed from below: "The terror in France could thus by its mighty hammer blows only serve to spirit away, as it were, the ruins of feudalism from French soil. The timidly considerate bourgeoisie would not have accomplished this task in decades. The bloody action of the people thus only prepared the way for it. In the same way, the overthrow of the absolutist monarchy would merely be temporary if the economic conditions for the rule of the bourgeois class had not yet become ripe."[47]

Marx's contrast between economic readiness and political vacillation suggest that the self-restraint of the bourgeoisie as a revolutionary class and the consequent need for representatives of another social class to substitute for it in the realm of political action did not begin in Germany in 1848 but had a longer lineage dating even further back in time than the French Revolution. The corollary is that the actors who do carry through the revolution on behalf of the bourgeoisie are likely to find their own goals impossible of attainment. A classic passage by Engels from 1850, on the role of Thomas Munzer in the German Peasant War of 1525, makes the essential point:

> The worst thing that can befall a leader of an extreme party is to be compelled to take over a government in an epoch when the movement is not yet ripe for the domination of the class which he represents and for the realization of the measures which that domination would imply. What he *can* do depends not upon his will but upon the sharpness of the clash of interests between the various classes, and upon the degree of development of the material means of existence, the relations of production and means of communication upon which the clash of interests of the classes is based every time. What he *ought* to do, what his party demands of him, again depends not upon him, or upon the degree of development of the class struggle and its conditions.

He is bound to his doctrines and the demands hitherto propounded which do not emanate from the interrelations of the social classes at a given moment, or from the more or less accidental level of relations of production and means of communication, but from his more or less penetrating insight into the general result of the social and political movement. Thus he necessarily finds himself in a dilemma. What he *can* do is in contrast to all his actions as hitherto practiced, to all his principles and to the present interests of his party; what he *ought* to do cannot be achieved. In a word, he is compelled to represent not his party or his class, but the class for whom conditions are ripe for domination. In the interests of the movement itself, he is compelled to defend the interests of an alien class, and to feed his own class with phrases and promises, with the assertion that the interests of that alien class are their own interests. Whoever puts himself in this awkward position is irrevocably lost. . . . Not only the movement of his time, but the whole century, was not ripe for the realization of the ideas for which [Munzer] himself had only begun to grope. The class which he represented not only was not developed enough and incapable of subduing and transforming the whole of society, but it was just beginning to come into existence.[48]

Engels is claiming that while Munzer represented the communist aspirations of the peasantry, these were unrealizable at the time since the only social force actually capable of achieving them, the working class, did not yet exist in sufficient numbers to act as an agency. As a result, all that Munzer could have hoped to achieve were the goals of the bourgeoisie, "the class for whom conditions are ripe for domination," even though they had signally failed to enter the field on their own behalf. In fact, it is questionable whether the German Lands were even ready for domination by capitalism at this period. Part of the case Engels wanted to convey is that the German bourgeoisie has always been vacillating and untrustworthy, in 1525 as in 1848, even though meant rather overemphasizing the possibility of their coming to power at the former date. Notwithstanding the weakness of the actual example, the essential point was sound and had been stated by Marx in 1847 in a passage I have already quoted in the previous chapter: "If therefore the proletariat overthrows the political rule of the bourgeoisie, its victory will only be temporary, only an element in the service of the *bourgeois revolution* itself, as in the year 1794, as long as in the course of history, in its 'movement,' the material conditions have not yet been created which make necessary the abolition of the bourgeois mode of production and therefore also the definitive overthrow of the political rule of the bourgeoisie."[49] In 1847 Marx appeared to believe that the material conditions did not exist for the proletariat to overthrow bourgeois rule; by 1850 he argued that if not already existent, they could be established in a very short time: this change of position was the basis of the new strategy of "permanent revolution."

The notion arose out the experience of the French Revolution, in which events took the form of a series of increasingly radical episodes, as the popular classes become more and more involved in the process. The effect was to propel the revolution beyond the limits of what the bourgeoisie considered acceptable, but the social forces involved were incapable of sustaining the new society, with the result that it fell back into what was historically possible at the time, in other words, a bourgeois regime. Thus "permanent revolution" meant something like a continuous or uninterrupted succession of escalating moments.[50] Marx and Engels may have been among the first people to refer to the notion in print in 1843 and 1844.[51] It was not, however, a concept exclusive to them but one common to members of "the Democracy," the alliance of the petty bourgeoisie, peasantry, and working class to the left of the bourgeois liberals. Their goal was the Social Republic—not socialism, but a regime modeled on the Jacobin state at its most radical; in other words one that went beyond the limits of bourgeois acceptability.

During the course of the German Revolution of 1848 Marx and Engels held three versions of permanent revolution, each successively more radical as the unwillingness of the bourgeoisie to confront the feudal absolutist regime grew more apparent. In the first, the bourgeoisie would ally with the Democracy to overthrow the existing regime, after which the Democracy removes the bourgeoisie to establish the Social Republic. The second, formulated when it became apparent that the bourgeoisie were more concerned with a potential threat to their property than with absolutism, involved the Democracy striking out on its own for the Social Republic—still remaining within the boundaries of capitalism, but intent on opening up the way for rapid capitalist development while a new revolution was being prepared. The third, formulated when it also became apparent that the leaderships of the non-working-class elements of the Democracy were no more willing to take the revolution forward than the bourgeoisie proper, involved the proletarian revolution as the only alternative to counterrevolution, but on the basis of an international movement led by the more advanced working classes, most importantly in France and Britain. Here finally is the idea that the escalation characteristic of the French Revolution would, in the new conditions of more advanced capitalist development, lead to the victory of the proletariat.[52]

It is the third and final version of permanent revolution that is incorporated in the most radical text written by Marx or Engels during this period: the "Address to the Central Committee of the Communist League" of March 1850. Two themes emerge from the main body of this work: first, that the liberal bourgeoisie and the social-reformist Democracy would be the most dangerous enemies of the working class when in power; second, and consequently, the working class needed to retain absolute organizational and political independence.[53]

> While the democratic petty bourgeoisie want to bring the revolution to an end as quickly as possible . . . it is our interest and our task to make the revolution permanent until all the more or less propertied classes have been driven from their ruling positions, until the proletariat has conquered state power and until the association of the proletarians has progressed sufficiently far—not only in one country but in all the leading countries of the world—that competition between the proletarians of these countries ceases and at least the decisive forces of production are concentrated in the hands of the workers.[54]

Many people have been mesmerized by the reference to "mak[ing] the revolution permanent" in this passage and the concluding sentence ("their battle-cry must be: The Permanent Revolution."), and drawn the conclusion that Marx anachronistically saw socialism as being on the immediate agenda. In fact, apart from this climactic rhetorical flourish, Marx argues for a more realistic agenda throughout. In the immediately preceding paragraph he writes: "Although the German workers cannot come to power and achieve the realization of their class interests without passing through a protracted revolutionary development, this time they can at least be certain that the first act of the approaching revolutionary drama will coincide with the direct victory of their own class in France and will thereby be accelerated."[55] German workers must maintain their organizational and political independence from the petty bourgeoisie, to push the latter class beyond the satisfaction of its own demands and to continue pressing their own class interests even after the feudal-absolutist state has been decisively overthrown. Marx confirmed this position later in the same year in *The Class Struggles in France*, the significance being that he had always pointed to France as being the most advanced workers' movement and the one to which German workers should look for inspiration. Yet even here further capitalist development was necessary:

> In general, the development of the industrial proletariat is conditioned by the development of the industrial bourgeoisie. Only under the rule of the bourgeoisie does it begin to exist on a broad national basis, which elevates its revolution to a national one; only under the rule of the bourgeoisie does it create the modern means of production, which also become the means of its revolutionary liberation. It is only the rule of the bourgeoisie which serves to tear up the material roots of feudal society and level the ground, thus creating the only possible conditions for a proletarian revolution.[56]

It is true that they assumed only a short period of time would be necessary for capitalism to develop to the point where the socialist revolution was possible. Toward the end of his life Engels concluded that they had been overoptimistic: "History had proved us, and all who thought like us, wrong. It has made clear that the state of economic development on the Continent at that time was not, by a long way, ripe for the elimination of capitalist production."[57]

Marx and Engels rarely considered the possibility that defeat might result from absolutist regimes, above all tsarist Russia, simply being more powerful and resourceful than their enemies. The main obstacle to the successful completion of a bourgeois revolution was for them the unwillingness or inability of the bourgeoisie to lead an effective struggle. But a subordinate element is the idea, mainly expressed by Engels, that some peoples as a whole are incapable of achieving development.

Bourgeois Revolution and the "Nonhistoric Peoples"

As we saw in the previous chapter, Engels had previously expressed what we would now regard as borderline racist attitudes toward the Highland Scots and the

Catholic Irish. These were not, however, the only peoples who apparently required the imposition of bourgeois civilization from outside. In an article written in 1847, Engels considered the suppression by the French of a prolonged rising of Algerian Bedouins: "The struggle of the Bedouins was a hopeless one, and although the manner in which brutal soldiers . . . have carried on the war is highly blameable, the conquest of Algeria is an important and fortunate fact for the fate of civilisation." Engels goes on to remind his readers that the Bedouins survived through robbing and enslaving more settled communities: "And after all, the modern *bourgeois*, with civilisation, industry, order and at least relative enlightenment following him, is preferable to the feudal lord or to the marauding robber, with the barbarian state of society to which they belong."[58] A similar attitude, but concerning Europeans rather than Africans or Latin Americans, permeates a more famous article, "The Magyar Struggle," written for and published in the *Neue Rheinische Zeitung* in January 1849. As the Europe-wide revolutionary movement of 1848 began to recede Engels tried to identify the social basis of the emergent reaction, and thought he had done so in the particular characteristics of certain national groups. Engels was particularly concerned with whether or not support for any particular national movement would help prepare the way for capitalism and ultimately the working class itself. From this perspective the Slav nationalism that Engels targets in his article is an obstacle to both. Indeed, for him it cannot even be described as a genuine national movement since it ultimately relies on the Russian absolutist state—then the main bastion of reaction in Europe—for its continued existence:

> There is no country in Europe that does not possess, in some remote corner, at least one remnant-people, left over from an earlier population, forced back and subjugated by the nation which later became the repository of historical development. These remnants of a nation, mercilessly crushed, as Hegel said, by the course of history, this *national refuse*, is always the fanatical representative of the counter-revolution and remains so until it is completely exterminated or de-nationalized, as its whole existence is in itself a protest against a great historical revolution.

There were, however, earlier examples of such "human refuse" than those that concerned Engels in 1848: "In Scotland, for example, the Gaels, supporters of the Stuarts from 1640 to 1745." Engels concludes by expressing his hopes for a revival of the revolutionary movement of the French proletariat and the German and Magyar peoples: "The general war which will then break out will scatter this Slav Sonderbund ["special path"], and annihilate all these small pig-headed peoples even to their very names. The next world war will not only cause reactionary classes and dynasties to disappear from the face of the earth, but also entire reactionary peoples. And that too is an advance."[59] This makes uncomfortable reading for contemporary socialists since we associate calls for "extermination" or "annihilation" of whole peoples—understandable if not forgivable even given the counterrevolutionary danger of time—with another political tradition altogether, namely fascism. The belief in the existence of "nonhistoric" peoples was closely linked in the thought of Marx and Engels with that of "races," including a distinctly "Celtic" race that included the Highlanders and native Irish, as opposed to the "Anglo-Saxon" Lowlanders and English. These notions are important in our context because they make clear that, contrary to what is claimed by Ephraim Nimni, Engels began his literary career by *including* the native Irish alongside the Highlanders in the "nonhistoric" category, which is clearly linked to the notion of racial groups ("peoples") discussed above.[60]

As the Ukrainian Bolshevik and Left Oppositionist Roman Rosdolsky wrote in his classic critique, nonhistoricity "represents a relic of the idealist interpretation of history and so has no place in Marxism."[61] To argue that particular national groups display *inherent*, and moreover, *eternal* characteristics, seems particularly idealist. Rosdolsky noted that "the reactionary conduct of the Highland Scots . . . proceeded . . . not from the reactionary character of their *nationality*, but from specific social, economic and political conditions that drove this "national refuse" into opposition to the revolution (and so their very nationality became an *expression* of this opposition)."[62] Unsurprisingly, these positions led Engels into wrong predictions. In a subsequent article, "Democratic Pan-Slavism," we are told:

> We repeat: apart from the Poles, the Russians, and at most the Turkish Slavs, no Slav people has a future, for the simple reason that all the other Slavs lack the primary historical, geographical, political and industrial conditions for independence and viability. Peoples which have never had a history of their own, which from the time when they achieved the first, most elementary stage of civilization already came under foreign sway, or which were *forced* to attain the first stage of civilization only by means of a foreign yoke, are not viable and will never be able to achieve any kind of independence.[63]

Many of the peoples that he attacks as incapable of forming nations, such as the Czechs, subsequently went on to do precisely that, while those that failed to do so, such as the Basques, were prevented then, and continue to be prevented now, by repression, not some congenital incapacity bred in the bone. In other words, the content of national movements changes over time. Whatever the role of the Basques in 1848, would any socialist argue that their struggle for independence was reactionary during the period of the Franco regime in Spain?

Were these perspectives peculiar to Engels alone? Did Marx take a different attitude? In the concluding passage of his famous article, "The British Rule in India," published on June 25, 1853, in the *New York Daily Tribune*, Marx makes comments that are strikingly similar to those written by Engels on Algeria. Both condemn colonial *methods*, rather than objectives, and endorse the civilizing role of colonialism, rather than support the colonized, and England is described as "an unconscious tool of history" in causing a "social revolution" in Asia.[64] In his critique of this article, Edward Said accused Marx of succumbing to an "orientalist" discourse that overtakes his human sympathy for the sufferings of Indians subject to British colonialism.[65] For other commentators Marx and Engels's work can be dismissed more generally as merely another Eurocentric defense of capitalism, no more concerned with the resulting impact on indigenous peoples and their civilizations than apologists for the World Trade Organization.

Marx and Engels seem to have originally taken the view that it was necessary for the European bourgeoisie to introduce capitalism into Asia and Africa because the supposedly "stagnant" nature of these societies acted as a block to indigenous development. Or, as Robert Young writes, "the dominant force of opposition to capitalism, Marxism, as a body of knowledge remains complicit with, and even extends, the system to which it is opposed."[66] Other writers have made more sweeping charges:

> For Marx the Indian uprising of 1857 was no more progressive than the resistance of the first nation Americans against the European settlers. In the triumph of European colonialism—including its genocide—Marx saw the progress of Capital and with it the creation of a working class that would put an end to it. To the victim of colonialism there was not much to choose between Marx's progress and the Imperialist conquest. Both represented Europe's power to destroy cultures and languages, introduce forms of slavery, and in the Americas and Australia, genocide. For these peoples there is little in Marx's talk of creating the material conditions for human liberation that contained much attraction. Human liberation appears more as European power built on their graves.[67]

Indeed, according to these critics, treating the extension of the capitalist mode of production as a necessary precondition for socialism necessarily led them to support the destruction of all obstacles to capitalist dominance, both retrospectively in their historical judgments and contemporaneously in their political interventions. And if those obstacles were people—Indians, Native Americans, or Scottish Highlanders—this was merely the unfortunate but unavoidable cost of human progress. In the following decades, it was this aspect of the concept of bourgeois revolution that would be most subject to revision.

10
MARX AND ENGELS (3) AFTER 1852: TRANSITIONS, REVOLUTIONS, AND AGENCY

Marx and Engels held three main positions on the conditions for the possibility for bourgeois revolution throughout the turbulent years between 1847 and 1852. First, capitalist productive forces had to develop to the point that they were prevented from further growth by the existing feudal class relations. Second, a revolution to remove these social relations required the existence of a social force capable of doing so, which need not necessarily be a section of the capitalist class itself. Third, some peoples or nations—including a minority located in Europe itself—were incapable of developing to the point where either development or revolution could take place on an endogenous basis. Did they subsequently change any of these positions after 1852?

FORCES OF PRODUCTION, RELATIONS OF PRODUCTION, AND THE SUPERSTRUCTURE

In *The Class Struggles in France*, one of the last major pieces written during the revolutionary period, Marx reaffirmed the connection between the development of the productive forces and the possibility of successful social revolution, in this case the socialist revolution in France: "While this general prosperity lasts, enabling the productive forces of bourgeois society to develop to the full extent possible with the bourgeois system, there can be no question of a real revolution. Such a revolution is only possible at a time when *two factors* come into *conflict*: the *modern productive forces* and the *bourgeois forms of production*."[1] Neither Marx nor Engels ever revised this position. The notebooks that we now call the *Grundrisse* (1857–58) have a special significance for political Marxists, equivalent to that which the "works of the epistemological break" have for structural Marxists of an earlier generation. It is here, they believe, that the new orientation on "social property relations" first appears. These claims are not, however, supported by the text itself. The following passage occurs in the course of a discussion of how landed proprietors can change the method by which they exploit their labor force:

The change in the form in which he obtains his revenue or in the form in which the worker is paid is not, however, a formal distinction, but *presupposes a total restructuring of the mode of production* (agriculture itself); it therefore presupposes conditions which rest on a certain development of industry, of trade, and of science, in short of the forces of production. Just as, in general, production resting on capital and wage labour differs from other modes of production not merely formally, but equally presupposes a total revolution and development of material production.[2]

Marx reiterated the same point directly after completing these notes, in that most profoundly unfashionable of texts, the "Preface" to *A Contribution to the Critique of Political Economy* (1859). This is sometimes treated simply as a summary of the unpublished *German Ideology* for the benefit of an audience that would never have the opportunity to read it. In fact, Marx uses the "Preface" to present, in highly condensed form, all the key aspects of historical materialism as it had developed since 1845 and to introduce an entirely new concept. First, he reaffirms the direction of influence between the forces and relations of production: "In the social production of their existence, men inevitably enter into definite relations, which are independent of their will, namely relations of production appropriate to a given stage in the development of their material forces of production." He then clarifies the notion of "social relations" first used in *The Poverty of Philosophy* by separating out those directly related to production from the others, which he assigns to the "superstructure": "The totality of these relations of production constitutes the economic structure of society, the real foundation, on which arises a legal and political superstructure and to which correspond definite forms of social consciousness." There are therefore two levels of correspondence: on the one hand, between the forces and relations of production (together forming the "structure") and, on the other, between those social relations and functions not directly connected with production and their ideological expressions (together forming the "superstructure"). The possibility for revolution opens when the first of these correspondences breaks down: "At a certain stage of development, the material forces of society come into conflict with existing relations of production or—this merely expresses the same thing in legal terms—with the property relations within the framework of which they have operated hitherto. From forms of development of the productive forces these relations turn into their fetters. Then begins an era of social revolution."[3] There are reasons specific to the German politics of the period why Marx emphasized structure rather than agency in these passages. Marx was anxious to make his work available to workers in the German lands, where he still considered his main audience to be, among whom his rival Ferdinand Lassalle appeared to be gaining support. In order to guarantee that *A Contribution to the Critique of Political Economy* would reach them, however, he had to ensure that it would not be banned from publication by the censors, hence the absence of reference to the class struggle in the somewhat mechanistic formulations in the "Preface."[4] Even so, it does not represent a fundamental break from the positions he and Engels had worked out in the late 1840s. The *Manifesto*, not usually thought of as a rigidly mechanistic or determinist work, describes the specific process of capitalist development within feudalism in very similar terms to the more general formulations of the "Preface": "At a certain stage in the development of these means of production and of exchange, the conditions under which feudal society produced and exchanged, the feudal organisation of agriculture and manufacturing industry, in one word, the feudal relations of property became no longer compatible with the already developed productive forces; they became so many fetters. They had to be burst asunder; they were burst asunder."[5]

What happens after "an era of social revolution" begins is indeterminate and can only be resolved at the level of the superstructure: "In studying such transformations it is always necessary to distinguish between the material transformation of the economic conditions of production, which can be determined with the precision of natural science, and the legal, political, religious, artistic or philosophic— in short, ideological forms in which men become conscious of this conflict and fight it out."[6] Again, there is nothing remotely deterministic about this, since a fight can end, in the words of the *Manifesto*, "either in a revolutionary reconstitution of society at large, or in the common ruin of the contending classes."[7]

The "Preface" is particularly important in the context of a discussion of bourgeois revolutions because Marx is taking the transition from feudalism to capitalism as his model for transitions and revolutions more generally. As we shall see, there are problems with this generalization since the working class, unlike the bourgeoisie, cannot become the bearer of new social relations prior to actually seizing political power. It does make clear, however, that Marx had not abandoned the view of the relationship between capitalist development and bourgeois revolution established with Engels between 1847 and 1852. The bourgeois-revolutionary locus is clearest in the passage that recalls the discussion in *The Eighteenth Brumaire* about the lack of self-awareness necessary for the bourgeoisie while it is acting as a revolutionary class: "Just as one does not judge an individual by what he thinks about himself, so one cannot judge such a period of transformation by its consciousness, but, on the contrary, this consciousness must be explained from the contradictions of material life, from the conflict existing between the social forces of production and the relations of production."[8]

By the time Marx began writing *Capital* in the 1860s he might justifiably have felt it unnecessary to repeat these formulations yet again. By then he had published several statements of his theory of socioeconomic development, both individually and with Engels, and could easily have simply referred to these before applying his general theory to the specific case of the capitalist mode of production without repeating the arguments yet again. Nevertheless, in chapter 1 of volume 1 Marx quotes the 1859 "Preface" in order explicitly to defend it from criticism that it is only applicable to the contemporary capitalist society.[9] At the very end of the notes that became volume 3 he summarizes the thesis yet again:

The sign that the moment of such a crisis [of a particular historical form of production] has arrived is that the contradiction and antithesis between, on the one hand, the relations of distribution, hence also the specific historical form of relations of production corresponding to them, and on the other hand, the productive forces, productivity, and the development of its agents, gains in breadth and depth. A conflict then sets in between the material development of production and its social form.[10]

It is, however, elsewhere in volume 3 that Marx gives what is perhaps the fullest statement of the position in his entire output:

The specific economic form in which unpaid surplus labour is pumped out of the direct producers determines the relationship of domination and servitude, *as this grows directly out of production itself and reacts back on it in turn as a determinant.* On this is based the entire configuration of the economic community arising from actual relations of production, and hence also its specific political form. It is in each case the direct relationship of the owners of the conditions of production to the immediate producers— *a relationship whose particular form naturally corresponds always to a certain level of development of the type and manner of labour, and hence to its productive power*—in which we find the innermost secret, the hidden basis of the entire social edifice, and hence also the political form of the relationship of sovereignty and dependence, in short the specific form of the state in each case. This does not prevent the same economic basis— the same in its major conditions—from displaying endless variations and gradations in its appearance, as the result of innumerable different empirical circumstances, natural conditions, racial relations, historical influences acting from outside, etc., and these can only be understood by analyzing these empirically given conditions.[11]

The phrases that Marx uses here—"the relationship of domination and servitude . . . grows out of production itself," the exploitative relationship "corresponds always to a certain level of the type and manner of labour, and hence to its productive power"—would appear to render this passage immune to misinterpretation, but alas no. Comninel quotes it and then goes on to give a textbook example of how to make a quotation mean the exact opposite of what it actually says:

For the "base" on which "the entire social structure" is founded is not said to be production in any general sense, but "the specific economic form in which unpaid surplus-labour is pumped out of direct producers." Even "the entire formation of the economic community" *grows up out of* these class relations of production, not the reverse. Admittedly, the exploitative relations are once again problematically said to be "always naturally corresponding to a definite stage in the development of the methods of labour and thereby its social productivity"—which, if we recognize technology to be a product of class society, seems once again to leave the horse behind the cart. Yet this assertion is something of an aside, and if allowance is made for Marx's inclination to associate historical materialism with liberal-scientific materialism—a tendency even more notable in Engels, and notably embraced by their followers—the statement poses no real problem. Indeed, the "direction" of this correspondence can be reversed from what is normally understood, and priority given to the *exploitative relationship*, as it relates to "the development of the methods of labour."[12]

An impressive performance—but consider again three aspects of the passage to which Comninel refers. First, the "social edifice" to which Marx refers is clearly intended as something separate from either the forces or the relations of production and, given that he immediately goes on to link it to the state, it fairly obviously corresponds to what he describes metaphorically in the 1859 "Preface" as the "superstructure." Marx does indeed write that the basis of "the entire social edifice" is found in the relations of production, but why does that rule out, as a conceptually prior process, the basis of the productive relations being found in the productive forces? Second, Comninel raises the bogey of "technology"—a familiar tactic for those who want to play down the significance of the productive forces, but one which in this case is difficult to play successfully since Marx is actually referring to (and I quote) "the development of the methods of labour," which is a rather broader concept. Finally, and most outrageously of all, Comninel simply tells us that he intends to reverse what Marx actually says in order to make the passage fit his own preconceptions. When Engels restated the argument on his own behalf in 1886 then, he was not deviating from what Marx had written, but reaffirming the joint understanding of historical development they had shared for the previous forty years:

> At a certain stage, the new forces of production set in motion by the bourgeoisie—in the first place the division of labour and the combination of many workers performing individual operations in one manufactory handling all stages of production—and the conditions and requirements of exchange, developed through these forces of production, became incompatible with the existing order [relations] of production handed down through history and sanctified by law, that is to say, incompatible with the privileges of the guild and the numerous other personal and local privileges (which were just as numerous fetters for the unprivileged estates) of the feudal order of society. The forces of production rebelled against the order [relations] of production represented by the feudal landlords and the guild masters.[13]

Why do these misconceptions persist, despite being in flat contradiction to what Marx and Engels actually wrote? Alex Callinicos has drawn our attention to the difference between "the abstract model of capitalist production outlined by Marx in *Capital*" and the concrete forms that capitalism has actually taken: "The first is intended to isolate the essential features of capitalism, common to all its variants; the second seek, within the limits set by these features, to identify the diverse historical forms they have assumed."[14] In effect, political Marxists do not seem to recognize that there *is* an abstract model in *Capital*. Apart from Brenner himself, they think that England was the only site of endogenous capitalist development and therefore assume that Marx takes English development as a model for the origin of capitalism because, in effect, it was the only example he had. It is not in dispute that England was the country where capitalism developed to the greatest extent. It was for this reason that Marx made it the basis of his analysis, in the same way that he always took the most developed form of any phenomena as the basis of his analysis. But in his mature work Marx repeatedly states that capitalist development took place beyond England in space and before England in time. In particular, he describes "the expropriation of the agricultural producer" as taking its "classic form" in England.[15] "Classic," status does, however, rather depend on the existence of other forms, which is presumably why passages of the following type occur throughout *Capital*: "Although we come across the first sporadic traces of capitalist production as early as the fourteenth or fifteenth centuries in certain towns of the Mediterranean, the capitalist era dates from the sixteenth century. Wherever it appears, the abolition of serfdom has long been completed, and the most brilliant achievement of the Middle Ages, the existence of independent city-states, has already been on the wane for a considerable time."[16] Confronted with quotations of this kind, some political Marxists simply deny that Marx meant what wrote, as we have already seen in the work of Comninel. Take, for example, the question of the "so-called primitive accumulation." Here is the famous passage from *Capital* where he traces the chronology of the different forms taken by this process:

> The discovery of gold and silver in America, the extirpation, enslavement and entombment in mines of the indigenous population of that continent, the beginnings of the conquest and plunder of India, and the conversion of Africa into a preserve for the commercial hunting of blackskins, are all things which characterize the dawn of the era of capitalist production. These idyllic proceedings are the chief moments of primitive accumulation. Hard on their heels follows the commercial war of the European nations, which has the world as its battlefield. . . . The different moments of primitive accumulation can be assigned in particular to Spain, Portugal, Holland, France and England, in more or less chronological order. These moments are systematically combined together at the end of the seventeenth century in England; the combination embraces the colonies, the national debt, the modern tax system, and the system of protection. These methods depend in part on brute force, for instance the colonial system. But they all employ the power of the state, the concentrated and organized force of society, to hasten, as in a hothouse, the process of transformation of the feudal mode of production into the capitalist mode, and to shorten the transition.[17]

Ellen Meiksins Wood is unhappy with this passage, with its unfortunate references to "Spain, Portugal, Holland and France"; so we are told:

> We should first take note that Marx . . . is explaining the "genesis of the *industrial* capitalist," not the origins of capitalism, nor the emergence of specifically capitalist "laws of motion," nor specifically capitalist social relations, a specifically capitalist form of exploitation, or the imperatives of self-sustaining economic development. Marx is trying to explain how the accumulation of wealth was converted in the right conditions—that is, in already capitalist social relations (in England), from simply the unproductive profits of usury and commerce into industrial capital. As for the origins of the capitalist system, the "so-called primitive accumulation"—in Marx's terms, the expropriation of the direct producers, in particular peasants—that gave rise to specifically capitalist social relations and the dynamic associated with them. Marx situates it firmly in England and in the countryside.[18]

Like the passage from Comninel discussed above, this is an extraordinary example of how to read a passage through a theoretical filter, translating as you go until its meaning is compatible with your own position. What does Marx actually say about "the expropriation of the direct producers, in particular peasants, that gave rise to specifically capitalist social relations and the dynamic associated with them"? Does he situate it "firmly in England and in the countryside"? "The history of this expropriation assumes different aspects in different countries," he writes in *Capital*, "and runs through its various phases in different orders of succession, and at different historical epochs." More than one time and more than one place then. A footnote continues: "In Italy, where capitalist production developed earliest, the dissolution of serfdom took place earlier than elsewhere."[19] Marx could of course have been factually wrong but, regardless of the accuracy of his views (which have in fact been confirmed by modern scholarship), it is not possible to claim, on the basis of either his early or his mature work, that he believed capitalist development was restricted to England, or even to England and the United Netherlands. He certainly believed that by 1640 the capitalist mode of production had become *dominant* in England to a greater extent than anywhere else, but that was perfectly compatible with believing that capitalist production had developed elsewhere, within otherwise fundamentally feudal economies. It was, after all, in the *Grundrisse*, not *The German Ideology*, that he wrote: "It must be kept in mind that the new forces of production and relations of production do not develop out of *nothing*, nor drop from the sky, nor from the womb of the self-positing Idea; but from within and in antithesis to the existing development of production and the inherited, traditional relations of property."[20] And it was in *Capital*, not the *Manifesto of the Communist Party* that he added, in less Hegelian tones: "The economic structure of capitalist society has grown out of the economic structure of feudal society. The dissolution of the latter set free the elements of the former."[21]

THE NONREVOLUTIONARY BOURGEOISIE AS RULE AND EXCEPTION

Did Marx and Engels display the same continuity of attitude toward bourgeois revolutions as they did toward the forces and relations of production? The term "bourgeois revolution" did not entirely disappear from their vocabulary after 1852, but they tended to use it in relation to revolutions that had occurred before 1848. As late as in volume 1 of *Capital* (1867), for example, Marx refers to total dominance of the money-form only being achieved "on a national scale" toward the end of the eighteenth century "during the French bourgeois revolution."[22] Were there then no further successful bourgeois revolutions after the Springtime of Peoples ended in unrelieved failure in 1849? In effect, the revolutionary duo treated two chronologically overlapping episodes of national transformation, both of which began in the early 1860s, as functionally equivalent forms of social revolution, although without applying the adjective "bourgeois" to them. One, analysis of which was overwhelmingly left to Engels, and conducted after the fact, was German Unification. The other, discussed mainly by Marx while it was still ongoing, was the American Civil War. The context for both was their changing perspective on the political capacity of the bourgeoisie.

Before 1852 Marx and Engels tended to exaggerate how revolutionary already-successful national bourgeoisies had been, partly as a means of shaming their German successors into decisive action. After 1852 their attitude displays not only a corrective rebalancing toward more realistic expectations, but also a real and growing skepticism, which Engels in particular expressed in general terms. Unlike previous ruling classes, he argued, the bourgeoisie had great difficulty in ruling on its own behalf, even in those cases where it had displayed a serious degree of revolutionary spirit:

> It seems a law of historical development that the bourgeoisie can in no European country get hold of political power—at least for any length of time—in the same exclusive way in which the feudal aristocracy kept hold of it during the Middle Ages. Even in France, where feudalism was completely extinguished, the bourgeoisie as a whole has held full possession of the Government for very short periods only. During Louis Philippe's reign, 1830–48, a very small portion of the bourgeoisie ruled the kingdom; by far the larger part was excluded from the suffrage by the high qualification. Under the Second Republic, 1848–51, the whole bourgeoisie ruled but for three years only; their incapacity brought on the Second Empire. It is only now, in the Third Republic, that the bourgeoisie as a whole have kept possession of the helm for more than 20 years; and they are already showing lively signs of decadence. A durable reign of the bourgeoisie has been possible only in countries like America, where feudalism was unknown, and society at the very beginning started from a bourgeois basis. And even in France and America, the successors of the bourgeoisie, the working people, are already knocking at the door.[23]

As the last sentence suggests, the problem was that the emergence of the working class on an organized basis forced the various national bourgeoisies to seek alliances with its former oppressors. It has long been accepted by Marx and Engels that the German bourgeoisie had arrived historically "too late": "The period of its florescence is occurring at a time when the bourgeoisie of the other West European countries is already politically in decline." By this Engels means that the bourgeoisie of Britain ("England") and France were already threatened by the working class and consequently had sought alliances with the former feudal ruling classes even where capitalism was already most developed:

> It is a peculiarity of the bourgeoisie, in contrast to all former ruling classes, that there is a turning point in its development after which every further expansion of its agencies of power, hence primarily of its capital, only tends to make it more and more unfit for political rule.... At a certain point—which is not necessarily reached everywhere at the same time or at the same stage of development—it begins to notice that its proletarian double is outgrowing it. From that moment on, it loses the strength required for exclusive political rule; it looks around for allies with whom to share its rule, or to whom to cede it entirely, as circumstances may require."[24]

Their new skepticism about the revolutionary capacities of the bourgeoisie was now applied to the historical record. "Since it is an army of officers," wrote Engels of the bourgeoisie in 1865, "it must ensure the support of the workers or it must buy political power piecemeal from those forces confronting it from above, in particular, from the monarchy."[25] As he subsequently noted, however, there were situations where money was insufficient and political action to advance the development of capitalism, which the bourgeoisie itself was unwilling or unable to take, and had to be taken by others for different reasons. Marx made the point more generally in *Capital*: "The knights of industry ... only succeeded in supplanting the knights of the sword by making use of events in which they had played no part whatsoever."[26] Marx is still thinking here of the plebeians and Engels's final (1882) amendments to the text of *Anti-Dühring* made these remarks concrete in relation to France: "The 'have-nothing' masses of Paris, during the Reign of Terror, were able for a moment to gain the mastery, *and thus to lead the revolution to victory in spite of the bourgeoisie themselves*. But in doing so, they only proved how impossible it was for their domination to last under the conditions then obtaining."[27] He later (1892) described this process as "a law of evolution of bourgeois society" in a discussion of the English case: "Had it not been for that yeomanry and the plebeian element in the towns, the bourgeoisie would not have fought the matter out to the bitter end, and would never have brought Charles I to the scaffold. In order to secure even those conquests of the bourgeoisie that were ripe for gathering at the time, the revolution had to be carried considerably further—exactly as in 1793 in France and 1848 in Germany."[28]

Yet whether they are actually describing a general law is open to doubt. It seems rather to be one specific to the early stages in the development of bourgeois society; for in later stages it was not only plebeians or proto-proletarians who cleared the way for capitalist development. Another route was where a newly established bourgeois state expanded outward, bringing new forms of economic, social, and political organization in its wake. Harrington and his contemporaries had observed the New Model Army do precisely this in Scotland during the 1650s. Schlegel saw the French Grande Armée perform a similar role across Europe during the Napoleonic Wars, before becoming the first person to describe this process as a "revolution from above." Marx and Engels too were born into a part of Germany shaped by the expansion of the French Revolution outside its national borders. Initially, it was the figure of Napoleon who is seen as decisive, as Engels explained to a Chartist audience during the mid-1840s: "Napoleon was in Germany the representative of the revolution, the propagator of its principles, the destroyer of old feudal society."[29] The first substantial discussion by Marx and Engels of the Napoleonic period in French history took place around the same time in *The Holy Family*:

> Napoleon represented the last battle of *revolutionary terror* against the *bourgeois society* which had been proclaimed by this same Revolution, and against its policy. Napoleon, of course, already discerned the essence of the *modern state*; he understood that it is based on the unhampered development of bourgeois society, on the free movement of private interest, etc. He decided to recognize and protect this basis. He was no terrorist with his head in the clouds. Yet at the same time he still regarded the *state* as

an *end in itself* and civil life only as a treasurer and his *subordinate* which must have no *will of its own*. He *perfected* the *Terror* by *substituting permanent war* for *permanent revolution*. He fed the egoism of the French nation to complete satiety but demanded also the sacrifice of bourgeois business, enjoyments, wealth, etc., whenever this was required by the political aim of conquest.[30]

The emphasis here is on how Napoleon turned the energies of the French Revolution, which had been so internally disruptive of the emergent bourgeois order, outwards. Whatever his own imperial delusions, he was unencumbered by the particular self-deceptions necessary for the Jacobin leadership to break the power of the absolutist state. The consolidation of French power in Europe required the imposition of bourgeois order in the countries subjected to French rule, if only in order to ensure French security. In *The Eighteenth Brumaire of Louis Bonaparte* Marx extended this assessment of Napoleon's role from Europe back to France itself:

> The first revolutionaries smashed the feudal basis to pieces and struck off the feudal heads that had grown on it. Then came Napoleon. Within France he created the conditions which first made possible the development of free competition, the exploitation of the land by small peasant property, and the application of the unleashed productive power of the nation's industries. Beyond the borders of France he swept away feudal institutions so far as this was necessary for the provision, on the European continent, of an appropriate modern environment for the bourgeois society in France.[31]

Here, it is Napoleon, a figure much further removed from the bourgeoisie than Robespierre, who actually establishes the necessary conditions for capitalist expansion within France. Yet even Napoleon was only able to act because he had inherited a state established by an earlier revolution from below.

Until the early 1850s then, the notion of "revolution from above" was still a subordinate aspect of their thinking about bourgeois revolution compared to their overwhelming stress on "revolution from below," a position that expressed the historical experience up to 1848. In so far as they did consider "revolution from above," they saw the process as largely being one conducted "from outside"—although Marx's comments on Napoleon's role within France hint at the possibility of it also being carried out, "from within." Engels was later to expand on these suggestions in response to subsequent developments summarized by Marx as: "Reaction carries out the programme of revolution." Marx wrote this in 1859, at the start of an astonishing twelve-year period that began with the first stages of Italian unification and ended with the Paris Commune, between which events state structures had been transformed across Central and Southern Europe, North America, and the Far East.[32] Looking back at this period in subsequent decades, Engels recalled: "The Revolution of 1848, not less than many of its predecessors, has had strange bedfellows and successors. The very people who put it down have become, as Karl Marx used to say, its testamentary executors. Louis Napoleon had to create an independent and united Italy, Bismarck had to revolutionize Germany and to restore Hungarian independence, and the English manufacturers had to enact the People's

Charter."[33] But as his comment suggests, in Italy and Germany at least, this involved an ironic reversal of roles: "The grave-diggers of the Revolution of 1848 had become the executors of its will."[34] The means by which this took place in Germany was considered in detail by Engels.

He argued that, in the aftermath of the revolution of 1848–49, there had been three possible ways in which Germany could have been unified and set on the path of unimpeded capitalist development, none of which involved bourgeois leadership. The first would have been the openly revolutionary road. Engels saw this as starting with an attempt by the Prussian princes to defend the territories on the left bank of the Rhine from France. Their inability to wage war to a successful conclusion would lead the people to unite in a liberation struggle that would overthrow the nobles and, since Louis Napoleon would no longer posture as the inheritor of the French Revolution in the face of such a genuinely popular insurrection, might also result in the overthrow of the French Second Empire. From the perspective of the working-class movement, this was the best possible solution, although, Engels ruefully conceded, it was never particularly likely to occur. The worst possible solution would have been if Germany had been unified under Austria, the most reactionary of all the larger states, the most classically absolutist in form and more concerned with its own imperial interests in Central and Southern Europe than with developing German capitalism. However, because of the general ineptitude of the Austrian regime, this was in some ways even more implausible than the scenario involving popular revolution. The actual solution came in a third way, under Prussian leadership, or rather, under the leadership of a fraction of the Prussian Junker class, led by Prince Otto von Bismarck, who became state chancellor in 1862.[35]

Essentially, the revolution took the form of a series of successful territorial wars against Denmark (1864), Austria (1866), and France (1870–1) leading to the expulsion of Austria from the Reich in 1871 and the proclamation of the king of Prussia as the German emperor. "Prussia fomented civil war and, with it, revolution. After its victory, it overthrew *three thrones 'by the grace of God'* and annexed their territories, together with the once free city of Frankfurt. If that was not revolutionary, then I don't know what the word means. Not content with that, it confiscated the private property of the princes it had driven out." As Engels points out, this was "not legal" and "hence revolutionary."[36] What led Bismarck and his supporters to undertake this brilliant series of military-diplomatic maneuvers? The Iron Chancellor stated his own motivation with admirable brevity in 1866: "If revolution there is to be, let us rather undertake it than undergo it."[37] Engels's own analysis is of fundamental importance to our understanding of bourgeois revolution after 1848:

> A person in Bismarck's position and with Bismarck's past, having an understanding of the state of affairs, could not but realize that the Junkers, such as they were, were not a viable class, and that of all the propertied classes only the bourgeoisie could lay claim to a future, and that therefore . . . his new empire promised to be all the stabler, the more he succeeded in laying the groundwork for its gradual transition to a modern

bourgeois state. . . . By leaving the larger part of the Junkers, who were beyond salvation anyway, to their inevitable doom, it still seemed possible to forge what remained of them with new elements into a class of independent big landowners, which would become only the ornamental elite of the bourgeoisie; a class to which the bourgeoisie, even at the height of its power, would have to grant state representation and with it the most lucrative positions and enormous influence. By granting the bourgeoisie political concessions, which anyway could not be withheld for any length of time (such at least should have been the argument from the standpoint of the propertied classes), by granting it in these concessions gradually, and even in small and rare doses, the new empire would at least be steered onto a course which would enable it to catch up with the other, politically far more advanced West-European states, to shake off the last remnants of feudalism and philistine traditions which still held a firm grip on the bureaucracy, and, above all, to stand on its own feet by the time its by no means youthful founders departed this life.[38]

In his analysis of German Unification Engels highlighted a characteristic of bourgeois revolutions that had not previously been present in their discussions, namely that they might involve a prolonged process lasting several decades. In his writings this is presented as an aspect of Prussian exceptionalism: "It was the peculiar feat of Prussia not only to culminate, by the end of this century, her bourgeois revolution begun in 1808–13 and continued in 1848, but to culminate it in the present form of Bonapartism. If everything goes well, and the world remains nice and quiet, and we all become old enough, we can still perhaps live to see—about 1900—the government of Prussia actually relinquishing all feudal institutions, and Prussia finally reaching a point where France stood in 1792."[39] It was in fact to take until 1918 for the republic to be proclaimed even though this passage was written the year before the founding of the German Empire in 1871, Engels did not doubt, then or subsequently, that the key moments of the revolution had occurred. However, as Eric Hobsbawm notes, "in the case of Bismarck's 'historically progressive' achievement of German unity, they did not fully work out its implications": There is a danger in supporting 'historically progressive achievements' irrespective of who carries them out, except of course *ex post facto*."[40] Hobsbawm is thinking here mainly of the divergence between Marx and Engels on the one hand and socialists based in Germany on the other over the correct attitude toward Bismarck; but a far deeper problem would later emerge, above all in Russia, over the question of whether "historically progressive" measures associated with the bourgeois revolution had to be supported by socialists at the expense of the socialist revolution.

Neither Engels nor Marx attempted to generalize from the German experience. The Risorgimento in Italy had taken a similar form to German Unification, with Piedmont playing the role of Prussia and Camilo Benso, the Count of Cavour, playing the role of Bismarck, and it involved popular participation in a way that its German sequel never did. Nevertheless, Marx and Engels were skeptical about what had been achieved. Engels wrote to one of the leaders of the Italian Socialist Party in 1894:

The *bourgeoisie*, which came to power during and after the national independence movement, would not and could not complete its victory. It neither destroyed the remains of feudalism nor transformed national production according to the modern capitalist pattern. Incapable of ensuring the relative and temporary *advantages* of the capitalist system to the country, they burdened it on the other hand with all the damage and the disadvantages of the system. And as if that were not enough, they forfeited the last remnant of respect and confidence by involving themselves in the dirtiest bank scandals.[41]

With one exception, the other revolutions from above which characterized the 1860s, whether great (the Meiji Restoration) or small (Canadian Confederation), were simply ignored by Marx and Engels. The exception, discussed mainly by Marx, was however of considerable importance: the American Civil War.

Care needs to be exercised in trying to extrapolate a general view of the Civil War from the contemporary writings of Marx and Engels. They expressed their views on the subject in three places: personal correspondence between the two men (much of which is taken up with analysis of the military conduct of the war, a subject over which they regularly disagreed until the very final stages); reports for the abolitionist Horace Greeley's paper the *New York Daily Tribune* and the Viennese *Die Presse*; and two public pronouncements, in the form of letters to Presidents Lincoln and Johnson, on behalf of the International Working Men's Association (IWMA).[42] Each of these presents its own difficulties. In the private letters, a number of shared assumptions were obviously taken for granted and this theoretical context has to be re-created by the reader. In the articles, certain complexities were omitted for a general newspaper audience, which tends to give an oversimplified picture of their views. In the open letters, the need to define a working-class position in relation to the conflict inevitably took precedence over the requirements of theory. In addition, the sources on which Marx and Engels based their analysis were limited to often inaccurate newspaper reports and a handful of books on the subject of the South, the two most important of which, by John Elliot Cairns and Frederick Law Olmstead, appeared only during the first year of the war. Their correspondence suggests that they also received updates from German émigrés in the North like August Willich, who fought for the Union.

The resulting inconsistencies and flaws in their writings have led to accusations of, among other things, their being oversympathetic to Lincoln, of neglecting the imperial dimension of Northern war aims on the one hand and the popular character of Southern smallholder resistance to them on the other; of exaggerating working-class opposition to slavery in the North and in Britain, and of succumbing to economic reductionism, and so on.[43] Much of this criticism commits precisely the error that I earlier noted in relation to their writings between 1847 and 1852, namely of treating their every statement as if it were a carefully prepared academic paper, rather than, as they were in this case, personal correspondence in which certain basic positions could be assumed, newspaper reports for the *New York Tribune* and *Die*

Presse in which certain complexities had to be omitted, or public pronouncements on behalf of the IWMA, which were intended for programmatic or propagandist purposes rather than presenting a fully rounded analysis. More sympathetic writers, above all in the Marxist humanist tradition associated with Raya Dunayevskaya, have tended to emphasize not so much the accuracy or otherwise of Marx and Engels's analysis of the war, but its impact on their political theoretical positions, claiming that the Civil War influenced the structure of *Capital*, volume 1, by providing the impetus for chapter 10, "The Working Day." These claims seem to me to be unproven at least and reliant on coincidence rather any demonstrable causal connection; the struggle for the eight-hour day, which erupted in the aftermath of the war, is more relevant here. Nevertheless, these writers are certainly correct to point to the way in which the Civil War made Marx and Engels reconsider the relationship between race and class, and the impetus it gave for the formation of the IWMA on a basis of working-class abolitionism and the labor movement to support the North—the issues to which Marx himself draws attention in *Capital*.[44] Three points are worth emphasizing in relation to their writing on this subject.

The first is that although Marx did not use the term *bourgeois revolution* in relation to the conflict, he did situate it within his conception of a struggle between two different societies, which he first raised in the *Economic and Philosophical Manuscripts* and made concrete in "The Bourgeoisie and the Counter-revolution." The society based on chattel slavery in the South was clearly not classically feudal in the way that Marx identified contemporary Japan as being.[45] But nor did it simply involve a variant of capitalism. In discussing the implications of a Confederate victory, Marx wrote:

> What would in fact take place would be not a dissolution of the Union, but a *reorganization* of it, a *reorganization on the basis of slavery*, under the recognized control of the slaveholding oligarchy. . . . The slave system would infect the whole Union. In the Northern states, where Negro slavery is in practice unworkable, the white working class would gradually be forced down to the level of helotry. This would fully accord with the loudly proclaimed principle that only certain races are capable of freedom, and as the actual labour is the lot of the Negro in the South, so in the North it is the lot of the German and the Irishman, or their direct descendants. The present struggle between the South and North is, therefore, nothing but a struggle between two social systems, the system of slavery and the system of free labour. The struggle has broken out because the two systems can no longer live peacefully side by side on the North American continent. It can only be ended by the victory of one system or the other.[46]

The second aspect is the attitude of the working class. Marx and Engels are here continuing their attitude developed during the German Revolution of 1848–49, in which the working-class movement, while retaining its independence , should support the bourgeoisie insofar as it was acting in a revolutionary way, and push for their own interests. "The working men feel sure that, as the War of Independence initiated a new era of ascendancy for the middle class, so the American Anti-Slavery War will do for working classes."[47] Here Lincoln is described as a "single-minded son of the working-class," a statement in which both attitude and origin are falsely ascribed.

The third is that for much of the war, the halfhearted conduct of the Northern bourgeoisie, their politicians, and their military commanders seemed to confirm all the suspicions that Marx and Engels had about the incapacity of that class to fight on their own behalf. The Northern bourgeoisie, to an even greater extent than the German bourgeoisie in 1848, were faced by a factory proletariat that had already demonstrated its militancy, a circumstance that Marx and Engels believed had rendered the latter incapable of fighting on its own behalf. In 1862 Engels wrote to Marx complaining about the "indolence" and "indifference" displayed in the North: "Where, amongst the people, is there any sign of revolutionary vigour?" So bad was the situation that Engels adds this, the most insulting comparison of which he was capable: "I've never encountered the like of it before, not even in Germany at the worst of times."[48] Marx believed that they would have to be rescued, not in this case by the proletariat but "a slave revolution."[49] In the end, some elements of this did occur in the formation and intervention of the black regiments, which involved two hundred and fifty thousand former slaves and signaled the long-delayed adoption of decisive revolutionary tactics by Lincoln. Indeed, one of the reasons for the somewhat exaggerated praise with which Marx and Engels regularly lauded Lincoln after the Emancipation Declaration may have simply been their relief at this development.[50]

In fact, Marx was in some respects too critical of the Northern bourgeoisie. The "social" nature of the impending conflict was well understood on both sides of the Mason-Dixon Line long before the Confederate attack on Fort Sumter. Southern ideologists were quite aware of the threatening historical precedents. One author, William Drayton, compared abolitionists to English puritans during the days of the Commonwealth: "Their columns are almost nasal with cant; and it might be supposed, from the aspect of their publications, that the days of Cromwell were revived, and that his fanatical followers, heated into tenfold fury, were abroad in the land." He argued that if abolitionists succeeded in freeing the slave population it would lead to a repetition of the Haitian Revolution: "Have they studied the history of St. Domingo; and are they prepared to let loose upon the refined and innocent ladies of the South, the savage Negro, incapable of restraint, and wild with ungovernable passions?" Finally, Drayton saw parallels with the French Revolution, claiming that once the opponents of slavery had established equality for blacks, the next stage in their madness would be to establish it for women! Naturally, a quotation from Burke fell to hand to support his case:

> The French revolutionists, from whom the fanatics derive their notions of abolition, directly undertook to assert the rights of women. The French legislature took up this subject in 1789. 'Succeeding Assemblies'; says Burke in his *Regicide Peace*, 'went the full length of the principle, and gave a license to divorce at the mere pleasure of either party, and at one months notice.' The reason alleged was 'that women had been too

long under the tyranny of parents and husbands.' To such lengths will these abstractionists carry their insane zeal. [51]

Interestingly, Georgian secessionists actually described the establishment of the Confederacy as a "political revolution," which had been made necessary to forestall the social revolution that the abolitionists would otherwise unleash upon them.[52] The more radical elements in the North were clear that a social revolution was exactly what they were planning, although they tended to hold the South responsible for forcing such a course of this action upon them. In the debates on confiscation of slaveholder property from the second session of the Thirty-Seventh Congress in 1862, for example, Senator Morrill of Maine offered a robustly materialist explanation for the conflict: "Sir, what we are witnessing and encountering is the old struggle of a class for power and privilege which has so often convulsed the world repeating itself in our history. A class identified with a local and exceptional institution, grown powerful through political representation, demands to govern."[53] The Northern military commander and twentieth president of the United States, James Garfield, referred to the revolutionary experience as an epochal process: "It will not do to speak of the gigantic revolution through which we have lately passed as a thing to be adjusted and settled by a change in administration. It was cyclical, epochal, century-wide, and to be studied in its broad and grand perspective, a revolution of even wider scope, so far as time is concerned, than the Revolution of 1776."[54] Garfield elsewhere drew an analogy between the events described in Thiers's *History of the French Revolution* and the Civil War and he was not alone among participants in treating the latter as a social revolution, as James McPherson recounts:

> The abolitionist Wendell Phillips was the most articulate spokesman for a revolutionary policy. He insisted that the Civil War "is primarily a social revolution. . . . The war can only be ended by annihilating that Oligarchy which formed and rules the South and makes the war—by annihilating a state of society. . . . The whole social system of the Gulf States must be taken to pieces." The congressional leader of the radical Republicans, Thaddeus Stevens, was equally outspoken. We must "treat this war as a radical revolution," he said. Reconstruction must "revolutionize Southern institutions, habits, and manners. . . . The foundations of their institutions . . . must be broken up and relaid, or all our blood and treasure have been spent in vain." The colonel of a Massachusetts regiment stationed in the occupied portion of South Carolina during 1862 said that the war could be won and peace made permanent only by "changing, revolutionizing absorbing the institutions, life, and manners of the conquered people."[55]

The role of the industrial bourgeoisie went beyond mere rhetoric. "Unpalatable as it is to many," writes Andrew Dawson of this class in Pennsylvania, "manufacturers constituted the revolutionary class and not their workforce":

> Industrialists threw themselves wholeheartedly into preserving the Union. They reserved jobs for volunteers, supported widows and orphans, sponsored the Great Sanitary Fair, and organized factory militias in case of invasion. Their finest political achievement, though, came in 1862 with the foundation of the Union League. The

League represented the demise of the merchant class and the ascent of manufacturing. Tirelessly publicizing the northern cause, the League raised regiments of soldiers, calling for the end of slavery and supported black civil rights in Pennsylvania.[56]

Outside of America, it was only among the dwindling band of bourgeois thinkers that still adhered to the principles of classical political economy that interpretations of the Civil War similar to Marx's own were to be found. The key figure here was one of Marx and Engels's authorities on the Confederacy, the Irish writer Cairnes, one of the last followers of Ricardo and a Liberal who regarded socialism as based on a mistake and consequently impossible to realize.[57] Nevertheless, Cairnes believed that "the course of history is largely determined by economic causes" and this formed the basis of his analysis of the American Civil War: "To causes of this description, it seemed to me, the futures of slavery in North America—its establishment in one half of the Union and its disappearance from the other—were directly to be ascribed; while to that institution, in turn, the leading differences in the character of the Northern and Southern people, as well as the antagonism of interests between the two sections which has issued in a series of political conflicts of interest over half a century, were no less traceable."[58] From these general principles, Cairnes was clear as to the reason for the war: "Whatever we may think of the tendencies of democratic institutions, or of the influence of territorial magnitude on the American Character, no theory framed upon these or any other brackets of the contesting poles, however ingeniously constructed, will suffice to conceal the fact, that it is slavery which is at the bottom of the quarrel, and that on this determination it depends whether the Power which derives its strength from slavery shall be set up with enlarged resources and increased prestige, or be now once for all effectively broken."[59]

Marx was therefore in the unusual situation, for once, of being in broad agreement with at least some of his bourgeois contemporaries in his interpretation of events.[60] In the case of Cairnes, who accepted "the influence of material interests on the destinies of mankind," it was because of a residual affiliation to the core beliefs of the Enlightenment and a political economy that had influenced Marx's thought in the first place; in the case of the Northern politicians it was because they were faced with a contest in which victory required an assessment of the situation based on materialist analysis. The peculiarities of American development meant that it was here, rather than Germany in 1848, that the bourgeoisie made its last stand as a revolutionary class. The self-understanding of its revolutionary role displayed by the US bourgeoisie was nevertheless exceptional by this period. How was it possible? The working class in the North was divided between those who supported the war on abolitionist grounds, those who supported it on anti-secessionist grounds (which could be quite compatible with racism toward the slaves), those who opposed it on grounds of opposition to the draft or the economic hardships it caused ("a poor man's fight") and those who opposed it on straightforwardly racist grounds. What the bourgeoisie did not face was a revolutionary working class attempting to drive the revolution forward *in the North* in a more radical direction, in the manner of the "permanent revolution" envisaged by Marx in 1850. Indeed, the biggest upheavals were directed against the war and the free black population in the shape of the New York antidraft riots of 1863. It is in this context that the territorial dimension assumes great importance. The fact that revolutionary violence could be directed outward to a now effectively external enemy, through the mechanism of disciplined state power, meant that a far greater degree of radicalism could be attempted than if the struggle had been a purely internal one conducted, as it were, by civilians. In other words, the Northern bourgeoisie were ultimately prepared to embrace the logic of total war rather than face defeat, even if this meant the emancipation of the slaves and deploying the freedmen against their former masters as part of the Union's military apparatus.

But these enabling conditions for the overthrow of the Confederacy also indicate reasons for the retreat from radicalism once the war was won. "Nothing renders society more restless than a social revolution but half accomplished," wrote Carl Schurz, veteran of the German Revolution of 1848, Northern commander and politician, at the end of the war. He continued: "The South will have to suffer the evil of anarchical disorder until means are found to effect a final settlement of the labour question in accordance with the logic of the great revolution."[61] Yet, once the Confederacy had been defeated, once the coherence of the South as a society had been shattered and its potential to dominate the United States ended, once actual slavery had been dismantled and the threat of subjugation to the former British colonial power removed, the majority of the Northern ruling class—many of whom were themselves racists—had no particular interest in ensuring equal rights and democratic participation for the black population. In the end, the "anarchy" invoked by Schurz—or the process of black liberation as we would see it—could not be endured when it was no longer absolutely necessary for the security of US capitalism, particularly if the possibility existed of black radicalism in the former South coinciding, or even overlapping with renewed worker militancy in the North. The necessary importance subsequently given by socialists to the question of racism in the United States has perhaps obscured the way in which this outcome was absolutely typical of the bourgeois revolutions from above to which the American Revolution in most respects belongs: the members of the Scottish Highland clans, supposedly liberated from their chiefs and feudal lords after 1746, were then subjected to the Clearances by a new capitalism that did not require their presence; the fate of the rural masses in the Italian Mezzogiorno remained unchanged after the Risorgimento, as they continued to labor on the same latifunda for the same landowners. Racism added another deeper level of oppression against the black population of the South, but their abandonment by a triumphant bourgeoisie, now safely in command of state power, was entirely typical: however distant sharecropping may have been from free labor as conceived in the ideology of the prewar Republican Party, it was not incompatible with capitalism.

Insofar as there is a problem with these analyses of German Unification and the American Civil War, it does not lie with the more expansive notion of bourgeois revolution implicit within them but rather in the fact that it was never integrated or consolidated into a general theory. The most substantial account of historical materialism as a whole attempted by either man, Engels's *Anti-Dühring*, does discuss bourgeois revolution, but mainly in relation to the period up to and including the French Revolution, excluding all subsequent events from discussion under this heading.[62] Engels retained this chronological delimitation until the end of his life, writing in 1892: "The long fight of the bourgeoisie against feudalism culminated in three great, decisive battles." He then specifically refers to the Reformation, the English Civil War, and the French Revolution, although he does not describe these as bourgeois revolutions.[63] In a letter of 1889 Engels makes the now conventional point about the bourgeoisie in the French Revolution as being "too cowardly in this case as always to uphold its own interests; that starting with the Bastille events the plebs had to do all the work for it; that without the intervention of the plebs on July 14, October 5–6, August 10, September 2, etc., the bourgeoisie would have succumbed to the *ancien régime* each time."[64] It is possible that in the former quote Engels was thinking less about revolutions as such and more about the advances in bourgeois self-confidence and influence that these moments represented: the Reformation was not, after all, an individual revolution and Engels identifies its importance as extending far beyond the German lands where it began, pointing instead to the establishment of a specific bourgeois ideology that informs the formation of parties in England and Scotland, and one postrevolutionary state in the United Provinces. Nevertheless, there is an ambiguity, or at least an unresolved tension running through these final formulations that was to contribute to many of the theoretical confusions that arose in the socialist movement after both Marx and Engels were dead.

Nonhistoricity and the Contradictions of Progress

To summarize the argument thus far: Marx and Engels retained and clarified the concepts of the forces and relations of production and of the superstructure, which they developed between 1847 and 1852, but modified their views on agency and outcome in the bourgeois revolutions that they had expressed during the same period. A third aspect of their thought, however, one which they had held for longer and carried intact into the revolutionary years, was completely abandoned by them from the mid-1850s: their belief in the existence of "non-historic" nations, and inability of certain peoples to achieve indigenous capitalist development more generally. This shift is disputed. Ephraim Nimni, for example, alleges that, for Marx and Engels, "historic nations" "are national communities capable of being agents of historical transformation, that will further the formation of a strong capitalist economy." Consequently: "The theory of "non-historic nations" is not a curiosity, a slip of the tongue, an ad hoc argument, or a regrettable mishap. It is rather the result of the rigid and dogmatic universal laws of social evolution that define the precise historical location of the 'modern nation' and by default render obsolete national communities that cannot fulfill this rigid Eurocentric political criterion."[65] In fact, opposition to the political aspirations of "non-historic nations" and qualified support for capitalist progress are not necessarily linked. Furthermore, Marx and Engels not only abandoned their belief in the former but never subscribed to the latter. Two factors seem to have been involved in leading Engels in particular to abandon the notion of "nonhistoricity" toward the end of his life. One was a refinement of his concept of the nation. In an unpublished manuscript written as late as 1882 Engels still treats nations as "primordial" constructs, the German nation apparently having existed as early as the first century BCE.[66] Two years later he situates their formation at a specific historical juncture—the emergence of the absolutist states out of the feudal estates monarchies during the fifteenth century.[67] Whatever one thinks of this later assessment—and I believe that Engels still places the process far too early in the development of capitalism—it clearly constitutes a break with the racialized conceptions of the nation that underpin the notion of nonhistoricity.

The other, connected, factor was the realization that supposedly "non-historic" nations could become "historic" through the process of struggle. The particular nation to illustrate this type of transformation was one that acquired ever greater significance for both men during their exile in Britain: Ireland. Engels fails to mention Ireland in "The Magyar Struggle," yet as we have seen, both he and Marx originally regarded its native inhabitants as equally "non-historic" as the Highland Gaels. And as Roman Rosdolsky correctly points out, the native Irish played as reactionary a role in the British Revolution as the Highlanders, and one of much greater political significance. Far from remaining so until the socialist millennium, however, they had, within a century, ceased to be the main basis of support for absolutist reaction in the British Isles and moved to the forefront of revolutionary republicanism in Europe, where their role was celebrated by, among other revolutionaries . . . Karl Marx and Frederick Engels.

By 1855, Marx was already expressing a more positive view of the Irish in *The People's Paper*: "It is a . . . very remarkable phenomenon that in the same measure as Irish influence in the *political* sphere grows in England, the Celtic influence on the *social* sphere decreases in Ireland." His explanation for the latter aspect contained elements of the same belief in English civilization that had characterized Engels's first comments on the question: "Irish society is being radically transformed by an Anglo-Saxon revolution."[68] By the occasion of his visit to Ireland in 1856, Engels too was emphasizing the effects of colonial rule on shaping the Irish character, "through systematic oppression, they have come to be a completely wretched nation and now as everybody knows, they have the job of providing England, America, Australia, etc. with whores, day laborers, maquereaux [pimps], pickpockets, swindlers, beggars and other wretches."[69] By the time Engels came to prepare notes for his uncompleted *History of Ireland*, after a second visit to that country in September 1868, his attitude has undergone a further shift. Now the stress was less on the oppressions that the Irish people had endured at the hands of the British, with the consequent degeneration of their national character, and more on their resistance to that oppression. More importantly for our purposes, he also notes that although "the English have been able to reconcile people of the most diverse races to their rule," including the Scottish Highlanders, there is a difference between the latter and the Irish, who alone "have proved too much for the English to cope with."[70] Ireland in this sense had national "advantages" that the Highlands lacked and their assertion by the Fenians led Marx and Engels to reassess the source of Irish liberation and consequently to change their attitude to the Irish people. From being a consequence, almost an offshoot, of the revolutionary movement in Britain, Marx and Engels came to regard the revolution in Ireland not only as being brought about by the Irish themselves but as preceding the revolution in Britain. Contrary to what is sometimes said, however, they did not believe that the former would *cause* the latter; rather they believed that it would weaken the British ruling class by removing from its control the land that was one of its main sources of wealth ("one *prerequisite* for the proletarian revolution in England"), ending the supply of cheap immigrant labour to British industry and ("most important of all!") resolving the hostility between the working classes of both countries caused by racism on the British side.[71]

The most important thing about this shift in position is that it involves the tacit abandonment of the theory of "historic nations" as a determining factor in deciding which national movement to support—for Ireland was originally not one of these—and an assertion instead of the centrality of politics. By mid-1870 Engels could draw definite conclusions from the failure of the Lowland Scots and the English to assimilate Ireland to Britain:

> If . . . assimilation has failed after seven hundred years of struggle; if instead all the intruders who swept in over Ireland in waves, one after the other, were assimilated by *Ireland*; if, even at present, the Irish are no more English or "West Britons," as they are called, than the Poles are "West Russians" after a mere century of oppression, if the struggle is still not yet at an end and there is *no* prospect of any end at all except through the extermination of the oppressed race—if all this is so, then all the geographical excuses in the world will not suffice to prove that England's calling is to conquer Ireland.[72]

As Engels wrote to Kautsky in February 1882, "I am of the opinion that *two* nations in Europe are not only entitled but duty bound to be national before they are international—Ireland and Poland."[73] To have attained parity with Poland—one of the nations described in "The Magyar Struggle" as having "actively intervened in history" and being "still capable of independent life"—can only mean that Engels had by this point completely, if implicitly, abandoned the notion of "non-historicity."[74]

More important than the attitude of Marx and Engels to "non-historic" nations is that toward the progressive role of capitalism in relation to the precapitalist world, since "non-historicity" was in effect a specific application of an unqualified support for capitalism in relation to the national question. Did Marx and Engels later abandon their earlier endorsement of capitalist progress? Eric Hobsbawm was perhaps the first writer to make this claim: "It seems probable that Marx, who had earlier welcomed the impact of Western capitalism as an inhuman but historically progressive force on the stagnant pre-capitalist economies, found himself increasingly appalled by this inhumanity."[75] Later writers ascribed this shift as the result of a more complex set of determinations. Teodor Shanin argues that four developments of the 1860s and 1870s helped produce what he calls the thought of the "Late Marx." First, the occurrence of the Paris Commune of 1871 suggested not only the actuality of the socialist revolution but the form that it might take. Second, the increasing availability of scientific knowledge about prehistoric communities by the middle decades of the century suggested that primitive communism had held sway over human society for a much longer period than had previously been accepted: it could therefore be argued that primitive communism, rather than relatively short-lived forms of class society, was the "natural" condition of human beings. Third, the growing awareness of contemporary noncapitalist communities suggested an existing link with primitive communism. Fourth, and finally, his interest in the revolutionary potentialities of Russian society brought together all three other developments, in "the theory and practice of Russian revolutionary populism" and the "rural communes," whose existence seemed to stretch from the primitive communist past to the present-day peasant mir. Shanin particularly stresses not only the negative impact of capitalism on tribal societies, but to the positive example that these societies offered as a model for contemporary socialists. "The Iroquois 'red skin hunter' was, in some ways, more essentially human and liberated than a clerk in the City and in that sense nearer to the man of the socialist future."[76] Similar views have been expressed by Franklin Rosemont, who claims that, after reading of the Iroquois described by Lewis Morgan, Marx's "entire conception of historical development, and particularly of precapitalist societies, now gained immeasurably in strength and precision," and that this new knowledge of tribal societies "sharpened his sense of the living presence of indigenous peoples in the world, and of their possible role in future revolutions."[77]

Both claims present difficulties for those who stand in the Marxist tradition. The original position supposedly held by Marx and Engels—which might be termed the "onward march of the productive forces"—undermines the moral authority of Marxism to speak on behalf of the oppressed and exploited, for it appears to imply that their needs must be sacrificed to those of capitalist development. The second—which might be called in the words of the Scottish Marxist John Maclean, "back to communism and forward to communism"—restores our image of Marx and Engels as defenders of the oppressed and exploited, but brings into question the explanatory power of Marxism to interpret human history, for it suggests that socialism is possible at any stage of development—indeed, perhaps the more backward the better, because nearer to the original state of primitive communism.[78] We are not, however, required to choose between these interpretations, which generally involve isolating individual fragments of their work and treating them as representative.

In fact, both Marx and Engels were always acutely aware of the contradictory nature of "progress" in relation to capitalism. In the work where historical materialism received its first fully scientific formulation, Marx wrote against Proudhon:

> Feudalism also had its proletariat—serfdom, which contained all the germs of the bourgeoisie. Feudal production also had two antagonistic elements which are likewise designated by the name of the *good side* and the *bad side* of feudalism, irrespective of the fact that it is always the bad side that in the end triumphs over the good side. It is the bad side that produces the movement which makes history, by providing a struggle. If, during the epoch of the domination of feudalism, the economists, enthusiastic over the knightly virtues, the beautiful harmony between rights and duties, the patriarchal life of the towns, the prosperous condition of domestic industry in the countryside, the development of industry organized into corporations, guilds and fraternities, in short, everything that constitutes the good side of feudalism, had set themselves the problem of eliminating everything that cast a shadow on the picture—serfdom, privileges, anarchy—what would have happened? All the elements which called forth the struggle would have been destroyed, and the development of the bourgeoisie nipped in the bud. One would have set oneself the absurd problem of eliminating history.[79]

If this dialectical understanding tended to be subordinated to a more one-sided celebration of capitalism, such as that enshrined in the *Manifesto of the Communist Party*, then the explanation seems to lie in the immediacy of the bourgeois revolution in Germany and the need to emphasize the necessity of the capitalist development that would follow for the prospects of socialism. In effect, this is an example of what Lenin would later call "stick-bending." Once the revolutionary period was over, however, their discussions regained their former balance. In a remarkable speech to celebrate the fourth anniversary of the Chartist periodical *The People's Paper* in 1856, Marx devoted the majority of his comments to the theme of the contradictions of progress:

> There is one great fact, characteristic of this our nineteenth century, a fact which no party dares deny. On the one hand, there have started into life industrial and scientific forces, which no epoch of former human history ever suspected. On the other hand, there exist symptoms of decay, far surpassing horrors recorded of the latter days of the Roman Empire. In our days everything seems pregnant with its contrary. Machinery, gifted with the wonderful power of shortening and fructifying human labour, we behold starving and overworking it. The new-fangled sources of wealth, by some strange weird spell, are turned into sources of want. The victories of art seem bought by the loss of character. At the same pace that mankind masters nature, man seems to be enslaved to other men or to his own infamy. Even the pure light of science seems unable to shine but on the dark background of ignorance. All our invention

and progress seem to result in endowing material forces with intellectual life, and in stultifying human life into a material force. This antagonism between modern industry and science on the one hand, modern misery and dissolution on the other; this antagonism between the productive powers and social relations of our epoch is a fact, palpable, overwhelming, and not to be controverted. Some parties may wail over it; others may wish to get rid of modern arts, in order to get rid of modern conflicts. . . . For our part, we do not mistake the shape of the shrewd spirit that continues to mark all these contradictions. We know that to work well the new-fangled forces of society, they only want to be mastered by new-fangled men—and such are the working men. They are as much the invention of modern time as machinery itself. In the signs that bewilder the middle class, the aristocracy and the poor prophets of regression, we do recognize our brave friend, Robin Goodfellow, the old mole that can work the earth so fast, that worthy pioneer—the Revolution.[80]

His understanding of how "everything seems pregnant with its contrary" was also present in his concrete analysis of particular societies. In this context, let us return to his writings on India.

As early as 1858 Marx wrote to Engels admitting that capitalism had a much longer future ahead of it than either man had thought possible in 1848, and this had obvious implications for the prospects for socialism in Europe: "Will it not necessarily be crushed in this little corner of the earth, since the movement of bourgeois society is still in the ascendant over a far greater area?"[81] What were the implications of "this little corner of the earth" bringing the rest of the world under colonial domination? Were Marx and Engels right that India, China, and the other colonial and semicolonial countries could only be dragged from their stagnation by colonial conquest? They certainly exaggerated the lack of socioeconomic development prior to colonization, particularly in relation to India. In this respect they retained the Enlightenment view of the East as immobile and subject to Asiatic despotism. It is possible that, with sufficient time and freedom from external interference, at least some of these countries might have seen the indigenous emergence of capitalism. But given the existence of the capitalist powers, and their need to secure territories for raw materials, markets, and investments, they were not to be given that time or that freedom. What might have been possible had India and the rest been situated in a dimension unreachable by the British Navy is a question for science fiction not historical materialism. Once colonization had taken place, the question was what attitude to take toward it. The assumption Marx and Engels made was that, whatever atrocities the colonial powers committed on the way, they would ultimately develop the countries over which they ruled, to the point where they would produce their own gravedigger in the same way they had in the existing capitalist countries. Neither man had any illusions in the means by which that bourgeoisie would accomplish this revolution. Nevertheless, this was their real error. The colonial powers had no intentions of hastening their own demise by developing the economies of the subject peoples, at least not in any systematic way. The implications of this for revolution in the colonial and semicolonial world only become apparent after their deaths.

As Aijaz Ahmad has written: "For buttressing the proposition that Marxism is not much more than a 'modes-of-production narrative' and that its opposition to colonialism is submerged in its positivistic 'myth of progress,' it is always very convenient to quote one or two journalistic flourishes from . . . 'The British Rule in India' and 'The Future Results of British Rule in India.'"[82] Edward Said is only one writer who availed himself of just such a convenience. Although he nowhere suggests that the first article is representative of Marx's views, his highlighting of particular passages from it implies that it can be treated as such.[83] It is not the case that the article is beyond criticism. As Callinicos notes, it suffers from at least three major defects: a teleological attitude to history implied by the notion of England acting as "an unconscious tool"; a reliance on the concept of an unchanging "Asiaticism" that—whatever its relevance for earlier periods in history—cannot be justified in relation to nineteenth-century India, and, most relevantly for this discussion, an unqualified acceptance of the progressive impact of capitalism in areas where it had not previously existed.[84] Ahmad argues, however, that these weaknesses were in part the result of shortage of accurate information on Marx's part, particularly with regard to the nature of the dominant mode of production, Marx's "sustained oppositional practice" leading his materialism "in a direction where it is impelled to assert universal laws of its own, different from those it opposes, but without sufficient evidence of its own." But this is not all that there is to the article. As Ahmad writes, the best reference point for the argument it contains is not the notion of "Orientalism," but his own writings on the development of *Western* capitalism,

> where the destruction of the European peasantry in the course of the primitive accumulation of capital is described in analogous tones, which I read as an enraged language of *tragedy*—a sense of colossal disruption and irretrievable loss, a moral dilemma wherein neither the old nor the new can be wholly affirmed, the recognition that the sufferer was at once decent and flawed, the recognition also that the history of victories and losses is really a history of material production, and the glimmer of hope, in the end, that something good might yet come out of this merciless history."[85]

This is very well said, yet it still does not come to terms with the full complexity of Marx's views; for these, we must turn to the second article to which Ahmad refers: "The Future Results of the British Rule in India."

Written on July 22, 1856, and published in the *New York Daily Tribune* on August 8, this second article clearly belongs to the same set of considerations as the first ("I propose . . . to conclude my observations about India."). That is to say, it is not a subsequent rethinking at a later date. Here the tragic dimensions of the Indian colonization are fully articulated: "All that the English bourgeoisie may be forced to do will neither emancipate nor materially mend the social condition of the mass of the people, *depending not only on the development of the productive powers, but on their appropriation by the people*." Marx holds out two possible ways by which British rule can be ended: proletarian revolution in Britain itself or a colonial rebellion by the native population in India, before ending ("I cannot part with the subject of India without some concluding remarks") with a passage that dwells on the "profound hypocrisy and inherent barbarism of bourgeois civilization" in the colonies. The best that can be said for bourgeois society is that it has "laid the material basis of a new world" in "the mutual dependency of mankind" and "the development of the productive powers of man and the transformation of material production." As a result: "When a great social revolution shall have mastered the results of the bourgeois epoch, the market of the world and the modern powers of production, and subjected them to the common control of the most advanced peoples, then only will human progress cease to resemble that hideous pagan idol, who would not drink the nectar but from the skulls of the slain."[86] Even this magnificent passage is not without its ambiguities ("domination of natural agencies," "the most advanced peoples"), but as Callinicos writes, it can scarcely be accused of evading the consequences of British rule for the Indians.[87] More positively, the concept of progress that Marx employs here is not merely the development of the productive forces as such, but insofar as this "represents an expansion of human capacities," the potential for which can only be realized by a revolution, a revolution which, it will be noted, Marx does not suggest will necessarily be achieved for the Indians from outside. In the drafts of his letter to the Russian revolutionary Vera Zasulich Marx makes his earlier change of perspective explicit: "As for the East Indies, for example, everybody except Sir Henry Maine and others of his ilk realizes that the suppression of communal landownership out there was nothing but an act of English vandalism, pushing the native peoples not forward but back."[88] It is clear from these comments that Marx not only refused to share the views of those who colonized India, but that his hostility to what they did there increased throughout his life. The final position of both Marx and Engels is perhaps best expressed by the latter in a response of 1882 to one of Karl Kautsky's endless requests for clarification:

> As I see it, the actual colonies, i.e., the countries occupied by European settlers, such as Canada, the Cape [South Africa], Australia, will all become independent; on the other hand, countries that are merely ruled and inhabited by natives, such as India, Algeria and the Dutch, Portuguese and Spanish possessions, will have to be temporarily taken over by the proletariat and guided as rapidly as possible towards independence. How this process will develop is very difficult to say. India may, indeed very probably will, start a revolution and, since the proletariat that is effecting its own emancipation cannot wage a colonial war, it would have to be given its head, which would obviously entail a great deal of destruction, but after all that is inseparable from any revolution. . . . Once Europe has reorganized, and North America, the resulting power would be so colossal and the example set will be such that the semi-civilized countries will follow suit quite of their own accord, their economic needs alone will see to that.

Engels closes his letter by stating the impossibility of saying how long it would take for the ex-colonies to reach socialism, only that it cannot be imposed upon them by a victorious proletariat in the metropolitan centers: "Only one thing is certain, namely that a victorious proletariat cannot forcibly confer any blessing whatever on another country without undermining its own activity in the process."[89]

But what of areas that were not colonies, that were among the Great Powers, while retaining precapitalist, perhaps even nonfeudal, social relations? In effect this meant Russia. In 1877 Marx wrote a letter to the Russian journal *Otechesivenniye Zapiski* criticizing the interpretation of *Capital* made in its pages by the populist N. K. Mikhailovsky. Marx makes two points in this epistle.[90] The first is that the Russian peasant commune *may* provide the launching pad for the advance to communism in Russia, but the possibility of that happening is *already* being undermined by the advance of capitalism. The second is that even if the latter development does come to fruition, it will not replicate exactly the earlier process in Western Europe, contrary to what is asserted by Mikhailovsky, who wants to turn a "historical sketch of the genesis of capitalism in Western Europe into a historic-philosophical theory of general development, imposed by fate on all peoples, whatever the historical circumstances in which they are placed, in order to eventually attain the economic formation that, with a tremendous leap of the productive forces of social labor, assures the most integral development of every individual producer." Marx was to repeat the first point in his March 8, 1881, letter to Zasulich. He affirms his conviction that "the commune is the fulcrum of social regeneration in Russia," but then adds the same rider as in his earlier critique of Mikhailovsky: "in order that it may function as such, it would first be necessary to eliminate the deleterious influences which are assailing it from all sides, and then ensure for it the normal conditions of spontaneous development."[91] Under what conditions might the peasant commune play the role that Marx has suggested for it?

These were outlined the following year in a preface, published under the names of both men, for the second Russian edition of the *Manifesto*: "The only possible answer today is this: if the Russian Revolution becomes the signal for a proletarian revolution in the West, so that the two complement each other, the present Russian common ownership of land may serve as the starting point for communist development."[92] That the victory of a revolutionary movement in the West could establish a socialist context for Russian development and thus avoid the fate of capitalism was in their view a possibility, but by no means a certainty. If this was an open question for them in relation to Russia, by January 1894 it had become clear which direction events had taken. In the afterword to "On Social Relations in Russia"—his last intervention on this subject—Engels attempts to compile a balance sheet that is clearly loaded against those who still expected the peasant commune to act as the social basis of the Russian Revolution. The Russian commune, he notes, "has already forgotten how to till its land for the common good"; its ultimate salvation must await "the industrial proletarians of the West." In response to the capitalist impositions all "lost more and more of their communistic character and dissolved into communities of mutually independent landowners." Primitive communism is incapable of producing out of itself "the future socialist society, this final and most intrinsic product of capitalism": "Any given economic formation has its own problems to solve, problems arising out of itself; to seek to solve those of another, utterly alien formation would be utterly absurd. *And this applies to the Russian commune no less than to the South Slav Zadruga, the Indian Gentile community or any other savage or barbaric form of society characterised by the common ownership of production.*" With typical generosity of spirit toward Russian revolutionaries of the time, Engels adds that "we do not blame them for regarding their Russian compatriots as the chosen people of the social revolution. But this does not mean that we need to share their illusions."[93]

What had led to the introduction of capitalist relations into Russia? Engels noted a process similar to that that had taken place in Germany occurring in Russia, although with less dramatic results. Here too war provided a major impetus to economic development: "The defeats of the Crimean war had exposed Russia's need for rapid industrial development. Above all railways were needed, and these are not possible on a broad footing without large- scale domestic industry. The precondition for this was the so-called emancipation of the serfs ... [94]

Yet it is clear what Engels is talking about here is an economic process, not a political one:

> When the old tsarist despotism continued unchanged after the defeats of the Crimean War and the suicide of Tsar Nicholas, only one road was open: the swiftest transition possible to capitalist industry. . . . Had the despotism of the tsars been replaced after the Crimean War by the direct parliamentary rule of nobles and bureaucrats, the process might have been slowed down somewhat; if the burgeoning bourgeoisie had taken the helm, it would certainly have been accelerated even more. As things were, there was no alternative.[95]

In other words, bourgeois revolution was still necessary and, unlike in Germany, it would have to be carried out from below:

> Capitalistic production works its own ruin, and you may be sure it will do so in Russia too. It may, and if it lasts long enough, it will surely produce a fundamental agrarian revolution—I mean a revolution in the condition of landed property, which will ruin both the *pomeshchik* [landlord] and the *muzhik* [peasant], and replace them by a new class of large landed proprietors drawn from the *kulaki* [kulaks] of the villages and the bourgeois speculators of the towns. At all events, I am sure the conservative people who have introduced capitalism into Russia will be one day terribly astonished at the consequences of their own doings.[96]

Marx wrote in the preface to *Capital* that "the country that is more developed industrially only shows, to the less developed, the image of its own future."[97] He was not suggesting that all countries would take the same length of time to reach the future as the original metropolitan powers, nor that arriving there would have the same implications for late developers, but neither was he suggesting that they could bypass sections of the road. As Kevin Anderson has pointed out, in the later French edition of *Capital*, volume 1, Marx replaced the phrase "to the less developed" with the words "to those that follow it on the industrial path," indicating that this was intended to apply to Europe rather than the world.[98] Yet although I share Anderson's view that Marx's "theory of social development evolved in a more multilinear direction" and that "his theory of revolution began over time to concentrate increasingly on the intersectionality of class with ethnicity, race, and nationalism," it is necessary to remember—as his final writings on Russia should force us to remember—that Marx thought multilinearity was only possible in the latter half of the nineteenth century because capitalism had been established in Western Europe over the previous three hundred and fifty years. If the framework adopted by Marx and Engels had been one that either uncritically welcomed the development of the productive forces under capitalism or unthinkingly expected socialism to circumvent capitalist development altogether through the agency of peasant communalism, it is unlikely that it would have been of much use to anyone, other than state capitalist bureaucrats on the one hand and Third World fantasists on the other; but they were involved in neither apologetics nor utopianism. They understood that the expansion of the productive forces brought about by capitalism was a necessary condition for the ultimate goal of human emancipation because without it there will be neither a working class to seize power from the capitalists nor a sufficient level of material resources with which to feed, clothe, house, or educate the world's population. It was also an insufficient condition, because unless the working class was conscious and organized it would not succeed in achieving its revolutionary potential. But the objective situation (the existence of capitalism) precedes the subjective (the conscious mobilization of the social classes that capitalism has brought into being) and the former required the bourgeois revolution.

Classical Marxism (1) 1889–1905: Bourgeois Revolution in the Social Democratic Worldview

The first incarnation of the capitalist states system emerged from the concentrated period of bourgeois revolution from above between 1859 and 1871. Within this temporarily stabilized international order the working-class movement now began to establish permanent party organizations. Accordingly, between the launch of the Portuguese Socialist Party in 1871 and the formation of the British Labour Party in 1906—essentially the period from the Paris Commune to the first Russian Revolution—virtually every country in Europe saw the emergence of what were variously called socialist, social democratic, labor, or workers' parties, internationally united through their adherence to the Second International, which was established in 1889 as the successor to the short-lived International Working Men's Association (1864–76).[1] And these parties were not confined to Europe: within the same period similar parties were also formed in Argentina, Chile, Australia, and the United States.

The extent to which the parties of the Second International were influenced by Marxism varied. Where the bourgeois revolution had still to be accomplished, or at least completed—a situation that tended to be accompanied by low levels of capitalist development and high levels of political repression—the greater the likelihood was that Marxism would dominate the local socialist movement. Consequently, the trajectory of ideological radicalism can be traced in an uneven but unmistakably ascendant line from West to East, as is suggested by a comparison of the British Labour Party with the Russian Social Democratic Labor Party.[2] The German Social Democratic Party and the smaller but structurally similar Austrian Social Democratic Party were perhaps the archetypal parties of the Second International: both had high levels of membership and electoral support, overwhelmingly drawn from the working class; both formally committed themselves to Marxism during the 1890s; both contained some of the most influential Marxist thinkers of the time; and both embodied the studied ambivalence over the question of whether revolution would be required to achieve socialism that—with antipodal exceptions like the British and Russian parties—was characteristic of the Second International as a whole.

Between the death of Marx in 1883 and that of Engels in 1895 there emerged as the intellectual counterpoint to these organizational developments what Isaac Deutscher called the "classical Marxist" tradition, "the body of thought developed by Marx, Engels, their contemporaries, and after them by Kautsky, Plekhanov, Lenin, Trotsky [and] Rosa Luxemburg." Deutscher distinguished the tradition from that of "'vulgar Marxism,' the pseudo-Marxism of the different varieties of European social-democrats, reformists, Stalinists, Krushchevites, and their like."[3] But classical Marxism cannot be contrasted with the vulgar tradition in quite such an uncomplicated manner, for, as the names listed by Deutscher indicate, the category of classical Marxism includes two different types of thinker.

These thinkers were not distinguished by their class origin. Of those who belonged to the tradition only the Scot, James Connolly, came from an unambiguously working-class background.[4] Others, such as Gramsci, certainly experienced poverty; but like Marx and Engels themselves their backgrounds tended to be solidly petit bourgeois or even bourgeois.[5] The distinction between them was not social but theoretical, based on their approach to historical materialism itself, and political, expressed in the political choices that they would ultimately make. On the one hand, the work of Kautsky and Plekhanov was characterized—to varying degrees—by a tendency toward economic determinism, in which socialism is regarded as inevitable, given a certain level of development of the productive forces; on the other, those like Connolly, Lenin, Luxemburg, and Trotsky had a more dialectical understanding of the relationship between inherited circumstances and human activity. One practical indication of the divergent approaches taken by these two groups was that while members of the former were always respected intellectuals within their respective parties, they tended not to be political leaders, while members of the latter usually performed both functions. Nevertheless, up to 1905 and in some respects beyond that date, the main protagonists all underwent a period of common development, in which they were united by shared intellectual assumptions, so that their essays in historical interpretation or discussions of contemporary strategy tended to involve differences in emphasis rather than total opposition.

The tensions within classical Marxism were partly exposed by the revolution of 1905, first in Russia itself, then increasingly in Germany, before two events finally destroyed the unity of the Second International: the First World War and the Russian Revolution of October 1917. These saw the different theoretical approaches within classical Marxism take the form of intense political differences which placed individual members of the tradition sometimes literally on opposite sides of the barricades in both imperialist and class wars. Those on the right, like Plekhanov in Russia, openly supported the imperialist states within which they were situated; those in the center, like Kautsky in Germany, refused to advocate revolutionary opposition to them; and both wings ultimately united in opposition to the Bolshevik experiment. It would however be absurd—indeed, a form of secularized Calvinism—to suggest that the political positions adopted by individuals in 1914 or 1917 were determined by their preexisting theoretical assumptions, so that if we study their pre-1914 works closely enough we will find evidence of attitudes that led to later betrayals. A figure like Franz Mehring, for example, opposed the First World War and supported the Russian Revolution, even though the methodology employed in his historical work was very similar to that of Kautsky. The combination of genetic inheritance, social environment, material interest, and personal commitment, which led individuals to choose one path rather than another, is far too complex for easy attribution of predestined membership of the revolutionary elect or the counterrevolutionary damned. What can be said, perhaps, is that a disposition to adopt certain theoretical positions is likely to indicate an affinity with particular political attitudes; but the former did not cause the latter.

The years 1914–17 are therefore a crucial turning point in the history of classical Marxism, to the extent that David Renton has even argued: "classical Marxism lasted from Karl Marx's death to the triumph of the Russian Revolution in 1917."[6] However, this periodization foreshortens the period during which it was still a living tendency within the socialist movement. It is untenable to claim that the era of classical Marxism concluded at the very moment of its greatest practical vindication, especially when this also led to an efflorescence of Marxist theory involving not only leaders of the Russian Revolution like Lenin and Trotsky but also thinkers who rallied to the banner of socialist revolution like Antonio Gramsci, Karl Korsch, Georg Lukács and, slightly later, Walter Benjamin. A far more plausible concluding date is the period around the opening of the Second World War, during which even those figures who had survived into the 1930s had their lives directly or indirectly ended by the regimes of Italian fascism, German Nazism, or Russian Stalinism.

SOCIAL DEMOCRACY
AND THE DIFFUSION OF MARXIST THEORY

The extent to which the mass of the Social Democratic rank and file workers as opposed to intellectuals were influenced by, let alone fully cognizant of, classical Marxist theory is unclear. Some historians, like Norman Stone, have drawn on analysis of the reading habits of the working-class membership to express skepticism about some of the grander claims made of the spread of a Marxist intellectual culture:

> Of books taken out of the Favoriten district headquarters of Vienna socialism, eighty-three per cent came under the heading *Belletristik*—i.e., "penny dreadfuls"—and that the pages of the heavier academic works were usually uncut after the first few, for it required real dedication for a man to get through works such as Karl Kautsky's *Peasant Question* [*sic*—Stone means *The Agrarian Question*]. Did this mean that the working classes were not as class conscious as their leaders expected them to be; or did it mean only that Kautsky was a crashing bore? Opinions divided.[7]

Yet, however off-putting Kautsky's more theoretical writings may have been to the average Berlin engineering worker, his popularizations of Marxist doctrine were printed and presumably bought in greater numbers than Marx and Engels's original works. In 1905, the Sozialdemokratische Partei Deutschlands (Social Democratic Party, SPD) published the *Manifesto of the Communist Party* in an edition of between two thousand and three thousand copies, while Kautsky's *The Social Revolution* was one of 21,500.[8] But to focus on books alone is to take too "intellectualist" or academic measure of Marxist influence. Many Marxist positions were transmitted not from books but from newspapers: "In Berlin in 1906, less than 3 per cent of the 48,352 SPD members were not reading *Vorwärts* (the daily paper) or another party paper, and elsewhere subscribers often outnumbered members." These views were also conveyed and reinforced through the institutions of the parties and the labor movement more generally. As Geoff Eley points out, the main parties of the Second International "broadly accepted the politics Marx pioneered so consistently in his final two decades": "If Marxism is defined like this rather than by detailed knowledge of *Capital*, popular socialist consciousness appears in a far more Marxist light."[9] What theoretical propositions informed this consciousness? Donald Sassoon claims that these could be condensed into three: first, "the present capitalist system is unfair"; second, "history proceeds through stages"; and third, "workers are a fundamentally homogeneous class, regardless of differences which might exist between them": "The first proposition embraces the Marxist theory of exploitation; the second is the so-called materialist conception of history; while the third, not really elaborated by Marx, was the product of the ideas and political practice of the leaders of European socialism (especially in Germany) after Marx's death."[10]

What were the implications of these developments—the creation of mass working-class parties, the codification of an orthodox interpretation of historical materialism (albeit one that concealed important theoretical differences), and the dissemination of the orthodoxy to party members in simplified form—for the concept of bourgeois revolution? The thinkers of the Second International who wrote most on the subject before 1905 were Kautsky and Plekhanov. As I have suggested above, the later renegacy of these figures does not invalidate their earlier insights, but in the case of bourgeois revolution their tendency toward mechanical materialism produced a version of the concept that was markedly more inflexible than had been the case in the writings of Marx and Engels. Nor was this the only problem. As we saw in the previous three chapters, Marx and Engels left only a series of fragmentary writings on the bourgeois revolutions. Compounding the resulting difficulties, and a specific example of a general limitation on a full understanding of Marxist theory at the time, was the limited availability of both the early texts in which they worked through their initial version of the concept and the later writings in which they implicitly modified it. In an autobiography written during the Second World War, the British Communist T. A. Jackson described his discovery of the *Manifesto of the Communist Party* in the early 1900s and the "blazing revelation" that it inspired, leading him "hot-foot in search of every line of Marx and Engels I could discover," only to find "there was surprisingly little." This seems to have been a common experience,

and not only in Britain where Marxism was relatively weak.[11] Until the third and
fourth decades of the twentieth century virtually nothing by Marx and Engels pertaining to the subject of bourgeois revolution and written before *The Poverty of Philosophy* (1847) or after *The Eighteenth Brumaire of Louis Bonaparte* (1852) was in print
in any language.[12] Consequently, the works that were most widely read tended to be
precisely those in which they used the French Revolution and—to a lesser extent—
its predecessors as models of bourgeois revolution, especially their polemics over the
situation in Germany. Insofar as Engels tried to systematically deal with the subject
of bourgeois revolution after Marx's death, his late and extremely authoritative cod-
ifications of historical materialism also focused very much on the earliest, most dramatic, but least typical examples, in England and France. Here, for example, is a
description of the process of bourgeois revolution, from one of the most sophisticated
works of Marxist theory produced before the First World War, the Austrian Social
Democrat Otto Bauer's *The Question of Nationalities and Social Democracy* (1907):

> During the revolutionary epoch, the bourgeoisie was locked in a struggle with the
> state, with the whole traditional legal system. The absolutist state had either preserved
> the feudal and guild legal forms or had not fully eliminated them, and was thereby
> impeding the development of capitalism; the small size of the economic regions had
> become an impediment to the development of the forces of production; the economic
> and political authority of the absolutist state had become insupportable for the now
> mature bourgeoisie, which wanted to govern itself; the traditional small state could
> not be protected from foreign domination. As a consequence, the bourgeoisie aimed
> everywhere to overthrow the prevailing legal order, to destroy the existing state. How-
> ever it did not want to destroy the state as such, but to replace it with another, one
> that met its requirements for the safeguarding of private property: from the bourgeois
> point of view, the state had dominated it long enough and should now become the
> instrument of bourgeois domination.[13]

Here the mixed nature of the inheritance is clearly visible. On the one hand,
Bauer rightly emphasizes the seizure and transformation of the state as the central
object of any revolutionary movement to break constraints on capitalist development. On the other, he wrongly assumes that the bourgeoisie is necessarily the conscious agency responsible for such a movement.

By the time Engels died in 1895 the concept of bourgeois revolution had become part of the general theoretical repertoire of both the socialist left and the
broader labor movement, extending far beyond those individuals and organizations
claiming adherence to Marxism of any sort. It was not the only concept to experience this fate. As Stuart MacIntyre writes of the reception of historical materialism
in Britain: "Labour Socialism and Marxism were drawing on a common set of
ideas; the former diffusing them into a loose synthesis, the latter preserving them
in a fundamentalist code."[14] In the particular case of bourgeois revolution, however,
it also underwent a gradual process of transformation, in which it retained some
of the original characteristics that it originally held for Marx and Engels while
adding others that they had never considered in this context. What were these?

RADICAL TRADITIONS, DEMOCRACY, AND "THE PEOPLE"

Each country possessed preexisting radical traditions that predated not only the widespread adoption of Marxism by the socialist movement but in many respects the existence of the socialist movement itself. These focused on the nation as the historical arena of struggle and, as a corollary, dissolved the changing nature of the class forces involved into binary oppositions between those for or against freedom. Instead of the successive struggles of slaves, peasants, artisans, and workers against their respective ruling classes, the historical periodizations, and the different class configurations present in each were suppressed in favor of an amorphous populism. Where Marxism distinguished between historical classes on the basis of different positions within the relations of production and consequently the different capacities that each possessed, this earlier tradition made "the people" the central category and "democracy" the unifying theme. It became important for activists to legitimate their goals by identifying past struggles that could be retrospectively endorsed and assimilated into a local narrative of democratic advance, which would only be completed with the achievement of socialism. One consequence of this was the search for predecessors from which to construct a native radical tradition stretching back through national history—a populist narrative alternative to what one early radical historian, John Richard Green, called "drum and trumpet" history.[15] Indeed, these traditions were often simply taken over wholesale from left liberalism, particularly in those countries such as Britain and, to a lesser extent, France, where Marxism was initially weak, hence the respective influence of the Whig interpretation of the English Civil War and the Jacobin interpretation of the French Revolution. In Britain, for example, the official ruling-class conception of "Our Island Story" highlighted the Magna Charta and the Bill of Rights as the foundations of English liberty; but in "the People's Story" it was the Peasant's Revolt and the Cromwellian commonwealth that feature as the crucial episodes.

Scotland can serve as an example of how certain types of historical moment came to become part of a useable past for the emergent radical movement, not least because it has so few of them. The fledgling working-class movement largely adopted aspects of the English radical tradition, but there were two local episodes of heroic struggle that recur in Scottish iconography from the 1790s on. One, from the late thirteenth and early fourteenth centuries, was the "Wars of Independence," a Scottish victory that ended serious English attempts at conquest for another two hundred years and ensured the survival of a separate feudal kingdom north of the border. The other, between the Restoration of 1660 and the Glorious Revolution of 1688, was the resistance by the extreme Presbyterians ("the Covenanters") to the ambitions of Charles II and James II and VII, at least in relation to religious issues. For the purposes of establishing a tradition it mattered not that neither episode was remotely concerned with "democracy" as it was understood in the era of the French Revolution: the Scottish lords celebrated their victory over Edward

TT by imposing even greater seignorial exactions on the peasantry than had their former English overlords; the Covenanters, heroic in the struggle against absolutism—a struggle that can be seen as a failed attempt at bourgeois revolution from below—nevertheless envisaged a sectarian theocracy in which there was no place for Catholics, Episcopalians, or even fellow Protestants "outside the Covenant."

Robert Burns, a complex figure whose own life ended as the age of the industrial working class was beginning, dealt with both of these subjects in his poetry.[16] In one poem, published anonymously in 1793, Burns's ostensible subject is a speech given by King Robert the Bruce prior to the decisive Scottish victory at Bannockburn in 1314, in which he invokes the memory of martyred patriot, Sir William Wallace:

> *Scots, wha hae wi' WALLACE bled,*
> *Scots, wham BRUCE has often led,*
> *Welcome to your gory bed,—*
> *Or to victory.—*[17]

The melody of this song is based on "Hey Tuttie Tattie," the march Burns believed Bruce had ordered to be played at Bannockburn. Burns himself described the composition of this song in a letter, saying that "I had no idea of giving myself any trouble on the subject, till the accidental recollection of that glorious struggle for Freedom, associated with the glowing ideas of the same nature, *not quite so ancient*, aroused my rhyming mania."[18] What were these more modern ideas to which Burns refers? The poem famously concludes with a line that is usually seen as paraphrasing the Tennis Court Oath sworn by members of the French National Assembly on June 20, 1789: "Let US DO—or DIE!!!" Read in this way Burns can be seen as linking two separate events to the Scottish political scene: the historical struggle for feudal state formation and the contemporary struggle to defend the French bourgeois republic. Despite his ambivalence toward the Calvinist tradition in Scotland, expressed in satires like "Holy Willie's Prayer," Burns was also prepared to honor the heroism of the Covenanters, writing on his copy of Sir John Sinclair's *The Statistical Account of Scotland*:

> *The Solemn League and Covenant*
> *Now brings a smile, now brings a tear.*
> *But sacred Freedom, too, was theirs:*
> *If thou'rt a slave, indulge thy sneer.*[19]

Thereafter, these two historical moments were often linked together, with the latter taking precedence. John Duncan, a weaver from Stonehaven and later self-educated botanist, told his biographer how, as a child in the first decade of the nineteenth century, he had explored the environs of Dunnottar Castle:

> But in all their long, changeful and fascinating story, what charmed his young imagination most was, not the halls where royalty had rested; not the place where the Scottish Crown, sword and scepter had lain and whence they had been cleverly borne to the neighboring church of Kineff; not even the stirring story of Wallace and his

gallant capture of the castle when he shook so grandly for Scottish Independence ... it was the "Whig's Vault," on the edge of the cliff, where the Covenanters were immured.... Nothing colored his whole existence more than the inspiring story of the struggle for Scottish religious freedom, which entered deep into his inner heart in after life, and infused his piety with the uncompromising fire of the old Covenanters.[20]

A decade later still, William Aiton, the Sheriff-Substitute at Hamilton, described how a crowd of perhaps ten thousand workers and their families marched from Strathaven to Drumclog on June 13, 1815: "They went first to the place where the Covenanters defeated Claverhouse, and from thence to a cairn of stones or tumulus, on the farm of Allanton, Ayrshire, about two miles from the field of Drumclog, where they imagined Sir William Wallace had fought his first battle with the English." Yet, despite his disapproval, the Sheriff plainly saw that the search for revolutionary ancestors was not primarily inspired by nationalist motives:

> Ever since the lower orders in Scotland gave up the study of religious opinion, and wrangling about abstruse points in divinity, and the purity of religious sects, and began to study politics, *too many of them have shown an inclination to notice and bring to view every occurrence, whether recent or ancient, wherein successive resistance has been opposed to any regular and established authority.* It can only be from such motives that the skirmish at Drumclog was pompously celebrated on the 13th June, 1815, by an assemblage of people, who marched to the field of action with military ensigns and music, for the purpose, as they said, of "Commemorating the Victory obtained by their ancestors, the Covenanters, over the Kings Troops, commanded by Captain Graham."[21]

The view of history as the unfolding of representative democracy on a national basis through a series of historical milestones was deeply influential within the emerging workers' movements over the second half of the nineteenth century—understandably, since gaining the male franchise was one of its main objectives. "Between the 1860s and the First World War," writes Geoff Eley, "socialist parties became the torchbearers of democracy in Europe."[22] And, of course, there was a Marxist justification for this emphasis since the *Manifesto* had argued that winning the "battle for democracy" was the means by which to achieve working-class power.[23] For this reason Marxist accounts of the bourgeois revolution tended to be interested in those aspects that could be interpreted as heralding the emergence or extension of parliamentary representation. Although the history of bourgeois revolution from below since 1830 was mainly one of heroic failure, it still formed a tradition to which the modern labor movement could relate. As Eric Hobsbawm reports: "The labor and socialist movement saw itself as the lineal continuation of this tradition. The Austrian Social Democrats celebrated March Day (anniversary of the victims of Vienna Revolution of 1848) before they celebrated the new May Day."[24]

The recollections of Social Democrats who later became Communists bear personal witness to the strength of these perceived lineages, as in these two examples relating to the years from immediately prior to the First World War. Joseph Freeman recalled his attitude to history as a young Socialist entering high school in

New York: "When I read about the Civil War, I was indignant with the slave-holding South and adored Lincoln; in the Revolutionary War I was on the side of Washington." Making these identifications with the heroes of local revolutionary history did not of course preclude doing so with those of other countries, even at this date. Freeman recalls: "But greater than all these was the brightest star of the French Revolution, the slayer of the *ancien régime* . . . Napoleon."[25] T. A. Jackson wrote of a similar attitude to the past that he formed in London while a member of the British Social Democratic Federation (SDF), although these relate to the left in the English Revolution, rather than the mainstream figures mentioned by Freeman: "I cannot shake off the conviction that an actual father-to-son organizational descent might be traced from SDF and ILP [Independent Labour Party] branches through the Chartists and the English Jacobins, to the Fifth-Monarchy Men, and the Leveller agitators of the New Model Army."[26]

Establishing these linkages did not in itself necessarily lead to theoretical difficulties as long as comparisons between different periods remained at the level of inspirational rhetoric. There were occasions, however, in which they collapsed into anachronism, which tended to take one of two forms. One was where actors in an earlier period were simply assimilated to those in the present day. Thus, the leading right-wing SPD intellectual Eduard Bernstein could conclude his account of socialist and democratic tendencies within the English Revolution from the 1890s with this back-projection from his own time: "We have seen how the struggle between two sections of the ruling classes for political dominion, in its sequel, brought upon the political stage the most advanced sections of the working classes of the period, and thus led to the formulation of demands which anticipate the programme of modern political democracy."[27] The other form of anachronism, while rejecting claims of class identity across the centuries, nevertheless found similarities in behavior of groups at even greater distances in time from one another. These groups were not necessarily part of any radical tradition but could often be obstacles to the achievement of democratic goals, as can be seen from the work of a figure from the same generation as Bernstein, the US socialist leader Daniel De Leon.

In his widely read brochure *Two Pages from Roman History* (1903), De Leon compares his own method to that which was supposedly commended by Marx in *The Eighteenth Brumaire of Louis Bonaparte*, namely "when man wants to interpret what is going on in his own day, he tries to find a parallel in the past." De Leon compares the process to that of translation: "In order to interpret the new language that is being spoken by modern events, let us translate it back into the well-known language of now well understood past events. We shall understand the new term "labor leader" when we recall the career of the old term "plebs leader" in Roman history."[28] There then follows an extraordinary comparison between, on the one hand, the plebeian representatives in the Roman Senate during the fifth century and the Gracchi brothers of the first century BCE, and, on the other, the US trade union bureaucracy of De Leon's own time. In 1908 a still-revolutionary Kautsky himself warned against these tendencies, sensibly urging caution against "two dangers" that faced historical investigators who were also engaged in contemporary politics: "In the first place, they may attempt to mould the past entirely after the image of the present, and, in the second place, they may seek to behold the past in the light of the needs of present-day policy."[29] Unfortunately his advice was not always heeded, and he eventually ignored it himself.

CAPITALISM AS A UNIVERSAL STAGE IN SOCIAL DEVELOPMENT

The radical tradition was important because of the way in which it informed the second of the core Marxist "propositions" identified by Sassoon, namely that "history proceeds through stages." The most important text in this respect was the 1859 preface to *A Contribution to the Critique of Political Economy* in which Marx wrote that "the Asiatic, ancient, feudal and modern bourgeois modes of production may be designated as epochs marking progress in the economic development of society."[30] Marx is not proposing a universal succession of modes of production. Those listed here are only chronological in two senses. One is that, as Eric Hobsbawm puts it, "each of these systems is in crucial respects further removed from the primitive state of man."[31] The other is that this is the order in which these modes of production arose historically. Neither sense suggests that every social formation is fated to pass under the dominance of each mode of production in succession. Slavery is the best example. All class societies have held slaves at some point, but very few have been based on the slave mode of production, except those of the Greek and Roman city-states, and later in parts of the territory of the Roman Empire. Slavery can therefore scarcely be considered a universal stage through which all societies have to pass. Nevertheless, this passage was interpreted within the mainstream of Social Democracy to mean that history should be understood as a universal succession of increasingly more developed modes of production—an understanding compatible with contemporary non-Marxist notions of evolutionary progress.[32] What determined whether one stage was ready for supersession by another? The answer lay in the same text by Marx: "No social order is ever destroyed before all the productive forces for which it is sufficient have been developed, and new and superior relations of production never replace older ones before the material conditions for their existence have matured within the framework of the old society."[33] This was not the only passage in which Marx appeared to argue that the full maturation of the productive forces within a particular mode of production had to precede its overthrow. In the preface to *Capital*, volume 1, he wrote: "The country that is more developed industrially only shows, to the less developed, the image of its own future. ... Even when a society has begun to track down the natural laws of its movement—and it is the ultimate aim of this work to reveal the economic law of motion of modern society—it can neither leap over the natural phases of its development nor remove them by decree. But it can shorten and lessen the birth pangs."[34] The final sentence of course introduces the possibility of human action speeding up the process and, as we have seen in relation to the revolutions of 1848, Marx by no means regarded the role of socialists as playing a waiting game until conditions were completely "mature." In fact, Marx's statements about development could be interpreted as describing a process that had to occur *either* within each individual society *or* across the system as a whole: the point being that the forces of production might not be developed sufficiently for the dominance of capitalism or socialism in the case of every individual country, but they might be on a global scale. The theoreticians of the Second International held the first interpretation, arguing that every country had to undergo the same pattern of development. Nor could the pace of history be forced. At the conclusion of a work discussing communist movements in Europe at the time of the Reformation, Kautsky wrote: "The direction of social development does not depend on the use of peaceful methods or violent struggles. It is determined by the progress and needs of the methods of production. If the outcome of violent revolutionary struggles does not correspond to the intentions of the revolutionary combatants, this only signifies that these intentions stand in opposition to the development of the needs of production." Kautsky does allow, however, that where changes are in conformity with the development of the productive forces, violence can "accelerate their pace."[35]

But the nation in which this position was articulated and upheld more rigorously than any other was not Germany but, appropriately enough, Russia, in whose future Marx and Engels had briefly glimpsed a possible alternative, before dismissing it. In Western Europe, Social Democratic theorists had far less reason to emphasize the necessity for societies to pass through the recognized stages of development: their own societies had done so, and consequently the debates, particularly in Germany, were over strategies for transcending a capitalism that was already achieved, not bypassing one still in the process of formation. Russia was different. The key figure on the Russian Marxist left until the end of the nineteenth century, Plekhanov, was perhaps the most sophisticated thinker of his entire generational cohort. His recognition of the necessity for capitalism in Russia was accompanied by an insistence that the working class, which it was bringing into being, had to struggle against the new bourgeoisie as hard as it did against the feudal-absolutist state to which the latter were also ostensibly opposed. Indeed, he was initially prepared to echo Marx's more unorthodox pronouncements concerning the prospects for Russian development: "To Marx's teaching is attributed the absurd conclusion that Russia must go through exactly the same phases of historical and economic development as the West."[36]

This element of his thought was however quickly submerged by the need to emphasize the necessity of capitalist development against the Populists. The ultimate outcome of the revolution in Russia, given the preponderance of land-hungry peasantry, could only be the more extensive implantation of a capitalist economy in the countryside, not the agrarian communism predicted by the Populists.[37] If this was true for Russia, then it was even more so for those states, like China, even further east in geographical terms and further behind in developmental terms:

> The West European revolution will be mighty, but not almighty. To have a decisive influence on other countries, the socialist countries of the West will need some kind of vehicle for that influence. "International exchange" is a powerful vehicle, but it is not almighty either. The Europeans have brisk trade with China, but one can hardly be confident that working class organisation in the West will very soon "impose" "socialist organisation in the sphere of home exchange" on China. Why? Because China's "social structure" seriously hinders European ideas and institutions in having decisive influence on it. . . . However powerful the possible influence of the European revolution may be, we must bother about providing the conditions which would render that influence effective.[38]

It is important to note that, for Plekhanov at least, this was not a racist or paternalist discourse. He maintained the same position in relation to the history of Western Europe: "Everywhere there has been imitation; but the imitator is separated from his model by all the distance which exists between the society which gave him, the *imitator*, birth and the society in which the *model* lived." Plekhanov correctly notes that Locke was the greatest influence on French philosophers of the eighteenth century: "Yet, between Locke and his French pupils there is precisely that same distance, which separated English society at the time of the 'Glorious Revolution' from French society as it was several decades before the 'Great Rebellion' of the French people." His conclusion was therefore: "*Thus* the influence of the literature of one country on the literature of another is directly proportional to the similarity of the social relations of those countries. It does not exist at all when that similarity is near to zero."[39] Similarly, Kautsky wrote: "Theory has never yet raced ahead of practice in any new major social development."[40]

The achievement of democracy, the underlying theme of all the pre-Marxist radical traditions, and the development of the productive forces, the prime mover of social change in mainstream Second International Marxism, were often synthesized, as in this early passage by Plekhanov:

> The degree to which a particular people is prepared for true and genuine democracy is determined by the degree of its economic development. Sharply defined economic relations define no less sharply defined political groupings, the antagonism between labor and capital gives rise to the struggle between workers' and bourgeois parties. And the development of the productive forces brings this struggle closer to its end and guarantees the victory of the proletariat. So it has been and still is in all the "Western" countries.[41]

The same point was made by non-Marxist socialists. Here is the French Socialist leader Jean Jaurès (1859–1914) in his classic *Socialist History of the French Revolution* (1901): "The French Revolution indirectly prepared the ground for the advent of the proletariat because it brought about the two essential prerequisites of socialism, democracy and capitalism."[42] But who made the French Revolution and its predecessors?

THE BOURGEOIS REVOLUTION
AS THE WORK OF THE BOURGEOISIE

The historical model in which human history was divided into stages, each characterized by an ever more developed mode of production, was accompanied by the notion that each successive stage would involve the triumph of a particular class associated with the new way of organizing economic life. Textual authority for this could be found in a famous passage from the first section of the *Manifesto of the Communist Party*: "The [written] history of hitherto existing society is the history class struggles."[43] In the paragraphs that follow, Marx and Engels give a list of pairs of antagonistic classes: "freeman and slave, patrician and plebeian, lord and serf, guild-master and journeyman." The list is so familiar, the rhetoric in which it is presented so overwhelming, that the difficulties it represents are often overlooked. Partly these stem from inconsistencies within the pairings: as Geoffrey de Ste. Croix has pointed out, insofar as the opposing classes are divided between exploiters and exploited, the first couple identified by Marx and Engels should be slaveowners and slaves, rather than freemen and slaves.[44] Nevertheless, with this exception, the pairs listed are indeed "exploiter and exploited." Marx and Engels, however, refer to them as "oppressor and oppressed." Furthermore, they claim that these are binary oppositions in which the victory of one side is associated with "either a revolutionary reconstitution of society at large, or in the common ruin of the contending classes."[45] This raises a number of questions, notably whether slaves or serfs were capable of "reconstituting society," and of the absence of the bourgeoisie from the list.[46] In a preface from the 1880s Engels compounded the existing confusion by making the "exploited" co-extensive with the "oppressed":

> In every historical epoch, the prevailing mode of economic production and exchange, and the social organization necessarily following from it, form the basis upon which it is built up, and from that which alone can be explained the political and intellectual history of that epoch; that consequently the whole history of mankind (since the dissolution of primitive tribal society, holding land in common ownership) has been a history of class struggles, contests between exploiting and exploited, ruling and oppressed classes. That the history of these class struggles forms a series of evolutions in which, nowadays, a stage has been reached where the exploited and oppressed class—the proletariat—cannot attain its emancipation from the sway of the exploiting and ruling class—the bourgeoisie—without, at the same time, and once and for all, emancipating society at large from all exploitation, oppression, class distinction, and class struggles.[47]

We are invited to view history, then, not only as involving a series of class struggles, but as involving a series of class struggles in which one hitherto subordinate class overthrows and takes over from its predecessor, until the working class, the

"universal class," overthrows the bourgeoisie and puts an end to the process by initiating the dissolution of all classes. The bourgeoisie therefore appear as the penultimate set of revolutionary actors in an unfolding drama that will climax in
communism. Bauer, for example, wrote in 1907: "Just as the bourgeoisie, once the
numerically poorest and most insignificant of the estates within feudal society, rose
up in this society, ultimately destroyed it, and built up its own society, so too there
is a class stirring in contemporary society with whose interests our social institutions are incompatible, the working class."[48] It is important to understand, however,
that this view was widely held by figures within the labor movement who were
otherwise far from being influenced by historical materialism. "We are imbued
with the idea that we are the last great class to march forward, to rise to power,"
said the very un-Marxist British trade union leader Ernest Bevin at the first annual
Conference of the Transport and General Workers' Union to follow the defeat of
the British General Strike in 1926.[49]

As a sophisticated adherent of this perspective, Plekhanov was certainly more
responsible for establishing the conventional "Marxist" conception of the bourgeois
revolutions than Marx and Engels themselves. The most systematic study of their
historical predecessors was undertaken by him in a work published in 1896, the
year after Engels's death and, as the title of the relevant chapter indicates, it focuses
almost entirely on "the French historians of the Restoration"; the only earlier
thinker to be considered was the Neapolitan, Giambattista Vico.[50] The following
passage from 1884 is characteristic:

> Nor will anyone deny that [the bourgeoisie's] stirrings have always had quite a definite
> economic character. But that did not prevent it from following the pack of political
> struggle and political gains. Now by arms, now by peace treaties, sometimes for the re-
> publican independence of towns, sometimes for strengthening of royal power, the rising
> bourgeoisie waged a hard, uninterrupted struggle against feudalism for whole centuries,
> and long before the French Revolution it could proudly draw its enemies' attention to
> its successes. "The chances were different and the successes varying in the great struggle
> of the burghers against feudal lords," the historian says, "and not only was the sum of
> privileges wrested from them by force or obtained by agreement not the same every-
> where, but even when the political forms were the same, there were different degrees
> of liberty and independence for the towns." Nevertheless, the sense of the movement
> was identical everywhere—it meant the beginning of the social emancipation of the
> third estate and the decline of the aristocracy, secular and ecclesiastical.[51]

Plekhanov invoked the French Liberal historians to support his own conclusions
to a far greater extent than Marx and Engels themselves ever did (he quotes here
from Thierry's *Essay on the History of the Third Estate*) and displayed an overestima-
tion of bourgeois revolutionary fervor ("the rising bourgeoisie waged a hard, uninterrupted struggle against feudalism for whole centuries") to which Marx and
Engels only succumbed in those moments when they wished to highlight the inadequacies of the Germans. Here he explicitly draws on the French example to illustrate the notion of the working class as the successors to the bourgeoisie:

When the representatives of the nobility and clergy, in one of the first sessions of the estates, fell back upon the foundation of their privileges—the historic right of conquest—the theoretician of the bourgeoisie, Abbé Sieyès, proudly replied: "*Rien que cela, messieurs? Nous serons conquérants à notre tour!*"—which means, "Nothing but that, gentlemen? Well, we too shall be conquerors in our turn!" And the working class must say just that to the advocates of bourgeois force.[52]

These comments, and others like them, led Plekhanov's first Western biographer to make this judgment on his fixation with the French Revolution as a model and an inspiration:

> In his quest for unity, simplicity, and certainty, he tended to lose sight of the substantial differences in the modern history of the various countries comprised in the "West." France, for example, had been the scene of the classic "bourgeois" revolution, whereas Germany's attempt at such a revolution ended in failure. Blurring this all-important distinction, Plekhanov arbitrarily took the French model to represent the Western pattern of development. Then, elevating the French experience into a universal, he projected for Russia a revolution of the same kind and a similar outcome. In reality, Russia in 1900 was much more like Germany before 1848 than France before 1789. Coming much later than the comparable campaign in Germany, the movement for the overthrow of Russian absolutism was even less likely than its predecessor to follow the French pattern.[53]

The problematic political implications of Plekhanov's position were to become clear in the first years of the twentieth century, during the debates over the nature of the forthcoming Russian Revolution. He argued that working-class revolutionaries should seek alliances with sections of the bourgeoisie who were opposed to the tsarist autocracy, in the same way that bourgeois revolutionaries had sought alliances with sections of the nobility who were opposed to French absolutism:

> When the ideologists of the French bourgeoisie in the XVIII century "went" among the aristocracy, recruiting fighters for a new social order, did they betray the *point of view of their own class*? Not at all. No such betrayal occurred, only a perfectly correct political calculation (or, if you will, instinct), which led to an even more consistent affirmation of exactly the same point of view. And will there be any betrayal if ideologists of the proletariat go among the "upper" classes with the goal of finding means and resources that might serve the interests of Social Democracy? It would appear that in this case, too, there will be no betrayal; here again, the "reaching out" will be a matter of political calculation.[54]

There is not, however, a fundamental antagonism between the capitalist bourgeoisie and the feudal nobility in the same way that there is one between the socialist proletariat and the capitalist bourgeoisie. Both the nobility and the bourgeoisie are actual or potential ruling classes within exploitative modes of production, the working class is not; more importantly, it is potentially possible for all members of the nobility to become capitalists, as many had done in England, but not for members of the proletariat to do so. In other words, leaving aside any other dissimilarity between the two cases, the class relations alone are too different for comparable strategies to be followed. But, even leaving these difficulties aside, had members of the bourgeoisie in any case ever played a revolutionary role in the revolutions that bear its name?

In his earlier and more reflective writings, Plekhanov argued that they tended not to be directly involved:

> Naturally, the representatives of that class do not come out into the streets, put up barricades or publish underground leaflets . . . the bourgeoisie in general do not like such "hazardous" means. Only in very rare cases were they the first to raise the banner of revolt even in Western Europe. . . . As for secret political propaganda, what kind of bourgeoisie would they have been had they not understood the significance of the division of labor? The bourgeoisie leave propaganda to the so-called intelligentsia and do not let themselves be distracted from the task of their own enrichment. They know that their cause is "certain" and that the political struggle begun by our intelligentsia will sooner or later clear the ground for their, the bourgeoisie's domination. Did not the Italian bourgeoisie let the revolutionaries pick out of the fire the chestnuts of political emancipation and unification and are they not now feeding on these chestnuts?[55]

Here, Plekhanov describes "the intelligentsia" as being responsible for bourgeois propaganda. The term is a peculiarly Russian one and he uses it in the context of a discussion of the Russian situation. Nevertheless, it points toward a more general issue, which Marx and Engels never systematically discussed, concerning which sections of the bourgeoisie actually provided leadership, in the cases where it did so.

The subject was explored in greater depth by Kautsky who, during the centenary year of 1889, established the first systematic Marxist account of the French Revolution in a series of articles published in *Die Neue Zeit*, which were later collected and reissued as a book. One section dealing with the Parisian sansculottes concluded that their contribution to the bourgeois victory was indispensable while their own victory was impossible—a conclusion that Engels had already reached during the previous decade, although Kautsky gave more emphasis to the fact that they were not wage-laborers. The most interesting aspect of Kautsky's discussion does not however concern the plebeians, but the bourgeoisie itself, which he described as divided and inconsistent: "The bourgeoisie did not constitute in any sense a homogenous revolutionary mass. Some fractions were directly interested, due to momentary advantages, in the preservation of privileged estates; others regarded the revolution with mistrust and aloofness; while others, who sympathized with it, lacked courage and force."[56]

In this text Kautsky makes essentially the same point in relation to France that Plekhanov had made in more general terms. As Bertel Nygaard points out, for Kautsky the key revolutionary section of the bourgeoisie was "the intelligentsia," consisting of "lawyers, journalists and others performing intellectual tasks": "It belonged to the capitalist bourgeoisie through family connections and its social position, yet remained aloof from those particular business interests and competitive relations that kept other parts of the bourgeoisie from acting concertedly in a revolutionary way." The importance of this fraction was that "it could formulate the general interests of the bourgeoisie as a whole and act on its behalf." It could of course only do so at the head of the sansculottes and peasants: "In other words, the French Revolution was bourgeois and capitalist in *spite* of the capitalist bourgeoisie."[57] Similar arguments were made by Mehring in 1897 in relation to Germany: "The literature and philosophy that had lifted Germany, politically and economically backward as it was, at least culturally onto a level with the other civilized western nations, had arisen in the eighteenth century from petty-bourgeois layers, from craftsmen and petty officials in church, school and state, not from the big and medium bourgeoisie."[58]

At certain points then, the leading figures of the Second International took a more complex view of bourgeois revolutions as a historical phenomenon than is often assumed, at least in relation to the role of the bourgeoisie. But these elements of their thought tended to be buried beneath their more conventional judgments and it was the latter that received the widest circulation among the Social Democratic rank and file. Furthermore, as with many other issues, their views were originally accepted on the left of the Second International until the impending outbreak of an actual bourgeois revolution in Russia forced the reconsideration of some key positions. The first Russian Revolution had an impact, even on the older generation of Social Democratic theorists, although it was certainly not uniform: Kautsky was temporarily radicalized by the experience, while Plekhanov was confirmed in his conservatism. It was among the younger generation, however, that the new breakthroughs were now to be made.

12

CLASSICAL MARXISM (2) 1905–24: THE RUSSIAN CRUCIBLE

T
he decisive impetus for the development of the concept of bourgeois revolution was, from the opening of the twentieth century, the looming presence of the Russian Revolution, first as an eagerly anticipated prospect, then as a deeply divisive result. From the early 1840s, debates over the nature of the forthcoming German Revolution led to the emergence of the concept of bourgeois revolution in the thought of Marx and Engels; from the early 1880s, debates over the nature of the forthcoming Russian Revolution saw a revival of the subject among the first and second generations of their followers. In both cases then, the impetus came from the need to orient the socialist movement in a particular national context where the bourgeois revolution had yet to occur. However, these latter-day discussions resulted in a more systematic conceptualization of bourgeois revolutions than had been attempted by Marx and Engels themselves. Unsurprisingly, Russian Marxists were at the forefront of these debates.[1]

THE GENERAL CONTEXT

By the end of the nineteenth century it was generally accepted within the Second International that the bourgeoisie was no longer the revolutionary force it had been, even in 1848. Specifically, this meant that it would not play a revolutionary role in Russia, where the next great revolution was expected. In a speech to the founding congress of the Second International in 1889, Plekhanov said that, in relation to the overthrow of the autocracy: "the revolutionary movement in Russia will triumph only as a working-class movement or else it will never triumph!"[2] The position was restated by Peter Struve in the 1898 Manifesto of the Russian Social Democratic Labor Party (RSDLP): "The further east one goes in Europe, the meaner, more cowardly and politically weak the bourgeoisie becomes, and the greater are the cultural and political tasks that fall to the proletariat." Struve was then at the beginning of a political descent that would see him move from "Legal" Marxism to Liberalism to supporting the White counterrevolutionary movement in the Russian Civil War.

Nevertheless, at this point, his conclusion was clear: "The Russian proletariat will cast off the yoke of autocracy, so that it may continue the struggle with capitalism and the bourgeoisie with still greater energy until the complete victory of socialism."[3] It was also generally accepted that a period of capitalist development would be necessary once the autocracy had been overthrown, in order to develop the productive forces to the point where socialism was achievable—a position that did not, of course, imply an uncritical attitude toward capitalism. In 1898, toward the end of an exhaustive study demonstrating that capitalism was already developing in Russia, Lenin wrote about the progressive role of capitalism: "Recognition of the progressiveness of this role is quite compatible . . . with the full recognition of the negative and dark sides of capitalism, with the full recognition of the profound and all-round social contradictions which are inevitably inherent in capitalism, and which reveal the historically transient character of the economic regime." His Narodnik opponents argued that "an admission of the historically progressive nature of capitalism means an apology for capitalism," but Lenin rightly denied this and argued that it was possible to welcome capitalism at the same time as fighting against its effects.[4]

It was in the context of these general perspectives that the term "permanent revolution" reentered Marxist debates. The first person to revive it seems to have been the Russian revolutionary David Ryazanov during his 1903 critique of the draft programme of *Iskra*, the paper of the RSDWP.[5] Within a year, however, it had once more become part of general discourse of the center and left wings of the Second International in Central and Eastern Europe, as a means of encapsulating how the working class would have to carry out the bourgeois revolution in Russia. In addition to Ryazanov, Kautsky, Lenin, Luxemburg, Mehring, Plekhanov, Parvus, and Trotsky all held this perspective, with only Lenin refusing the actual term "permanent revolution" and only Trotsky investing the term with a significantly different content. But even Lenin's refusal was semantic rather than substantive.[6] During a discussion about the need to prepare for a forthcoming struggle between the rural proletariat and the peasant bourgeoisie, written during the revolution of 1905, he wrote:

> For from the democratic revolution we shall at once, and precisely in accordance with the measure of our strength, the strength of the class-conscious and organized proletariat, begin to pass to the socialist revolution. We stand for uninterrupted revolution. We shall not stop half-way.[7]

It is important to insist on this relative unanimity, since there is a long-established tradition, widely held in the Trotskyist movement but also influential in some academic accounts, of reducing prerevolutionary views about the nature of the Russian Revolution into a tripartite structure established by Trotsky. In a late article he summarized the "three conceptions of the Russian Revolution" associated respectively with the Mensheviks, Lenin (in fact representing the collective Bolshevik position), and himself:

The Menshevik attitude towards the revolution, stripped of episodic encrustations and individual deviations, is reducible to the following: The victory of the Russian bourgeois revolution is conceivable only under the leadership of the liberal bourgeoisie and must hand over power to the latter. The democratic regime will then permit the Russian proletariat to catch up with its older Western brothers on the road of the struggle for socialism with incomparably greater success than hitherto. Lenin's perspective may be briefly expressed as follows: The belated Russian bourgeoisie is incapable of leading its own revolution to the end. The complete victory of the revolution through the medium of the "democratic dictatorship of the proletariat and the peasantry" will purge the country of medievalism, invest the development of Russian capitalism with American tempos, strengthen the proletariat in the city and country, and open up broad possibilities for the struggle for socialism. On the other hand, the victory of the Russian revolution will provide a mighty impulse for the socialist revolution in the West, and the latter will not only shield Russia from the dangers of restoration but also permit the Russian proletariat to reach the conquest of power in a comparatively short historical interval. The perspective of permanent revolution may be summed up in these words: The complete victory of the democratic revolution in Russia is inconceivable otherwise than in the form of the dictatorship of the proletariat basing itself upon the peasantry. The dictatorship of the proletariat, which will inescapably place on the order of the day not only democratic but also socialist tasks, will at the same time provide a mighty impulse to the international socialist movement. Only the victory of the proletariat in the West will shield Russia from bourgeois restoration and secure for her the possibility of bringing the socialist construction to its conclusion.[8]

This summary is accurate insofar as it deals with the division of opinion within Russia between the revolutions of 1905 and October 1917, but "Lenin's" position was in fact a variant of the dominant position of the center and left of the Second International, which, before the first of these dates at least, was also shared by the Mensheviks. Michael Löwy has attempted to add a fourth conception to this list, associated with Parvus and Luxemburg, and a fifth associated with Kautsky occupying a position halfway between those of Lenin and Luxemburg.[9] I do not find this approach, which could be extended until there are as many different "conceptions" as there were participants in the debate, particularly helpful. It might be more useful to see the second conception, between those of the Mensheviks and Trotsky, as involving a continuum of views, the main difference between these views being the extent to which they regarded the peasantry as capable of independent activity, the nature of the relationship between the working class and the peasantry, and whether one or both of these classes would either seek to form a postrevolutionary government or abdicate immediately in favor of representatives of the bourgeoisie.[10]

Some Marxists outside Russia were prepared to give the Russian bourgeoisie the benefit of the doubt. In an article first published in 1903 Kautsky wrote: "Today we can nowhere speak of a revolutionary bourgeoisie," adding, at the beginning of the revolution of 1905, "with the possible exception of Russia."[11] But the actual course of the 1905 revolution settled the matter. As Lenin wrote in the aftermath:

Nowhere else in the world, probably, has the bourgeoisie revealed in the bourgeois revolution such reactionary brutality, such a close alliance with the old regime, such "freedom" from anything remotely resembling sincere sympathy towards culture, towards progress, towards the preservation of human dignity, as it has with us—so let our proletariat derive from the Russian bourgeois revolution a triple hatred of the bourgeoisie and a determination to fight it.[12]

Within Russia, the Mensheviks now began to entertain precisely the illusions in the Russian bourgeoisie that the Russian movement and the Second International as a whole had previously rejected. At the beginning of 1905 their leader Julius Martov wrote: "We have the right to expect that sober political calculation will prompt our bourgeois democracy to act in the same way in which, in the past century, bourgeois democracy acted in Western Europe, under the inspiration of revolutionary romanticism."[13] Of course, the working class would be a participant in the bourgeois revolution, but under bourgeois leadership, which meant that it could not undertake any forms of struggle that might cause the bourgeoisie to retreat from their mission—although the very fact that this was a concern should have spoken volumes about the reliability of the bourgeoisie as a revolutionary force. "Social relations in Russia have not matured beyond the point of bourgeois revolution," said Pavel Axelrod. "History impels workers and revolutionaries more and more strongly towards bourgeois revolutionism, making them involuntary political servants of the bourgeoisie, rather than in the direction of genuine socialist revolutionism and the tactical and organizational preparation of the proletariat for political rule."[14] Their misplaced faith in the bourgeoisie, and the unwarranted assumption that the proletariat would exercise a self-denying ordinance, involved illusions that would ultimately lead the Mensheviks to substitute themselves for the former and attempt to restrain the latter. In the context of a discussion of the bourgeois revolution, the Menshevik conception was in many respects even less radical than the position held by Marx and Engels at the beginning of the revolutions of 1848, let alone the position they held at their end; it was certainly far less skeptical about the revolutionary capabilities of the native bourgeoisie. Lenin was scathing, denouncing "their doctrinaire and lifeless distortion of Marxism": "They argue that the revolution is a bourgeois one and therefore . . . we must retrace out steps in the same measure the bourgeoisie succeeds in obtaining concessions from Tsarism." Later in the same article he mocked "the magnificent principle: the revolution is a bourgeois revolution—therefore comrades, watch out lest the bourgeois recoil!"[15] The conceptions of the Russian Revolution associated with Lenin and Trotsky were not only politically more serious from a revolutionary socialist perspective but also of greater theoretical interest concerning the nature of bourgeois revolutions in general—indeed, until the 1920s most developments in relation to the concept were the work of one or the other of these men.

LENIN AND THE "BOURGEOIS-DEMOCRATIC" REVOLUTION

Tony Cliff once concluded, following a study of Lenin's early views on the revolutionary party: "If he is cited on any tactical or organizational question, the concrete issues which the movement was facing at the time must be made absolutely clear."[16] In fact, the warning issued by Cliff here can be applied more widely: no statements by Lenin can be fully comprehended outside of the context in which they were expressed. "Lenin cannot be understood just by reading Lenin," writes Lars Lih, by which he means that the meaning of any text by Lenin depends on the reader knowing, among other things, the theoretical level of the audience that he was addressing, how far certain assumptions were shared with other Social Democrats and therefore did not require to be openly stated, and the extent to which he was exaggerating a position in order to counteract a previous exaggeration in the opposite direction by his opponents ("bending the stick").[17] A further problem is that Lenin's relentless focus on the immediate matter at hand often gives his work the appearance of inconsistency, although it is rarely so in reality. "It is rather," Alasdair MacIntyre writes, "that Lenin tends to confront problems in isolation from each other"; MacIntyre is thinking here about the seemingly incompatible explanations for reformist class consciousness that Lenin advances in *What Is to Be Done?* (1902) and *Imperialism* (1916).[18] In other words, more than is the case with any other leading Marxist, consideration of any work by Lenin must always involve knowledge of the circumstances in which it was written and possibly also a number of other texts, the subject of which may ostensibly be quite different.

The problem of reconciling apparently contradictory positions occurs in relation to his discussion of the Russian Revolution, at least until April 1917, when he changed his assessment of its nature. Take, for example these two passages on the nature of prerevolutionary Russia, from adjoining pages of the same article. In the first Lenin argues that "since the entire economic life of the country has already become bourgeois in all its main features, since the overwhelming majority of the population is in fact already living in bourgeois conditions of existence, the anti-revolutionary elements are naturally extremely few in number, constituting truly a mere 'handful' as compared with the 'people.'" On this account the Russian economy is essentially capitalist, but only a few paragraphs later he seems to backtrack from this position:

> True, in Russia capitalism is more highly developed at the present time than it was in Germany in 1848, to say nothing of France in 1789; but there is no doubt about the fact that in Russia purely capitalist antagonisms are very, very much overshadowed by the antagonisms between "culture" and Asiatic barbarism, Europeanism and Tartarism, capitalism and feudalism; in other words, the demands that are being put first today are those the satisfaction of which will develop capitalism, cleanse it of the slag of feudalism and improve the conditions of life and struggle both for the proletariat and for the bourgeoisie.[19]

The inconsistency could be resolved if Lenin was in fact discussing two different aspects of Russian society, one being the dominant mode of production and the other the form of the state. Perry Anderson has plausibly claimed that, for Lenin: "The Russian social formation was a complex ensemble dominated by the capitalist mode of production, but the Russian state remained a feudal Absolutism."[20] There are certainly a number of historical examples, notably the United Netherlands and England, where bourgeois revolutions were made against foreign or native absolutist states in societies in which the transition to capitalism was all but complete. Russia was clearly nowhere near as advanced in capitalist terms as these forerunners; nevertheless we can accept Anderson's formulation as long as we understand that "dominance" by the capitalist mode of production does not mean that the majority of social relations of production have to be capitalist—Lenin rightly did not believe this to be the case—only that the economy as a whole is subject to capitalist laws of motion. As we shall see, however, this method of "confronting problems in isolation" recurs at several other points in Lenin's discussion of bourgeois revolution, particularly in relation to the question of democracy.

How then did Lenin conceive of the nature of the Russian Revolution? Like everyone else on the Marxist left apart from Trotsky he argued that it could only be a bourgeois revolution, but his writings contain by far the most detailed arguments for this claim of anyone in his or the preceding generation of revolutionaries. Here is a passage written during the 1905 revolution, which starts from the proposition "Marxists are absolutely convinced of the bourgeois character of the Russian revolution":

> What does this mean? It means that the democratic reforms in the political system and the social and economic reforms, which have become a necessity for Russia, do not in themselves imply the undermining of capitalism, the undermining of bourgeois rule; on the contrary, they will, for the first time, really clear the ground for a wide and rapid, European, and not Asiatic, development of capitalism; they will, for the first time, make it possible for the bourgeoisie to rule as a class.... The idea of seeking salvation for the working class in anything save the further development of capitalism is *reactionary*. In countries like Russia, the working class suffers not so much from capitalism as from the insufficient development of capitalism. The working class is therefore *decidedly interested* in the broadest, freest and most rapid development of capitalism. The removal of all the remnants of the old order which are hampering the broad, free and rapid development of capitalism is of decided advantage to the working class. The bourgeois revolution is precisely a revolution that most resolutely sweeps away the survivals of the past, the remnants of serfdom (which include not only autocracy but monarchy as well) and most fully guarantees the broadest, freest and most rapid development of capitalism. That is why a *bourgeois* revolution is *in the highest degree advantageous to the proletariat*. A bourgeois revolution is *absolutely* necessary in the interests of the proletariat. The more complete and determined, the more consistent the bourgeois revolution, the more assured will be the proletarian struggle against the bourgeoisie for Socialism.[21]

Who would lead these revolutions? In Lenin's own words: "Does not the very concept 'bourgeois revolution' imply that it can be accomplished only by the bourgeoisie?" As we have seen, he decisively rejected this implication and Menshevik attempts to base a strategy around it, arguing instead that the proletariat and peasantry would not only benefit from the success of a bourgeois revolution in Russia but would be responsible for making it:

A liberation movement that is bourgeois in social and economic content is not such because of its motive forces. The motive force may be, not the bourgeoisie, but the proletariat and the peasantry. Why is this possible? Because the proletariat and the peasantry suffer even more than the bourgeoisie from the survivals of serfdom, because they are in greater need of freedom and the abolition of landlord oppression. For the bourgeoisie, on the contrary, complete victory constitutes a danger, since the proletariat will make use of full freedom against the bourgeoisie, and the fuller that freedom and the more completely the power of the landlords has been destroyed, the easier will it be for the proletariat to do so. Hence the bourgeoisie strives to put an end to the bourgeois revolution half-way from its destination, when freedom has been only half-won, by a deal with the old authorities and the landlords.[22]

Members of the bourgeoisie were unwilling to wage a decisive struggle against the autocracy and everything associated with it, not because they feared the actual strength of the regime, but rather because they feared the potential strength of the proletariat which, growing in conditions of untrammeled capitalist development and political freedom, would pose a far greater threat to their property than the tsarist state. Kautsky, like the majority of the center and left of the Second International, agreed with Lenin that revolutionary leadership could no longer be provided by the bourgeoisie, and for essentially the same reasons:

The age of the bourgeois revolutions, i.e., of revolutions in which the bourgeoisie was the driving force, is over in Russia as well [as in Western Europe]. There too the proletariat is no longer an appendage and tool of the bourgeoisie, as it was in the bourgeois revolutions, but an independent class with independent revolutionary aims. But whenever the proletariat emerges in this way the bourgeoisie ceases to be a revolutionary class. The Russian bourgeoisie, insofar as it is liberal and has an independent policy at all, certainly hates absolutism but it hates revolution even more, and it hates absolutism because it sees it as the fundamental cause of revolution; and insofar as it asks for political liberty, it does so above all because it believes that it is the only way to bring an end to the revolution.[23]

Introducing this article to a Russian readership, Lenin was quick to assimilate Kautsky's position to his own: "A bourgeois revolution, brought about by the proletariat and the peasantry in spite of the instability of the bourgeoisie—this fundamental principle of Bolshevik tactics is wholly confirmed by Kautsky."[24] In fact, although tentative, the conclusions drawn by Kautsky as to the nature of the Russian Revolution are different from those of the Bolsheviks: "The bourgeoisie therefore does not constitute one of the driving forces of the present revolutionary movement in Russia and to this extent we cannot call it a bourgeois one." The assumption here is that bourgeois revolutions must be led by the bourgeoisie—a position that, as we saw in chapter 11, Kautsky had earlier rejected and that Lenin continued to reject. This is not, however, the most important difference. After confessing to being uncertain about the nature of the Russian Revolution, Kautsky eventually arrived at this formula:

We should most probably be fair to the Russian Revolution and the tasks that it sets us if we viewed it as neither a bourgeois revolution in the traditional sense nor a socialist one but as quite a unique process which is taking place on the borderline between bourgeois and socialist society, which requires the dissolution of the one while preparing for the creation of the other and which in any case brings all those who live in capitalist civilization a significant step forward in their development.[25]

The article from which these remarks are taken is one of a series written around the period of the 1905 Russian Revolution when Kautsky was temporarily under the influence of Luxemburg—it is, in other words, a position associated with the height of his radicalism, not one prefiguring his later collapse into reformism. Indeed, those who remained politically aligned with Lenin after the collapse of the Second International, like Luxemburg herself, displayed similar uncertainties to those of Kautsky in defining the nature of the Russian Revolution:

> *In its content*, the present revolution in Russia goes far beyond previous revolutions, and, in its methods, it cannot simply follow either the old bourgeois revolutions or the previous—parliamentary—struggles of the modern proletariat. It has created a new method of struggle, which accords both with its proletarian character and with the combination of the struggle for democracy and the struggle against capital—namely, the revolutionary mass strike. In terms of content and methods, it is therefore a completely new type of revolution. Being formally bourgeois-democratic, but essentially proletarian-socialist, it is, in both content and method, *a transitional form* from the bourgeois revolutions of the past to the proletarian revolutions of the future, which will directly involve the dictatorship of the proletariat and the realization of socialism.[26]

Although he did not directly engage with Kautsky and Luxemburg on this issue, Lenin insisted that there was no necessary contradiction between working-class agency and bourgeois outcome, and consequently no difficulty in identifying the nature of the Russian Revolution:

> Bourgeois revolutions are possible, and have occurred, in which the commercial, or commercial and industrial, bourgeoisie played the part of the chief motive force. The victory of such revolutions was possible as the victory of the appropriate section of the bourgeoisie over its adversaries (such as the privileged nobility or the absolute monarchy). In Russia things are different. The victory of the bourgeois revolution is impossible in our country *as the victory of the bourgeoisie*. This sounds paradoxical, but it is a fact. The preponderance of the peasant population, its terrible oppression by the semi-feudal big landowning system, the strength and class-consciousness of the proletariat already organized in a socialist party—all these circumstances impart to *our* bourgeois revolution a *specific* character. This peculiarity does not eliminate the bourgeois character of the revolution. [27]

Lenin situated these arguments within a longer-term historical context. Like Engels, he acknowledged that participation by the popular masses had been decisive in winning at least some of the earlier bourgeois revolutions, above all those in England and France, but that they had been unable to achieve their own objectives once the bourgeoisie or its representatives had been installed in power. The modern equivalent of these forces, the urban proletariat, was however in a position to do so, on account of its greater numeric strength, deeper implantation in the process of production, and higher cultural level: "Consequently, the specific feature of the Russian bourgeois revolution is merely that instead of the plebeian element of the towns taking second place as it did in the sixteenth, seventeenth and eighteenth centuries, it is the proletariat which is taking first place in the twentieth century."[28]

As I have previously emphasized, arguments for the leading role of the working class in the Russian Revolution were not unique to Lenin or the Bolsheviks more generally, but in many respects simply represented the clearest exposition of a positions common to the center and left of the Second International. In other respects, however, Lenin made a number of innovations in theorizing bourgeois revolutions, although, as tended to be the case, his generalizations sprang from consideration of the Russian experience. One of these, which made explicit a theme implicit in Engels's writings on Germany, was the notion of "consummation." For Lenin, bourgeois revolutions involved a prolonged process that ranged over decades rather than months or years. In the case of Russia, "the year 1861 begat the year 1905," and it was this period as a whole following the liberation of the serfs that constituted "the era of her bourgeois revolutions."[29] Such "eras" tended to involve several individual moments of revolutionary upheaval; they were not, however, completely open-ended, but concluded in a decisive episode that is the consummation of the entire process.

> Generally speaking, [consummation] may be taken to mean two things. If used in its broad sense, it means the fulfillment of the objective historical tasks of the bourgeois revolution, its "consummation," i.e., the removal of the very soil capable of engendering a bourgeois revolution, the consummation of the *entire cycle* of bourgeois revolutions. In this sense, for example, the bourgeois-democratic revolution in France was *consummated* only in 1871 (though begun in 1789). But if the term is used in its narrow sense, it means a particular revolution, one of the bourgeois revolutions, one of the "waves," if you like, that batters the old regime but does not destroy it altogether, does not remove the basis that may engender subsequent bourgeois revolutions. In this sense the revolution of 1848 in Germany was "consummated" in 1850 or the fifties, but it did not in the least thereby remove the soil for the revolutionary revival in the sixties. The revolution of 1789 in France was "consummated," let us say, in 1794, without, however, thereby removing the soil for the revolutions of 1830 and 1848.[30]

Consummation can therefore occur at two levels, both *at* the climax of individual episodes and *as* the concluding episode of the entire revolutionary process. We need to distinguish, however, between Lenin's general claim about the bourgeois revolution as a process and the examples he gives to illustrate it. In relation to France, for example, Luxemburg gave a similar but more detailed analysis, arguing that the convulsions which shook France after the Great Revolution resulted in successive sections of the bourgeoisie coming to power, from high finance (1815), to the industrial bourgeoisie (July 1830), to the middle and small bourgeoisie (February 1848), with June 1848 representing the moment when the working class understood its separation from the petty bourgeoisie. Yet for her too 1871 is the concluding episode: "In the shape of the contemporary Third Republic, modern bourgeois class domination reached its most highly developed and final form. . . .

Thus was first formed in France the modern bourgeois society, which completed the work begun by the Great French Revolution."[31] Yet the greater specificity of Luxemburg's account also exposes its weakness: the successive assent to state power by different elements of the bourgeoisie that she describes suggests a series of political revolutions on the basis of an already achieved bourgeois social revolution rather than different moments in the course of the latter. Whether the consummation of the French Revolution is represented by the advent of the Third Republic in 1871, or the Second Republic in 1848, or the July Monarchy in 1830, or even the Restoration of 1815 rather depends on what one thinks the historical objectives of that revolution, or any bourgeois revolution, actually are.

For Russian Marxists in particular, their forthcoming revolution had two key elements, which they summarized by describing it as *bourgeois-democratic* in nature—a compound term that had not appeared in the work of Marx or Engels, but by which they meant that the Russian Revolution would be both bourgeois in content (that is, it would establish the unimpeded development of capitalism) and that it would introduce democratic politics that the working class could use to further its own demands. The introduction of democracy as an objective in the bourgeois revolution introduced a certain conceptual instability to the concept that found expression in descriptions of the revolution went from being *bourgeois* to *bourgeois-democratic* to *democratic*. Here is an example of this slippage from Lenin: "This is a democratic revolution, i.e., one which is bourgeois as regards its social and economic content. This revolution is overthrowing the autocratic semi-feudal system, extricating the bourgeois system from it, and thereby putting into effect the demands of all the classes of bourgeois society—in this sense being a revolution of the whole people."[32] Similarly, in the first manifesto of the Russian Social-Democratic Labor Party to be issued after the outbreak of the First World War, Lenin wrote: "Since Russia is most backward and has not yet completed its bourgeois revolution, it still remains the task of Social-Democrats in that country to achieve the three fundamental conditions for consistent democratic reform, viz., a democratic republic (with complete equality and self-determination for all nations), confiscation of the landed estates, and an eight-hour working day."[33] The problem here is that democracy is a political concept that has no necessary connection to, still less equivalence with, "bourgeois . . . social and economic content." Democracy may be desirable, even essential, for the proletariat to develop ideologically and organizationally to the point where it could challenge for power, but that is precisely why the bourgeoisie was hostile toward it. In fact, the necessity of democracy for the working class existed whether or not the bourgeois revolution had been achieved, as in Germany, or whether it had not, as in Russia.[34] The sociologist Robert Michels, at the syndicalist stage of his journey from German Social Democracy to Italian Fascism, wrote in 1911 of how the German liberal bourgeoisie had mistaken "dreams for reality" in its conception of the outcome of unification:

> In this confusion rests the organic defect of all German liberalism, which since 1866 has continually endeavored to disguise its change of front (that is to say, its partisan struggle against socialism and its simultaneous and voluntary renunciation of all attempts to complete the political emancipation of the German bourgeoisie), by the fallacious assertion that with the unification of Germany and the establishment of the empire of the Hohenzollerns all or almost all of the aspirations of its democratic youth have been realized.[35]

Since, as Michels rightly says, the German Empire was scarcely a model of parliamentary representation, elevating democracy to a necessary outcome of the bourgeois revolution would then cast doubt on whether it had been completed in Germany, or any of the other areas characterized by revolutions from above.

Lenin did not make this move and seems in fact to have had two alternative conceptions of the path to bourgeois revolution in Russia, based on the "two types of bourgeois agrarian evolution" that had previously occurred in Europe and its overseas extensions. In the first, the "Prussian" or reformist path that had been under way in Russia since 1861, the landowners of the great estates would gradually replace feudal methods of exploitation with those of capitalism, retaining feudal instruments of social control over their tenants (at least in the medium term), but ultimately transforming themselves into large capitalist landowners or farmers. In the second, the "American" or revolutionary path, the landowners are overthrown, feudal or other precapitalist controls are removed and the estates redistributed among the previous tenants, who now emerge as a new class of medium capitalist farmers.[36] The point here is less the accuracy of Lenin's distinction between the Prussian and American paths—in fact his discussion of the former is accurate, that of the latter considerably less so—than these alternative paths to bourgeois revolution offered different sets of conditions for the proletariat and its peasant allies to conduct future struggles.[37]

In arguing that the proletariat could be the agent of bourgeois revolution in Russia, he had returned to the paradox, which Marx and Engels had noted from the 1860s onward, that at least some of the objectives of the revolutions of 1848 had eventually been carried out by their opponents: "If you want to consider the question 'historically,' the example of any European country will show you that it was a series of governments . . . that carried out the historical aims of the bourgeois revolution, that even the governments which defeated the revolution were nonetheless forced to carry out the historical aims of that defeated revolution."[38] The proletariat would not therefore be the first class to carry out the bourgeois revolution in the absence of the bourgeoisie, a fact that had specific implications for Russia. In his reflections on the fiftieth anniversary of the "peasant reform" of 1861, Lenin described it as "a bourgeois reform carried out by feudal landowners" at the instigation of the greatest feudal landowner of all, Tsar Alexander II, who, like Bismarck, had "to admit that it would be better to emancipate *from above* than to wait until he was overthrown *from below*." Lenin identified three main reasons for these initiatives: to control the growth of capitalist relations of production stimulated by the increase in trade, to overcome military failure in the Crimean War through the expansion of arms manufacture, and to pacify an upsurge of peasant insurgency in the countryside. But even the reforms were only achieved through "a struggle waged *within* the ruling class, a struggle waged for the most part *within the ranks of the landowner class.*"[39]

These arguments were liable to two different interpretations. One was that the Prussian path could begin the era of bourgeois revolution in Russia, but could not complete it, above all it could not achieve democracy; "consummation" would therefore have to be the work of the proletariat and peasantry. As we have seen, this was the interpretation that dominated in Lenin's writings. The other was that the entire bourgeois revolution in Russia could be carried out by following the Prussian path—an interpretation that inevitably meant accepting that it need not involve democracy at all. Lenin was clear that the type of revolution from above that had unified Germany during the 1860s had been begun during the same decade in Russia but nowhere near consummated. He was typically scathing about anyone who suggested otherwise, as in the following broadside against the unfortunate Comrade Y. Larin (then a Menshevik) from 1911:

> Our bourgeois revolution has not been completed. . . . That is why, in order to divert the Russian workers *from* socialism, the reformists, who are the captives of bourgeois ideas, *constantly* refer to the example of *Austria* (as well as Prussia) in the 1860s. Why are they so fond of these examples? . . . because in these countries, after the "unsuccessful" revolution of 1848, the bourgeois transformation was completed "*without any revolution.*" That is the whole secret! That is what gladdens their hearts, for it seems to indicate that bourgeois change is possible *without* revolution!! And if that is the case, why should we Russians bother our heads about a revolution? Why not leave it to the landlords and factory owners to effect the bourgeois transformation of Russia "without any revolution"! It was because the proletariat in Austria and Prussia was weak that it was unable to prevent the landed proprietors and the bourgeoisie from effecting the, transformation *regardless* of the interests of the workers, in a form *most prejudicial* to the workers, retaining the monarchy, the privileges of the nobility, arbitrary rule in the countryside, and a host of other survivals of medievalism. . . . Why were "crises" in Austria and in Prussia in the 1860s *constitutional*, and not revolutionary? Because there were a number of special circumstances which eased the position of the monarchy (the "revolution from above" in Germany, her unification by "blood and iron"); because the proletariat was at that time extremely weak and undeveloped in those countries, and the liberal bourgeoisie was distinguished by base cowardice and treachery, just as the Russian Cadets are in our day. . . . But that's the whole point—to the reformist the twaddle about the consummated bourgeois revolution . . . is simply a verbal screen to cover up his *renunciation of all revolution.*[40]

Lenin's central point here is that the existing German and Austrian ruling classes were able to carry though bourgeois revolutions from above—"bourgeois revolution" in this case meaning the transformation of the state in order to facilitate capitalist development—because of the weakness of the labor movement. Their equivalents in Russia, even assuming that they were interested in carrying through such a transformation, had not done so and could not do so without opening up the possibility of a working-class intervention that might destroy them—an intervention that reformists like Larin were threatening to divert with their claims that the bourgeois revolution had already been accomplished. Consequently, as Lenin wrote in another article from the same period, "you cannot *transfer* to Russia the German completion of the bourgeois revolution, the German history of a democracy that had spent itself, the German "revolution from above" of the 1860s, and the *actually* existing German legality."[41]

Nevertheless, there is an undertone of disquiet in Lenin's argument, which finds expression in the very ferocity of his polemic against Larin. (I have excluded several particularly vitriolic exclamation-marked passages from the last-but-one quotation.) There is a venerable right-wing argument that holds that Lenin thought the opportunity for revolution in Russia might be "missed" if the ruling class was capable of delivering a series of concessions and reforms sufficient to demobilize the working class in the short to medium term, and that this accounted for his insistence on making the revolution, no matter how "premature" it may have been in developmental terms. There is an element of truth in this assessment, namely that Lenin generally saw politics in terms of alternatives—this is after all, one of the ways in which his work is incompatible with any conception of historical inevitability.[42] It does not mean, however, that the alternative to revolution was a more consistent and wide-ranging version of the reforms tentatively initiated by the regime after the defeat of the 1905 revolution. In fact, no Russian politician or state manager had the necessary strategic insight to carry through such a program after the assassination of Prime Minister Pytor Stolypin in 1911 effectively put an end to agrarian reform. The real alternative to revolution in Russia was more likely to have been a slow-motion version of the internal disintegration, territorial dismemberment, and quasi-colonization that characterized China. But if there was, realistically, only one path to bourgeois revolution in Russia, Lenin did concede that there could be two elsewhere.

> Every peasant revolution directed against medievalism, when the whole of the social economy is of a capitalist nature, is a bourgeois revolution. But not every bourgeois revolution is a peasant revolution. If, in a country where agriculture is organized on fully capitalist lines, the capitalist farmers, with the aid of the hired laborers, were to carry out an agrarian revolution by abolishing the private ownership of land, for instance, that would be a bourgeois revolution, but by no means a peasant revolution. Or if a revolution took place in a country where the agrarian system had become so integrated with the capitalist economy in general that that system could not be abolished without abolishing capitalism, and if, say, that revolution put the industrial bourgeoisie in power in place of the autocratic bureaucracy—that would be a bourgeois revolution, but by no means a peasant revolution. In other words, there can be a bourgeois country without a peasantry, and there can be a bourgeois revolution in such a country without a peasantry. A bourgeois revolution may take place in a country with a considerable peasant population and yet not be a peasant revolution; that is to say, it is a revolution that does not revolutionize the agrarian relations that es-

pecially affect the peasantry and does not bring the peasantry to the fore as a social force that is at all active in creating the revolution. Consequently, the general Marxist concept of "bourgeois revolution" contains certain propositions that are definitely applicable to any peasant revolution that takes place in a country of rising capitalism, but that general concept says nothing at all about whether or not a bourgeois revolution in a given country must (in the sense of objective necessity) become a peasant revolution in order to be completely victorious.[43]

This extraordinarily torturous passage essentially makes two points. One is that successful bourgeois revolutions need not involve a peasant revolution either because a peasantry no longer exists or because the bourgeoisie has been able to bypass or sideline it in the process of seizing power from the absolutist state. The other is that a revolution that did involve the peasantry and the masses more generally was more likely to result in progressive social measures than one that did not, but their absence did not mean that a bourgeois revolution had failed to occur. Lenin made this explicit in one of his last discussions of bourgeois revolution as a general phenomenon:

> If we take the revolutions of the twentieth century as examples we shall, of course, have to admit that the Portuguese and the Turkish revolutions are both bourgeois revolutions. Neither of them, however, is a "people's" revolution, since in neither does the mass of the people, their vast majority, come out actively, independently, with their own economic and political demands to any noticeable degree. By contrast, although the Russian bourgeois revolution of 1905–07 displayed no such "brilliant" successes as at time fell to the Portuguese and Turkish revolutions, it was undoubtedly a "real people's" revolution, since the mass of the people, their majority, the very lowest social groups, crushed by oppression and exploitation, rose independently and stamped on the entire course of the revolution the imprint of *their* own demands, *their* attempt to build in their own way a new society in place of the old society that was being destroyed.[44]

Lenin also saw the bourgeois revolutions as having a second temporal dimension involving not individual chronology but collective periodisation. Portugal and Turkey, at opposite ends of Europe, were only the most "Western" of a series of events that indicated that the revolutionary tradition was acquiring a new spatial focus: "The epoch of bourgeois-democratic revolutions in Western, continental Europe embraces a fairly definite period, approximately between 1789 and 1871. This was precisely the period of national movements and the creation of national states. When this period drew to a close, Western Europe had been transformed into a settled system of bourgeois states, which, as a general rule, were nationally uniform states."[45] These revolutions did not have immediate sequels for, by 1871: "The West had finished with bourgeois revolutions. The East had not yet risen to them."[46] Over thirty years would elapse before the East would resume the sequence of revolutionary upheavals:

> In Eastern Europe and Asia the period of bourgeois-democratic revolutions did not begin until 1905. The revolutions in Russia, Persia, Turkey and China, the Balkan wars—such is the chain of world events of *our* period in our "Orient." And only a

blind man could fail to see in this chain of events the awakening of a *whole series* of bourgeois-democratic national movements which strive to create nationally independent and nationally uniform states.[47]

The first period of bourgeois revolutions therefore involved the consolidation and unification of states in those areas where capitalism had emerged earliest and was now the most developed. The second period involved those areas that were, with the partial exception of China, under the informal domination of those whose bourgeois revolutions had been consummated during the first. Now the bourgeois revolutions were increasingly concerned not with national unification but national liberation, often involving a movement in two directions: externally, for the declining tributary empires to put an end to Western interference; internally, for the subject peoples of these empires to free themselves from central control. In those countries for which the bourgeois revolution still lay in the future, capitalist development remained relatively progressive. It was for this reason that Lenin welcomed the victory over Russia of Japan, the only Eastern country to have consummated its revolutionary era between the end of the first period in 1871 and the opening of the second in 1905:

> Here again, as so often in history, the war between an advanced and a backward country has played a great revolutionary role. And the class-conscious proletariat, an implacable enemy of war—this inevitable and inseverable concomitant of all class rule in general—cannot shut its eyes to the revolutionary task which the Japanese bourgeoisie, by its crushing defeat of the Russian autocracy, is carrying out. The proletariat is hostile to every bourgeoisie and to all manifestations of the bourgeois system, but this hostility does not relieve it of the duty of distinguishing between the historically progressive and the reactionary representatives of the bourgeoisie."[48]

Russia occupied a contradictory role in the world system for Lenin. At one level it clearly belonged alongside China, Persia, and Turkey as one of the "Asiatic" empires; but it also played a role as one of the European Great Powers, and to a far greater extent than Turkey, the only other country that belonged to both groups. Membership of the Great Powers was, however, an indication of military capacity rather than economic development, and so bourgeois revolution was still necessary. Perhaps the greatest distinction that Lenin made between Russia and the other eastern areas was that in the latter he still expected the bourgeoisie to play a revolutionary role, writing in 1912:

> The East has definitely taken the Western path . . . new *hundreds of millions* of people will from now on share in the struggle for the ideals which the West has already worked out for itself. What has decayed is the Western bourgeoisie, which is already confronted by its grave-digger, the proletariat. But in Asia there is *still* a bourgeoisie capable of championing sincere, militant, consistent democracy, a worthy comrade of France's great men of the Enlightenment and great leaders of the close of the eighteenth century. The chief representative, or the chief social bulwark, of this Asian bourgeoisie that is still capable of supporting a historically progressive cause, is the peasant. And side by side with him there already exists a liberal bourgeoisie whose

leaders . . . are above all capable of treachery: yesterday they feared the emperor, and cringed before him; then they betrayed him when they saw the strength, and sensed the victory, of the revolutionary democracy; and tomorrow they will betray the democrats to make a deal with some old or new "constitutional" emperor.[49]

But these expectations extended beyond China. The following year he wrote, in more general terms: "Everywhere in Asia a mighty democratic movement is growing, spreading and gaining in strength. The bourgeoisie there is *as yet* siding with the people against reaction."[50] In this regard, as in so many others, there was a close correlation between Lenin and Luxemburg, who wrote:

> Revolution is an essential for the process of capitalist emancipation. The backward communities must shed their obsolete political organizations, relics of natural and simple commodity production, and create a modern state machinery adapted to the purposes of capitalist production. The revolutions in Turkey, Russia, and China fall under this heading. The last two, in particular, do not exclusively serve the immediate political requirements of capitalism; to some extent they carry over outmoded precapitalist claims while on the other hand they already embody new conflicts which run counter to the development of capital.[51]

In summary then, we can say that by the outbreak of the First World War, Lenin had greatly expanded on four aspects of the concept of bourgeois revolution that had remained underdeveloped in the work of Marx and Engels. First, bourgeois revolutions did not have to be carried out by the bourgeoisie. Second, and consequently, they were alternative paths to bourgeois revolution, depending on which class was the dominant social force involved. Third, bourgeois revolution involved a process, although one with a definite end point or moment of consummation; here too, the speed with which a bourgeois revolution was accomplished depended on the identity of the social class that was most involved in carrying it through. Fourth, in the colonial or semicolonial world, from Russia eastward, bourgeois revolutions were still necessary for development. On this last point Lenin was unshakeable, particularly in relation to his own nation: the bourgeois revolution in Russia could not be avoided or bypassed.

> The degree of Russia's economic development (an objective condition), and the degree of class consciousness and organization of the proletariat (a subjective condition inseparably bound up with the objective condition) make the immediate and complete emancipation of the working class impossible. . . . Whoever wants to reach socialism by any other path than that of political democracy, will inevitably arrive at conclusions that are absurd and reactionary both in the economic and political sense.[52]

Only one Marxist thinker among Lenin's contemporaries was prepared to consider the possibility that the Russian Revolution might lead not only to the overthrow of absolutism but to socialism, provided it was joined by the revolutionary movement in the advanced West: Trotsky.

His original position on the nature of the Russian Revolution was impeccably orthodox. In August 1904 he had written:

Only in the free Russia of the future, in which we (and not for example Messrs So-
cialist-Revolutionaries) will obviously be obliged to play the role of opposition and
not government, will enable the class struggle to develop to its full extent. But so that
the struggle of the proletariat in this "free Russia," under the leadership of Social
Democracy, may prepare the struggle for the dictatorship of the class, we must even
today oppose the proletariat to all institutions, permanent and temporary, of the class
which will tomorrow take the helm of the state.[53]

Yet, in little over a year, Trotsky had moved to a position far beyond what Marx
could possibly have envisaged in 1850, or what his fellow revolutionaries who had
revived the term "permanent revolution" did envisage in 1905. How?

TROTSKY: PERMANENT REVOLUTION RELOADED

Trotsky's own writings suggest that he had formulated his version of permanent revolution before the general strike and formation of the St. Petersburg Soviet in October 1905. In a 1919 preface to *Results and Prospects* he wrote that the pamphlet
was "conceived in its fundamental lines already in 1904."[54] In a letter from 1921 he
recalled the divisions that opened up among Mensheviks and Bolshevik leaders in
the soviet following the defeat of the strike. Even those Mensheviks who did not
move sharply to the right "refused to accept the theory of permanent revolution,"
which brought Trotsky closer to the Bolshevik group: "Although it, too, did not accept 'permanent revolution,' it stood firm against the penitential howling of Menshevism."[55] In his autobiography, written in 1929, Trotsky recalled his reaction to
the general strike itself: "The revolutionary leadership of the proletariat revealed itself
as an incontrovertible fact. I felt that the theory of permanent revolution had withstood its first test successfully. Revolution was obviously opening up to the proletariat
the prospect of seizing the power."[56] If these recollections are accurate, then Trotsky
must have arrived at his conception very soon before the strike began on October 9,
as there is no reference to it in his writings of 1905 prior to then. The first reference
occurs in an article from November in which he actually uses Lenin's preferred term:

Overcoming the mighty resistance of the autocratic state and the conscious inactivity
of the bourgeoisie, the working class of Russia has developed into an organized fighting
force without precedent. There is no stage of the bourgeois revolution at which this
fighting force, driven forward by the steel logic of class interests, could be appeased.
Uninterrupted revolution is becoming the law of self-preservation of the proletariat.[57]

Trotsky seems to have rapidly moved to his version of permanent revolution during the course of 1905. His initial position was essentially that common to the center
and left of the Second International, stressing the necessity for the proletariat to
play the leading role in the Russian bourgeois revolution. If anything distinguished
his position at this stage it was a particular emphasis on the centrality of the urban
areas in the struggle, a key theme of "Up to the Ninth of January," written toward
the end of 1904: "Above all else, we must clearly understand that the *main arena of*

events will be the city."[58] Decades later Trotsky claimed for tactical reasons that his conception of permanent revolution was the same as that used by Marx in 1850 and then by some of his contemporaries, particularly Mehring and Luxemburg.[59] In fact, two other figures were most responsible for Trotsky's radicalization of the concept and for rendering it quite different from that of anyone else in the Marxist tradition: Parvus and Kautsky.

Trotsky had a close intellectual and political partnership with Parvus during the latter half of 1904 and all through 1905. Parvus had recognized affinities with his own work in Trotsky's "Up to the Ninth of January" and wrote a preface for the first edition, which appeared early in 1905. Yet as Cliff notes, Parvus stood at this time in advance of Trotsky, in a relationship of teacher to pupil, as any honest comparison of his preface with Trotsky's article reveals.[60] In particular, Trotsky seems to have been influenced by what, in comparison to his own work at this time, was the far greater historical depth of Parvus's work, particularly in relation to the origins of the Russia state and, later, to the emergence of capitalism in Russia:

> ... during the precapitalist period in Russia the cities developed more along the lines of China than in accordance with the European pattern. They were administrative centers with a purely bureaucratic character and did not have the slightest political significance; in economic terms they were merely political bazaars for the surrounding gentry and peasantry. Their development had hardly progressed at all when it was interrupted by the capitalist process, which began to create cities in its own pattern, that is, factory cities and centers of world commerce. The result is that, in Russia, we have a capitalist bourgeoisie but not the intermediate bourgeoisie from whom political democracy in Western Europe emerged and upon whom it depended.

The latter point concerning revolutionary agency was of extreme importance. Parvus rightly rejected the notion that large-scale capitalists themselves had ever been revolutionary, but saw that previously the lower levels of the economic class, those closest to the petty bourgeoisie, had acted as a revolutionary force. In addition to its fear of the working class, the weakness of the Russian bourgeoisie as a historical latecomer was that it did not have this more plebeian wing to act as a stimulus and support for its "noneconomic" element. These consisted of either "the liberal professions ... those strata that stand apart from the relations of production" or those groups that were only beginning to be classified in Germany as the New Middle Class—"the technical and commercial personnel of capitalist industry and trade and the corresponding branches of industry such as insurance companies, banks, and so forth." The former had been important as a component of revolutionary movements between 1789 and 1848, and the latter would become an equally important component of revolutionary movements later in the twentieth century; but in the contemporary Russian context, Parvus pointed to their fragmentation and vacillation: "These diverse elements are incapable of producing their own class program, with the result that their political sympathies and antipathies endlessly waver between the revolutionism of the proletariat and the conservatism of the capitalists."[61] But why was the Russian proletariat so prone to "revolutionism"? Parvus offers the beginning of an explanation in his comments on the formation of "factory cities and centers of world trade":

> The very same pattern that hindered the development of petty-bourgeois democracy served to benefit the class consciousness of the proletariat in Russia, namely, the weak development of the handicraft form of production. The proletariat was immediately concentrated in the factories.[62]

Until the end of his life Trotsky continued to pay homage to the influence that Parvus exercised over him during this period. But, like everyone else apart from Trotsky himself, Parvus never "crossed the Rubicon," to arrive at the idea of a socialist outcome to the Russian Revolution.[63] As Trotsky wrote of Parvus's position during the 1905 Revolution: "His prognosis indicated, therefore, not the transformation of the democratic revolution into the socialist revolution but only the establishment in Russia of a regime of workers' democracy of the Australian type, where on the basis of a farmers' system there arose for the first time a labor government which did not go beyond the framework of a bourgeois state." Trotsky rejected this comparison (the only one available to Parvus at the time) on the grounds that Australia had developed within a capitalist framework from the start, that the government was based on a relatively privileged working class, and that neither of these conditions applied to Russia.[64]

Kautsky's *general* theoretical influence on Trotsky was great, as it was on most Marxists, at least until the end of the first decade of the twentieth century.[65] "Kautsky was undoubtedly the foremost theoretician of the Second International," wrote Trotsky in 1919, "and for the better part of his conscious life he represented and gave generalised expression to the *best* aspects of the Second International."[66] Kautsky's *specific* theoretical influence on Trotsky's version of permanent revolution seems to have been through two texts, one published before Trotsky had begun the process of rethinking the concept, the other after Trotsky had completed it but before he published a detailed presentation of his conclusions: in the latter case Kautsky was mainly responsible for deepening the historical and sociological foundations of Trotsky's argument. In the first text, "Revolutionary Questions," from November 1904, Kautsky argues the widely accepted case that a revolution in Western Europe would have a detonative effect in the eastern part of the continent:

> The political rule of the proletariat in Western Europe would offer to the proletariat of Eastern Europe the possibility of shortening the stages of its development and artificially introducing socialist arrangements by imitating the German example. Society as a whole cannot artificially leap over particular stages of development, but the backward development of some of its particular constituent parts can indeed be accelerated by the proximity of more advanced parts.

He then goes on to make the bolder and less conventional argument, in effect allowing that the spatial priority of influence might be reversed: "They [the Eastern

European nations] may even come to the foreground because they are not hindered by the ballast of traditions that the older nations have to drag along. . . . That *can* happen. But as we already said, we have gone beyond the field of discernible *necessity* and are at present considering only *possibilities*."[67]

The second text by Kautsky to have influenced Trotsky was an article of February 1906, "The American Worker," where the former attempts to establish the circumstances in which a working class can emerge without being "hindered" by "tradition." Here, Kautsky tried to establish, for the first time since the less developed remarks by Parvus the previous year, not only why the working class in Russia *is* politically militant but also why it is *more* politically militant than those areas of the West that are the most developed in capitalist terms:

> There are two states, which face each other as extremes, in which one of the two elements of [the capitalist] mode of production is disproportionately strong, i.e., stronger than it should be according to its level of development: *in America, the capitalist class; in Russia, the working class*. . . . It is certainly a peculiar phenomenon that the Russian proletariat [of all national sections of the working class] should show us our future—as far as, not the organization of capital, but the rebellion of the working class is concerned—because Russia is, of all the great states of the capitalist world, the most backward. This seems to contradict the materialist conception of history, according to which economic development constitutes the basis of politics. But in fact it only contradicts that kind of historical materialism of which our opponents and critics accuse us, by which they understand a *ready-to-hand model*, and not a *method of inquiry*.[68]

Kautsky then develops his argument with reference to the nature of the Russian absolutist state—again deepening the insights of Parvus. Here his comparison is not a more advanced state like the United States, but a more backward one: Turkey. In the case of both Russia and Turkey the state grew militarily, bureaucratically, and fiscally in order to compete in geopolitical terms with the Western European powers, accruing a massive national debt in both cases. There was, however, a major difference between Turkey and Russia:

> Turkey has become so helpless that it must inevitably submit to the dictate of foreigners. It exists as an independent state only thanks to the jealousy of the different powers, none of which can have the whole booty alone. They all agree, however, in plundering this unlucky land and forcing their own products onto it, thus hindering the development of any kind of local industry. As a result of this we see in the Turkish economy, as in the Russian, a progressive decay of agriculture and a growth in the number of proletarians, but in Turkey these proletarians can find no employment in capitalist industry. . . . But Russia was not as helpless as Turkey.

Russia had access to capital from the West where capitalists were looking for new areas of investment and provided the basis for a historically unprecedented process of industrialization: "This transformed a great part of the Russian proletarians from lumpen proletarians or indigent small peasants into wage-workers, from timid and servile beggars into decided revolutionary fighters. But this growth of a strong fighting proletariat was not paralleled by the growth of a similarly strong Russian capitalist class."The proletariat has the possibility of uniting all the most vital national forces around it in the struggle against foreign-based capital and the absolutist state that protects it: "In this way, the Russian workers are able to exert a strong political influence, and the struggle for liberation of the land from the strangling octopus of absolutism has become a duel between the Czar and the working class; a duel in which the peasants provide an indispensable assistance, but in which they can by no means play a leading role."[69] The nature of the Russian state helped condition the nature of the working-class response, as did the nature of the American state, but in the opposite direction:

> The Russian worker developed in a state which united the barbarism of Asiatic despotism with the means of coercion developed by modern absolutism in the eighteenth century: it is within this framework that the capitalist mode of production developed in Russia. As soon as the proletariat began to move, it immediately came across almost insuperable obstacles in every direction, experienced in the most painful way the insanity of the political situation, learned to hate it, and felt compelled to fight against it. It was impossible to attempt to reform this situation; the only possible course was a complete revolution of the established order. Thus, the Russian worker developed as an instinctive revolutionary, who enthusiastically adopted conscious revolutionary thought because only it stated in a clearer and more precise way what he had already obscurely felt and suspected. And he found a broad stratum of intellectuals which, like him, suffered under existing conditions; like him, were mostly condemned to live a wretched existence; like him, could only exist in a constant struggle against the existing order of things; and, like him, could only hope of deliverance through complete revolution.... Things are different in America. If Russia is the most unfree, America is the freest country of the capitalist world.... All the conditions were lacking that could suggest to the exploited classes the necessity of a decisive transformation of the state institutions; even the exploited classes themselves, as a mass phenomenon, were missing. And the mentality arising from these conditions has continued to exist to the present day. It is true that, in the meantime, a strong proletariat and the strongest capitalist class in the world have appeared in the United States, but, in spite of that, to this day the mass of the people can be divided, rather than between capitalists and proletarians, between those who are already capitalists, and those who want to become such.... The America worker has not been, up till now, forced to inquire into and oppose the *totality* of the existing social order.[70]

Trotsky's appreciation of these texts was partly methodological, partly substantive. In the first substantial work to present his version of permanent revolution, *Results and Prospects*, written in prison during 1906 following the suppression of the revolution, he enthusiastically cited Kautsky's defense of Marxism in "The American Worker" as a "method of inquiry": "We particularly recommend these lines to our Russian Marxists, who replace independent analysis of social relations by deductions from texts, selected to serve every occasion in life."[71] Trotsky's own formulation makes essentially the same point: "Marxism is above all a method of analysis—not analysis of texts, but analysis of social relations."[72] But Trotsky also relies on the same article to support his argument for why the working class was the dominant force in the Russian Revolution with the peasantry playing only play a subordinate role.[73]

Trotsky's expectations of the working class were not, however, derived solely from the theoretical insights gained from his Marxist teachers: at least as important was the practical influence of the 1905 revolution itself. Unlike Lenin, Trotsky was deeply involved in the process almost from the beginning: the revolution began in January; Trotsky returned to Russia in February; Lenin did not return until November. Most importantly, from October Trotsky played a leading role as chair of the most striking organizational innovation produced by the working class during the revolution: the St. Petersburg Soviet. In his speech to the court following the defeat of the revolution, Trotsky described the Soviet as "the organ of self-government of the revolutionary masses," "a new historical power" hitherto unknown.[74] No one had expected this development—certainly not the Bolsheviks who were initially suspicious of the soviet as a body not subject to party control—and it was only later that the Paris Commune came to be seen as a historical precursor. Trotsky argues that Kautsky's case for the "possibility" of a revolution breaking out in Russia in advance of the West in "Revolutionary Questions" had been rendered more likely by events:

> Later on, the Russian proletariat revealed a colossal strength, unexpected by the Russian Social-Democrats even in their most optimistic moods. The course of the Russian Revolution was decided, so far as its fundamental features were concerned. What two or three years ago was or seemed *possible*, approached to the *probable*, and everything points to the fact that it is on the brink of becoming *inevitable*.[75]

The very demonstration of working-class creativity and power demonstrated by the soviet and the general strike seems to have confirmed in Trotsky the view that it could indeed advance toward socialism, but only under one condition, the identification of which represents his most original contribution to these discussions: the international dimension.

It is in this context that Trotsky's differences with Kautsky are most marked. Here, in an article written in December at the climax of the 1905 revolution, the latter claimed that the growing interconnectedness of the world system would prevent external intervention in the Russian Revolution, in contrast with earlier bourgeois revolutions:

> During the seventeenth century, international intercourse was still so limited that the English Revolution remained a purely local event that found no echo in the remainder of Europe. It was not foreign wars but the long drawn-out civil war arising from the great power of resistance of the landed nobility that created the revolutionary military domination and finally led to the dictatorship of the victorious general, Cromwell. The end of the eighteenth century already found a more developed intercourse between European nations, and the French Revolution convulsed all Europe; but its liberating efforts found only a weak echo. The convulsion was a result of the war that in France led to the rise of a military regime and the empire of the victorious general, Napoleon. Now, at the beginning of the twentieth century, international relations have

become so close that the beginning of the revolution in Russia was enough to awaken an enthusiastic response in the proletariat of the whole world, to quicken the tempo of the class struggle, and to shake the neighboring empire of Austria to its foundations. As a consequence, any *coalition* of European powers against the revolution, such as took place in 1793, is inconceivable.[76]

It is true that the Russian Revolution did not provoke external intervention, but only because there was no need, the power of the tsarist state still being sufficient for the purpose of counterrevolution at this point; the experience of the Russian Revolution of 1917 was to demonstrate how extraordinarily complacent Kautsky was in relation to this threat. Here, the mechanistic aspects of his thought, his lack of dialectics, genuinely point toward his later collapse in a way that most of the passages from his work quoted in this chapter do not. Adopting his guise as arch-proponent of the inevitability of socialism, Kautsky assumes that working-class pressure against intervention would invariably be successful rather than involve a contest that, despite some successes for the labor movement (for example, the British "Hands of Russia" campaign of 1919), the bourgeoisie won to the extent that they were able to intervene in the Russian Civil War. But there is a greater problem with Kautsky's formulation than excessive optimism. His entire perspective on "the international" envisages a collection of national states in which an internal event in one, like a revolution, has an external effect on others by way of provoking opposition or support: there is no sense here that the international capitalist system has a collective reality of its own, or that individual revolutions are merely national manifestations of the general crisis of that system. Typically, Luxemburg had a far greater sense of how both bourgeois and proletarian revolutions since 1789 ("modern revolutions") were uncontainable within the framework of individual states:

> Nothing is more foolish and absurd than wanting to regard modern revolutions as national incidents, as events that display all their force only within the borders of the state in question and exert only a more or less weak influence on the "neighboring states" according to their "internal situation." Bourgeois society, capitalism, is an international, *world* form of human society. There are not as many bourgeois societies, as many capitalisms, as there are modern states or nations, but only *one* international bourgeois society, only *one* capitalism, and the apparently isolated, independent existence of particular states within their state frontiers, alongside the single and inseparable world economy, is only one of the contradictions of capitalism. That is why all the modern revolutions are also at bottom *international* revolutions. They are also one and the same violent bourgeois revolution, which took place in different acts over the whole of Europe between 1789 and 1848 and established modern bourgeois rule *on an international basis.*[77]

While this captures an important aspect of any revolution occurring in Russia and points east in the early twentieth century, Luxemburg still tends to retain the distinction between bourgeois and proletarian revolutions. It is this that Trotsky began to question, asking, "Is it inevitable that the proletarian dictatorship should be shattered against the barriers of the bourgeois revolution, or is it possible that in the given *world-historical* conditions, it may discover before it the prospect of victory on breaking through those barriers?"[78] What were these world-historical conditions? The key issue is the outcome of a bourgeois revolution that occurs in the period when capitalist laws of motion already operate across the world economy as a whole: "Imposing its own type of economy and its own relations on all countries, capitalism has transformed the entire world into a single economic and political organism."[79] The consolidation of capitalism as a global system permeates every aspect of Trotsky's argument, beginning with his discussion of the nature of the Russian Revolution:

> So far as its direct and indirect tasks are concerned, the Russian revolution is a "bourgeois" revolution because it sets out to liberate bourgeois society from the chains and fetters of absolutism and feudal ownership. But the principal driving force of the Russian revolution is the proletariat, and that is why, so far as its method is concerned, it is a proletarian revolution. Many pedants, who insist on determining the historical role of the proletariat by means of arithmetical or statistical calculations, or establishing it by means of formal historical analogies, have shown themselves incapable of digesting this contradiction. They see the bourgeoisie as the providence-sent leader of the Russian revolution. They try to wrap the proletariat—which, in fact, marched at the head of events at all stages of the revolutionary rising [1905]—in the swaddling-clothes of their own theoretical immaturity. For such pedants, the history of one capitalist nation repeats the history of another, with, of course, certain more or less important divergences. Today they fail to see the unified process of world capitalist development which swallows up all the countries that lie in its path and which creates, out of the national and general exigencies of capitalism, an amalgam whose nature cannot be understood by the application of historical clichés, but only by materialist analysis.[80]

Trotsky occasionally came close to suggesting that the victory of the Russian Revolution on a socialist basis was preordained ("becoming *inevitable*"); but in more considered passages he rightly highlighted that this was dependent on what happened after the overthrow of the absolutist regime. If the political representatives of the proletariat took state power, should they then hand it over to representatives of the bourgeois classes that had been unable and unwilling to do so? He argued that such a self-denying ordinance should be rejected by socialists:

> To imagine that it is the business of Social-Democrats to enter a provisional government and lead it during the period of revolutionary-democratic reforms, fighting for them to have a most radical character, and relying for this purpose upon the organized proletariat—and then, after the democratic programme has been carried out, to leave the edifice they have constructed so as to make way for the bourgeois parties and themselves go into opposition, thus opening up a period of parliamentary politics, is to imagine the thing in a way that would compromise the very idea of a workers' government. This is not because it is inadmissible "in principle"—putting the question in this abstract form is devoid of meaning—but because it is absolutely unreal, it is utopianism of the worst sort—a sort of revolutionary-philistine utopianism.[81]

For Trotsky, there were two reasons why a Social Democratic government would have to take more radical action than allowed for by the formula of "bourgeois-democratic" revolution. One was the relationship between that government and the Russian working class. As he put it: "Social Democrats cannot enter a revolutionary government, giving the workers in advance an undertaking not to *give way* on the minimum program and at the same time promising the bourgeoisie not to *go beyond* it."[82] To take the most obvious example: what attitude should a Social Democratic government take if workers began to take over factories, expropriate the owners, and run the enterprises themselves? Such actions would clearly be in breach of capitalist property relations—in other words they would go beyond the supposedly bourgeois limits of the revolution. If the government acted to restore the previous owners, it would be betraying its own supporters, thus weakening its social base and encouraging the bourgeoisie to resist any further attempts to dispossess them. "'Self-limitation' by a workers' government would mean nothing other than the betrayal of the interests of the unemployed and strikers—more, of the whole proletariat—in the name of the establishment of a republic."[83] But if the government did not restore the former owners and instead supported working-class seizures of private property, then it would openly be declaring itself in conflict with capitalism. Such a conflict would not be confined to the native bourgeoisie, since so much of Russian capital was foreign in origin, although ruling-class solidarity against the threat of revolution would impel other states to intervene regardless of any actual investments their national capitals might have had in Russia.

The inevitability of intervention is the second reason why the Russian Revolution would be forced to move in a socialist direction.

> Should the Russian proletariat find itself in power, if only as the result of a temporary conjuncture of circumstances in our bourgeois revolution, it will encounter the organized hostility of world reaction, and on the other hand will find a readiness on the part of the world proletariat to give organized support. Left to its own resources, the working class of Russia will inevitably be crushed by the counter-revolution the moment the peasantry turns its back on it. It will have no alternative but to link the fate of its political rule, and, hence, the fate of the whole Russian revolution, with the fate of the socialist revolution in Europe. That colossal state-political power given it by a temporary conjuncture of circumstances in the Russian bourgeois revolution it will cast into the scales of the class struggle of the entire capitalist world.[84]

The Russian Revolution will both act as an inspiration to the global working class and exert a powerful claim on their solidarity, the most effective form of which would be other working-class revolutions in those states where the bourgeois revolution was already a matter of history. The implications of this argument (which Trotsky made more explicit in later writings) are that these revolutions would not only be undertaken in support of the Russian Revolution, but also because workers in other countries would also seek to replicate its socialist aims on their own behalf. Revolutions cannot be initiated acts of will, however, they require in addition a series of crises, the existence of which outside of Russia was itself an indication of the way in which the world system formed a totality.

The final issue to be discussed by Trotsky was the fundamental one of Russia's socioeconomic backwardness. It was this reality, emphasized most strongly among his contemporaries by Lenin, that was the key factor in preventing any of them from accepting that socialism was possible in Russia, fixated as they were on Russia as an individual nation. Trotsky was aware of the problem that would face any Social Democratic government on the day after seizing power: "The revolutionary authorities will be confronted with the objective problems of socialism, but the solution of these problems will, at a certain stage, be prevented by the country's economic backwardness. There is no way out from this contradiction within the framework of a national revolution."[85] The solution therefore lay outside this framework, since "the objective pre-requisites for a socialist revolution have already been created by the economic development of the advanced capitalist countries."[86] The socialist revolution in the West was therefore necessary for the Russian Revolution to survive on a socialist basis, not only as a source of class solidarity in the struggle against counterrevolution—although this would be the most immediate requirement—but also as the mechanism that would make available to the new regime the financial, technological, and scientific resources that would enable it to overcome the inheritance of tsarist backwardness. Without these twin supports the Russian Revolution would, at best, start and finish as a bourgeois revolution: "If the proletariat is overthrown by a coalition of bourgeois classes, including the peasantry whom the proletariat itself has liberated, then the revolution will retain its limited bourgeois character. But if the proletariat succeeds in using all means to achieve its own political hegemony and thereby breaks out of the national confines of the Russian revolution, then that revolution could become the prologue to a world socialist revolution."[87]

Although one of the boldest innovations in historical materialism since the death of Marx himself—only Lenin's model of the revolutionary party really stands comparison—Trotsky's version of permanent revolution was essentially a strategic rather than a theoretical conception. His awareness of the international context in which the Russian Revolution would take place enabled him to envisage a different outcome than any of his peers; but he no more than they gave any detailed answer to the question of why the Russian working class displayed the militancy that would enable it to begin the process of international socialist revolution in these apparently unpropitious conditions. The nearest Trotsky came to providing an answer is in this passage from *1905*, in which he distills the work of Parvus and Kautsky into one aspect of what he called "the peculiarities of Russian development":

> When English or French capital, the historical coagulate of many centuries, appears in the steppes of the Donets Basin, it cannot release the same social forces, relations, and passions which once went into its own formation. It does not repeat on the new territory the development which it has already completed, but starts from the point at which it has arrived on its own ground. Around the machines which it has transported

across the seas and the customs barriers, it immediately, without any intermediate stages whatever, concentrates the masses of a new proletariat, and into this class it instills the revolutionary energy of all the past generations of the bourgeoisie—an energy which in Europe has by now become stagnant.[88]

It would be over twenty years before Trotsky provided the missing theoretical underpinning for his strategy of permanent revolution, in the form of the "law" of uneven and combined development.[89] As he left the subject toward the end of the first decade of the twentieth century, however, there was one aspect in which conception of the bourgeois revolution was narrower and less developed than that of Lenin: in both form and content it is almost entirely based on the French Revolution. His discussion moves from the success of 1789 in France, through to the failure of 1848 in Germany, to the prevision of future success revealed by 1905 in Russia.[90] He did not consider at this stage the very different way in which the German, Italian, or Japanese revolutions were eventually accomplished in the 1860s. The point, of which Lenin was only too aware, was that there might be another route to bourgeois revolution than through the agency of the working class, if not in Russia, then perhaps in other backward countries. The nearest Trotsky comes to considering this question is in his remarks on the Turkish Revolution that began in 1908:

> In Russia it was the proletariat that came forward as the chief fighter for the revolution. In Turkey, however . . . industry exists only in embryonic form, and so the proletariat is small in numbers and weak. The most highly educated elements of the Turkish intelligentsia, such as teachers, engineers, and so on, being able to find little scope for their talents in schools and factories, have become army officers. Many of them have studied in Western European countries and become familiar with the regime that exists there—only, on their return home, to come up against the ignorance and poverty of the Turkish soldier and the debased conditions of the state. This has filled them with bitterness; and so the officer corps has become the focus of discontent and rebelliousness.[91]

The absence of any further discussion of "revolution from above" is mitigated by the fact that Trotsky was at this point focused almost entirely on Russia and did not consider the wider implications of his version of permanent revolution. He was of course conscious of the way in which the Western bourgeoisie helped maintain precapitalist states: "It has avidly clung to every reactionary power without questioning its origins." The only criterion for support that any regime required was that it genuinely represented some effective form of social power, thus excluding, for example, the emperor of China, but including various Arab emirates: "In this way, the world's bourgeoisie has made the stability of its state system deeply dependent on the unstable pre-bourgeois bulwarks of reaction."[92] And in this respect there were comparisons with the way in which the West tolerated the continued existence of absolutism in Russia:

> The European financial bourgeoisie, whose political influence in parliamentary countries has grown uninterruptedly and has forced the commercial and industrial

capitalists into the background, converted, it is true, the Tsarist Government into its vassal; but it did not and could not desire to become a component part of the bourgeois opposition within Russia. . . . The European Stock Exchange was even directly interested in the maintenance of absolutism, for no other government could guarantee such usurious interest.[93]

Eventually Trotsky would make one of the most profound contributions to the Marxist understanding of revolution in the colonial and semicolonial world, but it would take the eventual success, then ultimate decline of the Russian Revolution, to provide the stimulus for his extension and theoretical grounding of permanent revolution.

Lenin and Trotsky Reconciled?

The second Russian Revolution began on February 23, 1917. Five days later the tsarist regime fell, to be replaced by a Provisional Government dominated by bourgeois politicians. On April 3, Lenin arrived at the Finland Station in St. Petersburg. Nothing he had written or said prior to that point fully prepared his fellow Bolsheviks, let alone the wider socialist movement, for the position that he now took. The last article that he wrote before leaving exile in Switzerland to return to Russia was notably cautious, emphasizing the backwardness, not only of Russian economy and society, but also—perhaps more unexpectedly—of the Russian labor movement, and still referring to the revolution then under way as bourgeois-democratic in nature:

> To the Russian proletariat has fallen the great honor of *beginning* the series of revolutions which the imperialist war has made an objective inevitability. But the idea that the Russian proletariat is the chosen revolutionary proletariat among the workers of the world is absolutely alien to us. We know perfectly well that the proletariat of Russia is less organized, less prepared and less class-conscious than the proletariat of other countries. It is not its special qualities, but rather the special conjuncture of historical circumstances that *for a certain, perhaps very short, time* has made the proletariat of Russia the vanguard of the revolutionary proletariat of the whole world. Russia is a peasant country, one of the most backward of European countries. Socialism *cannot* triumph there *directly* and *immediately*. But the peasant character of the country, the vast reserve of land in the hands of the nobility, *may*, to judge from the experience of 1905, give tremendous sweep to the bourgeois-democratic revolution in Russia and *may* make our revolution the *prologue* to the world socialist revolution, a *step* toward it.[94]

Apart from the potential link between the Russian Revolution and the world socialist revolution, this was not the perspective from which Lenin addressed his listeners and readers after stepping out of the sealed train that had borne him through Germany. Instead, he called on the party to prepare for the overthrow of the Provisional Government and, in effect, for the socialist revolution. The Menshevik Nikolai Sukhanov recalled hearing Lenin's two-hour speech to a mainly Bolshevik audience on the night of April 3: "Of how . . . his whole conception was to be reconciled with the elementary conceptions of Marxism (the only thing Lenin did not dissociate himself from in his speech)—not a syllable was said. Everything touching on what had hitherto been called scientific socialism Lenin ignored just as completely as he destroyed the foundations of the current Social-Democratic programme and tactics." And it was not only Sukhanov who was astonished—so too were most Bolsheviks. At a meeting of all the Social Democratic factions the next day, he noted the reaction of the audience: "They weren't only stunned: each new word of Lenin's filled them with indignation."[95] In the days and weeks that followed, Lenin was variously accused of being out of touch with Russian realities, with having abandoned Marxism for anarchism or syndicalism, or of simply having lost his mind. Yet the most obvious accusation that could have been made, although no one seems to have done so at the time, was that Lenin had adopted the position of permanent revolution for which Trotsky had argued during the 1905 Revolution.

During 1919, at the height of the Russian Civil War, Trotsky, a Bolshevik since July 1917 and now the People's Commissar for Military Affairs and commander in chief of the Red Army, republished *Results and Prospect* with a new preface in which he summarized the pattern of events his work had expected to take place:

> The Revolution, having begun as a bourgeois revolution as regards its main tasks, will soon call forth powerful class conflicts and will gain final victory only by transferring power to the only class capable of standing at the head of the oppressed masses, namely, to the proletariat. Once in power, the proletariat not only will not want, but will not be able to limit itself to a bourgeois democratic programme. It will be able to carry through the Revolution to the end only in the event of the Russian Revolution being converted into a Revolution of the European proletariat. . . . But should Europe remain inert the bourgeois counter-revolution will not tolerate the government of the toiling masses in Russia and will throw the country back—far back from the democratic workers' and peasants' republic. Therefore, having won power, the proletariat cannot keep within the limits of bourgeois democracy. It must adopt the tactics of *permanent revolution*, i.e., must destroy the barriers between the minimum and maximum programme of social democracy, go over to more and more radical social reforms and seek direct and immediate support in revolution in Western Europe.

Trotsky could perhaps be forgiven for expressing the degree of satisfaction he did at the accuracy of his predictions:

> The fact that it is possible for us now to re-issue without alteration this pamphlet written in 1906 and conceived in its fundamental lines already in 1904, is sufficient proof that Marxist theory is not on the side of the Menshevik substitutes for bourgeois democracy but on the side of the party which actually carries out the dictatorship of the working class. The final test of a theory is experience. Irrefutable proof of our having correctly applied Marxist theory is given by the fact that the events in which we are now participating, and even our methods of participation in them, were foreseen in their fundamental lines some fifteen years ago.[96]

Trotsky later claimed that, despite their earlier differences, Lenin had come to see the correctness of his version of permanent revolution, just as he had come to see the correctness of Lenin's model of the revolutionary party. "I consider that my assessment of the motive forces of the revolution was unreservedly correct," he wrote in letter late in 1921, "but that the conclusions I drew from it with regard to both fractions [Bolsheviks and Mensheviks] were unreservedly incorrect."[97] If Lenin had not shifted his position to that of Trotsky, he would have been unable to "rearm" the party during the course of 1917, with damaging consequences for the revolution. Trotsky later wrote in the diary he kept during his last exile:

> Had I not been present in 1917 in Petersburg, the October Revolution would still have taken place—*on the condition that Lenin was present and in command.* If neither Lenin nor I had been present in Petersburg, there would have been no October Revolution: the leadership of the Bolshevik Party would have prevented it from occurring—of this I have not the slightest doubt! If Lenin had not been in Petersburg, I doubt whether I could have managed to conquer the resistance of the Bolshevik leaders. The struggle with "Trotskyism" (i.e., with the proletarian revolution) would have commenced in May, 1917, and the outcome of the revolution would have been in question.[98]

In his autobiography Trotsky cited as evidence of their alignment an article he wrote in the Bolshevik press on September 7, 1917, in which he counterposed permanent revolution to the "permanent slaughter" being prepared by imperialism: "How could Lenin have tolerated my heretical propaganda in silence?" More importantly, he noted that at the meeting of the Petrograd committee on November 1, Lenin had declared that since Trotsky had decisively rejected the possibility of reuniting with the Mensheviks, "there had been no better Bolshevik." From these remarks Trotsky concluded that Lenin "proved very clearly—and not for the first time, either—that it had not been the theory of permanent revolution that had separated us, but the narrower, though very important question of the attitude towards Menshevism." His other evidence was the verbal testimony of Adolph Joffe, who told Trotsky that in a conversation with Lenin in 1919, the latter had said, "Yes, Trotsky proved to be right," a claim that Joffe repeated in his suicide note on November 16, 1927.[99]

Against this, a seemingly endless succession of Stalinists, beginning with the general secretary himself in 1924, repeated that Lenin did not change his position on the nature of the Russian Revolution during 1917 and that, furthermore, his unchanged perspective proved to be correct as a bourgeois revolution in February was "uninterruptedly" followed by a socialist revolution in October. There is support for this claim in some of Lenin's writings, particularly those from between April and June, in which we find claims such as this:

> Before the February–March revolution of *1917*, state power in Russia was in the hands of one old class, namely, the feudal landed nobility, headed by Nicholas Romanov. After the revolution, the power is in the hands of a *different* class, a new class, namely, the *bourgeoisie.* The passing of state power from one *class* to another is the

first, the principal, the basic sign of a *revolution*, both in the strictly scientific and in the practical political meaning of that term. To this extent, the bourgeois, or the bourgeois-democratic, revolution in Russia is *completed*.[100]

State power in Russia has passed into the hands of a new class, namely, the bourgeoisie and landowners who had become bourgeois. To this extent the bourgeois-democratic revolution in Russia is complete.[101]

But the context of this and other articles from these months has to be recalled. Statements to the effect that the bourgeois revolution had been accomplished were intended to make the dramatic turn in policy involved in abandoning the "democratic dictatorship of the proletariat and peasantry" more acceptable to Bolsheviks by suggesting that the objectives of their existing program had been achieved. Even so, Lenin's political honesty and sense of reality did not allow him to claim that that this had been accomplished in anything other than a very partial—indeed, minimal sense, as is suggested by the use of the qualifying phrase, "to this extent," in both passages quoted above. The dominant theme of Lenin's writings before 1917 was that a revolutionary alliance of the proletariat and peasantry would overthrow tsarism, but that this revolution would be followed by a prolonged period of bourgeois democracy and capitalist economic development, after which a second, socialist revolution would be possible. The length of the intervening period would be impossible to determine in advance, since it would depend on the speed with which capitalist industrialization proletarianized the peasantry and several other factors, but was certainly not coincident with the seven months between February and October. Why not? For the simple reason that none of the tasks that Lenin had identified as being the goals of the bourgeois revolution—agrarian reform, destruction of the tsarist state, even a stable bourgeois democratic polity—were achieved by the February Revolution; they were only achieved or, in the case of the last, superseded, by the October Revolution.[102] Lenin's final judgment on the short-lived bourgeois regime was delivered in a speech on the fourth anniversary of the October Revolution:

> The bourgeois-democratic content of the revolution means that the social relations (system, institutions) of the country are purged of medievalism, serfdom, feudalism. What were the chief manifestations, survivals, remnants of serfdom in Russia up to 1917? The monarchy, the system of social estates, landed proprietorship and land tenure, the status of women, religion, and national oppression. Take any one of these Augean stables, which, incidentally, were left largely uncleansed by all the more advanced states when they accomplished *their* bourgeois-democratic revolutions one hundred and twenty-five, two hundred and fifty and more years ago (1649 in England); take any of these Augean stables, and you will see that we have cleansed them thoroughly. In a matter of *ten weeks*, from October 25 (November 7), 1917, to January 5, 1918, when the Constituent Assembly was dissolved, we accomplished a thousand times more in this respect than was accomplished by the bourgeois democrats and liberals (the Cadets) and by the petty-bourgeois democrats (the Mensheviks and the Socialist-Revolutionaries) *during the eight months* they were in power. . . . Take religion, or the denial of rights to women, or the oppression and inequality of the non-Russian

nationalities. These are all problems of the bourgeois-democratic revolution. The vulgar petty-bourgeois democrats talked about them for eight months. In not a *single* one of the most advanced countries in the world have these questions been *completely* settled on *bourgeois-democratic* lines. In our country they have been settled completely by the legislation of the October Revolution. We have fought and are fighting religion in earnest. We have granted *all* the non-Russian nationalities *their own* republics or autonomous regions. We in Russia no longer have the base, mean, and infamous denial of rights to women or inequality of the sexes, that disgusting survival of feudalism and medievalism, which is being renovated by the avaricious bourgeoisie and the dull-witted and frightened petty bourgeoisie in every other country in the world without exception. All this goes to make up the content of the bourgeois-democratic revolution. A hundred and fifty and two hundred and fifty years ago the progressive leaders of that revolution (or of those revolutions, if we consider each national variety of the one general type) promised to rid mankind of medieval privileges, of sex inequality, of state privileges for one religion or another (or "religious *ideas*," "the church" in general), and of national inequality. They promised, but did not keep their promises. They could not keep them, for they were hindered by their "respect"—for the "sacred right of private property." Our proletarian revolution was not afflicted with this accursed "respect" for this thrice-accursed medievalism and for the "sacred right of private property."[103]

We can therefore accept Duncan Hallas's typically careful assessment that "Lenin, in effect although not in words, adopted the Permanent Revolution perspective," so long as we understand that Lenin arrived at his conclusions independently and by a partially different route than Trotsky.[104] As Trotsky himself acknowledged, it is not clear that Lenin read *Results and Prospects* even when it was republished in 1919. Prior to then, his only exposure to the text seems to have been secondhand, in an article by Martov in which the Menshevik leader—who could otherwise have had no sympathy with Trotsky's overall argument—favorably quoted certain passages critical of the "democratic dictatorship of the proletariat and peasantry" formula.[105] There is no evidence of Lenin being familiar with any of Trotsky's other works on the subject. Lenin's acceptance of permanent revolution was therefore based on a changed assessment of the nature of the Russian Revolution that brought him to the same conclusions as Trotsky rather than because he was persuaded by Trotsky's theoretical work.

A precondition for doing so was the study that Lenin undertook of Hegel following the outbreak of the First World War and the capitulation of the overwhelming majority of the Second International to social patriotism. In his *Philosophical Notebooks*, Lenin quotes from Hegel's *Science of Logic*:

> It is said that there are no leaps in nature; and ordinary imagination, when it has to conceive an arising or passing away, thinks it has conceived them . . . when it imagines them as a gradual emergence or disappearance. But we saw that the changes of Being were in general not only a transition of one magnitude to another, but a transition from the qualitative into the quantitative, and conversely: a process of becoming other which breaks off graduality and is qualitatively other as against Existent Being.

Against this passage Lenin writes that "gradualness explains nothing without leaps" and down the side of the page: "Leaps! Breaks in gradualness. Leaps! Leaps!"[106] And later, in his marginalia to Hegel's *Lectures on the History of Philosophy*, Lenin makes a similar interjection: "What distinguishes the dialectical transition from the undialectical transition? The leap. The contradiction. The interruption of gradualness. The unity (identity) of Being and Not-Being.[107] The conclusion that Lenin famously drew from his discovery of Hegel was that the entire socialist movement post-Marx had essentially retreated to a pre-Marxist position on the dialectic. The recovery of the dialectic therefore allowed Lenin to break from stageism on a different basis from Trotsky. Trotsky's own work before 1914 was more dialectical than Lenin's, perhaps reflecting the influence on him of Antonio Labriola, in whose writings Second International Marxism attained its most sophisticated level of expression.[108] Consequently, Trotsky's own "philosophical notebooks"—written in the mid-thirties apparently as preparatory material for a polemic with Max Eastman—do not have the same sense of a major intellectual breakthrough as those of Lenin.[109] In Lenin's case, however, the political implications of his intellectual reorientation were expressed in several areas of his thought: "from the category of sum-total to the theory of the weakest link in the imperialist chain; from the interpenetration of opposites to the transformation of the democratic revolution into the socialist revolution; from the dialectical conception of causality to the refusal to define the character of the Russian revolution solely by Russia's 'economically backward base'; from the critique of vulgar evolutionism to the 'break in continuity' in 1917."[110]

Yet these notes—important in Lenin's development as a thinker as they undoubtedly are—remain at the level of philosophical abstraction. Lenin did not arrive at the notion of a "leap" over the bourgeois-democratic stage or a "break" in Russian development leading to socialism as a result of recovering the dialectical method alone: it also required the application of that method to the contemporary situation. One aspect of this was his analysis of imperialism—or rather the political implications of that analysis. Neil Harding summarizes a central conclusion of Lenin's writings on this question:

> In Lenin's perspective, the imperialist bourgeoisie now occupied the same place which the nobility and landowners had occupied *vis-à-vis* the thrusting inventive entrepreneurs in the early phases of capitalist development. Superfluous to the modern productive process, bereft of energy or ideas, their only recourse was to conserve their huge privileges by employing a battery of monopolistic practices, none of which served to develop the productive forces of mankind. They also increasingly relied upon the naked power of a vastly augmented militarized state and administrative machine to protect their narrow interests. . . . The recklessness of imperialist aggrandizement portended nothing but war upon war, the destruction of the productive forces and of man on a huge scale, and the progressive degeneration not only of the imperialist bourgeoisie but even of the proletariat of the advanced countries.[111]

In other words, the bourgeoisie had already passed the point at which it could be classified as progressive; consequently the revolution that bore its name would deliver no benefits to the proletariat or the oppressed—and Lenin's scathing comments on the fourth anniversary of October, quoted above, list in some detail precisely which benefits the Russian bourgeoisie had failed to deliver, even when presented with the gift of state power.

But the bourgeoisie was not the only class whose capacities were affected by the advent of imperialism as a stage in capitalist development: so too was the proletariat—or at least, the Western proletariat. What Lenin called "opportunism" within the working-class movement had arisen first in Britain, then in all the nations that played an oppressive role within the imperialist system. According to Lenin, the bourgeoisie were able to use the superprofits from imperialism to "bribe" trade union officials and the upper strata of the working class into compromising with or openly capitulating to the system, leading to the phenomena of opportunism, social patriotism, and reformism more generally.[112] As a proposition based solely on the supposed effects of imperialist bribery, this was dubious. What were the mechanisms through which these payments would be made? Moreover, the experience of the First World War was that the so-called labor aristocrats—the engineers of Berlin, Glasgow, and Turin, as much as Petrograd—led the great contemporary labor upheavals and later formed a major component of the industrial cadres who joined the Communist parties in Europe.[113] If Lenin's explanation for the *existence* of reformism was flawed, his account of the *effect* of reformism in retarding socialist revolution in the West was, however, more realistic. In Russia, where the hold of reformism was weaker, workers could be won more easily to a revolutionary socialist perspective. As Lenin wrote in 1920, "it was easy for Russia, in the specific and historically unique situation of 1917 to *start* the socialist revolution, but it will be more difficult for Russia than for the European countries to *continue* the revolution and bring it to its consummation."[114] In this respect there is at least a difference in emphasis between Trotsky and Lenin. For Trotsky, the peculiar nature of Russian capitalist development—not least the fact that it took place within the context of a repressive, undemocratic absolutist state—the working class tended to be more politically militant and theoretically advanced than its Western counterparts. For Lenin, the Russian working class simply had, so to speak, fewer opportunities for opportunism, give that the Russian bourgeoisie had less capacity for "bribery." Russian workers had then benefited from the brittleness of the tsarist state, which, already under pressure from the war, had shattered relatively easily at the first manifestation of working-class and peasant resistance: the former were not necessarily better organized or more class conscious than their Western counterparts, they had been provided with an opening, in the form of a collapsing archaic state, that the latter had not:

> Any person who does not shut his eyes to the facts, who is not blind, knows that we are merely repeating what we have said earlier, and what we have always said: that we do not forget the weakness of the Russian working class compared to other

contingents of the international proletariat. It was not our own will, but historical circumstances, the legacy of the tsarist regime, the flabbiness of the Russian bourgeoisie, that caused this contingent to march ahead of the other contingents of the international proletariat; it was not because we desired it, but because circumstances demanded it. We must remain at our post until the arrival of our ally, the international proletariat, which will arrive and will inevitably arrive, but which is approaching at an immeasurably slower pace than we expect or wish.[115]

There were, however, two respects in which Lenin's reasons for arguing for a socialist outcome to the revolution were similar to those of Trotsky.

One was the nature of the institutions thrown up by the workers and soldiers themselves: the soviets or workers' councils. I argued above that Trotsky only completed his version of the conception of permanent revolution after experiencing the creativity and organizational élan demonstrated by the St. Petersburg soviet at whose head he stood during the general strike; yet Trotsky wrote relatively little about the nature of soviet rule, then or subsequently, even though he resumed his role as president of the Soviet of Workers' and Soldiers' Deputies during 1917. The soviets had a far more important role for Lenin. Once the revolution had begun, he realized very quickly the full significance of the innovation represented by the soviets and the possibilities opened up by the situation of "dual power": "This fact must be grasped first and foremost: unless it is understood, we cannot advance. We must know how to supplement and amend old "formulas," for example, those of Bolshevism, for while they have been found to be correct on the whole, their concrete *realization has turned out to be* different. *Nobody* previously thought, or could have thought, of a dual power."[116] In fact, Trotsky later discerned earlier experiences of dual power—involving different social classes and institutions—in the English and the French Revolutions: "The two-power regime arises only out of irreconcilable conflicts—is possible, therefore, only in a revolutionary epoch, and constitutes one of its fundamental elements." In the English and the French Revolutions the centers of dual power opposed to the absolutist state were in territories seized through military onslaught or urban insurrection by forces opposed to the regime—but not in Russia.[117] Here, Lenin was right that no one in the Russian context had foreseen the implications of a new form of dual power in which opposed state authorities struggled for mastery, not from different territorial locations, but competing social institutions. The "democratic dictatorship of the proletariat and peasantry," which Lenin now called to be abandoned, had assumed the continued existence of a bourgeois parliament, as befitted the capitalist society over which it would rule. The emergence of an alternative form of government meant that assumption could now be dropped:

> The specific feature of the present situation in Russia is that the country is *passing* from the first stage of the revolution—which owing to the insufficient class-consciousness and organization of the proletariat, placed power in the hands of the bourgeoisie—to its *second* stage, which must place power in the hands of the proletariat and the poorest sections of the peasantry.... Not a parliamentary republic—the return to a parliamentary republic from the Soviet of Workers' Deputies would be a retro-

grade step—but a republic of Soviets of Workers', Agricultural Labors' and Peasants' Deputies throughout the country, from top to bottom.[118]

Lenin did not support the *policies* of the soviets in the early months of 1917, since these reflected their then reformist composition, itself an expression of what he regarded as the "insufficient class consciousness" of the workers and soldiers at this point of the revolution. Instead he argued for the importance of the soviet *form* of government, which, given revolutionary class consciousness, could act as the democratic mechanism with which to overthrow and then replace the existing state. Typically, having arrived at these conclusions, Lenin sought theoretical justification in the writings of his Marxist teachers, and finding that the critique of the state was present in the later writings of Marx and Engels, notably on the Paris Commune and the origins of the family, but that these insights had been ignored or dismissed by the guardians of Social Democratic orthodoxy, just as surely as they had ignored or dismissed the Hegelian dialectic. In effect, the soviet was the socialist solution to the problem of the state in general and the capitalist state in particular, which had previously only been glimpsed in embryonic form in the commune. Thus, in *The State and Revolution* he writes of "the conversion of *all* citizens into workers and other employees of *one* huge 'syndicate'—the whole state—and the complete subordination of the entire work of this syndicate to a genuinely democratic state, *the state of the Soviets of Workers' and Soldiers' Deputies*."[119]

The other way in which Lenin's thought was compatible with that of Trotsky was over the significance of the international setting in which in the Russian Revolution had taken place. This too represented a shift in Lenin's thought. Although always insistent on the need for proletarian internationalism, he had not previously seen the Russian bourgeois revolution as being dependent on support from other revolutions. But, ever the realist, Lenin understood that a socialist revolution was a different matter: a bourgeois republic in Russia was acceptable to the global ruling class, a socialist republic was not. No matter how important the soviets were as examples of proletarian self-emancipation, they, and the revolution that rested upon them would not survive the combination of internal bourgeois opposition and external imperialist intervention. A recurrent theme of Lenin's writings, from October 25, 1917, on, was that without revolutions in the West—whether caused by the wartime crisis, or undertaken in emulation of the Russian example or some mixture of the two—the Russian republic could not survive.[120] One example, taken from early in the revolution, will suffice here: "We are far from having completed even the transitional period from capitalism to socialism. We have never cherished the hope that we could finish it without the aid of the international proletariat. We never had any illusions on that score. . . . The final victory of socialism in a single country is of course impossible."[121] It was therefore possible to accept that a socialist revolution had been accomplished in Russia without making the same assumptions as Trotsky. In fact, Trotsky's unique perspective never achieved universal or even widespread acceptance among his fellow Bolsheviks or other Communists, even before the consolidation of Stalinism: during the debates over permanent revolution later in the twenties he was truthfully able to point out that only Manuilsky had endorsed his position.[122] Among the leading non-Russian figures, Gramsci argued that the similarity between the positions taken by Trotsky and Lenin in 1917 was essentially coincidental:

> Bronstein [Trotsky] in his memoirs recalls being told that his theory had been proved true ... fifteen years later, and replying to the epigram with another epigram. In reality his theory, as such, was good neither fifteen years earlier nor fifteen years later [neither in 1905 nor in 1930]. As happens to the obstinate ... he guessed more or less correctly; that is to say, he was right in his more general practical prediction.

Gramsci claimed that Trotsky, in contrast to Lenin, "in one way or another can be considered the political theorist of frontal attack in a period in which it only leads to defeats."[123] The one important figure in the communist movement who seems to have absorbed the implications of the Russian Revolution for the future of the bourgeois revolution was Lukács, although ironically he did so in his classic 1924 distillation of Lenin's thought, rather than with reference to Trotsky:

> For the real revolution is the dialectical transformation of the bourgeois revolution into the proletarian revolution. The undeniable historical fact that the class which led or was the beneficiary of the great bourgeois revolutions of the past becomes objectively counter-revolutionary does not mean that those objective problems on which its revolution turned have found their social solutions—that those strata of society who were vitally interested in the revolutionary solution of these problems have been satisfied. On the contrary, the bourgeoisie's recourse to counter-revolution indicates not only its hostility towards the proletariat, but at the same time the renunciation of its own revolutionary traditions. *It abandons the inheritance of its revolutionary past to the proletariat.* From now on the proletariat is the only class capable of taking the bourgeois revolution to its logical conclusion. In other words, the remaining relevant demands of the bourgeois revolution can only be realized within the framework of the proletarian revolution, and the consistent realization of these demands necessarily leads to a proletarian revolution. Thus, the proletarian revolution now means at one and the same time the realization and the supersession of the bourgeois revolution.[124]

These remarks are taken from one of the rare moments in this great work in which Lukács does not merely express but extends the thought of his subject—indeed, as we shall see in chapter 13, not even Trotsky would have gone quite so far as Lukács did at this time.

More typical of communist attitudes was the widely read handbook by two leading Bolshevik theorists, Bukharin and Preobrazhensky's *The ABC of Communism* (1920), originally drafted as a commentary on the program adopted by the Eighth Party Congress in March 1919. Commenting on differences between the new program and its predecessor, the authors note that, when the latter was adopted in 1903, "the strength of the Russian working class was extremely small": "That is why no one then imagined that it would be possible to undertake the direct overthrow of the bourgeoisie. . . . No-one then dreamed that it would be possible to realize the rule of the workers once and for all, or immediately to dispossess the bourgeoisie of its factories and workshops." Furthermore, with the partial exception of Austria, the revolution of 1905 had found a response only in the undeveloped East. According to Bukharin and Preobrazhensky, what had changed in the intervening period was that, on the one hand, industry had grown and with it the working class, and on the other, that the revolutions of 1917 had been met with an upsurge of revolutionary activity in the developed West.[125] Trotsky had, of course, not imagined or dreamed but predicted the overthrow of the bourgeoisie and the rule of the proletariat in 1905–6 on the basis of a scientific assessment. Bukharin and Preobrazhensky did not retrospectively endorse that prediction, but claimed instead that the outcome predicted had only become possible as a result of subsequent developments that had made Russia more like the West in terms of its economic and class structure. Leaving aside the massive exaggeration involved in this claim, the point is that the only real overlap with Trotsky's position is over the need for an international revolution:

> If the question arises, in what way Russia can advance to the communist system in spite of the backward condition of the country, the answer will mainly be given by pointing to the international significance of the revolution. The proletarian revolution must today be a world revolution. . . . It is plain that Russia must become involved in the movement to socialism. Her backwardness, the comparatively undeveloped state of her industry, and so on, would all be overcome if Russia were to form part of an international, or even merely a European, soviet republic.[126]

The fact that other Bolsheviks converged on this position from a different direction than Trotsky did not necessarily indicate any overall political hostility to him or his conception of permanent revolution at this stage. Preobrazhensky became a supporter of Trotsky and the leading economist of the Left Opposition. Bukharin had been opposed to Trotsky from the left on a number of issues before writing *The ABC of Communism* and was subsequently to do so from the right, at which point he did indeed criticize the concept of permanent revolution, but this was still four years in the future. Nevertheless, the positions taken by Bukharin at this time are significant, since he was the only major Bolshevik theorist other than Trotsky to use the term "permanent revolution," although he meant something significantly different by it.

In 1918, while still in the "left" phase of his political development, Bukharin had written of the international nature of the Russian Revolution: "Thus the permanent revolution in Russia is sharply transformed into a European revolution of the proletariat, armed by this same imperialist state over whose head the gleaming blade of the guillotine is already raised."[127] Michael Haynes, who quotes this passage, notes that Bukharin did not share Trotsky's analysis, only his conclusions: "Whereas Trotsky's formulation of permanent revolution, whilst starting from the world revolution, pushed the emphasis onto the way in which the internal contradictions within Russia would force the revolution outwards to survive, Bukharin placed his emphasis on the way in which the Russian Revolution would be pulled outwards by the general crisis of capitalism of which it was a part."[128] Once the possibilities for revolution had temporarily receded by 1921 and the immediate accomplishment of international socialism was therefore no longer plausible, Bukharin was therefore able, starting from the same premises, to reverse the implications of his position and endorse that of socialism in one country instead; but these debates still lay several years in the future.

THE REGRESSIONS OF ORTHODOXY

How did the remaining thinkers of the Second International regard postrevolutionary Russia? Their question, as one young Menshevik, Boris Sapir, later wrote was: "Did not the level of development of productive forces fit the country only for a bourgeois revolution?" The answer for them was self-evident and consequently the Mensheviks "looked down on what they considered a lunatic attempt to implant integral socialism in a backward land." There could only be one outcome of such "lunacy": "Bolshevism was, so to speak, a stand-in for the bourgeoisie, playing the role the bourgeoisie failed to play. With the Bolsheviks the working class would not build a socialist society but only serve as a battering ram for that historically determined staged of Russia's development, the bourgeois revolution."[129] The Mensheviks had, so to speak, a vested interest in maintaining this position; but it was widespread among all those who maintained Social Democratic orthodoxy. Take, for example, the tiny propagandist sect, the Socialist Party of Great Britain (SPGB), which simultaneously refused to support trade unions on the grounds that this could only result in mere reformist palliatives and believed that it was possible to introduce socialism by electing SPGB members to Parliament, apparently without incurring any resistance from the state apparatus. David Widgery was only slightly exaggerating when he claimed that the SPGB "[d]enounced the Russian Revolution as state-capitalist within hours of hearing of it"—in fact it took a number of months to do so, but swiftly enough to suggest that the verdict did not require a great deal of consideration.[130] In the face of communist arguments that in Russia the working class exercised state power over an economic system that was in transition to socialism:

> The Socialist Party retorted that there was no such intermediate stage of social development. It pointed out that Russia was an undeveloped country with great submedieval tracts, and capitalism had taken hold only in the small, widely separated industrial areas ... the revolutionary act was the metamorphosis from private to communist ownership; a partial change meant no change at all, since common ownership in anything less than entirety was, by definition, not common ownership. It must be either socialism or capitalism.[131]

I quote this simply because it reproduces in chemically pure form the attitudes of the Social Democratic orthodoxy from which, whatever their internal differences, the leading Bolsheviks had all broken. A more intellectually substantial although not fundamentally different position was taken by Kautsky, the very thinker who had once so influenced Trotsky in relation to the nature of the forthcoming Russian Revolution. Nevertheless, it was he who now gave perhaps the most systematic expression to the view that the accomplished revolution simply could not be anything other than capitalist: "It is only the ancient feudal landed estate which exists no more. For its abolition conditions in Russia were ripe. But they were not ripe for the abolition of capitalism."[132] Against the arguments of the Bolsheviks that the international context of the Russian Revolution meant socialism there was at least a possibility, Kautsky simply refused to consider Russia as anything other than an individual state: "The Marxists [the Mensheviks] ... were convinced that the revolution which they were expecting in Russia could do nothing but open up the way for a complete development of capitalism, and that only when the latter had attained a high degree of development would a socialist community be possible. Thus the countries of industrialized Western Europe would have to precede the countries of Eastern Europe on the road to Socialism."[133] Kautsky is being typically disingenuous here, not least by rewriting his own past. The Bolshevik Karl Radek commented on similar passages: "This honest fellow here seeks to create the impression that he had been a Menshevik, so to speak, since birth." In fact, as Radek rightly points out (and as we saw earlier in this chapter), Kautsky originally "*went even further*" than the Bolsheviks "*by estimating as possible the passing over of the Russian Revolution to a direct struggle for socialism.*"[134] More to the point, the Mensheviks whom Kautsky supported in Russia were not prepared to carry through the bourgeois revolution that they themselves declared was the only one possible:

> They are recalling that they had envisaged for a long time that the Russian Revolution could only lead to the domination of the bourgeoisie, and that it would only be capable of overthrowing feudalism. But these representatives of the bourgeoisie in the revolution betrayed the Russian Revolution to forces which did not wish to liquidate feudalism. The Mensheviks, who supported the government of Prince Lvov and prevented the peasants from liquidating big feudal land ownership, have no reason to boast about having immediately recognized the bourgeois limits of the revolution. They did not even dare to push the Russian Revolution to its bourgeois limits.[135]

More significant than Kautsky's dishonesty, however, is his intellectual incoherence. On the one hand he claimed that the proletarian revolution would be totally unlike the bourgeois revolution in form, since it would take place under conditions of democracy:

> We Social Democrats, however, are decidedly not of the opinion that what has happened in the past must always happen in the future. We have shaped our ideas of the revolution from the examples of previous bourgeois revolutions. The proletarian revolution will be accomplished under quite different conditions. The bourgeois revolutions took place in States where a despotism relying on an army isolated from the people suppressed all free popular movements; countries in which there was no freedom of the Press, no freedom of assembly, no freedom of association and no universal suffrage,

and where no real representation of the people existed. In such circumstances the struggle against the government necessarily took the form of a civil war. The modern proletariat, at least in Western Europe, will come to power in countries where a certain measure of democracy, even if it is not "pure" democracy, has been deeply rooted for decades, and where the military are no longer so isolated from the people as they used to be. It remains to be seen how the proletariat will achieve the conquest of political power where it represents the majority of the people. There is no need for us to suppose that the course of the great French Revolution will be repeated in Western Europe. If Russia today shows so many similarities to the France of 1793, that only demonstrates how close Russia is to the stage of a bourgeois revolution.[136]

On the other hand, Kautsky argues that, under capitalism, democracy will allow the working class to develop the necessary maturity for it to rule, in an analogous way to that by which the bourgeoisie prepared itself for power under feudalism—alas, the Russian working class did not have this level of maturity, although he did patronizingly suggest that in part was a consequence of Bolshevik policies since 1917 rather than a congenital fault.[137] As Bukharin pointed out, the analogy was false since the bourgeoisie and the proletariat were "*absolutely dissimilar* in respect of culture" prior to their respective revolutions. Although the bourgeoisie were politically oppressed by the feudal landowners, they were not exploited by them and, as an exploiting class in their own right, were able to develop an alternative, superior culture: "*The non-exploited bourgeoisie was able to create in the bosom of feudalism a culture higher than its enemy which it was therefore able to overthrow.*"[138] This was not the case for the working class, regardless of whether it had the right to vote or not. The regression involved in Kautsky's position is all the more extraordinary if we recall that he was the person who first drew attention to the greater level of political culture possessed by Russian workers under the absolutist state than by American workers under what was—in the northern states at least—the most democratic polity in the world.

For Kautsky, democracy had become the sole guiding principle in politics; but his was a very particular form of democracy, namely the representative form practiced in the developed capitalist states of the West. He had initially welcomed the October Revolution, while expressing his concern that the Bolsheviks might not respect democracy in this sense, which meant, in a Russian context, the Constituent Assembly. However, once it became clear that the new regime would base itself on soviet rather than parliamentary forms, Kautsky began what Salvadori Massimo calls his "ideological crusade against Bolshevism." His views on direct democracy were virtually the same as those of the open counterrevolutionary Max Weber, who also believed that direct or plebiscitary democracy would either mutate into parliamentary democracy or be replaced by what he called Caesarism.[139] Similar too was his deep hostility to the German Revolution. Germany was a country that Kautsky believed, unlike Russia, *did* possess the material basis for socialism, but he nevertheless still opposed attempts by the Spartacists to base the revolution of 1918 on the workers' councils, and thus helped to bring about its defeat.[140] In other words, Kautsky was simply opposed to all attempts at socialist revolution, no matter how advanced the countries in which they took place. In this sense his attempts to compare bourgeois and socialist revolutions were supremely pointless, since he re-garded any form of insurgency as a throwback to the French Revolution and re-jected the genuinely distinctive characteristic of proletarian revolutions—the soviet form of collective self-organization. In effect, workers could vote for the socialist revolution, but any other form of activity was either illegitimate (because it was not "democratic") or at best demonstrative. For the Pope of Marxism, as for the fundamentalists of the SPGB, the state as guarantor of capitalist social relations of production simply vanishes from their analysis, if not, alas, from the world.

In 1927 Kautsky published his would-be magnum opus, *The Materialist Concep-tion of History*, a monument to scholastic irrelevance that demonstrates in exemplary form why we will not have to give further consideration to the views of Social Democracy in the present work. In many respects Kautsky retreated to his mecha-nistic formulations of the 1880s and 1890s, but now filtered them through his later polemics with the Bolsheviks so that any earlier suggestions that historical develop-ment might be sped up by revolutionary action have been discarded. Any such action was, he claimed, doomed to failure, no matter at what point in history it took place:

> Only in a class society can it happen that a dissatisfied class, when special historical conditions give it the strength to do so, makes the attempt to create new relations of production more favourable to it, even if the conditions for the existence of these new conditions have not yet matured in the womb of the old society. When this is not the case, however, the innovations will not be lasting . . . despite all decrees and also despite all terrorism by which the attempt is made to compensate for the lack of the historical preconditions for the new relations of production. This recognition is a sturdy bulwark against all utopian fantasies.[141]

The obvious question at this point is how a revolution could take place at all if the conditions that make it possible "have not yet matured"? The equally obvious answer might be that conditions have to be considered at a global or at least inter-national level rather than within national boundaries, but—as we saw in his remarks on the external context of the 1905 revolution—even at his most radical the inter-national never existed for Kautsky except as the sum total of individual states. Pre-mature revolutions are therefore simply irrational eruptions of frustration at existing conditions. Kautsky argues that the Bolsheviks, by taking advantage of this, were subject to the same form of self-delusion that Marx identified in the French rev-olutionaries of 1789, perhaps even in the millenarians of the radical Reformation: "They justify their completely new doctrine not with the quite unusual conditions in which it has arisen. Rather, as Luther and his followers supposed that what they were striving for was the return to primitive Christianity, which later generations had adulterated, Lenin and his followers claimed that what they taught and prac-ticed was nothing less else than the pure primitive communism of the *Communist Manifesto* . . . [which] had been adulterated by Social Democracy."[142]

At one point, Kautsky actually criticizes Marx's position in the 1859 "Preface"—an uncharacteristically bold move given that this text formed the theoretical underpinning of his entire version of historical materialism. Kautsky was unhappy with the famous passage stating that conflicts between the forces and relations of production would lead to an era of social revolution, which, he suggested, "was presumably formulated as a result of a study of the bourgeois revolutions."[143] The difficulty for Kautsky is not that Marx overgeneralizes from one set of examples—a legitimate complaint, although what Marx writes is at a high enough level of abstraction to allow for different *forms* of social revolution—but rather the implication that each great transition must involve crisis and class struggle, hence: "It is not from the conflict between the productive forces, for the application of which the capitalist mode of production has become too restrictive, and capitalist property that we expect the end of capitalism. . . . We believe that we have every reason to be confident that this end will be reached sooner."[144] In effect, Kautsky hopes the day-to-day injustices produced by capitalism will eventually persuade workers to vote for its abolition rather than the tendency to crisis inherent in capitalism forcing workers to rise up in revolution against it. Thus, when Marx identifies the sole common characteristic of all forms of social revolution—their origin in crises attendant on the internal contradictions of a mode of production—the once and otherwise orthodox Kautsky must now reject it, precisely because it implies that socialism must also be achieved by revolutionary means.

Although not specifically directed at Kautsky, the most devastating response to claims that October 1917 had never, and could never have been, anything other than a bourgeois revolution was given by Lukács in 1924. First, Lukács acknowledges the significance of the distinction between bourgeois and socialist revolutions: "One of Marx's greatest theoretical achievements was to distinguish clearly between bourgeois and proletarian revolution. This distinction was of the utmost practical and tactical importance in view of the immature self-delusions of his contemporaries, for it offered the only methodological instrument for recognizing the genuinely proletarian revolutionary elements within the general revolutionary movements of the time." He then moves on to argue that Social Democracy has erected a necessary analytical distinction into an untenably absolute division in political life:

> In *vulgar Marxism this distinction is, however, paralyzed into a mechanistic separation.* For opportunists, the practical consequence of this separation is the schematic generalization of the empirically correct observation that practically every modern revolution begins as a bourgeois revolution, however many proletarian actions or demands may arise within it. The opportunists conclude from this that the revolution is only a bourgeois one and that it is the task of the proletariat to support *this* revolution. From this separation of the bourgeois from the proletarian revolution follows *the renunciation by the proletariat of its own revolutionary class aims.*[145]

The attitudes expressed by Kautsky toward the Russian Revolution were not restricted to those who had moved to the right of the socialist movement; they were also prevalent on the ultraleft. These groups tended to retain their support for the Russian Revolution into the early 1920s until a combination of their opposition to the Third or Communist International (Comintern) policies externally (allying with non-working-class groups in the East, participating in bourgeois parliaments in the West) and Soviet policies internally (the suppression of the Kronstadt revolt, the introduction of the New Economic Policy), led them to revise their position. Their analysis of the Russian Revolution conducted by their theoreticians nevertheless tended to follow logic identical to that of the Social Democrats they otherwise despised.[146] Here, for example, is Otto Rühle on the nature of the Russian Revolution, following an impeccably orthodox discussion of the bourgeois revolutions prior to 1917:

> From the beginning, the Russian Revolution—in accordance with its historical conditions—could only be a bourgeois revolution. It had to get rid of Tsarism, to smooth the way for capitalism, and to help the bourgeoisie into the saddle politically. Through an unusual chain of circumstances the bourgeoisie found itself in no position to play its historical role. The proletariat, leaping on to the stage in its place, did make itself in a moment master of the situation by an unprecedented exertion of energy, daring, tactical readiness, and intelligence, but fell in the following period into a fatal predicament. According to the phaseological pattern of development as formulated and advocated by Marx, after feudal Tsarism in Russia there had to come the capitalist bourgeois state, whose creator and representative is the bourgeois class. But government power from 1917 was occupied not by bourgeois, but by proletarians who repudiated the bourgeois state and were ready to institute a new economic and social order following socialist theory. Between feudalism and socialism yawned a gap of a full hundred years, through which the system of the bourgeois epoch fell unborn and unused. The Bolsheviks undertook no more and no less than to jump a whole phase of development in Russia in one bold leap. Even if one admits that in doing so they reckoned on the world revolution which was to come to their aid and compensate for the vacuum in development within by support from the great fund of culture from outside, this calculation was still rashness because it based itself solely on a vague hope. Rash too was the experiment arising from this calculation.[147]

Ironically then, the same absolute division between bourgeois and proletarian revolutions recurs in the approach of those who occupied the opposite position from Kautsky in the spectrum of socialist thought. Lukács himself had been associated with ultraleft positions until 1921, but having broken with them was now able to identify the difficulties that they posed for revolutionaries by denying the continued relevance of the bourgeois revolution:

> But the radical left-wing analysis, which easily sees through the mechanistic fallacy of this theory and is conscious of the age's proletarian revolutionary character, is in turn subject to an equally dangerous mechanistic interpretation. Knowing that, in the age of imperialism, the universal revolutionary role of the bourgeoisie is at an end, it concludes—also on the basis of the mechanistic separation of the bourgeois and the proletarian revolution—that *we have now finally entered the age of the purely proletarian revolution*. The dangerous practical consequence of this attitude is that all those tendencies towards decay and fermentation which necessarily arise under

imperialism (the agrarian, colonial, and national questions, etc.), *which are objectively revolutionary within the context of the proletarian revolution,* are overlooked, or even despised and rebuffed. These theoreticians of the purely proletarian revolution voluntarily reject the most effective and most important of their allies; they ignore precisely that revolutionary environment which makes the proletarian revolution concretely promising, hoping and thinking in a vacuum that they are preparing a "purely" proletarian revolution.[148]

In his other great work from this period, *History and Class Consciousness*, Lukács made the point more concretely: "Kemal Pasha may represent a revolutionary constellation of forces in certain circumstances whilst a great 'workers' party' may be counter-revolutionary."[149] In other words, a Turkish nationalist movement that did not pretend to be socialist but genuinely challenged imperialism could be more important in advancing socialist goals than a Social Democratic organization that claimed to be socialist but actually supported imperialism.

THE FUTURE OF THE BOURGEOIS REVOLUTION IN THE EAST

Unsurprisingly, the aftermath of the Russian Revolution saw discussion of the bourgeois revolution continue the patterns of 1848 and 1905, in that it remained primarily focused on the contemporary relevance of the category. As Lukács's reference to Turkey suggests, this mainly concerned strategies in the colonial and semicolonial world. In effect, the issues here were similar to those that had faced Russian revolutionaries before 1905 and 1917, but in countries mainly under the direct rule of foreign imperialisms, in which capitalism was even less developed and the working class even smaller than in Russia. Were they capable of undergoing permanent revolution, or would they still have to undergo bourgeois revolutions followed by more or less extended periods of capitalist development?

In his remarks Lukács had drawn on the wide-ranging, but inconclusive debates on this very subject within the Comintern, the history of which essentially mirrors that of the Russian Revolution that gave it birth. In his classic history of the organization, written in the late 1930s, the former Stalinist Comintern functionary-turned-Social Democrat Franz Borkenau distinguished three periods in its history: 1919–23, in which it sought, however inadequately, to bring about world revolution; 1924–28, in which it became an aspect of the factional struggle within the Russian bureaucracy; and 1929–39, in which it had simply become an instrument of Russian foreign policy—a period that of course continued until Stalin dissolved the Comintern in 1943 as a gesture of solidarity with his erstwhile allies in the West. As Borkenau rightly notes, the three stages, and the policies associated with them overlapped.[150] Discussions of the bourgeois revolution as a contemporary rather than historical process are inextricably linked to these changes in the role of the Comintern.

In the early 1920s, during its unambiguously revolutionary period, the Comintern attempted to formulate a strategy for a colonial and semicolonial world that advocated the "bourgeois democratic" revolution that all Marxists except Trotsky had originally envisaged for Russia, on the grounds that the removal of imperialist domination was necessary for the internal expansion of capitalism and democratic rights provided the best conditions for the self-organization of the working class and other oppressed classes. At the Second Congress of the Comintern in 1920—the first at which the national and colonial question was addressed—delegates passed two different sets of theses, both with a general orientation on "bourgeois-democratic" goals, but with somewhat different emphases in relation to both the forces that would make the revolutions in the East and the significance of these revolutions for the West.

Moving the first set of theses, Lenin said: "There can be no doubt of the fact that any nationalist movement can only be a bourgeois-democratic movement, because the great mass of the population of the backward countries consists of the peasantry, which is the representative of bourgeois capitalist relations." Communists would have to support the peasantry, but the thesis referred to "national-revolutionary" rather than "bourgeois-democratic" to signify that Communists would only support bourgeois movements "if these movements are really revolutionary and if their representatives are not opposed to us training and organizing the peasantry in a revolutionary way." However, Lenin also posed the question of whether "capitalist development of the economy is necessary for those backward peoples who are now liberating themselves and among whom now, following the war, progressive movements have developed." His conclusion was: "If the victorious revolutionary proletariat organizes systematic propaganda, and the Soviet Government comes to its assistance with every means at its disposal, it is incorrect to assume that the capitalist stage of development is necessary for such peoples." Naturally this could not be accomplished overnight, but "with the help of the proletariat of the advanced countries the backward countries can arrive at soviet organization and, through a series of stages, and even avoiding the capitalist system, can arrive at Communism."[151]

The second set of theses, by the Indian Marxist Manabendra N. Roy, are sometimes seen as being more radical than the first, particularly when taken in the context of his other writings from the same period. "Cease to fall victim to the imperialist cry that the masses of the East are backward races and must go through the hell fires of capitalistic exploitation from which you are struggling to escape," he declared in one particularly militant text, also from 1920.[152] As Helmut Gruber points out, however, both theses "were substantially in agreement, especially about the need to forge strong links between oppressed peoples [of the East] and the revolutionary proletariat [of the West]."[153] Roy was also returning to the position that had characterized the Bolsheviks before the April theses: the proletariat and the peasantry would carry out the bourgeois revolution, after which there would be a relatively short period of capitalist development before socialism could be placed on the agenda. "In the first period the revolution in the colonies will not be communist. . . . In the first stage of development the revolution in the colonies must be carried out according to the programme of purely petty-bourgeois demands, such as distribution of the land and so on. But from this it must not be concluded that the leadership in the colonies can be allowed to fall into the hands of the bourgeois democrats."[154] Where Roy differed from Lenin was in his greater stress on the role of the working class alongside the peasantry as part of the "revolutionary forces," and—as this quote suggests—his greater skepticism about the role of the bourgeoisie, which he tended to regard as entirely focused on the achievement of national liberation and uninterested in social goals of even a democratic nature. Perhaps the way in which his "supplementary" theses differ most, however, is in the relative importance they ascribe to the West and the East in the process of socialist revolution. For Lenin the socialist revolution in the advanced West would be paramount in allowing the socialist transformation in the East, in the same way as it would for Russia itself; for Roy, the bourgeois-democratic (or "national-revolutionary") movement in the East would stimulate the socialist revolution in the West: "The loss of the colonies and the proletarian revolution in mother countries will bring the downfall of the capitalist order in Europe . . . revolutionary nationalism too will lead to the collapse of European imperialism, which is of enormous significance for the European proletariat."[155] These positions were not necessarily incompatible.[156] It was possible to envisage, for example, a revolutionary process in the East establishing nationalist but still capitalist regimes that broke the power of imperialism, thus assisting the revolutionary process in the West, which, after conquering power, would in turn help the Eastern countries to bypass a prolonged period of capitalist development. Yet, as Gruber writes, despite common elements that meant they could be fused into a single strategic vision, "what may only have appeared as subtle differences in the summer of 1920 in fact formed the basis of subsequent contradictions in the Comintern's national and colonial policy."[157] The essential difference was that Lenin saw the possibility of an alliance between the "revolutionary-nationalist" bourgeoisie and the peasantry, in which the former would tend to play a vacillating or equivocal role, while Roy was certain that the interests of the two groups were opposed. All sides agreed, however, that if nationalists attempted to accomplish the bourgeois-democratic revolution without peasant support, or in opposition to the peasantry and its demands, then the working class and its organizations—above all the local Communist Party and, through it, the Comintern—would side with the peasantry against them.

In the early 1920s the potential problems in Comintern policy did not arise from contradictions within its approach of supporting genuine anti-imperialist nationalisms while simultaneously building independent working-class communist parties, but rather from a contradiction between the diplomatic stance of the Soviet government in relation to these countries and the support of the Comintern for their Communist parties. Borkenau argued that this stemmed from naivete on the part of the Bolsheviks:

Thus, the Comintern would attempt at the same time to support Kemal [in Turkey], Riza [in Persia], and the Mufti of Jerusalem, and to overthrow them. The root of the later catastrophe in China lies in this duplicity, in this child-like conviction that your adversary will not understand your intentions, though you express them quite openly, and that he will cooperate with you as long as *you* want it, and allow himself to be overthrown when it suits *you*.[158]

The problem, however, was not the inability of the Bolsheviks to understand the ruling classes of the—very few—Eastern states that had by this point established a degree of independence from imperialism, but neither was it simply hypocrisy; it was rather the inherent tension of the situation within which they found themselves. On the one hand, as leaders of the only existing workers' state, they needed to ensure the survival of Russia within a hostile geopolitical environment, one aspect of which involved providing diplomatic, military, and economic support for nationalist regimes in Afghanistan, China, Persia, and Turkey in their attempts to expel or resist the reimposition of imperialist controls. On the other hand, as leaders of the international socialist movement, they were committed to building parties that ultimately sought to overthrow those self-same regimes. There is no doubt that there were several occasions when the former took precedence over the latter, most obviously in the case of the repression of Turkish Communists and the left more generally between December 1920 and January 1921, which resulted in many deaths and imprisonments, but provoked no response at the time from the Russian government, which was then engaged in cultivating a treaty with Kemal.[159] Once Bolshevik leaders had decided to survive rather than go do down to glorious defeat along the lines of the Paris Commune—a decision signaled by their signing the Treaty of Brest-Litovsk on March 3, 1918—this type of conflict was virtually inevitable. What did not exist, at this stage, was a consistent policy of privileging Russian state interests over those of the international movement. When this did take place, as it increasingly did from 1924 on, it was a sign that the Russian Revolution itself had entered terminal decline.

The tensions that existed before 1924 can be felt most sharply in the writings of Trotsky. Of all the Bolshevik leaders, he above all might have been expected to see the greatest possibility for socialist revolution in the colonial and semicolonial world, given his earlier arguments about the nature of the impending Russian Revolution. Many figures active in the 1920s and sympathetic to Trotsky, such as the Ukrainian novelist Mykola Khvylovy, regarded the East as a source of revolutionary regeneration.[160] However, not even Trotsky initially believed that a process comparable to that of permanent revolution in Russia was possible there. In 1919, early in the civil war, Trotsky had considered the possibility of the epicenter of revolution moving further east. In a memorandum to the Central Committee dated August 5, 1919, before the Comintern had even begun to consider these issues, he made several recommendations to help facilitate this shift, including building industrial capacity in the Urals, establishing a military academy either there or in Turkistan, and devoting political and military staff to give support to the revolutionary movements in Asia:

> We have up till now devoted too little attention to agitation in Asia. However, the international situation is evidently shaping in such a way that the road to Paris and London lies via the towns of Afghanistan, the Punjab, and Bengal. . . . Asia may become the arena of the next uprising. Our key task lies in effecting the necessary switch of the centre of gravity of our international orientation at an opportune moment. . . . In the period immediately ahead preparation of the "elements" of an Asian orientation and, in particular, preparation of a military thrust against India to aid the Indian revolution can only be of a preliminary, preparatory character.[161]

Yet these are tactical considerations, which see the colonial revolution aiding the ongoing proletarian revolution in the West ("Paris and London") through causing economic disruption at home and military diversions abroad, rather than the site of precocious socialist experiments. In this and similar communications written during the civil war Trotsky is writing very much as the people's commissar for military affairs, the role of national statesman overriding that of international revolutionary. At one point during the following year he even described the possibility that attempted socialist revolution in, among other countries, Afghanistan and Persia, "is going to cause us major difficulties at the present time": "Until the situation in the West is stabilized and until our industries and transport systems have improved, a Soviet expansion in the East could prove no less dangerous than a war in the West . . . a Soviet expansion in the East is today to our advantage principally as an important element in diplomatic relations with England." His conclusions were that the Soviet regime should concentrate on "political and educational work," urging "caution" where actions by local revolutionaries might lead to Soviet involvement, and making clear "our readiness to come to an understanding with England with regard to the East."[162]

Statements by Trotsky after the Red Army had emerged victorious from the civil war and the new regime had achieved a degree of stability contain more balanced assessments of the nature of possible revolutions in the East. In a speech to the Fourth Congress of the Comintern during 1922 he said:

> It is self-understood that the colonies—Asia and Africa (I speak of them as a unity), despite the fact that they, like Europe, contain the greatest gradations—the colonies, if taken independently and isolatedly, are absolutely not ready for the proletarian revolution. If they are taken isolatedly, then capitalism still has a long possibility of economic development in them. But the colonies belong to the metropolitan centers and their fate is intimately bound up with the fate of these European metropolitan centers.[163]

These remarks make the realistic assumption that any development toward socialism in the East will be dependent on the support and resources made available by a revolutionary West. His comments on specific countries did not indicate a belief that any of them could avoid a period of postrevolutionary capitalist development. Indeed, other revolutionaries like Roy were more skeptical of the willingness of the native Eastern bourgeoisie to struggle for national independence, as in these comments from 1924:

> In India where national capitalism is growing rapidly, the national bourgeoisie has been won over to support the empire and has even demanded in a recent manifesto that military power and foreign relations should remain in the hands of the British government. Because the Indian bourgeoisie knows better than anyone else that the discontent of the masses is economic and not nationalistic, the exploiting class in India demands protection from the exploited. Indian capitalism is running straight into the arms of British imperialism and the same tendency will soon be seen in other countries.[164]

By contrast, in April of the same year Trotsky addressed a meeting of the Communist University of the Toilers of the East in which he made these remarks on China:

> There is no doubt whatsoever that if the Kuomintang Party in China succeeds in uniting China under a national-democratic regime, the capitalist development of China will make enormous strides forward. And all this leads to the mobilization of countless proletarian masses which will immediately emerge from a prehistoric, semi-barbarian state and will be thrust into the whirlpool of industrialization. Therefore, in these countries there will be no time for the refuse of past centuries to accumulate in the minds of workers.[165]

The claim that Chinese workers would be radicalized by the speed and intensity of industrialization suggests parallels with the Russian experience, but still assumes that this will only take place after the bourgeois revolution has prepared the necessary conditions. But what if, in the course of the bourgeois revolution, the Communist Party, the leadership of the working class, itself sided with the bourgeois nationalists of the Kuomintang *against* the peasantry? The prospect was so inconceivable in Moscow during the early 1920s that no one even contemplated it as a hypothesis; yet, even as Trotsky was delivering his lecture, policy shifts were taking place that, before the decade was out, would produce exactly this result in China.

13

THE EMERGENCE
OF ORTHODOXY: 1924–40

The establishment of the Stalinist regime in Russia and the attendant assertion of complete Russian control over the international communist movement took place between 1924 and 1928. The majority of Stalin's own substantive writings are from these years, but unlike those of virtually every other significant figure featured in this book, they are completely devoid of any theoretical interest—although for students of a ruling ideology in the process of formation they are of course indispensable. As Nigel Harris explains:

> Stalinism is essentially deducible from practice, and Stalin's exiguous theoretical output is no longer any sort of guide to understanding that practice but is rather a rationale provided after the event to justify it—theory is not the guide to practice but its description after it has happened. The change is implicit in the fact that practice has become a tyranny of immense brutality and irrationality that needs to be concealed by, not theory, but ideology. As a result, Stalinism has an opaque quality. We can no longer see its direct connection with the acts of the Soviet State, and we are constantly if dimly aware of a background echo of real but unspoken purposes. Discussion within Stalinism, as befits a false consciousness, retreats into ritual, text-quoting, semantic quibbles, and terminological disputes. It is in essence idealist: it begins not with social reality, the facts of experience, but with ideas, the text, the axiom; facts, institutions, people, must be brought into conformity with the idea. Present intolerable practice must be brought into conformity with a past terminology of great hopes and vision that implicitly condemn that practice.... Stalin's writing is brief and poor in quality, but of central importance for the history of the Soviet Union since it dominated the entire intellectual scene. Its most interesting tendency is a groping for the characteristic forms of conservative thought, and its most striking characteristic, an immense unresolved contradiction ... between determinist theory and voluntarist practice.[1]

Since the intellectual domination to which Harris refers was eventually exercised over such unlikely areas as linguistics, it is perhaps unsurprising that a subject of immediate practical importance such as the nature of revolutions in the colonial and semicolonial world was one of the first to be pronounced upon by the fledgling dictator. Over a relatively short period of time, perhaps less than a decade, the Stalinist interpretation of bourgeois revolution became codified into an unchallenged orthodoxy, crucial to the maintenance of which were the resources of a powerful state and the prestige of the Soviet Union within the international labor movement. Within the Communist parties, on this issue as on all others, there were strict limits imposed on what it was permissible to think, or at least openly express, beyond which lay calumny and marginalization.

Yet the dominance of the orthodoxy was not possible solely because of the usurped authority of a once-great revolution. In many ways it reaffirmed the commonsense assumptions of Social Democracy before the First World War and the Russian Revolution, familiar to us from chapter 11, and which had only ever been partially dislodged by the Russian Revolutions and the debates surrounding them. Now they were revived, in even more dogmatic and inflexible terms, in particular the necessity for a "bourgeois-democratic" stage in the revolutionary process and the revolutionary role of the bourgeoisie within it—or at least of its "progressive" wing, the identity of which varied according to the requirements of Russian foreign policy. In an example of what might otherwise be described as "guilt transference," had Stalin not been immune to that emotion, he and his supporters accused their critics, above all Trotsky, of doing precisely what they themselves had done and adopting the positions associated with the Second International in general and the Mensheviks in particular.

As a result of this combination of authority and familiarity, Stalin exercised more influence over what is usually taken to be the Marxist theory of bourgeois revolution than anyone else, including Marx and Engels, and, extraordinary as it may seem, in many respects his influence in this respect has survived both him and the system he created.[2] Developments that began in the later part of the period discussed here may help explain this afterlife. For the period between 1924 and 1940 saw not only the codification of the theory of bourgeois revolution but also its bifurcation into two increasingly divergent domains: one pertaining to contemporary politics—the bourgeois revolution as a strategic goal; the other pertaining to the historical past—the bourgeois revolution as an academic subject. The rich body of historiography that only began to appear in the 1950s and whose first landmarks include such works as Christopher Hill's *Puritanism and Revolution* and Albert Soboul's *The Parisian Sans-Culottes and the French Revolution* (both 1958) did more to inspire interest in bourgeois revolutions than the instrumental formulations scattered through the collected writings of Stalin. The *theoretical* weakness of the orthodoxy means, however, that critics of the concept of bourgeois revolution—the various revisionists, world systems theorists, and political Marxists whose work we will encounter in detail in part 3 of this book—have an interest in claiming that it is the only possible version: it makes their job easier, so to speak. The effect is to render the complexities of the classical Marxist tradition, which offers a more substantial intellectual challenge, hidden from view. The first stage in reclaiming that tradition is therefore to understand how the orthodoxy originally emerged in direct opposition to it.

POLITICS: THE REVIVAL OF STAGES THEORY

In April 1924, Stalin, by now general secretary of the Communist Party of the Soviet Union and one of the "triumvirs" at the head of the state with Kamenev and Zinoviev, began a series of lectures at Sverdlov University. In these, his first substantial attempt to establish himself as the inheritor and continuer of Lenin's legacy, he criticized the concept of permanent revolution without naming Trotsky (referring instead to "the permanentists") and argued that the Russian Revolution had indeed proceeded according to the stages set out by the all-seeing genius of Vladimir Illych before 1905 and never subsequently revised.[3] In these initial forays, the main evidence for Trotsky's "anti-Leninism" was his supposed underestimation of the revolutionary potential of the peasantry. From December 1924, however, the concept of permanent revolution came under attack for another reason. Although hinted at in his earlier lectures, Stalin now explicitly unveiled the hitherto-unheard-of proposition that "socialism in one country" was possible in Russia. That the safety of the Russian Revolution required it to be joined by other revolutions, that socialism was only possible on a global scale—these positions had been universally accepted among the Bolsheviks and had been reaffirmed by Stalin himself in his lectures earlier that year. As we saw in chapter 12, these positions provided the main point of convergence between the views of the "old" Bolsheviks and those of the newcomer Trotsky in 1917. Stalin and the group that was beginning to coalesce around him nevertheless found it convenient to pretend that this was a particularly "Trotskyist" heresy, encapsulated in the concept of permanent revolution. Thus, the debate over permanent revolution did not initially focus on the possibility of the bourgeois revolution passing over to the proletarian revolution, but on the condition that Trotsky had identified for this possibility to be realized: the necessity for the revolution to spread beyond the borders of Russia.

Given the quasi-religious cultivation of textual authority deployed by Stalin, it was unfortunate for his new position that Marx and Engels had argued socialism was only possible on a global scale. Stalin therefore had to claim that uneven development was a "new factor" in world history, unknown to the founders of historical materialism:

> Engels' negative answer to the question: "Can this revolution take place in one country alone?" wholly reflects the epoch of pre-monopolist capitalism, the pre-imperialist epoch, when the conditions did not yet exist for the uneven, spasmodic development of the capitalist countries, when, consequently, the premises did not yet exist for the victory of the proletarian revolution in one country (as is known, the possibility of the victory of such a revolution in one country follows from the law of uneven development of capitalist countries under imperialism). . . . Genius though he was, Engels could not see what did not yet exist in the pre-monopolist period of capitalism, the forties of the last century, when he wrote his *Principles of Communism*, and which arose only later, in the monopolist period of capitalism.[4]

More specifically, inter-imperialist competition would allow revolutions to take place in even quite backward countries situated "at the weakest link in the imperialist chain."[5] Stalin credited Lenin with the discovery of uneven development, but the latter figure posed a further problem since, as we saw in chapter 12, he consistently rejected the idea that socialism was possible in any single country, particularly one as backward as Russia. The solution in this case was to ignore all but a handful of texts—and here Lenin's practice of "dealing with problems in isolation from each other" lent itself precisely to this type of misappropriation—where passages could, with some presentational work be offered as supporting Stalin's case, along with a great deal of hedging and semantic quibbling about what exactly constituted the "final victory" of socialism.[6] Stalin did not waste time in a serious engagement with Trotsky's position, but simply misrepresented it as "the universal theory of a simul taneous victory of the revolution in the principal countries of Europe."[7]

In 1925 Stalin opened a second line of attack against permanent revolution, of more direct relevance to our subject. The first had been concerned to refute any arguments against the transformation of Russia into an independent, supposedly socialist, component of the states system, rather the temporary advance-guard of a world revolution. The second sought to deflect criticisms of the kind of self-interested foreign policy that such a state would have to conduct, if it was to ensure its survival. The occasion was a dramatic upturn in the progress of the Chinese Revolution, which had been ongoing to varying degrees of intensity since 1911.

The Chinese Revolution was regarded by the Bolshevik leadership, including Trotsky, as "bourgeois-democratic" or "national-revolutionary" in character, the main foci being the military struggle of the nationalist Kuomintang against various regional warlords and their Western backers in order to unify the country. The Communist Party of China (CCP), which had only been formed in 1921, was instructed by the Comintern early in 1923 to join the Kuomintang, although to simultaneously maintain its own organizational identity and individual membership. At the same time, the Russian state provided the Kuomintang with military training, supplies, and political advisers. Initially, these dual strategies simply embodied the inevitable tension between the twin imperatives of defending the Russian state and fomenting the world revolution that, as we saw in the previous chapter, had been present since the founding of the Comintern in 1919. From the middle of the decade, however, it became apparent that the first was beginning to take systematic precedence. On May 30, 1925, a massive strike wave, sparked by the repressive tactics of British imperialism, erupted first in Shanghai then across the industrial cities of the coastal region. By the end of June the British concessions were effectively paralyzed. The CCP grew by tens of thousands, the trade unions by millions. But the insurgencies were not confined solely to the cities, nor directed solely at the foreign presence, since by the opening of 1926 the urban working-class revolt had been joined by a peasant rent strike against the native landlords. All at once it seemed possible that 1925 might be to 1911 in China what 1917 was to 1905 in Russia.

These colossal developments were deeply threatening to the leadership of the Kuomintang, who sought to form a unified capitalist nation-state by military means, after which more favorable terms could be negotiated with Western interests, not unleash worker and peasant insurgencies which threatened to overthrow class relations of both local and foreign origin. More to the point, they were also deeply inconvenient for the dominant faction in the leadership of the Communist Party of the Soviet Union. Leaving aside Stalin's organic suspicion of any kind of working-class self-activity, these upheavals disturbed the stability of the international environment in which socialism in one country was to be constructed. Against all the evidence that the Chinese working class was capable of achieving the same outcome as the Russian in 1917, the leading factions in the Russian state and the Comintern, which were by now indistinguishable, asserted the objectives of the revolution had to be limited to those of the "bourgeois-democratic" stage.

The climax was reached early in 1927. During March, as the Kuomintang army led by Chiang Kai-shek advanced on Shanghai, the workers rose against the local warlord and, after several weeks of street fighting, had effectively taken power. Chiang entered a city that had already been conquered by a working-class movement that he was determined to suppress—with the very weapons provided him by the Russians. Yet the CCP was ordered by the Comintern to hide its own weapons and not to warn its members and supporters about the impending attack, still less to mobilize them to resist it. On April 12, Chiang struck in a coup that cost the lives of tens of thousands of workers and began the process of destroying their trade unions. By the end of the decade the CCP had effectively ceased to be a working-class party, since its entire urban membership base in that class had been destroyed, and had become instead a rural guerrilla organization based on the peasantry—an extraordinary and unforeseen transformation the significance of which was not apparent at the time. More immediately, the defeat of the Chinese Revolution confirmed the international isolation of Russia and thus prepared for the complete ascendancy of the bureaucracy.

Faced with the initial wave of Stalinist attacks on permanent revolution, Trotsky denied that it had any contemporary relevance—not as an act of dissimulation, but because opposition to "socialism in one country" did not depend on affirming it. Simply the much more widely shared view that socialism could only involve international revolution: "I absolutely deny that the formula 'permanent revolution,' which applies wholly to the past, in any way caused me to adopt a careless attitude to the peasantry in the conditions of the Soviet revolution. If at any time after October I had occasion, for private reasons, to revert to the formula 'permanent revolution,' it was only a reference to party history, i.e., to the past, and had no reference to the question of present-day political tasks."[8] Nor did Trotsky immediately change position in response to the unfolding situation in China. In a speech to the Executive Committee of the Comintern at the end of 1926 he admitted to unspecified "inadequacies" of the concept and stated that he had "never considered it to be a universal doctrine applicable generally to all evolutions, a 'suprahistorical theory,' to use a phrase from Marx": "The concept of permanent revolution was applied by me to a definite stage in the historical development of Russia."[9] Again, this was not dissimulation. By subordinating the CCP and, through it, the trade unions to the Kuomintang, Stalin had already retreated to positions close to those of the Mensheviks in the Russian Revolution of 1917. Yet the very fact that the Russian Revolution of 1917 could be understood in "permanentist" terms was a standing rebuke to those who were engineering a quite different outcome in China. Nevertheless, for Trotsky the alternative to the Comintern policy in China was not permanent revolution but, in effect, the position of the Bolsheviks prior to "The April Theses" ("democratic dictatorship of the proletariat and peasantry") and the variants on it held by the Comintern before its Fifth World Congress:

China has no prerequisites whatever economically for an independent transition to socialism; that the revolution now unfolding under the leadership of the Kuomintang is a bourgeois-national revolution, that it can have as its consequence, even in the event of complete victory, only the further development of productive forces on the basis of capitalism. But it is necessary to develop no less forcefully before the Chinese proletariat the converse side of the question as well: The belated bourgeois-national revolution is unfolding in China in conditions of the imperialist decay of capitalism. As Russian experience has already shown in contrast, say, to the English—politics does not at all develop in parity with economics. China's further development must be taken in an international perspective. Despite the backwardness of the Chinese economy, and in part precisely due to this backwardness, the Chinese revolution is wholly capable of bringing to political power an alliance of workers and peasants, under the leadership of the proletariat. This regime will be China's political link with the world revolution. In the course of the transitional period, the Chinese revolution will have a genuinely democratic, worker-and-peasant character. In its economic life, commodity-capitalist relations will inevitably predominate. The political regime will be primarily directed to secure the masses as great a share as possible in the fruits of the development of the productive forces and, at the same time, in the political and cultural utilization of the resources of the state. The further development of this per- spective—the possibility of the democratic revolution growing over into the socialist revolution—depends completely and exclusively on the course of the world revolu- tion, and on the economic and political successes of the Soviet Union, as an integral part of this world revolution. If the Chinese revolution were to triumph under its present bourgeois-nationalist leadership, it would very quickly go to the right, demon- strate its good intentions to the capitalist countries, soon gain recognition on their part, offer them concessions on new bases, obtain loans, in a word, enter into the sys- tem of capitalist states as a less degraded, less colonial, but still profoundly dependent entity. Furthermore, the Chinese republic would hold in relation to the Soviet Union *in the best variant* the same position as the present Turkish republic. A *different* path of development can be opened up only if the proletariat plays the leading role in the national democratic revolution. But the first and most elementary precondition for this is the complete independence of the Communist Party, and an open struggle waged by it, with banners unfurled, for the leadership of the working class and the hegemony in the revolution.[10]

Even in the immediate aftermath of the coup Trotsky could still write: "That the Chinese revolution at this stage is national-democratic, i.e., bourgeois, is elementary for all of us."[11] Although the opportunity for successful revolutionary outcome had temporarily passed, Trotsky continued to argue throughout the spring of 1927 that what could be achieved would be the completion of the bourgeois revolution, albeit by a workers' and peasants' government. He conceded that this might only have a temporary existence, giving way to direct bourgeois rule before the possibility of socialist revolution became feasible:

> It is quite possible that China will have to pass through a relatively prolonged stage of parliamentarism, beginning with a Constituent Assembly. This demand is inscribed on the banner of the Communist Party. If the bourgeois democratic revolution does not grow into a socialist revolution in the near future, then in all probability the workers' and peasants' soviets will pass from the scene for a definite stage and give way to a bourgeois régime, which, depending on the progress of the world revolution, will in turn give way, at a new historical stage, to the dictatorship of the proletariat.[12]

As we shall see in the next chapter, Trotsky subsequently began to generalize the strategy of permanent revolution to most, if not all, parts of the colonial and semicolonial world, beginning with China itself. The point, however, is that during the events of 1925–27, although highly critical of the Comintern's policy, he still denied that permanent revolution had any relevance other than as a historical category applicable solely to Russia. His proposed strategy in relation to China was in fact closer to the Kautsky-Luxemburg-Lenin-Mehring-Parvus-Ryazanov center-left consensus in relation to *Russia* prior to 1905. Whether this would have been any more realistic in China in 1925 than it had been in Russia twenty years earlier is another question, but it was at any rate a position that emphasized the need for revolutionaries to maintain their organizational independence from the bourgeoisie, and for there to be no constraints on working-class activity, whatever the wishes of the bourgeois parties—in other words the opposite of what was actually being imposed on the CCP.

The Stalinist orthodoxy concerning bourgeois revolutions was first proclaimed in January 1926, early in the new phase of the Chinese Revolution, the occasion being the second installment of Stalin's attempt to remake Lenin in his own image. Although not directly concerned with events in China, the elaborate codification of the respective attributes supposedly possessed by bourgeois and proletarian revolutions cannot be abstracted from criticisms Trotsky and his allies voiced in what was by this point the United Opposition:

1) The bourgeois revolution usually begins when there already exist more or less ready-made forms belonging to the capitalist order, forms which have grown and matured within the womb of feudal society prior to the open revolution, whereas the proletarian revolution begins when ready-made forms belonging to the socialist order are either absent, or almost absent.
2) The main task of the bourgeois revolution consists in seizing power and making it conform to the already existing bourgeois economy, whereas

the main task of the proletarian revolution consists, after seizing power, in building a new, socialist economy.

3) The bourgeois revolution is usually *consummated* with the seizure of power, whereas in the proletarian revolution the seizure of power is only the *beginning*, and power is used as a lever for transforming the old economy and organizing the new one.

4) The bourgeois revolution limits itself to replacing one group of exploiters in power by another group of exploiters, in view of which it need not smash the old state machine; whereas the proletarian revolution removes all exploiting groups from power and places in power the leader of all the toilers and exploited, the class of proletarians, in view of which it cannot manage without smashing the old state machine and substituting a new one for it.

5) The bourgeois revolution cannot rally the millions of the toiling and exploited masses around the bourgeoisie for any length of time, for the very reason that they are toilers and exploited; whereas the proletarian revolution can and must link them, precisely as toilers and exploited, in a durable alliance with the proletariat, if it wishes to carry out its main task of consolidating the power of the proletariat and building a new, socialist economy.[13]

As a set of historical generalizations about bourgeois revolutions every one of these points was open to challenge. The first three are derived from the English and French experiences, and to refute them one need simply point to the contrasting experiences of Scotland, Germany, Italy, or Japan where capitalism was nascent or nonexistent before the revolutions, after which the state was used to initiate economic development; the fourth assumes that there is no difference between feudal-absolutist and capitalist states; the fifth is more defensible, even then, in the aftermath of a bourgeois revolution the new ruling class must still exercise what Gramsci would later call hegemony over the "toiling and exploited" in order to retain the stability necessary for bourgeois society to exist. Overall, Stalin was simply repeating the error criticized by Lukács only two years before of erecting an absolute distinction between bourgeois and proletarian revolutions—although to speak of "error" suggests ideas deployed as vehicles for theoretical understanding, however incorrectly, and not, as they are here, weapons of factional struggle. The following year, Stalin overlaid his initial historical distinction between different types of revolution with a further geographical distinction between different areas to which they were relevant in the contemporary world. Revolutionaries, he wrote, needed to maintain:

A strict distinction between revolution in imperialist countries, in countries that oppress other nations, and revolution in colonial and dependent countries, in countries that suffer from imperialist oppression by other states.... To fail to draw this distinction, to fail to understand this difference and identify revolution in imperialist countries with revolution in colonial countries, is to depart from the path of Marxism, from the path of Leninism, and to take the path of the supporters of the Second International.

Stalin then set out, in his habitual tone of liturgical simplicity, exactly what these stages have to be, making it quite clear that it was in fact he who was taking the path of the Second International, or more specifically that of the Mensheviks in 1917: "the first stage is the revolution of an all-national united front . . . the second stage is the bourgeois democratic revolution . . . the third stage is the socialist revolution."[14] The concept of the "bourgeois-democratic revolution" had by now decisively shifted from being one that advocated allying with bourgeois (or even pre-bourgeois) forces only where they were genuinely involved in fighting imperialism, and in alliance with revolutionary socialist movements in the West, to one in which support had to be given to the supposedly "revolutionary" bourgeoisie as a matter of course, as a necessary historical stage that each country has to experience individually in preparation for the subsequent stage of the socialist revolution.

But what if no section of the bourgeoisie was prepared to carry out the bourgeois-democratic stage? "The bourgeois-democratic revolution in China is a combination of the struggle against feudal survivals and the struggle against imperialism," wrote Stalin.[15] Unfortunately, in China, the political organization of bourgeois nationalism, the Kuomintang, had allied on the one hand with the very landlords who represented the main feudal survivals and, on the other, British (and ultimately US) imperialism: any bourgeois-democratic revolution ultimately would have to be made against the Kuomintang, although the situation was complicated by the Japanese invasion of Manchuria in 1931. By the late 1920s the working class had been heavily defeated and was in no position to resume even basic trade union activity. Meanwhile, the organization that had once sought to lead the Chinese working class, and for a brief period had actually done so, now based itself on a section of the rural bourgeoisie—albeit one that was profoundly dissatisfied with conditions in China—namely the peasantry. Whether the CCP had effectively become a peasant organization, representing the interests of that class, or was acting as an autonomous body, simply relying on peasants as a temporary resource was not clear in the 1930s, although by then it was certainly recruiting the overwhelming majority of its members from the countryside. What is absolutely clear is that it had ceased to be a working-class party in any sense that did not involve a kind of metaphysics whereby labels ("the party of the Chinese working class") assume a greater significance than material reality.

Mao Tse-tung had definitively established himself as the leader of the CCP by 1935. The language in which he attacked the strategy of permanent revolution was learned from Stalin, and sounded similar, as in this passage from 1937: "We are exponents of the theory of the transition to the revolution, and not of the Trotskyite theory of 'permanent revolution.' We are for the attainment of socialism by going through all the necessary stages of the democratic republic."[16] Two years later Mao elaborated on the implications of this position from the CCP base in Yenan:

> What, after all, is the character of the Chinese revolution at the present stage? It is now clear that Chinese society is still a colonial, semi-colonial, and semi-feudal society, that the principal enemies of the Chinese revolution are still imperialism and

the feudal forces, that the task of the Chinese revolution consists in a national revolution and a democratic revolution for overthrowing the two principal enemies, and furthermore that the bourgeoisie sometimes takes part in this revolution and that, even if the big bourgeoisie betrays the revolution and becomes its enemy, the spearhead of the revolution will still be directed at imperialism and feudalism rather than at capitalism and capitalist private property in general. That being so, the character of the Chinese revolution at the present stage is not proletarian-socialist but bourgeois-democratic.

According to Mao the bourgeois-democratic revolution under way in China and the rest of the colonial and semicolonial world was, however, of a new type, one that would climax in the dictatorship not of the bourgeoisie but of an alliance of the "revolutionary classes" led by the proletariat against "imperialists, collaborators, and reactionaries" whose property would be nationalized:

> While clearing the way for capitalism, this democratic revolution of a new type creates the precondition for socialism. The present stage of the Chinese Revolution is a transitional stage between putting an end to the colonial, semi-colonial, and semi-feudal society and establishing a socialist society—a process of new-democratic revolution. …China must go through this revolution before she can advance to a socialist society; otherwise she cannot advance to socialism.[17]

Stalinists in Russia had however quite different reasons for opposing permanent revolution than Stalinists in China. In the case of the former, it was partly to avoid the disruption to building socialism in one country that socialist revolutions elsewhere in the world system would involve and partly because any genuine working-class revolution would provoke unflattering comparisons with the situation that prevailed in Russia—particularly after the consolidation of the full totalitarian dictatorship during 1928–29—with implications for Russian influence over the international labor movement. In the case of the latter, the reasons were in a sense less duplicitous: they could only hope to achieve a bourgeois revolution because their new class basis would not support a socialist one. In effect, the CCP was substituting itself for a nonexistent revolutionary bourgeoisie.

The starting point of Stalin's argument, subsequently adopted by Mao, was the supposed inescapable differences between revolution in the West and the East. It might seem, therefore, that future bourgeois revolutions would at least be confined to the latter. Of course, most countries outside of northwestern Europe, Australasia, and North America still had either undemocratic regimes or quasi-feudal agrarian social relationships or both—and even in the minority of states where bourgeois democracy and capitalist economy were both firmly established, areas like Northern Ireland in the United Kingdom or the South in the United States of America existed as internal regional exceptions. Nevertheless, until the mid-1920s, no one had seriously proposed that anything other than the socialist revolution remained to be achieved west of Russia or north of the Balkans. However, at the same time as the CCP was being subordinated to the Kuomintang in China, the notion that bourgeois revolution was still conceivable in the West was adopted by the Communist Party of Poland (PCP).

On May 12, 1926, Joseph Pilsudski launched a successful coup against the elected center-right government dominated by the leader of the Peasant Party, Wincenty Witos. Pilsudski, a former member of the nationalist right wing of the Polish Socialist Party who had led the Polish military resistance to the Russian Red Army in 1920, was supported by the PCP. Isaac Deutscher, a member of the party at the time, later recalled the "tragicomic" nature of these events:

> Hardly five years had elapsed since Pilsudski had marched on Kiev, mainly in order to return the Ukrainian estates to their landowners, and the Communist Party was now calling back this man of destiny to head the army, in order to safeguard national independence. It is enough to describe the situation in these terms—and these are the only realistic (though grotesque) terms—to dispose of the theory according to which the comeback of Pilsudski was supposed to mark the beginning of the bourgeois revolution in Poland. How could the defender of the feudal estates of the *szlachta* (nobility and gentry) become transformed into the inspirer of the bourgeois revolution, the main task of which is usually to destroy feudalism, or what is left of it?[18]

Behind the grotesquery lay two political calculations. One was Russian foreign policy. During the entire period between 1924 and 1928, during which Stalin assumed complete control of the Russian state, the Comintern was involved in a search for allies to its right, such as the Kuomintang in China and the Anglo-Soviet Trade Union Committee in Britain, on a basis that combined unprincipled maneuvering and hopeless naivete in equal measure. As part of this orientation, it sought "unity" with various Social Democratic organizations, including the Polish Socialist Party; and since it supported its former member Pilsudski in his bid for power, so too did the PCP. The classification of Pilsudski's coup as the bourgeois revolution seems to have originated in the PCP itself, as the basis of a second calculation. The leadership of the PCP, formerly loyal to Zinoviev, had recently been ousted in favor of a Stalinist leadership anxious to demonstrate that it had no truck with Trotskyism or in a Polish context, Luxemburgism, which Stalin regarded as almost equally pernicious.[19] As Deutscher recalled:

> In their enthusiasm to fight and defeat the Luxemburgist tradition, the Party leaders suddenly discovered that in Poland history had put on the agenda the bourgeois democratic revolution, and not, as they had thought hitherto, the socialist revolution, which would complete our overdue and unfinished bourgeois revolution. . . . The situation was grotesque precisely because this *bourgeois* revolution [Pilsudski's coup] was designed to overthrow a government presided over by Witos, the leader of the kulaks, backed by the largest section—the peasant section—of the Polish bourgeoisie.[20]

As Deutscher rightly points out, unlike contemporary events in China, the so-called May mistake, was not imposed by the Comintern, which did not approve support for Pilsudski and censured the Polish leadership for doing so. The Comintern had, however, set the theoretical groundwork for errors of precisely this sort by the attacks on permanent revolution, with the implication that a bourgeois revolution was still required in any country where there remained any traces of precapitalist social relations in the countryside. And by the following decade this was precisely the position that it was imposing on the Communist parties.

At the beginning of the 1930s, neither the Comintern nor, consequently, the tiny Communist Party of Spain (PCE) had a coherent view of the course that any Spanish revolution might take; indeed, the very absence of a clear position—in stark contrast with China—indicates the irrelevance of Spain in Comintern thinking at the time. E. H. Carr summarizes the debates that took place within the PCE early in 1930:

> Everyone agreed that revolution was on the march in Spain. But controversy turned on the well-worn theme of the character of the revolution. If it was still in the stage of a bourgeois democratic revolution against the remnants of feudalism (whose existence in Spain could hardly be denied), it would be the duty of communists to lend support to bourgeois democratic parties. If on the other hand, the dictatorship of Primo de Rivera and Berenguer had reached the stage of finance capitalism, communists should already fix their sights on the coming proletarian revolution.[21]

The latter position was clearly more in line with the ultra-left "class against class" position adopted at the Sixth Congress of the Comintern in 1928, according to which socialism was on the agenda everywhere, regardless of specific national circumstances, and the main enemies of socialism were the reformist parties. Early in 1931, as the regime entered crisis and the dawn of the republic loomed, the Comintern explicitly moved to this position, declaring: "The presence in Spain of *deep survivals of feudalism*' did not justify the view that 'a typical bourgeois democratic revolution is ripening.' On the contrary, the regime was already 'bound up with the whole system of finance capital and imperialism,' and *'the moving forces of the Spanish revolution can only be the proletariat and the peasantry.'"[22] Although arrived at almost entirely inadvertently, this position more or less corresponded to the reality of Spanish conditions. In any event, the opportunity soon came to put it into practice.

The Popular Front alliance of socialists, communists, anarchists, Catalan nationalists, and others was elected on February 20, opening up four months of growing industrial unrest action and land seizures. Franco's rebellion against the Republican government began on July 17. In response, workers and peasants resisted the insurrection with guns in hand and began to set up institutions of self-government. A fascist coup to preserve bourgeois property against an imagined threat from the new reformist government and a real threat from workers and peasants had provoked a socialist revolution in response. What was the attitude of the Comintern? At the end of the month Dolores Ibarruri, soon to achieve fame as "La Pasionaria," made an announcement in the PCE newspaper on behalf of the Central Committee: "The revolution that is taking place in our country is the bourgeois democratic revolution which was achieved over a century ago in other countries, such as France, and we Communists are the front-line fighters in this struggle against the obscurantist forces of the past."[23] Regrettably, not everyone in Spain understood this. The leader in exile of the Communist Party of Italy, Palmiro Togliatti, then working in Spain as a Comintern agent under the alias of Ercoli, noted that one of the "extra difficulties" faced by the Spanish Popular Front during the civil war was "the influence of petty-bourgeois anarchism and of social democratic illusions, which have still not been totally overcome and are today expressed in a tendency to miss out the stage of the bourgeois democratic revolution."[24] In his classic oral history of the war, Ronald Fraser quotes a communist soldier who had absorbed the Ibarruri and Togliatti–approved positions:

> In accord with the communist party's pre-war political line, the revolutionary upsurge sweeping through the Popular Front zone was carrying through the bourgeois democratic revolution. This had to be completed before the socialist revolution could appear on the political agenda. The transformation of society which was indisputably taking place, thought Francisco Abad, a communist soldier, would eliminate feudalism on the land and in the economy. The stages in the political and economic development of a society could not be by-passed; the bourgeois democratic revolution had to precede the passage to socialism. Meanwhile, it was impermissible that the revolutionary situation should be used to take measures opposed to that revolution—like the workers seizing factories and running them.[25]

Many socialists instinctively understood that this policy was wrong, but were unable to muster coherent arguments against Stalinists. One of Fraser's interviewees, Socrates Gomez, then a member of the youth wing of the Partido Socialista Obrero Español, recalled: "When the communists talked about completing the bourgeois democratic revolution before being able to pass on to the socialist revolution we didn't know what to reply. Our political education was virtually nil, 98 percent of us had never read a word of Marx."[26] The problem was not the survival of quasi-feudal social relations in rural Spain, the existence of which everyone accepted, but the question of how they would be abolished and which social forces would do so. The alliance of the bourgeois and feudal classes at the economic level did not preclude deep divisions about how the country should be ruled—this was scarcely Spain's first civil war, after all. It did mean, however, that as in China, and despite all the other dissimilarities between the two countries, only the oppressed had an interest in abolishing these relations. The Comintern and its representatives in Spain imagined the Spanish Revolution as a bourgeois revolution in the interests of Russian foreign policy when in fact it was a combination of a civil war between two wings of the existing ruling class—a political revolution—and a potential socialist revolution against them both, which did not of course rule out temporary alliances with the less immediately threatening side. In effect, the Comintern opted for one wing of the bourgeoisie against the other and the PCE grew on precisely this basis. "The communist's vast gains, increasing their strength to 25,000 members in eight months, came from the middle class attracted by the Party's disciplined approach, from the ambitious and from right-wingers afraid of arrest," notes one modern historian.[27] But just as the CCP reliance on the Chinese peasantry did not necessarily mean that it had become a "peasant party," neither did the PSE reliance on the Spanish bourgeoisie mean it had become a "bourgeois party": it would only be possible to assess the nature of the Communist parties outside Russia, at least of those outside the heartlands of imperialism, at the end of the Second World War, when several were able to take power on a long-term basis in several states. As for the bourgeois revolution and its tasks, perhaps the most telling criticism of the PSE and its Russian backers is that these were not even attempted, or were reversed where they had been achieved against the wishes of the Republican government. As Franz Borkenau, an eyewitness to events in the summer of 1936 and winter of 1937 noted: "The communists, by orders from Moscow, had dropped every idea, not only of a proletarian, but even of a village revolution after the example of the French Revolution. . . . The communists put an end to revolutionary social activity, and enforced their view that this ought not to be a revolution but simply the defence of a legal government.[28]

By the time the Spanish Civil War had ended with the fascist victory in 1939 the entire notion of the bourgeois or bourgeois-democratic revolution as a process in which communists should participate, or even seek to lead, had become completely meaningless. It would have been at least arguable that in some parts of the East where the working class was very weak or nonexistent a "classic" bourgeois revolution was still a valid goal, but the argument was never put in terms of an actual assessment of class forces. The concept of bourgeois revolution had been transformed from an analytic category into a label that could be applied to a country in one period then withdrawn in another without any conditions having changed in the intervening period. In most cases, it was applied as a an ideological weapon to prevent working-class revolution from succeeding, even when it was in the process of doing so, as it had been in China in 1925 and Spain in 1936.

Less catastrophic, but still disabling for the labor movement were situations in which the same understanding of outstanding issues from an otherwise successful bourgeois revolution could be used as the basis for two entirely opposite political strategies. A particularly revealing episode in this respect took place in the United States, around the time the Spanish Civil War was beginning. It was generally agreed on the left that while slavery had been abolished and the threat that the Confederacy posed to capitalist industrialization removed, postbellum reconstruction had failed to transform the condition of the black population, which remained under the undemocratic and racially oppressive Jim Crow regime. In a book written at the tail end of the ultraleft Third Period, James Allen, the leading white expert on black issues for the Communist Party of the United States of America (CPUSA) and author of such pamphlets as *Negro Liberation* (1932) claimed that Reconstruction had ended with the return to power of the plantation owners, who had effectively restored the former system in the new guise of sharecropping. Leave aside the absurd contention that the plantation owners were "restored" to their former position as slaveowners after 1877, what political conclusions did Allen draw from this? The landowners would not allow the South to be industrialized, blacks would be prevented from migrating to the industrialized North, and no help could be expected from the northern capitalists who had allowed the restoration to take place: the only hope of improving their conditions in the interim before the inevitable collapse of capitalism was therefore the establishment of a state exclusively for African Americans in the "Black Belt" Southeast of the United States. By the time this work appeared in 1936, the Seventh Comintern Congress the preceding year had shifted position to one of support for the Popular Front, leading the CPUSA to abandon the policy of black self-determination and look for salvation from the "progressive" northern liberal bourgeoisie around Roosevelt, who had earlier been denounced as a proto-fascist, a term now mainly reserved for the southern landowners. Allen argued this position in another book that upheld exactly the same analysis of Reconstruction, while now arguing a diametrically opposite political line—one that extended this newfound admiration for the northern bourgeoisie back to Lincoln himself.[29] Productions of the sort written by Allen, which had equivalents in every country where Communist parties were established, were simply elaborations of the current party line, justified by historical examples that could be manipulated to support virtually any conclusion: they were not works of history in any recognizable sense. Nevertheless, around the same time a generation began to emerge that would be responsible for genuine historical work for which bourgeois revolution would be a central theme.

HISTORY: MODELS AND TRADITIONS

In the orthodox conception that Stalinism essentially inherited from the Second International, the bourgeois revolutions were part of a linear pattern of historical development, showing how new ruling classes rose and replaced their predecessors. In the words of a leading Stalinist textbook, first published in 1938: "the capitalist system can be replaced by the Socialist system, just as at one time the feudal system was replaced by the capitalist system."[30] The idea that this was a process which *would* rather than simply *could* happen was captured in the title of a book by the distinguished British scholar of Chinese science and technology Joseph Needham, published in the immediate aftermath of the Second World War: *History Is on Our Side*.[31] But orthodoxy did not only involve a particular view of history, it also began to affect how Marxist history was written—indeed, with the exception of a handful of earlier works, it could even be said that Marxist history only *began* to be written in any systematic way after the advent of Stalinism.

As we have seen, down to the 1920s, all the Marxists who had contributed to discussions about the bourgeois revolution, with the partial exception of Lukács, had been activists, not academics; even their bourgeois predecessors had been political actors like Roederer or at least public intellectuals like Smith. For Barnave in 1789, Marx in 1848, or Lenin in 1905, the bourgeois revolution was a living reality and historical considerations were intended to inform their response to it: they produced many great insights into history, but almost always in pursuit of contemporary political goals. (This of course is the opposite of the Stalinist approach, where contemporary political goals determined how history was understood.) From the 1930s, however, we begin to see for the first time the gradual emergence of a cohort of university-based professional historians, usually members of the Communist Party or at least influenced by Communist Party politics, beginning to explore their respective national histories, in which the bourgeois revolution featured as an important turning point, particularly in the cases of England, France, and America, where it was long over.[32] Leading Marxist historians like Eric Hobsbawm and Albert Soboul, who worked within the orthodox framework throughout their careers, albeit in increasingly sophisticated ways, were authoritative figures who could not be ignored even by ideologically hostile fellow-academics and who, above all, were widely read by a public that extended far beyond the left, however broadly defined. The quality of their historical writing contrasted strongly with the inadequacy of their historical theory that underlay it; but the former also had the contradictory effect of validating the latter, which provided a simple and schematic means of understanding historical development apparently untainted by any intrinsic connection with the nature of the Stalinist regimes.

Perhaps the most distinguished Marxist historians of any nation were those associated with the Historians Group of the Communist Party of Great Britain (CPGB), established in 1938, which included in its ranks Christopher Hill, Rodney Hilton, Victor Keirnan, Brian Manning, John Saville, Geoffrey de Ste. Croix, and Edward Thompson, among others. A memoir by Hobsbawm, one of its leading members, claims: "On the whole we did not feel any sense of constraint, of certain matters being off-limits, nor did we feel that the Party tried to interfere with or distort our work as communist historians." One reason for this may of course have been that the CPGB leadership were sure that members of the group had internalized Stalinist assumptions so thoroughly that no interference was required—a perspective that Hobsbawm partly, if tacitly, accepts: "Our arguments were sometimes designed *a posteriori* to confirm what we already knew was necessarily 'correct,' especially in our discussions on Absolutism and the English Revolution." He argues that there were three reasons "by and large, our work as historians did not suffer more from the contemporary dogmatism":

> First . . . even during the most dogmatic Stalinist period, the authorized versions of Marxist history were concerned with genuine historical problems, and arguable as serious history, except where the authority of the Bolshevik Party and similar matters were involved. . . . Second, there was no "party line" on most British history, and what there was in the USSR was largely unknown to us . . . Third, the major task we and the Party set ourselves was to criticize non-Marxist history and its reactionary implications, where possible contrasting it with older, politically more radical interpretations.[33]

Many of the historians associated with the Historians Group, not least Hobsbawm himself, went on to produce substantial and impressive works of lasting value, as the names listed above remind us. Nevertheless, he does rather play down the constricting effects of orthodoxy here, particularly during the period that he regards as the most creative in the group's existence, between 1946 and 1956, as we shall see in relation to its debates over the prerevolutionary English state.

The conception of bourgeois revolution deployed by these and subsequent generations of Marxist historians who received their political training during the period of High Stalinism were quite compatible with pre- or non-Marxist radical or "economic" interpretations of history. In the United States, for example, Charles and Mary Beard conceptualized the American Civil War as a "Second American Revolution," the first being the War of Independence, which finally allowed the unfettered expansion of capitalism on the basis of industrialization and free farming. The necessity for a "Second American Revolution" had been argued even before the event.[34] But even if the concept was not original to them, their version became the dominant explanatory framework through which the period was understood by the left: a comparison between the Beards' version of the Civil War in *The Rise of American Civilization* (1927–30) and the nominally Marxist account by Louis Hacker in *The Triumph of American Capitalism* (1940), for example, does not reveal any fundamental differences of approach.[35] Yet the Beards explicitly rejected Marxism for a politics that bridged Progressivism and moderate reformist socialism. Nevertheless, they embraced a brand of determinism quite as extreme as anything produced by theoreticians of the Second or Third Internationals.[36] Herbert Morais, the CPUSA member who edited the first collection of Marx and Engels's writings on the Civil War, criticized the "limitations inherent in the liberal bourgeois approach" of the Beards—by which he meant their neglect of the role of the working class and African Americans—but nevertheless hailed as "probably the best description of the Civil War."[37] But the influence of the Beards spread far beyond the ranks of orthodox communism, being accepted by later professional, if left-leaning, historians, independent Marxist scholars, and even Trotskyists.[38]

What then was this conception of the bourgeois revolution? In most cases the narrative that emerged took approximately the following, relatively simple form. From the sixteenth century, a class of urban capitalists began to develop within European feudalism, gradually laying the economic foundations of a new form of society. Despite their growing economic weight, these capitalists were consigned to a position of social inferiority by a rural class of feudal landowners and excluded from political power by the absolutist states. "Such a discrepancy never lasts forever," wrote Georges Lefebvre in 1939 of France: "The Revolution of 1789 restored the harmony between fact and law."[39] In order to release capitalism from its feudal restrictions, the absolutist states needed to be overthrown; but since the capitalist class was still only a minority of the population—albeit a bigger minority than the feudal class it hoped to supplant—it had to lead a coalition of the other oppressed classes in order to accomplish the revolution. As Hill wrote of the English Civil War in 1940 ("a class war"): "Parliament beat the king because it could appeal to the enthusiastic support of the trading and industrial classes in town and country-side, to the yeomen and progressive gentry, and to wider masses of the population whenever they were able by free discussion to understand what the struggle was really about."[40] Most of these historians accepted, as had Marx and Engels, that the popular movement had forced the bourgeois leadership to go further than the latter originally intended, but that it could not have achieved its own independent objectives. Soboul exemplified the overwhelming consensus here, writing in relation to France:

> Doubtless it was impossible for [the popular movement] to achieve its particular ob-jective—the egalitarian and popular republic towards which the sans-culottes were moving without any clearly defined programme—prevailing circumstances as well as its own contradictions raised far too many obstacles. Nevertheless, the popular movement has still contributed towards historical progress by its decisive intervention in support of the bourgeois revolution. Without Parisian sans-culotterie, the bour-geoisie could not have triumphed in so radical a fashion.[41]

Insofar as the bourgeois revolutions involved the people, they were seen as the high point to date of a tradition of popular struggle extending back through history, in which the oppressed resisted their ruling class oppressors, whichever class they happened to belong to at any time. As we saw in chapter 11, these traditions, which could be traced back to the very origins of the labor movement, had already been formalized by the parties of the Second International, so in this respect too Stalinism involved a reaffirmation of views that were already deeply embedded in the various labor movements, although before 1914 they had rarely been displayed in such nakedly nationalistic terms. The assimilation of the radical tradition received its greatest impetus from the turn to the Popular Front in 1935, which acted as a ref-erence point for many of the new breed of Marxist historians for the rest of their lives.[42] With short-lived oscillations back to bureaucratic ultraleftism in line with Stalin's foreign policy (between the signing of the Nazi-Soviet Pact and the launch of Operation Barbarossa, and again at the onset of the Cold War), the Popular Front position set the general tone of Communist Party and Communist Party–influenced work down to their dissolution in the early 1990s, with obvious implications for the intellectual framework within which research and writing were conducted.

At the opening of the Seventh Congress of the Communist International in 1935, soon-to-be Secretary General Georgi Dimitroff complained: "The fascists are rummaging through the entire *history* of every nation so as to be able to pose as the heirs and continuators of all that was exalted and heroic in its past, while all that was degrading or offensive to the national sentiments of the people they make use of as weapons against the enemies of fascism." They were being allowed to do so by Communists who indulged in "national nihilism": "Communists who suppose that all this has nothing to do with the cause of the working class, who do nothing to enlighten the masses on the past of their people in a historically correct fashion, in a genuinely Marxist-Leninist spirit, who do nothing *to link up the present struggle with the people's revolutionary traditions and past*—voluntarily hand over to the fascist falsifiers all that is valuable in the historical past of the nation, so that the fascists may fool the masses."[43] Taking his lead from Dimitroff, Maurice Thorez, leader of the Communist Party of France, similarly declared: "We will not abandon to our enemies the tricolor, the flag of the great French Revolution, or the Marseillaise, the song of the soldiers of the Convention."[44]

The British Communist Jack Klugman retrospectively noted that "God Save the King" presented rather more difficulties for the left than "Le Marseillaise," but nevertheless the embrace of "progressive national feelings" had benefits:

> It repossessed for the Marxist revolutionary of today his or her cultural heritage of the past. We became no longer just the critics of the insufficiencies of Wat Tyler seen through the eyes of a card-carrying peasant, or of the 1790 Jacobins, or of the moralistic limitations of Chartism. We became the inheritors of the peasants' revolt, of the left of the English Revolution, of the Chartist movement, of the women's suffrage movement from the 1790s to today. It set us in the right framework, it linked us with the past and gave us a more correct course for the future.[45]

Raphael Samuel's reconstruction of the British—or more precisely, English—Stalinist approach to popular memory can stand for that of the Communist parties more generally, each of which appealed to a similar national lineage:

> One of the more ambiguous legacies of radical-democratic history is that of English nationalism—the notion that the English people have been singled out for a special place in history, that the English language is superior to others, and that the liberty of the individual is more secure than it is abroad. It forms the groundwork of Green's *Short History*, with its brilliantly chosen but utterly arbitrary starting point of the "free" Anglo-Saxons. It is tentatively present in the historical work of H. M. Hyndman; it finds fugitive echoes in the work of the early Communist writers, notably T. A. Jackson; it reemerges as a major theme in Communist writings of the period of the Popular Front . . . Communists, in this period, set about deliberately fostering a sense of democratic heritage, and in those "March of History" pageants which the party organized in 1936, Cromwell's portrait was borne proudly aloft with those of John Ball and Wat Tyler. In line, historically, with the broad democratic alliance which the Party was attempting to build, class struggles—such as the Peasant's revolt and the English Civil War—were presented as fights for freedom, and, as in liberal-radical history, the focus was on "the common people" rather than the industrial working class.[46]

In the May Day 1938 marches in Scotland, CPGB members wore tartan sashes and carried banners displaying images of Sir William Wallace and King Robert the Bruce, just as the first Scottish working-class radicals had back in the second decade of the nineteenth century, but now with the addition of Calgacus, the Pictish warrior who supposedly led the Caledonians to defeat by the Roman Ninth Legion at the Battle of Mons Graupius in AD 79.[47] As these types of lineage suggest, the radical traditions to which bourgeois revolutions belonged were treated

almost exclusively in national terms. The local working-class movement had inherited the democratic heritage and had to defend it—if necessary against unpa-
triotic sections of the present-day bourgeoisie who threatened to betray it. This
aspect of the orthodox model did not only provide the left with a historical explanation but also political inspiration, which in many respects was the key to its appeal for militants and why it was hard to abandon for those raised in it: Anthony
Barnet recalls Hill ending a talk at the foundation of the History Workshop Centre
for Social History during the late 1980s by saying "it is an insult for those like
Thatcher who are destroying our industry to talk about patriotism—they don't
know the meaning of the word."[48]

There were of course differences of emphasis about the popular movement.
Dona Torr, like Hill a leading figure in the Historians Group of the CPGB, wrote
in 1956 of the English Revolution:

> There were therefore two revolutions brewing in 1640. The City merchants, the richer
> gentry wanted a "small" revolution, the overthrow of restrictions on free capitalist de-
> velopment, a seizure of control at the centre by classes who already possessed it locally:
> and then business as usual. But the people had other views. Continuous traditions
> linked them with the past struggles of the English peasantry. The theory of the Nor-
> man Yoke looked back to freer Anglo-Saxon times. Hostile pamphlets described
> Oliver Cromwell as a Wat Tyler, Lilburne as a Jack Straw.... So the ideas of the Lev-
> ellers and the Diggers have their place in the English revolutionary tradition which
> extends from John Ball to Tom Mann.[49]

But the instability within such a promiscuous embrace of heroic forerunners is
obvious from those listed by Torr. Cromwell and the Independents crushed Lil-
burne and the Levellers, who in turn had quite a different class base from Winstanley and the Diggers. It is obviously impossible to celebrate each of these equally,
at least not for the same reasons. We get some sense of this tension in Margaret
James's discussion of contemporary materialist interpretations of the English Revolution for the CPGB's tercentenary commemorative volume, in which Hill's famous essay first appeared. Naturally, some attention is paid to Harrington and his
followers like Baynes, but the bulk of the article is taken up with a discussion of
Winstanley, with whom James is clearly far more comfortable and sympathetic,
even though his influence and that of his followers was virtually nonexistent in
their own time.[50] On the one hand, then, the revolutionary nature of the historical
bourgeoisie had to be emphasized, partly in order to identify the idea of a succession
of revolutionary classes, partly because of the alliances that the Communists were
endlessly seeking with "progressive" sections of the contemporary bourgeoisie
against fascism, "monopolies," and so on; but on the other, the popular classes whose
goals could not be achieved, whose aspirations were suppressed by the self-same
revolutionary bourgeoisie, also had to be enshrined as precursors to the modern
socialist movement. The contradictions were intense, but usually avoided by oscil-
lating between different positions depending on the occasion.

However, while it was one thing to invoke the Levellers or the sansculottes from May Day platforms, it was quite another to foreground popular radicalism below the level of the bourgeoisie in ways that reflected on contemporary politics. At the end of the Second World War erstwhile Trotskyist Daniel Guérin invoked the strategy of permanent revolution in relation to France between 1793 and 1795.[51] Yet even Guérin, who wrote of the "coexistence of a bourgeois revolution and the embryonic form of a proletarian revolution," did not believe that the latter had any possibility of ultimate success at the time: "The objective conditions of the time did not allow the [sansculotte] vanguard to beat the bourgeoisie at their own game."[52] However, even this essential level of agreement with the orthodox tradition did not spare Guérin from severe criticism, not least because of his treatment of Robespierre, who features in his history as the suppressor of the popular masses and the leader most responsible for deradicalizing the revolution from 1793. Whatever the anachronistic exaggerations in Guérin's account, of which there are several, his real abiding sin in the eyes of the orthodox was refusing to subscribe to the myth of the entirely progressive nature of the bourgeois leadership and the implication that other forces in the contemporary world had performed the same role as Robespierre, in situations where working-class victories were possible.[53]

There were, however, more substantive problems with the orthodox model of bourgeois revolution than the question of how relevant their key events and personalities were to contemporary socialist concerns. It was essentially based on the experience of England between 1640 and 1660, and France between 1789 and 1815. A handful of other cases, notably the Dutch Revolt and the American Revolutionary and Civil Wars could be assimilated to it without undue conceptual stretching; but beyond them were either failed attempts, most of which occurred between 1820 and 1849, or a series of events that may have been decisive in establishing modern nation-states, but which bore little or no resemblance to the dominant Anglo-French amalgam. This need not have been an insurmountable theoretical problem, as long as the assumption had been dropped that every country had to undergo a bourgeois revolution on these lines; but this was impossible, for reasons that had little to do with scientific understanding of capitalist development and much to do with the ideological significance of bourgeois revolutions in Stalinist narratives of "the peoples' story." Consequently, in the West at least, attempts were made to identify a bourgeois revolution in every national history. As Perez Zagorin argues, the combination of a "monocausal class explanation" on the one hand, and a "teleology" of historical development on the other led Marxists to stretch the concept of bourgeois revolution so as to "absorb within its elastic boundaries events as different in nature as the German Peasant War and Reformation, the English and French Revolutions, almost all the revolutions of 1848, the Risorgimento, the American Civil War, the Russian revolutions of 1905 and February 1917, the Mexican Revolution, and the procommunist phase of the Chinese Revolution—a list that merely confirms its lack of usefulness as type in the empirical study of revolution."[54] Some of these events might indeed have been bourgeois revolutions, but the inclusion of all these events (and others) was not achieved by developing a new, more rigorous and inclusive concept, but by claiming that they actually conformed to the orthodox model, leading inexorably to massive historical distortions in two principal areas.

The first involved the question of the precapitalist state. Stalin had undertaken his attempt to define bourgeois revolutions in order to establish the differences between them and socialist revolutions; but one similarity was that both involved an attack on the state power, either to seize it (the bourgeois revolution) or smash and replace it (the socialist revolution). But in almost every case except those from which the model was constructed this had not happened. In a revealing episode involving the Historians Group of the CPGB, the argument was put that it had not happened even in England, one of the model bourgeois-revolutionary states. Jurgen Kuczynski's pseudonymous review of Hill's 1940 pamphlet on the English Revolution argued:

> While capitalism developed within the framework of dying feudalism within the fourteenth century it became the dominant element in the sixteenth and gave society as a whole a capitalist bourgeois character. Marx is right: the sixteenth century society is a bourgeois society. . . . Elizabeth was not a feudal monarch bowing to the demands of an oppressed capitalist class. She was the most prominent capitalist in a capitalist bourgeois society—comparable to Leopold of Belgium, one of the greatest colonial investors in the nineteenth century.

This does rather raise the question of what the Civil War was actually about. For Kuczynski it was essentially a mopping-up operation: "There still existed feudal strongholds in the country, and under Charles I there was a counter-revolutionary movement. . . . The Civil War of 1642 began as a war against this counter-revolution, was a necessary bloody suppression of feudalism joined by certain treacherous bourgeois groups (e.g., some monopolists) in order to keep the bourgeoisie in power."[55] A reply by Douglas Garman made the weak a priori argument that Kuczynski must be wrong because if no revolution was required to bring the bourgeoisie to power in England, then this opened the door to reformism. The possibility that, under certain conditions, the bourgeoisie might not require any sort of revolution does not seem to have occurred to him.[56] Nor did it to anyone else—or if it did the thought was quickly repressed. Kuczynski's rejoinder focused on the nature of the absolutist state: "Absolute monarchy was a product of bourgeois development in England at a time when this form of government and its institutions were a valuable safeguard against feudalism. With the progress of capitalism, absolute monarchy became a hindrance."[57] In the discussion that followed Kiernan similarly argued that the English Revolution had actually achieved very little that had not already been achieved by the Tudor and Stuart state, and that consequently the genuine radicalism of the years between 1640 and 1660 came from the petty bourgeoisie who were resisting the effects of capitalism, not feudalism.[58] Kiernan subsequently withdrew his more controversial positions, while urging a more balanced view of the Tudor state.[59] A statement of orthodoxy, probably written by Christopher Hill, Brian Pearce, and Dona Torr, reaffirming both the feudal-absolutist nature of the Tudor and Stuart state and the bourgeois-revolutionary nature of the events between 1640 and 1649 was published in the *Communist Review* during 1948, as the collective view of this section of the Historians Group.[60] (Alas, contrary to legend, the class nature of the Tudor and Stuart state does not appear to have been decided on by a vote.) As in Garman's original response to Kuczynski, Hill's position was ultimately based on political considerations. He compared those who doubted the feudal nature of the Tudor and Stuart state to the Russian historian Pokrovsky:

> This controversy is of great political importance, because the bourgeois revolution is still a real political issue in Asia, South East Europe, Spain, and other parts of the world. Pokrovsky, by ante-dating the Bourgeois Revolution [to a period earlier than 1640], in fact played into the hands of Trotskyism.... Pokrovskyism is fundamentally reformist because it assumes that a transfer of power is possible without revolution.[61]

The debate over British absolutism had an interesting coda during the international debate on the transition to capitalism stimulated by the publication of Maurice Dobb's *Studies in the Development of Capitalism* (1946), which ran from 1950 to 1955, Dobb reaffirmed that the only alternative to considering that the English ruling class and its state were still feudal was the one raised by Kuczynski and more tentatively by Keirnan, namely that the civil war was an attempted counterrevolution by a court and crown effectively excluded from power by the bourgeoisie. The US Marxist Paul Sweezy who, unconnected to his national Communist Party, was less susceptible to the claims of orthodoxy, rightly rejected this position as untenable and unnecessary: "Why isn't there another possibility which Dobb does not mention, namely, that in the period in question there was not one ruling class but several, based on different forms of property and engaged in more or less continuous struggle for preferment and ultimate supremacy?" This would involve treating the absolutist state as Engels had in *The Origins of the Family*, as an institution balancing between classes: "In this interpretation, the civil war was the bourgeois revolution in the straightforward sense that it enabled the capitalist class to master the state and achieve definitive mastery over the other classes."[62] This does not, however, answer the question of whether the feudal-absolutist state has to be overthrown in the same way as a capitalist state. In a commentary on this discussion, Keith Tribe has identified a further problem, arguing that the "formula 'feudal-absolutist' is deeply contradictory."[63] But this depends on seeing the feudal state in entirely static terms: it is perfectly possible to conceptualize absolutism as the typical form of the feudal state during the transition to capitalism; the problem is whether the state can simultaneously act in the interests of two distinct ruling classes.

As the outcomes of these discussions suggest, the idea that those social classes situated *above* the bourgeoisie might achieve a revolution to advance capitalism and, ultimately, the situation of the bourgeoisie was considered inconceivable. The lords might begin revolutions, as in France, but never complete them. "In the present case the Revolution was launched by those whom it was going to sweep away," wrote Georges Lefebvre in 1932, "not by those who were to be its beneficiaries."[64] Similarly, the absolutist states themselves acted to confine capitalism within existing feudal social relations. As Kohachiro Takahashi wrote in one of the most important contributions to the original debate on the transition to capitalism:

> These revolutions in Western Europe [England and France], by the independence and the ascent of the petty commodity producers and their differentiation, set free from among them the forces making—as it were *economically*—for the development of capitalist production; while in Prussia and Japan this "emancipation" was carried out in the opposite sense. The organization of feudal land property remained intact and the classes of free and independent peasants and middle-class burghers were undeveloped. The bourgeois "reforms" like the *Bauernbefreiung* and the *Chiso-kaisei* (agrarian reforms in the Meiji Restoration), contain such contrary elements as the legal sanctioning of the position of the Junker's land property and parasite land proprietorship of semi-feudal character. . . . The socio-economic conditions for the establishment of modern democracy were not present; on the contrary capitalism had to make its way within an oligarchic system—the "organic" social structure—designed to suppress bourgeois liberalism.[65]

Once again we can see the deleterious impact of envisaging bourgeois revolution as a series of tasks that existing feudal classes understandably had never shown any great willingness to implement. The inescapable consequence of doing so is shown in this succinct assessment by Eric Hobsbawm from around the bicentenary of the French Revolution: "After 1830 there were no further successful bourgeois revolutions."[66]

The other issue, to which Takahashi referred, was the question of democracy. Partly to justify current Stalinist foreign policy, the notion of a "bourgeois-democratic" revolutionary stage—contentious enough even in contemporary political terms—was now read back into history and applied to England, France, and the other countries where bourgeois revolutions had been identified, but with the emphasis on democracy. Democracy had been an aspect of popular intervention in a minority of the bourgeois revolutions, debated in the English Putney Debates of 1647 or embodied in the Parisian Sections from 1789 to 1794; but only in France was it a relatively stable legacy of the revolutions themselves, since its establishment almost always followed them, often at a considerable distance in time. In the Stalinist model, democracy became the most important of a checklist of "tasks" borrowed from the French Revolution—the others were the agrarian question and national unification—which had to be ticked off before the bourgeois revolution could be declared complete. In Japan, for example, the issue divided opinion in the Communist Party before the Second World War with one faction, the Rono-ha, taking the view that the Meiji could be described as a bourgeois revolution on essentially consequentialist grounds.[67] If these "tasks" were really taken seriously, then the Japanese revolution was incomplete until the agrarian reforms imposed by the US occupiers after 1945. Unfortunately this introduces further problems since the American Revolution itself was presumably unfinished until the black population achieved full formal civil rights with the passing of the 1965 Voting Rights Act, the 1967 Supreme Court judgment in the case of *Loving v. Virginia* allowing "mixed" marriages, and so on. The absurdity of such notions should be obvious.

Alternatively, if no plausible contender for the role could be found, the actual but apparently deviant history could be presented as the reason for failure to achieve normative levels of capitalist development or representative democracy, particularly where such failures that supposedly led the nation in question to succumb to fascism. In this way, even the absence of revolutions on the Anglo-French model confirmed its validity. Here, for example, is the by now long-orthodox Lukács in 1952 describing the supposed consequences for Germany of the irrationalism produced by "retarded capitalist development":

> The other major nations of the West, especially England and France, had already attained national unity under an absolute monarchy. . . . In Germany, on the other hand, the bourgeois revolution had first to fight for national unity and lay its corner-stones. (Only Italy experienced a similar development; moreover its intellectual consequences show, despite all the historical differences between the two countries, a certain affinity which has had notorious repercussions in the very recent past.)

But according to Lukács, the bourgeois revolution failed to occur, with the result that "the major upheavals . . . which laid the foundations for democratic developments in the West" were missing in Germany, where events produced in the masses only "an ideology of submission"; because "the German nation's unity was created not by way of revolution but from 'the top'. . . this side of the German's mentality remained virtually unchanged." Even the establishment of the Weimar Republic in 1918 did nothing to enlighten the "democratically uneducated masses": "Here again we can observe the big contrast between the German and the Franco-English development, where revolutionary democratic periods (Cromwell, the Great Revolution, etc.) were the periods of greatest national upsurge. The circumstances of the Weimar Republic's origin supported the old view of an anti-democratic development that was 'specifically German' and uniquely suited to 'Germany's essence.'"[68] It is notable that although Lukács begins by discussing the limited extent of German capitalism, the main burden of his argument actually falls on the absence of German democracy. That one of the great figures of the classical Marxist tradition should be reduced to these arguments, which essentially suggest that the German working class brought the punishment of fascism upon itself, is an indication of the malign power of Stalinism to corrupt even the finest minds.

These arguments had an influence among thinkers of the left who did not regard themselves as Marxists of however heterodox a nature. Take, for example, the arguments of the leading figure in North American radical sociology, Barrington Moore, in his classic work, *Social Origins of Dictatorship and Democracy* (1966). Moore characterized the orthodox position as involving:

A steady increase in the economic power of the commercial and manufacturing classes in the towns up to the point where economic power comes into conflict with political power still in the hands of an old ruling class based mainly on the land. At this point there supposedly occurs a revolutionary explosion in which the commercial and manufacturing classes seize the reigns of political power and introduce the main features of parliamentary democracy.

Although Moore regarded this picture as being "not altogether false," he added that "this meaning of bourgeois revolution is such a simplification as to be a caricature of what took place," giving three aspects of those events he accepted as bourgeois revolutions which contradicted orthodoxy:

The importance of capitalism in the English countryside that enabled the English landed aristocracy to retain control of political machinery right through the nineteenth century; . . . the weakness of any purely bourgeois impulse in France, its close ties with the old order, its dependence on radical allies during the Revolution, the continuation of peasant economy into modern times; . . . the fact that plantation slavery in the United States grew up as an integral part of industrial capitalism and presented an obstacle to democracy much more than capitalism.[69]

His own argument identified three possible paths to modernity, "bourgeois revolutions culminating in the Western form of democracy, conservative revolutions from above ending in fascism, and peasant revolutions leading to communism," constituted both "alternative routes and choices," and "successive historical stages."[70] The second category of "revolutions from above" opened up a promising line of argument. What Moore regarded as a central difficulty with the orthodox conception of bourgeois revolution also pointed toward an alternative:

Much of the confusion and unwillingness to use large categories comes from the fact that those who provide the mass support for the revolution, those who lead it, and those who ultimately profit from it are very different sets of people. As long as this distinction remains clear, it makes sense (and is even indispensable for the sake of drawing distinctions between as well as perceiving similarities) to regard the English Civil War, the French Revolution, and the American Civil War as stages in the development of *the* bourgeois-democratic revolution.

In short: "In discussing bourgeois revolutions the justification for the term rests on a series of legal and political consequences."[71] Moore noted that in Italy, Germany, and Japan, a factor in establishing the "social anatomy" of the regimes that emerged in the 1860s was "the retention of a very substantial share in political power by the landed elite, due to the absence of a revolutionary breakthrough by the peasants in combination with urban strata." Yet this did not mean that no development took place:

Some of the semiparliamentary governments that arose on this basis carried out a more or less peaceful economic and political revolution from above that took them a long distance toward becoming modern industrial countries. Germany traveled the furthest, Japan only somewhat less so, Italy a great deal less, Spain very little. Now, in the course of modernization by a revolution from above, such a government has to carry out many of the same tasks performed elsewhere with the help of a revolution from below. The notion that a violent popular revolution is somehow necessary in order to sweep away "feudal" obstacles to industrialization is pure nonsense, as the course of German and Japanese history demonstrates.[72]

It might appear therefore that Moore had arrived at a fully consequentialist position, complete with an understanding of what this implied in terms of agency and the category of "revolution from above"; but no. According to Moore, "Germany and, even more, Japan were trying to solve a problem that was inherently insoluble, to modernize without changing their social structure," which had terrible political consequences: "The only way out of this dilemma was militarism, which united the ruling classes. Militarism intensified a climate of international conflict, which in turn made industrial advance all the more imperative ... Ultimately these systems crashed in an attempt at foreign expansion, but not until they had tried to make reaction popular in the form of fascism."[73] In other words, although Moore goes very far toward breaking with orthodoxy, he too is unable to do so because of his adherence to the criteria of democracy: the failure to achieve a system of parliamentary democracy in time, together with the more general failure to achieve full-scale "modernization" doomed these countries to fascism—a position virtually indistinguishable from that of Lukács. Fortunately, the tradition to which the latter originally belonged does contain an alternative to the orthodoxy concerning bourgeois revolution, developed during the same period surveyed here. It is to that tradition that we now return.

14

CLASSICAL MARXISM (3) 1924–40: RETHINKING BOURGEOIS REVOLUTION—STRATEGY, HISTORY, TRADITION

Was there an alternative to the new orthodoxy and the tacit incorporation of the assumptions of Second International Marxism that it involved? From the late 1920s attempts to defend and develop the theory of bourgeois revolution, as with all the central themes of historical materialism, were increasingly carried out by politically defeated and geographically dispersed figures who had temporarily survived the twin catastrophes of Stalinism and fascism: Trotsky the exile, Gramsci the prisoner, Benjamin the wanderer. Although there were important overlapping areas in their thought, each of these three men produced a concept that explicitly or implicitly challenged an aspect of the orthodoxy—as contemporary strategy, as historical event, and as ideological tradition. With "uneven and combined development" Trotsky explained why a "bourgeois-democratic" stage was no longer necessary in revolutions that took place in the colonial and semicolonial world; with "passive revolution" Gramsci questioned how significant the role of the bourgeoisie had been in the majority of bourgeois revolutions that had already taken place; and with "the tradition of the oppressed" Benjamin exploded the idea of an unbroken chain of radicalism to which the proletariat could simply lay claim.

Vastly different in their relationships to fame and power, these figures were of course only three among the millions of individuals obliterated at what Victor Serge called "midnight in the century," as mainland Europe was divided between rival totalitarianisms and the world entered the most destructive war in history.[1] Like Trotsky, whom he once supported and for whom he always retained a critical respect, Serge lived out his final exile in Mexico and it was here, early in the Second World War, that he completed an account of his own life as an anarchist, Bolshevik, Left Oppositionist, "personalist," novelist, historian, and biographer. In the astonishing pages that recount his adventures in the first half of the twentieth century, Serge refers, in passing, to the fate of the three key figures whose work will be discussed in this chapter. In Paris during 1937 he takes part in a Popular Front demonstration, "when somebody pushed a Communist pamphlet into my hand: it contained a picture of Antonio Gramsci, who had died on 27 April of that year in an Italian prison hospital, after eight years of captivity." Still based Paris in 1940, but now under the collaborationist Vichy regime, he awaits the opportunity to escape to Central America and reads of more deaths in the newspapers. Serge did not know Benjamin (or the low opinion Benjamin held of his work) and simply records, "at this time, the poets Walter Hasenclever and Walter Benjamin commit suicide." Another death has, however, greater personal significance: "Trotsky murdered in Mexico. Yes, this is the hour for the Old Man to die, the blackest hour for the working classes: just as their keenest hour saw his highest ascendancy."[2]

In chronological sequence: Gramsci died of his many illnesses in a Roman hospital on April 27, 1937, shortly after being released from his fascist prison; Trotsky was assassinated in Mexico on August 21, 1940, victim of a Stalinist agent; Benjamin committed suicide on the Spanish border on September 25, 1940, to avoid being forcibly repatriated to France and the possibility of arrest by the Gestapo. When discussing their work I will also have occasion to refer to that of a fourth man, namely Lukács, who outlived these contemporaries, but only through his capitulation to Stalin, which in a different way can also be seen as tragic given the destructive effect it had on his theoretical powers. Serge also knew Lukács and recounts meeting him in Moscow "in 1928 or 1929," but at any rate after his capitulation: "He was then working at the Marx-Engels Institute; his books were being suppressed, and he lived bravely in the general fear. Although he was generally well-disposed towards me, he did not care to shake my hand in a public place, since I was expelled [from the Bolshevik Party] and a known Oppositionist. He enjoyed a physical survival, and wrote short, spiritless articles in Comintern journals."[3] In this chapter, however, we can step back to the work produced by Lukács before the Stalinist ascendancy when, at the height of his creativity, he produced several important insights into the structure of bourgeois revolutions that need to be integrated with those of Trotsky and Gramsci.

These then are our main protagonists. Other than the nature of their fate, did they have anything else in common? Trotsky unambiguously belonged to the classical Marxist tradition; so too did Gramsci and Lukács, although they are also often seen as contributing to the origins of what Perry Anderson called "Western" Marxism, to signal the shifting geographical axis of Marxist thought, from Eastern and Central Europe to Western Europe, after the rise of Hitler and consolidation of Stalinism. This tradition, according to Anderson, was "a product of *defeat*," it represented a version of Marxist theory that was divorced from the working class and had "migrated virtually completely into the universities"; the work of Western Marxism moved in the opposite direction to classical Marxism, "from economics and politics towards philosophy," took the form of a "second-order . . . discourse" or "esoteric discipline," and was characterized by "extreme difficulty of language."[4]

Anderson notes that both men were not only activists but leaders of their respective Communist parties whose theoretical work focused on the central political concerns of historical materialism. In both cases the presence in their later writings of the characteristic features of Western Marxism—an obscurity of expression in the case of Gramsci, a preoccupation with literature and philosophy in the case of Lukács—were not the result of personal preference but imposed on them by the respective conditions of imprisonment in fascist Italy and exile to Stalinist Russia.[5] Anderson assigns Benjamin to belong to the ranks of the Western Marxists without any equivocation, yet to me Benjamin appears as genuinely transitional figure between the classical and Western Marxist traditions in a way that Gramsci and Lukács were not. Benjamin's central focus on culture and his absence from direct political engagement tend to exclude him from the front rank of the classical Marxist tradition, as is suggested by a comparison with the career trajectory of Gramsci, the figure with whom he otherwise shares the most interests. Nevertheless, he belongs more to the classical Marxist tradition than to its successor for four reasons.

First, although Benjamin had ambitions to become an academic, he was never successful in obtaining a permanent post, with the result that he was forced to make a living through reviewing, public lecturing, translating, and other forms of intellectual odd-jobbery. In any case there is reason to believe that he would not have found the false impartiality and narrow specialization of academic life intolerable. Benjamin did publish in scholarly journals when he could, of course, but his non-academic status meant he was always more of a classical "man of letters" than, for example, the German Western Marxists with whom he is most often associated like Theodore Adorno, Max Horkheimer, or Herbert Marcuse. Isaac Deutscher was another Marxist from the subsequent generation who had to survive in similar ways outside the academy, although his style could scarcely have been more different from that of Benjamin. Their type barely survived the Second World War and hardly exists today. The group to which Benjamin had the greatest affinities was perhaps the left-wing New York intellectuals of the thirties and forties. There are many differences, of course. Their idiom was much clearer and more direct. And while many of them were also Jewish, even prior to their radicalization in the 1930s they tended to be secular, humanist, and, insofar as they were concerned with Judaism, it was mainly with defending distinctive aspects of the culture from assimilation. In other respects their outlook was cosmopolitan and the *doctrines* of Jewish mysticism, which play such a central role in Benjamin's work, were always alien to them.[6] Nevertheless, when allowances are made for their respective cultural particularities, it is clear that Benjamin and his New York contemporaries were the same type of intellectuals and that consideration of these affinities might be at least as productive as the attention that is endlessly paid to Benjamin's links with the Frankfurt School.[7]

Second, and partly because of his position outside the academy, Benjamin developed a literary style that was quite distinct from the clotted, constipated prose of the professors. It is not without its difficulties, of course. One of the reasons Anderson regards Benjamin as one of the representative figures of Western Marxism is a use of language involving "a gnomic brevity and indirection"—indeed, Anderson says that the famous passage from "On the Concept of History" invoking the Angel of History is expressed in language that would have been "virtually incomprehensible to Marx and Engels."[8] Anderson is simply wrong on the last point. If anything, it was Marx's own use of "sociological poetics" that may have provided Benjamin with one of the sources for his own style. When we consider some of the images that Marx employs—the capitalist as a sorcerer, conjuring up forces from the nether world that then escape his control; history as a theatrical performance, first tragic then comic; capital as a vampire, sucking the blood of living labor— the Angel of History does not seem so outlandish a concept as to present him with difficulties of comprehension.[9]

Third, although Benjamin was interested in what we now regard as high culture— above all in his obsessive, life-long engagement with the poet Charles Baudelaire— he also opened up entirely new areas for Marxist analysis in relation to folk, popular, and mass cultures. Because the babble about culture is now never-ending, and usually utterly valueless, it is important to understand both how innovative Benjamin's work was and how it differed from what followed. Although Benjamin was a modernist, his central emphasis was on the importance of new cultural forms that emerged *after* the ascendance of the bourgeoisie and bore limited resemblance to the historical novel or the classical symphony. Of his contemporaries, only Gramsci among the classical Marxists and George Orwell among the wider socialist movement had comparable interests in wider culture issues. In this respect, Benjamin took positions that were distinct from both the Frankfurt School and the New York intellectuals, both of which had considerably more pessimistic attitudes toward contemporary culture.

The fourth area of difference with Western Marxism places him closest to the classical tradition: his commitment to the socialist revolution. For, unlike all Western Marxists, Benjamin never adapted to Social Democracy, Stalinism, or any variation of socialism from above, nor did he lapse into political pessimism or despair. It is possible to interpret his suicide as an act of *personal* despair; but as Paul Wood writes, "it was undoubtedly an act of great courage."[10] It can also be interpreted as a final act of self-determination, by actively choosing death rather than surrender and so deny the Gestapo their victim. There is a parallel here with Trotsky, who, in a different context, wrote in his Testament that "threatened with a long-drawn out invalidism . . . I reserve the right to determine for myself the time of my death."[11] In any event, Benjamin retained to the end his belief in the possibility of socialist revolution on the basis of working-class self-activity. His final substantial work before his suicide, "On the Concept of History," and its preparatory notes, are the greatest theoretical affirmation, in the face of inconceivable adversity, of the actuality of the revolution in the entire Marxist canon. The difference between this work and outright renegacy of Horkheimer or even the evasiveness of Adorno could not be starker.

A common membership in the classical Marxist tradition, albeit with differing degrees of centrality, did not necessarily mean that the positions that our subjects took were always compatible. Benjamin read and admired several of Trotsky's works, but the two men neither met nor corresponded, so comparisons of their work can be made, as it were, on a purely intellectual level, based on the analysis of texts.[12] At first sight, nothing could be further from the materialist assessment involved in Trotsky's strategy of combining bourgeois and proletarian revolutions than the messianic impulse behind Benjamin's conception of the proletarian revolution as redeeming the dead generations of the oppressed: yet, in his own way Benjamin broke quite as dramatically with idea of historical stages as Trotsky. As Terry Eagleton puts it, what is a "political strategy" for Trotsky "remains an idea" for Benjamin; but nevertheless, what an idea: "A ripe moment of the homogenous time of bourgeois revolution becomes the strait gate through which the proletariat will enter, the *Jetztzeit* in which differential histories—feudalist, bourgeois-democratic, proletarian—are impelled into contradictory correspondence."[13]

In the case of Gramsci and Trotsky, however, where one might expect closer affinities, the relationship between their respective positions is actually more complex, precisely because it involved concrete political issues. Trotsky had sufficient respect for Gramsci as a cultural thinker to seek his advice on Italian Futurism and to publish the latter's response in the original Russian edition of *Literature and Revolution* (1923).[14] But as leaders of the international communist movement down to the mid-1920s, they differed over the controversies concerning Russian development and Comintern strategy. In addition, Gramsci famously misunderstood what Trotsky meant by permanent revolution and when he refers to it in a positive way it is always in relation to Marx's use of the term in and around 1848. At one point—in a prison note, which is in any case rendered opaque by the conflicting positions expressed within it—Gramsci compares permanent revolution with equal inaccuracy to both the pre-1914 Social Democratic strategy of waiting for a universal revolutionary upsurge (a Stalinist slander familiar to us from the previous chapter) and a "Napoleonic" strategy of imposing revolution from outside and above, one which would of course eventually be followed by Stalin in Eastern Europe between 1945 and 1948.[15]

Lukács did not know Gramsci personally, but retrospectively saw him as an ally in the ultimately unsuccessful struggle against the mechanical Marxism of the Second International: "We all inherited this problem, but none of us—not even Gramsci, who was perhaps the best of us—solved it."[16] On the other hand, Lukács did know Trotsky and seems to have had a personal antipathy toward him: "Trotsky I disliked immediately," he recalled toward the end of his life, "I thought him a poseur."[17] Lukács later recalled his choice in the mid-1920s: "Lenin died in 1924. The party struggles that followed his death were concentrated increasingly on the debate about whether socialism could survive in one country. . . . In the debates of the Russian

Party I agreed with Stalin about the necessity for socialism in one country and this shows very clearly the start of a new epoch in my thought."[18] It oversimplifies and compresses the process by which Lukács adopted Stalinist positions, however, to assume that this was complete by 1924 or 1926.[19] As late as 1928 he proposed a program of action (the "Blum Theses") for the Hungarian Communist Party (HCP) that involved essentially the same position he had set out in general terms four years earlier in his short book on Lenin. His theses were rejected by the other leaders of the HCP who promptly removed him from the Central Committee and his final capitulation to Stalinism, starting with the obligatory self-criticism, followed:

> I was indeed firmly convinced that I was in the right but I knew also—e.g. from the fate that had befallen Karl Korsch—that to be expelled from the Party meant that it would no longer be possible to participate actively in the struggle against Fascism. I wrote my self-criticism as an "entry ticket" to such activity as I neither could nor wished to continue to work in the Hungarian movement in the circumstances.[20]

Apart from the final documents written by Trotsky prior to his expulsion from the Bolshevik Party and then Russia itself, the "Blum Theses" were the last attempt from within the official communist movement to articulate a serious approach to dealing with precapitalist relations without accepting that this necessarily required a bourgeois revolution. For those who simply assimilate Lukács's position at this time to that of the Popular Front, which he enthusiastically adopted later in the 1930s and never abandoned, we have only to contrast the strategy he proposed for Hungary with the strategy that the Comintern was shortly to implement in Spain. Lukács accepted that the Stalinist regime was Thermidorian—on essentially the same grounds as Trotsky—but nevertheless thought it had to be accepted as an inevitable part of the revolutionary process.[21] Lukács had earlier argued against demarcating too closely between the bourgeois and proletarian revolutions; but here we can see the equally serious problems associated with failing to distinguish between their structural forms.

WAGERING ON REVOLUTION

What links all four figures together is something less concrete than a political strategy. It might rather be described as a subterranean *theme* within classical Marxism: commitment to a "wager" on the possibility of revolution. The concept of the wager was first introduced into Western culture by the Roman Catholic philosopher Blaise Pascal during the seventeenth century. Pascal's argument was that since we cannot know for certain whether God exists or not by way of our reason, we have to gamble, to wager, on his existence. Pascal argues that we have everything to gain and nothing to lose from wagering on the existence of God but everything to lose—that is, eternal life—from wagering against it.[22] Later Marxists secularized the argument, beginning with Lukács's pupil Lucien Goldmann in his classic study of Pascal and Racine, *The Hidden God* (1964), the title of which is taken from the former writer:

> Marxist faith is faith in the future which men make for themselves in and through history. Or more accurately, in the future that we must make for ourselves by what we do, so that this faith becomes a "wager" which we make that our actions will, in fact, be successful. The transcendental element present in this faith is not supernatural and does not take us outside or beyond history; it merely takes us beyond the individual.[23]

Alasdair MacIntyre further developed the theme in a brilliant discussion of Goldmann's book. He points out that "the wager of action" is not, or at least should not, be undertaken in a spirit of voluntarism: we understand that only certain actions are possible at any time with the possibility of success. But how do we acquire this knowledge?

> But if tragic thought and dialectical thought differ in . . . crucial respects, they also resemble each other at key points. Both know that one cannot first understand the world and only then act in it. How one understands the world will depend in part on the decision implicit in one's already taken actions. The wager of action is unavoidable. . . . Not eternity but the future provides a context which gives meaning to individual parts in the present. The future which does this is as yet unmade; we wager on it not as spectators, but as actors pledged to bring it into being.[24]

From the perspective of the 1960s MacIntyre advocated discovering a "Pascalian Marx" but in some respects he and Goldmann were recapitulating positions arrived at independently by different individuals within a shared tradition during the interwar period, in most cases without direct reference to Pascal.

Although Benjamin makes several passing references to Pascal, he does so without explicitly discussing the wager. Nevertheless, Michael Löwy has plausibly suggested that "On the Concept of History" is also infused with the belief that "the Marxist utopia of an authentic human community is of the order of a Pascalian wager":

> It is the engagement of individuals—or social groups—in an action that involves risk, the danger of failure, the hope of success, but to which one commits one's life. Any wager of this type is motivated by trans-individual values, whether these are immanent and secular, as in the Marxist wager on the achievement of the socialist community, or transcendent and sacred, as in the Pascal's wager on the existence of God, and is not susceptible of scientific proof or factual demonstration.[25]

Löwy does, however, cast Benjamin's position in an unnecessarily religious light, since there are as good Leninist as Jansenist grounds for seeing the wager on revolution as inescapable. Lenin tended to prefer more homely French wisdom than that of Pascal, encapsulated in Napoleon's phrase, "*on s'engage et puis . . . on voit*" [colloquially: "let's get stuck in . . . then we'll see"].[26] But however the idea is expressed, it surely informed Lenin's *practice* between his arrival at the Finland Station and the fall of the Winter Palace in 1917, above all in his relentless insistence that the specific moment has to be seized or the occasion may pass, no matter how propitious the general conditions may be. Moments had passed before: "It . . . is not every revolutionary situation that gives rise to a revolution; revolution arises only out of a situation in which . . . objective changes are accompanied by a subjective change, namely, the ability of the revolutionary *class* to take revolutionary mass action *strong* enough to break (or dislocate) the old government, which never, not even in a period of crisis, 'falls,' if it is not toppled over."[27] Benjamin inherited this heightened awareness of the need to act within the conjuncture:

> Definition of basic historical concepts:
> *Catastrophe*—to have missed the opportunity.
> *Critical moment*—the status quo threatens to be preserved.
> *Progress*—the first revolutionary measure taken.[28]

It is worth pausing at this stage to remember that Benjamin was a German Jew—that is, a member of a group on the verge of genocidal oppression from a country had had missed two "opportunities," in 1918–23 and 1929–33.

The very concept of an "opportunity" is incompatible with a voluntarist conception of revolution being possible in any and every set of conditions. But as Lukács wrote, revolutionaries, among whom Lenin was preeminent, should work from the principle that "the actuality of the proletarian revolution is no longer only a world historical horizon arching above the working class, *but that the revolution is already on the agenda.*" It is not of course that the revolution "is readily realizable at any given moment," but its actuality was "a touchstone for evaluating all the questions of the day": "Individual actions can only be considered revolutionary or counter-revolutionary when related to the central issue of revolution, which is only discovered by an accurate analysis of the socio-historic whole."[29] For Benjamin, Social Democracy—and implicitly Stalinism—is defined by its refusal to contemplate that "the revolutionary situation" will ever arrive:

> In reality, there is not a moment that would not carry with it its own revolutionary chance—provided only that it is defined in a specific way, namely as the chance for a completely new resolution of a completely new problem. For the revolutionary thinker, the peculiar revolutionary chance offered by every historical moment gets its warrant from the political situation. But it is equally grounded, for this thinker, in the right of entry which the historical moment enjoys vis-à-vis a quite distinct chamber of the past, one which up to that point has been closed and locked. The entrance into this chamber coincides in a strict sense with political action, and it is by means of such entry that political action, however destructive, reveals itself as messianic.[30]

What both Lukács and Benjamin are saying, in different ways, is not that revolutionaries should be declaring a state of permanent insurrection—which would indeed be voluntarism—but that they should behave in the knowledge that we are in the period in which revolution is historically possible and necessary. At certain places and times the overall contradictions of the era will lead to crises, to genuine "revolutionary situations," but the task of the revolutionary is not to passively wait for these to arise but to help bring them about and then take the opportunities they present.

Even under the best of objective conditions, a successful outcome cannot be guaranteed, only that our actions can make it more or less likely. In a passage from his prison notebooks, untranslated into English until 1971, Gramsci makes a similar point to MacIntyre:

> In reality one can "scientifically" foresee only the struggle, but not the concrete moments of the struggle, which cannot be the results of opposing forces in continuous movement which are never reducible to fixed quantities since within them quantity is continually becoming quality. In reality one can "foresee" to the extent that one acts, to the extent that one applies a voluntary effort and therefore contributes concretely to creating the result "foreseen." Prediction reveals itself thus not as a scientific act of knowledge, but as the abstract expression of the effort made, the practical way of creating a collective will.[31]

Lukács too was concerned to emphasize that political actors are part authors of their own performance: "In the dialectics of society the subject is always included in the reciprocal relationship in which theory and practice become dialectical with reference to each other."[32] In his defense of *History and Class Consciousness* from the mid-1920s he elaborated on the "moment of decision" that was involved: "The dialectical interaction of subject and object in the historical process consists in the fact that the subjective moment is, self-evidently . . . a product, a moment of the objective process." The "subjective moment" extends further back in time than the point at which revolution becomes a possibility: "If, of course, precisely in the decisive countries, the proletariat is subjectively too immature for revolution, then evidently that has objective, social causes, in whose ranks, however, an extraordinarily large role is played by subjective moments that have become objective moments."[33]

Both Lukács and Trotsky discussed the implications in more concrete terms in the context of Lenin's doctrine of the "art of insurrection." Lukács notes the way in which Lenin emphasizes "moments that are consciously *made*, that is to say brought into by the subjective side (by the conscious acting subject—groupings of forces, surprise attacks, etc.)": "Insurrection as an art is, then, one moment in the revolutionary process where *the subjective moment has a decisive predominance.*[34] Trotsky highlighted the way in which the missed opportunity affects not only the working class but also those other classes that fixed their hopes momentarily on the success of the working class: "A revolutionary situation is not long-lived. . . . If the proletarian party is not decisive enough to convert the hopes and expectations of popular masses into revolutionary action in good season, the flood-tide is quickly followed by an ebb."[35]

The greatest literary expression of the dilemma posed by the wager considered in political terms is Shakespearean rather than Pascalian, and involves the classic use of the tidal metaphor invoked by Trotsky. Shakespeare has Brutus say to Cassius on the eve of the Battle of Philippi (but imagine Lenin writing to the Bolshevik Central Committee during September 1917):

Our legions are brimful, our cause is ripe:
The enemy increaseth every day;
We, at the height, are ready to decline.
There is a tide in the affairs of men
Which, taken at the flood, leads on to fortune;
Omitted, all the voyage of their life
Is bound in shallows and in miseries.
On such a full sea are we now afloat;
And we must take the current where it serves,
Or lose our ventures.[36]

Yet Brutus and his fellow-conspirators lost that battle and their lives, an outcome that is in the nature of a wager played for such high stakes, as also in the case of revolution; but for all the unpredictability of the outcome, to refuse to play can lead to only one result. "Many potential revolutions fail for want of attempt," writes Andrew Abbott, "just as many attempted revolutions fail for want of structural opportunity."[37]

In the context of bourgeois revolutions the relevance of the wager in the work of these thinkers was twofold. On the one hand, if historical opportunities were missed in relation to a certain form of bourgeois revolution, one modeled on the experience of 1640 or 1789, then what consequences followed? In the absence of Cromwell and the Independents, Robespierre and the Jacobins, or Lincoln and the Radical Republicans, did the societies in question simply continue to stagnate, perhaps making superficial adjustments to their changing economic and political environment? Or did changed conditions imply that a different form of bourgeois revolution has become possible and may have even, unnoticed, taken place? This aspect was not purely historical since the question of whether "bourgeois-revolutionary tasks" or even the process as a whole still had to be undergone in certain countries was, as we have seen, a pressing political issue between the wars. But on the other hand, the same questions could be asked in situations where the possibilities of permanent revolution went unrealized either because the wager was refused or simply lost. In the absence of Lenin and the Bolsheviks, did the possibilities then revert to those of the bourgeois rather than proletarian revolution? In which case, which sections of the bourgeoisie would provide the agency if none had been able or willing to play this role before? These were some of the questions that the subjects of this chapter considered as the locomotive of world history began to rush toward catastrophe with the passengers unable, in Benjamin's words, "to activate the emergency break."[38]

"UNEVEN AND COMBINED DEVELOPMENT"

We left Trotsky in the previous chapter in the spring of 1927, as the policies of the Comintern were bringing the Chinese Revolution to defeat. Prior to March he had maintained virtually a year of silence on the subject and, even after reentering the debate, the content of his contributions indicated that he still conceived of the

Chinese Revolution as bourgeois-democratic in nature. Can we take these interventions at face value? His first and greatest biographer, Deutscher, concluded that they involved conscious concessions to his allies in the United Opposition, intended to maintain unity with those like Zinoviev and Radek who did not share his position on permanent revolution.[39] As I have already argued, however, there is no reason to assume that Trotsky was being evasive or insincere; as Tony Cliff argues: "It would be a mistake to assume that Trotsky was always absolutely clear about the role of the theory of permanent revolution in analyzing the prospects for the Chinese Revolution, and his formulations contradicting the theory appear long before the bloc with the Zinovievists."[40] The first occasion on which Trotsky unambiguously stated an alternative position seems to have been an article from September 1927 that concluded: "The Chinese revolution at its new stage will win as a dictatorship of the proletariat, or it will not win at all."[41] By this date the Chinese Revolution had already lost as a dictatorship of the proletariat, but Trotsky had nevertheless resumed adherence to the strategic position he had formerly advocated for Russia and he would never abandon it again: "In China the conception of the permanent revolution was confirmed once more," he wrote in 1938, "this time not in the form of victory, but of a catastrophe."[42]

Trotsky's initial adherence to the theory of bourgeois-democratic stages in China had been perfectly consistent and logical, as long as he continued to regard the conditions that produced the Russian Revolution as essentially unique. Once he dropped that assumption, and began to treat conditions in China as broadly comparable to those in Russia, the same argument for permanent revolution could be made for the former country and indeed for any other where these conditions applied. The wager on revolution could be made with an equivalent chance of success—provided of course these also included the subjective element of a revolutionary party committed to act in a revolutionary way. The events constitutive of the emergence of the Chinese labor movement, from the general strikes that immobilized coastal China during June 1925 to the insurrection that overthrew the warlord regime in Shanghai during March 1927, seems to have cumulatively demonstrated to Trotsky that it was no less a revolutionary social force than the Russian labor movement had been. This in turn implied that the Russian experience had not been exceptional after all, but only precocious, prefiguring the situation in still more backward social formations to the East that had been hastened by economic growth during and immediately after the First World War. In this perspective, what Trotsky referred to as Russian "peculiarities," first in *1905* then more famously in the opening chapter of *The History of the Russian Revolution*, must be seen as relating more to the particular *form* taken by the developmental process in Russian conditions rather than to its *nature*, which might have taken different forms in other countries. What was this process?

What had hitherto been missing from Trotsky's account of permanent revolution was any explanation for the *origin* of the revolutionary militancy of the Russian working class and, by extension, at least some of the other working classes in the underdeveloped world, such as in China. In identifying it, he finally provided permanent revolution with the theoretical basis that it had previously lacked, in the form of the law of uneven and combined development. To use the term "law" can give the wrong impression. Shortly after the term appeared in print for the first time in 1932, Trotsky himself shied away from doing so, writing: "As a law it is rather vague; it is more of a historical reality."[43] If it is a law, then it is of the type that Daniel Bensaïd has described as a "law of tendency": "In an open system, like political economy, the empirical regularities and constant conjunctions of events are in fact manifested as tendencies."[44] Bensaïd was thinking here of "the law of the tendency of the rate of profit to fall" introduced by Marx in the third volume of *Capital*. Trotsky himself gave an answer in general terms in his notebooks on dialectics from the mid-1930s:

> Some objects (phenomena) are confined easily within boundaries according to some logical classification, others present [us with] difficulties: they can be put here or there, but within stricter relationship—nowhere. While provoking the indignation of systematizers, such transitional forms are exceptionally interesting to dialecticians, for they smash the limited boundaries of classification, revealing the real connections and consecutiveness of a living process.[45]

The term "uneven and combined development" therefore simultaneously refers to a historical process and the attempt to theoretically comprehend that process in thought. This theoretical discovery, perhaps the most important in twentieth-century Marxism, took place between Chiang Kai-shek's coup in Shanghai during April 1927 and the completion of the first volume of *The History of the Russian Revolution*, the preface to which is dated November 14, 1930, where the term appears for the first time.

There is a tendency among Trotskyists to claim that the concept of uneven and combined development was already fully present rather than simply implicit in Trotsky's writings between 1905 and 1909, and that only the actual term is absent.[46] This seems to me to do a disservice to both historical accuracy and Trotsky, implying as it does that his thought failed to develop in any important respect after his initial breakthrough in the first decade of the twentieth century. It is true that there are isolated passages in his earlier work that foreshadow this or that aspect of uneven and combined development, and I will quote several of them in what follows; but they remain unsystematic intimations, the significance of which is only recognizable in retrospect. The most common mistake is to reduce uneven and combined development to, or confuse it with, uneven development, with the result that the radical *novelty* of what Trotsky meant by the former term is thereby diminished.[47] As Ernest Mandel once wrote, part of the "magnificent theoretical achievement" represented by the law of uneven and combined development is precisely that it is "quite distinct from the law of uneven development familiar to all Marxists."[48] Given the failure of so many Marxists to recognize the distinction, Mandel may have exaggerated how familiar the concept of uneven development actually was, or indeed still is.

Until the First World War uneven development had largely been a descriptive concept, without specific political implications. Marx and Engels, and indeed their Enlightenment predecessors used the concept, if not the term, and Trotsky in several places expressed his astonishment at claims by Stalin to the contrary.[49] But as Neil Smith notes, it "was first examined in any depth by Lenin, who tried to sketch some of the economic and geographical outlines of the process."[50] In *Imperialism: The Highest Stage of Capitalism* (1916) Lenin wrote that "the uneven and spasmodic development of individual enterprises, individual branches of industry and individual countries is inevitable under the capitalist system."[51] Essentially, he argued that by the beginning of the twentieth century uneven development had acquired three main aspects. One was the process by which the advanced states had reached their leading positions within the structured inequality of the world system. The pressure of military competition between the actual or aspirant great powers forced some of the absolutist states among them to adopt the level of economic and industrial development already achieved by their capitalist rivals: those who did so, in Germany, Italy, and Japan had leaderships that realized that this was a necessity if they were to have any chance not just of continuing to successfully compete in geopolitical terms but of surviving near the summit of the states system. In very compressed timescales they had been able to adopt the socioeconomic achievements of Britain to the extent that they became recognizably the same kind of societies, without necessarily reproducing every characteristic of the Anglo-Saxon pioneer: where backwardness remained it tended to be in the nature of the political regimes led by monarchs or emperors supported by a landowning aristocracy. By the outbreak of the First World War membership of the dominant states was essentially fixed. What remained was the second aspect of uneven development: the ongoing rivalry between the great powers that involved them constantly trying to catch up and overtake each other in a contest for both economic and geopolitical supremacy that would continue as long as capitalism itself. This rivalry led in turn to a third aspect: the developed imperialist states collectively but competitively asserting their dominance over two other types, described by Lenin as "the colonies themselves" and "the diverse forms of dependent countries which, politically are formally independent but in fact, are enmeshed in the net of financial and diplomatic dependence," like Argentina and Portugal.[52] Colonial expansion prevented some of the societies subject to it from developing at all, and in the case of the most undeveloped, the peoples involved suffered near or complete extermination and their lands were taken by settlers. More often the peoples survived, but their social systems were immobilized by imperial powers interested in strategic advantage or plunder, or both.

The most famous, and certainly the most often quoted passage in Trotsky's *The History of the Russian Revolution* is an expression of the first meaning of uneven development: "The privilege of historic backwardness—and such a privilege exists—permits, or rather compels, the adoption of whatever is ready in advance of any specified date, skipping a whole series of intermediate stages."[53] But if all that Trotsky had proposed was a schema in which the "advantages of backwardness" allowed less developed nation-states to adopt the most modern available technologies he would have remained within the limits of a well-established usage, widely acknowledged by many figures other than Lenin, some of whom were not Marxists. The radical American economist Thorstein Veblen, for example, wrote in 1915: "Measured by the rate of progression that had brought the English community to the point where it then stood [in 1870], the German industrial system was some two and half centuries in arrears—somewhere in Elizabethan times; its political system was even more archaic; and use and wont governing social relations in detail was of a character such as this economic and political system would necessarily foster." But unification enabled Germany to overcome some of this lag:

> Germany offers what is by contrast with England an anomaly, in that it shows the working of the modern state of the industrial arts as worked out by the English, but without the characteristic range of institutions and convictions that have grown up among English-speaking peoples concomitantly with the growth of this modern state of the industrial arts. Germany combines the results of English experience in the development of modern technology with a state of the other arts of life more nearly equivalent to what prevailed in England before the modern industrial revolution came on; so that the German people have been enabled to take up the technological heritage of the English without having paid for it in the habits of thought, the use and wont, induced in the English community by the experience involved in achieving it.

Like Japan, "Modern technology has come to the Germans ready-made."[54] Veblen did recognize, however, that such technologies would not necessarily overcome ideological or political backwardness, with which it could coexist for a period at least.

The Austro-Marxist Rudolf Hilferding formulated a similar position in more general terms immediately prior to the First World War, in his classic work *Finance Capital*:

> Capitalist development does not take place independently in each individual country, but instead capitalist relations of production and exploitation were imported along with capital from abroad, and indeed imported at the level already attained in the most advanced country. Just as a newly established industry today does not develop from handicraft beginnings and techniques into a modern giant concern, but is established from the outset as an advanced capitalist enterprise, so capitalism is now imported into a new country in its most advanced form and exerts its revolutionary effects far more strongly and in a much shorter time than was the case, for instance, in the capitalist development of Holland and England.[55]

Trotsky, like any serious Marxist of his generation, was familiar with *Finance Capital*, writing of its author that "he did, at any rate, write a serious book," before adding: "But the most scientific book cannot replace the absence of will, of initiative, of revolutionary instinct and political decision, without which action is inconceivable."[56]

Marxists like Gramsci who, unlike Hilferding, supported the Russian Revolution, identified the same process but also saw in it a means of avoiding capitalist development. Some of Gramsci's early comments on uneven development are merely banal, including such revelations as "capitalism is a world historical phenomenon, and its uneven development means that individual nations cannot be at the same level of economic development at the same time."[57] Gramsci did, however, make rather more penetrating comments in 1917 in an article entitled "The Revolution against *Capital*," in which he welcomed the October Revolution as a practical rejection of the stageism of the Second International:

> Why should [the Russian people] wait for the history of England to be repeated in Russia, for the bourgeoisie to arise, for the class struggle to begin, so that class consciousness may be formed and the final catastrophe of the capitalist world eventually hit them? The Russian people—or at least a minority of the Russian people—has already passed through these experiences in thought. It has gone beyond them. It will make use of them now to assert itself just as it will make use of Western Capitalist experience to bring itself rapidly to the same level of production as the capitalist world.

For Gramsci, the Russian experience of uneven development was a further extension of what had already occurred within the capitalist system: "In capitalist terms, North America is more advanced than England, because the Anglo-Saxons in North America took off at once from the level England had reached only after long evolution."[58]

The process of uneven development and its potential political implications were therefore relatively well established by the late 1920s. Trotsky continued to employ the term until 1930, most importantly in the articles collected in *The Third International after Lenin* and in *Permanent Revolution* and its various prefaces. In these texts his main emphasis is still distinguishing his use of uneven development from that of Stalin, for whom countries developed at different tempos and must therefore advance through a series of stages at their own individual pace until communism. Although Stalin emphasized all three senses of unevenness—the "advantages of backwardness," competition between the advanced countries, and the domination of the backward countries by the advanced—at different times, he always treated them in isolation from each other, emphasizing first one then another according to his political requirements. By contrast, Trotsky was concerned with establishing the inner connections between them on two levels: that of global capitalism as a totality—by which he meant *both* world economy *and* states system—and that of the individual countries located within it, in which the state might nevertheless still be precapitalist or colonial in form.

In relation to the first level, Trotsky was to emphasize, as perhaps no Marxist had done before, the nature of what would later tend to be called "the international": "If the historical process were such that some countries developed not only unevenly but even *independently of each other*, isolated from each other, then from the law of even development would undoubtedly follow the possibility of building socialism in one capitalist country—first in the most advanced country and then, as they mature, in the more backward ones."[59] But capitalism did not allow such independence and Marxist analysis had to begin with the reality it had created. Consequently: "Marxism takes its point of departure from world economy, not as a sum of national parts but as a mighty and independent reality which has been created by the international division of labor and the world market, and which in our epoch imperiously dominates the national markets. The productive forces of capitalist society have long ago outgrown the national boundaries. The imperialist war (of 1914–1918) was one of the expressions of this fact."

In the first place this had negative implications for the attempt to build "socialism in one country" in Russia:

> In respect of the technique of production socialist society must represent a stage higher than capitalism. To aim at building a *nationally isolated* socialist society means, in spite of all passing successes, to pull the productive forces backward even as compared with capitalism. To attempt, regardless of the geographical, cultural and historical conditions of the country's development, which constitutes a part of the world unity, to realize a shut-off proportionality of all the branches of economy within a national framework, means to pursue a reactionary utopia.[60]

But as Trotsky also made clear, it had implications for attempts to build socialism in one country in *any* country, even if they were more advanced than Russia or China:

> Not only backward China, but in general no country in the world can build socialism within its own national limits: the highly developed productive forces which have grown beyond national boundaries resist this, just as do those forces which are insufficiently developed for nationalization. The dictatorship of the proletariat in Britain, for example, will encounter difficulties and contradictions, different in character, it is true, but perhaps not slighter than those that confront the dictatorship of the proletariat in China.[61]

Trotsky highlighted instead the "unity" of the world economy and the "interdependence" of the imperial powers and the colonial and semicolonial world. Unevenness in this sense means simultaneously that individual countries could leap over the capitalist stage of development, as Russia was in the process of doing and as China might have, but would still be unable to complete the transition to socialism while the world economy as a whole remained dominated by the capitalist mode of production: the international system was both a spur at one moment (before the revolution) and a block at another (after the revolution).

The argument for permanent revolution as an international phenomenon has often been misrepresented either maliciously or as a result of sheer incomprehension. "Only counter-revolutionary Trotskyites talk such nonsense as that China has already completed her bourgeois-democratic revolution and that any further revolution must be socialist," wrote Mao Tse-tung in 1935, in an example of the first: "The revolution of 1924–27 was a bourgeois-democratic revolution, which was not carried to completion but failed."[62] Indeed—but Trotsky had never argued that the Chinese bourgeois-democratic revolution was completed in the 1920s, his point was rather that it had failed because the bourgeoisie had no interest in overthrowing the feudal and imperialist elements of the existing order, and the working class had been prevented from overthrowing them. Nicolas Krasso, in an example of the second, claimed that permanent revolution involved a vast socio-logical "schema" in which the intermediary institutions of political parties and na-tion-states is absent: "The refusal to respect the autonomy of the political level, which had previously produced an idealism of class action innocent of any party organization, now produced a global Gleichschaltung—a planetary social struc-ture, soaring above its articulations in any concrete international system." As a re-sult, Trotsky was apparently unable to distinguish between different countries and the strategies appropriate to them: "For him, capitalism was one and indivisible, and the agenda of revolution was one and indivisible, either side of the Vistula. This formal internationalism (reminiscent of that of Luxemburg) in fact abolished the concrete international differences between the various European countries." "History," Krasso—or possibly his editor—concluded, "kept different times in Paris, Rome, London or Moscow."[63] In fact, even a passing acquaintance with the volumes of Trotsky's writings devoted to Britain, China, Spain, or Germany would immediately reveal how insistent he was on identifying the particularity of each national trajectory, the care with which he assessed their comparative level of de-velopment. Nor does he imagine that the imminence of revolution could possibly be identical across every country:

> Does it follow from what has been said that all countries in the world, in one way or another, are already ripe for the socialist revolution? No, this is a false, dead, scholastic, Stalinist-Bukharinist way of putting the question. World economy in its entirety is indubitably ripe for socialism. But this does not mean that every country taken sep-arately is ripe. . . . One must not proceed from a preconceived harmony of social de-velopment. The law of uneven development still lives, despite the tender theoretical embraces of Stalin. The force of the law operates not only in the relations of countries to each other, but also in the mutual relationships of the various processes within one and the same country. A reconciliation of the uneven processes of economics and politics can be attained only on a world scale.[64]

In other words, far from existing in uniform readiness for socialist revolution, it would be the success of the socialist revolution that would even out the existing differences between nations. Before that point was achieved, however, the process of permanent revolution would establish connections among the oppressed in both the dominant and subordinate countries, just as the process of uneven capitalist development established connections between their oppressors.

> If we take Britain and India as polarized varieties of the capitalist type, then we are obliged to say that the internationalism of the British and Indian proletariats does not at all rest on an *identity* of conditions, tasks and methods, but on their indivisible *interdependence*. Successes for the liberation movement in India presuppose a revolu-tionary movement in Britain and vice versa. Neither in India, nor in England is it

possible to build an *independent* socialist society. Both of them will have to enter as parts of a higher whole.[65]

Thus far Trotsky had elaborated on the positions he had first established before the First World War, albeit now in relation to more than one country and with a far greater emphasis on the mechanisms through which the individual components of the international system were connected. It was, however, the second way in which he explored the interconnections between the three aspects of unevenness that found him on new theoretical terrain: not how the international bound together individual countries at different stages of development, but how different stages of development were fused within individual countries.

Other Marxists had noted the coexistence of different temporalities within the same social formations. In this context, we should note these remarks from 1896 by Labriola, Trotsky's most important philosophical influence, not least because of his emphasis on totality.[66] Russian industrialization, he wrote, "seems destined to put under our eyes, as in an epitome, all the phases, even the most extreme, of our history."[67] But even here Labriola suggests the coexistence of forms rather than their mutual interpenetration. A more important forerunner to Trotsky in this respect was Luxemburg in a brilliant article, also from 1896, on the Ottoman Empire.

Luxemburg noted that until the end of the eighteenth century, Turkey had been oppressive for the majority of the people but stable. These conditions changed during the nineteenth century: "Shaken by conflict with the strong, centralised states of Europe, but especially threatened by Russia, Turkey found itself compelled to introduce domestic reforms [that] abolished the feudal government, and in its place introduced a centralised bureaucracy, a standing army and a new financial system." The cost of these reforms was paid in taxation and duties by the population, burdens that went toward maintaining a hybrid form of state: "In a strange mixture of modern and medieval principles, it consists of an immense number of administrative authorities, courts and assemblies, which are bound to the capital city in an extremely centralised manner in their conduct; but at the same time all public positions are *de facto* venal, and are not paid by the central government, but are mostly financed by revenue from the local population—a kind of bureaucratic benefice." The effect was "a terrible deterioration in the material conditions of the people": "But what made them particularly unbearable was a quite modern feature that had become involved in the situation—namely, *insecurity*: the irregular tax system, the fluctuating relations of land ownership, but above all the money economy as a result of the transformation of tax in kind into tax in money and the development of foreign trade." As Luxemburg notes, these changes were "in a certain respect, reminiscent of Russia." But with one crucial difference, whereas in Russia the reforms of 1861 and after established the basis for capitalist development and industrialisation, "in Turkey an economic transformation corresponding to the modern reforms was completely lacking."[68] We do not know whether or not Trotsky was aware of Luxemburg's article. Given the extent of her influence on Kautsky prior to the Russian Revolution of 1905, Luxemburg's observations may well have inspired his brief contrast between Russia and Turkey in "The American Worker," a work that in turn influenced Trotsky's original formulation of permanent revolution.[69] Nevertheless, her discussion of the destabilizing effects of capitalist modernity was not reflected in Kautsky's article nor was it a central feature of Trotsky's argument at this point.

More relevant may be an article by Lenin that appeared chronologically closer to Trotsky's discovery of combined development. Written in early 1923 during the final months of his active life, Lenin took the publication of Sukhanov's memoir of the Russian Revolution as the occasion to restate, for the last time, his rejection of the undialectical basis of Second International Marxism: "Up till now they have seen capitalism and bourgeois democracy in Western Europe follow a definite path of development, and cannot conceive that this path can only be taken as a model only *mutatis mutandis* [changing what needs to be changed], only with certain amendments (quite insignificant from the standpoint of the general development of world history)." For Lenin, two factors in particular had rendered the Social Democratic position untenable. One was the First World War, which, although itself a product of imperialist competition and consequently of capitalism, disturbed social relations in ways that were unforeseeable under normal conditions of exploitation, even when these had formerly been accompanied by more limited forms of warfare. The other, more significant in this context, was that "while the development of world history as a whole follows general laws it is by no means precluded, but, on the contrary, presumed, that certain periods of development may display peculiarities in either the form or the sequence of this development":

> For instance, it does not even occur to them [Social Democrats] that because Russia stands on the border-line between the civilized countries and the countries which the war has for the first time brought into the orbit of civilization—all the Oriental, non-European countries—she could and was, indeed, bound to reveal certain distinguishing features: although these, of course, are in keeping with the general line of capitalist development, they distinguish her revolution from those which took place in the West-European countries and introduce certain partial innovations as the revolution moves on to the countries of the East. . . . Our European philistines never even dream that the subsequent revolutions in Oriental countries, which possess much vaster populations and a much vaster diversity of social conditions, will undoubtedly display even greater distinctions than the Russian revolution.[70]

Trotsky was certainly aware of this article and cited it on several occasions.[71] But while these remarks are suggestive they remain at a level of generality that made them assimilable to several different interpretations and political strategies, including that of "socialism in one country."

The final text that I want to consider here, drafted around the time *The History of the Russian Revolution* appeared in English in 1932, could not possibly have been an influence on Trotsky, since its very existence was unknown to anyone except perhaps one close relative of the author and his jailers. In an important note on the relationship between social classes and moments of state formation, Gramsci wrote:

> In real history these moments imply each other reciprocally—horizontally and vertically, so to speak—i.e. according to socio-economic activity (horizontally) and to country (vertically). Combining and diverging in various ways. Each of these combinations may be represented by its own organized economic and political expression. It is also necessary to take into account the fact that international relations intertwine with these internal relations of nation-states, creating new, unique and historically concrete combinations.[72]

The parallels with Trotsky's work are striking; unfortunately they are not developed in a concrete way and we never learn what these combinations might take or where they are to be found.[73] One reason for this may have been that in Gramsci's famous distinction between East and West, which supposedly demanded different revolutionary strategies, his object is always the state rather than society; the latter may bear a different relationship to the state in each area, but it remains undifferentiated across them. In this respect, therefore, for all the problems there are with Anderson's assessment of Gramsci, to which Peter Thomas has alerted us, his verdict here can still be upheld:

> For all the intensity and originality of his enquiry, Gramsci never finally succeeded in arriving at an adequate Marxist distinction between East and West.... For a simple geographical opposition includes by definition an unproblematic comparability of the two terms. Transferred to social formations, however, it implies something that can never be taken for granted: that there is a straightforward historical comparability between them. In other words, the terms East and West assume that the social formations on each side of the divide exist in the same temporality, and can therefore be read off each other as variations of a common category. . . . But this "natural" assumption is precisely what needs to be questioned.[74]

Trotsky's achievement here is therefore quite singular. The first indications of the direction in which he was now moving came in his speech to the executive committee of the Comintern in December 1926—one of the occasions in which he denied the relevance of permanent revolution—where he began to explore changes in the international system that would cause him to reconsider that verdict:

> On the whole, Lenin attributes unevenness to two things: firstly to rate, and secondly to the level of economic and cultural development of the various countries. With regard to the rate, imperialism has increased the unevenness to the highest degree; but with regard to the level of the various capitalist countries, it has called forth a leveling tendency precisely because of the variation of rate. Anyone who does not understand this does not understand the heart of the question. Take England and India. The capitalist development in certain parts of India is much more rapid than was the capitalist development in England in its beginnings. The difference, the economic distance between England and India—is this today greater or smaller than fifty years ago? It is smaller. Take Canada, South America, South Africa, on the one hand, and England

on the other. The development of Canada, South America, South Africa, has proceeded during the last period with gigantic strides. The "development" of England is
in stagnation, yes, even in decline. Therefore, the rate is uneven as never before in history, but the level of development of these countries has been more closely approxi-
mated than thirty or fifty years ago.[75]

What Trotsky is beginning to do here is consider the possibility that unevenness
does not simply involve structured inequality between countries, in a kind of league
table where areas are listed from the most backward to the most advanced, and in
which development occurs in a uniform manner. If an increasing "rate" of uneven
development implies a "leveling" *up* in certain areas of life, even in the backward
areas (like India) and a "leveling" *down* of certain others, even in the advanced areas
(like England), then in the former at least, aspects of life in the latter may appear
in a context that is otherwise quite different:

> Imperialism, thanks to the universality, penetrability, and mobility and the break-
> neck speed of the formation of finance capital as the driving force of imperialism,
> lends vigour to *both these tendencies*. Imperialism links up incomparably more rapidly
> and more deeply the individual national and continental units into a single entity,
> bringing them into the closest and most vital dependence on each other and render-
> ing their economic methods, social forms, and levels of development more identical.
> At the same time, it attains this "goal" by such antagonistic methods, such tiger-leaps,
> and such raids upon backward countries and areas that the unification and leveling
> of world economy which it has effected, is upset by it even more violently and con-
> vulsively than in the preceding epochs.[76]

The inability of uneven development to fully encapsulate these phenomena is what
appears to have made Trotsky search for a new concept, with a new name, starting
from and incorporating uneven development but deepening its content: "From the
universal law of unevenness thus derives another law which for want of a better name,
we may call the law of combined development—by which we mean a drawing together of the different stages of the journey, a combining of separate steps, an amalgam
of archaic with more contemporary forms."[77] The origin of combination in unevenness
is why Trotsky named his new concept "uneven and combined development" rather
than, as in the common misconception, "combined and uneven development": "I
would put *uneven* before *combined*," he wrote shortly before his assassination, "because
the second grows out of the first and completes it."[78] Almost from the start of his
revolutionary career, Trotsky had railed against the way in which the "systematizers"
of Social Democracy substituted for analysis the recitation of sentences from Marx,
and in the case of Stalinism also sentences from Lenin, to justify their embrace of
stages; but until now, although he had proposed a radically different *strategy* to that
proposed by these conservative bureaucracies, he had not explicitly supported it with
an alternative *theory*. With uneven and combined development he was now able to
show the historically conditional and limited nature of even Marx's greatest insights
and the consequent need to transcend them for theory to keep pace with reality:

"The industrially more developed country shows the less developed only the image of its own future." This statement of Marx which takes its departure methodologically not from world economy as a whole but from the single capitalist country as a type, has become less applicable in proportion as capitalist evolution has embraced all countries regardless of their previous fate and industrial level. England in her day revealed the future of France, considerably less of Germany, but not in the least of Russia and not of India. The Russian Mensheviks, however, took this conditional statement of Marx unconditionally. Backward Russia, they said, ought not to rush ahead, but humbly to follow the prepared models. To this kind of "Marxism" the liberals also agreed. Another no less popular formula of Marx—"No social formation disappears before all the productive forces have developed for which it has room"—takes its departure, on the contrary, not from the country taken separately, but from the sequence of universal social structures (slavery, medievalism, capitalism). The Mensheviks, however, taking this statement from the point of view of the single state, drew the conclusion that Russian capitalism has still a long road to travel before it will reach European or American level. But productive forces do not develop in a vacuum! You cannot talk of the possibilities of a national capitalism, and ignore on the one hand the class struggle developing out of it, or on the other its dependence upon world conditions.[79]

How then do "world conditions" lead to uneven and combined development within individual countries? This can be best illustrated by contrasting two alternative types of insertion into the global capitalist system that do not involve the same process or only do so in marginal ways.

One is the path of the advanced capitalist states. As we have seen, the pace of development was relatively faster in most of the countries that followed Holland and England, partly because of the urgency of acquiring the attributes of capitalist modernity, partly because the long period of experiment and evolution, characteristic of the two pioneers, could be dispensed with, as Trotsky noted: "Only a minority of countries has fully gone through that systematic and logical development from handicraft through domestic manufacture to the factory, which Marx subjected to such detailed analysis."[80] In the case of Scotland in the eighteenth century or Prussia in the nineteenth century, this led to enormous tensions, intensified in both cases by undemocratic state forms, which resolved themselves in moments of class struggle foreshadowing the process of permanent revolution, above all in the 1820 general strike in the former and the 1848 revolution in the latter. "Scotland entered on the capitalist path later than England," wrote Trotsky in 1925, "a sharper turn in the life of the masses of the people gave rise to a sharper political reaction."[81] Similarly, he wrote of the consequences "when the productive forces of the metropolis, of a country of classical capitalism . . . find ingress into more backward countries, like Germany in the first half of the nineteenth century."[82] But because these societies did make the transition to the ranks of the advanced societies, either as the center (Prussia/Germany) or a component part of another national formation (Scotland/Britain) these moments passed with the tensions that caused them.

The other was the path of the most backward areas to be made colonies or semi-colonies: "Commercial, industrial and financial capital invaded backward countries from the outside, partly destroying the primitive forms of native economy and partly subjecting them to the world-wide industrial and banking system of the West."[83] What Peter Curtin calls "defensive modernization" was not enough to protect these societies from Western incursions. In the case of the Merinian monarchs of Madagascar, for example: "They not only failed to modernize beyond adopting Christianity and superficial European fashions, they failed to build a kind of society and government administration that would perpetuate their own power."[84] Colonial rule could even throw societies backward, as in the case of British-occupied Iraq. Ruling through the Hashemite monarchy after 1920, the regime deliberately rejected any attempts at modernization, except in the oil industry. Instead, it reinforced disintegrating tribal loyalties and semifeudal tenurial relationships over the peasantry. Peter Gowan describes the British initiatives as "the creation of *new* foundational institutions of landownership in order to *revive* dying traditional authority relations, resulting in economically and socially regressive consequences, undertaken for thoroughly modern imperialist political purposes—namely, to create a ruling class dependent upon British military power and therefore committed to imperial interests in the region."[85]

A further group of states neither emulated the process of "catch up and overtake" among the advanced countries nor suffered that of "blocked development" within the backward, but instead experienced a collision between the two. These states embodied "combination," unable to reproduce the level of development attained by the advanced capitalist states, but nevertheless able to "unblock" themselves to the extent of making partial advances in specific areas. There were essentially three ways by which combined development came into effect. The first was where feudal-absolutist or tributary states, like Russia or Turkey, under pressure from the Western powers, were forced for reasons of military competition to introduce limited industrialization and partial agrarian reform. As Trotsky noted, "the Great War, the result of the contradictions of world imperialism, drew into its maelstrom countries of *different* stages of development, but made the same *claims* on all the participants."[86] The second was where still more backward states like China or regions like the post-Ottoman Arab Middle East had been broken by imperialist pressure, but instead of being colonized, were allowed to disintegrate while the agents of foreign capital established areas of industrialization under the protection of either their own governments or local warlords. The third was where the metropolitan power in colonial states like British India, and to a lesser extent French Algeria, were unwilling to allow full-scale industrialization in case it produced competition for its own commodities, but was prepared to sanction it in specific circumstances for reasons of military supply or where goods were not intended for home markets. The consequences in each case were similar: "Historical backwardness does not imply a simple reproduction of the development of advanced countries, England or France, with a delay of one, two, or three centuries. It engenders an entirely new 'combined' social formation in which the latest conquests of capitalist technique and structure root themselves into relations of feudal or pre-feudal barbarism, transforming and subjecting them and creating peculiar relations of classes."[87] In accord with his habitual emphasis on social totality, Trotsky was not saying that forms characteristic of different stages of development simply co-exist alongside each other in striking or dramatic contrasts, although that could be true.[88] Nor was he just emphasizing the existence of transitional modes of production, although he recognized that these did exist. Uneven and combined development usually involves what Michael Burawoy calls "the combination of the capitalist mode of production with pre-existing modes."[89] Jamie Allinson and Alexander Anievas too have written of how the "logics of different modes of production interact with one another in consequential ways in backward countries."[90] But a process that permeates every aspect of society, ideology as much as economy, must involve more than this. The "articulation" of capitalist and precapitalist modes had, after all, been progressing slowly in the Russian countryside since the abolition of serfdom in 1861, and had led to many complex transitional forms, as Lenin documented in great detail.[91] On the eve of the revolution of 1917 Lenin wrote of Russia as being "where modern capitalist imperialism is enmeshed, so to speak, in a particularly close network of pre-capitalist relations."[92] But this did not necessarily produce the type of situation Trotsky was seeking to explain.

The detonation of the process of uneven and combined development required sudden, intensive industrialization and urbanization. Burawoy is therefore right to describe uneven and combined development as a product of "the timing of industrialisation in relation to the history of world capitalism."[93] It is irrelevant in this context the motives for which industrialization is undertaken: "The [backward] nation ... not infrequently debases the achievements borrowed from outside in the process of adapting them to its own more primitive culture."[94] In some cases adaptation is merely decorative, as the Balkan states formerly part of the Ottoman Empire: "In the countries of the Near East, as of the Far East (and to some extent Russia too), one can observe in all spheres of life how ready-made European forms and ideas, or sometimes merely their names, are borrowed in order to give expression to the requirements of a very much earlier historical period. Political and ideological masquerades are the lot of all backward peoples."[95]

But in other cases, of which Russia was the most important, "debased adaptation" helped preserve the precapitalist state. From 1861 tsarism established factories using manufacturing technology characteristic of monopoly capitalism in order to produce arms with which to defend feudal absolutism; but by doing so they brought into being a class more skilled, more politically conscious than that faced by any previous absolutist or early capitalist state.[96] All subsequent non-Marxist theories of "the advantages of backwardness" assumed that technological transfers had a limited, or at least delayed, impact on other aspects of social life.[97] Trotsky agreed that these transfers certainly did allow Russia to attain higher levels of development than their established rivals in certain areas: "At the same time that peasant land-cultivation as a whole remained, right up to the revolution, at the level of the seventeenth century, Russian industry in its technique and capitalist structure stood at the level of the advanced countries, and in certain respects even outstripped them."[98] But at the same time they could quicken the pace of change more generally: uneven and combined development affects the totality of a national society, not merely the economy. "The hasty mixture of Edison and Confucius has left its mark in all Japanese culture," wrote Trotsky of Japan after the Meiji Restoration.[99] But uneven and combined development can also work, as it were, in reverse: "debased adaptation" is not only a feature of backward societies. Here too the opening of the age of imperialism is decisive. Between 1870 and 1914, for example, imperial Britain, Germany, and Japan all consciously emphasized the role of their monarch-emperors; in each case, the preexisting symbolism of the crown being used to represent national unity against two main challenges: external imperial rivalry and internal class divisions. But Trotsky saw this as a much more general phenomenon, necessarily caused by the need to maintain bourgeois hegemony over the exploited and oppressed in an era of revolution and which reached its apogee in the United States. In an address to the First All-Union Society of Friends of Radio in 1926 he warned of the counterrevolutionary possibilities of the technological form his listeners had come to celebrate: "It is considered unquestionable that technology and science undermine superstition. But the class character of society sets substantial limits here too. Take America. There, church sermons are broadcast by radio, which means that the radio is serving as a means of spreading prejudices.[100] Once the notion of combined development was available to him, Trotsky saw this appropriation of advanced technology as the obverse of the ideological advances made by Russian and Chinese workers. "In America we have another kind of combined development. We have the most advanced industrial development together with the most backward—for all classes—ideology."[101] In a striking passage in an essay of 1933 considering the nature of National Socialism, Trotsky commented on their persistence, not only in Nazi Germany but generally in the developed world:

> Today, not only in peasant homes but also in city skyscrapers, there lives alongside of the twentieth century the tenth or the thirteenth. A hundred million people use electricity and still believe in the magic power of signs and exorcisms. The Pope of Rome broadcasts over the radio about the miraculous transformation of water into wine. Movie stars go to mediums. Aviators who pilot miraculous mechanisms created by man's genius wear amulets on their sweaters. What inexhaustible reserves they possess of darkness, ignorance and savagery![102]

As early as his journalism from the Balkans immediately prior to the First World War, Trotsky traced how the process of combination, starting with the economy, begins to work through society as a whole:

> Like all backward countries, Bulgaria is incapable of creating new political and cultural forms through a free struggle of its own inner forces; it is obliged to assimilate the ready-made cultural products that European civilization has developed in the

course of its history. Whether particular ruling groups wish it or not, Bulgaria is obliged, and urgently, to build railways and to re-equip the army, and that means obtaining loans; in order to introduce proper accounting for these, parliamentary forms are required; European political programmes are imitated, the proletarianizing of the population is facilitated, and this means that social legislation has to be introduced.[103]

The archaic and the modern, the settled and disruptive, overlap, fuse, and merge in all aspects of the social formations concerned, from the organization of arms production to the structure of religious observance, in entirely new and unstable ways, generating socially explosive situations in which revolution became what Lukács termed "actual."[104] It is tempting to describe these as mutations, except that the inadequacy of the language led Trotsky to reject the biological metaphors in which stages of development had been described from the Enlightenment to the Third International in its Stalinist phase: "The absorptive and flexible psyche, as a necessary condition for historical progress, confers on the so-called social 'organisms,' as distinguished from the real, that is, biological organisms, an exceptional variability of internal structure."[105] In this context it is important to note that Trotsky recognized that uneven and combined development continued to operate in a postrevolutionary context. In a letter to the first issue of the journal *Under the Banner of Marxism* in 1922, Trotsky wrote: "The Soviet state is a living contradiction of the old world, of its social order, of its personal relations, of its outlooks and beliefs. But at the same time the Soviet state itself is still full of contradictions, gaps, lack of coordination, vague fermentation—in a word, of phenomena in which the inheritance of the past is interwoven with the shoots of the future."[106] And in a speech given the following year at the opening of the Karl Liebknecht Institute in Moscow, he noted that "the German working class moves on asphalt, but its hands and feet are bound in class slavery. We stride out over ruts, ditches, potholes and puddles, but our feet are free."[107] On a slightly less exalted note, Benjamin noted during his visit to Moscow in 1926: "And the complete interpenetration of technological and primitive modes of life, this world historical experiment in the new Russia, is illustrated in miniature by a streetcar ride."[108]

Prior to the revolution, however, the very existence of the undemocratic state that "debased adaptation" was intended to preserve helped provoke the working class into destroying it. Thus, for Trotsky, the most important consequence of uneven and combined development was the enhanced capacity it gave the working classes for political and industrial organization, theoretical understanding, and revolutionary activity: "when the economic factors burst in a revolutionary manner, breaking up the old order; when development is no longer gradual and 'organic' but assumes the form of terrible convulsions and drastic changes of former conceptions, then it becomes easier for critical thought to find revolutionary expression, provided that the necessary theoretical prerequisites exist in the given country."[109] As an example of this he drew attention to the greater implantation of Marxism among the working classes of Russia and, later, China than in that of Britain. In the case of Russia itself, "the proletariat did not arise gradually through the ages, carrying with itself the burden of the past, as in England, but in leaps involving sharp changes of environment, ties, relations, and a sharp break with the past. It was just this—combined with the concentrated oppressions of czarism—that made Russian workers hospitable to the boldest conclusions of revolutionary thought—just as the backward industries were hospitable to the last word in capitalist organization." But this was not a once-for-all process: "The Russian proletariat was forever repeating the short history of its origin."[110] In China too, where the state was part colonial enclave, part warlord fiefdom: "The fact that the students and workers ... are eagerly assimilating the doctrine of materialism, while the labor leaders of civilized England believe in the magic potency of churchly incantations, proves beyond a doubt that in certain spheres China has outstripped England." In these cases ideology outstrips economy, for "the contempt of the Chinese workers for the mediaeval dull-wittedness of [Ramsay] MacDonald does not permit the inference that in her general economic development China is higher than Great Britain."[111]

Yet there are also differences between the Russian and Chinese experiences. Trotsky believed that in Russia agrarian relations remained essentially feudal and consequently it was not only the social formation that embodied combined development but the revolutionary process itself:

> The law of combined development of backward countries—in the sense of a peculiar mixture of backward elements with the most modern factors—here rises before us in its most finished form, and offers a key to the fundamental riddle of the Russian revolution. If the agrarian problem, as a heritage from the barbarism of the old Russian history, had been solved by the bourgeoisie, if it could have been solved by them, the Russian proletariat could not possibly have come to power in 1917. In order to realize the Soviet state, there was required a drawing together and mutual penetration of two factors belonging to completely different historic species: a peasant war—that is, a movement characteristic of the dawn of bourgeois development—and a proletarian insurrection, the movement signaling its decline.[112]

When Trotsky argues that the socialist revolution will have to accomplish aspects of the bourgeois revolution he is thinking primarily of overthrowing the precapitalist state and replacing it with proletarian rather than bourgeois forms of democracy. As his comments about the Russian peasant war suggest, in a situation where the peasantry are overwhelmingly the majority class, victory can only be achieved if it moves into action simultaneously with the proletariat but to achieve its own goals:

> The strength of the agrarian-democratic and essentially bourgeois revolution was manifested in the fact that it overcame for a time the class contradictions of the village: the farm hand helped the Kulak in raiding the landlord. . . . The weakness of this belated bourgeois revolution was manifested in the fact that the peasant war did not urge the bourgeois revolutionists forward, but threw them back conclusively into the camp of reaction. . . . The peasant revolution, thus rejected by the bourgeoisie, joined hands with the industrial proletariat.[113]

In the Russian case then, at least one important aspect of the bourgeois revolution is actually carried out by the class that has traditionally aspired to do so (as in sixteenth-century Germany) or actually done so (as in eighteenth-century France). Here permanent revolution *incorporates* the bourgeois revolution in the countryside.

But Trotsky also believed that permanent revolution, again based on uneven and combined development, could also occur where the preexisting agrarian economy is dominated by capitalist social relations. Here the Chinese experience was important. Contrary to his position on Russia, Trotsky completely rejected Comintern claims that feudalism dominated either the Chinese economy or the remnants of the Chinese central state:

> Unless one is playing with words, there is no feudalism in China. In the Chinese village there are serf-owner relations which are crowned, however, not by feudal but by bourgeois property forms and a bourgeois sociopolitical order. This type of serf-owner relationship, which is the result of agrarian overpopulation, given the overall lag in capitalist development, can be found—of course in much more "mild" forms—in several Balkan countries, which have known neither feudalism nor the noble estates since their emancipation from the Turkish yoke.[114]

Trotsky was not arguing that China was the site of another precapitalist mode, usually described in Russian debates as "Asiatic," following the term used by Marx and Engels down to 1859. A conference in Leningrad during 1931 put an end to a debate that had been running in the Soviet Union since 1925, by declaring that the "Asiatic" mode was nonexistent. There seems to have been two reasons for this edict being issued. The first was that the possibility of an exploiting state that did not rest on private property was, to say the least, an embarrassment to the ideologues of Stalinism, whose state exploited the Russian working class and peasantry … without the existence of private property. The second was in relation to the contemporary situation in China, the "Asiatic" state par excellence. Since Stalin had been allied with what he imagined was the revolutionary bourgeoisie in the shape of the Kuomintang, and he took it as axiomatic that the bourgeoisie could only emerge out of feudalism, any attempt to declare that China was not feudal, but "Asiatic" undermined these assumptions and could obviously only be a Trotskyist attempt to criticize the alliance. The rejection of the Asiatic mode remained an article of faith in the Soviet Union virtually down to the end of the Stalinist regime.[115]

For Trotsky the latter reason was decisive for the emphasis Stalin and Bukharin placed on the supposedly feudal nature of China: "The attempt to create feudalism in China, still more its prevalence, relies not on facts, but on the naked desire to justify collaboration with the bourgeoisie."[116] In fact, he seems to have regarded China as a country that had essentially completed the transition from feudalism. "Of course, matters would be quite hopeless if feudal survivals did really *dominate* in Chinese economic life," he wrote in 1929: "But fortunately, survivals in general cannot dominate." Instead he emphasized the extent of market relations and influence of different forms of mercantile and banking capital. Rural social relations, "stem in part from the days of feudalism, and in part they constitute a new formation," but within this formation, "it is capitalist relations that *dominate* and not 'feudal' (more correctly, serf and, generally, pre-capitalist) relations. Only thanks to this dominant role of capitalist relations can we speak seriously of the prospects of proletarian hegemony in a national revolution."[117]

It should be clear from these passages that Trotsky does not view capitalist social relations as necessarily involving some vulgar normative model of free wage labor within the market. In a passage drawing the political conclusions of the interpenetration of the residual feudal and dominant capitalist modes under partial imperial control he points to the complexity of the forms involved:

> The Chinese revolution has a national bourgeois character principally because the development of the productive forces of Chinese capitalism collides with its governmental customs, dependence upon the countries of imperialism. The obstruction of the development of Chinese industry and the throttling of the internal market involve the conservation and rebirth of the most backward forms of production in agriculture, of the most parasitic forms of exploitation, of the most barbaric forms of oppression and violence, the growth of surplus population, as well as the persistence and aggravation of pauperism and all sorts of slavery. No matter how great the specific weight of the typically "feudal" elements in Chinese economy may be they can be swept away only in a revolutionary way, and consequently not in alliance with the bourgeoisie but in direct struggle against it. The more complicated and tortuous is the interlacing of feudal and capitalist relations, the less the agrarian question can be solved by legislation from above, the more indispensable is the revolutionary initiative of the peasant masses in close union with the workers and the poor population of the cities, the falser is the policy that clings convulsively to the alliance with the bourgeoisie and the large landowner and subordinates its work among the masses to this alliance.[118]

The issue here is not the correctness of Trotsky's assessment of social relations in the Russian and Chinese countryside (although in my opinion he both underestimates the extent of capitalist development in case of the former and overestimates it in that of the latter); it is rather that he regarded uneven and combined development as possible both in contexts where feudal social relations were dominant *and* in those where capitalist relations are dominant: what is decisive is that former levels of stability are disrupted by the irruption of industrial capitalism and all that it brings in its wake: rapid population growth, uncoordinated urban expansion, dramatic ideological shifts. Is permanent revolution, and consequently the completion of the bourgeois revolution, relevant in both these cases? The answer to this question depends on what one conceives as being involved in completion—or "consummation," to use Lenin's term. One way would be to focus on the question of the state. Justin Rosenberg writes of Russia: "Was this a capitalist state—or did it remain pre-capitalist? Trotsky's answer, in effect, was that it was neither. The international pressures of uneven development were driving Russia into a combined pattern of development. They were leading to a fusion of the old and new, an unstable amalgam of Western and Russian elements with its own peculiar developmental tendencies."[119]

Here Rosenberg confuses economy and society, which can be in transition between two different modes of production or combine elements of them both, and the state, which, in Marxist terms, cannot be "transitional," at least until a new class has taken control of it. As in the earlier cases of the United Netherlands and England—where capitalist development was at a far higher level than in either Russia or China—if the state remains pre-bourgeois, then the fundamental objective of the bourgeois revolution remains to be accomplished and then surpassed, as was clearly the case in Russia, which remained absolutist down to February 1917, but also in China, where it fragmented after 1911 into a incoherent structure of overlapping forms involving rival colonial powers, remnants of the tributary imperial regime, quasi-fascist warlord enclaves, and in some cases a complete governmental vacuum, filled by organized crime. Trotsky's preferred criteria for completion involved a series of "tasks," the most important of which for him seem to have involved national independence and unification, agrarian reform, and democracy.[120] This was the most conventional, "orthodox," aspect of Trotsky's approach to bourgeois revolution. In any event, it was not always clear what was meant by "agrarian reform," since the nature of the "task" depended on whether the objective was bourgeois or socialist revolution. Giving the land to the peasants or recognizing their seizure of it is one outcome; subjecting the land to commercial operations of the market is quite another. Peasant ownership is certainly a bourgeois aspiration, but the latter is more conducive to capitalist development. Early in the Second World War, one Chinese Trotskyist, Zheng Chaolin, took up the issue of "bourgeois democratic tasks," which he argued were essentially "national liberation and land reform," but noted the difficulty with the latter task: "To see agrarian reform as a reliable bourgeois democratic task is to want to resolve the Chinese land question as in the French Revolution—to ask the peasants to buy the land, to make land a commodity to be bought and sold. We do not need a revolution for this. This is already happening in China."[121] Assuming that peasant control was meant rather than commodification none of these tasks had been carried out in China, so any problems associated with using them as criteria for completion of the bourgeois revolution were not immediately apparent. On the contrary, in conditions where industrial capitalism was reaching further and further beyond the established centers of the system and bringing uneven and combined development in its wake, the continued existence of bourgeois revolutionary tasks, including transformation of the state, meant that Trotsky could now invoke permanent revolution as a general strategy for the colonial and semicolonial world:

> The lessons of the second Chinese revolution are lessons for the entire Comintern, but primarily for all the countries of the Orient. All the arguments presented in defense of the Menshevik line in the Chinese revolution must, if we take them seriously, hold trebly good for India. The imperialist yoke assumes in India, the classic colony, infinitely more direct and palpable forms than in China. The survivals of feudal and serf relations in India are immeasurably deeper and greater. Nevertheless, or rather precisely for this reason, the methods which, applied in China, undermined the rev-

olution, must result in India in even more fatal consequences. The overthrow of Hindu feudalism and of the Anglo-Hindu bureaucracy and British militarism can be accomplished only by a gigantic and an indomitable movement of the popular masses which precisely because of its powerful sweep and irresistibility, its international aims and ties, cannot tolerate any halfway and compromising opportunist measures on the part of the leadership.[122]

By 1938 Trotsky was to describe permanent revolution, even more sweepingly, as "the general trend of revolutionary development in all backward countries"[123] This should not be taken too literally. Trotsky was perfectly aware that what he called "the hierarchy of backwardness" involved enormously varied levels of development *across* the colonial and semicolonial world.[124] As a result, the size of the working class and its ability to influence events was also subject to massive differentiation. Trotsky was the opposite of a utopian voluntarist and accepted that a certain degree of social weight was necessary on the part of any working class before it could aspire to taking power; what was possible in India and China would not necessarily be possible in equatorial Africa or Afghanistan. Where the working class existed it was always necessary to establish organizational and political independence, but: "The relative weight of the individual and transitional demands in the proletariat's struggle, their mutual ties and their order of presentation, is determined by the peculiarities and specific conditions of each backward country and—to a considerable extent—by the *degree* of its backwardness."[125] Not every backward country experienced uneven and combined development, although ironically, those that had not tended to be those that had escaped colonization. Ethiopia, for example, "was a social formation that contained social relations analogous to feudalism," but until the Italian invasion of 1935 and the British occupation of 1941, "this pre-capitalist system remained almost untouched."[126] Trotsky argued that socialists should support Ethiopia against Italy—"the fight of an underdeveloped nation for independence against imperialism"—without pretending that the victory of Haile Selassie would be an example of permanent revolution.[127] But even in those countries where the working class was much smaller and weaker than the Russian or Chinese in relative terms, even where it was virtually nonexistent, the global nature of the socialist project would provide external mechanisms to overcome these internal obstacles.

Trotsky did not, however, restrict the relevance of permanent revolution to the colonial and semicolonial world, but to any country where there were still incomplete "democratic" tasks—using the term to refer, not only to the nature of the political regime, but to aspects like agrarian reform: "In backward nations, such *immediate* tasks have a democratic character: the national liberation from imperialist subjugation and the agrarian revolution, as in China; the agrarian revolution and the liberation of the oppressed nationalities, as in Russia. We see the same thing at present in Spain, even though in a different combination. . . . But after the working class has seized power, the democratic tasks of the proletarian regime inevitably grow over into socialist tasks."[128]

The specific tasks in Spain were actually similar to those in Russia ("the agrarian revolution and the liberation of the oppressed nationalities"). But Spain, although like Portugal and Greece, was clearly a backward country in Western European terms, it was nevertheless a backward *capitalist* country, not only in the sense that its economy was subject overall to capitalist laws of motion, but also because it was ruled by a capitalist state—an institution that Marxists should be able to recognize however unlikely the surroundings. "In Japan," Trotsky wrote in the 1930s, "we observe even today . . . correlation between the bourgeois character of the state and the semifeudal character of the ruling caste."[129] Consequently, Spain and similar countries were a qualitatively different case from Russia or China: there was no "bourgeois revolution" to accomplish—other than as a label applied by Stalinists to justify their refusal to argue for socialist goals, although feudal social relations still existed in the countryside. In discussions from later in the 1930s, Trotsky drew more general conclusions in relation to permanent revolution: "The Bolshevik point of view, clearly expressed only by the young section of the Fourth International, takes the theory of permanent revolution as its starting point, namely, that even purely democratic problems, like the liquidation of semi-feudal land ownership, cannot be solved without the conquest of power by the proletariat; but this in turn places the socialist revolution on the agenda."[130]

These positions were shared by Lukács in the "Blum Theses" of 1928, where he took account of surviving feudal relationships in Hungary without making any concessions to the notion that a separate bourgeois revolution was required to remove them. "The peculiarity of Hungarian development," Lukács wrote, "is that the feudal form of distribution of landed property remains unchanged alongside relatively highly developed and still-developing capitalism." But the integration of feudal landowners and industrial capitalists means that any expectation of the latter leading a bourgeois revolution is completely unrealistic:

> Here too, the HCP remains the only party which inscribes the consistent implementation of the demands of the bourgeois revolution on its banner: expropriation of the large landed-property owners without compensation, revolutionary occupation of the land, free land for the peasants! . . . All party members must understand that what is at issue is a question which is fundamental to the transition from the bourgeois revolution to the revolution of the proletariat; they must understand that the power of large-scale landed property and large-scale capital cannot be destroyed except by this kind of revolution, and that the remnants of feudalism cannot be wiped out except through the elimination of capitalism.[131]

Like his discussion of the interpenetration of bourgeois and proletarian revolutions in *Lenin*, this position is perfectly compatible with that being contemporaneously advocated by Trotsky in relation to China, even though Lukács himself described Trotskyism as "a position which I always rejected."[132]

On certain occasions Trotsky even suggested that permanent revolution might be applicable in the most advanced country of all, the United States, saying in a

discussion with his American supporters that "in a certain sense . . . the self-determination of the Negroes belongs to the question of the permanent revolution in
America."[133] It was of course still possible to find regional examples of uneven and
combined development in even the most advanced capitalist countries, including
the United States. Mandel writes that the southern states of the United States
"functioned as a reservoir of agricultural raw materials and as an 'internal colony'
in the sense that they formed a steady market for the industrial products of the
North and did not develop any large-scale industry within their own territory (this
was to change only with the Second World War)."[134] But within the South, and
before even the First World War, limited forms of industrialization gave rise to situations more typical of Saint Petersburg or Shanghai than Memphis, Tennessee.
One such area was around the Alabama coalfields. According to Brian Kelly:

> The region presents an almost classical example of what Marxists have described as
> "combined and uneven development": the turn-of-the-century South included a
> number of exceptional areas where large concentrations of industrial workers labored
> in mills, foundries, and manufacturing plants on a par with the most advanced in the
> North, but these stood like frontier outposts of a new age in a region overwhelmingly
> steeped in primitive agriculture, in some places little-changed from the way it had
> been conducted in the antebellum period.[135]

Yet neither Trotsky nor anyone else proposed that the socialist revolution in the
United States would be permanent in character on the basis of this highly localized
experience of uneven and combined development but on the need to extend
democracy to the black population as a whole. To refer to permanent revolution in
the context of the United States or any other advanced capitalist states is to detach
it from any basis in uneven and combined development, but more importantly to
deprive it of any specificity, since there is virtually no country in the world where
some precapitalist social form or pre-democratic political institutions cannot be
found. It would still have been possible to argue that only the working class would
be able to achieve abolition of such forms and institutions—although this would
in fact turn out to be false—without stretching the concept of permanent revolution
until it was virtually synonymous with that of socialist revolution as such. Trotsky
did not adopt this position, largely because, as the 1930s continued and defeats for
the working class accumulated, he came to believe that reforms were impossible: it
was socialism or barbarism and it was now or never.

The resulting ambiguities are encapsulated in Trotsky's classic statement of his
position: "The democratic revolution grows over directly into the socialist revolution
and thereby becomes a *permanent* revolution."[136] The term "democratic revolution"
can either be a synonym for bourgeois revolution, through a contraction of the
"bourgeois-democratic" formulation—a social revolution; or it can mean the accomplishment of outstanding democratic reforms by revolutionary means—a political revolution. In effect, from a position that began with the strategy of
permanent revolution being applicable only to Russia, Trotsky extended it in two

directions. In one direction were countries more *backward* than Russia, which also stood historically *before* the accomplishment of the bourgeois revolution (China, India) and were subject to uneven and combined development, one of the galvanic social effects of which tended to be the stimulation of revolutionary movements, even where the working class remained a minority. Here uneven and combined development generated "revolutionary situations" in ways that did not occur in countries where capitalism is long established, is relatively stable, and the working class is dominated by reformism. In the other direction were countries more *advanced* than Russia, which stood historically *after* the accomplishment of the bourgeois revolution (Spain, Japan), which were not subject to uneven and combined development—at least to anything like the same degree—but in which particular precapitalist social relations still remained, or where bourgeois democracy was still precarious or restricted. The distinction may seem unnecessarily pedantic since in both cases permanent revolution would remove any pre-bourgeois forms and result in the dictatorship of the proletariat. Trotsky also continued to maintain that it would be necessary to globalize the revolution *regardless of how backward or advanced the countries in which the proletariat and its allies first take power.* "The socialist revolution begins on the national arena, it unfolds on the international arena, and is completed on the world arena. Thus, the socialist revolution becomes a permanent revolution in a newer and broader sense of the word; it attains completion, only in the final victory of the new society on our entire planet."[137]

Trotsky's greatest contributions to the theory of bourgeois revolution—the strategy of permanent revolution and the law of uneven and combined development—were both related to the contemporary relevance of the category. Like the Social Democratic and Stalinist orthodoxy that he opposed, these interventions also had implications for how the historical bourgeois revolutions were understood, but in this respect Trotsky's theoretical legacy involves the same ambiguities that characterized his later use of the term permanent revolution, above all an unstable set of criteria for deciding whether or not a bourgeois revolution had been consummated. As a result, Gramsci—a figure whose thought is marked by its own ambiguities—is a more helpful historical guide than Trotsky, precisely because he is less fixated on the "classic" bourgeois revolutions whose significance is matched only by their exceptionalism.

"Passive Revolution"

Early in *The History of the Russian Revolution* Trotsky isolates one important characterization of revolutions in general: "The most indubitable feature of a revolution is the direct interference of the masses in historical events. . . . The history of a revolution is for us first of all a history of the forcible entrance of the masses into the realm of rulership over their own destiny."[138] The notion of "the masses" of course conceals different class configurations in each revolution, but taking this term simply to mean the majority of the population, the English, French, and

Russian Revolutions all involved their "direct interference" and "forcible entrance" into the historical process: "advancing from the sturdy artisans and independent peasants of the army of Cromwell—through the Sansculottes of Paris—to the industrial proletarians of St. Petersburg, the revolution had deeply changed its social mechanism, its methods, and therewith its aims."[139] Trotsky believed that there was a further common characteristic of all social revolutions and it was to be found in the means by which the masses achieved their goals: "Only mass insurrection has ever brought the victory of one social regime over another."[140] What distinguishes different types of social revolution, what marks one as bourgeois and the other as proletarian is not so much the different organizational forms represented by, for example, the Parisian sections and the Petrograd Soviet, as the outcome in terms of class power. In the French Revolution the masses were once again expelled from history once victory was achieved: "Such a stage is built into the mechanism of the bourgeois revolution insofar as the class that sacrifices most for its success and places the most hope in it receives from it least of all."[141] By contrast, in the Russian Revolution the masses—in theory at least—remained in control of their own destiny. As we have seen, in a contemporary context, Trotsky's refusal to draw an absolute demarcation between bourgeois and proletarian revolutions had a liberating effect on his theoretical approach, but in a historical context it imposed a real restraint upon it, as it also did on his political direction during the postrevolutionary period, when Trotsky sought to identify through which phase the Russian Revolution was passing by analogy with its Gallic predecessor.[142] These historical analogies with the French Revolution, above all the notion of "Thermidor"—that is, the coup of Thermidor [July] 9, 1794, which brought the most radical phase of the French Revolution to a close—added to Trotsky's confusions over the nature of the emerging Stalinist regime. His original position incorrectly identified Thermidor as a counterrevolution (it was in fact a conservative reaction within the framework of the revolution), but correctly identified the possibility of a counterrevolution taking place within Russia, although he assumed that this would be on the basis of restored private capitalism. His final position now correctly identified the French Thermidor as a conservative reaction, but incorrectly identified a similar process as having taken place in Russia (when in fact the Stalinist regime had conducted a counterrevolution on the basis of state, not private, capitalism).[143] The key issue, here as in a number of other areas, is how we understand the historical significance of the French Revolution.

As we saw in chapter 12, Trotsky always tended to treat the French Revolution as a model for bourgeois revolutions and he was far from alone in doing so among the most creative Marxist thinkers of his generation. Lukács, for example, wrote in *History and Class Consciousness*: "From the Great French Revolution on, all revolutions exhibit the same pattern with increasing intensity."[144] The French Revolution can indeed yield many insights into the dynamics of subsequent revolutionary movements in which mass mobilizations are central; but the most important of these cases, the Russian Revolution of 1917 and the Iranian Revolution of 1978–79, were not—or in the case of the first, not purely—bourgeois revolutions. In other words, the French Revolution illuminates the process of revolution from below in a general sense, but it cannot do so in relation to the underlying nature of the bourgeois revolutions as a specific category, precisely because one of the questions at issue is whether they necessarily involve popular mobilizations. The problem is compounded in Trotsky's case by his tendency to judge the completion of bourgeois revolutions on the basis of whether they had accomplished a set of "tasks" which were, once again, derived from the French experience.

Strict adherence to these two criteria—the decisive role of mass mobilizations on the one hand, the achievement of specific tasks on the other—would have left Trotsky with the same difficulties as supporters of the orthodoxy, namely restricting the completion of bourgeois revolutions to a very few cases. Some of his followers have accepted this logic. In relation to the United States, for example, Peter Camejo described Reconstruction as "part of the democratic revolution which was aborted in the eighteen-sixties and eighteen-seventies."[145] Fortunately, Trotsky did not consistently apply his own criteria, which in this case indicates creative thought breaching self-imposed barriers, rather than mere incoherence. At certain points he recognized that the forms taken by the bourgeois revolutions had varied over time. Unlike Lenin, however, this did not mean the existence of alternative paths to bourgeois revolution in the contemporary world—since the strategy of permanent revolution assumed that only the proletariat was any longer capable of accomplishing it, and even then only in the process of transcending it. He meant rather that historically there had been a succession of paths, each based on a different social class or alliance of social classes, of which the proletariat was the last. During the Chinese Revolution of the 1920s he noted:

> This movement provides an incontestable analogy with the struggle of the French Third Estate against particularism, or with the later struggle of the Germans and Italians for national unification. But in contrast to the first-born countries of capitalism, where the problem of achieving national unity fell to the petty bourgeoisie, in part under the leadership of the bourgeoisie and even of the landlords (Prussia!), in China it was the proletariat that emerged as the primary motive force and potential leader of this movement.[146]

One aspect of this position, shared with that of Lenin, was that bourgeois participation had never been a necessary condition for a revolution to qualify as bourgeois. In some writings, Trotsky came close to arguing that the bourgeoisie had never directly played a leading role: "When the movement of the lower layers overflowed and when the old social order or political regime was overthrown, then power dropped almost automatically into the hands of the liberal bourgeoisie." The bourgeoisie therefore had no need to consciously organize for the seizure of power: "The liberal bourgeoisie (the French in 1789, the Russian in 1917) can content itself with waiting for the elemental mass movement and then at the last moment throw into the scales its wealth, its education, its connection with the state apparatus, and in this way seize the helm."[147] "Bourgeois leadership," here, as in the *Manifesto of the Communist Party*, is expressed through the prerevolutionary economic, social, and cultural weight of the bourgeoisie that then ensures its dominance once the struggle for state power has been won by other forces, in these cases those beneath it in the social structures of France and Russia: "The bourgeoisie may win the power in a revolution not because it is revolutionary, but because it is bourgeois. It has in its possession property, education, the press, a network of strategic positions, a hierarchy of institutions. Quite otherwise with the proletariat. Deprived in the nature of things of all social advantages, an insurrectionary proletariat can count only on its numbers, its solidarity, its cadres, its official staff."[148] The point Trotsky makes here was still generally accepted in Russia during the mid-1920s. As Benjamin reported from Moscow in 1926: "The theoreticians of Bolshevism stress how widely the situation of the proletariat in Russia after the successful revolution differs from that of the bourgeoisie in 1789. At that time the victorious class, before it attained power, had secured for itself in struggles lasting decades the control of cultural apparatus. Intellectual organization, education, had long been pervaded by the ideas of the Third Estate, and the mental struggle for emancipation was fought out before the political."[149]

One key difference between bourgeois and proletarian revolutions is therefore the far greater need for organization and consciousness of the latter. In the former, provided the bourgeoisie has performed its role of establishing an economic, social, and cultural basis for a new society, it is in a sense irrelevant how the social forces involved in actually destroying the old regime are organized, what they believe, or what their motives are; the result will nevertheless be (and here Trotsky is clearly thinking of England after 1660 and France after 1815) that there can be no return to former conditions: "After the profound democratic revolution, which liberates the peasants from serfdom and gives them land, the feudal counterrevolution is generally impossible. The overthrown monarchy may reestablish itself in power and surround itself with medieval phantoms. But it is already powerless to reestablish the economy of feudalism. Once liberated from the fetters of feudalism, bourgeois relations develop automatically."[150]

The implication of passages like these is that the key issue is the transformation of the feudal-absolutist state, removing the obstacle that it represented to capitalist development and replacing it with a new nation-state form. This remains constant across the shifting patterns of bourgeois revolution:

> Whereas in nationally homogeneous states the bourgeois revolutions developed powerful centripetal tendencies, rallying to the idea of overcoming particularism, as in France, or overcoming national disunion, as in Italy and Germany—in nationally heterogeneous states on the contrary, such as Turkey, Russia, Austria-Hungary, the belated bourgeois revolution released centrifugal forces. In spite of the apparent contrariness of these processes when expressed in mechanical terms, their historic function was

the same. In both cases it was a question of using the national unity as a fundamental industrial reservoir. Germany had for this purpose to be united, Austria-Hungary to be divided.[151]

But as the variety of cases listed in this passage shows, history records several different means by which these transformations have been accomplished: "The semifeudal Prussian monarchy executed the most important tasks of the bourgeoisie, but executed them in its own manner, i.e. in a feudal, not a Jacobin style."[152] This, however, is where the question of inconsistency arises.

Although Trotsky referred several times to Prussian landlord leadership in the case of Germany, after "the belated German bourgeoisie proved incapable of achieving national unification through its own strength," he also wrote: "Bismarck only half-fulfilled this task, leaving almost intact the entire feudal and particularist rubbish."[153] The accuracy of this assessment is not in doubt; what is questionable is whether the survival of aspects of feudalism is incompatible with the completion of the bourgeois revolution. Gramsci was perhaps even more scathing about the leadership of the Italian Risorgimento: "Did they at least attain the end they set for themselves? They said that they were aiming at the creation of a modern state in Italy, and they in fact produced a bastard. They aimed at stimulating the formation of an extensive and energetic ruling class; and they did not succeed; at integrating the people into the framework of the new State, and they did not succeed."[154]

As we shall see, Gramsci nevertheless believed that the Italian bourgeois revolution was completed by the Risorgimento. Trotsky's ambivalence toward the parallel process of German Unification was once again inherited by at least some of his followers. The great French historian Pierre Broué, for example, argued that although Germany was "an advanced capitalist country," it was still the site of "an incomplete bourgeois revolution": "Indeed, we may regard the first result of the November [1918] Revolution as the fulfillment of the bourgeois revolution which as aborted midway through the nineteenth century."[155] In relation to the revolution of 1918, however, Trotsky himself maintained that the bourgeois revolution had already been completed: "As to the German Revolution of 1918, it was no democratic completion of the bourgeois revolution, it was proletarian revolution decapitated by the Social Democrats; more correctly, it was a bourgeois counter-revolution, which was compelled to preserve pseudo-democratic forms after its victory over the proletariat."[156] What led Trotsky to contradict himself in this way?

Trotsky seems to have treated processes like German Unification and the Meiji Restoration as substitutes for, or a means of avoiding, bourgeois revolutions, rather than bourgeois revolutions themselves, on the grounds that they did not involve mass insurrections and failed to achieve one or more of the designated "tasks," usually that of agrarian reform. Revolutions from above, on this reading, are not revolutions at all. In relation to Japan, for example, Trotsky correctly situates the Meiji Restoration within the context of the international transformations of the 1860s, but denies it the classification of bourgeois revolution: "The Japanese epoch of transformation, which opened in 1868—shortly after the epoch of reforms in Russia and the Civil War in the United States—constituted a reflex action on the part of the ruling classes expressing the instinct for self-preservation—it was not a 'bourgeois revolution,' as some historians say, but a bureaucratic attempt to buy off such a revolution."[157] These views are virtually identical to those expressed by the more sophisticated historians of the orthodox school. According to Eric Hobsbawm, for example:

> In Japan ... the initiative, the direction and the cadres of the "revolution from above" came from sections of the feudalists themselves. The Japanese bourgeoisie (or its equivalent) played a part only in so far as the existence of a stratum of businessmen and entrepreneurs made it practicable to install a capitalist economy on lines derived from the West. The Meiji Restoration cannot therefore be regarded in any real sense as a "bourgeois revolution," however aborted, though it can be regarded as the functional equivalent of part of one.[158]

In a similar vein, Albert Soboul rejected the notion that the Italian Risorgimento, German Unification, and *especially* the Meiji Restoration could be considered as bourgeois revolutions:

> The Japanese peasantry was still dominated by an oligarchy of the privileged upper bourgeoisie and the semi feudal *jinushi* landowners; the emergent capitalist society preserved the essential element in the feudal relations of production. It therefore becomes clear why, aided by the opening of the country under foreign pressure, the Meiji revolution ended in the formation of an absolutist, oligarchic monarchy. It thus differs completely from the French Revolution, which overthrew the absolutist state and allowed the emergence of a bourgeois democratic society.

The central problem is yet again made clear by Soboul in a subsequent passage: "The French Revolution, therefore, assumes a unique place in the history of the contemporary world."[159]

At least one Russian Marxist scholar of the pre-Stalinist era—who may have been one of the "historians" to whom Trotsky referred—saw no reason to deny the Meiji Restoration the title of bourgeois revolution. In a work of the early 1920s, *The History of the Meiji Era*, O. V. Pletner noted that although "the class of feudal lords remained in power" in Japan after 1868, they "rejected all outmoded feudal norms and started the rapid development of capitalism on the new economic basis." Pletner took the view that it was the consequences of the Meiji Restoration that were important rather than the role of the bourgeoisie: "Hence the term 'revolution' may be used in relation to the Meiji Ishin only conventionally. It may be called 'bourgeois' only from the viewpoint of its results, which does not mean at all that the bourgeoisie played the most important role at that time.[160]

Other Marxists associated with the early years of the Comintern advanced the analysis further. In this connection, Lukács made a number of important observations in *History and Class Consciousness*, at one point going beyond even the notion of "revolution from above":

The true revolutionary element is the economic transformation of the feudal system of production into a capitalist one so that it would be possible in theory for this process to take place *without a bourgeois revolution*, without political upheaval on the part of the revolutionary bourgeoisie. And in that case those parts of the feudal and absolutist superstructure that were not eliminated by "revolutions from above" would collapse of their own accord when capitalism was already fully developed. (The German situation fits this pattern in certain respects.)[161]

In fact, the "feudal and absolutist superstructures" rarely "collapsed of their own accord," but they certainly collapsed. When the Hapsburg Empire disintegrated under the weight of military defeat, and nationalist and working-class pressure, Austro-Hungary fragmented into several different states that were already dominated by the capitalist mode of production to a greater (Austria, Czechoslovakia) or lesser (Hungary) extent. No revolution was required and, indeed, the only ones that threatened were socialist revolutions that were in each case defeated by what Trotsky called "bourgeois-counter-revolutions." But the essential point made by Lukács is correct: not every country is required to undergo a bourgeois revolution. Once a sufficient number of countries had undergone the process to establish a capitalist world economy, the need to compete within it ensured that most ruling classes would implement a series of incremental adaptations to the new order. A capitalist world economy only emerged in the last quarter of the nineteenth century; indeed, the opening of the imperialist stage of capitalist development was itself indicative of the fact that such an economy had been formed.

At certain points, Trotsky himself seemed to accept this, noting, for example, that many parts of Latin America had never experienced a decisive bourgeois revolution, but only a succession of individually futile political revolutions, reflective of the slow pace of development: "Only mass insurrection has ever brought the victory of one social régime over another. Periodical conspiracies are commonly an expression of social stagnation and decay, but popular insurrections on the contrary come usually as a result of some swift growth which has broken down the old equilibrium of the nation."[162] What he called the "chronic 'revolutions' of the South American republics" were also characteristic of the former dominant imperial power, whose own trajectory all-too-closely paralleled that of its former colonies:

> The history of Spain is the history of continuous revolutionary convulsions. *Pronunciamentos* and palace revolutions follow one another. During the nineteenth and the first third of the twentieth century a continuous change of political regime occurred and within each one of them—a kaleidoscopic change of ministries. Not finding sufficiently stable support in any one of the propertied classes even though they were all in need of it—the Spanish monarchy more than once fell into dependence upon its own army. But the provincial dismemberment of Spain put its stamp on the character of the military plots. The petty rivalry of the *juntas* was only the external expression of the fact that the Spanish revolutions did not have a leading class. Precisely because of this the monarchy repeatedly triumphed over each

new revolution. However, sometimes after the triumph of order, the chronic crisis once more broke through with an acute revolt. Not one of the regimes that supplanted each other sank deep enough into the soil. Every one of them wore off quickly in the struggle with the difficulties growing out of the meagerness of the national income, which is incommensurate with the appetites and pretensions of the ruling classes.... All the Spanish revolutions were the movement of a minority against another minority: the ruling and semi-ruling classes impatiently snatching the state pie out of each other's hands.[163]

But both Spain and the South American republics nevertheless had capitalist—if backward—economies and were presided over by capitalist—if weak, corrupt, and unstable—states, the outcome of a twin process of gradual adaptation to the demands of the world economy alongside incremental adjustments to the state form. As Trotsky's references to the army suggest, however, the dominance of a capitalist economy did not mean that the bourgeoisie had to be in direct control of the state, a point also made by Lukács: "The necessary link between the economic premises of the bourgeoisie and its demands for political democracy or the rule of law, which—even if only partially—as established by in the great French Revolution on the ruins of feudal absolutism, has grown looser."[164] However, as Lukács explains elsewhere, the bourgeoisie, more than any previous ruling class, has never needed to take direct control of the state apparatus; all it required was that the apparatus functioned on its behalf:

> The bourgeoisie had far less of an immediate control of the actual springs of power than had ruling classes in the past (such as the citizens of the Greek city-states or the nobility at the apogee of feudalism). On the one hand, the bourgeoisie had to rely much more strongly on its ability to make peace or achieve a compromise with the opposing classes that held power before it so as to use the power-apparatus they controlled for its own ends. On the other hand, it found itself compelled to place the actual exercise of force (the army, petty bureaucracy, etc.) in the hands of petty bourgeois, peasants, the members of subject nations, etc.[165]

The most profound and systematic considerations on the nature of bourgeois revolutions that were neither "classic," like the French, nor unidentifiable, like the Spanish, were produced by Gramsci. For Lenin and Trotsky, arguments about the history of the bourgeois revolution were bound up with contemporary questions of socialist strategy, not a subject of academic study. This was also true of Gramsci but, trapped as he was in a fascist prison from the late 1920s, his otherwise unenviable circumstances allowed him the opportunity to develop arguments at much greater length than Russian Marxists of the previous generation. The cruel paradox of his incarceration was that while he was aware of emerging Stalinist orthodoxies, unlike Lukács he was freed from the requirement of conforming to them, while unlike Trotsky he did not have to devote his energies to directly confronting their political implications. As Serge put it: "A fascist jail kept him outside the operation of these factional struggles whose consequence nearly everywhere was the elimination of the militants of his generation. Our years of darkness were his of stubborn resistance."[166]

Gramsci shared the near-universal understanding of the French Revolution as the most important event in human history before the Russian Revolution. Some commentators, like Partha Chatterjee, have argued that for this reason he saw subsequent bourgeois revolutions as having failed in comparison: "Gramsci, of course, treats this as a 'blocked dialectic,' an exception to the paradigmatic form of bourgeois revolution he takes to be Jacobitism. It now seems more useful to argue, however, that as a historical model, passive revolution is in fact the general framework of capitalist transition in societies where bourgeois hegemony has not been accomplished in the classical way."[167] In fact, Gramsci does precisely what Chatterjee recommends and regards the French Revolution not as a model but as an exception, not a measure of the inadequacy of later bourgeois revolutions, a standard beneath which they had fallen but an event that helped to explain *why* the later bourgeois revolutions took the form that they did. This did not in any way diminish his respect for the Jacobins:

> The Jacobins . . . were the only party of the revolution in progress, in as much as they not only represented the immediate needs and aspirations of the actual physical individuals who constituted the French bourgeoisie, but they also represented the revolutionary movement as a whole, as an integral historical. They represented future needs as well, and, once again, not only the needs of those particular physical individuals, but also of all the national groups which had to be assimilated to the existing fundamental group.[168]

Nor did he regard the role of the bourgeoisie as being completed by 1815. Like Lenin and Luxemburg before him, he saw the final consummation of the French Revolution as coincident with the proclamation of the Third Republic:

> It was only in 1870–71, with the attempt of the Commune, that all the germs of 1789 were finally historically exhausted. It was then that the new bourgeois class struggling for power defeated not only the representatives of the old society unwilling to admit that it had been definitively superseded, but also the still newer groups who maintained that the new structure created by the 1789 revolution was itself already outdated; by this victory the bourgeoisie demonstrated its vitality *vis-à-vis* both the old and the very new.[169]

This perspective sees the French bourgeoisie playing an active and creative political role for far longer than conventional in Marxist historiography; but in doing so the question of why other bourgeoisies did not is thrown into even starker relief. This is Gramsci's great historical subject.

Focusing on the period of the Italian Risorgimento and the revolutions from above of the 1860s more generally, Gramsci first used the notion of "revolution without revolution" to describe them, a notion in which the parallels with Lukács are very strong. He later referred to "revolution-restoration" before finally, and most famously, settling on the term "passive revolution." The latter term, as we saw in chapter 7, was first used by Vincenzo Cuoco in two ways: as an explanation of the failure of the Parthenopean Republic to gain popular support and then as a strategy for avoiding the dangerous necessity of doing so, a strategy adopted by the Moderate Party in the Risorgimento. Gramsci used it in Cuoco's second sense, as filtered through the work of Edgar Quinet, who first used the phrase "restoration-revolution" in relation to Italy.[170] But Gramsci also refers to passive revolution, "not as a programme, as it was for the Italian Liberals of the Risorgimento, but as a criterion of interpretation"—an interpretation that he links, far more explicitly than any other classical Marxist discussion of the bourgeois revolution, to Marx's 1859 "Preface" to *A Contribution to the Critique of Political Economy*, describing it as "a necessary political corollary" to the latter text.[171]

In these writings Gramsci developed the analysis of Germany that had first been made by Engels:

> In Germany, the movement of 1848 failed as a result of the scanty bourgeois concentration (the Jacobin-type slogan was furnished by the democratic Far Left: "Permanent Revolution"), and because the question of renewal of the State was intertwined with the national question. The wars of 1864, 1866, and 1870 resolved both the national question and, in an intermediate form, the class question: the bourgeoisie obtained economic-industrial power, but the old feudal classes remained as the governing stratum of the political State, with wide corporate privileges in the army, the administration, and on the land. Yet at least, if these old classes kept so much importance in Germany and enjoyed so many privileges, they exercised a national function, became the "intellectuals" of the bourgeoisie, with a particular temperament conferred by their caste origin and tradition. In England, where the bourgeois revolution took place before that in France, we have a similar phenomenon to the German one of fusion between the old and the new.[172]

Here, Gramsci draws a comparison between the English and German revolutions that may appear counterintuitive to those who imagine that sociopolitical developments in the former country were unique. He did not regard events in Italy as an "isolated phenomenon": "it was an organic process which, as far as the formation of our [the Italian] ruling class was concerned, corresponded to what happened in France during the Revolution and what had happened in England under Cromwell."[173] In other words, for him the supposed differences between England, Italy, and, in some contexts, even France were less important than the similarities between them: "The concept of passive revolution, it seems to me, applies not only to Italy but also to those countries that modernize the state through a series of reforms or national wars without undergoing a political revolution of a radical Jacobin-type."[174] Gramsci also suggested that the concept could be extended geographically to include the Meiji Restoration, writing that "India and China should not be compared with Japan": "Japan comes close to the English and German type of development—that is, an industrial civilization that develops within a semifeudal framework—but as far as I can tell, more like the English than the German type."[175]

All bourgeois revolutions involve a "passive" element in the sense that they involve larger or smaller minorities taking power in the state—the masses may have played a role, but ultimately the transition is completed from above by the exercise of state power and not, as Trotsky thought, by mass insurrectionary movements. Nevertheless, after 1849 the top-down aspect of the bourgeois revolutions did become more dominant: "The period of passive revolution . . . is a period in search of [superior] forms because the content has already been established by the English and French revolutions and by the Napoleonic Wars."[176] The content had been established, but what made a new form necessary? The dominance of "passive revolution" after 1849 was the result of two related factors, both products of the growth and dynamism of the capitalist system.

The first was the creation of the working class. During the French Revolution even the most class-conscious members of the bourgeoisie drew back from the actions necessary to achieve victory over the old regime, paralyzed as they were by a fear of the urban plebeians who might—and in the event, did—push beyond the limits that the former considered acceptable. It was therefore inevitable that once the potentially even more dangerous working class appeared as a social force, as it did during the revolutions of 1848–49, the bourgeoisie would seek accommodation with the existing regimes rather than risk igniting a conflagration that might engulf them, too. Gramsci noted in relation to the behavior of the Action Party during the Risorgimento, for example, that "the atmosphere of intimidation (panic fear of a terror like that of 1793, reinforced by the events in France of 1848–49) . . . made it hesitate to include in its programme certain popular demands (for instance, agrarian reform)."[177] Gramsci was prepared to accept that some Risorgimento moderates opposed those "who with the excuse that the moment of authority is necessary and indispensable, would like to keep humanity forever in its 'cradle' and enslaved," but also added, "they would not go beyond certain limits, the limits of their social group which had to leave its 'cradle' behind in concrete terms; the composition was found in the 'revolution-restoration' conception, in other words in a tempered reformist conservatism."[178]

The second factor was the availability of agencies that could provide capitalist leadership in the place of this increasingly cautious bourgeoisie. The states that had undergone revolutions during the earlier cycle—preeminently Britain and France—were now not merely the competitors of those which had not but potential models for them to follow. This is a specific example of what Gramsci called "the fact that international relations intertwine with . . . internal relations of nation-states, creating new, unique, and historical concrete combinations."[179] Once the system of which these nation-states were the preeminent members had achieved a certain momentum, its very success became the most decisive argument in persuading sections of the noncapitalist ruling classes that they must effect internal self-transformation or be overtaken by their more developed rivals. Before the Risorgimento, "the Italian economy was very weak and capitalism was just emerging; a strong and extensive bourgeois class did not exist": "It was not so much a question of freeing the advanced economic forces from antiquated legal and political fetters but rather of creating the general conditions that would enable these economic forces to come into existence and to grow on the model of other countries."[180] Gramsci noted that during the Restoration period between 1815 and 1848 the European ruling class "'preserved' a large number of the conquests of the previous period; that is, it acknowledged the supremacy of the upper bourgeoisie and implemented its 'civil' programme." But while doing so in "actual reality" it also had to present these concessions "ideologically": "it had to develop a political philosophy of its own that would justify its position while criticizing the 'petty bourgeois' program of the revolution; that is, the ensemble of 'practical instruments' that had made possible the attainment of popular unity around the bourgeoisie itself (that is to say, that ensemble of ideological principles that are the most characteristic of French political rationalism and of the so-called principles of 1789)."[181]

Typically then, a fraction of the existing ruling class, under pressure from both nation-states that had already undergone bourgeois revolutions and the demands of the popular masses, simultaneously restructured the existing state from within and expanded its territorial boundaries through conventional military conquest. Gramsci wrote of "a period of small waves of reform rather than . . . revolutionary explosions like the original French one" which combined "social struggles, interventions from above of the enlightened monarchy type, and national wars—with the two latter phenomena predominating": "The period of 'Restoration' is the richest in developments of this kind: restoration becomes the first policy whereby social struggles find sufficiently elastic frameworks to allow the bourgeoisie to gain power without dramatic upheavals, without the French machinery of terror."[182] Gramsci identifies three specific characteristics of passive revolution in Italian history, although equivalents could also be found in the cases of Germany and Japan.

The first was a favorable geopolitical context: the very conflicts and rivalries that the emergent capitalist system engendered provided a space and opportunity for new participants to emerge:

> The Italian bourgeoisie succeeded in organizing its state not so much through its intrinsic strength, as through being favoured in its victory over the feudal and semi-feudal classes by a whole series of circumstances of an international character (Napoleon III's policy in 1852–60; the Austro-Prussian War of 1866; France's defeat at Sedan and the development of the German Empire after this event). The bourgeois State thus developed more slowly, and followed a process which has not been seen in many other countries.[183]

The second was the key role of a dynamic territorial area as the active core within the process of state formation. Gramsci wrote of the importance of Piedmont in the creation of Italy over the heads of the local bourgeoisie: "This fact is of the greatest importance for the concept of 'passive revolution'—the fact, that is, that what was involved was not a social group which 'led' other groups, but a State which, even though it had limitations as a power, 'led' the group which should have been 'leading' and was able to put at the latter's disposal an army and politico-diplomatic strength."[184]

The third was the formation of a new ruling class involving elements of the old. Gramsci wrote of Italian unification that it involved "the formation of an ever more extensive ruling class": "The formation of this class involved the gradual but continuous absorption, achieved by methods which varied in their effectiveness, of the active elements produced by allied groups—and even those which came from antagonistic groups and seemed irreconcilably hostile."[185] How was this achieved? The bourgeoisie as a class was open to permeation from above and beneath: the problem in Italy was that the emergence of a new class formation was not entirely in its power and consequently much depended on the existing feudal class. In previous periods it would have acted as a block: "The previous ruling classes were essentially conservative in the sense that they did not tend to construct an organic passage from the other classes to their own, i.e., to enlarge their class sphere 'technically' and ideologically: their conception was of a closed caste. The bourgeois class poses itself as an organism in continuous movement, capable of absorbing the entire society, assimilating it to its own cultural and economic level."[186] In some cases, however, the nobility was prepared to dedicate its class organization to the service of the new capitalist mode of production. In the case of England, a majority had already made the transition to capitalist forms of exploitation by the revolutionary era; in the case of Germany and Italy, a majority saw the necessity to make such a transition. "The old feudal classes are demoted from their dominant position to a 'governing' one, but are not eliminated, nor is there any attempt to liquidate them as an organic whole; instead of a class they become a 'caste' with specific cultural and psychological characteristics, but no longer with predominant economic functions."[187]

The concept of "passive revolution" is perhaps the most evocative one to describe the process of "revolution from above" developed within the classical Marxist tradition: the dignity of action is reserved, in the main, for the state and the forces that it can bring into play rather than the masses themselves. There is, however, one respect in which the demands of the masses are represented. Alongside the "reaction of the dominant classes to the sporadic, elementary, and non-organic rebelliousness of the popular masses" the "restorations" imposed by the former also "accepted a certain part of the demands expressed from below," which is one reason why "progressive restoration-revolution" can also be identified as "passive revolution."[188] As Peter Thomas writes in elaboration of this point:

> Passive revolution had not been necessitated by the economic structure of bourgeois society or inscribed in modernity as its telos. Rather its successful imposition had involved consciousness, political choices: on the one hand, the choice of the ruling classes to develop strategies to disaggregate those working classes and confine them to a economic-corporative level within the existing society; on the other, the political choices of the subaltern classes that resulted in a failure to elaborate their own hegemonic apparatuses capable of resisting the absorptive logic of the passive revolution.[189]

Could the concept of "passive revolution" be applied beyond the revolutions from above? Gramsci seems to have thought that it could be extended in two possible ways. One of these was in relation to the Italian fascist regime that had imprisoned him:

> The ideological hypothesis could be presented in the following terms: that there is a passive revolution involved in the fact that—through the legislative intervention of the state and by means of corporative organization—relatively far-reaching modifications are being introduced into the country's economic structure in order to accentuate the "plan of production" element; in other words that socialization and co-operation in one sphere of production are being increased, without however touching (or at least going beyond the regulation and control of) individual and group appropriation of profit.[190]

Elsewhere, and more tentatively, he considered the meaning of the ideological, social, and cultural aspects of "Fordist" mass production, which he called "Americanism," and wondered whether it could "constitute an historical 'epoch,' that is, whether it can determine a gradual evolution of the same type as the 'passive revolution' . . . typical of the last century, or whether on the other hand it does not simply represent the molecular accumulation of elements destined to produce an 'explosion,' that is, an upheaval on the French pattern."[191] Alex Callinicos notes that in these passages, "what had originally been conceptualized as a particular path *to* capitalist domination—from above, gradually, and without violent rupture—comes to be understood by Gramsci as a principal means of *maintaining* capitalist domination in an epoch of wars and revolutions." As Callinicos continues, "It is . . . legitimate to ask how useful a piece of concept stretching this is." In relation to Gramsci's original use of the term, "the *ancien régime* has given way to a society in which the capitalist mode of production prevails": "But precisely what doesn't happen in the case of fascism and Fordism is any kind of systematic transformation. . . . From [Gramsci's] perspective . . . these are *counter*-revolutionary projects that seek to manage the structural contradictions of the capitalist mode of production, not the accomplishment of socialist transformation by other means."[192] The dangers involved in this kind of concept stretching as suggested by attempts, ostensibly inspired by Gramsci, to use the concept of passive revolution as an *alternative* to those of social revolution in general and bourgeois revolution in particular. An article by Dylan Riley and Manali Desai, for example, compares the rise of fascism in Italy with the process of decolonization in India, as respective examples of "violent" and "nonviolent" passive revolution; as we have seen, consideration of the former as an example of passive revolution began with Gramsci himself, but in this case the difficulties associated with it are compounded by an attempt to weld Gramsci's category onto those derived from radical, but non-Marxist social science. The authors argue that passive revolutions involve projects of "conservative modernization," which certainly captures an aspect of passive revolution, but from here on confusion is total: "As in social revolutions, political organizations rather than bureaucrats and notables are the main actors. Yet, like revolutions from above and autocratic modernization, passive revolutions leave intact, and may even strengthen, the social and political power of pre-existing dominant classes."[193] Why are the categories of "social revolution" and "revolution from above" considered mutually exclusive? Can the first not take the form of the second? From the perspective of the bourgeois revolution—or even "modernization"—does it matter if "pre-existing dominant classes" retain their political and social *power*, so long as their political and social *role* changes? Gramsci thought that it did not, writing of "the phenomenon (especially in England and Germany) whereby the leading personnel of the bourgeois class organized into a State can be constituted by elements of the old feudal classes, who have been dispossessed of their traditional economic predominance (Junkers and Lords), but who have found new forms of economic power in industry and in the banks, and who have not fused with the bourgeoisie but have remained united to their traditional social group."[194] The problem is that Riley and Desai do not accept that—whatever else it may be—passive revolution is a form of bourgeois revolution. On the contrary, they argue that there are several conditions that explain the occurrence of passive revolutions: "Most important of these is the absence of a "'bourgeois revolution,' defined as the violent elimination of the landed elite accompanied by land redistribution."[195] But this definition is based on essentially arbitrary criteria, which would exclude, among other revolutions, the Dutch and the English.

Riley and Desai use as an epigram to their article a paraphrase of a famous passage from Giuseppe di Lampedusa's novel *The Leopard*. In the book, Fabrizio, prince of Salina and a leading member of the "pre-existing dominant class," discusses Garibaldi's incursion into Sicily with his beloved nephew and heir, Tancredi. Fabrizio urges support for the king, but Tancredi disagrees:

> The eyes began smiling again. "For the King, yes, of course. But which King?" The lad had one of those sudden serious moods which made him so mysterious and so endearing. "Unless we ourselves take a hand now, they'll foist a republic on us. If we want things to stay as they are, things will have to change. D'you understand?" Rather moved, he embraced his uncle. "Well, goodbye for now. I'll be back with the tricolor."[196]

The point, however, is that Tancredi and, insofar as he endorses his character's position, Lampedusa was wrong; things did not stay as they were and this surely was Gramsci's point.[197] Although he was alert to "differences between France, Germany, and Italy in the process by which the bourgeoisie took power (and England)," he was in no doubt that they had done so in each of those countries.[198] One of Gramsci's great achievements was to break free our conception of bourgeois revolution from narrow orthodox definitions; too many of his modern would-be admirers have simply used his work to reimpose them.

A more fruitful attempt to extend Gramsci's category has been undertaken by Jaime Allinson and Alexander Anievas, who retain the main conception of passive revolution as bourgeois revolution from above, and argue for the need to link it with Trotsky's theory of uneven and combined development to form a more complete explanatory framework. The idea that uneven and combined development might produce passive revolution as an outcome is a promising one, to which I am highly sympathetic. Unfortunately, the example that they use of the Meiji Restoration, although a key example of passive revolution, is perhaps one where this attempted theoretical fusion has the least purchase. Allinson and Anievas list three causal factors derived from Trotsky, "the whip of external necessity," "the privileges of backwardness," and—their own formulation rather than Trotsky's—"contradictions of sociological amalgamation."[199] The first two factors, which were certainly important in the decisions that led to the restoration of the emperor, are in fact aspects of *uneven* development; it is the third that really relates to *combination* but, on the basis of the evidence Allinson and Anievas themselves provide, the effects of this were only experienced after 1868. In other words, combined development was an effect of the revolution rather than, as in Russia and China, a cause, as Trotsky himself points on in a comparison of Japan and Russia:

> Even late developing Russia, which traversed the same historic course as the West in a much shorter length of time, needed three centuries to get from the liquidation of feudal isolation under Ivan the Terrible, through the Westernizing of Peter the Great, to the first liberal reforms of Nicholas II. The so-called Meji Restoration incorporated in a matter of a few decades the basic features of those three major eras in Russia's development.[200]

Nevertheless, even if this specific example cannot be sustained, others surely can, not least in Germany where one of the motivations for Bismarck's passive revolution was clearly the threat of the emergent working-class presence produced by uneven and combined development—one virtually nonexistent in Japan. Did passive revolution continue to have contemporary relevance? Gramsci never considered this except in the context of his overextension of the concept to Italian fascism and American Fordism; but as in the case of the antipodean strategy represented by permanent revolution, the answer depended on whether the bourgeois revolution was considered to have a future or not.

Gramsci expanded the range of historical events that could be considered as bourgeois revolutions, or perhaps—remembering the earlier positions taken by Engels and Lenin on German Unification—it might be more accurate to say that he restored the category to a former capaciousness from which it had been shrunk by the dictates of orthodoxy. His inclusion of relatively unheroic episodes such as the German and Italian unifications within the category did not, however, mean that he was dismissive of the role played by the avant-garde of the bourgeoisie in the "classic" examples, above all England and France. One issue that Gramsci does not address, however, was that of what, if any, emotional meaning the great bourgeois revolutions should hold for the labor movement. His discussions of the Jacobins tended to concentrate on their significance for subsequent movements of the bourgeois, rather than those of the proletariat. This was unfortunate, since one of the weaknesses of the classical Marxist tradition, from the founding of the Second

International on, was that it implied too close a comparison between the historical role of the bourgeoisie and that of the contemporary proletariat.

"THE TRADITION OF THE OPPRESSED"

As we have seen, Trotsky's views were as far from those of Plekhanov in relation to the Russian Revolution as it was possible to be on the spectrum of Social Democratic opinion. Yet in 1905, Trotsky also used the French example to attack the Russian bourgeoisie for displaying even greater political cowardice than the German bourgeoisie sixty years earlier. These modern liberals were repelled by their Jacobin ancestors, Trotsky noted, but the working class was not: "The proletariat, however radically it may have, in practice, broken with the revolutionary traditions of the bourgeoisie, nevertheless preserves them, as a sacred tradition of great passions, heroism, and initiative, and its heart beats in sympathy with the speeches and acts of the Jacobin Convention."[201] In addition to invoking the heroic bourgeois past, Trotsky also introduces a notion of "revolutionary traditions." These could be turned against not only the modern bourgeoisie but reformist tendencies within the working class. In "Where Is Britain Going?," for example, he was careful to state that Cromwell and the Independents are in no sense forerunners of socialism, but nevertheless uses their revolutionary example to expose claims by Ramsay MacDonald and others that British development is characterized by "gradualness." What emerges is the idea—which Trotsky elsewhere rejected—that Communists within the working-class movement play the same role as the Independents and Jacobins played within the bourgeoisie: "It can be with some justice said that Lenin is the proletarian twentieth-century Cromwell."[202] The danger was that, shorn of context or qualification, statements like these could be used to license not only an overly heroic view of the bourgeoisie's political role but the notion that the bourgeois revolution was essentially the same kind of experience as the socialist revolution, complete with political leadership and organization, the only real differences being in their respective class basis.

Benjamin took a more dialectical approach. He was hostile to the idea understood as an inevitable upward movement through successive modes of production, each one involving growth in the productive forces until the point is reached where socialism becomes possible. As we have seen, this view of progress also played an important ideological role for the Social Democratic and Stalinist bureaucracies, for whom the moment when sufficient progress has occurred for socialism to be on the agenda always seems to be beyond the next horizon: the productive forces were never quite developed enough (Kautsky), the "democratic stage" had still to be achieved (Stalin), and so on.

Benjamin was not alone in his suspicions. At the end of the Second World War the non-Marxist Orwell—a writer with whom Benjamin had far more affinities than is usually thought—disputed the very idea of capitalist progressiveness as understood by Stalinism: "The instance generally used is the overthrow of feudalism by the bourgeoisie, which is supposed to foreshadow the overthrow of capitalism by Socialism in our own age. Capitalism, it is argued, was once a progressive force, and therefore its crimes were justified, or at least were unimportant."

Orwell then specifically refers to an article by the then editor of the *New States-man* and Stalinist fellow traveler, Kingsley Martin, in which the latter compares Henry VIII and Stalin as progressive figures in their respective times:

> Now, Henry VII has not a very close resemblance to Stalin; Cromwell would provide a better analogy; but, granting the importance given to him by Mr. Martin, where does this argument lead? Henry VIII made possible the rise of capitalism, which led to the horrors of the Industrial Revolution and thence to a cycle of enormous wars, the next of which may well destroy civilization altogether. So, telescoping the process, we can put it like this: "Everything is to be forgiven Henry VIII, because ultimately he enabled us to blow ourselves to pieces with atomic bombs."[203]

In spite of the mock-naïve tone adopted here Orwell was of course perfectly aware that socialism—"the fully human life which is now technically achievable"—was only possible on the basis of the development of the productive forces made possible by capitalism.[204] His point here is that *in the absence of the socialist revolution,* "progress," whatever its incidental benefits, is always accompanied by new means of oppression and even possible destruction.

Benjamin's argument is more subtle and more politically focused, but displays the same skepticism. In his last great essay written before his suicide, "On the Concept of History," Benjamin focuses particularly on the illusions of Social Democracy:

> The conformism which has marked the Social Democrats from the beginning attaches not only to their political tactics but to their economic views as well. Nothing has so corrupted the German working class as the notion that it was moving with the current. . . . Social Democratic theory and to an even greater extent its practice were shaped by a conception of progress which bore little relation to reality but made dogmatic claims. Progress as pictured in the minds of the social Democrats was, first of all, progress of humanity itself (and not just advances in human ability and knowledge). Second, it was something boundless (in keeping with the infinite perfectibility of humanity). Third, it was considered inevitable—something that automatically pursued a straight or spiral course.

What these claims all had in common, according to Benjamin, was their vision of progress occurring "through a homogenous, empty time": "A critique of the concept of such a progression must underlie any criticism of the concept of progress itself."[205] Callinicos has argued: "Benjamin's hostility to the vulgar-Marxist faith in the growth of the productive forces as the motor of inevitable socialist revolution . . . leads him to ignore the aspects of capitalism on which Marx places such stress in the *Communist Manifesto,* its dynamic, restless, revolutionizing character, throwing society into flux from which the proletariat can draw the power and desire to seize power." Consequently, Benjamin displays a tendency to "to deny capitalism any progressive aspects."[206] While Marx (and Engels) certainly do emphasize the chaotic, exhilarating tendencies described by Callinicos, it is not clear to me that they link them with the possibilities for socialist revolution. Regardless of that, however, it is not the case that life under capitalism is always "dynamic, restless, revolutionizing": it may be so in areas of the Global South subject to uneven and combined development, considerably less so in, say, the suburbs of Edinburgh. For Marx, the fundamentally positive difference that capitalism has made in the human condition, the aspect that made socialism conceivable, is that for the first time in history the goal of overcoming scarcity, and consequently that of overcoming inequality, is now possible—possible, but not inevitable, and Benjamin's quarrel is with those who neglect this qualification, not with the existence of penicillin, electricity, or running water. As Esther Leslie comments in her outstanding study of Benjamin: "As the bourgeois class secures economic and political power, progress, a cardinal strand in Enlightenment political rhetoric and social theory, unfolds in actuality its class inflections as economic and social progress for one class, presented ideologically as the universally significant progression of humanity itself." Technological improvements themselves are not necessarily progressive: "The easy identification of technological development with progress overrides questions of social form or production relations." The problem, however, is not the technological aspect of the forces of production as such, but, as Leslie suggests, the relations of production within which they occur. Although both develop, the tendency is always for the latter to retard the former: "Every inch of progress on a technological level under these relations of production, the oppressed suffer regression on a social level: like Marx's understanding of machinery as potential liberator that in *this* moment under *this* organization of relations of production only intensifies our exploitation and, often, our discomfort."[207] Every discussion of progress must therefore start with the question, progress for whom? Although Benjamin's target in "On the Concept of History" is specifically Social Democracy, Leslie is right to describe it more generally as "Benjamin's reckoning with Social Democracy, Stalinism, and bourgeois thought, none of which were able to prevent the disaster of fascism."[208]

What are the implications of this stance for the notion of the revolutionary succession from bourgeoisie to proletariat? Benjamin was generally not impressed by the historical record of the bourgeoisie in political terms. "Goethe and Napoleon shared a similar vision," he wrote in an essay on the former, "the social emancipation of the bourgeoisie within the framework of political despotism."[209] This was written specifically of the German bourgeoisie, but even in relation to the supposedly exemplary French bourgeoisie Benjamin saw its revolutionary period as being much shorter than was conventional in the classical Marxist tradition. In particular Benjamin had a much more restricted—and in my opinion more defensible—view of the chronological extent of the French Revolution than Lenin, Luxemburg, or Gramsci: "With the July Revolution, the bourgeoisie realized the goals of 1789."[210] And with the realization of these goals came certain consequences: "The derogation of the critical spirit begins directly after the victory of the bourgeoisie in the July Revolution."[211] For him, the significance of 1871—for other Marxists the culmination of the French Revolution—lies elsewhere, in the shift of working-class consciousness represented by the Paris Commune: "It dispels the illusion that the task of the proletarian revolution was to complete the work of '89 in close collaboration with the bourgeoisie. This illusion had marked the period 1831–1871, from the Lyons riots to the Commune. The bourgeoisie never shared in this error. Its battle against the social rights of proletariat dates back to the great Revolution."[212] Benjamin's refusal to celebrate the bourgeoisie, his understanding of its revolutionary role in history as mainly contingent and always short-lived underlay his hostility to the contemporary Popular Front, which he described in the closing months of his life as possessing "intrinsic weaknesses."[213]

His approach involved considerably more than simply referring to a tradition of "past struggles" with which to inspire contemporary socialists: it questions the very nature of that tradition. One aspect of the theory of progress discussed above is an undialectical attitude toward the development of class society, in which those social forces that brought the capitalist world into being, and the culture they created, are treated to uncritical celebration. As Benjamin points out, in one of the very greatest passages in all of Marxism, this has certain ideological consequences:

> With whom does the historian actually sympathize? The answer is inevitable: with the victors. And all rulers are the heirs of prior conquerors. Hence, empathizing with the victor invariably benefits the current rulers. The historical materialist knows what this means. Whoever has emerged victorious participates to this day in the triumphal procession in which the current rulers step over those who are lying prostrate. According to traditional practice, the spoils are carried in the procession. They are called "cultural treasures," and a historical materialist views them with cautious detachment. For in every case these treasures have a lineage that he cannot contemplate without horror. They owe their existence not only to the efforts of the great geniuses who created them, but also to the anonymous toil of others who lived in the same period. There is no document of culture which is not at the same time a document of barbarism. And just as such a document is never free of barbarism, so barbarism taints the manner in which it was transmitted from one hand to another.[214]

To simply remember the achievements of the bourgeois revolution and bourgeois culture—Cromwell and Robespierre on the one hand, Milton and David on the other—without also holding in our minds the contradictions of the progress they represent is to forget the "anonymous toil" that made it possible: "It is more difficult to honor the memory of the anonymous than it is to honor the memory of the famous, the celebrated, not excluding poets and thinkers."[215] To put this in concrete terms: the peasants who revolted against the English monarchy in 1381 and their yeoman descendants of the New Model Army who overthrew it in 1649 are not part of the socialist tradition; they are the ancestors—in some cases quite distant ancestors—of the present capitalist class, of "the current rulers." Benjamin was of course perfectly aware that the ruling classes suppress aspects of their rise to power that have become inconvenient to them. Thus, in *The Arcades Project*, he writes: "The enshrinement or apologia is meant to cover up the revolutionary moments in the occurrence of history. At heart, it seeks the establishment of a continuity. . . . The parts where tradition breaks off—hence its peaks and crags, which offer footing to one who would cross over them—it misses."[216] But the answer to this is not to "claim" bourgeois revolutionaries for the socialist tradition: it is still possible to understand and celebrate their achievements and, in some cases, their heroism and self-sacrifice, without superimposing their struggles onto our own. The socialist tradition is what Benjamin calls "the tradition of the oppressed," the tradition of those who did not benefit from the victories over the precapitalist order, even though they participated in the struggle against it, and who *could not* have benefited from it, given the impossibility of establishing the socialist order much earlier than Benjamin's own lifetime. In some cases the distinction is less easy to draw, but without it, celebration of what we might call "the tradition of the victors" simply becomes celebration of the established fact, of where history has temporarily come to rest. It is only *after* the socialist revolution that we will be able to embrace this tradition without "cautious detachment": "only a redeemed mankind is granted the fullness of its past—which is to say, for only a redeemed mankind has its past become citable in all its moments."[217] If it is only the actual achievement of the socialist revolution that will finally allow us to *incorporate* previous revolutions into our tradition, it is only the struggle to achieve it that allows us to fully *understand* them. Outside of the future goal of a redeemed humanity the history of which they are part will remain a heap of fragments, the pile of rubbish against which the Angel of History turns its wings: "Without some kind of assay of the classless society, there is only a historical accumulation of the past."[218]

But if one aspect of Benjamin's approach is to narrow down the range of our tradition, another is to blow it wide open, to explode the conception of what he calls "empty, homogenous time" and replace it with "messianic, now-time," so that every moment in history is potentially of use to revolutionaries. Benjamin says that "nothing that has ever happened should be regarded as lost to history."[219] In the classic passage from *The Eighteenth Brumaire of Louis Bonaparte* discussed in chapter 10, Marx describes the ideology of the French revolutionaries of 1789: "Camille Desmoulins, Danton, Robespierre, Saint-Just, and Napoleon, the heroes of the old French Revolution, as well as its parties and masses, accomplished the tasks of their epoch, which was the emancipation and establishment of modern *bourgeois* society, in Roman costume and with Roman slogans." Marx argued that the "gladiators" of the bourgeois revolution "found in the stern classical traditions of the Roman republic the ideals, art forms, and self-deception they needed in order to hide from themselves the limited bourgeois content of their struggles and maintain the enthusiasm at the high level appropriate to great historical tragedy."[220] This assessment is not in dispute, but Benjamin argues that something else is also going on, in addition to the heroic "self-deception" of which Marx writes:

> To Robespierre ancient Rome was a past charged with now-time, a past which he blasted out of the continuum of history. The French Revolution viewed itself as Rome reincarnate. It cited ancient Rome the way a fashion cites a by-gone mode of dress. Fashion has a nose for the topical, no matter where it stirs in the thickets of long ago; it is the tiger's leap into the past.[221]

In other words, the characteristically austere qualities of Republican Rome— civic patriotism, "republican virtue," self-sacrifice, and so on—were *actually* relevant to the French revolutionaries in their struggle with the absolutist regime and were not—or were not only—a rhetorical ploy with which they sought to disguise their real objectives.

There are major structural differences between the bourgeois and socialist revolutions; above all in the fact that, unlike the bourgeoisie, the working class has to be fully conscious of what it is trying to achieve. In the context of socialist politics, Benjamin's demand that we ransack the whole of history for pasts "charged with now-time" is tantamount to saying that we do not and cannot know which aspects of our tradition or history more widely will be of most use to us in coming struggles. We inherit some general, historically demonstrable conclusions about the limits of reformism, the dynamics of revolution, the role of the revolutionary party, and so on; but every new situation is in some senses unique, for each there will be a moment or moments in history that help to illuminate them. The point is that these moments will not always be the ones we want or expect.

▣ ▣ ▣

I began this chapter with the figure of Victor Serge recording the deaths of his contemporaries in an autobiography written under conditions of terrible political and personal isolation, an attempt "to create in a void" during which he was always conscious of "writing for the desk-drawer alone."[222] But the work of those whose passing he noted—the most important of that by Benjamin, and virtually all of that by Gramsci   was also written in the knowledge that it might never be published or—in the case of Trotsky—reach an audience of any size if it did. Nevertheless, early in the year during which he would take his own life, Benjamin offered a justification for the effort involved in a letter to his friend Gershom Scholem: "Every line we succeed in publishing today—no matter how uncertain the future to which we entrust it—is a victory wrenched from the powers of darkness."[223]

The figures considered here were forced to rethink aspects of the theory of bourgeois revolution in opposition to both the preexisting Social Democratic orthodoxy and the recharged version associated with Stalinism. Their respective theoretical legacies, on this subject at least, have still to be fully absorbed into contemporary Marxist thought, and the process did not even begin until after Trotsky, Gramsci, and Benjamin had been in their graves for several decades. As Benjamin's locomotive of history went over the edge of a cliff in 1940, it might have appeared that their work had been interred with their bones. When the debate on bourgeois revolution resumed after the Second World War, the orthodoxy held dominion over the overwhelming majority of the left and challenges to it came not from upholders of the classical Marxist tradition advocating a more defensible conception of bourgeois revolution but from academic historians seeking to demonstrate that any conception of bourgeois revolution referred to a nonexistent subject.

THREE

REVISIONS, RECONSTRUCTIONS, ALTERNATIVES

15

REVISIONISM: THE BOURGEOIS REVOLUTIONS DID NOT TAKE PLACE

As we saw in chapter 7, bourgeois thinkers had with very few exceptions effectively abandoned the theory of social revolution by 1848, for essentially the same reasons as they had abandoned the labor theory of value: both invited members of the working class to draw radical conclusions about their position in capitalist society and how it might be changed. Toward the end of his life, Engels wrote a letter that revisited Marx's critique of the ahistorical conceptions of political economy in *The Poverty of Philosophy* ("Thus there has been history, but there is no longer any."), but now in relation to politics: "It is . . . in the nature of all parties and/or classes that have come to power by revolutionary means to demand that the fundamental laws newly created be unconditionally recognized and held sacrosanct. The right to revolution *has* existed—otherwise those who rule would, after all, not be entitled to do so—but from now on it is to cease to exist."[1]

Nevertheless, the events that Marx and Engels called bourgeois revolutions could not be totally disregarded, if only because they played such an important role in the founding national mythologies of several important states; commemorations therefore had to be carefully managed so as not to legitimate revolution as an acceptable means of resolving social crises. Revolutions had to be treated as purely historical phenomena of no contemporary relevance, at least in the West, since the expansion of representative democracy throughout the second half of the nineteenth century supposedly made recourse to the violent overthrow of governments unnecessary as a means of achieving social change. The explosive qualities of the various national pasts were defused in different ways, but each involved placing limits on what could be retrospectively endorsed. Trotsky once noted the differences between the British and French approaches: "The French bourgeoisie, having falsified the revolution, adopted it, and, changing it into small coinage, put it into daily circulation. The British bourgeoisie has erased the very memory of the seventeenth-century revolution by dissolving its past into 'gradualness.'"[2]

Even confined to history, however, social revolutions retained their power as examples, especially to more class-conscious workers who noticed that while democracy could change the composition of government, the capitalist system remained essentially unaltered. It is unsurprising, therefore, that attempts to minimize even the historical significance of the great bourgeois revolutions on capitalist development began to gather pace. It is equally unsurprising that they should first be formulated in Britain, the country with the most developed capitalist economy and the largest working class. There were of course rearguard actions. Although Samuel Gardiner is chiefly known for conceptualizing the English Civil War as the "Puritan Revolution," in a series of books published between 1883 and his death in 1902, his arguments were far closer to the historiography of the French Revolution produced during the Restoration, and indeed to Marxism, than most of his peers: "The laws by which the progress of human society is governed work not irrespective of human agency, but by the influence of surrounding conditions on human wills, whereby the activity of those wills is roused to react upon the conditions." But for Gardiner, it is human will rather than impersonal laws that has priority, for "unless the resolute will be there to struggle onwards and upwards towards an ideal higher still, the gift [of knowledge] will have been bestowed in vain":

> Every new social class as it rises to power needs, in proportion to its previous ignorance, a strictness of discipline which becomes unnecessary as soon as it has learned to bear lightly the responsibility of its new position. That discipline in England was afforded to the middle classes by rule, grasping, unscrupulous, and immoral as it was, of Henry VIII. In Scotland it was by the Presbyterian clergy that the middle classes were organized, and that organization thus given enabled them to throw of the yoke of the feudal nobles and ultimately to assert their own predominance.[3]

The point here is not the accuracy of the forces identified by Gardiner as providing the bourgeoisie with leadership, which can be questioned in relation to both England and Scotland, but rather that he still sees the social change as requiring revolutionary political leadership. At the other extreme were the views of the pioneering sociologist Herbert Spencer, expressed here in the course of a polemic against the encroachments of the state from 1860: "The failure of Cromwell permanently to establish a new social condition, and the rapid revival of suppressed institutions and practices after his death, show how powerless is a monarch to change the type of society he governs. He may disturb, he may retard, or he may aid the natural process of organization; but the general course of this process is beyond his control."[4]

A more typical approach than either Gardiner's voluntarism or Spencer's determinism was one that celebrated the period, not in relation to any social or economic changes that it might have consolidated or introduced, but instead for the political values and legal relationships that it bequeathed to prosperity. For the historian Lord Acton, writing at the turn of the twentieth century, the republic was indeed a failure, but an intellectually fruitful one: "The Commonwealth is the second stage on the road of revolution, which started from the Netherlands, and went on to America and France, and is the centre of the history of the modern world.

Seen from a distance the value of that epoch is not in that which it created, for it left not creations but ruins, but in the prodigious wealth of ideas which sent into the world. It supplied the [1688] English Revolution, the one that succeeded, the American, the French, with its material."[5] Two aspects of this argument are worthy of note. The first is that while Acton shares with Burke and Macaulay an emphasis on 1688 as the decisive turning point in English history, he is far more prepared than they to see it as a completion of the earlier revolution of 1640. This may be because, living in the twilight of bourgeois stability before the cataclysm of 1914, he felt less threatened by the potential for revolution and was consequently less concerned with denying any value to previous upheavals. The year 1688 is as devoid of socioeconomic content for Acton as it was for his predecessors, although the final sentence in the following passage has a refreshing honesty absent from their panegyrics on British exceptionalism: "The gentry who managed the affairs of the county managed the affairs of the country after 1688 as they had done before. There was no transfer of force from the aristocratic element of society to the democratic. . . . And yet it was the greatest thing done by the English nation. It established the State upon a contract . . . It was perfectly compatible with the oppression of class by class, and of the country by the State, as the agent of a class."[6] The second aspect is that Acton does not simply draw a connection between the two English revolutions, but between them and their Dutch predecessor and their American and French successors, all of which are treated as moments in the unfolding of a movement in history. In other words, Acton has taken the same sequence of events previously identified by thinkers from Harrington and Barnave to Marx and Engels; but instead of these revolutions establishing new types of society, Acton sees them as extending a particular notion of liberty.

The climax of this gradual shift to idealism occurs—as in so many other areas of intellectual life—in the work of the Austrian Marginalist wing of neoclassical economics, above all in the work of Friedrich von Hayek, not coincidentally an admirer of Acton.[7] For the Marginalists and those who shared their methodological principles, capitalism had always existed, it had simply not been the dominant form of economy until relatively late in human history—and here there is of course a direct link back to Adam Smith and his view of commercial society as corresponding to human nature.[8] Thus, we find Max Weber celebrating "the achievements of ancient capitalism" supposedly displayed by the early Roman Empire and Hayek claiming that the decline of Rome from the second century AD was due to the advance of "state socialism" following the supposed abandonment of free market economics and the rule of law.[9]

The same events that comprise the history of the bourgeois revolutions for Marxists reappear in Hayek's work, but now as episodes in the emergence of individualism, a movement with roots supposedly in classical antiquity and Christianity, but which, like the expansion of markets with which it is so closely linked in marginalist thought, only becomes generalized in Europe from the end of the Middle Ages:

From the commercial cities of Northern Italy the new view of life spread with commerce to the west and north, through France and the south-west of Germany to the
Low Countries and the British Isles, taking firm root wherever there was no despotic
power to stifle it. In the Low Countries and Britain it for a long time enjoyed its
fullest development and for the first time had an opportunity to grow freely and to
become the foundation of the social and political life of these countries. And it was
there that in the late seventeenth and eighteenth centuries it again began to spread
in a more fully developed form to the West and East, to the New World and the center of the European continent where devastating wars and political oppression had
largely submerged the earlier beginnings of a similar growth.

This could be a description of the progress of the bourgeois revolution, even
down to the identification of those areas where it initially failed, above all in Germany: "The most fateful of these developments," writes Hayek in a footnote to the
preceding passage, "pregnant with consequences not yet extinct, was the subjection
and partial destruction of the German bourgeoisie by the territorial princes in the
fifteenth and sixteenth centuries."[10] The British political philosopher Michael
Oakeshott regarded Hayek as too doctrinaire in economic theory, but nevertheless
similarly saw the emergence of human individuality as resulting from the same
process of territorial diffusion. Social relations based on kinship and characterized
by status reached their apogee in the twelfth century:

> It was modified slowly, sporadically, and intermittently over a period of about seven
> centuries, from the thirteenth to the twentieth century.... Italy was the first home of
> the modern individual who sprang from the break-up of the medieval communal life.
> ...North of the Alps, events took a different course, though they moved more slowly
> and had to contend with larger hindrances In England, in France, in the Netherlands,
> in Spain, in Switzerland, in Poland, Hungary, and Bohemia, and particularly in all
> centers of municipal life, conditions favourable to individuality, and individuals to
> exploit them, appeared."[11]

Effectively then, there existed a coherent alternative interpretation of the sequence of revolutionary events that Marxists regard as the bourgeois revolutions,
which, inverting the direction of the base-superstructure metaphor, emphasized
their role in generating ideas about the human personality and legal relationships
that these suggested. However, until the aftermath of the Second World War, adherents of the two interpretations rarely challenged each other. Conventional historians would occasionally register their dismay at what was usually referred to as
the "economic interpretation of history," which of course included much more than
Marxism. In the United States, for example, Charles Andrews criticized both
Marxist and Populist historians in the last volume of his *The Colonial Period of
American History* (1938) for arguing that the American War of Independence was
primarily inspired by economic motives on the part of the colonists:

> One may not doubt that behind the effort to obtain self-government and freedom from
> the restraints of British control there lay factors that were commercial, financial, legal,
> social, and industrial. But no one of these by itself would have brought the Revolution.

It is too great a simplification of history to regard the events of the past as nothing but a struggle of classes, a clash of economic interpretations, for such an oversimplification of the problem leads to an oversimplified solution. No amount of study of the social side of colonial life—much vaunted today as if it was something new—will explain the events of 1775 and 1776. To emphasize the economic aspects to the exclusion of all else is to interpret human affairs in terms of material things only, to say nothing of the spiritual power necessary to use these material resources for human welfare, to ignore the influence of sentiment and morality, and to underrate the rich and varied stuff of human nature, the distractions of statesmen, and the waywardness and uncertainties of events.[12]

But these and other comments like them are merely made in passing, in a tone of sorrow and incredulity that anyone would wish to reduce the manifold complexity of events to monocausal explanations: there is no real sense that the views being criticized constitute a threat. A series of overlapping developments were however to unsettle the serenity of the historical and cognate professions. One was not directly political and arose from the way in which academic reputations came to be established during the postwar expansion of higher education across the West. An important aspect of this was identified by US historian Crane Brinton while reviewing an early work of the tendency that he was the first to name:

There is the compulsion—no weaker term will do—on the historian, and particularly on the young scholar seeking to establish himself, to be original. This originality cannot be for the historian today merely something "rarely so well expressed"; nor, to be fair, can it be merely what critics of conventional Rankean historical work as displayed in doctrinal thesis or monographs complain that it is: the simple digging out of the sources of brand new "facts." The creative historian, like the creative artist, has in our time to produce something new as "interpretation." He has, in short, to be a *revisionist*.[13]

Yet even overturning established positions as a strategy of career furtherance would not necessarily determine the direction that revision would take. Historiographical traditions in both England and France were certainly still influenced by the radical Liberal and Jacobin interpretations of their respective revolutions and, as the repentant former Marxist Louis Hacker complained at a meeting of the proto-neoliberal Mont Pelerin Society in 1951, there was an analogously influential tradition of Jeffersonian democracy in the United States.[14] Those seeking to establish themselves as holders of new revisionist interpretations found these older positions still worth attacking, but only in France could the local variant be described as the dominant tradition and even there it had not gone unchallenged. The character of revisionism was in fact largely determined by a geopolitical context in which the Soviet Union had emerged from the Second World War as a major power and a threat to Western capitalism.

The period was a paradoxical one. Although the years from 1948 to 1973 tend to be associated with Keynesian demand management, relatively high levels of social provision and effective trade unionism, the intellectual tone—particularly in Britain, Germany, and the United States—was deeply conservative, combining hysteria over geopolitical rivalries of the Cold War with complacency over the social stability generated by the welfare state. The dominant political theorist was Sir Karl Popper, who in *The Open Society and Its Enemies* (1945) and *The Poverty of Historicism* (1957) provided justification for avoiding any consideration of the substantive claims made by Marx (and Freud) by declaring their methodology invalid. Popper himself relied on the methodological individualism associated in different ways with Weber and Hayek. In the latter book Popper identified the object of his critique as "an approach to the social sciences which assumes that historical prediction is their principal aim," which for him included attempts to formulate historical laws, such as the succession of stages culminating in Communism, supposedly upheld by Marx.[15] Popper's almost total ignorance of what Marx and Engels, or indeed any of the classical Marxists, actually believed was not an obstacle to the widespread acceptance of his argument.

At least some of the revisionists writers were themselves committed Cold Warriors—a position that was of course perfectly compatible with right-wing Social Democracy. Hugh Trevor-Roper was a traditional Conservative, "a true son of Tory Christchurch" as one admiring contemporary described him, famously elevated by Harold Macmillan to the Regius Chair of History at Oxford over the Labor-supporting A. J. P. Taylor.[16] But at the same time he was repelled by the fanatical anti-Communism expressed at the founding Conference of the Congress for Cultural Freedom in Berlin during June 1950 and wrote withering reports for the *Manchester Guardian*—then as now the daily paper of choice for the liberal British middle classes—expressing his disquiet, much to the annoyance of the CIA operatives who bankrolled the event.[17] Recoil from the hysterical excesses of anti-Communism did not of course prevent some academics from defending the West within their own professions. Since most Marxists belonged to their local Communist Party, their analysis of history was essentially treated as another aspect of communist subversion. Alfred Cobban, along with Trevor-Roper, the cofounder of revisionism, helped ensure that one of his own students, George Rudé, was blacklisted from lecturing in Britain.[18] But not even hostility to Stalinism guaranteed protection from the guard dogs of liberalism. In Britain, Isaac Deutscher was blocked from taking up a post at Cambridge by Isaiah Berlin on the grounds that he could not be trusted to "subordinate scholarship to ideology."[19] In the United States, the venerable historian Carl Becker—a figure far from Marxism of any sort—was attacked for "deliberate falsification" and of prostituting his scholarship in order to advance a left-wing agenda.[20] But the Cold War in the academy involved more than merely attempting to destroy the careers or reputations of Marxist scholars; it also meant, at some level, engaging with their work. What Christopher Hill wrote in relation to Britain was also true for the United States: "Those of us who had tenure before the cold war heated up were lucky to retain our positions: there was no promotion and no recruitment of Marxists into the profession in the fifties."[21]

As I noted in chapter 13, the classical Marxist discussions of the bourgeois revolutions, such as those that preceded the German Revolution of 1848 or the Russian

Revolution of 1905, tended to be strategic in nature, conducted by left-wing party leaders and activists, in which history was reviewed to guide contemporary socialist practice. Bourgeois economists would expect to read *Capital* and treat it as a serious contribution to their intellectual discipline, however much they regarded it as flawed by, for example, Marx's supposed inability to derive prices from values; bourgeois historians of the English Civil War, however, were unlikely to refer to Lenin's *Two Tactics of Social-Democracy in the Democratic Revolution* in order to engage with his theory of agency in the bourgeois revolution. At this stage, there were simply no regular points of intersection between the written work of professional historians and that of professional revolutionaries. Outside of France, there were very few substantial Marxist histories of the bourgeois revolutions, as opposed to popular pamphlets or journalistic accounts, mainly because prior to the postwar growth of higher education, there were very few Marxist academic historians who would have had the time and incentive to write them. Those Marxists who were established in the universities, like Maurice Dobb in Britain or Paul Sweezy in the United States, tended to be economists or economic historians. As Eric Hobsbawm wrote, reflecting on his own experience in Britain: "Outside the Party there was then no intellectual public which took Marxism seriously, or even who accepted or understood our technical terminology."[22] By the mid-1950s, however, a substantial number of books and scholarly articles by historians committed to historical materialism had appeared on the two most widely recognized bourgeois revolutions, in England and France, thus providing anti-Marxist historians with a body of work that they could criticize. From the early 1950s, therefore, the orthodox conception of the bourgeois revolution came under increasing attack from historians who were opponents of both Marxist theory and Stalinist reality, their assumption being that the former had led to the latter. The almost universal misidentification of Marxism with Stalinism by both supporters and opponents of the latter meant that revisionists were ignorant of the fact they were themselves criticizing a revision, a departure from the complexity of the original Marxist position.

Origins and Development

We encountered revisionism in chapter 1, in the work of Jonathan Clark and Blair Worden, two British representatives of the tendency in its self-confident, self-conscious maturity. However, the first, relatively isolated, expressions of the revisionist case were made during the 1950s, when two British historians, Trevor-Roper and Cobban, launched their respective attacks on Marxist interpretations of the English Civil War and the French Revolution—although unlike their successors, both men accepted that these revolutions had actually taken place and were significant historical turning points. The anti-Marxist aspects of their arguments were supported over the following decade, sometimes indirectly, by a diverse handful of other writers, the most important of whom were Norman Cohn, Geoffrey Elton, Jack Hexter,

Peter Laslett, George Taylor, and Jacob Talmon. "As with any revisionism," wrote Theodore Rabb in relation to the English Revolution, "the first few ventures set a permanent tone": "Rough spots may be polished in subsequent work, and details accumulated, but the main features of the argument are in place."[23] Most of the discussion in this chapter will be devoted to the arguments of these early figures since, as Rabb suggests, virtually all the themes characteristic of the subsequent revisionist movement—including those usually associated with postmodernism—can be found, at least in embryonic form, in their writings. Very little of note has since been added, at least in theoretical terms; indeed, as Bryan Palmer has written in relation to one of the twin founders of revisionism: "Cobban has been followed by a seemingly endless parade of well-trained parrots, each mouthing a slightly different rendition of the same rehearsed analytic one-liner."[24]

Trevor-Roper entered the field first and his target was the Christian Socialist, Labor Party member, and highly respected economic historian R. H. Tawney—one suspects because if he could successfully demolish the positions associated with this academically reputable figure, then the claims of the disreputable Marxists who held essentially the same views could be dismissed without requiring a similarly direct engagement. Tawney had published two articles in 1941: one, in the *Economic History Review* arguing that the rising gentry was the central revolutionary force in the civil war; the other, in the *Proceedings of the British Academy*, identifying Harrington as the key contemporary figure to have recognized this process.[25] According to Tawney:

> It was that the revolution of his day had been determined by changes in social organization which passed unnoticed till too late; and that the old regime had been destroyed neither by the errors of the ruler ... nor by the intransigence of the Parliament, but by impersonal forces too strong for both; and that political stability was not to be expected till political institutions were brought into accordance with realities. Forms must be adapted to social facts, not facts to forms. ... It was not the Civil War which had destroyed the old regime, but the dissolution of the social foundations of the old regime which caused the Civil War.[26]

His own account of the changes in class structure expanded on Harrington's argument with evidence drawn from both other contemporary witnesses and statistics on the holding of manors in Tudor and early Stuart England.

> The core consisted of the landed proprietors, above the yeomanry and below the peerage, together with a growing body of well-to-do farmers, sometimes tenants of their relatives, who had succeeded the humble peasants of the past as lessees of demesne farms; professional men, also rapidly increasing in number, such as the more eminent lawyers, divines, and an occasional medical practitioner; and the wealthier merchants who, if not, as many were themselves sons of landed families, had received a similar education, moved in the same circles, and in England, unlike France, were commonly recognized to be socially indistinguishable from them. ... The ruin of famous families by personal extravagance and political ineptitude; the decline of in the position of the yeomanry towards the turn of the [sixteenth] century, when long leases fell in;

the loss, not only of revenue, but of authority, by the monarchy, as crown lands melted; the mounting fortunes of the residuary legate, a gentry whose aggregate income was put even in 1600 at three hundred times that of peers, bishops, deans and chapters, and a richer yeomen altogether, and who steadily gathered into their hands church estates slipping from the grasp of the peasant, nobility, Church, and Crown alike—such movements and their consequences were visible to all.[27]

As his invocation of Harrington suggests, Tawney relied more on the insights of commentators who lived through the final stages of the events he described rather than subsequent Marxist attempts to theorize them. Indeed, he was skeptical about the explanatory power of the theory of bourgeois revolution in relation to the period between 1640 and 1660: "Was the Civil War a bourgeois revolution? Of course it was a bourgeois revolution. The trouble is the bourgeoisie were on both sides."[28]

For Trevor-Roper it was essential to reject the thesis of the rising gentry associated with Tawney and to dismiss the evidence of contemporary witnesses, which he proceeded to do in 1953, also in the pages of the *Economic History Review*. The much-disputed detail of the controversy need not concern us here; what is of greater relevance is the basis of Trevor-Roper's case. "According to [Tawney], the Great Rebellion was the logical, though violent culmination of the process which he imagines, a form of emphatic foreclosure by the creditor class of rising 'entrepreneur' gentry, City merchants and lawyers, upon the mortgaged estates of a half-bankrupt peerage, Church and Crown." This is how Trevor-Roper summarizes his opponent's position; but how, he asks, does this explain the leading role of the Independents, "Oliver Cromwell and his followers in arms and politics"? "They were not a 'rising' gentry; they were not a creditor class; nor were they a sudden phenomenon of the 1640's." What then were they? "The fanatical hatreds, the impossible demands, the futile foreign policy of the Independents were the culmination of a century of protests: the protests of the declining gentry." On the basis of this interpretation, the arguments advanced by Harrington and accepted by Tawney are not a scientific assessment but an ideological "doctrine" designed to justify and encourage the actions of the "mere gentry" in its struggle with the court: "The fact that they lost in that struggle is evidence of the falsity of the doctrine: for if power always follows property, and the gentry had all the property, the gentry should clearly have prevailed against the successive 'oligarchical' courts by which they were in fact ruled." Harrington's doctrines were in fact "slogans uttered, regardless of truth, to inspire waverers in a difficult and uncertain struggle"—very similar, as Trevor-Roper maliciously insinuated, to those used by the Nazis to claim victory during the Battle of Britain and Operation Barbarossa. More specifically, it amounted to "a political dogma whereby a class seeking power sought to sanctify its claims."[29]

The ferocity of Trevor-Roper's attack on Tawney was much commented on at the time, not least by Tawney himself. Yet what is at first sight more startling is the intensity of Trevor-Roper's animus toward Harrington, a figure who had been dead for nearly three hundred years. It is as if Trevor-Roper realized that Harrington was the inspiration behind not only Tawney's interpretation of the English Revolution but the entire theory of bourgeois revolution of which it was a specific example.[30] It may also be why, for all his criticism of Tawney's supposed scholarly inadequacies, Trevor-Roper's own critique of Harrington was factually inaccurate in virtually every respect, as C. B. MacPherson pointed out shortly afterward. Trevor-Roper erred by amalgamating Harrington's position with those of his followers and others who had independently arrived at similar conclusions to them, even though these differed from Harrington's in several respects. Furthermore, he misrepresented Harrington by claiming that the latter was ambiguous about the period during which the rise of the gentry took place, when in fact he was perfectly precise in dating the process. Most disabling of all for Trevor-Roper's case, however, was that contrary to his assertions, Harrington did not claim that the gentry as a whole had acquired most of the available land, mainly because he did not regard the gentry as a class but rather as an estate, or what would later be called a status group, divided in economic terms between those who were nearer to the nobility and those who were nearer to "the people," which in this context meant the yeomen farmers.[31] In short, Trevor-Roper's intervention was intellectually much weaker than the works by either Harrington or Tawney that he sought to dismiss.

Nevertheless, in an article published two years later in the popular magazine *History Today* Trevor-Roper unabashedly summarized his general conclusions: "Socially, as politically, the Revolution had been a failure, and the history of England after 1660 was a continuation of its history before 1640." The implications of this for the Marxist position—which it was now apparent was the ultimate target of this polemic—were clear for Trevor-Roper: "Thus I conclude that the Great Rebellion was not a 'capitalist' rising, nor did it 'succeed,' in any sense, nor in any way forward the advance of capitalism in England." We should note that Trevor-Roper did acknowledge that capitalism actually existed and that the "blind revolt of the gentry against the Court, of the provinces against the capital" was caused in part by an economic crisis:

> There were reformers; there were capitalists; there were political thinkers; and, had there been no rebellion of the gentry, these might well have achieved their aims by peaceful progress. But the rebellion of the gentry, a rebellion of mutinous, impoverished, backward-looking provincial squires, gave them no chance—at least until the rebellion had consumed itself and outlasted some of its causes. Perhaps indirectly the rebellion may have forwarded the undoubted change of mentality between the early and late seventeenth century in England: by burning up both itself and its mental fuel, it may have cleared the way for the progress of new very un-puritan ideas. But, equally, it may have impeded that progress for a generation. We cannot say. What we can say—at least, what I am prepared to say—is that it was not, in itself, a successful stage in the rise of the bourgeoisie.[32]

Around this time Trevor-Roper moved directly onto the offensive against his Marxist opponents, above all Christopher Hill, who he termed "the ablest Marxist historian who has sought thus to interpret the Puritan Revolution" and, more generally, Eric Hobsbawm.[33] He lamented the sterility and pedantry of Marxists who subordinated their activities to "barren arguments about the meaning of the fancy words they have themselves chosen to use (as if words like 'feudalism' or 'capitalism' had any real meaning other than what they are conventionally agreed to mean)."[34] Trevor-Roper's original antagonist, Tawney, had already given a splendid rebuttal of this argument thirty years earlier: "Verbal controversies are pointless; if an author discovers a more suitable term [than capitalism] by all means let him use it. He is unlikely however, to make much of the history of Europe during the past three centuries, if, in addition to eschewing the word, he ignores the fact."[35]

Some of Trevor-Roper's other criticisms however, were aimed more directly at the Stalinist orthodoxy and these hit their target. In particular, he identified the damaging intellectual consequences that followed the need of contemporary Marxists to establish themselves as the latest representatives of a national radical tradition:

> In the nineteenth century the "Whig" Protestant writer—Guizot in France, Macaulay in England—looking forward to change in the future, transferred their ideas into the past and saw the protestants of the sixteenth century, the Whigs of the seventeenth, not merely as the party of radical action (which is one thing), but also the party of economic, social, and intellectual progress (which is another). Today the same theory is a Marxist theory. The Marxists, having replaced the Whigs as the party of radical action, similarly look to their pedigree, and attach themselves to an older radical tradition. In order to replace the Whigs, they borrow their philosophy.... The Puritan Revolution in England, we are now assured, was not merely the "constitutional" revolution: it was the "*bourgeois*" revolution: and the bourgeois revolution was, in turn, the intellectual revolution.[36]

What then would a defensible Marxist account of the English Civil War as a bourgeois revolution have to prove? "If it is to be shown either that the English Puritan Revolution was a successful 'bourgeois revolution,' it is not enough to produce evidence that English capitalism was more advanced in 1700 than in 1600. It must also be shown either that the men who made the revolution aimed at such a result, or that those who wished for such a result forwarded the revolution, or that such a result would not have been attained without the revolution."[37] The criteria proposed here are not equally valid. It is legitimate to argue that any identification of the English Civil War as a bourgeois revolution must be able to show a causal connection between it and the subsequent domination of capitalism. It is not clear why it must also prove that revolutionaries *intended* such an outcome, only that their actions would tend toward such an outcome given the preexisting level of capitalist development. Trevor-Roper makes the error, repeated by virtually all subsequent revisionists, of refusing to contemplate what would have happened if Charles I had actually won the civil war and succeeded in imposing French-style absolutism on England and the British Isles more generally; for the resulting regime would not have resembled that of Charles II so much as that of Louis XII.

Indeed, it might be argued that the continuity that Trevor-Roper detects in English history before 1640 and after 1660, far from demonstrating the irrelevance of the Revolution to capitalism, actually demonstrates its indispensability in preventing such an outcome.

Ironically, in the same article in which Trevor-Roper set out his criteria of proof for demonstrating the bourgeois nature of the English Revolution, he also outlined an analysis, intended as an alternative to the Marxist conception of bourgeois revolution, but in fact quite compatible with the way it was conceived in the classical Marxist tradition (although certainly not in relation to the vulgar orthodoxy). The nature of the seventeenth-century crisis, he wrote, was: "Not of the constitution nor of the system of production, but of the State, or rather, of the relation of the State to society. Different countries found their way out of that crisis in different ways. In Spain the ancien regime survived: but it survived only as a disastrous, immobile burden on an impoverished country. Elsewhere, in Holland, France, and England, the crisis marked the end of an era: the jettison of a top-heavy superstructure, the return to responsible mercantilist policy." The parasitism of what Trevor-Roper calls the "Renaissance state," tolerable in a time of economic expansion, now became insufferable in one of economic contraction, leading to general arguments for "the self-reduction of an established, powerful, privileged bureaucracy." How was this achieved? "In fact, the change was nowhere achieved without something of a revolution. If it was limited to France and Holland, that was partly because some of the combustible rubbish had already, in a previous revolution, been consumed. In England there had been no such previous revolution, no such partial reform. There was also, under the early Stuarts, a fatal lack of political skill."

On this reading then, the distinctiveness of the English Revolution was not that it had the most advanced capitalist economy but because it had the most inflexible absolutist state: "In England therefore the storm of the mid-century, which blew throughout Europe, struck the most brittle, most overgrown, most rigid Court of all and brought it violently down."[38] By reintroducing the state so forcibly into the debate Trevor-Roper potentially made an important contribution to reconceptualizing bourgeois revolutions in a general sense, for if the state was the primary obstacle to economic expansion of a capitalist basis, then did it matter which social group destroyed it or what their motivation was for doing so, provided they did not erect new barriers? Trevor-Roper was scarcely interested in pursuing this line of argument but, more to the point, neither were his Marxist opponents, who at this held fast to the orthodox conception of conscious bourgeois agency.

In an intervention of 1958 first published, appropriately enough, in *Encounter*, the CIA-funded journal of the Congress for Cultural Freedom, the US historian Jack Hexter offered an adjudication that essentially and unsurprisingly supported Trevor-Roper. Hexter was alert to the wider implications of the debate: "Dividing the English landlords of the century before the Great Rebellion between rising court and declining mere gentry is a little like dividing the participants in the

French Revolution between aristocrats and *enragés*: it leaves out a lot of important people and makes it unduly hard to explain what actually happened."[39] Hexter complained of the distorting "necessity" for Marxists like Hill and *Marxistants* like Tawney to transform the English gentry into a bourgeoisie:

> The necessity becomes more pressing if one is committed to the belief that the Reformation was a bourgeois revolution. For then between the bourgeois revolution of the sixteenth century and the bourgeois revolution that broke out at the end of the eighteenth century in France, the English Revolution of the seventeenth century is egregiously out of line unless it, too, is bourgeois. But from the beginning of that revolution to the end the men with decisive power were landed folk not city folk, not *bourgeoisie* in the inconvenient etymological meaning of the term. Surely then the most expeditious means of bringing the English revolution into line with the other revolutions is to rechristen the seventeenth-century gentry and call them henceforth *bourgeoisie*, on the ground that was their right name all along. . . . Those who recall the magnificent and ambivalent sketch that Marx draws of his hero-villains, the bourgeoisie, in the *Communist Manifesto* will hardly fail to recognize the lineaments of Tawney's description.[40]

Hexter wanted to deny the bourgeoisie a leading role in the English Revolution but not, however, argue that the bourgeoisie had never taken part in revolution. In a paper first delivered and published in the late 1940s (but unnoticed until reprinted in his *Reappraisals in History* in 1961), he contrasted the attitudes of the English middle class in the sixteenth and seventeenth centuries with those of the French middle class in the eighteenth century:

> The Tudor middle class is no threat to aristocracy or monarchy because it has no ideology of class war or even of class rivalry. It does not seize on More's *Utopia* and the propaganda of the "commonwealth" group of social critics, as the man of 1789 seizes on the writings of Rousseau and the *philosophes*, to claim in the name of the people the right to power. To his own question, "What is the Third Estate?" Abbé Sieyès answered, "Everything." His answer spoke the mind of the revolutionary middle class in France in the last days of the *ancien régime*. That answer would have scarcely occurred to the members of the middle class in Tudor England; indeed that answer would not have been intelligible to them.[41]

Iconoclastic in relation to the English Revolution, Hexter was deeply conventional in relation to the French, which he depicted in terms that would not have been out of place in the most orthodox accounts:

> The middle class in Europe did not enter the Promised Land gently and gradually, by a sort of imperceptible oozing "development." It arrived in a holocaust, splattered with its own blood and the blood of its enemies. The only reason that could have convinced these enemies was the *ultima ratio*—the victorious exercise of force. Valmy, the great campaigns of the Army of the Republic, the blood-bath of the Terror, heralded the arrival of the middle class in a universal language that all Europe understood.[42]

Hexter accepted that the actual outcome of the French Revolution was not inevitable, at least in the short term; but because it did succeed it enabled the middle class to triumph even in those countries where it had not waged its own revolutionary struggle for power, as in England in 1832. The deflation of the significance of the English Revolution and the English bourgeoisie led to an even greater inflation of the significance of the French Revolution and the French bourgeoisie, by way of contrast. But what if the latter were also less revolutionary than had hitherto been accepted?

Cobban launched his critique of what he called the "social interpretation" of the French Revolution in his inaugural lecture as chair in French History at the University of London, subsequently published in 1955 as "The Myth of the French Revolution."[43] He then developed the argument at greater length in the Wiles Lectures at Queen's University in Belfast during 1962 and published as *The Social Interpretation of the French Revolution* in 1964. Cobban saw the possibilities of extending the critique of the English Civil War as a bourgeois revolution to France: "In the historiography of the English civil war the explosion has already occurred, and it has blown up the supposed bourgeois revolution, leaving aristocracy and gentry, royal officials, lawyers, merchants, people, rising and falling classes, feudal and bourgeois society, landowners and peasants, scattered in fragments about monographs and text-books."[44] In relation to France, Cobban made four main claims, all of which had a long life ahead of them.

First, France was no longer a feudal society by 1789. Some dues and services still survived, it is true, but insofar as they still had a function, it was because, as in the case of the *banalités*, they now involved commercial transactions: "There is at least some excuse for believing that the revolution in the French countryside was not against feudalism but against a growing commercialization; and that it was not a 'bourgeois' movement but on the contrary was directed partly against the penetration of urban financial interests into the countryside."[45] The significance of seigniorial rights and dues may therefore have been deliberately overemphasized by a reluctant Constituent Assembly under pressure from the peasantry, so that their abolition would at least not set a precedent that could then be extended to bourgeois property rights.

Second, the most active representatives of the Third Estate were not capitalists, and certainly not industrial capitalists. They were rather the venal office holders, functionaries and professional men—of whom lawyers were the most numerous—who used the revolution to ascend the state structure at the expense of both counterrevolutionary nobles and conservative capitalists. Prior to 1789 the latter had been in the ascendant: "As the commercial and financial classes were rising, so, it seems, the class of venal officers was declining." Here the parallels with Trevor-Roper's claims about the "declining gentry" are very strong indeed. "To a certain extent it would be justifiable," Cobban wrote of the conflict between capitalists and the professions, "to describe it as a struggle between a rising and a falling bourgeoisie." For Cobban then, "the revolutionary bourgeoisie was primarily the declining class of *officiers* and the lawyers and other professional men, and not the businessmen of commerce and industry," a characterization that he believed explained the economic outcome of the revolution.[46]

Third, both the formal abolition of feudal dues and the ascendancy of the bourgeois office holders had been achieved by 1791—the subsequent events were violent, but "little of what had been achieved by 1791 was to be lost, and most of what was subsequently done was to be undone." On this account everything that took place from Year One to the Eighteenth Brumaire is essentially irrelevant, since by 1799 the situation had simply reverted to that pertaining eight years earlier. Cobban was, of course, conscious that those "eight years of disorder and continuing revolution" still had to be accounted for. His own account downplayed the threat of counterrevolution ("moribund from birth") and discounted any continuing pressure from the peasantry, since they were now satisfied with the security they had gained early in the process. "But in the towns the poorer population suffered increasingly from inflation and the shortage of supplies, and constituted, therefore, a source of potential unrest that could be exploited by the political factions." These struggles were however transient, as "when it came to an end the difference between 1799 and 1791 was far less than that between 1791 and 1789."[47]

Fourth, the impact of the revolution on capitalist development was limited. As Cobban remarks, "Looking at the economic consequences as a whole, they seem astonishingly small for such a great social and political upheaval." By the end of the Revolution: "The woolen and metallurgy industries were stagnating. Capitalist concentration remained essentially commercial, under capitalists of the old type, employing domestic labour and combining commercial and banking activities with the organisation of manufacture. Above all, France remained essentially a rural country and its old agricultural methods remained unchanged."

Cobban recognized that the loss of export markets and foreign trade during the revolutionary and Napoleonic Wars had an impact, but this was not the underlying problem; it was rather that the class that had made the revolution was uninterested in commerce or manufacture. Nothing had transformed the condition of the biggest class of potential capitalists—indeed the revolution had consolidated their social inertia: "The peasantry, which held so much of the productive capacity of the country, was still largely self-sufficient and invested its savings in land, which attracted capital to the detriment of both industry and commerce." For Cobban, the situation was worse than mere stagnation, "at least in some fundamental respects, it may not have been a step forward at all, but rather one backwards, that instead of accelerating the growth of a modern capitalist economy in France, the revolution may have retarded it," perhaps until much later in the nineteenth century.[48]

All these points were open to challenge. The French economy may have ceased to be feudal by 1789; but did this mean that the absolutist state had similarly been transformed into a body compatible with the expansion of capitalism? The revolutionaries may not have been capitalists; but why is this significant if their actions led to the removal of obstacles to capitalist development? The main objectives of the revolution may have been achieved by 1791; but would they have been safe from reversal if the revolution had not radicalized in order to repulse its external opponents? The entrenchment of an independent peasant class may have slowed the pace of capitalist development in the countryside; but perhaps this was a necessary price to pay for peasant participation in removing institutional political obstacles to capitalist development across France as a whole?[49] These weaknesses notwithstanding, Cobban did nevertheless attempt to provide an alternative, more defensible explanation for the French Revolution in terms of social classes, as Trevor-Roper had attempted to do for the English Revolution. At least one historian, Norman Hampson, thought that Cobban had not gone far enough in attending to the social and intellectual motives of the revolutionaries, with the result that he had produced "a non-Marxist economic interpretation," which still sought to explain events in terms of material interests.[50]

Cobban had distinguished between a "bourgeois" as a member of a status group and a "capitalist" as a member of an economic class, and argued that the latter had not initiated the French Revolution. The most serious attempt to develop these arguments in the years immediately after Cobban launched his critique was made by the US historian George Taylor, whose first distinctively revisionist entry into the field in 1964 identified three different types of capitalism in prerevolutionary France—industrial, mercantile, and financial—of which the last was the most important, typically in the form of speculation. All were "relatively primitive" and involved the nobility and even the royal court.[51] A subsequent article went much further in attacking the very language in which the French Revolution had been hitherto discussed. Although drawing on Cobban, Taylor in some respects took a different position. He did not, for example, regard France as essentially capitalist by in 1789, referring instead to the dominance of what he termed "proprietary" wealth derived from "investments in land, urban property, venal office, and annuities," which produced a regular income, involved little risk, and, although originally the province of an aristocracy who abhorred vulgar entrepreneurial effort, by 1789 also involved a bourgeoisie who shared these attitudes. But although Taylor regarded proprietary wealth as noncapitalist, he did not assimilate it to feudalism, a system which—and here he does follow Cobban—he tends to equate with seigneurialism.[52] Any differences with Cobban over the nature of the French economy were however secondary when compared with the two central conclusions that Taylor wanted to draw, and that he saw as paralleling those made by Hexter in relation to England:

> The first is that when the word bourgeois is used to indicate a nonnoble group playing a capitalist role in the relations of production it includes less than half the well-to-do Third Estate and excludes the proprietary groups that furnished 87 per cent of the Third Estate deputation to the Estates-General.... The second conclusion is that we have no economic explanation for the so-called "bourgeois revolution," the assault of the upper Third Estate on absolutism and aristocracy.[53]

These conclusions indicated that the entire nature of the French Revolution had to be reconsidered. If the agents of revolution were overwhelmingly not bourgeois, then it was not a bourgeois revolution; if the revolution had no economic causes then it was not a social revolution of any sort: " ... it was essentially a political revolution with social consequences and not a social revolution with political consequences."[54] The article ended with a rallying call for abandonment of a tainted terminology: "The phrases 'bourgeois revolution' and 'revolutionary bourgeoisie,' with their inherent deceptions, will have to go, and others must be found that convey with precision and veracity the realities of social history."[55]

These arguments did however leave several questions unanswered: what then had led to the Jacobin dictatorship, the September Massacres, the Terror, and all those other supposedly pointless events that Cobban regarded with such fastidious British distaste and that Taylor largely ignored? In a history of the revolution by François Furet and Denis Richet originally published in 1965, the authors introduced the idea of "*le dérapage de la révolution*," variously translated into English as the "skidding," "sliding," or being "blown off course" of the revolution after August 10, 1792, a position close to Cobban's earlier claim that the real goals of the revolution had been achieved by 1791.[56] The term however, is suggestive of mere accident caused by inclement conditions. A more comprehensive and—given the Cold War dread of revolution then prevalent in the West—ideologically satisfactory answer had been earlier provided, not by Cobban or any other historian but by the political scientist Jacob Talmon in 1952, in a book based on his dissertation. His supervisor had been Cobban, but even he found the argument excessive, not least because of the way in which Talmon sought to identify Rousseau as the inspiration for the Terror and, less directly, for modern totalitarianism.[57]

Talmon focused on the Enlightenment beliefs that he claimed had taken on a life of their own and led to the Dictatorship of Virtue, an abstract set of truths that empowered the Jacobins and their supporters to kill in the name of ideological purity.[58] There had been earlier episodes in European history that foreshadowed these developments: "The extreme wing of English Puritanism at the time of the Cromwellian Revolution still bore the full imprint of religious eschatology. It had already acquired modern features however. It combined extreme individualism with social radicalism and a totalitarian temperament. Nevertheless this movement, far from initiating the continuous current of modern political Messianism, remained from the European point of view an isolated episode."[59] But the real "initiation" came with the French Revolution, which occurred against a background of economic centralization and mass mobilization inconceivable to the Independents or Levellers:

> Nothing could be easier than to translate the original Jacobin conception of a conflict endemic in society, between the forces of virtue and those of selfishness, into the Marxist idea of class warfare. Finally, the Jacobin and Marxist conceptions of Utopia in which history was destined to end were remarkably similar. Both conceived it as a

complete harmony of interests, sustained without recourse to force, although brought about by force—the provisional dictatorship.[60]

It was possible however to trace the origins of this supposed collective psychosis much further back in history, so that the English Civil War becomes not one of the first modern revolutions, bourgeois or not, but one of the last millenarian revolts. In 1957 Norman Cohn published his study of "revolutionary millenarianism and mystical anarchism" from the Tafurs of the First Crusade to the Ranters of the English Civil War, in which the links between these movements and modern communist movements were sharply drawn:

> One can indeed discern two quite distinct and contrasting tendencies. On the one hand working people have in certain parts of the world been able to improve their lot out of all recognition, through the agency of trade unions, co-operatives, and parliamentary parties. On the other hand during the half-century since 1917 there has been a constant repetition, and on an ever-increasing scale, of the socio-psychological process which once joined the Taborite priests or Thomas Munzer with the most disorientated and desperate of the poor, in phantasies of a final, exterminatory struggle against "the great ones"; and of a perfect world from which self-seeking would be for ever banished.[61]

Between them Talmon and Cohn had detached the bourgeois revolutions from any economic, social, or political context and reimagined them as examples of a recurring millenarian impulse, extending back to the peasant insurrections of the Middle Ages and forward to the Stalinist regimes of the twentieth century. The parallels they drew between "mystical anarchism" and "totalitarian democracy" of the millenarians and Jacobins, and the supposedly equivalent modern totalitarianisms of Fascism and Communism contributed toward the 'end of ideology' thesis during the 1950s that was itself part of what Alasdair MacIntyre calls the "general intellectual landscape" of the time, one which celebrated political apathy as "the precondition of the stability of democratic political orders."[62]

One final component of the revisionist repertoire still had to be added: the elevation of contingency to a decisive role in historical causation. For some historians it was not enough to reject Marxist or Marxist-influenced interpretations. Geoffrey Elton was as politically conservative as Trevor-Roper, but the latter was at least interested in constructing an alternative social explanation. For Elton, *any* sociological account that emphasized long-term structural trends was subject to suspicion. After surveying several attempts to provide long-term explanations for the English Revolution, of quite different theoretical inspiration, Elton concluded: "What these views have in common is a sense of inevitability, a feeling that so profound a disturbance as a civil war must have had roots so deep, causes so fundamental, that analysis can be expected to discover them clearly enough."[63] But all these views were mistaken: the English Civil War was the result of a combination of short-term, largely unpredictable events and might therefore never have taken place. Notwithstanding Elton's abhorrence of the way history had been contaminated by sociological theory, support for his position came from that very source. The occasion was another discussion of the English Civil War, but the implications were relevant to any historical event that had been described as a bourgeois revolution.

Peter Laslett had in the early 1960s turned from his pioneering reinterpretive work on Locke to the study of demography. In his book *The World We Have Lost* (1965) Laslett wrote, "It is necessary to analyse the reasons for the Civil War and ask whether the word Revolution can justifiably be used of seventeenth-century England, if anything of Social Revolution is intended." Laslett then listed the issues that concerned Marxist and other historians who sought a social explanation:

> Along with a request for the social origins of a particular political crisis, there is usually also a demand for a descriptive response of a kind which would relate the English Revolution with the long-term social transformation which finally gave rise to the modern industrialized world. Can any connection be traced, it is required to know, between Cromwell and his Roundheads on the one hand, and the social forces which led to the dethronement of the patriarchal family in economic organization on the other? Or between the Glorious Revolution of 1688 and the coming of the factories?[64]

Laslett himself did not speculate on these connections, but suggested elsewhere in the book that the questions involved were illegitimate and unnecessary:

> Political breakdown is only likely to come about when it happens that several sources of conflict become *superimposed* . . . each individual conflict, each individual pair of antagonistic forces, is regarded as an independent variable. None of them is taken as an "expression of" another, or as "underlying" one or all of the others. . . . this . . . excludes altogether any explanation which insists that the whole complex interaction was "really" religious, or "really" economic, or "really the rise of a social class," and that the "real" contradiction was somehow resolved in the process of open violence.

His conclusion was that "the notion of a social revolution is not permissible."[65] Although Laslett cited Ralf Dahrendorf in support of his use of the concept of superimposition, the real origins of his position on irreducibility, and those of all the other revisionists, is to be found in the methodology of Max Weber, particularly in his insistence on the irreducibility of different forms of social action to any one of them: "For the forms of social action follow "laws of their own" . . . and even apart from this fact, they may in a given case always be codetermined by other than economic causes." Weber does allow that "at some point economic conditions tend to be causally important, and often decisive," but almost immediately takes the point back by adding that "conversely, the economic is usually also influenced by the autonomous structures of social action within which it exists." Since "significant generalization" is impossible, the best we can hope for is to identify "the degree of elective affinity between concrete structures of social action and concrete forms of social organization."[66] In one sense it is unsurprising to find that classical sociology, the social theory most consciously developed as an alternative to historical materialism, should provide the theoretical basis for the rejection of one of historical materialism's component theories.

Revisionism in relation to the history of the United States took a different although analogous form. Although the Beards played a similar role to Tawney in England and Lefebvre in France as non-Marxist surrogates for actual Marxist historians, the continuing relative weakness of Marxist historiography in the United States meant that there was less of a target for revisionism than in England or France. In any case, neither the American Revolution nor the American Civil War had exactly the same status among the pantheon of bourgeois revolutions as the English and French Revolutions. The Civil War has tended to be of greater interest to American Marxists, not least because the unresolved issue of black civil rights clearly dated back to the failure of postwar Reconstruction to democratize the South: the Civil War therefore had immediate contemporary relevance that the earlier Revolutionary War against the British did not. Further, neither Marx and Engels nor any other key figures of the classical tradition discussed the eighteenth-century American Revolution, but the former pair did comment at length on the Civil War and their views were widely disseminated, largely through the CPUSA, although the general position was accepted more widely on the left. In his memoirs Bob Dylan recalls asking fellow-musician Dave Van Ronk about the influence of states' rights in the Civil War and receiving a "bemused" response:

> "The Civil War was fought to free the slaves," he said, "there's no mystery to it." . . . Van Ronk took the Marxist point of view. "It was one big battle between two rival economic systems was what it was."[67]

Around the time the young Zimmerman was being educated in orthodoxy by Van Ronk a US academic named Gerald Runkle produced one of the most comprehensive attempts by a non-Marxist to assess the writings of Marx and Engels on the subject of the Civil War, in an article that is effectively the US equivalent of the revisionist texts on the English and French Revolutions. Runkle argued that the very validity of historical materialism turned on whether the concept of revolution as understood by Marx and Engels was applicable to events between 1861 and 1865. What did Runkle understand this to involve?

> According to the basic Marxian theory, revolutions occur when the mode of production of a society becomes incompatible with the forces of production of that society. But that this was not so in the South is evident from the almost total absence of bourgeois development there. The "revolution" came from without, not from within. . . . The "class struggle" was indeed an unusual one, for one class was supreme in the South (and virtually non-existent in the North), another was powerful in the North (and virtually non-existent in the South). The great enemies of the privileged class in the South were not the people directly exploited by that class, the Negroes and the 'poor whites,' but the people in the North! . . . That great changes occurred in the North before, during, and after the war does not mean that the North was spear-heading a revolution in the Marxian sense. Marx's mistake here (and elsewhere) is to mistake the results of the war with the cause of the war. He anticipated very well the results of the war. A more capitalistic America did emerge. The "forces of production" developed rapidly during the war, industry grew, and fortunes were made. The bour-

geoisie entered into a period of almost unchallenged supremacy. The economy and society of America were indeed revolutionized. This does not mean, however, that the growing strength of industrial capitalism brought about the war. Many other factors operated with it to bring about the war, which was in turn a great causal factor for modern capitalism. In short, the advance of capitalism was a conspicuous, but not the only, result of a war which was brought about by many factors of which bourgeois development was only one.

Consequently, the question of why Marx did not continue to develop his analysis of the Civil War after it concluded presents no great mystery: "One suspects that the American Civil War did not, therefore, lend itself to the kind of interpretation that would enhance or confirm dialectical materialism. If this is so, then the war constitutes a tacit refutation of basic Marxian theory."[68]

In fact, the elements that Runkle claimed disproved historical materialism— the lack of internal class contradiction within southern society, the external imposition of revolutionary change, the lack of causal connection between the northern victory and subsequent capitalist development—only did so in relation to the orthodox conception; Marx and Engels did not find the absence of these factors a reason for disqualifying the Civil War as a social revolution. As Eugene Genovese pointed out: "In their terms . . . the Union as a whole was the relevant entity. . . . Runkle's distinction between internal and external contradictions ignores the first principle of dialectics—the interrelatedness of all phenomena—and is a false problem."[69] As was so often the case with revisionism, Runkle makes a series of wrong assumptions about what Marxism involves, then accuses Marx of inconsistency for not adhering to a set of positions that were never his in the first place.

If discussions about the Civil War in the early years of revisionism reflected those about the English and French Revolutions, those concerned with the American Revolution were significantly different. Instead, an argument began to emerge—or perhaps it might be better to describe the argument as being finally made explicit—to the effect that, precisely because the American Revolution had *not* been a social revolution, it should best serve as a model for any subsequent revolutions. Typically, the first formulation of this case was made, not by a member of the US historical profession, but by the German émigré and former leftist, Hannah Arendt, in the early 1960s. Despite the multiple layers of incoherence from which her book *On Revolution* suffers, and its tangential relationship to the subject of bourgeois revolution, since it does not attain the level of specificity required to identify the concept, her central distinction between the American Revolution and all the other great revolutions was to prove deeply influential, even though it did not directly engage with Marxist views of the former.

"It was the French and not the American Revolution that set the world on fire," notes Arendt, "and it was consequently from the course of the French Revolution, and not from the course of events in America or from the acts of the Founding Fathers, that our present use of the word 'revolution' received its connotations and overtones everywhere, the United States not excluded." For Arendt, this was all deeply regrettable: "The sad truth of the matter is that the French Revolution, which ended in disaster, has made world history, while the American Revolution, so triumphantly successful, has remained an event of little more than local importance." As the reader will notice, there are several unargued assumptions here, and these are not argued anywhere else in this extraordinarily weightless text. Nevertheless, at various points Arendt gestures toward two main differences between the French Revolution and the American. The first was the distinction between "liberation and freedom." The French Revolution involved the first, the mere violent overthrow of the existing regime, the American Revolution the second, the establishment of a new and permanent constitutional order: "There is nothing more futile than rebellion and liberation unless they are followed by the constitution of the newly won freedom." Arendt saw twentieth-century parallels with the French Revolution: "The first of these alternatives ['liberation'] clearly applies to the revolutions in Russia and China, where those in power not only admit the fact but boast of having maintained indefinitely a revolutionary government; the second alternative ['freedom'] applies to the revolutionary upheavals which swept nearly all European countries after the First World War, as well as to many colonial countries that won their independence from European rule after the Second World War." Arendt was explicit as to the nature of the constitutional settlements in the latter cases: "Their purpose was to stem the tide of revolution, and if they too served to limit power, it was the power of the government as well as the revolutionary power of the people whose manifestation had preceded their establishment." But what was the reason for these different revolutionary outcomes? Arendt at least does not ascribe this to the malign authoritarianism of the Jacobins and Bolsheviks on the one hand, and of the benign libertarianism of the Founding Fathers on the other, but rather to the nature of the states that they sought to overthrow:

> Historically speaking, the most obvious and the most decisive distinction between the American and the French Revolutions was that the historical inheritance of the American Revolution was "limited monarchy" and that of the French Revolution was an absolutism which reached back into the first centuries of our era and the last centuries of the Roman Empire. Nothing, indeed, seems more natural than that a revolution should be predetermined by the type of government it overthrows; nothing, therefore, appears more plausible than to explain the new absolute, the absolute revolution, by the absolute monarchy which preceded it, and to conclude that the more absolute the ruler, the more absolute the revolution will be which replaces him. The records of both the French Revolution in the eighteenth century and the Russian Revolution which modeled itself upon it in our own century could easily be read as one series of demonstrations of this plausibility. [70]

Arendt's relentless fixation on the political at the expense of the socioeconomic allows her to elide the differences between social revolutions, as if only time separated the French and Russian Revolutions rather than a century of capitalist development and a new constellation of class forces. From our perspective, however, the key problem with her work is that, in effect, she is claiming that the only revolutions that have an acceptably "constitutional" outcome are essentially those that did not involve social revolutions in the first place, because they are simply correcting an oppressive deviation from an existing political norm. This normative approach may explain her reluctance to discuss the American Civil War, since, whatever else one may wish to say about it, was far more obviously "social" than the American Revolution, but not directed against a preexisting absolutist state.[71] Arendt concedes that the English constitution that the Americans sought to restore was itself a product of social revolutionary upheaval, the implication being that America was an exception.[72]

Arendt's arguments were later mobilized by the ex-Trotskyist, now neoconservative Irving Kristol, in a lecture delivered in 1973, one of a series sponsored by the American Enterprise Institute for Public Policy Research in the run-up to the bicentennial of the American Revolution and subsequently published in 1976. As befits someone with his former political allegiance Kristol had a much sharper focus than Arendt, as can be seen from his elaboration of her typology of revolutions:

> By her criteria the French and Russian revolutions should more properly be called "rebellions," whereas only the American Revolution is worthy of the name. A rebellion, in her terms, is a meta-historical event emerging out of a radical dissatisfaction with the human condition as experienced by the mass of the people, demanding instant "liberation" from this condition, an immediate transformation of all social and economic circumstances, a prompt achievement of an altogether "better life" in an altogether "better world." The spirit of rebellion is a spirit of desperation—a desperate rejection of whatever exists, a desperate aspiration toward some kind of utopia. A rebellion is more a sociological event than a political action. It is governed by a blind momentum which sweeps everything before it, and its so-called leaders are in fact its captives, and ultimately its victims. The modern world knows many such rebellions, and all end up as one version or another of "a revolution betrayed." The so-called "betrayal" is, in fact, nothing but the necessary conclusion of a rebellion. Since its impossible intentions are unrealizable and since its intense desperation will not be satisfied with anything less than impossible intentions, the end result is always a regime which pretends to embody these intentions and which enforces such false pretensions by terror.[73]

This is the world turned upside down indeed. The type of event that Marxists—and not only Marxists—had regarded as the most important type of revolution, a social revolution, is reduced to a mere rebellion in pursuit of unattainable ends. The obliteration of any distinction between revolutions that have led to capitalism and those that potentially could lead to socialism deprives them of all specificity. So, although Kristol refers to them as "sociological," the implication is that they are more "pathological" expressions of the ahistorical millenarian impulse identified by Cohn and Talmon two decades earlier. A genuine revolution for Kristol is therefore essentially political:

> It aims to revise and reorder the political arrangements of a society, and is therefore the work of the political ego rather than of the political id. A revolution is a practical

exercise in political philosophy, not an existential spasm of the social organism. It requires an attentive prudence, a careful calculation of means and ends, a spirit of sobriety—the kind of spirit exemplified by that calm, legalistic document, the Declaration of Independence. All this is but another way of saying that a successful revolution cannot be governed by the spirit of the mob. Mobs and mob actions there will always be in a revolution, but if this revolution is not to degenerate into a rebellion, mob actions must be marginal to the central political drama.

At this point in his argument, Kristol made explicit a conclusion implicit in Arendt's original discussion: "This is almost like saying that a successful revolution must be accomplished by a people who want it but who do not desperately need it—which was, indeed, the American condition in 1776. One may even put the case more strongly: a successful revolution is best accomplished by people who do not really want it at all, but find themselves reluctantly making it. The American Revolution was precisely such a reluctant revolution."[74] Consequently, the constitutions set up by the ex-colonies had three features in common:

> First, they involved few basic changes in existing political institutions and almost no change at all in legal, social, or economic institutions; they were, for the most part, merely revisions of the preexisting charters. Secondly, most of the changes that were instituted had the evident aim of weakening the power of government, especially of the executive; it was these changes—and especially the strict separation of powers—that dismayed Turgot, Condorcet, and the other French *philosophes*, who understood revolution as an expression of the people's will-to-power rather than an attempt to circumscribe political authority. Thirdly, in no case did any of these state constitutions tamper with the traditional system of local self-government. Indeed, they could not, since it was this traditional system of local self-government which created and legitimized the constitutional conventions themselves.[75]

As befitted the occasion of their delivery, Kristol's arguments are essentially celebratory, and in that sense betray their source. As Richard King points out, Arendt was "hardly an uncritical champion of the American experiment." In particular, what she saw as the "institutionalization" of political freedom was for her "an essentially tragic story of precious achievement and then loss."[76] Both Arendt and Kristol wanted to offer America as a model for other countries, and it is difficult to see how this could be possible, since they were not in the fortunate position of conducting their revolutions against the background of England's "matchless" constitution.

The answer had been provided in one of the other key texts produced in the United States during the late 1950s and early 1960s, the economic historian W. W. Rostow's *The Stages of Economic Growth* (1960)—a book in which, like Laslett's *The World We Have Lost*, the influence of Weber can be strongly felt, in this case at one remove in the bastardized form of "modernization" theory. Edward Thompson has described the "eerie timelessness" of the vocabulary of "traditional" or "pre-industrial" societies, the latter term in particular being "a tent within whose spacious folds there sit beside each other the West of England clothiers, Persian silversmiths, Guatemalan shepherds, and Corsican bandits" and this is certainly the case here.[77]

Rostow undertook to set out the conditions of "self-sustaining economic growth." Rostow claimed that there were two pathways to this condition. One, which applied "not merely to the evolution of most of Europe but also the greater part of Asia, the Middle East, and Africa . . . required fundamental changes in a well-established traditional society: changes which touched and substantially altered the social structure and political system as well as techniques of production." The other applied to a much smaller group of countries, those described by Rostow, following Louis Hartz, as "born free": "the United States, Australia, New Zealand, Canada, and, perhaps, a few others." The connection between them was self-evident: "These nations were created mainly out of a Britain already far along in the transitional process."[78] Communism is therefore a "disease" of the transition from traditional to modern society, likely to emerge where the process had been stalled by conflicts, not only among opponents and supporters of change, but also among the latter themselves. In this context, it is clear why there is no need to distinguish between different types of social revolution: it is because they are ultimately all focused on carrying out "modernization":

> Communism is by no means the only form of effective state organization that can consolidate the preconditions in the transition of a traditional society, launch a take-off, and drive a society to technological maturity. But it may be one way in which this difficult job can be done, if—and this remains to be seen—it can solve the problem of agricultural output in the take-off decades. Communism takes its place, then, besides the regime of the Meiji Restoration in Japan, and Ataturk's Turkey, for example, as one particularly inhumane form of political organization capable of launching and sustaining the growth process in societies where the preconditions period did not yield a substantial and enterprising commercial middle class and an adequate political consensus among the leaders of society. It is the kind of disease which can befall a transitional society if it fails to organize effectively those elements within it which are prepared to get on with the job of modernization.[79]

This may seem very far removed from debates over whether the gentry were rising or falling in prerevolutionary England, or the extent of aristocratic involvement in commerce in prerevolutionary France, but in fact it provided an overall developmental framework for which the anti-Marxist aspects of revisionism, which some revisionists explicitly adopted. Taylor, for example, explicitly relied on Rostow for the concept of traditional society, and the fatalistic economic attitudes it supposedly engendered, which he applied to France.[80] The central point was that revolutions were unnecessary for capitalist development in the contemporary world; moreover, they had never been necessary, since the evolutionary schema set out by Rostow had and would lead to "take-off" proving certain attitudes were cultivated and certain political approaches rejected. The nature of the latter was obvious from the subtitle of Rostow's book, which accurately declared it to be a "non-Communist manifesto." Rostow argued that currently backward states could be expected to follow the same path to "take-off" as England. "It is here, then, that in 1959, writing in the democratic north, the analysis of the stages-of-growth comes to an end: not with the age of affluence; not with the automobile and hire purchase; not with the problem of secular spiritual stagnation; not even with the United States and its vast baby crop; but with the dilemmas and worries of the men in Djakarta, Rangoon, New Delhi, and Karachi; the men in Tehran, Baghdad, and Cairo; the men south of the desert too, in Accra, Lagos, and Salisbury." Why? "For the fate of those of us who now live in the stage of high mass-consumption is going to be substantially determined by the nature of the preconditions process and the take-off in distant nations, processes which our societies experienced well over a century ago, in less searching and difficult forms."[81] The "disease" of communism and an alternative, "humane" path to take-off and "high mass-consumption" could only be achieved by an alignment with—in fact, complete subordination to—US foreign policy. As one of Rostow's critics, whom we shall encounter again in chapter 17, remarked of this assertion in the late 1960s:

> [Rostow] wrote of these stages at the CIA financed Center for International Studies on the Charles River and has been operationalizing them on the Potomac as President Kennedy's Director of Policy and Planning in the State Department and President Johnson's chief adviser on Vietnam. . . . As to the efficacy of the policy recommended by Rostow, it speaks for itself: no country, once underdeveloped, ever managed to develop by Rostow's stages. Is that why Rostow is now trying to help the people of Vietnam, the Congo, the Dominican Republic, and other underdeveloped countries to overcome the empirical, theoretical, and policy shortcomings of his manifestly non-communist intellectual aid to economic development and cultural change by bombs, napalm, chemical and biological weapons, and military occupation?[82]

Rostow stood at the opposite end of the spectrum of bourgeois economic theory from Hayek and the Marginalists, but he similarly portrayed a historical process to which revolution was irrelevant: the Onward March of Economic Liberty has been replaced by the Onward March of Economic Development, although the latter was no more relevant to those whom the recommendations were offered.

ASCENDANCY AND CLIMAX

The origins of revisionism can therefore be dated to the 1950s. Most of the pioneering works had been published by the mid-1960s, immediately prior to the revolutionary insurgencies that erupted in 1968 and continued until 1975, overlapping in their final throes with the first intimations of neoliberalism in Chile, New York City, and Jamaica. The ascendancy of revisionism dates from the late 1970s, nearly thirty years after Hexter had first questioned the role of the Tudor middle class in 1948; timing that suggests that this new influence owed much to the changed political context in which historiographical debates were now taking place. Jonathan Clark and Alan Macfarlane, two openly ideological exponents of what Ellen Meiksins Wood calls "no great transformation" models of English development— the first emphasizing the persistence of the English ancien régime and the other the perennial nature of English capitalism—were both very conscious that the rise of revisionism involved a change of the political as well as the historical guard.[83] Macfarlane, writing from the vantage point of Margaret Thatcher's second term in office, argued that in relation to England a mistaken "revolutionism" arose from several reasons: "The need to make the past very different in order to make it problematic, the influence of European sociologists and particularly Marx and Weber, the self-questioning doubt induced by comparative anthropological knowledge." But more than any other reason was a contemporary political stance:

> If all that exists now can be shown to be the result of a recent "revolution," then it is easier to consider changing present institutions. What exists around us can be seen to be an artificial, almost accidental, creation. It is part of culture, not nature. If the family system or the capitalist ethic is only a few hundred years old, it is easier to feel that it may not last long either. The vision of numerous revolutions in the recent past is essentially optimistic, utopian. The premise of continuity can conversely be attractive to those who wish to stress enduring values, who dislike profound change.[84]

Clark, at much the same time, wrote of "the change of mood in the late 1970s," one aspect of which was the falling out fashion of the ideas of the "Old Guard," "that cohort of scholars whose minds were formed in the matrix of inter-war Marxism," and the "Class of '68," "those writers whose world view took shape in euphoric approval of the radicalism and unrest of the late 1960s and early 1970s."[85]

Much of the doctoral work that would dispute the ideas of the Old Guard and the Class of '68 was in fact carried out during the very same period of "radicalism and unrest" that inspired the latter group. (One imagines revisionist students diligently working in the library while trying to block out the sound of their revolutionary peers noisily defending the barricades outside.) In relation to England, the crucial year was 1976, which saw a cluster of publications by Paul Christianson, John Morrill, and Conrad Russell.[86] At least one surviving members of the first cohort of revisionists understood immediately that the work of their successors, with their denial that the civil war had any long-term causes or involved any principled divisions among the participants, and their emphasis on the local and contingent, was as much directed at the modified social interpretations of the 1950s as the original Marxist and *Marxistant* subjects of the original revisionist critique. Hexter in particular launched a ferocious response in which he denounced revisionist interpretations as both intellectually and morally bankrupt.[87]

In relation to France, the comparably decisive contributions arrived at the end of decade in the form of books by Furet (1978, English translation 1981) and William Doyle (1980).[88] Challenges to the theory of bourgeois revolution in relation to either country had hitherto largely been confined to Anglo-Saxon academics, but as the presence of Furet indicates, these were now being issued by French historians in relation to their own country and this was of great ideological significance: "Paris today is the capital of European intellectual reaction" wrote Perry Anderson in the early 1980s, "in the same way that London was thirty years ago."[89]

The most obvious standard-bearers for reaction were by a group of renegades from the generation of 1968, the self-styled "new philosophers." One, the ex-Maoist André Glucksmann, accused twentieth-century Marxist revolutionaries of not "transcending" the Great French Revolution, but instead of "reproducing" the experience, at most replacing the guillotine with the firing squad. Glucksmann argued that these revolutions were not ascribable to particular classes at all, and he mocked Marxist analysis of the French Revolution that involved "a bourgeoisie able to control an economy which did not come into existence until a hundred years later and popular masses who were already resisting this control by a non-existent market." His heroes were the peasantry, or more precisely, the "plebs" whose resistance is eternal, no matter what the nature of the economy, society or the state: "A thousand scattered insurrections, fantastically condensed into a 'seizure of power,' a variety of revolts by oppressed people obliterated by the bourgeois revolution—this entire optical device proves incapable of suppressing the great opaque mass at the center of the X-ray picture of the events of 1790."[90]

The central figure, however, was Furet, who had been a member of the Communist Party of France until 1958, but now referred to the orthodoxy adhered to by his former party as a "'Marxist Vulgate."[91] If his earlier work with Richet had contained themes first elaborated in Cobban, notably the "skidding off course of the revolution" in 1791, his new contributions recalled Talmon's emphasis on ideology. In the key chapter of *Interpreting the French Revolution*, "the French Revolution is over." For Furet, the term *bourgeois revolution* was not a "concept" but a "mask," which was used to conceal "two propositions . . . the inevitability of the event and . . . a radical break in time". "Hence the confused notion of 'bourgeois revolution' inseparably designates both a historical content and a historical agent, arising out of the fore-ordained explosion of the last few years of the eighteenth century."[92] Furet specifically attacked the connections that the French left in particular drew between the French and Russian Revolutions. He was, however, concerned less with the historical accuracy of this claim than with highlighting what he thought the real connections were, namely the comparable totalitarian systems embodied in the Terror and the Gulag. The declassing of revolutions allowed for comparisons to be made between those that might otherwise have been allocated to distinct historical periods, such as the French and Russian Revolutions. The similarity is supposedly that both revolutions began as the achievable and constructive struggle for liberty, in 1789 and February 1917, but then declined into the futile and destructive quest for equality, in 1793 and October 1917. As Furet writes, the French Revolution "became the mother of a real, dated, and duly registered event: October 1917."

> At the very moment when Russia—for better or worse—took the place of France as the nation in the vanguard of history, because it inherited from France and from nineteenth-century thought the idea that a nation is *chosen* for revolution, the historiographical discourses about the two revolutions became fused and infected each other.

The Bolsheviks were given Jacobin ancestors, and the Jacobins were made to antici-pate the Bolsheviks.

This reflected with reasonable accuracy the orthodox position in which the clas-sic bourgeois revolution in France is succeeded by the classic proletarian revolution in Russia. What Furet then did, however, was to assert a *real* underlying connection between the two revolutions, not because both involved the overthrow of one class by another, but because both involved the violent imposition of a revolutionary truth on unwilling societies: the Jacobin and Stalinist experiences were not "devi-ations" from the otherwise unsullied purity of the revolutionary ideas of 1789 and 1917 but their inescapable essence:

> In 1920, Mathiez justified Bolshevik violence by the French precedent, in the name of comparable circumstances. Today the Gulag is leading to a rethinking of the Terror precisely because the two undertakings are seen as identical. The two revolutions remain connected: but while fifty years ago they were systematically absolved on the basis of excuses related to "circumstances," that is, external phenomena which had nothing to do with the nature of the two revolutions, they are today, by contrast, accused of being, consubstantially, systems of meticulous constrain over men's bodies and minds.[93]

In 1989, the official celebrations of the bicentenary of the French Revolution were accompanied and paralleled by the climax of revisionism. A continuing em-phasis on the irrelevance of the category of bourgeois revolution to the event in question was increasingly supplemented by attempts to dismiss it as merely a tech-nologically inhibited precursor to later episodes of sustained violence against hu-manity: the September Massacres as the antechamber to the Holocaust and the Gulag Archipelago. We can find examples of the new consensus in relation to both claims from a work of synthesis published during the bicentenary by the British historian Simon Schama. Unlike most revisionist texts, *Citizens* was bought by rel-atively large numbers of people outside academia. This is what they read:

> How did [the French Revolution] happen? The long-hallowed explanation is that, at the last minute, aristocratic expectations of succession [to the monarchy] were con-founded by the sudden appearance of a new political class—the bourgeoisie. Thwarted in their efforts at upward mobility and the possession of office, this Third Estate seized political leadership to destroy not just the monarchy but the entirety of the old "feudal" regime and installed themselves as the lords of the nineteenth century.

"The wholly imaginary nature of this explanation hardly needs repeating here," concludes Schama, showing in this one sentence how far the dominant interpre-tation of the French Revolution had changed by the bicentenary of 1789.[94] In a survey of the literature that had influenced his account, Schama wrote that his "own emphasis . . . in many respects follows the path first tracked by Albert Cobban . . . once thought so scandalous" but which has "since become a classic of historical interpretation." He also paid homage to Furet's *Interpreting the French Revolution* as being "of fundamental importance in redirecting revolutionary history back towards politics."[95] In the claim that there was not an early, defensible stage of the revolution before violence became endemic the shift from the views of the former to those of the latter is clearly discernible:

> The notion that, between 1789 and 1791, France basked in some sort of liberal pleasure garden before the erection of the guillotine is a complete fantasy. From the very beginning, the violence which made the revolution possible in the first place created exactly the brutal distinctions between Patriots and Enemies, Citizens and Aristocrats, within which there could be no human shade of gray.... The Terror was merely 1789 with a higher body count. From the first year it was apparent that violence was not just an unfortunate side effect from which enlightened Patriots could selectively avert their eyes: it was the Revolution's source of collective energy. It was what made the Revolution revolutionary.[96]

Revisionism has tended to fragment into two main camps. One, found in the work of North American historians like Donald Sutherland, still involves a materialist interpretation. Here, the theme is the underlying continuity of peasant life, its imperviousness to new Enlightenment notions, and, above all, its explosive violence. Sutherland describes peasant land seizures as involving: "Chiliastic calls for a massive bloodletting ... more reminiscent of medieval notions of the end of days than of the red dawn of the future." In the end, the shape of the post-revolutionary state was determined by "the vast weight of ancient peasant France," which "imposed itself upon the government, at the expense of many of the ideals of 1789."[97] In accounts like these, continuity is all, the revolution a meaningless surface disturbance eventually becalmed by peasant immobility. The other, more idealist interpretation was initiated by Furet but is perhaps epitomized by Mona Ozouf. This excludes any social interpretation of events and emphasizes the emergence of a new political culture of deracinated intellectuals that apparently led to the Terror. For Ozouf, in the beginning there was not even the Word, but only the Thought. David Bell, an admirer, claims that the revisionists have demonstrated the impossibility of identifying either "a 'bourgeois' social group possessing a distinct relationship to the means of production" or "a group united by a common assertion of 'bourgeois' identity" in 1789.[98] Conclusions concerning continuing socioeconomic stability on the one and explosive ideological frenzy on the other were quite familiar by the 1960s at the latest; only the vocabulary in which they are expressed, and the methodology by which they were reached was different. These had two sources.

One was the tradition of social history, which hitherto had been regarded—and to a large extent actually was—a left-wing tradition, in the sense that it was written about the oppressed or exploited by people who identified or at least sympathized with them: some of its finest achievements had been concerned with the role of these groups in the bourgeois revolutions. But it transpired that it was not only, as Edward Thompson thought, "the poor stockinger, the Luddite cropper, the 'obsolete' handloom weaver, the 'utopian' artisan, and even the deluded follower of Joanna Southcott" who needed to be rescued from "the enormous condescension of history."[99] So too did the rich tax farmer, the conspiratorial Royalist exile, the former mistress of the Queen's bedchamber, the misunderstood grain speculator, the former San Dominican slave owner, and many more besides. If the focus was on individual experience, then the techniques of social history could be applied to anyone, even figures at the summit of society against whom the revolutions were directed—not in order to understand the relationship between the human personality, social role, and historical context, but to set their experience in relation to "their calendar of birth, love, ambition, and death imprinted on the calendar of great events," and doing so enables "the Revolution" to be treated, "not as a march of abstractions and ideologies but as a human event of complicated and often tragic outcomes."[100]

The other, even more politically ambivalent source was postmodernism. The central claims of postmodernism were summarized by one of its earliest ideologues, Jean-François Lyotard, for whom "modern" involves "any science that legitimates itself with reference to a metadiscourse . . . making an explicit appeal to some grand narrative, such as the dialectics of Spirit, the hermeneutics of meaning, the emancipation of the rational or working subject, or the creation of wealth." In contradistinction to the modern: "I define postmodern as incredulity towards metanarratives."[101] The concept of bourgeois revolution and the Marxist theory of history more generally were obviously grand narratives as defined by Lyotard, deserving of incredulity. Once this was understood, even the most apparently obvious questions were simply impossible to answer. Here, for example, is Keith Jenkins explaining why it was impossible to establish the origins of the Great French Revolution:

> If, say, Marxism lays down a method of proceeding (crudely, economic conditions must be considered as basic determinants of superstructural changes within the thesis of class struggle; crudely, by involving methodological abstraction, etc.), then how far do you work this in detail? For example, how far do you (have to?) take the influence of economics (to 1783, 1760, 1714, 1648?) and what, exactly, do you include in this category of the economic? How, within, the economic, do you know when aspects of it play a decisive role and then lie dormant again, determining "in the last instance"? Again, how far afield will you go: is France metaphorically an island or inextricably caught up within a general European trajectory? What counts as Europe in the eighteenth century? Does America? Again, how do you measure the various levels and degrees of interpenetration between, say, the economic, the cultural, the ideological; and what goes into these categories? . . . the question of "Why 1789?" means "What are the causes of 1789?" such causes apparently being an infinite chain spreading backwards and outwards which you somehow have to cut into despite that fact that no method (and no amount of experience) can provide you with any logical or definitive cut in (or "cut out") points in order to give a sufficient and necessary explanation.[102]

Even works that acknowledged no formal adherence to postmodern principles shared the mood of skepticism over the possibility of providing coherent historical explanation. "In *Citizens*," writes Richard Evans, "the French Revolution of 1789–94 becomes almost meaningless in the larger sense, and is reduced to a kind of theatre of the absurd; the social and economic misery of the masses, an essential driving force behind their involvement in revolutionary events, is barely mentioned; and the lasting significance of the Revolution's many political theories and doctrines for modern European and world history more or less disappears."[103] Similarly, the discrediting of "grand narratives" was celebrated by those whose sensibilities were antipodean to those of avant-garde enthusiasts for the latest trends in relativist irrationalism. "The collapse of grand theories originating elsewhere in the academic world has allowed the effective reassertion of scholarly standards generated from within the historical profession," wrote Jonathan Clark in 1986: "the revival of narrative is an important consequence in respect of method."[104] No one would accuse Clark of postmodernism—there is no place for gratuitous insult here—and he has been deeply critical of the tendency that he sees (quite wrongly) as "allied" to Marxism in practice even though "incompatible, indeed antithetical" in methodological terms.[105] There are, however, clearly elective affinities with his own conservative defense of tradition, which could be traced back to the very origins of revisionism: "The postmodernist cult of the fragment bears a suspicious resemblance to the traditional empiricist hostility to historical theory. Both Cold War liberals like Karl Popper and G. R. Elton and contemporary postmodernists like Lyotard ... seek to ban an attempt to understand societies as developing totalities because they believe that such large-scale theorizing leads inevitably to totalitarian dictatorship."[106]

But perhaps the most striking characteristic of revisionist texts, particularly those relating to France, is the way in which they simply echo what conservatives since Burke had said on the subject. Not unexpectedly, one of the clearest political expressions of this perspective was given by Margaret Thatcher in her memoirs:

> For me as a British Conservative, with Edmund Burke the father of Conservatism and the first great perceptive critic of the Revolution as my ideological mentor, the events of 1789 represent a perennial illusion in politics. The French Revolution was a Utopian attempt to overcome a traditional order—one with many imperfections, certainly—in the name of abstract ideas, formulated by vain intellectuals, which lapsed, not through chance but through weakness and wickedness, into purges, mass murder and war. In so many ways it anticipated the still more terrible Bolshevik Revolution of 1917. The English tradition of liberty, however, grew over the centuries: its most marked features are continuity, respect for law and a sense of balance, as demonstrated by the Glorious Revolution of 1688.

Thatcher then recalled an interview she had given with *Le Monde* at the time of the 1789 bicentennial in which she had pointed out that the origins of human rights lay not in the French Revolution but in "a mixture of Judaism and Christianity" and extolled the superiority of "our quiet revolution, where Parliament exerted its will over the King."[107]

At the same time as Thatcher was lecturing her French hosts an editorial appeared in the *Economist* setting out what was currently considered acceptable in terms of historical revolutions. Writing in the serene transatlantic tones characteristic of the leading Western forum for neoliberal thought—and quite different from the antirevolutionary hysteria then emanating from Paris—the anonymous author identifies the problems with the French Revolution: "True, the revolution put paid to feudalism in France, but in doing so it ushered in not democracy but dictatorship." This comment is remarkable in actually registering the existence of feudalism, but a more conventional train of thought is soon resumed, with the identification of an alternative—the only revolution which never succumbed to the temptations of equality as a goal: "America, by contrast, has been a model of stability since its revolution, the only hiccup being a civil war, fought to resolve the main ambiguity left by the founding fathers: the ultimate resting place of sovereignty in the American federation." The same impulse that demotes the English Civil War in favor of the Glorious Revolution here elevates the War of Independence over the American Civil War: in both cases—from this perspective the War of Independence is in most respects an extension of the Glorious Revolution—events that did not involve significant levels of social transformation are celebrated over those that did. Indeed, 1776 is taken to be the missing pivot of global history, for "it is tempting to believe that the world would have been a happier place had the seminal revolution of the eighteenth century been not the French but the American one." Nevertheless it is possible that the Eastern Europeans, whose societies were at this point clearly on the eve of major reforms, might now learn the lessons ignored over the previous two hundred years, even if the extent could not yet be foreseeable:" If they [the Eastern Europeans] are ever to abandon the philosophical underpinnings of the Bolshevik Revolution and its Chinese equivalent (most of the communist "revolutions" were imposed from above), they would be wise not to be seduced by 1789 and all that but to go back to 1776. It is a pity they did not do so in 1917.[108]

Similar views were being expressed contemporaneously in Russia itself, during the final stages of glasnost and perestroika. The US historian Eric Foner reported from Moscow: "The concept of 'revolution' is being rethought—turned on its head, really." By 1990 one former Soviet historian, E. B. Chernyak, was arguing: "Revolutions (like the French and Russian) that attempt to abolish the existing order entirely should be deemed less radical than 'organic revolutions' (like the American), which build on existing institutions rather than destroying them. The reason? By reducing future social conflict, revolutions of the second sort create more favourable conditions for economic growth."[109]

When the Eastern European regimes fell at the end of the year, any passing embarrassment supporters of Western capitalism might have felt about celebrating the overthrow of Stalinism by the hated method of revolution—including in the Romanian case an armed insurrection and brief civil war—was quickly overcome by delight at this apparently clear demonstration of the superiority of markets and the arrival of a future in which neoliberal globalization could proceed unimpeded by opposition from an existing rival or the possibility of a future alternative. Revisionists seized this opportunity to explicitly link the supposed failures of Marxism both as a means of understanding history and of organizing society. The theoretical interpretation of, for example, the English Civil War as a bourgeois revolution and the practical example of the Russian Revolution as a communist society had, it seemed, both been exploded. Conrad Russell, who when not revising the English Revolution out of existence sits as a peer of the realm on the Liberal Democrat benches of the British House of Lords, drew the connections. In an article published between the fall of the Berlin Wall and the dissolution of the Soviet Union he asked: "If the English Civil War was not a bourgeois revolution we have to consider whether it happened at some other time, or whether it never happened at all." Having restated his position that it was not, Russell went on to reject 1688 and 1832 as alternative dates. Russell proposed instead that we abandon the attempt to identify a bourgeois revolution in English history and seek the origins of the civil war in ideas, particularly of a religious nature: "If we once accept that Marx and all his works were a colossal wrong turning in the intellectual history of the West (and now of the East also), then we may be in a position to start again."[110]

The fashion has now extended to denying the existence of bourgeois revolutions in regions that had few claims to having experienced one in the first place. The following comments about the supposed non-occurrence of a Québécois revolution illustrate both the logic of the revisionist case and the centrality of the French Revolution to it:

> If the French Revolution of 1789 was not meaningfully bourgeois, need we expect other nations to achieve that historical development? If the grand sources of our historical narratives can no longer lay claim to a bourgeois revolution, we probably cannot expect revolution-less Quebec or Canada to do so either. If the French Revolution is no longer bourgeois, need other countries experience such a transition in political, economic, and social structures all at once? Are we not assuming a historiographical precedent where one does not exist?[111]

To illustrate how diffuse these positions became, here is the late Arthur Marwick, principally a social historian of twentieth-century Britain, writing during the 1990s in a book that at no point deals with the issue of bourgeois revolution: "In reality the society we live in has evolved through complex historical processes, very different from the Marxist nonsense about 'the bourgeoisie' overthrowing the feudal aristocracy." And there is of course a contemporary moral: "Just as [society] was not formed by the simple overthrow of the aristocracy by the bourgeoisie, so, in its contemporary form, it does not simply consist of a bourgeois ruling class and a proletariat."[112] As this implies, Marwick thought that "our society" could also do without Marxist nonsense about the proletariat overthrowing the bourgeoisie. In the case of Marwick—a legendary philistine even by the exacting standards of the British historical profession—one suspects that he did not have to read the revisionists in order to arrive at this conclusion. But in many other cases, revisionism provided an intellectual basis for the conclusions that people now found it convenient to draw.

But revisionist ideas also began to penetrate the wider culture beyond the academy. Here, for example, is a passage from a comic novel published in 1987, in which the hero, who is researching what he believes to be real cases of witchcraft during the English Civil War, criticizes a colleague:

> "People like Rick," I went on, pulling out a bottle of Côtes de Provence from under the tomatoes, "are determined to prove that reality is as grey and unchanging as they are. I didn't dare tell him what I was doing. He would have condemned it as unhistorical. But I don't see why my vision of the seventeenth century is any less valid than his lists and statistics and fragments of court reports, all of which are there simply to bolster up a theory derived from a nineteenth-century German Jew."[113]

By the end of the twentieth century then, the preexisting orthodoxy had been replaced by a new consensus that can be summarized as follows: prior to the so-called bourgeois revolutions, the bourgeoisie was not "rising" and may even have been indistinguishable from the feudal lords; during the so-called bourgeoisie revolutions was not in the vanguard of the movement and may even have been found on the opposing side; after them, the bourgeoisie was not in power and may even have been further removed from control of the state than it had previously been; above all, these revolutions had nothing to do with either the emergence or consolidation of capitalism. Depending on which version of the argument was in use at any time, this was either because capitalism had already fully developed before the revolutions and so did not require them or because capitalism only developed too many years after the revolutions for there to be any causal connection between them, or even (a particularly British theme) because it was impossible to define feudalism or capitalism in the first place. Instead, revisionists claimed, these revolutions—if indeed they could be called revolutions—were just what they appeared to be and what participants said they were: expressions of inter-elite competition for office, differences over religious belief and observance, or movements in defense of regional autonomy.

The non-Marxists, anti-Marxists, and ex-Marxists who made up the ranks of the revisionists had, of course, no interest in providing alternative explanations for the dominance of capitalism, since the majority of them evidently regarded it as natural, inevitable, and, in some cases, eternal. Indeed, so far had the abandonment of "grand narratives" gone that one important revisionist contributor to the debates over the French Revolution was moved to ask, in a work first published in 1980, whether it was adequate to "wallow in fragmented chaos" or whether those who had "reveled in the joy of destruction" did not need to "declare what they now think the general picture to be."[114] But those who believe that the world is shaped by radical contingency do not require a social interpretation of historical developments. As Mary Fulbrook noted, "revisionists feel no great compulsion to develop a comprehensive explanation, since they consider that the object of explanation has been misinterpreted: the English Revolution was not a world historically important event requiring a commensurate scale of explanation, but rather represents, at least in origins, a somewhat bloody tiff between a specific monarch and certain fractions among his subjects."[115] In fact, the credibility of revisionist arguments almost always depended more on the weaknesses of the orthodox model than on their own strengths.

Revisionists generally proved incapable of proposing any coherent explanatory alternative of their own and with the exception of a very few early figures, of which Trevor-Roper was the most important, they disdained the attempt. But was revisionism left in possession of a field from which their opponents had entirely fled?

ORTHODOX RESPONSES TO REVISIONISM

Initially, left responses to revisionism insisted on the validity of the orthodoxy and questioned instead the empirical content of revisionist claims. As a strategy this was doomed to failure, not because the revisionists were invulnerable to challenge on factual grounds but because it failed to counter what they had correctly identified as the central weakness of the theory: the absence from the historical record of a bourgeois class subject consciously seeking to establish its own rule by revolutionary means. Over the years these defenses became more sophisticated. For some of the orthodox responding to revisionism involved taking a more nuanced view of the French Revolution. Hobsbawm, for example, argued in an important essay simply called "Revolution" (1986) that it was unnecessary

> To accept the simple-minded model of "bourgeois revolution" as a conscious political operation by a "bourgeoisie" conscious of itself as a class and formed as such under the old regime, which struggled for power against an old ruling class standing in the way of the establishment of the institutions of a "bourgeois society." As the never-ending debate on the French Revolution shows, this model is plainly inadequate. Paradoxically, it may tell us more about the later nineteenth-century revolutions, taught by the French Revolution what a "bourgeois revolution" should be like, and in which self-conscious entrepreneurial groups like liberal bourgeois, with something like a coherent politico-economic program, played a part—e.g., in Germany in and after 1848.[116]

But the later revolutions to which Hobsbawm alludes, during which participants consciously attempted to emulate the French revolutionary model, were all failures, so this shift in position is less significant than it appears: it allows a more subtle analysis of those revolutions that are already accepted as forming the canon, not for extending it.

The last two decades in particular have seen the publication of an important body of work, in both England and France, which challenges revisionist claims, often through the study of local rather than national developments—a case of engaging the enemy on their own ground, since regional or provincial studies are widely seen as an area of revisionist strength. The authors of these works have tended to avoid drawing wider conclusions from their research, often quite properly; but even those more general accounts that seek to defend aspects of the orthodox model only do so in relation to the two countries from which it was originally generalized.

The work of the North American historian of France, Henry Heller, is representative here in relation to both the key issues. One is the specific nature of the

French Revolution—what caused it, who was involved, what were their motivations, and so on. The other is whether it is possible to produce a general theory of bourgeois revolution that can encompass not only the French example but also the quite different experiences of countries as distinct as, for example, Scotland, Mexico, or China. Heller has made a considerable contribution to the first issue, but tends to avoid the second, upholding the view that the French Revolution was bourgeois primarily because it was led by the bourgeoisie.[117] With some qualifications this is a defensible position in relation to France; but if direct bourgeois leadership is the main criterion of classification, then there have been precious few other bourgeois revolutions. Indeed, Heller echoes the conventional view of the fate of countries that failed to repeat the French experience: "We must acknowledge that transitions to capitalism occurred in Japan and Germany without such a rupture, albeit at an ultimately tragic historical cost in the form of fascism."[118]

In many ways Heller's work resembles that of the late Brian Manning, a historian who defended the bourgeois nature of the English Revolution in his work as vigorously as Heller does that of the French Revolution. Manning was, however, suspicious of Marxist reappraisals of the bourgeois revolution that downplayed the conscious role of the bourgeoisie, seeing this as moving away from notions of class struggle.[119] I think Manning was wrong about this, since the view that revolutions do not *have* to be carried out by the bourgeoisie does not commit one to the claim that they are *never* carried out by the bourgeoisie, as in their different ways both the English and French Revolutions were. It is surely possible to defend a conception of bourgeois self-emancipation while still holding that this was not the only or the most common route to capitalist domination. In short, while orthodox counterarguments were effective in refuting specific points; but whatever victories were gained against the revisionists in local empirical battles, as long as their opponents continued to defend the untenable proposition that bourgeois revolutions *necessarily* involved the bourgeoisie in a conscious attempt to remake society in its own image, the revisionists were bound to win the global conceptual war.

The long retreat by the left, from the defeat of the movements of 1968 to the fall of the Stalinist regimes in 1989–91, together with the concomitant rise of neoliberalism, led many socialists to lose confidence in Marxist theory and its central concepts. Take the following exchange, from a roundtable discussion held by a group of British socialist historians in 1999:

> David Parker: So the bourgeois revolution completely disappears?
>
> Jim Sharp: Yes.
>
> David Parker: And you think we have to live with that?
>
> Jim Sharp: Something changed between 1500 and 1800. There was a developing bourgeoisie in England, but the idea that what happened in the middle decades of the seventeenth century was a bourgeois revolution is not sustainable. We are looking at shifting patterns of relationships between central authority and elites—an English version of what is going on in continental Europe.[120]

The vagueness of "something changed between 1500 and 1800," compared to the confident pronouncements of Hill or Soboul in an earlier era suggests the scale of the retreat involved. Other responses to revisionism did however recognize that the inadequacies of the orthodoxy could not be overcome simply by accumulating more supporting empirical detail: the concept had either to be reconstructed on a defensible basis or replaced by an alternative explanatory framework.

16 FROM SOCIETY TO POLITICS; FROM EVENT TO PROCESS

T he first attempt at reconstruction retained the term *bourgeois revolution*, but tended to both change the meaning it had previously conveyed and reduce the historic significance of the events that it described. There are two variants of this approach. In the first, the content of bourgeois revolutions is diluted until it becomes almost entirely political in nature: from referring to decisive turning points that removed obstacles to capitalist development, the concept is stretched to include subsequent alterations in existing capitalist states that bring them into more perfect alignment with the requirements of competitive accumulation—realignments to which there can be no foreseeable end this side of the socialist revolution. A second variant extends the bourgeois revolutions in time until they become indistinguishable from the general course of capitalist development in the countries concerned, encompassing economic, political, social, and cultural changes—a view with strong affinities to those of the French Annales School of historiography, a tradition that has always been distrustful of event-based history and emphasized instead the *longue durée*. According to Fernand Braudel, in his classic dismissal of "the history of events," they merely recount "surface disturbances, crests of foam that the tides of history carry on their strong backs."[1] Whatever the virtues of this approach, it is clearly incompatible with any conception of bourgeois revolution as an epochal moment of transition.

Over time, these two shifts in meaning, from the social to the political and from event to process, have tended to intertwine so that what emerged was a single position with alternating emphases, concentrating at some times on a succession of individually inconclusive political upheavals in which different class fractions have vied for control of the state (France in 1789, 1815, 1830, 1848–51, 1871, 1940, 1958, 1968 . . .), highlighting at other times the reconfigurations of capital that follow the onset of major economic crises (the world after 1873, 1929, 1973, 2008 . . .), then back. And, while there is nothing inherently implausible about bourgeois revolutions taking a prolonged form, extending their conceptual and chronological boundaries to such an extent makes it difficult to see how the term *revolution* can be applied in any meaningful way, other than perhaps as a metaphor. And to do so is, in effect, to tacitly concede the revisionist argument.

The first move in this direction took place during the early 1960s in the course of a dispute about English historical development, the opening salvos of which saw the logic of the orthodox conception being taken to its inescapable conclusion. Following his installation as editor of *New Left Review* (*NLR*) in 1962, Perry Anderson began to produce a highly influential series of essays that, together with complementary pieces by fellow editorial board member Tom Nairn, constituted the basis of what has since become known as the Anderson-Nairn thesis on the backwardness of the English social formation. (Scotland was symptomatically absent from these debates.) Writers in the *NLR* had expressed skepticism about the bourgeois revolution before Anderson himself addressed the subject. Victor Kiernan, a veteran if occasionally dissident member of the CPGB Historians Group, wrote in the course of reviewing Eric Hobsbawm's magnificent but highly orthodox *The Age of Revolution* (1962):

> We have been rather too much in the habit of referring to the Bourgeois Revolution as though to a firm and fixed historical category. In reality it is more in the nature of a speculation, or theoretical construct, or political fiction, or piece of shorthand; it has affinities variously with the ether, the square root of minus one, and the Abominable Snowman. Apart from those very hybrid affairs in 16th century Holland and 17th century England, there is practically speaking only one example, 1789; and 1789 not only ruled out any imitators, but also cancelled itself out, by damping capitalism down instead of gingering it up. Germany later on, even Japan, without any benefit of rev-olutionary baptism, industrialized more rapidly and wholeheartedly than France.[2]

This was not Anderson's position: rather than casting doubt on the category of bourgeois revolution, he wanted instead to argue that England's case had not in-volved a sufficiently decisive experience. Anderson therefore tended to accept the emerging revisionist case in relation to England, particularly as it appeared in the work of Hugh Trevor-Roper and J. H. Hexter; his main concern at this point being to undermine what he saw as the illusions of his fellow left-wingers, an end to which these writers were also committed, albeit from the opposite political stand-point. Anderson claimed that the supposedly archaic aspects of the modern British state and society could be explained by the limited and incomplete nature of the English Revolution: "*England had the first, most mediated, and least pure bourgeois revolution of any major country.*" Since both sides in the civil war consisted of sec-tions of the landowning classes, "it was a 'bourgeois revolution' only by proxy." And here the paradoxes come thick and fast. It was "a supremely successful *capitalist* revolution" that nevertheless "left almost the entire social structure intact," a feat accomplished "by transforming the roles but not the personnel of the ruling class."[3] There are two substantive difficulties with Anderson's position, both due to his ac-ceptance, at this point, of the orthodox conception of bourgeois revolution.

The first is the role of the bourgeoisie. The key reason Anderson gives for the "impurity" of the English Revolution is the absence of an urban bourgeois leadership among the Parliamentarians and the consequent unaltered political, social, and cultural dominance of the landed aristocracy over the representatives of banking and mercantile capital. Similar claims had first been expressed by Ricardo during the Napoleonic Wars and subsequently became part of the standard repertoire of liberal complaint during the following century.[4] Within a decade of Anderson launching his argument in 1964, however, these had come to be associated far more with the intellectually literate members of the New Right. In 1975, Sir Keith Joseph, then playing John the Baptist to Margaret Thatcher's Jesus Christ, noted the incompleteness of the British bourgeois revolution with the result that Britain "never had a capitalist ruling class or stable *haute bourgeoisie*": "The great feudal families, together with the landed gentry, court, church, and legal profession set their stamp so firmly on post-medieval British society that the merchant classes sought acceptance rather than challenging it, as they did in France."[5] Nevertheless, mere association with the class enemy is not a sufficient basis on which to establish the truth or otherwise of a historical interpretation. The issue is not the accuracy of Anderson's claim for aristocratic hegemony but rather its significance. As Edward Thompson argued at the time in his response, "The Peculiarities of the English" (1965), English landowners were fully fledged agrarian capitalists by 1688 and, even though many of them possessed a title indicating their membership in the peerage, it was their economic position that conferred their social power.[6] For Marxists, capitalists exist as "capital personified," their actions constituting "a mere function of capital."[7] Whether the culture of their life world expressed aristocratic or bourgeois values is less important than their integration into the process of competitive accumulation, which imposes its own, deeper cultural logic. In other words, it is precisely the question of the transformation of "roles," rather than the replacement of individuals, which is at stake. Otherwise, the implications of the argument are that there is a politico-socio-cultural element to the bourgeois revolution that must be achieved before it can be considered complete, even in the heart of the West during the latter half of the twentieth century. This, at any rate, is implied by the extraordinarily ambiguous rallying cry with which Anderson concludes the penultimate paragraph of "Origins of the Present Crisis": "The unfinished work of 1640 and 1832 must be taken up where it was left off."[8]

The second problem was the comparator that Anderson implicitly used to illustrate the inadequacies of the English Revolution, namely France. For earlier British Marxists, like Christopher Hill, "the English Revolution of 1640–60 was a great social movement like the French Revolution of 1789."[9] Their comrades on the other side of the Channel tended to feel this comparison insufficiently recognized the greater significance of the latter event. "In England, though there have been political revolutions, social evolution has gone on in relative calm, wrote Lefebvre: "The French Revolution was realized by violence."[10] Soboul, recalling the earliest socialist historian of the French Revolution, similarly argued: "The English Revolution was far less sweeping than its French counterpart: in the words of Jean Jaurès in his *Historie socialiste de la Révolution Française*, it was 'strictly bour geois and conservative' when compared with its 'mainly bourgeois and democratic French counterpart.'"[11] By implication at least, France now single-handedly as sumed the role of model bourgeois revolution; but if France was the only country that could unambiguously be described as having undergone a "pure" bourgeois revolution, if even England—the most significant country whose experience was remotely comparable—was inadequate in this respect; then what did this imply for those "major European countries" in which social classes had not even attained English levels of revolutionary activity?

The source of both these problems lay in the particular interpretation of Gram sci. In the early 1960s the availability of material from Gramsci's prison notebooks was dependent on what his successor as leader of the Communist Party of Italy (PCI), Palmiro Togliatti, was prepared to authorize for publication. He had been deeply concerned by the incompatibility of much of their contents with Stalinist orthodoxy. "The notebooks of Gramsci, which I have finished studying, contain material which could be utilized only after a proper processing," he wrote to Georgi Dimitroff in 1941· "Without such treatments the material cannot be utilized and, in some parts, if the contents were found in their unexpurgated form, it would not be in the party's best interest."[12] It was in this spirit that Togliatti "oversaw" the editing of the original Italian edition, which appeared between 1948 and 1951, as part of a strategy that simultaneously emphasized Gramsci's supposed but in fact wholly imaginary adherence to Stalinist doctrine and his role as a distinctively "na tive" intellectual ornament for the PCI. Access to Gramsci's work was even more limited for those reliant on English translations—a narrow selection from work already censored. The relevant works of Gramsci that were available in English were two short US-edited selections of his writings, both published in 1957.[13] Nor were there a great number of serious commentaries. Gramsci appears in US histo rian Stuart Hughes's 1958 survey of European intellectual trends between 1890 and 1930, but is subject to a relatively sophisticated Cold War treatment empha sizing the supposedly "totalitarian" implications of his theory.[14] A pioneering article from 1960 on Gramsci's use of hegemony by the Welsh Communist Gwyn Williams was misleading and subsequently disowned by its author on these grounds.[15] These two works were drawn on by Thompson who was subsequently criticized by Anderson precisely for relying on such dubious secondary sources.[16]

Nairn had read Gramsci in the original Italian while he was studying at the Scuola Normale Superiore in Pisa, during 1957–58. One of Nairn's first published articles, "La nemesi borghese," appeared in the PCI's cultural journal *Il Contemporeano* during 1963, the bourgeoisie whose nemesis he recounted in Gramscian terms being that of England.[17] That the PCI should have exercised an influence on the hitherto apo litical Nairn was unsurprising: it was the largest communist party in Western Europe, had the most sophisticated theoretical approach and a highly developed cultural ap paratus, in many ways comparable to that of the Central European Social Democracy before the First World War. The contrast with the CPGB would have been obvious even in Nairn's native Fife, which had a strong communist tradition by British standards. On his return to the United Kingdom, Nairn maintained his contact with the PCI as British correspondent for its daily paper *Unita* and joined the editorial board of *NLR*. His partnership with Anderson produced the articles that form the basis of their famous "thesis" on the backwardness of the English social formation.[18] In "La nemesi borghese" Nairn had invoked Gramsci's notion of "delegated authority," in the sense of the bourgeoisie passing responsibility for political rule onto the established landowning class.[19] It reappears in Anderson's "Origins of the Present Crisis," where Gramsci is invoked at the beginning of the section on "History and Class Consciousness: Hegemony."[20] The irony of this was that Marxists in other countries, notably in Germany, had long argued that their national peculiarities were precisely due to their not having had the benefit of what they supposed was the common Anglo-French experience. A decade beforehand, for example, Georg Lukács had written that, in contrast to nineteenth-century Germany (and Italy): "The other major states of the West, especially England and France, had already attained to national unity under an absolute monarchy, i.e., in their cases, national unity was one of the first products of the class conflicts between bourgeois and feudal life."[21] Far from making a case for English exceptionalism, Anderson was actually making one for France, to a degree that not even French Marxists had hitherto attempted, with the result that the achievements of all other bourgeois revolutions were implicitly called into question. As I have argued in chapter 14, this was not in fact Gramsci's intention and the position expounded by Anderson is closer to that of Hexter—indeed Anderson upbraids Thompson for not attending to his article "The Myth of the Middle Class in Tudor England."[22]

Anderson later admitted that these early writings lacked a "general theory" of bourgeois revolution: "A condition of further enquiry was clearly a critical reflection on the category of bourgeois revolution itself."[23] His main collaborator at the *NLR* was more immediately willing to explicitly draw the necessary conclusions concerning what Thompson called Other Countries. Nairn wrote of "late-developing nations like Germany and Japan" where "a new, forced industrialism was entering partnership with more genuinely archaic landlord classes—with social orders that had never gone through an equivalent of 1640, let alone a 1789."[24] At first sight the point being made here seems clear enough: Germany and Japan did not experience bourgeois revolutions, even incomplete variants comparable to the English. Elsewhere in the same article, however, Nairn compares England with the "new, state-ordered, nationalist capitalisms which developed in the course of the nineteenth century," noting that it was protected from their fate only be the existence of the empire, without which: "It too would have been compelled to suffer a second, modernizing revolution and the logical reorganization of its constitution and its state: precisely that second political upheaval whose absence has been the constant enigma and despair of modern Britain."[25] On the one hand then, Germany, Japan and (presumably) Italy had not experienced bourgeois revolutions; on the other, they had become the beneficiaries of not one but two such revolutions—although it is not clear when either of these events is supposed to have taken place in the case of any of the nations concerned. Ultimately it would be the latter interpretation that would prevail and become the default position expressed by authors associated with the *NLR*.

Meanwhile, Thompson's formidable response to the Anderson-Nairn thesis suggested an alternative characterization of the English Revolution. Rather than identifying it with the "episode" of the civil war, which could then be compared unfavorably with the French Revolution, it should be reconceptualized as an extended process running from the introduction of commercial sheep-rearing in the late eleventh century through to the political consolidation of agrarian and mercantile capitalist supremacy in 1688. Thompson invited his readers to imagine this history as if the civil war had not taken place: "In this event the model-builders would be wholly at a loss for the Revolution; and, paradoxically, might perforce be better historians, for they would have to construct, from the Wars of the Roses, the Tudor Monarchy . . . the attainder of royal ministers, the religious conflicts of the sixteenth and seventeenth centuries, and from 1832, pieces of the great arch which in fact, make up the bourgeois revolution."[26] Yet although Thompson questioned the relevance of the French Revolution as a standard against which the English should be judged, he did not propose an alternative general model that did not rely on the experience of a single country—indeed, he questioned whether this could be done.[27]

Thompson's view of English development was subsequently much elaborated by Phillip Corrigan and Derek Sayer in *The Great Arch* (1985), a work whose title derives from the passage quoted in the preceding paragraph. In relation to events in England during the seventeenth century they ask: "Does all this, then, amount to a 'bourgeois revolution'"?

> The question is a difficult one to answer. Yes, if we mean—and in itself this is a lot—that the events of 1640 through to 1688–9 deserve to be called revolutionary, and facilitated the development of capitalism and a wider embourgeoisement of culture and society; on either point there can be little dispute. But the appropriateness of the concept, whether as a description or explanation, may in other respects be doubted. The notion of a "bourgeois revolution" popularly conveys the idea of a set-piece struggle between clearly defined class groupings, with the victorious bourgeoisie emerging in secure possession of political power. This clearly was not the situation in seventeenth-century England. It encourages overly neat identification of political actors with conflicting social and economic class interests. . . . Finally, and from our point of view most seriously, the very notion of *a* bourgeois revolution suggests a momentary rupture, a defined and dated event, in which power visibly changes hands. Not only is this an implausible description of the events that culminated in the Restoration of 1660 and the "readjustment" of 1688–[8]9. It also seriously obscures, and massively oversimplifies, the complex and protracted history of state formation and transformation through which capitalist classes did come finally to achieve political dominance in England.[28]

Although Corrigan and Sayer refer explicitly to "Thompson's Great Arch" (and indeed to the Braudelian notion of *longue durée*) in the passages that follow, they also refer to the English revolution of the seventeenth century as being "incomplete" and one which "stopped half-way."[29] These terms suggest a position actually closer to that of Anderson, since one of Thompson's arguments was precisely that the revolutions of 1640–60 and 1688–89 could *only* be understood as part of an entire centuries-long process and *not* as isolated events. In effect, Corrigan and Sayer, like Thompson himself sidestepped the implications of Anderson's argument for the concept of bourgeois revolution by focusing instead on the supposedly exceptional nature of English development. Nevertheless, by the early 1980s, all the elements were in place with which to reconstruct the concept of bourgeois revolution, in both variants.

A SUCCESSION OF POLITICAL REVOLUTIONS?

That the possibilities of the bourgeois revolution might involve a succession of events was suggested by the Swedish sociologist and *NLR* contributor Goran Therborn in 1976:

> The bourgeois revolution was not, of course, a single event but a historical process of economic, political, juridical, and ideological ruptures between old social institutions and new bourgeois forms. In this revolutionary process a capitalist market emerged, the political power of feudal landowners was defeated and a state representing the bourgeoisie and furthering the development of capitalism was created, in which feudal privileges were abolished and equality before the law established. In every country a particular event can normally be singled out as decisive. . . . These events, however, constituted neither the first nor the last important moments of the bourgeois revolution in each country, as the long persistence of the power of the land-owning aristocracy in England, Italy and Germany makes clear.[30]

The most comprehensive version of the argument was however first provided by the US historian Arno Mayer in two works that effectively generalized the Anderson-Nairn thesis about English development for Europe as a whole.[31] Mayer claimed that the landed ruling classes of Europe effectively remained in power until nearly halfway through the twentieth century, long after the events usually described as the bourgeois revolutions took place. Until the end of what he calls "the Thirty Years War of the general crisis of the twentieth century" [1914–45], Europe was still dominated by an order "thoroughly preindustrial and prebourgeois": "The Great War was an expression of the decline and fall of the old order fighting to prolong its life rather than the explosive rise of industrial capitalism bent on imposing its primacy." Mayer extends his analysis to what had once seemed the obvious exceptions, writing that, "Neither England nor France had become industrial-capitalist and bourgeois civil and political societies."[32] During the thirty years between 1914 and 1945:

> The elites and institutions of Europe's embattled old regime were locked in a death struggle with those of a defiant new order: in the economic sphere merchant and

manufactural capitalism against corporate and organized industrial capitalism; in civil society prescriptive ruling classes against university trained elites; in political society land-based notables and establishments against urban-based professional politicians; in cultural life the custodians of historicism against the champions of experimentation and modernism; and in science the guardians of established paradigms against the pioneers of the world's second great scientific and technological revolution.

By the end of the Second World War the struggle was over: "Throughout most of Europe the old regime was either decimated or cast off by 1945."[33] But the imposition of the "defiant new order" was not achieved through the victory of its indigenous representatives. On the contrary, the European old regimes were actually overthrown by external state intervention, crushed between the armed might of the United States and the Soviet Union, the rival powers that were, in their different ways, the bearers of industrial modernity. In fact, the claim that landowning dominance continued into the twentieth century, upon which Mayer's account depends, is open to criticism on two grounds.

First, what was the actual role of the nobles in European society? They certainly occupied important posts as monarchical advisers, in the diplomatic corps, in (mainly nontechnical) army posts, and as representatives in the various regional assemblies. But their preponderance had already been eroded by 1914. In this perspective, the 1914–18 war, rather than its successor, sealed their fate: "By the eve of World War I—the great caesura of modern European history—the nobility had to share its leadership with men of common origin." In part, this was because there were too few nobles to fill the posts required by the modern bureaucratic state and still fewer of them capable of competently filling them: "In 1804 none of the major posts in the Austrian foreign office had a bourgeois incumbent; by 1918 burghers held 66 per cent of these appointments." In the Austrian army the number of burghers among the officer class rose from around 5 per cent in 1808 to 68 per cent in 1918.[34]

Second, and more importantly, did the nobles represent feudal or capitalist landowning interests? If the latter, then, as in the case of England, whatever influences the nobility did possess should more properly be regarded as one of culture and style, rather than one that conflicted with the interests of the industrial or financial bourgeoisie. Heide Gerstenberger notes: "If the 'bourgeois revolution' was achieved through a process of forced reform, the economic, cultural as well as political hegemony of those groups which occupied the ranks of the social hierarchy in societies of the Ancien Regime type could persist long after the capitalist form of exploitation had become dominant."[35] One supporter of the Mayer thesis writes of "a landowning elite [that] survived from the days of feudalism through the ages of absolutism and nationalism and into the twentieth century."[36] The question, however, is whether they survived as representatives of the same socioeconomic interests as they did in "the days of feudalism." As Eric Hobsbawm notes, the economic orientation of the landlords was expressed with increasing ideological clarity:

Never has there been a more overwhelming consensus among economists and indeed among intelligent politicians and administrators about the recipe for economic growth: economic liberalism. The remaining institutional barriers to the free movement of the factors of production, to free enterprise and to anything that could conceivably hamper its profitable operation, fell below a world-wide onslaught. What made this general raising of barriers so remarkable is that it was not confined to the states in which political liberalism was triumphant or even influential. If anything it was even more drastic in the restored absolutist monarchies and principalities of Europe than in England, France, and the Low Countries, because so much remained to be swept away there.[37]

Indeed, as Norman Stone has written of this period, with the important exception of Russia, all the major states of Europe also had "a large, educated, energetic middle class with enough money for its support to be essential to any state that wished to develop," but it was the state that acted as the main agent of development. Britain was also different, but not because the middle class was incapable of influencing the state:

> In Great Britain, that class existed so strongly, even in the eighteenth century, that liberal reforms were introduced piecemeal there, and often without formal involvement of parliament. Existing *ancien-régime* institutions, such as the old guilds or corporations, would be gradually adapted to suit a changing era. Thus, in form, England (more than Scotland) is the last of the *ancien régimes*; she did not even have a formal law to abolish serfdom. . . . . In the 1860s, states, short of money, had to follow the British example by formal legislation.[38]

The terminology of the *ancien régime* might make it appear that Stone is making a similar case to that of Anderson and Nairn; but in fact, this deeply conservative historian is actually inviting us to do what Marxists should perhaps be doing anyway, namely probing beneath the surface appearances of phenomena to observe the underlying realities.

Despite the superficiality of Mayer's work, Anderson responded to it by adopting his periodization, commending him for his "formidable empirical demonstration of agrarian paramountcy in the ruling orders of every European power down to the First World War itself" and concluding that "the English landowning class" as he had originally conceived it now had to be situated "in a wider European panorama."[39] What then explained the specificity of English development? Here is where the concept of bourgeois revolution, absent in Mayer, reenters. Although Britain shared many characteristics in common with other European states, its experience in the twentieth century diverged in one crucial respect:

> Among them, Britain alone had now never experienced a modern "second" revolution, abruptly or radically remolding the state inherited from the first. For between the initial bourgeois revolution that breached the old order and the final completion of bourgeois democracy as the contemporary form of the capitalist state, there typically lay violent intervening convulsions that extended the work of the original upheaval and transformed the political framework of the nation.[40]

Although the Revolution of 1688 did constitute such a revolution, it came too soon after the "original upheaval" of 1640 to lead to any significant further structural change to the English state.

In applying this analysis to mainland Europe Anderson draws out what is only hinted at in Mayer's work: that the completion of the bourgeois revolution, in Japan, Germany, Italy and even France, was the result of invasion and occupation by the American-led Allies during the Second World War: "Allied victory brought agrarian reform to Japan, partition to Germany, the republic to Italy, universal suffrage to France. The final clearance of the social and political landscape that had prevailed down to the First World War—the whole scenery surveyed by Mayer—was only accomplished in the Second."[41] Anderson does not deny that, for example, Germany had a capitalist economy and a capitalist state by 1914, let alone 1945, any more than he does that England had a capitalist economy and capitalist state by 1688. The wider conclusion, only implied in his earlier work, is therefore that the bourgeois revolution should not be restricted to the initial process of establishing a state conducive to capitalist development, but should be expanded to include subsequent restructuring in which the bourgeoisie assume political rule directly, rather than indirectly through the landowning classes. But if the concept can be extended in this way, why confine it to the aftermath of the Second World War, when direct bourgeois rule had still to be achieved across most of the world?

In *The Enchanted Glass* (1988), Nairn also drew on Mayer's work to date the triumph of capitalism still later in the twentieth century:

> The European Ancien Régime still isn't ancient and is only just history . . . and the dust has only really settled since the 1950s. . . . It would really be safer and more accurate to say "since the 1960s" or "the 1970s," to allow for France's last fling with the quasi-Monarchy of General de Gaulle, and the end of military dictatorship in Spain, Portugal, and Greece. If the "triumph" of the bourgeois class and industrial capitalist values is taken to mean the formation of fairly homogeneous societies regulated by these norms—a stable and pacific state-*system* at approximately the same level of development—then it has only just come about.[42]

If the definitive "triumph" of capitalism requires the internationalization of a particular set of political institutions, then it had still not been achieved at the time these words first appeared in print, above all in the Stalinist states. By the time the second edition of Nairn's book was published in 1994, however, the Eastern European variants had either collapsed or been overthrown by their own populations, events that had clear parallels with the end of the Mediterranean dictatorships during the 1970s.

Does this then mean that bourgeois revolutions will continue until capitalism is superseded? Some Marxists have indeed drawn this conclusion. During the 1970s one Russian Marxist dissident, Leonid Plyushch, regarded the regime that had imprisoned him in a psychiatric hospital as presiding over a form of state capitalism in which even the limited forms of representative democracy were denied. As a result, he argued, the political tasks facing the Russian opposition were "paradoxical": "We still have to make our bourgeois-political revolution even though we have already destroyed private property: it is history back to front."[43] After the fall of the Stalinist regimes, Colin Barker and Colin Mooers claimed that this is effectively what had taken place: "The East European revolutions ... make sense as a species of 'bourgeois revolution.'" Barker and Mooers were rightly insistent that capitalism was already the dominant mode of production in Eastern Europe, with the states themselves acting as collective capitalists. Why then were bourgeois revolutions required? "Bourgeois revolutions may also occur *within* already constituted capitalist relations. Because capitalist development is both 'uneven and combined' nations not only leap over stages of development, they also fall backward. Capitalism not only revolutionizes the means of production, it revolutionizes the political conditions of its own existence. Specific state and regime forms become impediments to further capitalist advance."[44]

Clearly, the events of 1848 or 1989 were revolutions of *some* kind, but which? We should note that the notion of a succession of "corrective" bourgeois revolutions, although not central to the orthodox model, has a venerable Stalinist lineage, usually applied in cases where revolutions could not be easily categorized in class terms, as in this late example referring to the French Revolution of 1848: "Feudalism had already been swept away in France by the revolution of 1789–94. But another bourgeois revolution became inevitable when the rapacious rule of the financial aristocracy, the top crust of the bourgeoisie, and the political monopoly it enjoyed began to hamper the further development of capitalism.[45]

Rather than describe them as bourgeois revolutions, they seem to me to be far better understood as examples of the broader category of *political* revolution inherited by Marx and Engels in the early 1840s from the first generation of socialist radicals.[46] In the capitalist epoch, as Barker and Mooers correctly point out, revolutions are sometimes required to move from one form of capital accumulation to another: "Such were the 19th century revolutions in France, the German political transformations of 1918–19, 1933, and 1945, the Iberian revolutions of the 1970s and the Latin American 'democratic transitions' of the 1980s."[47] But precisely because these all remained within the confines of the capitalist mode of production, they can only be defined as political, no matter how extreme the consequences in this respect might be. As I have emphasized throughout this book, social revolutions are epochal events involving change from one type of society to another and certainly not only changes of government, however violently achieved. Take, for example, 1933, the date of one of the "German political transformations" to which Barker and Mooers allude. The Nazi seizure of power is sometimes described as a counterrevolution, but, in the absence of a successful revolution to counter, this designation is hopelessly misleading. The Nazis and their supporters certainly feared a socialist revolution, which had threatened at various points between 1918 and 1923, but their political goal was preemptive, not reactive: they wanted to end the possibility of socialist revolution ever happening. In response to these problems of definition, some writers have attempted to define the Nazi seizure of power as a social revolution, comparable in scope, if different in kind to that desired by their Communist rivals.[48] However, as even writers sympathetic to this view have had to acknowledge, "neither the [Italian] Fascist nor Nazi state wanted to abolish capitalist economics and private property."[49] This verdict corresponds to that of Trotsky in 1933: "The Nazis call their overturn by the usurped title of revolution. As a matter of fact, in Germany as well as in Italy, fascism leaves the social system untouched. Taken by itself, Hitler's overturn has no right even to the name counter-revolution. But it cannot be viewed as an isolated event; it is the conclusion of a cycle of shocks which began in Germany in 1918."[50] In fact, as Richard Evans reports, "Hitler himself seems to have thought of the Revolution as a changeover of personnel in positions of power and authority."[51]

ENDLESS RESTRUCTURING OF CAPITALISM?

The second variant of this reconstructed concept of bourgeois revolution, originally suggested by Thompson's metaphor of the "great arch" of the English Revolution, invoked process rather than an event or series of events. It retained the sense of an extended period of economic, social, and political change, but where Thompson and his followers did at any rate envisage the process in England as having an end point at which capitalism was definitively established, more recent versions have, as in the first variant, dispensed with any concluding episode. In this respect a comment by Anderson is appropriate: "This particular arch is a rainbow, which has no end."[52] Bourgeois revolutions are no longer even political transformations that bring the state into line with the needs of capital but can be detected in every restructuring of the system. It was of course possible to find justifications for such an approach further back in the Marxist tradition than Thompson, above all in the work of Gramsci at least insofar as he suggested that the concept of "passive revolution" could be used to mean more than bourgeois revolution from above. As Adam David Morton writes: "A theory of passive revolution is pivotal in demonstrating how Italian and wider European state formation was shaped by the causal conditioning of 'the international,' whether through developments linked to the French Revolution; social forces associated with Fascism; or the growing dominance of Anglo-Saxon capitalism."[53] Understood in this over-capacious way, "bourgeois revolution" can either refer to the trajectory of individual social groups, of individual capitalist states, of regions, or even of the capitalist states system as a whole.

In relation to individual social groups, Hester Eisenstein, in the course of an otherwise perceptive book on the relationship between second-stage feminism and neoliberalism, wrote that "the women's movement created a successful 'bourgeois revolution' for women in the United States":

> Whereas the English, French, and American revolutions of the seventeenth and eighteenth centuries replaced feudal relations with the rule of the white bourgeoisie, these revolutions notoriously did not extend to the rights of women, people of color, and

those without property. Whereas bourgeois men freed themselves from the rule of kings, and freed working-class men from feudal relations of servitude, both bourgeois and working-class women remained subject to the rule of men within the family. It took the nineteenth- and twentieth-century women's movements to claim the rights of women as full citizens. This unfinished revolution now seems complete.[54]

In the case of individual states, Robert Stern has for example described the Indian bourgeois revolution as being "the development *together* . . . of capitalism and parliamentary democracy," joint developments that constitute "the dominant pattern of change" since 1947. Although starting as "a revolution from the top down," by the postcolonial state, it has now acquired a popular base: "Increasingly as it proceeds . . . combining and incorporating elements in a society that long antedates it, it has become as well a revolution upward from expanding middle classes."[55] As we shall see, there is indeed a way in which the various movements against colonialism can be considered the last episodes in the bourgeois revolution, considered in global terms; but in that respect the founding of the independent nation-state signals the end of the process in India, not the beginning.

In regional terms, Ian Roxborough has argued that it is futile to seek the precise momentat which bourgeois revolutions took place in the Latin American states:

> The change from an export-orientation to ISI [import substitution industrialization] and then to the dominance of the multinationals are examples of the principal transformations which have taken place in Latin America. Each structural shift in the economy brought with it a changing realignment of class forces and political turmoil. In this sense, the bourgeois revolution has been a continuous process in Latin America. One cannot therefore give it a precise date, one can only point to the various phases of the process.[56]

In terms of the system as a whole, the term was quickly adopted to describe the imposition of neoliberalism on a global scale. Leo Panitch has written of "the bourgeois revolution from above of the 1980s" and of how "the restructuring of the past few decades reveals the limits of this new bourgeois revolution."[57] Gary Teeple describes neoliberal globalization as "a second bourgeois revolution."[58] Some writers have even tried to identify neoliberal globalization as the only genuine bourgeois revolution. In the mid-1980s, for example Adam Przeworski wrote:

> For the first time in several decades, the Right has a historical project of its own: to free accumulation from all the fetters imposed upon it by democracy. For the bourgeoisie never completed its revolution. Just as it freed accumulation from the restraint of the feudal order, the bourgeoisie was forced to subject it to the constraint of popular control exercised through universal suffrage. The combination of private property with universal suffrage is a compromise, and this compromise implies that the logic of accumulation is not exclusively the logic of private actors. What is involved in the current offensive of the Right is not simply a question of taxes, government spending, or even the distribution of income. The plans for relaxing taxation of profits, abolishing environmental controls, eliminating welfare programs, removing government control over product safety and conditions of work, and weakening the labor unions add

up to more than reorientation of the economic policy. They constitute a project for a new society, a bourgeois revolution.[59]

In the work of writers such as David Harvey and Naomi Klein this analysis of neoliberalism has led to the extraordinary conclusion that the Great Boom between 1948 and 1974, the period of greatest growth in the history of capitalism, was a time of deep frustration for multinational capital, constrained as it was by New Deal and Great Society programs in the United States and welfare state provision in Western Europe. Neoliberalism is therefore the full maturation of capital, the ultimate realization of the hitherto unfulfilled ambitions of its representatives. At their most extreme, such arguments involve a conception of capital in which it is inherently opposed to the state. In effect, arguments of this nature deny that there are capitalist states at all—there is only "the state," which acts to prevent the complete imposition of capitalist social relations, understood here entirely in market terms.[60] For David Lockwood "the state" involves an alternative set of social relations:

> If this analytical framework—the state as a productive relation, separate from and increasingly in competition with the capital production relation—is applied to the period since the first stirrings of the bourgeois revolution, it can explain why, in the course of the bourgeois revolution, the state has not (up to this point) been reduced to an "executive committee" of the bourgeoisie—and why in fact for much of that period in much of the world the state has managed to dominate social development. And it might also explain why the ongoing development of capitalism—the mighty increase in the development of the productive forces known as globalization—weakens the national state, and why the successful conclusion of the bourgeois revolution globally must mean the liberation of capital from the fetters of state policy. . . . The extent to which that domination is preserved, or weakened, or eventually destroyed is a measure of the success of the bourgeois revolution.

For Lockwood, following the Russian Revolution, "the process of bourgeois revolution was halted for at least the next half century" until the onset of globalization: "It was only with the advances in technology that made possible a genuine world manufacturing system and a world market, and in turn gave rise to globalization, that the advance of the bourgeois revolution was resumed. The advance of globalized (and globalizing) capital will remove the state as the dominant production relation and allow for the completion of the bourgeois revolution."[61]

States certainly involve social relations, embedded in the various institutions of which they consist; states can also embody specific social relations of production, as in the case of the tributary state or under state capitalism; but to describe the state as a "social relation" is both meaningless and ahistorical unless one specifies which classes are involved. Otherwise, this simply reproduces the ideology (although not, of course, the reality) of neoliberalism with a Marxist patina. Indeed, former Marxists have been at the forefront of mobilizing their past vocabulary for the purposes of supporting their neoliberal present. Nigel Harris, for example, denies that there was a bourgeois revolution during the period when they were generally supposed to have occurred: "There was certainly a progressive extension of suffrage (and the rights associated with this) and steady increase in the constraints on the prerogatives of the crown (leading in some cases to the establishment of republics), but this process was far from establishing business control of the state." We note here that bourgeois revolution has become direct possession of the state by capitalists, a process that had to wait until the end of the twentieth century: "Thus, it is only now that we can see the real 'bourgeois revolution,' the establishment of the power of world markets and of businessmen over the states of the world."[62] Since this process remains incomplete even now, we can expect yet more of such revolutions—but by now enumeration is clearly meaningless, since "bourgeois revolution" has simply become a metaphor for an ongoing process of capitalist restructuring that will continue as long as the system exists. "What is intended," writes Stuart Hall of neoliberalism, "is a permanent revolution."[63]

Faced with both an inadequate orthodoxy and the equally unsatisfactory alternatives of overextension or dilution, many Marxists and other anticapitalist radicals have completely abandoned the theory of bourgeois revolution for two alternative explanations of capitalist ascendancy. Whatever their many other differences, these theories both reject the development of the productive forces as the central dynamic behind the emergence of capitalism—a convergence that leads them to display what Chris Harman called the "unity of opposites."[64]

17 "THE CAPITALIST WORLD-SYSTEM"

The first alternative that I want to consider is an aspect of the once-influential "capitalist world-system" theory associated with Andre Gunder Frank, Immanuel Wallerstein, and their cothinkers. In relation to contemporary capitalism the theory overlapped with those of "dependency" and "underdevelopment"; in relation to its historical development it shifted focus completely from bourgeois revolution onto the transition from feudalism to capitalism itself. Three aspects of capitalist world-system theory have strong affinities with the work of the American Marxist, Paul Sweezy, and in some respects were inspired by it. The first is a shared rejection of Marx's view that feudalism contained internal contradictions that at least opened up the possibility for the emergence of capitalism. As Sweezy noted during the original 1950s debate on the transition, "the feudal system contains no internal prime mover and when it undergoes genuine development—as distinct from mere oscillations and crises which do not affect its basics structure—the driving force is to be found outside the system."[1] The second, which provided the missing internal "driving force," is an emphasis on the expansion of trade and commerce as the "prime mover" in the development of capitalism: "We see . . . how long-distance trade could be a creative force, bringing into existence a *system* of production for exchange alongside the old feudal system of production for use."[2] Dependency theorists tend to see this process not only as how the capitalist mode of production came to dominate the world economy but also how the nations of the periphery were originally fixed into their current position in the world states system. The third involves the most direct connection: the notion of "dependency" itself formulated by Sweezy's collaborator Paul Baran in *The Political Economy of Development* (1957) and developed by both men jointly in *Monopoly Capital* (1966). The key issue here is the means by which Baran and Sweezy see the peripheral nations freeing themselves from the system: "The highest form of resistance is revolutionary war aimed at withdrawal from the world capitalist system and the initiation of social and economic reconstruction on a socialist basis."[3]

The principal theorist of the dependency school, Frank did not claim to be a Marxist, although he acknowledged it as an influence.[4] In particular he drew a number of conclusions from the starting points established by Baran and Sweezy. First, repetition of the original transition to capitalism was impossible: "It is fruitless to expect the underdeveloped countries of today to repeat the stages of economic growth passed through by modern developed societies, whose classical capitalist development arose out of pre-capitalist and feudal society." It was also unnecessary, since the underdeveloped countries were already capitalist (albeit "underdeveloped") formations, by virtue of their participation in the world market.[5] The nearest equivalents to the European or North American bourgeois revolutions might appear to be the various Latin American civil wars between 1825 and 1860, but these were fought simply to establish the precise way in which the countries involved would be integrated into the world system; in effect they involved what Frank called a "lumpenbourgeois counter-revolution."[6] Frank therefore rejected—in my view, correctly—the notion that the contemporary bourgeois in these countries could be in any way "revolutionary": they had found a position for themselves within the system and had no material reason to challenge it. Consequently—and here we part company—the bearers of "historical progress" were instead that rather less specific group of beings collectively known as "the people." Equally problematic, Frank, like Baran and Sweezy, saw the solution for the underdeveloped countries in terms of individual national liberation, in this passage for the countries of Latin America: "Only by the destruction of the capitalist structure itself and the liberation of Brazil from the world imperialist–capitalist system as a whole—only by the rapid passage to socialism—is it possible to begin to solve the crisis and underdevelopment of Brazilian agriculture, Brazil, and Latin America."[7] Several critics pointed out, however, that the retreat from the world system into autarchy would, quite contrary to the wishes of those proposing such a course, reproduce precisely the features of socialism in one country that they found objectionable in the Stalinist regimes, as had happened for example in Cuba.[8] As Jairus Banaji wrote, such a policy "is tantamount to a program of isolationist state capitalism, and has nothing at all to do with the revolutionary interests of the working class, which at all stages are bound up with the world market and its further development."[9]

In one important respect, the position adopted by Wallerstein was infinitely more realistic than that of Frank. Although never entirely consistent, Wallerstein and his followers tended to see the Stalinist and semi-Stalinist regimes as being internally socialist, but rendered functionally capitalist by their participation in the world capitalist economy. As his colleague Christopher Chase-Dunn writes:

> The socialist states, like the earlier forms of socialist opposition (such as labor unions) arise as weapons of resistance to the logic of capitalism and they force capitalism to expand and reorganize itself. But eventually they become functional parts of the capitalist system rather than forces for its transformation. At least until now, the scale of the market system has expanded faster than the scale of those oppositional move-

ments that arise to socialize it.

The implications of this are that simply adding new "socialist" states in a piecemeal or "domino" strategy is unlikely to lead to a cumulative increase in the socialist content of the world economy. Chase-Dunn even goes so far as to claim that "a world-system composed of nation-states that are internally 'socialist' but that continue commodity production for exchange on the world market would not constitute a socialist mode of production."[10] Some critics of Wallerstein, such as Frank Fitzgerald, have accused him believing that "the world capitalist market . . . constrains socialist governments to behave as collective capitalists": "Without using the terminology, Wallerstein is a consistent advocate of the state capitalist thesis."[11] Unfortunately Wallerstein never attains the coherence of the state capitalist thesis, or at least of the version developed by Tony Cliff to which Fitzgerald refers. According to Wallerstein: "The fact that all enterprises are nationalized in [the Stalinist] countries does not make the participation of these enterprises in the world-economy one that does not conform to the mode of operation of a capitalist world market-system: seeking increased efficiency of production in order to realize a maximum price on sales, thus achieving a more favourable allocation of the surplus of the world economy."[12] In spite of the torturous sentence construction here it is clear that for Wallerstein, as for Chase-Dunn, the sole factor determining the capitalist nature of the so-called socialist countries is the insertion into the world market; in other words, through the process of circulation. The theory of state capitalism, to which we will return in chapter 19, takes as its starting point the process of competitive accumulation generated externally through geopolitical rivalry between state capitals, east and west, and expressed internally through social relations of production that involve wage labor and (state) capital. So far is Wallerstein from this perspective that at one point he even invokes the Great Proletarian Cultural Revolution—a title in which every single word is a lie—and the justification for it offered by Mao Tse-tung in support of his position:

> Mao is asserting that even if there is the achievement of political power (dictatorship of the proletariat) and economic transformation (abolition of the private ownership of the means of production), the revolution is still far from complete. . . . Mao Tse-tung is arguing for viewing "socialist society" as a process rather than structure. Like Frank and Sweezy . . . implicitly rather than explicitly, he is taking the world-system rather than the nation-state as the unit of analysis.[13]

Given the collapse of the majority of the Stalinist states and the embrace of the market by both their successors and China, the only major one still formally committed to "Marxism-Leninism" as an ideology, the argument is effectively over for the present, although it will undoubtedly surface again as soon as the possibility of socialist revolution reemerges on a global scale. The reason for raising this aspect of world-system theory, apparently far removed from our subject, is because Wallerstein regards the feudal states of the sixteenth century, like the nominally socialist states of the twentieth, as inherently capitalist through their participation in the world economy; indeed, he explicitly links the two:

> We have insisted that the modern world economy is, and can only be, a capitalist-world economy. It is for this reason that we have rejected the appellation of "feudalism" for the various forms of capitalist agriculture based on coercive labor which grew up in a world-economy. Furthermore . . . it is for the same reason that we . . . regard with great circumspection and prudence the claim that there exist in the twentieth century socialist national economies within the framework of the world-economy (as opposed to socialist movements controlling certain state-machineries within the world-economy).[14]

Like Frank, Wallerstein thinks that bourgeois revolutions are no longer necessary, but his position is also more extreme, and more directly relevant to our theme, in that he thinks bourgeois revolutions have *never* been necessary. Why not?

MARKETS AND THE SELF-TRANSFORMATION OF THE FEUDAL LORDS

For Wallerstein, bourgeois revolutions are not irrelevant because they failed to completely overthrow the feudal landed classes but because, long before these revolutions took place, the lords had already transformed themselves into capitalist landowners. Capitalism apparently arose because the existing class of lords made a conscious decision to transform the basis on which they exploited their tenants and laborers; but if they were already in such a commanding position, why did they feel the need to change? Wallerstein tends to argue that, rather than being a voluntaristic decision, it was a conscious response by the lords to the fourteenth-century crisis of feudalism, the social collapse that followed, and the adoption, by the oppressed and exploited, of ideologies hostile to lordly rule. The lords therefore changed the basis on which they extracted surplus value over an extended period lasting two centuries. By around 1650, however:

> The basic structures of historical capitalism as a viable social system had been established and consolidated. The trend towards egalitarianism of reward had been drastically reversed. The upper strata were once again in firm control politically and ideologically. . . . The image of historical capitalism having arisen via the overthrow of a backward aristocracy is wrong. Instead, the correct basic image is that historical capitalism was brought into existence by a landed aristocracy which transformed itself into a bourgeoisie because the old system was disintegrating. Rather than let the disintegration continue to uncertain ends, they engaged in radical structural surgery themselves in order to maintain *and significantly expand* their ability to exploit the direct producers.[15]

The key social actors are therefore the very class of feudal lords regarded as the enemy to be overthrown in the conventional model of bourgeois revolution. Although Wallerstein and his school do not deny the existence of a bourgeoisie proper, it is the self-transformation of the lords that is decisive, not the actions of the preexisting bourgeoisie: "To insist that France is primarily involved in a capitalist world-economy at this time [the seventeenth century] does not necessarily involve arguing, however, that the bourgeoisie wielded substantial political power. Obviously it did not. In Eastern Europe, the aristocrats were capitalist farmers and the indigenous commercial bourgeoisie was on the way to extinction."[16]

The nature of the capitalist world system that the lords are responsible for bringing into being is defined by the dominance of commercial relationships. Indeed, Wallerstein defines "the essential feature of the capitalist world economy" as "production for sale in a market in which the object is to realize the maximum profit."[17] Although wage labor certainly exists at the core, it is insertion into the world market that defines the system as a whole as capitalist, since productive relations in the periphery continue to include modified forms of slavery and serfdom, in addition to wage labor: "The point is that the 'relations of production' that define a system are the 'relations of production' of the whole system, and the system at this point in time is the European world-economy. Free labor is indeed a defining feature of capitalism, but not free labour throughout the productive enterprises."[18] According to Wallerstein, anyone who produces for the market can therefore be described as a capitalist: "Once [the world-economy] is capitalist, relationships that bear certain resemblances to feudal relationships are necessarily redefined in terms of the governing principles of a capitalist economy."[19]

The strengths of this position should not be underestimated. It treats the question—so important for Arno Mayer and those influenced by him—of whether the ruling classes possessed land and title or not as less significant than whether income from these sources was derived from feudal or capitalist methods of exploitation. It also gives due weight to the fact that the advanced nature of the "core" of the system is at least partly dependent on the enforced backwardness of the "periphery." But there are also problems with the theory, above all whether capitalism can be defined as the realization of profit through trade on the world market. Robert Brenner, who more than anyone else has placed this issue on the agenda, is therefore correct to draw attention to the problem with this definition:

> Now, there is no doubt that capitalism is a system in which production for a profit via exchange predominates. But does the opposite hold true? Does the appearance of widespread production for "profit in the market" signal the existence of capitalism, and more particularly a system in which, as a characteristic feature, "production is constantly expanded and men constantly innovate new ways of producing." Certainly not, because production for exchange is perfectly compatible with a system in which it is either unnecessary or impossible, or both, to reinvest in expanded improved production in order to "profit."[20]

There is no need to agree with Brenner's own extraordinarily narrow definition of capitalism to see that he has identified a real problem. As he pointed out, the argument that expansion of trade is the prime mover in generating capitalist development is often assumed to be that of Marx himself, but it is in fact derived from Adam Smith. Hence, despite their differences, Brenner can legitimately describe Sweezy, Frank, and Wallerstein all as "neo-Smithian" Marxists.[21]

What then was the nature of societies in the periphery? One attempt to define them, by Ernesto Laclau, involved arguing that "the world capitalist system . . . includes, *at the level of its definition*, various modes of production." In the context of the debate of the nature of the post-Columbian Americas, he argued that those, like Wallerstein, who regard these territories as having been capitalist from their absorption into the world market, "have constantly confused the two concepts of *the capitalist mode of production* and *participation in a world capitalist system*."[22] Perhaps surprisingly, given Laclau's Althusserian background, the Trotskyist Ernest Mandel took a similar position, writing "the capitalist world economy is an *articulated system of capitalist, semi-capitalist, and pre-capitalist relations of production linked to each other by capitalist relations of exchange and dominated by the capitalist world market*."[23] Frank himself latterly tended to oscillate between his original position and one proposed by Laclau.[24] Banaji defines these alternatives as "incorporation," where all pre-capitalist relations of production are labeled "capitalist" simply by production for the capitalist world market, and "dualism," where precapitalist relations of production retain a separate form but coexist with and are subordinated to capitalist relations of production, again where production is for the world market. The latter position is superior because it recognizes, for example, that plantation slave labor could not be described as capitalist simply because it produced cotton for the British textile industry; but it is also inadequate as plantation slave labor cannot be described as simply representing "the slave mode of production" either.

> An epoch whose historical tendency is given by the transformation of precapitalist into capitalist relations of production (hence also by primitive accumulation of capital) cannot simultaneously be one in which capitalism "coexists with," much less "maintains" or "intensifies" non-capitalist modes of production. Far from the penetration of capital occurring "on the basis of" precapitalist modes, it arises out of their dissolution—the proletarianization of the mass of independent producers.

The real issue here is a completely formalist understanding of what wage labor involves. Both Frank and Laclau (and Mandel) see it as "free" labor in the marketplace; but the real definition of wage labor is that which provides labor-power for capital, a process that can take a number of forms:

> Either one sticks to the dead formalism which defines wage-labor not in terms of the relation of *living* labor to *capital* but through images derived from the sphere of circulation . . . and in this case capitalism is exonerated of the massive brutalities which it inflicted on mankind prior to the birth of the modern working class (modern industry) and of the society shaped by its struggles. Or one accepts that capitalism is compatible with the most brutal and barbaric forms of labor, that wage-labor, labor which produces capital, can take a series of unfree forms implying various degrees of coercion and bondage.[25]

The "dissolution" of pre-capitalist modes of production and the reconstitution of labor on a capitalist basis, whatever the specific form, did not take place immediately. One of the difficulties of Banaji's otherwise impressive discussion is an uncertainty about the historical period by which this occurred. As Michael Haynes has noted, the economies that emerged in colonial Latin America immediately after 1492 were "complex transitional forms" produced by uneven development: "They are not totally subordinate to the dictates of the full cycle of capital reproduction because the system is weak and as yet partially formed."[26] In this respect they were comparable to forms that were to be found in parts of Europe, as Robert Duplessis highlights: "The slave agriculture of the Americas resembled eastcentral European neoserfdom in that both fused the raising of commodities for the market with coercive productive relations, resulting in economic systems that were neither fully capitalist nor wholly seigniorial."[27] There was still a transition to be undergone, in other words, but the central point is correct: these societies became capitalist not because they produced for the world market but because production was carried out by wage labor for capital under conditions of competitive accumulation.

The question of the bourgeois revolution is not, however, rendered irrelevant simply by the existence of capitalism. Societies in Latin America and Eastern Europe were clearly very backward forms of capitalism and politically dominated by the more advanced countries, sometimes directly, sometimes not (this is the basis in reality of the distinction between "colonial" and "semi-colonial" popularized by the Comintern). The issue here is therefore one of the state. Where a country was still colonized by another, or where the existing, nominally independent, state was incapable of developing capitalism beyond a certain point, then bourgeois revolution was still on the agenda—although by the twentieth century the possibility had arisen of it being overtaken by permanent revolution. From a socialist perspective, Frank was therefore right to argue that the stages strategies typical of the Communist parties in Latin America were irrelevant; the difficulty, as suggested above, is what Frank conceived to be socialism.

In relation to the historical events known as bourgeois revolutions, supporters of capitalist world-system theory want to dissociate them from the ascendancy of capitalism. Teshale Tibebu once asked whether "bourgeois revolution [is] necessary for the development of capitalism." He answered that, since capitalism can only survive as a global system: "There was only one 'Original Sin,' only one transition, only one 'bourgeois revolution'—the rise of the capitalist world-economy in the sixteenth century. What came after that is a history of incorporation."[28]

But the rise of a particular mode of production is even less of a revolution than the combination of economic and political events proposed by Thompson in his concept of "the great arch" of English history. Wallerstein himself continues to use the term, "bourgeois revolution," but it has lost all relation to the creation of a capitalist world economy: "The bourgeois revolution would come in 1789, at another epoch, for another purpose, and in some ways too late." Too late for what? "By then, the world economy had evolved and it would be too late for France to achieve primacy within it."[29] In this respect, Wallerstein also accepts the revisionist case. At one point he seems prepared to consider the Dutch Revolt under this heading: "To begin with, was it a revolution? And if it was a revolution, was it a national revolution or a bourgeois revolution? And is there any difference between these two concepts? . . . It seems to me that this question is no more ambiguous (and to be sure no more clear) in the case of the Netherlands 'Revolution' than in the case of any of the other great 'revolutions' of the modern era."

His conclusion was that: "The significance of the Netherlands Revolution is not that it established a model of national liberation." Was it a bourgeois revolution then? Wallerstein cannot quite bring himself to concede the point, but this appears to be what he is describing: "The importance lies in the economic impact on the European world-economy. The Netherlands Revolution liberated a force that could sustain the world-system as a system over some difficult years of adjustment, until the English and the French) were ready to take the steps necessary for its definitive consolidation."[30] In effect, Wallerstein is prepared to at least countenance that the Dutch Revolt might be a bourgeois revolution precisely because it took place before the consolidation of the world economy. This is not true in the case of the other "classic" bourgeois revolutions. For him, "there was no significant difference between England and France in the whole period of around 1500 to 1800." Insofar as there were struggles near the top of society, they were between sections of the same class, and "this was as true of the Glorious Revolution of 1688–1689 as it was of the revolution of 1640; and it was true of the Fronde as well, and even of the French Revolution of 1789": "We must do away with the ahistorical idea that the bourgeoisie and the aristocracy were two radically different groups, particularly in this period of time. They were two heavily overlapping social groups that took on different contours depending on whether one defined the dominant stratum in terms of social status or in terms of social class. It made a lot of difference which definition was used. The social and political struggles were real, but they were internal to the ruling strata."[31] The struggle between aristocracy and bourgeoisie, in so far as it existed at all, was a "diversion" in both senses: "fun and games; and a displacement of the attention of others, in this case, the peasants and the sans-culottes."[32] This was written of the French Revolution and "fun and games" is certainly an interesting new way of viewing, say, the September Massacres or the Battle of Valmy. In fact, later in the same book Wallerstein gives three reasons for why the French Revolution was important but not bourgeois:

> First, it was a relatively conscious attempt by a diverse group of the French ruling capitalist strata to force through urgently needed reforms of the French state in light of the perceived British leap forward to hegemonic status in the world-economy. . . .
> Second, the Revolution created the circumstances of a breakdown of public order sufficient to give rise to the first significant antisystemic (that is, anti-capitalist) movement in the history of the modern world-system, that of the French "popular masses."

. . . Third, the revolution provided the much needed shock to the modern world-system as a whole to bring the cultural-ideological sphere at last into line with the economic and political reality.[33]

Insofar as Wallerstein is concerned with the French ruling classes, he draws on the work of revisionists from Cobban to Furet who deny that they were divided on socioeconomic terms; insofar as he is concerned with the popular masses, he draws on the work of radicals like Guérin who claim that they were primarily involved in a struggle with the bourgeoisie. The popular masses themselves, above all the peasantry, were of course convinced that feudalism was their principal enemy. Wallerstein follows his great influence Fernand Braudel, in arguing that they had in fact misidentified their adversary. The seigniorial reaction in the latter half of the eighteenth century to raise the level of peasant exploitation in France was not "a return to tradition," but a yielding to "capitalist temptation," at least in certain areas like the Northeast: "Might it not be thought that it was at least because the language of capitalism had not found the vocabulary to handle a new and surprising situation, that the French peasant reverted to the familiar language of anti-feudalism?"[34] The key general significance of the French Revolution for Wallerstein is however the third one he lists, the realm of ideology: "The French Revolution marked neither basic economic nor basic political transformation. Rather, [it] was, in terms of the capitalist world-economy, the moment when the ideological superstructure finally caught up with the economic base. It was the consequence of the transition, not its cause nor the moment of its occurrence."[35]

Regrettably, the "capitalist" nobilities of Europe failed to understand the great service of ideological clarification that the French bourgeoisie were performing for them.

The notion that bourgeois revolutions can be reduced to ideological struggles between different capitalist groups has gained traction outside the ranks of the capitalist world-system theorists. Take for example John Ashworth's outstanding two-volume work on the origins of the American Civil War, an important attempt to deal with the sources of the conflict in explicitly Marxist terms. His first volume traces the growing divergence between North and South and concludes by anticipating the outcome of their antagonism: "The result would be war, emancipation, social upheaval—and the consolidation of capitalist relations of production in the United States. In other words the result would be a bourgeois revolution."[36] Yet in his second volume, an element of ambiguity enters. Ashworth shifts his focus from consequences of the war ("the consolidation of capitalist relations of production") to the motivations of those who defended the Union, highlighting in particular their ideological support for wage labor and opposition to slavery: "Slavery was criticised, condemned, and finally destroyed in the United States essentially because by the norms of northern society it was increasingly unacceptable. These were the norms of northern free-labor society, one characterised by 'bourgeois social relations,' as they are often termed, with wage labor at their core."[37]

According to Ashworth, in economic terms the North was not in crisis before the war (although there was a high level of internal class struggle) and the further development of industrial capitalism would not have been constrained by the continued existence of agrarian slavery in the South, however much of an abomination many Northerners found it. Indeed, as far as the South itself was concerned, conditions after the war were scarcely more advantageous to capitalism than before—a situation that would take decades to overcome. The triumph of the bourgeois revolution in the United States was therefore coextensive with the ascendancy on a national scale of a hitherto sectional ideology encapsulated in the prewar Republican Party slogan of free soil, free labor, and free men.

Not all capitalist world-system theorists share a totally dismissive attitude toward bourgeois revolutions. James Blaut, for example, was prepared to acknowledge the significance of the "Glorious Revolution" in 1688 as a "symbol" of the political triumph of capitalism in Holland and England.[38] In his view, however, this was only possible on the basis of an earlier date, namely 1492, symbolizing in its turn the beginning of the colonial domination of the Americas and then the entire non-European world. Without what he calls "colonial capital," "the sluggish late-medieval economy of pre-1492 days would have continued its slow progress out of feudalism and towards capitalism (or something like capitalism), but there would have been no Seventeenth-Century Bourgeois Revolution."[39] However, on the basis of the "accumulation of wealth from the mines and plantations of America and from trade in Asia and Africa" on the one hand, and "the huge enlargement of markets outside of western Europe" on the other, a new political process was able to take place: "This, the bourgeois revolution, allowed the emerging capitalist class-community to mobilize state power towards its further rise, such that the entire society contributed to the underwriting of colonial adventures and to the preparation of infrastructure such as cities and roads, while the state's police and military power could now be mobilized to force people off the land and into wage work, and to conscript people and resources for advantageous wars abroad."[40] As will become apparent in the context of this argument over the Global South, the dangers of a definition of capitalism based exclusively on the existence of that world market are not exhausted in relation to history since the sixteenth century.

ABOLISHING MODES OF PRODUCTION

One argument that has emerged from the fragments of capitalist world-system theory is that a world market and, by implication, capitalism, has existed since the previous millennium at least. According to veteran anthropologist and former Marxist Jack Goody:

> What the Eurocentric historians do not allow for is the occurrence of "bourgeois revolutions" led by merchants and by "professionals" (specialists whose work depended on written procedures, such as lawyers, doctors, teachers) in other parts of the world

that had seen mercantile expansion. . . . Goitein, the great historian of the medieval Jewish communities of the Geniza in the Cairo of the eighth and ninth centuries, writes of a "bourgeois revolution." It was marked by the presence of the scholar-merchant, who sought both knowledge and fortune, spreading down both lines of communication, between North and South and between East and West.[41]

Elsewhere in the same work Goody claims that these processes were not confined to the Near East but were also present in China, so often regarded as the epitome of unchanging stagnation. It is true, Goody writes, that "the dominant ideology despised trade, yet the mercantile economy grew under its own impetus and gradually changed the whole socio-cultural system": "This was the 'bourgeois revolution' that was not confined to one part of the world, for all operated in a world economy."[42]

Frank also accepts that the rise of the West was made possible by the Global South, or more specifically, Asia.[43] For in his later writings even Wallerstein is too Eurocentric, even Blaut makes too many concessions to the notion of bourgeois revolutions constituting a break. Following Tibebu, he argues that both the bourgeois and proletarian revolutions are "imaginary," both examples of "wishful thinking," but: "So are, I submit, both transitions [from feudalism to capitalism and from capitalism to socialism]."[44] The implications of this are that: the Asiatic mode of production did not exist, there is nothing exceptional about European development, a world economy has existed since circa 5000 BC, and consequently there is no significant break in world history in or around 1492. He notes that his former world-system colleagues can accept the first two, or even—in the case of Braudel—the first three, but not the fourth: "Yet all four of these conclusions inexorably render questionable to say the least the very concept of a 'capitalist mode of production' and the supposed significance of its alleged spread from Europe to the rest of the world." And if there is no transition to capitalism, if indeed there have been no fundamental transitions at any time in history of civilization, then what need is there for the notion of "mode of production"? As Frank says, "this received conceptualization has continued to divert our attention away from the much more significant world systemic structure and processes, which themselves engendered the organizational forms that were then misleadingly termed 'feudal' and 'capitalist' modes of production.'"[45] The same point has been made, rather more elegantly, by Goody, who writes in relation to capitalism that, given the universal existence throughout history of "widespread mercantile activity": "Can we not therefore dispense with this pejorative term drawn from nineteenth-century Britain and recognize the element of continuity in the market and in bourgeois activities from the Bronze Age until modern times?"[46] His alternative is evolutionary:

> But supposing the development of human society from the Bronze Age is regarded in different terms, as an ongoing elaboration of urban and mercantile culture without any sharp breaks involving categorical distinctions of the kind suggested by the use of the term "capitalist." . . . If "capitalism" is seen as characterizing all these societies,

its uniqueness inevitably disappears and so too does the problem of explanation. One is left with explaining increasing intensity, with elaboration rather than categorical change. Indeed, the situation might be clarified by the abandonment of the term "capitalism" altogether, since its use will always tend to suggest some kind of long-term, privileged position for the West.[47]

There is a certain logic at work here. If markets have operated for as long as civilization, defining capitalism as coextensive with them can only end in similarly detecting the existence of capitalism throughout human history. However, if it has existed throughout history, clearly it has no separate existence from that history and might well be seen as constitutive of it; it certainly does not need to be identified by a distinct name—but neither, of course, do any other modes of production, the existence of which must similarly be in doubt. Wallerstein may deny being a Smithian, but some of his more extreme cothinkers have taken the process of naturalizing capitalism-as-commercial-markets much further than even Smith. And here again we simply encounter an understanding of capitalism that can be traced back to the Marginalist counterrevolution in economic thought, where capitalism is posited as an eternal if sometimes suppressed aspect of human existence. The other attempt to find an alternative to bourgeois revolution in the prior process of the transition has followed an entirely different and opposite path.

18

"CAPITALIST SOCIAL PROPERTY RELATIONS"

The second alternative approach that I want to consider is associated with political Marxism and above all with the work of Robert Brenner. In the chapters dealing with Marx and Engels we saw how writers belonging to this theoretical tendency opposed the concept of bourgeois revolution and claimed Marx had effectively abandoned it by the late 1850s. In purely negative terms, therefore, their position overlaps with that of the capitalist world-system theorists. Like Wallerstein, Brenner treats bourgeois revolution as irrelevant and does so for essentially the same reasons, namely that capitalist development—albeit confined to a much more limited number of countries than those that constitute Wallerstein's "core"—occurred prior to and independently of the events that are usually described in this way. Like Wallerstein, Brenner sees the self-transformation of feudal lords as a key moment in the development of capitalism, although he sees this as taking place across a single country rather than the world system as a whole. Unlike Wallerstein, however, Brenner does not see the mechanism by which capitalist development occurs as being the expansion of trade and commerce but rather the introduction of a distinctive set of "capitalist social property relations," the term he uses in place of the more conventional Marxist concept of "capitalist relations of production." The two are by no means synonymous. As Brenner explains, he prefers the former for two reasons:

> First, the term social relations of production is sometimes taken to convey the idea that the social structural framework in which production takes place is somehow determined by production itself, i.e., the form of cooperation or organization of the labor process. This I think is disastrously misleading. Second, I think it is necessary not only to lay bare the structuring or constraining effects of *vertical* class, or surplus extraction, relations between exploiters and direct producers, which is generally what is meant by social relations of production. It is, if anything, even more critical to bring out of the structuring or constraining effects of the *horizontal* relationships among the exploiters themselves and of the direct producers themselves.[1]

Brenner is clearly right to emphasize the multiple levels of oppression, cooperation, and competition involved in social relations of production; but as we shall see in due course, his replacement of the word "production" with "property" involves a fundamental shift in how Marxists—not least Marx himself—have understood the way in which these relations emerged. For the moment, it is enough to note that Brenner regards capitalist social property relations to be so distinctive that, rather than encompassing the entire world by the sixteenth century, as capitalism does for Wallerstein, they were still restricted to a handful of territories even a hundred years later. Where Wallerstein is broad, Brenner is narrow.

I regard the Brenner thesis as by far the more serious of the two alternatives to the theory of bourgeois revolution. No attempt to construct a defensible version of the theory can avoid responding to the challenge it poses. I think the thesis is wrong, but in a stimulating and productive way that has forced even those of us who disagree with it to think rather more seriously than we might otherwise have done about the very nature of capitalism. Discussion of the thesis is, however, complicated by two factors. One is that Brenner's work is not entirely consistent. Although he and his followers deny it, there seems to be a disjunction between his discussion of the differential class bases of agrarian society in early modern Europe, which began the "Brenner debate," and his work on merchant involvement in the English Civil War. (Interestingly, the former is a synthesis of secondary materials; the latter is mainly based on primary research.) The other is that there is far from complete unanimity among the self-proclaimed political Marxists who follow Brenner—George Comninel, Charles Post, Benno Teschke, and Ellen Meiksins Wood—who in many respects have taken more extreme positions than Brenner himself. We cannot hold Brenner directly responsible for every interpretation they have made of his original thesis, or even assume that he is necessarily in agreement with all of them. In what follows, I will therefore try to distinguish between Brenner's own positions, those that are common to the entire school, and those that are held by individual members. When discussing positions common to political Marxism, I will take Wood as their representative. Despite my extensive disagreements with her, over this issue at least, she writes with a clarity and comprehensibility that is all too rare among Marxist academics. She also has a helpful tendency to take Brenner's arguments to extremes in ways that reveal their inner logic.

Perhaps more than any other Marxist tendency since Althusserianism, a rival body of thought that—as we shall see—it resembles to a surprising degree, political Marxism claims to have discovered a unique insight into the meaning of Marx's writings, a meaning undisclosed to previous generations of Marxists and perhaps even to Marx himself. I regard these claims as wholly illusionary, but they have been accepted by people who fail to understand the extremity of what is implied. If the Brenner thesis—and certainly the version associated with Wood—is correct, then any aspirations we may have for a socialist future are solely dependent on the outcome of the voluntarist clash of class wills. It is possible that they are right and

Marx was wrong. We should be clear, however, that these are incompatible positions, and that if Marx had held the positions that political Marxism ascribes to him, then he would effectively have abandoned not merely the less precise early formulations found in, for example, *The German Ideology*, but the entire theoretical basis of historical materialism.

THE BRENNER THESIS

In the essay that began the entire Brenner debate, "Agrarian Class Structure and Economic Development in Pre-industrial Europe" (1976), Brenner attempted to demonstrate, in my view successfully, the inadequacies of the demographic and commercialization models that he identified as the two dominant explanations for capitalist economic development.[2] It is important to be aware of the extent of the claims that Brenner makes in relation to the latter, especially in his subsequent essays. In effect, Brenner argues that virtually *all* Marxist interpretations of the transition to capitalism prior to his own, from the early Marx to Sweezy and from Sweezy to Wallerstein, are either open or hidden variations on the commercialization model, in that they look to the expansion of trade and commerce as the external "prime mover" in the development of capitalism.

The very few exceptions are, however, deficient in other ways. Brenner acknowledged a debt to Maurice Dobb, an early opponent of the commercialization thesis for whom the class struggle plays an important role in the development of capitalism, and several writers have simply treated Brenner's work as updating, although perhaps simplifying, Dobb's position.[3] In fact, Brenner has made clear that he did not regard Dobb's explanation as adequate.[4] Dobb argued that, in England, increased exactions by the lords during the crisis of the fourteenth century provoked a level of peasant militancy that ended serfdom and allowed a class of small producers and yeoman farmers to emerge. These groups then evolved into capitalists in response to the opportunity presented by the removal of feudal dominance. A capitalist class therefore coexisted with its feudal opponent until the bourgeois revolution of 1640–60 resolved the contest in favor of the former.[5] For Brenner these claims are open to two major criticisms. On the one hand, Dobb offers no motivation for peasants who had been freed from serfdom to transform themselves into capitalists since they were under no compulsion to do so: Dobb simply assumes that this transformation was inevitable given certain conditions. On the other hand, Brenner argues that feudalism no longer existed anywhere in England by 1640 and could therefore scarcely have been overthrown by the bourgeoisie after that date. Capitalism had emerged from somewhere in the three hundred years between the fourteenth-century crisis and the opening of the English Civil War, but from where?[6] In order to answer this question, we need to return to Brenner's premises.

Brenner argues that "modern economic growth," the systematic growth associated with capitalism and with no other exploitative mode of production, only takes place when two conditions are satisfied. One is that the direct producers are separated from both their means of production and their means of subsistence, and therefore have no alternative but to satisfy their needs by recourse to the market. The other is that the exploiters can no longer sustain themselves by simply intensifying extra-economic pressure on the direct producers, but instead have to increase their efficiency. Unlike in precapitalist economic formations, both sides are compelled to be competitive, most importantly by cutting costs. Without these conditions there is no incentive for either class to innovate. Any direct producers who attempted to introduce new techniques would meet resistance from their fellow agriculturalists who would regard it as a breach of collective solidarity. Any exploiters who attempted to introduce new techniques would require a labor force motivated to adopt them and, in its absence, they would be more likely to invest instead in more effective methods of coercion. Even if new methods were successfully adopted by individuals of either class, there is no reason to expect that they would be adopted by anybody else, not least because technical advances introduced once and for all do not themselves bring economic development or the compulsion to innovate with a view to reducing costs. Brenner is of course aware that, for example, peasants adopted more efficient ploughs from the eleventh century onward, but denies that this had any significant impact on social relations because community control resisted systematic improvement, specialization, and market dependence. "The only significant method by which the feudal economy could achieve real growth was by opening up new land for cultivation."[7] Nor was the situation different in the towns, since they were also unable to act as spontaneous generators of capitalism: "their potential for growth was strictly limited because urban industry was almost entirely dependent upon lordly demand (as subsistence-oriented peasants had only limited ability to make market purchases) and lordly demand was itself limited by the size of agricultural surplus, which was in turn constrained by the limited growth potential of the agrarian productive forces."[8]

How could this closed circuit, in which the same feudal relations of production are endlessly reproduced according to a given set of "rules," ever be broken? In the case of peasant communities where the means of production were collectively owned, Brenner thinks that they would never have been. Where peasants possessed the means of production individually, he proposes three possible alternatives, all unintended consequences of actions designed to produce quite other results. First, peasants could lose land through selling it or through demographic growth. Second, the lords could increase the level of surplus extraction to such an extent that peasants could no longer pay their rent or, if they could pay it, could no longer retain enough produce for their own subsistence. Third, the lords might be forced to expropriate those peasants who had asserted their independence to such an extent that they were virtually defining themselves as owners, not merely in effective possession. From the enormous difficulties involved in subverting feudal "rules for reproduction," Brenner draws two conclusions: "The first is that pre-capitalist economies have an internal logic and solidity which should not be underestimated. The second is that capitalist economic development is perhaps an historically more limited, surprising and peculiar phenomenon than is often appreciated."[9] If Brenner is right, peasant small production could have carried on almost indefinitely beneath the surface of precapitalist social structures had it not been for the unhappy accident that gave rise to capitalism. What was the nature of this apparently unfortunate series of events?

Recall the two sets of economic actors that Brenner claims must be present and compelled to accumulate capital: an exploited class of direct producers who are forced to sustain themselves through the market and an exploiting class of property owners who cannot sustain themselves through forcible extraction of a surplus. In England, both classes become simultaneously subject to these conditions. Following the non-Marxist historian Lawrence Stone, Brenner argues that, by the accession of the Tudor dynasty in 1485, non-economic coercion was of declining significance to the English lords, since the peasantry were no longer subject to the serfdom that required it and, in the aftermath of the Wars of the Roses, an exhausted nobility faced a strengthened state that would no longer tolerate magnate insubordination. But they could increase their incomes through the exploitation of their lands, or more precisely, the exploitation of commercial tenants who increasingly came to occupy their lands.[10] We are offered an explanation here for why the lords were increasingly compelled to turn to systematic commercialization of their estates, but what allowed the peasants to abolish serfdom while preventing them from successfully resisting when the lords attempted to turn them into commercial tenants? Brenner has a twofold answer to this question, both of which involve comparisons with nations that did not take the road to capitalist development at the same time as England.

The first part concerns different outcomes of the class struggle in Eastern and Western Europe. After the period of demographic collapse during the second half of the fourteenth century, the lords attempted to discipline a numerically reduced peasantry that was consequently in a much stronger bargaining position. Successful peasant resistance to these impositions permanently ended serfdom in Western Europe, but failed to do so in Eastern Europe, where it was either reimposed in areas where it had been weakened or imposed for the first time in areas that had previously escaped subjugation. Brenner later added a further regional variant across the Ottoman Empire in southeastern Europe, which from the mid-fourteenth century abolished the existing feudal aristocracies and replaced them with a centralized tax-raising state. The relationship of the bureaucracy to the peasantry shifted over time in response to the external pressures on the Ottomans. At first, the state reduced the extractive burden on the cultivators while guaranteeing them possession; on the other hand, while this contributed to the essentially subsistence character of agriculture and the block to systematic political accumulation, such as was undertaken by the feudal classes elsewhere in Europe. What Brenner calls a "command economy in grain" exercised to ensure food supplies to the cities, acted as a disincentive to the peasants to expand production. Ultimately, state officials began to increase levels of exploitation of the peasantry in response to two needs. First, to pay for militias to replace the increasingly obsolescent cavalry upon which the Ottoman state had hitherto relied. Second, as the empire reached its territorial limits, the officials who had previously been able to rely on the spoils of expansion now turned inward, to extort these from the existing subjects. In short, by around 1600, this region had reached the same developmental impasse as the rest of Eastern Europe, albeit through a different route. Brenner rejects the relative weight of the urban sector as the main explanation for the divergence between East and West.[11] Instead he identifies another factor as decisive: "The development of peasant solidarity and strength in Western Europe—especially as this was manifested in the peasant's organization at the level of the village—appears to have been far greater in western than in eastern Europe; and this superior institutionalization of the peasant's class power in the west may have been central to its superior ability to resist seigniorial reaction." But outcomes were by no means uniform even within Western Europe.[12]

The second part of his answer identifies the source of this further divergence as the extent to which the various peasantries of Western Europe were able to retain possession of the land won during the late feudal revolts from actual or potential exploiters:

> This is not to say that such outcomes were arbitrary, but rather that they tended to be bound up with certain historically specific patterns of the development of the contending agrarian classes and their relative strength in the different European societies: their relative levels of internal solidarity, their self consciousness and organisation, and their general political resources—especially their relationships to the non-agricultural classes (in particular, potential urban class allies) and to the state (in particular, whether or not the state developed as a class-like competitor of the lords for the peasants surplus).[13]

It is the last point that is crucial for Brenner in explaining the difference between England and France. The English feudal state was centralized, but not in the sense that it drew in power from the periphery. It was established with the consent of the feudal ruling class and largely ruled in alliance with it. As a result its power was less than the French state, which centralized later on an absolutist basis and in opposition to the individual interests of the lords. In England, the absolutist project was aborted, leaving the peasants free from the burden of state taxation, but also without protection from the lords: "It was the English lord's inability either to re-enserf the peasants or to move in the direction of absolutism (as had their French counterparts), which forced them in the long run to seek novel ways out of their revenue crisis."[14] In France, "the centralised state appears to have developed (at least in large part) as a class-like phenomenon—that is as an independent extractor of the surplus, in particular on the basis of its arbitrary power to tax the land."[15] The very success of the French peasantry in resisting the power of the lords left them exposed as potential sources of taxation by a much more powerful opponent—the absolutist state—which was in competition with the lords for surplus that the peasants produced. Paradoxically, however, the French state also protected the peasants from lordly impositions, in rather the same way as a farmer protects his chickens from the fox. The English lords, constrained by neither peasant ownership nor absolutist restriction, were able to consolidate their lands in the interest of economies of scale by forcing some peasants to accept competitive leases. Those peasants who were unsuccessful in gaining leases were either compelled to become wage laborers for now-capitalist farmers or to leave the land altogether in search of work elsewhere. In both cases their labor power had become a commodity to be bought and sold on the market. But England is not the only country or region in Western Europe in which Brenner claims capitalist social property relations were successfully established. There are two others.

The one to which Brenner has devoted the most attention is the Northern Low Countries (roughly equivalent to present-day Netherlands, the name that I will use from now on). In his response to the original debate, Brenner followed Jan de Vries in noting that, in the absence of both peasants and lords, Dutch agriculture had been characterized virtually from the beginning by competition, internal class differentiation, and specialization. He also noted, in a separate context, that because of its integration into the European feudal markets, the Dutch economy as a whole was, unlike the English, unable to continue expanding during the crisis of the seventeenth century.[16] The latter point is not particularly controversial and has been made by a number of writers who by no means share all or indeed any of Brenner's views.[17] It was the former that seemed to contradict his overall thesis; but Brenner had an explanation. In the case of the Netherlands the decisive factor leading to capitalist social relations was not the outcome of class struggle but peasant interaction with the environment. These maritime regions are ecologically unique in Europe. In the medieval period, before alternative occupations were available, peasants were forced to reclaim land from the sea and then protect it through a network of dykes and ditches in order to farm at all. Not unexpectedly, feudal lords were not particularly interested in laying claim to territories that required such effort to make viable. As a result, lordship tended to involve the assertion of juridical authority rather than actual tenurial relationships with the peasants and by the fourteenth century even this had largely been abandoned. Essentially, the peasants had transformed themselves into independent, self-sufficient small farmers. However, the very transformation of their environment had an unintended consequence. The reclaimed peat marshes were subject to subsidence—an effect of oxidization that reduced the land available for cultivation to such an extent that farmers were no longer able to provide for their own subsistence. As a result they were forced to turn to the market in order to sustain themselves. The Golden Age of the Dutch peasantry had coincided with the period of maximum oppression for the peasantry elsewhere in Western Europe. From the late fourteenth century, as the Western

European peasantry entered its own Golden Age of relative freedom, the Dutch peasantry entered a phase of ecologically determined crisis. To put it as starkly as possible, in order to afford to buy the bread they could no longer produce for themselves, they had to sell other goods: cattle, dairy, and grain for the growing beer industry. Some were unable to do this and had to leave the land to survive—in other words to become fully-fledged proletarians in the towns. In the Southern Low Countries, which had an evolution similar to Western Europe as a whole, farmers entered market relations in order to supplement or maintain income levels, but the northern farmers had to specialize to survive. Eventually the crisis led to the formation of large farm units that alone could provide the basis for long-term investment and economies of scale. Holland therefore possessed a capitalist farming sector in the countryside alongside urban industries with plentiful supplies of labor at relatively low wages, although sustainable because of comparably low food prices made possible by the import of cheap grain from Eastern Europe.[18]

In both the English and Dutch cases, the decisive moment for Brenner in the formation of a capitalist economy is where both peasants and (where they exist) lords are forced to turn to the market, not as a supplement to their income, or as a means of acquiring nonessential goods, but as the principal means of survival. "Market dependence" is therefore the defining feature of the "capitalist social property relations," which in turn are constitutive of the capitalist mode of production. Some of his supporters are unhappy with the addition of Holland to the pantheon of endogenous capitalist development. Wood has accused Brenner of not being sufficiently consistent in upholding his own thesis, writing that "in his analysis of economic developments in the Low Countries, [Brenner] has perhaps departed from, or at least not elaborated enough, his own insights on the nature and consequences of market dependence as a social-property relation." She asks: "At what point does a quantitative difference become a qualitative one? For that matter, precisely how does the economic logic of the Dutch farmer differ from that of craft producers, even more dependent on the market for their basis food needs, in a commercial centre like Renaissance Italy?"[19]

Wood is evidently concerned to avoid the discovery of capitalist social property relations in other areas, since the more examples multiply the less credible appear claims for their exceptional nature. Given their nervousness about recognizing capitalism anywhere else but England, it is surprising that Brenner's supporters do not appear to have noticed that the third area that Brenner himself claims has experienced capitalist development poses greater problems for the thesis than even the United Netherlands.

Catalonia was one of the three principalities of Aragon that combined with Castile to form the Spanish monarchy in 1469. In "Agrarian Class Structure and Economic Development in Pre-Industrial Europe" Brenner followed Pierre Vilar in pointing out that of all peasant movements the late fifteenth-century *remensas* revolt in Catalonia which effectively ended serfdom in that region was simultaneously the best organized, the least dependent on urban support and, ultimately, the most successful, in that it saw the formal abolition of serfdom and the legal recognition of freehold rights over the land. What emerged at the end of the fifteenth century was an "equally capitalist system" to that of England, but involving large-scale owner cultivation using wage labor without the intermediation of tenant farmers. On this basis Catalan capitalist farmers were able to increase productivity to the extent that they avoided the economic crisis of the seventeenth century and the resulting demographic collapse. In the latter respect Catalonia resembled England far more than it did Holland.[20] Why was Catalonia able to make the transition? Brenner has not returned to the subject in any detail, but in a later essay he implies that the answers lie in the form of the state. Catalonia—again, like England—had a strong monarchical system in which the crown collaborated with the local lords and did not need to protect the peasantry from them in an attempt to establish its own tax base.[21] Catalonia therefore seems to have occupied a position that combined characteristics of both England (cooperation between crown and lords) and France (a peasantry with secure possession of the land). Catalan constitutional autonomy, which survived incorporation into the Spanish kingdom, was ultimately suppressed in 1714 with the accession of the Bourbons and the final consolidation of the centralized absolutist state.[22] Yet none of these changed political circumstances acted to retard Catalan development or prevented it from becoming the first and, for many years, the only area in Spain to undergo industrialization.[23] How did market compulsion come into effect in Catalonia? It would be open to Brenner to argue that the significance of Catalan capitalism was limited because, unlike England, it failed to achieve statehood, or because, like Holland, it was tied to the surrounding feudal environment; but neither of these points explains how it came into existence in the first place. Jaime Torras has argued that capitalist development began in Catalonia before the *remensas* revolt, that it did not subsequently depend on the extent of large-scale farming, which Brenner in any case exaggerates, and that much of the impetus for capitalist development came not from the rural but the urban sector; the experience of Catalonia does not, in other words, support his thesis.[24]

Despite their suspicion of claims for indigenous capitalist development anywhere other than England, political Marxists have been prepared to accept one other case: the northern states of the United States of America, in the aftermath of the American Revolution. Post writes:

> The unintended consequences of closing off access to free or inexpensive land on the frontier, levying burdensome taxes, and enforcing the payment of debt in gold and silver, was the transformation of the conditions under which farmers in the North obtained, expanded, and maintained landed property. The burdens of mortgages, taxes, and debts ensured that Northern farmers marketed both their surplus and portions of their subsistence-output. Put simply, northern-US farmers became dependent upon successful market-production for their economic survival—they became agrarian petty-commodity producers who had to specialize output, accumulate land and capital, and introduce new tools and methods in order to obtain, maintain, and expand

landed property. . . . As rural households became dependent on the market for their economic survival, Northern agriculture became a massive home-market for industrially produced capital- and consumer-goods, sparking the US industrial revolution in the nineteenth century. In sum, *the transformation of social-property relations in Northern agriculture led to the shift from extensive growth to intensive development—the development of capitalism—in the US-North.*[25]

But what was the role of the class struggle in these developments? According to Post, it was primarily initiated by merchants and speculators through the state:

> In the 1780s and 1790s, the merchants, with the support of the planters after Shays's Rebellion, constructed state-institutions and a standing army that was capable of enforcing their legal claims to landed property—not in order to establish capitalist production, but to allow themselves to reproduce themselves as buyers and sellers of land. The unintended consequence of the speculator's successful struggle to enforce legal titles on land—the creation of a monopoly of land—was to fundamentally alter the conditions under which Northern households obtained, maintained, and expanded landholdings.[26]

The key phrase here, as it is in Brenner's own explanation for the emergence of capitalist social property relations in England and the Netherlands, is "unintended consequences." I will return to these issues below, but regardless of the criticisms that I will subsequently make, it should be clear that the Brenner thesis is an intellectual achievement remarkable for its internal consistency and explanatory power. If elements of the thesis are less original than some of Brenner's more adulatory supporters appear to realize, it is also true that these elements have never before been brought together into such a coherent synthesis.[27] Originality may in any case be an overrated virtue in these days of instant revisionism. What is more important is that Brenner and his followers have rightly challenged several positions that Marxists have carelessly adopted in common with their intellectual opponents.

One of these is the assumption that capitalism is somehow innate, always existing in some subordinate form and only waiting to be released from feudal or other constraints. Many Marxists make this assumption by default through their inability to explain how capitalism comes into existence, thus inadvertently aligning themselves with the position of Adam Smith and his contemporaries, for whom the emergence of capitalism is, in Brenner's own words, "human nature reassert[ing] itself."[28] The continuing influence of "the commercialization model," and hence the need to guard against it, should not be underestimated. If it were true that capitalism had existed virtually since the emergence of civilization, then the possibility of socialism, at least in the form of anything but a totalitarian dictatorship, would be nonexistent, for capitalism would indeed have been shown to be congruent with human nature—a point that bourgeois ideologues have been making with increasing stridency since the fall of Stalinism in 1989–91. The insistence of political Marxism on the radical break that capitalism involves in human history therefore retains all its relevance. On a less obviously ideological level, Brenner's work has made it more difficult—if not, alas, impossible—for historians of the late medieval or early modern periods to write about "economic development" or "economic growth" as if these automatically involved capitalist economic development and growth, and without specifying the social relations within which economic activity took place. As he himself has noted, his approach "obliges" historians to distinguish between "change within the system versus change of the system, or alternatively stated, the evolution of a society of a given type versus the transition from a society of one type to a society of a qualitatively different type."[29]

These qualities have ensured that Brenner's work has received an acceptance that is wide, but often not, I think, very deep. Indeed, so dominant has this interpretation become, that the Brenner thesis is often treated as if it was "the Marxist position." In her recent history of capitalism, for example, Joyce Appleby presents the case for developments in the forces of production leading to changes in the relations of production, then writes the following:

> These may sound like innocuous statements, but they challenge the Marxist position that the conversion of agriculture from primitive reproduction to enhanced productivity began with farsighted landlords who coerced their tenants into commercial leases with rents set in response to harvest yields that exposed tenants to the competitive forces of the market. In this analysis tenants are assumed to have resisted cooperating with their landlord's improvement plans because they feared becoming dependent on the market and losing the independence that fixed rents gave them.

"I believe that the reverse of the Marxist position is true," writes Appleby, "that new social relations were the consequence, not the cause, of the transformation of English farming."[30] But what Appleby is arguing here *is* the Marxist position, and what she identifies as the Marxist position is that of Brenner and his followers.

Beyond the fairly narrow ranks of political Marxism Brenner's thesis is often cited approvingly, but without the full implications necessarily being understood. James Holstun has drawn on Brenner's conclusions about non-inevitability of capitalism to encourage revolutionaries to look back to the period "when precapitalist economies did not yet seem doomed, when capitalist ones did not yet seem foreordained."[31] Yet Brenner believes that capitalism was already firmly established during the mid-seventeenth-century period to which Holstun refers. In fact, in its initial form at least, the thesis is not one that can be accepted in part or synthesized with other interpretations. On the contrary, its rigor and internal consistency is such that the positive alternative that it offers can really only be accepted or rejected in full. One reason why Perry Anderson's once-promised volume on the bourgeois revolutions never materialized may have been due to a loss of confidence following his acceptance of the Brenner thesis, and an understanding that it could not simply be incorporated into his existing schema.[32]

But Brenner has also received support from sources that are hostile to the Marxism that he sees as central to his method. Stephen Rigby, for example, has commended Brenner because his work "allows empirical complexity and diversity" and particularly because it shows that "the relations of production cannot be explained in terms of the needs of society's productive forces."[33] These comments were made in the course of a book in which the main purpose is to dismiss most of the Marxist theory of history. More sweepingly still, Alastair MacLachlan has used political Marxism to argue that historical materialism as such was an incoherent attempt to fuse incompatible intellectual traditions:

> Scottish economics and French politics did not cohere. . . . But the harnessing of Scottish economics to German philosophy proved every bit as artificial as it had to French politics; and when the composite explanatory model of world history which combined a Smithean sociological chassis and a Hegelian motor left the workshop of pure theory in the 1840s, it hit the road as the familiar double-decker Marxism of base and superstructure, with its "techno-functionalist" explanation of class and property relations, its "meccano-set" version of dialectical contradiction, and its clumsy and incompletely synchronized gearbox of political revolution and structural transformation: the ill-assorted mechanism of a model which combined evolutionary inevitabilism with revolutionary struggle—a mechanism given further rigidity by the naturalistic determinism and scientism of second generation assembly workers like the later Engels, Kautsky and Plekhanov.[34]

Comments of this sort seem to indicate that, although Brenner has correctly identified major problems with the way historians, including Marxist historians, have dealt with the development of capitalism, his alternative involves a different set of problems. I want to discuss these in some detail, before turning to how Brenner and his supporters deal with the question of bourgeois revolution.

Critique: Theory and History

Political Marxists are fond of emphasizing their reliance on the *Grundrisse* and Marx's subsequent critiques of political economy. Edward Thompson argued that, in many respects, the *Grundrisse* and, to the extent that it remained within the same framework, *Capital*, constituted an anti–Political Economy that reproduced the same terms of reference as the bourgeois original while reversing its value judgments. I think that Thompson was mistaken in relation to Marx's own work, but his claims are apt to describe the way in which political Marxists ignore "activities and relations . . . which are not the concern of Political Economy, and for which it has no terms."[35] By focusing almost exclusively on what they call social property relations, they "have no terms" to explain events that lie outside these relationships. As Rigby points out, Brenner is one of those "Marxist theorists" who "constantly slip towards an implicit pluralism by which Marxism dies the death of a thousand qualifications." Rigby is quite happy with this, of course; his only concern is that Brenner has failed to recognize the need to abandon not just "the primacy of the economic," but "any attempt to ascribe objective primacy in historical explanation": "In other words, whatever our explicit theory may be, we cannot help, in practice to be pluralists."[36]

The problem here is not that Brenner's Marxism is unable to explain every historical event. It is in any case indicative of a rather oversocialized notion of human existence if our struggle with, for example, the non-human aspects of nature is treated as an extraneous factor. As Sydney Hook noted long ago: "An earthquake is a natural event which has definite *geological* causes. It has, however, definite historical *effects*. . . . The causes of the earthquake are historically irrelevant; its effects are not, for the social consequences of an earthquake will be different in one economic situation from what it will in another."[37] What Marxism can do, as Hook suggests, is explain why non-human aspects of nature have a lesser or, in this case, greater impact on human society. Take the Black Death, an example relevant to Brenner's explanation for the changed balance of class forces at the end of the fourteenth century. It is far from being the contingent factor that pluralists like Rigby seek to make. The rodent carriers of the pestilence arrived in Europe through the ports of the Italian Peninsula on ships engaged in extended trade with the East. The extent of its impact was a function of the weakened resistance to disease of a population who were already suffering from reduced caloric intake as a result of the feudal economic crisis. The problem is rather that political Marxism has difficulty in explaining aspects of human society that are not directly reducible to "social property relations."

In the Brenner thesis the emergence of capitalism, in England at least, is an unintended outcome of the actions of the two main feudal social classes, peasants and lords. Holstun has written that this position provides socialists with an approach that "resists the binary blackmail threatened by revisionists or postmodernists, for the results are neither inevitable nor purely contingent."[38] But contingency is precisely what is involved. Brenner conceives of feudalism as a self-enclosed, self-perpetuating system that cannot be undermined by its own internal contradictions. The parallels with Althusserianism are very strong in this respect.[39] Indeed, Post, the one leading political Marxist to have been previously influenced by Althusser, cites Balibar and Brenner as authorities on the definition of social labor.[40] Consequently, in order to explain the actual appearance of either capitalism in one country (for Brenner) or socialism in one country (for Althusser), both rely on what Althusser called an overdetermined conjuncture. Compare, for example, Brenner's explanation for why capitalism only appeared in England with Althusser's explanation for why revolution was successful only in Russia.[41] These similarities are curious, given that Brenner is a revolutionary whose own political beliefs and practice are firmly within the Trotskyist tradition. Nevertheless, there are also strong overlaps in content, such as the belief in a "break" in Marx's theoretical development.

It is in the work of his followers like Wood and Comninel, however, that the tone and approach of the Althusserianism echoes most loudly—ironically, since they oppose it more strenuously than any other school in Marxist thought.[42] The parallels are, however, almost exact. Just as texts were once investigated for any signs of "humanism," "empiricism," or "economism," now Wood stands guard against any hint of "the bourgeois paradigm" or "the commercialization model." There is a similarly selective reading of Marx, in which every element that cannot be used to support the thesis is either ignored or willfully misinterpreted, and a similar refusal to engage with inconvenient historical evidence. Wood, who seems unaware of the notion of falsification, simply matches any argument—with whatever evidential base—against the thesis, declares that the former is incompatible with the latter and must therefore be discarded. She shows no sign of recognizing that, since the thesis itself is based on a number of factual claims about England, France, and Eastern Europe, it might possibly have to be reconsidered in the light of evidence that contradicts these claims. Brenner himself has conceded that he is working with a model of capitalism that is effectively an ideal type, not one that can be found in the history of any country or region: "I do not contend that such economies ever existed in pure form, though rough approximations can be found in seventeenth-century England and seventeenth-century northern Netherlands. But, it is useful to posit the model to see more clearly the social-property relations that underpin the tendency to accumulate capital, as well as to understand the tendency to act like capitalists of the owner-operators who constitute often significant segments of capitalist societies, notably farmers."[43] Wood rightly admires Thompson; perhaps she should recall his comment on the earlier schematics of Anderson and Nairn: "Minds which thirst for a tidy Platonism very soon become impatient with actual history."[44]

It is claimed that Brenner has an explanation for the—in his terms, highly unlikely—appearance of capitalism: the class struggle. Indeed, this is one of the reasons why some of Brenner's followers were puzzled by his abandonment of the class-struggle model in his writings on Holland. As Post notes, "Brenner's earlier analysis of the rural transition privileged the role of class conflict over either the growth of commodity production or demographic changes" and, on the basis of this analysis, "ecological crisis of the sort which affected northern maritime agriculture would not be a sufficient condition for a transition to capitalist or petty bourgeois agriculture."[45] Even outside the Brenner school proper the claim is repeated by writers with quite different attitudes to the thesis; by friendly critics like Rigby, by hostile critics like Chris Harman, and by more ambivalent critics like Rodney Hilton, who enshrined it in his introduction to *The Brenner Debate* itself.[46] Consequently, many socialist readers must have gone to Brenner's key articles, eagerly anticipating detailed accounts of peasant resistance to the lords, only to be disappointed by the scant attention that he actually devotes to the subject. In fact, it is the outcome of such class conflicts that Brenner is interested in, not the conflicts themselves. De Vries has written:

> If I understand it correctly, Brenner's basic argument has changed over time: what began as an assertion of the primacy of the class struggle—relatively autonomous processes where history seems to be up for grabs—has become an assertion of the primacy of social-property relations, where nothing can change except by some strong, unintended disturbance to the system, some exogenous shock. We have moved from Marxism—which explains how capitalism necessarily emerges from feudalism—to

Brennerism—which explains how it can't.[47]

But there has been no change. Brenner has always held the second position, it is simply that in the case of England, the outcome of the rural class struggle acted as a mechanism ("an exogenous shock") for establishing capitalist social relations of production, but in the United Netherlands ecological pressures played the same role. Why does Brenner need such a mechanism in the first place?

Marxists have previously argued that capitalism emerged in the countryside through a series of transitional forms, initially combining different modes of production, but progressively becoming more purely capitalist in nature. Lenin's discussion of Russian agriculture after the abolition of serfdom in 1861, in *The Development of Capitalism in Russia*, is one of the most outstanding examples of this type of analysis: "With all the endless variety of forms characteristic of a transitional epoch, the economic organisation of contemporary landlord farming amounts to two main systems, in the most varied combinations—the *labor-service* system and the *capitalist* system." These were not absolute differences: "Life creates forms that unite in themselves with remarkable gradualness systems of economy whose basic features constitute opposites. It becomes impossible to say where 'labor-service' ends and where 'capitalism' begins."[48]

Brenner might well agree with this assessment in relation to nineteenth-century tsarist Russia. He points out in a footnote that the direct producers can be involved in a system where exchange value predominates without themselves being wage laborers:

> Examples of such "transitional forms" would be the peasant producer of industrial crops, without landed property enough to provide him means of subsistence (especially food), as well as the independent urban artisan (with no guild protection). Other examples would be systems of free tenantry (without wage labor), where the tenants hold on terminable money lease from the landlord, as well as "putting out" systems, where the producers are dependent on merchant suppliers for raw materials. What determines that all these forms are "transitional" is that they allow for a *more or less* direct transition to formally capitalist class relations and co-operative labor under the pressures of competition on the market.[49]

From his perspective such gradual transformations were possible because the system that began in England established an international context in which other countries were both pressured into adopting capitalist social property relations and provided with a model to which they could aspire. Russian landowners therefore have a motivation for introducing capitalism, albeit under tightly controlled conditions. But since English landowners and peasants were the first to be subject to these relations they could have had no such motivation. The outcome of class struggle provides Brenner with the situation in which the necessary determinations come into effect. Now, as Brenner himself admits: "[Marx] did not explain exactly why the English landlords did not desire or lacked the capacity to maintain or reconstruct serfdom (as did their contemporaries in East Elbian Europe). Nor did he make clear what made it possible for the English lords to succeed in expropriating the peasants from their means of subsistence and in reducing them to commercial farmers and wage laborers, when their contemporaries in France could not accomplish this."[50] This was not an omission on Marx's part; he saw no need for a special mechanism with which to explain the appearance of capitalism in England because he did not think that the development of capitalism was unique to England, but a general phenomenon, at least in Europe. Consequently, if Marx was correct in his assessment, the entire elaborate hypotheses about the different outcomes of the class struggle and the impact of environment are totally unnecessary.

If, as I have suggested, the argument from contingency is a speculative answer to a non-question, then it may explain why Brenner has some difficulty explaining why the class struggle resulted in such different outcomes across Europe. His attempts to deal with this problem are among the least convincing aspects of the entire thesis. Brenner points to the different capacities deployed by the classes involved: these lords had better organization, those peasants displayed less solidarity; but without an explanation for the prior processes by which these classes acquired their organizational or solidaristic qualities, these are mere descriptions which, to borrow a favorite expression of Wood's, "assume precisely what has to be explained." His inability to explain the differing levels of peasant resistance to the lords (as opposed to the consequences of that resistance) means that he has to fall back on what Rigby calls "a host of particular historical factors which cannot be reduced to expressions of class structure or of class struggle."[51] It was for this quite specific reason that Guy Bois described Brenner's Marxism as involving "a voluntarist vision of history in which the class struggle is divorced from all other objective contingencies."[52] Colin Mooers makes a similar point when he writes that if "ruling classes could choose not to introduce capitalist methods," then we lose sight of the way "in which ruling-class choices are constrained and shaped by changes in the forces and relations of production."[53] But Brenner is only a voluntarist in relation to that part of the period before the different settlements of the land question occurred. After, precisely the opposite applies and his interpretation becomes overly determinist. In the case of England, far from being free to opt for a particular course of action, he sees no alternative for either the lords or the peasants but to become market dependent. As soon as the mechanism has produced the required result, the element of choice disappears from his account, to be replaced by that of constraint.

However, let us accept, for the sake of argument, that capitalist social property relations arose only in the English countryside and that they did indeed do so as a result of the indeterminate outcome of the class struggle. There are still other problems. Brenner is surely right to reject the counterposition of a supposedly feudal countryside to supposedly capitalist towns, but are we not being asked to accept an equally implausible reversal of these terms? Indeed, it is difficult to envisage how there could have been an inescapable "market compulsion" in the countryside in the first place while the urban economy remained untouched by capitalist social property relations, given that the former was not and could not have been isolated from the latter. Furthermore, it is by no means clear how capitalist social property relations were then extended to the towns, which presumably remained feudal, or post-feudal, or at any rate noncapitalist until something—but what?—brought about the introduction of these relations.

Political Marxists are either silent on these issues or apparently fail to realize that it represents a problem. Wood, for example, writes: "Without England's industrial capitalism, there would have been no dispossessed mass obliged to sell its labor-power for a wage." I agree—but to whom did the dispossessed sell their labor power, given that Wood believes that no capitalist class existed outside of the landlords and tenant farmers in the English countryside? We are further told that: "Without the dispossessed non-agrarian work force, there would have been no mass consumer market for the cheap everyday goods—such as food and textiles— that drove the process of industrialization in England."[54] Again, I agree, but in order to buy the commodities they required the new workforce needed jobs. Who employed them? Could it be that enterprising merchants or artisans saw—whisper who dares—an *opportunity*? For, on the basis of Wood's own arguments, urban employers could not, at this stage, have been subject to market compulsion: "The self-sustaining development unique to capitalism requires not just the removal of obstacles to development but a positive compulsion to transform the forces of production and this comes only in competitive conditions, where economic actors are both free to move in response to those conditions and obliged to do so."[55] At the very least there is a missing link in the chain of argument here.

I am not suggesting, of course, that agrarian capitalism had no effect on other sectors of the economy. Thompson, who was probably the first person to use the term, described the broader impact of agrarian capitalism coming "fully into its inheritance" in the eighteenth century: "Ascendant agrarian capitalism involved not only rent-rolls, improvement, enclosures, but also far-reaching changes in marketing, milling, transport, and in the merchanting of exports and imports; while the gentry were able to employ a professional servant-class, in the lesser clergy, country lawyers, surgeons, surveyors, tutors, etc."[56] Thompson is obviously right that it both transformed the existing service sector and generated a requirement for new services, but this does not explain the emergence of capitalist production in the towns or—for that matter—the non-agricultural areas of the countryside. I understand how Brenner accounts for the establishment of capitalism in the English countryside; I also understand how Brenner accounts for the spread of capitalism beyond Britain: I do not understand how capitalist social property relations spread from the English countryside to the rest of England. Nor, for that matter, how the same process took place in the Netherlands or Catalonia, the other areas where Brenner himself thinks that capitalism existed.

This is not a problem in Marx's own discussions of the rise of capitalism. In a section of the *Grundrisse* ("The Chapter on Capital") much admired by political

Marxists, Marx argues that "the dissolution of the old relations of production" has to take place in both the towns and the countryside, and that the process in the former is partly responsible for it in the latter: "Urban labor itself had created means of production for which the guilds became just as confining as were the old relations of landownership to an improved agriculture, which was in part itself a consequence of the larger market for agricultural products in the cities etc."[57] In other words, Marx conceptualizes an uneven but broadly simultaneous development across the rural and urban sectors with mutually reinforcing results. Such an explanation is impossible for political Marxism, however, as it would involve conceding that, in some circumstances at least, people could willingly choose to become capitalists rather than do so only when the role was imposed on them. As a result they have no explanation at all for urban capitalist development, other than by osmosis.

When confronted with those (very extensive) sections of Marx's writings that contradict their views, political Marxists either pretend that they mean something else, as Wood does in relation to primitive accumulation, or issue disapprovingly admonitions about Marx's failure to understand his own theory. Comninel complains of "Marx's very loose usage of the concepts of 'capital' and 'capitalism' in the historical sections of *Capital*, in contexts where he clearly does not mean the capitalist mode of production."[58] Rather than speculate on what Marx really meant, would it not be simpler for Comninel to accept that Marx means exactly what he says and that, consequently, he and his cothinkers have a different theory of capitalism than that of Marx? For political Marxists, capitalism is defined by the existence of what they call market compulsion—the removal of the means of production and subsistence from the direct producers so that they are forced to rely on the market to survive. There is of course a venerable tradition of thought that defines capitalism solely in market terms, but it is not Marxism, it is the Austrian economic school whose leading representatives were Ludwig von Mises and Frederick von Hayek. In the Hayekian version of their argument the reductionism involved has a clear ideological purpose. It is to declare any forms of state intervention or suppression of market mechanisms, from the most modest public provision of welfare services through to full nationalization of the economy, as socialist, incompatible with capitalism and consequently liable to lead down "the road to serfdom." Political Marxists are obviously on the other side of the intellectual barricades from Hayek and his followers, but this is precisely why I find it so curious that they similarly define any kind of economic activity that does not involve "market compulsion" as noncapitalist, particularly since Hayek's position is extreme even by the standards of contemporary bourgeois ideology. It might be worth recalling, in this connection, what John Maynard Keynes said of Hayek, since the remark evidently has wider application: "It is an extraordinary example of how, starting with a mistake, a remorseless logician can end up in Bedlam."[59]

For Marx, capitalism was defined not as a system of market compulsion, but as one of *competitive accumulation based on wage labor*. "What all capitals have in common is their capacity for expanding their value," writes Roman Rosdolsky, "the fact that they appropriate (directly or indirectly) the surplus-value created in the capitalist production process."[60] Both aspects are equally important, but Marx starts with wage labor. Rosdolsky writes, "if the basic presupposition of the capital relation is to be understood, i.e., the relation of capital to labor and the role of surplus value as the driving force of capitalist production, we must begin not with 'many capitals,' but with capital or 'capital in the whole society' i.e., with 'capital in general.'"[61] But we need not take his word for it; here is Marx himself on the subject in 1847:

> How then, does any amount of commodities, of exchange values, become capital? By maintaining and multiplying itself as an independent social power, that is, as the power *of a portion of society*, by means of its *exchange for direct, living labor [power]*. The existence of a class which possesses nothing but its capacity to labor is a necessary prerequisite of capital ... *capital presupposes wage labor; wage labor presupposes capital. They reciprocally condition the existence of each other: They reciprocally bring forth each other.*[62]

Again, these are not simply the juvenile effusions of the young Marx. He writes in *Capital*, Volume I, that the emergence of capital as a social relation is the result of two types of commodity owners: on the one hand, "the owners of money, means of production, means of subsistence" and "on the other hand, free workers, the sellers of their own labor power, and therefore the sellers of labor." He concludes: "With the polarization of the commodity market into these two classes, the fundamental conditions of capitalist production are present."[63] Toward the end of *Capital*, Volume 3, in a passage originally written in the mid-1860s, Marx gave what must, unfortunately, be one of his least accurate predictions: "It is unnecessary after the argument already developed to demonstrate once again how the relationship of capital and wage-labor determines the whole character of the mode of production."[64]

Wage labor was by no means universal in England by 1789, let alone by 1688. As Ricardo Duchesne notes, in the countryside: "The real dispossession of the peasantry occurred in the second half of the eighteenth century when landlords stopped renewing copyhold and beneficial leases for life, or for long terms of years and amalgamated small yeomen farmers into large estates."[65] Similarly in the towns: "One can say that wage labor is completely realised in form in England only at the end of the eighteenth century," wrote Marx, "with the repeal of the law of apprenticeship."[66] Yet we have to be clear what wage labor means. In the latter quote Marx is clearly referring to wage labor in its classic "free" form, but as we saw in the previous chapter, this is not the only or even the most typical form it can take. Shahid Amin and Marcel van der Linden argue that the notion of "free wage labor" is essentially an ideal type, "an analytic core surrounded by numerous rings of labor relations that we would like to call intermediary." Their conclusion, which I share, is that: "It probably makes more sense to regard the intermediary forms of wage labor not as relationships existing outside the true working class, but as articulations of a worldwide segmentation of labor."[67] There are numerous examples of how even nominally free labor has historically been constrained:

> The British Master and Servants Acts, which were extended into the legal codes of
> most of the British colonies in the nineteenth century . . . made the leaving of a job
> by free workers before the expiration of an agreed-upon time-period a criminal of-
> fence, analogous to theft and punishable by imprisonment. . . . Similar restrictions on
> quitting could be seen in some critical industries even in the twentieth century. For
> example, a British worker who left a munitions factory without permission in the
> First World War would be forced to suffer several weeks' unemployment. In the
> United States, during the Second World War, a worker failing to remain in a specified
> job could be threatened by being drafted into the military, and provisions were made
> to reduce "pirating" by employers.[68]

These are all examples taken from societies in which there is no doubt that capitalism is the dominant mode of production, but as we shall see in due course the
argument has implications for forms of labor prior to the full establishment of capitalism. As Jarius Banaji writes: "In short, historically, capital accumulation has been
characterised by considerable flexibility in the structuring of production and in the
forms of labor used in producing surplus-value. The liberal conception of capitalism
which sees the sole basis of accumulation in the individual wage-earner conceived
as free laborer obliterates a great deal of capitalist history, erasing the contribution
of both enslaved and collective (family) units of labor power." Banaji suggests that,
"instead of seeing wage-labor as one form of exploitation among many, alongside
share-cropping, labor tenancy, and various kinds of bonded labor, these specific individual forms of exploitation may just be ways in which paid labor is recruited,
exploited, and controlled by employers."[69]

Political Marxists would probably dispute these arguments, given the relentless
formalism of their conception of capitalism, but the point is that they do not even
accept that wage labor—however this is understood—is necessary for capitalism.
Teschke writes: "Capitalism denotes a social system predicated on determinate
social property relations between direct producers, who have lost unmediated access to their means of subsistence and become subject to market imperatives, and
non-producers, who have come to own the means of production."[70] These direct
producers are not necessarily workers, not necessarily wage laborers. For Wood:
"Brenner's history shows how economic units became market-dependent, in historically unprecedented ways, not because of the relation between capital and
labor but before the widespread proletarianisation of the workforce and as a precondition to it." Workers are therefore unnecessary to the existence of capitalism:
"A tenant could, for instance, remain in possession of land, but his survival and
his tenure could nonetheless be subject to market imperatives, whether he employed wage labor or was himself the direct producer." The logic of this position
is that the origins of capitalism need not involve wage labor. Wood in particular
has followed this logic through to its conclusion and claimed that, rather than
being constitutive of capitalism, as Marx had thought, wage labor is in fact a

consequence of it:

> In the specific property relations of early modern England, landlords and their tenants became dependent on the market for their self-reproduction and hence subject to the imperatives of competition and increasing productivity, whether or not they employed wage-labor. . . . The fact that market-dependence and competition preceded proletarianisation tells us something about the relations of competition and their autonomy from the relations between capital and labor. It means that producers and possessors of the means of production, who are not themselves wage-laborers, can be market-dependent without employing wage-labor.[71]

For Wood, the removal of the means of *subsistence* from the direct producers is the fundamental moment in their subjection to market compulsion.

It is true, of course, that in a context where the economy is already dominated by the capitalist mode of production, tenant farmers can play the role of capitalists whether or not they employ wage labor, but this has nothing to do with whether or not they possess the means of subsistence. Independent farmers in the Southwest of Scotland, and even in parts of the Highlands, were already dependent on the market long before the transition to capitalism was imposed during the second half of the eighteenth century for the simple reason that they were restricted by environmental constraints to pastoral farming and could not meet their needs in any other way. If capitalism is based on a particular form of exploitation, on the extraction of surplus value from the direct producers through wage labor, then I fail to see how capitalism can exist in the absence of wage laborers. How is surplus value produced in a model that contains only capitalist landlords and capitalist farmers? It may be *realized* through market transactions, but it can scarcely be *produced* by them. The only means by which Wood proposes that surplus value can be extracted is the competition for leases among tenant farmers (that is, in that the latter compete to hand over the greatest proportion of their output to the landlord in order to acquire or retain a tenancy). But there is nothing distinctly capitalist about this mechanism. In late-seventeenth-century Scotland, which political Marxists regard—rightly in this case—as feudal, it was common for feudal landlords to conduct a "roup" or auction of leases that included the full panoply of labor services as part of the rent. Indeed, pioneering improvers like Fletcher of Saltoun and Seton of Pitmedden regarded this as one of the main means through which the peasantry was exploited.[72]

In fact, there have never been capitalist societies, even mid-Victorian Britain or the United States today, where all economic relations been market determined. In some cases this has been because of the retention of precapitalist relations such as led to the reassertion of "moral economy" against "political economy," of the "just price" against the "market price," which occurred in England and Lowland Scotland as late as the end of the eighteenth century. (Indeed, if capitalist social relations of production were already in place before the English Civil War, then what were these great social struggles actually about?) But more commonly it has been the imposition of public or state provision and regulation by capitalist states. One writer who is sometimes credited by Wood with having some—although still, alas, imperfect—understanding of the specificity of capitalist economy is Karl Polanyi.[73] Yet she tends to misunderstand his central point. Writing during the Second World War, Polanyi argued that:

> To allow the market mechanism to be the sole director of the fate of human beings and their natural environment, indeed, even of the amount and use of purchasing power, would result in the demolition of society. . . . Robbed of the protective covering of cultural institutions, human beings would perish from the effects of social exposure; they would die as the victims of acute social dislocation through vice, perversion, crime, and starvation. Nature would be reduced to its elements, neighbourhoods and landscapes defiled, rivers polluted, military safety jeopardized, the power to produce food and raw materials destroyed.

It was in response to these outcomes that state intervention had increasingly become the norm throughout the nineteenth century: "While on the one hand markets spread all over the face of the globe and the amount of goods involved grew to unbelievable proportions, on the other hand a network of measures and policies was integrated into powerful institutions designed to check the action of the market relative to labor, land and money."[74] There are problems with Polanyi's analysis. As Colin Leys points out, "the state, which in his model regularly reasserts the interests of society against those of capital ('the self-regulating market'), itself rests on class forces, and his disinclination to specify these forces leaves this salutary historical function of the state ultimately unexplained."[75] However, his central point is absolutely correct: as Vivek Chibber has recently reminded us, "the essential lessons of Marx and Polanyi" are that in a capitalist economy "the choice is over *how* to have the state intervene in the economy, not *whether* to have it intervene."[76] In other words, "pure" capitalist social property relations have never been completely dominant anywhere, nor—unless socialists completely fail in their objectives—will they ever be.[77]

An overemphasis on markets as the defining characteristic of capitalism is not the only curious affinity between political Marxism and Marginalism: there also appears to be a common conception of human nature. Hayek focused on the emergence of a market order—"the spontaneous extended human order created by competitive capitalism"—and held that it was a formation that evolved over several thousands of years with the gradual development of institutions, rules and laws which are quite contrary to the instincts of human beings.[78] These instincts remain essentially egalitarian and collectivist, biological remnants of the attitudes that were appropriate to tribal groups of foragers but are destructive of the market order if they were given free reign, as he believed would happen under socialism:

> That rules become increasingly better adjusted to generate order happened not because men better understood this function, but because these groups prospered who happened to change them in a way that rendered them increasingly adaptive. The

evolution was not linear, but resulted from continued trial and error, constant "experience," in areas wherein different orders contended. Of course there was no intention to experiment—yet the changes in rules thrown forth by individual accident, analogous to genetic mutations, had something of the same effect.[79]

According to Hayek, the very amorality of the market order, the fact that it often rewards the worst and penalizes the best, means that it runs counter to the instincts of the mass of people. But the market is the only rational means of economic organization, and so these instincts must be suppressed in the interests of what Hayek calls, following the terminology of Adam Smith, "the Great Society." For Hayek, capitalism is only possible through the transformation of human nature; or rather the suppression of the behavior characteristic of human nature from almost the entire period since we completed our evolution from the primates.[80]

Political Marxists obviously reject the positive value that Hayek ascribes to the overthrow of these supposedly ancient human characteristics, but it nevertheless makes very similar assumptions. Duchesne writes: "[Wood] thinks that capitalism is too unnatural and too destructive of human relations for anyone to have wanted it, least of all a collectivist peasantry."[81] But there are as many problems with a conception of human nature that sees it as being uninterested in economic development as there are with a definition of capitalism based on the existence of market compulsion. The rejection of one form of bourgeois ideology should not blind us to the dangers of accepting another, albeit with the inversion of its value system; there is no advantage to us in rejecting Smithian Marxism only to embrace Hayekian Marxism instead. No mode of production is intrinsically alien to human nature. This is not to imagine that human nature is infinitely plastic or malleable, and has no stable qualities at all. As Norman Geras argues:

> Historical materialism itself, this whole distinctive approach to society that originates with Marx, rests squarely upon the idea of a human nature. It highlights that specific nexus of universal needs and capacities which explain the human production process and man's organized transformation of the material environment; which process and transformation it treats in turn as the basis both of the social order and of historical change.... If human beings have a history which gives rise to the most fabulous variety of social shapes and forms, it is because of the kind of beings they, all of them, are ...[82]

In other words, human beings may not have a "certain propensity in human nature . . . to truck, barter and exchange one thing for another," as Smith thought, but they can develop such a propensity under certain conditions and without compulsion.[83] What I am suggesting, therefore, is that the entire elaborate edifice of the Brenner thesis is based upon a conception of human nature in which it is seen as innately opposed to capitalism—indeed, in which it is seen as innately opposed to economic development as such—and will only be induced to accept capitalist relations under duress. While this may allow us the comforting thought that capitalism need not have happened, it also has certain other implications. For if capitalism is essentially a contingent or accidental historical outcome, then so too is the possibility of socialism. One does not have to accept, in Second International or Stalinist style, that human social development has gone through a succession of inevitable stages to reject the ascription of absolute randomness to key historical turning points as a viable alternative. Marx's own position lends support to neither of these positions.

IMPLICATIONS FOR THE THEORY OF BOURGEOIS REVOLUTION

If, as I have suggested, Brenner is wrong about the geographically limited and socially contingent nature of capitalist development, then this has certain implications for his critique of the theory of bourgeois revolution. Brenner claims that the theory of bourgeois revolution is "based on a mechanically determined theory of transition" that "renders revolution unnecessary in a double sense": "First, there really is no transition to accomplish: since the model starts with bourgeois society in the towns, foresees its evolution as taking place via bourgeois mechanisms, and has feudalism transform itself in consequence of its exposure to trade, the problem of how one type of society is transformed into another is simply assumed away and never posed. Second, since bourgeois society self-develops and dissolves feudalism, the bourgeois revolution can hardly play a necessary role."[84] The first point is valid as a criticism of many accounts of the transition from feudalism to capitalism, but the second is not, although it is endlessly repeated by Brenner supporters such as Wood:

> The concept of bourgeois revolution is confusing for several reasons. Was a revolution necessary to bring about capitalism, or simply to facilitate the development of an already existing capitalism? Was it a cause or an effect of capitalism? Although much has been claimed for the bourgeois revolution as the critical moment in the transition to capitalism, no conception of bourgeois revolution exists in which the revolution explains the emergence of capitalism or capitalists. All of them must assume the prior existence of fairly well-developed capitalist formations, which themselves create revolutionary pressures as they find their own development thwarted by pre-capitalist classes and institutions. The bourgeois revolution, then, seems to be more effect than cause, and we are still without an explanation of the social transformations that brought capitalism into being.[85]

The theory of bourgeois revolution is not, however, about the origins and development of capitalism as a socioeconomic system but the removal of backward-looking threats to its continued existence and the overthrow of restrictions to its further expansion. The source of these threats and restrictions has, historically, been the pre-capitalist state, whether estates-monarchy, absolutist, or tributary in nature. It is perfectly possible for capitalism to erode the feudal social order in the way Brenner describes while leaving the feudal state intact and still requiring to be overthrown if the capitalist triumph is to be complete and secure. Fortunately, there is no need for me to pursue this argument because Brenner himself has already done so.

Brenner's first major publication was a study of the London merchant community during the civil war period, which drew on his doctoral research and was at least compatible with the concept of bourgeois revolution.[86] In his critique of the work of Maurice Dobb, Brenner suggested in a footnote that an interpretation of the English Civil War as bourgeois revolution was not "ruled out": "The anti-capitalist effects of Caroline fiscal policies (e.g., industrial monopolies, prerogative taxes), the monarchy's alliance with the leading strata of city financiers and monopoly merchants, and the close connection with the church hierarchy might be viewed from such a vantage point."[87] Similarly, in his 1989 essay, "Bourgeois Revolution and Transition to Capitalism," Brenner argued that it "would be premature" to conclude "that social interpretations of the English revolution are bound to fail" and "that there is no connection between the rise of agrarian capitalism within an aristocratic and landlord shell and the mid-seventeenth-century conflicts."[88] The postscript to his massive monograph, *Merchants and Revolution*, is essentially an attempt to substantiate these hints.

The now capitalist landowning classes no longer required the state for economic purposes, that is to say, they had sources of income that reduced the need for the salaries for filling official posts. They did, however, require it to act to protect their property and to regulate manufactures, particularly of cloth, in which many of them had a growing interest. They therefore filled state offices voluntarily, acting to support the monarchy and controlled the levels and nature of taxation through Parliament. The state was, however, dominated by the monarchy, whose incumbents continued to play the role of patrimonial lord, supported by a "patrimonial group" of courtiers. Moreover, the monarch held sole access to military force in an increasingly centralized state, since following their abandonment of extra-economic compulsion the lords no longer exerted power over distinct territorial areas. There were, however, two linked areas where the central state and the ruling class were divided. The first was over religion. A majority of the lords had come to see some variety of Calvinist Protestantism as an essential part of their ideology, since their ascendancy had been opposed by sections of the nobility, peasant uprisings (the Pilgrimage of Grace) and foreign invasions (the Spanish Armada) had all been associated with Catholicism. In particular, the spread of Protestantism and the English influence seemed to be intertwined. For the monarchy, however, Protestantism was problematic in two ways. On the one hand, the emphasis on the duty of Christians to interpret the Bible and act according to that understanding was not compatible with the level of obedience to the Crown. On the other hand, a commitment to Protestantism not only precluded certain advantageous dynastic marriages, but was also virtually certain to involve the state in destructive wars. Conflicts between Crown and Parliament were therefore likely to combine both issues of religion and foreign alliance. The second area of division was over taxation. The Crown sought to build up support by creating courtiers whose incomes came from state revenues and by appointing religious leaders who wanted to retain those aspects of the Reformed Faith closest to Catholicism. His attempts to raise money from taxation inevitably hit those areas which were most vulnerable, which were not the land, but trade, which in turn required military protection from rival states. There was therefore a logic pushing the two sides to conflict, since their interests could not be resolved within the framework of the existing state.[89]

How convincing is this attempt at a new "social explanation"? In order to maintain consistency with his earlier work, Brenner has to maintain that feudal relations had been virtually overcome in England by 1640 and that the civil war was essentially fought between two wings of the same class. This was a venerable theme in revisionist writings. Peter Laslett argued in 1965 that England was a "one class society' in which conflicts were the result of "the internal contradictions of capitalism" and that any class conflicts were therefore between those with little or no property (that is, the Levellers and the Diggers) and the capitalist class above them.[90] Similarly, Wallerstein argued, that, despite inevitable complexities, a key aspect of the civil war was the conflict "between those who emphasized the role of the monarchy, who hoped thereby to hold on to a slipping system of privilege and deference, whose fears of social revolution outweighed other considerations, who were somewhat paralyzed before the forced choices of world economy, and those, on the other hand, who gave primacy to the continued commercialization of agriculture, who welcomed some change in social patterns, who saw little virtue in the extravagance of the Court, who were orientated to maximizing England's advantage in the world-economy."[91] In these cases as with Brenner the effect is that the English state has to be treated virtually as an autonomous body. It apparently has interests opposed to that of the dominant capitalist class, but these neither embody those of a feudal class nor balance between the capitalist and feudal classes, since the latter no longer exists. There were, of course, states based on what Brenner calls "politically constituted property" at this stage in history, but these were the great tributary empires of China, Byzantium, and Russia. But in these cases the state acted as a collective feudal overlord, exploiting the peasantry through taxation and, where capitalist production had begun to emerge (as it had in China), successfully preventing it from developing to the point where a capitalist class might challenge the political rule of the dynastic regime. Any serious comparison of the resources available to the Ming emperors and the Stuart kings would show the sheer *absence* of autonomous state power available to the latter. Hobbes made the point at the time of the civil war: "In such a constitution of people, methinks, the king is already ousted of his government, so as they needed not have taken arms for it. For I cannot imagine how the king should come by any means to resist them."[92]

According to Brenner, Charles I relied for support on three forces with which "to resist them," his courtiers, the High Anglican, and the traditional merchants; but it is difficult to believe that the war would have lasted longer than a handful of months if this was all that he could muster. "What requires explanation is the very existence of a significant Royalist party under these circumstances," writes Wood: "The irony is that, with a ruling class largely united in its anti-absolutist interests, the case of support for the Crown would not have sufficed to create a substantial Royalist alliance if the revolutionary threat unleashed by popular agitation and Parliamentary mobilization had not driven many propertied Parliamentarians back into the arms of the king."[93] Brenner also places great emphasis on the fear of popular intervention in forcing capitalist aristocrats into supporting the Crown. This certainly took place and Charles consciously played on these fears in his search for support among the nobility and gentry. Yet this will not do as a complete explanation.

First, Charles had already assembled formidable forces to his side before the interventions of the London crowd in December 1641. Second, Parliament was just as anxious as the Crown to gain the support of the unambiguously feudal Scottish Covenanting armies after hostilities broke out, precisely as an alternative to relying on the people. Third, even after the Independents had taken over from the moderate Presbyterians, Cromwell was ultimately prepared to crush the Levellers, who were the largest, but by no means the most radical of the social movements. In short, distrust and opposition to the mass movement was quite compatible with support for Parliament, even after its radicalization and militarization. The most obvious answer to the question of where royal support came from, but one that Brenner is unable to accept, is that at least part of it came from sections of English society whose socioeconomic position derived from local "patrimonial" (feudal) interests comparable to those of Charles himself. Charles did not, after all, simply invoke the general threat of disorder in his search for support, but the fact that any weakening of the monarchy, even such as that proposed by Parliament prior to the outbreak of the civil war, would lead to commensurate weakening of the aristocracy. But weakening in what sense? Not the position of capitalists, surely.

Even with these difficulties, Brenner's complex argument shows why a revolution—let us leave aside for the moment whether the designation of "bourgeois" is appropriate or not—was necessary in England, even though the economy was already largely capitalist. However, Brenner's position *only* allows for revolutions under such conditions. Effectively, this reduces the field to England and the similarly capitalist Holland, where the threat to capitalism came not from the native dynasty, but from the foreign rule of the Spanish Hapsburgs. What happened in the rest of the world? Brenner has not explicitly dealt with this question, but his fellow-thinkers have offered answers based on his theoretical framework. According to Wood: "Without English capitalism there would probably have been no capitalist system of any kind: it was competitive pressure emanating from England, especially an industrialized England, that, in the first instance, compelled other countries to promote their own economic development in capitalist directions." As with Brenner, the autonomous role of the state is decisive, although in the opposite direction from that of the English state under the Stuarts: "The state became a major player. This was true most notably in Germany, with its state-led industrialisation, which in the first instance was undoubtedly led by older geopolitical and military consideration than by capitalist motivations."[94]

A similar answer has been given by Teschke, who claims that European capitalist development was entirely due to the competitive pressure of the British state on other states and did not, even to a limited extent, emerge from processes internal to the latter. Teschke talks about "revolutions from above," but not bourgeois revolutions, presumably on the grounds that the bourgeoisie was not involved in these events, although they did lead to the development of capitalism. His timing, however, closely resembles that of the Mayer thesis: "This long period of transformation lasted from 1688 to the First World War for Europe, and beyond for the rest of the world."[95] In short, Brenner's insistence that the transition to capitalism was virtually complete by the time of the English (and possibly Dutch) Revolutions is matched by his followers' insistence that it had barely begun by the time of subsequent "revolutions from above."

Yet, as I have already discussed in relation to the theory of "process" discussed earlier, it is difficult to say whether the notion of "revolution" (even if "from above") is appropriate when dealing with such an extended period of time. There are difficulties too with the periodization. Identifying the crucial period as between 1688 and 1918, as Teschke does, rather elides the inconvenient fact that, outside of Scotland, the major transitions to capitalism occurred not after 1688 but after 1789. And here we come to the elephant in the room or, if you prefer an allusion to the Scottish Play, the ghost at the feast. I say inconvenient, because every political Marxist, without exception, is committed to the proposition that the Great French Revolution had nothing to do with the development of capitalism either at home or abroad—and this is of course another respect in which they are at one with Wallerstein and the capitalist world-system theorists. Why? Because the people who made the revolution were not capitalists. In the words of Comninel:

> It is hard to see how any sense can be made of bourgeois revolution, in its usual form, from the perspective of class exploitation. For the peasantry, who might be expected to be opposed to the feudal aristocracy, are not included at all.... The enduring struggle is that of the bourgeois and the urban people against the aristocracy. Where do relations of *exploitation* figure among these classes—particularly when it is always emphasised that the sans-culottes were not proletarians? And if the bourgeoisie were to be taken as capitalists, whom do they exploit? If no one (or so few as not to count), on what grounds do they become a ruling class?

One response might be that at least some of the revolutionaries were people who *wanted* to exploit peasants and artisans in new capitalist ways but were prevented from doing so by the Old Regime. Marx described the Physiocratic dream as being where "all taxes are put on rent, or in other words, landed property is in part confiscated" and noted that this "is what the legislation of the French Revolution sought to carry through and which is the final conclusion of the fully developed Ricardian political economy."[96] Comninel will have none of this: "The French Revolution was essentially an *intra-class* conflict over basic political relations that at the same time directly touched on relations of surplus extraction." By "intra-class conflict" Comninel means that the Revolution involved a struggle over the possession of state offices between different wings of a ruling class that combined both nobles and bourgeoisie. So, the most cataclysmic event of the eighteenth century, perhaps of human history down to that point, whose effects were felt across the world from Ireland to Egypt, and which, until 1917 at least, defined the very nature of revolution itself, was . . . a squabble over who gets to be the local tax farmer in Picardy. I cannot forebear to point out that once again the parallels with structural Marxism are very strong here. Althusser himself claimed that "it was not until 1850–70 that capitalism established itself firmly in France" and suggested that the bourgeoisie of 1789 were not connected with capitalism: "What if the bourgeoisie, far from being the contrary product of the feudal class, was its culmination and, as it were, acme, its highest form and, so to speak, crowning perfection? This would enable us to resolve many problems which are so many dead-ends, especially the problems of the bourgeois revolutions, such as the French Revolution, which are supposed, come hell or high water, to be capitalist, yet are not."[97]

Wood has argued for the incoherence of the concept of bourgeois revolution, on the grounds that it appears to encompass quite different types of event:

> If capitalism pre-exists the revolution, it can, of course, still be argued that bourgeois revolution is an effect of capitalist relations and a factor in their further development. Yet the concept of bourgeois revolution is called upon to explain both cases (like England) in which revolution occurs precisely because capitalist property relations are already well developed and an already dominant capitalist class must sweep away obstructions in the state, while subduing subordinate classes that stand in its way; and also cases (like France) in which, on the contrary, revolution occurs because aspiring capitalists (or a bourgeoisie we must assume to consist of aspiring capitalists) must defeat a dominant non-capitalist class. Contrasting these two cases, we may be forced to conclude that revolutions can be "bourgeois" without being capitalist and capitalist without being bourgeois.[98]

Teschke has also claimed that the distinctiveness of the English and French experiences means that they cannot be contained within the same category:

> We need to stop subsuming the English and French, and many other, revolutions under the common heading of "bourgeois revolution." In this respect, the assimilation of France and England as two variants of one path towards modernity, with the former achieving political centralization a bit earlier while lagging behind in economic development, and the latter being economically precocious while having to catch up politically, needs to be rejected. In contrast, we need to embed the respective nature of the French and English revolutions in the specificities of the long-term dynamics of their sharply diverging class relations and trajectories from the Middle Ages onwards.

"In short, while the English Revolution was not bourgeois, it was capitalist; and while the French Revolution was bourgeois, it was not capitalist."[99] The parallels between the course of the English Revolution, which took place in a society where capitalism was supposedly almost fully developed, and that of the French Revolution, which took place in a society where capitalism had supposedly not developed at all, are remarkable, even down to quite specific incidents; yet these must presumably be coincidental, if the societies were as different as political Marxists would have us believe.

Are there any states then in which bourgeois revolutions might be legitimately said to have occurred? For political Marxists there is only one, or rather two, both of which took place within the same state territory. Post argues:

> The American Revolution and Civil War can, at best, be viewed as bourgeois revolutions because they helped secure the political and juridical conditions for the development of capitalism in the US. Only the unintended outcomes of a revolution led by a non-capitalist merchant-class—the development of petty-commodity production and capitalist manufacturing in the North and the preservation of plantation-slavery in the South—allowed the US Civil War to assume the form of a "classic" bourgeois revolution led by a self-conscious class of capitalist manufacturers and commercial farmers struggling to remove the obstacle posed by the geographical expansion of plantation-slavery.[100]

Post is arguing two different positions on the nature of bourgeois revolutions here, which sit uneasily together. The first is that the American Revolution was a bourgeois revolution because a set of "unintended outcomes" resulting from it led, over the subsequent decades, to capitalist development in the North. Leave aside for the moment the question of whether capitalism existed or not in the United States before 1776: if a revolution can be declared bourgeois because it unintentionally led to capitalism, then why can this logic not also be applied to France, where the same indirect connections traceable to the aftermath of 1784 in the United States can made with the outcomes of 1815? The second and completely antipodean position is that the American Civil War was a bourgeois revolution in the literal sense in that it involved the Northern industrial capitalist class waging war on a pre- or at any rate very backward capitalist formation in the South. The problem with this position, which is more logically consistent with the insistence of political Marxism that there be absolute alignment between actors, intentions, and outcomes, is that it would leave the American Civil War as the only bourgeois revolution in history, even though one could point to events during the same decade that led effectively to the same outcomes without involvement of an industrial bourgeoisie.

In relation to bourgeois revolutions, therefore, the Brenner thesis can lead in two equally unproductive directions. On the one hand, it can lead to the abandonment of Marxist conceptions of totality and the adoption of pluralist explanations for conflicts where apparently they do not involve issues of class exploitation (as Brenner effectively does by explaining the English Civil War on the basis of ideological and political differences between Crown and Parliament). On the other, it can lead to a retreat to vulgar Marxism in which conflict between social groups is explained with reference to their direct "economic interests" (as Comninel does by explaining the French Revolution as a dispute between two wings of the same ruling class over access to state property). I find both these arguments deeply unsatisfactory. Behind the theory of bourgeois revolution is the particular way of understanding changes in human social development that we know as historical materialism, of which it is a specific application. To dispense with the theory therefore has far wider implications than merely abandoning an over-hasty formulation. Arguments, like those of political Marxism, which seek to be *plus Marxiste que le Marx* tend to begin by denigrating one of the sources and component parts of historical materialism (typically Hegel and German idealist philosophy) and to end by generating new versions of historical materialism the main characteristic of which is the abandonment of any conception of society as a mediated totality. And in this respect, political Marxism is once more aligned with the structural Marxism to which it is otherwise so opposed. If there is no necessary connection between the dominance of the capitalist mode of production on the one hand and revolution, war, religion, or art on the other, then the concept of totality is redundant and those aspects of life that do not form part of capitalist social property relations will have to be analyzed on their own terms. If feudalism did not generate an internal dynamic tending toward its breakdown, then we can forget about the inherent contradiction of class societies, including our own. The difficulties here are therefore not reducible to empirical questions about England in the seventeenth century or France in the eighteenth, but about both Marxism itself and the system that it seeks to understand.

19

"CONSEQUENTIALISM"

enno Teschke claims that there have been "two sharply diverging responses" to the revisionist critique of bourgeois revolution: "One, associated with the orthodoxy, retained the concept while making substantive empirical concessions; the other, associated with political Marxism, dismissed the concept while re-interpreting the empirical on the basis of a new class analysis."[1] As we have seen, there were more than two responses, but leave that aside. It is the first response to which Teschke refers, and which he correctly calls "consequentialism," that is the subject of this chapter. Contrary to what he says, however, it is only partly a response to revisionism since, far from being "associated with the orthodoxy," it is a *critique* of the orthodoxy, a return to the classical Marxist position that, unlike the alternative that Teschke supports, does not involve abandoning central components of historical materialism. The rediscovery of the original consequentialist meaning of bourgeois revolution is in one sense a "fundamentalist" project—not involving an unthinking acceptance of traditional authority, but rather, as Oliver Roy puts it, "clearing away the obfuscation of tradition."[2] To return to fundamentals in the case of bourgeois revolution involves excavating the theory from under the multiple layers of rubble—first Stalinist, then revisionist—beneath which it has been buried since the 1920s.

The notion that bourgeois revolutions might be assessed or even defined by their consequences reemerged more or less concurrently with revisionism and the various responses to it that I discussed in the previous four chapters. Although consequentialism attained systematic and consolidated form only in the 1980s at the hands of a widely divergent group of writers, it had a more or less direct link to classical Marxism through debates within the Trotskyist movement in the 1940s. And it is with Trotsky himself that we must begin, as he assesses the prospects for revolution on the eve of the Second World War.

PROSPECTS AND RESULTS

In *The History of the Russian Revolution* Trotsky wrote: "A revolution only takes place when there is no other way out."[3] From the mid-1930s onwards, particularly in the two years between the launch of the Fourth International in 1938 and his assassination in 1940, he had come to accept three interrelated propositions about the world situation that, together, pointed to only one conclusion: without world revolution in the immediate future, civilization would relapse into barbarism as a result of economic collapse and the impact of an even more destructive imperialist war than that of 1914–18. There was no other way out.

His first and most unqualified proposition concerned the future of the capitalist system. In the early 1920s Trotsky had argued that capitalism would continue to "live by crises and booms, just as a human being lives by inhaling and exhaling." But, also like human beings, these cycles had a history and it was necessary for revolutionaries to identify where in their history the current period was situated, "to establish whether it is still developing or whether it has matured or whether it is in decline." His conclusion was that capitalism had long passed through the stage of maturity: "Cyclical fluctuations will continue to take place but, in general, the curve of capitalist development will slope not upwards but downwards." Consequently, the possibility of "restoration of capitalist equilibrium" or a "capitalist upswing in the next few years" was "absolutely impossible under the conditions of modern economic stagnation."[4] Trotsky maintained this position until the mid-1930s at least, denying that the Great Depression that opened in 1929 was "the final crisis" foreseen in the *Internationale*: "There is no final crisis which can be, by itself, fatal to capitalism. The oscillations of the business cycle only create a situation in which it will be easier, or more difficult to overthrow capitalism."[5] In relation to the system as a whole, Trotsky retained the organic metaphors that he had abandoned in relation to societies affected by uneven and combined development. Rising unemployment and falling national income, "pertain internally to the present phase of capitalism just as gout and arteriosclerosis pertain to certain ages of man." "Mitigations and flickers of better times are possible in the process of decline," he wrote in 1936, but even if these were "inevitable," they were also "purely episodic."[6]

By the late 1930s, he seems to have reached the more extreme conclusion that even temporary periods of growth were impossible; consequently, global capitalism had entered a period of permanent and irreversible decline. The title of the Transitional Program with which Trotsky launched the Fourth International in 1938 proclaimed that capitalism was in its "death agony" and the opening sentences embellish the point in the most dramatic possible terms: "The economic prerequisite for the proletarian revolution has already in general achieved the highest point of fruition that can be reached under capitalism. Mankind's productive forces stagnate. Already new inventions and improvements fail to raise the level of material wealth."[7]

Trotsky may have been encouraged to cultivate such an apocalyptic scenario by an unconscious desire to rule out any prospect of reformism, whether of the Social Democratic or Stalinist variety. In any event it was a position from which he never subsequently retreated. The previous year, in an article for the ninetieth anniversary of the *Manifesto of the Communist Party* he compared capitalism in Marx's time and his own:

> Marx taught that no social system departs from the arena of history before it exhausts all its creative potentialities. The [*Communist*] *Manifesto* excoriates capitalism for retarding the development of the productive forces. During that period, however, as well as in the following decades, this retardation was only *relative* in nature. Had it been possible in the second half of the nineteenth century to organize economy on socialist beginnings, its tempo of growth would have been immeasurably greater. But this theoretically irrefutable postulate does not invalidate the fact that the productive forces kept expanding on a world scale right up to the [first] world war. Only in the last twenty years, despite the most modern conquests of science and technology, has the epoch of out-and-out stagnation and even decline in world economy begun. Mankind is beginning to expend its accumulated capital, while the next war threatens to destroy the very foundations of civilisation for many years to come.[8]

In fact, the world economy was by no means subject to as uniform a decline as Trotsky thought. By 1937–38 manufacturing output in Europe (excluding the Soviet Union) was 12 percent higher than it had been in 1929 and across the world as a whole it was 20 percent higher. Partly as a result of the generalized turn to autarchy, world trade certainly collapsed and had not recovered to 1929 levels by the outbreak of the Second World War; but even here individual countries dramatically improved their positions: Japan doubled its share of international textile exports after 1929, accounting for 20 percent of the world total by 1938.[9] These shifts had been noted by Marxist economists early in the 1930s and one, Fritz Sternberg, even drew Trotsky's attention to the figures, but did not succeed in changing his assessment.[10]

Trotsky's second proposition concerned the future of the Stalinist regime in Russia. He changed his position on the type of political action required to regenerate the Russian Revolution at least four times between 1923 and 1940, each shift signaling increasingly radical opposition to the emergent regime.[11] His initial approach to reversing the bureaucratic degeneration of the Russian Revolution, before Stalin had consolidated his power, envisaged workers reforming the apparatus through the medium of the existing soviets; his final position recognized that Soviet democracy had in reality long been completely suppressed and advocated working-class political revolution to overthrow the bureaucracy. Why only a political as opposed to a social revolution? Because, according to Trotsky, the continued existence of nationalized property meant that Russia remained a workers' state; the coming revolution would therefore resemble the political revolutions that followed the great bourgeois revolutions such as the French:

> The revolution which the bureaucracy is preparing against itself will not be social, like the October revolution of 1917. It is not a question this time of changing the economic foundations of society, of replacing certain forms of property with other forms. History has known elsewhere not only social revolutions which substituted the bourgeois for the feudal regime, but also political revolutions which, without

destroying the economic foundations of society, swept out an old ruling upper crust (1830 and 1848 in France, February 1917 in Russia, etc.). The overthrow of the Bonapartist caste will, of course, have deep social consequences, but in itself it will be confined within the limits of political revolution.[12]

The bureaucracy was a group parasitic on these socialist "economic foundations," and was therefore a historically transient formation. "Might we not place ourselves in a ludicrous position," he asked his uncertain followers in 1939, "if we affixed to the Bonapartist oligarchy the nomenclature of a new ruling class just a few years or even a few months prior to its inglorious downfall?"[13] Trotsky therefore regarded the Stalinist regime as a historically unique and inherently unstable formation: the socialist property relations he thought were embodied in nationalized property had to be defended, but the regime was doomed to collapse under the impact of the coming world war, either by bourgeois counter-revolution and capitalist restoration, or by proletarian political revolution—although, as we shall see, he did allow in his last writings that there might also be a third alternative in which the bureaucracy transformed itself from a parasitic caste into a new ruling class.

His characterization of the bureaucracy also had implications for how he expected it to behave outside Russia—an expectation amply supported by its role in China, Germany, and Spain, to list only the sites of the most spectacular catastrophes in which it had been implicated: "The bureaucracy which became a reactionary force in the USSR cannot play a revolutionary role in the world arena."[14] He did allow, however, that there was one possible way in which the bureaucracy might inadvertently do so. At the opening of the Second World War in September 1939 the Soviet Union invaded and forcibly incorporated eastern Poland and western Ukraine, imposing identical property relations to its own in the process. In the ensuing war between the Soviet Union and Finland it seemed possible that the latter country would also be subject to what some Trotskyists would later call "structural assimilation" to the Soviet Union.[15] In assessing what Stalin had done in these cases, Trotsky drew a specific analogy with the latter stages of the bourgeois revolution in France:

> The first Bonaparte halted the revolution by means of a military dictatorship. However, when the French troops invaded Poland, Napoleon signed a decree: "Serfdom is abolished." This measure was dictated not by Napoleon's sympathies for the peasants, nor by democratic principles but rather by the fact that the Bonapartist dictatorship based itself not on feudal, but on bourgeois property relations. Inasmuch as Stalin's Bonapartist dictatorship bases itself not on private but on state property, the invasion of Poland by the Red Army should, in the nature of the case, result in the abolition of private capitalist property, so as thus to bring the regime of the occupied territories into accord with the regime of the USSR.[16]

The assumption here is that these "revolutions from above" would only occur at the margins of the global struggle, on the "debatable lands" that bordered Russia itself: Trotsky did not speculate on what would happen if these types of transformations began to play a more central role—if quantity, so to speak, was transformed into quality.

The third proposition was that the bourgeoisies of the colonial and semi-colonial world had irreversibly moved into the camp of counterrevolution. They were too intertwined with native pre-capitalist classes or foreign imperialist interests or both to lead a struggle against either; but even had they the inclination to do so they were too frightened of the working class to attempt to realize their objectives in practice. The coming revolutions—which, to be sure, would have to encompass bourgeois tasks—could only be led to victory by working classes following the strategy of permanent revolution, as the Russian had during 1917:

> As evidenced by the entire subsequent course of development in Europe and Asia [since 1848], the bourgeois revolution, taken by itself, can no more in general be consummated. A complete purge of feudal rubbish from society is conceivable only on the condition that the proletariat, freed from the influence of bourgeois parties, can take its stand at the head of the peasantry and establish its revolutionary dictatorship. By this token, the bourgeois revolution becomes interlaced with the first stage of the socialist revolution, subsequently to dissolve in the latter. The national revolution therewith becomes a link of the world revolution. The transformation of the economic foundation and of all social relations assumes a permanent (uninterrupted) character. For revolutionary parties in backward countries of Asia, Latin America, and Africa, a clear understanding of the organic connection between the democratic revolution and the dictatorship of the proletariat—and thereby the international socialist revolution—is a life or death question.[17]

He saw the Stalinist parties increasingly supporting these counterrevolutionary bourgeoisies. In Spain, he wrote, Stalin "placed the technique of Bolshevism at the service of bourgeois property."[18] Indeed, both in Spain and beyond members of the bourgeoisie and petty bourgeoisie were actually being incorporated into membership of the Communist parties:

> The ... degeneration of the Comintern transformed its sections in colonial and semi-colonial countries, especially in Latin America, into a left agency of European and American imperialism. Parallel with this, a change occurred also in the social basis of the colonial "Communist" parties. ... Stalinism has in recent years become the party of [the] labor "aristocracy" as well as the "left" section of the petty bourgeoisie, the office holders in particular. Bourgeois lawyers, journalists, teachers, etc., adapting themselves to the national revolution and exploiting the labor organizations to make careers for themselves, find in Stalinism the best possible ideology. ... Stalinism— under all its masks—is the chief obstacle in the path of the liberating struggle of backward and oppressed peoples.[19]

Unchecked—and after Stalin's complicity in the rise of Hitler to power Trotsky believed it would continue unchecked—the changing composition of the Stalinist parties might even lead to open class conflict between them and genuine revolutionary movements based on the working class: "The struggle between the two

Communist factions, the Stalinists and the Bolshevik-Leninists ... bears in itself an inner *tendency* toward transformation into a class struggle. The revolutionary development of events in China may draw this tendency to its conclusion, i.e., to a civil war between the peasant army led by the Stalinists and the proletarian van-guard led by the Leninists."[20]

As in the case of the revolutionary role of the Russian bureaucracy, however, Trotsky made what seemed at the time to be a minor qualification to his assessment of both bourgeois and Stalinist incapacity. Even where foreign dominance was "concealed by the fiction of State independence" the ruling bourgeoisie was capable of resisting imperialism, at least up to a certain point.[21] This tended to be the case in countries that had never been formal colonies or had ceased to be during the era of classic bourgeois revolutions. The most obvious examples of this were those that were the first and last destinations of his final exile: Turkey and Mexico.

During the early stages of the Turkish Revolution, immediately prior to the First World War, he had written:

> In the tasks before it (economic independence, unity of nation and state, political freedom), the Turkish revolution constitutes self-determination by the bourgeois na-tion and in this sense it belongs with the traditions of the 1789–1848. But the army, led by its officers, functioned as the executive organ of the nation, and this at once gave events the planned character of military maneuvers. It would, however, have been utter nonsense (and many people were guilty of this) to see in the events of last July a mere *pronunciamento* and to treat them as analogous to some military-dynastic coup d'etat in Serbia. The strength of the Turkish officers and the secret of their suc-cess lie not in any brilliantly organized "plan" or devilishly cunning conspiracy, but in the active sympathy shown them by the advanced classes: the merchants, the crafts-men, the workers, sections of the officials and of the clergy and, finally, the countryside as embodied in the peasant army.[22]

Even here the emphasis is on popular support for the Young Turks, in the form of strikes by "bakery workers, printers, weavers, tramway employees ... tobacco workers ... as well as port and railway workers," and these had played a major role in the boycott of Austrian goods.[23] Yet once the regime had stabilized in the mid-1920s it began to accommodate to imperialism, despite the best efforts of Russian diplomacy, subsequently making only the most token gestures toward independence.

Mexico presented a more complex picture. In 1938, shortly after Trotsky arrived, the regime nationalized the foreign-owned oil industry. In this context he described the Mexican Revolution as an ongoing process that was carrying on "the same work as ... the United States of America accomplished in three-quarters of a century, be-ginning with the Revolutionary War for independence and finishing with the Civil War for the abolition of slavery and for national unification," and even made some-what exaggerated comparisons between the Mexican leader Cárdenas with the lead-ers of the American Revolution.[24] But later that year, in more reflective discussion, he described the period of the 1930s as generally being one "in which the national bourgeoisie searches for a bit more independence from the foreign imperialists" and that revolutionaries were "in permanent competition with the national bourgeoisie as the one leadership which is capable of assuring the victory of the masses in a fight against the foreign imperialists." As the notion of "competition" suggests, although the organizations of the national bourgeoisie were in some senses "the Popular Front in the form of a party," they played a different role from the entirely reactionary popular fronts in Europe and North America: "It can have a reactionary character insofar as it is directed against the worker; it can have an aggressive attitude insofar as it is directed against imperialism."[25]

In relation to the Stalinists Trotsky also allowed that, although "highly improbable" a "workers' and farmers' government" might be created: "one cannot categorically deny in advance the theoretical possibility that, under the influence of completely exceptional events (war, defeat, financial crash, mass revolutionary pressure, etc.), the petty bourgeoisie parties, including the Stalinists, may go further than they themselves wish along the road to a break with the bourgeoisie." Trotsky was nevertheless clear that this "would represent merely a short episode on the road to the actual dictatorship of the proletariat."[26] Given the uses to which these brief remarks were subsequently used by some of his followers it is important to note that Trotsky is not claiming that there are circumstances in which Social Democrats or Stalinists would establish a soviet regime, merely that they might be forced into a more radically reformist stance prior to actual revolutions taking place. However, given that the type of "completely exceptional events" listed by Trotsky were precisely what he *expected* to take place and consequently exercise their "influence," this passage contained sufficient ambiguity to sustain several different interpretations.

These caveats raised issues whose implications would only become apparent after Trotsky's death. He had written off the possibility of decolonization without permanent revolution, seeing the relative freedom of states like Turkey or Mexico as exceptional; but what were the implications of states with a similar relationship to the world system (that is, backward capitalism) multiplying? Similarly, he had imagined that revolutions in the more advanced states, or in those that had experienced uneven and combined development would come to the aid of those that were too backward or inert even to begin the revolutionary process; but this assumed that future revolutions would be based on an internationalist working class: what if the objective changed from international socialist revolution to national capitalist development?

In a biography of Stalin left unfinished at his death he searched for comparisons that would clarify the historical role of his subject: "In attempting to find a historical parallel for Stalin, we have to reject not only Cromwell, Robespierre, Napoleon and Lenin, but even Mussolini and Hitler. [We come] closer to an understanding of Stalin [when we think in terms of] Mustapha Kemal Pasha or perhaps Porfirio Díaz."[27]

Kemal and Díaz were of course the respective dictators of Turkey and Mexico in their first periods of top-down modernizing development. In one sense the comparison underestimates the scale of what Stalin achieved in these terms and is intended to belittle him in relation to a list of truly great revolutionary leaders of varied class origin. But in another sense, given that Trotsky thought the Turkish Revolution that Kemal came to lead had to solve the tasks of 1789–1848, it also suggested another series of unsettling questions. What if the Stalinist regime in Russia was in effect a bureaucratic substitute for the bourgeoisie? What if the Communist parties in the colonial and semi-colonial world were not merely reformist adjuncts to the bourgeoisie, but could in certain circumstances perform its former revolutionary role?

As we saw in chapter 14, Trotsky, like Benjamin and Gramsci, understood that revolution involved a wager and, like them, he was one of the very few Marxists prepared to look into the abyss that opened up once it was acknowledged that the wager could be lost:

> If this war provokes, as we firmly believe, a proletarian revolution, it must inevitably lead to the overthrow of the bureaucracy in the USSR and regeneration of Soviet democracy on a far higher economic and cultural basis than in 1918. In that case the question as to whether the Stalinist bureaucracy was a "class" or a growth on the workers' state will be automatically solved. To every single person it will become clear that in the process of the development of the world revolution the Soviet bureaucracy was only an *episodic* relapse. If, however, it is conceded that the present war will provoke not revolution but a decline of the proletariat, then there remains another alternative: the further decay of monopoly capitalism, its further fusion with the state and the replacement of democracy wherever it still remained by a totalitarian regime. The inability of the proletariat to take into its hands the leadership of society could actually lead under these conditions to the growth of a new exploiting class from the Bonapartist fascist bureaucracy. This would be, according to all indications, a regime of decline, signalizing the eclipse of civilization. An analogous result might occur in the event that the proletariat of advanced capitalist countries, having conquered power, should prove incapable of holding it and surrender it, as in the USSR, to a privileged bureaucracy. Then we would be compelled to acknowledge that the reason for the bureaucratic relapse is rooted not in the backwardness of the country and not in the imperialist environment but in the congenital incapacity of the proletariat to become a ruling class. Then it would be necessary in retrospect to establish that in its fundamental traits the present USSR was the precursor of a new exploiting régime on an international scale. . . . The historical alternative, carried to the end, is as follows: either the Stalin regime is an abhorrent relapse in the process of transforming bourgeois society into a socialist society, or the Stalin regime is the first stage of a new exploiting society. If the second prognosis proves to be correct then, of course, the bureaucracy will become a new exploiting class. However onerous the second perspective may be, if the world proletariat should actually prove incapable of fulfilling the mission placed upon it by the course of development, nothing else would remain except only to recognize that the socialist programme, based on the internal contradictions of capitalist society, ended as a Utopia.[28]

It is important to understand the full enormity of what Trotsky is proposing here: if capitalism and Stalinism were not both swept away by revolution, then the latter, far from being a historical anomaly, would actually become the model for a totalitarian fusion of capital and the state in the West and the East ("the precursor of a new exploiting régime on an international scale").

Between the end of the Second World War in 1945 and the opening of the Korean War in 1950 it became clear that none of Trotsky's propositions had withstood the verdict of history. First, capitalism had not collapsed but had entered what would ultimately prove to be the greatest period of economic growth in history. Second, Stalinist Russia had not only survived but emerged stronger and expanded territorially into Eastern and Central Europe where it created states in its own image. Third, permanent revolution had not occurred in the colonial and semi-colonial world, but indigenous Stalinist parties based mainly on the peasantry had instead founded new states in the Balkans and Southeast Asia that, in all essentials, followed the Russian model. How did Trotskyists respond to these developments and what did their responses mean for the theory of bourgeois revolution?

One response, adopted by adherents of what US Trotskyist James P. Cannon called "orthodox Trotskyism," was effectively to revise reality so that it corresponded with the claims that Trotsky had made before the Second World War. In Alasdair MacIntyre's words, "It transformed into abstract dogma what Trotsky thought in concrete terms at one moment in his life and canonized this."[29] This was a necessary consequence of treating his judgments as beyond falsification, but one that also meant losing contact with the principle of working-class self-emancipation that had been at the heart of both Trotskyism and the classical Marxist tradition it sought to continue. An alternative response to the falsification of Trotsky's claims was taken by the "unorthodox," whose ranks included Cornelius Castoriadis, Tony Cliff, Raya Dunayevskaya, C. L. R. James, and Max Shachtman. Some of these figures continued to consider themselves Trotskyists, some did not; but all of them, whatever their other differences, attempted to revise Trotsky's final positions in the light of reality by holding fast, not to his specific judgments but to the central tenets and methods of historical materialism that underpinned the latter's greatest achievements. And, initially at any rate, they all cleaved to the self-activity of the working class, not as an optional if desirable extra but as the indispensable core of Marxism as a theory of socialist revolution.[30]

The key issue at stake, the one which—to quote Henry Cockburn on the French Revolution—affected "not this thing, or that thing, but literally every thing," was the validity of Trotsky's definition of Russia as a "workers' state." Accompanying Trotsky's shift from reformist to revolutionary conclusions in relation to the Stalinist regime was a related shift in his understanding of why Russia supposedly remained a workers' state, albeit a necessary one if he was to maintain that the forthcoming revolution could only be political in nature. The original position of the Bolsheviks was quite clear. "I have no illusions about our having only just entered the period of transition to socialism," said Lenin in January 1918, "about not yet having reached socialism."[31] Four months later, he noted that the Russian economy still contained five intermingled "socio-economic structures"; patriarchal or "natural" peasant farming, small commodity production, private capitalism, state capitalism, and socialism. His point was that Russia was not a socialist state, it was a workers' state, defined not by state ownership of the economy but by whether the working class exercised political rule, by whether "the Soviet state is a state in which the power of the workers and the poor is assured."[32] In May 1918, this was still true, if only just; but by the Eighth Congress of the Soviets in 1920 Lenin had to point out to Trotsky that not only the economy involved non-socialist character-istics: the workers' state itself was becoming increasingly subject to non-proletarian class influences:

> Comrade Trotsky speaks of a "workers' state." May I say that this is an abstraction. It was natural for us to write about a workers' state in 1917; but it is now a patent error to say: "Since this is a workers' state without any bourgeoisie, against whom then is the working class to be protected, and for what purpose?" The whole point is that it is not quite a workers' state. That is where Comrade Trotsky makes one of his main mistakes. . . . This will not do. For one thing, ours is not actually a workers' state but a workers' and peasants' state. And a lot depends on that.

Following this passage in Lenin's speech, *Bukharin shouted from the floor:* "What kind of state? A workers' and peasants' state?"[33] Bukharin was expressing incredulity toward the idea that such a hybrid formation could exist. Shortly after this discussion, Lenin returned to the subject, taking account of Bukharin's interjection:

> I must correct another mistake of mine. I said: "Ours is not actually a workers' state but a workers' and peasants' state." Comrade Bukharin immediately exclaimed: "What kind of a state?" In reply I referred him to the Eighth Congress of Soviets, which had just closed. I went back to the report of that discussion and found that I was wrong and Comrade Bukharin was right. What I should have said is: "A workers' state is an abstraction. What we actually have is a workers' state, with this peculiarity, firstly, that it is not the working class but the peasant population that predominates in the coun-try, and, secondly, that it is a workers' state with bureaucratic distortions."[34]

It is possible, of course, to debate the extent to which the working class exercised political rule between 1918 and 1920, but the basis of the definition itself is un-ambiguous and was accepted by Trotsky who wrote, again in 1920, that a workers' state was defined by what he called "the class nature of the government."[35]

As summarized by Cliff, Trotsky's initial position depended on "whether the proletariat has direct or indirect control, no matter how restricted, over the state power; that is, whether the proletariat can get rid of the bureaucracy by reform alone, without the need for a revolution." In his subsequent definition, however: "No matter how independent the state machine is from the masses, and even if the only way of getting rid of the bureaucracy be by revolution, so long as the means of production are statified the state remains a workers' state with the proletariat the ruling class."[36] On this basis of his revised definition, Stalin's "Second Revolu-tion" after 1928 could be deemed far more revolutionary than October 1917 be-cause it introduced the nationalized property relations upon which the "workers' state" was supposed to depend—indeed, Isaac Deutscher was subsequently to write that in terms of "scope and immediate impact . . . the second revolution was even more sweeping than the first."[37] Furthermore, if the decisive criterion was nationalized property, then why did it matter which class or social force introduced it? What need was there for the revolutionary party, the working class, or indeed any of the tenets of classical Marxism? The Red Army would be sufficient.

The anti-Marxist implications of shifting from working-class power to nationalized property relations were largely held in check in Trotsky's own work. He was careful to emphasize in his last writings that nationalized property was a remnant, a last remaining vestige of the workers' state, and that the progressive content of nationalization would only be realized after the overthrow of the bureaucracy. For orthodox Trotskyists nationalized property was now transformed from being a residual characteristic to the only relevant factor. On this basis, of course, several new, albeit "deformed," "workers' states" had been created—although the working classes had not been involved in the revolutions that had created them, did not in any sense control them, and were subjected to ruthless police dictatorships while being forced to participate in the process of primitive accumulation. As long as these were simply extensions of Stalinist Russia, as in Eastern Europe and North Korea, it was more or less possible to retain Trotsky's analysis—even though this level of expansion contradicted his claims for the weakness and instability of the regime; but as soon as identical states emerged through indigenous Stalinist movements in Yugoslavia and China, as soon as Stalinism was revealed to be, not an accident of history but an emergent tendency within the world system, the category of workers' state either had to be abandoned or its original meaning transformed. The latter course involved a kind of metaphysics that equated a set of juridical relations with the class nature of the state, which in turn led, logically enough, to the reimagining—or perhaps one should say the rebranding—of social classes themselves. A party-army led by petty-bourgeois intellectuals and consisting of militarized ex-peasants could, for example, be described as representing, or perhaps even consisting of, "the Chinese working class," and its victory in 1949 hailed as a socialist revolution: whether one accepted this or not determined whether Trotskyists entered the orthodox or unorthodox camp.

Nevertheless, in relation to developing a consequentialist position on bourgeois revolution both tendencies made important contributions, albeit in different areas. Two figures in particular, one from each camp, are important here, although in most respects they were as far apart from each other as it is possible to be while still claiming an affinity with Trotsky's thought: Deutscher and Cliff. After the outbreak of the Second World War—or rather, after Russia's entry into the Second World War—Deutscher never again seems to have considered active participation in a political organization; Cliff spent his entire life trying to build one. In 1951 Deutscher reviewed *The God That Failed*, a collective confessional by ex-Communist Party writers justifying their abandonment of revolution for various forms of social democracy. His alternative was revealing:

[The ex-Communist] cannot join the Stalinist camp or the anti-Stalinist Holy Alliance without doing violence to his better self. So let him stay outside any camp. Let him try to regain critical sense and intellectual detachment. . . . This is not to say that ex-communist man of letters, or intellectual at large should retire into the ivory tower. (His contempt for the ivory tower lingers in him from his past.) But he may withdraw into a watchtower instead. To watch with detachment and alertness this heaving chaos of a world, to be on sharp lookout for what is going to emerge from it, and to interpret it *sine ira et studio*—this is now the only honorable service the ex-communist intellectual can render to a generation in which scrupulous observation and honest interpretation have become so sadly rare.[38]

Cliff argued that Deutscher was effectively describing his own situation, but that in practical terms his position in the watchtower was no different from one in the ivory tower that he ostensibly rejected.[39] In fact, there is evidence that Deutscher descended from the watchtower toward the end of his life.[40] During the period in which his major works were written, however, there is no doubt that Cliff's criticism was substantially correct. Deutscher joined neither the Fourth International nor of any of the dissident organizations that split from it after Trotsky's death. Indeed, his attitude to Trotskyism was deeply dismissive and Trotskyists paid him back in the same coin, attacking his work while simultaneously plagiarizing his scholarship.[41] These opposing attitudes to organization and activity were inseparable from their different interpretations of Stalinism. Nevertheless, it was precisely Deutscher's support for Stalin's "revolution from above" in Eastern Europe that informed his insights into the nature of the historical bourgeois revolutions, while Cliff's opposition to the same process allowed him to comprehend the formation of new Stalinist states in the Balkans and Asia as the modern equivalents of these revolutions.

DEUTSCHER ON THE STRUCTURE OF THE BOURGEOIS AND PROLETARIAN REVOLUTIONS

Like the orthodox Trotskyists, Deutscher accepted that Russia and its satellites and imitators were all "workers' states" because they were based on nationalized property. Yet, his description of *The Revolution Betrayed* (1937) became "the Bible of latter-day Trotskyist sects and chapels whose members piously mumbled its verses long after Trotsky's death," conveys his impatience with the religious veneration they accorded Trotsky's last writings. Why? Not because they clung to its definition of a "workers' state," but because most refused to abandon their formal commitment to political revolution.[42] Deutscher described himself as "[f]ree from loyalties to any cult," by which he meant Trotskyism as much as Stalinism.[43] From 1948 the dominant tendency within the Fourth International, associated with Michael Pablo, had successfully argued that the Stalinist states in Eastern Europe and China were "workers' states." But even Pablo had assumed that it would be Stalinist parties that would—under "exceptional circumstances," "pressure from the masses," and the like—carry out future revolutions. Deutscher was able go much further than orthodox Trotskyists could without rendering their existence completely redundant and claim that Stalinist Russia was not only capable of internal self-reform, but that, even unreformed, it was the major force for world revolution. At one level this is, of course, merely the logic of the orthodox Trotskyists taken to its conclusion. For many of them, therefore, their rage at Deutscher was that of Caliban at seeing his own face in the mirror.

Deutscher's position does at least have the benefit of consistency. Unfortunately it is consistently wrong. "We need not doubt," he wrote, "that . . . the logic of [Trotsky's] attitude would have compelled him to accept the reality of the revolution in Eastern Europe, and despite all distaste for the Stalinist methods, to recognize the 'People's Democracies' as workers' states."[44] I do doubt this, for the simple reason that it is entirely incompatible with Trotsky's view of Stalinism. Deutscher undoubtedly thought it would be desirable for these property relations to be supplemented by democracy, but that was not decisive. "No one can foresee with certainty whether the conflict will take violent and explosive forms and lead to the new 'political revolution' which Trotsky once advocated, or whether the conflict will be resolved peacefully through bargaining, compromise, and the gradual enlargement of freedom."[45] This leaves the question open, but effectively concedes that the bureaucracy is capable of self-transformation, of bringing the degeneracy of the political superstructure into line with the purity of the socialist economic base, so to speak. At no point, even before his exile, did Trotsky ever believe that the bureaucracy could reform *itself*. Even further from Trotsky's own positions, Deutscher believed that the working class should refrain from any activity that might threaten this self-reformation or open the door to the return of capitalism: "Eastern Europe (Hungary, Poland, and eastern Germany) . . . found itself almost on the brink of bourgeois restoration at the end of the Stalin era; and only Soviet armed power (or its threat) stopped it there."[46]

The theoretical roots of these attitudes can be found in Deutscher's inability to distinguish between different types of revolution or, more precisely, his assumption that bourgeois and proletarian revolutions shared a common structure. In his case this was because he thought that the proletarian revolution could be assimilated to the bourgeois revolution, rather than—as is more commonly the case—the other way around. Paradoxically, however, this allowed him to take a much clearer position on bourgeois revolutions than almost any other Marxist in the postwar period, his only rivals being the dissident "unorthodox" Trotskyists who opposed him in virtually every other way.

In some respects Deutscher held the same assumptions as those of the Stalinist orthodoxy. In an interview for Hamburg Television in 1967, for example, he opined that "since the Reformation the tragedy of Germany consists in the fact that it has not advanced with the times, and that Germany has never fought through its own revolution." There then follows the standard evocation of the English and French experiences, against which Germany has been tried and found wanting:

Germany in many respects has remained fixed in the sixteenth century and at the catastrophe of the Thirty Years War. Every revolution has failed. Germany did not merely invent the *ersatz* industrially, it produced it socio-politically as well: the ersatz-revolution of a Bismarck, the ersatz revolution of 1918 and the ersatz-revolution of 1945—none of them were made by Germans, but by conquering foreign armies. That is the tragedy, the guilt and the misfortune of Germany.[47]

This passage, delivered in the German media at the beginning of a period of the first real era of radical insurgency since the Second World War may have been exaggerated for polemical purposes, and it does not necessarily imply that Germany was unsuccessful in achieving capitalism. The underlying theme of an external model to which Germany had failed to reproduce is, however, all too orthodox and quite compatible with more sophisticated Stalinist positions, such as those associated with the postwar writings of Lukács and with those of radical sociologists like Moore. Elsewhere, Deutscher contributed more compelling reflections, specifically in two lengthy passages separated by twenty years.

The first is from his 1949 biography, *Stalin*. Deutscher begins by making a distinction within types of *socialist* revolution, "*revolution from below*, such as the upheaval of 1917 had been" and the Stalinist takeover of Eastern and Central Europe, "primarily a *revolution from above*." Deutscher justified this argument by analogy with the spread of the bourgeois revolutions, with Stalin playing the role of Napoleon or Bismarck:

> Europe, in the nineteenth century, saw how the feudal order, outside France, crumbled and was replaced by the bourgeois one. But east of the Rhine, feudalism was not overthrown by a series of upheavals on the pattern of the French Revolution, by explosions of popular despair and anger, by revolutions from below, for the spread of which some of the Jacobins had hoped in 1794. Instead, European feudalism was either destroyed or undermined by a series of revolutions from above. Napoleon, the tamer of Jacobitism at home, carried the revolution into foreign lands, to Italy, to the Rhineland, and to Poland, where he abolished serfdom, completely or in part, and where his code destroyed many of the feudal privileges. *Malgré lui-meme*, he executed parts of the political testament of Jacobitism. More paradoxically, the Conservative Junker, Bismarck, performed a similar function when he freed Germany from many survivals of feudalism which encumbered her bourgeois development. The second generation after the French Revolution witnessed an even stranger spectacle, when the Russian Tsar himself abolished serfdom in Russia and Poland, a deed of which not so long before only "Jacobins" had dreamt. The feudal order had been too moribund to survive; but outside France the popular forces arrayed against it were too weak to overthrow it "from below"; and so it was swept away "from above."[48]

The second passage comes from the 1967 George Trevelyan lectures, which formed the basis of his last book, *The Unfinished Revolution*. Here Deutscher anticipates the revisionist critique that clinging to the orthodox conception invited:

> The traditional view [of the bourgeois revolution], widely accepted by Marxists and non-Marxists alike, is that in such revolutions, in Western Europe, the bourgeois played the leading part, stood at the head of the insurgent people, and seized power.

This view underlies many controversies among historians; the recent exchanges, for example, between Professor Hugh Trevor-Roper and Mr. Christopher Hill on whether the Cromwellian revolution was or was not bourgeois in character. It seems to me that this conception, to whatever authorities it may be attributed, is schematic and unreal. From it one may well arrive at the conclusion that bourgeois revolution is almost a myth, and that it has hardly ever occurred, even in the West. Capitalist entrepreneurs, merchants, and bankers were not conspicuous among the leaders of the Puritans or the commanders of the Ironsides, in the Jacobin Club or at the head of the crowds that stormed the Bastille or invaded the Tuileries. Nor did they seize the reins of government during the revolution nor for a long time afterwards, either in England or in France. The lower middle classes, the urban poor, the plebeians and *sans culottes* made up the big insurgent battalions. The leaders were mostly "gentlemen farmers" in England and lawyers, doctors, journalists and other intellectuals in France. Here and there the upheavals ended in military dictatorship. Yet the bourgeois character of these revolutions will not appear at all mythical, if we approach them with a broader criterion and view their general impact on society. Their most substantial and enduring achievement was to sweep way the social and political institutions that had hindered the growth of bourgeois property and of the social relationships that went with it. When the Puritans denied the Crown the right of arbitrary taxation, when Cromwell secured for English shipowners a monopolistic position in England's trading with foreign countries, and when the Jacobins abolished feudal prerogatives and privileges and, they created, often unknowingly, the conditions in which manufacturers, merchants, and bankers were bound to gain economic predominance, and, in the long run, social and even political supremacy. Bourgeois revolution creates the conditions in which bourgeois property can flourish. In this, rather than in the particular alignments of the struggle, lies its *differentia specifica*.[49]

In these passages Deutscher identifies two different types of revolutions from above. One is where states established by revolutions from below, like those of Cromwell or Napoleon, spread the revolution externally by military intervention. The other is where the ancien régime itself—or elements within it—imposes capitalist social relations of production internally through their control of the existing state apparatus. The second type of revolution from above is important in relation to his more general argument concerning the definition of bourgeois revolutions. These cannot be defined by reference to class position of the social forces that carried them out, since in neither case were these composed of capitalists or even members of the bourgeoisie. Nor can they be defined by their intentions, since neither the English Independents nor the French Jacobins were primarily motivated by establishing capitalist relations of production; the Prussian Junkers and Japanese samurai were concerned with this outcome, but more as a means of strengthening the international political and military positions of their respective states than with the profitability of their individual estates.

Deutscher was not alone in identifying two characteristics of bourgeois revolutions as being "revolution from above" as a possible means of achieving them, and their outcomes as being the decisive factor in assessing whether they had occurred. Several other writers from the Trotskyist tradition—including those who were the most critical of his views on Stalinism, above all Cliff and Shachtman—took essentially the same positions. In relation to the first, Cliff wrote in 1949, that those like Deutscher who saw "the revolution that took place in Eastern Europe and [the] Bismarckian path of capitalist development in Germany" were adopting a position that "if thought out, leads to the most shocking conclusions," namely the abandonment of the self-activity of the working class as the basis of socialism. Nevertheless, Cliff's position on the nature of the bourgeois revolutions is similar to Deutscher's: "As a matter of fact it was only in one case that they carried through to the end a revolutionary struggle against feudalism—this was in France. In the case of England they compromised with the feudal landowners. In Germany and Italy, Poland and Russia, China and South America, they came to power without a revolutionary struggle. In the USA the almost complete non-existence of feudal remnants enabled the bourgeoisie to avoid an anti-feudal revolutionary struggle." Cliff is underestimating the level of struggle involved with France, not least in England and—in relation to the Civil War at least—America, presumably as an exercise in "stick-bending" for the purposes of his argument; nevertheless, his conclusion is apt: "The 'Bismarckian' path was not the exception for the bourgeoisie, but the rule, the exception was the French revolution."[50] Shachtman wrote during the same year: "The Great French Revolution was great—the greatest of all the bourgeois revolutions, the classic among bourgeois revolutions—precisely because it was not organized and led by the French bourgeoisie!" There then follows a discussion of the different social forces at work in England, France, and by Napoleon in Europe. Unlike Deutscher, but like Cliff, Shachtman sees Germany as the paradigmatic case: "In Germany it was not the bourgeoisie that unified the nation and leveled the feudal barriers to the expansion of capitalism, but the iron representative of the Prussian Junkers, Bismarck. He carried out bourgeois revolution in the interests of the feudal Junkers, and made his united Germany a powerful capitalist country, but without the bourgeoisie and against it. Much the same process developed in distant Japan." Again, there is a degree of polemical understatement involved here: the bourgeoisie may have been unwilling or even incapable of waging their own revolution, but Bismarck could scarcely be said to be acting *against* their interests. The point that Shachtman makes next is however of major importance:

Once the fetters of feudalism were removed from the capitalist mode of production, the basic victory and the expansion of the bourgeoisie and its social system were absolutely guaranteed. Once the work of destruction was accomplished, the work of constructing bourgeois society could proceed automatically by the spontaneous expansion of capital as regulated automatically by the market. To the bourgeoisie, therefore, it could not make a fundamental difference whether the work of destruction was begun or carried out by the plebeian Jacobin terror against the aristocracy, as in France, or by the aristocracy itself in promotion of its own interests, as in Germany. Neither the revolutionary French plebeians nor the Napoleonic empire builders could replace feudalism with a special economic system of their own, or create any social system other than bourgeois society.[51]

These remarks, which echo those of Lukács in *History and Class Consciousness*, were made in the course of a very critical review of Deutscher's *Stalin*; but on this point both the criticized and the critic were as one. What this indicates, I think, is that in this, as in so may other respects, Trotskyism was responsible for preserving important elements of the classical Marxist tradition that would otherwise have been even more deeply buried than they were. In this respect, Cliff and Shachtman were still closer to each other at this date, despite their different assessments of the nature of Stalinism, than either was to orthodox Trotskyism.

In terms of Deutscher's own work the problem arises when he extends his model from bourgeois to proletarian revolutions, whose structures are necessarily quite different. He argued in *Stalin* that his subject "does not stand alone in modern European history" but had been preceded by "Napoleon and Bismarck." Indeed: "It is mainly in Napoleon's impact upon the lands neighboring France that the analogy is found for the impact of Stalinism upon eastern and central Europe."[52] In several places Deutscher argues that all the "great revolutions" (English, French, Russian) follow the same pattern. First comes the rising against the old regime, which unites the majority of the oppressed. Then follows the civil war, which exhausts the new society and leads to the supposedly temporary suppression of many of the freedoms for which the revolution was made. Finally, the new ruling class entrenches itself and decisively abandons the egalitarian dreams of the popular masses, leading the most radical elements to cry "the revolution betrayed" before their ultimate suppression.[53] The only real difference he sees in the case of Russia is that, unlike the Independents and Jacobins, the Bolshevik Party formed prior to the outbreak of revolutionary crisis: "This enabled it to assume leadership in the revolution and, after the ebb of the tide, to play for many decades the part the army had played in revolutionary England and France, to secure stable government and to work towards the integration and remodeling of national life."[54] In all other respects, Deutscher finds the parallels exact, even down to the role of the leader who eventually emerges. "What appears to be established is that Stalin belongs to the breed of the great revolutionary despots, to which Cromwell, Robespierre, and Napoleon belonged."[55] If Hegel saw Napoleon as the World Spirit mounted on horseback then, reading this passage, one has the impression that Deutscher saw Stalin as the World Spirit mounted on a tank. As we saw in chapter 14, Trotsky rejected Cromwell, Robespierre, Napoleon, Lenin, Mussolini, and Hitler as useful parallels for Stalin, comparing him instead with Kemal and Díaz, the Turkish and Mexican modernizing dictators. Deutscher was evidently disturbed by the fact that Trotsky did not support his view of Stalin: "Here the lack of historical scale and perspective is striking and disturbing."[56] In fact, Trotsky is far nearer the truth, and it is a matter of regret that he did not live to pursue these comparisons further; for a parallel with the bourgeois revolutions is relevant, but not the one Deutscher imagined.

Deutscher's influence was immense during the 1960s and for some radicals at least, it was possible to be a Deutscherist without being a Trotskyist.[57] In 1965

Perry Anderson, perhaps the leading exponent of "non-Trotskyist" Deutscherism, wrote about "Deutscher's masterly writings on the subject" of "the grandeur and servitude of Leninism," and the following year described him as "the only Marxist historian of world eminence working in Britain today."[58] In his memoir of the sixties Tariq Ali recalls Anderson being "sympathetic to the positions of the pro-Moscow CPs in Western Europe . . . moderated by a particular interpretation of Isaac Deutscher's writings on the USSR."[59] Here is Anderson during this period defending the idea that the Stalinist states are not merely workers' states but actually socialist, in classic Deutscherist terms: "Socialism in its full critical and philosophical sense—the realm of freedom, the final triumph of man over necessity and alienation—has, of course, not remotely been realized in Russia or any other Eastern country. . . . At the same time, it is pedantic, and parochial, to refuse a certain historical truth to the description: in a minimal-ideal sense, these countries are socialist—their economies are socially and not privately appropriated, and the ideology which regulates their operation is a socialist one." To refuse to recognize this on the grounds that the Stalinist states are undemocratic was, according to Anderson, "a form of blindness." The conclusion to which this led was that Stalin's crimes "were socialist, not liberal crimes—a violence consciously decided and willed, a deliberate reproduction and magnification of the violence inherent in an environment of scarcity."[60] The obscene suggestion that any socialism worthy of the name could be responsible for the death and enslavement of millions of people flows from the reduction of socialism (albeit in a "minimal-ideal sense") to a set of property relations, which can of course be introduced by any number of social forces—as Anderson did not fail to point out:

> Capitalism does not automatically or everywhere require a victorious industrial bourgeoisic to launch it—any more than socialism necessarily requires a victorious industrial proletariat to impose it; although in time capitalism inevitably creates an industrial bourgeoisie, just as socialism in our century has always created an urban proletariat. Only a parochial historian (or Marxist) will be surprised by this. Japanese capitalism was promulgated as a national destiny by the rural warlords of the Satsuma and Choshu clans. Chinese socialism was launched by the Hunan and Yenan peasantry in arms. Modern Brazilian capitalism is the accidental product of an import-substitution process dictated by the interests of the patrimonial coffee oligarchy of São Paulo. Cuban socialism was won by a handful of revolutionary intellectuals supported by the subsistence farmers of the Sierra Maestra. There is no simple, technical fatality which allocates mandatory roles univocally to social groups. Within certain limits (obviously, no bourgeoisie will ever lay the foundation-stones of socialism), objective roles are separable from their agents.[61]

Here the consequences of failing to draw a distinction between the structure of bourgeois and socialist revolutions is all too apparent: the abandonment of any conception of the latter as being *constituted* by the process of working-class self-liberation.

If the working class is irrelevant to the accomplishment of socialism, then what remains? What great impersonal historic forces can take their place? As we saw in chapter 11, Deutscher claimed to uphold what he had termed classical Marxism against the vulgar Marxism practiced by Stalin, Mao, and their epigones, and the virtues of his works confirm that this was no idle boast. Yet, as we have also seen, within the category of classical Marxism he included many of the thinkers of the Second International, like Kautsky and Plekhanov, whose work was characterized—to different degrees—by an extreme determinism. Reading Deutscher's trilogy it is difficult to avoid the conclusion that the experience of the defeat of the Russian Revolution led him to revive the determinism of the Second International. If defeat is too overwhelming, if the prospect of starting again is too difficult, then the temptation can be to present it, through the application of pseudo-dialectical voodoo, as a victory—or at least in the process of being transformed into a victory. Hence the title of the postscript to *The Prophet Outcast*, "Victory in Defeat": "The Soviet Union emerged as the world's second industrial power, its social structure radically transformed, its large industrial working class striving for a modern way of life, and its standards of living and mass education rising rapidly, if unevenly. The very preconditions of socialism which classical Marxism had seen as existing only in the highly industrialized countries of the West were being created and assembled within Soviet society."[62] There is a name for the social system that produces "the preconditions of socialism": it is capitalism. Other thinkers would draw the necessary conclusions.

CLIFF ON THE CONTEMPORARY FORM OF THE BOURGEOIS REVOLUTION

In his autobiography, Cliff recounted how, starting from a perspective of working-class self-emancipation, he "devoted a lot of time and effort to developing three interlinked theories to deal with the three areas of the world" where Trotsky's predictions had proved false, "Russia and Eastern Europe, advanced capitalist countries, and the Third World." "The three theories were: state capitalism, the permanent arms economy, and deflected permanent revolution." This "troika," Cliff writes, "make[s] a unity, a totality, grasping the changes in the situation of humanity after the Second World War." As he also noted, however, "the troika was not conceived as a unity . . . it was only at the end of the process that the inter-relationships between the different spheres of research became clear." He wrote of himself and his collaborators: "Our criticism of orthodox Trotskyism was conceived as a return to classical Marxism."[63] This was, however, classical Marxism conceived in far less deterministic fashion than Deutscher.

First, if capitalism was not in terminal decline, then the possibility existed of it continuing to expand to new areas and consequently of bourgeois revolutions taking place to remove structural obstacles to its local development. One reason for Trotsky's unwillingness to reconsider his expectations of imminent economic and social collapse was the false theoretical assumption that, once the material basis for socialism had been attained under capitalism, it would automatically begin to regress if socialism was not established in the immediate future. As Cliff argued in 1948, even before the full extent of the postwar boom had become apparent:

> A social order which is necessary to develop the productive forces and prepare the material conditions for a higher order of society, is progressive. We must emphasize the *material conditions*, because if we include all the conditions (class consciousness, the existence of mass revolutionary parties, etc., etc.) then any social order will be progressive, as its very existence proves that *all the conditions* for its overthrow are not there. It does not follow that when a social order becomes reactionary, becomes an impediment to the development of the productive forces, that these productive forces cease to advance, or that the rate of advance falls absolutely. There is no doubt that feudalism in Europe became reactionary in the thirteenth to eighteenth centuries, but this did not prevent the productive forces developing at the same rate as before or indeed of developing at an even faster rate.[64]

In other words it was theoretically perfectly possible for the prerequisites for socialism to be present but for capitalism to continue to expand as it did after the Second World War. In 1947, Cliff argued on behalf of the majority of the unified British Trotskyist organization that this was in fact happening, although neither he nor anyone else foresaw how spectacular growth would ultimately be.[65] It was in fact unprecedented. Trotsky noted that growth had been significant in the thirteen years before the First World War, with the rate averaging 4.5 percent per year; but between 1950 and 1970 it averaged 5.5 percent per year, and from a productive base of such increased size that the absolute figures were beyond comparison.[66] "Individual performances have been very different," wrote Michael Kidron, "and most countries have had bursts of speed then suffered hold-ups, but the system as a whole has never grown so fast for so long as since the war—twice as fast between 1950 and 1964 as between 1913 and 1950 and nearly half as fast again as during the generation before that."[67] Nor did the growth stop in 1964: "By 1973 output in the advanced capitalist countries was 180 per cent higher than in 1950—almost three times as great. More was produced in that quarter century than in the previous three quarters, and many more than in any comparable period in human history."[68]

A return to recession after the Second World War was averted by an unintended consequence of the Cold War. Henryk Grossmann in 1929 identified in passing the distinctive effect of military spending on retarding accumulation within classical Marxism.[69] During the 1940s and early 1950s a writer using the pen name of T. N. Vance, associated with the Schachtmanite wing of American Trotskyism, began to argue that what was emerging was a "permanent war economy."[70] Cliff adopted this concept, which was subsequently renamed the "permanent arms economy" by Kidron in recognition of how it was not the use value of armaments that was the key issue but rather the way in which expenditure on what was—in strictly economic terms—waste absorbed capital that would otherwise have reentered the circuit of accumulation. This led to important constraints on the growth of the organic composition of capital and, consequently, counteracted the tendency of the rate of profit to fall.[71] Other mechanisms had performed the same function earlier in the history of the system, notably investment in colonial possessions outside the re-productive circuits of capital and luxury spending by the ruling class, but none of these involved expenditure on a comparably massive scale. And, like these earlier mechanisms, it was assumed that arms expenditure too would ultimately fail as a stabilizer; this was not a theory that assumed, as many from Crosland to Castoriadis did, that Keynesian demand management had permanently abolished the cycle of boom and slump; but for the meantime, during the fifties and sixties, talk of a return to crisis conditions was simply delusional.

Nevertheless, preventing a slump is not the same as causing a boom, although high levels of arms spending did contribute toward it by feeding through to other sectors of the economy through the so-called "multiplier effect." Leaving aside the short-term effects of postwar reconstruction, two other processes were required. One was the generalization of "Fordist" high-productivity, mass-consumption regimes across the core of the system, above all in the production of cars and electrical house-hold goods.[72] The other was the industrialization of those areas of Europe and North America that had previously been based on small-scale, family-based agriculture or petty commodity production, effectively bringing millions of new productive workers into the labor process and consumers into the market for mass-produced commodities.[73] In the Stalinist regimes of Eastern Europe very similar processes were at work as in the West, including industrialization, economic growth, and, less often noticed, the increased availability of consumer goods.[74] Eventually, the expansion and attendant restructuring of the world economy extended, unevenly and inconsistently, to the "newly industrializing countries" of what was from the 1950s known as the Third World; first to Brazil and Mexico in Latin America, then to Hong Kong, Singapore, South Korea, and Taiwan in East Asia, then beyond: "Once the internationalized core was created, the effects spread outwards, involving increasing numbers of less developed countries, so that now there are new newly industrializing countries."[75]

The second area that Cliff addressed was the nature of the Stalinist states. Like everyone else, Cliff recognized the importance of the "Second Revolution," but he saw its significance in diametrically opposite terms from Deutscher:

> The inauguration of the Five-Year Plan has been a turning point in the development of the relations of distribution, in the relations between accumulation and consumption, between the productivity of labor and the standard of living of the workers, in the control over production, in the legal rights of the workers, in the institution of forced labor, in the relation of agriculturalists to the means of production, in the tremendous swelling of the turnover tax, and finally, in the structure and organization of the army, which is a main sector of the state machine. The reality of industrialization and collectivization turned out to be in absolute contradiction to the hopes the masses had in them, and even to the illusions which the bureaucracy themselves held. They thought the Five-Year Plans would take Russia many strides forward to the building of socialism. This is not the first time in history that the results of human

actions are in outright contradiction to the wishes and hopes of the actors themselves. Why was the First Five-Year Plan such a turning point? For the first time the bureaucracy now sought the rapid creation of the proletariat and accumulation of capital, in other words, as quickly as possible to realize the historical mission of the bourgeoisie. . . . Thus industrialization and technical revolution in agriculture ("collectivization") in a backward country under conditions of siege transforms the bureaucracy from a layer which is under the direct and indirect pressure and control of the proletariat, into a ruling class. . . . Dialectical historical development, full of contradictions and surprises, brought it about that the first step the bureaucracy took with the subjective intention of hastening the building of "socialism in one country" became the foundation of the building of state capitalism.[76]

Two points are of key importance here. First, although Cliff saw the bureaucracy as carrying out the economic role of the bourgeoisie, he did not claim that the Stalinist bureaucrats consciously regarded themselves as members of a new collective capitalist class and deliberately attempted to conceal this from the exploited; on the contrary, he argued that they genuinely believed that their actions were leading to the establishment of socialism. This may have been the greatest and most complete example of false consciousness in history, but it is scarcely unprecedented in the history of bourgeois revolutions. Trotsky had considered the possibility that, in China after 1927 at least, Communist Party membership could become dominated by individuals from outside the working class, who would—in the sincere belief that they represented socialism—infuse the organization with their own petty bourgeois interests and values:

> But aren't there communists at the head of the Chinese Red armies? Doesn't this by itself exclude the possibility of conflicts between the peasant detachments and the workers' organizations? No, that does not exclude it. The fact that individual communists are in the leadership of the present armies does not at all transform the social character of these armies, even if their communist leaders bear a definite proletarian stamp. How do matters stand in China? Among the communist leaders are many declassed intellectuals and semi-intellectuals who have not gone through the school of proletarian struggle. For two or three years they live the lives of partisan commanders and commissars; they wage battles, seize territories, etc. They absorb the spirit of their environment. Meanwhile the majority of the rank-and-file communists in the Red detachments unquestionably consists of peasants, who assume the name communist in all honesty and sincerity but who in actuality remain revolutionary paupers or revolutionary petty proprietors. In politics he who judges by denominations and labels and not by social facts is lost.[77]

This is a passage that continues to cause some embarrassment to Trotsky's latterday orthodox followers. Michael Löwy, borrowing a concept from his adversary, Nicolas Krasso, accused Trotsky of "sociologism" for deducing the political nature of the Red Army from its class composition, although Trotsky is then awarded marks because he elsewhere "avoided this sociologistic reductionism and interpreted the concept of proletarian leadership in more specifically political terms as the leadership of a proletarian organization." Löwy then quotes, as evidence, a comment by Trotsky from *Permanent Revolution*, written three years previously: "The realization of the revolutionary alliance between the proletariat and the peasantry is conceivable only under the political leadership of the proletarian vanguard, organized in the Communist party."[78] Trotsky's "sociologism"—or, as I prefer to think of it, his historical materialism—did of course involve the existence of an *actual* proletarian vanguard, not simply a group of petty bourgeois who have been awarded this label because of their supposed adherence to allegedly "proletarian" but in fact Stalinist ideas.

Second, Cliff accepted that the classification of the Soviet Union as a "degenerate workers' state" was valid until 1928, while some increasingly mediated elements of working-class rule remained; but from that date, the state is turned into a weapon against the working class and peasantry *at the same time as property relations were decisively changed by a complete nationalization program.* Cliff's point was that we should be concerned not with relations of property, not with "the juridical illusion," but with relations of production, which were now constituted by wage labor and capital, where the state managers had assumed the role of a "collective capitalist." Trotsky had of course been perfectly aware that *partial* forms of state capitalism existed, particularly in those parts of the semi-colonial world with a "degree of independence":

> The nationalization of railways and oil fields in Mexico has of course nothing in common with socialism. It is a measure of state capitalism in a backward country which in this way seeks to defend itself on the one hand against foreign imperialism and on the other against its own proletariat. The management of railways, oil fields, et cetera, through labor organizations has nothing in common with workers' control over industry, for in the essence of the matter the management is effected through the labor bureaucracy which is independent of the workers, but in return, completely dependent on the bourgeois state. This measure on the part of the ruling class pursues the aim of disciplining the working class, making it more industrious in the service of the common interests of the state, which appear on the surface to merge with the interests of the working class itself.[79]

Trotsky even discussed the possibilities of a "total" state capitalism in *The Revolution Betrayed* and came to this conclusion:

> Theoretically to be sure, it is possible to conceive a situation in which the bourgeoisie as a whole constitutes itself a stock company which, by means of the state, administers the whole economy. The economic laws of such a regime would present no mysteries. . . . Such a regime never existed, however, and, because of profound contradictions among the proprietors themselves, never will exist—the more so since, in its quality of universal repository of capitalist property, the state would be too tempting an object for social revolution.[80]

Trotsky therefore regarded state capitalism as a *practical*, not as a *theoretical*, impossibility, primarily on the contingent grounds that, within particular states, intercapitalist competition will prevent the necessary integration from taking place. But in many ways this type of integration had already taken place. One of the first Marxists to use the actual term, "state capitalism" (the concept goes back to Engels) was

Bukharin during the First World War. He pointed out that, under the imperialist state dominated by finance capital and state capitalist trusts, competition between individual capitals within a national territory was superseded by competition between national capitals at the level of the international, through military as well as economic means.[81] Bukharin exaggerated the extent to which inter-capitalist rivalry could be overcome within nation-states; but the tendency itself was unmistakable and—as we saw earlier in this chapter—Trotsky himself had predicted the increasingly universal fusion of state and capital as a consequence of the failure of proletarian revolution.

Even if we accept that an integral state capitalism could never be established through the normal processes of capitalist development, the question still remained whether there were other routes by which this could be reached. One—exceptional—route, Cliff argued, was the internal degeneration of a proletarian revolution under the external pressure of the capitalist world system. In one of the debates on the nature of the Soviet Union, Ernest Mandel claimed that Stalinist bureaucracy was not compelled to accumulate but sought to retain its collective managerial position "as a means of achieving the optimum standard of consumption available under given conditions. . . . *The consumption desires of the bureaucracy* (like the consumption desires of pre-capitalist classes) *and not the need to maximize accumulation and output*, are the motive force behind bureaucratic management."[82] But whatever motivations brought individual members of the bureaucracy to seek those roles (and the material benefits of a place among the ruling class would obviously have exercised attractions, regardless of the risks), and whatever post hoc justifications they may have used to rationalize their behavior, once in post they were indeed compelled to behave in such a way as to enable Russia to match American military spending or face being overwhelmed by their Western imperial rival.[83] The theme of harnessing the process of uneven development recurs obsessively in speeches and articles by Stalin in the early 1930s, as the murderous process of industrialization was getting under way: "The necessity of putting an end to the technical and economic backwardness of the Soviet Union, which doomed it to an unenviable existence; the necessity of creating in the country the prerequisites that would enable it not only to overtake but in time to outstrip, technically and economically, the advanced capitalist countries."[84] His most famous invocation of the need to "catch up and overtake" is made in even more extreme terms:

> It is sometimes asked whether it is not possible to slow down the tempo somewhat, to put a check on the movement. No, comrades, it is not possible! The tempo must not be reduced! . . . To slacken the tempo would mean falling behind. And those who fall behind get beaten. But we do not want to be beaten. No, we refuse to be beaten! One feature of the history of old Russia was the continual beatings she suffered because of her backwardness. . . . We are fifty or a hundred years behind the advanced countries. We must make good this distance in ten years. Either we do it, or we shall go under.[85]

Trotsky's failure to understand what was implied by statements like this and the reality that they signified was explained by Cliff in these terms: "*Past experience* was

Trotsky's main impediment in grasping that a triumph for reaction does not always mean a return to the original point of departure, but may lead to a decline, in a spiral form, in which are combined elements of the pre-revolutionary and of the revolutionary pasts, the latter subordinated to the former; the old capitalist class content will then emerge in a new 'socialist' form, thus serving as a further confirmation of the law of combined development which Trotsky himself did so much to develop." Cliff described this as "a conservative attachment to formalism," a formalism that subsequently infected his orthodox supporters like Mandel.[86]

Early adherents of the theory of state capitalism tended to focus, for perfectly understandable reasons, on "the Russian question": one of the great strengths of Cliff's version was, however, precisely that it did not treat Russia as an exception, but only as the most extreme example of a global tendency. Rather than view these societies as being fundamentally different from those of the West, as was endlessly declared in the Cold War propaganda of both sides, it was therefore better to see them as existing on a continuum of state intervention, with two extremes, the United States and the Soviet Union, at opposite ends of the scale. This point was originally made by other adherents of the state-capitalist position from quite different theoretical tendencies. As the Council Communist Paul Mattick wrote in the late 1960s: "Arising at the same time as the mixed economy, the state-capitalist system may be regarded as Keynesianism in its most developed and consistent form."[87] Between the two extremes lay many states that combined elements of both, most in the postcolonial world, particularly in those that were to be classified as the newly industrializing countries. Nigel Harris later noted that South Korean development "was as state capitalist as any East European economy and as Keynesian as any West European social democracy" and, although a major contributor to the growth of world trade, "as regards the role of the state," it was "as 'socialist' as most of the countries that applied that term to themselves."[88]

Nevertheless, the question still remains of *why* the United States and the Soviet Union and their respective allies—"the two camps"—were in such potentially lethal opposition if both were fundamentally capitalist, but the answer is less obscure than is sometimes supposed. Capitalist nation-states, after all, had been known to go to war with each other before the onset of the Cold War, notably in 1914 and 1939. In this case, however, there was an additional reason. Mattick noted that the displacement of "the market system by the planned system" or the complete supersession of private capital by state capital, would be experienced by individual capitalists as "their death warrant," and would not be accepted by them without opposition or even, as Mattick suggested, "civil war."[89] The same is also true on the other side, as any attempt to reintroduce private capital into wholly state capitalist economies would mean that some sections of the bureaucratic ruling class would lose their privileged positions in a situation of market competition—as many did after 1991, particularly in former East Germany, although in Russia perhaps as much as 80 percent still managed to transform themselves into private capitalists or managers.[90] The transition for the bureaucracy as a whole was enabled by the beginnings of "privatization from above" from the mid-1980s: "The opposition's gradual adoption of an unalloyed precapitalist ideology (and concomitant abandonment of such earlier ideals as 'socialism with a human face' and workers' self-management) served to undermine whatever opposition that technocrats and professionals within the nomenklatura might otherwise have mounted against 'radical' change."[91]

The final question we have to address is the relationship of the "Great Change" from 1928 to the bourgeois revolutions. "The distinguishing feature of this revolution is that it was accomplished *from above*, in the initiative of the state," wrote the propagandists of the regime in 1938, under the guidance of Stalin himself.[92] Does this mean then that we are looking at a further example of the type of revolution that was characteristic of the 1860s? We are not. As Michael Haynes has pointed out, there is a word missing from the description offered above: What occurred was not a revolution, but a *counter*revolution from above.[93] The process of permanent revolution had already achieved and surpassed the bourgeois revolution, then established the political preconditions for the transition to socialism, although beyond these it never succeeded in going. Russia after 1928 had regressed to a capitalist stage that it had already transcended, albeit in a new form. The process, starting from much earlier in the 1920s, was certainly reminiscent of the bourgeois revolutions. As Chris Harman noted:

> It is not always the case that the transition from one sort of society to another always involves a single sudden change. This is the case for the transition from a capitalist to a workers' state, because the working class cannot exercise its power except all at once, collectively, by a clash with the ruling class in which, as the culmination of long years of struggle, the latter's forces are defeated. But in the transition from feudalism to capitalism there are many cases in which there is not one sudden clash, but a whole series of different intensities and at different levels, as the decisive economic class (the bourgeoisie) forces political concessions in its favor. The counter-revolution in Russia proceeded along the second path rather than the first.[94]

But, as I noted above, Russia was the exception—the only country to have experienced a temporarily triumphant socialist revolution and subsequent bureaucratic counterrevolution. There was, however, another route to state capitalism. In backward countries where capitalism was weak or nonexistent, where the state was colonial or pre-capitalist, the imposition of a state capitalist regime had a different historical meaning, which can be considered as a continuation of the earlier bourgeois revolutions. This was Cliff's third major contribution and the one most directly relevant to our subject. As with the question of state capitalism, it is important to understand the type of position against which he was arguing. For Orthodox Trotskyists, the bourgeois revolutions had simply been over since February 1917. If this were not the case: "Then Trotsky was deadly wrong with his theory of permanent revolution, and his denial of any possibility for capitalism to solve the historic tasks of the bourgeois revolution in underdeveloped countries."[95] Since Trotsky could obviously not have been wrong in any respect, reality would once again have to be adjusted to conform to the theory. There were, however, several ways of doing so. Two different types of case were involved here.

One was where authoritarian radical nationalist regimes had been established in the former colonial or semi-colonial countries. These were typically aligned with the Soviet Union in diplomatic terms and had undertaken substantial but rarely total nationalization of the economy. In orthodox Trotskyist doctrine these regimes were merely "Bonapartist" and not afforded the dignity of the label "workers' states"; but neither could it be allowed that they had accomplished the bourgeois revolution. In relation to these cases, Anderson's position during the 1970s of Trotskyist sympathizer rather than a paid-up member of the Fourth International enabled him to make some sensible observations based on well-known facts:

> The two main accomplishments always cited as impossible for any colonial bourgeoisie were the achievement of national independence and a solution of the agrarian question. Postwar historical experience was to be more ambiguous. The example of the Algerian Revolution appears to contradict the former assessment; the case of the Bolivian Revolution the latter. A third criterion, not so often mentioned, was the establishment of representative (parliamentary) democracy: thirty years of the Indian Union suggests that this too may be possible.[96]

In a chapter ("The Unfinished Bourgeois Revolution") from his 1981 book on permanent revolution, Michael Löwy rejected this type of criticism:

> Some countries—Mexico, Bolivia, Algeria, Peru, etc.—have implemented relatively radical agrarian reforms, while others—Mexico, India, Venezuela, etc.—have established more or less stable parliamentary democratic states. Finally, some countries have attained a significant degree of political and economic independence in relationship to imperialism: Algeria, Burma, Egypt (at least in Nasser's time), Mozambique, etc. Yet these results must be qualified in two ways: first, each of these accomplishments has been incomplete, limited and often ephemeral; secondly, no country has so far succeeded in successfully combining all three revolutionary-democratic transformations, and, as a result, explosive and unresolved contradictions have persisted in the core of their social formations.[97]

But Anderson had in fact anticipated these arguments:

> Secondary lines of defence might argue that no ex-colonial country has ever met all three criteria, or that true independence, agrarian settlement and democracy have never been gained in any country, because of the role of imperialism, usury and corruption in them. But any undue extension of the criteria for a bourgeois revolution of this sort tends to make the theory of permanent revolution itself into a tautology (only socialism can by definition subtract a country completely from the world market, or solve all the problems of a peasantry), or demands credentials of it which would never have been met by the advanced capitalist countries themselves (which took centuries to achieve bourgeois democracy, for example, with regressions similar to those of contemporary India). The axiom of "permanent revolution" must therefore be deemed so far unproven as a general theory.[98]

One of the most important general points that Anderson makes here is the way in which a far higher standard of achievement is expected of contemporary bourgeois revolutions than of those that provided the model in the first place, which suggests that the model itself is inadequate.

The "workers' states" had, however, supposedly surpassed the bourgeois revolution. One version of this argument was that various Stalinist (China, Yugoslavia, Vietnam) or initially radical nationalist (Cuba) regimes were forced to obey "the logic of the situation," or "under pressure from the masses" had moved in practice to strategies of permanent revolution, whatever the unfortunate associations the term held with the doctrines of a person they believed to be a counterrevolutionary traitor to socialism, Judas Trotsky.[99] As veteran Chinese Trotskyist Peng Shu-tse wrote: "Under the irresistible pressure of objective conditions the CCP [Chinese Communist Party], in order to protect itself, was forced to yield to the laws of permanent revolution and nationalize the property of the bourgeoisie, thereby making China a workers' state. This, then, proves that Trotsky's prediction regarding the permanent revolution was basically correct." Alas, the CCP had only acted thus in an "unconscious and empirical" way, "thus greatly distorting the natural development of the permanent revolution."[100] Livio Maitan claimed that "during the very first stages of the anti-Soviet polemics Chinese theoreticians formulated ideas very close to Trotsky's permanent revolution and Lenin's ideas of 1917." He quotes Lu Ting-i: "Lenin set out the principle that the proletariat should obtain the leadership in the bourgeois democratic revolution and transform the revolution without interruption into the socialist revolution."[101] There were of course significant differences between Lenin and Trotsky even in 1917, but what Maitan appears to mean is that the Chinese leadership claimed that it was establishing its own variant of the "democratic dictatorship of the proletariat and peasantry," now involving a Bloc of Four Classes in a "New Democracy" under which capitalism would flourish for a prolonged period. Although New Democracy ostensibly existed until 1956, it had in reality been abandoned before the CCP even came to power, since "practice tends to brush aside eclecticism and ambiguity: during the crucial years of 1946–47 the revolutionary pressure of the land hungry peasants and the intransigence of the Kuomintang and the old ruling classes ruled out the possibility of collaboration and compromise, and the Communist party had to place itself at the head of an impetuous mass movement which was developing in an anti-capitalist, not merely in an anti-imperialist and anti-feudal direction."[102]

The idea that Mao or his fellow Stalinists had any intention of maintaining multiclass regimes with a private capitalist economy is quite extraordinary in its naiveté: as with Stalin's strategy in Eastern Europe between 1945 and 1948, bourgeois politicians would have provided the illusion of plurality until such time as the bureaucratic dictatorship was perfected, although Ho, Mao, and Tito had less reason to do this since they achieved power by the efforts of their own party-armies rather than the Russian Red Army. Their intention however was always to create states that replicated the structures of Stalinist Russia—this was their model, after all. It defies belief that "mobilizations" by the "masses" in four separate countries—and subsequently several more—were uniformly able to force the new regimes into expropriating private capital against their wishes, but were simultaneously unable to prevent the same regimes from creating murderous police-states that then forced them to labor in factories and fields over which they exercised no control. In any event, these remarkably consistent outcomes across three continents enabled the conclusion to be drawn that Trotsky's confidence in the imminence of permanent revolution had been vindicated:

> The theory of permanent revolution . . . was largely able to predict, explain and illu-
> minate the red threat that runs through the twentieth century: the social revolutions
> in the peripheral capitalist countries. . . . What happened in Russia, Yugoslavia, China,
> Vietnam and Cuba corresponds closely to Trotsky's central thesis: the possibility of
> an uninterrupted and combined (democratic/socialist) revolution in a "backward,"
> dependent or colonial country. The fact that, by and large, the leaders of the post-
> October revolutionary movements did not acknowledge their "permanent" character,
> or only did so *a posteriori* and with a different terminology, does not alter the unmis-
> takably permanentist character of these revolutions.[103]

In fact, some Stalinist leaderships, above all the Chinese, did talk about "permanent revolution," although what they meant by this was quite different from Trotsky. The term was first used in a positive sense by Lui Shao-ch'i in a speech of May 5, 1958, at the CCP Congress and was included in a resolution of the Central Committee that December included not only the rather startling claim: "We are partisans of the Marxist-Leninist theory of permanent revolution," but also: "We are equally partisans of the Marxist-Leninist theory of stages in the revolution."[104] How can these positions be reconciled? The draft Constitution of the CCP, "elaborated on the basis of suggestions by Mao Tse-tung and submitted at his request to the Twelfth Plenum of the Central Committee in October 1968," contained a passage that made the meaning of permanent revolution clear:

> Classes, class contradictions, and class struggle will exist from beginning to end of
> this historical stage as will the struggle between the two roads of socialism and cap-
> italism, the danger of capitalist restoration, and the threat of subversion and aggres-
> sion from imperialism and modern revisionism. These contradictions can only be
> resolved by relying on the theory and practice of Marxist permanent revolution. The
> great proletarian cultural revolution in our country is precisely a great political revo-
> lution under conditions of socialism, in which the proletariat opposes the bourgeoisie
> and all exploiting classes.[105]

In other words, Mao and his faction in the CCP Central Committee were using permanent revolution in the common-sense meaning of a revolution that never ends, which constantly has to be reignited and waged because the bourgeoisie (or sometimes, reflecting Mao's proclivity for outright philosophical idealism, "bourgeois ideas") never sleep, are never completely defeated. This, needless to say, has nothing in common with Leon Trotsky, but—not unexpectedly—quite a lot in common with the positions taken by Joseph Stalin during the Great Purges of the 1930s: "We must cast aside the rotten theory that with every advance we make the class struggle will die down more and more, and that in proportion as we achieve success the class enemy will become more and more tractable.... On the contrary, the farther we advance, the greater will be the fury of the remnants of the exploiting classes, the sooner will they resort to the sharper forms of struggle."[106] In fact, in one respect Mao was more extreme than Stalin. As Slavjo Žižek remarks: "It was once fashionable to claim that the irony of Stalin's politics from 1928 onwards was that it *was* in fact a kind of 'permanent revolution,' a permanent state of emergency in which revolution repeatedly devoured its own children. This claim, however, is misleading: the Stalinist terror was the paradoxical result of the attempt to stabilize the Soviet Union into a state like any other, with firm boundaries and institutions— that is to say, terror was a gesture of panic, a defence reaction against the threat to state stability."[107]

For Mao, on the other hand, recurrent states of emergency, the most extreme of which was the Cultural Revolution, were a way of making dramatic shifts in policy that would otherwise have been opposed by sections of the Chinese ruling class. One ex-Maoist noted that "Stalin's codification of Leninism and his repressive practices marked a shift away from Lenin and popularized the idea that struggle against dissenters was a battle against enemy agents," but Mao had gone beyond even this: "even Stalin's conception of a monolithic party did not include the idea that the development of a bourgeois headquarters within it was inevitable."[108]

We can dispense therefore with the notion that Stalinist parties in the Third World were compelled to carry out actions that they would not otherwise have taken. Nor was the occasional utterance of the words "permanent" and "revolution" in conjunction with each other anything other than a terminological coincidence. Some orthodox Trotskyists, above all Mandel, understood that any attempt to found an assessment of whether or not a worker's state had come into being on the actions of the masses, even mediated through mysteriously malleable Stalinist parties, introduced an element of inconsistency into the definition, since it had to be able to be applied anywhere nationalized property had been introduced regardless of its origin. During an internal debate within the Fourth International following the Vietnamese invasion of Kampuchea in 1978 Mandel attempted to set out "the unchanged majority position" on the class nature of the Stalinist regimes since 1948: "where a radical agrarian revolution has occurred, where the existing bourgeoisie has lost state power and is no more a ruling class, where private property has been essentially suppressed, where the economy obviously does not operate any more on the basis of capitalist production and property relations and does not function any more according to the laws of motion of capitalism, a workers' state has come into being, independently of the conditions under which this has occurred."[109] Mandel held this position quite consistently. Asked the following year how one could determine whether a workers' state had been established, he produced a list of criteria, all of which in different ways involve the suppression of private property, before concluding: "Lastly, there is another factor which, though it is not at all decisive in determining the class character of the state from the analytical point of view, is often crucial in deciding in which direction a particular underdeveloped country will evolve once the structures of the old state apparatus has been seriously shaken. I am speaking of the combination of the degree of mass mobilization and its consciousness and leadership."[110] John Molyneux has rightly described this as "one of the most extraordinary passages ever penned by a self-proclaimed Trotskyist," not only in its denial of the self-emancipatory role of the working class but its relegation of the working class to part of the "masses" who may, or may not, be mobilized for the walk-on part Mandel envisages for them.[111] However extraordinary this passage may be in relation to the classical Marxist tradition of working-class self-emancipation, it is, alas, not unique, or even rare.

In fact, although they used a different vocabulary, figures from the Social Democratic or even Liberal Democratic traditions were often far clearer than orthodox Trotskyists about who had led the "communist" revolutions and to what end. Here is the British labor politician Richard Crossman in the early 1950s:

> *The carriers of communism in Asia are a tiny, educated minority, who form the social conscience and who have been personally wounded by the insolence of Western imperialism and white ascendancy.* The coolie in Malaya, or for that matter the tribesman in Nigeria, does not want *either* liberty, equality and fraternity, *or* the dictatorship of the proletariat. He is below the level of such political aspirations. Not so the minor civil servant, the university professor and the lawyer. The affronts perpetrated by the white man on this social conscience are a far more important communist lever than the economic condition of the masses. Communism enlists the conscience and idealism of this elite and offers it a "career open to the talents" in its totalitarian society. In the twentieth-century democracy is no longer, as it was in the period of Marx, a *necessary* stage on the way to industrialization. Unless trained in the Western tradition, as Indians were, the elite does not desire it: and the masses do not desire it, since they can be modernized, taught to drive tractors, fly airplanes and worship Stalin without any democratic liberation. For fighting a modern war, for working on a collective farm, or for repetitive work in a factory, the Chinese coolie is more malleable material and more expendable than a Western European worker, or a New England farmer. So too, the colonial intelligentsia are more suitable members of a communist managerial class than Westerners, imbued with democratic traditions.[112]

The racist undertone here is palpable, but Crossman was nevertheless correct to identify the type of impulse that led sections of the Third World middle class to identify with Stalinism and how it potentially enabled them to manipulate the mass of the population. Similarly, from early in the following decade, the Weberian sociologist Ernest Gellner observed of the same class: "They are interested in [Marxism] as an ideology which might best steel them and their countries and their elites for the ardors of the road to industrialization. Marxism is not intended for the overcoming of the ills of industrialization: its role is to bring it about."[113] There are many problems with Gellner's approach to human history, but his understanding of it as a "Trinitarian" progression from hunter-gather societies through "agraria" to "industria" at least meant that he is able to see the similarities between different types of industrial—from our perspective, industrial capitalist—societies, without inventing imaginary distinctions between them on the basis of a scholastic metaphysics.[114]

On the one hand, the Trotskyists who should have been able to explain the Third World revolutions were unable to do so; on the one hand, where bourgeois post-colonial regimes had taken power, they denied that bourgeois revolutions had occurred by imposing an impossibly high and previously unattained standard of completeness upon them. On the other, where Stalinist parties had taken power, they claimed that these revolutions were—semantic quibbles aside—socialist, typically by pretending that the middle-class leaderships and their peasant followers were actually working class. On the other hand, the non-Marxists who were not self-deceived about the class nature of the Stalinist leaderships in the Third World nevertheless accepted the regimes at their own self-identification as "communist," either as undemocratic competitors to Social Democracy or as a variant of the wider category of industrialized societies. Cliff's achievement was to transcend the problems associated with both positions on the basis of classical Marxism. He did so by introducing the notion of "deflected" permanent revolution in a seminal article published in *International Socialism* during 1963. From the evidence of Cliff's autobiography, China seems to have been the main model for deflected permanent revolution; indeed he describes the 1963 article as being a "distillation" of his earlier book *Mao's China* (1957), with additional material on Cuba which, at that time, was the most recent addition to the roster of state-capitalist regimes.[115]

Trotsky saw permanent revolution as a process that would enable the less developed countries to decisively break with feudal, tributary, or colonial rule under working-class leadership and move directly to socialism as components of an international revolutionary movement, as in Russia in 1917. Cliff saw deflected permanent revolution as the process that ensues when the working class does not carry through that strategy and another social force takes on the role of leadership, enabling the break with pre-capitalist modes of production or foreign domination to take place, but only in order for the countries in question to become parts of the capitalist world system, as in China in 1949. Although Cliff did not use the term "bourgeois revolutions," he effectively treated deflected permanent revolutions as the modern version or functional equivalent. Both the original and the revised concept therefore involved fundamental social transformations leading to either socialism (permanent revolution) or state capitalism (deflected permanent revolution).

Cliff was therefore able to contrast the original Russian Revolution of October 1917 with all the other supposedly socialist revolutions that followed it; but he was also able to compare these revolutions to others that did not have Stalinist leadership, using the categories of "norm" and "deviation." The norm was established by those revolutions that had resulted in the most complete state capitalist outcomes under Stalinist leadership independently of Russia, particularly those in China and Cuba, although at the time when Cliff was writing in the early 1960s he could also have referred to North Vietnam, Albania, or Yugoslavia. The deviations were those—actually the majority of cases—where the outcome was a mixture of state and private capitalism under radical nationalist leadership that may have been influenced by Stalinist ideas and organizational methods but often—as in the cases of Egypt or Iraq—oscillated between trying to incorporate the local Communist Party and trying to suppress it. With the very important exception of India, the most typical examples of the "deviations" were to be found in North Africa and the Middle East.

What allowed deflection to take place? The background was one of intensifying peasant revolt, the opening up of spaces for maneuver by small nations as a consequence of inter-imperialist rivalry, and the growing importance of the state in the process of capital accumulation. But state power is not autonomous: it must be exercised by, or on behalf of a class. Trotsky had made two assumptions about the capacities of the main social classes, only one of which was valid:

> While the conservative, cowardly nature of a late-developing bourgeoisie . . . is an absolute law, the revolutionary character of the young working class . . . is neither absolute nor inevitable. . . . Once the constantly revolutionary nature of the working class, the central pillar of Trotsky's theory, becomes suspect, the whole structure falls to pieces . . . the peasantry cannot follow a non-revolutionary working class, and all the other elements follow suit. But this does not mean that nothing happens.

"It is one of the tricks of history that when a historical task faces society, and the class that traditionally carries it out is absent, some other group of people, quite often a state power, implements it."[116] Cliff identified the "revolutionary intelligentsia" as a substitute for the revolutionary bourgeoisie in the Global South. No summary can substitute for actually reading his exemplary analysis of this group, perhaps the finest passages he ever wrote, but the main characteristics that he ascribed to it are important to note here. As non-specialists, members of the intelligentsia could offer to represent the "nation" against other, merely sectoral, groups. The backwardness of their nation offended them, not simply as a matter of civic pride, but because in material terms it meant they are unable to find work—or at least work in the state apparatus at a level appropriate to their education. As the traditional aspects of their society were increasingly destabilized by the irruption of capitalist development, they found it hard to maintain its values, but looked instead to those of efficiency, modernization, industrialization, all of which were apparently embodied in the Soviet Union. They claimed to love "the people," but simultaneously felt guilty at their relative privilege and distrustful of those less educated or intelligent than themselves. Above all, they are hostile to democracy and strove to exclude the masses from their strategies of transformation, except in a subordinate or supportive role, which is why their preferred method was one of military struggle on a guerrilla or even conventional basis.[117]

Cliff's arguments were developed by Nigel Harris, originally in relation to one of Cliff's deviant cases, India.[118] By the late seventies, however, Harris had conducted a major study of the Chinese case, which provided Cliff with his norm. In doing so he made explicit the argument about the modern form of the bourgeois revolution. In the same way that Cliff had done for Russian Stalinists in and after 1928, Harris emphasized the disjunction between what their Chinese contemporaries thought they were doing and what they were actually doing. The difference was that the Chinese did not have state power in their hands: "Without a popular revolution, a "peasant war," how were the revolutionaries to come to power? Only through the army or a comparably disciplined instrument, a mass party. If such instruments could be rendered independent of the interests of existing classes, there was no need to demand liberty. At the moment when history required it, a model was found." Leaving aside the Hegelian flourish in the final sentence, there is no doubt that Harris is right. The model had in fact two aspects: one was the Stalinist party as the quasi-autonomous agent of revolutionary transformation; the other was the Russian state after the "Second Revolution" as the means of achieving development. In effect, the CCP had retreated from the goals of the Russian Revolution to those of the French Revolution:

> The "switching of the points" from the aspirations of 1917 to those of 1789 (as reshaped by capitalism in the twentieth century) afflicted the Communist Party just at the moment when it found itself leading a genuine working-class movement, between 1925 and 1927. There was no time to make a smooth adjustment. The contradiction between the interests of the new Russian ruling class and those of the Chinese working class wrecked the party, uprooting it from the traditions of the October revolution. It was re-created, slowly and painfully, but only in isolation from the class it claimed to be leading. The task of the partisans would have been unsupportable if they had been encumbered with the interests of an urban working class. The partisans were no more rooted in the peasants of the localities in which they operated, although they were dependent upon them for food supplies and manpower. The party was *independent* of the entrenched classes of China, the embodiment of a future national ruling class appropriate to the demands of *national* survival today. The experience of the Soviet Union in the 1930s illustrated that, if the Chinese Communists could only secure power, they could create an independent State. But it was a very long process, a "protracted struggle," because the party insisted upon its independence, insisted on not leading the independent initiative of the exploited of China lest that jeopardize its own *party* freedom. . . . Once in power, the party showed its ability to eliminate its erstwhile allies, the landlords, "patriotic gentry" and capitalists, and to limit the activities of small property owners. Its main task—to accelerate accumulation—was triumphantly accomplished in the early years.

"Could this be seen as, in reality, 'building socialism'?" It could and was, and in some places still is; but as Harris notes, it could be done: "Only by ignoring the material reality, and seeing only the ideology."[119] And, as Harris insisted, it was the ideology of the revolutionary bourgeoisie as much as its developmental goals that were echoed by the CCP. In the case of the revolutionary plebeians during the

French Revolution, membership of the People was decided by one's patriotism; in the case of "Chairman Mao thought" membership of the working class was awarded on the basis of having the "correct" attitude to work or the state.[120] In both cases the underlying moralism extended far beyond China. Here, for example, is Che Guevara speaking to Cuban trade unionists in 1960 about "obligations that even conflict with the common denominator the working class has made of its aspirations and its struggles against the ruling class, because one of the great obligations of today's working class is to produce well":

> When I say "produce," the workers can say, "that is just what the bosses said, and the more we produced, the more money we gave them, and the less they needed some comrade and we caused the unemployment and increased concentration of wealth." That is true. That is why there is an apparent contradiction. But production right now has got to be, precisely, the production of wealth so that the state can invest more in the creation of sources of work, and it has got to be the type of production that does not cost anyone his job. . . . Change the mentality of the union leader, whose job is not to shout against the boss or to set up absurd rules within the order of production, rules that sometimes lead to featherbedding. The worker who today collects his salary without earning it, without doing anything, is really conspiring against the nation and against himself.[121]

The issue here is not to question the individual heroism displayed by Guevara, nor is it to accuse him of hypocrisy—in fact his personal behavior contrasted strongly and favorably with that of, for example, Mao. "In their private lives these men may be ascetic," wrote Ian Roxborough in one of the few academic texts of the sixties or seventies to show Cliff's influence, "but that is irrelevant."[122] Considered in the light of a project to introduce state capitalism by revolutionary means, Guevara's speech is that of a manager trying to persuade workers to set aside their vulgar material interests for the benefit of the accumulation program of a capitalist state. Lukács noted in 1968, "A man like Guevara was a heroic representative of the Jacobin ideal—his ideas were transported into his life and completely shaped it." Lukács expressed his "reverence" for the "nobility" of this human type: "But their idealism is not that of the socialism of everyday life, which can only have a *material* basis, built on the construction of a new economy."[123]

The relentless refusal of Cliff, Harris, and the writers who shared their analysis to judge people and eras "by what they thought of themselves," their materialist insistence on privileging social content over ideological form meant they were free from the multiple contradictions that entrapped orthodox Trotskyism; while in political terms it was possible to support deflected permanent revolutions on the grounds of anti-imperialism or national liberation without pretending that they had anything to do with socialism. Nevertheless, the analysis suggested at least four issues that required further clarification. First, it is not entirely clear that "intelligentsia" is sufficiently broad a category to include all the leading social forces involved in these revolutions, above all the military: the two cases led by Nasser in

Egypt and Mengitsu in Ethiopia were after all among the most important of the "deviations from the norm" of deflected permanent revolution.

Second, even if we accept the category of intelligentsia, was the class fraction it describes a new development in the history of capitalism? Are the leaders or ideologues of the "deflected" revolutions so very different from those who led the bourgeois revolutions between 1789 and 1848? In some respects the parallels are nearly exact. John Rees once observed that the intelligentsia "had, in an earlier incarnation, often been a crucial element of the practical leadership of the classical bourgeois revolutions," without however drawing any conclusions.[124] What is new in these situations was not therefore the existence or activity of a "revolutionary intelligentsia" hitherto unknown: both were already familiar from the history of the nineteenth century. It was rather that this class fraction felt able to take action in the knowledge that they did not need to fear the working class. Why not?

This question requires us to address the third issue. Cliff offers a number of reasons why the working class in the Global South did not play the role envisaged by Trotsky, down to the early 1960s. Of these, the general influence of ruling-class ideas and the illiteracy and inexperience of the workers are clearly relevant but were also true of Russia in 1917 and China in the 1920s; they are not in themselves an explanation. Other reasons have genuine explanatory power and remain extremely pertinent even today. Many workers in urban industry retained links to smallholdings in the countryside, to which they returned in times of unemployment, making the permanent formation of class consciousness and organization difficult. Conversely, those workers who were in stable employment could have relatively higher living standards than the rural masses, making the possibility of alliances with them less likely. Those trade unions or community groups that do exist are often led by non-working-class elements, "outsiders," with different interests and political goals, and are heavily reliant on support from the developmental state, which tends to impose an apolitical agenda acceptable to the regime. Both these leaderships and the personnel who run the state apparatus are influenced by Stalinist politics, the key subjective element in controlling and lowering the aspirations of the working class.[125] But many of these characteristics were also present in pre-revolutionary Russia: workers with links to the countryside; trade unions established by agents of the state; and industries where trade unions did not exist even before the ban that followed the revolution of 1905.[126] Some deeper level of explanation is required. The absence of the revolutionary party is clearly part of it, but parties themselves can only have a meaningful existence where certain determinate conditions allow them to form and grow. Lack of revolutionary leadership can explain the outcome in China during the 1920s or in Iran in 1978–79, where major upheavals took place and Cliff's other inhibiting conditions were overcome, but not where such situations did not arise. At the end of his discussion of workers in the Global South, Cliff wrote: "An automatic correlation between economic backwardness and revolutionary political militancy does not exist."[127] The same point has been subsequently made of Russia by conservative but materialist historians otherwise completely distant from Trotskyism.[128] But Trotsky never argued that such an automatic correlation did exist; for him it was conditional and Cliff does not refer to, let alone discuss, the enabling condition that Trotsky saw as fundamental to its establishment: uneven and combined development.

The fourth issue is concerned not with agency but outcome. "Deflection" originally involved shifting from proletarian to bourgeois revolutionary objectives, but what can it mean if the real task of the bourgeois revolution has largely been accomplished on a global scale? The root of the problem is illustrated by the two main cases that Cliff discusses: China and Cuba. Before 1949 China stood historically before the completion of the bourgeois revolution: there was effectively no central state, the agrarian sector still contained tributary and feudal relations, and it was subject to oppression by several competing imperialist powers. Cuba by 1959, on the other hand, was a bourgeois state—a very weak one, of course, overawed by the US state and penetrated by organized crime, but it seems to be an abuse of language to say that it was in any sense pre-capitalist, nor was the working class striving for power in the 1950s in the way that the Chinese working class had in the 1920s. In effect, the difference between these two revolutions is that between social and political revolutions. China experienced a social revolution in 1949: it could have been the socialist revolution, if the movements of the mid-twenties had succeeded, but ended up instead as the functional equivalent of the bourgeois revolution instead, a lesser but still decisive systemic shift. Cuba only experienced a political revolution, which did not fundamentally change the nature of the economic system, which moved from being a highly corrupt market capitalist economy to one on the state capitalist model, although—leaving aside the obvious absence of democracy—this initially benefitted many Cubans in relation to health and welfare. The extent of the move would have been less dramatic had US paranoia about encroaching "communism" not effectively forced the new Cuban regime to ally with Russia and adopt fully state capitalist forms of organization—which was certainly not Castro's original intention. There were, in other words, two different types of revolution encompassed by the term "deflected permanent revolution" from the very beginning and this has implications for the contemporary relevance of permanent revolution as both a social process and a political strategy.

As capital increasingly sweeps away even the remnants of previous modes of production and the social formations that include them, the pattern of revolutions has increasingly tended toward the "political" rather than the "social" type, starting with the revolutions of 1989 in Eastern Europe that swept away the Stalinist regimes and began what Chris Harman called the "sideways" movement from Eastern state capitalism to an approximation of the Western trans-state model.[129] The subsequent displays of "people power" in the Philippines, Thailand, and Serbia, the "color revolutions" in the former Republics of the Soviet Union, and perhaps now the revolutions associated with the Arab Spring—the issue is still undecided at the time of writing—are all of this type. Capitalism endlessly reproduces "unevenness"—differences in power and autonomy; but except in a handful of cases (Afghanistan, Nepal, Tibet) the unstable but structured inequality that results is not an unresolved issue from an earlier period, not a remnant of feudalism or colonialism, but a result of the normal operation of competitive accumulation expressed at the level of the states system. At least one of Cliff's leading cothinkers did argue that none of the cases of deflected permanent revolution involved social revolutions, although without using the latter term. Discussing the same examples as Cliff, Harman noted:

> In none of these cases was there a shift from one mode of production to another. In each case those who had control of the exiting state apparatus used it to reorganise industry, reducing internal competition to a minimum to accumulate in the face of external pressures. That does not mean that there was never any opposition to such a move—"police" actions of various sorts were often taken against old, "private" capitalist interests who resisted the changes. But these were possible without any mobilisation of the mass of the population for full-blooded social revolution, indeed in some cases without any mobilisation of the mass of the population at all.[130]

This perhaps goes too far, not only in respect of the Chinese Revolution of 1949 but a minority of the revolutions that followed it. Before the Ethiopian Revolution of 1974, for example, feudal social relations were still dominant and the state was the nearest to the European absolutist model of any remaining in the world.[131] Nevertheless, Harman's central point about the nonsocial nature of the majority of these revolutions was correct. The relevance of this argument in the context of our subject is that at a certain point in the twentieth century—and it would be absurd to pretend that the date can be established with scientific exactitude—the bourgeois revolution ceased to be a possible outcome in revolutionary situations, because for all practical purposes it had been universally achieved everywhere except in the most peripheral formations. From the opening of the neoliberal era at the very latest, the only social revolutions that it is possible to imagine have been socialist.

THE REEMERGENCE OF A CONSEQUENTIALIST GENERAL THEORY

Between them, the two very different versions of Trotskyism represented by Deutscher and Cliff provided the arguments with which to resolve the issues of agency and outcome that had so confused discussions of bourgeois revolution since the suppression of the classical Marxist tradition. Cliff's positions would eventually be transmitted to a wider audience through the more academically embedded intellectuals associated with his "unorthodox" Trotskyist tendency in Britain known in successive incarnations as the Socialist Review Group, International Socialism, and the Socialist Workers Party. But it was Deutscher whose influence was felt first—unsurprisingly perhaps, given that his lack of awkward organizational affiliations and more sympathetic view of the Soviet Union made his views easier to accept for those politically educated in the Stalinist tradition. Indeed, the first historian to recognize the importance of his comments on the bourgeois revolution—and the conduit through which his views reached wider acceptance—was Christopher Hill, a leading figure in the Historians Group of the CPGB until his resignation from the party in the aftermath of 1956.

As we have seen, Hill was a proponent of the orthodox model of bourgeois revolution and his early writings, particularly his classic essay of 1940, "The English Revolution," are in this mode. Yet it is also true that Hill abandoned this aspect of his interpretation, and more quickly than is usually thought. In writings of the 1950s, such as *Economic Problems of the Church* and "Recent Interpretations of the Civil War" (both 1956), he had already separated capitalism and democracy. In the former work he wrote that prior to the Revolution: "The advance of capitalism had been slow, but its standards had begun to influence men's actions before it changed their conscious thought. . . . Yet the Puritan and democratic revolution was defeated: it was the bourgeois revolution that succeeded."[132]

Here the separation between capitalism and political democracy has already been made. In an essay written at the same time he hinted at the type of outcomes that should be considered important instead: "And if we put it at its lowest, one could argue that to create the conditions for free capitalist development in England then did open up wide vistas for increasing production, for a Baconian relief of man's estate; whereas the regime of Laud and Charles I offered only a Spanish stagnation."[133] But both of these early remarks were only made in passing and cannot be considered a full theoretical reorientation.

The first suggestion of a substantial shift in Hill's position came in 1969 in the revised "Introduction" to the collection of texts on the English Revolution, *The Good Old Cause*, where Hill announced, quite unexpectedly: "'Bourgeois revolution' signifies a revolution which—whatever the subjective intentions of the revolutionaries—had the effect of establishing conditions favourable to the development of capitalism."[134] It was in an essay of 1971 commemorating Deutscher's work as a historian of revolution, however, that Hill noted the significance of his conception of "revolution from above" ("although he never seems to have worked it out fully") and his consequentialism, commenting that "Deutscher was quite right to say that historians of seventeenth-century England have spent too much time in analyzing the participants rather than the consequences of the Revolution."[135] By 1974 Hill came to regard Deutscher's comments in *The Unfinished Revolution* on his own earlier work as legitimate criticism and subsequently quoted them in defence of his revised definition, in which "the Marxist definition of a bourgeois revolution, which I find the most helpful model for understanding the English Revolution, does not mean a revolution made by the bourgeoisie."[136]

By the time of a paper given in 1976, but only published in 1980, Hill had virtually abandoned any perspective involving the conscious role of the bourgeoisie. In support he cited Deutscher not as an innovator but alongside Lenin ("who may perhaps be allowed to know something about the subject") as a representative of the classical Marxist tradition:

> The English Revolution, like all revolutions, was caused by the breakdown of the old society; it was brought about neither by the wishes of the bourgeoisie, nor by the leaders of the Long Parliament. But its *outcome* was the establishment of conditions far more favorable to the development of capitalism than those which prevailed before 1640. The hypothesis is that this outcome, and the Revolution itself, were made possible by the fact that there had already been a considerable development of capitalist relations in England, but that it was the structure, fractures, and pressures of the society, rather than the wishes of leaders, which dictated the outbreak of revolution and shaped the state which emerged from it.[137]

In his discussion Hill drew parallels between the English Revolution and the two successors that in different ways it most resembled: "In its ultimate outcome the English Revolution was closer to the Prussian model than the French, though in the 1640s the radicals played a part which hints at that of the French Jacobins." Here, Hill is perhaps echoing Gramsci, but goes on to suggest that the main difference between the English and French Revolutions was in the stage at which they stopped rather than any fundamental dissimilarity: "The point of stabilization under the bonapartism of Oliver Cromwell was less radical than the point of stabilization under the bonapartism of Bonaparte."[138] By now Hill was even prepared to claim— somewhat implausibly at this date—that his new position was the one held by "proponents" of the theory of bourgeois revolution more generally, linking it back to the thinker who first developed the concept, if not the term:

> At all points then, I wish to disclaim the imputation of conscious will, which the opponents, but not the proponents, of the idea of bourgeois revolution attribute to it. Bourgeois revolution is not possible until capitalist relations of production have developed within a country; it comes on the agenda only when the traditional government cannot go on ruling in the old way. The inability is itself the indirect consequence of social developments, as James Harrington realized was the case for England in the 1650s.[139]

By the time Hill gave the fullest presentation of his case in 1988 it was more accurate to say that the consequentialist position had indeed gathered significant support. After listing the ways in which the English Revolution had been responsible for capitalist expansion, he emphasized their unintended nature:

> Nobody in 1640 intended any of these things. The Revolution was not planned, not willed. Some historians think there can have been no revolution if it was not planned, just as all strikes are made by wicked agitators. But Parliament did not make the Revolution; no one advocated it. In the 1640s defenders of parliament's cause had to make do with sixteenth-century Calvinist theories of revolt led by the lesser magistrate, or with the rights of freeborn Englishmen against the Norman Yoke. In the course of struggle theories of popular sovereignty and the rights of man were evolved, which later revolutionaries drew upon. But there was no Bolshevik party in England in 1640. For that matter, neither the French nor the Russian Revolutions were willed

in advance by anyone. By 1917 the Bolsheviks, building on the English and French experience, were able to take advantage of a revolutionary situation; but they did not *make* the Revolution. A revolutionary situation developed when the Tsarist state collapsed, just as the English state collapsed in 1640; and the Bolsheviks were prepared to take advantage of it. Great revolutions are not made by conspiratorial minorities.[140]

This passage suggests some of the potential difficulties with consequentialism: claiming that no one organized the revolution in order to establish a capitalist republic does not commit one to the position that no one organized the revolution for any reason at all. For perfectly understandable and supportable reasons Hill wanted to oppose conceptions of revolution as a mere coup d'état ("wicked agitators," "conspiratorial minorities"), but in doing so he tended to abandon any conception of revolutionary leadership. It is legitimate to argue that, during the English and French revolutions at any rate, the Independents and Jacobins only emerged in the course of events—in the Russian case the Bolsheviks obviously existed beforehand; but in all these cases it was only the initial stage of the revolution—1640, 1789, February 1917—that was accomplished without a conscious leadership; the decisive moments—1649, 1792, October 1917—required the intervention of these radical and focused minority groups.

Here and in subsequent writings Hill was mainly concerned with outcomes; the implications that this had for questions of agency—above all the possibility of "revolution from above" conducted by fractions of the feudal ruling class—remained unexplored in his work, apart from a brief discussion in his early tribute to Deutscher, largely because this was not decisive in relation to the English Revolution. The first person since Deutscher to explicitly use the concept seems to have been Perry Anderson in *Lineages of the Absolutist State* (1974): "In the West, the Spanish, English, and French monarchies were defeated or overthrown by bourgeois revolutions from below; while the Italian and German principalities were eliminated by bourgeois revolutions from above, belatedly."[141] Anderson elaborated on this distinction in a talk given at Cambridge University in 1976 (but only published in 1992), which presumably summarizes the promised but unpublished sequel to *Lineages*.[142] The idea of revolution from above was adopted by US radical sociologist Ellen Kay Trimberger in an important book of that title published in 1978, which took the discussion into events of the twentieth century. Working in the tradition of Barrington Moore and her sometime collaborator Theda Skocpol, Trimberger used both Weberian and Marxist concepts to, in her words, "develop a model of revolution from above by military bureaucrats as distinct from either coup d'etat or mass bourgeois or socialist—revolution from below."[143] Trimberger identified the Meiji Restoration as the first revolution to be made by "autonomous military bureaucrats," although she saw parallels with the less complete revolutions associated with Ataturk in Turkey from 1923, Nasser in Egypt from 1952, and Velasco in Peru from 1968.[144] Her conception of revolution from above as a means of achieving at least partial industrialization on a capitalist basis implied that these were bourgeois revolutions, particularly since she tended to argue—in terms derived from Immanuel Wallerstein and capitalist world-system theory—that there were no socialist states and (presumably) that there have therefore been no socialist revolutions. Trimberger does not in fact draw this conclusion; her emphasis on the autonomy of the forces involved denies the societies they created any specific social content—indeed, at one point she suggested that future revolutions of this type could be moved in left-reformist directions, particularly in Latin America: "In those countries where the prospects for revolution from below look bleak, radicals and Marxists may have no choice but to support military revolution from above and to try to force it in more progressive directions." However, although Trimberger expected revolutions from above to continue, she did not expect them to result in full-scale industrialization: "Analysis of revolution from above . . . leads to the conclusion that the use of state bureaucracy to foster capitalist development through sponsorship of either an independent or state capitalist class will be ineffective."[145] In fact, the last significant revolution from above—the Ethiopian revolution of 1974—had already occurred by the time Trimberger's book appeared in print, and the pattern for the subsequent decades of political revolution from below was being set in Iran.

Nevertheless, despite her own avoidance of the category of bourgeois revolution, Trimberger's work could be interpreted as describing late examples of precisely this process. In particular, the parallels that she drew between the Meiji Restoration—which several Marxists had identified as one of the great bourgeois revolutions from above—and subsequent, less decisive revolutions potentially allowed the category to be applied to near-contemporary events, rather than concluding as Anderson tended to do, that the era of bourgeois revolutions had ended in 1871 or February 1917. In many respects Trimberger's post-Meiji examples fall into the category of Cliff's "deviations from the norm" of deflected permanent revolution and one of Cliff's cothinkers, the English sociologist Colin Barker, drew on her work on Japan in an unpublished but much cited paper of 1982 on the Meiji Restoration. Barker noted that the process in Japan had parallels not only with future events in Turkey, Egypt, and Peru but also with contemporaneous events in Germany. But this was not all: "More controversially, parallels might also be drawn with Stalin's industrialization of Russia—although there the state and social structure that was displaced by a section of the bureaucracy was a decayed popular state that had emerged from an earlier full-blown social revolution."[146] Barker's actual discussion of the Meiji Restoration is full of interest, but for our purposes what is most interesting about it are the general conclusions that he draws from this case. One was that revolutions from above were not restricted to societies in which feudalism was the dominant mode of production; if, as Trimberger and her authority, Samir Amin, believed, Japan was a tributary formation, then clearly we are considering a path to capitalist industrial development that was potentially available to precapitalist modes more generally. The other was his denial that the Meiji

Restoration represented a social revolution. Following Skocpol's definition of social revolution, Barker argued that, on the one hand, events in Japan lacked "the element of 'class upheaval'" that she saw as essential, but on the other, "they also amount to more than a political revolution, since the Meiji Restoration eventuated in more than a change in the structure of the state alone: the social structure itself was transformed in significant ways." Barker at this point invokes Trimberger's notion of revolution from above as an alternative to both political and social revolution:

> Japan presents us with an example of a transition, accomplished in politics, from a pre-capitalist mode of production, without benefit of a social revolution. What the Japanese case shows is that the process of restructuring the social relations of production in the shift from a "feudal" or tributary" mode of production to a capitalist mode need not involve the active political participation of the lower classes. Indeed, the "social revolutionary" method of transition from pre-capitalist to capitalist relations is, historically, not necessarily the most common form. . . . The masses are not necessarily active or organized agents in the process of transformation which initiates capitalist social relations. A moment's reflection suggests why this should be so. The shift from a "feudal" to a "tributary" (or "Asiatic," etc.) mode to a capitalist one is a shift from one form of social production which the majority of society is an object of exploitation and oppression to another form in which the same is true.[147]

Barker's point about the transition from one exploitative system to another not necessarily having to involve the masses is well made. It is not clear, however, why this should be denied the term "social revolution," unless it is through a desire to retain a particular notion of process—in this case involving mass participation—within the definition. But if the transformation of the social relations of production is central—and Barker accepts that this occurred after 1868—then this is an entirely arbitrary classification. Part of the difficulty here is that Barker does not use, or even discuss, the concept of bourgeois revolution in this context, but employs instead the less specific concepts of social revolution and revolution from above as respectively defined by Skocpol and Trimberger. Nevertheless, his paper made explicit what had been implied in Cliff's earlier discussion of the intelligentsia—the wide range of possible social forces that could be responsible for establishing capitalist nation-states:

> There is a crude version of "Marxism" (though not one found in Marx and Engels) which supposes that, since the problem is reducible to the problem of capitalist development, then a capitalist class—a bourgeoisie like that of Holland or England—must play the revolutionary part, and unify the nation as a "definable national entity." In a small number of countries, the revolutionary role was assumed by something like a classic bourgeoisie, but elsewhere the same role might be played, with of course individual variations, by other actors. Here a self-transformed monarchy; there a populist political leader; here a cohesive group of civil or military bureaucrats; there a bunch of religious fanatics; here an autocrat; there a democrat; here a "liberal"; there a "communist."[148]

The idea of revolution from above was not welcomed by all Marxists, even those who had in other respects departed from the orthodoxy. Trimberger had referred in passing to Gramsci's concept of passive revolution, suggesting that revolution from above "may be similar," but declined to pursue the issue on the grounds of her ignorance of Italian history.[149] In a collection published in 1979, the British Marxist historian of Italy Paul Ginsborg became one of the first writers since Anderson and Nairn to discuss in English Gramsci's notion of "passive revolution" in relation to the bourgeois revolutions. His reasons for doubting the utility of "revolution from above" are important for highlighting a further distinction, that between process and moment. Drawing on Lenin's concept of an "era" of bourgeois revolution, Ginsborg wrote that it "can perhaps be best characterised in terms of a twofold process, both economic and political. In economic terms, the period witnesses the definitive triumph of capitalism as the dominant mode of production. In the political sphere, the absolutist state comes to be replaced by one founded on the principles of bourgeois democracy."[150] These are processes leading to specific outcomes, although we can see the persistence of the orthodox notion in his invocation of democracy as the alternative to the absolutist state. On this basis, depending on how thorough "democracy" is expected to be, the final date of the bourgeois revolution in Britain would be set back until working-class men or women received the vote. Presumably Ginsburg did not mean that it remained unconsummated until the interwar years of the twentieth century, but that is a potential effect of this characterization. Later in the same article he expanded his definition from focusing solely on achievements, arguing further that "a successful bourgeois revolution" was also defined by "its course": "Its course, like that of all revolutions, is marked by a violent social upheaval which overthrows the existing social order. Its achievements, specific to bourgeois revolution alone, lie in the creation of a state power and institutional framework consonant with the flourishing of bourgeois property relations, and with the development of bourgeois society as a whole." It is on this basis that Ginsborg cast doubt on the viability of the concept of "bourgeois revolution from above," describing it as an "unpromising" idea. In relation to Italy and Germany, he concedes that the term describes an important aspect of nation-state formation: "The formative process of the bourgeois national state in Italy and Germany was, it is true, carried through from above (though Garibaldi's exploits in southern Italy are hardly to be forgotten in this respect). But to describe this process as a "bourgeois revolution from above" is to risk lumping together process and moment indiscriminately. It also implies the abandonment of any idea of defining bourgeois revolution in terms of its course, i.e., as a moment of violent social upheaval which overthrows the existing political order."[151]

Ginsborg assumes that revolution from above is essentially a process of incremental change, rather than an event leading to a decisive shift. Whether this is necessarily the case is open to question, but there is no doubt that the dissolution of moment into process had attractions for other members of the generation of Marxist historians who had come of age in the 1960s. "If the definition of a bourgeois revolution is restricted to the successful installation of a legal and political framework in which the free development of capitalist property relations is assured," writes Gareth Stedman Jones in 1977, "there is then no necessary reason why a 'bourgeois revolution' need be the direct work of a bourgeoisie." For Jones, "the triumph of the bourgeoisie should be seen as the global victory of a particular form of property relations and a particular form of control over the means of production, rather than the conscious triumph of a class subject which possessed a distinct and coherent view of the world." These reflections were inspired by a critical reading of Eric Hobsbawms's *The Age of Capital* (1975), in which the author discussed the great "revolutions from above" of the 1860s, but only in relation to nation-state formation and war. For Jones the conventional use of the term that denied it to events in Japan, Germany, Italy, and the United States was "unsatisfactory and precise," not least because of the way in which it afforded only "secondary significance" to struggles between labor and capital, or even treated these as the decisive moments in the bourgeois revolutions: "There is even a quasi-Hegelian way of writing about revolutions, in which, by pushing the revolution to the left, the pressure of small producers unwittingly takes the 'bourgeois revolution' to its logical conclusion. Thus, by a formidable feat of ventriloquism, measures pushed through in the teeth of bitter opposition from the grande bourgeoisie become essential 'hallmarks' of the 'bourgeois revolution.'"[152]

By the beginning of the 1980s, consequentialism had begun to establish itself as a valid alternative to the orthodoxy, but still in ways that indicated that it was novel position, which required defense. In a textbook on social and political theory published in 1981 Andrew Gamble wrote of how, in discussing the "profound upheaval" involved in the bourgeois revolution, "an image is easily conjured up of a militant, self-confident, expanding capitalist class which found its economic activities blocked by a landowning aristocracy." But as Gamble adds, "only a little historical knowledge is necessary to see that there is hardly an instance where capitalism was established by such an independent bourgeoisie," including in France.

> The important point to grasp therefore is that a "bourgeois revolution" does not imply a revolution made by a self-conscious and self-confident bourgeois class. In the great political revolutions that ushered in the bourgeois era the bourgeoisie as an identifiable class was more often noted for its absence than for its active participation. What the term bourgeois revolution came to signify is not a straightforward duel between a landed aristocracy and an industrial bourgeoisie with clearly opposed economic interests, but a long-drawn-out conflict within the ranks of the property owners, a conflict in which the participation of other classes was often crucial. Its eventual outcome was to make the economic, social, and political conditions of existence of the bourgeoisie predominant in every social formation of the West.[153]

Perhaps the most serious attempt to bring together these different strands of argument into a fully elaborated consequentialist position was made by two British Marxist historians of Germany, David Blackbourn and Geoff Eley, in separately written but thematically linked essays, first published as a book in German in 1980, then in revised form in English in 1984. Of the two, Eley's essay is the most important, since Blackbourn, while working within the same general frame of reference was, we shall see, more skeptical about the need to retain a concept of bourgeois revolution: "It is possible that we should actually be better off without the label bourgeois revolution at all."[154]

Their joint starting point was the paradox that, while revisionists were questioning orthodox interpretations of the English and French Revolutions, in Germany both Marxists and—more importantly—non-Marxists still clung to the orthodox model. Their reason for doing so was to argue that Germany had failed to undergo the Anglo-French experience and the so-called *sonderweg* or "special path" undertaken instead condemned the country to an illiberal political culture that ultimately led to Nazism. We have already encountered this position in the work of Deutscher, Lukács, and Moore, but even Marxists who did not explain National Socialism in these terms tended to deny the existence of a German bourgeois revolution. In his first major work, *Political Power and Social Classes* (1968), Nicos Poulantzas expressed this view with (for him) unusual clarity:

> The bourgeois revolution in Prussia (and generally in Germany) *simply did not take place.* The 1848 movement and the issuing of a constitution by the king did not mark an important turning-point in the process of the transformation of the relations of production; and they did nothing to alter the state's superstructure or the occupier of political power. . . . The landed nobility still retained political power and the Prussian state was to remain for a long time dominated by feudal structures. It was in fact this state which under Bismarck undertook to bring the bourgeoisie to political domination. . . . Under Bismarck, this state transformed itself from within, as it were, in the direction of the capitalist state.[155]

For Blackbourn and Eley the tragedy of fascism arose not because the German bourgeois revolution was incomplete or unsuccessful or nonexistent but as the result of the crisis of the Weimar Republic in the years immediately preceding the Nazi seizure of power.[156] The irony was therefore that the orthodoxy was being maintained in one of the major countries where it was clearly inapplicable but only as a negative comparator. The German bourgeoisie was "historically weak and immature": "yet it was clear that no one any longer, and for good reason, believed in a 'rising middle class'—except, perhaps in Germany, where the exception still seemed to prove the rule." It was therefore necessary "to reconsider the definition of bourgeois revolution."[157] Eley made his case in three moves.

First, he spectacularly reversed the terms of the debate. Instead of trying to oppose the revisionist critiques of the orthodox conception, he effectively accepted them. For Eley, the orthodoxy involved "a set of changes forced through by the bourgeoisie itself, acting collectively in its own class interests, in direct confrontation with feudal or 'pre-industrial' ruling class":

> We should be clear what this definition implies. It encourages stress on motivations and the social identity of the participants in revolutionary events, suggesting that the

bourgeoisie would itself be at the head of the revolutionary movement in an authentic bourgeois revolution, leading the masses and seizing the helm of state. Now aside from the empirical objections to this conception which should be clear enough from work on the English and French Revolutions (the revolutionaries were not only or even mainly "bourgeois," their opponents were not "aristocratic" in same straightforward sense, the "bourgeoisie" was on both sides of the barricades, the conscious aims of the revolutionaries were not particularly "revolutionary," and so on), this raises some serious theoretical problems. For one, it presumes that the bourgeoisie can be conceptualized in the first place as a corporate political actor, with a collective class interest traceable through particular events and ideas in a directly expressive way, speaking through the acts of individual politicians.

"Though Marxist in origin," Eley drily noted, "this is not a conception that many Marxists would now want to defend."[158] Germany did not fail to conform to the model because the model itself did not correspond to historical reality. Consequently, "we can make a reasonable case for arguing that Germany did, after all, experience a successful bourgeois revolution in the nineteenth century. This did not take the form of a pitched battle between bourgeoisie and aristocracy, in which the former seized state power from a traditional monarchy and replaced it with parliamentary democracy. But then it didn't anywhere else in Europe either, certainly not in Britain in the seventeenth century and certainly not in France in 1789." In effect, Eley argued that revisionist critiques of the orthodoxy are not so much wrong as beside the point: there was no need for Marxists to defend the indefensible orthodox "myth" because an alternative conception was available.

Second, Eley argued that the alternative conception of bourgeois revolution was that of a process leading to a specific outcome: unimpeded capitalist development. This did not necessarily involve democracy or any other specific tasks. Instead, we should "associate bourgeois revolution with a larger complex of change—instead of a narrowly defined political process of democratic reform—which cumulatively established the conditions of possibility for the development of industrial capitalism, then there are good reasons for seeing the process of "revolution from above" between the 1860s and 1870s as Germany's distinctive form of bourgeois revolution, so that we focus more on the material or objective consequences of events than their motivational origins."[159] One consequence of this approach was that Eley saw the bourgeois revolution in Germany as a process that occurred over two key periods, first involving the top-down agrarian reforms between 1807 and 1812, then more decisively the period of nation-state formation between 1862 and 1871.

Third, and perhaps most boldly of all, Eley claimed not only that the German Revolution was as complete as the English and French ("the German pattern of 'revolution from above' was just as capable of securing bourgeois predominance as the different experiences of Britain and France"), but that it might be considered *more* bourgeois than them: "In some ways it was more closely linked to the realization of specifically bourgeois interests than elsewhere, because in Britain and France the latter was complicated by the unruly interventions of the subordinate classes ('plebeians,' *menu people*). Arguably, the the greater progress of democratic forms in those two countries owed far more to these intrusive popular conflicts than to the spontaneous liberalism of a 'rising bourgeoisie.'"[160]

Eley did not consider this analysis as it applied only to Germany, but as part of a general pattern of development characteristic of the emergence of the second wave of capitalist "Great Powers" under conditions of geopolitical competition:

> There is a case for treating German Unification, the Italian Risorgimento, and the Meiji Restoration in Japan as directly comparable experiences. Each might be described as a "bourgeois revolution from above," in the specific sense that in a concentrated space of time and through a radical process of political innovation it delivered the legal and political conditions for a society in which the capitalist mode of production could be dominant. This was achieved by often quite farsighted and visionary interventions by the existing states (or at least by the radical pragmatism of "modernizing" tendencies within them), but without the social turbulence and insurrectionary extravagance which marked the earlier Franco-British pattern. Of course in neither Germany nor Italy (the Japanese case is more difficult to judge) was the action of the state wholly autonomous or unrelated to wider processes of social change, although the latter might easily be imposed from outside, as in the Napoleonic occupations of Germany and parts of Italy, or the threatening incursion of Western influences into Japan.

In this context Eley invokes what he calls "the classical Marxist concept of uneven and combined development," although what he appears to mean is the concept of uneven development. Eley is scarcely alone in this error, however, and terminology apart, he is clearly right to distinguish between the historical conditions under which the "revolutions from above" occurred and those of their predecessors:

> On the one hand, German and Italian unifications occupied a distinct temporality when compared to the earlier sequence of the Dutch, British, American, and French Revolutions. Where the latter occurred before the global victory of capitalist relations on a European, let alone a world, scale—the former actively presupposed the triumph of capitalism; where the earlier revolutions were driven forward by broad coalitions of large and small property-owners, the later ones lost this popular impetus to an intervening stage of social differentiation which . . . set the bourgeoisie proper against the mass of pauperized small producers and the infant working class.[161]

The joint work of Blackbourn and Eley was immediately recognized as a major Marxist contribution to the understanding of German history. Another leading left-wing British Germanist, Richard Evans, hailed their book as doing "so much to get away from the old Comintern dogmas which have informed so much Marxist work in this field—dogmas whose empirical foundation historians of Germany have increasingly revealed to be extremely shaky."[162] In more general terms however, Evans asked: "How persuasive are the author's claims that the term "bourgeois revolution" should refer solely to the triumph of the capitalist mode of production?" Like Ginsborg, Evans was concerned that the distinction between moment and process was being elided:

Marx and Engels certainly used the term "bourgeois revolution" to encompass both the change in relations of production which brought the bourgeoisie to a position where it displaced the feudal aristocracy as the dominant owner of property and labor power; and the consequent political changes by which the bourgeoisie secured the adaptation of "superstructural" elements to conform more closely to its interests (e.g., the abolition of guilds, the establishment of a free market in property, the restrictions on labor supply such as serfdom, the ending of mercantilist restrictions on trade and manufacture, the creation of a political system that would be responsive to its needs; and so on). There is no doubt that they considered it necessary for the bourgeoisie, defined in its broadest sense, to act in some degree as the agent of the latter process, though usually in alliance with other classes.[163]

As we saw in our earlier discussion of Marx and Engels there is in fact considerable doubt that they "considered it necessary for the bourgeoisie ... to act in some degree as the agent" of bourgeois revolution; but Evans had nevertheless identified a genuine problem, namely whether the type of approach adopted by Eley in particular merely dissolved the moment of bourgeois revolution into the longer-term process of the transition from feudalism to capitalism.

If Eley's work started from a particular case study and then proceeded to draw general conclusions, that of Alex Callinicos was an attempt to formulate a general theory. As in the case of Cliff, Callinicos first began to consider the problem of bourgeois revolution in relation to Trotsky's unfulfilled expectations about the prospects for permanent revolution. In a review of Löwy's *The Politics of Combined and Uneven Development* (1981) Callinicos noted the problem of making "an identification of bourgeois-democratic revolution with merely one of its cases," which is of course the French, "and making its specific features—the abolition of the monarchy, national unification and independence, the division of estates among the peasantry—necessary components of any 'genuine' bourgeois revolution": "The process which led to the establishment of most of the main capitalist powers did not fit this model—the main beneficiary of the English revolution was a quasi-capitalist agrarian class which kept firm hold of its land and got rid of kings rather than monarchy, while Germany, Italy and Japan experienced what Gramsci called 'passive revolutions' in which the feudal landowners gradually accommodated themselves to industrial capitalism, leaving many of the structures of the old society intact." As Anderson had noted the previous decade, applying such a rigorous set of criteria for contemporary revolutions in the Third World would retrospectively mean that all the "classic" bourgeois revolutions would fail them, with the possible exception of the French, the implication being that virtually every bourgeois revolution was still incomplete: "Surely it is more sensible, rather than invoke the metaphysical concept of a 'complete and genuine solution' [to the tasks of the bourgeois revolution], to judge a bourgeois revolution by the degree to which it succeeds in establishing an autonomous center of capital accumulation, even if it fails to democratize the political order, or to eliminate feudal social relations."[164] The notion of achieving "an autonomous center of capital accumulation" is central to any serious consequentialist definition of bourgeois revolution, but these remarks were not at this stage integrated into a general position. It was possible that Callinicos did not feel it was necessary to argue the position: in an article for *New Left Review* in 1988 he claimed that "use of the French Revolution as a normative model has rightly been abandoned by Marxist historians," before going on to quote from Jones and reference Hill's later writings.[165] But given the limited number of historians whom Callinicos was able to invoke in his support (although he also drew on the work of Blackbourn and Eley), this was by any standard an over-optimistic assertion.[166]

Callinicos returned to the question of bourgeois revolution as such in *Making History* (1987) in the context of a discussion about structure and agency.[167] But this amounted to a sketch for his major attempt to reconstruct the theory. In 1989, the journal *International Socialism* devoted a special issue to the bicentenary of the French Revolution, against the backdrop of the revisionist climacteric. Drawing on both the classic tradition (Lenin, Lukács, and Gramsci), and some specific contributions (Eley on Germany, the later Hill on England, Barker on Japan, and Jones more generally), Callinicos's contribution was both the culmination and systematization of forty years of fragmentary and often passing observations by writers who were often ignorant of or in other respects in opposition to each others' positions. One passage in particular contains the classic presentation of the consequentialist argument:

> Bourgeois revolutions must be understood, not as revolutions consciously made by capitalists, but as revolutions which promote capitalism. The emphasis should shift from the class which makes a bourgeois revolution to the effects of such a revolution—to the class which benefits from it. More specifically, a bourgeois revolution is a political transformation—a change in state power, which is the precondition for large-scale capital accumulation and the establishment of the bourgeoisie as the dominant class. This definition requires then, a political change with certain effects. It says nothing about the social forces which carry through the transformation.[168]

One of the organizing principles of his argument was the dual model of bourgeois revolution in which the key distinction, familiar from Deutscher and Anderson, is whether the impetus for change came from "from below" or "from above."[169] Treated not as an absolute distinction but as an indication of two tendencies within the overall trajectory of bourgeois revolution, the demarcation is helpful; but nevertheless qualifications need to be introduced. These are necessary not so much because of the existence of elements "from below" in the later revolutions, since the exploits of Garibaldi's Legion were not decisive in the Italian Risorgimento nor were Japanese peasant revolts a major factor in the Meiji Restoration. The issue is rather the far more weighty contribution "from above" in the earlier revolutions. The decisive moment in the English Revolution, for example, was the military coup by the New Model Army between December 1648 and January 1649; in other words, the exercise of state power by its most characteristic institution. Similarly, if we take the French Revolution as a whole from 1789 and 1815, then the entire process from 1794 at the latest is mainly state directed. And, as we have seen, in both cases the consolidation of the regime was accompanied by the externalization of the revolution, not only from above but "from outside"; to Scotland in the case of Cromwell, Central and Western Europe in that of Napoleon. The central paradox of this shifting trajectory is that as the outcome of capitalist and particularly industrial capitalist development becomes more explicit, the agents of revolution become further and further removed from the capitalist class.

Unlike most of the earlier contributors to the discussion, however, Callinicos did not treat the issue as solely a historical one. Following Cliff, he situated the revolutions that accompanied postwar decolonization into the overall trajectory of the bourgeois revolution: "Nationalist movements, often marching under 'Marxist-Leninist' colors but dominated by the urban petty bourgeoisie, were able to lead and organize successful peasant wars against imperialism and its allies. The regimes brought to power by these revolutions proceeded to construct state capitalist social orders, in which the task of capital accumulation was assumed by a state bureaucracy recruited from the victorious movement and collectively exploiting workers and peasants alike." What is the position of the deflected permanent revolutions in relation to the "revolution from above" or "revolution from below" distinction? Callinicos wrote that "the Meiji Restoration occupies a borderline between the 'revolutions from above' of the mid-19th century and a third variant of bourgeois revolution prevalent in the present century."[170] One way of assessing this "third variant" would be to treat the revolutions described by Cliff as the "norm" (China) as "revolutions from below" and those he described as "deviations" (Egypt) as "revolutions from above," although there are of course many intermediate cases such as India. The problem here is what is meant by the notion of revolution from below. It is true that Mao and Castro had to overcome the existing state power with arms in hand, but their revolutions did not involve the self-activity of revolutionary masses that had occurred at various points in bourgeois revolutions from below, especially the French, although their foreign supporters were happy to delude themselves that this was so. In the case of China in particular, the party-army led by Mao was the framework of a new state, and acted as such, to the point of instructing workers not to go on strike as the Red Army approached Shanghai and Beijing. For these workers and their equivalents elsewhere in the Third World who were, at best, manipulated as a stage army by an emergent bureaucratic ruling class, revolutions imposed by military force were as much revolutions from above as those emanating from within the existing state machine.

As had previously been suggested by Cliff and Barker, the development represented by the twentieth-century revolutions from above was simply the last phase of a long historical sequence in which a succession of social forces that had accomplished bourgeois revolutions, indicating their structural dissimilarity from socialist revolutions:

The historical irony that movements claiming the inspiration of Marxism should do the work of capitalism, merely underlines the fundamental difference between bourgeois and socialist revolutions. Bourgeois revolutions are characterized by a disjunction of agency and outcome. A variety of social forces—Independent gentry, Jacobin lawyers, *Junker* and *samurai* bureaucrats, even "Marxist-Leninists"—can carry through political transformations which radically improve the prospects for capitalist development. No such disjunction characterizes socialist revolutions.[171]

Several authors have explicitly adopted Callinicos's definition.[172] Others have independently arrived at essentially the same position. In a recent statement of the consequentialist case, first published in 1990, Heide Gerstenberger has written:

> As a structural category . . . bourgeois revolution does not refer . . . to a particular form of historical change. Whether conflicts leading to a change in power culminated in open civil war and events that contemporaries already viewed as the start of a whole new epoch, or whether they led to successive rounds of reform until personal power was eventually eliminated, does not affect bourgeois revolution as a structural category. Finally, the concept also says nothing about the groups who waged the conflicts that led to personal power being regulated, limited and abolished.[173]

Echoes of it can even be found in the work of otherwise unsympathetic historians opposed to accounts which privilege bourgeois agency. "The revolution might be seen as being made not by the bourgeoisie but for the bourgeoisie," William Beik tentatively proposed in 2010, as if this was a startling new idea.[174]

But the consequentialist position has also been misunderstood. David Lockwood, for example, accepts the distinction Callincos makes between revolutions from above and below, but draws two erroneous conclusions. One concerns the incapacity of the bourgeoisie: "A study of bourgeois revolutions, of both the 'classical' variety . . . and those 'from above' . . . reveals that the foundations of the bourgeois revolution and for a capitalist economy are not laid by the bourgeoisie itself. In fact, it may be the case that prior to the revolution a bourgeoisie proper does not exist at all. Not only is the bourgeoisie not fully formed before the bourgeois revolution, and not in its vanguard, it also does not emerge immediately in its wake."[175] This is not a new argument. Nicos Poulantzas, for example, argued that all bourgeois revolutions displayed a common feature: "namely *the bourgeoisie's lack of political capacity (because of its class constitution) successfully to lead its own revolution in open action*."[176] But the consequentialist argument does not claim that the various bourgeoisies have *never* played revolutionary roles and such a claim would be unsustainable. The earliest successful examples of bourgeois revolution, in the United Netherlands and England, did involve leadership by mercantile, agrarian, and even industrial capitalists, although the latter tended to be based in the colonies rather than the metropolitan centers. As Callinicos himself notes, "the French Revolution was carried through under bourgeois leadership," although he rightly accepts that this was "exceptional."[177] The point is simply that there is no *necessity* for the bourgeoisie to play this role in order for a revolution to qualify as bourgeois. Lockwood's other error is to reify the state as the agent of revolution in the absence of the bourgeoisie:

> The competition between states, and the military needs it engendered, created beneficial conditions for the emergence of capitalism. The state, however, did not set out to "create" capitalism. Its emergence was a by-product of the need of states to make the best use of their military investments. Instead of seizing the wealth of the emerging capitalist classes, states found it more effective to protect property rights and to tax property owners. In establishing its supremacy over a national territory, the state at the same time marked out and defended a national market.[178]

Lockwood uses the examples of the Meiji Restoration and tsarist industrialization as examples, but later makes it clear that he sees all bourgeois revolutions as essentially state led. This seems to me to be completely mistaken. For one thing, there is no such thing as "the state," or even "states," but only feudal estates-monarchy states, feudal-absolutist states, tributary states, and so on; these may have had a more or less mediated relationship to the classes whose interests they represented, they were scarcely autonomous from them. For another, even if the historical role of the bourgeoisie is contingent on an outcome-based definition of bourgeois revolution, then it should be clear from the preceding discussion that the *transformation* of the state was necessary in each case, regardless of whether those carrying out the transformation were previously external to the state apparatus (as in France) or formed a fraction of the existing state-managerial bureaucracy (as in Germany).

Consequentialism has been criticized, in some cases by Marxists who regard positions such as those taken by the later Hill and Callinicos that downgrade bourgeois agency as capitulations to revisionism.[179] What these critics fail to understand is that consequentialism involves a redefinition of bourgeois revolution that is equally unacceptable to revisionists, since it still involves a notion of social crisis and transformation utterly hostile to their obsession with short-term contingencies.[180] The strongest opponents of consequentialism have been those who wished to dispense with the theory of bourgeois revolution in any form. Wood claimed that the term "bourgeois revolutions" has "undergone many redefinitions" that we have now reached the point where it means "any revolutionary upheaval that, in one way or another, sooner or later, advances the rise of capitalism, by changing property forms or the nature of the state, irrespective of the class forces involved."[181] The real issue is whether it can be empirically demonstrated that a particular sequence of events ("a bourgeois revolution") led, not "sooner or later," but *directly* to an outcome (the establishment of "an independent centre of capital accumulation"), which would not otherwise have taken place at that point in history. It is not clear to me why this is a problem. Curiously, it is one of Wood's fellow-political Marxists, Charles Post, who has given the most extreme example of the very approach she criticizes, although she tactfully refrains from mentioning this in her introduction to his book:

The first American Revolution, at best, fits a minimal definition of the bourgeois revolution—a revolution that creates state-institutions capable of promoting the development of capitalist property-relations. This definition requires no prior development of capitalist social-property relations, no precapitalist obstacles to capitalist development, nor a class-conscious capitalist class in the lead of the revolution. A revolution is bourgeois only to the extent that it, *intentionally or unintentionally*, advances capitalist development in a given society.[182]

There are certainly important issues raised by Post's work, including the questions of whether the American Revolution did in fact lead directly to the development of capitalist property relations and whether the social forces that eventually carried out this development did so with this outcome in mind (on the latter point Post is an orthodox political Marxist who finds the idea of anyone willingly embracing capitalism inconceivable); but the theoretical framework is a perfectly valid one for carrying out such research and debate needed to answer them.

Nevertheless, although Callinicos has constructed the strongest and most comprehensive version of the consequentialist argument, it also raises a number of issues that require further discussion. The most important of these is the relationship, identified by both Ginsborg and Evans, between "process" and "moment," or more precisely between the transition to capitalism and the bourgeois revolution. A tendency to dissolve the latter into the former was certainly present in some of the writers who influenced Callinicos, notably Jones, but Blackbourn too shifted the emphasis from the politico-social onto underlying socioeconomic processes, describing the German case as a prolonged "silent revolution."[183] This position has acquired support from writers who "would identify bourgeois revolution with the long, slow and often 'silent' process by which a particular mode of production and its concomitant property relations place their stamp on human relations."[184] The problem here is that if one is simply applying the label to a process, then it is difficult to see how this differs from the arguments of those revisionists who oppose the entire concept of bourgeois revolution. In the case of Spain, for example, Jesús Cruz has argued against the notion of bourgeois revolution in that country on the grounds that Spain did not become fully capitalist until the late 1960s and early 1970s, so that no event can be identified as leading to this outcome:

> If what we mean by bourgeois revolution is a violent change that causes political, social, and economic upheaval, then there were, indeed, very few bourgeois revolutions. In most countries capitalist transformation has occurred slowly and unevenly, the entire process sometimes lasting over a century.... In the case of Spain this process has lasted some one hundred and sixty years. Applying the term "revolution" to the process is, then, simply making historical pieces fit into a puzzle that is in itself a poor tool for the study of history.[185]

Against these positions, which effectively reduce the notion of revolution to a metaphor, Callinicos argued that "the term 'revolution' should not be dissolved into the long-term socio-processes involved in the development of capitalism" and quoted Anderson in support of his contention that all social revolutions involved "episodes of convulsive political transformation."[186] If the word "revolution" meant the destruction of the existing state and the construction of a new one, then it could scarcely occur gradually (or silently) in the way that the word "process" implied. For Gerstenberger too, one reason for retaining the term "bourgeois revolution" is precisely because "it offers the great advantage of rejecting all theoretical concepts that analyse the modern state as the result of gradual change: the outcome of increasing strength and rationalization, accompanied by long-run processes of cultural transformation."[187] However, there are two difficulties here.

The first is in part a result of Callinicos's reliance on Anderson. Both the context of Anderson's remarks and their subsequent elaboration ("a punctual break with the order of capital"), however, show that he is specifically discussing the socialist revolution, not revolutions in general and certainly not bourgeois revolutions; but bourgeois revolutions do not have to take the same form as proletarian revolutions—that is, a frontal assault on the state apparatus. With the exceptions of the English and French absolutist regimes, the feudal states against which the bourgeois revolutions were directed differed in several ways from their capitalist successors, most significantly in that they were not all unitary machines against which such an operation could be mounted. Some revolutions, such as the Dutch, took the form of extended wars against foreign dynasties, gradually liberating territories where the capitalist mode of production was already dominant over a period of decades. Others, such as the German, took the form of unification movements incorporating different regions at varying levels of development within the most advanced. At least one, the Scottish, took the form of an existing central state dismantling elements of dual power represented by the feudal jurisdictions and military tenures retained after the Union of Parliaments in 1707. In all these cases the establishment of unified states committed to capital accumulation was the result of more or less prolonged periods in which revolution equaled the cumulative effect of conventional military operations supported by juridical enactments—a "process," in other words.

The other, and greater, problem is that the vast majority of nation-states in the world—now amounting to nearly two hundred—have not experienced "convulsions" even of those associated with the revolutions from above. The danger here is that of falling into one of the dilemmas of orthodoxy, of seeking to discover a "revolution," however disguised, in the development of every country, with all the resultant historical distortions this involves. Tom Lewis, for example, has used Callinicos's arguments to rebut the type of adopted revisionism associated with Cruz: "Both intellectually and politically, I find the idea that capitalism and bourgeois rule were not fully functional in Spain before the 1960s, in the economic realm, and the late 1970s, in the political realm, to be absurd."[188] This is a position with which I am in complete agreement; but Lewis then identifies the period between 1834 and 1843, and that of the Carlist Wars more generally as the decisive period in the Spanish bourgeois revolution.[189] The former position does not depend on the latter: in the case of Spain an equally convincing case could be made for 1820, 1854, or 1868, and a more defensible argument might be that the dominance of capitalism in Spain—as in Sweden, Brazil, or Iran—was a cumulative process in which no single episode can be identified as decisive. It is clear that some countries had to undergo bourgeois revolutions in order to liberate capitalist relations of production from their precapitalist bonds at an international level; but once this has reached a certain point, what follows is a process in which nation-states adopt and adapt to economic, social, and political forms, except in situations of outright colonial domination. We might then say that the notion of a Great Arch, which I criticized in chapter 16, while not generally applicable to the history of capitalism, is relevant once the capitalist system passed a certain developmental stage.

These issues are indicative of a problem that has recurred throughout this book: the need to identify what is distinct about the bourgeois revolutions compared to other forms of social revolution. The bourgeois revolutions lie between the polar extremes represented by the transition to feudalism and the socialist revolution. To emphasize "process" is to force them into the same mold as their feudal predecessors; to highlight "moment" is to make them over in the image of their socialist successors. Neither is adequate: in some respects bourgeois revolutions look back to the former, in others they look forward to the latter, and in still others are distinct from them both. What then is specific to them? In the final part of this book I will attempt to answer this question by way of reconstructing the theory of bourgeois revolution from, as it were, the first principles of historical materialism.

FOUR

THE SPECIFICITY OF THE BOURGEOIS REVOLUTIONS

20

Between Two
Social Revolutions

The concept of bourgeois revolution is a specific application of the materialist conception of history that provides an explanation for the consolidation, extension, and ultimate domination of society by capitalism. In doing so, it links together events otherwise distant from each other in terms of time, space, and form. There are alternative explanations for these events, most of which would make no conceivable connection between, for example, the sixteenth-century wars of religion and the twentieth-century wars of national liberation; but these explanations also involve theories. It was no Marxist but Frederick von Hayek, a supporter of one of these alternatives (the Marginalist variant of neoclassical economics) and a virulent opponent of historical materialism, who wrote:

> The idea that you can trace the causal connections of any events without employing a theory, or that a theory will emerge automatically from the accumulation of a sufficient amount of facts, is of course sheer illusion. The complexity of social events in particular is such that, without the tools of analysis which a systematic theory provides, one is almost bound to interpret them; and those who eschew the conscious use of an explicit and tested logical argument usually merely become the victims of the popular beliefs of their time.[1]

Any theory is of course open to misuse. Perez Zagorin has argued, with specific reference to our subject: "Marxist historical scholarship has too often had to impose a mutilating pressure on the facts and in the face of recalcitrant evidence to resort to excessively ingenious methods of interpretation, which causes its procedures to resemble the addition of epicycles to the Ptolemaic hypothesis in order to 'save the phenomena.'"[2] In effect he claims that, in this respect at least, Marxists respond to the threat of empirical refutation by resorting to auxiliary hypotheses in order to protect the inner core of the concept, the type of procedure that the philosopher of science Imre Lakatos once identified as characteristic of a "degenerating research programme."[3] Like every other historical concept, that of bourgeois revolution must ultimately be assessed on the basis of whether or not it makes the past more comprehensible to us, in ways that are compatible with the available evidence. MacIntyre once outlined the tasks that any successful social theory must accomplish. How, he asked, did Charles Darwin demonstrate the validity of "evolution by natural selection"?

> Darwin states his own thesis [in *The Origin of Species*] with remarkable brevity. He then takes hard case after hard case and shows how in fact all can be fitted into the evolutionary picture. How many hard cases does he need to dispose of before his case is established? Clearly there is no simple answer, but at a certain point conviction becomes overwhelming. Equally historical materialism is established by showing the amount of history that is made intelligible by it; and once again there is no hard and fast rule as to the point at which such a view becomes plausible.[4]

A defensible concept of bourgeois revolution must also be able to explain "hard cases" in a way that makes history "intelligible," without adjusting the concept to fit the evidence or misrepresenting the evidence to fit the concept. Henryk Grossman once wrote that Marx was attempting to understand social phenomena, not by focusing on their "superficial attributes ... at any given moment or period," but "in their successive transformations, and thus to discover their essence."[5] What is the essence of a bourgeois revolution? Or, to put it more prosaically, how would we recognize that one has taken place?

The general method of Political Economy described by Marx in the *Grundrisse* as "obviously ... scientifically correct" begins with an abstract conception, proceeds by moving back and forth between it and concrete examples in a process that deepens the original concept and eventually arrives at a view of the concrete as "a rich totality of many determinations and relations."[6] The usefulness of this approach is not, however, restricted to Political Economy or, as in Marx's case, its critique. MacIntyre once suggested an example in relation to one of the most famous claims by Marx and Engels: "The history of all hitherto existing history is the history of class struggles."[7] As MacIntyre writes, this "is not a generalisation built up from instances, so much as a framework without which we should not be able to identify our instances; yet also a framework which could not be elaborated without detailed empirical study."[8] But formulating a concept ("elaborating a framework" in MacIntyre's terms) is only possible through abstracting from the essential qualities present in a range of cases. The difficulty in relation to bourgeois revolutions is precisely that there is no agreement about what the essential qualities of the concept are. Domenico Losurdo, for example, has written that, as a category, bourgeois revolution "is at once too narrow and too broad":

> As regards the first aspect, it is difficult to subsume under the same category of bourgeois revolution the Glorious Revolution and the parliamentary revolt that preceded the upheavals that began in France in 1789, not to mention the struggles against monarchical absolutism, explicitly led by the liberal nobility, which developed in Switzerland and other countries. On the other hand, the category of bourgeois revolution is too broad: it subsumes both the American Revolution that sealed the advent of a racial state and the French Revolution and San Domino Revolution, which involved complete emancipation of black slaves.[9]

One solution might be to adopt the more specific procedure Marx outlined in the "Preface" to the first edition of *Capital*, Volume 1:

> The physicist either observes physical phenomena where they occur in their most typical form and most free from disturbing influence, or, wherever possible, he makes experiments under conditions that assure the occurrence of the phenomenon in its normality. In this work I have to examine the capitalist mode of production, and the conditions of production and exchange corresponding to that mode. Up to the present time, their classic ground is England. That is the reason why England is used as the chief illustration in the development of my theoretical ideas.[10]

In other words, we should select the "classic" case where the fundamental characteristics of the concept are most fully developed. In one sense this is exactly what Marx and Engels did in relation to bourgeois revolutions. In a note to the *Manifesto of the Communist Party* added in 1888, forty years after it was first published, Engels wrote: "Generally speaking, for the economic development of the bourgeoisie, England is taken here as the typical country; for its political development, France."[11] Three years earlier he had explained the centrality of the French experience to historical materialism in greater detail:

> France is the land where, more than anywhere else, historical class struggles were each time fought out to a decision and where, consequently, the changing political forms within which they move and in which their results are condensed have been stamped in the sharpest outlines. The focus of feudalism in the Middle Ages, the model country of unified estate monarchy since the Renaissance, France demolished feudalism in the Great Revolution and established the unalloyed rule of the bourgeoisie in a classical purity unequalled by any other European land. And the struggle of the rising proletariat against the ruling bourgeoisie manifested itself here in an acute form unknown elsewhere.[12]

Eric Hobsbawm developed Engels's point by setting out a detailed case for the "typical" status of the Great French Revolution. By 1794, he wrote:

> The main shape of French and all subsequent bourgeois-revolutionary politics were now clearly visible. This dramatic dialectical dance was to dominate the future generations. Time and time again we shall see the moderate middle-class reformers mobilizing the masses against die-hard resistance or counter-revolution. We shall see the masses pushing beyond the moderates' aims to their own social revolutions, and the moderates in turn splitting into a conservative group henceforth making common cause with the reactionaries, and a left wing group determined to pursue the rest of the as yet unachieved moderate aims with the help of the masses, even at the risk of losing control over them.

Hobsbawm does note that "in most subsequent bourgeois revolutions the moderate liberals were to pull back, or to transfer into the conservative camp, at a very early stage," which already introduces a distinction between the French Revolution and those which followed it.[13] More problematic is the fact that the process Hobsbawm describes is not in fact characteristic of most subsequent bourgeois revolutions: France in 1830, certainly; Germany in 1848, perhaps (although it failed); but beyond them?

The key problem, however, is the procedure outlined by Marx and Engels. It is certainly appropriate when discussing the capitalist mode of production, which by definition has certain indispensable characteristics, such as generalized commodity production or the self-expansion of capital. It would be equally appropriate in a discussion of any other embodiment of a structured social relationship, like the absolutist state ("unified estate monarchy"), in relation to which France before 1789 can, as Engels says, be treated as the "classic" case. But the bourgeois revolution is not the embodiment of a structured relationship, like those of wage labor to capital or of peasants to the tax collector; it is the enactment of a process. Consequently, to treat the characteristics of the French case as the highest level of bourgeois revolutionary development is to imply that countries that do not display these characteristics have either undergone an incomplete experience or failed to undergo the experience at all, with all the political and theoretical confusions that follow.

Perhaps another revolution might be more suitable as a "classic" case then? Tony Cliff wrote: "The 'Bismarckian' path was not the exception for the bourgeoisie, but the rule, the exception was the French revolution."[14] Geoff Eley similarly argued that the German experience, in avoiding the "volatile scenario of the English and French Revolutions," is actually a better model than them: "In some ways—the sharpness of the rupture with the past, the definitive character of the legal settlement, the commanding strength of capital in the new national economy—German Unification was more specifically 'bourgeois' in its content and more resoundingly 'bourgeois' in its effects than either the English or the French Revolutions had been, precisely because significant popular interventions failed to occur."[15] But is Otto von Bismarck any more of a representative figure than Maximilien Robespierre? In fact, the German experience of territorial expansion by military conquest at the hands of an internally transformed absolutist state has close parallels only with the contemporary events of the Italian Risorgimento, although more distant comparisons can be found in the American Civil War and Canadian Confederation.

In response to these difficulties some Marxists have simply abandoned any attempt to establish a "classic" case. In 1968 Nicos Poulantzas wrote, "though the transition to feudalism throughout Western Europe presents common tendential characteristics, no paradigm case of the bourgeois revolution can be found."[16] In his 1976 lecture on the subject Perry Anderson similarly emphasized the difficulties involved in identifying a common set of constitutive elements for the bourgeois revolutions: "Here the exception was the rule—every one was a bastard birth."[17] As long as attempts to establish a definition depend on aspects of the bourgeois revolutions as a process, they are bound to end up with a series of national "peculiarities" that, as Anderson himself noted in a related context, lead "into the sands of an interminable nominalism."[18] In fact, the problem is irresolvable so long as we treat "bourgeois" as referring to the dominant agency and "revolution" as taking a particular form. A more useful approach is therefore to place the concept of bourgeois revolution on the terrain of what Andrew Abbott calls "turning point" analysis, in which "neither the beginning nor the end of the turning point can be defined until the whole turning point has passed, since it is the arrival and establishment of a new trajectory . . . that defines the turning point itself." Consequently, "turning point analysis makes sense only after the fact."[19] To establish the nature of the turning point in relation to bourgeois revolutions we need temporarily to pull back from specific detail of their form and survey instead the general pattern of revolution in history.

POLITICAL REVOLUTIONS, SOCIAL REVOLUTIONS, AND VARIETIES OF CLASS STRUGGLE

I began this book by noting that, in one sense, the entire debate about the events conventionally known as bourgeois revolutions centered on whether they were political or social in character, and the distinction has recurred repeatedly throughout the subsequent pages. If we are to identify what is specific to bourgeois revolutions, then we need first to clarify the distinction, which has by no means received universal support. Steve Pinkus, for example, argues that it is not "useful" to distinguish between political and social revolutions, and that the former must be understood simply as "civil wars, rebellions, or coups d'état." In effect, Pinkus seems to believe that *all* genuine revolutions are social in nature:

> Revolutions must involve both a transformation of the socioeconomic orientation and of the political structures. That transformation must take place through a popular movement, and the transformation must involve a self-consciousness that a new era has begun. The distinction drawn in the literature between social and political revolutions, it seems to me, is normative as much as analytical. Scholars draw a bold line in the sand between social and political revolutions because they admire some revolutionary outcomes and disdain others. Analytical language has been used to disguise political preferences.[20]

There are certainly works where revolutions have been described as either political or social on the basis of political preference, but this book is not one of them. On the one hand, I "admire" the popular movements for greater democracy involved in the American War of Independence, although I regard it as a political revolution. On the other hand, the Meiji Restoration is scarcely the kind of event to inspire admiration in democrats, although I regard it as a social revolution and historically progressive in the sense that it brought an end to the tributary regime in Japan. The assertions that Pinkus himself makes about the character of social revolutions involve elements that are entirely arbitrary. I would be prepared to accept that they "must involve . . . transformation of the socioeconomic orientation and of the political structures," but why "must" these transformations be achieved by a self-conscious popular movement?

In fact the distinction between political and social revolutions is perfectly valid, as is indicated by the way it has been used by writers from Harrington and Locke onward, even only in implicit ways. As we saw in chapter 8, the dominant position on the left between the Conspiracy of the Equals in 1795 and the Springtime of the Peoples in 1848 was that all previous revolutions, including the Great French Revolution, had been merely political revolutions; the social revolution had yet to occur and when it did it would be socialist in content. It was only while formulating the principles of historical materialism that Marx and Engels began to argue, from late in 1845, that the revolutions that had brought about the dominance of capital, and were still doing so, were also social: the bourgeois revolutions. Yet even within the later classical Marxist tradition there was by no means complete unanimity on this question.

In one passage from his great work, *History and Class Consciousness*, Lukács suggested that the French Revolution could be a bourgeois revolution *without* being a social revolution:

> A political revolution does no more than sanction a socio-economic situation that has been able to impose itself at least in part upon the economic reality. Such a revolution forcibly replaces the old legal order, now felt to be "unjust" by the new "right," "just" law. There is no radical reorganization of the social environment. (Thus conservative historians of the Great French Revolution emphasize that "social" conditions remained relatively unchanged during the period.) Social revolutions, however, are concerned precisely to change this environment.[21]

Leave aside, for the moment, the accuracy of any judgment that claims that the French Revolution failed to "change the social environment"; Lukács has effectively retreated here to the pre-Marxist position that only socialist revolutions are truly social, since they are not the culmination of previous socioeconomic changes, but the mechanism by which such changes are put into effect. The problem is that these transformative powers are not exclusive to socialist revolutions: the establishment of capitalism in Scotland followed the suppression of the last Jacobite Rebellion in 1746; to a still greater extent, the establishment of capitalism in Japan followed the Meiji Restoration of 1868. The implications of his argument are therefore that these bourgeois revolutions from above were more significant ("social") than the French bourgeois revolution from below—an extraordinary conclusion given the way in which Lukács elsewhere treats the French Revolution as an exemplar for all modern revolutions.

The identification of social revolutions only with those events that initiate a process of socioeconomic transformation has also been made—albeit from a completely different theoretical starting point—by Theda Skocpol:

> Social revolutions are rapid, basic transformations of a society's state and class structures; and they are accompanied and in part carried through by class-based revolts from below. Social revolutions are set apart from other sorts of conflicts and transformative processes above all by the combination of two coincidences: the coincidence of societal structural change with class upheaval and the coincidence of political with social transformation. . . . Political revolutions transform state structures but not social

structures, and they are not necessarily accomplished through class conflict.... What is unique to social revolution is that basic changes in social structure and in political structure occur together in a mutually reinforcing fashion. And these changes occur through intense sociopolitical conflicts in which class struggles play a key role.[22]

This is a good example of how writers can arrive at an inadequate model by arbitrarily isolating features from a handful of cases (a problem that also affects her critic Pinkus). Skocpol rightly argues that the French, Russian, and Chinese Revolutions were all social revolutions, a fact that is more significant in this context than their specific class character; but her definition also leads to other key modern revolutions being excluded from the category. She notes that the course of the English Revolution involved episodes "very similar indeed to the developments that would mark the trajectory of the French Revolution 150 years later":

> Partly because of such similarities and partly because both Revolutions happened in countries that became capitalist, liberal democracies, the English and the French Revolutions are often labeled "bourgeois revolutions." Whatever the appropriateness of this label for either revolution, it should not blind us to the very important differences between them. Though the English Revolution was certainly a successful revolution, it was not a *social* revolution like the French. It was accomplished not through class struggle but through a civil war between segments of dominant landed class (with each side drawing support from all of the other classes and strata). And whereas the French Revolution markedly transformed class and social structures, the English revolution did not. Instead it revolutionized the political structure of England.[23]

The assumption here is that, in a social revolution, the relationship between state and socioeconomic transformation must be unidirectional from the former to the latter; but this leads to the conclusion that two societies that are essentially of the same type, have undergone very similar revolutionary experiences, and in both cases led to the transformation of the state—all of which Skocpol accepts with respect to England and France—must nevertheless be deemed to have undergone different types of revolution, simply because the extent of prior socioeconomic transformation was different in degree.

If the categories of political and social revolution are to be helpful in terms of historical understanding, then I think we have to narrow the scope of political revolutions so that they are not about transformation but control of the state and broaden the scope of social revolutions so that transformations of the state can be both an effect and a cause of socioeconomic transformation. Political revolutions therefore take place *within* a socioeconomic structure and social revolutions involve a *change from* one socioeconomic structure to another. Hal Draper has perhaps made the clearest distinction between these two types of revolution:

> *Political* revolution ... puts the emphasis on the changes in governmental leadership and forms, transformations in the superstructure.... If ... social boundaries are burst by the change, then we have a different sort of revolution, which is of special importance to Marx's theory.... The outcome is a revolution involving the transference of political power to a new class; and this change in ruling class tends to entail a basic

change in the social system (mode of production). It is this kind of revolution which is most properly called a *social* revolution.[24]

To this very helpful distinction Draper then adds what I regard as an unnecessary complication:

> If we decide to define social revolution as a basic transformation in the social system involving its class base, then it is apparent that such a sweeping change cannot be conceived as a mere act or event, but as a process more or less extended in time. . . . Moreover, it is clear that in some case in the past, social systems have changed basically, and classes have risen and fallen, in a secular movement of history which can be described as a social revolution   at least in historical retrospect, even though no one may have been aware that a revolution was going on.

Draper argues that "such a long-term or secular transformation in society, however achieved," has no widely accepted name leading him to the "desperate recourse of inventing one." His invention is "a *societal revolution*, meaning that it denotes a change from one type of society to another."[25] Some writers, like Joseph Choonara, have found this distinction meaningful, but I remain unconvinced.[26] By "societal" Draper seems to have been thinking of two processes. One is the specific case of the transition from slavery to feudalism, a process of which it could certainly be said, "no one may have been aware that a revolution was going on." If, however, we understand that social revolutions take different forms, I see no reason why this transition cannot also be accommodated under that rubric, without the need for desperate terminological recourse. The other process Draper seems to mean by "societal" is the more general one of transition from one mode of production to another. The extent to which these take place before, during, or after a revolution will vary depending on which type of social revolution and, in the case of the bourgeois revolution, which period in their development we are discussing. Again, the existing notion of transition is perfectly adequate to identify processes of long-term change with moments of social revolution at their core, without confusing matters by also describing the former as revolutions. As Eley writes of the bourgeois revolutions, we have in each case to distinguish "between two levels of determination and significance":

> Between the revolution as a specific crisis of the state, involving widespread popular mobilization and a reconstitution of political relationships, and on the other the deeper processes of structural change, involving the increasing predominance of the capitalist mode of production, the potential obsolescence of many existing practices and institutions, and the uneven transformation of social relations. How these two levels became articulated together in the revolutionary conjuncture of a 1789 or 1848—change at the level of the state, change in the social formation—is a matter for detailed historical transformation.[27]

A focus on fundamental change at the level of the state seems to be the best means of distinguishing between the process of modal transition and the moment of social revolution.

In summary then, we can say the following: Political revolutions are struggles within society for control of the state, involving factions of the existing ruling class, which leave fundamental social and economic structures intact. These revolutions have been relatively frequent in history and include: the Roman Civil Wars, which led to the abandonment of Republican rule for the Principate in 27 BCE; the victory of the Abbasid over the Umayyad dynasty in 750, which led to the opening up to all Muslims the elite offices of the Caliphate formerly held exclusively by Arabs; and the Eastern European Revolutions of 1989–91, which swept away the Stalinist regimes and began the transformation of Eastern state capitalism into an approximation of the Western trans-state model. Political revolutions may involve more or less popular participation, may result in more or less improvement in the condition of the majority, can introduce democracy where it has previously been absent; but ultimately the ruling class that was in control of the means of production at the beginning will remain so at the end (although individuals and political organizations may have been replaced on the way), and the classes that were exploited within the productive process at the beginning will also remain so at the end (although concessions may have been made by the winning faction to secure their acquiescence or participation).

The absence of fundamental social change associated with political revolutions means that there is far less distinction between them and processes of accelerated reform. Take, for example, the Great Reform Act of 1832 in Britain. For Mark Neocleous, "the fundamental issue" is this: "Was it a reform for the bourgeois class, *the completion of the bourgeois revolution*, or merely a hacking at the old aristocratic structure to avoid bourgeois power?"[28] In fact the surgery was neither as invasive nor as cosmetic as these alternatives suggest. The bourgeois revolutions in Britain had been completed by 1688–89 in England and by 1745–46 in Scotland: the Great Reform Act was a successful attempt by the industrial bourgeoisie to achieve the franchise for itself and thereby gain more direct access to an already-capitalist British state. If a revolution had actually taken place, as Edward Thompson believed was possible between February 1831 and May 1832, then British society might have been more thoroughly democratized than it in fact was, but—given that socialism was not on the agenda at this early date—such a revolution would still have remained within the realm of the political.[29]

Social revolutions, however, are not merely struggles for control of the state, but struggles to transform it, either in response to changes that have already taken place in the mode of production, or in order to bring such changes about. As Perry Anderson notes, "modes of production change when the forces and relations of production enter into decisive contradiction with one another": "The maturing of such a contradiction need involve no conscious class agency on either side, by exploiters and exploited—no set battle for the future of economy and society; although its subsequent unfolding, on the other hand, is likely to unleash relentless social struggles between opposing forces."[30] Only three epochal processes fall into the category of social revolution. At one extreme is the transition from slavery to feudalism. At the other extreme is the socialist revolution, to date a possibility rather than a reality, but which, if achieved, will begin the transition from capitalism to socialism. Between these two extremes lie the bourgeois revolutions and, as we shall see, their intermediacy is not simply chronological. As Alex Callinicos writes: "The balance between the role played by structural contradictions and conscious human agency in resolving organic crisis has shifted from the former to the latter in the course of the past 1,500 years. The transition from feudalism to capitalism occupies an intermediate position in this respect between the fall of the Roman Empire and the Russian Revolution."[31] The relationship between political and social revolutions is complex. Some political revolutions have social implications and all social revolutions have political implications. Some revolutions, taken by themselves, appear to be merely political revolutions, are in fact the opening or concluding episode of a more extended social revolution. In relation to the bourgeois revolution, the English Revolution of 1688 has this relationship to the revolution of 1640.[32] Reversing the chronological order of importance, the American Revolution of 1776 has this in relation to the Civil War of 1861–65. More importantly in the context of this discussion, some revolutions conclude as political revolutions because they fail as social revolutions. In relation to the socialist revolution, this is clearly the case with the German Revolution of 1918. A similar case could also be made for the Bolivian Revolution of 1952, the Portuguese Revolution of 1974–75 and indeed most of the so-called democratic revolutions to have taken place since, most recently in Indonesia (1998) and Serbia (2000); it is still unclear whether the revolutions of the Arab Spring (2011–?) will also be halted within the confines of the political. Finally, as the "turning point" analysis I referred to earlier would suggest, it is only after a revolutionary process has concluded that it is possible to say whether it has involved political or social revolution. As Jeffery Webber writes: "One way out of the quandaries of process and consequence that arise in defining revolution is to separate the notion of *revolutionary epoch* from *social revolution*. The concept of revolutionary epoch provides us with a way of understanding that revolutionary transformative change is possible but not predetermined in a certain period, stressing the uncertainty—and yet not wide openness—of alternative outcomes."[33]

Because social revolutions are so rare, it is difficult to make generalizations about their nature. It is not even possible to say that in every case social revolution involves the replacement of one ruling class with another, since in some cases the personnel of a former ruling class remained in place while their role in the social relations of production changed—where, for example, slave owners became feudal lords or feudal lords became capitalist landowners. As this suggests, not all social revolutions are brought about by the direct triumph of one class over another through the class struggle, for "the history of all hitherto existing society" has involved two different types of class struggle, "two different categories of historical process."[34] Claudio Katz has identified these as exemplifying, respectively: "The antagonism within a class system and that between class systems."[35]

The first type, "within a class system," is where the classes involved are exploiter and exploited. The issues here are relatively straightforward. Slave owners extract surplus value from slaves, feudal lords and tributary bureaucrats do the same to peasants, and capitalists do the same to workers. In each case the exploited class resists to the extent that material conditions allow, but it is not always possible for them to go beyond resistance to create a new society based on a different mode of production. Alvin Gouldner writes of the one "unspoken regularity" of the series of class struggles listed in the *Manifesto of the Communist Party*: "The slaves did not succeed the masters, the plebeians did not vanquish the patricians, the serfs did not overthrow the lords, and the journeymen did not triumph over the guild-masters. The lowliest class never came to power. Nor does it seem likely to now."[36] We need not accept this dismal conclusion; nevertheless, it is true that exploited classes do not always have the structural capacity to make a social revolution: slaves did not; the majority of peasants did not; the working class does, and in this respect—among several others—it is unique among the exploited classes in history.

The other type of class struggle, "between class systems," is where those involved are oppressor and oppressed. The issues here are considerably more complex. For one thing, while all exploited classes (slaves, peasants, workers) are oppressed, not all oppressed classes are exploited and they may even be exploiters themselves. The number of oppressed classes that have the capacity to remake society is as limited as the number of exploited classes with that capacity. Among oppressed classes it is the bourgeoisie that is unique. Anthony Giddens writes:

> The struggle between the feudal nobility and rising bourgeoisie, in fact, does not appear in the classification of conflicting classes which Marx offers. . . . Here the criterion for the identification of class conflict is obviously that of the "exploitative dependence" of one class upon the other in the dichotomous model; there is a direct conflict of interest having its source in the appropriation of surplus value by a nonproductive class. In the case of the nobility and the bourgeoisie, however, conflict of interest derives from the need of the latter to dissolve the social and economic relationships characteristic of the feudal order, and of the former to maintain them. Thus although the bourgeoisie is in one sense a "subordinate" class within post-feudal society, in an other sense it constitutes a "dominant" class, in terms of the exploitative relationship in which it stands with wage-labor.[37]

The class struggle can therefore be not only between exploiters and exploited but also between exploiter and exploiter: it can nevertheless still be the means of bringing about social revolution, provided that the modes of production represented by these classes are different and one is more "progressive," in the Marxist sense of involving the greater development of the productive forces. Louis Althusser described "the central contradiction of the French Revolution, and of bourgeois revolution in general," as being that it involved "a struggle for state power *between two equally exploitative classes*, feudal aristocracy and bourgeoisie."[38] The notion of "equality" is misleading here since, before the bourgeois revolution, the former class could rely on the state to act in its interests, and the latter could not, that is why revolutions were required; but both classes were certainly exploitative.

The class struggle in history has therefore taken multifaceted forms. It is a permanent feature of the relationship between exploiting and exploited classes, but can also occur between dominant and subordinate exploiting classes, or between existing and potential exploiting classes. And these different class struggles have taken place simultaneously, intertwining and overlapping. The precise combinations have been or (in the case of socialism) will be different in relation the case of each of the great social revolutions. What form did they take in those that came before and may yet come after the bourgeois revolutions?

FROM SLAVERY TO FEUDALISM, FROM CAPITALISM TO SOCIALISM

In parts of the north and far west of Europe, such as Scandinavia and Scotland, feudalism evolved spontaneously out of primitive communism and through the Asiatic mode, understood here as a general term for the transitional process through which all pre-capitalist class societies first evolved.[39] The rise of feudalism in the former territories of the Roman Empire in the West from the 470s therefore represents the first direct passage in history from one exploitative mode of production to another. But was there a "feudal revolution"? George Duby was perhaps the first writer to refer to one occurring around 1000 and in doing so invoked an explicit parallel with the bourgeois revolution.[40] The concept was taken up by other, mainly French historians, above all by Guy Bois.[41] However, despite the endorsement of distinguished names like these, it seems more accurate to treat the transition to feudalism as a whole *as* the feudal "revolution," since there was no seizure of power and members of the former slave-owning ruling class simply changed their roles and added to their ranks from those of the former "barbarian" tribal chiefs. The transition from slavery to feudalism on the former territories of the Roman Empire in the West was unintended in the sense that no one consciously set out to establish the latter system; it emerged through a series of pragmatic adaptations in the ways production and exploitation took place. The peasants had to try new methods of production since their own subsistence—or at least continued tenure—now depended on doing so in a way that it did not for slaves; their success in achieving greater productivity encouraged the slave-owners-cum-lords to orient still further toward non-slave agriculture: "Slavery became extinct against a background of almost continuous and increasingly more marked development of the forces of production."[42] Feudalism is an integrated system in which, unlike capitalism, the economic, the social, the political, and the ideological are not separable in either appearance or reality; it is not therefore that socioeconomic change preceded the formation of new political and ideological forms (the estates monarchy, the "three orders") that we now regard as characteristic of feudalism, so much as that these were consolidated and formalized between c. 700 and c. 1000.[43]

If the feudal "revolution" was a process of socioeconomic transition out of whose completion new political forms eventually emerged, then the socialist revolution will be a socio-political struggle for power whose completion will allow a new economic order to be constructed. The precondition for socialism is the development of the productive forces by capitalism. As Marx and Engels wrote early in their careers, "development of productive forces . . . is an absolutely necessary practical premise, because without it privation, *want* is merely made general, and with *want* the struggle for necessities would begin again, and all the old filthy business would necessarily be restored."[44] Because the working class is non-exploitative there is no prior development of an alternative socialist or communist mode of production. As Lukács noted:

> It would be a utopian fantasy to imagine that anything tending towards socialism could arise within capitalism apart from, on the one hand, the *objective economic premises that make it a possibility* which, however, can only be *transformed* in to the true elements of a socialist system of production after and in consequence of the collapse of capitalism; and, on the other hand, the development of the proletariat as a class. . . . But even the most highly developed capitalist concentration will still be qualitatively different, even economically, from a socialist system and can neither change into one "by itself" nor will be amenable to such change "through legal devices" within the framework of capitalist society.[45]

The process of transition therefore *begins* with the destruction of capitalist states and the substitution of transitional soviet "states that are not states"—but only as the prelude to their ultimate self-dissolution, as capitalist (and in some cases residual pre-capitalist) productive relations are replaced by socialist ones. In that sense the transition to socialism involves the withering away of both the market *and* the state: "The foundations of capitalist modes of production and with them their 'necessary natural laws' do not simply vanish when the proletariat seizes power or even as a result of the socialization, however thoroughgoing, of the means of production. But their elimination and replacement by a consciously organized socialist economics must not be thought of only as a lengthy process but as a consciously conducted, stubborn battle. Step by step the ground must be wrested from this 'necessity'."[46]

Socialist productive relations will potentially allow even greater growth of the productive forces than under capitalism, but would only do so on the basis of a democratic decision taken by inhabitants of the new society after careful consideration of the all the implications, not least those concerning the environment. But even if growth was desired, it is unlikely to be achieved immediately. Bukharin's account of the postrevolutionary economic collapse inevitably generalized too much from the Russian Revolution, given it was the only experience available to him, but even in more advanced countries there can be little doubt that a combination of physical destruction, deskilling, the dislocation of the factors of production and necessary redistribution into nonproductive consumption will initially lead to a temporary decline of the productive forces before they can be reconstituted on a higher basis.[47] Clearly we are at a disadvantage in discussing the details of the transition to socialism since, unlike the transition to feudalism, we are discussing a process that has still to occur: the precise characteristics of socialist society are still obscure to us and, although some interesting work has now been done on what a genuine socialist economy would involve, these necessarily have a speculative character.[48] The only socialist revolution to have sustained itself for years rather than months, the Russian Revolution of October 1917, was thrown into reverse by the triumph of the Stalinist counterrevolution by 1928 and the transition it initiated has still to be successfully resumed. Nevertheless, from that experience and those of the brief but illuminating moments in failed socialist revolutions both before (the Paris Commune) and after (Germany 1918–23, Spain 1936–37, Hungary 1956, Portugal 1974–75, Iran 1978–79, Poland 1980–81, Egypt 2011–?), it is possible to see how the working class can establish new democratic institutions that have taken over the running of the economy, society, and the state. And these have never ceased to emerge, the most recent being the Argentinean *piqueteros* and *asembleas* of the crisis of 2000–01.

The experience of the Russian Revolution highlights another important difference between these two social revolutions. The societies that were transformed on feudal lines occupied a relatively small region of Western and Central Europe. Feudalism did not contain an inherent tendency toward expansion and therefore did not require a world or even continental system either for exploitation (the territorial acquisitions of the Crusaders in the Middle East were—to adopt a term associated with political Marxism—"opportunities" rather than "necessities") or for self-defense, since the great tributary states of the East were almost completely uninterested in these undeveloped formations, so obviously inferior to them in every respect except that of warfare, as they would eventually find to their cost. Feudalism had centuries to develop and expand outwards from its initial heartlands in what are now parts of France and Belgium; it was only in its later period of crisis that individual feudal states seriously sought to expand beyond Europe, most obviously in the irruption of the Hispanic states into the Americas. The socialist revolution, on the other hand, is necessarily a global event. As long as it remains isolated it remains susceptible to counterrevolution, either from without, as in most cases from the Paris Commune onward, or from within, as was the case in Russia. The latter point perhaps bears some elaboration. The threat to the Russian Revolution, which was eventually realized, was not simply the backwardness of the economy, but the fact that in the capitalist world system, the pressures of competitive accumulation would ultimately make themselves felt, to the point of determining what happened in Russian factories. Greater levels of economic development might enable a state to hold out from internal degeneration longer than Russia was able, but cannot ultimately protect against this process. That is why the international nature of the socialist revolution is a necessity, not a desirable but optional extra. Space has implications for time: the territorial extent of the socialist revolution exercises severe restraints over its temporality.

The final contrast lies between the different types of agency and their associated levels of consciousness. The exploited class on which the dominant slave mode of production was based was not responsible for overthrowing the slave owners. Indeed we know of only three major slave revolts in Roman history, two on Sicily during the second century BCE, and the most famous, that of Spartacus, on the Italian mainland during the first century BCE. Some other, smaller revolts have more recently come to light, but the fundamental picture remains unchanged. The absence of slave rebellion is at least partly the result of the extreme difficulty that the conditions of slavery posed, but it also worth considering what "success" might have meant. The leaders of the Sicilian slave revolts were intent on taking over existing institutions—including slavery—and establishing a Hellenistic kingdom on the Syrian Seleucid model. "The tragedy and moral of the whole episode is that no conceivable alternative existed."[49] Slaves dreamed, not of replacing slavery with a different system, but of escaping from it, either in order to return to the societies from which they had been captured (which were themselves in the process of transition to full-blown class societies) or by setting up their own communities outside of the Roman domains: even the Spartacists' final attempt on Rome seems to have been an effort to achieve this rather than to establish a new regime in Rome itself.[50] The class struggle in the Roman world was conducted between the free citizens, over an overwhelmingly passive slave population. But the inheritors were no more the peasants and plebeians of Ancient Rome than they were the slaves (although the slaves who obtained their freedom clearly benefited). Despite several important risings from early in the fifth century, the role of peasants was not principally as participants in open class struggle.

The new ruling class was in fact an alliance of the two forces that were actually responsible for ending the empire in the West: from within, the landowners who withdrew support for the state in opposition to its increasing demands for taxation; from without, the tribal chiefs and their retinues who led the barbarian invasions. The decline of slavery began toward the end of the second century, as the territorial limits of the empire were reached. In circumstances where new supplies of slaves could not simply be seized, the only way in which landowners could maintain numbers was by the more expensive business of physically reproducing the existing labor force—breeding new slaves, in other words. Similarly, if new territorial gains were excluded, the only mechanism through which landowners could expand their estates was by acquiring land from other, usually smaller landowners who would then be reduced in status. But the more land was acquired the greater the liability for tax, which landowners tried with increasing success to evade, thus reducing the resources available to the state. The main recipient of state funding was the army, engaged in increasingly futile attempts to repel the Germanic invasions—attempts whose lack of success provided an even greater incentive to tax evasion. Meanwhile the German invaders began to appear an attractive alternative to supporting a declining but increasingly acquisitive state apparatus. The triumph of the barbarians did not immediately lead to total transformation. Taxation continued, but without the need for a centralized army—since the new states raised armies from their own landowners and retainers—the main purpose for raising taxation no longer existed. Tax collection became increasingly fragmented: inessential for supporting monarchs, whose wealth derived from their own estates, it became principally used for securing support through gifts or bribes. Previously, members of the ruling class had sought to acquire land in order to gain access to control of the state apparatus, but now it became an end in itself. Simultaneously, from the reign of Augustus (27BCE–14AD), the freedom of the peasant-citizen began to be eroded as the state no longer permitted him to vote or required him to fight, with the restriction of the franchise to what were now openly called the *honestiores* ("upper classes") and the recruitment of armies by enlistment rather than as a duty of citizenship. Increasingly taxed to pay for the wars and the burgeoning bureaucracy, including that of the Church, peasants also inadvertently hastened the internal disintegration of the empire by placing themselves under the protection of landowners, effectively renouncing their independence on the assumption that not only would their new status as tenants not carry tax liabilities, but their new lords would be capable of avoiding such responsibilities themselves and consequently would not pass them on. In other words, an unfree labor force now began to emerge that rendered slavery redundant. The former slave owners changed the relations of production by lifting up the slaves they owned to the status of serfs while forcing down the free peasants tenanted on their land to the same level, as a response to the growing shortage of captured slaves and the expense of raising them. The tribal chiefs were meanwhile evolving into settled communities with stable and inherited social divisions between the warrior caste and the peasantry, a process hastened by the establishment of permanent settlements on the former territories of the empire. Both were moving from different directions toward what would become, over several hundred years, a new feudal ruling class. There was also a two-way movement of the exploited, particularly between the ninth and eleventh centuries. On the one hand, the supply of slaves dried up and those that remained were settled as serfs. On the other, the previously free peasants were increasingly brought into a servile condition.[51]

Peasant resistance continued during the transition, but these revolts were different from predecessors under the Roman Empire and successors under the consolidated feudal regime after 1000. Earlier peasant revolts, above all those of the Bagaudae against the Roman Empire in Gaul, were essentially directed against taxation and injustice at a time when the state was weakened and therefore the possibility of change beneficial to the peasantry became possible. Later peasant revolts too were conducted against the state in relation to "military service, laws on status and, above all, taxation."[52] In this period, revolts have a different impetus.

Chris Wickham argues that aristocratic hegemony did function in certain areas where the peasants had to rely on aristocrats for external support, as in eighth-century Lucchesia (in modern Italy), although this did not, of course exclude "small-scale signs of disobedience," but these are compatible with overall acceptance of ruling values. At the other end of the spectrum, as in eighth-century Paris, the aristocrats dominated through "overwhelming physical force" and did not require peasant acceptance of their rule, which they in any case did not receive. Between these lies a third type of area, such as sixth-century Galatia, where neither situation prevailed; that is, where aristocrats could rely on neither ideology nor violence to secure compliance. As Wickham notes, the latter situation is where revolts are most likely to take place, but: "The absence of hegemony is only one reason why peasants revolt, of course; they have to have something concrete to oppose as well."[53] In this case peasant revolts are signs of resistance to attempts by the emergent ruling class to impose serfdom. England is exceptional in its lack of peasant revolt, which seems to have two causes. First, because initially landowners had less control over the peasantry than in any other part of Europe, while at the same time they exercised superiority over exceptionally large territories. Second, when the lords did move to subject or expropriate peasant communities they did so slowly and in piecemeal fashion, attacking the weakest and while leaving the strongest and wealthiest untouched until the basis of possible collective resistance was eroded.[54] Elsewhere, the gradual encroachments of the emergent feudal state led to what Wickham calls "frequent small scale resistance," which erupted into one the great risings of the period: the Stellinga revolt in Saxony during 841–42, a revolt that took the opportunity of a civil war among the local Saxon ruling class to launch a program for the return to the pre-aristocratic social order.[55] I earlier quoted the distinction made by Katz between class struggle within class systems and class struggle between class systems; the types of class struggle enumerated by Wickham for the period of the transition to feudalism are essentially examples of the former. Insofar as they could have resulted in revolutionary changes they were of the sort that would have restored society to what it had been (or what revolutionaries imagined it had been) before the imposition of feudal social relations. If they are such, then they were revolutions in the Aristotle and Polybius would have understood them: as attempts to restore a former condition, not attempts to establish a new form of society.

The exploited class under capitalism, the working class, will have to achieve the socialist revolution, or it will not be achieved at all. The working class is the first exploited (as opposed to oppressed) class in history that is able to make a revolution on its own behalf. Unlike the peasantry, the working class is structured collectively and is therefore the basis of a new form of social organization in a way that the former can never be. Unlike the bourgeoisie, the working class itself has the numeric size and structural capacity to rebuild society without using another class as an instrument to destroy the existing system. The working class is not an alternative exploiting class to the bourgeoisie and it will not be transformed into one by victory. Even those writers who believe that socialism is impossible and that revolution will only lead to a new form of managerial or bureaucratic society do not claim that the proletariat itself will constitute the ruling class, but rather that it will consist of a technocratic elite or "new class." Consequently, the "everyday" class struggles between exploiters and exploited, and the "transformative" struggles for social revolution are linked by the fact that the same classes are involved: the former always contains the possibility of the latter. To this conception of working-class agency we need to add two qualifications.

First, not all workers will participate in the revolution, at least on the revolutionary side. Gramsci showed that most members of the subordinate classes have highly contradictory forms of consciousness, the most characteristic being a reformist inability to conceive of anything beyond capitalism while opposing specific effects of the system.[56] The alternatives are not, however, restricted to active rejection at one extreme and passive acceptance at the other: there can also be *active* support, the internalization of capitalist values associated with the system to the point where they can lead to action. Marxists and other anticapitalist radicals rightly point out that, rather than men benefiting from the oppression of women, whites from the oppression of blacks, straights from the oppression of gays, and so on, it is capitalism or the bourgeoisie that does so. This is a necessary corrective to the approach typical of many left-wing social movements in which every form of oppression is seen as separate from the others and none have any necessary connection to the capitalist system. Nevertheless, it fails to take seriously the distinction made by Lukács between "what men *in fact* thought, felt and wanted at any point in the class structure" and "the thoughts and feelings which men would have in a particular situation if they were *able* to assess both it and the interests arising from it in their impact on immediate action and on the whole structure of society."[57] We cannot assume that members of the working class are not only capable of the thoughts and feelings "appropriate to their objective situation," but do in fact *have* these thoughts and feelings, and are only prevented from taking the action that these feelings imply because of reformist mis-leadership, lack of confidence due to temporary defeats, or a deeper acceptance that, however desirable an outcome socialism might be, the world can nevertheless not be changed in any fundamental way. But what if workers do not have this level of consciousness? Many of them have either been unaware of "the standpoint of the working class" or have simply refused to adopt it. Instead, a significant minority have taken positions supportive of, for example, racial oppression, which may not have benefited them compared with the benefits they would have received by struggling for racial, let alone full social equality. Without some degree of class consciousness, however, they need not ever consider this alternative: in the immediate context of their situation a stance that is detrimental to working-class interests as a whole may make sense to particular individual members of the working class. Lukács once wrote of revisionism, which in this context can be taken to mean reformism more generally, that: "It always sacrifices the genuine interests of the class as a whole . . . so as to represent the immediate interests of specific groups."[58] In a revolutionary situation, some working-class people will take this a stage further, by sacrificing even the interests of specific groups in favor of their immediate individual interests, usually equated with a supra-class national interest.[59]

Second, the central role of the working class does not mean that it will be the only force involved in the socialist revolution. Lenin wrote in 1916 against those who had criticized the Eastern Rising in Ireland: "So one army lines up in one place and says, 'We are for socialism,' and another, somewhere else and says, 'We are for imperialism,' and that will be a social revolution! . . . Whoever expects a 'pure' social revolution will never live to see it. Such a person pays lip service to revolution without understanding what revolution is."[60] The potential allies of the working class have changed in the course of the last hundred years—if the Russian Revolution had successfully spread after 1917, then the peasantry would have played a far greater role, even in Europe, than they will now, just as sections the "informal" sector in the developing world and the "new" middle or technical-managerial class in the developed will play a far greater role now than they would have in 1917. Similarly there are oppressed groups—of which in the West today the most significant are Muslim communities—whose situation makes them open to argument about the root cause of their oppression. Lenin's notion that socialists must be "tribunes of the oppressed" is as relevant as it ever was—at any rate, any socialism worthy of the name will not succeed without that spirit.[61]

Because the transition to socialism starts with the seizure of power, it must be a conscious process. No socialist economy will blindly emerge from the struggle to develop the productive forces, or to find new ways of exploiting the direct producers who set those forces to work. The struggle for power by the working class requires organization to awaken, consolidate, and maintain class consciousness, but organization is also required as the basis for an alternative form of state power. In short, what the proletariat has to match is not the organizational structures within which the bourgeoisie conducted their struggle for power (in the minority of examples where they did in fact did so), but the centralizing role the state and ideological forms established by the bourgeoisie after its ascendancy. The role of organization in consolidating and maintaining class consciousness is of crucial importance here, from the most basic forms of trade unionism through to revolutionary organization. "The [working] class, taken by itself, is only material for exploitation," wrote Trotsky in 1932: "The proletariat assumes an independent role only at that moment when from a class *in itself* it becomes a political class *for itself*. This cannot take place other than through the medium of a party. The party is that historical organ by means of which the class becomes conscious."[62] The distinction Trotsky draws here between a class in itself (a social group occupying an economic role) and a class for itself (a social group that has become conscious of its own position and what is required to change it) is usually but incorrectly thought to originate with Marx who actually distinguishes between a class "against capitalism" and a class "for itself."[63] The original formulation is preferable in that it suggests not an idealized shift from complete political unconsciousness to consciousness—as few workers accept every aspect of the system as reject every aspect of it, at least before a revolutionary situation emerges—but a process of clarification through struggle.

Socialism would represent the greatest transformation in the human condition since the emergence of class society itself. Indeed, so enormous is the task, so vast is the gulf between the realities of capitalism and the possibilities of socialism, that many on the left have envisaged their goal as simply being a modified version of capitalism, not an entirely new form of human society. The two models of socialism that dominated the twentieth century, Social Democracy and Stalinism, exemplify the problem. Precisely because they have, respectively, defended a modified version of private capitalism where it existed and introduced state capitalism where it did not, any new socialist project for the twenty-first century has to begin by rejecting them both: the dream of human freedom is not realized in either Attlee's Britain or Castro's Cuba, whatever their other admirable qualities. As Draper once pointed out in a rightly celebrated essay, both Social Democracy and Stalinism are examples of "socialism from above": "What unites the many different forms of Socialism-from-Above is the conception that socialism (or a reasonable facsimile thereto) must be *handed down* to the grateful masses in some form or another, by a ruling elite which is not subject to their control in fact." The result is not socialism at all and Draper contrasts it with "socialism from below": "The heart of Socialism-from-Below is its view that socialism can only be realized through the self-emancipation of activised masses 'from below' in a struggle to take charge of their own destiny, as actors (not merely subjects) on the stage of history."[64] Democracy is not merely a desirable feature but a necessity for socialism. Indeed, it will be defined by the way in which democracy becomes the basis for those aspects of human existence from which either the market or the bureaucratic state currently exclude it. It is only through the transformative process of taking power that workers can throw off the legacy of years of enforced servility or misdirected anger that capitalism inculcates: "Both for the production on a mass scale of . . . communist consciousness, and for the success of the cause itself, the alteration of men on a mass scale is necessary, an alteration which can only take place in a practical movement, a *revolution*; the revolution is necessary, therefore, not only because the *ruling* class cannot be overthrown in any other way, but because the class *overthrowing* it can only in a revolution succeed in ridding itself of all the muck of ages and become fitted to found society anew."[65]

With these antipodal examples of social revolution in mind we can now return to the bourgeois case. As we saw in chapter 12, Lenin used two concepts in connection with bourgeois revolution, that of an *era* during which the process unfolds and that of a moment of *consummation* with which it concludes.[66] The following two chapters are structured around these two concepts; more specifically, they ask what makes the former possible and how we know that the latter has taken place.

21

PRECONDITIONS FOR AN ERA
OF BOURGEOIS REVOLUTION

"For Marxists," writes Robert Lochhead, "bourgeois revolutions cover a period of nine centuries."[1] On the basis of this assessment the first episodes of bourgeois revolution took place in the second half of the twelfth century with the communal risings that established the independence of the German and Italian city-states from the Holy Roman Empire. The difficulty with this periodization is that no permanently successful bourgeois revolution took place until four hundred and fifty years later with the consolidation of the Dutch Republic, which suggests that the preconditions for successful bourgeois revolution did not exist until much later than the rise of the towns. Before identifying these preconditions, it is worth clarifying what I mean by the term.

In his famous discussion of the origins of the English Revolution, Lawrence Stone divided the causes into three successive groups, increasingly concentrated in time, which he classified as "long-term preconditions" (1529–1629), "medium-term precipitants" (1629–39), and "short-term triggers" (1640–42).[2] Stone's long-term preconditions were the factors he saw as leading to instability and disequilibrium in the Tudor and Stuart polity. While some of these were rather unspecific ("economic growth," "social change"), others did highlight more concrete aspects of the English situation—the decline of external threats, a crisis of ruling-class confidence, the rise of a parliamentary opposition, and the spread of new ideas and values.[3] My conception of "preconditions" differs from his in three respects. First, they are not a series of loosely connected explanatory factors; instead they take the form of a determinate historical sequence, with each one setting the conditions for emergence of the next. Second, their successive emergence occurred across a longer time-scale, broadly between the arrival of the Black Death in Europe in the 1340s and the beginning of the Reformation in the 1510s. Third, they involved tendencies within the European feudal system as a whole and consequently occurred at a deeper and more general level than those identified by Stone in relation to England—in effect, they constitute an additional, chronologically prior grouping of causes, the impact of which had to be registered before the factors specific to England could begin to take effect from 1529.

These preconditions signaled that what Marx called "an era of social revolution" had begun. Since Marx was clearly thinking of the bourgeois revolutions in the 1859 "Preface" from which this phrase is taken, we can use this classic (and unfairly maligned) text as the starting point for our discussion: "At a certain stage of development, the material productive forces of society come into conflict with the existing relations of production or—this merely expresses the same thing in legal terms—with the property relations within the framework of which they have operated hitherto. From forms of development of the productive forces these relations turn into their fetters. Then begins an era of social revolution."[4] Conflict between the forces and relations of production indicates the emergence of the first precondition: a crisis of feudalism, which became apparent from the late thirteenth century. In this passage Marx, as it were, leaps over several stages of the process by saying that crisis in and of itself necessarily introduces an era of social revolution; in fact, several other preconditions are necessary. A crisis may simply lead to collapse and retrogression, as had happened to earlier societies, such as that of the Maya.[5] Also required is the emergence, from the crisis of feudalism, of a second precondition: capitalism as a potential alternative system with the capacity to resume the development of the productive forces:

> No social order is ever destroyed before all the productive forces for which it is sufficient have been developed, and new superior relations of production never replace older ones before the material conditions for their existence have matured within the framework of the old society. Mankind thus inevitably sets itself only such tasks as it is able to solve, since closer examination will always show that the problem itself arises only when the material conditions for its solution are already present or at least in the course of formation.[6]

But at what level—national, international, or global—do these new relations of production have to be present? Ellen Meiksins Wood once asked: "Was a revolution necessary to bring about capitalism, or simply to facilitate the development of an already existing capitalism? Was it a cause or an effect of capitalism?"[7] The answer is that bourgeois revolutions could be *either* cause *or* effect. Lukács wrote that during "the transition from feudalism to capitalism": "The rival systems of production will . . . co-exist as already perfected systems (as was seen in the beginnings of capitalism within the feudal order)."[8] In fact, there are no examples where a perfect equilibrium between feudalism and capitalism existed prior to the bourgeois revolution taking place. Bourgeois revolutions are the only types of social revolution that have occurred *during* the transition from the dominance of one mode of production to another; consequently, they were neither the culmination of a socioeconomic process like the feudal "revolution" nor a moment of politico-social transformation like the socialist revolution. The extent to which individual bourgeois revolutions tended toward either the former or the latter varied depended on the stage in the transition to capitalism during which they took place. In some cases, bourgeois revolution was primarily a means of facilitating the further development of capitalism in conditions where key aspects of the transition had taken place before the revolutions began: these cases resemble the transition to feudalism. In other, later cases, bourgeois revolution was primarily a precondition for the emergence of capitalism in conditions where key aspects of the transition had still to take place after the revolutions ended: these cases resemble the socialist revolution.[9] One reason the later bourgeois revolutions took place in less developed conditions was that once the initial breakthroughs had taken place in the United Provinces and England, European absolutism mobilized to prevent any similar revolutions taking place. Consequently, in no other country after England did a capitalist economy grow up relatively unhindered until the point where the classes associated with it could lead an assault on feudal absolutism. But in neither set of cases was capitalism internally either completely dominant (even in England) or completely nonexistent (even in Japan). In the latter cases, however, revolutions took place in a context where capitalist laws of motion were much stronger across the world economy as a whole; indeed, it was this that made them possible. In other words, to speak of a "capitalist alternative" does not mean that one necessarily existed within each individual state territory, but rather that one existed at the level of the world system as a whole. The result was an apparently paradoxical trajectory: the earliest bourgeois revolutions took place where there were high levels of local capitalist development but low levels of global capitalist development; the later bourgeois revolutions took place where the balance was, if not reversed, then strongly weighted in the opposite direction.

Apart from a brief reference to "ideological forms in which men become conscious of this conflict and fight it out," agency is famously absent from Marx's highly compressed and—for reasons discussed in chapter 10—deeply structural formulations.[10] Taking the 1859 "Preface" as his starting point, Gramsci later explored the question of who would be involved in attempting or preventing a solution to what he called "organic" crises:

> A crisis occurs, sometimes lasting for decades. This exceptional duration means that incurable structural contradictions have revealed themselves (reached maturity), and that, despite this, the political forces which are struggling to conserve and defend the existing structure itself are making every effort to cure them, within certain limits, and to overcome them. These incessant and persistent efforts (since no social formation will ever admit that it has been superseded) form the terrain of the "conjunctural," and it is upon this terrain that the forces of opposition organize. These forces seek to demonstrate that the necessary and sufficient conditions already exist to make possible, and hence imperative, the accomplishment of certain historical tasks (imperative, because any falling short before an historical duty increases the necessary disorder, and prepares more serious catastrophes).[11]

As with Marx's original remarks, these general considerations yield quite specific preconditions in the context of the bourgeois revolutions. Capitalism was not brought into existence by victory or defeat in the class struggle, nor—as political Marxists believe—by an indeterminate outcome of the class struggle in England. The outcome of the class struggle did, however, determine whether or not capitalism would be consolidated on a particular territory once it *had* emerged. Christopher Bertram has noted that "class struggle may impede productive development in many different ways," the most important of which from our perspective is the top-down variety where "a dominant class whose domination is absolute may be tempted to derive its wealth simply from greater exploitation of subordinate classes rather than through any development of technique (indeed its exploitation of unfree labor may preclude the development of more sophisticated techniques)."[12]

The third precondition was therefore that the states that acted as the focus for the pre-capitalist ruling classes had—for whatever reason—to be unable to prevent capitalism developing as an alternative means of social organization. Where the state was strong enough to prevent what Marx and Engels called "the revolutionary reconstitution of society," then it could result in what they called "the common ruin of the contending classes."[13] More frequently, however, it did not reach this stage, because the state was able to prevent what Chris Wickham calls "minimum conditions" for the transition to capitalism ever being reached. Wickham is thinking of China in this context, as an example of "high-level equilibrium which can happily continue for centuries, its contradictions, if any in practice dealt with without difficulty, feudal reproduction being not less creative than capitalist reproduction in our own day."[14] When ruin ultimately occurred it tended, as in the case of China, to be the result of the invasions and impositions invited by its social stagnation and weakness, rather than directly through internal conflict and collapse. "As exposure to the atmosphere reduces all mummies to instant dissolution," wrote Marx, "so war passes supreme judgment upon social organizations that have outlived their vitality."[15]

But, like the existence of an organic social crisis, a relatively weak state is a negative precondition. Capitalism is not a disembodied social force and must be liberated or imposed through political action, a fact that implies a fourth precondition: the existence of revolutionary agencies, associated with capitalism but not necessarily consisting of capitalists, with the capacity to remove structural impediments to its ascendancy. The earliest successful examples of bourgeois revolution, in the United Provinces and England, involved leadership by mercantile, agrarian, and—in the case of the latter country—even industrial capitalists, although these tended to be based in the countryside and the colonies rather than the metropolitan centers. There was a difference between the French Revolution and these earlier examples of bourgeois revolution from below. As a consequence of the relative success of the absolutist regime in retarding the development of capitalism, France was internally less developed in 1789 than England had been in 1640. But even those capitalists who had emerged in France were more inclined to reform than their predecessors, not least because of the risk that revolution posed to their property, which tended to be more industrial than agrarian or mercantile. From 1789 on, therefore, the nature of leadership in the bourgeois revolutions became increasingly removed from capitalists in the class structure: Robespierre was a lawyer, Danton a journalist, Roux a priest; only a very few of the leading French revolutionaries, of whom Roederer was the most important, could seriously be described as capitalists. With the exception of the period between 1859 and 1871 during which fractions of the existing feudal classes came to the fore, these noncapitalist sections of the bourgeoisie dominated the leaderships of the bourgeois revolutions until the cycle was complete on a global scale; indeed, as the twentieth century wore on, the social roles that they occupied tended to shift even further from the economic core toward those of military and party bureaucrats.

The fifth and final precondition concerns the motivations of these agencies and here again we need to return to Marx's original discussion: "Just as one does not judge an individual by what he thinks about himself, so one cannot judge such a period of transformation by its consciousness, but, on the contrary, this consciousness must be explained from the contradictions of material life, from the conflict existing between the social forces of production and the relations of production."[16] If this insight had been taken more seriously, we might have been spared much subsequent confusion about the role of consciousness and ideology in the bourgeois revolutions. In fact, the agents of bourgeois revolution displayed a range of different levels of consciousness, depending on the classes involved and the periods during which each took place, but all required an ideology that motivated them to move from being a theoretical to an actual revolutionary leadership. In no bourgeois revolution did the revolutionaries ever seek to rally popular forces by proclaiming their intention to establish a new form of exploitative society—a goal that peasants, small commodity producers, and workers might have been understandably reluctant to support—but did so instead by variously raising demands for religious freedom, representative democracy, national independence, and, ultimately, socialist reconstruction, although by the last named the dissociation between being and consciousness, between reality and representation, had become almost total. Of all the successive, if overlapping, ideologies under which the bourgeois revolutions were waged, only that of the Enlightenment can be genuinely described as originating within the bourgeoisie, rather than being adopted and adapted for bourgeois purposes. And of all the victorious bourgeois revolutions, only the French can be said to have been inspired by Enlightenment thought, which is one reason why this greatest of all examples is also the most exceptional.

Initially at least—that is to say in the cases of the United Provinces and England—all of these preconditions had to be present before a bourgeois revolution had the possibility of success. The specifics of how the various preconditions were met differed from country to country. Each had their own specific versions of what Stone termed, in the English context, "long-term preconditions," "medium-term precipitants" and "short-term triggers," but these variations belong to the individual histories of the successive revolutions. What can be said in an overview of this sort is that in every case opening of a period of social revolution is usually unmistakable, involving a moment of what Teodor Shanin calls "alternativity," when all their pre-conditions are met and the fuse of political crisis is lit:

> Long periods pass during which material circumstances (as well as our images of them) and social institutions (reflected in individual cognitions) facilitate the high consistency of social reproduction and foreclose fundamental changes. During these well-patterned, repetitive, socialization-bound and sociologically explicable stages the historical processes behave themselves in a nicely predictable manner, the "alterna-tivity" of history is low. Then, once in a while, comes a period of major crisis, a revo-lution, an "axial" stage. The locks of rigidly pattered behavior, self-censored imaginations, and self-evident stereotypes of common sense are broken, and the sky seems the limit, or all hell seems let loose. The "alternativity" of history, the significance of consciousness, and particularly the scope for originality and choice, increase dra-matically. The "turning" taken then by a society establishes the pattern of development for decades or centuries.[17]

When historical development accelerates to the point where the outbreak of revolution is inescapable three alternatives are then posed: victory for the revolu-tion on a transformative social basis; defeat and the reassertion of the existing order, or—less straightforwardly—confinement within the limits of political rev-olution. Of course, no revolution can be guaranteed success, even if it is objectively feasible, because of the element of subjectivity—the revolutionary forces may lack effective leadership while the defenders of the existing order may possess precisely this quality. And, as we shall see in the next chapter, even success could prove tem-porary in the face of counterrevolution from without. But even victory could take two forms—there are, in other words, also "alternatives" in this respect. Here I think we have to take seriously the implications of the first of the three "symptoms" declared indispensible by Lenin for a "revolutionary situation": "When it is im-possible for the ruling class to maintain their rule without any change; when there is a crisis, in one form or another, among the 'upper classes,' a crisis in the policy of the ruling class, leading to a fissure through which the discontent and indigna-tion of the oppressed classes burst forth. For a revolution to take place, it is usually insufficient for 'the lower classes not to want' to live in the old way; it is also nec-essary that 'the upper classes should be unable' to live in the old way."[18] The point, as Lenin was quite aware, is that in the case of the bourgeois revolution, the hith-erto feudal ruling class could under certain conditions successfully attempt to rule in a "new" way, involving capitalist social relations, but only after a certain point in history had been reached, the point at which capitalism had become an un-stoppable economic force. Thereafter, ultimate victory may have been assured, but the question then became not whether the world would be capitalist but what form would be taken by the bourgeois revolutions and the capitalist nation-states they would create. But these considerations point us toward the end of an era; we must first understand how it began.

THE ACTUALITY OF THE FEUDAL CRISIS

Until the Japanese Meiji Restoration of 1868 all successful bourgeois revolutions were made against European feudal states or their overseas extensions in the Americas; we therefore need to begin with the mode of production upon which they were based. Non-Marxist historians have tended to identify feudalism with a relatively short-lived episode in its development, namely the establishment of land tenure based on military service ("vassalage") during the tenth century in parts of what are now Belgium and France. Under this system, the vassals, themselves members of the ruling class, were obliged to provide military service to the monarch and attend his court in return for land granted directly from the crown. Sub-vassals had the same relationship to their superiors, and so on down the chain of seigniorial command. In Marxist terms, however, feudalism is more than a political relationship between different sections of the ruling class. It is rather a distinct mode of production compatible with several different forms of political rule. Feudalism in this sense is fundamentally defined by the existence of an exploitative social relationship between a class of landowners and another, vastly more numerous, class of peasants, who were by no means always serfs tied to a specific piece of land or a particular master. This relationship had two distinguishing features.

The first was that the main source of income for the landowners was appropriated, in the form of rent, from the surplus produced by the peasants, rather than from the work of slaves or wage laborers.[19] Members of the feudal ruling class did, of course, own slaves or employ wage laborers at different periods in the development of the system but merely to supplement an income already guaranteed by the exploitation of their tenants. Moreover, as Jairus Banaji reminds us, within an economy subject to feudal laws of motion: "The slaves and hired laborers who intervened in this kind of economy were as much part of specifically *feudal relations of production* as the serf population itself."[20]

The second distinguishing feature was the process by which the surplus was extracted. Since the peasants had effective possession of the means of production (land, tools, animals), and would not have handed over part of their produce without external pressure, the relationship between lord and peasant was inevitably coercive, involving either the threat or actual application of force. As a result, the political and judicial institutions through which this pressure was exerted are inseparable from economic relations and must be included in any definition of the system. Key among these institutions were the territorial jurisdictions through which local lords could bring tenants to their own court of law.[21] The general commutation of servile dues and the attendant shifts from labor rent through rent in kind to money rent refined the system without bringing about the domination of capitalist relations of production—the existence of money being a necessary but insufficient condition for this to take place.

The first period of feudal development, following the consolidation of the system early in the eleventh century, saw increases in productivity, measurable by increased

crop yields, through the application of technological innovation and direct seigniorial supervision of the labor process.[22] The evidence of these centuries demonstrates
that feudalism was capable of developing the productive forces, to a degree, without
the relations of production posing an obstacle—the capitalist component of the
European economy was in any case of minor importance at the time, except in
parts of northern Italy and Flanders. The significance of this period of development
can be seen by the end of the twelfth century: "This was the first time that one
could begin to speak of a 'European economy,' at least since the Roman Empire,
and certainly the first time that such a trans-regional economy was not dependent
on a trans-regional state."[23] The existence of such an economy means that it is possible to speak of a *general* crisis of feudalism, spreading unevenly but inescapably
across Europe from the late thirteenth to the early fourteenth century, bringing an
end to this period of expansion. Guy Bois has highlighted the extent to which the
crisis represented a qualitative shift:

> The watershed at the beginning of the fourteenth century is not simply one episode
> among the many dramatic conflicts that punctuate the history of feudalism. It must
> be seen at a deeper level, as the beginning of the crisis of a mode of production. What
> does this mean? First, that the system had exhausted its possibilities of expansion,
> having completely occupied all cultivatable land. . . . The economic impasse became
> a social one. The end of expansion precipitated the fall in seigniorial revenue. How
> could the lord compel his subjects to make additional contributions when he no
> longer possessed sufficient powers over them? The impasse was at once political, in-
> stitutional, and moral. It is this general character of the crisis (which affected all as-
> pects of social life) that we denote by the expression "crisis of feudalism."[24]

The feudal crisis is usually taken to consist of the following elements, some of
which are mentioned by Bois. First, a population that had grown significantly
through the centuries of expansion began to reach the territorial limits of lands
that could be colonized for clearance or reclamation. In areas of existing settlement,
crop yields first stagnated and then began to fall through exhaustion of the land,
in part as a result of it being used mainly for arable rather than pastoral purposes,
leading to a lack of manure for fertilization. A similar stalling in forces of production can be detected in the mining industry, which extracted the silver used for
monetary exchange: once the near surface seams of the metal had been exhausted,
existing levels of technique were unable to penetrate sufficiently far underground
to reach new reserves, which inevitably led to the increasing debasement of the
currency on the one hand and the hoarding of older, purer coins on the other. The
combined effect on the lords of declining rural productivity and currency inflation
was to reduce their income at a time when their socially determined levels of expenditure were rising.[25]

These causes of crisis varied in intensity across feudal Europe, but there was one
further block to development, which had a more universal impact. This lay not in
the forces of production but rather in the way in which the relations of production

and the state were inseparable under feudalism. As Stephen Epstein has pointed out, "the principle threat to feudalism did not come from trade; up to a point, feudalism thrived on trade," not least because lords "did not exclude markets, they regulated and taxed them for income." As Epstein notes:

> The lords' and towns' main purposes in stimulating trade was to maximize income streams from their fiscal and jurisdictional rights, and those rights were a fundamental aspect of their social and political powers. In other words, "free trade" would have reduced both feudal and urban revenue, and challenged the jurisdictional superiority of lord over peasant and town over country. Consequently, strong feudal jurisdiction was incompatible with long-run economic growth. Not surprisingly, agricultural innovation appears to have been inversely correlated with the intensity of seigniorial rights, and rural industry was inversely correlated with the jurisdictional powers of towns. The fundamental constraint in the feudal economy was not technological inertia, but the market monopolies and other coordination failures arising from political and jurisdictional parcellization.[26]

There was no capitalist solution available to resolve the feudal crisis: indeed, it was only the effect of the latter that generated the possibility of capitalism as an alternative form of society in the first place. It is important to understand the implications of this sequence of developments, in particular it means that any claim that capitalism—as opposed to merchants' and usurers' capital—existed before the fourteenth century involves a form of misrecognition. Feudalism involved economic relationships other than those between lords and peasants. Like all precapitalist modes of production it necessarily involved markets, trade, and consequently the existence of a class of merchants who were integral to its functioning. Throughout early modern Europe mercantile capitalism played an ambiguous role in the development of the system. They drew their profits, not from realizing the value added to commodities in the process of production, but from the discrepancy in price between their initial outlay and the ultimate selling price at the end of long-distance trade routes. Fernand Braudel is right to say: "With few exceptions, the capitalist, that is in this period, the 'important merchant' with many undifferentiated activities, did not commit himself wholeheartedly to production." His central interests made him "a man of the market": "Above all in distribution, marketing—the sector in which real profits were made."[27] Marx noted that even by taking control of production, the merchant "cannot bring about the overthrow of the old mode of production itself, but rather preserves and retains it as its own precondition." More specifically, where "the merchant makes the small masters into his middlemen, or even buys directly from the independent producer he leaves him nominally independent and leaves his mode of production unchanged": for capitalism to develop required either the industrialist to directly become a merchant or the merchant to directly become an industrialist.[28] For all these reasons, their activities were, as Alex Callinicos writes, a "necessary but not sufficient" condition for the dominance of capitalist relations of production: "As long as capitalism did not conquer production it was forced (and indeed largely content) to co-exist with feudalism."[29]

This assessment of the merchant class fraction also has implications for how we understand the territorial bases from which they undertook many of their activities: the towns. Adam Smith was the first thinker to regard these as the spatial embodiment of what he called "commercial society," as opposed to the parcelized feudal authority dispersed throughout the countryside.[30] Subsequently, his position has been endorsed by several important non-Marxist thinkers including Weber and Braudel. It is perhaps best summarized by Michael Postan: "Medieval towns . . . were non-feudal islands in the feudal seas; places in which merchants could not only live in each other's vicinity and defend themselves collectively but also places which enjoyed or were capable of developing systems of local government and principles of law and status exempting them from the sway of the feudal regime."[31] Several Marxists have also accepted this position, often in the form expressed by Postan.[32] Eric Mielants's statement of the case is representative: "Because of the nobility's weakness, division and inability to adequately (re)generate primitive accumulation based on extraeconomic coercion, the elites in charge of the European city-state system were capable of constructing strategies that furthered the ceaseless accumulation of capital (with subsequent reinvestment in their companies)."[33] But like the merchants who dominated them, the towns had an ambiguous position within the feudal system that cannot be treated as one of uncomplicated opposition.

The struggle for urban autonomy during the eleventh and twelfth centuries was not in any sense "anti-feudal"; it was rather an attempt by the local patriciates to establish their own distinct position within the feudal ruling class. Similarly, the urban "revolutions" that pitched the merchant guilds against the magnates were not struggles between "capitalist" and feudal classes but struggles for office within the latter; at most these were political revolutions, as defined in the previous chapter. Unsurprisingly then, in their capacity as corporate bodies the towns often acted as institutional seigneurs for the surrounding countryside, with the burgesses playing the role of collective exploiters of the peasantry, no different in this respect from individual nobles or the Church. As a result, in Italy in particular, peasants would often ally with the lords against the authority of the towns, above all that of imposing and collecting taxes. It was not the role of towns as corporate entities that helped to undermine feudalism, but the fact that they constituted independent spaces of relative freedom—"islands," in Postan's terminology—where lordly jurisdictions did not hold sway. As such, they allowed a forum for the collective exchange of new opinions concerning everything from agricultural production or religious observance, which would have been impossible in more isolated or scattered rural communities; they provided places of physical safety for peasants fleeing the land and their masters (although runaway peasants were by no means always welcomed by the urban guilds, whose function was precisely to restrict entry into the occupations they organized, not open them up to unskilled rural refugees). Did they also play a more directly political role? Here too the record is uneven. The great series of peasant revolts that stretched from maritime Flanders in the 1320s to Catalonia in the 1480s effectively ended serfdom in the West, although not, of course, feudalism itself. Although never themselves instigators of these revolts, towns sometimes contributed to their success, either through empathetic risings of the urban plebeians against their own oppressors (as in Canterbury and London during the English Peasant Revolt of 1381) or the more calculated support of the towns themselves as feudal corporate bodies with their own reasons for opposing the lords (as Paris did during the French *Grande Jaquerie* of 1359). During the most successful of all peasant revolts, in Catalonia between 1462 and 1472, however, the urban patriciate of Barcelona actually allied with the feudal nobility *against* the *Remenscas* peasants.[34] The last example in particular demonstrates that Trotsky was simply wrong to claim, as a general position, that: "In Europe, beginning with the close of the Middle Ages, each victorious peasant uprising did not place a peasant government in power but a left urban party. To put it more precisely, a peasant uprising turned out victorious exactly to the degree to which it succeeded in strengthening the position of the revolutionary section of the urban population."[35] Indeed, the most decisive alliance between peasants and towns (involving both individual burghers and the commune as a collective actor) demonstrates how it was possible for areas to escape from feudal domination without necessarily doing so on a capitalist basis.

The Swiss cantons, largely for reasons of geographical inaccessibility, retained on a greater scale than elsewhere most of the individual peasant freedoms that had been lost elsewhere in Western Europe by the end of the thirteenth century. Alpine society was both effectively (although not always formally) free of feudal lordship and organized communally for certain activities like the sale of dairy products, the protection of mountain passes, and mercenary activity. The importance of the Swiss valleys as a trade route between southern Germany and northern Italy also encouraged the growth of independent towns based on the model of the Italian communes. The difference between the Swiss and, for example, the Italian city-states was that the former retained the alliance with the peasantry who remained armed and in certain circumstances were granted citizenship, while the urban guilds did not seek to undermine rural production. The reliance of the towns on the surrounding countryside also had ideological effects in that the burghers could not celebrate their superior position to that of the peasantry or the urban poor, as their counterparts in the Italian and German lands did, without risking their security.[36] One consequence was that "no large number of dispossessed peasants was available as a source of cheap labor and of any large urban proletariat."[37] When the Austrian Habsburgs attempted to subject the Swiss lands to their seigniority (or rather to extend their seigniority across the entire territory), they were met by an alliance of free burgesses and peasants that established the Swiss Confederation between 1291 and 1393, a process that coincided with the most devastating period of the first crisis of feudalism. The fact that the feudal overlords were external ("foreign" would be anachronistic here) meant that their removal stripped out the ruling class, leaving other relationships in place. Progress toward capitalism was slow. The first cantons to join the confederation in 1291 had thrown off a foreign feudalism before capitalism had a chance to develop, leaving a population of small commodity producers in possession of their land. Although this example is the nearest one we have to a "revolutionary road to simple commodity production," the situation did not remain static but saw the forest cantons and cities either fall under the domination of the various feudal courts of the German crown in the North or develop toward capitalism in South, but without any effective superstructure. By the time Calvin set up his dictatorship in Geneva during the sixteenth century this land of free peasants and urban oligarchs was the very opposite of a centralized nation-state. Divided by language, a fragmented canton structure, and, after the Reformation, opposed religious affiliations, it made much of its wealth by hiring out the population as mercenaries to the very regimes that were stifling capitalist development elsewhere in Europe. If this, "the first independent republic in Europe" was in any sense "a bourgeois republic," it was only in the sense that, as Engels put it, "the Swiss . . . *turned* their fame as warriors *to cash*."[38] Feudal crisis on its own could lead to revolution, but not to bourgeois revolution.

The Possibility of a Capitalist Alternative

The crisis did not of course last uninterruptedly from the late thirteenth to the late eighteenth century, "There is no doubt that feudalism in Europe became reactionary in the thirteenth to eighteenth centuries," writes Tony Cliff, "but this did not prevent the productive forces developing at the same rate as before or indeed of developing at an even faster rate."[39] But in so far as the productive forces did resume their growth after the first crisis it was only to the extent that capitalism had begun to establish itself. How did this new way of organizing production first emerge? The elements that would eventually combine to create the capitalist mode of production—not only market competition but also wage labor and commodity production—preexisted it by many centuries. Political Marxists are therefore right to insist that the existence of these elements does not in itself indicate the existence of capitalism as such. One can further agree with them that the socioeconomic activities that ultimately ended up producing capitalism were not, initially at any rate, necessarily undertaken with capitalism as a conscious goal. Neither of these observations should be taken to mean, however, that capitalism was an unlikely outcome.

There are very few ways in which exploitation or the social relations of production more generally can be organized. "Slavery, serfdom and wage labor are historically and socially different solutions to a universal problem which remains fundamentally the same," writes Braudel.[40] Given this highly restricted range of options, the chances of something like capitalism arising were actually rather high, given certain conditions. Alan Carling has argued that it originally emerged as a result of what he calls "feudal fission": "It was probable that something like English agricultural capitalism would arise out of something like European feudalism." Why? Carling identifies two characteristics of feudalism as crucial to this outcome: political decentralization and the demographic cycle. The first meant that no state was in a position to impose a uniform system of production, with the result that new systems could develop in the spaces where sovereignty did not hold sway. The second meant that population collapse was regularly of such severity that it left spaces of this type (following the desertion of hitherto occupied land, for example), which could be filled by property and productive relations of an ultimately capitalist nature: "If there are 10 or 20 independent fission experiments in each demographic cycle, the probability of at least one 'English' outcome is very high, even if the probability is very low of an English outcome in any single experiment.... And England only has to happen once for capitalism to become established. That is why it is not as fanciful as one might suppose to suggest that the transition from feudalism to capitalism was almost inevitable—almost indeed a natural necessity of history."[41]

It is not the demographic cycle in general that is significant here, but rather the specific downturn associated with the general crisis of the fourteenth century, which was in turn massively intensified by the incidence of the Black Death. If capitalism did not preexist the feudal crisis, why did this catastrophe lead people to turn to new ways of economic organization? In order to answer this question we must first revisit some fundamental tenets of historical materialism.

Marxism treats the social world as a whole, or what Lukács calls a "mediated totality." To be part of a totality is to be part of "a total social situation caught up in the process of social change"; to say that a totality is mediated is to overcome "the mere immediacy of the empirical world," in which moments are "torn ... from the complex of their true determinants and placed in artificial isolation."[42] Two claims are being made here: one is that societies constitute totalities (and Lukács rightly believed that capitalist societies are the most "totalizing" of all); the other is that our method for understanding specific aspects of a society must involve treating them as constituents of a greater whole.[43] For Bertell Ollman, Marxism conceives of reality "as a totality composed of internally related parts" so that each of these parts "in its fullness can represent the totality" and for each aspect "the conditions of its existence are taken to be part of what it is": "Capital, for example, is not simply the physical means of production, but includes potentially the whole pattern of social relations that enables these to function as they do."[44] David Harvey has spelled out the implications of this approach for the type of disciplinary boundaries that became characteristic of academic inquiry after the Enlightenment:

> Put simply, the Marxian method accepts fragmentation and separation for purposes of analysis only on the condition that the integrity of the relation between the whole and the part is maintained intact. The Marxian theory thus starts with the proposition that everything relates to everything else in society and that a particular object of

inquiry must necessarily internalize a relation to the totality of which it is a part. The focus of the inquiry is, then, on the relations of the epistemological object to the enquiry—as Marx does when he commences his analysis of capitalism by an examination of the commodity—is to discover the relations within it that reveal the real nature of the capitalist mode of production. . . . Marx did not disaggregate the world into "economic," "sociological," "political," "psychological," and other factors. He sought to construct an approach to the totality of relations within capitalist society.[45]

And yet, stating "everything relates to everything else in society" without further elaboration is simply to affirm a truism from which few but the most extreme Nietzschians would dissent. Different aspects of the totality form what Derek Sayer calls "a hierarchy of conditions of possibility."[46] In his mature work (that is, post-1847) Marx argued that there were three different forms of human practice, which together explain how societies emerge, develop, and transform themselves. One, the most fundamental, involves those activities that bring together natural and technological capacities and qualities into the cooperative activities that directly produce and reproduce human existence. These activities entail the social relationships of exploitation and conflict within which they take place. These in turn entail those institutions of which the states system is fundamental—and ideologies by which these relationships are justified, defended, and challenged.[47] For Marx then, "the anatomy of . . . civil society . . . has to be found in political economy" and the anatomy of the state has to be found in turn in civil society.[48]

These three practices have usually been identified by the terms "forces of production" and "relations of production"—together constituting the "base" (or "infrastructure")—and the superstructure. As Benjamin puts it, the superstructure is not a "reflection" of the base, but its "expression": "The economic conditions under which society exists are expressed in the superstructure—precisely as, with the sleeper, an overfull stomach finds not its reflection but its expression in the content of dreams, which, from a causal point of view, it may be said to 'condition.'"[49] I do not intend to use the term "base and superstructure" here, but not because I object to the use of metaphor. As Andrew Collier points out, most abstract terms, like "wave" in physics or—more relevant to this discussion—"market" in economics, start out as metaphors, but tend to lose their metaphoric quality whenever they are closely defined within the particular branch of science.[50] My objection is rather that it is not a very helpful metaphor and, on the contrary, it positively encourages undialectical forms of thought: a building is constructed from the base up, but there is no point at which a society does not have both a base and a superstructure, nor do buildings change their superstructure once constructed. Indeed, outside of the 1859 "Preface" Marx and Engels themselves used the metaphor on less than a dozen occasions and several of these were in explanatory letters by Engels warning against the mechanistic uses to which it was already being put within the Second International.

The underlying concept that the metaphor inadequately seeks to express—of a hierarchy of practices in which a causal chain ascends from the productive forces through the productive relations to the various aspects of the superstructure—is however essential to historical materialism, providing this is understood in properly epochal terms: it is not a mechanism for explaining every historical event that has taken place or every social institution that has arisen. In one of the late letters to which I have already referred, Engels tried to clarify some of the key propositions of historical materialism against trivial applications, noting, for example, the impossibility, "without making oneself ridiculous, to explain in terms of economics the existence of every small state in Germany, past and present."[51] But both Marx and Engels were in no doubt that the productive forces had to develop to a certain extent before capitalism itself could come into existence. For Marx, the core human quality, the one that distinguishes us from the rest of the animal world, is the need and ability to produce and reproduce our means of existence. This is why production, not property, is the *sine qua non* of Marx and Engels's own Marxism, and why their theory of social development privileges the development of the productive forces over productive relations. As Marx wrote in *Capital* Volume 1: "For capitalist relations to establish themselves at all presupposes that a certain level of historical production has been attained. Even within the framework of an earlier mode of production certain needs and certain means of communication and production must have developed which go beyond the old relations of production and coerce them into the capitalist mould."[52] Given the high levels of abstraction at which these debates tend to be conducted, including my own discussion thus far, it might be useful to examine the process through a concrete micro-example from the epoch of the Scottish bourgeois revolution. As late as the Anglo-Scottish Union of 1707, coal mining, lead mining, and salt panning north of the border were activities dominated by the lords, who supplemented their income from feudal rent by exporting the mineral wealth of their lands. The minerals were extracted by men who were legally serfs (although the Scottish Enlightenment reformers tended to refer to them as "slaves," by analogy with plantation labor in the Americas). By the last quarter of the eighteenth century the class position of the men operating this machinery had, however, undergone a decisive change: they were no longer legally bound as serfs to the coal they dug, but were wage laborers whose terms and conditions were at least partly determined by their collective organization. The process discussed here therefore went in sequence from changes to the forces of production (introduction of the new mining technology to increase output), leading to long-term changes in the relations of production (gradual transition to wage-labor to ensure workforce availability), overlapping with the conclusion of the Scottish bourgeois revolution (defeat and abolition of localized military-feudal "dual power" in the last Jacobite Rising of 1745–46), and leading directly to still longer-term changes in the legal-ideological region of the superstructure (juridical recognition and formalization of the shifts in relations of production with Acts of Parliament of 1775 and, more decisively, of 1799).[53]

Despite the existence of this type of historical example, sections of the left have for several decades now tended to downplay or deny altogether this aspect of his thought. In part this has been inspired by an understandable revulsion at the mechanistic and determinist formulae typical of Social Democracy and Stalinism. A passage from the most famous of all Stalinist textbooks, displaying the general secretary's distinctive approach to literary production, provides a classic example: "First the productive forces of production of society change and develop and then, depending on these changes and *in conformity with them*, men's relations of production, their economic relations, change."[54] The critique of what is usually, if wrongly, called "productive force determinism" has two aspects.

One is that it has no explanatory power and fails to square with the known facts. Unsurprisingly, given its emphasis on social property relations, political Marxism has played a leading role in providing intellectual support for this tendency. According to Wood, "the proposition that history is propelled forward by the inevitable contradictions between forces and relations of production" is, in her view, "scarcely less vacuous than the general law of technological development in its simpler form."[55] "Productive force determinism is of little use in explaining the crisis of pre-capitalist modes of production and is redundant in Marx's model of the crisis of capitalism," writes Stephen Rigby: "Neither is the theory of any use in explaining transitions from one mode of production to another, a central issue in Marxist historiography."[56] Only slightly less dismissive is Carlos Castoriadis, who at least accepts that the development of the productive forces may explain one important historical process:

> It more or less faithfully describes what took place at the time of the transition from feudal society: from the hybrid societies of Western Europe from 1650 to 1850 (where a well-developed and economically dominant bourgeoisie ran up against absolute monarchy and the remains of feudalism in agrarian property and in legal and political structures) to capitalist society. But it corresponds neither to the breakdown of ancient society and the subsequent appearance of the feudal world, nor to the birth of the bourgeoisie, which emerged precisely outside of and on the fringes of feudal relations.[57]

The other aspect of the critique of "productive force determinism," often articulated by the same people, concerns the way in which it supposedly diminishes human agency. James Young complains that: "There has long been a tendency amongst some 'Marxist' historians to portray any expansion of the productive forces as being the key to human emancipation from either nature or feudal oppression."[58] Joseph Ferraro claims that Marx and Engels did not give primacy to the productive forces but to "human activity" and apparently finds it necessary to tell us: "It is humans who are the principal protagonists in history, not the productive forces; and not humans in the abstract, but humans divided into antagonistic classes."[59]

These are not new arguments but ones that have existed in different forms since Marxism began to acquire a mass following, as the following comment from the 1880s suggests: "When the average Russian intellectual hears that in Marx 'everything is reduced to the economic foundation' (others simply say 'to the economic') he loses his head, as though someone had suddenly fired a starting pistol."[60] The local allergic reaction reported here by Plekhanov in the 1880s has more recently acquired global epidemic proportions, but it is no more appropriate now than it was then. The forces and relations of production are not a synonym for "the economic" and study of their interrelation does not correspond to the bourgeois academic discipline of "economics," even though Marx and Engels occasionally used these terms or referred to the "economic element" as a conventional means of expression. A central theme of Marxism is the critique of political economy, and this at times overlaps with consideration of the forces and relations of production (as in Marx's discussions of the "formal" and "real" subordination of labor, or of "primitive accumulation"); but these discussions belong to different regions in the totality of Marxist thought. Insofar as we allow these distinctions at all, the forces and relations of production are aspects of "the social" rather than "the economic," since they are essentially about the organization of cooperation and exploitation within and between classes. In one sense then, Ferraro is quite correct: the productive forces do not "develop" themselves: they are not sentient, nor are they even independent variables, "calling forth" this or "selecting" that response from the relations of production. To say that forces of production have developed is simply to say that human beings have been motivated to change them and have then successfully done so in such a way that the social productivity of labor has risen as a result.[61] Human agency is quite as decisive here as it is in the class struggle.

Eric Olin Wright has argued that, as a general proposition, there is a "weak" tendency for the productive forces to be developed, from the transition to class society onward. Unlike tools or equipment, productive techniques will tend to be retained once they are acquired: no one has a positive interest in causing labor productivity as such to fall, although it may still do so through the effects of war, as in central Europe during the first half of the seventeenth century. On the contrary, ruling classes have a general interest in sustaining or increasing labor productivity, if only to ensure the availability of the surplus that they must appropriate to maintain itself. But more generally, developing the productive forces will create new needs—for types of manufactured clothing, say—whose continued satisfaction depends on the level of development being maintained, so that there are people from more than one class with positive interests in doing so.[62] When people develop the productive forces it creates a situation in which they, or other people, can adopt new, more compatible productive relations, of which there are not an infinite number. As John Torrance argues in his "Darwinian" reading of Marx, "mutations in production relations are not random, but experimental":

> They arise as deliberate attempts to adapt to perceived conditions. To that extent the mechanism resembles the breeding of new strains under domestication. But it also differs from artificial selection, where only desired traits are allowed reproductive success in a controlled environment. For development of the productive forces limits variation in productive relations in much the same way as the natural environment limits biological variation: those variants most capable of reproducing themselves persist while others die out.

Torrance suggests a parallel with "feral species, bred experimentally, but surviving in the wild," which seems appropriate for class societies.[63] But although developing the productive forces makes certain types of society possible, it does not make them inevitable. Here again the role of human agency is decisive. Ruling classes are never passive. By successfully preventing people from developing the productive forces to the point where they can lead to changes in productive relations, they have either ensured centuries of relative stagnation or the repetition of developmental phases that never progress beyond a certain point. In other relatively rare cases, this type of blocking maneuver led to outright regression, as it did across Western Europe in the fifth century, in the fourteenth, and again—although on a more regionalized basis—in the seventeenth; but even in these cases, the "anti-development" of the productive forces also led to transformations in productive relations: change does not always go in one direction. As Alasdair MacIntyre once noted, "it is no use treating the doctrine that the basis determines the superstructure as a general formula in the way Stalinism has done": "For the difference between one form of society and another is not just a difference in basis, and a corresponding difference in superstructure, but a difference also in the way basis is related to superstructure."[64] The process by which human beings first make progressive changes to the productive forces, then the productive relations and ultimately the superstructures can explain the two greatest social transformations that have occurred in human history: the transition from pre-class society ("primitive communism") to various forms of class society (slave, feudal, tributary).[65] The other was the transition to capitalism.

As we saw in chapter 18, political Marxists do not believe that anyone under pre-capitalist modes of production has any incentive to develop the productive forces. Or as Robert Brenner puts it, the process whereby "individual economic actors adopt more effective techniques in bringing in new relations of production simply because the techniques are more productively effective decisively depends on the existence of capitalist property relations." Why? Because only under capitalism "will the individual economic actors necessarily have the motivation . . . to adopt new techniques."[66] Wood appears to believe that saying human beings have the desire and capacity to improve their material conditions is the same as saying that they have always been subjugated by the needs of competitive accumulation. One consequence of this denial that there might have been any positive incentives to embrace capitalist production is a tendency to portray peasant life before capitalism as essentially based on a natural economy of self-governing communities, which have no incentive to develop the productive forces, and into which the lords or the Church only intrude superficially and occasionally in order to acquire their surplus. I do not recognize this picture. In a great passage from one of the early classics of Scottish vernacular literature, *The Complaynt of Scotland*, written by Robert Wedderburn but published anonymously in 1549, the character of "the laborer" [peasant] rages against the misery of his life: "I labor night and day with my hands to feed lazy and useless men, and they repay me with hunger and the sword.

I sustain their life with the toil and sweat of my body, and they persecute my body with hardship, until I am become a beggar. They live through me and I die through them."[67] Four centuries later the power of that final sentence is undiminished. Developing the productive forces seems to me to be at least as rational a response to the feudal exploitation it so vividly describes as the alternatives of "fight or flight" that are usually posed. People have wanted to do the former since the transition to agriculture; they have only had to do the latter since the transition to capitalism. The wish to better the circumstances in which we live has been one the main impulses behind the attempts to develop the productive forces and it is intimately bound up with class society, not least because in situations where the direct producers have to hand over part of what they have produced to someone else, there is a very real motive—one might almost say, an imperative—to increase their output, a motive that need have initially nothing to do with market compulsion. As Peter Musgrave writes:

> The search for profit maximization is as valid an economic objective for early modern Europeans as it is in the modern world. It would certainly be wrong to argue that at no time and at no place in early modern Europe did people or families set out to improve the performance of their own private economies by seeking and following the sort of opportunities which were to lead on to the industrial developments of the nineteenth and twentieth centuries. This economic aim could be followed sensibly in an early modern context only in certain limited and specific circumstances.

Musgrave, like Brenner, assumes that risk is the main factor preventing peasants from opting for profit maximization. What could overcome these concerns? Musgrave argues that it could only have been such insecurity that the risk was worth taking because it could scarcely be worse than current conditions.[68] Increasing production, if it leads to greater disposable income, might give peasants the wherewithal to buy their way out of performing labor services, to hire wage labor to carry out work that would otherwise destroy the health and shorten the life of family members, or perhaps even to acquire heritable property which would remove them from feudal jurisdictions altogether. "Rather than retreating from the market," writes Jane Whittle, "peasants used the market to escape from serfdom."[69] And in conditions of crisis, such as those that shook European feudalism in the fourteenth century, the pressure on the ruling class to raise the level of exploitation, and consequently on the peasantry to look for ways of escape, was of course heightened still further.

The result was a prolonged process of class differentiation among the peasantry. In England, it led to the emergence of a class of richer peasants who were at least as important to English agrarian development as the lords. As several writers—by no means all hostile to the Brenner thesis—have pointed out, without the existence of such a relatively prosperous class it is difficult to see where the lords would have found a sufficient number of tenants, or how these tenants could have afforded the investment that the landlords demanded.[70] Terence Byres writes: "The possibility ... exists for the peasant to produce surpluses, whether deliberately or adventitiously, and to market those surpluses. This is so given that the lords, their powers of extra-economic coercion notwithstanding, are unable to extract everything above sub-sistence, even though they may well wish to." Rich peasants "had less restricted resources than middle and poor peasants; had larger plots and greater investment funds, and would, therefore, have been able to produce surpluses and better able to take attendant risks." Not to recognize the existence of this prior process of differ-entiation, like Brenner, is to assume: "Without explanation the existence of a class with the capacity and strength to take on commercial leases, to cope with and re-spond to market dependence, to compete in production and so, ultimately, become a class of capitalist farmers. Where did this class come from?"[71]

The period in which this class began to form fell between the onset of crisis and the arrival of the Black Death. Whittle writes of Norfolk: "The active land market, the litigious and market-orientated nature of Norfolk peasants, the large numbers of hired workers and rural craftsmen, not to mention the development of socialized rural industry in the form of worsted weaving, all dated from the late thirteenth and early fourteenth centuries, if not earlier."[72] Nevertheless, population decline and consequent labor shortages from the 1340s strengthened these tendencies. Rodney Hilton writes of Forncett, an estate to the southwest of Norwich, prior to 1381:

> A peasant society governed by customs in which serfdom and labor services played an important part was shattered by uncontrollable peasant mobility and the com-mercialization of all transactions in land. In 1378 on the very eve of the rebellion about a quarter of the free-holdings and three-quarters of villein holdings on this es-tate had been abandoned. The remaining tenants, many of them in theory unfree, were dealing briskly and commercially in the available land, taking parcels of, on an average, three to four acres on lease for short terms.

Nor is this the only example: "In Essex, the market in peasant land was devel-oping a social differentiation among inhabitants of villages, dividing the landless and the cottagers from the few well-to-do."[73]

We are in short looking at a general phenomenon, at least across the southern half of England: "Whether we look at peasant life in the south-east, in the Thames Valley, in East Anglia or in the Midlands, we find standing out from the ordinary run of tenants with the fifteen or twenty-acre holdings, a small group of families sometimes free, more often serf, holding a hundred acres or more." These holdings would usually be composites, pieced together from a range of sources, and rarely consolidated. There were inevitably major tensions between the legal status of these larger peasants and their economic position, the former preventing them carrying out the activities which the latter would otherwise have made possible, notably the lack of freedom to buy and sell land, even if they had acquired surpluses. In contrast to the smaller peasants: "Most irritating to them must have been the hindrances to accumulation, rather than the fear of starvation."[74] This class of farmers existed because peasants had already put themselves under the discipline of the market in a situation where they were under no compulsion to do so. "[Brenner] assumes that lords were able to find tenants to take land on lease at a time when we also know that lords were granting land on increasingly favorable terms—without [entry] fines, with rent reductions—because of the overall shortage of tenants."[75] And why was there a shortage of tenants? "Clearly," writes Jaime Torras, "any explanation of the singularity of the English case must take into account those other sectors of the economy, absent from Brenner's model, which may have absorbed available labor and, by vying for it against the agricultural entrepreneurs, may have made wage-saving improvements attractive to them."[76]

These other sectors involved both non-agrarian rural and urban activity. R. B. Outhwaite writes: "The English countryside accommodated nearly one and one half million extra inhabitants before 1650, and by no means were all of them landless agricultural or industrial laborers." Far from being absorbed into large farming units from the mid-fourteenth century, there was a growth in the number of small farms, particularly in fenland, forest, woodland, and pastoral areas:

> The rapid growth of small farms became a problem in some places, a problem that was "solved" by these small farmers and cottagers turning their attentions increasingly to industrial pursuits, such as spinning or weaving of wool or hemp, the knitting of stockings, the making of lace or fishing nets, the manufacture of nails, basket-making or straw-plaiting. Whether such activities developed depended primarily on the availability of local raw materials, the proximity both of markets and of rival manufacturers, and the interest or lack of interest of merchant organizers. Where such activities developed, however, they accentuated many of the tendencies already noted: they became an additional inducement for local populations to stay and an extra attraction perhaps to immigrants; they may have encouraged early marriage—for both sexes; they made small-holdings viable; they may, in some cases, have enabled some landlords to secure higher rents, by permitting the proliferation of small units, than they could by encouraging the process of amalgamation.[77]

The same combinations occur in the towns. Indeed, the basis of the combination often was the connection with the countryside. Donald Woodward writes of the relationship between building craftsmen and agriculture that it "was close in many areas and that, like laborers, building craftsmen often supplemented their craft-earnings by farming both for subsistence and the market." Neither group was composed of pure wage-laborers. "Their modern equivalents are not wage-earning factory workers, but, rather, jobbing joiners, plumbers and electricians." In fact, their modern equivalents are more accurately identified as the semi-proletarians of the Global South who return to farms to work part-time during the year, or who maintain smallholdings to supplement their income or food intake. Nevertheless, Woodward is right to conclude: "English society during the sixteenth and seventeenth centuries had not yet become a predominantly wage-earning society ... it was above all still a society in which the small unit of production and the small unit of ownership and control prevailed in most trades."[78]

The tripartite class structure of agrarian capitalism in England—capitalist landlord, capitalist tenant farmer, landless laborer—was achieved by a two-way process involving, on the one hand, divisions among the exploited and, on the other, changes from above in the functions of the exploiters. The former began first and may have been the inspiration for the latter. "Would it be too far-fetched to suggest that it was the example of substantial copyholders and the like, with their strictly commercial attitude to their land and produce, that gave lords the idea of adopting commercial rather than feudal relationships, when the former became more promising?"[79] Take, as a specific example of change from the bottom up, the process of enclosure, which Brenner tends to see as imposed on peasant communities by the lords. What is enclosure? The most useful definition, by Wordie, defines it as a situation of "land held in severalty, fell completely under the power of one owner to do with as he pleased, whether or not he chose to enclose his land in the literal sense with hedges and ditches." The essential point is that the land no longer carried common rights.[80] "He" was of course occasionally "she," but more importantly was often a collective, since the dispossession of common land was by no means only carried out by individuals. When did the bulk of enclosures take place? As Wordie carefully explains, making "every effort to err on the side of enclosure where doubt exists," by 1500 England at most 45 percent enclosed and only 47 percent enclosed by 1600, but 75 percent enclosed by 1760, meaning "there was almost twice as much enclosure in seventeenth-century England as in any other century, including the eighteenth."[81]

Who carried out the enclosures? Robert Duplessis has noted that this was in fact often initiated by peasants themselves with the consequence of increasing divisions within the community: "Members of the existing yeoman elite—freeholders on lands their ancestors had acquired after the Black Death or tenants with long-term renewable leases at fixed rents—were often in a position to take on or create enclosed farms." For example: "On the manor of Cheshunt (Hertfordshire), where 20 per cent of the tenants already held slightly more than half the land in 1484, but boosted their share to 70 per cent in 1562, the trend towards concentration was due essentially to transfers among tenants."[82] These changes were in response to market "opportunities": "For example, in order to take advantage of the potentially higher profit margins of pastoral farming, village communities should ideally have rearranged their fields and introduced some form of convertible husbandry. But in order to facilitate this process, they often had to discard the communal features of the open field-system and enclose fields, in other words, alter the property and institutional framework of the entire township."[83]

But even after the lords began to adopt commercial relationships, they were not capable of doing so completely on their own terms, precisely because of the existence of a class of capitalist farmers. As Mark Overton points out:

> There is mounting evidence to show that there was not a coordinated relationship between landlord power, tenure ownership, farm size and capitalist farming. Landlords were frequently unable to exercise the power that Brenner attitudes to them: customary tenancies and leases could give legal protection to tenants, whose rights

were upheld by the courts. In general, economic differentiation was a process which took place among the tenantry. Moreover landlords, especially in the sixteenth century, showed little interest in developing their estates for capitalist tenant farming, and as a rule they were not very adventurous in promoting innovation in agriculture. The pioneers of new methods in the seventeenth and eighteenth centuries (at least in Norfolk) were not the great landowners but smaller farmers, both tenants and owner-occupiers ... the most dramatic advances in output and land productivity came in those areas (such as Norfolk) where leadership was relatively weak.[84]

On the basis of her study of Norfolk during the fifteenth and sixteenth centuries, Whittle writes: "There is no evidence that lords tried to transfer customary or copyhold land to leasehold in the sixteenth century. While considerable amounts of formerly customary or demesne lands were held by leasehold in Norfolk manors during the fifteenth century, this appears to have been because tenants preferred leasehold to customary tenure. It was untainted by the vestiges of serfdom, and its rents were sometimes lower."[85] The number of peasants who were able to achieve security of tenure ("freehold") was generally far greater than Brenner allows. These were often proprietor-tenants who exercised competitive pressure for increased rents on their subtenants and acquired far greater levels of income from doing so than the manorial lord himself. In Rossendale, for example, copyhold tenants were paying three to four times less to the manorial lord than the subtenants on the same holding were paying them.[86]

But what was true for England was also true, if to a lesser extent, of France. According to political Marxist orthodoxy: "Agrarian capitalism did not develop in France, since neither peasants, who formed subsistence communities based on unmediated access to their means of production, nor the upper classes (nobles and bourgeois), which reproduced themselves through land-rents and the spoils of political offices were subject to capitalist imperatives."[87] We should by now be wary about magical incantations involving the term "capitalist imperatives." As Phillip Hoffman comments of seventeenth-century France: "The poor often favored the dissolution of the commons, and in the one instance in which the poor did fight for common grazing rights—in Varades—it was to protect their stake in what was clearly capitalist agriculture."[88] The episode to which Hoffman refers is full of interest. For virtually a hundred years after 1639 the peasants of Varades fought with the local marquis to retain use the commons against his attempts to enclose it. As Hoffman comments, at first glance this looks like another example of enterprising capitalist aristocrat in conflict with traditional peasant agriculture—which would in itself cast doubt on the supposed unwillingness of the French landed classes to improve, but the situation was more complex than this. There was indeed a capitalist interest here, but it lies not with the landowner—in this case we can confirm the stereotype—but with the peasants themselves. For as Hoffman explains, they were attempting to continue to use the common to graze sheep, but as "a commercial enterprise raised for sale because they could be transported over long distances." The problem is where we conceive of "the commons" as invariably being associated with the spaces of peasant collectivity under feudal or tributary modes of production. In this case, at least: "The common pasture was not the preserve of subsistence farming. Rather, it was the meeting place for nascent rural capitalism, the locus for a curious alliance between modest peasants and the agents of commercial agriculture."[89]

Braudel points out, again in relation to the seventeenth century, that large estates up in Brie, near Paris, were being bought by urban owners who generally did not work the land themselves but let it out to tenant farmers who would often hire from several different proprietors at once: "All the signs indicate a 'capitalist' organization, such as the English revolution had instituted: the landowner, the rich tenant and the agricultural laborers."There were differences with England, notably in the absence of technological innovation, but nevertheless, "this tenant-farmer was a new feature of the landscape, the owner of a slowly accumulating capital which was already turning him into an entrepreneur." One indication is the way in which peasant anger was turned against these tenant farmers during the so-called Flour Wars of 1775, an indication of the resentment the latter provoked by raising himself above his class and the way in which they dominated the village life, not least by carrying out the wishes of the proprietors.[90]

Henry Heller has accepted that even the vast expansion of banking and commercial capital, together with the less significant but still not negligible investment in productive technology, can define seventeenth-century France as capitalist. He argues, however, drawing on the work of Le Roy Ladurie and Bois, that in Languedoc and Normandy a differentiation—indeed, a polarization—was already taking place by the first half of the sixteenth century, resulting in people leaving the land to work in the Isle-de-France, Le Havre, and Paris for whatever wages they could get—a factor that meant there was less of a need to develop or invest in labor-saving devices than there was in England.[91] There were changes following the crisis of the seventeenth century: "Thenceforth, intensification did not merely amount to extending the acreage of the land under cultivation, but it also began to affect the structures of agricultural production as a whole." In particular, the expropriation of the French peasantry began to intensify from the 1740s:

> Whereas the peasants were more or less successful in defending the "occupancy" of the land against outside attempts to take it away from them, the landlords also tried to enlarge their estates mainly at the expense of the common land. Thus, common rights were carved up, forests were closed and grazing rights superseded. Production on the estates became more rationalized, also in the sense that the landlords tended to rely on the *gros fermiers*. The latter in turn usually leased the land to the peasants, thus interposing themselves between the landlords and the mass of the peasants.

Clearly this is not exactly the same as the process in England, since an element of both feudal rent and payment in kind was retained within the peasant relationship to the landowners or larger tenants.[92] The dispossession of the French peasantry was a fact, as the area around Toulouse demonstrates. On the one hand, there was "a global decline in the amount of land left in Peasant hands": "In the Toulousian and the Lauragais although [the peasants] constituted between 60 and 70 per cent of the population, they held only a fifth or less of the land by the early eighteenth century." On the other, there was "a dramatic decline in the size of the tenures that survived": More than a third of the peasantry of the Toulousian had less than six-tenths of a hectare (1.48 acres) and, 84 percent less than three hectares (7.41 acres). The French peasants were considerably less secure than Brenner claims: "yet, as the French experience shows, the simple process of proletarianization, albeit a general precondition of capitalist development, was not a sufficient one." Apart from anything else, it is insufficient by itself to create the size of home market necessary for the self-expansion of capital.[93] Nevertheless, we can perhaps conclude this part of our survey in the words of Richard Hoyle: "Whereas Brenner suggested a single road to the capitalist farms of the eighteenth century, it may perhaps be seen that there were several ways in which these forms emerged."[94] Marx himself was clear that not only capitalist agriculture but the capitalist mode of production as a whole had multiple points of origin: "The feudal system, for its part, foundered on urban industry, trade, modern agriculture (even as results of individual inventions like gunpowder and the printing press)."[95] Two examples will illustrate how feudalism helped to generate from within itself the social forces that could potentially destroy it and the social forms that could potentially replace it.

In a critique of Carling's "feudal fission thesis," Vivek Chibber notes that he "is surprisingly vague on what the mechanism is that can serve to transmit new, more congenial production-relations across the terrain of stagnating productive forces, but it appears that the two most likely candidates are, first, their simple imposition through military conflict; and second, through some kind of demonstration-effect." Chibber argues that there are difficulties with both mechanisms. In the case of military victory: "Such transformations of the productive structure presume a capacity on the part of the victors that far exceeds the power required to simply win in war." In the case of demonstration-effect, the rulers of less developed systems may desire to emulate their more developed rivals, but "since the rival economic systems rest on different productive relations, a transition to those production-relations will involve the dismantling of the very social relations on the basis of which these rulers maintain their power."[96] In fact, as we shall see, some ruling classes did consciously choose to adopt different and more productive social relations in circumstances where not to do so would lead to their destruction or subordination. The question of military imposition is more complex. Although I agree with Chibber that the ability to conquer a territory does not necessarily imply the ability to transform the productive relations that are dominant there, the process of making war itself seems to have been more generally important: even in relation to states that sought to restrict further capitalist development, military competition also inadvertently helped to stimulate it.

During the First World War Bukharin wrote in general terms of war that "as a function of state power and a 'non-economic' factor" it was "one of the key factors of the economic process."[97] More recently, Erica Schoenberger has written more specifically of how absolutist states may either create or extend markets as a response to "the problems generated by processes of territorial conquest and control": "Without planning to promote the commercialization of society, the state's efforts to convert fixed and lumpy resources into flows across territory may spur the formation or further development and generalization of markets." These processes were built into the very act of state formation: "This proposition is incompatible with a view that warfare is purely destructive. It is compatible with the argument that one possible outcome of wars—territorial integration—provides a favorable context for market development, but goes further to suggest that the process of fighting wars in itself may spur commercialization."[98]

To anticipate one objection: the point here is not that markets themselves equate with capitalism, but the type of changes that shifts toward extensive production lead to in terms of social relations of production. Prior to the emergence of the absolutist states toward the end of the fifteenth century, for example, the manufacture of armor was subcontracted out by the dominant nobles to artisan workshops that specialized in making individual components, such as helmets or breastplates. Throughout Europe guild regulations forbade any increase in the size or number of workplace units to meet demand: "Until 1507 no more than the master himself, two qualified journeymen and a single apprentice were supposed to work in a single workshop. It is not surprising that such tiny workshops each concentrated on supplying single items of armor . . . to the merchants who put them together."[99] By the end of the fifteenth century, outside of two cities in the German Lands (Cologne and Nuremburg) and another two in Northern Italy (Milan and its satellite, Brescia): "There were no other major production centers for armor elsewhere in Europe, not in France, nor in the British Isles, nor in Scandinavia, nor in Eastern Europe, nor in Southern Italy, nor in any of the kingdoms of the Iberian Peninsula." Christopher Duffy notes: "Artillerymen entered the Age of Reason in medieval guise."[100] They did not leave it in the same way. As military competition intensified, all were forced to varying degrees to produce their own armor and weaponry more generally rather than rely on actual or potential enemies. Ordinance had previously been produced on a diverse, localized basis. The demand for interchangeable parts, whose design was based on practical experimentation and that incorporated technical improvements derived from other parts of the economy (horse harnesses, sights, elevating mechanisms) implied the need for systematic manufacture.

The process of production could not remain untouched by these new demands. "It is not possible to put a blast-furnace—even a seventeenth-century one—in a cottage" writes Donald Coleman, "or to disperse the assembly process inherent in the building of a great house or a great ship."[101] Marx refers to the emergence of forms of production—paper or saw mills, metal works, glass factories—which from the beginning require industrial manufacture on a scale for which the number of workers, extent of investment or size of market was impossible under the guild system could not be conducted.[102] In relation to military competition, change was partly the result of the increased quantities required. During the 1440s the French royal artillery consumed 20,000 pounds of gunpowder a year; by the 1540s this had risen to 500,000. Prussian powder production rose from 448,000 pounds in 1746 and rose to 560,000 pound in 1756. But it was also a qualitative difference. As Sheilagh Ogilvie notes, "military and strategic considerations led central and north Italian states to grant industrial privileges to remote, frontier, or mountainous parts of their territories, enabling the rise of rural proto-industries in the teeth of urban guild privilege."[103] During the reign of Louis XIV (1638–1715) the French army adopted the use of mobile field artillery that would be as effective in the field as in sieges: "Under the enlightened direction of Jean Baptiste de Gribeauval, the calibers, carriages and equipment of the French artillery were standardized, and their parts were made interchangeable (thanks to the ability of industrial plants to mass-produce identical, precise and highly durable metalwork)."[104] Here there are genuine continuities between the pre- and post-revolutionary economy in France. In what can retrospectively be seen as early measures of state capitalism, the Committee of Public Safety effectively nationalized the existing armories and organized the building of new ones in Paris and elsewhere. The majority of forges (about a thousand) were confiscated from their noble and ecclesiastical owners and transformed into state property, leased out to the *maitres de forges* who had previously run them, Under the Directory and Napoleon they were ultimately sold off to the same individuals who, over the entire revolutionary period, began through a process of internal competition to centralize ownership and control: "The stage was set for a future transformation of this industry—key to the development of nineteenth-century industrial capitalism—under the auspices of these *maitres de forges* who now operated these means of production as their private property." Steel production nearly doubled between 1789 and 1801. And the new owners prospered too: by 1811 more than a dozen of the *maitres de forge* had assets of between one and three million francs.[105]

Not every state was capable of producing its own equipment. Portugal remained dependent on imported guns from other, rival states; but at the opposite extreme, Sweden underwent three phases of development in gun manufacture in the middle years of the sixteenth century, from wrought-iron to cast bronze to cast iron. Carlo Cipolla notes of this striking micro-example of uneven development: "Sweden was concentrating into a few decades the evolutionary process that the Continent had taken centuries to accomplish."[106] Three centuries later tsarist Russia saw the most spectacular examples of military development, but the central dynamic was similar. After 1861 an industrialization program was principally undertaken to strengthen the ability of the tsarist autocracy to participate in military competition with rival (and more advanced) states in Western Europe. Clive Treblicock notes, "from 1861 until 1917 Russian industrialization was pursued always in part for military purposes and always within a framework rigidly defined to minimize domestic upheavals."[107] The latter aspect was not destined to be successful other than in the short term, as Peter Gatrell points out: "To promote industrial expansion was to introduce a Trojan horse into the camp of imperial Russia in the shape of new social forces, possessed of their own agenda and aspirations."[108] This Trojan horse contained both a bourgeoisie and—unlike in earlier centuries—an organized working class that threatened the state from within.

It was in relation to shipping, however, that the greatest steps toward capitalist social relations were made: "Power, the ability of the states and the dynasty to impose its will on other states, depended on guns, including guns on board ship, if effectively deployed. In order to pay for the guns, states needed the kind of money which, in the sixteenth century, could only be obtained from trade."[109] The threefold task of protecting the mercantile marine, raiding blockade, and interception saw a massive shipbuilding campaign, particularly after 1588. This affected all the competing states, capitalist and absolutist alike, for war imposes its own symmetry on the participants, if they are capable of taking part. By the 1680s, the French state possessed 221 ships; during the Wars of the British and Irish Succession between 1689 and 1697 they captured 4,000 enemy ships.[110] Where did these ships come from? To an even greater extent than blast furnaces, ships cannot be built by a handful of artisans and their journeymen in a backyard. It requires a dry dock for construction, a steady supply of materials and a large number of laborers—wage laborers. It was not only construction that involved wage labor, however, but the organization of maritime workforce. The following comments by Marcus Rediker are made of Britain after the Glorious Revolution, but the same logic applied in the absolutist states:

> As capital came to be concentrated in merchant shipping, masses of workers, numbering 25,000 to 40,000 at any one time between 1700 and 1750, were in turn concentrated in this vibrant branch of industry. The huge numbers of workers mobilized for shipboard labor were placed in relatively new relationships to capital—as free and fully waged laborers—and to each other: seamen were by their experiences in the maritime labor market and labor process, among the first collective laborers. . . . The completely contractual and waged nature of maritime work represented a capital-labor relation quite distinct from landlord-tenant, master-servant, or master-apprentice relationships. The seaman was both a free wage-laborer located in a critical sector of the economy and a collective laborer located among an unprecedented number of men such as himself.[111]

There was of course one important difference between Britain and its imperialist rivals, but this did not lie in the realm of the labor process in the shipyards or on the vessels themselves. During the early eighteenth century, the suggestion was made by French state managers that one way to raise sufficient taxes to pay for improvements to the French Navy that would enable it to compete with that of Britain was to extend the tax base to those, above all the nobles, who were currently exempt but responsible for collecting it from the peasantry. "Politically," Bruce Lenman dryly observes, "this was not practical."[112] This conception of practicality indicating the self-imposed developmental limits of states where the bourgeois revolution had not yet been achieved.

Where conquest was important in nurturing capitalist development was not in Europe itself but through the establishment of colonies, above all in the Americas. There was of course a connection between the enhanced ability to make war and the expansion of empires beyond Europe, as Smith noted in 1776: "In modern war the great expense of fire-arms gives an evident advantage to the nation which can best afford that expense; and consequently, to an opulent and civilized, over a poor and barbarous nation. In ancient times the opulent and civilized found it difficult to defend themselves against the poor and barbarous nations. In modern times the poor and barbarous find it difficult to defend themselves against the opulent and civilized."[113] Paradoxically, the major contribution of Western European colonization to the transition may have been in the creation of forms transitional to wage labor, rather than from what is normally thought of as the primitive accumulation in its external aspect. James Blaut claimed: "The massive flows of wealth into Europe from colonial accumulation in America and later in Asia was the one basic force that explains the fact that Europe became rapidly transformed into a capitalist society, and the complimentary fact that Asian and African protocapitalist centers began to decline first in relative then in absolute importance." The validity of any theory that ascribes the outcome of world history to "Europe's location near America and because of the immense wealth obtained by Europeans in America and later in Asia and Africa" must be in doubt.[114] As Robin Blackburn points out: "The simple amassing of wealth is a secondary aspect of "primitive accumulation," since capitalist industrialization required an appropriate framework of institutions and production relations capable of converting wealth into capital."[115] The same is true for the clearance of "surplus" populations from the land. As Braudel notes in relation to the Mediterranean region, the persecution of vagbonds and vagrants, usually seen as part of the primitive accumulation in England, was in fact common across Europe, but did not produce the same economic results.[116] In other words, enforced transfers of wealth in and of themselves will not necessarily lead or even contribute to capitalist development: in some cases it simply acted as a life-support mechanism for the most economically backward absolutist states. Pierre Vilar described Spanish imperialism as "the highest stage of feudalism": "Occupying land, enslaving the inhabitants, looting treasure—there were no preparations for 'investment' in the capitalist sense of the word."[117] These actions were intended to rescue the existing class structure, as Banaji explains:

> At its inception the colonization of Latin America was a *feudal* colonization, a response to the crisis of feudal profitability which all the landowning classes of Europe were facing down to the latter half of the sixteenth century. In the Baltic and Easter Europe this crisis was partly overcome by territorial expansion into contiguous areas, and then displaced by the production of grain for export; but in the maritime periphery of Europe, in Spain and Portugal where this feudal crisis recurred with peri-

odic sharpness, it expressed itself in a movement of *overseas* colonization. The Spain which launched this movement of expansion was a Spain dominated by feudalism, but a feudalism in crisis.[118]

Similarly, Portugal began from a situation of limited material resources and skilled manpower, which placed great difficulties in the way of creating a large enough military and salaried bureaucracy to efficiently run the empire. Consequently, the crown had to make participation attractive to the nobility—the only class capable of carrying out these roles. But in doing so, the crown also had to allow them to plunder resources to make it worthwhile for themselves and to ensure the participation of their own followers. The effect was to both decentralize and thus diminish royal authority and ensure that resources were endlessly recycled into maintaining military control over the imperium. Unable to control noble expectations and lacking central mechanisms to bring them under control, the crown was reduced to granting offices on short tenures and leasing trading rights on short leases, but these moves only encouraged the noble recipients to exploit the opportunities for short-term gain. "By the end of the sixteenth century the pattern of social and economic behavior had destroyed any burgeoning Portuguese capitalism and left the empire with all the strengths of a decentralized and locally deep-rooted feudalism, but without the financial resources and central authority to further strengthen its armed forces for a long drawn-out struggle to survive in a new and mercantile competition with the Dutch and English."[119]

It might even be said that the plundering of the colonies did more to preserve feudal social relations and absolutist states than it necessarily did to enhance capitalist social relations and states. Colonies established for geopolitical reason such as several of the British possessions in Asia may have been essential for imperial security but were net drains on the exchequer. Mike Davis has rightly argued against "the claim that the Industrial Revolution necessarily depended upon the colonial conquest or economic subjugation of Asia; on the contrary, the slave trade and the plantations of the New World were much more strategic streams of liquid capital and natural resources in boosting the industrial take-off in Britain, France and the United States." Only the industrialization of the United Provinces seems to have been based on the extraction of tribute from the colonies. For Britain in particular, it was only in the latter half of the nineteenth century that India became an important market for Dundonian jute, Lancastrian cotton, or Sheffield steel: "The coerced levies of wealth from India and China were not essential to the rise of British hegemony, but they were absolutely crucial in postponing its decline."[120]

It was trade with the colonial settlers rather than the expropriation of the colonized peoples that provided the greatest impetus to capitalist development in the colonizing states. In the original debate on the transition, both Maurice Dobb and Paul Sweezy noted the importance of long-distance trade was that, to put it in Hegelian terms, quantity eventually changes into quality. Once the demand for commodities expanded beyond a certain point, it had implications for, not simply the division of labor nor the labor process more generally, but how production itself was organized.[121] Marx wrote that trade with the colonies and the consequent expansion of commercial capital "were a major moment in promoting the transition from the feudal to the capitalist mode of production": "The sudden expansion of the world market, the multiplication of commodities in circulation, the competition among the European nations for the seizure of Asiatic products and American treasures, colonial system, all made a fundamental contribution towards shattering the feudal barriers to production."[122] In particular, from the mid-seventeenth century the plantation colonies became major new markets for merchandise that was produced in the European metropolitan centers: "The demands of the new colonial markets could not be satisfied by the relatively small number of urban workers handed down from the Middle Ages, and the manufactures proper opened out new fields of production to the rural population which had been driven from the land by the dissolution of the feudal system."[123] The so-called triangular trade involved merchant exchange of commodities for slaves in the African markets, the slaves were then taken to the Americas to work on plantations to produce the agricultural commodities that were exported back to Europe where they were worked up for re-export. Finally, commodities were traded directly with the plantations, which relied on the imperial homelands for goods they could not produce themselves. It is certainly true that in some cases, like those of the cotton manufacturers at Nantes in relation to West Africa, it tied producers into stable markets that in time became their sole markets, nevertheless it allowed new industries to emerge or new ways of organizing industry were considered in order to meet these new demands.[124]

The most important impacts may, however, have occurred in the colonies themselves, where the most important experiments were under way. In the cases of Portugal or Spain there may have been greater movement toward capitalist relations of production in their imperial possessions than in the metropolitan centers themselves. Before the Spanish conquest of Peru, for example, the native inhabitants worked what they called a *mit'a*, or turn, which was in effect a form of community labor. The Spanish kept the name for this practice, but during the sixteenth century transformed it into a form of forced labor, turning the peasants into temporary workers, "*mitayos*," for set periods during which they had to leave the community— often with their families in train—for the silver mines of Potosi, ranches, agricultural estates, or even as craftsmen in workshops. Were the mitayos slaves? In fact, they were examples of a transitional form of wage labor and this was not their only relationship to the market:

> From the moment his service began a mitayo contended with pressures to enter commercial transactions which reduced his net pay. If daily rations and the foodstuffs brought from home communities proved insufficient to support the mitayo and his relatives who accompanied him, the peasant would need to purchase the remainder from his temporary master or in the market at large.... Even without a food deficit,

mitayos had good reason to turn to the market. Rations did not generally include coca, an indispensable source of sustenance during Andean labor.[125]

The Brazilian sugar plantations of the Portuguese Empire displayed comparable transitional forms. By the end of the seventeenth century these had become something like a model for the rest of the plantation colonies of the Americas, regardless of the nature of the colonial state. The merchants who owned the plantations were involved in the process of production, from cultivation to processing to ultimate transportation to market, to an extent that they very rarely were in the metropolitan centers. And the same process would often happen in reverse, with planters becoming merchants in their turn. Plantations, although often smaller than the average area owned by landowners in Europe, occupied labor forces up to ten times as large. These were more akin to later factories than to the actual manufacturing as it existed in most of Europe at the time in the form of the largely unsupervised putting-out process. Moreover, some of the processes involved skilled labor, but even those that did not saw massive coordinated physical effort on the part of male slaves, which had the same effect upon the laborers as factory work did on a latter generation of wage laborers: it united them as a class—something of which the slave owners were only too aware.[126] Brazil was not unique. Slaves on the sugar plantations of the French Caribbean were in some ways like peasants, both in the fact that they worked the land for subsistence and in the elemental violence with which they rose against their oppressors given the opportunity; but not in others. As C. L. R. James noted, "working and living together in gangs of hundreds on the huge sugar factories which covered the North Plain [of San Domingo], they were closer to a modern proletariat than any group of workers in existence at the time."[127] These similarities between Brazilian and San Dominican slave plantations extended to those of their British rivals in the Caribbean. Of these classically "combined" forms Blackburn writes: "It would . . . be wrong to propose a sharp contrast between English 'bourgeois' colonization and French 'feudal' colonization, since the social forces involved in both—merchants and colonists—were comparable."[128] Although the possession of colonies led to variable outcomes in the imperial centers, in the colonies themselves transitional forms of social relations of production were emerging that tended to converge. These emergent social relations and the trading links connecting them to Europe would form part of a network through which capitalist laws of motion could become operative on a global scale, once the existing states system was overthrown.

Following the resumption of economic growth in the mid-fifteenth century then, increases in productivity ceased to be generated by feudalism itself, but by the now expanding sectors based on capitalist production. As Bois puts it:

There was not a sort of continuous transition from one mode of production to another, simply through the growth of the "new" within the "old." On the contrary, there were successive waves of accumulation (in the twelfth, thirteenth, sixteenth, and eighteenth centuries) separated by phases of ebb. For obvious reasons, each of these waves broke further on than the last, since the structures of the feudal system, weakened by the irreversible erosive action (both socially and psychologically) of earlier thrusts of accumulation, offered less resistance.

Capitalist impulses were initially "auxiliary," "but the role of the new impulses, of a capitalist type, grew ever stronger," leading ultimately to a situation in which "the auxiliary becomes the main motor force."[129] When the second general crisis began, nearly three hundred years after the first, it was no longer a purely feudal crisis, but one occurring within a transitional economy in which capitalism was a still subordinate, widely uneven, but growing component. Peter Coveney has summarized the components of this second wave as: "population growth and food crisis in an unreformed agrarian economy; economic stagnation or recession affecting the great majority of the European population; under-employment, pauperism and vagrancy; over-crowded cities becoming the forcing houses of epidemic disease; the states with their wars and oppressive fiscalism, increasing social distress and de-stabilizing the traditional political structures of late medieval Europe."[130]

These afflictions were, however, also experienced outside Europe and its overseas extensions. Jack Goldstone has argued that during the middle decades of the seventeenth century similar underlying causes lay behind the crises of Stuart England, Ottoman Turkey, and Ming China. These arose from the growth of population leading to pressure on resources, price inflation, initial shortfalls in tax revenue as a result of levels being fixed, subsequent dramatic increases in taxation to compensate, rigorous state intervention to enforce monarchical control, resistance, and division among the ruling and popular classes, leading finally to the emergence of ideologies that justified resistance to the ruler. The main differences, according to Goldstone were ideological, rather than economic, social, or political. Puritanism in England was "apocalyptic" and pointed toward an interventionist role for a reconstructed English state in world affairs. Sufism in Turkey and T'ai-chou neo-Confucianism in China were "cyclical" and demanded a return to the uncorrupt ways of some earlier period: "After 1650, the Ottoman and Chinese empires became more rigidly orthodox and conservative than they had been earlier; they turned more inward and eschewed novelty, while rewarding conformity to past habits. State reconstruction on these lines was successful in restoring a measure of prosperity and prolonging the life of these states, but they entered the late-seventeenth and eighteenth centuries without the dynamism of England."[131] If, however, England had been no different in terms of development from Turkey and China, then it is unlikely that the overthrow of the state would have been anything other than temporary, no matter how interventionist the Puritan ideology of the revolutionaries. Here we can agree with Brenner and Christopher Isett that "England's path of economic evolution diverged decisively from that of the Yangtze delta over the course of the early modern period (1500–1750), as it also did from that of most of the rest of Europe at the same time." There was, in other words an *already existing divergence*" in economy, which had led to the divergence in ideology, and which meant that the crisis in England could potentially lead to a different outcome than those that occurred further east.[132] Where and when capitalism shifted from the periphery to the center of economic life was in very large part dependent on the nature of the pre-capitalist state, to which we now turn.

THE STRUCTURAL CAPACITIES OF PRECAPITALIST STATES

The question of pre-capitalist state power is central in answering the question of why it was not in the hitherto most advanced areas, like the Ottoman and Chinese Empires, that the potentiality of capitalism was first realized but in relatively backward territories of Europe. As Mielants has argued, even if "all the relevant features necessary to ensure a gradual transition from feudalism to capitalism were available" this may still be insufficient unless the situation also involves "the lack of other features," among which he includes "the construction of a well-organized 'world empire' or the recurring destructive raids of pastoral nomads on the emerging centers of capital accumulation."[133] It is in this context that Carling's argument concerning the ability or otherwise of states to maintain noncapitalist modes of production is of decisive importance, if we understand the state to be the complex of institutions and social relations through which existing ruling classes conduct the class struggle. What kind of states were these that acted as obstacles to the establishment of viable nation-states dominated by capitalist laws of motion? As Epstein points out, "the most significant effect of the demographic shock [after 1348] was sharply to accelerate the process of political centralization inherent to the feudal-tributary mode of production"; this was in turn accompanied by greater territorial integration and both processes were "strongly contested by the more powerful feudal lords and towns."[134] Let us leave aside the question of whether we can speak of a "feudal-tributary" mode of production for the moment and focus first on the states that emerged in territories that were unambiguously feudal.

The replacement of the feudal estates-monarchy by absolutism followed the first crisis of feudalism.[135] Under conditions of generalized economic contraction the landowning classes had only two means of maintaining—let alone increasing—their level of income. One was by extending the area controlled by the state to which they owed allegiance and so increasing the number of peasants under their seigniorial control. The other was by intensifying the level of exploitation for both long-standing and these newly conquered peasant communities. The first brought conflict between those states that encroached on each other's territories, a process exemplified by the Hundred Years' War between England and France (1337–1453). The second brought conflict within states, between the lords and the peasants themselves. The latter violently opposed these increased exactions in a great series of risings that began in maritime Flanders in the 1320s and ended, in Western Europe at least, in Catalonia in the 1470s. Both the effective pursuit of external military aggression and the suppression of internal revolt required the agency of a centralized coercive state power greater than the territorially dispersed structures typical of military feudalism. For our purposes two main characteristics of this emergent state form are of central importance.

One was the relative autonomy of the absolutist states from their class base—the feudal lords. The latter did not, in the main, directly control the state apparatus, either through inherited membership of their estate or appointment to regal office. On the contrary, since they regularly went to war with each other and, less regularly, combined to make war on the monarch, it was essential that the state apparatus be operated by a bureaucracy directly responsible to the Crown. Only thus could the collective interests of the feudal ruling class be secured. Inseparable from this strengthening of central power was a twofold weakening of both the collective and individual powers exercised by the lords. Collectively, they were the dominant estate within any parliament, and could still use this position to thwart the wishes of the Crown. The relative success of individual absolutisms therefore depended on (and could almost be measured by) the extent to which they managed to suppress their particular national assembly—the longevity of French absolutism compared to the English variant being very marked in this respect. Individually, the lords held jurisdictional authority within their own superiorities, which provided, on the one hand, a (theoretically) untrammeled supremacy over the peasants and, on the other, a territorial base for resistance to the monarch, particularly when combined with a system of military land tenure. Aspirant absolutists therefore sought to dominate the peasantry directly, without relying on local intermediaries. Where this displacement of power was successfully achieved—as it was in Sweden, France, Spain, Prussia, Austria, and Russia—the responsibility for extracting the surplus from the peasantry had largely been assumed by the central state and the mechanism of surplus extraction changed from rent to tax. The local autonomy of the lords was thereby greatly reduced.

The other main characteristic of absolutist states was the hegemony that they exercised over the class that would eventually supersede the lords—the bourgeoisie. For the bourgeoisie, the absolutist state was important both as a means of controlling civil disorder within the towns and of protecting the towns themselves from the demands of individual lords. For the absolutist state, the bourgeoisie were important as a source of revenue, of personnel to fill the offices of state and, most importantly, as a social force that the monarchy could muster in the face of collective opposition by the lords. Yet this dependent relationship left the bourgeoisie as an influence upon the state, not a codeterminate (with the lords) of its class nature. Absolutism placed the bourgeoisie in a protected but subordinate place within the social order, which had the paradoxical effect of allowing socioeconomic advance while imposing political retardation.

Were absolutist states still feudal? Jane Whittle has argued: "Royal taxes became the early modern equivalent of the feudal exactions of the early modern period."[136] Bois similarly claims, on the basis of the French experience: "The two basic classes of society remained face to face. Only the methods by which one exploited the other had changed. The power of the prince henceforth protected that of the lord, extracting from peasant production whatever was needed to maintain the ruling class. Coexistence between the two forms of levy had become necessary, but it was difficult."[137] Brenner, however, has argued that absolutist France was not feudal. The "difficulty" to which Bois refers is indicative of two different forms of exploitation corresponding to the "two forms of levy." For Brenner, the state in prerevolutionary France "developed . . . as a class-like phenomenon . . . an independent extractor of the surplus."[138] It is difficult, however, to see how this position can be held for France alone, given that it was merely the most developed example of a general tendency. Characteristically, Wood has taken Brenner's position to its logical conclusion, arguing that absolutism was not only "class-like," but a distinct mode of production in its own right: "In some Western European cases, feudalism gave way not to capitalism but to absolutism, with its own non-capitalist modes of appropriation and politically constituted property."[139] More specifically: "The absolutist state was a centralized instrument of extra-economic surplus extraction, and office in the state was a form of property which gave its possessors access to peasant produced surpluses."[140] Absolutism then, is a pre-capitalist mode of production, not a state form characteristic of the transition from feudalism to capitalism. Benno Teschke has made a similar generalization: "[Absolutism] was a *sui generis* social formation, displaying a specific mode of government and determinate pre-modern and pre-capitalist domestic and international 'laws of motion.'"[141] There is, of course, a mode of production in Marxist theory that the state acts as the prime extractor of the surplus: the tributary mode. Was absolutism effectively its Western variant?

The concept of a tributary mode, if not the actual term, originates with Marx himself: "In the case of the slave relationship, the serf relationship, and the relationship of tribute (where the primitive community is under consideration), it is the slaveowner, the feudal lord or the state receiving tribute that is the owner of the product and therefore its seller."[142] Samir Amin, the figure most responsible for popularizing the concept of the tributary mode, characterizes it as "the separation of society into two main classes: the peasantry, organized in communities, and the ruling class, which monopolizes the functions of the given societies, political organization and exacts a tribute (not in commodity form) from the rural community."[143] Wickham subsequently elaborated on this basic definition, writing that the tributary mode involves a "'state class' based on a public institution, with political rights to extract surplus from a peasantry that it does not tenurially control." Although he subsequently changed his position, Wickham originally argued that the crucial distinction between the tributary and feudal modes lay in the means by which the surplus is collected from the peasantry. In the former, it is through payment of taxation to the state; in the latter, through payment of rent to private landowners.[144] For Wickham, there are two further differences between the tributary mode and the feudal. The first is that a tributary state taxes landowners in addition to peasants. The second is that the tributary mode allows far greater autonomy for the peasantry in the process of production than the feudal mode. As a result: "They represent two different economic systems, even if they can come together in some exceptional circumstances. Their differences, their antagonisms, lie in their divergent interventions in the peasant economy, just as their convergences lie in the fact that both are rooted in it. The same productive forces, however, can, be seen as giving rise to two separate modes of production."[145] Eric Wolf gives an example of this convergence from pre-colonial India, where the operation of the tributary mode involved domination of the direct producers by the local agents of the state—either military bureaucrats with lifetime grants of land (*jagirdars*) or hereditary chiefs (*zamindars*)—responsible for collecting the tribute, part of which went toward their own revenue, part to the central state. "The critical difference from the later English practice was that these rights were not, properly speaking, rights of property in land, but rather claims on people's labor and the products of that labor." In some cases the central state by-passed the zamindars completely to extract the surplus directly. In others the za-mindars had a feudal relationship with the peasants.[146]

One key question is therefore whether extraction of surplus as rent by a landowning class on the one hand and extraction of surplus as tax by a state on the other constitute different modes of production. Marx himself had suggested that there was no essential difference between the feudal and tributary modes. He noted that where peasants form what he called a "natural community," then "the surplus labor for the nominal landowner can only be extorted from them by extra-economic compulsion, whatever the form this might assume": "If there are no private land-lords but it is the state, as in Asia, which confronts them directly as simultaneously landowner and sovereign, rent and tax coincide, or rather there does not exist any tax distinct from this form of ground-rent."[147] In response to Wickham, Halil Berk-tay and John Haldon similarly pointed out that, in terms of the central exploitative relationship with the peasantry, there was no difference between these; the differ-ence lay in the extent and nature of state power.[148] The most serious theoretical at-tempt to argue this case was subsequently made by Haldon in relation to the tributary states of the East. He argues that there is no fundamental difference be-tween tax and rent such as would allow us to regard them as constituent of different modes of production: "The fundamental difference between these two forms of the same mode of surplus extraction lies in fact in a political relation of surplus appro-priation and distribution." On this basis the relationship of peasants to feudal land-lords on the one hand and to tributary states on the other is essentially the same, even down to the level of day-to-day interference:

> The forms of intervention vary quantitatively, to a degree; but states and their agents could also be just as involved in the process of production and extraction of surplus as landlords (indeed, in Mughul India, for example, tax-farmers also involved them-selves in these relationships). Where both exist it does not imply that there are two

different ruling classes (for the state represents the landlords), merely that the state bureaucracy and the landlords represent different factions of the same ruling class and their conflicts are not based on a different relationship to the direct producers, but over the distribution of the surplus extracted from them.[149]

In other words, the tributary and feudal modes are variations on the same mode of production, but it is the tributary variant that has been the most widespread, both in the sense that it embraced the majority of the world's population after the fall of the Roman Empire and that these areas remained the most economically developed until the eighteenth century. However, it is perfectly possible to accept that there is no fundamental difference between tax and rent without also accepting that there is no fundamental difference between the tributary and feudal modes.

The problem with the latter position is that it restricts the concept of a mode of production solely to relations of exploitation; but as Perry Anderson has pointed out: "*All* modes of production in class societies prior to capitalism extract surplus labor from the immediate producers by means of extra-economic coercion." His solution is to argue "pre-capitalist modes of production cannot be defined *except* via their political, legal and ideological superstructures, since these are what determine the type of extra-economic coercion that specifies them."[150] But this argument too presents problems. As Paul Hirst explains, it "*means that there can be as many modes of production as there are distinct legal-political constitutions and forms of extra-economic sanction which follow on from them.*"[151] There is, however, no need to distinguish between pre-capitalist modes solely on the basis of their superstructural forms. Even if the process of exploitation is essentially the same, modes of production also involve relations between the exploiters themselves, crucially how their relations are mediated by the state. Curiously, Wickham has noted this while retaining his later belief that two modes are identical:

> The basic economic division inside class societies thus becomes simply that between societies based on taking surpluses from peasants (or, for that matter, household-based artisans) and those based on withholding surplus from wage laborers. . . . It does not mean that the Chinese or Roman empires, the Frankish kingdoms, and the feudal world of the eleventh century were exactly the same, for an essential *structural* difference remains between the first two, and tax-raising state systems (with aristocracies subject to them), and the second two, polities dominated by aristocratic rent-taking and Marc Bloch's politics of land.[152]

It is because of these different relationships between their respective ruling classes and their states that Banaji has argued that the tributary mode has to be seen as distinct from feudalism:

> The tributary mode of production may be defined as a mode of production where the state controls *both the means of production and the ruling class*, and has "unlimited disposal over the total surplus labor of the population." . . . The relations of production of the tributary mode . . . involved *both* the control of peasant-labor by the state (the state-apparatus as the chief instrument of exploitation) *and* the drive to forge

a unified imperial service based on the subordination of the ruling class to the will of the ruler. . . . The bond between the ruler and the ruling elite within the wider circles of the ruling class was the basis on which *new* states were constructed, and the state itself bureaucratized to create an efficient tool of administration. The autocratic centralism of the tributary mode and its backbone in the recruitment of a pliant nobility were not just "political superstructures" to some self-contained state, they were essential moments of the structuring and organization of the economy (*of the relations of production*).[153]

The feudal mode of production was a peripheral, mainly Western European mode of production. According to Janet Abu-Lughod: "By definition . . . restructuring is said to occur when *players who were formerly peripheral* begin to occupy more powerful positions in the system and when *geographical zones formerly marginal to intense interactions* become foci and even control centers of such interchanges."[154] The restructuring of the medieval regional systems in favor of the hitherto marginal and peripheral region of Western Europe began from the second half of the fourteenth century, co-extensive with the emergence of capitalism. Abu-Lughod explains this by reference to the "disarray" of the Orient as a result of the "progressive fragmentation" of hitherto unified trading routes and the greater impact of the Black Death in the East, as it was carried along the far more developed urban sea routes.[155] There were however more general problems in the tributary world, some of which have been identified by Haldon:

> Tributary relations of production can in fact only be transformed or replaced by capitalist relations of production when there takes place a proletarianization of the peasantry, that is, when a large proportion of the producing population is separated from their means of production, hence creating a free and available supply of labor which can then be exploited within capitalist production relations. . . . The "capital" available to merchants and traders is always only potentially capital, insofar as, without a proletariat whose labor-power can be transformed into relative surplus value, it functions merely as a medium of simple exchange.

The proletariat began to form in Europe, but not in the Eastern tributary empires:

> Partly this was because expansionist European traders arrived in time to dominate Asian trade and to invert the pre-existing relations of commercial exploitation between the Indian sub-continent and its periphery. In addition, the different ways in which the institutional forms of tributary relations were structured in India—in particular, the self-contained and semi-autonomous nature of rural production relations, the integration of merchant and trading groups into a balanced set of social relationships through lineage identities and demands—are central elements in this picture.[156]

The most serious obstacle to capitalist development—and here we return to the first of Carling's enabling conditions—lay however in the very nature of these states. The significance of the distinction between feudal and tributary modes lies in their relative ability to prevent the development of capitalism beyond a certain point and consequently the possibility of overthrow by a potential new ruling class based on that mode of production. Mielants rightly warns: "One must be careful to avoid the construction of a new and more sophisticated version of typical Oriental Despotism vs. European free-market orientated and democratic urban communities. It seems unlikely that the European nobility as a whole was less 'despotic' than the non-European nobility."[157] The European nobility was not intrinsically less oppressive than its Asian equivalents, but simply operated within a different structural context. Notwithstanding his belief in the identity of the feudal and tributary modes, Wickham has rightly emphasized how the state under the latter enjoys two advantages over that in the former. First, "tax-based states were ... richer and more powerful than rent-based, land-based, states." Second, and more important even than wealth, was stability, which Wickham illustrates with the Byzantine example:

> Even at the weakest point of the eastern empire, roughly 650–750, Byzantine political structures were more coherent than those of even the best-organized land-based states, such as Lombard Italy in the same period; tax-based structures had more staying power, and the risk of decentralization, a feature of all land-based states, was less great. If taxation disappeared as the basis of any given state, then, no matter how much cultural, ideological, or legislative continuity there was ... it would not prevent fundamental changes in political resources, infrastructure and practice.[158]

Callinicos too has emphasized the effectiveness of the Asian tributary states in preventing the growth of an independent class of lords and their transformation into capitalist landlords or manufacturers while, at the other end of the class spectrum, preserving the peasantry as a source of tax income. It is therefore precisely the weakness of feudal compared to tributary societies that provides capitalism with the most fertile ground to develop, notably through the greater direct involvement of the lords in the productive process and the existence of fragmented power structures which encourage the flow of commodities.[159]

The spaces that allowed the emergence of capital should not be understood as synonymous with the towns but instead identified with what Patricia Crone refers to as the "extreme dispersal of power" characteristic of feudal Europe.[160] In fact, as I have already argued, towns were no more intrinsically capitalist than the countryside was intrinsically feudal. In the case of both town and country the issue was how far capitalist production had been established and to what extent those controlling that production had achieved political power on their own behalf. Examples of this could be found in England, Flanders, and the Netherlands where, as Ogilvie notes, "craft guild and merchant companies could easily be evaded by moving industry outside the towns," because in all these cases either "the state was too weak to provide support or enforcement for the institutional privileges of towns over the countryside," or "the large number of cities created too much inter-urban competition for effective capture by a single city of state enforcement for its privileges against all the other cities."[161] Medieval cloth production in England was policed by both guilds and local governments that were also dominated by the guilds, which inspired the flight of production to the countryside: "Free of borough and guild taxes, and with easy access to cheap wool and a good water supply, rural cloth workers in Yorkshire increased production.

As early as 1300, York and Beverley were facing competition from at least eight other cities. Thereafter, and at an accelerating pace, the manufacturing and finishing, especially of the cheaper kerseys, was undertaken away from, and at the expense of, the older urban centers."[162] Ironically, in some parts of England in particular, rural industry was established in the "common" areas, which fell outside feudal control altogether: "The heath and woodland system were often outside the parochial system, or their large parishes were left with only a distant chapelry, so there was freedom from parson as well as squire. . . . In such areas feudal ties of subordination hardly existed, and there was little obstacle to the intrusion of rural industry in search of cheap part-time labor."[163]

There were of course regional variations even within Western Europe; those areas that remained decentralized had the advantage here, at least in the period before the bourgeois revolution. Bois has argued that feudalism both originated in and reached its highest level of development in France. England, on the other hand: "Sufficiently near to the most advanced feudal societies to have high levels of technical resource at her disposal, she was also sufficiently underdeveloped to have escaped the consequences of the fossilization of social relations which feudal reorganization induced." What Bois is in fact describing is the operation of uneven development, "the relative backwardness of England's social evolution as compared to France was to prove its trump card in the transition from feudalism to capitalism."[164] But if "the advantages of backwardness" were indeed decisive, then there is no need to invoke such ahistorical causations as the "luck" invoked by John Hobson to explain how in Western Europe the last came to be first.[165] The tributary world was hampered precisely because the greater level of development had produced a state capable of preventing systemic challenges—as opposed to, say, periodic peasant revolts—from emerging.

The Chinese Empire encompassed a great civilization with important scientific and technical accomplishments, surpassing those of Europe. As Chris Wickham has pointed out, there is no reason to suppose that Europe, even Western Europe, was in a privileged position to begin development toward industrial capitalism during the early feudal period. Similar and, in some areas, superior, levels of development can be found in Song China at exactly the same time: "Chinese ploughs were in many respects more sophisticated than European ones until the eighteenth century." Rice yields were far higher than cereal yields (50–100:1 compared to 4:1):

> Furthermore, no one could claim that the sophisticated and complex irrigation techniques of the Yangtze Delta were not intensive, or that they did not need highly organized local collective cooperation, at least on the level of the northern European common field and probably rather more so. By the twelfth century, several substantial areas of China specialized in cash crops such as tea or fruits that could be exchanged for staples in a structured market system. The social division of labor was developing, and merchant capital was based on a complex credit system. Under the Sung, population density was higher than Europe's with no signs of Malthusian dangers (new strains of rice could crop twice or three times a year). Artisanal work was flourishing, and in

the crucial areas of textiles and ceramics was technologically highly sophisticated, well above European levels.[166]

"Overall," claims Kenneth Pomeranz, "China was closer to market-driven agriculture than was most of Europe, including most of Western Europe."[167] It was closer, but it never arrived and the key reason was political. As Mark Elvin points out, from the advent of the Song dynasty in AD 960, China also began to "diverge significantly" from Europe, not only in respect of its inventiveness and productivity, but in the development of the state: "Chinese society, like that of Europe at this time, developed in the direction of manorialism . . . but since the state retained control over defense functions, as it did not in Europe, there was no feudal superstructure . . . in the sense of a dominant specialist military class disposing of fiefs granted in return for military service and ruling these as more or less unquestioned lords."[168] It is important to understand that these developments did not lead to absolute retardation of the economy. John Hall writes: "For market relations to gain autonomy, extensive networks are needed. In China, such extensive networks were provided by the polity. However, imperial rule was, perhaps could only be, based upon the negative tactics of horizontal linkages that it could not control, and it was because of this that bureaucratic interference eventually proved deleterious for the economy."[169] But "market relations" did exist in China; as we have already seen, markets and merchants are quite compatible with non- or, more precisely, precapitalist modes of production and may even have been essential to them, as was certainly the case in China.[170] What did not exist were capitalist social relations. The Chinese bureaucratic tributary state acted to suppress emergent class forces and the dangerous ideas associated with them. As late as the eighteenth century critical writings were censored or destroyed. The high point of this "literary inquisition," as it was known, ran between 1779 and 1789—the events of the latter year showing the distance that had opened up between China and Europe.[171] Reading the work of one leading intellectual in seventeenth-century China, Wang Fu-Chih (1619–92), it is difficult not to see him as a predecessor to Smith in Scotland or Barnave in France; but unlike them, his thoughts led to no immediate results.[172] "China has been long one of the richest, that is one of the most fertile, most cultivated, most industrious and most populous countries in the world," wrote Smith himself in 1776: "It seems, however, to have been long stationary." Yet as he also noted, "Though it may perhaps [have] stood still, [it] does not seem to go backwards."[173] These comments embody the contradictions in the late eighteenth-century Enlightenment view of China: in many ways admiring, but in others seeing it as an example of the stationary state that Political Economy most feared. Adam Ferguson noted that China was an exception to the pattern of stadial development he and his cothinkers detected in Europe: "The succession of monarchs has been changed; but no revolutions have affected the state."[174] It was not that revolutions failed to take place: China had seen dynasty after dynasty fall to successive peasant revolts, to an extent quite unknown in Europe. The point, however, is that although the dynasties may have fallen, tributary relations of production, and the state associated with them, continued unaffected in any fundamental way. After initially welcoming the Taiping rebellion in China on its outbreak in 1851, Marx was subsequently to see this as another manifestation of the recurrent Chinese dilemma of "constant immobility in their social substructure, with unceasing change in the persons and clans that gain control of the political superstructure."[175]

The Ottoman imperial state did not display the same underlying continuities of the Chinese, and may only have achieved its final form, like the Austrian and Russian, in response to the second crisis of feudalism during the seventeenth century.[176] Nevertheless, the empire imposed severe restrictions on private property in land and therefore little space for new approaches to production and exploitation to arise. There is nothing in the either the Koran or the Sunnah that is intrinsically hostile to capitalism.[177] Nor is there anything inherently stagnant about Islamic societies; but they stand as further examples of how ruling classes are consciously able to use state power, "the superstructure," to prevent new and threatening classes from forming, with all that implies about the thwarting of intellectual developments. Abbasidic relations were never classically feudal, since the state refused to grant land in perpetuity, but only in the form of the *iqta*, by which it was held for a limited period of time, thus preventing both the establishment of local sovereignty and the possibility of hereditary possession but also discouraging improvement: "The grantees, who lived in the cities and knew that before long the estates would be taken from them or that they themselves would ask for a change, did not look after their maintenance."[178] There was a period toward the end of the twelfth century when the urban bourgeoisie did manage to take advantage of the temporary fragmentation of the empire to assume a political role and even establish city-republics comparable to those in Central and Southern Europe, but also like their European counterparts they fell to a combination of local princes and the imperial state. With the reassertion of tributary power came the suppression of the intellectual and technological advances that had been characteristic of the Arab-Islamic world during the European "Dark Ages": "The great technological progress had been made when freedom of enterprise and the *tiraz* system—factories which were great industrial enterprises—was flourishing. These great enterprises could afford experiments which resulted in technological innovations. In the age of the Seldjukids and the Ayyubids the princes curtailed freedom of enterprise, established monopolies, and impose heavy taxes on the workshops."[179]

As representatives of the main exploiter, state officials displayed a quite conscious hostility to potential alternative sources of power, hence the bias it displayed toward small-scale commerce and the hostility it displayed toward large mercantile capital. Consequently, merchants tended to be from external "nations," Jews, Greeks, or Armenians—not from the native Arab or Turkish populations. As Mielants writes, "the socioeconomic splendor of the medieval Islamic society cannot be denied" and merchant capitalists contributed toward it: "But the presence of capitalists does not necessarily imply the successful creation of an endurable capitalist system in the long run."[180] "Asking why the Scientific Revolution did not occur in Islam," writes Pervez Hoodbhoy, exaggerating only slightly, "is practically equivalent as asking why Islam did not produce a powerful bourgeois class."[181] Take the example of the Tunisian writer Ibn el Khaldun (1332–1402), author of the *Kitab Al-Ilbar* or *Book of Examples* (usually referred to in English as *The Muqaddimah* or *Introduction to History*). His sociological insights identified the continuing struggle between civilizations based on the one hand on towns and traders (*hadarah*) and on the other on tribes and holy men (*badawah*), the two endlessly alternating as the dominant forces within the Muslim world.[182] Smith and his colleagues in the Historical School of the Scottish Enlightenment could develop a theory that saw societies develop and progress upward from one "mode of subsistence" to another because they had seen this movement in England, and wished to see it reproduced in Scotland. Ibn el Khaldun saw only cyclical repetition in the history of Islamic society and could not envisage any way to break the cycle. His work could not transcend the society it sought to theorize.

Of all the great tributary states the Mughal Empire was perhaps the one in which progress toward capitalist relations of production were most advanced. By the seventeenth century, several changes to Indian economic life, including the increased monetary basis of commercial activity, had established the necessary conditions for capitalist development to at least the same extent as those areas of Western Europe still under absolutist rule. Irfan Habib makes this assessment:

> We find that in both agricultural and non-agricultural production, production for the market formed a very large sector. In agriculture, there existed *khwud kast* cultivation, based on hired labor, representing an advance, in form, towards capitalist farming. In handicrafts, merchant capital had developed considerably and had brought artisans under control through forms of the putting-out system. But manufacturing as an established form was yet largely outside of the sphere of commodity production. In other words, capital was by and large merchant capital, and though the economy was fairly highly monetized, domestic industry still predominated.[183]

A merchant class with large amounts of money capital had emerged, particularly along the western coastal regions, tied closely to the Mughal rulers and the markets provided by their empire. But Christopher Bayly has argued that capitalist relations, if anything, became more dispersed with a range of different actors including "the petty kings, the revenue and military entrepreneurs, the great bankers and warrior peasant lords of the villages" at their centers.[184] The decline of the Mughals between 1680 and 1750 did not in itself lead to the dissolution of indigenous Indian capitalism, but it did mean that there was no longer a central authority to balance or mediate between these different competing interests, which were now overlaid with princely political rivalries:

> Rulers and revenue farmers needed credit to tide them over the periods between harvests as they were required to equip and pay armies month by month throughout

the year. This encouraged them to squeeze the merchants and village magnates. Merchants for their part avoided direct management of agrarian taxation and were reluctant to disburse resources which they might need in commodity trades. It was in the interest of the village magnates to construct their own networks of credit in the countryside. Above all, the successor states to the Mughals were often in conflict with each other, fighting for cash revenues and for the still limited pool of agricultural and artisan labor.[185]

It is quite conceivable that, undisturbed, at least part of the former Mughal Empire could have developed into a fully developed capitalist economy, initially in the spaces which were opening up across this increasingly fragmented society, in the same way as had happened in parts of Western Europe. But its inhabitants were not permitted the time in which the process might have taken place, and into the void entered the Western Europeans themselves, in the form of the British East India Company. As Satish Chandra concludes: "It is not necessary to enter into the controversy whether Indian society was capable, on its own, of developing from merchant capitalism to industrial capitalism. What is significant is that the growth of merchant capitalism itself was arrested in the eighteenth century, and industrial capitalism hardly showed any signs of developing till the third quarter of the nineteenth or the early twentieth century."[186]

The consequences of failing to make the breakthrough to capitalism then left these societies vulnerable to the predations of those that had. As John Darwin has written, from around 1830, the peoples of what he calls the "Outer World" beyond Europe and North America "found themselves in a race against time: a race to 'self-strengthen' before European power and wealth could overwhelm their defenses."[187] One indication of their decline consequent on a failure to win this race can be seen in the increasing ability of these states to cope with natural disaster. Davis has shown that in 1743 and 1744 the Qing regime in China was able to provide relief to the northern area of Hebei after an El Niño event had caused the monsoon to fail, with consequent drought and crop failure, at the same time as millions in feudal Europe were dying. "Whereas in 1876 the Chinese state—enfeebled and demoralized after the failures of the Tongzhi [T'ung-chih] Restoration's domestic reforms—was reduced to desultory cash relief augmented by private donations and humiliating foreign charity, in the eighteenth century it had both the technology and political will to shift grain massively between regions and, thus, relieve hunger on a larger scale than any previous polity in world history." Even the Mogul regime in India, although weaker and lacking the resources of the Qing, was able to provide grain and to hold the price down to the extent that starvation was avoided: "Although the British insisted that they had rescued India from 'timeless hunger,' more than one official was jolted when Indian nationalists quoted from an 1878 study published in the prestigious *Journal of the Statistical Society* that contrasted thirty-one serious famines in 120 years of British rule against only seventeen recorded famines in the entire previous two millennia."[188]

The Chinese "restoration" to which Davis refers—the T'ung-chih or "union for order," might seem comparable with the Japanese Meiji or "enlightened rule,"but as the outcome he describes suggests, the former in reality was quite different. "What this great effort could not achieve (and was not meant to achieve) was the transformation of China into a modern state on the Western model,"writes Darwin: "It might even be argued that the real priority of the 'restoration' was precisely that: to restore the authority of the Confucian state and its ethos of frugality and social discipline, not to break the Confucian mold."[189] The only example of a tributary state that was overthrown before any significant capitalist development had taken place therefore remained Japan, largely because it contained a social group capable of recognizing that what was happening to China could foreshadow their own fate, if no challenge to the existing order was successfully mounted, enabling the transition to capitalism to be achieved. But no matter which societies had developed capitalism first, they would have been compelled to respond in the same way to the imperatives of the system. There is no basis for thinking that a Chinese or Turkish capitalism would have been immune to these imperatives any more than Japanese capitalism was: cultural "difference" is of little significance before the demands of competitive accumulation.

All the great tributary empires were venerable when absolutism was a novelty. "Unlike Asiatic monarchy,"writes Victor Kiernan, "absolutism was an unstable transitional form, even if over a wide area it was prolonged for centuries."[190] There is then a connection between the tributary and absolutist states. Russia, in particular, might best be considered not as an example of what Anderson called "the Eastern variant" of absolutism, but rather of "the Western variant" of the tributary state.[191] Indeed, the emergence of absolutism can be seen as an attempt to introduce into Europe the mode of production and corresponding state form typical of Asia, the Middle East, North Africa, and even parts of Latin America (Mexico and Peru), in order to impose a similar "fetter on production."Amin suggests that absolutism would have been the Western variant of the tributary mode, but that it arrived too late to arrest the development of capitalism in the same way that the Chinese state repeatedly succeeded in doing after 1300.[192] Capitalism already existed in Western and Central Europe— albeit unevenly and with varying degrees of implantation—at the point when the absolutist states were in the process of formation. It was this lag that created the conditions of possibility for the initial breakthroughs in those territories where capitalism was strongest and absolutism weakest. Nevertheless, even if the absolutist states were incapable of completely containing capitalism, they could still prevent it from achieving dominance unless they were overthrown. Who achieved this task?

THE BOURGEOISIE AS A REVOLUTIONARY LEADERSHIP

In his book, *Categories and Methods of Historical Science* (1984), the Russian historian Mikhail Barg distinguished three "projects" in the bourgeois revolutions, past, present, and future. These have been summarized by Christopher Hill:

In the German Reformation and Peasant War "the project of the past" mobilized a medieval-type social movement—peasantry and burghers: it was the culmination of past history. The "project of the present" was that of the capitalist class forces grown up within feudal society. Two modes of production were in conflict, and so the revolution turned into a national political struggle for *national* ends. This was a new type of *class war*, distinct from peasant revolts which had great destructive force but no constructive national policy. The peasantry *could* not change the social structure. Hence the bourgeoisie could claim to be genuinely "national" in a way the peasantry could not. The "project of the present" represented the maximum possible at the time: hence bourgeois hegemony. It was transcended only by the "project of the future"— the leveling aspirations of the plebs, which would have led to the most complete clearing of the country from the Middle Ages. The "project of the future" emerged at the highest point of the revolution (Diggers, Babeuf), but it was not feasible at that stage in history.[193]

Although Barg's model involves the schematicism typical of Stalinist Russian historiography, his assessment of the capacities of the various classes is essentially correct. As we saw in the previous chapter, not every class is capable of making a social revolution. We can see these limitations most clearly in relation to the peasantry. Even after the dissolution of serfdom in Western Europe, which had been accomplished by the late fifteenth century, the peasantry remained the central exploited class in feudal society, the class upon whose labor that society was based. Yet although the peasants certainly continued to struggle against the landowners who exploited them, they were not ultimately victorious in the sense of replacing the landowners as a new ruling class within a new society based on a new mode of production. The peasants may have attempted to moderate or remove the effect of the feudal system, but they had no alternative to it, simply a desire to escape the source of their exploitation. In this sense peasant revolts resemble those of slaves, although the former were of course vastly more numerous. There were three main obstacles to the peasantry becoming an independent revolutionary force during the transition to capitalism.

The first was that where collective activity by peasants did take place it was not always directed toward their masters but sometimes against other exploited or oppressed groups. When Pope Urban II preached a crusade to drive the Seljuk Turks from Asia Minor in 1095 the call was not only answered by feudal knights intent on plunder, land, and, of course, enacting God's will. The preaching of itinerant *prophetae* like Peter the Hermit also aroused thousands of the insecure peasant masses living in overcrowded, disease-ridden conditions to set off for Jerusalem and retake it from the infidels. At the heart of this movement—the so-called People's Crusade—was certainly deflected class anger: the cry of the quasi-mythical leader King Tafur—"Where are the poor folk who want property? Let them come with me!"—encapsulates the rational core of their religious enthusiasm. The way this was expressed, however, was not only in the massacre of Muslims in Jerusalem—for in this they were matched death-for-death by the knightly crusaders themselves—but in the massacres of Jews. In May and June 1096 the Episcopal towns of the Rhine, from Speyer to Worms to Mainz to Cologne and beyond were attacked by three armies of popular crusaders. The Jewish communities, which had been settled there for many centuries, were massacred, often against the wishes of the local ruling class, who found them useful. One group led by the itinerant preacher Gottschalk, entered Hungary where they began to pillage the local peasantry until they were massacred in turn by royal troops at Stuhlweissenburg.[194] And this was followed by four further explosions of anti-Semitic persecution "from below" between 1200 and 1450, as far north as Flanders and as far south as Spain.[195] When Marx and Engels wrote of the "idiocy of rural life," they were not suggesting that this was all there was to peasant existence, but neither was it simply a gratuitous insult.[196]

The second obstacle was that, even when collective activity was directed at the ruling class rather than convenient scapegoats, the lack of a societal alternative proved a fatal weakness. The local nature of the peasant vision, their inability to conceptualize the system as a whole, has led them, historically, to exonerate the ruler from the crimes of his officials. The peasants of 1381 in England believed the false promises of Richard II, but even if they had not, what could they have done with London? Even the examples of peasant success prove the point. None of the great European peasant revolts actually overthrew a state; but as Jean Chesneaux writes of China:

> The most important contribution of peasant movements in the historical play of forces in imperial China was in the overthrow of dynasties. The Ch'in regime (221–207 BC) was destroyed by peasant revolts; their leader Liu Pang proclaimed himself emperor and founded the Han dynasty (206–23 BC). In their turn, the later Han (AD 25–220), the T'ang and the Sung (AD 960–1279) were overthrown or irreparably weakened by great waves of peasant discontent. The Ming dynasty (1368–1644), which achieved power through popular revolts against the Mongols, was itself brought to an end by peasant rebellions under Chang Hsien-chung and Li Tzuch'eng, which were subsequently suppressed by the Manchus.[197]

As we saw in the previous section, none of these huge convulsions resulted in any fundamental change. As Trotsky observed:

> In ancient China revolutions brought the peasantry to power, or rather, the military leaders of peasant insurrections. That led each time to a redivision of the land and the establishment of a new "peasant" dynasty, after which history would begin again from the beginning with new concentration of land, a new aristocracy, a new system of usury, and a new uprising. So long as the revolution maintained its purely peasant character, society is incapable of emerging from these hopeless and vicious circles. Such was the basis of ancient Asiatic history, including ancient Russian history.[198]

We can see a similar pattern near the end of the era of bourgeois revolution. During the Mexican Revolution the armed Zapatista peasantry had succeeded in taking control of Mexico City by December 1914: six months later they had abandoned it, without establishing a new governmental apparatus. Eric Wolf writes of the "tragic ineptitude" revealed by both Villa and Zapata in their failure to "create a political machine that could govern the country." In one sense this is unfair: not personal inadequacy but class incapacity lay behind the incomprehension of the Mexican revolutionaries.[199] Adolfo Gilly explains why the conquest of the Mexican capital involved not the seizure of state power but the creation of a power vacuum: "The exercise of power demands a program. The application of a program requires a policy. A policy means a party. The peasants did not have, could not have, any of these things."[200]

The third obstacle was that 'the peasantry' were not homogenous, but internally differentiated with often opposed interests; indeed, one of the major effects of peasant success in ending serfdom, in both Western Europe after the crisis of the fourteenth century and Russia after 1861, was to allow a layer to emerge whose interests were separate from both the tenants below them and the great landowners above them. We have already discussed this process in England and France: did the Russian *mir* develop in a different way? There is in fact some doubt as to whether it ever existed in the form that is usually thought. The idea of the peasant commune seems to have originated with the German Catholic nobleman, August von Haxthausen, a major figure in the Romantic Movement in the German Lands.[201] Haxthausen claimed that the commune was the basis of peasant economy and society in a book published in 1846 after his travels in Russia, and his views were subsequently adopted by early populists like Herzen and Chernychevsky. Partly as a result of his influence over Russian reformers the Emancipation Act of 1861, which formally ended serfdom, introduced collective ownership of the land, but this was an innovation or, at best, a generalization from a geographically limited form of social organization. Recent investigation into one average estate, Voshchazkniko, in Yaroslav province, has produced the following conclusions:

> Communal land was not the basis of a self-sufficient household economy, its repartition was far from being harmonious, and the larger shares allocated to richer peasants seem to have been a form of progressive taxation. There was no correlation between family size and size of communal holding. There was no communal property in anything but land. The commune was not "patriarchal" either in the sense that its eldest members ran it, or in the sense that an unusually high proportion of households were headed by men. Communal offices were shirked or avoided; those elected often hired others in their place. Poverty was far from impossible and in some cases extreme, though welfare provision was resisted by the commune and had to be enforced by the landlord. Private property in land and dwellings was widespread. Far from avoiding market transactions, serfs were active participants in land, labor and credit markets. Equality was neither aimed at nor achieved; social stratification was at least as pronounced as in pre-industrial or early industrial western and central Europe, and was reinforced trans-generationally through inheritance.[202]

In the Russian case as in the English, a minority had effectively left their peasant origins behind to become part of the rural capitalist class. It was this minority, rather than the peasantry as a whole, which would provide part of the leadership of the bourgeois revolutions, which observation brings us back to the question of the bourgeoisie itself.

As we saw in chapter 15, skepticism over the revolutionary capacity of the bourgeoisie has of course become the stock-in-trade of revisionism, particularly in relation to the French Revolution. Sarah Maza argues that in "a society in crisis," where "new sources of social order and cohesion had to be sought . . . the bourgeoisie in either its narrow or wider senses would have been a most unlikely place to start."[203] Other historians have been more generally dismissive. According to Murray Bookchin:

> In the Marxist and liberal view of these [bourgeois] revolutions, it was bankers, merchants, manufacturers, and other entrepreneurs—the predatory men who were amassing enormous wealth in the eighteenth century—who formed the class vanguard of the great revolutions, presumably in spite of themselves. . . . But if it is true that capitalism is globally supreme today, no class in history has been more craven, cowardly, and fearful of social change (especially change involving the "dark people," as they called the underprivileged) than the entrepreneurs who peopled the commercial centers of Europe and America during the eighteenth century. As a class the bourgeoisie has *never* been politically revolutionary, let alone insurgent.[204]

There have indeed been liberals who have held this view; but as we saw in Part Two, from Marx onwards thinkers in the classical Marxist tradition took a much more nuanced view of the bourgeoisie than Bookchin suggests, without dismissing altogether its role as a revolutionary class.[205] Nevertheless, it is true that several different social groups or fractions other than the bourgeoisie have been responsible for leading the transformation in pre-capitalist or colonial states in ways conducive to capitalist development. In this context it may be worth temporarily refocusing the title of this book to ask another, related question: how revolutionary were the bourgeoisie in the bourgeois revolutions?

We first need to establish what it meant to be a member of the bourgeoisie during the feudal era. Paul Corcoran writes:

> In France the term "bourgeois" originally had a reasonably precise meaning, dating back to the period of feudal consolidation and referring to the inhabitants of the enclosed or fortified area surrounding the castle of the local lord for whom they also performed particular duties and for which they were afforded a certain legal status. It is from this point of origin that the notion of bourgeois as a town-dweller derives.[206]

Most European languages have analogous terms to *burgeis* in the original Old French: *burgerij* in Dutch, *burgher* in German, *borgesia* in Italian, *burzuazja* in Polish, and *burguesía* in Spanish. Some Marxists appear to believe that these etymological origins remove any need for further discussion. "A bourgeoisie, if the term is to mean anything at all, is a class based on towns; that is what the word means," wrote Anderson in 1966: "It is ludicrous to call a landowning class a 'bourgeoisie'—one might as well call artisans a peasantry.[207] Wood agrees: "The burgher or bourgeois is, by definition, a town dweller."[208] But, as Corcoran further notes, over time the original topographical terms began to be used in an additional, normative sense: "As feudal society developed and the capitalist element within, the term also took on a pejorative meaning in the mouths of the aristocrats, for whom the bourgeois were avaricious, hypocritical, servile, uncultivated and interested in money above all."[209]

For revisionists, it is this lack of social definition that characterizes the bourgeoisie. Maza writes that "bourgeois" is "an extremely slippery term"; to be bourgeois was to be consigned to a "holding category," both the term and the social experience it suggested were "unstable": "To be bourgeois was to be in transit, uncomfortable about your social identity, with workers muttering against you and noblemen sneering at your manners."[210] The bourgeoisie apparently had no internal coherence as a class "for itself," but was defined instead almost entirely by forces external to it. David Bell claims that the revisionists have demonstrated the impossibility of identifying either "a 'bourgeois' social group possessing a distinct relationship to the means of production," or "a group united by a common assertion of 'bourgeois' identity" in 1789.[211] Maza, for example, writes: "Unlike both aristocracies, whose existence usually rests on a combination of legal distinctions and kinship patterns, and rural and urban working classes, which are united by common forms and objects of labor, the middle class exists only in relation to other groups." In fact, *all* social classes exist, "only in relation to other groups," or more precisely, in relation to other social classes. Nevertheless, the supposed exceptionalism of the bourgeois case allows Maza to reduce its existence to a question of "discourse": "whether and how it is named and invested with social, political, moral, or historical importance."[212]

For political Marxists the bourgeoisie is in any case irrelevant: our attention should be focused instead on capitalism and capitalists. This is a subject that has particularly exercised Wood:

> We have got so used to the identification of bourgeois with capitalist that the presuppositions secreted in this conflation have become invisible to us ... in its French form, the word used to mean nothing more than someone of non-noble status who, while he worked for a living, did not generally dirty his hands and used his mind more than his body for work. That old usage tells us nothing about capitalism, and is likely to refer to a professional, an office-holder, or an intellectual no less than to a merchant.[213]

Neal Wood summarizes the supposed distinction in this way: "One can be bourgeois, in the narrow traditional sense, without being a capitalist, and the converse is also true."[214] On this basis, Benno Teschke can claim that, "while the English revolution was not bourgeois, it was capitalist; and while the French Revolution was bourgeois, it was not capitalist."[215] Do these authors then see the bourgeoisie as a distinct class in its own right, separate from but overlapping with the capitalist class? If so, given that Marxists do not treat class as culturally defined, what socioeconomic role does the bourgeoisie play, if not that of personified capital? In effect, they seem to regard the bourgeoisie either as a Weberian status group or as a residual (or as Maza has it, a "holding") category for those who do not fit into one or other of the main economic classes. For supporters of capitalism the elevation of capitalists above the bourgeoisie poses no difficulties, theoretical or otherwise. "The dramatic difference between the two classes is obscured by Marxist periodization," writes Liah Greenfield:

> But the fact is that these two classes had nothing in common (or, at least, as little as any two different classes in society): One [the bourgeoisie] was docile, interested in security, ashamed of its social position; the other [the capitalist class] adventurous, achievement-orientated, and self assertive. Their collective tempers, their interests, outlooks, and styles—everything that could characterize them as communities, that is, classes in a meaningful sense—were different. Moreover, in distinction to the bourgeoisie, which was many centuries old, the capitalist class was only emerging in France in the late eighteenth century. It evolved out of the bourgeoisie, it is true, but also out of sectors of the nobility, and, in any case, like other new social groups, such as the intellectuals, it did not cultivate collective memory that would emphasize its genetic lineage: there was a break in continuity.[216]

In fact, the kind of theoretical convolutions implied by the distinction between "bourgeois" and "capitalist" are quite unnecessary. As Elizabeth Fox Genovese and Eugene Genovese point out: "The use of a single term for ... different social entities causes problems, but when most Marxists speak of the [French] Revolution as bourgeois they are referring specifically to the national consolidation of bourgeois social relations of production in the sense that all the great nineteenth-century social theorists understood them, not to the specific careers of a small merchant from Arles, or a *rentier* from Nimes."[217] By the time Marx and Engels—surely two of the "great nineteenth-century social theorists"—used the term "bourgeoisie" in the 1840s, it stood, in relation to town-dwellers, for something both shallower than previously (because it excluded the new class of urban industrial laborers) and wider (because it included rural capitalists). There is therefore no inherent contradiction in Edward Thompson referring to the rule of an "agrarian bourgeoisie" in England after 1688.[218] In part then, "bourgeoisie" meant capitalists, both urban and rural, in the literal sense of those who owned or controlled capital; but it also meant something wider.

In what is by far the most sensible discussion of this issue, Hal Draper describes the bourgeoisie as a whole as involving "a social penumbra around the hard core of capitalists proper, shading out into the diverse social elements that function as servitors or hangers-on of capital without themselves owning capital."[219] It is important to understand that the components of this "penumbra" are *not* members of the petty bourgeoisie, who stand outside the capital-labor relationship and "earn their living by dint of their own labor and their own property."[220] On the contrary: according to Anderson, membership of the non-capitalist bourgeoisie "is typically composed ... of the gamut of professional, administrative and technical groups that enjoy life-conditions similar to capitalists proper—everything customarily included in the broader term 'bourgeoisie' as opposed to 'capital.'"[221] One way of thinking about the bourgeoisie is therefore to divide the notion of a socioeconomic class into its constituent parts: the bourgeoisie in general comprise the class in its "social" aspect; the section of the bourgeoisie who specifically own or control capital comprise the class in its "economic" aspect; the connection between capitalist and non-capitalist sections of the bourgeoisie is that both derive their income, directly or indirectly, from the extraction of surplus value from the proletariat.[222]

As we have seen, the bourgeoisie was originally as necessary, as intrinsic to feudalism as the peasantry—not in the sense that it was similarly exploited, but in the sense that the system required bankers and merchants as well as lawyers and bureaucrats to function. Once capitalism, as distinct from merchants' or usurers' capital, came into existence, it changed the nature of the bourgeoisie: the center of gravity of the class shifted. And if nothing else, the various fractions of the capitalist bourgeoisie can be credited, with recombining the preexisting elements of the feudal economy in an entirely new way. In this sense, as Louis Althusser wrote, the capitalist bourgeoisie "is indeed nothing other than the element predestined to unify all the other elements of the mode of production, the one that will transform it into another combination, that of the capitalist mode of production."[223] One might say that the decisive moment in the transformation of the bourgeoisie into a potential ruling class was when the non-capitalist sections began to either derive, or at least see the possibility of deriving, their income from the exploitation of workers rather than of peasants. It was not inevitable however that these possibilities would result in revolutionary consciousness.

Braudel long ago identified "the defection of the bourgeoisie" in Spain and Italy, areas in which crises took place in conditions where capitalism had either never developed or had regressed: "The bourgeoisie in the sixteenth century, committed to trade and the service of the crown, was always on the verge of disappearing." Their lack of self-consciousness was in part due to the very insecurities of commerce, in part because their relatively small numeric size made it difficult to see themselves as a distinct class, and in part because they wished to avoid the hostility of the nobles who constituted a major part of their market. Their impulse was always to compromise, to attempt to join the minor ranks of the aristocracy and invest in landowning, to accumulate capital, but because of the guaranteed return that land promised. "The bourgeoisie was not always pushed out, brutally liquidated," writes Braudel: "It turned class traitor."[224] Henry Kamen points out, however, that this was not the result of a moral failing on its part, because "if sectors of the bourgeoisie failed, it was because external conditions, rather than a conscious defection, determined their situation." In these conditions "the bourgeoisie felt that they belonged ultimately not to their present condition but to the rank which they aspired," which was that of the existing ruling class—although Kamen notes that the adoption of aristocratic ideals "did not necessarily lead to the withdrawal of capital from wealth formation."[225]

> There is indeed nothing to indicate that the sixteenth-century Castilian was congenitally unsuited to a business life.... All the signs ... seem to indicate that in the early sixteenth century there were very fair prospects for the development of a dynamic

"capitalist" element in Castille, which—like its equivalents in England and Holland—might gradually have imposed some of its ideas and values on the rest of society. The fact that these prospects were not realized would suggest that at some point adverse circumstances proved too strong, and that the enterprise of the north Castilian *bourgeoisie* failed to withstand a serious change for the worse in the country's economic and social climate.[226]

The decline of the Castilian bourgeoisie was not simply a consequence of the government incompetence and mismanagement that Elliott identifies as occurring in the sixteenth century, which need not itself have proved fatal; it was instead a purposive process undertaken with the intention of subduing bourgeois power. This was accomplished in part through the depletion of liquid capital in order to pay for Spanish participation in the Thirty Years' War, the accompanying forced reduction of interest rates and the consequent restoration of feudal land ownership as the primary source of income; in part through the conscious intervention of the monarchy to strengthen traditional aristocratic hierarchies by blocking social mobility.[227] "The contempt for commerce and manual labor, the lure of easy money from investment in *censos* and *juros* [taxes and mortgages], the universal hunger for titles of nobility and social prestige—all these, when combined with the innumerable practical obstacles in the way of profitable economic enterprise, had persuaded the bourgeoisie to abandon its unequal struggle, and throw in its lot with the unproductive upper class of society."[228]

John Berger has painted an evocative portrait of the type of bourgeoisie that remained in the condition of subalternity, drawn specifically from the Spanish case. Here the bourgeoisie was a creation of the imperial state and played the role of an economically unproductive bureaucracy, which could be sustained only as long as wealth flowed from the Americas and Flanders. Once this ceased:

> Chronic impoverishment set in; there was no attempt to develop the economy because this so-called middle class did not understand the link between capital and production: instead they sank back into provincial improvidence, proliferating only their "connexions."... The Spanish middle class ... had—even if they wore the same clothes and read some of the same books—little in common with their French or English or German contemporaries. Such middle-class virtues as there were in Spain were not created of necessity: if they existed they were cultivated theoretically. There had been no successful bourgeois revolution. In an absolutist state the middle class had no independent power and so the virtues of initiative, industriousness, non-conformism, thrift, scientific curiosity, had no reason to exist. On the contrary the history of the Spanish middle class had encouraged the very opposite traits.... The state bureaucracy had discouraged initiative and put a premium on safe laziness. It came to be thought that to work hard was to lose one's dignity. The energy of the Spanish middle class was turned to ritual, which bestows on events a significance gathered from the past and precludes innovation or the thought of it.[229]

But not all territorially based bourgeoisies could be accommodated and consequently adapt themselves to the pursuit of heroic inertia. Some made the shift from incorporation to at least partial independence. Hans Baron notes that the early Florentine bankers and financiers did not represent a threat to the feudal order: "Forming, as they did a foreign body in the noble feudal world and yet living at its expense, they were not the potential bearers of a new outlook on economic life." A distinction, however, needs to be drawn between them and the merchants who entered into production, thus—potentially at least—embodying a new form of social organization: "The new industrial merchant class of the woolen gild, whose interests were bound up with the majority of the population, was socially much more consistent than [the financiers] and had an outlook on life more independent of the traditions of the feudal world." Baron summarizes the difference as being that, "merchants and bankers in the thirteenth century had lived on the edge of the feudal world; in the fifteenth-century Florence they lived on the edge of an industrial society."[230] Jürgen Habermas writes in similar terms of the Hamburg bourgeoisie before the disasters of the Thirty Years' War:

> The "capitalists," the merchants, bankers, entrepreneurs, and manufacturers (at least where, unlike Hamburg, the towns could maintain their independence from the traditional rulers) belonged to that group of the "bourgeois" who, like the new category of scholars, were not really "burghers" in the traditional sense. . . . Unlike the great urban merchants and officials who, in former days, could be assimilated by the cultivated nobility of the Italian Renaissance courts, they could no longer be integrated *in toto* into the noble culture at the close of the Baroque period.[231]

As Habermas suggests with his reference to "scholars," as the bourgeoisie began to take shape as a potential alternative ruling class to the feudal nobility, new professions and social categories arose that immediately became part of it: journalists, doctors of medicine, public intellectuals who were not—or not necessarily—clerics or theologians.

In neither Italy nor Germany did the bourgeoisie succeed in making a revolution and consequently was forced backward into a position reminiscent of its earlier dependence. In those states where members of the bourgeoisie at least managed to retain an independent position in feudal society, they underwent a common experience of individual pride in their own achievements and class humiliation at the restrictions still imposed upon them. Members of the bourgeoisie in the broad sense were both conscious of and angered by the discrepancy between their growing wealth and their exclusion from certain social positions, let alone their distance from the exercise of political power. The contempt of the absolutist rulers was palpable. Here is James VI (of Scotland) and I (of England) writing in his late sixteenth-century guide to kingcraft, *Basilicon Doron*, nominally a letter to his eldest son, Henry. James refers to "our third and last estate, which is our Burgesses" as being "composed of two sorts of men; Merchants and Craftsmen": "The Merchants think the whole common-wealth ordained for making them up; and accounting it their lawful gain and trade, to enrich themselves upon the loss of all the rest of the people, they transport from us things necessary; bringing back sometimes necessary things, and at other times nothing at all. . . . And the Craftsmen think, we should be content with their work, how bad and dear soever it be: and if in any thing they be controlled, up goeth the blue blanket."[232] When James's successor Charles I attempted to prevent movement between social classes during the period of his personal rule after 1629, "the inspiration came from the old-fashioned noble and gentry families, who were resisting bitterly the aspirations of well-to-do middle sort of people—yeoman farmers as well as clothiers—to be regarded as gentlemen": "The achievement of the formal title of 'gentleman' could not ensure a man of acceptance as a gentleman by the leading county families, who ostracized or cold shouldered the *nouveaux riches*."[233]

One factor was necessary to channel resentment into the active pursuit of social change. As Eric Olin Wright has argued, feudalism was in its own way as hegemonic a system as capitalism, at least in relation to the subaltern capitalist class: "So long as they were able to 'feudalize' their capitalist exploitation (that is, buy into the feudal class in various ways) they generally supported feudalism. It was only in the period of the long crisis of late feudalism, in part perhaps stimulated by the expansion of capitalism itself, that the bourgeoisie became stridently antifeudal."[234] In other words, once the crisis of feudalism made the possibility of being satisfactorily incorporated into the existing system a diminishing possibility, at least some sections of the bourgeoisie began to see the social relations in which they were involved as an alternative to, rather than a subordinate component of feudalism. David Harvey has argued that the oppositional bourgeoisie operated across "seven different activity spheres":

> Capitalism did not supplant feudalism by way of some neat revolutionary transformation resting on forces mobilized within only one of these spheres. It had to grow within the interstices of the old society and replace it bit by bit, sometimes through main force, violence, predation and seizure of assets, but at other times with guile and cunning. And it often lost battles against the old order even as it eventually won the war. As it achieved a modicum of power, however, a nascent capitalist class had to build its own alternative social relations, administrative systems, mental conceptions, production systems, relations to nature and patterns of daily life as these had long been constituted under the preceding feudal order.[235]

These spheres might be seen as aspects of the transition as a social rather than purely economic process. The key issue then is the role the bourgeoisie did play in what Harvey calls "main force, violence, predation and seizure of assets"; in short, revolution. As Thompson once noted: "Mill-owners, accountants, company-promoters, provincial bankers, are not historically notorious for their desperate propensity to rush, bandoliers on their shoulders, to the barricades. More generally they arrive on the scene when the climatic battles of the bourgeois revolution have already been fought. . . . What need did these bourgeois have of courage when their money served them better?"[236] But in some cases money would not serve and it was in these cases that the distinction between the capitalist and noncapitalist sections of the bourgeoisie acquired decisive significance, since sections of the latter were less adverse to bandoliers and barricades, and tended to form the revolutionary leaderships. Which sections?

There is a famous schema, widely but erroneously ascribed to Lenin, in which ideological leadership could only be provided to the working class "from outside."[237] In his discussion of the formation of the seventeenth-century French Jansenism, Lucien Goldmann suggested, without direct reference to Lenin, that the formation of an "external" leadership might explain the influence of this movement for reform of the Catholic Church:

> The ideology is first of all elaborated outside the social group by a few professional politicians, and essentially, by ideologists . . . It is the circles which are outside the main group which combine to provide both the ideologues and the extremist leaders . . . However, shortly after the birth of the movement, it is the *élite* or vanguard of the group itself which takes control, providing the leaders of the main body of opinion, and offering the real resistance to the king's authority. What might, in modern times, be called the sympathizers or fellow travelers come from the *officiers* and in particular from the *Cours souveraines* and the *parlements*. It is thanks to them that the ideas of the *élite* produce the great effect which they do upon the rest of the country.[238]

Generalizing from Goldmann's work, Michael Mann argued that the process he described was applicable to the way in which leaderships were formed for the bourgeoisie. On the one hand: "Left to itself the bourgeoisie was only capable of economism—in the eighteenth century of segmental manipulative deference." But on the other: "An ideological vanguard might articulate best the experience and needs of other power actors (economic, military, and political), but its ideology was then appropriated by them."[239] The difficulty with Mann's argument is that of "externality": leaderships came from outside the capitalist wing of the bourgeoisie, but were part of it in the wider "non-economic" sense. The notion of an "ideological vanguard" has a family resemblance to Gramsci's notion of "organic intellectuals," but the latter conveys greater sensitivity to the integral nature of this group to the bourgeoisie: "Every social group, coming into existence on the original terrain of an essential function in the world of economic production, creates together with itself organically, one or more strata of intellectuals which give it homogeneity and an awareness of its own function not only in the economic but also in the social and political fields. The capitalist entrepreneur creates alongside himself the industrial technician, the specialist in political economy, the organizers of a new culture, of a new legal system, etc."[240]

The most decisive bourgeois leaderships therefore tended to emerge from those sections of the class without direct material interests in the process of production. What made it possible for this section of the bourgeoisie to provide leadership to the class as a whole? One way of answering this question is to take a negative example; where a group of highly developed capitalist societies failed to complete the bourgeois revolution: the Italian city-states.

The republics of Northern and Central Italy displayed the same ambivalence toward the feudal system as elsewhere in Europe.[241] Nevertheless, the Italian experiment may have proved to be a historical dead end, not because of the extent to which it remained part of feudalism, but because of the extent to which it did not. For, in one important respect, they displayed a characteristic of the mature capitalist system even in this formative period: competition raised to the level of state rivalry. Giovanni Arrighi noted that, historically, there have been two kinds of competition between capitals. The first is more "a mode of regulating relationships between autonomous centers which are in fact *cooperating* with one another in sustaining a trade expansion from which they all benefit, and which the profitability of each centre is a condition of the profitability of all the centers." The second is not restricted to firms, but is carried on by states, beginning with the behavior of the Italian city-states during the Hundred Years' War when "an overaccumulation of capital leads capitalist organizations to invade one another's spheres of operation; the division of labor that previously defined the terms of their mutual cooperation breaks down; and, increasingly, the losses of one organization are the condition of the profits of another." The situation ceases to be "positive-sum" and becomes "zero-sum."[242] This level of economic competition prevented the city-states from forming a unified nation-state under Frederick II and led to the resultant submission of the communes, over several centuries, to the feudal barons of the surrounding countryside; a defeat compounded by conquest at the hands of the Spanish Habsburgs at the end of the fifteenth century.

It was not simply capitalism that then went into retreat but everything associated with it. John Breuilly takes two essays by Dante to argue that national consciousness could be found as early as the thirteenth century, although not yet nationalism. In one, "On Vernacular Language" Dante claims to have discovered an Italian language, which he in turn identifies with the Italian nation and argues for its use by poets. In the other, "On the Monarchy," Dante argues for the establishment of a universal monarchy to establish harmony across Christendom as a whole, not only in the Italian Peninsula. Breuilly argues that the divergence between these two positions is proof of both "the existence of some kind of national consciousness and concern with national language and cultural identity in late thirteenth and early fourteenth-century Europe" and "the non-existence of nationalist consciousness."[243] The "illustrious vernacular" of which Dante spoke was in fact the Florentine dialect adopted by intellectuals like himself who belonged to the bourgeoisie of the most advanced Italian city-state. As Gramsci rhetorically asked: "Does not this mean that two conceptions of the world were in conflict: a bourgeois-popular one expressing itself in the vernacular and an aristocratic-feudal one expressing itself in Latin and harking back to Roman antiquity?"[244] With the decline of the Communes and the reimposition of feudalism, the attempt to establish a vernacular means of expression was destroyed along with its social basis: "After a brief interlude (the communal liberties) when there is a flourishing of intellectuals who come from the popular (bourgeois) classes, the intellectual function is reabsorbed into the traditional caste, where the individual elements come from the people but where the character of the caste prevails over their origins."[245] In other words, the proto-national consciousness expressed above all by Dante was linked to the very early development of capitalism in Italy, whose defeat meant that the possibility of national unification was taken off the historical agenda. The failure to make Italy meant that no Italians would be made for another five hundred years. In these circumstances the aspiration for a universal monarchy was an *alternative* to a nationalism that had been blocked, and whose literary manifestations would soon themselves be abandoned. National consciousness could not flourish, or even take root, where the conditions for capitalist development were no longer present, and for it to be consolidated across Europe, even if only among the bourgeoisie, there had to be at least one case where it successfully made the transition to nationalism and then became embodied in a nation-state. Insofar as identification with the state did take place, it was with the existing city-states: "This identification then led to the relatively easy outbreak of warfare between different city-states, which perceived their competitors as dangerous rivals (as do modern nation-states)."[246]

Drawing on the Italian example, we might therefore say that existence of capitalism and capitalists was not enough to guarantee that a bourgeois revolution would even be attempted. The non-economic bourgeoisie were therefore central for three reasons. First, precisely because they were not subject to competitive economic divisions within their class, these groups were often more able to express the common interests of the bourgeoisie as a whole than capitalists: they were tactful cousins smoothing over the tensions between the hostile band of warring brothers. Second, and conversely, they were also prepared to temporarily transgress capitalist property rights in order to better permanently enshrine them. Third, because these revolutionaries still belonged to a minority exploiting class, albeit one broader than their feudal predecessor, they needed to involve other social forces to expel the Spanish and overthrow the English absolutist states. As I noted earlier, the bourgeoisie should not be confused with the petty bourgeoisie, but the former did have a close *relationship* with the latter, which, until 1848 at least, invariably provided the foot soldiers for the struggle with feudal absolutism. Anderson writes that the bourgeoisie "will normally lack a clear-cut frontier with layers of the petty bourgeoisie below it, for the difference between the two in the ranks of the small employer is often quantitative rather than qualitative."[247] These links are strongest before the transition from agrarian and mercantile capitalism to industrial capitalism, as Gareth Stedman Jones explains: "In general, the more industrial capitalism develop, the stronger was the economic power of the *grande bourgeoisie* in relation to the masses of small producers and dealers from which it had sprung, and the greater the distance between their respective aims. Conversely, the less developed the bourgeoisie, the smaller the gulf between "bourgeois" and "petit bourgeois," and the greater the preponderance and cohesion of the popular movement."[248]

The capacity of these organic intellectuals to represent a collective bourgeois interest, to abandon when necessary the immediate economic manifestations of that interest, and to unite classes outside the bourgeoisie were only possible because they tended to act from motives that were not strictly economic in nature. These motives varied over time but tended to be more concerned with religious or constitutional liberties than with removing absolutist impediments to the exploitation of wage labor. What ideologies then helped shape the revolutionary consciousness of the bourgeoisie?

THE FIRST IDEOLOGY OF TRANSFORMATION

Mikulas Teich has described a series of three "historically demarcated sequences" encompassing "the long-drawn-out transition from feudalism to capitalism": the Renaissance, the Reformation, and the Enlightenment.[249] Yet the relative importance of these sequences is quite different. In the initial cases of the United Provinces and England, opposition to absolutism was at least partly expressed in terms of religious belief; in the later case of France, far more consistently in grounds of Enlightenment rationality; the link between England and France in particular was provided by nationalism, which was compatible with both positions. As this suggests, in the context of our discussion the Renaissance is the least significant. In part this was because a movement primarily concerned with aesthetics and philosophy the Renaissance was the most removed from questions of state power, at least until the late figure of Machiavelli who, as I argued in chapter 1, was not a bourgeois revolutionary. Perhaps more to the point, however, there is a respect in which, as we shall see, the Renaissance period was expressive precisely of the absence of the bourgeois revolution in the Italian city-states. This absence gives the great productions of humanist culture a retrospectively elegiac quality, as if the achievements of Michelangelo were compensation for the unwillingness or inability of his Medici patrons to unify the peninsula. Ultimately, the visual arts too would decline into the decadence of Mannerism, the aesthetic equivalent of the static formalism characteristic of the feudal courts that began to dominate Italy from the late fifteenth century. It is, as they say, no accident that the emergence of Mannerism can be dated to the same decade of the 1520s that saw the final assertion of Spanish royal power in Italy, even over Rome itself.[250] Gramsci wrote of there being "two currents" in the Renaissance, "one progressive and the other regressive, and that in the final analysis the latter triumphed after the general phenomenon had reached its full splendor in the sixteenth century (though not as a national and political fact, though, but as a prevalently but not exclusively cultural fact)." As he also notes, "the people were preparing the reaction against this splendid parasitism in the form of the Protestant Reformation" and it was this process that constituted the first ideology of bourgeois revolution.[251]

The revolt begun by Luther in 1517 was by no means predestined for success. There was, after all, nothing new in schisms within the Catholic Church taking a political form. After the Great Schism of 1378 Christendom divided between two (and at one point three) different contenders for the papal throne. Yet neither this nor any of the lesser schisms had threatened to lead to the creation of a new faith to rival the established church. Nor was heresy previously unknown. Heresies, often millenarian in content and drawing their main support from peasants and urban plebeians, had given ideological focus to several of the most explosive social movements of the Middle Ages. Yet no actual or potential ruling class in Europe, with the partial exception of the Bohemian, embraced these doctrines. The fifteenth-century Hussite Revolt, which led to the independence of the kingdom of Bohemia, is in fact of great relevance to our theme, since it presents a picture of what could happen when a great revolutionary movement arose, united by a radical religious ideology, but which lacked the socioeconomic basis that would enable it to develop into a bourgeois revolution.

The Hussite movement between 1419 and 1434 was, in effect, a proto-Reformation, a form transitional between the various forms of medieval heresy and Protestantism.[252] Like the establishment of the Swiss Confederation, the Hussite Revolt was successful because it involved an alliance between peasants, individual burgesses, and the towns as corporate bodies. Indeed, the Bohemian case had an even wider class base in that it also involved additional forces in the form of the minor nobility and the lesser gentry. Like the Swiss Confederation, the Kingdom of Bohemia sought to overthrow the local authority of the Austrian Habsburgs, but the key antagonist of the Hussites was the church—as landowner, as secular power, and as the source of religious authority. The success of the revolt established the first territorially based, schismatic church in Western Europe, based on recognition of the Bible as the final authority in all matters of religion, yet this did not directly lead to similarly novel developments in economics and politics. If anything, the nobles and gentry consolidated their positions through expropriation of church lands and property, and acquisition of Crown domains on what amounted to permanent leasehold, while the Crown itself was reduced to a relatively weak form of elected estates-monarchy.[253] Ironically, insofar as the Hussite Revolt contributed toward capitalist development in the longer term it was through the one feature that it shared with the earlier peasant revolts: the effective ending of serfdom.

Even the Reformation proper did not in and of itself lead to capitalist development. Attempts to explore the relationship between Protestantism (the Calvinist variant in particular) and capitalism often involve a pair of false alternatives. One is a supposedly Marxist position that sees the capitalist economy producing Protestantism as a form of ideological legitimation. The other is a supposedly Weberian position that sees Protestantism as an independent factor that inadvertently provided the psychological motivation for believers to undertake capital accumulation. Neither position accurately represents the views held respectively by Marx or Weber: both men have been ill-served in respect of this subject, often as much by their supporters as by their opponents. It is therefore necessary briefly to review what they actually had to say on the role played by the ideologies of the Reformation.

Many writers start from a set of wrong assumptions about Marxist theory and how it explains the nature of Calvinism. In a defense of Weber, exemplary in the accuracy with which it represents his thought, Gordon Marshall writes: "[Marxism] states that since ideas, such as those conveyed by Calvinist doctrines, are merely 'reflections' of underlying economic conditions, then Calvinism (indeed the Reformation in general) was a historically necessary development following upon prior economic changes. In other words, the new capitalist class utilized Calvinist beliefs in order to excuse their prior class interests, these being to accumulate capital in the manner prescribed by the 'spirit of capitalism' as conceived by Weber."[254] On reading this passage, one wishes that Marshall would show the same scrupulousness of exposition when discussing Marx that he does when discussing Weber. What he outlines here is not classical Marxism, but the crude reductionism characteristic of the Second International at its worst and Stalinism at its most typical. Furthermore, although one might suppose that Marshall is summarizing Marx on the subject of Calvinism, he is not, for Marx nowhere wrote a systematic account of any aspect of the Reformation. His contributions on the subject were in fact restricted to a number of suggestive but unsystematic observations, the two most relevant of which both appear in *Capital*, Volume 1.

One observation is specifically concerned with the—largely unintended—economic consequences of the Henrican dissolution of the monasteries and seizure of church property in England after 1537. Church land acquired during this process by "speculating farmers and townsmen" was subject, in some cases, to consolidation and the introduction of commercial agriculture, and often accompanied by the eviction of existing church tenants who then went on to form part of the rural proletariat.[255] In other words, Marx sees one economic aspect of the Reformation—the expropriation of church wealth—as contributing in England to primitive accumulation and the formation of capitalist relations of production in the countryside. Marx says nothing here about ideology, but notes the economic effects of the establishment of the Anglican Church, which in all of Protestant Europe was the one doctrinally closest to Catholicism. Theoretically, the insight could be generalized to take account of similar events in any other countries that did have Calvinist reformations. In practice, it simply does not square with the evidence. In the case of Scotland, church wealth was simply squandered by the rapacious feudal nobility and consequently contributed nothing toward capitalist development. In the case of the United Provinces, capitalist development certainly took place, but the wealth of the Catholic Church seized during the Eighty Years' War with Spain was more often used to pay for the Dutch military effort rather than to invest in production.[256]

The other observation is a generalization and deserves to be quoted in full: "For a society of commodity producers, whose general social relations of production consists in the fact that they treat their products as commodities, hence as values, and in this material form bring their individual, private labors into relation with each other as homogeneous human labor, Christianity with its religious cult of man in the abstract, particularly in its bourgeois development, i.e., in Protestantism, Deism, etc., is the most fitting form of religion."[257] Here Marx emphasizes the ideological appropriateness not of Calvinism specifically, nor even of Protestantism more generally, but of Christianity *per se* as the confessional counterpoint to generalized commodity production.[258]

Neither of these observations therefore deals specifically with Calvinism. The only direct suggestion that Marx makes concerning a homology between accumulation of capital and the Protestant worldview is in the *Grundrisse*: "The cult of money has its asceticism, its self-denial, its self-sacrifice—economy and frugality, contempt for mundane, temporal and fleeting pleasures; the chase after the *eternal* treasure. Hence the connection between English Puritanism, or also Dutch Protestantism, and money-making."[259]

It was in fact Weber who introduced the supposed affinity of Protestantism with capital accumulation, in the essays written in 1904 and 1905, which comprise *The Protestant Ethic and the Spirit of Capitalism*.[260] But Weber makes clear that he is indeed referring to "the *spirit* of capitalism," which he defines as an "ascetic compulsion to save" or more generally as "rational conduct on the basis of a calling," and specifically denies as "foolish and doctrinaire" the idea that only the Reformation could have produced this type of *mentalité*, "or even that capitalism as an economic system is a creation of the Reformation."[261] Weber was of course aware that capitalist production pre-dated the October 31, 1517, when Luther pinned his ninety-five thesis to the door of the castle church in Wittenberg; indeed, as we saw in chapter 15, he believed it had existed to some degree in virtually every previous form of human society. The notion of a calling could even be found in the work of Petrarch and the Humanist school of the Renaissance, as Baron notes: "The claims that man should indeed wish for more than to fill his traditional station, that he should be a miser of his time and contemplate his life in the light of continuous progress and unlimited activity—these claims seemed to the men of the Renaissance a cultural as well as an economic need."[262] Weber's point was rather that the adoption of the form of rationality associated with Calvinism and the other Puritan sects, in certain concrete circumstances, assist in the consolidation of capitalism as a systematic method of organizing economic life. This is a much weaker and more defensible claim than Weber is often thought to have made and, as such, it is compatible with a Marxist account of the origins of capitalism.[263] Where capitalist production was weak, as it was in most areas of Europe in the sixteenth century, the capitalist spirit alone was not enough to transform the conditions of action.[264]

What then is the source of the view that Marxism sees Calvinism as the ideological reflection of capitalism? It would appear to be a handful of relatively late comments by Engels.[265] But these see the importance of the Reformation to capitalism primarily in political rather than economic terms, as in the later Weberian tradition. Engels himself described the Reformation as a whole as "the No. 1 bourgeois revolution" that had "triumphed in Switzerland, Holland, Scotland, England," and adding that it had also been successful "to a certain extent" in Sweden and Denmark.[266] His claims for the extent of the bourgeois revolution here are simply unsustainable, as the massive differences between Switzerland and Scotland on the one hand and the United Provinces and England on the other suggest. His more considered verdict treated England as "the second act of the bourgeois revolution" after the United Provinces: "Here Calvinism justified itself as the true religious disguise of the interests of the bourgeoisie of that time, and on this account did not attain full recognition when the revolution ended in 1689 in a compromise between one part of the nobility and the bourgeoisie."[267] The problem with this formulation is the unnecessarily conspiratorial image of a "religious disguise" masking other, economic interests. The Reformation in fact provided the first ideology for "non-economic" bourgeois revolutionary leadership, although in several respects it was less intrinsically bourgeois than the Renaissance had been.

The crisis of feudalism had generated an enormous uncertainty concerning the human condition that the Catholic Church, committed as it was to the existing and supposedly unchanging order of Estates, could not address. Protestantism was the first movement of international significance that sought to provide assurance of salvation in a world where assurance was gone, and it did so by asking believers to look into their hearts for proof that they were among the saved. By proclaiming that everyone had as much (or, more plausibly, as little) chance of salvation, regardless of the Estate to which they belonged, Protestantism represented a relatively democratic element in European feudal society. The general nature of the spiritual crisis meant that Protestantism appealed to individuals among many different social groups—German knights and Scandinavian peasants as much as Dutch merchants. It was only bourgeois elements like the last named, however, who experienced new social tensions specifically produced by the clash between their own practice as capitalists and the teachings of the Catholic Church. As Mann writes, these tensions took three forms:

> First, there was a tension between the centralized authority of the Catholic Church and the decentralized decision-making required in a market system by those who owned the means of production and exchange. Second, there was a tension between a fixed order of statuses legitimated by the church and the requirements of commodity production, in which nothing apart from property ownership is given a fixed and authoritative status. . . . Third, a tension existed between the social duty of the rich Christian to be "luxurious" (i.e., to maintain a large household, provide extensive employment, and give to the poor) and the capitalist's need to claim private ownership rights over the surplus so as to provide a high level of reinvestment.[268]

The Reformation, however, saw both a successful and permanent split in the church, and the adoption of the new religion by significant sections of both the existing and potentially alternative European ruling class. In essence, the Reformation consisted of three related developments; the spread of Protestantism as a personal faith among individual believers, the formation of new "national" churches, which provided the doctrinal basis and congregational structure for the practice of that faith, and the adoption of these churches as the religious arm of the local state—although all three developments were subject to reversal. Ultimately, however, the success or failure of Protestantism in a particular area did not depend on the extent of individual conversion, or the motivation behind it. As Ewan Cameron writes: "To become established the Reformation had to 'affiliate' itself to some social unit."[269] More precisely, it had to affiliate itself to a series of states. But which states? In feudal terms, the wealthiest and most developed areas of Europe lay to the west and the south, in France, Italy, and Spain. These powers were the main contenders in the struggle for control over the papacy and, through that institution, exploitation of those areas of Europe that fell within the Holy Roman Empire. There was no reason for these ruling classes to embrace the new religion, since they had the potential to dominate the Catholic world from inside and therefore had no need to escape from its control.[270] The center of the Reformation lay, not in the most developed economic regions of Europe but in the most backward.

Those actual or potential ruling classes that embraced one or other variety of Protestantism fell into three broadly identifiable types. The first was typical of the north German principalities and Scandinavia, where Lutheranism, the initial ideological and organizational form of Protestantism, first established a base. The Lutheran creed was quite compatible with feudalism (as the German peasantry discovered to their cost in 1525), but it fulfilled a function for those states that wanted to escape the respective financial and political demands of the pope and the emperor. It provided an ideological banner for those princes with no hope of competing for control of the papacy to make themselves independent from its control instead. The second consisted of only one case: England. Here the state under Henry VIII retained many of the organizational and ceremonial forms of Catholicism, while detaching from Rome as a source of doctrinal authority and political allegiance. Initially, the greater geographical inaccessibility of England meant that even the limited gestures toward popular acceptance adopted by Lutherans on the continent were unnecessary to the regime. In time, England would eventually give rise to the most socially radical Protestant sects in Europe, but until the reign of Mary Tudor forged a lasting association between Protestantism, English protonational consciousness and the defense of state sovereignty, it was the most conservative reformation of all.

There was, however, a third type, linked by adherence to what Trevor-Roper calls "the Calvinist International."[271] The more conservative types of reformation, the Anglican and Lutheran, were those where the state itself imposed Protestantism (regardless of the initial degree of popular support) for reasons of domestic and, more importantly, foreign policy. "The more hostile the state," writes Owen Chadwick, "the more likely that the Protestants would be Calvinist, for Calvinism established an authority of the ministry free from the spiritual subjection of the state authorities."[272] As we saw in chapter 1, where the state was hostile, Calvinists either attempted to free the church of state control or, failing that, to overthrow the state. For this reason, as late as 1616 the Catholic propagandist Kaspar Schoppe could claim that Calvinists were the "worst enemies" of the Holy Roman Empire and desired to turn Germany into either a "tyrannical oligarchy" or a "revolutionary democracy."[273] Yet, as Quentin Skinner has argued, there is no Calvinist theory of revolution as such; indeed the Calvinist doctrine of resistance is very similar to that of the Lutherans (Luther did not oppose all resistance to princes, only popular resistance) and both drew from the existing Conciliar tradition. Skinner draws attention, in the context of Scottish political theory, to the influence of the Catholic John Major on the Protestant George Buchanan, but this was an example of a more general continuity: Calvinist theorists attempted to win over Catholics by appealing to a tradition which the latter recognized as legitimate.[274] The real distinctive feature of Calvinism was in its attitude toward the state—not equality in different realms, but superiority of the church over the state.

The relationship between Calvinism and the bourgeois revolution is therefore a complex one. All bourgeois revolutionary movements down to and including the English Revolution involved Calvinism, but very few Calvinist movements down to and including the English Revolution led to bourgeois revolutions. Calvinism was a doctrine that gave support to those who wished to overthrow a state, but there were many different social forces seeking to overthrow states in mid-sixteenth-century Europe, very few of them remotely bourgeois in composition. It was the need to challenge state power that explains why sections of the Scottish or Transylvanian nobilities embraced Calvinism rather than the Lutheranism favored by, for example, the German knights and princelings to which they were otherwise quite similar in social terms. The class content of Calvinism therefore varied from country to country. In France, for example, as Henry Heller has pointed out, Calvinism "was essentially a movement of artisans and bourgeoisie," but one in which the latter "were eager to subordinate themselves to the nobility," a minority of whom had turned to Calvinism for quite other reasons. Heller explains that the reasons for noble hegemony over French Calvinism were, on the one hand, that the bourgeoisie "had been unable to develop at this time an economic basis strong enough to enable it to make a stand independently of the nobility" and, on the other, that no consistent allies could be found among popular social classes: "apart from a minority of the more literate and skilled artisans," most small producers were as hostile to the bourgeoisie as they were to the nobility and clergy.[275]

Those societies most faithful to the teachings of Calvin himself were generally the least compatible with capitalist development. As Gramsci noted: "The Lutheran Reformation and Calvinism created a vast national-popular movement through which their influence spread: only in later periods did they create a higher culture ... the phase of popular development enabled the protestant countries to resist the crusade of the Catholic armies tenaciously and victoriously."[276] There is no doubt that Calvinism represented a retreat from the sophistication of late Renaissance Humanism, as exemplified by Erasmus, but by weakening the power of the Catholic Church, and providing the ideology for of the first successful bourgeois revolutions, it paved the way for later intellectual advances, without necessarily contributing directly to them. The point is well made by Trevor-Roper: "If Calvinism was intellectually retrograde and repressive, a positive, vindictive enemy of enlightenment, politically it nevertheless performed an essential service. . . . Politically, therefore, Calvinism may well have been necessary to the intellectual progress of Europe in the seventeenth century . . . but the fact that Calvinist resistance was necessary to the continuation and development of an intellectual tradition does not entail any direct or logical connection between them."[277] Once victorious, the Dutch bourgeoisie did not allow Calvinism to constitute an obstacle to the operation of capitalist economy. Baruch Spinoza, in many ways the most radical figure of his time, attacked the "dogma" of organized religion in 1670 for "degrading rational man to a beast, completely inhibiting man's free judgment and his capacity to distinguish true from false. . . . Men who utterly despise reason, who reject and turn away from the intellect as naturally corrupt . . . are believed to possess the divine light!"[278] In this respect at least Spinoza was expressing the beliefs held tacitly by the most advanced sections of the Dutch bourgeoisie, albeit in more vigorous terms than most were prepared to use. Calvinism could be a siege engine for destroying the fortifications of feudal absolutism; it was not scaffolding for constructing a capitalist economy. As Luciano Pellicani writes:

> The entrepreneurial bourgeoisie . . . had no intention of seeing Calvinist bigotry substitute [for] Catholic bigotry. . . . Thus it was the spirit of Erasmus, not of Calvin, which in the end set the tone of economic and cultural life in Dutch society, which became the most capitalist nation of Europe. And it succeeded in this precisely in that it institutionalised the typically bourgeois separation between business and religion: a separation which, to the custodians of Calvinist orthodoxy, seemed blasphemous, but against which they could do nothing.

Pellicani notes that, unlike the English, the Scots failed to adopt this separation, but embraced instead the views of "the bigoted and anti-capitalist Holland," which had been vanquished in its country of origin: "Thus, whereas England started down the road that was to lead her to become the main capitalist power in the world, Scotland remained immersed in the stagnant waters of Calvinist orthodoxy and underdevelopment."[279] But Pellicani reverses the actual causal order. Even if Protestantism offered ideological support to those who felt economically confined by Catholicism, it could not by itself ensure that capitalism would become the dominant mode of production in any given area. As Gordon Marshall has argued, the reason why Scottish capitalism failed to develop in the seventeenth century did not lie in "the worldview or motivation of the capitalists themselves"—for in his view they were indeed motivated to accumulate capital—but were "frustrated by the backwardness of the economic structure of the country . . . by the conditions of action that circumscribed their activities."[280] Marshall exaggerates the number of "capitalists" operating in Scotland in the seventeenth century, but the point is well made: Protestantism, even in its Calvinist form(s) was not an independent factor in the transition to capitalism. Its efficacy in this respect depended not only on whether members of the bourgeoisie adopted it as their religion, but also on the circumstances under which they did so.

The potential for this discrepancy between ideological intention and practical result lies in the very fusion of the economic, political, and ideological, which was characteristic of feudalism, and which reached its apogee under the absolutist state. One aspect of Bertram's notion of "evolution by international competition" is relevant here in relation to the overcoming of precapitalist state forms or, in his terms, the adoption of a capitalist "legal and political superstructure": "The proximate cause may be religious or political.... But those countries or cultures that fail to select structures conducive to the development of the productive forces will either be eliminated (or assimilated) by their rivals, or will undergo a crisis that will force them to select anew their basic structures. In either case, the unsuccessful, if they survive, will tend to adopt structures resembling those of their successful rivals."[281] There are two aspects to this claim: one about how "structures" are adopted in the first place and other about how they are then spread. I will return to the latter in the next chapter, but it is the former that concerns us here. Let us assume that Bertram's "social structure" includes the state: the establishment of a social structure "that permits a high rate of development may be the consequence of the class struggle, of military adventure, of religious doctrine, or anything else."[282] Regardless of what motives various groups had for opposing absolutism then, if they were successful in destroying it, the integrated structures associated with that state form would also be removed, making it possible for capitalism in all its initial myriad forms to experience unimpeded expansion. Under these conditions, government could always be delegated, provided the state was rededicated to the accumulation of capital. In England between 1649 and 1660, for example, the New Model Army could act as a substitute for a capitalist class, which, although economically dominant within society, was not yet capable of assuming political leadership within the state. The "new" colonial merchants who ruled in alliance with the major-generals during the 1650s were "significantly below, or outside, the traditional governing classes," and unrepresentative of the capitalist class in general: "The alliance of ... moderate republican forces that governed nationally and in London under the Commonwealth exerted an influence that could not possibly be justified by its real social weight within English society."[283]

But the discrepancy between intention and outcome is also what produces the sense of "the revolution betrayed." I mean by this not simply that the interests of the petty bourgeoisie, small commodity producers, and laborers were ignored or attacked, although was obviously the case in the English Revolution; but also that the ideological aims under which the bourgeoisie *themselves* went into battle had come to nothing. The ascendancy of King Jesus over King Charles is a different matter from the ascendancy of the English East India Company over the Dutch East India Company. The problem was perhaps first recognized after the Restoration by Milton in *Paradise Lost* (1667), in what is quite possibly the first major literary work to express these postrevolutionary feelings of betrayal. As Tom Paulin writes, Milton's Archangel Michael "voices the embattled puritan sense of how the written record can be falsified by the forces of reaction."[284] But he also voices the sense in which the inheritors have assumed the outward forms of revolutionary ideology while availing themselves of material benefits that were never the original goals of the movement:

> *Their Ministry performed, and race well run,*
> *Their doctrine and their story written left,*
> *They die; but in their room, as they forewarn,*
> *Wolves shall succeed for teachers, grievous Wolves,*
> *Who all the sacred mysteries of Heaven*
> *To their own vile advantages shall turn*
> *Of lucre and ambition, and the truth*
> *With superstitions and traditions taint,*
> *Left only in those written Records pure,*
> *Though not but by the Spirit understood.*
> *Then shall they seek to avail themselves of names,*
> *Places and titles, and with these to join*
> *Secular power, though feigning still to act*
> *By spiritual, to themselves appropriating*
> *The Spirit of God, promised alike and given*
> *To all Believers; and from that pretense,*
> *Spiritual Laws by carnal power shall force*
> *On every conscience; Laws which none shall find*
> *Left them enrolled, or what the Spirit within*
> *Shall on the heart engrave . . .*

Inevitably, those who maintain the original motivations of the revolution can no longer be tolerated by those who have emerged victorious:

> *Whence heavy persecution shall arise*
> *On all who in the worship persevere*
> *Of Spirit and Truth; the rest, far greater part,*
> *Well deem in outward Rites and specious forms*
> *Religion satisfied; Truth shall retire*
> *Bestuck with slanderous darts, and works of Faith*
> *Rarely be found: so shall the World go on,*
> *To good malignant, to bad men benign,*
> *Under her own weight groaning till the day*
> *Appear of respiration to the just,*
> *And vengeance to the wicked . . .* [285]

And so did the world go on indeed, down to the last days of the bourgeois revolution. But if they did not bring about what their organic intellectuals sought, what did they achieve?

22

Patterns of Consummation

According to Eric Hobsbawm, the seizure and maintenance of state power is not enough to bring a revolution to an end: "Revolutions cannot be said to "conclude" until they have either been overthrown or are sufficiently safe from overthrow."[1] This observation is accurate with regard to political revolutions, but profoundly misleading in relation to social revolutions, which are liable to be overturned by a mixture of external pressure and internal subversion as long as they remain isolated in a world where different and hostile systems prevail. Only when the cumulative impact of several revolutions has established a new social system can safety be assured; as Perry Anderson rightly notes, in relation to the bourgeois revolutions: "The idea of capitalism in one country, taken literally, is only a bit more plausible than that of socialism [in one country]."[2] What Alexander Chistozvonov calls the point of "irreversibility" must therefore be understood in relation, not only to the overthrow of individual precapitalist states and the removal of the obstacles they posed to internal capitalist development, but also the cumulative effect of these events: an international environment in which individual revolutions could no longer be suppressed, undermined, or simply contained by external feudal-absolutist or tributary counterrevolution.[3]

Necessary Outcomes

Understanding that the earliest bourgeois revolutions were never fully secure until this point of systemic irreversibility had been reached, we can nevertheless identify the two main characteristics of a post-bourgeois revolutionary society: an economy subject to capitalist laws of motion and a state committed to competitive accumulation. Take capitalist laws of motion first: do they necessarily involve the complete removal of all feudal (or other pre-capitalist) relations of production? A famous passage by Marx from the *Grundrisse* suggests that this is not necessarily the case: "In all forms of society there is one specific kind of production which predominates over the rest, whose relations thus assign rank and influence to the others. It is a

general illumination which bathes all the other colors and modifies their particularity. It is a particular ether which determines the specific gravity of every being
which has materialized within it."[4]

The succession of metaphors that Marx employs here are intended to convey a
more complex relationship than simple quantitative "dominance." "I doubt," writes
Ashok Rudra, "that it may be possible to establish scientifically which mode is
dominant over what other mode in a particular context." Nevertheless he has a try,
suggesting that "one can count the number of persons entering into a particular
productive relation (say, tenancy) and find out whether that is more or less than
the number of persons entering into another production relation (say, wage labor)
and settle which is more important."[5] "Tenancy" is not a productive relation in and
of itself, but no matter, the entire premise is wrong. As Geoffrey de Ste. Croix has
pointed out, the key issue in determining the class nature of any society is not necessarily how most labor is performed but rather how the labor that produced the
surplus accruing to the ruling class is performed.[6] Just as a precapitalist society can
contain—in the sense of both "including" and "limiting"—capitalist relations of
production, so too can a capitalist society contain pre-capitalist social relations. In
the latter case these might even involve a majority of the direct producers, as long
as the ruling class, which by definition includes those in ultimate control of the
state, occupied their position through the competitive accumulation of capital based
on wage labor.

But although different precapitalist modes of production (such as slavery and
petty commodity production) have coexisted in the type of dual economy discussed
by Ste. Croix, capitalist and precapitalist modes cannot, at least after the bourgeois
revolutions. Once consolidated, the former contextualizes and structures ("bathes,"
"modifies," "determines") the latter, so that their constitutive relations of production
acquire a new content. For example, Marx emphasized that, during the transition
to capitalism, small independent producers involved in agriculture or handicrafts
or both could carry on production in their traditional manner, but on behalf of the
usurer or merchant, even though the latter pair may play no direct role in organizing
the labor process. He referred to this process as the "formal subsumption of labor,"
in contrast to the "real subsumption of labor," which occurred when the capitalist
began to organize production and the labor process, culminating in large-scale factory manufacture.[7] As Preobrazhensky noted, until that point it might appear that
independent small commodity production continued: "Finally, as a last transitional
stage to genuinely capitalist surplus value we may cite the work of handicraft men
in their homes, for a buyer [putter-out], when they work up the customer's raw
material, with tools belonging to him, and are in essentials already actual wage-
workers, even though they retain the external attributes of independent producers."[8]
The central point, as Lenin explained, was that during the period when formal subsumption is maintained, "capital always takes the technical process of production
as it finds it and only subsequently subjects it to technical transformation."[9] Taking

over the existing labor process also involves taking over the form of property to which it corresponds: "Capital finds the most diverse types of medieval and patriarchal landed property—feudal, 'peasant allotments' [the holdings of bonded peasants]; class, communal, state, and the other forms of land ownership."[10]

Jairus Banaji has drawn a series of general conclusions from these and similar observations by figures from the classical Marxist tradition. He argues that Marx used the term "mode of production" (*produktionsweise*) in two ways: one to refer to the technical process of production, or the labor process more generally; the other to encompass an entire epoch in the history of the social organization of production, in which particular laws of motion predominate. The existence of wage labor, for example, does not necessarily signify the emergence of the capitalist mode of production; wage labor also took place under feudalism, but primarily as a means of meeting the consumption requirements of the lords rather than contributing to the self-expansion of capital. It is rather that the existence of the capitalist mode of production determines that wage labor becomes the central means through which surplus extraction takes place. Equally, however, various types of unfree labor associated with precapitalist modes of production, including slavery itself, can also take place within the context of the capitalist mode of production and, in the terms Marx uses in the *Grundrisse*, both posit and produce capital.[11]

The relevance of this argument to our theme is that it is perfectly possible for feudal, absolutist, or tributary states to be overthrown, thus removing the last obstacle to establishing what Alex Callinicos calls "an independent centre of capital accumulation," while some social relations remain, initially at least, those associated with precapitalist modes in the purely technical sense.[12] The decisive fact is that these technical relations are subordinated to capitalist laws of motion. Political Marxists repeatedly highlight the radical difference between capitalism and preceding modes of production. This emphasis is useful up to a point, but beyond it we lose all sense of what capitalism has in common with other exploitative class systems. Indeed, if capitalism did not possess this commonality, then it is difficult to see how it could have successfully incorporated aspects of these earlier modes, as it has in most of the world outside of a handful of countries at the core of the system where, quite exceptionally, capitalism exists in more or less pure form. Feudal lords were able, in some circumstances, to transform themselves into capitalists, just as ancient slave owners before them were able, in other circumstances, to transform themselves into feudal lords. The continuing fact of exploitation is what makes these adaptations possible. In this respect, as in many others, it will surely be socialism rather than capitalism that is distinct from all previous modes of production.

What then of the capitalist nation-state? Heide Gerstenberger writes: "The concept of 'bourgeois state' . . . implies an idea of 'bourgeois revolution.' This means nothing more—though nothing less—than the assertion that the emergence of bourgeois state power does not simply involve a change in organizational structures or modes of behavior in the exercise of 'state' power, but the creation from scratch of a public instance."[13] Gerstenberger claims that there is a complete break between the "personal" power of the absolutist state and the "public" power of the capitalist state, which suggests that the latter should not bear any traces of the former. In fact, this is no more necessary than it is for a capitalist economy to eliminate all traces of feudal social relations.

There are certain activities that capitalist states must perform, of which three are particularly important. The first is the imposition of a dual social order: horizontally over competing capitals so that market relations do not collapse into "the war of all against all"; and vertically over the conflict between capital and labor so that it continues to be resolved in the interest of the former. The second is the establishment of "general conditions of production," which individual competing capitals would be unwilling or unable to provide, including some basic level of technical infrastructure and welfare provision.[14] These are mainly "internal" to the territory of the state; the third is the way in which each capitalist state has to represent the collective interests of the "internal" capitalist class "externally," in relation to other capitalist states and classes. Capitalism is a system of competitive accumulation based on wage labor and these two defining aspects point to the reasons for the persistence of the states system: the first because of the need for capitals to be territorially aggregated for competitive purposes; the second because of the need for that territory to have an ideological basis—nationalism—which can be used to bind the working class to the state and hence to capital.

There are of course complex issues involved in identifying collective ruling class interests, especially given that one central characteristic of capitalism is competition between capitals; but the state managers who have to resolve this do not need to be themselves capitalists any more than the revolutionaries who created the state in the first place; indeed, in some respects it is essential that they are not. If policies were framed for the benefit of sectional capitalist interests this would constitute a problem for the local capitalist class as a whole. In other words, whatever their own origins or inclinations, state managers and politicians have to identify their interests, not with *specific* national capitals or even specific *sectors* of national capital, but with national capital as a whole. In the case of those bourgeois revolutions, such as the Japanese, which were carried out to develop capitalism from a minimal preexisting base, this was in any case unavoidable, since a capitalist class barely existed. Bertell Ollman comments: "The *samurai* who made the Meiji Revolution refused to become new feudal rulers (as happened after earlier successful revolts), opting instead to make themselves into a capitalist ruling class. But before they could do that they had to create capitalism and a capitalist class of which they could be part." Ollman includes in "capitalist class," not only capitalists but also "the higher state bureaucrats and the leading politicians in the ruling party," with the former group initially playing the most important role.[15] What happened to the pre-Meiji ruling class? As Ann Waswo records, the former *daimyo* or feudal lords "no longer exercised political control over the land they owned, and although they were represented in the

House of Peers, that body was at no time the center of political power": "Unlike England, then, where the landed aristocracy maintained its political influence and by means of the Corn Laws protected the agricultural income on which its power was based until a relatively advanced stage of industrial development, Japan in the decade after the Meiji Restoration was ruled by bureaucrats, the former Samurai who had led the Restoration movement and who had been divorced de facto from the land for centuries."[16] The differences are in fact less significant than they at first appear. The British landed aristocracy after 1688 in effect played the same role as the Japanese samurai bureaucrats after 1868, as Hobsbawm points out: "A plainly bourgeois society—nineteenth-century Britain—could, without serious problems, be governed by hereditary peers."[17] What is it about a capitalist state that makes the absence of direct capitalist rule possible, perhaps even essential?

Under all precapitalist modes of production exploitation took place visibly through the extraction of a literal surplus from the direct producers by the threat or reality of violence: economics and politics were "fused" in the power of the feudal lord or the tributary state. Under the capitalist mode of production exploitation takes place invisibly in the process of production itself through the creation of surplus value over and above that required in reproducing the labor force. Ellen Meiksins Wood identifies a "resulting division of labor in which the two moments of capitalist exploitation—appropriation and coercion—are allocated separately to a 'private' appropriating class and a specialized 'public' coercive institution, the state: on the one hand, the 'relatively autonomous' state has a monopoly of coercive force; on the other hand, that force sustains a private 'economic' power which invests capitalist property with an authority to organize production itself." Furthermore, unlike previous exploiting classes, capitalists exercise economic power without "the obligation to perform social, public functions." "Capitalism is a system marked by the complete separation of private appropriation from public duties; and this means the development of a new sphere of power devoted completely to private rather than social purposes."[18] This is the reason for what Hal Draper calls "the political inaptitude of the capitalist class" compared to other ruling classes in history: feudal lords combine an economic and political role; capitalists perform only the former— although the necessity for capitalists to devote their time to the process of accumulation and their own multiple internal divisions also militate against their functioning directly as a governing class.[19] This is quite compatible with the exercise of bourgeois hegemony over society as a whole, although even in this respect, some sections of the bourgeoisie tend to play a more significant role than others. Adam Smith shrewdly remarked of merchants and manufacturers:

> Their superiority over the country gentlemen is not so much in their knowledge of the public interest, as in their having a better knowledge of their own interest than he has of his. It is by this superior knowledge of their own interests that they have frequently imposed on his generosity, and persuaded him to give up both his own interest and that of the public, from a very simple but honest conviction that their interest,

and not his, was the interest of the public. The interest of the dealers, however, in any particular branch of trade or manufactures, is always in some respects different from, and even opposite to, that of the public.[20]

But the failure of the bourgeoisie to transcend their self-absorbed pursuit of profit drove some conservative supporters of capitalism to despair. Carl Schmitt complained that, unlike working-class ideologues, members of the bourgeoisie no longer understood the friend-enemy distinction, which was central to "the political"; the spirit of Hegel, he thought, had moved from Berlin to Moscow.[21] More prosaically, Bernard Porter notes that capitalists "tend to be hostile to 'government' generally, which they see mainly as a restraint on enterprise and, on a personal level, don't find 'ruling' half so worthwhile or satisfactory as making money."[22]

THE MOMENT OF SYSTEMIC IRREVERSIBILITY

We can now return to the process of bourgeois revolution at a global level. Immanuel Wallerstein has claimed: "By 1650 the basic structures of historical capitalism as a viable social system had been established and consolidated."[23] In fact, in many cases, these structures had been dismantled at a local level. Bohemia, for example, was less developed than the Italian city-states that had been re-feudalized during the previous century, but unlike them it was a coherent territorial state with a population ideologically bound together by the Hussite protoreformation of the fifteenth century. Defeat and reversal came suddenly at the hands of the armed counterreformation during the early stages of the Thirty Years' War. After the Battle of White Mountain in 1620 the Austrian Habsburgs abolished the defeated estates, expropriated the lands of the disloyal nobility, reestablished the Catholic religion for the population as a whole and reimposed serfdom on the peasantry.[24] More importantly, however, even the two states that were fully founded on capitalist relations of production by 1650 were not entirely secure. It is true, as Victor Kiernan writes: "In England and Holland social relations, immobilized over most of Europe, were relatively free to evolve in accordance with what may be termed Europe's historic logic."[25] Yet this was far from signaling the consolidation of the capitalist system. In fact, it was by no means certain that capitalism would survive in those territories where it had been realized until the new mode of production and the emergent states system associated with it had achieved stability at the international level. Even by the 1690s, when both the United Provinces and England had achieved irreversibility in relation to their own individual territories and united under the Orange monarchy, they were still within a world dominated by hostile absolutist and tributary states in which France, the most powerful of the former, sought to undo them from without and within. What then determined whether these new capitalist nation-states would survive in a still hostile environment long enough to transform it? The decisive issue was the type of capitalist state that had emerged from the bourgeois revolution. The Italian city republics had been unequal to the task; did their Dutch and English successors prove more capable?

The Dutch Revolt was the first permanently successful bourgeois revolution. Marcel van der Linder has rightly opposed attempts to reduce it "to a series of rebellions which had little to do with each other," noting that "it has been proved time and time again ... that the same group and class specific motives are consistently present: freedom of religion, anti-absolutism, and revolt against economic misery."[26] Nevertheless, the United Provinces by no means escaped the trajectory of its Swiss and Italian predecessors, as its wealth also depended partly on servicing the existing feudal regimes—not, like Switzerland, through the supply of military manpower, but like the Italian city-states, through its vast trading and financial networks.[27] Yet there was also a difference with Italy, as Gramsci pointed out: "In the Netherlands and only in the Netherlands was there an organic passage from the commune or city-state to a regime that was no longer feudal."[28] After the Swiss Confederation, the United Provinces was the second example of "city-state consociationalism," an alliance of independent political communities who cooperate jointly on a contractual basis while preserving their separate rights and privileges: "The republic of the Seven United Provinces emerged relatively early as an independent political unit, from what was in fact little more than an accidental, military alliance of seven separate territories which successfully rebelled against their common Hapsburg Overlord."[29] Yet, as Liah Greenfield writes: "The political organization of the Dutch Republic was the very opposite of a centralized state."[30] An unwieldy compromise between a federal and confederate polity was one of the structural reasons it was unable to sustain its pre-eminent economic position.[31] The governments of the main provinces, especially Holland, were too closely aligned with particular capitalist interests for the central apparatus of the States General to make decisions that could advance their collective interest. The other reason was that the Dutch Republic suffered from both the crises of feudalism—at second hand via the absolutist regimes that it serviced—and the risks associated with capitalism. As Pepijn Brandon has pointed out, the stagnation of the Dutch economy in the latter half of the seventeenth century did not mean re-feudalization, as it had in the case of the Italian city-states; it meant decline in capitalist terms:

> Although the strength of merchant-capital went hand-in-hand with substantial changes to production, the core of the capitalist class always remained focused primarily on trade. This started to become a serious hindrance to further capitalist development once the Dutch were outcompeted or forced out of international markets by political means from the 1650s onwards. Financialization, based on the strong integration in international capital-flows, proved the easier option for the Dutch ruling class over a restructuring of production, leading to the long eighteenth-century depression. Meanwhile, the consistent localism and small-scale of production meant that drawing up the walls of urban protectionism remained the preferred answer to increased competition for much of the urban middle classes. The federal state-apparatus, probably more directly populated and controlled by the leading families than

any state before or afterwards, could never act as a counterweight to these trends. Instead, it helped to enforce economic policies that were characterized by the absence of protectionism on a national scale and strong protectionism on a local scale.[32]

It is in respect of competition at the level of the state that the parallels between the United Provinces and the Italian city-states are perhaps strongest. The three Anglo-Dutch Wars of the seventeenth century, in 1652–54, 1665–67 and 1672–74, saw the two regions most advanced in capitalist terms in the world—on the one hand Holland and Zeeland in the United Provinces, on the other London, the southeast counties and East Anglia in England—pitched against each other, but although they "provided the sinews of war in material, money, and personnel, they were not responsible for the outbreak of any of the wars." There were economic reasons for the wars, but mediated through the geopolitical interests of the only two capitalist states in the world: "From the Dutch perspective the English aim in all three wars was no less than the conquest of the seas, and the reduction of the Dutch to a state of total and helpless submission."[33] The United Provinces were to remain a bulwark against French expansionism, but that role was also played by such notably non-bourgeois regimes as Austria. It was not to be at the center of a new world system. Brandon is right to reject Hobsbawm's description of the United Provinces as "a feudal business economy," but the latter's verdict is surely correct: "If the only 'capitalist' economies available in the seventeenth century had been like the Dutch, we may doubt whether the subsequent development of industrial capitalism would have been as great or as rapid."[34]

The English state did not simply play Venice to the Dutch state's Genoa: it suffered from none of the disabilities associated with its Italian predecessors or its Dutch rival. Indeed, as a result of the reversals and accommodations they had experienced England was by 1688 the only surviving source of a systemic alternative to feudal absolutism. "The absolute power of the sovereign has continued ever since its establishment in France, Spain, etc.," Smith told his students in the 1760s: "In England alone a different government has been established from the natural course of things."[35] Peter Coveney writes of the European political landscape at the opening of the eighteenth century:

> For all the turbulence of the mid-seventeenth century, when the stabilization came, when the European ancien regime consolidated in the later seventeenth century, the old social structure remained remarkably intact. . . . The Europe of 1700 was still in a very real sense more "medieval" than "modern." The large majority of the population still lived within a seigniorial framework or within medieval municipalities still largely untransformed. It was a society still stratified, formally, in terms of "feudal" hierarchy, of medieval "orders." . . . In most states some form of *modus vivendi* between centralizing authority and "reactionary" interests, usually landed and aristocratic but sometimes mercantile, established itself as the social and political basis of the European ancien regime.[36]

From Marx himself onward, the majority of Marxist historians have claimed that the events of 1688–89 in England ended the revolutionary process begun in

1640 by confirming a new capitalist ruling class in power and establishing a state geared to the accumulation of capital.[37] In these accounts it is accepted that the state had still to undergo several subsequent transformations, largely to accommodate the process of industrialization and the classes that it produced, but on the essential point—that there was no longer any question of a retreat to feudal economic relations or absolutist political rule in England—the decisive nature of the Glorious Revolution has never seriously been in doubt. In his outstanding history of the revolution of 1688–89, Steve Pinkus asks whether it can be considered as a bourgeois revolution and answers his own question thus: "Not in the sense that a self-conscious class, the bourgeoisie, overthrew another class to place itself in power." His conclusion, however, is quite compatible with the consequentialist position taken here:

> The Whig revolutionary triumph brought with it a new bourgeois culture. The revolution in political economy brought with it a revolution in cultural values. Political economic transformation—new tax structures, new institutions, and a new imperial agenda—encouraged the new cultural dominance of the urban middle classes. . . . The Revolution of 1688–89 represented the victory of those who supported manufacturing, urban culture, and the possibilities of unlimited economic growth based on the creative potential of human labor. The effect of the revolution meant that traders felt no need to aspire to the culture and estates of the landed elite. In fact, the aristocracy and the gentry began to act more bourgeois in the wake of the Revolution of 1688–89.[38]

Yet there is a difficulty associated with this virtually unanimous verdict. In fact, as Roy Porter writes, "1688 could in nowise be a final solution."[39] The finality usually ascribed to that year is only possible if events in England are treated in complete isolation. As Fred Halliday has noted:

> There is an extensive literature on the origins of the English revolution and indeed the character of this, the second—after the Dutch—"bourgeois" revolution. The overwhelming majority of this literature focuses on changes in the social and economic structure of Britain prior to the 1640s and on variant interpretations of the social character of the parliamentary cause. One can, indeed, say that virtually the whole of this literature is written as if England was not just an island, but was a closed entity, separate from the political, economic and intellectual world of the rest of Europe.[40]

More specifically, it is not possible to separate developments in England from either the wider struggle with France for European and colonial hegemony, or the impact of that struggle on the other nations of the British Isles, as the English ruling class themselves were only too well aware at the time. Counterrevolution can have both external and internal sources.

The external danger to England after 1688 mainly lay in France. Benno Teschke sees the unintended consequences of the British pursuit of "security and order" during the eighteenth century as "forcing continental states to respond to and finally adjust to the superior socio-political British model, especially under the impact of the Industrial Revolution."[41] This was eventually the case, but the first response of this greatest of the absolutist powers was not to accept the existence of England/Britain and emulate it, but to attempt to overthrow the new state form. Frank McLynn writes: "Britain and France were for the entire Jacobite period [1688–1746] engaged in a titanic economic and commercial struggle, waged worldwide." At the heart of this struggle lay the fundamental difference between the two states, "the divine right of kings versus the divine right of property."[42] The essential difference between Britain and France is however perhaps best illustrated by focusing on a subject that in different ways was dear to the hearts of both ruling classes: money.

Far from occurring "prematurely," the English Revolution took place in time to prevent the absolutist state consolidating and acquiring the massive state debts and parasitic bureaucracies that characterized its European rivals. John Brewer writes: "In this respect, the *timing* of the emergence of the English fiscal-military state is crucial." And here the English then British states did draw on the most useful aspects of the Dutch experience: "When its mobilization occurred, it happened under the auspices of a regime which not only exploited the techniques of Dutch finance but also, though parliamentary scrutiny placed a rein on the more egregious instances of venality."[43] As Colin Mooers has stressed, the nature of taxation and office holding in England were unique in Europe at the time. The principle form of taxation was the Land Tax, which was self-imposed on the landowners by the Parliament that they controlled, then assessed and collected by the lower levels of that class and their tenants. This preference for a land tax over customs and excise was conditioned by the connections there had always been under the Stuarts between custom and excise, the financial independence of the Crown, and its attempts to impose absolutist rule. There was, however, another aspect of the Land Tax that marked it as bourgeois in nature. English landowners were taxed on capitalist ground rents paid to them by tenants whose incomes derived from the employment of wage labor.[44] In this respect Britain had an advantage over France.

The internal threat to Britain lay in Scotland. After the new constitutional monarchy was established in 1688 the English ruling class regarded Scotland as a disruptive element to be contained rather than a potential ally to be transformed. But as long as Scotland remained untransformed, there was always the possibility that the feudal lords who had found it convenient to remove James VII and II might, through a further change in circumstances, wish to bring him back, and with him his French backer—the global rival of the English state. Neither the English Revolution nor the new world system that it promised (or threatened) to bring into being would be secure while this possibility remained. The oft-stated desire of the exiled Stuarts to reclaim all their previous kingdoms, combined with the French need to remove their opponents from the international stage, meant that the English ruling class was faced, not only with impoverishment, but also with a threat to its continued survival on a capitalist basis. Had the Jacobites, and through them, absolutist France, been victorious, Britain, the most dynamic economy in the new system and the only significant state geared to capitalist accumulation, would have been severely weakened and its greatest opponent given a further lease on life. The Jacobites would have been incapable of reimposing feudalism over the whole of Britain—the relative economic weight of Scotland was still too slight, and the development of capitalist agriculture elsewhere too great for that to be possible—but they could have established a regime more subservient to French absolutism than even that of Charles II during the previous century. In practical terms this would have removed the main obstacle to French hegemony in Europe, allowed France to inherit British colonial possessions and, at the very least, reversed the land settlement—particularly in Ireland—that resulted from the Revolution. Britain would have necessarily been reduced to a satellite of France, for the very lack of a firm social base in England would have forced the new regime to rely on the force of French arms for its existence.

These internal and external threats were overcome during the 1740 and 1750s. First, with the defeat of the Jacobites at the Battle of Culloden in 1746, then with a spectacular series of victories directly over the French state in the Seven Years' War, most decisively in India and Canada during 1759. As McLynn writes:

> The entire history of the world would have been different but for the events of 1759. If the French had prevailed in North America, there would have been no United States (at least in the form we know it), for it is inconceivable that France would ever have ceded any of its North American possessions and, without the Louisiana Purchase of 1803, even if we assume the thirteen British colonies had revolted successfully against their French overlords—a questionable assumption—they would have been hemmed in on the Atlantic seaboard, unable to expand westwards to the Pacific. If France had won in India, the global hegemony of the English language could never have happened. . . . The consequences of 1759 really were momentous; it really was a hinge on which all of world history turned.[45]

Similarly, Wallerstein writes that "the Treaty of Paris of 1763 marked Britain's definitive achievement of superiority in the 100 years struggle with France."[46] Lenman has criticized the ascription of decisive significance to the Treaty, writing specifically of Wallerstein:

> The attempt to reconcile this particular peace with conviction that somehow, somewhere, there has to be a "Bourgeois Revolution"—however complex and veiled in form—and that this is part of a predetermined pattern of global social evolution, no longer even serves to over-simplify world history conveniently (as the convoluted nature of Wallerstein's material shows), and is much better dumped in historiography's rubbish bin. Apart from anything else, the Peace of Paris was not the irreversible conclusion of a century of predictable evolution. It was a new balance of power between the Crowns of France and Great Britain, much of it based on remarkable successes for British arms in the previous five or six years. The balance was extremely fragile, indeed arguably self-destructive, and it was to be shattered within twenty years.[47]

There was nothing remotely premeditated about the result of the Anglo-French conflict between 1688 and 1763, nor was Wallerstein claiming that it involved a bourgeois revolution of any sort. Yet for once we can agree with him that it was more than another temporary shift in the balance of power, not because it saw Dutch hegemony replaced by British—as Wallerstein and those who have followed him like Arrighi believe—but because it marked a global turning point or moment of irreversibility for the emergent capitalist system as a whole.[48]

The ultimate global dominance of capitalism may now have been assured, but colossal struggles were still to follow, involving not so much the survival of the new system as the relationship it would have with surviving precapitalist modes of production and the nature of the capitalist states that would comprise the nation-stat system. In classifying the bourgeois revolutions we have hitherto distinguished between them on the basis of whether their main impetus came from below or above; but to this must be overlaid another, nonsynchronous feature: whether they took place before or after this moment of systemic irreversibility. The vast majority fell afterward and took the form of revolutions from above. "It was," writes Anderson, "the world *economic* strength of the capitalist mode of production—its spontaneous power of social transformation—which rendered possible the limited political thrust of these revolutions."[49] There was one exception, the last and greatest of all the bourgeois revolutions from below and the only one to occur after the moment of systemic irreversibility had passed: the French Revolution.

TOWARD INTERNATIONAL STRUCTURAL ADAPTATION (1): THE UNIQUENESS OF THE FRENCH REVOLUTION

The editors of one recent collection of essays may be justified in resetting the beginning of the Age of Revolution back from 1789, or even 1776, to the conclusion of the Seven Years' War in 1763; but their new endpoint—the commencement of the Anglo-Chinese Opium War in 1839—while commendably avoiding Eurocentrism, also demonstrates the difficulties attendant on a refusal to differentiate between revolutions on the basis of their class nature or relationship to the state.[50] In fact, of all the revolutionary upheavals that shook the world in this period of nearly eighty years, only the French Revolution and those associated with it, above all in San Domingo, constituted even temporarily successful *bourgeois* revolutions.

How did the preconditions for bourgeois revolution combine in the French case? Here the feudal crisis and the capitalist solution were both simultaneously manifest, but the latter as an external model to be adopted rather than a set of internal developments ready to be imposed. For, if the French bourgeoisie had any conception of the society to which they aspired, then it was one very like Britain.[51] This is not to succumb to the myth that there was no capitalist development in France before 1789 (or 1830, or 1848, or 1871, or 1959 . . .); but as a consequence of the relative success of the absolutist regimes in retarding the development of capitalism, France was internally less developed in 1789 than England had been in 1640, although the global environment was more developed. The crisis of the

French state therefore took a different form, not least in that it involved geopolitical competition to a far greater extent than in the latter and it was the latter that revealed the structural incapacity of the state to prevent revolution from beginning.

The American War of Independence took place against a backdrop of a naval arms race in which the absolutist monarchies of France and Spain collaborated, particularly from the late 1760s, to overwhelm the British. Although they attained superiority (sixty-six French and Spanish ships facing forty-four British ones across the Channel) it was never on the kind of overwhelming scale that could have guaranteed victory.[52] It was an example, however, of the kind of military spending that strained the French state to the limits of its capacity: "It was through state military competition that the backwardness of French productive relations was initially, and disastrously, demonstrated. The coercive force of England's more advanced system of social relations was experienced by France in a succession of military defeats and the ultimate bankruptcy of the absolutist state."[53] The fiscal crisis of the state, particularly as a result of the increased share of taxation falling on the commoners, was a major precipitant of the revolution. Not only were the nobles largely exempt from these taxes, but they also increased their own income levels by squeezing greater rents from their tenants. Henry Heller has insisted, however, that the financial crisis was simply a manifestation of a more all-embracing economic crisis, which had two other aspects. In industry and commerce there was a shortage of investment capital, "because too much of the economic surplus was drained off in the form of agricultural rents": "In the final analysis the paralysis of the leading sectors of an emergent capitalism reflected the ongoing stranglehold of the seigniorial class over the economy." In agriculture itself: "The growth in population rendered the holdings of many of the peasants progressively smaller and increasingly fragile." Both aspects were connected by the limitations of French development: "The domestic market was clearly inhibited by growing rural poverty. But the market was also blocked by the persistence of tolls and tariffs, local systems of weights and measures, a lack of adequate means of transport, and the burden of indirect taxes. Such a situation encouraged the persistence of too large a degree of domestic or local subsistence inhibiting urbanization and the commercialization of agriculture." In short, the Revolution had three underlying economic causes. Two of these, the crisis of industrial underinvestment in the capitalist manufacturing sector and "a classic Malthusian" crisis of subsistence in feudal agriculture, triggered by a combination of population increase and harvest failure, were primary. They set the context for the third, "the financial insolvency of the state," which in turn "led to an ultimate political crisis."[54] The alignment of the joint crises of capitalism, feudalism, and the absolutist state suggest the transitional, combined nature of the French economy, but also that the transition had reached the point where it would be increasingly difficult for the process to continue without radical political change: "The crisis of absolutism, rooted in the collision of two quite contradictory sets of productive relations, left the bourgeoisie with only one way forward: the abolition of seigneurialism, the creation of legal equality and guaranteed property rights, and the unification of France into a single economic market—all of which were central to capitalist development."[55]

What then of the two remaining preconditions: bourgeois leadership and its ideology? Elizabeth Fox Genovese and Eugene Genovese described the French revolutionaries as "those who, for whatever reasons, could no longer tolerate the national backwardness, social degradation, and political corruption and injustice attendant upon the contradiction between the emerging social relations of production and the entire 'superstructure' of legal relations and moral sensibilities, indeed of the very idea of humanity, could launch a successful assault on the state because possessed of an emerging ideology rooted in new productive forces and class relations."[56] By 1789 this intolerance on the part of the French bourgeoisie had increased in intensity, not least because its members were aware of the quite different and more favorable status afforded their equivalents in the United Provinces and Britain. Heller points out that, in terms of social weight, there were many more members of the bourgeoisie in the broad sense by the end of the eighteenth century than at the beginning: "It is estimated that the size of the bourgeoisie grew from 700,000 to 800,000 at the beginning of the eighteenth century to perhaps 2.3 million in 1789, vastly outnumbering the 120,000 or so nobles." Partly because of this, from 1720 onward the nobility began to force through measures that excluded the bourgeoisie from joining them, including the ending of ennoblement through office in 1728. The bourgeoisie were opposed to the tax exemptions of the nobility, particularly as taxation increased, although membership of the nobility based on merit was still their goal. As this suggests, the development of their class consciousness was subject to contradictory pressures. Further, their capacity for collective self-organization was limited, for fairly obvious reasons: "Before the onset of the Revolution, the sphere of autonomous political activity was quite circumscribed by the authorities of the ancien regime as a matter of policy." Nevertheless, a bourgeois way of life involving distinct forms of dress, manners, and speech began to develop, associated with which were semi-clandestine organizations like the Freemasons in which new ideas could be discussed and economic activities undertaken: "The meeting of the lodges became sites not only for philosophical discussions but for the creating and financing of new business partnerships." It was clear to many young bourgeois the careers were not open to their talents: "As a result, late eighteenth-century France produced a large stratum of alienated intelligentsia who played an important role in the Revolution."[57] As William Sewell points out:

> Revisionist historiography has tended to assume that if the bourgeois and the aristocracy were not distinct classes in a Marxist sense and if wealthy commoners could still rise into the nobility, then there was no reason for relations between the nobility and the bourgeoisie to be fraught with conflict. The French Revolution, therefore, could only be a political, not a social, revolution. I think this line of reasoning is based on a false premise. While it is certainly true that Old Regime society was much more

fluid than the classical Marxist historians of the Revolution claimed, it remained profoundly hierarchical. Where elaborate hierarchy was combined with fluid social relations, social status was never secure. Even those bourgeois who had wealth, education, and good social position had to be constantly vigilant to preserve their honor against threats from above and below. Social intercourse, consequently, was bathed in a continual cascade of disdain. Each group was subjected to multiple, if often petty, humiliations from above and returned the favor to those immediately below. In Old Regime society, disdain—and its inevitable complement, resentment—were produced abundantly by the ordinary experiences of bourgeois life. And although these resentments were by no means generated solely by slights at the hands of the nobles, the nobility and its privileges remained the pinnacle and the paradigm of hierarchy.[58]

If Calvinism was a non-bourgeois ideology that could, in certain conditions, be adopted by the bourgeoisie for revolutionary purposes, the Enlightenment was more closely connected to capitalist development. Critics of the Enlightenment have no doubt that there is a connection, although they are less certain what it is. For Michel Foucault the Enlightenment-as-regime-of-truth "was not merely ideological or superstructural; it was a condition of the formation and development of capitalism."[59] If Foucault credits the Enlightenment with giving rise to capitalism, Partha Chatterjee sees the Enlightenment as dependent upon it: "For ever since the Age of Enlightenment, Reason, in its universalizing mission has been parasitic upon a much less lofty, much more mundane, palpably material and singularly invidious force, namely the universalist urge of capital."[60] Faced with reductive arguments of this sort, it is tempting to deny that any connection exists. This is the strategy pursued by Wood, who writes of such criticisms: "We are being invited to jettison all that is best in the Enlightenment project—especially its commitment to a universal human emancipation—and to blame these values for destructive effects we should be ascribing to capitalism."[61] In fact, like the bourgeois revolutions themselves, the Enlightenment was both a product of capitalist development and a contributor to its further expansion. The transition displayed marked geographical and temporal unevenness between initiation and completion across, or even within the nations. In an early example of uneven development, Enlightenment thought tended to manifest itself simultaneously, or after only a brief delay, on the different components of the international scene. As a result, their class content and social meaning differed depending on whether the nation in question was nearer to the beginning or the end of the process of transition. In this respect, the Enlightenment shared two characteristics with the Reformation. "First, individual Enlightenments almost always involved a combination of different classes: The promoters of the Enlightenment were socially a heterogeneous group, and from that point of view, the Enlightenment was a mixed 'aristocratic-bourgeois' movement. Insofar as it is possible to ascribe to it a common program it was reformist. Insofar as it was undermining the reigning feudal order it was revolutionary."[62] The cross-class nature of Enlightenment thought manifested itself in these different programmatic orientations, although the dividing lines were often indistinct and the bourgeoisie itself was divided. The latter position recognized the logic of seeking to transform the absolutist state, as Jonathan Israel indicates: "Since the royal absolutism against which radical thinkers reacted could not easily be reformed or corrected piecemeal, this, in turn, and for the first time in European history, engendered an implicit and incipient, but nevertheless real and enduring preoccupation with revolution."[63] Israel has distinguished between a "radical" enlightenment on the one hand and a "conservative or "moderate" enlightenment on the other: "For the difference between reason alone and reason combined with faith or tradition was a ubiquitous and absolute difference."[64] The distinction captures an important truth, but here too the dividing line is also less distinct than Israel perhaps allows. The categories of "reformist" and "revolutionary" may roughly correspond to those of "moderate" and "radical," but much depended on context. According to Israel's classification, the Scottish Enlightenment was largely a moderate, reformist affair, and in purely intellectual terms so it was; but insofar as it was concerned with Political Economy, it also provided a program for the most rapid and decisive agrarian transformation in European, perhaps world, history down to the second half of the eighteenth century. Moderate theoretical positions could in certain circumstances lead to radical social effects.

The second similarity with the Reformation is that there was no necessary correspondence between prior capitalist development and the extent of Enlightenment radicalism. The Scottish case itself indicates the extent to which the Enlightenment was subject to the law of uneven development. Enlightenment thought was originally expressed in the context of the most developed capitalist economies, the Dutch and the English, but once it had emerged as a set of ideas they became available to anyone who aspired to live under the same conditions—in some cases backwardness acting as a spur to their adoption, producing forms of thought more focused on social change than that of the forerunners. Franco Venturi contrasts England with Scotland to the advantage of the latter: "It is tempting to observe that the Enlightenment was born and organized in those places where the contrast between a backward world and a modern one was chronologically more abrupt, and geographically closer."[65] But whether or not Enlightenment thought, conceived in these conditions, would actually become a material as well as intellectual force was by no means assured. As John Robertson has pointed out, Enlightenment thought in both Scotland and Naples was based on "Epicurean intellectual foundations," furthermore, "those foundations were of much longer and securer standing in Naples than they were in Scotland," but: "There was no high road from Enlightenment to revolution in Naples, any more than from Enlightenment to industrial revolution and empire in Scotland."[66] Again, in both cases the geopolitical context was decisive.

Where did the French bourgeoisie stand along the reformist-revolutionary axis? Pamela Pilbeam has written of "the real revolutionary impulse of the bourgeoisie in 1789 and subsequent years" that it "sought institutional, never violent change"; in other words it was primarily reformist in orientation.[67] This assessment tends to be supported by historians who see the real revolutionary social class as being the petty bourgeoisie; in these accounts the bourgeoisie is entirely consistent and consistently moderate:

> It is misleadingly simple to think of this process in terms of a bourgeoisie moving to the right and "betraying" its "mission" in face of the rise of a proletariat, for its opposition to the old order had always been moderate. In the first French Revolution, it was not a nascent class of capitalists, but the pressure and relative strength of small men that produced Jacobitism, revolutionary defense, the terror, democratic politics and revolutionary religion. These were not the essential components of a "classic" bourgeois revolution, but the results of a specific constellation of social forces at a particular historical juncture.[68]

There are two problems with this analysis. First, it fails to allow for the possibility of class differences between the leadership and the rank and file; in other words, views of the bourgeoisie might well have been temporarily congruent with those of the petty bourgeoisie—or at least the former might have persuaded the latter that this was the case. Sarah Maza accuses Marxists of believing that members of the bourgeoisie were "promoting their own class interests under the cover of something broader and nobler sounding," but, she asks: "Why should the bourgeoisie, if it existed, refuse to name itself, why should it feel compelled to conceal its own existence and purpose?"[69] But insofar as members of the revolutionary bourgeoisie were conscious of the underlying economic aims of their class as a whole, they could scarcely declare these openly to their allies among the other classes, who were the very ones likely to find themselves simply with a change of masters at the end of the process. This is not to suggest that the bourgeoisie necessarily engaged in deliberate deceit: their cadres required some "ethico-political" justification for their actions and had at least to try to convince themselves that what they were doing was in a greater "national" interest, even if it was primarily in their own. In this respect the role of the noncapitalist "professional" bourgeoisie was particularly important: "In its civic form, professionalism legitimated the attack on privilege, even when the latter was defended by corporative values. It stimulated a conception of the state as something which was not so much embodied in the dynast as present in the "nation," an ideological construct which developed *pari passu* with the growth and elaboration of the market."[70]

The identification of the bourgeoisie with the emerging modern concept of "the nation" was a decisive ideological maneuver. Greenfield argues that "the results" of the French Revolution "were favorable to capitalism because capitalism was consistent with nationalism, and the Revolution, which owed to nationalism its character, direction, and the very fact of its occurrence (though not timing), established nationalism as the foundation of the social order."[71] In his study of the thousand or so pamphlets published in France between January 1788 and June 1789, Boyd

Shafer identified the way in which the grievances of the opposition were treated as violations of the French national interest:

> The commercial treaty of 1786 with England was denounced on the ground that it harmed French industry, and Frenchmen were urged to use only French products. The nobles were asked to abandon privileges which harmed French agriculture and commerce, in order "to save the country," as England with machines was outstripping France. Economic freedom was demanded by an "awakening bourgeois" because "true liberty, as well as the interests of the nation," did not permit the continuation of restrictions on commerce, such as internal tariffs, and *jurades* and *maitreses*. The "passion of regulating everything to oppress everything," this writer complained, had not only produced "absurd annoyances to business," but had sapped the "sources of national wealth" as well.[72]

The second problem with foregrounding the role of the petty bourgeoisie is that claims for bourgeois moderation wrongly treat that bourgeoisie as a homogenous bloc. It is true that those capitalists who had emerged in France were more inclined to reform than their Dutch or English predecessors, not least because of the risk that revolution posed to their property, which tended to be more industrial than agrarian or mercantile. In this respect, Ralph Miliband's claim that "extreme bourgeois class consciousness appears to impose severe limits upon successful political practice" can be sustained, but is only true if we understand "bourgeois class consciousness" to mean something like: "extreme awareness of the potentially destructive short-term effects of revolution from below on capital accumulation and the personal safety of individual capitalists."[73] Full class consciousness might even have been an obstacle to adopting the necessary revolutionary conclusions, as it ultimately was for Barnave, but not for Robespierre, even though he had a similar class position. If my claims for the decisive role of the noncapitalist bourgeoisie are correct then, precisely because they were not directly involved in the process of production and hence of exploitation, they could potentially adopt more extreme revolutionary positions than the majority of actual capitalist members of their class, positions more typical of the small producers to whom Stedman Jones refers, which allowed members of both classes to unite under the banner of Jacobitism. Colin Lucas has written of how the "professional men" of the Third Estate became the leaders of the revolution as a result of two "confusions." First, because they presented their own grievances in general terms, as those of the entire estate, they were able to ideologically focus peasant and artisan hostility onto the noble landowners, rather than onto the ruling classes in general, deflecting attention from the fact that they belonged to one of those classes. In any circumstances other than revolution they would not have been able to make these connections. Second, the professionals first identified the nobility as a distinct privileged group, and then further identified the interests of the nobles with those of the absolute monarchy—a task made easier precisely by the way in which sections of the nobility rejected the Revolution. The constitution of 1791 defined the ruling class by possession of landed property, which in turn made the possessors eligible for election to public office: "The Revolution did therefore provide a social framework within which the acquisition of nobility was to be increasingly irrelevant and which allowed elite status to develop into the attribute of men of wealth however acquired and however expressed. In this sense, we may say that the Revolution made the bourgeoisie even if it was not made by the bourgeoisie."[74]

The noncapitalist bourgeoisie began to temporarily detach themselves from the economic goals of their class only when the revolution itself came under existential threat and could not be defended by means acceptable to businessmen. "Citizens," Robespierre asked members of the Convention in 1792, "did you want a revolution without a revolution?"[75] Many of them wanted precisely this; their difficulty was that it was not on offer. It was at this point, in 1792, that the rhetoric of Classical Republicanism was adopted by the Jacobin leaders to fill the ideological void. The recourse to antiquity, which Marx famously identified in *The Eighteenth Brumaire of Louis Bonaparte* as an example of the general tendency of bourgeois revolutions to clothe themselves in the garb of earlier historical periods, was in fact a much more specific response to the threat of counterrevolution, as Sewell explains:

> During the relative calm of 1789 to 1791, the revolutionaries needed no self-deception to mask their establishment of the legal conditions for capitalist enterprise. They promulgated revolutionary transformations of the nation's administrative, constitutional, and juridical structures under the banner of enlightened reason, efficiency, and natural law, without significant recourse to Roman and Greek masks. But when the affairs of the Revolution grew desperate, when the very survival of the Revolution was threatened by external war and internal revolts and the legislature was faced with the awful task of trying and executing the king for treason, the language of political economy—indeed the language of Enlightenment rationalism more generally—no longer sufficed. Political economy, whose leading advocate in the French Revolution was Sieyes, lacked a heroic vision.[76]

Sewell's point about the limitations of Enlightenment rationalism as a mobilizing ideology is true but underestimates the extent to which some leading Jacobins came to actively reject it:

> Robespierre delivered a keynote speech to the assembly condemning what he called the arid materialism of the *encyclopédistes* (Diderot and d'Holbach in particular), *philosophes*, who waged war not just upon the great Rousseau but on sentiment, common opinion, and the simple virtue and beliefs of common people.... Here, ironically, Robespierre's Jacobinism closely converged with royalist Counter-Enlightenment ideology, both propagating the myth of the Enlightenment as a coldly clinical, unfeeling machine of rational ideas, brutalizing natural sentiment and destroying instead of furthering what is best in human life.[77]

Nevertheless, the extremity of Robespierre's position was precisely why it was only tolerated by the majority of his class as a response to a moment of danger. The majority of the Jacobins saw political dictatorship, economic centralization, the Law of the Maximum, and similar measures as temporary in nature, made necessary by civil war and invasion. Only at the outer edges of Jacobinism did members see them as being anticapitalist in themselves, and this was the anticapitalism of the small producers, not workers.

When was the moment of irreversibility for France? Here the national experience was different from those of earlier bourgeois revolutions. In the case of Britain the Restoration of 1660 involved a reaction within the revolutionary process, rather than outright counterrevolution, although the latter remained a threat until both the second English revolution of 1688–89, the climax of the Scottish Revolution in 1745–46, and victory over France abroad during the 1750s and 1760s. In the case of France the restoration of 1815 effectively signaled the end of the bourgeois revolution. Several revolutions followed, of course, but they were either political, involving the redistribution of power within the bourgeoisie (1830), or failed socialist revolutions (1871) or a combination of both (1848). To argue that the French state underwent further changes as a result of these events and indeed into the twentieth century is not to declare the Great Revolution incomplete, it is merely— as I argued in chapter 15—to notice something important about the nature of all capitalist states, namely that they never attain a condition of perfection, but are regularly subject to restructuring in response to forces unleashed by capitalist accumulation. The point is that after 1815 the French state was compatible with capital accumulation whereas before 1789 it was not.

Higher levels of economic growth have often taken several decades to achieve in the aftermath of bourgeois revolutions and, in the French case, productivity actually fell in ways that might be more characteristic of the aftermath of socialist revolutions. Nevertheless, the revolution put in place a juridical superstructure, itself a crucial component of the state, which enabled such growth to take place, not least by encouraging initiatives that would have previously not been worth undertaking, rather than acting as a barrier to them: "Under the Old Regime, it would have paid to drain marshes or to irrigate the soil, but the path was blocked by overlapping property rights and a judicial system that encouraged debilitating court suits." The Revolution changed these conditions: "Once the local and administrative reforms were securely in place, water projects proliferated." Not every region of France was capable of benefiting from innovations of this kind, but where they did "the economic consequences proved dramatic."[78] There were of course more dramatic examples of how the legal framework was changed to facilitate capitalist production, most notably in the legislative program of the Convention during the first half of 1791: under the Law of Allaire of March 2, feudal guilds were abolished and restrictions on businesses removed; the decree on agrarian property rights of June 5, the most important of a series of enactments concerning agriculture, established freedom of ownership, including the right to enclose common land; and finally, the Le Chapelier Law of June 14–17, banned combinations and industrial action.[79] In other words, as David Parker asks, can the French Revolution not simultaneously have "removed the legal and institutional impediments to the operation of the free market" *and* temporarily "deepened and prolonged the economic crisis of most sectors of the economy".[80]

As we saw in chapter 15, revisionists have claimed that the existence of a mass of peasant smallholders left in secure possession of their holdings after the French Revolution acted as an economic break, thus casting doubt on the connection between the Revolution and the subsequent development of capitalism. Similar claims have subsequently been made by political Marxists like George Comninel. There are, however, perfectly good reasons why this might have occurred that have nothing to do the nature of social relations in postrevolutionary France. As we saw in the previous chapter, preparation for war had the effect of stimulating capitalist development in feudal-absolutist Europe; but war itself could lead to catastrophic retrogression. The effect of the Thirty Years' War on the north German lands is perhaps the best example of this, despite the tendency among modern historians to downplay the consequences for economy and society. Even when allowance has been made for the fact that economic development in the German lands had already stalled in the years directly before 1618, the overall impact of the war was to throw it into reverse. Conservative estimates suggest that the German population may have fallen from between 15 to 20 percent or from twenty million people to sixteen or seventeen million. In the areas directly affected by the fighting, such as Mecklenburg or Pomerania, the population may have fallen by as much as 50 percent. The majority of these deaths were not directly due to the war, but the result of famine or epidemic disease on a population weakened by food shortages and other privations. Of equal importance was the massive burden of municipal debt that afflicted cities required to pay both for the upkeep of their own forces and "contributions" toward enemy troops in order to spare themselves from occupation (debts that were often owed to wealthy noblemen), the abandonment of land by formerly independent peasants, and the formation of large-scale estate farming based on serfdom.[81]

France did not suffer the same levels of devastation as the German lands, but as Phillip Hoffman points out, the cumulative effect of the revolutionary years was to retard economic development. Hoffman also argues, however, that expecting otherwise is indicative of a rather unrealistic conception of what revolution and revolutionary war involve:

> That the Revolution harmed farming should come as no surprise, given what we know about the effects of warfare on agricultural productivity. Warfare and troop movements nearly always jolted farming. They did so during the Revolution, just as they had during the Wars of Religion. Requisitions were hardly beneficial either. When we add how the Revolution cut off sources of agricultural capital and dissipated trade—the great source of productivity growth under the Old Regime—the deleterious effects on the economy are almost predictable.[82]

And in this respect the French experience was scarcely unique. Productivity did not instantaneously increase after the American Civil War either; indeed, the decade of the 1860s saw the lowest growth in the entire century between the 1830s and

1930s, but these figures include the South, and therefore completely ignore the devastation of its economy and this too has more general implications. The North was eventually prepared to wage total war in order to destroy the social order based on slavery, even though the South would be an integral part of the reconstituted United States. It took the South nearly a hundred years to recover and for at least part of that period precapitalist or noncapitalist social relations of production—in the "technical" sense discussed above—continued to exist, at least in the countryside.[83] In other words, the survival and ultimate expansion of the capitalist system across the subcontinent was more important to Northern politicians than immediately achieving either uniformly intensive growth or "real subsumption" in the vanquished South.[84]

To return to the French Revolution, it is by no means clear that the small peasant agriculture sustained by the French Revolution *did* retard capitalist economic development other than in the very short term. Following the work of the Russian historian Anatoli Ado, Heller argues that Jacobin encouragement for "petty commodity production as a prelude to primitive accumulation, social polarization, and the emergence of a vibrant agrarian and industrial capitalism" was an attempt to reproduce the American version of capitalism rather than that of the Britain: "The short-lived Jacobin state may be seen as a bold if unsuccessful attempt to install such a capitalism from below." The division of the land did indeed initially retard capitalist development: "But under free market conditions it would have speeded primitive accumulation over the medium term by unleashing the path of small-scale commodity production in both town and country." This position was actually theorized under the Directory from 1795 by the proponents of what James Livesey calls "commercial republicanism," who saw it as a conscious alternative to the British path of "enclosure, tenant farming, and agricultural innovation": "Comparing Great Britain to France, the commercial republicans argued that Britain could not fulfill the promise of economic liberty, because unlike the republican French, the British under their monarchy did not enjoy full political liberty." But these were a minority. The post-Thermidorian reaction refused the demands of the peasants for land and upheld the ownership and dominance of "nobles, bourgeoisie, and rich peasants." We therefore may have to revise the traditional view of the agrarian settlement and consider whether it was not "the persistence of large property and the burden of rent, not small peasant property, which inhibited a more rapid development of French capitalism." In turn, this might suggest "the popular revolution based on the petty producers ought to be seen as an essential element of the capitalist dynamic characteristic of this upheaval." Heller agrees with Livesey that "revisionist attempts to measure the economic consequences of the Revolution in terms of short-term costs and benefits are historiographically misconceived." This does not mean that there were no benefits. In particular, Heller questions the conventional view that British manufacturing was superior to the French in the immediate aftermath of the Revolution. First, Britain was actually less mechanized during this period than is traditionally thought; only in the latter half of the nineteenth-century did machinofacture come to dominate production. Second,

mass production was not the only method of industrialization: "With its higher quality production, France inserted itself differently into the international division of
labor . . . [growing] at a rate comparable to that of its neighbors but based its secondary sector on small craft and manufacturing enterprises."[85] These arguments have
by no means achieved general acceptance, but they demonstrate that it is possible to
interpret the continued existence of small-scale peasant agriculture in France without
simply repeating the narrative of precapitalist backwardness.

The French Revolution was one of the great turning points in human history, as
every intelligent contemporary, friend or foe, recognized at the time. Yet, paradoxically, the cataclysmic force it unleashed also ensured that nothing like it would ever
happen again. Even at the time the French Revolution had no successful imitators
with the exception of the revolution in San Domingo; yet this extraordinary process,
the significance of which is only now being fully realized, was at least partly directed
against the French Republic, to the extent that it refused to apply in the colonies
the principles that it declared in the metropolis. Nor was it capable of leaping over
the material constraints within which it took place. "Given the immediate historical
context of a slave labor based world-system, from the moment Napoleon abandoned
the revolutionary ideals of 1789 and decided to reinstate French slavery, it is doubtful
if an entire nation composed solely of small farmers could have remained free from
slavery beyond 1802. . . . No true freedom, one that would allow for the sustained
development of both liberty and social equality, was ever possible for Haitians in
such an unfree totality as was Western modernity in 1804."[86]

In Europe, those who sought to emulate the French Revolution were either defeated, as in Ireland or, more commonly, a minority within their own societies who
relied on the external support of the French in order to achieve power and who
consequently could not retain it. Indeed, the next revolution to bear any real comparison to the French in terms of its internal dynamic and pattern of development
was the Russian Revolution of 1917, which had a quite different class basis. "The
French Revolution was and remained *sui generis*," writes Tim Blanning: "It was the
war which brought it to the outside world, and it did so with shattering impact."[87]
The revolutionary and Napoleonic Wars to which Blanning refers directly contributed to capitalist development by attacking feudalism outside the borders of
France. The intervention of the New Model Army in Scotland between 1651 and
1660 had been the first example of "externalizing" the bourgeois revolution; far
more significant, however, were these attempts by the French "people's armies" to
crush the local nobility, abolish feudal tenures and jurisdictions, and generally rationalize the economy and society throughout Europe, even after the internal reaction began with Thermidor. Their failure to do so permanently was an important
factor in determining why capitalist stabilization had to take place on the conservative basis of a restored monarchy, as it had in England beforehand.

The extent to which the French were able to establish sister republics in conquered Europe depended on whether indigenous forces existed that were willing

to be involved in the process of reform; but precisely because of their isolation, their minority status, they were not necessarily those with popular followings, as the Spanish rebellion against France and its local supporters after 1808 was to prove. Although the Napoleonic armies that invaded Spain in 1809 were clearly the bearers of a more advanced social system than the Bourbon monarchy they sought to overthrow, the fact that change was being imposed at bayonet point provoked a popular resistance that ultimately aided the reactionary alliance against France. Where there were social forces committed to republican politics, it tended to be in those areas, principally Holland, where bourgeois revolutions had already taken place and consequently where these forces were opposed to the imperial role of the French armies.[88] In Britain, the most advanced of all, the majority of the ruling class were violently opposed to France and prepared to ally with absolutist reaction to defeat her, partly because the British bourgeoisie feared a successful rival—as they had the Dutch in the 1650s—and partly because the very violence of the Revolution had acted as an inspiration to nascent working-class forces in England and Scotland and to bourgeois revolutionaries in Ireland. In some territories, like Hanover and Westphalia in 1807, the French abolished serfdom only for it to be restored after Napoleon withdrew in 1813. In other parts of the German lands, notably in the Rhineland, it proved impossible to restore seigniorial rights, but these examples were too few to be the immediate basis for a Europe of independent states on the French model.

Nevertheless, as I noted in chapter 7, Europe after 1815 was not "a world restored." François Crouzet argues that the preconditions for industrialization "existed thanks to the French Revolution and its exportation to neighboring centers, especially by Napoleon": "A whole deadwood of time-honored institutions (such as guilds or the manorial system), which had been hampering economic progress had been wiped out; and a bourgeois laissez-faire social and economic system, much more akin to the British system than to that of the Ancien Regime had been established—and was not much tampered with by the post-Waterloo 'Restorations.'"[89] It is important to note that the discrepancy between intention and result, which I highlighted in the previous chapter in relation to the English Revolution, also applies to the Napoleonic period of the French Revolution. Chateaubriand, a survivor, comes close to capturing the full complexity of Bonaparte's role in his memoirs "from beyond the grave":

> That Bonaparte, continuing the successes of the Republic, sowed everywhere the principle of independence, that his victories helped loosen the links between peoples and kings, tore those peoples free from the power of old customs and old ideas: that in this sense he pursued social liberation, all that I can in no way contest: but that of his own will, he consciously worked for the political and civil liberation of nations; that he established the most narrow despotism with the idea of giving Europe, and France in particular, the broadest constitution; that he was only a tribune disguised as a tyrant, that is a supposition it is impossible for me to adopt: the revolution, which was Napoleon's source, soon appeared to him as an enemy; he fought it ceaselessly.[90]

Between 1815 and 1848, no revolution comparable to that of 1789–94 took place, although liberal conspiracies and military coups were relatively commonplace. The difficulty was simple enough: the French, indeed the European bourgeoisie as whole, had a reasonably clear program of demands before 1789; but as Marx asked, "had any eighteenth-century Frenchman the faintest idea *a priori* beforehand of the way in which the demands of the French bourgeoisie would be accomplished?"[91] He had not. Revolutionaries invented the practices and structures that we associate with the French Revolution in response to events; but in situations where quite different conditions prevailed would-be revolutionaries could repeat the familiar slogans to virtually no effect. The idea of the French Revolution dominated the first half of the nineteenth century, but it had no successful imitators.

Toward International Structural Adaptation (2): From Revolution to Reform

Earlier in this chapter I noted how, by the conclusion of the Seven Years' War, the British capitalist-constitutional state form had triumphed over its French feudal-absolutist competitor. The very same British capitalist-constitutional state form had by the end of the Napoleonic Wars also triumphed over its French Jacobin rival and this was to prove equally decisive, for the results of the next phase of revolutionary state formation resembled the conservatism of England after 1688 rather more than the radicalism of France after 1789. It was highly compressed, beginning with the launch of the first Italian War of Independence in 1859 and ending with the Franco-Prussian War of 1870–71, with an aftermath in the form of the Paris Commune pointing toward the possible socialist future. From this period almost nothing resembles the great popular insurgencies of 1567, 1642, or 1792; instead we find that negotiated constitutional settlements (Canada), military-bureaucratic coup d'état (Japan), and above all, conventional warfare (Italy, Germany, United States) were the methods by which these transformations were accomplished. The only revolutionary movement comparable to the earlier movements from below was the Polish Insurrection of 1863, not coincidentally the one significant failure of the entire period. More successful bourgeois revolutions were carried out in these years than in any other, but as these formal shifts suggest, the significance of the individual preconditions discussed in the previous chapter had also changed—indeed, in many respects they were no longer distinguishable as separate factors. The outcomes, however, remained constant.

The expansion of capitalism beyond Europe and consequently the increased pressure for states to adapt to the new system was the indirect result of British victory over France in the Napoleonic Wars: the collapse of the European empires in the Americas, the substitution of informal British influence and influx of British manufactures; the end of existing trade monopolies with Asia; the global domination of British sea power—all these developments contributed to the establishment of the world capitalist economy dominated by Britain and policed by the Royal Navy.[92] By the middle of the century the momentum began to sweep all before it: "The drive to exchange more, to seek out new markets, to find 'new' products and commodities, and to draw the commerce of the world into one vast network centered on the great port cities of the West . . . was the main dynamic behind the gradual formation between the 1860s and the 1880s of a 'world economy'—a single system of global trade."[93] As far as the balance between feudal crisis and capitalist alternative was concerned, the attempts to establish unified nation-states in the 1860s were made on the basis of economies that were internally less developed in capitalist terms than even France had been in 1789, but which now existed within the overall context of a rapidly developing world capitalist economy. As a consequence Prussia and Piedmont suffered from the economic slump that had helped stimulate the revolutions of 1848, but were not able to participate fully in the boom of the 1850s that followed. Within the absolutist states feudalism was no longer so much in crisis as subject to the slow, inexorable collapse and reconstruction of its constitutive social relations on a capitalist basis, often without any conscious decisions having been taken to achieve this end. These were the outcome of long-term trends dating back to the French Revolution, which had forced some of the absolutist state bureaucracies and even some individual members of feudal ruling classes to begin the process of reform that would ultimately culminate in the revolutions from above between 1859 and 1871.

Scotland provides an interesting precursor, since the actions of the Scottish lords in the latter half of the eighteenth century inadvertently provided the prototype for the top-down transitions that would follow in mainland Europe during the nineteenth. The former process was the first transition to agrarian capitalism to be carried out almost entirely by an existing class of feudal landowners who realized that the only way to reverse their decline was to adopt the very methods of the capitalist agriculture that they had hitherto resisted. In this way they could at least remain members of a dominant class, albeit within a new set of social relations, using new methods of exploitation. There are obviously major differences between what might be called the Scottish path and, for example, its better-known Prussian successor. The Scottish landlords took part in a ferment of theoretical exploration during the Enlightenment that was unprecedented in the history of Europe or its overseas extensions; their Prussian successors merely inherited the operational conclusions without experiencing the liberatory intellectual process by which they were produced. The Scottish landlords were able to begin reform safe in the knowledge that they would not be met with widespread peasant resistance; their successors began reform in part to prevent peasant revolt from assuming the terrifying proportions that it had already done during the French Revolution.[94]

These differences aside, however, two striking similarities remain. One is that military defeat precipitated the reform process. In the case of Scotland, it was the Jacobite defeat at Culloden in 1746. In the case of Prussia, it was defeat by the Napoleonic armies at Jena and Auerstadt in 1806, the outcomes of which seemed to demonstrate the superiority of free peasants over serfs as a source of manpower, while the indemnities imposed by the victorious French demanded an increase in revenues that was unlikely to be produced as long as serfdom endured. The other similarity is that, because of a comparable primitiveness of economic relations, both landlord classes appropriated the peasant surplus in the form of labor rent. One unintended consequence of the reassertion of absolutist power in Central and Eastern Europe after the failure of the bourgeois revolutions of 1848 was to accelerate this process, as Jerome Blum points out:

> It is difficult to imagine, much less to document, the thesis that bourgeois capitalists in Russia or Romania or Hungary, or, in fact any of the servile lands, had sufficient influence to persuade governments to end the servile order, or that governments freed the peasants out of their concern for the needs of bourgeois capitalism. . . . The final reforms that freed the peasants from their servility, and afforded them civil equality with the other strata in society, were the last great triumph of royal absolutism over nobility—and, in truth, its last great achievement.

The revolutionary regimes of 1848–49 passed legislation that was never implemented, but "when the absolutists gained control, as they quickly did, they carried out the revolution's agrarian reforms because these reforms suited their own interests." What were these? One was "reducing the power of the nobility" and the other "enabled the throne to hold the loyalty and support of the peasantry": "These men, advocates of the bureaucratic sovereign state, opposed the traditional order because it interfered with and impeded the welfare and power of the state."[95] But in an environment in which capitalist market conditions increasingly prevailed, the slackening of feudal agrarian social relations could only result in adaptation to it. Hobsbawm has described how in Bohemia and Hungary in the latter half of the nineteenth century: "The large noble estates, sometimes helped by injections of finance from the compensation payments for the loss of labor services, transformed themselves into capitalist undertakings."[96] This was a general trend after 1848, in Latin America and East Asia as much as Central Europe and it meant that landowners now came to have new expectations and requirements of the state. "The landowners were trying to maximize profits by turning themselves into big local agro-business or efficient tax-collectors," writes Christopher Bayly, who mentions "Prussian junkers, Mexican *hacendados*, and Javenese *regenten*" as examples. "Entrepreneurial landed interests like this needed the government to put in roads, railways, and canals for them. Equally, the administrators needed the support of big landowners, provided they could be persuaded to reform sufficiently to head off peasant revolt and the hostility of urban dwellers."[97]

But very few of the existing states had the structural capacity to make these provisions on the scale required. Pressure therefore began to be exerted by emergent capitalist landowners for, at the very least, reform; what made at least some fractions among the existing feudal ruling class opt for revolution was the need to respond to more immediate danger: defeat in war:

The impetus towards these reforms had been the success of Great Britain and the failure of most of the continental countries in the middle of the century. In 1856, Russia had been humiliated in the Crimean War's outcome. Austria had been defeated in 1859 by the French and the Piedmontese, who established the kingdom of Italy in 1861. Prussia had been humiliated in 1850 by the Austrians. In the 1850s, most countries experienced financial confusion, and needed serious reforms and considerable loans to make good. But financiers would not give money unless there were reforms. One of these was that the running of the state should be entrusted, not to a Court and its hangers-on, but to experts, with the backing of law.[98]

The untransformed state therefore acted as a block to supporting capitalist expansion, restoring military capability, and achieving the financial stability necessary for either. "To be a Great Power—and in Central Europe or Japan merely to survive—it was useful to have a central government wielding infrastructural coordination of its territories than confederal regimes could muster. Self-styled Modernisers everywhere regarded this as essential. Neither German nor Japanese confederations nor transnational dynasties could provide this. Their survival in war or anticipated war was in jeopardy, and so they fell."[99] They fell, or at least some did; but who pushed them? Not the bourgeoisie, for reasons that once again can be traced back to the French Revolution. When pan-European revolutionary upheaval took place in 1848, the non-capitalist bourgeoisie would not reprise the audacity of the Jacobins. Why?

One reason, already extensively discussed in part 1 of this book, was their fear of the consequences of popular insurgency, now heightened by the greater social presence of the working class among the ranks of "the people," a presence that was also indicative of the larger levels of capitalist fixed investment that stood to be destroyed. The necessity for alliances brought with it the danger that, even if these peasant and plebeian allies were unable to achieve their own goals, they might still push matters further than any section of the bourgeoisie was willing to go. The English capitalist class had learned the lesson as early as 1688, when it called on an invasion by the regime of their Dutch predecessors to complete their revolution for them and thus exclude or minimize the threat of popular interventions of the sort had characterized the years from 1640–48. For the European bourgeoisies that developed later, it was the Great French Revolution that provided the same lesson. This assessment should not be historically foreshortened: the problem in 1848 was not that members of the bourgeoisie were unwilling to take part in the revolutions, but rather that they were unwilling to conduct the revolutions in the only ways that would overthrow the absolutist regimes. The radicalism of the French Revolution was inherited, not by the bourgeoisie, but by the emergent working-class movement. "If the bourgeoisie no longer thought in terms of 1789–1794," writes Hobsbawm, "the democratic and social-revolutionary radicals still did."[100]

Another factor contributed to these levels of self-defeating restrain, one that also concerned the role of the popular masses. In this case it was not, however, fear of their radicalism, but instead fear of their potential for reaction or, more precisely, the way in which elements of the ancien régime were able to mobilize popular feel-ing against religious or agrarian reforms.[101] "The bourgeoisie is naturally bound to fear the stupidity of the masses as long as they remain conservative," wrote Marx, "and the discernment of the masses as soon as they become revolutionary."[102] It is important in this context to remember that the Parisian sansculottes were not the only and certainly not the most typical participants "from below" in the upheavals between 1789 and 1815. During the Napoleonic Wars the French occupying armies attempted to impose bourgeois revolution "from above and outside" on the absolutist regimes of Western and Southern Europe, in alliance with local Liberals. Yet in at least two important cases, those of Spain and Naples, the republics estab-lished by Napoleon were resisted, not merely by representatives of the feudal ruling class, using conscripts and mercenaries but by popular uprisings dedicated to restor-ing church and king, often operating completely outside the command or control of the elites. It is meaningless to describe these revolts as nationalist in inspiration, since the kingdoms of Spain and Naples that the insurgents sought to defend were, in their different ways, the antithesis of modern nation-states. Indeed, in both cases modern nation-states were precisely what the hated Liberals were attempting to construct. Yet the mass of the population, who might have benefited from the over-throw of feudalism, were isolated from the Liberals by the latter's bourgeois status and relative wealth. The Liberals then heightened their social distance from the masses by their reliance on a foreign power and by offering no positive reforms to the peasantry. Presented by a mere change in the mechanism of exploitation, but one that would nevertheless destroy the only aspects of society that offered stability and consolation, and simultaneously offered the opportunity to exercise a power normally denied them, the masses rejected the new order arms in hand.[103]

There were deep contradictions within a popular resistance dedicated to restoring one of the most reactionary regimes in Europe, contradictions captured by Goya in *The Disasters of War* in a way that expressed both his awareness of the tragedy and his ambivalence toward the forces involved. Yet if the meaning of the movement was ambiguous, that of the outcome was not in doubt: the restoration of church and king.[104] A similar story could be told of events in Naples, where the French-es-tablished republic failed to abolish feudal relations on the land and instead raised taxes on the peasants and urban poor. The retaking of Naples by Calabrian forces and the British involved a slaughter that continued for two weeks in which Repub-licans were massacred by the urban poor and the lumpenproletariat.[105] The Spanish peasants and Neapolitan urban masses, faced with the choice of two evils, actively embraced the one that was familiar to them and at least preserved their existing life world. Nevertheless, these struggles, the Spanish in particular, involved self-sacrifice and collective organization linked to overt forms of class hostility, albeit one focused almost entirely on the external foreign enemy and its internal supporters, who were seen as both betraying the kingdom and seeking to impose new forms of exploita-tion. The liberal revolutionaries could offer the masses nothing, and the resulting absence of popular opposition to the old regimes was one reason the bourgeois revolutions in both Spain and what would eventually become Italy were delayed for so long after these initial top-down attempts. Nevertheless, in spite of their awareness of these historical episodes the French bourgeoisie supported the coup by Napoleon III, which brought revolutionary period begun in 1848 to an end, even though Bonaparte was supported in this and the subsequent referendum precisely by the reactionary elements of the peasantry which it most feared. More than anything else, this accommodation demonstrated which social force the bourgeoisie now regarded with the greatest dread, with all the attendant consequences for its own role as a revolutionary class.

At least sections of the bourgeoisie had participated in the revolutions of 1848. Hobsbawm notes of the motivations of students and intellectuals in that year: "It was largely based on the (as it turned out temporary) inability of the new bourgeois society before 1848 to provide enough posts of adequate status for the educated whom it produced in unprecedented numbers, and whose rewards were so much more modest than their ambitions."[106] In the decades that followed the noncapitalist sections of the bourgeoisie, which had previously given revolutionary leadership, might have been less paralyzed by fear of working-class radicalism and more prepared to face down peasant reaction, were increasingly integrated into a society in which their former frustrations and humiliations were rapidly becoming things of the past.

Leadership would therefore have to come from sections of the existing ruling classes of Europe and Japan, such as the Prussian landlords led by Bismarck, which had previously resisted revolution but now embraced a top-down version in order to make their states capable of military competition from their rivals—or in the case of Japan, to avoid the fate of colonization and dismemberment which had befallen China. They had models to follow, and here again uneven development, "the advantages of backwardness," was central, as Crouzet notes of the European powers:

> They had to *transform* existing industries, to "modernize" them by large scale introduction of the new techniques which had been invented and perfected in England, and did not need to build up completely new industries from scratch....The Continentals, once peace and normal relations with Britain had been established in 1815, were theoretically able to take advantage of the experience accumulated by the British during the preceding decades, to tap the reservoir of technical expertise and borrow straight away the best British practice.[107]

If industrial Britain provided a model for the organization of production, Napoleonic France and its European Empire provided a model for the formation of the nation-state: "The same techniques of administrative uniformity, linguistic imposition, and pressure for social integration that had marked Bonaparte's attempt to remold Europe were transferred by the statesmen of the new states of Europe within their national boundaries in order to eliminate what were regarded as the disaggregative forces of local identities."[108] The contrast between the German (1871) and Austro-Hungarian (1867) empires is illustrative in this respect. In the former:

"The regime was strengthened. The bourgeoisie mobilized behind it, disparaging federalism as reactionary. The opposite was occurring in Austria, where modernizing ideologies were snatched from centralizing liberals by regional 'nationalists.'"[109]

The postrevolutionary states in Italy, Germany, and Japan continued to be ruled by kings or emperors but, in terms of capitalist development, this is of less significance than it at first appears. An analogy can be drawn here with the distinction between the formal and real subsumption of labor that we have already discussed in relation to the socioeconomic transition from feudalism to capitalism. As we have seen, capital initially took over the existing technical mode of production and only later created the labor process anew in factories specially designed for this purpose; in a similar way, state managers took over the outer forms of the existing absolutist states, but internally transformed them into apparatuses capable of building an autonomous center of capital accumulation. Between 1870 and 1918, virtually all the great powers consciously emphasized the archaic, imperial role of their monarchies. Bayly has noted that these "were useful to the political forces trying to mediate an increasingly complex society." The role played by Kaiser William II is typical in this respect: "By astute manipulation of the press and acquiescence in the views of elected politicians, he could serve the interests of the new middle classes of Germany's industrial cities. As commander of the forces and descendant of Frederick the Great, he was the symbolic leader of the junkers of East Germany and of their brothers and sons in the imperial army. As emperor of German, he could pacify the interests of the states and regions, both Catholic and Protestant, that had seemed locked in battle at the time of Bismarck." Bayly makes the obvious comparison with the Japanese emperor, but also another that is perhaps less obvious: "The real parallel with late-imperial Germany was not imperial Russia . . . it was Britain," where "the royal ritual of coronations, parades, and state openings of Parliament became more elaborate and more beautifully choreographed as the century wore on."[110]

To the inattentive this may look like the assertion of "feudal" elements within the state, indicating an incomplete transition. Tom Nairn, for example, claims that in the earlier case of the British state after 1688, "an in-depth historical analysis shows that, while not directly comparable to the notorious relics of the 20th century, like the Hapsburg, Tsarist, or Prussian-German states, *it retains something in common with them.*" What is the basis of this commonality? "Although not of course an absolutist state, the Anglo-British system remains a product of the general transition from absolutism to modern constitutionalism; it led the way out of the former, but never genuinely arrived at the latter."[111] These arguments confuse form and content. In fact, the enhanced eminence of the British monarchy after 1870 was consciously engineered by the representatives of the capitalist ruling class for the same reasons and in much the same way as their equivalents did in imperial Germany and imperial Japan. There was only one respect in which Britain was exceptional: unlike the American president on the one hand or the German kaiser on the other, its monarch wielded no real power.[112] In all these cases the preexisting symbolism of the Crown was imbued with a sense of national unity against two main challenges: internal class divisions and external imperial rivalry. The point was well made by Bukharin, writing of the ideology of the imperialist powers in the First World War:

> These sentiments are not "remnants of feudalism," as some observers suppose, these are not debris of the old that have survived in our times. This is an entirely new socio-political formation caused by the birth of finance capital. If the old feudal "policy of blood and iron" was able to serve here, externally as a model, this was possible only because the moving springs of modern economic life drive capital along the road of aggressive politics and the militarization of all social life.[113]

In other words, Britain could indeed be compared with Germany and Japan: all three were capitalist states that could be strongly contrasted with feudal absolutist Austria-Hungary or Russia, even down to the role of the emperor and empresses: "Russia represented the opposite pole to Japan within the spectrum of authoritarian monarchy—no corporate regime strategy, much depending on the monarch himself."[114] The most striking contrast is however between Japan and China, the two states that, until the mid-1800s had been most inaccessible to Western power. Superficially, the Japanese revolutionaries had taken a reactionary position of restoring a previous form of rule ("Revere the Emperor!"); but as Ben-Ami Shillory notes, "the Meiji leaders, wishing to make Japan the leading force of East Asia, adopted Chinese Imperial trappings which had not previously existed in Japan."[115] But unlike the Chinese imperial attempts to "expel the barbarians," the Japanese also derived their new method of socioeconomic organization from these self-same barbarians. Success or failure in the case of any bourgeois revolution can therefore be determined by assessing whether or not it has achieved the essential changes in the nature of the state required by capital, regardless of formal continuities.

A further cluster of transformations occurred more or less contemporaneously with the revolutions from above in Germany, Italy, and Japan; those in the white colonial-settler states. Marx noted that, although mercantile capital existed in both, two distinct types of production prevailed in these territories. The first is where the colonists are essentially subsistence farmers who do not carry out capitalist production, the majority of whose products are not traded as commodities.[116] The key to the retention of small-commodity production in these circumstances is the superabundance of one of the most fundamental forces of production: land. In these circumstances it is impossible for the expropriation of the producers to take place: "In the colonies the separation of the worker from the conditions of labor and from the soil, in which they are rooted, does not yet exist, or only sporadically, or on too limited a scale."[117] But this is not the case everywhere. The second type, where plantation slave labor (and often varying degrees of unfree peasant labor) is used to produce commodities like sugar and cotton for the world market, is formally nearer to that of capitalism, even though wage labor is not involved.[118] With one great exception to which I will return, none of the societies in either variant required a bourgeois revolution in the form we have hitherto discussed.

Colonial settlements in which small-commodity production was initially dominant tended to be British. Samir Amin has discovered this pattern, "in New England between 1600 and 1750, in the South Africa of the Boers between 1600 and 1880, and in Australia and New Zealand from the beginning of white settlement to the rise of modern capitalism." What is interesting about these societies was that, historically, they were the *only* ones to be based on this mode of production, which was otherwise coexistent and subordinate to another modes: "These societies of small farmers and free craftsmen, where the simple commodity mode of production was not tacked on to tribute-paying or slave-owning modes constituted the principal mode of social organization, would be inexplicable if one did not know that they were a by-product of the break-up of feudal relations in England (and, secondarily, in the Netherlands and France)." Amin adds: "Such formations have a strong tendency to develop into full-fledged *capitalist* formations."[119] But did they require revolutions to do so? The settlers were not required to overthrow feudalism, which was marginal in North America and nonexistent in Australasia and Southern Africa, but against the indigenous populations, which were subjected to genocidal onslaught in the former two areas and to systematic racial subordination in the latter. Can these also be regarded as bourgeois revolutions? Rosa Luxemburg once noted:

> A natural economy thus confronts the requirements of capitalism at every turn with rigid barriers. Capitalism must therefore always and everywhere fight a battle of annihilation against every historical form of natural economy that it encounters, whether this is slave economy, feudalism, primitive communism, or patriarchal peasant economy. The principal methods in this struggle are political force (revolution, war), oppressive taxation by the state, and cheap goods; they are partly applied simultaneously, and partly they succeed and complement one another. In Europe, force assumed revolutionary forms in the fight against feudalism (this is the ultimate explanation of the bourgeois revolutions in the seventeenth, eighteenth and nineteenth centuries); in the non-European countries, where it fights more primitive social organizations, it assumes the forms of colonial policy. These methods, together with the systems of taxation applied in such cases, and commercial relations also, particularly with primitive communities, form an alliance in which political power and economic factors go hand in hand.[120]

This suggestive passage compares the bourgeois revolutions against feudal-absolutist states with "colonial policy" against indigenous societies in which the state was still in the process of formation. The latter, despite the savagery involved in displacing and exterminating the Native American and aboriginal peoples, and partly because it was not directed against a state, took the form of a more prolonged process than the former, even when they involved more than one episode. There is no law, however, which states that bourgeois revolutions can only be conducted against states associated with the feudal and tributary modes of production out of which capitalism emerged; in a context where a capitalist world economy was consolidating they could also be conducted against tribal societies still in the "Asiatic" stage transitional to full class society. The decisive periods in the destruction of these indigenous social structures and the seizure of the land that had previously been occupied—"owned" would be anachronistic here—overlapped with those of the revolutions of above, unsurprisingly, since the pressures of the world market was decisive in both cases. In New Zealand, for example, the wars between the colonial settlers and the Maori population reached their climax in the 1860s, after which the construction of the bourgeois order began: "Between 1870 and 1914 central government policy was designed to create a modern state, with a balanced population structure, the infrastructure for a primary producing and trading economy, a streamlined political system, and the administrative and social institutions necessary for a maturing society."[121] A unified nation-state still had to be created, but in the absence of a precapitalist state to be overthrown, this was essentially a technical and administrative task rather than a political and social one.

Colonial settlements based on slavery and other forms of unfree agricultural labor tended to be formerly Spanish and Portuguese. The Latin American revolutions that spread through these territories after the fall of the Bourbons in 1808 are sometimes referred to as the wars of independence, and the allusion to the US revolution of the previous century is apt, since the former were also ultimately political revolutions and left the social structures essentially intact following the expulsion of the Iberian powers. Although the rhetoric of the Latin American revolutions was derived from that of the French Republic their real reference point was 1776 rather than 1789, still less 1792. "The new nationalism was almost devoid of social content," writes John Lynch:

> The creoles [white colonialists] were haunted by the specter of caste war. And to some degree the chronology of their conversion to independence depended on two factors—the strength of popular agitation, and the capacity of the colonial government to control it. In Mexico and Peru, where viceregal authority had the nerve and the means to govern effectively, the creoles did not hasten to desert the shelter of imperial government. But where the colonial regime was thought to be weak and social explosion imminent—in northern South America—then the obsession of the creoles with law and order and their anxiety to preserve the social structure persuaded them to make a bid for power from the very beginning. . . . There was therefore, a causal connection between the radicalism of the masses and the conservatism of independence. Spanish America retained its colonial heritage not because the masses were indifferent to the creole revolution but because they were a threat to it.[122]

Although each country had its individual peculiarities, Lynch's general analysis is applicable in the specific cases of all the successor states of the Spanish and Portuguese Empires; thus Luis Tapia writes of Bolivia after 1825: "The constitutions of the nineteenth century acknowledged a political change—the replacement of Spanish colonial rule by a new state that responded to the dominant economic and social power groups within it—but brought no social change as such. That independence took place without changing the social structure is reflected in the constitutions of the time, conceived as these were more as a political transformation than a social one."[123]

Revolutions, albeit of a mainly top-down variety, had still been necessary where a coherent territorial state needed to be formed from preexisting, precapitalist fragments (as in Italy and Germany) or where a centralized precapitalist state was incapable of defending its territory against imperialist incursions as in Japan). The history of the former colonies of Latin America (and indeed that of their former colonial powers) suggests, however, that by the middle decades of the nineteenth century and the formation of the capitalist world economy, bourgeois revolutions were no longer essential for either the initiation or consolidation of capitalist development on any given territory, provided it was formally independent of external control. Under these conditions a prolonged process of adaptive reform, perhaps punctuated by a succession of political revolutions, could achieve the same result that had previously required a social revolution. Joseph Choonara writes, again in relation to Bolivia:

> As the system develops on a world scale and capitalist political domination becomes the norm, subsequent "bourgeois revolutions" can take on an even more disjointed and episodic form in late developing capitalisms. Often it is difficult to specify a moment or even a decisive period in which quantity transformed into quality. At what point, for example, did Bolivia cease to be "feudal" and become "capitalist"? Along with a long societal process of economic development, a whole series of upheavals were required, combining blows struck from below and maneuvers at the top, through successive political revolutions with a social dimension. This must include the great indigenous struggles of 1780–82 and the liberation from colonial rule in the early 19th century, the various coups and countercoups at the start of the 20th century to the great popular nationalist revolution of 1952 and beyond.[124]

Although I do not believe that identifying capitalist states and laws of motion is quite so difficult as Choonara suggests, this type of approach is nevertheless likely to prove more fruitful than attempts to play the game of "Hunt the Bourgeois Revolution." Alan Knight, for example, writes in relation to the Mexican Revolution of 1910–20 that, insofar as it produced "new circumstances" that "involved market production, labor mobility, and capital accumulation, it is entirely valid to regard the Mexican Revolution as, in some sense, a bourgeois revolution," above all, "because it gave a decisive impulse to the development of Mexican capitalism and of the Mexican bourgeoisie, an impulse which the preceding regime had been unable to give."[125] However, even in cases where a single decisive moment of bourgeois revolution is impossible to identify, it is important not to move so far from turning point analysis that we are left with a process without beginning or end. According to Enrique Semo, Mexico experienced three waves of bourgeois revolution: the wars of independence after 1810; the mid-century reform wars against the Catholic Church, the native inhabitants and the French; and the revolution of 1910–20. For

Semo the Mexican bourgeoisie remained progressive until 1940 but were only able to play this role in "the absence of the proletariat."[126] In fact, the decisive period in the transformation of most Latin American states was concentrated into decades rather than the centuries invoked by Choonara in relation to Bolivia or Semo in relation to Mexico.[127]

In relation to Mexico, Adolfo Gilly argues that the transition to capitalism began in 1867 after the decisive victory of the Liberals over the Conservatives and their French allies in the "Reform War." The difference with France was that "the barely nascent Mexican bourgeoisie had to rely upon mass support and Jacobin methods in order to sweep away the institutions and structures inherited from colonial times that now impeded its development," but it—or its representatives—did so from a position of state power that they used to crush resistance. Political change through the state set the conditions for economic change: on the one hand the nationalization of feudal church property (and the separation of church and state); on the other, the division of indigenous Indian land into individual and unsustainable plots, both types of property bought or simply seized by great landowners to establish latifundia:

> Just, as in the struggle to liquidate the feudal structures of Church property, it had been compelled to lean on the masses and employ the plebeian forms and methods of Jacobinism, so, in its struggle against the peasant masses, the bourgeoisie had to rely upon the barbaric methods of appropriation and plunder everywhere characteristic of primitive capitalist accumulation. In other words, it had to combine its own backward capitalist relations of production with other, still more primitive forms: pre-capitalist relations of peon-type dependence upon the hacienda. . . . Unlike the original period of capitalist accumulation, however, this process of accelerated accumulation at the expense of pre-capitalist economic forms took place during the worldwide expansion of capitalism. In some ways then, it resembled the plunder of the North American Indians, and in other ways the colonial wars conducted by imperialist countries. But the colonial war was waged by the Mexican landowner-bourgeois government in its own country and against its own people.[128]

The experience of Argentina, at the opposite end of the subcontinent is similar. Here too is the struggle against foreign aggression, in this case from the navies of the British and the French; here too the primitive accumulation, in this case by the clearing of the Pampas Indians for the privatized cattle herds of the great ranches. Both processes were associated with the rancher and general José Manuel Rosas. The turning point in transforming the state began in 1852:

> The laborious process of national organization begins with the defeat of Rosa's army by Urquiza's federal troops, continues with the passing of the first effective national constitution, and ends in 1881 when Buenos Aires becomes the nation's capital. During this period of time, a unified state structure is set up, the Buenos Aires customs houses are nationalized, the internal customs are eliminated, a single national currency is issued, a national legal code is established and a single army is organized. Simultaneously . . . a major boost is given to primary education, immigration, and the construction of new railways with public capital.[129]

There was however one great revolution during the 1860s that was in other respects quite distinct from those contemporary with it: the American Civil War. Barrington Moore described it as "the last revolutionary offensive on the part of what one may legitimately call urban or bourgeois capitalist democracy."[130] In fact, it is even more distinctive than this suggests. The Civil War resembled the German and Italian experiences in that it took the form of a conventional war for unification (or, more precisely, reunification); but unlike them and indeed every other bourgeois revolution of whatever period it involved the leadership of an industrial capitalist class. In this respect, as Charles Post points out, "the social origins of the US Civil War indicates that it, almost alone among the 'bourgeois revolutions' identified by the historical materialist tradition, actually fits the classical schema." Leaving aside what may or may not be involved in the "classical schema," the essential point is correct; in this case: "Capitalist manufacturers and commercial family-farmers, organized in the Republican Party, take the lead in organizing the political and military struggle to remove the impediment posed by slavery and its expansion."[131] Why did the United States not simply follow the general pattern of development in white colonial-settler regimes? It was, after all, already more developed in capitalist terms than any of them by midcentury. The answer lies in the fact that the social basis for opposition to capitalism was also more highly developed than elsewhere. George Novack once outlined the forces that US capitalism had to overcome:

> The three most important powers based on precapitalist forms of labor were the Indian tribes, the semifeudal proprietors, and the slaveholding planters. All contributed to the building of the bourgeois order in its formative stages: the Indians through the fur trade; the landed proprietors by importing capital, labor, tools, and provisions into the new settlements; the planters through the crops they grew and the wilderness areas their forced laborers cleared and cultivated. But, after performing useful services, they were themselves cleared away as they became obstacles to the further expansion of bourgeois property, production, and power. . . . The Indians were wiped out; the British overlords and their feudal dependants were expelled; the insurrectionary slaveholders were "gone with the wind" of the Civil War.[132]

The destruction of Native American tribal society, already well advanced before 1861, was essentially completed in the quarter century after 1865, as the colonization of the West drove them from their remaining lands. Feudalism was never of any great significance, even before 1776; the real obstacle to capitalist development was the existence of slavery in the South. Why did the Southern planters not simply adopt the same adaptive attitude as the Prussian Junkers toward the introduction of wage labor? Why, in other words, did members of the latter class not similarly transform themselves into capitalist landlords? Not only did they recognize no comparable necessity to do so, the pressures upon them were pushing in the opposite direction.

Both forms of white-settler colonial production identified by Marx existed in the southern United States before 1865, but they were neither separate nor equal in their relationship. Slavery was widespread in the South, but in most cases, relatively small scale. On the eve of war, over 97 percent of slaveholders owned fewer than fifty slaves and only 0.1 percent had estates with more than two hundred.[133] But the majority of Southerners were not slave owners and there were major class differences between the former and the latter. As Barbara Fields explains: "The domination of plantation slavery over Southern society preserved the social space within which the white yeomanry—that is, the small farmers and artisans who accounted for about three-fourths of the white families in the slave South just before the Civil War—could enjoy economic independence and a large measure of local self-determination, insulated from its characteristic form of capitalist market society."[134] The problem for the ruling class was not so much with the yeomen, however, as with the whites below them in the social structure, those who did not own slaves and who had little or no chance of ever owning them. As Theodore Allen has pointed out, it was in order to prevent the emergence of solidarity between this group and black slaves that the condition of racialized slavery had to be absolute.[135]

Both Prussian Junkers and the Southern planters understood that commercial success was essential if they were to continue as landed classes, but the Prussian serfs were not a group distinct from the rest of their society and the Junkers were consequently more vulnerable to the threat of a democratic movement uniting all the oppositional forces against them, perhaps in the form—long hoped-for by Marx—of a repetition of the Peasant War of 1525 alongside an urban insurrection by the modern working class.[136] In one sense, the Southern planters were in a stronger position than their German contemporaries, precisely because the slaves had been absolutely separated from all other subordinate social groups and were not in a position to make common cause with them. But the paradox of this position was that, unlike serfdom, slavery was not a system that could be reformed out of existence because the entire social structure was based on the position that blacks were racially inferior, incapable of any other role than as slaves, and could be expected to revert to savagery and exact revenge if freed from the supposedly paternalistic but firm restraints imposed by their masters.[137] There was manufacturing, but it too was constrained by slavery. Firms tended to be smaller and less productive than in the Midwest, and were often operated on a part-time basis as a supplement to income mainly derived from agriculture. There is no reason to suppose that Southern manufacturers were intrinsically less capable of being successful capitalists than their Northern cousins, but the restricted market characteristic of the Southern economy acted as a barrier to them, both in terms of the limited consumption demands of the large proportion of the workforce who were slaves and the fact that the larger farms and plantations produced their own small-scale goods for use.[138] It is not that the Southern slave economy was incapable of either dynamic spurts of growth or of adaptation to changing conditions, in fact it displayed both characteristics at different times between 1783 and 1861. It is rather that a system of absolutely racialized slavery tended toward self- imposed limits on expansion. Was there any way for the South to circumvent them?

The fact that social relations of production were based on an absolute connection between skin-color racism and exploitation might have been overcome if the South had been an imperial or colonial outpost of a metropolitan power; but it *was* the metropolitan power. These two factors made reform impossible and consequently made the South different not only from other societies with slaves but other slave societies. In these, like other societies with unfree labor, slaves were closer to peasant status in that they generally had their own land with which to cultivate crops, thus providing for their own subsistence and perhaps even giving them the opportunity to sell any surplus in local markets. In the South, even this was much restricted, as the masters suspected any arrangements that would diminish slave dependence upon them.[139] More importantly, while there was undoubtedly racism toward the enslaved blacks who worked on the sugar plantations in, for example, the British colony of Jamaica, whether or not they remained enslavesd or became wage laborers and peasants was not crucial to the survival of the British state and society. In the end, slavery was abolished in Jamaica in 1838 as a result of calculations over profitability and the reproduction of the labor force, together with concerns over a repetition of the slave rebellion of 1831.[140] In both of the other slave societies of the Americas, Cuba and Brazil, the state began to lessen the necessity for slave labor by introducing other types of unfree labor, which formed a bridge between slavery and free labor, in Cuba these involved Chinese and even Spanish coolies.[141] In Brazil free blacks and mulattoes could serve in the militia and, crucially, could own slaves themselves.[142] None of this was possible in the South.

Individual plantations could only grow by moving or adding new land; but the same was true of the society that they supported. Slavery in one society was never going to remain viable unless it could be guaranteed further territory. In the North, capital expanded, labor productivity grew and, potentially at least, both could continue indefinitely. In the South, increased productivity was achieved from moving operations to or extending existing plantations into more fertile soil, a process to which there were limits.[143] Those limits could of course be overcome if the boundaries of Southern slave society were widened, up into the Northwest or south and east into the Caribbean and the Americas beyond the United States. "If the Northern capitalist system was an expansive one, so too was the Southern slave system," writes Morris Berman: "The fight was at least in part a conflict of two expansionist systems, and it was not possible for both of them to win."[144] Robert Fogel has pointed out that the Confederacy could have dominated Central and South America, and even formed alliances further afield with other slave-trading nations, although this might have brought it into conflict with Britain that was still applying diplomatic pressure on Brazil and in Africa.[145] But given Britain's reliance on Southern cotton, and her tacit support for the Confederacy during the Civil War, it is very likely that British state managers would have overlooked these transgressions in the spirit of compromise on which they tended to rely when their material interests were in conflict with their moral values. There was, however, a much more serious obstacle to territorial expansion, emblematic of a tension between the in-dividual and collective interests of the slave owners.

Individual slave owners may have wanted to increase cotton production in order to boost their income; but collectively they had an interest in restricting it on the grounds that generalized increased supply would have the effect of lowering prices. Similarly they did not want the slave population to grow too quickly as this would have a comparable downward impact on the relatively high price of slaves. As Gavin Wright notes, "these attitudes had roots in their property interest and reflected the kind of economy which that property interest had created": "By slowing the growth of the regional population, both free and slave, that property interest also retarded territorial expansion and political weight. Since this political weight was a factor in secession, and since sheer manpower was a factor in the South's military defeat, in these ways we may say that the economics of slavery contributed to its own de-mise."[146] It was therefore important for the Southern slave owners to move into areas where other crops than cotton could be produced on the basis of slavery; the crucial failure of that class was to delay establishing a state until its Northern op-ponent was in a position to defeat it.

What then was the nature of the Old South? What mode of production exer-cised its laws of motion there? The societies over which the slave owners ruled can-not be directly assimilated to those of the ancient world; the insertion of the South into the emergent capitalist world economy meant the context for the social rela-tions of master and slave was unimaginably different from that of the tribal and tributary formations in which the Greek and Roman city-states developed. But nor can the South simply be regarded as a peculiarly backward variant of the cap-italist societies that were consolidating in Western Europe, Australasia, and the rest of North America; the surplus accruing to the landowners did derive from the exploitation of slaves. Perhaps the solution is to regard the South as a society tran-sitional to capitalism, but one in which the transition had never been able to progress beyond a certain point. The South therefore retained a form of production with the accompanying social relations, namely chattel slavery, which elsewhere had been merely one, albeit crucial, element in the primitive accumulation of capital. In other transitional societies the importance of slavery and other forms of unfree labor diminished over time, but in the South it remained and indeed became more central to the economic and social structure rather than less.

Nevertheless, this case of arrested development might simply have led to the South remaining, like the Scottish Highlands or the Italian Mezzogiorno, as the more backward component of a "dual economy," within a nation-state in which the laws of motion were set by the capitalist mode of production. It did not. In order to survive, the Southern ruling class established, on the basis of this retarded early stage in the transition to capitalism, a new and expansionist state, the Confederate States of America and it did so with the support of the overwhelming majority of the inhabitants who were not themselves slaves. In most societies where the economy was transitional from precapitalist modes of production to the capitalist mode, states remained under the control of the precapitalist ruling class, although they adapted to the new conditions, most typically in the emergence of absolutism: society became increasingly opposed to the state. As we have seen, these tensions were resolved either by a direct external challenge to the state from the new social classes created by capitalism or, in order to avoid this outcome while enabling the ability to compete in geopolitical terms, by internal pressure from sections of the existing ruling class who themselves undertook the process of transforming the state—or some combination of these two paths, with one predominating. None of these options was possible in the South. There was no alternative ruling class capable of overthrowing the plantocracy, but, because of the unbreakable divisions associated with racialized slavery, neither could the slaveowners engage in self-transformation without unleashing the very social conflicts that, in Europe, the process had been undertaken to avoid.

Strictly speaking, the South was therefore *sui generis* and its ideologues were more justified than they knew in referring to the "peculiarity" of Southern institutions. The South was exceptional; very few other societies—effectively only Cuba and Brazil—were so absolutely dependent on one particular transitional form of labor exploitation and no other society became both developmentally "frozen" at such a fundamental level while embodying that stage of development in the state form. The South was exceptional; but it is not therefore inexplicable in Marxist terms—providing we reject the assumption that all immediately precapitalist states have to map tidily and conveniently onto our categories of tributary, feudal estates, or feudal absolutist monarchy.

Within the North as a whole the dominant reason for opposition to slavery was the perception that its citizens were potentially or actually oppressed by what they called the "slave power," an attitude that involved hostility to the slave owners without necessarily displaying any sympathy for the slaves. Accordingly, attitudes within the working class were complex, dividing those who supported the war on abolitionist grounds, those who supported it on anti-secessionist grounds (which could be quite compatible with racism toward the slaves), those who opposed it on grounds of opposition to the draft or the economic hardships it caused ("a poor man's fight"), and those who opposed it on straightforwardly racist grounds. What the bourgeoisie did not face was a revolutionary working class attempting to drive the revolution forward *in the North* in a more radical direction, in the manner of the "permanent revolution" envisaged by Marx in 1850. Indeed, the biggest upheavals were directed against the war and the free black population in the shape of the New York anti-draft riots of 1863. It is in this context that the territorial dimension assumes great importance. The fact that revolutionary violence could be directed outward to a now effectively external enemy, through the mechanism of disciplined state power, meant that a far greater degree of radicalism could be attempted than if the struggle had been a purely internal one conducted, as it were, by civilians. In other words, the Northern bourgeoisie were ultimately prepared to embrace the logic of total war rather than face defeat, even if this meant the emancipation of the slaves and harnessing the freedmen against their former masters as part of the Union's military apparatus.

According to Charles and Mary Beard: "The main economic results of the Second American Revolution would have been attained had there been no armed conflict for the census returns with rhythmic beats were recording the tale of the fates."[147] James McPherson concludes in perhaps the greatest single-volume history of the Civil War with essentially the same argument: "Of course the northern states, along with Britain and a few countries in northwest Europe, were cutting a new channel in world history that would doubtless have become the mainstream even if the American Civil War had never happened. Russia has abolished serfdom in 1861 to complete the dissolution of ancient institutions of bound labor in Europe."[148] What McPherson ignores here is that it took the Russian Revolution of 1917 to complete the liberation of the serfs. The assumption, which I used to accept, is that, even if the Confederacy had won that battle and gone on to win the Civil War, the ultimate victory of industrial capitalism across the entire territory of what is now the United States of America would sooner or later have followed, either through a renewed attempt by the North or adaptation by the Confederate plantocracy to the new order, in the manner of the Prussian Junkers or Japanese Samurai.[149] But this view ignores the fact that a Confederate victory or—what amounts to the same thing—a Northern refusal to oppose the expansionist drive of the South in the first place, would have altered the conditions under which capitalism would then have developed, on a continental and ultimately global scale. John Ashworth notes that "the ending of slavery in the American South was part of a broader movement transcending national boundaries by which unfree labor systems were dismantled across the long nineteenth century" and lists the extensive number of countries and territories, many of them in the Americas, in which slavery was abolished before 1861. He then argues that "the same processes or factors that doomed unfree labor systems elsewhere on the globe resulted in the collapse, on the battlefield, of the South's slaveholding Republic and the ultimate triumph of the Union armies": "The fundamental, inescapable fact is that throughout much of the developed and even semideveloped world unfree labor systems were being dismantled partly because they were thought to obstruct or impede economic growth and development."[150] The Confederacy, after all, was not intent on preserving a compromise with the North but imposing a new and—in the literal sense of the word—reactionary settlement on the United States as a whole. The American Civil War was therefore the most decisive and significant of all the nineteenth-century bourgeois revolutions.

The exceptional nature of events in the United States can be illustrated by comparing the process of bourgeois revolution to the north in Canada. Successive British governments had considered combining the remaining colonies in British

North America into a single nation-state, but had never acted, partly because there was little demand within Canada itself, except as a lever to gain concessions from the British. The main pressure to do so was the developmental block posed by the remnants of feudalism in the former French colonies. Three quarters of the population of Lower Canada (now Quebec) lived on the countryside under a tenurial arrangement called the "seigniorial system," which the British had preserved after the conquest in 1763. The ruling class in the province resisted attempts to integrate Lower Canada with the other major territory, Upper Canada (now Ottawa) because of the threat this posed to the system: "The French Canadians masquerading in the fashionable hues of liberal democracy, were heart and soul in defense of the *ancien regime*. When . . . the British government made possible, though not obligatory, the commutation of feudal tenures in the province, the assembly protested in the name of the priceless heritage of feudalism which had been secured for all eternity by the Quebec Act."[151] The rebellion of 1837 has been described by two French Canadian historians as "an attempted bourgeois revolution . . . without the presence of a true bourgeoisie in its midst."[152] The Act of Union between the two provinces that followed in 1840 was intended to numerically overwhelm the French-speaking population with British colonists, but misfired in that allowed greater cooperation between radicals of both French and British origin. However, the seigniors maintained their hostility: "The French Canadians were determined to resist immigration, for immigration would inevitably affect the law, the agricultural system and the static culture of the lower St. Lawrence. . . . The *patriotes* preferred to save subsistence agriculture on feudal lines at the expense of large-scale trade in the new staples."[153] In the end the British abolished the seigniorial system in 1854 in order to allow English-speaking immigration into Lower Canada, since no British colonist would willingly submit to tenurial arrangement that has disappeared in England by 1688 and in Scotland after 1746; as was often the case by this stage in history, the impulse was tactical rather than embodying a principled opposition to feudalism. And, although there is a parallel here with the United States, in which Quebec plays the role of the South, these should not be taken too far, since the former territory was an obstacle rather than the existential threat posed by the latter.

As in the cases of Piedmont in Italy, Prussia in Germany, and the North in the United States, one area within the territories themselves took the initiative in the unification process. "Fundamentally, Confederation was the creation of a vigorous and confident Upper Canada, which saw it as the best way of escaping from the political log-jam of the existing province and as an acceptable framework for the prosecution of other projects."[154] This underestimates the colonial interest. By the 1850s at least some important political figures in Britain began to see unification as essential in order to act as a counterweight and ally against the power of the United States, not least by enabling the construction of the intercolonial railway, which would act as a carrier of both commodities and troops. The threat of US annexation became more intense as it became clear that the Union would win the Civil War. The Quebec Conference of September 1864 at which confederation was first systematically discussed coincided with the beginning of the end for the Confederacy. Donald Creighton writes of the majority of the delegates: "They did not realize that the war was coming to an end and that their long immunity from possible external danger was over."[155] As one historian of the event notes, by this stage, "the British government . . . was in favor of strengthening the central government even more than the delegates were ready to do."[156] The American abrogation of the reciprocity treaty of 1854 was intended to force Canadian politicians to apply for incorporation into the United States; instead it pushed them in the other direction: "The acceptance of the 'federal' principle against their own political traditions and wishes was the great concession that the English-speaking delegates at Quebec were prepared to make to French Canada; but they agreed to make it only on the clear understanding that the resulting British American union was to be a strongly centralized federation, a federation radically different from that which had helped to precipitate the American Civil War.[157]

In the achievement of Confederation in Canada, the key players were civil servants rather than military commanders and the stage was the conference chamber rather than the battlefield. It highlighted the diminishing need for revolutionary transformation in Europe and its overseas extensions: a process of cumulative structural adaptation had become the rule, even before the decade of the 1860s was out. With the exception of Britain's Irish colony, which liberated most of its territory between 1916 and 1921, the location of the bourgeois revolutions after 1871 shifted inexorably east and south of Europe, beginning with the old feudal absolutist and tributary empires, the Russian (1905), Persian (1905), Ottoman (1908), and Chinese (1911). But the failure or incompleteness of these revolutions indicated how difficult it now was to establish new capitalist formations in an established nation-states system already structured around the imperialist powers: the possibility of escape from precapitalist stagnation that had briefly been available between 1848 and 1871 closed after the latter date, with only Japan having taken the opportunity it presented.

The End of an Era

In one sense, that of historical possibility, the moment when the era of the bourgeois revolution ended can be timed and dated with some precision to around 9:00 p.m. on November 8 (October 25, old calendar) 1917, when Lenin began his report to the Second All-Russian Congress of Soviets with the words: "We shall now proceed to construct the socialist order."[158] The majority of the world still lay under the domination of colonial or precapitalist states, or some combination of the two; consequently, these societies were still required to liberate themselves, but the Russian Revolution now offered an alternative way of achieving their liberation. In other words, bourgeois revolutions were still possible, but they were no longer necessary, because the process of permanent revolution, at least in the form identified by Trotsky, opened up the possibility of an alternative path out of imperial domination, leading not toward occupying a subordinate position of formal independence within the capitalist nation-states system, but toward a socialist world in which both capitalism and nation-states would be historical relics.

But in another sense, that actually inscribed onto the historical record, the bourgeois revolutions now entered the period of their greatest proliferation, adding many more to the roster in the two and a half decades between the proclamation of the People's Republic of China in 1949 and the fall of Haille Salassie in 1974 than had been achieved in the three and a half centuries between the Dutch Revolt of 1567 and the Russian Revolutions of 1917. The former events are, however, rarely categorized as bourgeois revolutions. One reason is that, within little more than a decade of the Bolshevik leader rising to address delegates at the former Smolny Institute for Noble Girls, an extraordinary form of collective false consciousness had arisen, first in Russia itself, then spreading to the colonial and semicolonial world. Starting in China, twentieth-century bourgeois revolutionaries began to adopt the language and symbols—in Milton's terms, the "outward rites and specious forms"—of the socialist tradition. Their inspiration was not however the society promised by the Bolshevik revolution of 1917, but the one delivered by the Stalinist counterrevolution of 1928. False consciousness had been a characteristic of almost all previous bourgeois revolutions, but the level of cognitive dissonance here was of quite a different order, because it did not involve an ideology that was merely tangential to capitalism but one that was supposed to represent the society that would succeed capitalism. Puritanism in revolutionary England sought to establish the rule of the Saints and ended up facilitating the rule of a very unsaintly landed, mercantile, and banking elite; outside of Russia, Stalinism sought to establish state capitalist societies and succeeded in doing so, but mistook—in most cases it appears quite sincerely—what they had achieved for socialism.

These modern bourgeois revolutionaries were not necessarily organized in national Communist parties formally affiliated to the Soviet Union—in Africa in particular they tended not to be—nor did they necessarily look to full state capitalism on the Russian model as a goal; hybrids involving both state and private capital, often combined with long-standing forms of petty-commodity production, were common as decolonization was achieved. In many ways these revolutionaries were not particularly different in class terms from their predecessors between 1789 and 1848. In the colonial and semicolonial world after 1945, the local capitalists tended to be very weak and, even when not closely linked to the colonists, inherited the long-standing class fear of mass involvement in any revolution. Members of the "revolutionary intelligentsia" and the noncapitalist bourgeoisie more generally tended to treat the capitalist bourgeoisie with contempt, which is one reason the former looked to the state as an alternative. Frantz Fanon's discussion of the inadequacies of native African capitalist bourgeoisie is classic:

The bourgeoisie of an under-developed country is a bourgeoisie in spirit only . . . it will always reveal itself as incapable of giving birth to an authentic bourgeois society with all the economic and industrial consequences this entails. . . . It does not go in for investments and it cannot achieve that accumulation of capital necessary to the birth and blossoming of an authentic bourgeoisie. At that rate it would take centuries to set on foot an embryonic industrial revolution. . . . If the government wants to bring the country out of its stagnation and set it well on the road towards development and progress, it most first nationalize the middle-man's trading sector.[159]

The hostility between the capitalist and noncapitalist bourgeoisie in the colonial world during the twentieth century was far greater than in Europe and the Americas during the nineteenth. What remained similar was the sense of humiliation, and consequently hatred, felt by members of the revolutionary noncapitalist bourgeoisie for their oppressors in the old or colonial regime—so obviously inferior to them in every respect. The point was well expressed in an autobiographical passage by the leading figure in the revolutionary movement of Guinea-Bissau, Amilcar Cabral: "To take my own case as a member of the petty bourgeois group who launched the struggle in Guinea, I was an agronomist working under a European who everybody knew was one of the biggest idiots in Guinea; I could have taught him his job with my eyes shut, but he was the boss: this is something which counts a lot, this is the confrontation that really matters. This is of major importance when considering where the initial idea of struggle came from.[160]

This final phase in the history of the bourgeois revolutions involved two main variants: one involved the overthrow of precapitalist states, preserved beyond their natural life by one or other of the imperialist states for reasons of geopolitical strategy or access to raw materials, usually oil; the other involved the dismantling of actual colonial regimes that had constrained local capitalist development in order to meet the economic requirements of the metropolitan power. In the former, the process of transformation was initiated by an army coup, as in Egypt in 1952, Libya in 1969, or Ethiopia in 1974—although the first example actually occurred before the advent of Stalinism with the opening of the second phase of the Turkish Revolution in 1919. In the latter variant, the option of a coup did not exist and the revolutions therefore tended to combine elements of earlier bourgeois revolutions from below *and* above: "from below" in relation to the existing state, since it required an external military force—usually waging guerrilla warfare in the initial phases—to overcome it; but "from above" in relation to the popular masses, whose self-activity was either suppressed, minimized, or channeled into individual membership in an instrumentally organized party-army apparatus. This was the pattern in China between 1928 and 1949, North Vietnam between 1945 and 1954, and Algeria between 1956 and 1962.

Yet it would be wrong to identify every episode of national liberation that followed the Second World War as a bourgeois revolution. In some cases, such as Czechoslovakia from 1945 to 1948 and Cuba after 1959, external or internal forces replaced one model of capitalism with another. In others cases, such as that of India, liberation movements contributed toward making the position of colonialists untenable, but the successor regimes simply inherited the state apparatus bequeathed by the colonial power; native elites occupied the offices vacated by the departing Westerners, while peasants and workers returned to fields and factories as before. All these cases and many others were examples of political revolutions, in which the class basis of the state remained essentially unchanged. In still other cases, such as Malaya from 1947 to 1957 and Kenya from 1952 to 1963, liberation movements were actually defeated prior to British withdrawal, with independence then being granted on imperialist terms; but the states and societies that emerged were no more or less capitalist than those in which the movements had succeeded. It is perfectly possible for nation-states to be weak players within the world system and their economies to have little impact on the world market, as was the case in most of the former colonies, without this having the slightest bearing on whether or not they are capitalist nation-states with capitalist economies.

The Russian Revolution should have signaled the end of the era of bourgeois revolution and the opening of its proletarian successor. Given that it did not, the era finally came to an end in 1973–75, when the feudal-absolutist regime of Ethiopia was overthrown, the Portuguese colonies of Guinea-Bissau, Angola, and Mozambique were liberated, and the United States was defeated in Indochina with the fall of its client states in Cambodia, Laos, and South Vietnam. The climax of the bourgeois revolutionary era coincided with the retreat from, and in the case of Eastern Europe and the Societ Union, the collapse of the state capitalism model that had been the characteristic outcome of its last phase. It was in China, home of the greatest of these revolutions, that one important entry point to the neoliberal era was first opened, when Deng announced the Four Modernizations to the Third Plenum of the Eleventh Central Committee Congress of the Chinese Communist Party in December 1978.[161] When Deng looked back from 1992 on the transformation he had initiated in China he used the slogan "to get rich is glorious"; the echo of Guizot advising disenfranchised French citizens to "enrich themselves" if they wanted to be able to vote was unlikely to be accidental. And perhaps this is appropriate. Regardless of the vast differences between them in most respects, what the Frenchman and his Chinese successor had in common was that they represented not counterrevolution, but the consolidation of the bourgeois revolution that brought them to power and that is now over.

Is There a Future for Permanent Revolution?

If, as I have suggested, the bourgeois revolution is now a purely historical category— and no one seriously contends that there are still outstanding bourgeois revolutions waiting to be accomplished, other than perhaps at the very margins of the world system—is there any sense in which "permanent revolution" continues to be relevant?

Does retaining the term and the cognate notion of "deflection" have any benefits for Marxists other than providing the consolations of familiarity? It is possible, of course, to explicitly detach permanent revolution from the "tasks" of the bourgeois revolution, real or imagined, and instead focus on other characteristics associated with the term. The difficulty with this strategy is that these characteristics tend not to be specific to permanent revolution.

Take, for example, the following claim by Paul D'Amato: "All countries . . . need a permanent revolution, because though the material prerequisites for socialism exist on an international scale, they do not within a purely national framework."[162] While this is true, it is irrelevant to an argument for retaining the concept of permanent revolution. The claim that socialism was only possible on the basis of a global revolution had been central to historical materialism since its origins in the mid-1840s, antedating even the original (pre-Trotsky) concept of permanent revolution.[163] The reason Trotsky originally emphasized the requirement for the international extension of the Russian Revolution in his writings during and immediately after 1905 was precisely because he conceived it as developing into a proletarian revolution rather than remaining within the confines of a bourgeois revolution. Had it been the latter, as virtually everyone else in the Second International expected, the necessity for internationalization would not have arisen since, long before the early twentieth century, individual bourgeois revolutions had been able to survive because they were entering a preexisting capitalist environment. The reason permanent revolution is associated with international revolution is because Stalin chose to counterpose it to the doctrine of Socialism in One Country in the debates from 1924 onward; but in this context the debate was initially about the conditions of survival for the revolution in Russia, not about the character of the revolution in China. Stalin was of course ostensibly attacking a deviation peculiar to Trotsky, but he was in fact abandoning a central tenet of Classical Marxism as such. International revolution is simply a necessary condition for the existence of socialism anywhere in anything other than the very short term, but the first major countries in which opportunities to achieve this were aborted or squandered were, after all, Germany (1923) and Britain (1926): to argue that revolutions in these heartlands of developed capitalism would, if successful, have been "permanent" is to denude the concept of any specificity and consequently of any meaning.

A further argument for the continued relevance of permanent revolution emphasizes the necessity for it to be retained as a strategic alternative to Stalinist conceptions in which socialism is preceded by a "bourgeois-democratic" or—where democracy was restricted but state and economy were already clearly capitalist—a "national-democratic" phase. Here is a late but typical example of this type of argumentation by a leading figure in the South African Communist Party: "At this, the stage of the national democratic revolution the main component of which in the South African context is the national liberation of the African people, the main thrust of the revolutionary forces is to forge the broadest possible unity of the masses and of all the strata of the people for the overthrow of the hated racist regime."[164] Two points are worth making in this connection.

First, no Stalinist organization, certainly none that was in a position to take state power, ever genuinely intended the revolution to pass through a "democratic" stage of any sort—this was rhetoric designed to disarm or incorporate bourgeois opponents of colonial and precapitalist regimes or right-wing dictatorships by pretending adherence to representative democracy; the real intention was always to establish exclusive party regimes and state capitalist economies as soon as possible. In some countries, notably in India, Stalinist parties have either been unable or unwilling to challenge for total power and here the necessity for stages during which outstanding "tasks" will be accomplished is simply a justification for parliamentary deals. Achin Vanaik writes: "The Indian left that still speaks of semi-feudalism and semi-colonization or believes in a stage-ist approach—and hence rationalizes electoral-political alliances with non-Congress and non-BJP parties—is unprepared to recognize that India is a sub-imperialist, regional power."[165] Since 1917 at least the counterposing of "permanent revolution" to "stages," has therefore always been slightly unreal, since only adherents of the first position have actually been presenting their genuine position. The only situation in which a democratic stage seems to have been put forward in good faith was in South Africa, where the normal Stalinist methods of manipulation were less effective because of the size, combativity, and democratic traditions of the working class.

Second, and more important, whatever may have been the case before 1989–91, since then the basis for the entire strategy of stages has been removed. With the fall of the Stalinist regimes and the neoliberal turn in China, those who formerly argued this, with whatever degree of honesty, no longer believed that a socialist "stage" was possible: there was now nothing beyond capitalism, although there could be varieties of capitalism and they could be more or less democratic. Today the African National Congress exudes this sense of curtailed possibilities. Writing in 1976, Joe Slovo argued that the black bourgeoisie in South Africa was "pathetically small" and had "arrived too late on the historical scene to play a classic role either as a leading element in the national struggle or as the main beneficiary of mass revolutionary sacrifice": "Indeed, for a black bourgeoisie to gain ascendancy, the whole "normal" process would have to be reversed, in the sense that *its real class formation would have to follow and not precede political power.*" The trajectory outlined by Slovo in which bourgeois economic formation postdates the revolution was in fact historically far more common than he suggests, but in any case he thought it implausible in a South African context: "Since the aspirations of all the main classes among the oppressed majority can, at the moment, only be served by the destruction of the economic and political power of the existing ruling class, the question which remains is whether the all-white bourgeoisie could conceivably be assumed by a black equivalent in the future which could act to stop the revolution in its tracks and subvert the social aims of real national emancipation."[166] What Slovo does not seem to have considered is that blacks could join the existing white bourgeoisie as a new component of the South African ruling class, still less that this would be made possible by the organizations to which he belonged, the ANC and the SACP.[167] In an interview with Paul Kingsnorth from 2003, the former organization's then head of policy and research Michael Sachs explained why it had been so conservative since the overthrow of apartheid:

> "You know," he says, gesturing at nothing in particular, "you can't just go and redistribute things, in this era. Maybe if we had a Soviet Union to defend us we could do that but, frankly, you've got to play the game—you've got to ensure that you don't go on some adventure—you know, you *will* be defeated. They were defeated in Chile, they were defeated in Nicaragua . . . you can't do it now . . ."[168]

Sachs makes clear that it is not only socialism in the sense in which that was once understood that is impossible, but even social democratic reformism: "I have no doubt that if we had embarked on some kind of Keynesian socialist project in 1994, we would have been defeated by now, as the ANC."[169]

In effect, what has been constructed in South Africa is a version of what Jeffery Webber has called, in the context of Bolivia post-2006, "reconstituted neoliberalism."[170] Unsurprisingly then, leading figures in the government of Evo Morales have drawn similar conclusions to those of Mandela, Mbeki, and Zuma. When the Bolivian vice-president, Álvaro García Linera, was asked by Trotskyist interlocutors whether he thought that socialism was viable in Bolivia today, he replied:

> There are two reasons why there is not much chance of a socialist regime being installed in Bolivia. On the one hand, there is a proletariat that is numerically in a minority and politically non-existent, and you cannot build socialism without a proletariat. Secondly, the potential for agrarian and urban communities is very much weakened. There is an implosion of community economies into family structures, which have been the framework within which the social movements have arisen. In Bolivia, 70 percent of workers in the cities work in family-based economic structures, and you do not build socialism on the basis of a family economy.

The goal of the Morales government, he said, was to build an "Andean capitalism," and this was a long-term perspective: "Bolivia will still be capitalist in 50 or 100 years."[171] Choonara cites this interview as an example of the type of position against which permanent revolution is intended to offer an alternative.[172] It is true that the argument for internationalization could be used to rebuff García Linera's claims for the incapacity of Bolivia to achieve socialism in one country, but as I have already argued, that argument is not exclusive to permanent revolution. The main point, however, is that García Linera, like his equivalents in South Africa, is not seriously proposing a stage beyond capitalism but rather how it might, in the fullness of time, be restructured and reformed: the real question is whether socialism is conceivable as an alternative system at all.[173]

There is however a more plausible extension of the concept, which also involves the question of democracy and can claim some support from Trotsky himself: permanent revolution as the transition from democratic to socialist revolution. As I argued in chapter 14, there are texts in which Trotsky used this formulation, but in many of these all that is involved is a contraction from "bourgeois-democratic" to "democratic"; on other occasions, Trotsky more accurately contracted the former term in the opposite direction, that is, to "bourgeois," and this is usually what he means. It would be possible, however, to drop the misleading notion of "democratic revolution" with its Stalinist overtones and substitute that of "political revolution," as defined in chapter 20. As Choonara explains:

> Permanent revolution in this conception involves the combination of democratic and socialist challenges to the existing order of things. The former cover a range of potential demands, including the dissolution of large landed estates across much of the Global South, the introduction of parliamentary democracy in Egypt or Tunisia today, the resolution of the "indigenous question" in Bolivia in the struggles of 2003 or 2005, or the overthrow of colonialism in India in 1946–47. None of these demands are, in themselves, incompatible with capitalist social relations, but achieving these in the context of uneven and combined development can lead to an anticapitalist dynamic raising the possibility of social revolution.[174]

Trotsky himself changed the meaning of the term permanent revolution and it could be argued that doing so again simply involves a creative response to new circumstances. Furthermore, political revolutions for democracy are likely to increase. Jeff Goodwin has argued that "revolutionary movements are rather less likely to arise and social revolutions less likely to occur during the contemporary period than during the Cold War era—especially, but not exclusively, movements and revolutions that would seriously challenge the capitalist world system." Rejecting both the argument that globalization has reduced the power of individual states—thus rendering them less meaningful as the site of revolutionary overthrow—and the removal of the Soviet Union as a support for revolutionary movement as explanations, Goodwin claims instead that the real reason is the spread of representative democracy, which he regards as inimical to social revolution, although not to "political radicalism and militancy," which seek to influence the state, but not to seize it, still less to transform it.[175] The problem with this analysis, which may have been superficially plausible in the early years of the third millennium, is that representative democracy is now in retreat. A key characteristic of the Global South is relative and in some cases absolute poverty and it is this that leads to the absence or precariousness of democracy; under conditions of economic crisis this is unlikely to change. Moreover, the tendency has been for the crisis to lead to technocratic restrictions on democracy within the weaker areas of Europe, in Greece and even Italy. Nevertheless, there are several reasons I think that a further change in meaning of permanent revolution to encompass these developments is likely to lead to confusion.

What tends to happen is that the new meaning is "read back" into an earlier period in which the term meant something quite different (as in the case of terms like "nation" or "revolution" itself), with the effect of distorting the historical record. Trotsky's reworking of permanent revolution is a case in point as it produced numerous attempts by Trotskyists of a devotional persuasion to demonstrate that his conception in 1905 was essentially the same as that of Marx in 1850. A further objection concerned with historical understanding is that no social revolution from below, from the Dutch Revolt onward, has ever begun with a majority of the participants intending to totally transform the society, but rather by making ("political") demands for reform within the existing system. Wim Klooster writes of the "Atlantic" revolutions of the half century after 1776: "Overthrow of the old regime was not even necessarily the *initial* goal of the aggrieved."[176] In that sense it is only possible to identify revolutions as being either political or social once they are over: the English and French Revolutions began as the former and ended as the latter, but to describe them as examples of permanent revolution is effectively to say that all modern social revolutions (bourgeois or proletarian) can be described in these terms, which is once again to divest it of any specificity.

The most important reason for not adopting this new meaning of permanent revolution is that it misrepresents the nature of contemporary revolutions by assuming that socialism is their normal or expected outcome under current conditions, so that when it does not occur this must be a process of "deflection." As we saw in chapter 19, Cliff introduced the concept of "deflection" in the early 1960s to explain how, instead of permanent revolution leading to socialism, the postwar period had been characterized by modern forms of the bourgeois revolution leading to partial or total forms of bureaucratic state capitalism. This represented a real theoretical advance, but it nevertheless involved several difficulties that subsequent attempts to cling to the concept of permanent revolution and its "deflected" variant effectively reproduce. It elided the difference between two types of revolution: social—in this case bourgeois—revolutions that created new capitalist states in place of the existing precapitalist or colonial states and political revolutions that reconstructed the existing capitalist state, even though the rhetoric of "socialism" and national liberation may have been the same in both cases. In a sense the issue became clearer when the non-working-class actors no longer used the rhetoric of socialism. In an important article on political Islam, Chris Harman claimed that although Cliff had originally used the category with reference to "Stalinism, Maoism, and Castroism," it was equally applicable to "the Islamist intelligentsia around Khomeini in Iran," who "undertook a revolutionary reorganisation of ownership and control of capital within Iran while leaving capitalist relations of production intact."[177] Iran was a capitalist state before the revolution, during the revolution the working class was defeated, and consequently one wing of the bourgeoisie emerged triumphant over another on the basis of a different strategy for accumulation. But at least in the case or Iran there was a serious workers' movement that was in a position to challenge for power; this was not always the case.

Looking back from the mid-1980s Peter Binns observed, in relation to the Nicaraguan Revolution of 1978–79, that "the rise to power of a state capitalist ruling class on the back of a popular revolution in which the working class had become subordinated to a layer of petty bourgeois intellectuals" had not occurred. Instead, "in spite of the severity of the crisis, both economic and military, that has beset the Nicaraguan Revolution, this by now classic trajectory along the path of a 'deflected permanent revolution' toward state capitalism has itself been interrupted." Binns referred to this process, which he saw occurring in Angola and Mozambique as well as Nicaragua, as "doubly deflected permanent revolution," in which the beneficiaries were a section of the traditional bourgeoisie rather than a state bureaucracy.[178] This is conceptual overstretch with a vengeance. By 1978 the moment of state capitalism had passed. The Nicaraguan Revolution began as an attempt to replace a state run as a murderous, corrupt personal dictatorship with a constitutional bourgeois-democratic regime committed to a degree of social reform and ended by achieving this goal. The bourgeoisie did not seek a state capitalist outcome and the working class—although it participated heroically in the insurrection that overthrew Somoza—did not attempt to seize power on its own behalf. The second point is central here. Political revolutions, changes of regime by nonconstitutional methods, are a fact of life in the Global South and likely to remain so, but these can take place without involving any independent working-class intervention. For deflection to take place there must first be, not simply the potential for proletarian revolution in the abstract, but an *actual* working-class movement engaged in self-activity to the extent that the conquest of power is possible. This was true in China in the 1920s and Iran in the 1970s, but in many cases between and since there was no such movement and consequently nothing to be deflected.

Permanent revolution and, consequently, deflected permanent revolution may now be historical concepts, but uneven and combined development, the underlying process that made the former possible is not, with important implications for the possibility of socialist revolution beginning in the Global South. Following Trotsky, Tim McDaniel argues that there were four reasons why what he calls "autocratic capitalism" of tsarist Russia tended to produce a revolutionary labor movement. First, it eliminated or reduced the distinction between economic and political issues. Second, it generated opposition for both traditional and modern reasons. Third, it reduced the fragmentation of the working class but also prevented the formation of a stable conservative bureaucracy, thus leading to more radical attitudes. Fourth, it forced a degree of interdependence between the mass of the working class, class-conscious workers and revolutionary intellectuals.[179] McDaniel claims that a comparable situation has arisen since only in Iran, but this seems to unnecessarily restrict the applicability of the model to situations that resemble prerevolutionary Russia closely in formal terms.[180] In fact, the relentless expansion of neoliberal globalization, and the consequent irruption of industrialization and urbanization into areas they had previously bypassed, often under conditions of intense state repression, means that the responses identified by McDaniel are being reproduced in places as distinct as China and Dubai.[181] But these are only the most extreme examples of a general trend that is the most characteristic of the current phase of capitalist development. Two points need to be made in relation to the process.

One is that it is not limited to the Global South but to the relatively undeveloped parts of the First and former Second Worlds. As Beverley Silver writes:

> Strong new working-class movements had been created as a combined result of the spatial fixes pursued by multinational capital and the import substitution industrialization efforts of modernizing states. In some cases, like Brazil's automobile workers; labor militancy was rooted in the newly expanding mass production consumer durable industries. In other cases, like the rise of Solidarność in Poland's shipyards, militancy was centered in gigantic establishments providing capital goods. In still others, like Iran's oil workers, labor militancy was centered on critical natural resource export industries.[182]

Take, for example, the Italian Mezzogiorno, where Italian unification was followed by a pronounced process of deindustrialization, which led to a steady drain of capital to the North, with a long-term reservoir of cheap labor power, cheap agricultural products, and a docile clientele in the South; here the process of uneven and combined development led to similarly high levels of militancy to that seen in countries characterized by more general backwardness, the key episode being the revolt of the Italian in-migrants against their living conditions and low pay during the "industrial miracle" of the late fifties and early sixties. What is interesting about the Italian example, however, is that the process has continued, in different forms until the present day.[183]

The second point to be made is that, in the Global South proper at least, it is still unable completely to transform those societies. The state "containers" within which the process of uneven and combined development unfolds, including China, will never achieve the type of total transformation characteristic of the states that formed the original core of the capitalist world system, at least in any foreseeable timescale. One intelligent conservative commentator, Edward Luttwak, has referred to "the perils of incomplete imitation" whereby developing world ruling classes "have been importing a dangerously unstable version of American turbo-capitalism, because the formula is incomplete." What is missing? On the one hand, the legal regulation to control what he calls "the overpowering strength of big business" and on the other the internal humility by the winners and acceptance of the essential justice of their personal situation by the losers from the system.[184] Uneven and combined development is therefore likely to be an ongoing process, which will only be resolved by either revolution or disintegration. But in the meantime, China and other states like India and Brazil where growth has been less dramatic remain both inherently unstable in their internal social relations and expansive in their external search for markets, raw materials, and investment opportunities. It is in this inherent instability that the possibilities for permanent revolution lie. This does not mean that wherever uneven and combined development exists today the working-class movement will automatically adopt what Trotsky called the "boldest conclusions of revolutionary thought." In circumstances where Marxist ideas (and those of secular radicalism more generally) are either unavailable or discredited after the experience of Stalinism, movements will reach for whatever ideas seem to assist them in their struggle, regardless of their antiquity—but they will transform them in the process, contrary to what is asserted by reactionaries in the West.

◘ ◘ ◘

The late Fred Halliday once expressed his own disillusionment after the fall of the Soviet Empire, rejecting the revolutionary possibilities of uneven and combined development:

> The insight of Trotsky was that of locating the history and revolution of any one country in a broader, contradictory context, in seeing how ideas, and forms of conflict, like forms of technology or economic activity, could be transposed to contexts very different from that in which they originated. The mistake of the Marxist approach was to conclude that, in the end, the combination would prevail over the unevenness. The unevenness, evident above all in the widening income gaps between rich and poor on a world scale, has continued to grow, and is replicated dramatically in an era of capitalist globalization. But because of the fragmentary character of states, the spatial and political distributor of that unevenness, the combination, *the world revolutionary cataclysm*, did not occur.[185]

To this we reply: combination is not "the world revolutionary cataclysm," it is one of the objective enabling conditions for it to take place. And if the cataclysm has not yet occurred, this is largely because of the absence of the missing subjective condition, which Trotsky recognized in 1917, and which Cliff highlighted back in the 1960s: the revolutionary organization capable of giving focus to the social explosions that the process of uneven and combined development brings in its wake. In that respect, whatever else may have changed since both men wrote, the necessity for the party remains, if the incredible energies unleashed by uneven and combined development are not to be wasted yet again, with terrible consequences for the world and those who live in it. If we are not successful, matters will not simply continue in the old oppressive way, perhaps getting a bit better, perhaps getting a bit worse. Socialism is necessary simply to remove the threats to existence for millions from starvation, epidemic, and war, and for everyone, including the capitalists themselves, of environmental catastrophe. And this perhaps is the fundamental difference between the bourgeois and socialist revolutions, beyond all questions of structure, agency, and organization, important though they are. In the case of the bourgeoisie, to quote one of its greatest poets: "The world was all before them."[186] The working class does not have this luxury. The point was well made by W. H. Auden in relation to Spain during the 1930s, one of the supposedly "bourgeois democratic" but in fact potentially socialist revolutions of the twentieth century:

The stars are dead. The animals will not look.
We are left alone with our day, and the time is short, and
History to the defeated
May say alas but cannot help or pardon.[187]

The task of socialist revolutionaries is to arrive at a situation where they do not need history to help or pardon.

TO PRESERVE
THE JEWEL OF LIBERTY
IN THE FRAMEWORK OF
FREEDOM
ABRAHAM LINCOLN

IN MEMORY OF SCOTTISH AMERICAN SOLDIERS

Old Calton Cemetery, Edinburgh. Photograph by the author

EPILOGUE: REFLECTIONS
IN A SCOTTISH CEMETERY

A ll the great cities that have their origins in medieval Europe and the colonial Americas display the physical traces of the bourgeois revolutions if you know where to look. Edinburgh is no exception and many local examples are revealed by a short walk, of no more than a mile, between two graveyards in the Old Town. The second of these will provide the occasion for some reflections on the meaning of the bourgeois revolution today. Even on the short journey to this location, the final destination of many a Scottish luminary, the contradictions of the bourgeois revolutions are clearly visible.

We begin in Greyfriars Kirk on Candlemaker Row. Here, on February 28, 1638, public endorsement of the National Covenant signaled the onset of the revolutionary challenge to Charles I across Britain, the ignition of a multinational conflagration that was, until relatively recently, all too often subsumed within the episode known as the English Civil War. At the most southern part of the same kirkyard we find the prison where over a thousand artisan and peasant Covenanters were thrown after their uprising against Charles II was defeated at Bothwell Brig on June 22, 1679.[1] Leaving the kirk, we turn right onto George VI Bridge then left onto the High Street and the site of the old Parliament House where, in the dying months of 1706, crowds of several thousand Scots petitioned, demonstrated, and rioted against the political leaders and their clients within who were preparing to ratify the Treaty of Union with England in their own, essentially feudal, class interests.[2]

The High Street also contains modern representations of key figures of the Scottish Enlightenment, whose full flowering followed the defeat of the last Jacobite rising at Culloden on April 16, 1746. Outside the High Court is the statue of David Hume completed by Alexander Stoddard in 1995. We will visit the tomb in which the philosopher's remains are interred at the end of our journey, and so have no need to dwell on this depiction of him in classical garb, holding a scroll and looking suspiciously less portly than contemporary portraits would lead us to believe. The ludicrous effect is partly offset by the same sculptor's companion piece of Adam Smith, situated across the High Street and outside Saint Giles Cathedral.

Smith at least is represented in the costume of his age, standing in front of a scythe and sheaf of corn, symbols that rightly reflect the agricultural focus of *The Wealth of Nations*. Funded by private subscription and unveiled on July 4, 2008, this first statue to Smith in the Scottish capital seems unexceptional—certainly compared to the travesty of Hume across the street—until we notice among the list of subscribers listed on the back the name of Dr. Eamonn Butler of the Adam Smith Institute, a body whose views bear as much resemblance to those of Smith as the views of the Institute of Marxism-Leninism of the Central Committee of the Communist Party of the Soviet Union bore to those of Marx and Lenin. This hints at some of the issues we will have to consider at the end of our tour.

Continuing across North Bridge and further down the High Street we encounter a fine example of what Donald Horne calls "the tourism of the bourgeois revolution," relating in this case to its very earliest Scottish manifestation: the reformation of 1560. Here we find a sixteenth-century building, now operating as a souvenir shop falsely purporting to be "John Knox's House," where the unbending founder of Scottish Calvinism has, in Horne's words, been "reduced to tourist coziness."[3] Turning back up the High Street, right onto North Bridge and hence to Princes Street, we discover another respect in which Edinburgh has been marked by the bourgeois revolution: the organization of space. For Princes Street conveniently divides the city in two. To the south, where the sites described so far are situated, lies the old Edinburgh of tenements and wynds and open sewers that had grown chaotically but organically throughout the feudal period. To the north lies the New Town, the ultimate spatial expression of Enlightenment rationality and conscious design.[4] North Bridge, leading out of Edinburgh's feudal past and pointing toward the capitalist future, was itself one of the first examples of the new architecture, signs of how Edinburgh was as much shaped by the particularities of the Scottish Revolution as Paris was by those of the French.[5] Heading east along the last few yards of Princes Street, we pause only briefly to glance leftward at the bronze statue of the Duke of Wellington, designed by Sir John Steele and erected in 1852 to commemorate the victory of Britain and its allies over Napoleon at Waterloo on June 18, 1815. Inadvertently, of course, it also symbolizes the victory of a model of bourgeois revolution derived from 1688 over one derived from 1789. Passing onto Regent Road we arrive at our destination, the entrance to what has been, since 1718, the Old Calton Cemetery or Burial Ground.

Old Calton Cemetery contains many monuments, the most arresting of which is the great obelisk commemorating the martyrs of the first Scottish reform movement, the Friends of the People. Funded by public subscription, it was completed in 1844, a full fifty years after Fyshe-Palmer, Gerrald, Margarot, Muir, and Skirving were transported to Australia for daring to campaign for manhood suffrage. Yet these heroes of the 1790s were already operating in a post–bourgeois revolutionary context, their struggles linking the possibility of a cross-class political revolution to democratize the British state and—at that time—the more distant prospect of proletarian social revolution to overthrow it. Two other monuments, only feet away from each other, are more relevant to our theme and, in their different ways, suggest both the promise of the bourgeois revolution and how it was broken, how it was always destined to be broken.

⊡ ⊡ ⊡

One of these monuments is Hume's mausoleum, a squat cylindrical tower designed by Robert Adam and built in 1778, two years after the philosopher's death. As we saw in chapter 3, Hume is an important thinker for anyone concerned with the theory of bourgeois revolution, both as a historian of the English case and as a political economist working at the very moment in which capitalism achieved systemic irreversibility. But it is perhaps in his work as a philosopher that most clearly illustrates not only the limits of even the most radical bourgeois thought but also the way in which those radical qualities that it did possess have been abandoned; until what remains today can be used for purposes quite different from those that the thinkers originally intended.

The distinction between "reason" and "the passions" long preexisted Hume. In the British tradition of political philosophy these two terms were usually seen as standing in opposition to each other—Hobbes and his critics, for example, both thought that to succumb to the passions was to surrender the ability to reason, although this led them to different political conclusions.[6] For Hume the relationship was different. If we understand the passions as corresponding to "needs" or "desires," then, Hume wrote: "Reason is, and ought only to be the slave of the passions, and can never pretend to any other office than to serve and obey them."[7] In other words, we can act rationally in response to our passions, but the passions themselves are not susceptible to rational analysis. In some ways Weber was later to reformulate Hume's distinction between reason and "the passions" as that between instrumental rationality and value rationality. For Weber values (ends) were fundamental beliefs that may themselves be irrational (the "warring gods" between whom he believed we all have to choose), but to which adherence can be given by rational means. Weber thought that capitalist accumulation is a rational end, although one that may be chosen for irrational reasons, such as his famous "Protestant ethic."[8] Hume had already identified one consequence of the influence the passions exercised over reason: "Men often act against their interest; for which reason the view of the greater possible good does not always influence them."[9] There is however a more fundamental difficulty with reason that becomes apparent precisely when people *do* act in their own interests, as Max Horkheimer explains: "The difficulties of rationalist philosophy originate from the fact that the universality of reason cannot be anything else than the accord among the interests of all groups alike, whereas in reality society has been split up into groups with competing interests. . . . Reason's claim to be absolute presupposes that a community of interests exists among men."[10]

But there is no community of interests in class societies. Capitalists follow their class interests and in doing so pursue courses of action that, however rational they may be for individual members of their class, can be terrifyingly irrational for everybody else. The tobacco companies that are currently opening up huge new markets in Southeast Asia for their drugs will, in due course, be responsible for a cancer epidemic which will in turn put intolerable pressures on the fragile health services of those countries, the costs of which will be borne by the working class and peasantry. A similar logic applies to the nuclear fuel and oil companies lobbying Congress to resist even the most limited attempts to reduce gas emissions; the waters rise in Bangladesh and Mozambique, condemning thousands to homelessness or death, but not until shores of the United States are covered by the Pacific Ocean will this be factored into their calculations—and, if the recent experience of New Orleans is anything to go by, perhaps not even then. The overleveraged risk-taking of financial institutions prior to 2008 requires no further comment. These are all examples of what George Ritzer calls "the irrationality of rationality," the term that he uses for how McDonald's and its competitors promote the efficient delivery of food while destroying the environment and human health.[11] Once accumulation is engaged upon it is not a choice, rational or otherwise, because there are no alternatives, other than ceasing to be a capitalist: if this option is rejected, then capitalists are subject to a compulsion terrible, severe, and inescapable. "The seventeenth and eighteenth centuries opened the way for reason into technical areas and, in part, into the governmental sphere," wrote Trotsky: "But the bourgeois revolution proved incapable of bringing reason into the realm of economic relations."[12]

There is, however, another way of understanding the different aspects of rationality apart from counterposing ends and means, and it is one that suggests how Hume's own reasoning has been abandoned by his self-proclaimed admirers. This alternative is presented most clearly by Fredrick von Hayek, a thinker influenced by Weber, but whose fanatical insistence on the necessity of the market lacks any of the ambiguities of his predecessor. Hayek described himself as an "anti-rationalist," by which he did not mean that he considered himself irrational. On the contrary, Hayek believed that there two types of rationalism. Adherents of the first, "constructivist rationalism" "believe that human societies can be mastered by human beings and remodeled according to rational criteria. Human societies can be organized so as to abolish social evils such as poverty and violence." Adherents of the second, "evolutionary rationalism," among whom he numbered himself, show "a distrust of the powers of human reason, a recognition of the extent of human ignorance about the social and natural worlds, and therefore a stress upon the unexpected, unintended consequences of social action." According to Hayek, constructivists included Bacon, Condorcet, Godwin, Hobbes, Jefferson, Paine, Priestley, Price, Rousseau—and Marx; evolutionists had among their number Burke, Constant, Ferguson, Mandeville, Smith—and Hume. Leaving aside the question of whether this classification is accurate in respect of these thinkers (it is not), Hayek did identify a real distinction, for it is clear that Marxism and socialist thought more generally belongs to the constructivist camp. Hayek rejects constructivism on the grounds that it is not really rational at all, since any attempt to assert human control over the market will ultimately result, not simply in failure, but in social regression to a state of premodernity in which an economically unfree population is ruled by a dictatorship—although Hayek is inconsistent on this point since he does not object to dictatorships as such, only those that abolish or constrain the market.[13] In effect, Hayek is saying that only the rationality of market-based economic activity—capitalism, in his definition—is really rational. Beyond this, Hayek's evolutionary rationality is quite compatible with religious mystification: "Mythical beliefs of some sort may be needed to bring [the construction and spread of traditions] about, especially where rules of conduct conflicting with instinct are concerned." The traditions to which Hayek refers are of course those of the market order: "We owe it partly to mystical and religious beliefs, and, I believe, particularly to the main monotheistic ones, that beneficial traditions have been preserved and transmitted long enough to enable those groups following them to grow, and to have the opportunity to spread by natural or cultural selection."[14] In effect, Hayek is saying that it is irrelevant how irrational a belief may be, so long as it leads the holder to accept the market order.

We should be clear that it is not by holding this instrumentalist position on religion that Hayek has broken with the Enlightenment tradition. As Jonathan Israel has documented, one of the divisions between what he calls the moderate and the radical wings of the Enlightenment was precisely over whether their views were compatible with religious belief. But there is a further aspect of this issue that united at least some members of both wings, namely the extent to which it was safe for doubts about the existence of God to be the held among the masses. Spinoza, a radical, wrote that "the masses can no more be freed from their superstition than from their fears ... they are not guided by reason."[15] There was no point, therefore, in the common people reading his work, since they would not understand it.[16] Voltaire, a moderate (and himself a believer), wrote in a letter of 1768: "We have never intended to enlighten shoemakers and servants—this is up to apostles."[17] As Paul Siegel astutely remarks, Voltaire's attitude to the dissemination of Enlightenment ideas to the masses lies behind one of his best-known slogans: "If God did not exist, it would be necessary to invent him."[18] Religion was "necessary" for the common people, who might otherwise seek to apply reason to areas quite as uncomfortable to denizens of the coffee shops of Paris as habitués of the Palace of Versailles. Spinoza and Voltaire were both brilliant and courageous men, but there is no need to deceive ourselves that they saw the Enlightenment—in this respect at least—as extending much beyond their own class. Although also a moderate according to Israel's classification, Hume was probably nearer to Spinoza with respect to religion than to Voltaire. It would be wrong, however, to describe him as an atheist in the way that we can contemporary figures like Richard Dawkins or Christoplier Hitchens: Hume's skepticism prevented him from holding any position so dogmatic. Nevertheless, his essay "Of Miracles" makes it clear that, because of the indispensability of the miraculous to all religions, including Christianity, he regarded them as incompatible with reason.[19] In the terms that Hume uses elsewhere in the *Treatise of Human Nature*, religious belief is a form of passion.

Surprising though it may seem, the point at which Hayek breaks with Hume and with the Enlightenment more generally is over their attitude to capitalism. In fact, Hume and his contemporaries argued for what they called "commercial society," in very conditional terms and on the assumption that it would indirectly provide social benefits. Hume himself argued: "Commerce increases industry, by conveying it readily from one member of the state to another, and allowing none of it to perish or become useless. It increases frugality, by giving occupation to men, and employing them in the arts of gain, which soon engage their affection, and remove all relish for pleasure and expense. It is an infallible consequence of all industrious professions, to beget frugality, and to make the love of gain prevail over the love of pleasure."[20] As Albert Hirschman notes, in "Hume's statement . . . capitalism is here hailed by a leading philosopher of the age because it would activate some benign human proclivities at the expense of some malignant ones   because of the expectation that that, in this way, it would repress and perhaps atrophy the more destructive and disastrous components of human nature."[21] Ever since the end of the Middle Ages, and particularly as a result of the increasing frequency of national and civil wars in the seventeenth and eighteenth centuries, the search had been on for a behavioral equivalent for religious precept, for new rules of conduct and devices that would impose much needed discipline and constraints on both rulers and ruled, and the expansion of commerce and industry was thought to hold much promise in this regard. Drawing also on the work of Montesquieu in France and Sir James Steuart in Scotland, Hirschman shows that "the diffusion of capitalist forms" were not, as Weber had claimed, incidentally the consequences of the desperate Calvinist "*search for individual salvation*," but "the equally desperate search for a way of avoiding society's ruin, permanently threatening at the time because of precarious arrangements for internal and external order." But the effects of capitalism were anything but peaceful and conducive to order, and consequently the reasons these arguments were raised in the first place have been "not only forgotten but actively repressed." For Hirschman, this is necessary for the legitimacy of the capitalist order: "what social order could long survive the dual awareness that it was adopted with the firm expectation that it would solve certain problems and that it clearly and abysmally fails to do so?"[22] What actually happened, as Hirschman notes with entirely justifiable distaste, is that intellectual defenders of the system, as different in other ways as Keynes and Schumpeter, continued to argue as if the failure of capitalism was not apparent, the first by claiming that the acquisition of wealth was still less damaging than the pursuit of power, the second by claiming that imperialism was the result of the domination of European states by precapitalist ruling elites.[23]

Hayek and the neoliberal thinkers who have followed him show the same bad faith. Of all the things that might be said about the effects of capitalism, that it promotes "benign human proclivities" is evidently not one of them; yet faced with the resumption of economic crisis on a greater scale than at any time since the 1930s, neoliberal defenders of the system argue that, far from demonstrating its inherently destructive nature, it is a consequence of the constraints and distortions to which markets are still subject in the form of government regulation, trade union bargaining, and environmental campaigning.[24] It is not their passions that have overcome their reason but their interests. Indeed, faced with impending environmental crisis, to name only one potentially irreversible consequence of capitalism, it may be that support for it is increasingly incompatible with reason in *any* form other than a blinkered cost-benefit calculation of individual short-term personal benefits.

As we saw in chapter 6, Hume's friend Adam Smith also based his support for commercial society on a hypothesis concerning its likely positive effects compared to those associated with feudal absolutism. The hope, which Lukács rightly describes as being universal among bourgeois intellectuals at this time "that this democratic, bourgeois freedom and the supremacy of economics would one day lead to the salvation of all mankind" was not to be fulfilled:

> The glory and the pathos of this faith does more than fill the history of the first bourgeois revolutions—above all the Great French Revolution. It is this, too, which confers upon the great scientific pronouncements of the bourgeois class (e.g., the economics of Adam Smith and Ricardo) their forthrightness and the strength to strive for the truth and to reveal what they have discovered without cloaking it. The history of bourgeois ideology is the history of the destruction of this faith in its mission to save the world by making the whole of society bourgeois.[25]

The revolutionary thinkers of the bourgeoisie were grappling with a new phenomenon and can therefore be forgiven for not fully comprehending their subject. Now that the consequences of "actually existing capitalism" have been experienced for more than two hundred years, and it is clear that, for the majority of humanity, the dehumanizing effects of the division of labor already identified by Smith were not an unfortunate by-product but the very essence of the system, there is less excuse for such misrecognition. Political economy was the central discipline of the Enlightenment, the greatest intellectual achievement of the bourgeois revolutions.[26] The expectations that political economists like Hume and Smith had of capitalism have been disappointed, the predictions they made for it have been falsified; to defend capitalism now, to further claim these thinkers in support of such a defense while ignoring the discrepancy between their models and our reality is to attack Enlightenment values quite as comprehensively as did the feudal obscurantists to whom Hume and Smith were opposed.

◫ ◫ ◫

In front of Hume's mausoleum stands the Emancipation Monument, designed by George E. Bissell and built in 1893 to commemorate the Scottish soldiers who fought for the North during the American Civil War, six of whom are interred under or near it. It is the only memorial dedicated to any national group of combatants outside the United States, and depicts in bronze Abraham Lincoln with a freed slave crouching at his feet, the latter lifting one hand in gratitude at his redemption and with the other holding a book—we assume it to be the Bible—to demonstrate his newly acquired literacy. Several companies and regiments of Scottish immigrants were raised to fight for the Union and some, such as the Highland Scots of the 79th New York, adorned themselves in the full regalia of kilted dress uniforms, in their case consciously modeled on the 79th Cameron Highlanders of the British Army.[27] But resources that the Scots provided for the Union cause extended beyond manpower and the invented fashion accoutrements of Highland warriors to the expressions of radical Enlightenment political thought. Writing after the Civil War about the unity of humanity beyond race or nation, Frederick Douglass expressed the hope that "the American people will one day be truer to this idea than now, and will say with Scotia's inspired son: 'a man's a man for a' that'"—a line from Robert Burns he had previously used in arguing for black men to enlist in the Union army.[28]

It would be disingenuous to pretend that Scots did not also fight on the Confederate side. Moreover, if the North used Burns to support their struggle, the South too could draw on another of Scotland's literary giants, although of a very different political persuasion. Mark Twain was being his usual hyperbolic self when he held Sir Walter Scott personally responsible for the Civil War.[29] There is no doubt, however, that Scott's romanticism contributed to the self-identity of the southerner, as did the entire mythical heritage of Scottish clanship, not least in the formation of the Ku Klux Klan in December 1865.[30] One young Confederate, the son of a South Carolina planter, wrote to his mother during the War: "I am blessing old Sir Walter Scott daily, for teaching me, when young, how to rate knightly honor, and our noble ancestry for giving me such a State to fight for."[31] There is a double irony here. One is that Scott, for all his conservatism, was a characteristic figure of the Scottish Enlightenment whose novels were intended to demonstrate to his contemporaries that no matter how heroic Scottish feudal society had been, the warlike pursuit of honor was rightly doomed to be replaced by commerce and the peaceful pursuit of money: in the South his elegies were misunderstood as celebrations. The other is that, in due course, the Southern planters were to be destroyed in the way that in history most closely corresponded to the demise of the Highland chiefs and feudal lords traced by Scott in the Waverley novels.

But could the Civil War have gone further simply destroying the planters as a rival ruling class to that of the North? "Nothing renders society more restless than a social revolution but half accomplished," wrote Carl Schurz, veteran of the German revolution of 1848, Northern commander, and politician, at the end of the war: "The South will have to suffer the evil of anarchical disorder until means are found to effect a final settlement of the labor question in accordance with the logic of the great revolution."[32] Yet the Northern politicians, including figures like Schurz himself, are usually seen as "leaving the social revolution unfinished" and in some cases the Republican Party is accused of "betraying" the former slaves.[33] This seems to involve a misunderstanding of what bourgeois revolutions in general and this one in particular involve.

Once the Confederacy had been defeated, once the coherence of the South as a society had been shattered and its potential to dominate the United States ended, once actual slavery had been dismantled and the threat of subjugation to the former British colonial power removed, the majority of the Northern ruling class—many of whom were themselves racists—had no particular interest in ensuring equal rights and democratic participation for the black population. In the end, the "anarchy" invoked by Schurz—or the process of black liberation as we would see it—could not be endured when it was no longer absolutely necessary for the security of US capitalism, particularly if the possibility existed of black radicalism in the former South coinciding, or even overlapping with renewed worker militancy in the North. "The North's conversion to emancipation and equal rights was primarily a conversion of expediency rather than conviction," writes James McPherson: "It became expedient for Northern political and business interests to conciliate Southern whites and end to federal enforcement of Negro equality in the South was part of the price of that conciliation."[34] The necessary importance given by socialists to the question of racism has perhaps obscured the way in which this outcome was absolutely typical of the bourgeois revolutions from above to which the American Revolution in most respects belongs. The fate of the rural masses in the Italian Mezzogiorno, for example, remained unchanged after the Risorgimento, as they continued to labor on the same latifundia for the same landowners. Indeed, in many respects the South resembled the Mezzogiorno in that they were both effectively economic dependencies of the Northern regions of their respective nations.[35] Racism added another deeper level of oppression to the black population of the South, but their abandonment by a triumphant bourgeoisie, now safely in command of state power, was entirely typical. Free labor as conceived in the ideology of the prewar Republican Party was very distant from the types of labor into which blacks were now forced, such as sharecropping, let alone a prison system in which inmates were forcibly conscripted into production; but the latter were perfectly compatible with capitalism—as indeed, were several other identity-based restrictions on the freedom of labor. As Lisa Lowe notes: "In the history of the US, capital has maximized its profits not through rendering labor 'abstract' but precisely through the social production of 'difference,' restrictive particularity and illegitimacy marked by race, nation, geographical origins, and gender. The law of value has operated, instead, by creating preserving and reproducing the specifically racialized and gendered character of labor power."[36] And in that sense, the actual outcome of Reconstruction foreshadowed how US capitalism has developed ever since.

Was there the potential for a more democratic outcome to Radical Reconstruction? We are not dealing with a situation in which the objective was literally impossible to realize, like Anabaptist or Digger attempts to achieve communism in sixteenth-century Germany or seventeenth-century England. The issue is rather one of balance between objective and subjective conditions. Those who refer to "betrayal" by Northern politicians have to accept the implications of this position, which is that the achievement of equality was dependent on the actions of the reunified state and its military and juridical apparatus. For the reasons given in chapter 22, the Northern bourgeoisie was always collectively going to be more influenced by the necessity for social stability than the desirable but, from its point of view, optional quest for political equality. This is virtually an objective condition. In these circumstances the decisive issue was whether the former slaves could form an alliance with the majority of non–ruling-class whites, and both groups then allying with the organized working class in the North and forcing through a democratic (that is, political) revolution "from below." Obviously the Southern ruling class did everything they could to prevent such an outcome. The question—and this still seems to me to be an open question—is whether its success in doing so was preordained by the strength of a racism that was impossible to dislodge in the decade following Lee's surrender, or whether a different strategy on the part of the Radicals could have overcome it. This at least introduces the possibility that the subjective element might have been determinate here. The issues that it left unresolved could not have been resolved by the bourgeoisie and cannot now: they will have to be accomplished by a genuine second American Revolution, which can only be socialist in nature.

◻ ◻ ◻

The abandonment of the former slave population was not the only aspect of the Civil War that casts doubt on the extent to which the bourgeois revolutions could be harbingers of liberation. Another was the way in which, even before the Northern victory, the final onslaught against the societies of the indigenous population began. In March 1862 John M. Chevington led Union troops in the most important Civil War battle to be held in the Far West, at Glorietta Pass in New Mexico. Virtually as soon as the possibility of Confederate control of the Southwest was ended, the Union forces were turned against the Apache and Navajo peoples. Chevington himself commanded the Third Colorado Volunteers in the infamous massacre at Sand Creek on November 29, 1864, where a camp of five hundred Cheyenne, who believed that a peace treaty had been secured, were attacked while they slept, one hundred and fifty killed, and their bodies mutilated: "The volunteers returned to Denver to cheering crowds that admired the scalps and severed genitals displayed like trophies of battle."[37]

Analogous horrors can be found even in those classic revolutions from below that have provided most of images of bourgeois heroism. During the French Revolution, a counterrevolutionary peasant rising in the Vendée began in March 1793.

After it had been defeated in December, the terror unleashed on the area continued for six months, involving the destruction of houses and crops, in addition to people, many of whom were drowned in the River Loire, due to the inability of the guillotine to kill the numbers involved with sufficient speed. How many died will never be known, since it is difficult to separate out mortality from, on the one hand, those killed in battle during the rising itself and, on the other, the reduction in birth rates and increase in death rates, but between two thousand and three thousand may have died between December and January alone, and the final total may have reached tens of thousands.[38] During the English Revolution, Cromwell and the New Model Army stormed the Irish town of Drogheda on September 11, 1649, massacring twenty-six hundred members of the garrison and perhaps as many as a thousand civilians and clergy, an action that seemed to have been inspired partly by a desire for revenge and partly in order to frighten other towns into surrendering. A month later, Wexford fell while negotiations were still ongoing, leaving as many as two thousand dead, including civilians as well as soldiers.[39]

All bourgeois revolutions contain episodes of this sort. The English Revolution cannot be separated from the massacre at Drogheda. The French Revolution cannot be disassociated from the slaughter of the Chuans. The American Revolution cannot be cordoned off from the genocide committed against the Native Americans. These events are the other side of the coin to the popular insurgencies that characterized the cycle of bourgeois revolutions from below. There are therefore great difficulties involved in ascribing a progressive role to the system responsible for such events, and these difficulties are not a new discovery by contemporary radicals but ones that have troubled socialists of any sensitivity for many generations. Raymond Williams expressed the essential point:

> For it has been commonplace since Marx to speak, in some contexts, of the progressive character of capitalism, and with it of urbanism and of social modernization. The great indictments of capitalism, and of its long record of misery in factories and towns, have co-existed, within a certain historical scheme, with this repeated use of "progressive" as a willing adjective about the same events. We hear again and again this brisk, impatient, and as it is said realistic response: to the productive efficiency, the newly liberated forces, of the capitalist breakthrough; a simultaneous damnation and idealization of capitalism, in its specific forms of urban and industrial development; an unreflecting celebration of mastery—power, yield, production, man's mastery of nature—as if the exploitation of natural resources could be separated from the accompanying exploitation of men. What they say is damn this, praise this; and the intellectual formula for this emotional confusion is, hopefully, the dialectic. All that needs to be added, as the climax to a muddle, is the late observation, the saving qualification, that at a certain stage—is it now?; it was yesterday—capitalism begins to lose this progressive character and for further productive efficiency, for the more telling mastery of nature, must be replaced, superseded, by socialism.[40]

Williams was both reacting against a Stalinist attitude that saw as unproblematic the suffering caused by economic development, either historically (in the case of capitalism) or contemporaneously (in the case of what was mistakenly believed to be socialism in Russia). Stalinism died as a coherent ideology in 1991 with the state that gave it birth. Since then, defenders of the role played by capitalism in the past have tended to come from the ranks of those who defend the system in the present and who wish to see all remaining barriers to its dominance swept way. This alone may explain why campaigners against neoliberal globalization and imperialist war are dismissive of claims concerning capitalist progressiveness. Classical Marxism might seem to be the obvious source of an alternative to these beliefs, but it has fallen under deep suspicion precisely because of its supposedly uncritical attitude to progress. Immanuel Wallerstein expresses surprise that: "Even so stalwart a denouncer of historical capitalism as Karl Marx laid great emphasis on [capitalism's] historically progressive role."[41] Wallerstein was writing in the early 1980s and his tone suggests that the enthusiasm displayed by Marx for capitalism was a blind spot in an otherwise valuable body of work. Today, the prevailing attitude is far more hostile to Marx's work as whole, to the point that his praise for the achievements of capitalism is held to be, not a regrettable inconsistency, but an all-too-consistent indication of his willingness to sacrifice whole peoples and ways of life to the imperatives of modernity and development.

A unifying theme unites these criticisms. For want of anything better I will refer to it as "ahistorical anticapitalism," meaning a rejection of contemporary capitalism that is then read back into the historical record, so that the system is deemed always to have played a simply negative role in human affairs. Marxists see capitalism as a tragedy but a necessary one in that it establishes the material basis for socialism—understood as a society of free and equal human beings without exploitation or oppression. Ahistorical anticapitalists see only the tragedy. For them, the enclosures, clearances, and penal laws directed against people at the core of the system and to an even greater extent the extermination, enslavement, and colonial oppression of the people at its periphery were crimes of such magnitude that they render any notion of capitalism being "progressive," in however relative a way, an obscenity. There are two versions of ahistorical anticapitalism.

One concludes that the scale of the suffering caused by capitalism was so great that humanity would have been better off without it, regardless of whether it has made socialism possible or not. Indeed, adherents of this version tend to argue, on the basis of the Stalinist experience, that socialism is simply another example of Western industrialization and therefore not worth achieving. From this perspective, Marxism and neoliberalism are simply different sides of the same coin, both representing the counterfeit currency of progress. Jay Griffiths, for example, writes that:

> Progress is a one-word ideology and one which has suited both the Marxist worldview and also that of the Neoliberal far right of multinationals and global free marketeers. . . . Those who stand in the way of progress are called ridiculous, backwards, and reactionary. . . . Progress has an enormous appeal for ideologues, of both left and right and for ideologues-of-technology, all of whom use its highly political character,

while pretending that it is non-political. . . . Progress, described as inevitable, is thus not only treated as non-political but also subtly denoted as "only natural," as if it works like a law of nature, which is perverse indeed, considering how modernity's progress destroys nature. . . . For, as in the first colonizing era, it was the non-white races who suffered from the European definition of Progress-As-Genocide: so in this second era of corporate—or Marxist–colonialism, it is people of the land who suffer from modernity's progress away from nature.[42]

Griffiths is right to oppose the Chinese occupation of Tibet—one of the supposed examples of "Marxist colonialism" to which she alludes—but there is no reason to disguise the fact that Tibet before 1957 was a feudal theocracy and not some happy Hobbit-land where peasant and yak harmoniously communed with nature. Roger Burbach makes essentially the same point as Griffiths in more theoretical terms: "Capitalism in this century vied with the communist parties and the national liberation movements primarily over which system could best introduce or carry forward the project of modernization." He laments "the failure of many Marxists and neo-Marxists to recognize the heavy toll that modernism has taken on the third world, where modernization and development marked the discourse that the capitalist powers and the Soviet Union used to impose on the so-called underdeveloped world."[43]

The other form of ahistorical anticapitalism concludes that the suffering caused by capitalism had actually led to socialism it might ultimately have been, if not acceptable, then at least bearable, but it did not, will not, and has therefore been completely pointless. Murray Bookchin expresses well the logic of this position: "It is quite unclear that an industrial capitalist development of the kind that exists today was ordained by history. That capitalism greatly accelerated technological development, at a rate that had no equal in history hardly requires detailed discussion. . . . But capitalism, like the nation-state, was neither an unavoidable "necessity," nor was it a "precondition" for the establishment of a cooperative or socialist democracy."[44] Wallerstein similarly states the basic position concerning capitalist development with admirable clarity: "Not only do I believe that the vast majority of the populations of the world are objectively and subjectively less well off than in previous historical systems . . . I think it can be argued that they have been politically less well off also. So imbued are we all by the self-justifying ideology of progress which this historical system has fashioned, that we find it difficult even to recognize the vast historical negatives of this system."[45]

As the two versions tend to overlap, I do not distinguish between them in the argument that follows. Ahistorical anticapitalists tend to regard the system, from its genesis in Europe during the sixteenth century to the present day, as what Wallerstein calls a "virus," infecting other—presumably healthy—societies and preventing them developing in alternatives ways.[46] From this perspective the only difference between the genocide conducted by Spanish or Portuguese conquistadors against Native Americans while the system was still in embryo and the genocide conducted by the Nazis against European Jewry in its maturity is the extent of the destructive power at their disposal: "Capitalism in both its infancy and dotage is a terrifying social system," writes Alan Armstrong.[47] And at one level this is incontestable: for the victims the experience of suffering and death was the same. The issue is not simply an existential one, however, but one of historical meaning and of the possibility of historical alternatives. There was an alternative to the rise of Hitler in that the German working class objectively had the power, the structural capacity, not only to politically reverse the rise of fascism but to transcend the capitalist society from which it arose. Was there an alternative in this sense to the Hispanic conquest of the Americas and comparable events? Ahistorical anticapitalists tend to claim that two alternatives did exist, even when the system was only in the process of becoming dominant and that these continued to be available throughout the period of that dominance.

The first was found in the societies that fell victim to Western expansion. These supposedly embodied different and more egalitarian social structures to those of the West, as Bookchin explains: "It is important to remember that class society is not the creation of humanity as a whole. In its most ruthless form, it is the "achievement" of that numerically small proportion of "advanced peoples" who were largely confined to Europe. By far, the great mass of human beings who occupied the planet before the Age of Exploration had developed alternatives of their own to capitalism, even to class society."[48]

The second alternative is said to be inside Western Europe itself. Traditions of communal agriculture, supposedly comparable to those of the Native Americans, had survived within the feudal system but were threatened by the emergence of capitalism. Bookchin writes that "capitalism as we know it today was not predestined to gain the supremacy it presently has; rather ... popular revolutionary movements offered, and fought for, more rational and democratic social alternatives to the present society and to so-called 'bourgeois revolutions,' to use the label that has so often been given to the English, American, and French Revolutions."[49] Different paths of development would have been possible if at some point, often identified as the mid-seventeenth century, forces based on these "commons," forces other than the bourgeoisie, forces which in fact cleared the way for the bourgeoisie had taken power instead in alliance with the indigenous peoples. According to Peter Linebaugh and Marcus Rediker English seamen returning from the Americas in the early seventeenth century reported how the native peoples lived "without property, work, masters, or kings," and claim that by so doing "brought together the primitive communism of the New World and the plebeian communism of the Old":

> There existed a particular English open-field system of agriculture, including provision for common fields, which seems to have been replicated successfully in Sudbury, Massachusetts, until it, too, was overcome by the onslaught of private accumulation. Yet the commons were more than a specific English agrarian practice or its American variants; the same concept underlay the clachan, the sept, the rundale, the West African village, and the indigenous tradition of long-fallow agriculture of Native Americans—in other words, it encompassed all those parts of the earth that remained

unprivatized, unenclosed, a noncommodity, a support for the manifold human values of mutuality.[50]

John McMurtry draws similar parallels. The economics of what he calls "the real market" have their social equivalent in "the civil commons," which is not composed of natural resources themselves, but the social process by which they are protected and husbanded by the peoples who rely on them as, for example, the Turkana people of the Turkwel River in northwest Kenya treated the acacia trees as a common resource before they were enclosed and turned into commodities:

> In fact, the traditional village commons of England—before they were enclosed by early agribusiness capitalism—were regulated like the Kenyan acacia trees of the Turkwel River. That is, there were strict village rules or customs to ensure both that the natural resources were preserved and that there was continued access of all members of the community to their life-wealth (for example, the rule that a commoner could only turn out as many head of livestock to the shared pasture as were kept in the household corral over the winter).... The civil commons is society's long-evolving system of conscious human protection of the larger life-host humanity lives from. We saw it in early form in the commons of Kenya and English villages before their destruction.[51]

Here, once again, the connection is drawn between the socioeconomic organization of the indigenous peoples of Africa and the Americas, and those of Europe before the victory of capitalism; but as Robin Blackburn points out, the later often suffered from a form of misrecognition in relation to the former, one that apparently still occurs today: "Given the manifold uncertainties and frequent obscurity of the new market order, and the novel encounters on which it was based, it is not surprising that it bred new anxieties and truncated perceptions. Thus early modern Europeans, encountering Native Americans or Africans, believed them to be living outside culture and morality in some 'wild' or 'natural' state. This aroused both phobic fears and fantasies, and utopian longings and projections."[52] Bookchin at least suggests that some non-European societies had developed different forms of class society to that of European capitalism. In which case the argument is whether the alternative forms of exploitation on which they were based had comparable potential to ultimately lead to human liberation. Bookchin does not answer the question, but many do not even pose it. Thomas Patterson, for example, writes: "Assertions that [Western] civilization is desirable, beneficial, or superior to societies that lack similar hierarchical social relations merely perpetuate and promote the views of the powerful, self-proclaimed bearers and arbiters of culture and knowledge."[53] Here we simply have the conventional neoconservative polarization between the West and the Rest, but with plus and minus signs interchanged, so that latter are now presented as noble primitives untouched by class society. Neil Young gives this idea classic expression in his great song "Cortez the Killer," in which he describes the Aztec kingdom of present-day Mexico prior to the Spanish conquest:

Hate was just a legend
And war was never known

The people worked together
And they lifted many stones

They carried them to the flatland
But they died along the way
And they built up with their bare hands
What we still can't do today[54]

Now, it so happens that Patterson has written an important scholarly work on the other main pre-Columbian empire in the Americas, the Inca kingdom of present-day Peru, in which he presents a less attractive picture: "The Inca empire and the Andean states that preceded it were based on coercion and violence and on their capacities to construct and sustain political systems that allowed the group defined as the conquerors to expropriate land and extract surplus Labor from the subjugated communities." The Spanish inherited the empire from the Incas after their arrival in the 1530s and effectively maintained the same mode of production: "Like the Incas, the Spaniards were also outsiders who, by virtue of the *encomiedas* they received, claimed the right to appropriate surplus Labor and tribute from local communities."[55] Let us therefore leave unresolved for the moment the question of external alternatives, while noting that there is at the very least a question mark over their freedom from exploitative and oppressive social relations. "Plebeian communism" or the "civic commons" in seventeenth-century Western Europe were in any case radically different from native social organization in the Americas. Although "no land without its master" was the slogan of the feudal ruling class, communal village lands still existed in spaces between the competing jurisdictions claimed by different masters—the urban communes, churches, lords, and monarchs. In some cases, particularly in the North, these were descended from pre-feudal tribal properties; in others, mainly in the West and the South, they were more recent institutions won from the nobility before the system was consolidated at the end of the first millennium. Whatever their point of origin, however, these forms of property were for the feudal system as a whole both marginal (the bulk of production was not carried out there) and functional (it allowed the peasants to retain more of their product than they would otherwise have been able), not islands of communism opposed to it.[56] This was not the basis of an alternative system.

Was there then an alternative to the actual outcome? Christopher Hill has argued that there was:

> There were, we may oversimplify, two revolutions in mid-seventeenth-century England. The one which succeeded establishing the sacred rights of property (abolition of feudal tenures, no arbitrary taxation), gave political power to the propertied (sovereignty of Parliament and common law, abolition of prerogative courts), and removed all impediments to the triumph of the ideology of the men of property—the protestant ethic. There was however another revolution which never happened, though from time to time it threatened. This might have established communal property, a far wider democracy in political and legal institutions, might have disestablished the state church and rejected the protestant ethic.[57]

Hill's formulations were still phrased with care (the other revolution only "threatened," and that "from time to time"). Contemporary historians, including those working within a Marxist framework, have been less careful. In the most important recent example, *Ehud's Dagger*, James Holstun has produced what is probably the most determinedly theoretical work of Marxist history for the last twenty years, and one that every socialist can learn much from reading. Nevertheless, at several points Holstun goes beyond merely recognizing the importance of popular involvement to implying that they might have been successful in their own right, rather than on behalf of the bourgeoisie.

On the one hand, he argues like Thompson against "three sorts of teleological error," which he refers to as "necessitarian," "meliorist," and "winner's teleology." In other words, errors that see history as inevitable, progressive, and justifiable:

> Some Marxists, and Marx himself, insofar as he subscribed to a rigorous modes-of-production narrative inherited from Adam Smith, fall into all three sorts. Necessity comes with the "stageist" movement from feudalism to capitalism. Meliorism is trickier, since Marxism sees no smooth increase in human happiness, but it is at least implied in the promise that class struggle and the development of the productive forces will eliminate most human suffering. And winner's teleology appears when some misty-eyed but stiff-lipped emissary of Stalin or the Shining Path contemplates the "inevitable" (and therefore hastenable) demise of tribal peoples, monks, aristocrats, peasants, kulaks, and small producers inhabiting the soon to be superseded modes of production.[58]

On the other hand, Holstun argues like Hill that "the English Revolution" was "the first capitalist and anti-capitalist revolution."[59] The triumph of Parliament during the first phase of the civil war was followed by an increasing division between two factions: "A capitalist faction struggling to prevent the resurgence of absolutism, establish capitalist state forms, and stifle a popular faction that struggled in turn to create a genuine social revolution enfranchising a political nation of male small producers."[60] Taken together, the implication is clearly that "the popular faction" could have emerged victorious, and the course of history changed. More recently, Holstun has moved the date of the first anticapitalist rising back in time to Kett's Rebellion in 1549, which he also describes as the "greatest" in English history: "But perhaps because its particular form of anticapitalism resisted assimilation to the long-dominant 'bourgeois-revolution' model of social change, it has drawn surprisingly little attention from the British Marxist historians."[61] The key moment of possibility is however still more generally seen as occurring one hundred years later, as Peter Linebaugh makes clear in a rather ungenerous review of Robin Blackburn's book, *The Making of New World Slavery*:

> The destruction of the Diggers' experiments of agrarian organization without commodity exchange, or servile bondage, at the time of the campaign against the Levelers was a defeat of liberty which reverberated across the common lands of England, not to mention elsewhere. It was the consolidation of the bourgeois state from, say, the execution of Charles I to the compromise of 1689 which unleashed not only the Slave Codes, but the Penal Code in Ireland, Albion's bloody code, and the martial laws of

army and navy. 1649 was a hinge in world history, a point of turning. There were actual alternatives to the development of slavery, to the development of addictive drugs as the "exotic luxury" or "dynamo of colonial development," to the promotion of greed as a principle of distribution, to the instrumental rationality which replaced commonism, to the nationalism and racism, all of which Blackburn takes to define "modernity." But the door was shut upon these alternatives.

With the failure (as Linebaugh would have it) of these alternatives, capitalism, although always contested, was able to consolidate its dominance, first within England, then Western Europe, before extending its reach across the rest of the globe. Both sets of "commons" suffered as a result.[62] When history failed to turn, capitalism, although always contested, was able to consolidate its dominance, first within England, then Western Europe, before extending its reach across the rest of the globe. The question that has to be asked here, however, is whether the proffered alternatives were feasible at the time, or are simply exercises in counterfactual history by modern radicals unwilling to acknowledge that historical actors have not always had the choices we might wish for them? Holstun, for example, has argued that agrarian communism was possible in seventeenth-century England on the basis of the communities established by Gerrald Winstanley and the Diggers: "Any sincere critic of the Whig theory of history should be very nervous about the leap from saying 'the state and the gentry crushed the Diggers' to saying 'the Diggers couldn't have succeeded.'"[63] But why should we be nervous, if the latter statement is true? The Levelers and the Diggers are often spoken of together, but were of course quite different in ideology, class composition, size of membership, and virtually every other respect. The former group had members who represented numerically significant sections of the petty bourgeoisie, an organization with roots in both the army and urban society, especially in London, and held beliefs that were relatively unencumbered by religious ideology. They failed to achieve a more democratic outcome to the English Revolution, but the possibility of them doing so was not completely implausible. This is not true of the Diggers. We know of fewer than a dozen settlements in the southern half of England, none with more than a hundred inhabitants, all faced with apathy or even hostility from the local populations from whom they would have had to rely on for support.[64]

According to these authors the fact that capitalism has continued the process of expropriation down to the present day means that a resumption of the failed seventeenth-century alliance between Western "commons" and primitive communism also remains an ongoing possibility. Accordingly, the significance of 1649 (or 1792, or 1848, or whatever date is taken as emblematic of the bourgeois triumph) is that victory for the "commons" then would have prevented the system from arising in the first place, not that defeat ruled out the possibility of overturning it afterward. Armstrong claims that Marx—a "late Marx," apparently remorseful of his youthful enthusiasm for capitalism—saw the victory of popular radicalism as predicated on an alliance with survivals of primitive communism within Western Europe itself:

"Marx saw that where communal property still existed, it might be possible to move directly to higher stages of social organization, without passing through the capitalist stage. It increasingly depended on an alliance with the new popular forces, which also had an interest in opposing private property relations."

Armstrong gives a series of examples scattered across time and space. England in 1649: if the Levelers had continued their mutiny against being sent to Ireland and, as representatives of the "new democracy" of smallholders and artisans, allied with the "old democracy" of clan society. France in 1792: "If the French revolution had lived up to its original ideas and set up a commune state, the counter-revolutionary Chuan movement might not have made much headway in Brittany." Central Europe in 1848: if German revolutionaries had been able to "transcend their own national and middle-class backgrounds" they might have prevented "Slav peasants moving to the side of counter-revolution." Russia in 1921: if the Bolsheviks had maintained the alliance with the Makhnovists against the Whites and supported the re-creation of the rural *mir* they might not have alienated the peasants and produced the tensions that led Stalin to eliminate them as a class.[65] Leaving aside Armstrong's seeming inability to distinguish between bourgeois and proletarian revolutions, one is tempted to ask how plausible an "alliance" this was, if it so consistently failed to materialize in every situation.

At their most radical, above all in France, the petty-bourgeois component of the bourgeois revolutionary movements were aiming for an egalitarian republic based on commodity exchange between small property owners, a society based on what Marx called "simple commodity production."[66] But how feasible was this? Simple commodity production was based neither on communal property nor on cooperative production, nor yet did it involve the redistribution of the product; it rather "supposes private property, a social division of labor, and production for sale by individual producers (and their families) who own the means of production." More to the point, Marx did not treat simple commodity production as a mode of production with a historically independent existence but as a concept by which he could identify what was specific to capitalism: "It is commodity production without wage labor and capitalist profit."[67] Insofar as simple commodity relations have ever existed, they have usually been subsumed within another dominant mode of production. Wherever capitalism has become dominant this process of subsumption, partial under feudalism, becomes total. As Rosa Luxemburg wrote:

> We must distinguish three phases: the struggle against natural economy, the struggle against commodity economy, and the competitive struggle on the international stage for the remaining conditions of accumulation.... Since the primitive associations of the natives are strongest protection for their social organizations and for their material bases of existence, capital must begin by planning for the systematic destruction and annihilation of all non-capitalist social units which obstruct its development. With that we have passed beyond the stage of primitive accumulation; this process is still going on.... Natural economy, the production for personal needs, and the close connection between industry and agriculture must be ousted and a simple commodity

economy substituted for them. Capitalism needs the medium of commodity economy for its development, as a market for its surplus value. But as soon as simple commodity production has superseded natural economy, capital must turn against it. No sooner has capital called it to life than the two must compete for means of production, labor power, and markets. The first aim of capitalism is to isolate the producer, to sever the community ties which protect him, and the next task is to take the means of production away from the small manufacturer. . . . The general result of the struggle between capitalism and simple commodity production is this: after substituting commodity economy for natural economy, capital takes the place of simple commodity economy. Non-capitalist organizations provide a fertile soil for capitalism; more strictly; capital feeds on the ruins of such organizations, and although this non-capitalist milieu is indispensable for accumulation, the latter proceeds at the cost of this medium nevertheless, by eating it up.[68]

A position that holds that it would have been better if capitalism had been avoided is understandable, given the daily disasters for which the system continues to be responsible. Marxists must nevertheless reject it. Without capitalism, we would have no possibility of developing the forces of production to the extent that will enable the whole of the world's population to enjoy what is currently denied most of them—a fully human life. In fact, without capitalism there would be no "us"—in the sense of a working class—to seriously consider accomplishing such a goal in the first place. To me, at any rate, it seems to be completely implausible to think that if only capitalism had not come into existence we could all be living in a world of free peasants, independent small producers, and tribal commons. It is true that capitalism was not inevitable, of course, but the alternative was a world divided between endlessly warring feudal-absolutist and tributary states without even the possibility of escape that capitalism provides.

What then should our attitude be to the society that emerged from the bourgeois revolutions? Consider these descriptions of the same events, at the beginning of the capitalist world economy, from two different sources. The first is from Marx and Engels in the *Manifesto of the Communist Party* (1848):

The discovery of America, the rounding of the cape, opened up fresh ground for the rising bourgeoisie. The East indian and Chinese markets, the colonization of America, trade with the colonies, the increase in the means of exchange and in commodities generally, gave to commerce, to navigation, to industry, and impulse never before known and thereby, to the revolutionary element in the tottering feudal society, a rapid development.[69]

The second is from Marx alone in *Capital* (1867):

The discovery of gold and silver in America, the extirpation, enslavement, and entombment in mines of the indigenous population of that continent, the beginnings of the conquest and plunder of India, and the conversion of Africa into a preserve for the commercial hunting of blackskins, are all things which characterize the dawn of the era of capitalist production. . . . The treasures captured outside Europe by undisguised looting, enslavement, and murder flowed back to the mother country and were turned into capital there.[70]

The tone is very different. Which is the real position? The answer is that they both are; each reflects a different aspect of the same reality. There is no inconsistency. Marx early on criticized Proudhon precisely for trying to distinguish between the "good" and "bad" side of a social system, since it is out of the antagonism between them, the contradictory whole, that progress comes.[71] Fredric Jameson has captured this duality well:

> Marxism powerfully urges us to do the impossible, namely, to think this development positively and negatively all at once; to achieve, in other words, a type of thinking that would be capable of grasping the demonstrably baleful features of capitalism along with its extraordinary and liberating dynamism simultaneously within a single thought, and without attenuating any of the force of either judgment. We are somehow to lift our minds to a point at which it is possible to understand that capitalism is at one and the same time the best thing that has ever happened to the human race and the worst.[72]

For as long as class societies have existed, human beings have dreamed of and fought for a world without inequality. But these attempts were impossible to consummate as long as the historical basis of inequality, relative material scarcity, prevailed. It is interesting, in this context, to survey the highlights from the period of what Linebaugh and Rediker call "the revolutionary Atlantic," with which they end their book:

> English sailors and commoners wanted to stay in Bermuda rather than sail on to Virginia, and some, after they got there, deserted to Algonquinian villages. Diggers built communes upon the "earthly treasury" on George's Hill as the light shone in Buckinghamshire. Resistance to slavery extended from Putney Common to the estuarial waters of the river Gambia. Renegades who fought with Bacon against slavery in Virginia escaped to the swampy commons of Roanoke. Pirate rovers of the deep hindered the advance of West African slaving and offered occasional refuge. The outcasts gathered at John Hughson's tavern in New York for laughter and hospitality. Black preachers searched the Atlantic for a place to build a new Jerusalem. Sheffield cutlers pocketed the "wasters." Colonel Edward Marcus Despard redistributed land in Belize. Elizabeth Campbell staged a little Jubilee in Jamaica. The mutineers escaped the regimen of the *Bounty* for the beautiful ecology and people of Tahiti.[73]

Most of these examples are concerned with escape from the encroaching world of capital or the defense of the old world, not the creation of a world beyond. The fundamental difference that capitalism has made to the human condition is that for the first time in history the goal of overcoming scarcity, and consequently that of overcoming inequality is now not inevitable (despite what Marx and Engels may have said in their more unguarded or exhortatory moments) but possible, which it was not for Spartacus, John Ball, or—more importantly in this context— Gerrard Winstanley or Gracchus Babeuf. How then should we regard these figures and the movements they led?

Edward Thompson famously wrote of his disagreement with the "orthodox" historiography of the early labor movement because of the way in which "the period is ransacked for forerunners-pioneers" and the orthodoxy "reads history in the light of subsequent preoccupations and not in fact as it occurred": "Only the successful (in the sense of those whose aspirations anticipated subsequent evolution) are remembered. The blind alleys, the lost causes, and the losers themselves are forgotten. . . . Our only criterion of judgment should not be whether or not a man's actions are justified in the light of subsequent evolution. After all, we are not at the end of social evolution ourselves."

These are important considerations, but Thompson's own concern for "the poor stockinger, the Luddite cropper, the 'obsolete' hand-loom weaver, the 'utopian' artisan, and even the deluded follower of Joanna Southcott" did not involve the claim that they posed an alternative to actual course of events, merely that we should reject "the enormous condescension of history" that ignored or marginalized their struggles.[74] Thompson was not involved in writing counterfactual history but with bringing to light that which had been hidden from history, a quite different project from asserting the type of position set out here by Bookchin:

> In general, Marx's views tend to render the historical process highly fatalistic, obliging us to assume that in all the great movements for freedom over the past four centuries, there was never an alternative to the ultimate triumph of capitalism—in my view an unacceptable use of historical teleology. We would be obliged to assume that the German peasants who revolted in the 1520s were "reactionaries" because they were trying to retain their archaic village life; that the Roundhead yeomanry who formed Cromwell's new model army historically "doomed" as a social stratum by industrial inventions and forms of production that had yet to be developed; that the radical Minutemen farmers had to disappear like their English yeoman cousins; and that the sans-culottes who established the first French republic were déclassé riffraff or mere "consumers," as more than one historian has called them—and so on, up to fairly recent times.[75]

Here Bookchin elides two different questions: our understanding of the historical process on the one hand and our attitude toward historical actors on the other. It has been the case that thinkers or movements whose goals could not be realized or whose impact was negligible in their own time can be—in Walter Benjamin's terms—"torn" from their historical context and given new and vibrant meaning in ours; the contemporary struggle for socialism may be precisely the terrain in which their significance is finally comprehensible, as is certainly the case for Winstanley and the Diggers. Daniel Bensaïd has captured the attitude that is actually expressed in Marx's work:

> No pre-set course of history, no predestination, justifies resignation to oppression. Non-current, untimely, "mal-contemporaneous," revolutions cannot be assimilated to the pre-established schemas of "supra-history" or "pallid, supra-temporal models." Their occurrence does not observe the dispositions of a universal History. They are engendered at ground level, out of suffering and humiliation. It is always right to rebel. If "correspondence" has the force of normality, should we embrace the cause of the victors in opposition to impatience construed as a provocation? Without hesitation or reservation, Marx was on the side of the beggars in the German peasants' war, the Levelers in the English Revolution, the Equals in the French Revolution, the communards set to be crushed by Versailles.[76]

It seems to me to be both mistaken and unnecessary to pose the question in either/or terms. In *Discovering the Scottish Revolution* I argue that we have to distinguish between two different sets of historical actors in the bourgeois revolutions. One set consists of our socialist *predecessors*—that is, those who looked toward collectivist solutions that were unachievable in their own time, like the Diggers in England or the Conspiracy of Equals in France. The other set consists of our bourgeois *equivalents*—that is, those who actually carried the only revolutions possible at the time, which were, whatever their formal goals, to establish the dominance of capital.[77] Clearly, our attitude to these groups is very different. But since one aspect of bourgeois revolutions is to establish the most successful system of exploitation ever seen, it is scarcely surprising that the people who carried them through should, like Cromwell or Robespierre or Lincoln, leave a complex and contradictory legacy. Given the type of exploitative system that capitalism is, however, could we expect it to have come into being in any other way than, as Marx put it, "dripping from head to toe, from every pore, with blood and dirt"?[78]

☒ ☒ ☒

At the end of his great trilogy on the Enlightenment, Jonathan Israel asks whether radical thought could respond to "today's fundamentalism, anti-secularism, Neo-Burkeanism, Postmodernism, and blatant unwillingness to clamp down on powerful vested interests," before concluding: "There are few grounds for optimism."[79] Given the history of the twentieth century, to go no further back, that conclusion is perfectly comprehensible and has at least one well-known Marxist precedent. "I'm a pessimist because of intelligence," wrote Gramsci in a prison letter to his brother, "but an optimist because of will."[80] But being conscious of the likelihood of failure does not remove from us the responsibility to continue wagering on the possibility of success. Did the bourgeois revolutions contribute any resources that can be used to enhance this possibility? Or, to put the question in another way: did our bourgeois equivalents do any more for the possibility of human liberation than simply provide the material basis for future socialist development? These questions return us to the starting point for our reflections, beside Hume's mausoleum in Old Calton Cemetery where we can consider for a second time the trajectory of the movement to which he made such a central contribution.

Enlightenment thought did not simply involve a wager on the future benefits of commercial society. As Daniel Gordon writes, it was already subject to massive internal tensions since it "was designed not merely to convince people to regard commercial society as the best regime, but also to dramatize the personal qualities of courage, patriotism, and refinement that one should cultivate in opposition to the very same regime." In this "double-edged mentality . . . we should see the dialectic as a process internal to the Enlightenment—a process in which a certain degree of historical optimism immediately produced doubts about the completeness of the society desired."[81] From these doubts came the radicalized Enlightenment at the heart of Marxism.[82] In the *Manifesto of the Communist Party* Marx and Engels summarized the role of the Enlightenment in the bourgeois revolution: "When Christian ideas succumbed in the eighteenth century to rationalist ideas, feudal society fought its death battle with the then revolutionary bourgeoisie." Capitalism needed to free the power of rational thought, but reason is not the possession of single class, and once it became apparent that human beings had the power to transform their world along capitalist lines, the question inevitably arose of a further transformation. "The weapons with which the bourgeoisie felled feudalism to the ground are now turned against the bourgeoisie itself."[83] The weapons of which Marx and Engels write included the universalism of Enlightenment thought at its best.

The complexities of the doctrine of universality are best expressed in the American Declaration of Independence. Along with the French Declaration of Rights of Man and Citizen, this is one of the most famous political expressions of Enlightenment thought. In the immortal words of the second paragraph: "We hold these truths to be self-evident, that all men are created equal, that they are endowed by their Creator with certain unalienable Rights, that among these are Life, Liberty and the pursuit of Happiness."[84] Anyone wanting to raise an ironic postmodern chuckle at the supposedly fraudulent claims of Enlightenment universalism need only quote the opening passage and then point out everyone it excludes: all women, Native Americans, slaves, so on. From this, some people conclude that the oppression is endemic to the Enlightenment itself. Michael Bérubé points out, "Poststructuralism tends to argue that the emancipatory narratives of the Enlightenment are in fact predicated on—and compromised by—their historical and social origins in eighteenth century racism and sexism" and "the social violence of the last two centuries of American society is not something to be corrected by a return to the Enlightenment rhetoric of rights but is, rather, a fulfillment of the symbolic violence constitutive of the Enlightenment itself."[85]

Is it true that universality is 'tainted' in this way? In fact, as Terry Eagleton remarks, it is "one of the greatest emancipatory ideas in world history . . . not least because middle-class society could now be challenged by those it suppressed, *according to its own logic*, caught out in a performative contradiction between what it said and what it did."[86] This is certainly the attitude taken by one famous former black slave whose work I have already quoted: Frederick Douglass. In a speech given during the crisis decade before the Civil War Douglass began by pointing out the "performative contradiction":

> What, to the American slave, is your 4th of July? I answer; a day that reveals to him, more than all other days of the year, the gross injustice to which he is the constant victim. To him, your celebration is a sham; your boasted liberty, an unholy license; your national greatness, swelling vanity; your sounds of rejoicing are empty and heartless, brass fronted impudence; your shouts of liberty and equality, hollow mockery;

prayers and hymns, your sermons and thanksgivings, with all your parade and solemnity, are, to Him, mere bombast, fraud, deception, impiety, and hypocrisy—a thin veil
to cover up crimes which would disgrace a nation of savages. There is not a nation on
earth guilty of practices more shocking and bloody than are the people of the United
States, at this very hour. ... You invite to your shores fugitives of oppression abroad,
honor them with banquets, greet them with ovations, cheer them, toast them, salute
them, and pour out your money to them like water; but fugitives from your own land
you advertise, hunt, arrest, shoot, and kill.

But later in the same speech Douglass returned to the Declaration of Independence in a way that suggested that different meanings could be found there:
"In that instrument I hold that there is neither warrant, license, nor sanction of the
hateful thing; but interpreted as it ought to be interpreted, the Constitution is a
glorious liberty document. ... While drawing encouragement from 'the Declaration
of Independence,' the great principles it contains, and the genius of American Institutions, my spirit is also cheered by the obvious tendencies of the age."[87] In another speech from the same period Douglass discussed the Constitution in the
same connection: "Its language is 'we the people,' not we the white people, not even
we the citizens, not we the privileged class, not we the high, not we the low, but we
the people; not we the horses, sheep, and swine, and wheel-barrows, but we the
people, we the human inhabitants; and, if Negroes are people, they are included in
the benefits for which the Constitution of America was ordained and established."[88]
During the bourgeois revolutions there were occasions when those on the revolutionary side were forced to register their own failure to uphold the values associated
with their cause and acted accordingly. Susan Buck-Morss gives examples from
the Haitian Revolution of how such an awareness could lead to "clarity in action":
"The French soldiers sent by Napoleon to the colony who, upon hearing these former slaves singing the 'Marseillaise,' wondered aloud if they were not on the wrong
side; the Polish regiment under Leclerc's command who disobeyed orders and refused to drown six hundred captured Saint-Dominguans."[89]

William Morris's novel *A Dream of John Ball* is set during the English Peasants
Revolt of 1381, the first great breach in the feudal order in that country. To paraphrase the most famous line, the thing that at least some of the bourgeoisie fought
for turned out to be not what they meant, and other people have since had to fight
for what they meant under another name.[90] But what we fight for is not to accomplish outstanding "tasks of the bourgeois revolution" in the sense I have rejected
throughout this book. We fight rather for those universal principles of freedom
and justice that the bourgeois revolutions brought onto the historical agenda but,
for all their epochal significance, were unable to achieve. We should therefore remember the bourgeois revolutionaries in the hour of their greatness, which often
struck in the most unexpected places. During the 1790s William Ogilvie declared,
in that combination of the Promethean and the prosaic that characterizes the "practical" improvers of the Scottish Enlightenment: "There is no natural obstacle to

prevent the most barren ground from being brought by culture to the same degree of fertility with the kitchen garden of a villa, or the suburbs of a great town."[91] Behind these reflections on cultivation lies an attitude that rejects all forms of determinism, that affirms the unlimited possibilities for human beings to transform their world—possibilities that their wretched bourgeois descendants have long since abandoned—and are best summarized in these great words by Adam Ferguson, from *An Essay on the History of Civil Society*: "If we are asked therefore, where the state of nature is to be found? We may answer, it is here; and it matters not whether we are understood to speak in the island of Great Britain, at the Cape of Good Hope, or the Straits of Mallegan. While this active being is in the train of employing his talents, and of operating on the subjects around him, all situations are equally natural."[92]

NOTES

A NOTE ON THE REPRODUCTIONS

1. Hobsbawm, *The Age of Revolution*, 268. This edition of Hobsbawm's book features a reproduction of the entire painting on the front cover.
2. There were attempts to publicize the painting by inventing a real model for Liberty, in the person of a laundress, Anne-Charlotte D., who finding the body of her brother Antoine riddled with ten bullets, supposedly promised to kill as many Swiss Guards but was herself shot on the barricades as she was about to claim her tenth victim. See Pointon, *Naked Authority*, 64. It is possible that the model was actually based on the cover illustration from the 1725 Dutch edition of Charles Johnson's *General History of the Pyrates*, which depicts the cutlass-wielding female pirates Anne Bonny and Mary Read beneath the Jolly Roger. See Rediker, *Villains of All Nations*, 121–26.
3. Timothy J. Clark, *The Absolute Bourgeois*, 16–20; Paul Wood, "The Avant-Garde from the July Monarchy to the Second Empire," 36–39.
4. Fraser, *Napoleon's Cursed War*, 470–75; Gwyn A. Williams, *Goya and the Impossible Revolution*, 141–63.
5. See the classic discussions in Greenberg, "Avant-Garde and Kitsch," 6–11 and "Towards a Newer Loacoon," 27–30. See also the commentary in Timothy J. Clark, "Clement Greenberg's Theory of Art," 52–55.
6. Crow, "The Tensions of Enlightenment," 78–80, 83, 94–96.

PREFACE

1. Eagleton, *Why Marx Was Right*, 182.
2. Acemoglu and Robinson, "Why Did the West Extend the Franchise?," 1182–86; Therborn, "The Rule of Capital and the Rise of Democracy," 4, 17.
3. Appleby, *The Relentless Revolution*, 433–34.
4. Gordon S. Wood, "No Thanks for the Memories."
5. Lepore, *The Whites of Their Eyes*, 14.
6. Benjamin, "On the Concept of History," 391.
7. Orwell, *Nineteen Eighty Four*, 199.
8. Norman Stone, "Owning Up to a Revolution."
9. Denyenko, "Middle Class Backs Orange Revolution."
10. Kurlantzick, "The Bourgeois Revolution."
11. Hitchens, "The Old Man," 52.

12. Hitchens, "A Liberating Experience," 469.
13. Hitchens, *Regime Change*, 30.
14. Ibid., 48.
15. Ibid., 56.
16. Ibid., 101.
17. Douglass, "West India Emancipation," 428, 436, 437.
18. Davidson, *Discovering the Scottish Revolution*, 9–15, 73–76, 170, 182, 272–79, 290–94.
19. Holstun, *Ehud's Dagger*, 9–140; Ste. Croix, *The Class Struggle in the Ancient Greek World*, 3–111.
20. Davidson, "How Revolutionary Were the Bourgeois Revolutions?"; Davidson, "How Revolutionary Were the Bourgeois Revolutions? Continued." A rather more abbreviated version of the lecture appeared as "Bourgeois Revolution: On the Road to Salvation for All Mankind."
21. Davidson, "The Prophet, His Biographer and the Watchtower," 97–99, 101–8.
22. Thomas M. Devine, *Scotland's Empire*, 10–13.
23. Smout, "The Culture of Migration," 109–10. Poles later migrated to Scotland in their turn. The first influx consisted of the miners who settled in the Lanarkshire coalfields between the 1870s and the First World War. The second comprised those members of the Polish Army who stayed in Scotland after the Second World War: Deutscher served with that army and was briefly imprisoned for opposing the anti-Semitism of some of his compatriots. See Tamara Deutscher, "Isaac Deutscher, 1907–1967," vii. The third migration is currently under way, following the accession of Poland to the European Union in 2004.
24. Harrington, "The Commonwealth of Oceana," 159.
25. Clerk, *Memoirs of the Life of Sir John Clerk*, 49.

1. THE CONCEPT OF "REVOLUTION"

1. The first reference to "the revolution of the bourgeoisie" occurs in Marx, *The Poverty of Philosophy*, 212, written in the first half of 1847, followed by "the bourgeois revolution" in Marx, "Moralizing Criticism and Critical Morality," 319, 323, 333, written in late October 1847. See chapter 8.
2. For overviews of how Marx and Engels regarded these events see, respectively, Linden, "Marx and Engels, Dutch Marxism and the 'Model Capitalist Nation,'": 161–66; Christopher Hill, "The English Civil War," 133–56; and Löwy, "The Poetry of the Past."
3. Lenin, "The Three Sources and Component Parts of Marxism," 23–24. As we shall see, many of the leading figures in "English" political economy were of course Scottish. Apart from Marx and Engels themselves, only Trotsky among the classical Marxists showed any real awareness of the fact that "England" could not be used as a synonym for Britain and that it did not include Scotland. See Davidson, *Discovering the Scottish Revolution*, Annex, "Marx and Engels on Scotland"; Trotsky, "Where Is Britain Going?," 35–37, 45; *Trotsky's Diary in Exile*, 120. In what follows, the reader can be assured that where I write "England" it is solely to that nation that I refer.
4. See, for example, Meek, *Studies in the Labor Theory of Value*, ii–xxvi, 45–156; and, more recently, Milonakis and Fine, *From Political Economy to Economics*, 46–70.
5. Draper, *Karl Marx's Theory of Revolution*, vol. 3, 111–83; Draper, The *"Dictatorship of the Proletariat" from Marx to Lenin*, 11–26.
6. An increasingly confident group of adherents first began to identify themselves as members of a revisionist movement with this name in the early 1980s although, as we shall see in chapter 11, the arguments were first raised in the aftermath of the Second World War. See, for example, the declarations of revisionist intent in Jonathan C. D. Clark, *English Society*, 1; and Furet, "The Revolutionary Catechism," 116. The work of the re-

visionists is discussed at greater length in chapter 13.

7.   Gramsci, "Problems of Marxism," 382–83, Q16§2. See also Gramsci, *Prison Notebooks*, vol. 2, 137, Q4§1. Here and in subsequent citations from Gramsci's prison notebooks I have followed the modern convention of accompanying them with a reference to their location within the notebooks themselves, by notebook (Q), then note (§).

8.   Perry Anderson, *Considerations on Western Marxism*, 59–67, 91–92, note 40.

9.   Marx, "Preface to a Contribution to *The Critique of Political Economy*," 425.

10.   Ste. Croix, *The Class Struggle in the Ancient Greek World*, 35.

11.   Finley, *The Ancient Economy*, 21.

12.   Alasdair MacIntyre, *A Short History of Ethics*, 2.

13.   Marx, *Grundrisse*, 105. See also Lukács, "What Is Orthodox Marxism?," 9 and Lukács, "The Changing Function of Historical Materialism," 238–39.

14.   Pocock, "Virtue and Commerce in the Eighteenth Century," 119.

15.   Jonathan C. D. Clark, *Revolution and Rebellion*, 3–4, 101, 106–7.

16.   Ibid., 107.

17.   Holstun, *Ehud's Dagger*, 33.

18.   Luther, *Conversations with Luther*, 113.

19.   Hobbes, *Leviathan*, 624–25.

20.   Winstanley, "The Law of Freedom in a Platform," 307–8.

21.   Hobbes, *Leviathan*, 627–715.

22.   Christopher Hill, "Parliament and People in Seventeenth-Century England," 119. See also Christopher Hill, *Change and Continuity in Seventeenth-Century England*, 279.

23.   Christopher Hill, "The Word 'Revolution,'" 116–20.

24.   Skinner, *The Foundations of Modern Political Thought*, vol. 1, 349–58.

25.   Ellen Meiksins Wood, *Citizens to Lords*, 8–9; Neal Wood, *John Locke and Agrarian Capitalism*, 10–12.

26.   Jonathan C. D. Clark, *Revolution and Rebellion*, 4, note 5.

27.   Ste. Croix, *The Class Struggle in the Ancient Greek World*, 35, 79. For a discussion of the Aristotelian concept of class, see ibid., 69–80.

28.   Ellen Meiksins Wood, *Citizens to Lords*, 17–21. Moses Finley argues that the invention of politics should be extended chronologically backward from the Romans to the Etruscans and spatially eastward from the Greeks to the Phoenicians, but this does not affect my argument here. See Finley, *Politics in the Ancient World*, 50–52.

29.   Calvert, *Revolution*, 16–28; Norman Cohn, *Cosmos, Chaos and the World to Come*, 3–30.

30.   Finley, "Revolution in Antiquity," 49–50; Hatto, "'Revolution,'" 498–501; Malia, *History's Locomotives*, 299.

31.   See, for example, Aristotle, *The Politics*, 61–62 and Polybius, *The Rise of the Roman Empire*, 304.

32.   Finley, "Revolution in Antiquity," 54, 56.

33.   Halliday, "'The Sixth Great Power,'" 130. Halliday is here following the arguments of the East German writer Karl Griewank, from his 1955 book, *Der Neuzeitliche revolutionsbegriff: Entstehung und Entwicklung.*

34.   Augustine, *Concerning the City of God against the Pagans*, 488, 489.

35.   Malia, *History's Locomotives*, 289.

36.   Norman Cohn, *The Pursuit of the Millennium*, 108–13; Malia, *History's Locomotives*, 30–32.

37.   Hobsbawm, *Primitive Rebels*, 11.

38.   Skinner, *The Foundations of Modern Political Thought*, vol. 1, 109–10.

39.   Machiavelli, *The Discourses*, 106, 109, and 104–9 more generally.

40.   Machiavelli, *The Prince*, 135.

41.   Althusser, *Machiavelli and Us*, 70–71; Althusser, "The Underground Current of the Materialism of the Encounter," 171–72.

42.   Kamenev, "Preface to Machiavelli," 40.

43. Machiavelli, *The Prince*, 128–29.
44. Gramsci, *Prison Notebooks*, vol. 3, 39, Q6§52.
45. Balakrishnan, "From Florence to Moscow," 257–58.
46. Althusser, *Machiavelli and Us*, 118–20.
47. Locke, "An Essay Concerning the True Original, Extent, and End of Civil Government," 301, paragraph 48.
48. Bacon, *The New Organon*, 68–69, aphorism 84.
49. Pascal, "Preface to the Treatise on the Vacuum," 365–67. Two hundred years later, Marx was to draw another contrast between the same pair of creatures, emphasizing not the growth of human knowledge but the capacity of human imagination: "A bee would put many a human architect to shame by the construction of its honeycomb cells. But what distinguishes the worst architect from the best of bees is that the architect builds the cell in his mind before he constructs it in wax." Marx, *Capital*, vol. 1, 284. Here, Marx is probably following the ideas of Hermann Samuel Reimarus as expressed in his *Drives of Animals* (1760), rather than those of Pascal. See Bellamy Foster, Clark, and York, *Critique of Intelligent Design*, 89–90.
50. Gamble, *An Introduction to Social and Political Thought*, 25.
51. Israel, *Enlightenment Contested*, 5, 7.
52. Brunner, "Feudalism," 36–37; Mukherjee, "The Idea of Feudalism," 28–31; Pocock, *Ancient Constitution and the Feudal Law*, 70–123.
53. Craig, *The Jus Feudale*, 585–86.
54. Ibid., 145.
55. James Dalrymple, *The Institutions of the Laws of Scotland*, 359. For his reference to Craig, "our learned countryman," see ibid., 332.
56. David Stewart, *Sketches of the Character, Institutions and Customs of the Highlanders of Scotland*, 58.
57. Spelman, "The Original Growth, Propagation and Condition of Feuds and Tenures," 2, 4, 5.
58. Christopher Hill, "The Norman Yoke," 64.
59. Oakley, "On the Road from Constance to 1688," 1–11.
60. Skinner, *The Foundations of Modern Political Thought*, vol. 1, xv; Skinner, "Origins of the Calvinist Theory of Revolution," 314–26.
61. Israel, *Enlightenment Contested*, chapter 13; Skinner, *The Foundations of Modern Political Thought*, vol. 2, 338–48.
62. Hotman, *Francogallia*, 286–87.
63. Buchanan, *De Jure Regni Apud Scotos*, 91–92, 93, 117–18.
64. Prynne, *The Soveraigne Power of Parliaments and Kingdoms*, 5–7.
65. Burnet, *The History of My Own Time*, 70–71.
66. Brenner, *Merchants and Revolution*, 618–25.
67. Braudel, *Capitalism and Civilization*, vol. 2, 234–35; Greenfeld, *The Spirit of Capitalism*, 80.
68. Jardine, *Going Dutch*, 349.
69. Shaftesbury to Le Clerc, March 6, 1705.
70. Hatto, "'Revolution,'" 501–6, 510–12; Christopher Hill, "The Word 'Revolution,'" 101–16; Snow, "The Concept of Revolution in Seventeenth-Century England," 167–71.
71. Gelderen, *The Political Thought of the Dutch Revolt*, 263.
72. "Political Education," 233.
73. Israel, *Radical Enlightenment*, 77.
74. See, for example, Gowan, "The Gulf War, Iraq and Western Liberalism," 144–45; and Miéville, *Between Two Rights*, 189–92.
75. Court, "The True Interest, and Political Maxims of the Republick of Holland and West Friesland," 14.

2. INTERPRETING THE ENGLISH REVOLUTIONS

1. Bacon, *The History of the Reign of King Henry VII*, 66.
2. Bacon, "De interpretatiiore naturae prooemium," reproduced in Fulton H. Anderson, *The Philosophy of Francis Bacon* , 11.
3. Hobbes, *Leviathan*, 241.
4. Ibid., 185.
5. Ibid., 728.
6. Ibid., 186.
7. MacPherson, *The Political Theory of Possessive Individualism*, 78–105; MacPherson, "Introduction," 37–39, 51–63.
8. Hobbes, *Behemoth*, 3–4.
9. Ibid., 126.
10. Ibid., 25.
11. Shakespeare, *King Lear*, Act I, Scene II.
12. Ibid., Act IV, Scene III.
13. Hobbes, *Leviathan*, 227.
14. Oakeshott, "Introduction to *Leviathan*," 282. This is a rare moment of clarity in an otherwise completely ahistorical discussion during which the civil war is alluded to precisely once. Ibid., 226.
15. Hobbes, *Leviathan*, 272.
16. Hobbes, *Leviathan*, 273–74.
17. Ibid., 719.
18. Harrington, "The Prerogative of Popular Government," 423.
19. Harrington, "The Commonwealth of Oceana," 161.
20. Ibid., 196.
21. Stubbe, *A Letter to an Officer of the Army*.
22. Harrington, "The Commonwealth of Oceana," 163–64.
23. Ibid., 197–98.
24. Harrington, "The Prerogative of Popular Government," 405–6.
25. Ibid., 439. It is in the next sentence that Harrington expresses, in negative terms, the slogan ("power follows property") for which he is most remembered: "This is the national balance; for the provincial, there power does not follow property, but to the contrary."
26. Pocock, *The Machiavellian Moment*, 389. The reference to a "tradition of inheritance" is an allusion to Henry Ireton and his famous declaration at the Putney debates: "All the main thing that I speak for, is because I would have an eye to property." *Puritanism and Liberty*, 57; *The Clarke Papers*, 306.
27. Perry Anderson, "The Antinomies of Antonio Gramsci," 6.
28. Harrington, "The Commonwealth of Oceana," 163.
29. Zagorin, *A History of Political Thought in the English Revolution*, 135.
30. *Diary of Thomas Burton Esq.*, 133.
31. Ibid., 147, 148.
32. Pocock, "Historical Introduction," 43–44.
33. The far left of the English Revolution was of course still concerned to remove the vestiges of feudalism, particularly in relation to the laws concerning agrarian property. See, for example, Winstanley, "The Law of Freedom in a Platform," 372–74.
34. Pocock, *The Ancient Constitution and the Feudal Law*, 131.
35. Harrington, "The Commonwealth of Oceana," 331.
36. [Marten, Overton and Walwyn], *A Remonstrance of Many Thousand Citizens*, 123.
37. [Margetts], "[News-letter from Scotland]," 46.
38. *Mercurius Politicus* 28 (June 13–June 20, 1650): 21–22.
39. *Acts of the Parliament of Scotland and the Government of the Commonwealth*, vol. 6, part 2, 809.

40. Jones to Stane, November 19, 1651.
41. *Calendar of State Papers 1654, Domestic Series*, 90–91.
42. Cromwell, "Speech XVII," 119.
43. Harrington, "The Commonwealth of Oceana," 159.
44. It is interesting that even the founder of the revisionist movement in relation to the English Civil War, the author who originally insisted that it should not be considered as a bourgeois revolution, took it for granted that the aim of the New Model Army in Scotland was to destroy feudalism, although apparently without realizing that this had certain implications for his argument concerning England. See Trevor-Roper, "Scotland and the Puritan Revolution," 418, 430.
45. Tawney, "The Rise of the Gentry, 1558–1640," 36.
46. Ashton, *The English Civil War*, 73.
47. Clarendon, *Selections from* The History of the Rebellion, 3.
48. Ibid., 229–30.
49. Dryden, "Absalom and Achitophel," 202, lines 496–500.
50. Worden, *The English Civil Wars*, 165.
51. Dryden, "Prologue, Epilogue, Song and Secular Masque from the Pilgrim," 838, lines 63–70, 839, lines 86–91.
52. Winn, *John Dryden*, 510–12.
53. Cominges to Louis, February 4, 1664.
54. Aubrey, "James Harrington," 125.
55. Christopher Hill, "The Word 'Revolution,'" 120.
56. Laslett, "The English Revolution and Locke's 'Two Treatises of Government'," 45–66.
57. Locke, "An Essay Concerning the True Original, Extent, and End of Civil Government," 412, paragraph 222.
58. Ashcraft, *Locke's* Two Treatises of Government, 219, 228, and 216–28 more generally.
59. Israel, *Radical Enlightenment*, 73; Israel, *Enlightenment Contested*, 331–34.
60. Snow, "The Concept of Revolution in Seventeenth-Century England," 172–74.
61. Locke to Clarke, February 8, 1689.
62. Locke, "An Essay Concerning the True Original, Extent, and End of Civil Government," 414, paragraph 223.
63. Ibid., 326, paragraph 90.
64. Locke, "John Locke on the Glorious Revolution," 395.
65. Davenant, *Essays Upon: I. The Balance of Power. II. The Right of Making War, Peace and Alliances. III. Universal Monarchy*, 28.
66. Neal Wood, *John Locke and Agrarian Capitalism*, 114.
67. Ellen Meiksins Wood and Neal Wood, *A Trumpet of Sedition*, 115–16 and chapter 6 more generally.
68. Locke, "An Essay Concerning the True Original, Extent, and End of Civil Government," 290–91, paragraph 32.
69. Ibid., 296, paragraph 40.
70. Ibid., 322, paragraph 85.
71. See, for example, Duby, *The Early Growth of the European Economy*, 192–99 and Kitsikopoulos, "Technological Change in Medieval England," 406–10.
72. Locke, "The Fundamental Constitutions of Carolina," 215, articles 20–23. See the discussion of this episode in Byres, *Capitalism from Above and Capitalism from Below*, 169–76; and McNally, "Locke, Levellers and Liberty," 22–23, 31–32, 39–40.
73. Christopher Hill, *The World Turned Upside Down*, 183.
74. Roy Porter, *Enlightenment*, 243.
75. Marx to Lassalle, January 16, 1861.
76. Ellen Meiksins Wood and Neal Wood, *Trumpet of Sedition*, 96.
77. Pocock, *The Machiavellian Moment*, 477.

78.   Roy Porter, *Enlightenment*, 30–31. Contrary to the myths that always portray English intellectual life as forever lagging behind that of France, the historical record shows that French intellectuals of the eighteenth century openly and gratefully drew on the pioneering work of their English predecessors and contemporaries. See ibid., 6–12; Israel, *Radical Enlightenment*, 515–27; Israel, *Enlightenment Contested*, 356–64; and Spadafora, *The Idea of Progress*, 384.

3. STAGES OF DEVELOPMENT

1.   Fletcher to Russell, January 8, 1689.
2.   Ferguson, *Scotland's Relations with England*, 171.
3.   Fletcher, "A Discourse of Government with Relation to Militias," 2, 6–7.
4.   Fletcher, "Two Discourses Concerning the Affairs of Scotland," 68–69.
5.   Ibid., 76–79.
6.   Pocock, *The Machiavellian Moment*, 431–32.
7.   Ibid., 477.
8.   Marx, *Theories of Surplus Value*, vol. 1, 49–50.
9.   Montesquieu, *The Spirit of Laws*, 246.
10.   Quoted in Meek, "Introduction," 9.
11.   Turgot, "A Philosophical Review of the Successive Advances of the Human Mind," 42, 41.
12.   Rousseau, "Preface to *Narcissus*," 190.
13.   Turgot, "Reflections on the Formation and Distribution of Wealth," 176–77.
14.   Fox-Genovese and Genovese, "Physiocracy and Propertied Individualism," 276.
15.   McNally, *Political Economy and the Rise of Capitalism*, 85–90; Rubin, *A History of Economic Thought*, 101–10.
16.   Rousseau, *A Discourse on Inequality*, 131. For Rousseau's turn to moderation on 1757–58, see Israel, *A Revolution of the Mind*, 157.
17.   See Davidson, *Discovering the Scottish Revolution*, 73–285 and, for a summary account, Davidson, "Scotland: Birthplace of Passive Revolution?," 348–58.
18.   Dalrymple, *An Essay towards a General History of Feudal Property in Great Britain*, 344.
19.   Pascal, "Property and Society," 179.
20.   Noble, "Version of Scottish Pastoral," 285.
21.   Emerson, "The Social Composition of Enlightened Scotland," 321.
22.   Compare, for example, Locke, "An Essay Concerning the True Original, Extent, and End of Civil Government," 329, paragraph 94 and Smith, *The Wealth of Nations*, Book V, chapter 1, 236, on the primary role of the state to defend private property. Typically, Smith is more explicit in stating that this necessarily involves protecting the rich against the poor.
23.   Hont, "The Language of Sociability," 273, 276.
24.   Jones, "Introduction," 165, note 233, 171.
25.   Grotius, *Of the Rights of War and Peace*, vol. 2, 29.
26.   Meek, *Social Science and the Ignoble Savage*, 15, 16.
27.   Pufendorf, *On the Duty of Man and Citizen According to Natural Law*, 95.
28.   Moore and Silverthorne, "Gershom Carmichael and the Natural Jurisprudence Tradition," 75–76.
29.   Ferguson, *An Essay on the History of Civil Society*, 81–82.
30.   Meek, *Social Science and the Ignoble Savage*, 99; Meek, "Smith, Turgot and the 'Four Stages' Theory," 22–28.
31.   Smith, *Lectures on Jurisprudence*, 114.
32.   Kames, *Historical Law Tracts*, 56.
33.   Berry, *Social Theory and the Scottish Enlightenment*, 96.

34. Hont, "The Language of Sociability and Commerce," 254.
35. Kames, "Preface," xii.
36. [Wedderburn], "Preface," ii.
37. William Robertson, *The History of America*, vol. 2, 50.
38. Ibid., vol. 1, 111.
39. Mukersie, "Parish of West Calder," 193.
40. Montesquieu, *Spirit of Law*, 622. Montesquieu thought that origins of the feudal law lay with the barbarians, rather than the Romans. For his entire discussion, see ibid., 622–726.
41. Ibid., 183, 619. Chalcedon was a small maritime town in Asia Minor, which was situated directly opposite Byzantium.
42. Adam Smith, *The Wealth of Nations*, Book III, chapter 4, 435–36.
43. Rubin, *A History of Economic Thought*, 208, 209; Salter, "Adam Smith on Feudalism," 227–29.
44. Adam Smith, *The Wealth of Nations*, Book III, chapter 4, 433.
45. Jameson, "Postmodernism and the Market," 273.
46. Kames, *Essays upon Several Subjects Concerning British Antiquities*, [1].
47. Ibid., 154–56.
48. Dalrymple, *An Essay towards a General History of Feudal Property in Great Britain*, 338–39.
49. Hume, "Of Refinement in the Arts," 111–12.
50. Hume, *The History of England*, vol. 6, 384.
51. Harrington, "The Commonwealth of Oceana," 201.
52. Hume, "Whether the British Government Inclines More to Absolute Monarchy or to a Republic," 28. For one of many modern versions of this argument, which similarly fails to distinguish between form and content, see Pocock, "1776," 208.
53. Millar, *The Origin of the Distinction of Ranks*, 234–35.
54. Adam Smith, *The Wealth of Nations*, Book III, chapter 4, 437, 440.
55. Adam Smith, *Lectures on Jurisprudence*, 264.
56. Marx, *Theories of Surplus Value*, vol. 1, 288, 300.
57. Adam Smith, *Lectures on Jurisprudence*, 264. My italics.
58. Millar, *The Origin of the Distinction of Ranks*, 236.
59. Millar, *An Historical View of English Government*, 295.
60. Meek, "The Rehabilitation of Sir James Steuart," 6.
61. Winch, "Adam Smith's 'Enduring Particular Result,'" 268.
62. Gramsci, "Notes on Italian History," 119, Q10II§61.
63. Steuart, *An Inquiry into the Principles of Political Economy*, vol. 1, 24.
64. Ibid., 214–15.
65. Ibid., 171. See also ibid., 176.
66. Perelman, *The Invention of Capitalism*, 166, 170.
67. For other examples, see Steuart, *An Inquiry into the Principles of Political Economy*, vol. 1, 108, 122, 167, 200, 276, 290–91, etc.
68. Adam Smith, *The Wealth of Nations*, Book V, chapter 1, 225.
69. Gibbon, *The Decline and Fall of the Roman Empire*, vol. 1 [5], 17. See also ibid., 332.

4. THE AMERICAN THEORY OF POLITICAL REVOLUTION

1. Paine, *Common Sense*, 120.
2. Madison, "The Federalist, No. 14," 79.
3. Paine, "To the Citizens of the United States," 956.
4. For an overview of the debates, see Alfred Young, "American Historians Confront 'the

Transforming Hand of Revolution'."

5.   Gordon S. Wood, *The Radicalism of the American Revolution*, 175–76.

6.   For recent presentations of the left-wing interpretation, see Nash, *The Unknown American Revolution*; Raphael, *The American Revolution*; and Zinn, *A People's History of the United States*, 59–101.

7.   Nash, *The Unknown American Revolution*, 453.

8.   Jefferson, et al., "The Unanimous Declaration of the Thirteen United States of America," 4.

9.   Maier, *American Scripture*, 71.

10. See, for example, Lipset and Marks, *It Didn't Happen Here*, 21–22, 30–31.

11. Frankel, "Class Forces in the American Revolution," 93. Frankel was a pseudonym for Harry Braverman.

12. Murrin, "A Roof Without Walls," 334–36.

13. Berthoff and Murrin, "Feudalism, Communalism, and the Yeoman Freeholder," 261–86; Byres, *Capitalism from Above and Capitalism from Below*, 165–86.

14. Berthoff and Murrin, "Feudalism, Communalism, and the Yeoman Freeholder," 264–65.

15. *Independent Chronicle*, September 5, 1776, quoted in Douglas, *Rebels and Democrats*, 153.

16. Adams, "A Dissertation on the Canon and Feudal Law," 454–55.

17. Ibid., 464.

18. Hamilton, "The Federalist, No. 17," 97–99.

19. Merrill, "The Anticapitalist Origins of the United States," 481–93.

20. McDonald, *Alexander Hamilton*, 3.

21. Jefferson to Jay, August 23, 1785.

22. Murrin, "The Great Inversion," 376.

23. Madison, "The Federalist, No. 52," 322.

24. Bailyn, *The Ideological Origins of the American Revolution*, 35–36 and 22–54 more generally.

25. Dunn, "The Politics of Locke," 75, 79–80.

26. Locke, "An Essay Concerning the True Original, Extent, and End of Civil Government," 4.

27. Wills, *Inventing America*, 169–76.

28. Fleischacker, "The Impact on America," 328–33; Howe, "Why the Scottish Enlightenment Was Useful to the Framers of the American Constitution," 580–86.

29. Shklar, "Ideology Hunting," 686, 688, and 686–91 more generally.

30. Rush, "Observations on the Government of Pennsylvania," 78.

31. Madison, "The Federalist, No. 54," 334–35.

32. Quoted in Hofstadter, *The American Political Tradition*, 16.

33. Madison, "The Federalist, No. 10," 52, 53.

34. Brendel, "Introduction," 2.

35. Bradley, "The British Public and the American Revolution," 141–53.

36. Adam Smith, *The Wealth of Nations*, Book V, chapter 3, 485–86.

37. Israel, *A Revolution of the Mind*, 40.

38. Perry Anderson, "Postscript to Marshal Berman," 46. Anderson alludes to the legendary exchange between the Duc de la Rouchefoucauld-Liancourt and Louis XVI on July 15, 1789, the day after the storming of the Bastille: "Is it a revolt?" "No Sire, it is a revolution."

39. D'Houdetot to Jefferson, September 3, 1790.

40. Cockburn, *Memorials of His Time*, 73.

5. CONTRADICTIONS OF THE FRENCH REVOLUTION (1): BARNAVE AND HIS CONTEMPORARIES

1.   Quoted in Sewell, *A Rhetoric of Bourgeois Revolution*, 72.

2.   Ellen Meiksins Wood, *The Origin of Capitalism*, 183, 184.

3.   Malherbe, "The Impact on Europe, 299, 302.
4.   Rothschild, *Economic Sentiments*, 53.
5.   B-de, *Reflections on the Causes and Probable Consequences of the Late Revolution in France*, 44, 100, 103–4, 116.
6.   Morrison, "Parish of Canisbay," 149.
7.   Reproduced in Sagnac, *La législation civile de la révolution française*, 401–2.
8.   Scurr, "Inequality and Political Stability from the Ancien Regime to Revolution," 413–17.
9.   Webster, "J. Barnave," 58–63.
10.   Bates, "Political Pathologies," 437.
11.   Barnave, "Introduction to the French Revolution," 76–77.
12.   Ibid., 81–82.
13.   Ibid., 76–77, 82.
14.   Ibid., 121–22.
15.   Soboul, "Class and Class Struggle during the Revolution," 22.
16.   Quoted in Webster, "J. Barnave," 53.
17.   Clouatre, "The Concept of Class in French Culture Prior to the Revolution," 244.
18.   Quoted in Soboul, *The French Revolution*, 15.
19.   Miliband, "Barnave," 40.
20.   Barnave, "Introduction to the French Revolution," 100–01.
21.   Quoted in Braudel, *Capitalism and Civilization*, vol. 2, 237.
22.   Miliband, "Barnave," 46.
23.   Heller, *The Bourgeois Revolution in France*, 75–76; Heller, "Marx, the French Revolution, and the Specter of the Bourgeoisie," 208–9.
24.   Roederer, "The Spirit of the Revolution," 4.
25.   Ibid., 5, 6.
26.   Ibid., 8.
27.   Ibid., 7.
28.   Roederer, "The Impact of the Philosophical Ideas of the Revolution," 95.
29.   Margerison, "P-L. Roederer," 474.
30.   Roederer, "The Spirit of the Revolution," 52–53.
31.   Scurr, "Pierre-Louis Roederer," 263.
32.   Bell, "Class Consciousness, and the Fall of the Bourgeois Revolution," 329.

6. CONTRADICTIONS OF THE FRENCH REVOLUTION (2): BURKE AND HIS CRITICS

1.   Barruel, *Mémoires pour server a l'histoire du Jacobinisme*, vol. 1, 452–53.
2.   Marx, *Capital*, vol. 1, 926, note 13.
3.   Burke, "A Letter from the Right Honorable Edmund Burke to a Noble Lord," 276.
4.   McNally, *Political Economy and the Rise of Capitalism*, 256–57. For an earlier version of this argument, see Koebner, "Adam Smith and the Industrial Revolution," 389–91.
5.   Teichgraeber III, "Less Abused Than I Had Reason to Expect," 339, 340.
6.   Burke, *Reflections on the Revolution in France*, 270. Barnave himself was contemporary with Arthur Young, who in 1792 complained of "moneyed men, or capitalists, escaping all taxation" in France. See *Travels During the Years 1787, 1788 and 1789*, 529.
7.   Burke, *Thoughts and Details on Scarcity*, 25–26.
8.   Adam Smith, *The Wealth of Nations*, Book IV, chapter 5.
9.   Hirschman, *The Passions and the Interests*, 69–70.
10.   Ibid., 100.
11.   Dwyer, *The Age of the Passions*, 103.
12.   See, for example, Adam Ferguson, *An Essay on the History of Civil Society*, 181. The con-

nections are explored in: Buchan, *Adam Smith and the Pursuit of Perfect Liberty*, 5–7, 9; Davidson, "The Scottish Path to Capitalist Agriculture 3," 47–53, 62–64; and Göçmen, *The Adam Smith Problem*, 114–18.

13. Adam Smith, *The Wealth of Nations*, Book I, chapter 1, 7–16.
14. Adam Smith, *The Wealth of Nations*, Book V, chapter 1, 302–3.
15. Ibid., 303.
16. Ibid., 305, 306.
17. Rothschild, *Economic Sentiments*, 63.
18. McPherson, *Burke*, 63.
19. Adam Smith, *The Wealth of Nations*, Book I, chapter 10, 143–44 and chapter 11, 278. The Austrian Marginalist Carl Menger was only exaggerating slightly when he wrote in 1891: "Smith placed himself in all cases of conflict of interest between the strong and the weak, *without exception* on the side of the latter." Quoted in Rothschild, *Economic Sentiments*, 65.
20. Burke, *Reflections on the Revolution in France*, 128–31.
21. Ibid., 311.
22. Ibid.
23. Ibid, 311–312.
24. Pocock, "Edmund Burke and the Redefinition of Enthusiasm: the Context as Counter-Revolution," 29.
25. Burke, *Reflections on the Revolution in France*, 314.
26. Ibid., 315.
27. Blakemore, "Burke and the Fall of Language," 287.
28. Burke to Fitzwilliam, November 12, 1789.
29. See Chandler, *Wordsworth's Second Nature*, 58–59.
30. Burke, *Reflections on the Revolution in France*, 345–49.
31. The place of the Illuminati in the bourgeois imagination was eventually taken by the Communist World Conspiracy and, more recently, by Islamic fundamentalism. The contemporary equivalents of Robison's ravings can be found in those of the B-52 liberals who justify their Islamophobia with fantasies about the restoration of the Caliphate "from the Philippines to Gibraltar." See, for example, Nick Cohen, "I Still Fight Oppression." A world empire is certainly being constructed, not by Muslims, however, but by the very American state whose military apparatus writers like Cohen are constantly exhorting to bomb, invade, and occupy more countries in the Global South. In this context, one passage from Burke retains its relevance: "You are terrifying yourself with ghosts and apparitions, whilst your house is the haunt of robbers." Burke, *Reflections on the Revolution in France*, 248–49.
32. Burke, *Reflections on the Revolution in France*, 92.
33. Burke, "Thoughts on French Affairs," 13–14.
34. Burke, "Three Letters Addressed to a Member of the Present Parliament," 143–44.
35. Burke, "A Letter from the Right Honorable Edmund Burke to a Noble Lord," 141–42. It is not clear whether or not Burke was aware of the influence Harrington exercised over at least some French revolutionary thinkers, but we can safely assume that it would not have surprised him. See *A French Draft Constitution of 1792 Modeled on James Harrington's Oceana*.
36. Wordsworth, *The Prelude*, 192, lines 512–13.
37. Ibid., 193, lines 523–30.
38. Priestley, "Letters to the Right Honorable Edmund Burke," 83–89.
39. Burke, *Thoughts and Details on Scarcity*, 32. Marx comments: "No wonder then that, true to the laws of God and Nature, he always sold himself in the best market!" Marx, *Capital*, vol. 1, 926, note 13. Burke was in fact more principled than this suggests.
40. Edward P. Thompson, *The Making of the English Working Class*, 100.

41. Paine, *Rights of Man*, Part I, 162 and Part II, 193. Paine acknowledges that not all republics are fully representative: in his view, Holland ("an ill-constructed Republic") had regressed by reintroducing the hereditary principle in the role of the Stadholder. See ibid., Part I, 167 and Part II, 197.

42. Ibid., Part I, 69.

43. Ibid., Part I, 168.

44. Ibid., Part II, 183.

45. Ibid., Part I, 166.

46. Edward P. Thompson, *The Making of the English Working Class*, 104–5. At one point Paine suggests that Burke has failed to properly understand Smith. See *Rights of Man*, Part I, 97.

47. Paine, *Rights of Man*, Part II, 291–92.

48. Mackintosh, *Vindiciae Gallicae*, 128–31.

49. Ibid., 136–37.

50. Ibid., 366.

51. Reproduced in Lehmann, *John Millar of Glasgow*, 339.

52. Hirschman, *The Passions and the Interests*, 91–92.

53. Carlyle, *Autobiography of the Reverend Doctor Alexander Carlyle*, 492.

54. Israel, *A Revolution of the Mind*, 9–10, 16–17, 179–85.

55. *Asmodeus*, 2–3.

56. Reproduced in Lehmann, *John Millar of Glasgow*, 355.

57. Dugald Stewart, *Elements of the Philosophy of the Human Mind*, 228.

58. Quoted in Veitch, "Memoir of Dugald Stewart," lxxi.

59. Quoted in ibid., lxxiii–lxxiv.

60. Cockburn, *Memorials of His Time*, 78, 95.

61. Saville, *The Consolidation of the Capitalist State*, 36.

62. Teichgraeber III, "Less Abused Than I Had Reason to Expect," 366.

63. Sydney Smith, "Preface," iv.

64. Saville, *The Consolidation of the Capitalist State*, 38–39.

65. Rothschild, *Economic Sentiments*, 48.

66. Paine to Burke, January 17, 1790.

67. Adams to Jefferson, November 13, 1815.

68. Maier, *American Scripture*, 187–89.

69. See, for example, the standard account of the Congress by a modern master of self-defeating realpolitik, Kissinger, *A World Restored*.

70. Royer Collard, *Opinion sur le project de loi relative à la répression dit délits de presse*, 2.

7. THE BOURGEOISIE AND THE CONCEPT OF SOCIAL REVOLUTION

1. Maza, *The Myth of the French Bourgeoisie*, 5.

2. Guizot, *General History of Civilization in Europe from the Fall of the Roman Empire to the French Revolution*, 98.

3. Perry Anderson, "France I," 163.

4. Mellon, *The Political Uses of History*, 6.

5. Staël, *Considerations on the Principal Events of the French Revolution*, 2.

6. Guizot, *Essais sur l'histoire de France*, 75–76.

7. Guizot, "The History of Civilization in Europe," 194–95.

8. Ibid., 206–7.

9. Birchall, *The Specter of Babeuf*, 133–60.

10. Heller, "Marx, the French Revolution, and the Specter of the Bourgeoisie," 202–6.

11. Gruner, "The Revolution of July 1830 and the Expression 'Bourgeoisie'," 462.
12. Saint-Simon, "[From Feudalism to Industrialism]," 227, 228.
13. Saint-Simon, "[On the Intermediate (Bourgeois) Class]," 251.
14. Saint-Simon, "[From Feudalism to Industrialism]," 228.
15. Saint-Simon, "Consideration on Measures to Be Taken to End the Revolution," 211.
16. Maza, *The Myth of the French Bourgeoisie*, 6.
17. Staël, *Considerations on the Principal Events of the French Revolution*, 8–9.
18. Saint-Simon and Thierry, "The Reorganization of the European Community," 66.
19. Guizot, "Preface," xv, xvi, xviIsaac
20. Mignet, *History of the French Revolution from 1789 to 1814*, 1.
21. Saint-Simon, "Letters on the Bourbons," 222.
22. Balzac, "The Duchess de Langeais," 187.
23. Saint-Simon, "On the Political History of Industry," 178.
24. Macaulay, "Parliamentary Reform," 6–7.
25. Blanqui, *Histoire de l'economie politique*, x. It seems unlikely that the resemblance between this passage and the opening of the *Manifesto of the Communist Party* is accidental, and Marx does in fact refer to this work on several occasions. See, for example, *Theories of Surplus Value*, vol. 1, 174.
26. Lockhart, *The Life of Sir Walter Scott*, 720.
27. Scott, *Old Mortality*, 400.
28. Scott, *Redgauntlet*, 309–10.
29. Scott, *Anne of Geierstein*, 321. In the same novel Scott invented the notion of "the Wars of the Roses" to describe the conflict between the Yorkists and Lancastrians.
30. Robespierre, "Sur la guerre," 81–82.
31. Quoted in Kouvelakis, *Philosophy and Revolution*, 11, 354, note 5.
32. Fraser, *Napoleon's Cursed War*, 125.
33. John Robertson, *The Case for Enlightenment*, 403.
34. There is no biography of Cuoco available in English, but see the discussion of his career in Duggan, *The Force of Destiny*, 24–29 and, more briefly, Hoare and Goeffrey Nowell Smith, in Gramsci, "Notes on Italian History," 59, editorial note 11.
35. Cuoco, *Saggio storico sulla rivoluzione napoletana del 1799*, 83, 90.
36. Saint-Simon and Thierry, "The Reorganization of the European Community," 55.
37. Hegel, "Preface," in *The Philosophy of Right*, 42.
38. Hegel, *The Philosophy of History*, 19.
39. Ibid., 54.
40. Hegel, "Preface," in *The Phenomenology of Mind*, vol. 1, 10.
41. Perry Anderson, "The Ends of History," 285–94.
42. Hegel, *The Philosophy of History*, 453.
43. Quoted in Ladendorf, *Historisches Schlagwörterbuch*, 271–72.
44. Hegel, "Preface," in *The Philosophy of Right*, 3.
45. Braudel, *Capitalism and Civilization*, vol. 2, 237–39; Greenfeld, The Spirit of Capitalism, 149-50; Hobsbawm, *The Age of Capital*, 1; Raymond Williams, "Capitalism," 42.
46. List, *The National System of Political Economy*, 144.
47. Meek, *Social Science and the Ignoble Savage*, 222.
48. Adam Smith, *The Wealth of Nations*, Book I, chapter 2, 17.
49. Mommsen, *The History of Rome*, vol. 1, 461. Marx was later to dismiss the views of one unfortunate, Wilhelm Kiesselbach, on these grounds: "He has not the slightest suspicion of the modern meaning of capital. As little as Herr Mommsen when he speaks of 'capital' and the rule of capital in his *Romische Geschichte*." Marx, *Capital*, vol. 3, 44–445, note 46. See also Marx, *Grundrisse*, 512–13.
50. Marx, *Capital*, vol. 1, 873–74.
51. Babeuf, "Manifesto of the Equals," 54, 55.

52. Marx, "Postface to the Second Edition," in *Capital*, vol. 1, 97.
53. Macaulay, "The People's Charter," 195–99.
54. Macaulay, *Napoleon and the Restoration of the Bourbons*, 44–45.
55. Macaulay, *The History of England*, vol. 1, 1, 29.
56. Ibid., vol. 2, 661, 663.
57. It was on the basis of passages like this that Marx later described Macaulay "a systematic falsifier of history" and described him as a "Scottish sycophant and fine talker" who "falsified English history in the interests of the Whigs and the bourgeoisie." *Capital*, vol. 1, 38, note 88, 877, note 1. Trotsky later wrote of how: "The great 'national' historian Macaulay vulgarizes the social drama of the seventeenth century by obscuring the inner struggle of forces with platitudes which are sometimes interesting but always superficial. The French conservative Guizot approaches events more profoundly." His point, however, is that "the man who knows how to read and is capable of discovering under the shadows of history real living bodies, classes and factions" can find the truth about the English Revolution in these works. "Where Is Britain Going?," 87. His own account of the English Revolution relies on these two authorities. See ibid., 88–89 (Guizot) and 90 (Macaulay).
58. Arblaster, *The Rise and Decline of European Liberalism*, 221–22. See also Arblaster's more detailed discussion of these operas in *Viva la Libertad!*, 133–41, 245–50.
59. Cobban, "The Myth of the French Revolution," 94.
60. Tocqueville, *Recollections*, 68.
61. Jardin, *Tocqueville*, 419.
62. Furet, "The French Revolution Is Over," 14–23.
63. Siedentop, *Tocqueville*, 30.
64. For a comparison of their differing attitudes to and interpretations of the French Revolution of 1848, see Nimtz, *Marx and Engels*, chapter 5.
65. Tocqueville, *The Ancien Régime and the French Revolution*, 44.
66. Ibid., 49.
67. Ibid., 50–51.
68. Ibid., 61.
69. Ibid., 196. Marxists subsequently expressed similar positions on the conditions for revolution without reference to Tocqueville. See, for example, Trotsky, "Flood Tide," 82; and Gramsci, *Prison Notebooks*, vol. 2, 182, Q4§38.
70. Tocqueville, *Recollections*, 2–3.
71. Wolin, *Tocqueville between Two Worlds*, 402.
72. Desmond and Moore, *Darwin*, 21–44. Stephen Jay Gould has argued that the struggle for individual reproductive success in Darwin's work is derived from a particular reading of the role of economic competition in Adam Smith. As Gould writes, the great irony of this particular influence is that "Adam Smith's system ... does not work in economics, and it cannot. We are moral agents, we cannot bear the incidental loss involved in letting laissez-faire work in untrammeled ways. There is too much death and destruction. But nature does not care. . . . And so Adam Smith's system works in nature but does not work in society." Gould, *The Individual in Darwin's World*, 23.
73. Veitch, "Memoir of Dugald Stewart," lvi, note.
74. Ridpath, *Diary of George Ridpath*, 165–66, note 1.
75. Wedgwood to Bentley, October 1, 1766.

8. MARX AND ENGELS (1) 1843–47

1. Meek, "The Scottish Contribution to Marxist Sociology," 50.
2. The term was originally used by Guy Bois as a criticism of Robert Brenner's approach,

but was later adopted, first by Ellen Meiksins Wood, then more generally as a form of self-identification. See Bois, "Against the Neo-Malthusian Orthodoxy," 115; and Ellen Meiksins Wood, "The Separation of the Economic," 75–78. For a more detailed discussion of their work, see chapter 17 below.

3. Brenner, "The Social Basis of Economic Development," 40–51; Brenner, "Bourgeois Revolution and Transition," 280–85; Comninel, *Rethinking the French Revolution*, 56; Teschke, *The Myth of 1648*, 165–67; Ellen Meiksins Wood, *The Pristine Culture of Capitalism*, 2–8; Ellen Meiksins Wood, *The Origins of Capitalism*, 35–37.

4. See chapter 3 above.

5. Gareth Stedman Jones, "Introduction," 170–71.

6. Viliesis, "Der unbekannte Beitrag Adam Ferguson's zum materialistischen Geschichtsverstandnis von Karl Marx."

7. Meek, "The Scottish Contribution to Marxist Sociology," 48–49; Rubel, "Fragments sociologiques dans les inédits de Marx," 132.

8. Gareth Stedman Jones, "Introduction," 172–73.

9. Lukács, *The Young Hegel*, 171–76, 328–34, 402, 406–8; Alasdair MacIntyre, *Marxism: An Interpretation*, 27; Waszek, "The Division of Labor"; Waszek, *The Scottish Enlightenment and Hegel's Account of "Civil Society."*

10. Lisa Hill, "Adam Smith, Adam Ferguson and Karl Marx on the Division of Labour," esp. 356–57. Hill reads Smith and Ferguson through Hayekian spectacles and consequently underestimates the extent of their ambivalence towards commercial society.

11. Eleanor Marx, "Recollections of Mohr," 150.

12. Lafargue, "Recollections of Marx," 152.

13. Marx, *Theories of Surplus Value*, vol. 1, 43.

14. Marx, *A Contribution to the Critique of Political Economy*, 294, 295.

15. See chapters 2 and 5 above.

16. See, for example, Comninel, *Rethinking the French Revolution*, 55–56.

17. Engels to Borgius, January 25, 1894.

18. Marx to Weydemeyer, March 5, 1852.

19. Of these authors, Wade is probably the least known to modern readers. A former radical and editor of the *Gorgon*, he moved to the right from the 1820s onward and ended as a pensioner of Lord Palmerston. Of his works known to Marx and Engels the most significant was the comprehensively titled *History of the Middle and Working Classes with a Popular Exposition of the Economical and Political Principles which Have Influenced the Past and Present Condition of the Industrious Orders, also an Appendix of Prices, Rates of Wages, Population, Poor-Rates, Mortality, Marriages, Crimes, Education, Occupations, and Other Statistical Information, Illustrative of the Former and Present State of the Agricultural, Commercial, and Manufacturing Classes* (London: Effingham Wilson, 1833). See, for example, the reference to Wade in Engels, "The Condition of England," 433.

20. Marx to Engels, July 27, 1854.

21. Ricardo, *The Works and Correspondence of David Ricardo*, vol. 1, 35, 132.

22. Lenin, "The State and Revolution," 417.

23. The British Conservative politician Nigel Lawson once compared government preparations for the British miners' strike of 1984–85, with which he had been heavily involved as energy secretary, with rearmament prior to the Second World War. See Milne, *The Enemy Within*, 7. Peregrine Worsthorne, then associate editor and columnist with the ultraconservative London *Daily Telegraph* wrote in response to a survey conducted on the centenary of Marx's death: "Being very conscious of the existence of the class-war, I have to admit to being very influenced by Marx without whose writings this idea would never have become so all pervasive. . . . I am a Tory-Marxist, in the sense of accepting the need to take sides in the class war, even if, so to speak, on the other side." Townsend and Webster, "What Does Marx Mean to You?," 28. More recently,

Niall Ferguson has commented in an interview: "Something that's seldom appreciated about me ... is that I am in sympathy with a great deal of what Marx wrote, except that I'm on the side of the bourgeoisie." Skidelsky, "Empire State of Mind."

24. Marx, "Review of Guizot's Book on the English Revolution," 254.
25. Ibid., 250, 255.
26. Gruner, "The Revolution of July 1830 and the Term 'Bourgeoisie'," 468–70.
27. Blanc [1839], *Organisation du travail*, 68.
28. Thomas, *The Gramscian Moment*, 361.
29. Compare ibid., 359–62 with Gramsci, "Problems of Marxism," 399–402, Q10II§9.
30. See, in particular, Draper, *Karl Marx's Theory of Revolution*, vol. 1, 31–234; Kouvelakis, *Philosophy and Revolution*, 232–36; and Löwy, *The Theory of Revolution*, 23–117.
31. Wallerstein, *Historical Capitalism*, 106.
32. Perry Anderson, "The Notion of a Bourgeois Revolution," 108. For similar comments, see Tibebu, "On the Question of Feudalism," 122; and Zapperi, *Per la critica del concetto di rivoluzione borghese*, 91.
33. See chapter 6 above.
34. O'Brien, "A View of Social Development," 161.
35. Mazzini, "Thoughts on the French Revolution," 251.
36. Herzen, "To an Opponent," 549.
37. Quoted in Hofmann, *Ideengeschichte Der Sozialen Bewegung*, 90.
38. Engels, "The Internal Crises," 374.
39. Engels, "Outline of a Critique of Political Economy," 419.
40. Engels, "The Condition of England," 473.
41. Ibid., 469.
42. Engels, "Speeches in Elberfeld," 262.
43. Ibid.
44. Engels, *The Condition of the Working Class in England*, 319.
45. Ibid., 319, 391.
46. Ibid., 559.
47. Marx, "Critique of Hegel's Doctrine of the State."
48. Quoted in Löwy, *The Theory of Revolution in the Young Marx*, 43.
49. Marx, "On the Jewish Question," 221.
50. Ibid., 232.
51. Ibid., 222.
52. Marx, "Critique of Hegel's Philosophy of Right," 253–54.
53. Ibid., 256.
54. Ibid., 257.
55. Marx and Engels, *The Holy Family*, 36–37.
56. Marx and Engels, *The German Ideology*, 48.
57. Ibid., 52–53.
58. Ibid., 486.
59. Lukács, "Reification and the Consciousness of the Proletariat," 149–209.
60. Marx, "Critical Notes on 'The King of Prussia,'" 419–420.
61. Engels, "The Festival of Nations in London," 3.
62. Marx, *The Poverty of Philosophy*, 174.
63. Marx, "Preface to *A Contribution to the Critique of Political Economy*," 427.
64. Carver, "*The German Ideology* Never Took Place," 115–27.
65. See, for example, Callinicos, *Marxism and Philosophy*, 48–49; and Therborn, *Science, Class and Society*, 368–69.
66. Marx and Engels, *The German Ideology*, 41–42.
67. Ibid., 42. See also ibid., 55.
68. Ibid., 31–32.

69. Therborn, *Science, Class and Society*, 363.
70. Marx and Engels, *The German Ideology*, 32. My emphasis.
71. Ibid., 32–33.
72. Ibid., 85.
73. Ibid..
74. Ibid., 54.
75. Ibid., 74–75.
76. Ibid., 48–49.
77. Ibid., 432.
78. Marx, *The Poverty of Philosophy*, 166.
79. Ibid., 174. See also ibid., 204.
80. Ibid., 197.
81. Marx, *Wage-Labour and Capital*, 211.
82. Marx, *The Poverty of Philosophy*, 212.
83. Marx, "Moralizing Criticism and Critical Morality," 319.
84. Blanc [1850], *Organisation du travail*, 161–1622. Dislike of Bastiat was one of the few points upon which Blanc and Marx were agreed. Marx refers to him at one point as the author of "impertinent and superficial rubbish . . . doled out with self-important complacency." Marx, *Capital*, vol. 1, 999.
85. Thackeray, *The Newcomes*, 488.
86. Marx, *Capital*, vol. 1, 126; Marx, "Postface to the Second Edition," in ibid., 96.
87. Marx, "The General Council to the Federal Council," 86.
88. Marx and Engels, "The Manifesto of the Communist Party," 73,
89. Marx, *Capital*, vol. 1, 884–85.

9. MARX AND ENGELS (2) 1847–52

1. For the difficulties involved in identifying the status of individual works by Marx and Engels, see Draper, *Karl Marx's Theory of Revolution*, vol. 2, 1–5 and Thomas, *The Gramscian Moment*, 43. Thomas rightly points out that even *Capital*, volume 1 cannot be considered completely definitive. See also the discussion in Kevin B. Anderson, *Marx at the Margins*, 172–76.
2. Dunayevskaya, *Marxism and Freedom*, 27–29.
3. Engels, "The Campaign for the German Imperial Constitution," 155.
4. Blackbourn, *The Fontana History of Germany*, 61–62, 65–66, 70–74; Kouvelakis, *Philosophy and Revolution*, 243–46. The significance of location for Marx is stressed by most of his major biographers. See McLennan, *Karl Marx*, 1–2; Nicolaievsky and Maenchen-Helfen, *Karl Marx*, 1–4; Wheen, *Karl Marx*, 9–10.
5. Engels, "Introduction to Karl Marx's *The Class Struggle in France*," 509.
6. Heller, *The Bourgeois Revolution in France*, 11.
7. Ibid., 149.
8. Marx, "The Bourgeoisie and the Counter-Revolution," 192, 193.
9. Löwy, "The Poetry of the Past," 115.
10. Comninel, *Rethinking the French Revolution*, 29.
11. Marx and Engels, "The Manifesto of the Communist Party," 80.
12. Ibid., 98. Indeed, some writers seem to believe that the *Manifesto* does not refer to the bourgeois revolution at all. See, for example, Perry Anderson, "The Notion of a Bourgeois Revolution," 107.
13. Marx, "Review of Guizot's Book on the English Revolution," 252.
14. Marx, "The Bourgeoisie and the Counter-Revolution," 189.
15. Engels, "The Condition of England," 472–73.

16. Comninel, *Rethinking the French Revolution*, 202.
17. Ibid., 202–3.
18. Marx, "The Eighteenth Brumaire of Louis Bonaparte," 242.
19. Marx, "The Civil War in France," 208.
20. Ibid., 238; Marx, "First Draft of 'The Civil War in France,'" 246–50.
21. Marx, "The Eighteenth Brumaire of Louis Bonaparte," 174.
22. Engels, "The Civil War in Switzerland," 368, 369.
23. Marx and Engels, *The German Ideology*, 411.
24. Marx, "The Bourgeoisie and the Counter-Revolution," 192.
25. Marx, "Review of Guizot's Book on the English Revolution," 253.
26. Linden, "Marx and Engels, Dutch Marxism and the 'Model Capitalist Nation of the Seventeenth Century'," 163.
27. Marx, "Economic and Philosophical Manuscripts," 340.
28. Marx, "The Bourgeoisie and the Counter-Revolution," 192–93.
29. Marx, "The Trial of the Rhineland District Committee," 250, 259.
30. See, for example, Corcoran, "The Bourgeoisie and Other Villains," 477–79, 485.
31. Ellen Meiksins Wood, *The Origins of Capitalism*, 32.
32. Marx and Engels, "The Manifesto of the Communist Party," 69, 70.
33. Higonnet, "Terror, Trauma and the 'Young Marx' Explanation of Jacobin Politics," 190–91.
34. Marx and Engels, *The Holy Family*, 122.
35. Marx, "The Eighteenth Brumaire of Louis Bonaparte," 146.
36. Hegel, *The Philosophy of History*, 313.
37. Marx, "Critique of Hegel's Philosophy of Right," 247–48.
38. Marx, "The Eighteenth Brumaire of Louis Bonaparte," 146–48. See the useful summary of this argument in Althusser, *Machiavelli and Us*, 49–50.
39. Marx, "The Eighteenth Brumaire of Louis Bonaparte," 173–74.
40. Engels, "[The Constitutional Question in Germany]," 84, 86.
41. Marx, "Moralizing Criticism and Critical Morality," 333.
42. Ibid., 332. See also Marx, "The Bourgeoisie and the Counter-Revolution," 193.
43. Marx, "Counter-Revolution in Berlin," 15–16.
44. Marx, "Moralizing Criticism and Critical Morality," 333.
45. Marx, "The Paris *Reforme* on the Situation in France," 494.
46. Marx, "The Bourgeoisie and the Counter-Revolution," 192.
47. Marx, "Moralizing Criticism and Critical Morality," 319.
48. Engels, "The Peasant War in Germany," 469–70.
49. Marx, "Moralizing Criticism and Critical Morality," 319. Marx and Engels were not alone in taking this view. Herzen made the same point in relation to Russia in the late 1860s: "Even if the whole bourgeois world were blown to bits, *some sort of bourgeois world* would arise after the smoke had dissipated and the ruins had been cleared away, though somewhat modified, because that world *is not yet dead* internally and *also because neither the world* that builds nor the new organization are yet so ready as to be able to perfect themselves as they come into being." Herzen, "To an Old Comrade," 578.
50. Draper, *Karl Marx's Theory of Revolution*, vol. 2, 201–6.
51. Marx, "On the Jewish Question," 222; Marx and Engels, *The Holy Family*, 123.
52. Draper, *Karl Marx's Theory of Revolution*, vol. 2, 229–58.
53. Ibid., 259–63; Day and Gaido, "Introduction," 9–10; Nimtz, *Marx and Engels*, 102–7.
54. Marx, "Address of the Central Committee to the Communist League," 323–24.
55. Ibid, 330.
56. Marx, "The Class Struggles in France," 45–46.
57. Engels, "Introduction [to Karl Marx's *The Class Struggle in France 1848*]," 513.
58. Engels, "Extraordinary Revelations – Abd-El-Kader – Guizot's Foreign Policy," 471–72.
59. Engels, "The Magyar Struggle," 221–22, 225–26.

60.   Nimni, "Marx, Engels and the National Question," 314.
61.   Rosdolsky, *Engels and the "Non-Historic Peoples"* 129
62.   Ibid, 12. For an earlier, less developed version of this argument, see Kautsky, "The Slavs and Revolution," 61–62.
63.   Engels, "Democratic Pan-Slavism," 231.
64.   Marx, "The British Rule in India," 306–7.
65.   Said, *Orientalism*, 155.
66.   Robert J. C. Young, *White Mythologies*, 3.
67.   Strawson, "Culture and Imperialism," 69–70.

10. MARX AND ENGELS (3) AFTER 1852

1.   Marx, "The Class Struggles in France," 131.
2.   Marx, *Grundrisse*, 277.
3.   Marx, "Preface to *A Contribution to the Critique of Political Economy*," 425–26.
4.   Prinz, "Background and Alternative Motive of Marx's 'Preface' of 1859."
5.   Marx and Engels, "The Manifesto of the Communist Party," 72.
6.   Marx, "Preface to *A Contribution to the Critique of Political Economy*," 426.
7.   Marx and Engels, "The Manifesto of the Communist Party," 68.
8.   Marx, "Preface to *A Contribution to the Critique of Political Economy*," 426.
9.   Marx, *Capital*, vol. 1, 175, note 35.
10.   Marx, *Capital*, vol. 3, 1024. This passage is from chapter 51, "Relations of Distribution and Relations of Production"—one cited by Robert Brenner as the basis of his interpretation. See, for example, "Agrarian Class Structure and Economic Development in Pre-Industrial Europe," 11, note 3.
11.   Marx, *Capital*, vol. 3, 927–28.
12.   Comninel, *Rethinking the French Revolution*, 167. See also Teschke, *The Myth of 1648*, 55–56.
13.   Engels, "Ludwig Feuerbach and the End of Classical German Philosophy," 390. The term "relations" appeared in the original articles in *De Neue Zeit* in 1886; "order" in the pamphlet edition published in 1888.
14.   Callinicos, *Theories and Narratives*, 134–35.
15.   Marx, *Capital*, vol. 1, 90, 876.
16.   Ibid., 876.
17.   Ibid., 915–16. See also individual statements such as: "Liverpool grew fat on the basis of the slave trade. This was its method of primitive accumulation." Ibid., 924.
18.   Ellen Meiksins Wood, *The Origin of Capitalism*, 48.
19.   Marx, *Capital*, vol. 1, 876, note 1.
20.   Marx, *Grundrisse*, 278.
21.   Marx, *Capital*, vol. 1, 874, 975.
22.   Ibid., 183.
23.   Engels, "Introduction to the English Edition (1892) of *Socialism, Utopian and Scientific*," 297.
24.   Engels, "Preface [to the Second Edition of *The Peasant War in Germany*]," 97.
25.   Engels, "The Prussian Military Question," 122.
26.   Marx, *Capital*, vol. 1, 875.
27.   Engels, "Additions to the Text of *Anti-Dühring*," 636. Compare Engels, *Anti-Dühring*, 245.
28.   Engels, "Introduction to the English Edition (1892) of *Socialism, Utopian and Scientific*," 291–92.
29.   Engels, "The State of Germany," 19.
30.   Marx and Engels, *The Holy Family*, 123.

31.   Marx, "The Eighteenth Brumaire of Louis Bonaparte," 147.

32.   Marx, "Erfurtery in the Year 1859," 404.

33.   Engels, "England in 1845," 297.

34.   Engels, "Introduction [to Karl Marx's *The Class Struggle in France 1848*]," 513.

35.   Engels, "The Role of Force in History," 464–66.

36.   Engels to Bebel, November 18, 1884.

37.   Quoted in Gall, *Bismarck*, vol. 1, 305.

38.   Engels, "The Role of Force in History," 501–2.

39.   Engels, "Supplement to the Preface of 1870 for *The Peasant War in Germany*," 627.

40.   Hobsbawm. "Marx, Engels and Politics," 71.

41.   Engels to Turati, January 26, 1894. See also Engels, "The Future Italian Revolution," 437.

42.   A third letter from the IWMA, "To the People of the United States," emphasizing the need for blacks to be granted full equality, was not written by Marx but by one of the international's trade unionist leaders, William Cremer. See Kevin B. Anderson, *Marx at the Margins*, 193–94.

43.   Perry Anderson, "The Notion of a Bourgeois Revolution," 106; Fernbach, "Introduction," 31–32; Genovese, "Marxist Interpretations of the Slave South," 321–35.

44.   Kevin B. Anderson, *Marx at the Margins*, chapter 3, 193–95, 238–39; Dunayevskaya, *Marxism and Freedom*, chapter 5; Marx, *Capital*, vol. 1, 414–15.

45.   Marx, *Capital*, vol. 1, 878.

46.   Marx, "The Civil War in the United States," 351.

47.   Marx, "To Abraham Lincoln," 20. Virtually the same phrase recurs in *Capital*, vol. 1, 91.

48.   Engels to Marx, May 12, 1862.

49.   Marx to Lion Phillips, May 6, 1861.

50.   The most balanced assessment of Lincoln can be found in Marx, "Comments on the North American Events," 249–51.

51.   Drayton, *The South Vindicated from the Treason and Fanaticism of the Northern Abolitionists*, 179, 180, 181.

52.   *Macon Telegraph*, November 8, 1860, quoted in Johnson, *Towards the Patriarchal Republic*, 46.

53.   *Congressional Globe*, new series, 68, March 6, 1862, 1077.

54.   Garfield, *Garfield's Words*, 161.

55.   James M. McPherson, "The Second American Revolution," 5–6.

56.   Dawson, "Northern Manufacturers and the Coming of the American Civil War," 115.

57.   Eagleton, *Why Marx Was Right*; Milonakis and Fine, *From Political Economy to Economics*, 32.

58.   Cairnes, *The Slave Power*, ix–x.

59.   Ibid., x.

60.   There are other parallels between Marx and the Northern radicals. The former slave and abolitionist Frederick Douglass, for example, wrote in 1852 on the impact of capitalism: "Long established customs of hurtful character could formerly fence themselves in, and do their evil work with social impunity. Knowledge was then confined and enjoyed by the privileged few, and the multitude walked on in mental darkness. But a change has now come over the affairs of mankind. Walled cities and empires have become unfashionable. The arm of commerce has borne away the gates of the strong city. Intelligence is penetrating the darkest corners of the globe. It makes its pathway over and under the sea, as well as on the earth. Wind steam and lightning are its chartered agents. Oceans no longer divide, but link nations together. From Boston to London is now a holiday excursion. Space is comparatively annihilated." Douglass, "The Meaning of July Fourth for the Negro," 201. The last sentence of this passage from 1852 foreshadows the more famous declaration by Marx later in the decade: "Thus, while capital must on one side strive to tear down every spatial barrier to intercourse, i.e. to exchange, and conquer the

whole earth for its market, it strives on the other to annihilate this space with time, i.e. to reduce to a minimum the time spent in motion from one place to another." Marx, *Grundrisse*, 539.

61.   Schurz, "Report on the Condition of the South," 354.
62.   See, for example, Engels, *Anti-Dühring*, 152–53.
63.   Engels, "Introduction to the English Edition (1892) of *Socialism, Utopian and Scientific*," 290.
64.   Engels to Kautsky, February 20, 1889.
65.   Nimni, "Marx, Engels and the National Question," 314, 324.
66.   Engels, "[On the Early History of the Germans]," 30.
67.   Engels, "[The Decay of Feudalism and the Emergence of National States]," 559–61.
68.   Marx, "Ireland's Revenge," 80.
69.   Engels to Marx, May 23, 1856. Earlier in the same letter Engels refers to the low productivity of land, with one notable exception, "towards Limerick, the hills are excellently cultivated, mostly by Scottish farmers." These were the descendants of Protestant settlers from the Scottish Lowlands.
70.   Engels, "Plan of Chapter Two, and Fragments for *The History of Ireland*," 312.
71.   Marx to Meyer and Vogt, April 9, 1870.
72.   Engels, "[*The History of Ireland*]," 147–48.
73.   Engels to Kautsky, September 12, 1882.
74.   Engels, "The Magyar Struggle," 217.
75.   Hobsbawm, "Introduction," 50.
76.   Shanin, "Late Marx," 6–8, 15.
77.   Rosemont, "Karl Marx and the Iroquois," 210.
78.   Maclean, "All Hail, the Scottish Workers' Republic!," 218.
79.   Marx, *The Poverty of Philosophy*, 174–75.
80.   Marx, "Speech at the Anniversary of *The People's Paper*," 299–300.
81.   Marx to Engels, October 8, 1858.
82.   Ahmad, "Marx on India," 226.
83.   Said, *Orientalism*, 155.
84.   Callinicos, *Theories and Narratives*, 154.
85.   Ahmad, "Marx on India," 241, 227–28.
86.   Marx, "The Future Results of the British Rule in India," 319, 323, 324–25.
87.   Callinicos, *Theories and Narratives*, 154–60.
88.   Marx, "[Third Draft]," "[Drafts of the Letter to Vera Zasulich]," 365.
89.   Engels to Kautsky, February 7, 1882.
90.   Marx, "[Letter to *Otechesivenniye Zapiski*]," 199, 200.
91.   Marx to Zasulich, March 8, 1881.
92.   Marx and Engels, "Preface to the Second Russian Edition of 'The Manifesto of the Communist Party'," 42.
93.   Engels, "Afterword (1894) [to *On Social Relations in Russia*]," 423, 424, 425–26, 431.
94.   Ibid., 427.
95.   Ibid., 430–31.
96.   Engels to Danielson, September 22, 1892.
97.   Marx, *Capital*, vol. 1, 91.
98.   Kevin B. Anderson, *Marx at the Margins*, 178.

11. CLASSICAL MARXISM (1) 1889–1905

1.   Eley, *Forging Democracy*, 63, table 4.1; Sassoon, *One Hundred Years of Socialism*, 10, table 1.1.

2.   Hobsbawm, *The Age of Empire*, 116–18, 129–36; Renton, *Classical Marxism*, 20, 25–28.
3.   Isaac Deutscher, "Marxism in Our Time," 8 and 17–20 more generally.
4.   See, for example, Keiran Allen, *The Politics of James Connolly*, 5.
5.   Perry Anderson, *Considerations on Western Marxism*, 7–8.
6.   Renton, *Classical Marxism*, 10.
7.   Norman Stone, *Europe Transformed*, 114.
8.   Hobsbawm, "The Fortunes of Marx's and Engels' Writings," 181.
9.   Eley, *Forging Democracy*, 44, 45.
10. Sassoon, *One Hundred Years of Socialism*, 6.
11. Jackson, *Solo Trumpet*, 59.
12. See, in general, Renton, *Classical Marxism*, 34–39 and, with specific reference to Britain, Stuart MacIntyre, *A Proletarian Science*, appendix to chapter 3, 91–92.
13. Bauer, *The Question of Nationalities and Social Democracy*, 154.
14. Stuart MacIntyre, *A Proletarian Science*, 109.
15. John R. Green, *A Short History of the English People*, xviii.
16. Davidson, *The Origins of Scottish Nationhood*, 154–59.
17. Burns, "Robert Bruce's Address to His Troops at Bannockburn – or Scots Wha Hae," 466.
18. Burns to Thompson, August 1793, 639.
19. Burns, "The Solemn League and Covenant," 875.
20. Jolly, *The Life of John Duncan*, 16–17.
21. Aiton, *A History of the Rencounter at Drumclog*, 7–8, 99.
22. Eley, *Forging Democracy*, 109.
23. Marx and Engels, "The Manifesto of the Communist Party," 86.
24. Hobsbawm, *The Age of Empire*, 117.
25. Freeman, *An American Testament*, 49.
26. Jackson, *Solo Trumpet*, 57–58.
27. Bernstein, *Cromwell and Communism*, 279.
28. De Leon, *Two Pages from Roman History*, 8.
29. Kautsky, *Foundations of Christianity*, 10.
30. Marx, "Preface to *A Contribution to the Critique of Political Economy*," 426.
31. Hobsbawm, "Introduction," 38.
32. See, for example, the comparison between Kautsky and Herbert Spencer as evolutionists in Callinicos, *Social Theory*, 108–15.
33. Marx, "Preface to *A Contribution to the Critique of Political Economy*," 425–26.
34. Marx, *Capital*, vol. 1, 91, 92.
35. Kautsky, *Vorläufer der neueren Soziulismus*, Erster band, *Der Kommunismus in der Deutschen Reformation*, 365. The sections of this work from which these quotations are taken have yet to be published in English.
36. Plekhanov, "Socialism and the Political Struggle," 79.
37. Plekhanov, "Our Differences," 364–66.
38. Ibid., 357–58.
39. Plekhanov, "The Development of the Monist View of History," 704, 705.
40. Kautsky, *The Agrarian Question*, vol. 1, 325.
41. Plekhanov, "Our Differences," 327–28.
42. Jaurès, "General Introduction to *The Socialist History of the French Revolution*," 164.
43. Marx and Engels, "The Manifesto of the Communist Party," 67.
44. Ste. Croix, *The Class Struggle in the Ancient Greek World*, 66.
45. Marx and Engels, "The Manifesto of the Communist Party," 68.
46. The bourgeoisie was included in an earlier version of this list. See Marx and Engels, *The German Ideology*, 432.
47. Engels, "Preface to the English Edition of 1888 [of "The Manifesto of the Communist Party"]," 65.

680 NOTES TO PAGES 194–207

48. Bauer, *The Question of Nationalities and Social Democracy*, 88.
49. Quoted in Bullock, *The Life and Times of Ernest Bevin*, vol. 1, 379.
50. Plekhanov, "The Development of the Monist View of History," chapter 2.
51. Plekhanov, "Socialism and the Political Struggle," 84.
52. Plekhanov, "How the Bourgeoisie Remembers its Own Revolution," 24.
53. Samuel H. Baron, *Plekhanov*, 354 and 354–58 more generally.
54. Plekhanov, "'Orthodox' Pedantry," 148–49.
55. Plekhanov, "Our Differences," 240.
56. Kautsky, "The *Sans-Culottes* of the French Revolution," 539.
57. Nygaard, "Constructing Marxism," 459–60. Nygaard presumably intends the final quoted sentence to mean: "in *spite* of the absence of leadership from the capitalist bourgeoisie as a whole," not "in *spite* of the obstacle posed by the capitalist bourgeoisie."
58. Mehring, "Conditions in Germany," 169.

12. CLASSICAL MARXISM (2) 1905–24

1. Perry Anderson, "The Notion of a Bourgeois Revolution," 107.
2. Plekhanov, "Speech at the International Workers' Socialist Congress," 454.
3. Struve, "The Manifesto of the Russian Social Democratic Party (March 1898)," 224.
4. Lenin, *The Development of Capitalism in Russia*, 596.
5. Ryazanov, "Iskra and the Tasks of Russian Social Democrats," 131.
6. Day and Gaido, editorial introduction to Trotsky, "Social Democracy and Revolution," 447–50.
7. Lenin, "Social Democracy's Attitude towards the Peasant Movement," 237–38.
8. Trotsky, "Three Conceptions of the Russian Revolution," 71–72.
9. Löwy, *The Politics of Combined and Uneven Development*, 43.
10. For these debates, see Day and Gaido, "Introduction," 32–54; Geras, "Between the Russian Revolutions," 252–304; and Löwy, *The Politics of Combined and Uneven Development*, chapter 2.
11. Kautsky, "To What Extent Is the *Communist Manifesto* Obsolete?," 176.
12. Lenin [1907], "Notes of a Publicist ," 72–73.
13. Quoted in Isaac Deutscher, *The Prophet Armed*, 99.
14. Axelrod, "Axelrod's Speech at the Fourth Party Congress," 60.
15. Lenin, "Lessons of the Moscow Events," 382, 383.
16. Cliff, *Lenin*, vol. 1, 67.
17. Lih, *Lenin Rediscovered*, 21.
18. Alasdair MacIntyre, "How to Write about Lenin – and How Not to," 358.
19. Lenin, "The Socialist Party and Non-Party Revolutionism," 75, 76.
20. Perry Anderson, *Lineages of the Absolutist State*, 355.
21. Lenin, "Two Tactics of Social-Democracy in the Democratic Revolution," 48–50.
22. Lenin, "The Agrarian Question and the Forces of the Revolution," 334–35.
23. Kautsky, "The Driving Forces of the Russian Revolution," 605.
24. Lenin, "Preface to the Russian Translation of K. Kautsky's Pamphlet *The Driving Forces and Prospects of the Russian Revolution*," 411.
25. Kautsky, "The Driving Forces of the Russian Revolution," 607.
26. Luxemburg, "The Russian Revolution," 526.
27. Lenin, "The Assessment of the Russian Revolution," 56–57.
28. Lenin, "The Aim of the Proletarian Struggle in Our Revolution," 377–78.
29. Lenin, "The 'Peasant Reform' and the Proletarian-Peasant Revolution," 128.
30. Lenin [1910], "Notes of a Publicist," 202–3.
31. Luxemburg, "The Russian Revolution," 523–24.

32. Lenin, "The Socialist Party and Non-Party Revolutionism," 75.

33. Lenin, "The War and Russian Social-Democracy," 33.

34. Lih, *Lenin Rediscovered*, 98–100.

35. Michels, *Political Parties*, 10.

36. Lenin, The *Development of Capitalism in Russia*, 239; Lenin, "The Agrarian Programme of Social-Democracy in the First Russian Revolution, 1905-1907," 238–41.

37. On the respective historical accuracy of Lenin's assessment of the Prussian and American paths, see Byres, *Capitalism from Above and Capitalism from Below*, 428, 433.

38. Lenin, "Two Tactics of Social-Democracy in the Democratic Revolution," 42.

39. Lenin, "The 'Peasant Reform' and the Proletarian-Peasant Revolution," 120–22, 125.

40. Lenin, "Reformism in the Russian Social-Democratic Movement," 231, 234–35, 241.

41. Lenin, "A Conversation between a Legalist and an Opponent of Liquidationism," 187.

42. In this respect, as MacIntyre points out—heretically, but I think accurately—Lenin was actually nearer to the arch-revisionist Bernstein than the orthodox mainstream of Social Democracy represented by Kautsky. See "How to Write about Lenin – and How Not to," 356–57.

43. Lenin, "The Agrarian Programme of Social-Democracy in the First Russian Revolution," 351–52.

44. Lenin, "The State and Revolution," 421.

45. Lenin, "The Right of Nations to Self-Determination," 405.

46. Lenin, "The Historical Destiny of the Doctrine of Karl Marx," 583.

47. Lenin, "The Right of Nations to Self-Determination," 406.

48. Lenin, "The Fall of Port Arthur," 52.

49. Lenin, "Democracy and Narodism in China," 165.

50. Lenin, "Backward Europe and Advanced Asia," 99.

51. Luxemburg, *The Accumulation of Capital*, 419.

52. Lenin, "Two Tactics of Social-Democracy in the Democratic Revolution," 28, 29.

53. Trotsky, *Our Political Tasks*, 70.

54. Trotsky, "Preface to the Re-issue of This Work [*Results and Prospects*]," 32.

55. Trotsky, "Trotsky's Letter to Ispart," 119.

56. Trotsky, *My Life*, 185.

57. Trotsky, "Social Democracy and Revolution," 455.

58. Trotsky, "Up to the Ninth of January," 329.

59. Trotsky, "Summary and Perspectives of the Chinese Revolution," 308 (Marx); Trotsky, "Marxism and the Relation between Proletarian and Peasant Revolution," 349–51 (Marx); "The New Course," 102 (Mehering); *My Life*, 209 (Luxemburg).

60. Cliff, *Trotsky*, vol. 1, 80–87.

61. Parvus, "What Was Accomplished on the 9th of January," 265. For the German debates on the New Middle Class, see Burris, "The Discovery of the New Middle Class," 324–34; and Carter, *Capitalism, Class Conflict and the New Middle Class*, 16–36.

62. Parvus, "What Was Accomplished on the 9th of January," 268; for an alternative translation of this passage, see Trotsky, "Three Conceptions of the Russian Revolution," 67–68.

63. Löwy, *The Politics of Combined and Uneven Development*, 40 and 40–43 more generally.

64. Trotsky, "Three Conceptions of the Russian Revolution," 68–69.

65. The circumstances under which Kautsky first began to display the characteristics of what Lenin would later call opportunism are interesting, not least because only Luxemburg appears to have noticed at the time. In 1910 Kautsky took part in a debate with Luxemburg in which he used the work of the German military historian Hans Delbruck to counterpose a "war of attrition" in the West (in which he included Germany) and a strategy of overthrow in the East (by which he meant Russia). Luxemburg broke with Kautsky on this issue, arguing that it represented a disguised capitulation to electoralism, and that he misidentified the Russian strike movement as the inchoate expression of

primal volatility when in fact it was the most highly class-conscious movement yet seen among the European proletariat. In Russia both Martov for the Mensheviks and Lenin for the Bolsheviks tried to claim Kautsky's position as vindication of their own in 1905, neither seeing what was so obvious to Luxemburg, although Lenin was later to recognize it in retrospect. For these debates, see Perry Anderson, "The Antinomies of Antonio Gramsci," 61–69.

66.   Trotsky, "Karl Kautsky," 29–30. See also Trotsky, *1905*, 9–10.
67.   Kautsky, "Revolutionary Questions," 219.
68.   Kautsky, "The American Worker," 620–21.
69.   Ibid., 624.
70.   Ibid., 642–43.
71.   Trotsky, *Results and Prospects*, 66.
72.   Ibid., 64.
73.   Ibid., 65–66. Trotsky, "Preface to the Re-issue of This Work [*Results and Prospects*]," 33–34.
74.   Trotsky, *1905*, 399, 400.
75.   Trotsky, *Results and Prospects*, 105–6.
76.   Kautsky, "Old and New Revolution," 535.
77.   Luxemburg, "The Russian Revolution," 524.
78.   Trotsky, *Results and Prospects*, 67.
79.   Trotsky, "Introduction to *Ferdinand Lassalle's Speech to the Jury*," 444. See also Trotsky, *Results and Prospects*, 107.
80.   Trotsky, *1905*, 66.
81.   Trotsky, *Results and Prospects*, 77.
82.   Ibid., 80.
83.   Trotsky, *1905*, 333.
84.   Trotsky, *Results and Prospects*, 115.
85.   Trotsky, *1905*, 333.
86.   Trotsky, *Results and Prospects*, 100.
87.   Trotsky, *1905*, 303–4.
88.   Ibid., 68.
89.   The classification of permanent revolution as a strategy rather than a theory is one of the very few issues on which I find myself in agreement with the late Ernest Mandel. See *Revolutionary Marxism Today*, 84–94.
90.   Trotsky, "Introduction to *Ferdinand Lassalle's Speech to the Jury*," 437–45; Trotsky, *Results and Prospects*, 52–61.
91.   Trotsky, "The Turkish Revolution and the Tasks of the Proletariat," 4.
92.   Trotsky, "Introduction to *Ferdinand Lassalle's Speech to the Jury*," 445. See also Trotsky, *Results and Prospects*, 108.
93.   Trotsky, *Results and Prospects*, 50.
94.   Lenin, "Farewell Letter to Swiss Workers," 371.
95.   Sukhanov, *The Russian Revolution 1917*, 284–85, 286.
96.   Trotsky, "Preface to the Re-issue of This Work [*Results and Prospects*]," 31.
97.   Trotsky to Ol'minskij, December 6, 1921.
98.   *Trotsky's Diary in Exile*, 53–54. See also Trotsky, *The History of the Russian Revolution*, 343–44.
99.   Trotsky, *My Life*, 346, 558, 560.
100.   Lenin, "Letters on Tactics," 44.
101.   Lenin, "The Tasks of the Proletariat in Our Revolution," 57.
102.   Geras, "Between the Russian Revolutions," 94–98; Löwy, *The Politics of Combined and Uneven Development*, 62–63.
103.   Lenin, "Fourth Anniversary of the October Revolution," 52–54.

104. Hallas, *Trotsky's Marxism*, 18. For a similar judgment by someone at the opposite end of the spectrum of Trotskyist opinion from Hallas, see Isaac Deutscher, *The Prophet Armed*, 211–13.

105. Lenin, "The Aim of the Proletarian Struggle in Our Revolution," 370–74; Trotsky, *Permanent Revolution*, 166–67.

106. Lenin, "Conspectus of Hegel's Book, *The Science of Logic*," 123–24.

107. Lenin, "Conspectus of Hegel's Book, *Lectures on the History of Philosophy*," 284.

108. Trotsky, *My Life*, 123–24, 133.

109. Trotsky, "The Notebooks in Translation." In his discussion of Trotsky as a dialectician, John Rees sensibly traverses his entire career rather than focusing on these fragments. See chapter 6, "Trotsky and the Dialectic of History," in *The Algebra of Revolution*.

110. Löwy, "From the Great Logic of Hegel to the Finland Station," 11 and 8–12 more generally.

111. Harding, *Lenin's Political Thought*, vol. 2, 68–69.

112. Lenin, "Imperialism, the Highest Stage of Capitalism," 193–94, 301–2. See also, for a more detailed exposition of the argument, Zinoviev, "The Social Roots of Reformism."

113. For the definitive refutation of the "labor aristocracy" thesis, see Post, "Exploring Working-Class Consciousness.'"

114. Lenin, "'Left-Wing' Communism," 320, 330.

115. Lenin, "Report on Foreign Policy Policy Delivered at a Joint Meeting of the All-Russia Central Executive Committee and the Moscow Soviet," 377.

116. Lenin, "The Dual Power," 38.

117. Trotsky, *The History of the Russian Revolution*, 223, and 223–32 more generally.

118. Lenin, "The Tasks of the Proletariat in Our Revolution," 22, 23.

119. Lenin, "The State and Revolution," 475.

120. Lenin's comments to this effect are legion but, for a selection, see Trotsky, *The History of the Russian Revolution*, 1227–38. The most complete list of quotes is given in Black, *Stalinism in Britain*, 43–50, a work of sectarian dementia unparalleled even in the highly competitive annals of orthodox Trotskyism.

121. Lenin, "Report on the Activities of the Council of People's Commissars, January 11 (24)," 464–65, 470.

122. Trotsky, "Speech to the Seventh (Enlarged) Plenum of the ECCI, December 9, 1926," 177.

123. Gramsci, "State and Civil Society," 237, 238, Q7§16.

124. Lukács, *Lenin*, 48–49.

125. Bukharin and Preobrazhensky, *The ABC of Communism*, 63, 64.

126. Ibid., 207.

127. Bukharin, *De la dictature de l'impérialisme a la dictature du prolétariat*, 6.

128. Haynes, *Nikolai Bukharin and the Transition from Capitalism to Socialism*, 55 and 50–55 more generally.

129. Sapir, "The Conception of the Bourgeois Revolution," 372, 373.

130. Widgery, *The Left in Britain*, 500.

131. Baltrop, *The Monument*, 62–63.

132. Kautsky, *Terrorism and Communism*, 201.

133. Kautsky, *Bolshevism at a Deadlock*, 17.

134. Radek, "The Paths of the Russian Revolution," 40.

135. Ibid., 72.

136. Kautsky, "Dictatorship and Democracy," 121.

137. Kautsky, "Communists at Work," chapter 8 in *Terrorism and Communism*.

138. Bukharin, "Bourgeois Revolution and Proletarian Revolution," 162.

139. Kautsky, *Terrorism and Communism*, 229. Compare Max Weber, "Suffrage and Democracy in Germany," 126–27 and "Parliament and Democracy in Germany under

a New Political Order," 209–33. There is a useful discussion of Weber's views on democracy, contrasting his with those of Lenin, in Eric Olin Wright, "Bureaucracy and the State."

140.   Salvadori, *Karl Kautsky and the Socialist Revolution*, 218–339.

141.   Kautsky, *The Materialist Conception of History*, 457.

142.   Ibid., 175.

143.   Ibid., 455.

144.   Ibid., 456.

145.   Lukács, *Lenin*, 47–48.

146.   Linden, *Western Marxism and the Soviet Union*; compare the discussion on 12–23 (Kautsky) with 36–43 (Gorter, Pannekoek, and Rühle).

147.   Rühle, *From the Bourgeois Revolution to the Socialist Revolution*, 13.

148.   Lukács, *Lenin*, 48.

149.   Lukács, "Towards a Methodology of the Problem of Organisation," 311.

150.   Borkenau, *World Communism*, 419.

151.   Communist International [1920], "Fourth Session, July 28," 110–1, 112–13, 118.

152.   Manabendra N. Roy, "An Indian Communist Manifesto," 164.

153.   Gruber, *Soviet Russia Masters the Comintern*, 251–52.

154.   Communist International [1920], "Fourth Session, July 28," 118.

155.   Ibid., 116, 120.

156.   Both positions shared a mistaken assumption—although one common to virtually all Marxists at the time—that Western capitalism would be badly weakened without imperialist control of the colonies and semicolonies; in fact the greatest boom in capitalist history, between 1948 and 1974, coincided with decolonization and the retreat from empire. For one of the earliest attempts to explain why capitalism could survive without colonialism, see Kidron, "Imperialism: Highest Stage but One," 19–21.

157.   Gruber, *Soviet Russia Masters the Comintern*, 253.

158.   Borkenau, *World Communism*, 292–93.

159.   For this episode, see Carr, *The Bolshevik Revolution*, vol. 3, 294–304; and Dumont, *Du socialisme ottoman à l'internationalisme anatolien*, 183–85.

160.   Hirik, "'The Permanent Revolution' and 'Asian Renaissance,'" 188–90.

161.   Trotsky to the Central Committee of the Russian Communist Party, August 5, 1919.

162.   Trotsky to the People's Commissariat of Foreign Affairs, June 4, 1920.

163.   Trotsky, "Report to the Fourth World Congress," 316–17.

164.   Manabendra N. Roy, "Beware the Nationalist Bourgeoisie; Support the Class Struggle," 319.

165.   Trotsky, "Prospects and Tasks for the East," 201.

13. The Emergence of Orthodoxy: 1924–40

1.   Harris, "Marxism: Leninism-Stalinism-Maoism," 14.

2.   Perhaps the only other aspect of Stalin's thought which is treated with a comparable degree of indulgence is his famous, if highly misleading, definition of a nation. See Stalin, "Marxism and the National Question," 307 and 303–13 more generally. For a critique, see Davidson, *The Origins of Scottish Nationhood*, 7–11.

3.   Stalin, "The Foundations of Leninism," 106–9, 157–59.

4.   Stalin, "Letter to Comrade Yaroslavsky," 237–38. The passage to which Engels refers is Engels, "Principles of Communism," 351–52. For an earlier version of this argument, unknown during these debates, see Marx and Engels, *The German Ideology*, 48–54.

5.   Stalin, "The October Revolution and the Tactics," 386–89, 415–16.

6.   Stalin, "The Results of the Work of the Fourteenth Conference," 110–22. The two texts to which Stalin refers most often, here and in his other writings, are Lenin, "On the

Slogan for a United States of Europe," 342 and "On Co-operation," 467–68. The former refers to the conquest of state power, not the achievement of socialism and the latter discusses—in uncharacteristically tentative ways—the establishing preconditions for building socialism in a postrevolutionary situation: neither seriously support the interpretation Stalin imposes on them.

7. Stalin, "The October Revolution and the Tactics of the Russian Communists," 414. These claims were still being repeated forty years later by writers who were by no means all Stalinists. Nicolas Krasso, for example, thought that Trotsky envisaged revolution taking place not only across Europe but the entire world, in "a continuous conflagration at all times and all places—a metaphysical carnival of insurrection," remarks that suggest a limited acquaintance with Trotsky's actual writings. See Krasso, "Trotsky's Marxism," 68.

8. Trotsky, "Letter to the Plenum of the Central Committee," 305.

9. Trotsky, "Speech to the Seventh (Enlarged) Plenum," 176. The reference is to Marx's critique of the Russian Populist Mikhailovsky, who aspired to turn a "historical sketch of the genesis of capitalism in Western Europe into a historic-philosophical theory of general development, imposed by fate on all peoples, whatever the historical circumstances in which they are placed." See "[Letter to *Otechesivenniye Zapiski*]," 201.

10. Trotsky, "Class Relations in the Chinese Revolution," 142–43.

11. Trotsky, "On the Slogan of Soviets in China," 156.

12. Trotsky, "The Chinese Revolution and the Theses of Comrade Stalin," 162.

13. Stalin, "Concerning Questions of Leninism," 22–23.

14. Stalin, "The International Situation and the Defence of the USSR," 11–12, 15.

15. Stalin, "The Revolution in China and the Tasks of the Comintern," 292.

16. Mao, "Strive to Win over Millions upon Millions of the Masses to the Anti-Japanese National United Front," 290.

17. Mao, "The Chinese Revolution and the Chinese Communist Party" 96–97.

18. Isaac Deutscher, "The Tragedy of the Polish Communist Party," 130.

19. Stalin was apparently unable to decide whether Luxemburg was partly responsible for the theory of permanent revolution or not, as can be seen by comparing his original position ("It is not true that the theory of "permanent revolution" . . . was advanced in 1905 by Rosa Luxemburg and Trotsky. Actually, this theory was advanced by Parvus and Trotsky.") with his subsequent comically pedantic "clarification" ("It was not Trotsky but Rosa Luxemburg and Parvus who *invented* the theory of "permanent" revolution. It was not Rosa Luxemburg but Parvus and Trotsky who in 1905 *advanced* the theory of "permanent" revolution and actively fought for it *against* Lenin. Subsequently Rosa Luxemburg too, began to fight actively against the Leninist plan of revolution. But that was *after* 1905.") See Stalin, "The October Revolution and the Tactics of the Russian Communists," 397 and Stalin, "Reply to Oekhnovich and Aristov," 134.

20. Isaac Deutscher, "The Tragedy of the Polish Communist Party," 139.

21. Carr, *Twilight of the Comintern*, 290–91.

22. Ibid., 294.

23. *Mundo Obrero*, July 30, 1936, quoted in Bolloten, *The Grand Camouflage*, 87.

24. Togliatti, "Sulle particularita della rivoluzione Spagnola," 196.

25. Fraser, *Blood of Spain*, 323.

26. Ibid., 563.

27. Beevor, *The Battle for Spain*, 102.

28. Borkenau, *The Spanish Cockpit*, 285, 289.

29. Compare James Allen [Auerbach], *The Negro Question in the United States* and *Reconstruction*.

30. Commission of the C.C. of the C.P.S.U. (B.), *History of the Communist Party of the Soviet Union (Bolsheviks)*, 110.

31.   Needham, *History Is on Our Side.*

32.   The non-academic but scholarly tradition was maintained—although certainly not exclusively—by Trotskyists, starting with Trotsky's own *History of the Russian Revolution* (1932–34) and including such landmarks as Groves's *But We Shall Rise Again* (1938), C. L. R. James's *The Black Jacobins* (1938), and Isaac Deutscher's *Stalin* (1949).

33.   Hobsbawm, "The Historians Group of the Communist Party," 30–32.

34.   See, for example, Redpath, *The Roving Editor*, 300–1.

35.   Compare Beard, *The Rise of American Civilization*, 52–121 and Hacker, *The Triumph of American Capitalism*, 280–400.

36.   Novick, *That Noble Dream*, 95–96, 155.

37.   Enmale [Morais], "Introduction," xiii.

38.   See, for example, Camejo, *Racism, Revolution, Reaction, 1861–1877*, 13; Bernard Mandel, *Labour Free and Slave*, 202; McPherson, "The Second American Revolution," 10–22; and Novack, "Introduction," 16.

39.   Lefebvre, *The Coming of the French Revolution*, 2.

40.   Christopher Hill, "The English Revolution," 9.

41.   Soboul, *The Parisian Sans-Culottes and the French Revolution*, 259–69.

42.   For the most extreme example of the Popular Front as a political reference point, see Hobsbawm, *Interesting Times*, 218, 322–24.

43.   Dimitroff, "The Fascist Offensive and the Tasks of the Communist International," 77, 78.

44.   Quoted in Carr, *Twilight of the Comintern*, 407.

45.   Klugman, "Introduction: Crisis in the Thirties," 25.

46.   Samuel, "British Marxist Historians I," 41–42.

47.   *Scots Independent*, vol. 3, no. 10, June 1938. The only source for the existence of Calgacus is the Roman writer Cornelius Tacitus, in his account of how his father-in-law, Julius Agricola ruled Britain in the AD 70s and 80s. Tacitus has Calgacus address the Caledonians in a speech that ends in the famous line: "To robbery, butchery, and rapine, they give the lying name of 'government'; they create a desolation and call it peace." But this has as much relation to historical fact as the speech Shakespeare gives to Henry V on the eve of the Battle of Agincourt. See Tacitus, "Agricola," 81 and 73–90 more generally.

48.   Barnet, "After Nationalism," 147.

49.   Torr, *Tom Mann and His Times*, vol. 1, 109, 110.

50.   Margaret James, "Contemporary Materialist Interpretations of Society in the English Revolution," 85–88 (Harrington et al.), 88–100 (Winstanley).

51.   Guérin, *Class Struggle in the First French Republic*, 4–5.

52.   Guérin, *La lutte de classes sous la Première République*, vol. 1, 2, 405.

53.   See Rudé, *Interpretations of the French Revolution*, 26; and Soboul, "Class and Class Struggle during the Revolution," 43. For a balanced account of Guérin's work that seeks to defend him from undeserved Stalinist (and Trotskyist) critcism, see Carlin, "Daniel Guérin and the Working Class in the French Revolution."

54.   Zagorin, *Rebels and Rulers*, vol. 1, 44–45.

55.   P.F., "England's Revolution," 558–59.

56.   Garman, "A Reply to P.F.," 651–53.

57.   P.F. "A Rejoinder," 654.

58.   Keirnan, "Theses for Discussion on Absolutism no. 2," 97–98.

59.   Keirnan, "Postscript (Absolutism)."

60.   Sixteenth and Seventeenth Century Section of the Historians Group of the Communist Party, "State and Revolution in Tudor and Stuart England." For this attribution of authorship, see David Parker, "Introduction," in ibid., 39.

61.   "Minutes 10/11 January 1948: Discussion on Absolutism (cont)," 134. These accusations of Trotskyism were grossly unfair. In fact, the ultra-loyal Pokrovsky was a consistent critic of Trotsky's historical views, on the same grounds that he criticized the

orthodox view of the English Revolution, namely that they supposedly downplayed the extent of Russian and English capitalist development by the sixteenth century. For Trotsky's response to this criticism, see *The History of the Russian Revolution*, appendix 1 to vol. 1.

62. Sweezy, "A Rejoinder," 108; Engels, *The Origin of the Family, Private Property and the State*, 270–71.

63. Tribe, *Genealogies of Capitalism*, 22 and 18–23 more generally.

64. Reproduced in Hobsbawm, *Echoes of the Marseillaise*, 133.

65. Takahashi, "A Contribution to the Discussion," 96 and 94–97 more generally.

66. Hobsbawm, *Echoes of the Marseillaise*, 38.

67. Allinson and Anievas, "The Uneven and Combined Development of the Meiji Restoration," 474–75; Hoston, "Conceptualizing Bourgeois Revolution," 555–67; Itoh, *Value and Crisis*, 22–26.

68. Lukács, *The Destruction of Reason*, 46, 59, 75. Lukács maintained this position for the rest of his life. See, for example, *Conversations with Lukács*, 49–51.

69. Moore, *The Social Origins of Dictatorship and Democracy*, 428.

70. Ibid., 413–14. See also xiv.

71. Ibid., 427, 429.

72. Ibid., 438.

73. Ibid., 442.

14. CLASSICAL MARXISM (3) 1924–40

1. Serge, *Midnight in the Century*, 143. Ironically, Benjamin was unflattering about the literary qualities of the novel from whence the term derives: "His book has no literary value, and holds the attention only for its picturesque descriptions of Stalinist terror." See Benjamin, "Survey of French Literature," 44; and Leslie, *Walter Benjamin: Overpowering Conformism*, 209.

2. Serge, *Memoirs of a Revolutionary*, 188, 364–65.

3. Ibid., 188.

4. Perry Anderson, *Considerations on Western Marxism*, 42, 49–50. The actual term, "Western Marxism" seems to have been first used by Maurice Merleau Ponty in 1955, although almost exclusively in relation to Lukács. See *Adventures of the Dialectic*, 30–58.

5. Perry Anderson, *Considerations on Western Marxism*, 29–32. Anderson rightly includes Korsch alongside Gramsci and Lukács at the "advent" of Western Marxism; but the work of this important, if lesser, figure is not relevant to the subject of this book.

6. Wald, *The New York Intellectuals*, 27–31, 42–45.

7. Balibar is right to say that, despite some formal similarities in approach, in relation to Adorno and others, Benjamin "was merely a reticent, little understood 'fellow traveler.'" *The Philosophy of Marx*, 86.

8. Perry Anderson, *Considerations on Western Marxism*, 54, 89–90.

9. Marx and Engels, "The Manifesto of the Communist Party," 72; Marx, *The Eighteenth Brumaire of Louis Bonaparte*, 147–49; Marx, *Capital*, vol. 1, 342.

10. Paul Wood, "Marxism and Modernism," 124.

11. *Trotsky's Diary in Exile 1935*, 140–41.

12. See, for example, Eagleton, *Walter Benjamin*, 173–79; Leslie, *Walter Benjamin*, 228–34;

13. Eagleton, *Walter Benjamin*, 178.

14. Gramsci, "[A Letter to Trotsky on Futurism]."

15. Gramsci, "State and Civil Society," 240–41, Q14§68. Peter Thomas performs heroic labors in trying to make sense of these passages, in my view unsuccessfully, but also unnecessarily, since our appreciation of Gramsci does not depend on pretending that his

prison writings always possess an inner coherence that is manifestly absent from many of them. See *The Gramscian Moment*, 213–17. For Thomas's broader discussion of Trotsky and Gramsci, see ibid., 203–20.

16.   Lukács, "On His Life and Work," 51.

17.   Ibid., 54. To be fair, Lukács also describes himself as "antipathetic" toward the entire Bolshevik leadership with the exception of Lenin.

18.   Lukács, "Preface to the New Edition (1967)," xxvii–xxviii.

19.   As I believe Löwy does in *Georg Lukács*, 193–96.

20.   Lukács, "Preface to the New Edition (1967)," xxx. See also Lukács, "On His Life and Work," 55–56.

21.   Lukács, "Hölderlin's *Hyperion*," 137–39. For a discussion that argues that this article was a coded response to Trotsky, see Löwy, *Georg Lukács*, 196–98.

22.   Pascal, *Pensées*, 149–55.

23.   Goldmann, *The Hidden God*, 90 and 89–102, 283–302 more generally.

24.   Alasdair MacIntyre, "Pascal and Marx," 314.

25.   Löwy, *Fire Alarm*, 137.

26.   See, for example, Lenin, "On Co-operation," 480.

27.   Lenin, "The Collapse of the Second International," 214.

28.   Benjamin, "Convolute N," 474.

29.   Lukács, *Lenin*, 12–13.

30.   Benjamin, "Paralipomena to 'On the Concept of History,'" 402.

31.   Gramsci, "Problems of Marxism," 438, Q11§15.

32.   Lukács, "Reification and the Consciousness of the Proletariat," 207.

33.   Lukács, "Tailism and the Dialectic," 56, 60.

34.   Ibid., 58.

35.   Trotsky, *The History of the Russian Revolution*, 1025.

36.   Shakespeare, *Julius Caesar*, Act 4, Scene 3.

37.   Abbott, "On the Concept of Turning Point," 257.

38.   Benjamin, "Paralipomena to 'On the Concept of History,'" 402.

39.   Isaac Deutscher, *The Prophet Unarmed*, 274–83.

40.   Cliff, *Trotsky*, vol. 3, 216. Unfortunately, Cliff then goes on to write: "The theory of permanent revolution dominated his thinking even when he gave lip service to the rotten compromise with Zinoviev and Co"—a claim that contradicts his earlier correct assessment and for which there is no evidence. See ibid., 223 and 213–24 for his entire discussion.

41.   Trotsky, "New Opportunities for the Chinese Revolution, New Tasks, and New Mistakes," 269.

42.   Trotsky, "Revolution and War in China," 588.

43.   Trotsky, "Uneven and Combined Development and the Role of American Imperialism," 116.

44.   Bensaïd, *Marx for Our Times*, 282.

45.   Trotsky, "The Notebooks in Translation," 77.

46.   See, for example, Choonara, "The Relevance of Permanent Revolution," 175.

47.   For examples of these mistakes, see Davidson, "From Uneven to Combined Development," 10; and Davidson, "Putting the Nation Back into 'the International'," 10–11. For a more detailed discussion, see Davidson, *Violating All the Laws of History*, chapter 1.

48.   Ernest Mandel, *Trotsky as Alternative*, 1.

49.   Davidson, "From Uneven to Combined Development," 10–17; Trotsky, "The Draft Programme of the Communist International," 15; Trotsky, "Uneven and Combined Development and the Role of American Imperialism," 116.

50.   Neil Smith, *Uneven Development*, xiv.

51.   Lenin, *Imperialism, the Highest Stage of Capitalism*, 241.

52.   Ibid., 263–64.

53   Trotsky, *The History of the Russian Revolution*, 27.
54.   Veblen, *Imperial Germany and the Industrial Revolution*, 65–66, 85–86.
55.   Hilferding, *Finance Capital*, 322–23.
56.   Trotsky, *Terrorism and Communism*, 185–86.
57.   Gramsci, "The Return to Freedom," 69.
58.   Gramsci, "The Revolution against *Capital*."
59.   Trotsky, "The Draft Programme of the Communist International," 17.
60.   Trotsky, "Introduction to the German Edition," 146.
61.   Trotsky, *The Permanent Revolution*, 255.
62.   Mao, "On Tactics against Japanese Imperialism," 172.
63.   Krasso, "Trotsky's Marxism," 80–81. This passage, especially the final sentence, betrays what Gregory Elliot calls an "unmistakably Andersonian" tone, reflecting the contributory role of the *New Left Review*'s then editor in preparing the article for publication. See *Perry Anderson*, 57 and 56–58 more generally.
64.   Trotsky, *Permanent Revolution*, 254–55.
65.   Trotsky, "Introduction to the German Edition [of *The Permanent Revolution*]," 150.
66.   Trotsky, *My Life*, 123–24, 133.
67.   Labriola, "Historical Materialism," 133.
68.   Luxemburg, "Social Democracy and the National Struggles in Turkey," 38–40.
69.   Kautsky, "The American Worker," 621–25.
70.   Lenin, "Our Revolution (Apropos of N. Sukhanov's Notes)," 477, 480.
71.   See, for example, Trotsky, "The Draft Programme of the Communist International," 161; Trotsky, "Summary and Perspectives of the Chinese Revolution," 326.
72.   Gramsci, "The Modern Prince," 182; *Prison Notebooks*, vol. 2, 180, Q13§17.
73.   Gramsci continues the passage cited above: "A particular ideology, for instance, born in a highly developed country, is disseminated in less developed countries, impinging on the local interplay of combinations." The example of religion could quite easily be replaced by Marxism, which Gramsci had previously discussed in these terms in "The Revolution against *Capital*," but this type of transfer is explicable in terms of uneven development as such.
74.   Perry Anderson, "The Antinomies of Antonio Gramsci," 50. For Thomas's critique of Anderson, see *The Gramscian Moment*, 41–83.
75.   Trotsky, "Speech to the Seventh (Enlarged) Plenum of the ECCI, December 9, 1926," 180.
76.   Trotsky, "The Draft Programme of the Communist International," 16.
77.   Trotsky, *The History of the Russian Revolution*, 27–28.
78.   Trotsky, "A Serious Work on Russian Revolutionary History," 858.
79.   Trotsky, *The History of the Russian Revolution*, 1219. For the internal quotes by Marx, see, respectively, *Capital*, vol. 1, 91 and "Preface to *A Contribution to the Critique of Political Economy*," 425–26.
80.   Trotsky, "Karl Marx," 41.
81.   Trotsky, "Where Is Britain Going?," 37. For Scotland, see Davidson, *The Origins of Scottish Nationhood*, 167–86; and Davidson, "Class Consciousness and National Consciousness in the Scottish General Strike of 1820," 135–44.
82.   Trotsky, "Prospects and Tasks in the East," 199. For Prussia see, for example, Ludtke, "The Role of State Violence."
83.   Trotsky, "Karl Marx," 41.
84.   Curtin, *The World and the West*, 150.
85.   Gowan, "The Gulf War, Iraq and Western Liberalism," 167.
86.   Trotsky, "Prospects and Tasks for the East," 199.
87.   Trotsky, "Revolution and War in China," 583.
88.   This aspect was captured by Orwell in *The Theory and Practice of Oligarchic Collectivism*, the book attributed to the Trotsky figure, Emmanuel Goldstein, in *Nineteen Eighty-Four*, 156:

"The fields are cultivated with horse ploughs while books are written by machinery."

89. Burawoy, *The Politics of Production*, 99.
90. Allinson and Anievas, "The Uses and Misuses of Uneven and Combined Development," 52.
91. Lenin, *The Development of Capitalism in Russia*, 191–210.
92. Lenin, *Imperialism, the Highest Stage of Capitalism*, 694.
93. Burawoy, *The Politics of Production*, 99.
94. Trotsky, *The History of the Russian Revolution*, 27.
95. Trotsky, "Stojan Novakovic," 83.
96. Trotsky, *The History of the Russian Revolution*, 55. For modern academic support for Trotsky's argument see, for example, Gatrell, *Government, Industry and Rearmament in Russia*, 15 and Treblicock, *The Industrialisation of the Continental Powers*, 208.
97. See, for example, Gerschenkron, *Economic Backwardness in Historical Perspective*, 27–128. Ben Selwyn has argued that Gershenkron was in fact more aware of the wider impact of technological transfers than is often supposed, largely as a result of his earlier exposure to Trotsky's work. See "Trotsky, Gerschenkron and the Political Economy of Late Development," 433.
98. Trotsky, *History of the Russian Revolution*, 30. And see, for example, Reiber, *Merchants and Entrepreneurs in Imperial Russia*, 224.
99. Trotsky, "Japan Heads for Disaster," 291.
100. Trotsky, "Radio, Science, Technology and Society," 257.
101. Trotsky, "Uneven and Combined Development and the Role of American Imperialism," 117.
102. Trotsky, "What Is National Socialism?," 413. In this respect Trotsky's analysis has affinities with the notion of "nonsynchronism" introduced by that most engagingly eccentric of Western Marxists, Ernest Bloch, in 1932. The term itself is compatible with the (by comparison) everyday concept of combination, but it is important to understand what the focus of Bloch's argument is. For him the key example of nonsynchronism was Germany: "Germany in general, which did not accomplish a bourgeois revolution until 1918, is, unlike England, and much less France, the classic land of non-synchronism, that is, of unsurmounted remnants of older economic being and consciousness." According to Bloch, this condition was "not dangerous to capitalism": "on the contrary, capital uses that which is nonsynchronously contrary, if not indeed disparate, as a distraction from its own strictly present-day contradictions: it uses the antagonism of a still living past as a means of separation and struggle against the future that is dialectically giving birth to itself in the capitalist antagonisms." See Bloch, "Nonsynchronism and the Obligation to its Dialectics," 29, 32.
103. Trotsky, "In a Backward Country," 49.
104. Lukács, *Lenin*, chapter 1.
105. Trotsky, "In Defence of the Russian Revolution," 251.
106. Trotsky, "Attention to Theory!," 271.
107. Quoted in Volkogonov, *Trotsky*, 411.
108. Benjamin, "Moscow," 32.
109. Trotsky, "Prospects and Tasks in the East," 199.
110. Trotsky, *The History of the Russian Revolution*, 33.
111. Ibid., 1220.
112. Ibid., 72.
113. Ibid., 888.
114. Trotsky, "New Opportunities for the Chinese Revolution, New Tasks, and New Mistakes," 263.
115. For the early Russian debates, see Sawer, "The Soviet Discussion of the Asiatic Mode of Production," and, for the later, see Gellner, "Soviets against Wittfogel." The Stalinists were able to point to the fact that Marx never again used the term "Asiatic" after 1859, and that

both Engels and Lenin explicitly referred to only three exploitative modes of production: "Slavery was the first form of exploitation, peculiar to the world of antiquity; it was followed by serfdom in the Middle Ages, and by wage labour in modern times." Engels, *The Origins of the Family, Private Property and the State*, 274. Engels was at this point under the influence of Morgan, whose *Ancient Society* posits a direct transition from primitive communism to class society without any intervening "Asiatic" stage. See Godelier, "The Concept of the 'Asiatic' Mode of Production,'" 231–35. Lenin followed Engels in referring to "these great periods in the history of mankind, slave-owning, feudal and capitalist." In a lecture to students at Sverdlov University in 1919, Lenin states four times in the space of one page of the printed version that mankind has passed or is passing through slavery to feudalism to capitalism. Lenin, "The State," 477. For his reliance on Engels, see ibid., 473, 485.

116. Trotsky, "New Opportunities for the Chinese Revolution, New Tasks, and New Mistakes," 264.
117. Trotsky, "The Draft Programme of the Communist International," 159–60; "Summary and Perspectives of the Chinese Revolution," 324–25.
118. Trotsky, "The Chinese Revolution and the Theses of Comrade Stalin," 163.
119. Rosenberg, "Isaac Deutscher and the Lost History of International Relations," 8.
120. Perry Anderson, *Considerations on Western Marxism*, 118–19; Cliff, "Permanent Revolution," 188; Löwy, *The Politics of Combined and Uneven Development*, 89.
121. Zheng, "On the Nature of Revolution," 30, 31.
122. Trotsky, "The Draft Programme of the Communist International," 162; Trotsky, "Summary and Perspectives of the Chinese Revolution," 327.
123. Trotsky, "The Death Agony of Capitalism and the Tasks of the Fourth International," 138.
124. Trotsky, "Revolution and War in China," 582.
125. Trotsky, "The Death Agony of Capitalism and the Tasks of the Fourth International," 138.
126. Halliday and Molyneux, *The Ethiopian Revolution*, 65 and 54–74 more generally.
127. Trotsky, "The Italo-Ethiopian Conflict," 41.
128. Trotsky, "The Spanish Revolution and the Dangers Threatening It," 123.
129. Trotsky, "Not a Workers' State and Not a Bourgeois State?," 66.
130. Trotsky, "The Lessons of Spain," 307.
131. Lukács, "Blum Theses (Extracts)," 250, 251.
132. Lukács, "Preface to the New Edition (1967)," xxix.
133. Trotsky, "The Negro Question in America," 25.
134. Ernest Mandel, *Late Capitalism*, 87–88.
135. Kelly, "Materialism and the Persistence of Race in the Jim Crow South," 11.
136. Trotsky, *Permanent Revolution*, 278.
137. Ibid., 279.
138. Trotsky, *The History of the Russian Revolution*, 17.
139. Ibid., 34.
140. Ibid., 1017.
141. Trotsky, "The Spanish Revolution and the Dangers Threatening It," 125.
142. For general surveys, see Bergman, "The Perils of Historical Analogy," 83–98; and Isaac Deutscher, *The Prophet Unarmed*, 260–63, 286–91, 366–68, 388–89.
143. Compare, Trotsky, "Thermidor," 261–63 with "The Workers' State, Thermidor and Bonapartism," 168, 174. In his posthumous and uncompleted biography of Stalin, Trotsky refers to the 1927 work on the original Thermidor by Georges Lefebvre, one of the first Marxist-influenced professional historians of the French Revolution and a rare reference to any of them by a figure from the Classical Marxist tradition. See Trotsky, *Stalin*, 401 and, for the passages to which Trotsky refers, Lefebvre, *The Thermidorians*, 7, 17.
144. Lukács, "Towards a Methodology of the Problem of Organization," 308.
145. Camejo, "Introduction," 16.
146. Trotsky, "Revolution and War in China," 583–84.

147.   Trotsky, "Can a Counter-Revolution or a Revolution Be Made on Schedule?," 348.

148.   Trotsky, *The History of the Russian Revolution*, 1018.

149.   Benjamin, "Moscow," 37.

150.   Trotsky, "The Workers' State, Thermidor and Bonapartism," 179.

151.   Trotsky, *History of the Russian Revolution*, 890.

152.   Trotsky, "Not a Workers' State and Not a Bourgeois State?," 66.

153.   Trotsky, "A Fresh Lesson," 56.

154.   Gramsci, "Notes on Italian History," 90; Gramsci, *Prison Notebooks*, vol. 1208–9.

155.   Broué, *The German Revolution*, 2–5, 289. This was also the view of at least some of the German revolutionaries during the November Revolution of 1918. See ibid., 131.

156.   Trotsky, "Introduction to the First (Russian) Edition [of *Permanent Revolution*]," 131. A similar view was actually taken in 1957–58 by internal KPD critics of the Stalinist interpretation of November 1918. See Broué, *German Revolution*, 844–45.

157.   Trotsky, "Japan Heads for Disaster," 291.

158.   Hobsbawm, *The Age of Capital*, 151.

159.   Soboul, *A Short History of the French Revolution*, 167–68.

160.   Quoted in Mikhailova, "Soviet Japanese Studies on the Problem of the Meiji Ishin and Development of Capitalism in Japan," 33–34.

161.   Lukács, "Critical Observations on Rosa Luxemburg's 'Critique of the Russian Revolution,'" 282.

162.   Trotsky, *The History of the Russian Revolution*, 1017.

163.   Trotsky, "The Revolution in Spain," 71–72.

164.   Lukács, *Lenin*, 20.

165.   Lukács, "Towards a Methodology of the Problem of Organisation," 307.

166.   Serge, *Memoirs of a Revolutionary*, 187.

167.   Chatterjee, *The Nation and Its Fragments*, 211.

168.   Gramsci, "Notes on Italian History," 78; Gramsci, *Prison Notebooks*, vol. 1, 147, Q1§44.

169.   Gramsci, "The Modern Prince," 179; Gramsci, *Prison Notebooks*, vol. 2, 178, Q4§38 and Q13§17.

170.   Gramsci, "Notes on Italian History," 59, Q19§24; Gramsci, "Reference Points for an Essay on B. Croce," 341–43, Q10I§6.

171.   Gramsci, "Notes on Italian History," 114, Q10II§61.

172.   Ibid., 83, Q10§24.

173.   Gramsci to Tania, June 6, 1932.

174.   Gramsci, *Prison Notebooks*, vol. 2, 232, Q4§57.

175.   Ibid., 207, Q4§49.

176.   Gramsci, *Prison Notebooks*, vol. 3, 381, Q8§240.

177.   Ibid., 61, Q19§24.

178.   Gramsci, "Reference Points for an Essay on B. Croce," 343, Q10I§6.

179.   Gramsci, "The Modern Prince," 182, Q4§38, Q13§17.

180.   Gramsci, *Prison Notebooks*, vol. 3, 60, Q6§78.

181.   Gramsci, *Prison Notebooks*, vol. 2, 163, Q4§24.

182.   Gramsci, "Notes on Italian History," 115; Gramsci, *Prison Notebooks*, vol. 1, 230–31, Q10II§61.

183.   Gramsci, "Origins of the Mussolini Cabinet," 129. The importance of this passage was first highlighted in Morton, "Disputing the Geopolitics of Global Capitalism," 599.

184.   Gramsci, "Notes on Italian History," 105, Q15§59.

185.   Ibid., 58–59, Q19§24.

186.   Gramsci, "State and Civil Society," 260, Q1§47.

187.   Gramsci, "Notes on Italian History," 115; Gramsci, *Prison Notebooks*, vol. 1, 231, Q10II§61.

188.   Gramsci, "The Philosophy of Benedetto Croce," 373–74, Q1II§41xiv.

189. Thomas, *The Gramscian Moment*, 156–57.
190. Gramsci, "Notes on Italian History," 119–20, Q10II§61. See also Gramsci, "Passive Revolution and Planned Economy," 277; and Gramsci, *Prison Notebooks*, vol. 3, 378, Q8§236.
191. Gramsci, "Americanism and Fordism," 278–79, Q22§1.
192. Callinicos, "The Limits of Passive Revolution," 492, 498.
193. Riley and Desai, "The Passive Revolutionary Route to the Modern World," 816–17.
194. Gramsci, "State and Civil Society," 269–70, Q15§3.
195. Riley and Desai, "The Passive Revolutionary Route to the Modern World," 817.
196. Lampedusa, *The Leopard*, 27–28.
197. In Luchino Visconti's great Marxist film of the book, although the original dialogue is retained, the significance of the exchange between Fabrizi and Tancredi is invested with precisely the opposite meaning, one which corresponds more closely to the interpretation of the Risorgimento endorsed here—in effect, "everything will appear to stay the same, but in reality important aspects of it will change." Admittedly this is less compelling epigrammatic material.
198. Gramsci, "Notes on Italian History," 82, Q10§24.
199. Allinson and Anievas, "The Uneven and Combined Development of the Meiji Restoration," 479–80 and see 470–74, 479–85 more generally.
200. Trotsky, "Japan Heads for Disaster," 291.
201. Trotsky, *Results and Prospects*, 54.
202. Trotsky, "Where Is Britain Going?," 86.
203. Orwell, "Catastrophic Gradualism," 34.
204. Orwell, "Looking Back on the Spanish War," 305.
205. Benjamin, "On the Concept of History," 393, 394–95.
206. Callinicos, *Making History*, 220.
207. Leslie, *Walter Benjamin: Overpowering Conformism*, 178, 231.
208. Leslie, *Walter Benjamin*, 212.
209. Benjamin, "Goethe," 177.
210. Benjamin [1935], "Paris, Capital of the Nineteenth Century," 8.
211. Benjamin, "Convolute N," 475.
212. Benjamin [1939], "Paris, Capital of the Nineteenth Century," 24.
213. Benjamin, "Survey of French Literature," 39.
214. Benjamin, "On the Concept of History," 392.
215. Benjamin, "Paralipomena to 'On the Concept of History,'" 406.
216. Benjamin, "Convolute N," 474.
217. Benjamin, "On the Concept of History," 390.
218. Benjamin, "Paralipomena to 'On the Concept of History,'" 407.
219. Benjamin, "On the Concept of History," 390. Benjamin seems to have derived this idea from the German late-Enlightenment figure Carl Gustav Jochman. See "'The Regression of Poetry,' by Gustav Jochman," 363. Ironically, given Benjamin's distaste for at least some of Serge's novels, "nothing is ever lost," was also a favorite slogan of the latter. See Serge, *The Birth of Our Power*, 182 and chapter 23 more generally.
220. Marx, "The Eighteenth Brumaire of Louis Bonaparte," 147, 148.
221. Benjamin, "On the Concept of History," 395.
222. Quoted in Sedgwick, "Introduction," xvii.
223. Benjamin to Scholem, January 11, 1940.

15. REVISIONISM: THE BOURGEOIS REVOLUTIONS DID NOT TAKE PLACE

1. Engels to Bebel, November 18, 1884.

2.   Trotsky, "Where Is Britain Going?," 87.

3.   Gardiner, *History of the Great Civil War*, vol. 1, 226.

4.   Spencer, "The Social Organism," 198.

5.   Acton, "The Puritan Revolution," 205.

6.   Acton, "The English Revolution," 231–32. Acton concluded this essay on the revolution of 1688 with a reference to "another and a more glorious Revolution, infinitely more definite and clear cut," usually taken to mean the French Revolution, which Acton was unusual at this date in regarding as a positive development, even down to supporting Napoleon. See, for example, Evans, *Cosmopolitan Islanders*, 82–91 or Hobsbawm, *Echoes of the Marseillaise*, 69–70, 72–75.

7.   As Andrew Gamble points out in his brilliant study of Hayek: "Acton, Tocqueville, and Burckhardt are the three patron saints of Hayek's liberal international." *Hayek*, 130.

8.   Contrary to the widespread misconception, there are few other respects in which Smith's thought should be associated with that of Hayek. See Davidson, "What Was Neoliberalism?," 3–6.

9.   Hayek, *The Constitution of Liberty*, 167; Max Weber, *The Agrarian Sociology of Ancient Civilizations*, 355.

10.   Hayek, *The Road to Serfdom*, 11.

11.   Oakeshott, "The Masses in Representative Democracy," 365–66.

12.   Andrews, "A Note on the Economic Interpretation," 20–21.

13.   Brinton, "Review of *The Social Interpretation of the French Revolution*," 317.

14.   Hacker, "The Anticapitalist Bias of American Historians," 81.

15.   Popper, *The Poverty of Historicism*, 3.

16.   Annan, *Our Age*, 273.

17.   Saunders, *Who Paid the Piper?*, 78–79, 80, 84, 91, 111–12, 165.

18.   Hobsbawm, *Echoes of the Marseillaise*, 109.

19.   Shamefully, but typically, Berlin's biographer Michael Ignatieff defends his hero in these terms: "The difficulty lay in supposing that Deutscher could be trusted to teach non-Marxist concepts with the fairness requisite in a university teacher." Berlin's sabotaging of Deutscher's chance for an academic career is therefore "a fair enough application of the standards of liberal tolerance in a university." See *Isaiah Berlin*, 235. This probably tells us all we need to know about "liberal tolerance." Actually, Deutscher's scholarship, at least in his serious historical work, was usually impeccable—unlike, one might add, that of the sainted Sir Isaiah, whose *Karl Marx* (1939 and 1960), particularly the first edition, is a byword for factual inaccuracies and elementary theoretical misunderstandings.

20.   Brown, *Carl Becker on History*, 39.

21.   Christopher Hill. "Foreword," x.

22.   Hobsbawm, "The Historians Group of the Communist Party," 32.

23.   Rabb, "Revisionism Revised," 58.

24.   Palmer, *Descent into Discourse*, 89.

25.   Tawney had previewed these arguments in a less developed form during the 1920s. See Tawney, "Introduction."

26.   Tawney, "Harrington's Interpretation of His Age," 207, 212.

27.   Tawney, "The Rise of the Gentry," 4, 5.

28.   Quoted in Terrill, *R. H. Tawney and His Times*, 244. See also Tawney, "The Rise of the Gentry," 18.

29.   Trevor-Roper, "The Gentry," 33, 34, 43, 50.

30.   Trevor-Roper did at any rate recognize that there was a link between Harrington, Marx, and Tawney, which was the source of his hostility to Harrington. The same point was strenuously denied in conventional political science at the same time. See, for example, Shklar, "Ideology Hunting."

31.   MacPherson, *The Political Theory of Possessive Individualism*, 169–74.

32. Trevor-Roper, "The Social Causes of the Great Rebellion," 204, 205.
33. Trevor-Roper, "Karl Marx and the Study of History," 293–95.
34. Ibid., 295.
35. Tawney, "Preface to the 1937 Edition," vii.
36. Trevor-Roper, "The Religious Origins of the Enlightenment," 193–94.
37. Trevor-Roper, "The General Crisis of the Seventeenth Century," 65.
38. Ibid., 95.
39. Hexter, "Storm over the Gentry," 131.
40. Ibid., 140–41.
41. Hexter, "The Myth of the Middle Class in Tudor England," 113–14.
42. Ibid., 116.
43. Cobban, "The Myth of the French Revolution."
44. Cobban, *The Social Interpretation of the French Revolution*, 9.
45. Ibid., 52.
46. Ibid., 59, 60–61, 67.
47. Cobban, "The Myth of the French Revolution," 99, 105–6.
48. Cobban, *The Social Interpretation of the French Revolution*, 77, 78, 79.
49. This claim in particular was not as startlingly original as Cobban evidently thought. Engels and indeed leading proponents of the orthodoxy were quite aware of the retarding effects of peasant property-holding on rural capitalist economic development. See Engels, "The Peasant Question," 486; Lefebvre, *The French Revolution*, 306, 311; and Soboul, *The French Revolution*, 558–60.
50. Hampson, "Review of *The Social Interpretation of the French Revolution*," 192.
51. Taylor, "Types of Capitalism in Eighteenth-century France."
52. Taylor, "Noncapitalist Wealth and the Origins of the French Revolution," 471 and 471–82 more generally.
53. Ibid., 489–90.
54. Ibid., 491.
55. Ibid., 496.
56. The phrase, "skidding off course of the revolution" sounds rather more elegant in the original French, that is, "*le dérapage de la révolution*." Furet and Richet, *La révolution française*, 126.
57. Kates, "Introduction," 8.
58. Talmon, *The Origins of Totalitarian Democracy*, 80.
59. Ibid., 10–11.
60. Ibid., 252.
61. Norman Cohn, *The Pursuit of the Millennium*, 286.
62. Alasdair MacIntyre, "The End of Ideology and the End of the End of Ideology," 4.
63. Elton, "A High Road to Civil War?," 327.
64. Laslett, *The World We Have Lost*, 159, 160.
65. Ibid., 172, 173.
66. Max Weber, *Economy and Society*, vol. 1, 224.
67. Dylan, *Chronicles: Volume 1*, 76. Later Dylan defines the Civil War on his own terms, in a brilliant passage that suggests he is much less of the political naif that he is sometimes made out to be: "In the North, people lived by the clock. The factory stroke, whistles and bells. Northerners had to be 'on time.' In some ways the Civil War would be a battle between two kinds of time." Ibid., 86.
68. Runkle, "Karl Marx and the American Civil War," 138–41.
69. Genovese, "Marxist Interpretations of the Slave South," 350–51, note 16. For Marx and Engels's views on the American Civil War as a social revolution, see chapter 10 in this book.
70. Arendt, *On Revolution*, 55–56, 142, 144, 156.
71. King, "Hannah Arendt and the Concept of Revolution," 33–34, 43–45.

72. Arendt, *On Revolution*, 43, 158.
73. Kristol, *The American Revolution as a Successful Revolution*, 8.
74. Ibid., 8–9.
75. Ibid., 11–12.
76. King, "Hannah Arendt and the Concept of Revolution," 32.
77. Edward P. Thompson, "The Patricians and the Plebs," 19.
78. Rostow, *The Stages of Economic Growth*, 17. Hartz had argued in the 1950s that the United States had lacked a serious socialist movement because the absence of feudalism had established liberal hegemony early in national history. Interestingly, Hartz saw this as an indirect confirmation, in reverse, of the theory of uneven and combined development: "If an understanding of the American liberal world led to the grim conclusions for socialism we have uncovered here, why should hopeful activists look them in the face? After all, Trotsky's law of combined development, which stressed the skipping of the liberal stage by Russia, was designed to rationalize that country's immediate plunge into the socialist revolution. Would he have developed the same law if it had led to the opposite conclusion?" Hartz, *The Liberal Tradition in America*, 236–37. See also ibid., 308.
79. Rostow, *The Stages of Economic Growth*, 163–64.
80. Taylor, "Noncapitalist Wealth and the Origins of the French Revolution," 482. For the source of these arguments, see Rostow, *The Stages of Economic Growth*, 33, 34.
81. Rostow, The *Stages of Economic Growth*, 165–66.
82. Frank, *Sociology of Development and Underdevelopment of Sociology*, 9, 26.
83. Ellen Meiksins Wood, *The Pristine Culture of Capitalism*, 117–60.
84. Macfarlane, "Socio-economic Revolution in England and the Origin of the Modern World," 164.
85. Jonathan C. D. Clark, *English Society, 1688–1832*, ix; Jonathan C. D. Clark, *Revolution and Rebellion*, 2. Clark had a third target, the "Old Hat school," consisting of "Whig or Liberal historians," like Gardiner; but these were all dead, and their work requiring refutation only to the extent that their assumptions about progress and directionality had been incorporated into the Marxist and more broadly sociological approaches that followed.
86. Christianson, "The Causes of the English Revolution"; Morrill, *The Revolt of the Provinces*; Russell, "Perspectives in Parliamentary History."
87. Hexter, "Power Struggle, Parliament and Liberty in Early Stuart England," 4–5.
88. Doyle, *Origins of the French Revolution*; Furet, *Interpreting the French Revolution*.
89. Perry Anderson, *In the Tracks of Historical Materialism*, 32.
90. Glucksmann, *The Master Thinkers*, 45–47, 282–84.
91. See, for example, the reference to "the vulgate according to Mazauric and Soboul," in Furet, "The Revolutionary Catechism," 131.
92. Furet, "The French Revolution is over," 19–20.
93. Furet, "The French Revolution is over," 5–6, 12.
94. Schama, *Citizens*, 290.
95. Ibid., 906.
96. Ibid., 436, 447.
97. Sutherland, *France*, 140, 442.
98. Bell, "Class, Consciousness, and the Fall of the Bourgeois Revolution," 333.
99. Edward P. Thompson, *The Making of the English Working Class*, 12.
100. Schama, *Citizens*, xvi, xvi. Compare ibid., 51–60, 203–27, 356–68 and Trotsky, *The History of the Russian Revolution*, 73–84, 112–20.
101. Lyotard, *The Postmodern Condition*, xxiii–xxiv.
102. Jenkins, *Re-thinking History*, 62–63.
103. Evans, *In Defence of History*, 245.
104. Jonathan C. D. Clark, *Revolution and Rebellion*, 23.
105. Jonathan C. D. Clark, *Our Shadowed Present*, 19 and 1–32 more generally.

106. Callinicos, "Marxism and the Crisis in Social History," 34.
107. Thatcher, *The Downing Street Years*, 753.
108. "The Trouble with Revolutions," *The Economist*, July 8, 1989, 14.
109. Foner, "The Russians Write a New History," 79.
110. Russell, "The Bourgeois Revolution," 8, 9.
111. Coates, "The Rebellion of 1837–38 and the Other Bourgeois Revolutions in Quebec History," 28–29.
112. Marwick, *The Sixties*, 10.
113. Nigel Williams, *Witchcraft*, 29–30.
114. Doyle, *Origins of the French Revolution*, 2.
115. Fulbrook, "The English Revolution and the Revisionist Revolt," 252.
116. Hobsbawm, "Revolution," 26.
117. Heller, *The Bourgeois Revolution in France*, 7.
118. Ibid., 65.
119. See, for example, Manning, "The English Revolution," 46 and 44–46 more generally.
120. Evans et al., "History Today," 3.

16. From Society to Politics; from Event to Process

1.   Braudel, *The Mediterranean and the Mediterranean World*, vol. 1, 21.
2.   Keirnan, "Revolution and Reaction," 74.
3.   Perry Anderson, "Origins of the Present Crisis," 17, 18–19.
4.   Richard Johnson, "Barrington Moore, Perry Anderson and English Social Development," 21.
5.   Joseph, "Is Beckerman Among the Sociologists?," 501–2.
6.   Edward P. Thompson, "The Peculiarities of the English," 315–19.
7.   Marx, *Capital*, vol. 1, 739.
8.   Perry Anderson, "Origins of the Present Crisis," 47.
9.   Christopher Hill, "The English Revolution," 9.
10. Lefebvre, *The Coming of the French Revolution*, 2.
11. Soboul, *The French Revolution, 1787-1799*, 5.
12. Quoted in Vacca, *Togliatti sconosciuto*, 144–45.
13. Gramsci, *The Modern Prince and Other Writings*; Marzani, *The Open Marxism of Antonio Gramsci*.
14   Hughes, *Consciousness and Society*, 96–104.
15. Gwyn A. Williams, "The Concept of 'Egomania.'" For Williams's retraction, see "The Making and Unmaking of Antonio Gramsci," 12.
16. Edward P. Thompson, "The Peculiarities of the English," 345–46; Perry Anderson, "Socialism and Pseudo-Empiricism," 27–28.
17. Nairn, "La nemesi borghese."
18. Perry Anderson, "Foreword," 3; Forgacs, "Gramsci and Marxism," 75–77; Willie Thompson, "Tom Nairn and the Crisis," 307–11.
19. Nairn, "La nemesi borghese," 139.
20. Perry Anderson, "Origins of the Present Crisis," 30 and see 30–43 more generally.
21. Lukács, *The Destruction of Reason*, 46. See also ibid., 55. Anderson refers to this book while acknowledging the general influence of Lukács on his early theoretical formation, but it is unclear from the context whether he was aware of this particular work in the early 1960s. See "Foreword," 3–4.
22. Perry Anderson, "Socialism and Pseudo-Empiricism," 8.
23. Perry Anderson, "Foreword," 8.
24. Nairn, "The Twilight of the British State," 18.

25.   Ibid., 10. See also ibid., 25.

26.   Edward P. Thompson, "Peculiarities of the English," 321.

27.   Ibid., 321–22, 349–40.

28.   Corrigan and Sayer, *The Great Arch*, 85.

29.   Ibid., 85–86 and 72–86 more generally.

30.   Therborn, *Science, Class and Society*, 117–18.

31.   In the first of these, Anderson is one of the people thanked by Mayer for offering "detailed criticisms and suggestions." See Mayer, *The Persistence of the Old Regime*, x.

32.   Ibid., 3–4, 11.

33.   Mayer, *Why Did the Heavens Not Darken?*, 3, 32.

34.   Blum, *The End of the Old Order*, 421.

35.   Gerstenberger, "The Bourgeois State Form Revisited," 169.

36.   Halperin, *In the Mirror of the Third World*, 23.

37.   Hobsbawm, *The Age of Capital*, 35–6.

38.   Norman Stone, *Europe Transformed*, 18–19.

39.   Perry Anderson, "The Figures of Descent," 129.

40.   Ibid., 155.

41.   Ibid., 156.

42.   Nairn, *The Enchanted Glass*, 375.

43.   Plyushch, "Forward Together or Down Together," 44. According to Plyushch's fellow-dissident Boris Weil, the theory of state capitalism was widely accepted among the opposition at this time. See "Marx and Lenin Read in the Camps," 94.

44.   Barker and Mooers, "Theories of Revolution in the Light of 1989 in Eastern Europe," 35, 36.

45.   Vasilyeva, "Preface," xv.

46.   See, in relation to Eastern Europe, Callinicos, *The Revenge of History*, 50–66.

47.   Barker and Mooers, "Theories of Revolution in the Light of 1989 in Eastern Europe," 36.

48.   Eugene Weber, "Revolution? Counter-revolution? What Revolution?," 509.

49.   Griffin, "Revolution from the Right," 198.

50.   Trotsky, "What Is National Socialism?," 410.

51.   Evans, *The Coming of the Third Reich*, 457–58 and 456–61 more generally.

52.   Perry Anderson, "Socialism and Pseudo-Empiricism," 9.

53.   Morton, *Unravelling Gramsci*, 41.

54.   Eisenstein, *Feminism Seduced*, 64.

55.   Stern, *Changing India*, 3.

56.   Roxborough, *Theories of Underdevelopment*, 147.

57.   Panitch, *Renewing Socialism*, 21, 40.

58.   See, for example, Teeple, "Globalisation as the Second Bourgeois Revolution."

59.   Przeworski, *Capitalism and Social Democracy*, 219.

60.   Davidson, "What Was Neoliberalism?," 10–21, 65–70; Davidson, "Many Capitals, Many States," 77–88.

61.   Lockwood, "Historical Materialism and the State," 173, 178.

62.   Harris, *The Return of Cosmopolitan Capital*, 89, 264.

63.   Stuart Hall, "The Neoliberal Revolution,"26.

64.   Harman, "From Feudalism to Capitalism," 50–52.

17. "The Capitalist World-System"

1.   Sweezy, "A Rejoinder," 106.

2.   Sweezy, "A Critique," 42.

3.   Baran and Sweezy, *Monopoly Capital*, 365.

4. Frank, "Dependence Is Dead: Long Live Dependence and the Class Struggle," 96. An equally important influence was the work of Raúl Prebish in developing the theory of unequal exchange with the United Nations Economic Commission for Latin America during the 1950s and 1960s. See Love, "Raúl Prebish and the Origins of the Doctrine of Unequal Exchange."

5. Frank, *Capitalism and Underdevelopment in Latin America*, 16, 17.

6. Frank, *Lumpenbourgeoisie—Lumpendevelopment*, 15, 31.

7. Frank, *Capitalism and Underdevelopment in Latin America*, 305.

8. See, in general, Brenner, "The Origins of Capitalist Development," 91 and, with specific reference to Che Guevara's version of the argument for autarchy, Alasdair MacIntyre, "Marxism of the Will," 376.

9. Banaji, "Gunder Frank in Retreat?," 518.

10. Chase-Dunn, "Socialist States in the Capitalist World Economy," 48, 49.

11. Fitzgerald, "Sociologies of Development," 21.

12. Wallerstein, "The Rise and Future Demise of the World Capitalist System," 413.

13. Ibid., 396, 397.

14. Wallerstein, *The Modern World-System I*, 351.

15. Wallerstein, *Historical Capitalism*, 42, 105–6.

16. Wallerstein, "The Rise and Future Demise of the World Capitalist System," 289.

17. Ibid., 398.

18. Wallerstein, *The Modern World-System I*, 127.

19. Ibid., 92.

20. Brenner, "The Origins of Capitalist Development," 32.

21. Ibid., 27–41. We should note, however, that world systems theorists themselves deny being Smithians, in the case of Wallerstein, on the grounds that 1) Smith believed that capitalism ("commercial society") was an integral part of human nature and he does not, and 2) that Smith understands capitalism to be based on the operation of a free market and he understands it to be based on proletarianization of labor and the commercialization of land. See Wallerstein, "From Feudalism to Capitalism," 273, 280. Ironically, at one point Wallerstein argued that Marx himself "was a little too Smithian (competition is the norm of capitalism, monopoly a distortion)." *The Modern World-System III*, 51.

22. Laclau, "Feudalism and Capitalism in Latin America," 40, 41.

23. Ernest Mandel, *Late Capitalism*, 48–49. This is in fact less surprising than it seems. Whatever the other virtues of Mandel's work, it was characterized by a combination of severe formal adherence to the letter of Trotsky's writings while continuously supplementing them with an eclectic mix of theories with which they were often incompatible.

24. Frank, *World Accumulation*, 240–41 and 241–51 more generally.

25. Banaji, "Gunder Frank in Retreat?," 515, 516 and 514–18 more generally. See also "Modes of Production in a Materialist Conception of History," 61–66.

26. Haynes, "Columbus, the Americas and the Rise of Capitalism," 70.

27. Duplessis, *Transitions to Capitalism in Early Modern Europe*, 200.

28. Tibebu, "On the Question of Feudalism, Absolutism, and the Bourgeois Revolution," 85–86, 132.

29. Wallerstein, *The Modern World-System I*, 296, 297.

30. Ibid., 201–2, 210.

31. Wallerstein, *The Modern World-System II*, 120.

32. Wallerstein, *The Modern World-System III*, 52.

33. Ibid., 111.

34. Braudel, *Capitalism and Civilization*, vol. 2, 295, 297. For Wallerstein's use of this argument, see *The Modern World-System III*, 51.

35. Wallerstein, *The Modern World-System III*, 52.

36. Ashworth, *Slavery, Capitalism, and Politics in the Antebellum Republic*, vol. 1, 498.

37.   Ashworth, *Slavery, Capitalism, and Politics in the Antebellum Republic*, vol. 2, 647.
38.   Blaut, *The Colonizer's Model of the World*, 165, 187.
39.   Ibid., 199.
40.   Ibid., 201.
41.   Goody, *Capitalism and Modernity*, 61–62.
42.   Ibid., 107.
43.   Frank, *ReOrient*, 276–83.
44.   Frank, "The Modern World System Revisited," 187; Tibebu, "On the Question of Feudalism, Absolutism and the Bourgeois Revolution," 122.
45.   Frank, *ReOrient*, 330–31.
46.   Goody, *The Theft of History*, 211.
47.   Ibid., 305.

18. "Capitalist Social Property Relations"

1.   Brenner, "Property and Progress," 58. For an earlier, less developed version of the distinction, see Brenner, "The Social Basis of Economic Development," 46.
2.   Brenner, "Agrarian Class Structure and Economic Development in Pre-Industrial Europe," 13–29.
3.   See, for example, Harman, "From Feudalism to Capitalism," 44–45 and Tribe, *Genealogies of Capitalism*, 27–29.
4.   Brenner, "Dobb on the Transition from Feudalism to Capitalism," 121–25.
5.   Dobb, *Studies in the Development of Capitalism*, 50–70.
6.   Brenner, "Dobb on the Transition from Feudalism to Capitalism," 127–28, 131–39.
7.   Brenner, "Property Relations and the Growth of Agricultural Productivity in Late Medieval and Early Modern Europe," 23.
8.   Ibid., 25.
9.   Brenner, "The Social Basis of Economic Development," 53.
10.   Brenner, "Bourgeois Revolution and Transition to Capitalism," 300–301.
11.   Brenner, "Agrarian Class Structure and Economic Development in Pre-Industrial Europe," 30–63; Brenner, "Dobb on the Transition from Feudalism to Capitalism," 130; Brenner, "Economic Backwardness in Eastern Europe in Light of Developments in the West," 45–47.
12.   Brenner, "Agrarian Class Structure and Economic Development in Pre-Industrial Europe," 40–41.
13.   Ibid., 36.
14.   Brenner, "The Agrarian Roots of European Capitalism," 293.
15.   Brenner, "Agrarian Class Structure and Economic Development in Pre-Industrial Europe," 55.
16.   Brenner, "The Agrarian Roots of European Capitalism," 319–20, 325–26.
17.   See, for example, Hobsbawm, "The Crisis of the Seventeenth Century," 41–43 and Kreidte, *Peasants, Landlords and Merchant Capitalists*, 87–91.
18.   Brenner, "Property Relations and the Growth of Agricultural Productivity in Late Medieval and Early Modern Europe," 35, 40–41; Brenner, "The Low Countries and the Transition to Capitalism," 308–15.
19.   Ellen Meiksins Wood, "The Question of Market Dependence," 52, 55.
20.   Brenner, "Agrarian Class Structure and Economic Development in Pre-Industrial Europe," 35, 40, 49, note 81 and 52, note 88.
21.   Brenner, "The Rises and Declines of Serfdom in Medieval and Early Modern Europe," 264–72, 276.
22.   Perry Anderson, *Lineages of the Absolutist State*, 82–83; John H. Elliott, *Imperial Spain*,

376–77.
23. See, for example, Duplessis, *Transitions to Capitalism in Early Modern Europe*, 55, 161–62.
24. Torras, "Class Struggle in Catalonia," 255–59.
25. Post, "Agrarian Class-Structure and Economic Development in Colonial-British North America," 191–92.
26. Post, "Social Property Relations, Class Conflict and the Origins of the US Civil War," 250.
27. Some examples: on the specificity of economic rationality under feudalism, see Kula (1962), *An Economic Theory of the Feudal System*, 165–75; on the integration of the towns into the feudal economy and the misidentification of markets for capitalism, see Merrington (1974), "Town and Country in the Transition," 173–87; on the distinction between Eastern Europe ("East Prussia in particular"), France, and England, see Tawney (1941), "Rise of the Gentry," 13–14; on the differences between English and French agriculture, see Max Weber (1919–20), *General Economic History*, 69–70, 72, 76–77, 85–86; on the capitalist nature of English society before 1640, see PF (Jurgen Kuczynski) (1940), "England's Revolution," 558–59; and, on the uniqueness of English economic development, see Perkin (1968), "Social Causes of the Industrial Revolution," 135–36.
28. Brenner, "The Agrarian Roots of European Capitalism," 281.
29. Brenner, "Property and Progress," 59.
30. Appleby, *The Relentless Revolution*, 77, 78.
31. Holstun, *Ehud's Dagger*, 432.
32. Perry Anderson, *Lineages of the Absolutist State*, 11; Gregory Elliot, *Perry Anderson*, 79–80.
33. Rigby, *Marxism and History*, 169.
34. MacLachlan, *The Rise and Fall of Revolutionary England*, 16. And see ibid., 11–19 and the associated references for MacLachlan's reliance on Comninel and Brenner. For his substantive discussion of Ellen Meiksins Wood and Brenner, see ibid., 301–5.
35. Edward P. Thompson, "The Poverty of Theory or an Orrery of Errors," 254.
36. Rigby, *Marxism and History*, xi, xiii.
37. Hook, *Towards the Understanding of Karl Marx*, 173, 174.
38. Holstun, *Ehud's Dagger*, 119.
39. Compare Balibar, "The Basic Concepts of Historical Materialism," 292 and Brenner, "The Social Basis of Economic Development," 53.
40. Post, "The Agrarian Origins of US-capitalism," 49, note 31. See also the autobiographical note in Post, "Introduction," 4.
41. Althusser, "Contradiction and Overdetermination," 19–21; Brenner, "The Agrarian Roots of European Capitalism," 291–99.
42. See, in general, Ellen Meiksins Wood, *The Retreat from Class*, 18–19 and, specifically in relation to the French Revolution, Comninel, *Rethinking the French Revolution*, 82–84, 90–102.
43. Brenner, "Competition and Class," 44.
44. Edward P. Thompson, "The Peculiarities of the English," 321.
45. Post, "Comments on the Brenner-Wood Exchange on the Low Countries," 92.
46. Rigby, *Marxism and History*, 166; Harman, "From Feudalism to Capitalism," 44–6, 50–51; Hilton, "Introduction," 8.
47. Vries, "The Transition to Capitalism in a Land without Feudalism," 69.
48. Lenin, *The Development of Capitalism in Russia*, 194, 197.
49. Brenner, "The Origins of Capitalist Development," 52, note 43.
50. Brenner, "Bourgeois Revolution and Transition to Capitalism," 294. For a more general argument about Marx's supposed explanatory failures, see Ellen Meiksins Wood, "Horizontal Relations," 175.
51. Rigby, *Marxism and History*, xii.
52. Bois, "Against the Neo-Malthusian Orthodoxy," 115.

53.   Mooers, *The Making of Bourgeois Europe*, 37.
54.   Ellen Meiksins Wood, "The Question of Market Dependence," 142.
55.   Ibid., 57.
56.   Edward P. Thompson, "The Peculiarities of the English," 317.
57.   Marx, *Grundrisse*, 508. Here he also refers to the tenants of the landed proprietors as "already semi-capitalists," albeit "still very hemmed in ones."
58.   Comninel, *Rethinking the French Revolution*, 92. Again, this approach is comparable to that of the Althusserians. First define what "Marxism" is allowed to be, and then dismiss anything that fails to conform to it, even if it includes the majority of Marx's actual work.
59.   Keynes, "A Pure Theory of Money," 243.
60.   Rosdolsky, *The Making of Marx's Capital*, 44.
61.   Ibid.
62.   Marx, "Wage-Labor and Capital," 213, 220.
63.   Marx, *Capital*, vol. 1, 874, 975. See also Marx, *Grundrisse*, 505.
64.   Marx, *Capital*, vol. 3, 1019.
65.   Duchesne, "Rodney Hilton and the Peasant Road to 'Capitalism' in England'," 144.
66.   Marx, *Capital*, vol. 3, 770.
67.   Amin and Linden, "Introduction," 3, 4.
68.   Engerman, "Slavery, Serfdom and Other Forms of Coerced Labor," 32.
69.   Banaji, "The Fictions of Free Labor," 145.
70.   Teschke, *The Myth of 1648*, 140–41.
71.   Ellen Meiksins Wood, "Horizontal Relations," 176, 177.
72.   Davidson, *Discovering the Scottish Revolution*, 25–26.
73.   See, for example, Ellen Meiksins Wood, *The Origin of Capitalism*, 21–26.
74.   Polanyi, *The Great Transformation*, 73, 76.
75.   Leys, *Market-Driven Politics*, 218.
76.   Chibber, *Locked in Place*, 243.
77.   Toward the end of his life Engels noted that the law of value and distribution of the surplus value by means of the rate of profit "attain their most complete realization only on the presupposition that capitalist production has been reduced to the modern classes of landowners, capitalists (industrialists and merchants) and workers—all intermediate stages having been got rid of. This condition does not exist yet even in England and never will exist—we shall not let it get that far." Engels to Schmidt, March 12, 1895. For similar comments, see Trotsky, *Results and Prospects*, 86–88.
78.   Hayek, *The Fatal Conceit*, 7.
79.   Ibid., 20. For similar claims about the unnaturalness of capitalism, see Sombart, *The Quintessence of Capitalism*, 13.
80.   In Freudian terms, capitalism is the triumph of the market Super-Ego over the collectivist Id.
81.   Duchesne, "On *The Origin of Capitalism*," 135.
82.   Geras, *Marx and Human Nature*, 107–8.
83.   Adam Smith, *The Wealth of Nations*, Book 1, chapter 2, 17.
84.   Brenner, "Bourgeois Revolution and Transition to Capitalism," 280.
85.   Ellen Meiksins Wood, *The Origin of Capitalism*, 118–19.
86.   Brenner, "The Civil War Politics of London's Merchant Community."
87.   Brenner, "Dobb on the Transition from Feudalism to Capitalism," 139, note.
88.   Brenner, "Bourgeois Revolution and Transition to Capitalism," 303.
89.   Brenner, *Merchants and Revolution*, 647–66.
90.   Laslett, *The World We Have Lost*, 35–39, 172–73.
91.   Wallerstein, *The Modern World-System I*, 283.
92.   Hobbes, *Behemoth*, 3–4.
93.   Ellen Meiksins Wood, "Capitalism, Merchants and Bourgeois Revolution," 219.

94   Ellen Meiksins Wood, "The Question of Market Dependence," 142, 175.
95.   Teschke, *The Myth of 1648*, 12.
96.   Marx, *Theories of Surplus Value*, vol. 1, 52.
97.   Althusser, "The Underground Current of the Materialism of the Encounter," 201.
98.   Ellen Meiksins Wood, *The Origins of Capitalism*, 119.
99.   Teschke, "Bourgeois Revolution, State Formation and the Absence of the International," 11, 12.
100. Post, "Social Property Relations, Class Conflict and the Origins of the US Civil War," 250–51.

19. "Consequentialism"

1.   Teschke, "Bourgeois Revolution, State Formation and the Absence of the International," 5.
2.   Oliver Roy, *Islam and Resistance in Afghanistan*, 4.
3.   Trotsky, *The History of the Russian Revolution*, 1017.
4.   Trotsky, "Report on the World Economic Crisis and the Tasks of the Communist International," 252, 259, 262–63, and 231–64 more generally.
5.   Trotsky, "Once Again, Whither France?," 53.
6.   Trotsky, "France at the Turning Point," 124, 125.
7.   Trotsky, "The Death Agony of Capitalism and the Tasks of the Fourth International," 111.
8.   Trotsky, "Ninety Years of the Communist Manifesto," 22.
9.   Pinder, "Europe in the World Economy," 338, 339.
10.   Alasdair MacIntyre notes: "When, in the early 1930s, Trotsky was confronted with the facts of this growth by the Marxist economist Fritz Sternberg he remarked that he had no time recently to study the statistics; that on the truth or falsity of the statements involved much else that was committed to depended he does not seem to have noticed." See *Marxism and Christianity*, 90–91. For an example of Trotsky's discussions with Sternberg, see Trotsky, "After Talks with Fritz Sternberg." It is not the case that Trotsky was generally neglectful of the need for accurate data, as can been seen from this comment in a series of notes not intended for publication: "The dialectic does not liberate the investigator from painstaking study of the facts, quite the contrary; it requires it." See Trotsky, "The Notebooks in Translation," 92.
11.   For two brief but useful summaries of these shifts, which take quite different and opposed attitudes toward Stalinism, see Perry Anderson, "Trotsky's Interpretation of Stalinism," 49–54 and Alasdair MacIntyre, "Trotsky in Exile," 269–70.
12.   Trotsky, *The Revolution Betrayed*, 288.
13.   Trotsky, "The USSR in War," 17.
14.   Trotsky, "The Death Agony of Capitalism and the Tasks of the Fourth International," 146–17.
15.   Wohlforth, "The Theory of Structural Assimilation."
16.   Trotsky, "The USSR in War," 22.
17.   Trotsky, "Ninety Years of the Communist Manifesto," 24–25. See also, "The Death Agony of Capitalism and the Tasks of the Fourth International," 137–39.
18.   Trotsky, "The Lessons of Spain," 322.
19.   Trotsky, "A Fresh Lesson," 73.
20.   Trotsky, "Peasant War in China and the Proletariat," 530.
21.   Trotsky, "Revolution and War in China," 581, 582–83.
22.   Trotsky, "The New Turkey," 11.
23.   Ibid., 13.
24.   Trotsky, "Mexico and British Imperialism," 359.

25. Trotsky, "Latin American Problems," 784–85.
26. Trotsky, "The Death Agony of Capitalism and the Tasks of the Fourth International," 135.
27. Trotsky, *Stalin*, 413. The phrases in brackets are editorial interjections.
28. Trotsky, "The USSR in War," 10–11.
29. Alasdair MacIntyre, "Trotsky in Exile," 275.
30. For a discussion of these individuals and their organizations from a position supportive of Cliff, see Callinicos, *Trotskyism*, 55–85.
31. Lenin, "Report on the Activities of the Council of People's Commissars, January 11 (24)," 464.
32. Lenin, "'Left Wing' Childishness and the Petty Bourgeois Mentality," 335–36, 339.
33. Lenin, "The Trade Unions, the Present Situation and Trotsky's Mistakes," 24.
34. Lenin, "The Party Crisis," 48.
35. Trotsky, *Terrorism and Communism*, 178.
36. Cliff, "The Nature of Stalinist Russia," 3–4 and 3–17 more generally.
37. Isaac Deutscher, *Stalin*, 296.
38. Isaac Deutscher, "The Ex-Communist and His Conscience," 20.
39. Cliff, "The End of the Road," 189.
40. Davidson, "The Prophet, His Biographer and the Watchtower," 114–15.
41. Isaac Deutscher, *The Prophet Outcast*, 45–49, 342–48. See, for example, his response to criticism from the American SWP in *The Prophet Unarmed*, 449, note 64.
42. Isaac Deutscher, *The Prophet Outcast*, 266.
43. Isaac Deutscher, *The Prophet Armed*, x.
44. Isaac Deutscher, *The Prophet Outcast*, 241.
45. Isaac Deutscher, *The Great Contest*, 21–22.
46. Isaac Deutscher, *The Prophet Unarmed*, 429, note 69. See also Isaac Deutscher, "Russia in Transition," 44–46.
47. Isaac Deutscher, "Germany and Marxism," 169.
48. Isaac Deutscher, *Stalin*, 539–40.
49. Isaac Deutscher, "The Unfinished Revolution, 1917–1967," 21–22; Isaac Deutscher, *The Unfinished Revolution, 1917–1967*, 27–28.
50. Cliff, "The Class Nature of the People's Democracies," 65–66.
51. Shachtman, "Isaac Deutscher's *Stalin*," 230–231.
52. Isaac Deutscher, *Stalin*, 539, 540.
53. Ibid., 179–82, 337–38; Isaac Deutscher, *Unfinished Revolution*, 27.
54. Isaac Deutscher, *The Prophet Unarmed*, 10.
55. Isaac Deutscher, *Stalin*, 550. See also 554–55.
56. Isaac Deutscher, *The Prophet Armed*, 372. Deutscher's views are here influenced by those of Christian Rakovsky in his "Letter to Valentinov" published in the United Opposition press in 1928. In effect, Rakovsky described the opposition as being "between a demoralized, treacherous bureaucracy on the one side, and a hopelessly apathetic and passive working class on the other": "It followed (although Rakovsky did not say it) that the bureaucracy, such as it was, would remain, perhaps for decades, the only force capable of initiative and action in the reshaping of Russian society." See ibid., 434 and Rakovsky, "The 'Professional Dangers' of Power."
57. Davidson, "The Prophet, His Biographer," 108–14.
58. Perry Anderson, "Problems of Socialist Strategy," 227 and note; Perry Anderson, "Socialism and Pseudo-Empiricism," 23.
59. Ali, *Street Fighting Years*, 151. Anderson was subsequently to supplement his Deutscherist interpretation of Trotsky with the influence of Mandel, by the mid-1970s counterposing these figures and Roman Rosdolsky to the tradition of Western Marxism. See Perry Anderson, *Considerations on Western Marxism*, 96–101. For this shift in his thought, see Blackledge, *Perry Anderson, Marxism and the New Left*, 3–4, 50–51, 60–66

and Gregory Elliot, *Perry Anderson*, 30, 56–59, 95–110.

60. Perry Anderson, "Problems of Socialist Strategy," 227. Ali recalls Anderson rebuking Ralph Schoenman for reducing Stalinism to "a moral question" and receiving this response: "Stalin killed millions including the majority of old Bolsheviks and you say this is a fucking moral question. We're talking about one of the biggest crimes against socialism this century." Ali, *Street Fighting Years*, 151.

61. Perry Anderson, "Socialism and Pseudo-Empiricism," 9. It is only fair to note that Anderson has reprinted neither this essay nor "Problems of Socialist Strategy."

62. Ibid., 422–23.

63. Cliff, *Trotskyism after Trotsky*, 23, 79; Cliff, *A World to Win*, 42, 48.

64. Cliff, "The Nature of Stalinist Russia," 78.

65. Cliff, "All That Glitters Is Not Gold." "Germain" was Ernest Mandel.

66. Harris, *Of Bread and Guns*, 31.

67. Kidron, *Western Capitalism since the War*, 11. For details of the growth achieved by individual countries during this period, see Maddison, *Phases of Capitalist Development*, 96–97.

68. Armstrong, Glynn, and Harrison, *Capitalism Since World War II*, 167.

69. Grossmann, *The Law of Accumulation*, 157–58.

70. Vance, "After Korea—What?"; Vance, "The Permanent War Economy." Vance had earlier published under the names Frank Demby and Walter T. Oakes.

71. Cliff, "Perspectives for the Permanent War Economy'"; Harman, *Explaining the Crisis*, 78–84; Kidron, *Western Capitalism since the War*, chapter 3. For an overview of the development of the theory, see Pozo, "Reassessing the Permanent Arms Economy."

72. Davis, "The Political Economy of Late-imperial America," 195–201. As Davis has suggested elsewhere, the theories of the Permanent Arms Economy à la Kidron and the Regulation School à la Aglietta complete each other: "Each holds a different part of the elephant of contemporary capitalism, mistaking it for the whole." See Davis, "'Fordism' in Crisis," 251.

73. For one outstanding national case study of his process, see Ginsborg, *A History of Contemporary Italy*, 210–35.

74. Maddison, "Economic Policy and Performance," 491; Therborn, *European Modernity and Beyond*, 131–46.

75. Harris, *The End of the Third World*, 192.

76. Cliff, "The Nature of Stalinist Russia," 55–56. For non-Trotskyist accounts by writers of East European origin that support the assessment that 1928–29 saw a qualitative change in the Soviet Union, see Lewin, "Society, State, and Ideology," and Reiman, *The Birth of Stalinism*, especially 102–22.

77. Trotsky, "Peasant War in China and the Proletariat," 524–25.

78. Löwy, *The Politics of Combined and Uneven Development*, 94–95; Trotsky, *Permanent Revolution*, 277.

79. Trotsky, "Trade Unions in the Epoch of Imperialist Decay," 43.

80. Trotsky, *The Revolution Betrayed*, 245–46 and 245–48 more generally.

81. Bukharin, "Towards a Theory of the Imperialist State," 18. For Cliff's use of Bukharin's later writings on state capitalism, see "The Nature of Stalinist Russia," 105–7.

82. Ernest Mandel, "The Inconsistencies of State Capitalism," 17.

83. Cliff, "The Nature of Stalinist Russia," 90–92; Harman, *Explaining the Crisis*, 71–74, 84–86.

84. Stalin, "The Results of the First Five-Year Plan," 175.

85. Stalin, "The Tasks of Business Executives," 41.

86. Cliff, *Russia*, 145.

87. Mattick, *Marx and Keynes*, 279–80.

88. Harris, *The End of the Third World*, 42.

89. Mattick, *Marx and Keynes*, 284.

90. Haynes, *Russia*, 210–14.
91. Goodwin, *No Other Way Out*, 282.
92. Commission of the C.C of the C.P.S.U., *History of the Communist Party of the Soviet Union (Bolsheviks)*, 305.
93. Haynes, *Russia*, 88–95.
94. Harman, "How the Revolution Was Lost," 116. See also Cliff, "The Nature of Stalinist Russia," 55–56.
95. Ernest Mandel, "The Inconsistencies of State Capitalism," 21. For similar remarks, see Maitan, *Party, Army and Masses in China*, 355.
96. Perry Anderson, *Considerations on Western Marxism*, 118.
97. Löwy, *The Politics of Combined and Uneven Development*, 164.
98. Perry Anderson, *Considerations on Western Marxism*, 118–19.
99. Löwy, *The Politics of Combined and Uneven Development*, 124–27.
100. Peng Shu-tse, "Introduction," 91.
101. Maitan, *Party, Army and Masses in China*, 312.
102. Ibid., 313–14.
103. Löwy, *The Politics of Combined and Uneven Development*, 198.
104. Quoted in Schram, *The Political Thought of Mao*, 98, 99.
105. Reproduced in ibid., 327–28.
106. Stalin, "Report and Speech in Reply to Debate at the Plenum of the Central Committee of the C. P. S. U. (3–5 March 1937)," 263.
107. Žižek, "Afterword," 335, note 199.
108. Elbaum, *Revolution in the Air*, 156.
109. Mandel, quoted in Goodwin, "Razor Sharp Factional Minds," 110.
110. Ernest Mandel, *Revolutionary Marxism Today*, 112 and 108–13 more generally.
111. Molyneux, *Leon Trotsky's Theory of Revolution*, 207–8.
112. Crossman, "Towards a Philosophy of Socialism," 13–14.
113. Gellner, *Thought and Change*, 137.
114. Gellner, *Plough, Book and Sword*, 16–23.
115. Cliff, *A World to Win*, 227.
116. Cliff, "Permanent Revolution," 194.
117. Ibid., 196–98.
118. Harris, "India." For his explicit acknowledgment of Cliff's influence, see 4, note 1.
119. Harris, *The Mandate of Heaven*, 269, 280–81 and 261–82 more generally.
120. Ibid., 290–92.
121. Guevara, "On Sacrifice and Dedication," 159–60, 162.
122. Roxborough, *Theories of Underdevelopment*, 155.
123. Lukács, "On His Life and Work," 50.
124. Rees, "The Democratic Revolution and the Socialist Revolution," 28; Rees, *Imperialism and Resistance*, 155.
125. Cliff, "Permanent Revolution," 194–95.
126. Gatrell, *Government, Industry and Rearmament in Russia*, 93; Koenker and Rosenberg, *Strikes and Revolution in Russia*, 103–10; Schneiderman, *Sergei Zubatov and Revolutionary Marxism*, 69–140.
127. Cliff, "Permanent Revolution," 196.
128. See, for example, Norman Stone, *The Eastern Front*, 284.
129. Harman, "The Storm Breaks," 64–71.
130. Ibid., 38.
131. Halliday and Molyneux, *The Ethiopian Revolution*, 62–74.
132. Christopher Hill, *Economic Problems of the Church*, 352.
133. Christopher Hill, "Recent Interpretations of the Civil War," 30.
134. Christopher Hill, "Introduction," 20.

135. Christopher Hill, "The Theory of Revolutions," 124–25, 127–28.
136. Christopher Hill, *Change and Continuity in Seventeenth-Century England*, 279–80.
137. Christopher Hill, "A Bourgeois Revolution?," 110, 111.
138. Ibid., 130–31.
139. Ibid., 131.
140. Christopher Hill, "The Place of the Seventeenth-Century Revolution," 31–32.
141. Perry Anderson, *Lineages of the Absolutist State*, 431.
142. Perry Anderson, "The Notion of a Bourgeois Revolution," 110–11, 116–18.
143. Trimberger, *Revolution from Above*, vi.
144. Ibid., 4–5, 41–45.
145. Ibid., 173, 174.
146. Barker, "Japan," 67.
147. Ibid., 39–40. See also Skocpol, *States and Social Revolutions*, 4–5.
148. Barker, "Japan," 39.
149. Trimberger, *Revolution from Above*, 11, note 8.
150. Ginsborg, "Gramsci and the Era of Passive Revolution," 34.
151. Ibid., 36, 40.
152. Gareth Stedman Jones, "Society and Politics at the Beginning of the World Economy," 86–87.
153. Gamble, *An Introduction to Modern Social and Political Thought*, 26, 29.
154. Blackbourn, "The Discreet Charm of the Bourgeoisie," 174 and 174–75 more generally.
155. Poulantzas, *Political Power and Social Classes*, 180.
156. Eley, "The British Model and the German Road," 85, 154. These conclusions are supported by most serious contemporary histories of Nazi Germany. See, for example, Evans, *The Coming of the Third Reich*, 2–21 and Kershaw, *Hitler, 1889–1936*, 73–75.
157. Eley, "The British Model and the German Road," 13.
158. Ibid., 55–56.
159. Ibid., 144.
160. Ibid., 84.
161. Ibid., 84–85.
162. Evans, "The Myth of Germany's Missing Revolution," 93. This acknowledgment makes all the more incomprehensible later claims by Evans that Marxism had no way of explaining the rise of Nazism: "So if you cannot explain [the rise of the Third Reich] by a deficit in bourgeois values or a failure of the bourgeoisie to gain social and political hegemony, then that whole class and Marxist way of trying to explain the disasters in the first half of this century in Germany really collapses." But one key aspect of Blackbourn and Eley's work is precisely that conceptions of an unfulfilled German bourgeois revolution are unnecessary to explain the Third Reich. See Evans et al., "History Today," 27–28.
163. Evans, "The Myth of Germany's Missing Revolution," 77–78 and 73–74, 77–81 more generally.
164. Callinicos, "Trotsky's Theory of 'Permanent Revolution,'" 109–110.
165. Callinicos, "Exception or Symptom?," 99 and 98–102 more generally.
166. One reason may have been that this position was generally agreed upon within the Socialist Workers Party, in which Callinicos was and is a leading figure, without it ever being openly articulated. The only other occasion on which these arguments were made was in a short near-contemporary article by Hallas, "Bourgeois Revolution," which stretches from fourteenth-century Switzerland to twentieth-century Nicaragua covering most important points between with what Callinicos later rightly described as "exemplary panache and brevity." I was present in London the previous year when Hallas gave the dazzling talk upon which this article was based, and recall being deeply impressed—as I often was by this speaker—but in this case at least partly because I had never heard the argument against the necessity of bourgeois agency put in such comprehensive terms before. There was a ten-

dency within the SWP, represented by Ian Birchall, Norah Carlin, and Neil Faulkner, which essentially evaded the question of agency by focusing on the struggle of the working class and the classes below the bourgeoisie more generally. In Carlin's case this extended further back than the earliest bourgeois revolutions to the medieval period proper. See Carlin, "Medieval Workers and Permanent Revolution," and "Marxism and the English Civil War."

167. Callinicos, *Making History*, 229–33.

168. Callinicos, "Bourgeois Revolutions and Historical Materialism," 124.

169. Ibid., 136–59.

170. Ibid., 159.

171. Ibid., 160.

172. See, in general, Mooers, *The Making of Bourgeois Europe*, 34–35; in relation to the Netherlands, Linden, "Marx and Engels, Dutch Marxism and the 'Model Capitalist Nation of the Seventeenth Century'," 187–88; in relation to Scotland, Davidson, *Discovering the Scottish Revolution*, 8–12; and in relation to Spain, Lewis, "Structures and Agents," 13–14.

173. Gerstenberger, *Impersonal Power*, 662. Benno Teschke has tried to enlist Gerstenberger into the ranks of his theoretical tendency: "While Heide Gerstenberger retained the concept of bourgeois revolution, her explanatory framework is much closer to the theoretical program of political Marxism." See "Bourgeois Revolution, State Formation and the Absence of the International," 5, note 6. Gerstenberger's work is complex and liable to a number of interpretations although, as her presence in this chapter indicates, I disagree with Teschke about her affinities. Readers can decide for themselves; they should note, however, that Gerstenberger has specifically pointed out that "Teschke's theoretical concepts . . . only bear to a limited extent on the explanatory approach taken here" and her passing references to Brenner and Comninel scarcely suggest wholehearted adoption of political Marxist principles. See *Impersonal Power*, xi, 451. Elsewhere she writes, "contrary to Robert Brenner's assumptions, the concrete forms in which the generalization of personal domination developed have to be interpreted not so much as the *result* of struggles over direct exploitation but rather as one of the most decisive conditions under which such struggles had to be fought." See "The Bourgeois State Form Revisited," 169. It is not clear to me how taking the opposite position to Brenner places Gerstenberger "much closer to the theoretical program of political Marxism."

174. Beik, "Response to Henry Heller's 'The Longue Durée of the French Revolution,'" 122.

175. Lockwood, "Historical Materialism and the State," 172–73. Gerstenberger has a more generalized version of this argument in which no social classes can be said to exist before the triumph of the bourgeois revolution: "In this perspective, the 'bourgeois revolution' was not the victory of a 'bourgeois' over a 'feudal' class, but rather—indeed, quite the contrary—the historical structural change by which classes first acquired the systemic importance that they have in bourgeois society." She does not, however, argue that bourgeois revolutions were carried out by precapitalist states. See Gerstenberger, *Impersonal Power*, 21.

176. Poulantzas, *Political Power and Social Classes*, 183. Poulantzas's italics.

177. Callinicos, "Bourgeois Revolutions and Historical Materialism," 125.

178. Lockwood, "Historical Materialism and the State," 171.

179. See, for example, Carlin, "A New English Revolution," 126–27 and Manning, "The English Revolution," 44–46.

180. See, for example, J. C. D. Clark, *Revolution and Rebellion*, 26, where he argues that Hill's later positions involve mere "cosmetically amended" versions of the orthodoxy.

181. Ellen Meiksins Wood, *The Origin of Capitalism*, 118.

182. Post, "Social Property Relations, Class Conflict and the Origins of the US Civil War," 249–50.

183. Blackbourn, "The Discreet Charm of the Bourgeoisie," 176–205. The concept of a "silent revolution" was also used by Walter Makey, immediately prior to publication of the initial German version of Blackbourn's article, to describe the disintegration of feudal economy

and society in Scotland prior to 1637. See *The Church of the Covenant*, 1–15. This book is one of the few genuinely great works of Scottish history to have been written in the twentieth century, not least because Makey, against the empiricist traditions that dominate Scottish historiography, established a rigorous theoretical conception of feudalism as a framework within which his extensive primary source material could be understood.

184.   Neocleous, *Administering Civil Society*, 108 and 107–10 more generally. Here Neocleous specifically draws on the work of Blackbourn.
185.   Cruz, *Gentlemen, Bourgeois, and Revolutionaries*, 267.
186.   Callinicos, "Bourgeois Revolutions and Historical Materialism," 126, 152; Perry Anderson, "Marshall Berman," 44.
187.   Gerstenberger, *Impersonal Power*, 662–63.
188.   Lewis, "Structures and Agents," 15, note 2.
189.   Ibid., 12, 14, 15.

20. BETWEEN TWO SOCIAL REVOLUTIONS

1.   Hayek, "History and Politics," 23–24.
2.   Zagorin, *Rebels and Rulers*, vol. 1, 16.
3.   Lakatos, "Falsification and the Methodology of Scientific Research Programmes," 117–18.
4.   Alasdair MacIntyre, "Notes from the Moral Wilderness," 54.
5.   Grossman, "The Evolutionist Revolt against Classical Economics· II," 517.
6.   Marx, *Grundrisse*, 100–102.
7.   Marx and Engels, "The Manifesto of the Communist Party," 67.
8.   Alasdair MacIntyre, "Breaking the Chains of Reason," 151. MacIntyre had evidently read the *Grundrisse* by the mid-1960s, before it had been translated into English. See, for example, "Marxist Mask and Romantic Face," 322–23.
9.   Losurdo, *Liberalism*, 321.
10.   Marx, "Preface to the First Edition," in *Capital*, vol. 1, 90.
11.   Marx and Engels, "The Manifesto of the Communist Party," 69, note 15.
12.   Engels, "Preface to the Third German Edition of *The Eighteenth Brumaire*," 302–3.
13.   Hobsbawm, *The Age of Revolution*, 62.
14.   Cliff, "The Class Nature of the People's Democracies," 65–66.
15.   Eley, "The English Model and the German Road," 85.
16.   Poulantzas, *Political Power and Social Classes*, 183.
17.   Perry Anderson, "The Notion of a Bourgeois Revolution," 113.
18.   Perry Anderson, "Foreword," 6.
19.   Abbott, "On the Concept of Turning Point," 250.
20.   Pinkus, *1688*, 32.
21.   Lukács, "Legality and Illegality," 258.
22.   Skocpol, *States and Social Revolutions*, 4–5.
23.   Ibid., 141.
24.   Draper, *Karl Marx's Theory of Revolution*, vol. 2, 19–20.
25.   Ibid., 19.
26.   Choonara, "The Relevance of Permanent Revolution," 179–80.
27.   Eley, "The British Model and the German Road," 82–83. See also Hobsbawm, "Revolution," 10.
28.   Neocleous, *Administering Civil Society*, 94.
29.   Edward P. Thompson, *The Making of the English Working Class*, 889 and 887–915 more generally.
30.   Perry Anderson, "Geoffrey de Ste Croix and the Ancient World," 17. See also Perry Anderson, *Arguments within English Marxism*, 55–56.

31.   Callinicos, *Making History*, 229.

32.   I agree with Pinkus that the two episodes are inseparable: "Because the mid-seventeenth century crisis and the Revolution of 1688–89 were part of the same process, they need to be integrated into a single story." *1688*, 486. But taken seriously, this would mean treating 1637 or 1640 as the beginning of "the first modern revolution," rather than, as he insists, 1688.

33.   Webber, "Rebellion to Reform in Bolivia, Part II," 58; Webber, *From Rebellion to Reform in Bolivia*, 46.

34.   Ossowski, *Class Structure in the Social Consciousness*, 84.

35.   Katz, *From Feudalism to Capitalism*, 181.

36.   Gouldner, *The Future of Intellectuals and the Rise of the New Class*, 93.

37.   Giddens, *The Class Structure of the Advanced Societies*, 91–92.

38.   Althusser, *Machiavelli and Us*, 50.

39.   Godelier, "The Concept of the 'Asiatic Mode of Production and Marxist Models of Social Evolution'," 241.

40.   Duby, *The Three Orders*, 147–66.

41.   Bois, *The Transformation of the Year One Thousand*, 152, 171. Although the term "feudal revolution" is not used, the same concept and chronology can also be found in Dockes, *Medieval Slavery and Liberation*, 105–10 and Poly and Bournazel, *The Feudal Transformation*, 2–3, 118–40, 351–57. Duby was later to reject both the term and the notion. See *France in The Middle Ages*.

42.   Bonnassie, "The Survival and Extinction of the Slave System in the Early Medieval West," 43 and 38–46 more generally.

43.   Wickham, *Framing the Early Middle Ages*, 207; Harman, "Change at the First Millennium," 94–95.

44.   Marx and Engels, *The German Ideology*, 48–49.

45.   Lukács, "Critical Observations on Rosa Luxemburg's 'Critique of the Russian Revolution'," 283.

46.   Ibid., 281.

47.   Bukharin, "The Economics of the Transition Period," 125–28.

48.   See, for example, Albert, *Parecon*; Callinicos, *An Anti-Capitalist Manifesto*, chapter 3; and Pat Devine, *Democracy and Economic Planning*.

49.   Peter Green, "The First Sicilian Slave War," 24.

50.   Dockes, *Medieval Slavery and Liberation*, 17, 219. For an attempt to imagine how a victory by the Spartacus revolt might have led to the emergence of capitalism by c. 500 AD, see MacLeod, *The Restoration Game*, 188–93, an example of the type of speculation which is entirely appropriate for science fiction, but not for historiography,

51.   Finley, *Ancient Slavery and Modern Ideology*, 132–49; Ste. Croix, *The Class Struggle in the Ancient Greek World*, 226–59, chapter 8; Wickham, "The Other Transition," 12–30.

52.   Wickham, *Framing the Middle Ages*, 529–33.

53.   Ibid., 441.

54.   Ibid, 350–51.

55.   Ibid., 578–88.

56.   Gramsci, "The Study of Philosophy," 333–34, Q11§12.

57.   Lukács, "Class Consciousness," 51.

58.   Lukács, *Lenin*, 56.

59.   Rees, *The Algebra of Revolution*, 260, note 134.

60.   Lenin, "The Debate on Self-Determination Summed-Up," 355.

61.   Lenin, "What Is to Be Done?," 423 and 412–17, 421–36 more generally.

62.   Trotsky, "What Next?," 134.

63.   Marx, *The Poverty of Philosophy*, 211. The first use of the distinction between class "in itself" and class "for itself" seems to be in Bukharin, *Historical Materialism*, 292–93.

64.   Draper, "The Two Souls of Socialism," 3.

65.   Marx and Engels, *The German Ideology*, 52–53.
66.   In this context the terms "era" and "epoch" (as used, for example, by Webber) can be treated as interchangeable.

21. PRECONDITIONS FOR AN ERA OF BOURGEOIS REVOLUTION

1.   Lochhead, *The Bourgeois Revolutions*, 5.
2.   Lawrence Stone, "The Causes of the English Revolution," 57–58.
3.   Ibid., 58–117.
4.   Marx, "Preface to *A Contribution to the Critique of Political Economy*," 425–26.
5.   For an explanation that usefully synthesizes the current state of our knowledge about the Maya, see Diamond, *Collapse*, 157–77.
6.   Marx, "Preface to *A Contribution to the Critique of Political Economy*," 426.
7.   Ellen Meiksins Wood, *The Origin of Capitalism*, 118.
8.   Lukács, "The Changing Function of Historical Materialism," 242–43.
9.   I therefore disagree with Daniel Bensaïd when he rejects any comparison between bourgeois and proletarian revolutions, since this judgment is only sustainable if the Dutch or English revolutions are taken as paradigmatic of the former. See *Marx for Our Times*, 29–31.
10.   Marx, "Preface to *A Contribution to the Critique of Political Economy*," 426.
11.   Gramsci, "The Modern Prince," 178, Q13§17.
12.   Bertram, "International Competition in Historical Materialism," 122.
13.   Marx and Engels, "The Manifesto of the Communist Party," 68.
14.   Wickham, "Productive Forces and the Economic Logic of the Feudal Mode of Production," 20.
15.   Marx, "Another British Revelation," 516. This aphorism was actually made of Britain, during its disastrous performance in the Crimean War, but the point is of wider application.
16.   Marx, "Preface to *A Contribution to the Critique of Political Economy*," 426.
17.   Shanin, *Russia*, vol. 1, 312.
18.   Lenin, "The Collapse of the Second International," 213–14.
19.   Ste. Croix, *The Class Struggle in the Ancient Greek World*, 52.
20.   Banaji, "Modes of Production in a Materialsit Conception of History," 93.
21.   Hilton, "Feudalism in Europe," 2; Kula, *An Economic Theory of the Feudal System*, 9.
22.   Duby, *The Early Growth of the European Economy*, 192–99; Kitsikopoulos, "Technological Change in Medieval England," 406–10.
23.   Wickham, "Productive Forces and Economic Logic of the Feudal Mode of Production," 17.
24.   Bois, *The Crisis of Feudalism*, 4056.
25.   Perry Anderson, *Passages from Antiquity to Feudalism*, 197–209, 246–64; Bois, *The Crisis of Feudalism*, 263–99; Hilton, "Was There a General Crisis of Feudalism?"
26.   Epstein, "The Late Medieval Crisis as an 'Integration' Crisis," 34.
27.   Braudel, *Capitalism and Civilization*, vol. 2, 372.
28.   Marx, *Capital*, vol. 3, 452–54.
29.   Callinicos, "Bourgeois Revolutions and Historical Materialism," 134.
30.   Adam Smith, *The Wealth of Nations*, vol. 1, Book I, 138–43; Book III, 420–45.
31.   Postan, *The Medieval Economy and Society*, 239.
32.   See, for example, Katz, *From Feudalism to Capitalism*, 88.
33.   Mielants, *The Origins of Capitalism and the "Rise of the West"*, 80–81.
34.   Brenner, "Agrarian Class Structure and Economic Development in Pre-Industrial Europe," 38–40; Samuel K. Cohn, *Lust for Liberty*, 42–52, 109–11; Hilton, *Bond Men Made Free*, 119–34, 186–207; Merrington, "Town and Country in the Transition to Capitalism," 177–78,

180–2, 191–92; Mollat and Wolff, *The Popular Revolutions of the Middle Ages*, 297.

35.   Trotsky, "Three Conceptions of the Russian Revolution," 60.

36.   Perry Anderson, *Lineages of the Absolutist State*, 301–2; Steinberg, *Why Switzerland?*, 17–26.

37.   Deutsch and Weilenmann, "The Swiss City Canton," 406.

38.   Engels, "[On the Decline of Feudalism the Emergence of National States]," 563. See also Luxemburg, "The National Question and Autonomy," 118–20 and the passages from Engels and Kautsky quoted there.

39.   Cliff, "The Nature of Stalinist Russia," 78.

40.   Braudel, *Capitalism and Civilization,* , vol. 3, 63.

41.   Carling, "Analytic Marxism and Historical Materialism," 52–54. See also Carling, *Social Division*, 62–65.

42.   Lukács, "Reification and the Consciousness of the Proletariat," 162–63. See also Lukács's "The Marxism of Rosa Luxemburg," 27–29.

43.   One of the reasons I find Trotsky's notion of "differentiated unity" less compelling than that of "mediated totality" is because it refers solely to our method of analyzing the world rather than to the world itself. The other is that the idea of mediation implies movement, the process of becoming, and is consequently more dialectical. See Trotsky, "The Notebooks in Translation," 97.

44.   Ollman, "Marxism and Political Science," 139 and 138–44 more generally.

45.   Harvey, "On Countering the Marxian Myth—Chicago-Style," 75, 78.

46.   Sayer, *Marx's Method*, 101.

47.   I owe the notion of "entailment" to Colin Barker.

48.   Marx, "Preface to *A Contribution to the Critique of Political Economy*," 425; Marx, *Grundrisse*, 108.

49.   Benjamin, "Convolute K," 392.

50.   Collier, *Marx*, 46.

51.   Engels to Bloch, September 21, 1890.

52.   Marx, *Capital*, vol. 1, 1064.

53.   Davidson, *Discovering the Scottish Revolution*, 31–34, 207–9.

54.   Commission of the C.C. of the C.P.S.U. (B.). *History of the Communist Party of the Soviet Union (Bolsheviks)*, 122.

55.   Ellen Meiksins Wood, "Marxism and the Course of History," 101–2.

56.   Rigby, *Marxism and History*, 131.

57.   Cardan, *History and Revolution*, 6; Castoriadis, "Marxism and Revolutionary Theory," 18–19. "Cardan" was the pseudonym under which Castoriadis worked as an activist in the French post-Trotskyist group Socialism or Barbarism.

58.   James D. Young, *The Rousing of the Scottish Working Class*, 46.

59.   Ferraro, *Freedom and Determination in History According to Marx and Engels*, 118, 190.

60.   Plekhanov, "The Development of the Monist View of History," 697.

61.   See, for example, Bukharin, "The Economics of the Transition Period," 121 or Lenin, *The Development of Capitalism in Russia*, 596.

62.   Eric Olin Wright, "Gidden's Critique of Marx," 27–28. See also Wright, Levine, and Sober, *Reconstructing Marxism*, 80–83.

63.   Torrance, "Reproduction and Development," 398.

64.   Alasdair MacIntyre, "Notes from the Moral Wilderness," 55.

65.   Diamond, *Guns, Germs and Steel*, 93–156, 264–92. The emergence of classes is brought out more clearly in an earlier work by the same author, *The Rise and Fall of the Third Chimpanzee*, 169–71. As two reviewers have noted, although Diamond "seems blithely unaware" of the fact, he has nevertheless made "a major contribution to historical materialist scholarship," See Carling and Nolan, "Historical Materialism, Natural Selection," 216, 259.

66.   Brenner, "The Social Basis of Economic Development," 45.

67. [Wedderburn], *The Complaynt of Scotland*, 123. I have here translated the Middle Scots in which Wedderburn wrote into modern English.

68. Musgrave, *The Early Modern European Economy*, 51.

69. Whittle, *The Development of Agrarian Capitalism*, 310.

70. Byres, *Capitalism from Above and Capitalism from Below*, 28, 66–68; Manning, "The English Revolution and the Transition from Feudalism to Capitalism," 81–83; McNally, *Political Economy and the Rise of Capitalism*, 5–7; Mooers, *The Making of Bourgeois Europe*, 36–37.

71. Byres, "Differentiation of the Peasantry under Feudalism and the Transition to Capitalism," 55, 57, 64.

72. Whittle, *The Development of Agrarian Capitalism*, 309–10.

73. Hilton, *Bond Men Made Free*, 169.

74. Hilton, "Peasant Movements in England before 1381," 61.

75. Hoyle, "Tenure and the Land Market in Early Modern England," 5.

76. Torras, "Class Struggle in Catalonia," 261.

77. Outhwaite, "Progress and Backwardness in English Agriculture," 9, 12.

78. Woodward, "Wage Rates and Living Standards in Pre-Industrial England," 178–79.

79. Croot and Parker, "Agrarian Class Structure and the Development of Capitalism," 88.

80. Wordie, "The Chronology of English Enclosure," 484.

81. Ibid., 494–95, 502.

82. Duplessis, *Transitions to Capitalism in Early Modern Europe*, 67. See also McNally, *Political Economy and the Rise of Capitalism*, 6.

83. Kitsikopoulos, "Technological Change in Medieval England," 113.

84. Overton, *Agricultural Revolution in England*, 205.

85. Whittle, *The Development of Agrarian Capitalism*, 308.

86. Hipkin, "Property, Economic Interest and the Configuration of Rural Conflict in Sixteenth and Seventeenth-Century England," 71, 77.

87. Teschke, "Bourgeois Revolution, State Formation and the Absence of the International," 19.

88. Hoffman, *Growth in a Traditional Society*, 201.

89. Ibid., 23.

90. Braudel, *Capitalism and Civilization*, vol. 2, 282–83.

91. Heller, *Labor, Science and Technology in France*, 28–36.

92. Kriedte, *Peasants, Landlords and Merchant Capitalists*, 107–8, 111.

93. David Parker, *Class and State in Ancien Regime France*, 53, 54, 237, 272. On the last point see also Heller, *Labor, Science and Technology in France*, 36: "Historically, expropriation and dependence on wages are quite distinct phases. The loss of land through expropriation is not automatically followed by the offer or the acceptance of wage employment."

94. Hoyle, "Tenure and the Land Market in Early Modern England," 18.

95. Marx, *Grundrisse*, 540.

96. Chibber, "What Is Living and What is Dead in the Marxist Theory of History," 76, 77 and 73–78 more generally. Christopher Bertram also invokes "emulation or conquest" as the means of diffusion. See "International Competition in Historical Materialism," 120.

97. Bukharin, "The Economics of the Transition Period," 71.

98. Schoenberger, "The Origins of the Market Economy," 689, 690.

99. Spufford, *Power and Profit*, 260, 265 and 258–66 more generally.

100. Duffy, *The Military Experience in the Age of Reason*, 231.

101. Coleman, *Industry in Tudor and Stuart England*, 35.

102. Marx, *Capital*, vol. 1, 511.

103. Ogilvie, "Social Institutions and Proto-Industrialization," 35.

104. Geoffrey Parker, *The Military Revolution*, 24, 148, 151.

105. Heller, *The Bourgeois Revolution in France*, 96, 103, 119, 129.

106. Cipolla, "Guns and Sails," 52 and 52–55 more generally.

107. Treblicock, *The Industrialization of the Continental Powers*, 208.
108. Gatrell, *Government, Industry and Rearmament in Russia*, 15.
109. Unger, *The Ship in the Medieval Economy*, 275.
110. Geoffrey Parker, *The Military Revolution*, 102–3.
111. Rediker, *Between the Devil and the Deep Blue Sea*, 78, 114.
112. Lenman, *Britain's Colonial Wars*, 167.
113. Adam Smith, *The Wealth of Nations*, vol. 2, Book IV, 230–31.
114. Blaut, *The Colonizer's View of the World*, 152–53, 206.
115. Blackburn, *The Making of New World Slavery*, 527–28.
116. Braudel, *The Mediterranean and the Mediterranean World in the Age of Phillip II*, vol. 2, 739–43.
117. Vilar, "The Age of Don Quixote," 65.
118. Banaji, "Modes of Production in a Materialist Conception of History," 93.
119. Newitt, "Plunder and the Rewards of Office in the Portuguese Empire," 27 and 24–27 more generally.
120. Davis, *Late Victorian Holocausts*, 296.
121. Dobb, *Studies in the Development of Capitalism*, 218; Sweezy, "A Critique," 39–40.
122. Marx, *Capital*, vol. 1, 450.
123. Ibid., 556.
124. Duplessis, *Transitions to Capitalism in Early Modern Europe*, 241; Hobsbawm, "The Crisis of the Seventeenth Century," 50–53; Kriedte, *Peasants, Landlords and Merchant Capitalists*, 123–27.
125. Stern, *Peru's Indian Peoples and the Challenge of Spanish Conquest*, 85–86.
126. Blackburn, *The Making of New World Slavery*, 332–35.
127. C. L. R. James, *The Black Jacobins*, 85–86.
128. Blackburn, *The Making of New World Slavery*, 300–301.
129. Bois, *The Crisis of Feudalism*, 389.
130. Coveney, "An Early Modern European Crisis?," 22.
131. Goldstone, "East and West in the Seventeenth Century," 133.
132. Brenner and Isett, "England's Divergence from China's Yangzi Delta," 613.
133. Mielants, *The Origins of Capitalism and "the Rise of the West"*, 159.
134. Epstein, "Late Medieval Crisis as an 'Integration' Crisis," 45.
135. The following discussion of absolutism derives, in broad outline, from Perry Anderson, *Lineages of the Absolutist State*, 16–24 [taking into account the critical comments in Miliband, "Political Power and Historical Materialism," 56–62] and Brenner, "The Agrarian Roots of European Capitalism," 288–90. Anderson refers to Western Europe in general and Brenner to France in particular. The similarity of their positions is not in this case because Anderson has taken France as a normative model for developments elsewhere but because Brenner fails to see the extent to which the development of absolutism in France was simply the most advanced case of a general process. As we shall see below, this leads him to treat France as if it was dominated by an "absolute" mode of production.
136. Whittle, *The Development of Agrarian Capitalism*, 311
137. Bois, *The Crisis of Feudalism*, 407.
138. Brenner, "Agrarian Class Structure and Economic Development in Pre-Industrial Europe," 55.
139. Ellen Meiksins Wood, *The Pristine Culture of Capitalism*, 159.
140. Ellen Meiksins Wood, *The Origin of Capitalism*, 184.
141. Teschke, *The Myth of 1648*, 191.
142. Marx, *Grundrisse*, 443.
143. Amin, *Unequal Development*, 15–16.
144. Wickham, "The Uniqueness of the East," 48–50.
145. Ibid., 72.

146. Wolf, *Europe and the Peoples without History*, 247. See also Engels to Danielson, June 10, 1890.
147. Marx, *Capital*, vol. 3, 925–27.
148. Berktay, "The Feudalism Debate," 301–10; Haldon, "The Feudalism Debate Once More," 9–15.
149. Haldon, *The State and the Tributary Mode of Production*, 67, 84 and 63–69, 75–109 more generally. See also Wolf, *Europe and the Peoples without History*, 79–88. Wickham has now accepted this, writing that "it now seems to me that both [feudalism and the tributary mode] are sub-types of the same mode of production, in that both are based on agrarian surplus extracted, by force if necessary, from the peasant majority." See *Framing the Early Middle Ages*, 60.
150. Perry Anderson, *Lineages of the Absolutist State*, 404.
151. Hirst, "The Uniqueness of the West," 110 and 106–19 more generally. See also Wickham, "The Uniqueness of the East," 47.
152. Wickham, "Uniqueness of the East," 75 ["Additional note to Chapter 2" of *Land and Power*].
153. Banaji, "Introduction: Themes in Historical Materialism," 24, 25, and 23–40 more generally. See also "Modes of Production: A Synthesis," 354–56.
154. Abu-Lughod, *Before European Hegemony*, 367.
155. Ibid., 18–19, 359–66.
156. Haldon, *The State and the Tributary Mode of Production*, 257, 260.
157. Mielants, *The Origins of Capitalism*, 80.
158. Wickham, *Framing the Early Middle Ages*, 145.
159. Callinicos, *Theories and Narratives*, 171–76. This argument does not involve the—clearly unsustainable—claim that these conditions are in themselves sufficient to produce capitalism: the European feudal societies in which the central state was weakest—Scotland in the West and Poland in the East—experienced even less capitalist development than China.
160. Crone, *Pre-industrial Societies*, 156.
161. Ogilvie, "Social Institutions and Proto-Industrialization," 25.
162. Kermode, *Medieval Merchants*, 203.
163. Christopher Hill, *The World Turned Upside Down*, 46.
164. Bois, "Against the Neo-Malthusian Orthodoxy," 114.
165. Hobson, *The Eastern Origins of Western Civilization*, 313.
166. Wickham, "Historical Materialism, Historical Sociology," 73–74.
167. Pomeranz, *The Great Divergence*, 70.
168. Elvin, *The Pattern of Chinese History*, 69.
169. John A. Hall, "States and Societies," 37–38.
170. Arrighi, *Adam Smith in Beijing*, 314; Callinicos, *Imperialism and Global Political Economy*, 120–23.
171. Gernet, *A History of Chinese Civilization*, 475.
172. Needham, *The Shorter Science and Civilization in China*, vol. 1, 253–254.
173. Adam Smith, *The Wealth of Nations*, Book I, 80, 81.
174. Adam Ferguson, *An Essay on the History of Civil Society*, 111.
175. Marx, "Chinese Affairs," 216. This article is one of the very few occasions where Marx actually uses the base (or "substructure") and superstructure metaphor outside of the 1859 "Preface."
176. Barkey and Batzell, "Comparisons across Empires," 230–33.
177. Rodinson, *Islam and Capitalism*, 11–19.
178. Ashtor, *A Social and Economic History of the Near East in the Middle Ages*, 180.
179. Ibid., 247.
180. Mielants, *The Origins of Capitalism*, 143.

181.   Hoodbhoy, *Islam and Science*, 132.

182.   Khaldun, *The Muqaddimah*, 137, 142–42.

183.   Habib, "Potentialities of Capitalist Development in the Economy of Mughal India," 231.

184.   Bayly, *Indian Society and the Making of the British Empire*, 47.

185.   Ibid., 48.

186.   Chandra, "Some Aspects of the Growth of a Money Economy in India during the Seventeenth Century," 244, 246.

187.   Darwin, *After Tamerlane*, 224.

188.   Davis, *Late Victorian Holocausts*, 285, 287 and 280–88 more generally. It is possible to exaggerate the degree to which these precolonial states or communities other than the Chinese could withstand vast climatic changes. Michael Watts, a friendly critic of Davis, has noted that, although the Qing state was capable of protecting the Chinese population from starvation, this was not necessarily true of his other main examples: "Faced with the sorts of shortfall induced by severe El Niño events—half to three-quarters of the harvest wiped out over wide areas, near-total decimation of livestock—it seems implausible that either the Mughal state or the lineaments of a moral economy in the [Brazilian] *sertao* could have held off disaster." See "Black Acts," 132.

189.   Darwin, *After Tamerlane*, 275–76.

190.   Kiernan, *State and Society in Europe*, 270.

191.   Perry Anderson, *Lineages of the Absolutist State*, 221–35; Barkey and Batzell, "Comparisons across Empires," 229–30.

192.   Amin, *Class and Nation Historically and in the Current Crisis*, 88.

193.   Christopher Hill, "The Bourgeois Revolution in Soviet Scholarship," 11–12.

194.   Norman Cohn, *The Pursuit of the Millennium*, 61–70; Runciman, *A History of the Crusades*, vol. 1, 134–41.

195.   Samuel K. Cohn, *Lust for Liberty*, 102–3, 214–17.

196.   Marx and Engels, "The Manifesto of the Communist Party," 71.

197.   Chesneaux, *Peasant Revolts in China*, 21.

198.   Trotsky, "Three Conceptions of the Russian Revolution," 60.

199.   Wolf, *Peasant Wars of the Twentieth Century*, 37.

200.   Gilly, *The Mexican Revolution*, 147 and 147–81 more generally.

201.   For Engels's acknowledgement of Haxthausen's supposed discovery of the *mir*, see Engels to Danielson, June 10, 1890.

202.   Dennison and Carus, "The Invention of the Russian Rural Commune," 580.

203.   Maza, "Luxury, Morality, and Social Change," 212.

204.   Bookchin, *The Third Revolution*, vol. 1, 13.

205.   Indeed, even in the texts where Marx is most insistent on the virtues of the English and French bourgeoisies compared to the German, he does not suggest that they consciously prepared for their revolutions. Marx is often represented as holding a more positive view of the bourgeoisie than he in fact did through the way in which his words are rendered in translation. A famous passage from 1848 is now usually given as: "In both revolutions, the bourgeoisie was the class which was *genuinely* to be found at the head the movement." The original German reads: "In beiden Revolutionen war die Bourgeoisie die Klasse, die sich *wirklich* an der Spitze der Bewegung befand." This can be translated as: "In both revolutions the bourgeoisie was the class which *effectively* found itself located at the head [or forefront] of the movement." The former implies that the bourgeoisie consciously sought this position; the latter that it was at least partly unintended. Compare Marx, "The Bourgeoisie and the Counter-Revolution," in *The Revolutions of 1848*, 192 and "Die Bourgeoisie und die Kontrerevolution," 107. I owe this point to Kevin Wooten.

206.   Corcoran, "The Bourgeoisie and Other Villains," 479.

207.   Perry Anderson, "Socialism and Pseudo-Empiricism," 8.

208. Ellen Meiksins Wood, *The Origin of Capitalism*, 14.
209. Corcoran, "The Bourgeoisie and Other Villains," 479.
210. Maza, "Luxury, Morality, and Social Change," 210–11.
211. Bell, "Class Consciousness, and the Fall of the Bourgeois Revolution," 333.
212. Maza, "Luxury, Morality, and Social Change," 201–2.
213. Ellen Meiksins Wood, *The Origin of Capitalism*, 14.
214. Neal Wood, *John Locke and Agrarian Capitalism*, 20.
215. Teschke, "Bourgeois Revolution, State Formation and the Absence of the International," 11, 12.
216. Greenfeld, *The Spirit of Capitalism*, 147–48.
217. Fox Genovese and Genovese, "On the Social History of the French Revolution," 225–26.
218. Edward P. Thompson, "The Patricians and the Plebs," 83–84.
219. Draper, *Karl Marx's Theory of Revolution*, vol. 2, 169.
220. Ibid., 289.
221. Perry Anderson, "The Notion of a Bourgeois Revolution," 112.
222. Marx, *Capital*, vol. 3, 1025–27.
223. Althusser, "The Underground Current of the Materialism of the Encounter," 202.
224. Braudel, *The Mediterranean and the Mediterranean World*, vol. 2, 725, 729 and 725–34 more generally.
225. Kamen, *European Society*, 144.
226. John H. Elliott, *Imperial Spain*, 198.
227. Dennassai, "Consommation, Investissemento, Mouvements de Capitaux"; Jago, "The 'Crisis of the Aristocracy,'" 60–63, 89–90; Maravall, *La Cultura del Barroco*, 71–74.
228. John H. Elliott, *Imperial Spain*, 311. See also "A Non-Revolutionary Society," which concludes: "The price of revolution may have been high, but the price of non-revolution was perhaps even higher." Ibid., 91.
229. Berger, *Success and Failure of Picasso*, 20.
230. Hans Baron, "A Sociological Interpretation of the Early Renaissance," 431, 432, 433.
231. Habermas, *The Structural Transformation of the Public Sphere*, 23.
232. King James VI and I, "Basilicon Doron," 29, 30. Raising the blue blanket was the signal for a riot by the Scottish craft guilds.
233. Manning, *The English People and the English Revolution*, 235.
234. Eric Olin Wright, "Exploitation, Identity, and Class Structure," 203.
235. Harvey, *The Enigma of Capital*, 135.
236. Edward P. Thompson, "The Peculiarities of the English," 325, 326.
237. For Lenin's actual position, see Draper, "The Myth of Lenin's 'Concept of the Party'," 188–94, 198–201 and. Lih, *Lenin Rediscovered*, 644–67.
238. Goldmann, *The Hidden God*, 117.
239. Mann, *The Sources of Social Power*, vol. 2, 229, 230.
240. Gramsci, "The Intellectuals," 5–6, Q12§3.
241. Perry Anderson, *Lineages of the Absolutist State*, 154–62; P. J. Jones, "Communes and Despots," 82–85, 92–94.
242. Arrighi, *The Long Twentieth Century*, 227.
243. Breuilly, *Nationalism and the State*, 3–4.
244. Gramsci, "The Renaissance," 226; Gramsci, *Prison Notebooks*, vol. 2, 366, Q5§123.
245. Gramsci, "The Question of the Language and the Italian Intellectual Classes," 169; Gramsci, *Prison Notebooks*, vol. 2, 74, Q3§76; Larner, *Italy in the Age of Dante*, 1–9.
246. Mielants, *The Origins of Capitalism and "the Rise of the West,"* 157.
247. Perry Anderson, "The Notion of a Bourgeois Revolution," 112.
248. Gareth Stedman Jones, "Society and Politics at the Beginning of the World Economy," 87.
249. Teich, "Afterword," 216.
250. Koenigsberger, "Republics and Courts in Italian and European Culture in the Sixteenth

and Seventeenth Centuries," 36–39, 54; Nauert, *Humanism and the Culture of the Renaissance*, 93–94.

251.   Gramsci, "The Renaissance," 229–230; Gramsci, *Prison Notebooks*, vol. 2, 369, Q5§123.

252.   Leff, *Heresy in the Later Middle Ages*, 606–707.

253.   Betts, "Social and Constitutional Development," 38–45; Norman Cohn, *The Pursuit of the Millennium*, 205–22; Klassen, "The Disadvantaged and the Hussite Revolution," 264–67. For a brief but useful discussion of the Hussite movement with the wider context of European peasant revolt, see Graus, "From Resistance to Revolt," 5, 7.

254.   Marshall, *Presbyters and Profits*, 250.

255.   Marx, *Capital*, vol. 1, 881–83.

256.   Israel, *The Dutch Republic*, 176.

257.   Marx, *Capital*, vol. 1, 172.

258.   Interestingly, Michael Mann, a sociologist who—the rhetoric of transcendence aside—owes far more to Weber than Marx, has claimed that Christianity in general, as an "ideological power network," began to play this role in Western Europe during the feudal epoch through a program of "normative pacification": "Without this ecumenical reorganization, neither markets, nor property ownership, nor 'rational restlessness' would have flowed so within these territories." See *The Sources of Social Power*, vol. 1, 506. See also the more extended discussion on 381–85. One of the problems with this claim, as Perry Anderson has remarked, is that Christianity was not coterminous with Western Europe: the Byzantine Church was also engaged in "normative pacification," yet it did not oversee a level of economic development comparable to the Roman Catholic Church. See "Michael Mann's Sociology of Power," 84–85.

259.   Marx, *Grundrisse*, 232.

260.   According to Karl Löwith, he did not engage directly with what Marx wrote (unsurprisingly, given the absence of such writing) but rather with the work of Rudolf Stammler, who had attempted to apply a Marxist analysis to the history of religion. See *Max Weber and Karl Marx*, 101.

261.   Max Weber, *The Protestant Ethic and the Spirit of Capitalism*, 172, 180, 91.

262.   Hans Baron, "A Sociological Interpretation of the Early Renaissance in Florence," 437.

263.   Marshall is quite right to insist, however, that in terms of their methodology, Marx and Weber cannot be reconciled. See *Presbyters and Profits*, 247–51. Interestingly, Weber goes out of his way to praise the work of the arch-revisionist, Eduard Bernstein, particularly in comparison with the "schematicism of [Karl] Kautsky." See *The Protestant Ethic and the Spirit of Capitalism*, 219, 258, 278.

264.   The position that holds that Protestantism was a justification for capitalism was introduced into the debate, not by a Marxist, but by the Christian Socialist Tawney in *Religion and the Rise of Capitalism*, first published in 1926. According to Tawney, "whatever its theological merits or defects, [Protestantism] was admirably designed to liberate economic energies, and to weld into a disciplined social force the rising bourgeoisie, conscious of the contrast between its own standards and those of a laxer world, proud of its vocation as the standard bearer of the economic virtues, and determined to indicate an open road for its own way of life by the use of every weapon, including political revolution and war, because the issue at stake was not merely convenience or self-interest, but the will of God." Tawney concludes his discussion with an aphorism that excellently summarizes his position: "Calvin did for the bourgeoisie of the sixteenth century what Marx did for the proletariat of the nineteenth." See *Religion and the Rise of Capitalism*, 119–20. It was this position, superimposed on Engels's claims for Calvinism as a revolutionary ideology, which became almost by default accepted as the Marxist interpretation of the Reformation. And not only by opponents of Marxism (who can usually be relied on to denounce it for "economic determinism"), but many who considered themselves to be Marxists, or at least influenced by Marxist theory. This was relatively easy in Britain, where Marxism

remained theoretically underdeveloped until after 1956, and where Tawney's powerful interpretation filled the gap in this area of intellectual history for decades.

265. The sources cited by Marshall regarding "Marx's and Engels' account of the relationship between Reformation and the rise of capitalism" are in fact both by Engels: *Socialism: Utopian and Scientific* and *Ludwig Feuerbach and the End of Classical German Philosophy*. See *Presbyters and Profits*, 367, note 55.

266. Engels, "On the Peasant War," 554.

267. Engels, *Ludwig Feuerbach and the End of Classical German Philosophy*, 396. Engels rightly takes the period of the English Revolution to span the events of both 1640–1660 and 1688–89. The notion that the latter ended in a "compromise" is, however, to assume that the nobility were still in some sense a feudal class, rather than one whose members were already largely engaged in capitalist landownership.

268. Mann, *The Sources of Social Power*, vol. 1, 465.

269. Cameron, *The European Reformation*, 199.

270. See the two classic accounts produced by Marxists of the Second International: Mehring, "The German Reformation and Its Consequences," 8, 23–24 and Kautsky, *Thomas More and His Utopia*, 59–60.

271. Trevor-Roper, "Religion, the Reformation and Social Change," 33.

272. Chadwick, *The Reformation*, 137.

273. Nischan, "Confessionalism and Absolutism," 181. The occasion for this outburst was the public declaration by Elector John Sigismund of Brandenburg on Christmas Day, 1613, of his conversion to Calvinism. Brandenburg was virtually the only German state where the ruler moved from Lutheranism to Calvinism, a transition that seems to have been inspired by his alliance with the Dutch and Palatine Calvinists, whose support he needed in the Julich-Cleves succession dispute. Such shifts in allegiance were only possible, however, once the initial division of the European state system on the denominational basis outlined above had taken place. See ibid., 181–85.

274. Skinner, "The Origins of the Calvinist Theory of Revolution," 314–26.

275. Heller, *The Conquest of Poverty*, 240, 247. It is in any case by no means certain that the Huguenot cause in France was the only one supported by "capitalist" elements in French society. Indeed, there is a good case for arguing that the Catholic Holy League, which seized power in Paris during 1584, had a more plebeian base and radical agenda than the Huguenots ever did. One analysis of the leadership of the Catholic League, "the Sixteen," shows them "to have been widely representative of the middle classes, with particular strength among the middle and lower ranks of the legal profession." See Salmon, "The Paris Sixteen," 549–50. For examples of their radicalism, see ibid., 552–53.

276. Gramsci, "Problems of Marxism," 394–95, Q16§9.

277. Trevor-Roper, "The Religious Origins of the Enlightenment," 233–35.

278. Spinoza, *Tractatus Theologicus-Politicus*, 53.

279. Pellicani, "Weber and the Myth of Calvinism," 72, 73, note 77. It is indicative that, during the latter half of the eighteenth century, when Scottish capitalism did begin its remarkable ascent, local Enlightenment thinkers were forced to reject the Calvinist legacy as much as the absolutist obscurantism of the Jacobites. See Davidson, "The Scottish Path to Capitalist Agriculture 3," 17–21.

280. Marshall, *Presbyteries and Profits*, 276.

281. Bertram, "International Competition in Historical Materialism," 119–20.

282. Ibid., 122.

283. Brenner, *Merchants and Revolution*, 708–9.

284. Paulin, "Introduction," 32.

285. Milton, *Paradise Lost*, Book XII, lines 506–24, 529–42. Christopher Hill argues that, taken in conjunction with Milton's other writings, these passages must be understood as referring to the emergence of apostasy at some—never exactly specified—point be-

tween the death and resurrection of Christ and the reign of the Emperor Constantine. But given that Milton had expected the English Revolution to produce the Rule of the Saints, there is no reason why the notion of betrayal could not embrace both the original apostasy and the subsequent failure of the English Revolution to reestablish the pristine purity of the church at the time of the Apostles. See *The Experience of Defeat*, 292–95.

22. Patterns of Consummation

1. Hobsbawm, "Revolution," 23–24.
2. Perry Anderson, "Civil War, Global Distemper," 251.
3. Chistozvonov, "The Concept and Criteria of Reversibility and Irreversibility of an Historical Process," 9–10.
4. Marx, *Grundrisse*, 106–7.
5. Rudra, "Pre-Capitalist Modes of Production in Non-European Societies," 366.
6. Ste. Croix, *The Class Struggle in Ancient Greek World*, 52.
7. Marx, *Capital*, vol. 1, 645–46, 1019–38.
8. Preobrazhensky, *The New Economics*, 185–86.
9. Lenin, "The Economic Content of Narodism and the Criticism of It in Mr. Struve's Book (The Reflection of Marxism in Bourgeois Literature)," 466.
10. Lenin, "New Data on the Laws Governing the Development of Capitalism in Agri-
culture," 22.
11. Banaji, "Modes of Production in a Materialist Conception of History," 50–52, 92–94; Marx, *Grundrisse*, 463. For a helpful summary of Banaji's occasionally opaque position, see Bakan, "Plantation Slavery and the Capitalist Mode of Production," 75–77. For a related analysis, but which emphasizes the benefits for capital of retaining precapitalist rural social relations of production, rather than the assimilation by the former of the latter, see Bernstein, *Class Dynamics of Agrarian Change*, 92–95.
12. Callinicos, "Trotsky's Theory of 'Permanent Revolution' and Its Relevance to the Third World Today," 110.
13. Gerstenberger, *Impersonal Power*, 7.
14. Barker, "The State as Capital," 20–23.
15. Ollman, "Why Does the Emperor Need the Yakuza?," 200.
16. Waswo, *Japanese Landlords*, 13.
17. Hobsbawm, "Revolution," 27.
18. Ellen Meiksins Wood, "The Separation of the Economic and Political in Capitalism," 81–82.
19. Draper, *Karl Marx's Theory of Revolution*, vol. 1, 321–24.
20. Adam Smith, *The Wealth of Nations*, Book I, 278.
21. Schmitt, "The Concept of the Political," 63 and 62–65, 71–72 more generally.
22. Bernard Porter, *Empire and Superempire*, 49.
23. Wallerstein, *Historical Capitalism*, 42.
24. Wilson, *Europe's Tragedy*, 347–61; Polisensky, *The Thirty Years' War*, 137–50, 244–53.
25. Kiernan, *State and Society in Europe*, 273.
26. Linden, "Marx and Engels, Dutch Marxism and the "Model Capitalist Nation of the Seventeenth Century'," 187.
27. Brenner, "The Agrarian Roots of European Capitalism," 325–26; Brenner, "The Low Countries and the Transition to Capitalism," 330–34; Hobsbawm, "The Crisis of the Seventeenth Century," 41–43; Kreidte, *Peasants, Landlords and Merchant Capitalists*, 87–91.
28. Gramsci, "The Renaissance," 223; Gramsci, *Prison Notebooks*, vol. 2, 363, Q5§123.
29. Daalder, "Consociationalism, Center and Periphery in the Netherlands," 182.
30. Greenfeld, *The Spirit of Capitalism*, 91.

31   Israel, *The Dutch Republic*, 276–84.
32.   Brandon, "Marxism and the 'Dutch Miracle,'" 141 and 135–41 more generally.
33.   James R. Jones, *The Anglo-Dutch Wars of the Seventeenth Century*, 7, 12.
34.   Hobsbawm, "The Crisis of the Seventeenth Century," 43.
35.   Adam Smith, *Lectures on Jurisprudence*, 265.
36.   Coveney, "An Early Modern European Crisis?," 21.
37.   Marx, *Capital*, vol. 1, 884. For a typical reaffirmation of this position, see Saville, *The Consolidation of the Capitalist State*, 6.
38.   Pinkus, 1688, 483, 484, 485.
39.   Roy Porter, *Enlightenment*, 27.
40.   Halliday, *Revolution and World Politics*, 185.
41.   Teschke, *The Myth of 1648*, 263.
42.   McLynn, *The Jacobites*, 29.
43.   Brewer, *The Sinews of Power*, 24 and 27–217 more generally. For an example of how Brewer's analysis of the British fiscal-military state has now entered mainstream historiography, see Hoppit, *A Land of Liberty?*, 124–31.
44.   Mooers, *The Making of Bourgeois Europe*, 161–62.
45.   McLynn, *1759*, 1, 391 and passim. For a more sober but essentially concurrent account, see Simms, *Three Victories and a Defeat*, chapter 16.
46.   Wallerstein, *The Modern World-System II*, 257.
47.   Lenman, *Britain's Colonial Wars*, 3.
48.   In fact, as Alex Callinicos argues, Britain was the last truly hegemonic capitalist power. See *Imperialism and Global Political Economy*, 142–44.
49.   Perry Anderson, "The Notion of a Bourgeois Revolution," 118.
50.   Armitage and Subrahmanyam, "Introduction: The Age of Revolutions," xiii and xii–xvi more generally. For a critique of earlier refusals to differentiate between revolutions, in this case those of the 1640s, see Lublinskaya, *French Absolutism*, 101.
51.   Israel, *Radical Enlightenment*, 515–27; David Parker, *Class and State in Ancien Regime France*, 208; Roy Porter, *Enlightenment*, 6–12.
52.   Lenman, *Britain's Colonial Wars*, 258–59.
53.   Mooers, *Making of Bourgeois Europe*, 93–94.
54.   Heller, *The Bourgeois Revolution in France*, 67–69, 70, 147.
55.   Mooers, *The Making of Bourgeois Europe*, 95.
56.   Fox-Genovese and Genovese, "The Political Crisis of Social History," 229.
57.   Heller, *The Bourgeois Revolution in France*, 54–60.
58.   Sewell, *A Rhetoric of Bourgeois Revolution*, 64.
59.   Foucault, "Truth and Power," 133.
60.   Chatterjee, *Nationalist Thought and the Colonial World*, 168.
61.   Ellen Meiksins Wood, *The Origin of Capitalism*, 190.
62.   Teich, "Afterword," 217.
63.   Israel, *Radical Enlightenment*, 71–72.
64.   Ibid., 11.
65.   Venturi, *Utopia and Reform in the Enlightenment*, 133.
66.   Robertson, *The Case for Enlightenment*, 391, 405.
67.   Pilbeam, *The Middle Classes in Europe*, 233.
68.   Gareth Stedman Jones, "Society and Politics at the Beginning of the World Economy," 87.
69.   Maza, *The Myth of the French Bourgeoisie*, 6, 7.
70.   Colin Jones, "Bourgeois Revolution Revivified."
71.   Greenfeld, *The Spirit of Capitalism*, 148.
72.   Shafer, "Bourgeois Nationalism in the Pamphlets on the Eve of the French Revolution," 47–48.
73.   Miliband, "Barnave," 46.

74.   Lucas, "Nobles, Bourgeois and the Origins of the French Revolution," 124–26.

75.   Robespierre, "Extracts from 'Answer to Louvet's Accusation,'" 43.

76.   Sewell, *A Rhetoric of Bourgeois Revolution*, 189; Marx, "The Eighteenth Brumaire of Louis Bonaparte," 146–50.

77.   Israel, *A Revolution of the Mind*, 232–33.

78.   Hoffman, *Growth in a Traditional Society*, 194.

79.   Heller, *The Bourgeois Revolution in France*, 88, 89.

80.   David Parker, *Class and State in Ancien Régime France*, 217.

81.   Friedrichs, "The War and German Society," 208–15.

82.   Hoffman, *Growth in a Traditional Society*, 198.

83.   Charles Post argues that capitalist plantation-agriculture was only established in the South by the end of the nineteenth century. See "Social Property Relations, Class Conflict and the Origins of the US Civil War," 275–77.

84.   McPherson, "The Second American Revolution," 10–11, 16.

85.   Heller, *The Bourgeois Revolution in France*, 94, 101, 102, 113, 137. See also Ado, *Paysans en révolution*, 433–34, 437; and Livesey, *Making Democracy in the French Revolution*, 101–2, 130.

86.   Nesbitt, *Universal Emancipation*, 172.

87.   Blanning, *The Pursuit of Glory*, 351.

88.   Schama, *Patriots and Liberators*, 12–15.

89.   Crouzet, "Western Europe and Great Britain," 342–43.

90.   Chateaubriand, *Memoires D'outre-Tombe*, vol. 3, 647.

91.   Marx to Nieuwenhuis, February 22, 1881.

92.   O'Brien, "The Impact of the Revolutionary and Napoleonic Wars," 383; O'Rourke, "The Worldwide Economic Impact of the French Revolutionary and Napoleonic Wars," 148–49.

93.   Darwin, *After Tamerlane*, 237 and 237–45 more generally.

94.   Davidson, "The Scottish Path to Capitalist Agriculture 2;" Davidson, "The Scottish Path to Capitalist Agriculture 3;" Davidson, "Scotland: Birthplace of Passive Revolution?"

95.   Blum, *The End of the Old Order in Rural Europe*, 372, 373, 376.

96.   Hobsbawm, *The Age of Capital*, 188.

97.   Bayly, *The Birth of the Modern World*, 298.

98.   Norman Stone, *Europe Transformed*, 17–18.

99.   Mann, *The Sources of Social Power*, vol. 2, 354.

100.   Hobsbawm, *Echoes of the Marseillaise*, 46.

101.   Beales, "Social Forces and Enlightened Policies," 9–10; Outram, *The Enlightenment*, 122–23.

102.   Marx, "The Eighteenth Brumaire of Louis Bonaparte," 241.

103.   Torras, "Peasant Counter-Revolution?," 74, 75.

104.   Fraser, *Napoleon's Cursed War*, 480.

105.   Duggan, *The Force of Destiny*, 121, 123.

106.   Hobsbawm, *The Age of Empire*, 21.

107.   Crouzet, "Western Europe and Great Britain," 344–45.

108.   Woolf, "The Construction of a European World-View in the Revolutionary-Napoleonic Years," 101.

109.   Mann, *Sources of Social Power*, vol. 2, 311.

110.   Bayly, *Birth of the Modern World*, 426–30.

111.   Nairn, "The Twilight of the British State," 49.

112.   Cannadine, "The Context, Performance and Meaning of Ritual," 120–50.

113.   Bukharin, *Imperialism and World Economy*, 128. These remarks were probably made in response to the Austrian attempts to explain imperialism as an effect of aristocratic influence on international politics. See, for an example, which postdates Bukharin's work,

Schumpeter, "The Sociology of Imperialisms," 84–97.

114. Mann, "Ruling Class Strategies and Citizenship," 200.

115. Shillory, "The Meiji Restoration," 20.

116. Marx, *Theories of Surplus Value*, vol. 2, 302.

117. Marx, *Capital*, vol. 1, 935 and see 931–40 more generally.

118. Marx, *Theories of Surplus Value*, vol. 2, 303.

119. Amin, *Class and Nation Historically and in the Current Crisis*, 21.

120. Luxemburg, *The Accumulation of Capital*, 369.

121. Dalziel, "Southern Islands," 589. The situation in South Africa was different from North America and Australasia in that the native population was not economically marginalized but became enmeshed in capitalist social relations, again during the last third of the nineteenth century. Some Marxists have claimed that the Zulu Kingdom in South Africa had become fully dominated by capitalist laws of motion by the end of the 1880s. See, for example, Guy, "The Destruction and Reconstruction of Zulu Society," 189–90.

122. Lynch, *The Spanish American Revolutions*, 340, 341.

123. Tapia, "Constitution and Constitutional Reform in Bolivia," 160.

124. Choonara, "The Relevance of Permanent Revolution," 181.

125. Knight, "The Mexican Revolution," 26.

126. Semo, *Historia Mexicana*, 299–315; Semo, "Reflexiones Sobre la Revolución Mexicana," 147, 148.

127. One of the problems with Semo's analysis is that he regards the Mexican experience as distinct from the rest of the continent, writing, "The difference between the Mexican bourgeoisie and that of other Latin American countries is that the former lost its revolutionary faculties after making ample use of them, while the others have never led and will never lead a bourgeois revolution." See *Historia Mexicana*, 305.

128. Gilly, *The Mexican Revolution*, 13, 15 and 11–17 more generally.

129. Dabat and Lorenzano, *Argentina*, 12 and 10–12 more generally.

130. Moore, *The Social Origins of Dictatorship and Democracy*, 112.

131. Post, "Social Property Relations, Class Conflict and the Origins of the US Civil War," 249. For similar arguments about the conformity of the Civil War to the orthodox model of bourgeois revolution, see Kulikoff, "Was the American Revolution a Bourgeois Revolution?," 64.

132. Novack, "Introduction," 15–17.

133. Kolchin, *American Slavery*, 99–105.

134. Fields, "Slavery, Race and Ideology in the United States of America," 108.

135. Allen, *The Invention of the White Race*, vol. 2, 249.

136. "The whole thing in Germany will depend on whether it is possible to back the proletarian revolution by some second edition of the Peasants' war. In which case the affair should go swimmingly." Marx to Engels, April 16, 1856.

137. Bowman, "Antebellum Planters and Vormarz Junkers in Comparative Perspective," 783, 785–86, 795, 806–7.

138. Tchakerian, "Productivity, Extent of Markets, and Manufacturing in the Late Antebellum South and Midwest," 519–20.

139. Kolchin, *American Slavery*, 153.

140. Bakan, "Plantation Slavery and the Capitalist Mode of Production," 86–91; Gavin Wright, "Capitalism and Slavery on the Islands," 865–73.

141. Turley, "Slave Emancipations in Modern History," 187–89.

142. Blackburn, *The Overthrow of Colonial Slavery*, 492–93.

143. Ransom and Sutch, "Capitalists without Capital," 138–39.

144. Berman, *Why America Failed*, 132.

145. Fogel, *Without Consent or Contract*, 414–15.

146. Gavin Wright, "Capitalism and Slavery on the Islands," 863.

147. Beard, *The Rise of American Civilization*, vol. 2, 115.
148. McPherson, *Battle Cry of Freedom*, 861.
149. Davidson, *Discovering the Scottish Revolution*, 272–75.
150. Ashworth, *Capitalism, and Politics in the Antebellum Republic*, vol. 2, 639, 640.
151. Creighton, *The Commercial Empire of the St. Lawrence*, 222.
152. Bernier and Sallee, *The Shaping of Quebec Politics and Society*, 100.
153. Creighton, *The Commercial Empire of the St. Lawrence*, 273.
154. Martin, *Britain and the Origins of Canadian Confederation*, 294.
155. Creighton, *The Road to Confederation*, 110.
156. Whitelaw, "Reconstructing the Quebec Conference," 134.
157. Creighton, *The Road to Confederation*, 145.
158. Reed, *Ten Days That Shook the World*, 129; Trotsky, *The History of the Russian Revolution*, 1168.
159. Fanon, *The Wretched of the Earth*, 143–44.
160. Cabral, "A Brief Analysis of the Social Structure in Guinea," 52.
161. Davidson, "China: Unevenness, Combination, Revolution?," 216–22; Harvey, *A Brief History of Neoliberalism*, 120–35.
162. D'Amato, "The Necessity of Permanent Revolution."
163. Marx and Engels, *The German Ideology*, 48–54.
164. Dadoo, "Introduction," xvii–xviii.
165. Vanaik, "Subcontinental Strategies," 113.
166. Slovo, "South Africa—No Middle Road," 142–43.
167. See, for example, Johnson, "False Start in South Africa," and the response by Patrick Bond, "In Power in Pretoria?"
168. Kingsnorth, *One No, Many Yeses*, 119.
169. Ibid., 118.
170. Webber, *From Rebellion to Reform in Bolivia*, 153–236.
171. García Linera, "The MAS is of the Center-Left."
172. Choonara, "The Relevance of Permanent Revolution," 174–75.
173. In an article published in English around the time of his appointment to the Bolivian vice-presidency, García Linera set out alternative outcomes of a "revolutionary epoch": one "a restoration of the old regime (coup d'etat)," the other, "a negotiated and peaceful modification of the political system through the partial or substantial incorporation of the insurgents and their proposals for change into the power bloc." The relevance of the second outcome to his situation scarcely needs emphasis. See "State Crisis, Popular Power," 82.
174. Choonara, "The Relevance of Permanent Revolution," 182.
175. Goodwin, *No Other Way Out*, 298, 302, and 293–306 more generally.
176. Klooster, *Revolutions in the Atlantic World*, 158.
177. Harman, "The Prophet and the Proletariat," 344.
178. Binns, "Revolution and State Capitalism in the Third World," 42–43.
179. McDaniel, *Autocracy, Capitalism and Revolution in Russia*, 41–47.
180. Ibid., 407.
181. Davis, "Sand, Fear and Money in Dubai," 53–54. Indeed, in the case of China, it might be said that the neoliberal turn after 1978 actually resumed the process of uneven and combined development originally detected by Trotsky in the 1920s, which had been consciously halted by a Maoist leadership only too conscious of the explosive effects of uncontrolled urban expansion. See Davidson, "China: Unevenness, Combination, Revolution?" 214–16.
182. Silver, *Forces of Labor*, 164.
183. Ginsborg, *A History of Contemporary Italy*, 47–53, 223–29; Hardt and Negri, *Empire*, 287–89.

184.   Luttwak, *Turbo-capitalism*, 25–26.
185.   Halliday, *Revolution and World Politics*, 320–21.
186.   Milton, *Paradise Lost*, Book XII, line 646.
187.   Auden, "Spain," 136.

EPILOGUE: REFLECTIONS IN A SCOTTISH CEMETERY

1.   Campbell, *Standing Witnesses*, 90, 91.
2.   Davidson, *Discovering the Scottish Revolution*, 131–56.
3.   Horne, *The Great Museum*, 74.
4.   Ibid., 80–81.
5.   For Edinburgh, see Youngson, *The Making of Classical Edinburgh*, 59–65; for Paris, see Benjamin, "Convolute E," and Harvey, *Paris*, 125–40, 142–44.
6.   Robin, "The First Counter-revolutionary," 67–73.
7.   Hume, *A Treatise of Human Nature*, 156. See also ibid., 193.
8.   Max Weber, *Economy and Society*, vol. 1, 24–26.
9.   Hume, *A Treatise of Human Nature*, Books 2 and 3, 159.
10.   Horkheimer, "The End of Reason," 30. This is not the only aspect of Hume's work that depends on assuming a community of interest; so too does his moral philosophy and it is consequently open to the same critique. Alasdair MacIntyre writes: "We have moral rules because we have common interests. Should someone succeed in showing us that the facts are different from what we conceive them to be so that we have no common interests, then our moral rules would lose their justification. Indeed, the initial move of Marx's moral theory can perhaps be understood as a denial that there are common interests shared by the whole of society in respect of, for instance, the distribution of property meets Hume on his own ground." See "Hume on 'Is' and 'Ought,'" 116.
11.   Ritzer, *The McDonaldization of Society*, 121–42. This was a venerable theme of the Frankfurt School. See, for example, Marcuse, "Industrialization and Capitalism," 207.
12.   Trotsky, "Fragments from the First Seven Months of the War," 879.
13.   Gamble, *Hayek*, 32–33.
14.   Hayek, *The Fatal Conceit*, 136.
15.   Spinoza, *Tractatus Theologicus-Politicus*, 297.
16.   Ibid., 56.
17.   Voltaire to D'Alembert, September 2, 1768, 112.
18.   Siegel, *The Meek and the Militant*, 22.
19.   Hume, *A Treatise of Human Nature*, chapter 10.
20.   Hume, "Of Interest," 130–31.
21.   Hirschman, *The Passions and the Interests*, 66.
22.   Ibid., 130, 131.
23.   Ibid., 132–35.
24.   Peck, *Constructions of Neoliberal Reason*, 7–8.
25.   Lukács, "The Changing Function of Historical Materialism," 225. For a more recent judgment along similar lines, see Gerstenberger, *Impersonal Power*, 686.
26.   Robertson, "The Enlightenment above National Context," 697; Rothschild, *Economic Sentiments*, 16.
27.   McPherson, *Battle Cry of Freedom*, 326.
28.   Douglass, "The Future of the Colored Race," 196. See also, Douglass, "Why Should a Colored Man Enlist?," 341. For the original poem, see Burns, "A Man's a Man," 512–16.
29.   Twain, *Life on the Mississippi*, 46.
30.   Hook, "Scott and America," 103–10; Hook, "The South, Scotland, and William Faulkner," 193–201.

31. McPherson, *For Cause and Comrades*, 27.
32. Schurz, "Report on the Condition of the South," 354.
33. See, for example, Foner, *Reconstruction* ("unfinished revolution") and Camejo, *Racism, Revolution, Reaction* ("Republican betrayal").
34. McPherson, *The Struggle for Equality*, 430–31.
35. Luraghi, "The Civil War and the Modernization of American Society," 233–34, 242.
36. Lowe, *Immigrant Acts*, 27–28.
37. Milner II, "National Initiatives," 179–80.
38. Furet, "Terror," 458–59; Soboul, *The French Revolution*, 342.
39. Corish, "The Cromwellian Conquest," 339–42; Ohlmeyer, "The Civil Wars in Ireland," 98–99.
40. Raymond Williams, *The Country and the City*, 50–51.
41. Wallerstein, *Historical Capitalism*, 40.
42. Griffiths, *Pip Pip*, 185, 193–95.
43. Burbach, *Globalization and Postmodern Politics*, 85, 86–87.
44. Bookchin, *Remaking Society*, 89.
45. Wallerstein, *Historical Capitalism*, 40.
46. Wallerstein, "Eurocentrism and Its Avatars," 104–5.
47. Armstrong, "Back to the Future—Part Two," 35.
48. Bookchin, *The Ecology of Freedom*, 87.
49. Bookchin, *The Third Revolution*, vol. 1, ix.
50. Linebaugh and Rediker, *The Many-Headed Hydra*, 26.
51. McMurtry, *The Cancer Stage of Capitalism*, 204–5, 213.
52. Blackburn, *The Making of New World Slavery*, 15.
53. Patterson, *Inventing Western Civilization*, 132.
54. Neil Young with Crazy Horse, "Cortez the Killer."
55. Patterson, *The Inca Empire*, 157–65.
56. Perry Anderson, *Passages from Antiquity to Feudalism*, 148–50; Graus, "From Resistance to Revolt," 3; Marx, *Capital*, vol. 1, 885.
57. Christopher Hill, *The World Turned Upside Down*, 15.
58. Holstun, *Ehud's Dagger*, 24–25.
59. Ibid., ix.
60. Ibid., 89.
61. Holstun, "Utopia Pre-empted," 40. In this text Holstun is more circumspect about the ability of what he calls "monarcho-populism" to "graft a progressive small production onto a benevolent despotism that would help check capitalist forces." See ibid., 41.
62. Linebaugh, "Review of *The Making of New World Slavery*," 192.
63. Holstun, "Communism, George Hill and the *Mir*," 137.
64. Manning, *1649*, 109–34.
65. Armstrong, "Back to the Future—Part Two," 36.
66. Gareth Stedman Jones, "Society and Politics at the Beginning of the World Economy," 87.
67. Ennew, Hirst, and Tribe, "'Peasantry' as an Economic Category," 309–10.
68. Luxemburg, *The Accumulation of Capital*, 368–71, 402, 416.
69. Marx and Engels, "The Manifesto of the Communist Party," 68.
70. Marx, *Capital*, vol. 1, 915, 918.
71. Marx, *The Poverty of Philosophy*, 174–78.
72. Jameson, "The Cultural Logic of Late Capitalism," 47.
73. Linebaugh and Rediker, *The Many-Headed Hydra*, 352–53.
74. Edward P. Thompson, *The Making of the English Working Class*, 12.
75. Bookchin, *The Third Revolution*, vol. 1, 12–13. As a example of Bookchin's rather uncertain grasp of the Marxist attitude to these revolutions, it is worth noting that, in relation to the German Peasant War, Lukács certainly highlighted the tactical inadequacy

of the peasants, which he ascribed to problems in forming a fully revolutionary consciousness, but which scarcely suggests that he regarded them as "reactionaries." See Lukács, "Class Consciousness," 53 and "Tailism and the Dialectic," 86–94.

76. Bensaïd, *Marx for Our Times*, 54.
77. Davidson, *Discovering the Scottish Revolution*, 290–94.
78. Marx, *Capital*, vol. 1, 926.
79. Israel, *Democratic Enlightenment*, 951. Unfortunately this final volume appeared in print too late for me to make full use of it here.
80. Gramsci to Carlo, December 19, 1929. See also, Gramsci, "The Modern Prince," 175 and Gramsci, *Prison Notebooks*, vol. 3, 73, Q6§86. It should be noted that this was a personal credo, not the voluntaristic slogan—"pessimism of the intellect, optimism of the will"—it has subsequently become.
81. Gordon, "On the Supposed Obsolescence of the French Enlightenment," 204.
82. Callinicos, *Social Theory*, 56.
83. Marx and Engels, "The Manifesto of the Communist Party," 85, 73.
84. Jefferson, "The Unanimous Declaration of the Thirteen United States of America," 4.
85. Bérubé, "It's Renaissance Time," 205.
86. Eagleton, *The Illusions of Postmodernism*, 113.
87. Douglass, "The Meaning of July Fourth for the Negro," 192, 200, 201.
88. Douglass, "The Constitution of the United States," 477.
89. Buck Morss, "Hegel and Haiti," 865.
90. Morris, "A Dream of John Ball," 31. A. C. Bradley, a very different Victorian thinker than Morris, saw the inevitability of people to accomplish their intended goals as the very essence of tragedy: "The tragic world is a world of action, and action is the translation of thought into reality. We see men and women confidently attempt it. They strike into the existing order of things in pursuance of their ideas. But what they achieve is not what they intend; it is terribly unlike it. . . . They fight blindly in the dark, and the power that works through them makes them the instrument of a design which is not theirs." Bradley, *Shakespearean Tragedy*, 27.
91. Ogilvie, *An Essay on the Right of Property in Land*, 191.
92. Adam Ferguson, *An Essay on the History of Civil Society*, 8.

BIBLIOGRAPHY

Works are listed chronologically by date of original publication. Where this differs from the edition cited, it is shown after the author's first name in square brackets, except in the case of Gramsci's prison notebooks, where precise dating is not always possible. Where the date of composition significantly differs from the date of publication, as in the cases of Smith's *Lectures on Jurisprudence* or Marx's *Grundrisse*, I have used the former, but not where only a few years are involved. Author's names have been given in the style that was in use at the time a work was published, even if this has subsequently changed (hence Georgi Dimitroff and Mao Tse-tung rather than Georgi Dimitrov and Mao Zedong). In the case of unsigned newspaper or magazine articles, state documents, or records of meetings, the publication is listed as the author. URLs have been listed here only where an item exists solely in electronic format, otherwise the published version has been given. In keeping with tradition, I have not included specific editions of works by William Shakespeare or John Milton.

A French Draft Constitution of 1792 Modeled on James Harrington's Oceana: *Theodor Lesueur, Idées sur l'étendue et de la population présume de la France*, edited by S. B. Liljegren. Lund and London: C. W. K. Gleerup and Oxford University Press, 1932.

Abbott, Andrew [1997]. "On the Concept of Turning Point." In *Time Matters: On Theory and Method*, 240–60. Chicago: Chicago University Press, 2001.

Abu-Loghod, Janet L. *Before European Hegemony: The World System, 1250–1350*. New York: Oxford University Press, 1989.

Acemoglu, Daron and James Robinson. "Why Did the West Extend the Franchise? Democracy, Inequality, and Growth in Historical Perspective," *Quarterly Journal of Economics* (November 2000): 1167–99.

Acton, Lord (John E. E. D.) [1899–1901]. "The Puritan Revolution." In *Lectures on Modern History*, edited by John Neville Figgis and Reginald Vere Lawrence, 195–205. London: Macmillan, 1906.

———. "The English Revolution." In *Lectures on Modern History*, edited by John Neville Figgis and Reginald Vere Lawrence, 219–32. London: Macmillan, 1906.

Acts of the Parliament of Scotland and the Government of the Commonwealth, vol. 6, part 2, *1648–1660*, edited by Thomas Thomson and Cosmo Innes. Edinburgh: General Register House, 1872.

Adams, John [1765]. "A Dissertation on the Canon and Feudal Law." In *The Works of John Adams, Second President of the United States: With a Life of the Author, Notes and Illustrations, by His Grandson Charles F. Adams*, vol. 3, *Autobiography, Diary, Notes of a Debate in the Senate, Essays*, edited by Charles F. Adams, 447–62. Boston: Charles C. Little and James Brown, 1851.

——— [1815]. Adams to Jefferson, November 13, 1815. In *The Adams-Jefferson Letters: The Complete Correspondence between Thomas Jefferson and Abigail and John Adams*, vol. 2, edited by Lester J. Capon. Chapel Hill: University of North Carolina Press, 1959.

Ado, Anatoli [1971]. *Paysans en révolution: terre, pouvoir et jacquerie, 1789–1794*. Paris: Société des Etudes Robespierristes, 1996.

Ahmad, Aijaz. "Marx on India: A Clarification." In *In Theory: Classes, Nations, Literature*, 221–42. London: Verso, 1992.

Aiton, William. *A History of the Rencounter at Drumclog and the Battle of Bothwell Bridge in the Month of June, 1679, with an Account of What Is Correct, and What Is Fictitious in* The Tales of My Landlord *Respecting These Engagements, and Reflections on Political Subjects*. Hamilton: W. D. Borthwick, 1821.

Albert, Michael. *Parecon: Life after Capitalism*. London: Verso, 2003.

Ali, Tariq. *Street Fighting Years: An Autobiography of the Sixties*. London: Collins, 1987.

Allen, James [Sol Auerbach]. *The Negro Question in the United States*. New York: International Publishers, 1936.

———. *Reconstruction: The Battle for Democracy, 1865–1876*. New York: International Publishers, 1937.

Allen, Keiran. *The Politics of James Connolly*. London: Pluto Press, 1990.

Allen, Theodore. *The Invention of the White Race*, vol. 2, *The Origin of Racial Oppression in Anglo-America*. London: Verso, 1997.

Allinson, Jamie and Alexander Anievas. "The Uses and Misuses of Uneven and Combined Development: An Anatomy of a Concept," *Cambridge Review of International Affairs* 22, no. 1 (March 2009): 47–67.

———. "The Uneven and Combined Development of the Meiji Restoration: A Passive Revolutionary Road to Capitalist Modernity," in *Capital and Class* 34, no. 3, special issue on *Approaching Passive Revolutions*, edited by Adam David Morton (October 2010): 469–90.

Althusser, Louis [1965]. "Contradiction and Overdetermination," *New Left Review* 1, no. 41 (January–February 1967): 15–35.

——— [1976]. *Machiavelli and Us*. London: Verso, 1999.

——— [1982–83]. "The Underground Current of the Materialism of the Encounter." In *Philosophy of the Encounter. Later Writings, 1978–1987*, edited by Francois Matheron and Olivier Corpet, 163–207. London: Verso, 2006.

Amin, Samir [1973]. *Unequal Development: An Essay on the Social Formations of Peripheral Capitalism*. Hassocks: Harvester Press, 1976.

———. *Class and Nation Historically and in the Current Crisis*. New York: Monthly Review Press, 1980.

Amin, Shahid and Marcel van der Linden. "Introduction," *International Review of Social History* 41, Supplement 4, *Peripheral Labor: Studies in the History of Partial Proletarianization* (June 1997): 1–7.

Anderson, Fulton H. *The Philosophy of Francis Bacon*. Chicago: University of Chicago Press, 1948.

Anderson, Kevin B. *Marx at the Margins: On Nationalism, Ethnicity, and Non-Western Societies*. Chicago: Chicago University Press, 2010.

Anderson, Perry [1964]. "Origins of the Present Crisis." In *English Questions*, 15–47. London: Verso, 1992.

———. "Problems of Socialist Strategy." In *Towards Socialism*, edited for the *New Left Review* by Perry Anderson and Robin Blackburn, 221–90. London: Fontana, 1965.

———. "Socialism and Pseudo-Empiricism," *New Left Review* 1, no. 35 (January–February 1966): 2–42.

———. *Passages from Antiquity to Feudalism*. London: New Left Books, 1974.

———. *Lineages of the Absolutist State*. London: New Left Books, 1974.

——— [1976]. "The Notion of a Bourgeois Revolution." In *English Questions*, 105–18. London: Verso, 1992.

———. *Considerations on Western Marxism*. London: New Left Books, 1976.

———. "The Antinomies of Antonio Gramsci," *New Left Review* 1, no. 100 (November 1976–January 1977): 5–78.

———. *Arguments within English Marxism*. London: Verso, 1980.

———[1983]. "Trotsky's Interpretation of Stalinism," *New Left Review* 1, no. 139 (May/June 1983): 49–58.

———. *In the Tracks of Historical Materialism: The Wellek Library Lectures*. London: Verso, 1983.

——— [1983], "Geoffrey de Ste Croix and the Ancient World." In *A Zone of Engagement*, 1–24. London: Verso, 1992.

——— [1983–85]. "Marshall Berman: Modernity and Revolution" and "Postscript." In *A Zone of Engagement*, 25–55. London: Verso, 1992.

——— [1986]. "Michael Mann's Sociology of Power." In *A Zone of Engagement*, 76–86. London: Verso, 1992

———[1987]. "The Figures of Descent." In *English Questions*, 15–47. London: Verso, 1992.

———. "Foreword." In *English Questions*. London: Verso, 1992.

———. "The Ends of History." In *A Zone of Engagement*, 279–375. London: Verso, 1992.

——— [2004]. "France I." In *The New Old World*, 137–87. London: Verso, 2009.

Andrews, Charles M. [1938]. "A Note on the Economic Interpretation." In *The Causes of the American Revolution*, edited by John H. Wahlke, 18–21. Revised edition, Boston: D. C. Heath and Company, 1966.

Annan, Noel. *Our Age: Portrait of a Generation*. London: Weidenfeld and Nicolson, 1990.

Appleby, Joyce. *The Relentless Revolution: A History of Capitalism*. New York: W. W. Norton, 2010.

Arblaster, Anthony. *The Rise and Decline of European Liberalism*. Oxford: Basil Blackwell, 1984.

———. *Viva la Libertad! Politics in Opera*. London: Verso, 1992.

Arendt, Hannah [1963]. *On Revolution*. Harmondsworth: Penguin, 1973.

Aristotle, *The Politics*, edited by Stephen Everson. Cambridge: Cambridge University Press, 1988.

Armitage, David and Sanjay Subrahmanyam. "Introduction: The Age of Revolutions, c. 1760–1840—Global Causation, Connection and Comparisons." In *The Age of Revolutions in Global Context, c. 1760–1840*, xii–xxxii. London: Palgrave Macmillan, 2010.

Armstrong, Alan. "Back to the Future—Part Two: 1492 and 1992—Redemption, Improvement and Progress," *Cencrastus* 51 (Spring 1995): 35–40.

Armstrong, Phillip, Andrew Glynn, and John Harrison. *Capitalism since World War II: The Making and Breakup of the Great Boom*. London: Fontana, 1984.

Arrighi, Giovanni. *The Long Twentieth Century: Money, Power and the Origins of Our Times*, London: Verso, 1994.

———. *Adam Smith in Beijing*. London: Verso, 2007.

Ashcraft, Richard. *Locke's Two Treatises of Civil Government*. London: Unwin Hyman, 1987.

Ashton, Robert [1978]. *The English Civil War: Conservatism and Revolution, 1603–1649*. Second edition, London: Weidenfeld and Nicolson, 1989.

Ashtor, Eliyahu. *A Social and Economic History of the Near East in the Middle Ages*. London: Collins, 1976.

Ashworth, John. *Slavery, Capitalism, and Politics in the Antebellum Republic*, vol. 1, *Commerce and Compromise, 1820–1850*. Cambridge: Cambridge University Press, 1995.

————, *Slavery, Capitalism, and Politics in the Antebellum Republic*, vol. 2, *The Coming of the Civil War, 1850–1861*. Cambridge: Cambridge University Press, 2007.

Asmodeus: Or, Strictures on the Glasgow Democrats: In a Series of Letters Several of Which Were Lately Published in the Glasgow Courier. Glasgow: Printed and Sold by D. Niven, 1793.

Aubrey, John [1669–1996]. "James Harrington." In *Aubrey's Brief Lives*, edited by Oliver Lawson Dick, 124–27. London: Secker and Warburg, 1949.

Auden, W. H. [1937]. "Spain." In *Poetry of the Thirties*, edited by Robin Skelton, 133–36. Harmondsworth: Penguin, 1964.

Augustine [c. 420]. *Concerning the City of God against the Pagans*. Harmondsworth: Penguin, 1972.

Axelrod, Pavel B. [1906]. "Axelrod's Speech at the Fourth Party Congress." In *The Mensheviks and the Russian Revolution*, edited by Abraham Ascher, 59–64. London: Thames and Hudson, 1976.

Babeuf, Gracchus [1796]. "Manifesto of the Equals." In *Revolution from 1789 to 1906*, edited by Raymond Postgate, 54–56. London: Grant Richards, 1920.

Bacon, Francis [1620]. *The New Organon*, edited by Lisa Jardine and Michael Silverthorne. Cambridge: Cambridge University Press, 2000.

———— [1622]. *The History of the Reign of King Henry VII*, edited by Brian Vickers. Cambridge: Cambridge University Press, 1999.

Bailyn, Bernard. *The Ideological Origins of the American Revolution*. Cambridge, MA: Harvard University Press, 1967.

Bakan, Abigail. "Plantation Slavery and the Capitalist Mode of Production: An Analysis of the Development of the Jamaican Labour Force," *Studies in Political Economy* 22 (1987): 73–99.

Balakrishnan, Gopal. "From Florence to Moscow." In *Antagonistics: Capitalism and Power in an Age of War*, 253–62. London: Verso, 2009.

Balibar, Étienne [1965]. "The Basic Concepts of Historical Materialism." In Louis Althusser and Étienne Balibar, *Reading Capital*, 199–308. London: New Left Books, 1970.

———— [1995]. *The Philosophy of Marx*. London: Verso, 2007.

Baltrop, Robert. *The Monument: The Story of the Socialist Party of Great Britain*. London: Pluto Press, 1975.

Balzac, Honoré de [1833–1835]. "The Duchess de Langeais." In *History of the Thirteen*, 157–308. Harmondsworth: Penguin, 1974.

Banaji, Jairus [1977]. "Modes of Production in a Materialist Conception of History." In *Theory as History: Essays on Modes of Production and Exploitation*, 45–102. Leiden: E. J. Brill, 2010.

————. "Gunder Frank in Retreat?" *Journal of Peasant Studies*, 7, no. 4 (July 1980): 508–21.

———— [2003]. "The Fictions of Free Labour: Contract, Coercion, and So-Called Unfree Labour." In *Theory as History: Essays on Modes of Production and Exploitation*, 131–54. Leiden: E. J. Brill, 2010.

————. "Introduction: Themes in Historical Materialism." In *Theory as History: Essays on Modes of Production and Exploitation*, 1–44. Leiden: E. J. Brill, 2010.

————. "Modes of Production: A Synthesis." In *Theory as History: Essays on Modes of Production and Exploitation*, 349–60. Leiden: E. J. Brill, 2010.

Baran, Paul and Paul M. Sweezy, *Monopoly Capital: An Essay on the American Economic and Social Order*. New York: Monthly Review Press, 1966.

Barker, Colin. "The State as Capital," *International Socialism*, second series, 1 (July 1978): 16–42.

————. "Japan: Background and Significance of the Meiji Restoration of 1868," unpublished paper, Department of Social Science, Manchester Polytechnic, February 1, 1982.

Barker, Colin and Colin Mooers. "Theories of Revolution in the Light of 1989 in Eastern Europe," *Cultural Dynamics* 9, no. 1 (March 1997): 17–43.

Barkey, Karen and Rudi Batzell. "Comparisons across Empires: The Critical Social Structures of the Ottomans, Russians and Habsburgs during the Seventeenth Century." In *Trib-*

utary Empires in Global History, edited by Peter Fibiger Bang and Christopher A. Bayly, 227–61. Houndmills: Palgrave Macmillan, 2011.

Barnave, Antoine-Pierre-Joseph-Marie [1792–3]. "Introduction to the French Revolution." In *Power, Property and History: Barnave's* Introduction to the French Revolution *and Other Writings*, edited by Emanuel Chill, 75–131. New York: Harper Torchbooks, 1971.

Barnet, Anthony. "After Nationalism." In *Patriotism: The Making and Unmaking of British National Identity*, vol. 1, *History and Politics*, edited by Raphael Samuel, 140–55. London: Routledge, 1989.

Baron, Hans. "A Sociological Interpretation of the Early Renaissance in Florence," *South Atlantic Quarterly* 38, no. 4 (October 1939): 427–48.

Baron, Samuel H. *Plekhanov: The Father of Russian Marxism*. London: Routledge and Kegan Paul, 1963.

Barruel, Augustin. *Mémoires pour Server a l'histoire du Jacobinisme*, vol. 1. London: printed for T. Burton, 1798.

Bates, David. "Political Pathologies: Barnave and the Question of National Identity in Revolutionary France," *Canadian Journal of History* 36, no. 3 (December 2001): 427–52.

Bauer, Otto [1907]. *The Question of Nationalities and Social Democracy*, edited by Ephraim. J. Nimni. Minneapolis: University of Minnesota Press, 2000.

Bayly, Christopher A. *Indian Society and the Making of the British Empire*, vol. 2.1 of *The New Cambridge History of India*. Cambridge: Cambridge University Press, 1988.

———. *The Birth of the Modern World, 1780–1914: Global Connections and Comparisons*. Oxford: Blackwell, 2004.

B-de, Monsieur. *Reflections on the Causes and Probable Consequences of the Late Revolution in France, with a View of the Ecclesiastical and Civil Constitution of Scotland, and of the Progress of Its Agriculture and Commerce*. Dublin: W. Wilson, et al., 1790.

Beales, Derek E. D [1987]. "Social Forces and Enlightened Policies." In *Enlightenment and Reform in Eighteenth-Century Europe*, 7–27. London: I. B. Tauris, 2005.

Beard, Charles and Mary Beard [1927]. *The Rise of American Civilization*. 2 volumes in 1, new edition, revised and enlarged, New York: Macmillan, 1935.

Beevor, Anthony [1982]. *The Battle for Spain: The Spanish Civil War, 1936–1939*. second, expanded edition, London: Weidenfeld and Nicolson, 2006.

Beik, William. "Response to Henry Heller's 'The Longue Durée of the French Revolution,'" *Historical Materialism* 18, no. 2 (2010): 117–22.

Bell, David. "Class Consciousness, and the Fall of the Bourgeois Revolution," *Critical Review* 16, nos 2/3 (2004): 323–51.

Bennassar, Bartolomé. "Consommation, Investissements, Mouvements de Capitaux en Castille aux XVI' et XVII' Siècles." In *Conjoncture Economique, Structures Socials: Hommage a Ernest Labrousse*, edited by Fernand Braudel et al., 139–55. Paris, Mouton, 1974.

Benjamin, Walter [1927–40]. "Convolute E: [Haussmannization, Barricade Fighting]." In *The Arcades Project*, edited by Rolf Tiedemann, 120–49. Cambridge, MA: Belknap Press of Harvard University Press, 1999.

——— [1927–40]. "Convolute K: [Dream City and Dream House, Dreams of the Future, Anthropological Nihilism, Jung]." In *The Arcades Project*, edited by Rolf Tiedemann, 388–415. Cambridge, MA: Belknap Press of Harvard University Press, 1999.

——— [1927–40]. "Convolute N: [On the Theory of Knowledge, Theory of Progress]." In *The Arcades Project*, edited by Rolf Tiedemann, 456–88. Cambridge, MA: Belknap Press of Harvard University Press, 1999.

——— [1928]. "Goethe." In *Selected Writings*, vol. 2, part 1, *1927–1930*, edited by Michael W. Jennings, Howard Eiland, and Gary Smith, 161–93. Cambridge, MA: Belknap Press of Harvard University Press, 2003.

——— [1927]. "Moscow." In *Selected Writings*, vol. 2, part 1, *1927–1930*, edited by Michael

W. Jennings, Howard Eiland, and Gary Smith, 22–46. Cambridge, MA: Belknap Press of Harvard University Press, 2003.

——— [1935]. "Paris, Capital of the Nineteenth Century." In *The Arcades Project*, edited by Rolf Tiedemann, 3–13. Cambridge, MA: Belknap Press of Harvard University Press, 1999.

——— [1939]. "Paris, Capital of the Nineteenth Century." In *The Arcades Project*, edited by Rolf Tiedemann, 14–26. Cambridge, MA: Belknap Press of Harvard University Press, 1999.

——— [1940]. Benjamin to Scholem, January 11, 1940. In *The Correspondence of Walter Benjamin and Gershom Scholem, 1932–1940*, edited by Gershom Scholem, 262–64. Cambridge, MA: Harvard University Press, 1992.

——— [1940]. "'The Regression of Poetry,' by Carl Gustav Jochman." In *Selected Writings*, vol. 4, *1938–40*, edited by Howard Eiland and Michael W. Jennings, 356–78. Cambridge, MA: Belknap Press of Harvard University Press, 2003.

——— [1940]. "On the Concept of History." In *Selected Writings*, vol. 4, *1938–1940*, edited by Howard Eiland and Michael W. Jennings, 389–400. Cambridge, MA: Belknap Press of Harvard University Press, 2003.

———[1940]. "Paralipomena to 'On the Concept of History.'" In *Selected Writings*, vol. 4, *1938–40*, edited by Howard Eiland and Michael W. Jennings, 401–11. Cambridge, MA: Belknap Press of Harvard University Press, 2003.

———[1940]. "Survey of French Literature," *New Left Review* 2, no. 51 (May/June): 31–45.

Bensaïd, Daniel. *Marx for Our Times: Adventures and Misadventures of a Critique*. London: Verso, 2002.

Berger, John. *Success and Failure of Picasso*. Harmondsworth: Penguin, 1965.

Bergman, Jay. "The Perils of Historical Analogy: Leon Trotsky and the French Revolution," *Journal of the History of Ideas* 48, no. 1 (January–March 1987): 73–98.

Berktay, Halil. "The Feudalism Debate: The Turkish End—Is 'Tax-versus-Rent' Necessarily the Product and Sign of a Modal Difference?" *Journal of Peasant Studies* 14, no. 3 (April 1987): 291–333.

Berman, Morris. *Why America Failed: The Roots of Imperial Decline*. Hoboken, NJ: John Wiley and Sons, 2012.

Bernier, Gerald and Daniel Sallee. *The Shaping of Quebec Politics and Society: Colonialism, Power, and the Transition to Capitalism in the 19th Century*. Washington DC: Taylor and Francis, 1999.

Bernstein, Henry. *Class Dynamics of Agrarian Change*. Halifax, Nova Scotia and Sterling, Virginia: Fernwood Publishing and Kumarian Press, 2010.

Bertram, Christopher. "International Competition in Historical Materialism," *New Left Review* 1, no. 183 (September/October 1980): 116–28.

Bernstein, Edward [1895]. *Cromwell and Communism: Socialism and Democracy in the Great English Revolution*. Nottingham: Spokesman, 1980.

Berry, Christopher J. *Social Theory and the Scottish Enlightenment*. Edinburgh: Edinburgh University Press, 1997.

Bérubé, Michael. "Its Renaissance Time: New Historicism, American Studies, and American Identity." In *Public Access: Literary Theory and American Cultural Politics*, 203–24. New York: Verso, 1994.

Betts, R. R. "Social and Constitutional Development in Bohemia in the Hussite Period," *Past and Present* 7 (April 1955): 37–54.

Binns, Peter. "Revolution and State Capitalism in the Third World," *International Socialism*, second series, 25 (Autumn 1984): 37–68.

Birchall, Ian H. *The Specter of Babeuf*. Houndmills: Palgrave Macmillan, 1997.

Black, Robert. *Stalinism in Britain: A Trotskyist Analysis*. London: New Park, 1970.

Blackbourn, David. "The Discreet Charm of the Bourgeoisie: Reappraising German History in the Nineteenth Century." In David Blackbourn and Geoff Eley, *The Peculiarities of*

German History: Bourgeois Society and Politics in Nineteenth-Century Germany, 157–292. Oxford: Oxford University Press, 1984.

———. *The Fontana History of Germany, 1780–1918: The Long Nineteenth Century.* London: Fontana Press, 1997.

Blackburn, Robin. *The Overthrow of Colonial Slavery, 1776–1848.* London: Verso, 1988.

———. *The Making of New World Slavery: From the Baroque to the Modern.* London: Verso, 1997.

Blackledge, Paul. *Perry Anderson, Marxism and the New Left.* London: Merlin, 2004.

Blakemore, Steven. "Burke and the Fall of Language," *Eighteenth Century Studies* 17, no. 3 (Spring 1984): 284–307.

Blanc, Louis [1839]. *Organisation du travail.* Fifth edition, Paris: Au Bureau de la Société de L'Industrie Fraternelle, 1847.

———. *Organisation du travail.* Ninth edition, revised with a new chapter, Paris: Au Bureau du *Nouveau Monde,* 1850.

Blanning, Tim C. W. *The Pursuit of Glory: Europe, 1649–1815.* Harmondsworth: Penguin, 2008.

Blanqui, Jérôme-Adolphe. *Histoire de l'Economie Politique en Europe depuis les anciens jusqu'à nos jours.* Paris: Guillaumin, 1837.

Blaut, James M. *The Colonizer's View of the World: Geographical Diffusion and Eurocentric History.* New York: Guilford Press, 1993.

Bloch, Ernst [1932]. "Nonsynchronism and the Obligation to Its Dialectics," *New German Critique* 11 (Spring 1977): 22–38.

Blum, Jerome. *The End of the Old Order in Rural Europe.* Princeton, NJ: Princeton University Press, 1978.

Bois, Guy [1976]. *The Crisis of Feudalism: Economy and Society in Eastern Normandy, c. 1300–1550.* Cambridge and Paris: Cambridge University Press and Editions de la Maison des Sciences de L'Homme, 1991.

——— [1978]. "Against the Neo-Malthusian Orthodoxy." In *The Brenner Debate: Agrarian Class Structure and Economic Development in Pre-Industrial Europe,* edited by T. H. Aston and C. H. E. Philpin, 107–18. Cambridge: Cambridge University Press, 1985.

Bolloten, Burnett [1952/1961]. The *Grand Camouflage: The Spanish Civil War and Revolution, 1936–39.* London: Pall Mall, 1968.

Bond, Patrick. "In Power in Pretoria? Reply to Johnson," *New Left Review* 2, no. 58 (July/August 2009): 77–88.

Bonnassie, Pierre [1984]. "The Survival and Extinction of the Slave System in the Early Medieval West (Fourth to Eleventh Centuries)." In *From Slavery to Feudalism in Southeast Europe,* 1–59. Cambridge and Paris: Cambridge University Press and Editions de la Maison des Sciences de L'Homme, 1991.

Bookchin, Murray. *Remaking Society: Pathways to a Green Future.* Montreal: Black Rose Books, 1989.

———. *The Ecology of Freedom: The Emergence and Dissolution of Hierarchy.* Revised edition, Montreal: Black Rose Books, 1991.

———. *The Third Revolution,* vol. 1, *Popular Movements in the Revolutionary Era.* London: Cassell, 1996.

Borkenau, Franz [1937]. *The Spanish Cockpit: An Eyewitness Account of the Political and Social Conflicts of the Spanish Civil War.* London: Pluto: 1986.

——— [1939]. *World Communism: A History of the Communist International.* Ann Arbor: University of Michigan Press, 1962.

Bowman, Shearer Davis. "Antebellum Planters and Vormarz Junkers in Comparative Perspective," *American Historical Review* 85, no. 3 (1980): 779–808.

Bradley, Andrew C. *Shakespearean Tragedy: Lectures on Hamlet, Othello, King Lear [and] Macbeth.* London: Macmillan, 1904.

Bradley, James E. "The British Public and the American Revolution: Ideology, Interest and

Opinion." In *Britain and the American Revolution*, edited by H. T. Dickinson, 124–54. London: Addison, Wesley Longman, 1998.

Brandon, Pepijn. "Marxism and the 'Dutch Miracle': The Dutch Republic and the Transition Debate," *Historical Materialism* 19, no. 3 (2011): 106–46.

Branson, Noreen. *History of the Communist Party of Great Britain, 1941–1951*. London: Lawrence and Wishart, 1997.

Braudel, Fernand [1949]. *The Mediterranean and the Mediterranean World in the Age of Phillip II*, volume 2. London: Fontana, 1973.

———. *Capitalism and Civilization, 15th–18th Centuries*, vol. 2, *The Wheels of Commerce*. London: Fontana, 1982.

———. *Capitalism and Civilization, 15th–18th Centuries*, vol. 3, *The Perspective of the World*. London: Fontana, 1985.

Brendel, Cajo. "Introduction." In *Theses on the Chinese Revolution*, 2–9. London: Solidarity, 1974.

Brenner, Robert. "The Civil War Politics of London's Merchant Community," *Past and Present* 58 (February 1973): 53–107.

——— [1976]. "Agrarian Class Structure and Economic Development in Pre-Industrial Europe." In *The Brenner Debate: Agrarian Class Structure and Economic Development in Pre-Industrial Europe*, edited by T. H. Aston and C. H. E. Philpin, 10–63. Cambridge: Cambridge University Press, 1985.

———. "The Origins of Capitalist Development: A Critique of Neo-Smithian Marxism," *New Left Review*, 1, no. 104 (July–August 1977): 25–92.

———. "Dobb on the Transition from Feudalism to Capitalism," *Cambridge Journal of Economics* 2 (June 1978): 121–40.

——— [1982]. "The Agrarian Roots of European Capitalism." In *The Brenner Debate: Agrarian Class Structure and Economic Development in Pre-Industrial Europe*, edited by T. H. Aston and C. H. E. Philpin, 213–327. Cambridge: Cambridge University Press, 1985.

———. "The Social Basis of Economic Development." In *Analytical Marxism*, edited by John Roemer, 23–53. Cambridge: Cambridge University Press, 1986.

———. "Bourgeois Revolution and Transition to Capitalism." In *The First Modern Society: Essays in English History in Honor of Lawrence Stone*, edited by A. L. Beier, David Cannadine, and J. M. Rosenheim, 271–304. Cambridge: Cambridge University Press, 1989.

———. "Economic Backwardness in Eastern Europe in Light of Developments in the West." In *The Origins of Backwardness in Eastern Europe: Economics and Politics from the Middle Ages until the Early Twentieth Century*, edited by Daniel Chirot, 15–52. Berkeley and Los Angeles: University of California Press, 1989.

———. *Merchants and Revolution: Commercial Change, Political Conflict, and London's Overseas Traders, 1550–1653*. Princeton, NJ: Princeton University Press, 1993.

———. "The Rises and Declines of Serfdom in Medieval and Early Modern Europe." In *Serfdom and Slavery: Studies in Legal Bondage*, edited by Michael L. Bush, 247–76. London: Longman, 1996.

———. "Property Relations and the Growth of Agricultural Productivity in Late Medieval and Early Modern Europe." In *Economic Development and Agricultural Productivity*, edited by Amit Bhaduri and Rune Skarstein, 9–41. Cheltenham: Edward Elgar, 1997.

———. "Competition and Class: A Reply to Foster and McNally," *Monthly Review* 51, no. 7 (December 1999): 24–44.

———. "The Low Countries and the Transition to Capitalism." In *Peasants into Farmers? The Transformation of Rural Economy and Society in the Low Countries (Middle Ages–19th Century) in Light of the Brenner Debate*, edited by Peter Hoppenbrouwers and Jan Luiten van Zanden, 275–338. Turnhout: Brepols, 2001.

———. "Property and Progress: Where Adam Smith Went Wrong." In *Marxist History-writing for the Twenty-First Century*, edited by Chris Wickham, 49–111. Oxford: Oxford

University Press for The British Academy, 2007.

Brenner, Robert and Christopher Isett, "England's Divergence from China's Yangtze Delta: Property Relations, Microeconomics, and Patterns of Development," *Journal of Asian Studies* 61, no. 2 (May 2002): 609–62.

Breuilly, John [1982]. *Nationalism and the State*. Second edition, Manchester: Manchester University Press, 1993.

Brewer, John. *The Sinews of Power: War, Money and the English State, 1688–1783*. London: Unwin Hyman, 1989.

Brinton, Crane. "Review of *The Social Interpretation of the French Revolution*," *History and Theory* 5, no. 3 (1966): 315–20.

Broué, Pierre [1971]. *The German Revolution, 1917–1923*, edited by Ian Birchall and Brian Pearce. E. J. Brill, Leiden, 2005.

Brown, Robert E. *Carl Becker on History and the American Revolution*. East Lansing, Michigan: Spartan Press, 1970.

Brunner, Otto [1958]. "Feudalism: The History of a Concept." In *Lordship and Community in Medieval Europe: Selected Readings*, edited by Fredric L. Cheyette, 32–61. New York: Holt, Reinhart and Winston, 1968.

Buchan, James, *Adam Smith and the Pursuit of Perfect Liberty*. London: Profile Books, 2006.

Buchanan, George [1567]. *De Jure Regni Apud Scotos: Or a Dialogue, Concerning the Due Privileges of Government in the Kingdom of Scotland Betwixt George Buchanan and Thomas Maitland, by the Said George Buchanan*. Edinburgh: no publisher identified, 1680.

Buck-Morss, Susan. "Hegel and Haiti," *Critical Inquiry* 26, no. 4 (Summer 2000): 821–65.

Bukharin, Nikolai I [1915]. *Imperialism and World Economy*. London: Merlin, 1972.

——— [1915]. "Towards a Theory of the Imperialist State." In *Selected Writings on the State and the Transition to Socialism*, edited by Richard B. Day, 6–37. Armonk: M. E. Sharpe, 1982.

——— [1918]. *De la dictature de l'impérialisme a la dictature du proletariat* (Genève: Edition Universa, 1918.

——— [1920]. "The Economics of the Transition Period." In *The Politics and Economics of the Transition Period*, edited by Kenneth J. Tarbuck, 53–175. London: Routledge and Kegan Paul, 1979.

——— [1922]. "Bourgeois Revolution and Proletarian Revolution." In *Put' k sotsializmu v Rossii. Izbrannye proizvedeniia N. I. Bukharina/The Path to Socialism in Russia: Selected Works of N. I. Bukharin*, edited by Sidney Heitman. New York: Omicron Books, 1967.

———. *Historical Materialism: A System of Sociology*. New York: International Publishers, 1925.

Bukharin, Nikolai I and Evgenii A. Preobrazhensky [1920]. *The ABC of Communism*, edited by Edward H. Carr. Harmondsworth: Penguin, 1969.

Bullock, Alan. *The Life and Times of Ernest Bevin*, vol. 1. London: Heinemann, 1960.

Burbach, Roger. *Globalization and Postmodern Politics: From Zapatistas to High-Tech Robber Barons*. London: Pluto Press, 2001.

Burke, Edmund [1789]. Burke to Fitzwilliam, November 12, 1789. In *The Correspondence of Edmund Burke*, vol. 6, edited by Alfred Cobban and Robert A. Smith. Cambridge: Cambridge University Press, 1967.

——— [1790]. *Reflections on the Revolution in France and on the Proceedings in Certain Societies in London Relative to that Event*. Harmondsworth: Penguin, 1968.

——— [1791]. "Thoughts on French Affairs." In *The Works of the Right Honorable Edmund Burke*, vol. 8, 9–85. London: F. and C. Rivington, 1801.

——— [1795]. *Thoughts and Details on Scarcity: Originally Presented to The Right Honorable. William Pitt, in the Month of November, 1795, by The Right Honorable Edmund Burke* London: F. and C. Rivington and J. Hatchard, 1801.

——— [1796] "Three Letters Addressed to a Member of the Present Parliament, on the Proposals for Peace with the Regicide Directory of France: Letter II: On the Genius and

Character of the French Revolution as It Regards Other Nations." In *The Works of the Right Honorable Edmund Burke*, vol. 9, 137–190. London: F. and C. Rivington, 1801.

———— [1796]. "A Letter from the Right Honorable Edmund Burke to a Noble Lord, on the Attacks Made upon Him and his Pension in the House of Lords, by the Duke of Bedford and the Earl of Lauderdale." In *The Works and Correspondence of the Right Honorable Edmund Burke*, vol. 5, *Charge against Warren Hastings Concluded. Political Letters*, 110–151. London: George Bell and Sons, 1902.

Burnet, Gilbert [1705]. *The History of My Own Time*, part 1, edited by Osmund Airy. Oxford: Clarendon Press, 1897.

Burns, Robert [1793]. "Robert Bruce's Address to His Troops at Bannockburn—or Scots Wha Hae." In *The Canongate Burns: the Complete Poems and Songs of Robert Burns*, ed. Andrew Noble and Patrick Scott Hogg, 466–468. Edinburgh: Canongate, 20001.

———— [1793]. Burns to Thompson, August 1793, in *The Complete Letters of Robert Burns*, ed. James A. Mackay. Ayrshire: Alloway, 1987.

———— [1794]. "The Solemn League and Covenant." In *The Canongate Burns: The Complete Poems and Songs of Robert Burns*, ed. Andrew Noble and Patrick Scott Hogg, 875. Edinburgh: Canongate, 2001.

————[1795]. "A Man's a Man for a' That." In *The Canongate Burns: The Complete Poems and Songs of Robert Burns*, edited by Andrew Noble and Patrick Scott Hogg, 512–16. Edinburgh: Canongate, 2001.

Burris, Val. "The Discovery of the New Middle Class," *Theory and Society* 15, no. 3 (May 1986): 317–49.

Burton, Thomas [1659]. *Diary of Thomas Burton Esq.*, vol. 3, *January–March 1659*, edited by John T. Rutt, 118–52. London: Henry Colburn, 1828.

Byres, Terence J. *Capitalism from Above and Capitalism from Below*. Basingstoke: Macmillan, 1996.

————. "Differentiation of the Peasantry under Feudalism and the Transition to Capitalism: In Defence of Rodney Hilton," *Journal of Agrarian Change* 6, no. 1 (January 2006): 17–68.

Cabral, Amilcar [1964]. "Brief Analysis of the Social Structure in Guinea." In *Revolution in Guinea: An African People's Struggle*, 46–61. London: Stage 1, 1969.

Cairnes, John E. *The Slave Power: Its Character, Career, and Probable Designs: Being an Attempt to Explain the Real Issues Involved in the American Contest*. New York: Carleton, 1862.

Calendar of State Papers 1654, Domestic Series, Preserved in State Paper Department of Her Majesty's Public Record Office, edited by Mary A. E. Green. London: Longman, 1886.

Callinicos, Alex. "Trotsky's Theory of 'Permanent Revolution' and Its Relevance to the Third World Today," *International Socialism*, second series, 16 (Spring 1982): 98–112.

————. *Making History: Agency, Structure, and Change in Social Theory*, Cambridge: Polity, 1987.

————. "Exception or Symptom? The British Crisis and the World System," *New Left Review* 1, no. 169 (May/June 1988): 97–106.

————. "Bourgeois Revolutions and Historical Materialism," *International Socialism*, second series, 43 (Summer 1989): 113–71.

————. *Trotskyism*. Milton Keynes: Open University Press, 1990.

————. *The Revenge of History: Marxism and the East European Revolutions*. Cambridge: Polity Pres, 1991.

————. *Theories and Narratives: Reflections on the Philosophy of History*, Cambridge: Polity, 1995.

————. "Marxism and the Crisis in Social History." In *Essays on Historical Materialism*, edited by John Rees, 25–40. London: Bookmarks, 1998.

————. *Social Theory: A Historical Introduction*. Cambridge: Polity Press, 1999.

————. *An Anti-Capitalist Manifesto*. Cambridge: Polity, 2003.

————. *Imperialism and Global Political Economy*. Cambridge: Polity, 2009.

————. "The Limits of Passive Revolution," *Capital and Class* 34, no. 3, special issue on *Approaching Passive Revolutions*, edited by Adam David Morton (October 2010): 491–507.

Calvert, Peter. *Revolution*. London: Macmillan, 1970.

Campbell, Thorbjorn. *Standing Witnesses: An Illustrated Guide to the Scottish Covenanters and Their Memorials with a Historical Introduction*. Edinburgh: Saltire Society, 1996.

Cameron, Ewan. *The European Reformation*. Oxford: Clarendon Press, 1991.

Camejo, Peter. "Introduction." In *The Permanent Revolution* and *Results and Prospects*, 7–23. Third edition, New York: Pathfinder, 1969.

———. *Racism, Revolution, Reaction, 1861–1877: The Rise and Fall of Radical Reconstruction*. New York: Monad Press, 1976.

Cannadine, David. "The Context, Performance and Meaning of Ritual: The British Monarchy and the 'Invention of Tradition,' c. 1820–1977," in *The Invention of Tradition*, edited by Eric J. Hobsbawm and Terence Ranger, 101–64. Cambridge: Cambridge University Press, 1983.

Cardan, Paul (Carlos Castoriadis) [1964]. *History and Revolution: A Revolutionary Critique of Historical Materialism*. London: Solidarity pamphlet no. 38, 1971.

Carlin, Norah. "Medieval Workers and Permanent Revolution," *International Socialism*, second series, 1, (July 1978): 43–54.

———. "Marxism and the English Civil War," *International Socialism*, second series, 10 (Winter 1980/81): 106–28.

———. "Daniel Guérin and the Working Class in the French Revolution," *International Socialism*, second series, 47 (Summer 1990): 197–223.

———. "A New English Revolution," *International Socialism*, second series, 58 (Spring 1993): 119–29.

Carling, Alan H. *Social Division*. London: Verso, 1991.

———. "Analytic Marxism and Historical Materialism: The Debate on Social Evolution," *Science and Society* 57, no. 1 (Spring 1993): 31–65.

Carling, Alan H. and Paul Nolan, "Historical Materialism Natural Selection and World History," *Historical Materialism* 6 (Summer 2000): 215–64.

Carlyle, Alexander [1800]. *Autobiography of the Reverend Dr Alexander Carlyle, Minister of Inveresk Containing Memorials of the Men and Events of His Time*. Edinburgh: William Blackwood and Sons, 1860.

Carr, Edward H [1953]. *The Bolshevik Revolution, 1917–1923*, vol. 3. Harmondsworth: Penguin, 1966.

———. *Twilight of the Comintern, 1930-1935*. New York: Pantheon, 1982.

Carter, Bob. *Capitalism, Class Conflict and the New Middle Class*. London: Routledge and Kegan Paul, 1985.

Carver, Terrell. "*The German Ideology* Never Took Place," *History of Political Thought* 31, no. 1 (Spring 2010): 107–27.

Castoriadis, Carlos [1964–65]. "Marxism and Revolutionary Theory." In *The Imaginary Institution of Society*, 113–230. Cambridge: Polity, 1987.

Chadwick, Owen. *The Reformation*, vol. 3 of *The Pelican History of the Church*. Revised edition, Harmondsworth: Penguin, 1968.

Chandra, Satish [1966]. "Some Aspects of the Growth of a Money Economy in India during the Seventeenth Century." In *Essays on Medieval Indian History*. New Delhi: Oxford University Press, 2003.

Chase-Dunn, Christopher [1980]. "Socialist States in the Capitalist World Economy." In *Socialist States in the World System*, edited by Christopher Chase-Dunn, 21–56. Beverly Hills: Sage Publications, 1982.

Chateaubriand, François-René de [1848]. *Memoires D'outre-Tombe*, Tome 3. Paris: Flammarion, 1950.

Chatterjee, Partha. *Nationalist Thought and the Colonial World: A Derivative Discourse?* London: Zed, 1986.

———. *The Nation and Its Fragments: Colonial and Postcolonial Histories*. Princeton, NJ: Princeton University Press, 1993.

Chesneaux, Jean. *Peasant Revolts in China, 1840–1949*. London: Thames and Hudson, 1973.

Chibber, Vivek. *Locked in Place: State-Building and Late Industrialization in India*. Princeton, NJ: Princeton University Press, 2003.

———. "What Is Living and What Is Dead in the Marxist Theory of History," *Historical Materialism* 19, no. 2 (2011): 60–91.

Chistozvonov, Alexander. "The Concept and Criteria of Reversibility and Irreversibility of an Historical Process", *Our History* 63 (Summer 1975).

Choonara, Joseph. "The Relevance of Permanent Revolution: A Reply to Neil Davidson," *International Socialism*, second series, 131 (Summer 2011): 173–87.

Christianson, Paul. "The Causes of the English Revolution: A Reappraisal," *Journal of British Studies* 15, no. 2 (Spring 1976): 40–75.

Cipolla, Carlo M. [1965]. "Guns and Sails." In *European Culture and Overseas Expansion, 1400–1700*. Harmondsworth: Penguin, 1970.

Clarendon, Earl of (Edward Hyde) [1646–74]. *Selections from* The History of the Rebellion *and* The Life by Himself, edited by Gertrude Huehns. Oxford: Oxford University Press, 1978.

Clark, Jonathan C. D. *English Society, 1688–1832*. Cambridge: Cambridge University Press, 1985.

———. *Revolution and Rebellion: State and Society in England in the Seventeenth and Eighteenth Centuries*. Cambridge: Cambridge University Press, 1986.

———. *Our Shadowed Present: Modernism, Postmoderism and History*. London: Atlantic, 2003.

Clark, Timothy J. *The Absolute Bourgeois: Artists and Politics in France, 1848–1851*. London: Thames and Hudson, 1973.

——— [1982]. "Clement Greenberg's Theory of Art." In *Pollock and after: The Critical Debate*, edited by Francis Frascina, 47–63. London: Harper and Row, 1985.

Clarke, William [1647–49, 1651–60]. *The Clarke Papers: Selections from the Papers of William Clarke, Secretary to the Council of the Army, 1647–1649, and to General Monck and the Commanders of the Army in Scotland, 1651–1660*, edited by C. H. Firth. London: Royal Historical Society, 1992.

Clerk, John [1703]. *Memoirs of the Life of Sir John Clerk of Penicuik, Baronet, Baron of the Exchequer, Extracted by Himself from His Own Journals, 1676–1755*, edited by John M. Gray. Edinburgh: Scottish History Society, 1892.

Cliff, Tony [1947]. "All That Glitters Is Not Gold: A Reply to Germain's 'From the ABC to Current Reading: Boom, Revival or Crisis?'" In *Marxist Theory after Trotsky*, vol. 3 of *Selected Writings*, 139–54. London: Bookmarks, 2003.

——— [1948]. "The Nature of Stalinist Russia." In *Marxist Theory after Trotsky*, vol. 3 of *Selected Writings*, 1–138. London: Bookmarks, 2003.

——— [1950]. "The Class Nature of the People's Democracies." In *Neither Washington nor Moscow: Essays on Revolutionary Socialism*, 40–85. London: Bookmarks, 1984.

———[1955]. *Russia: A Marxist Analysis*. Revised edition, London: International Socialism, 1964.

——— [1957]. "Perspectives for the Permanent War Economy." In *Marxist Theory after Trotsky*, vol. 3 of *Selected Works*, 169–75. London: Bookmarks, 2003.

——— [1963] "Permanent Revolution." In *Marxist Theory after Trotsky*, vol. 3 of *Selected Works*, 187–201. London: Bookmarks, 2003.

——— [1964–5]. "The End of the Road: Deutscher's Capitulation to Stalinism." In *Neither Washington nor Moscow: Essays on Revolutionary Socialism*, 166–91. London: Bookmarks, 1984.

———. *Lenin*, vol. 1, *Building the Party*. London: Pluto, 1975.

———. *Trotsky*, vol. 1, *Towards October, 1879–1917*. London: Bookmarks, 1987.

———. *Trotsky*, vol. 3, *Fighting the Rising Stalinist Bureaucracy, 1923–1927*. London: Bookmarks, 1991.

———. *Trotskyism after Trotsky: The Origins of the International Socialists*. London: Bookmarks, 1999.

————. *A World to Win: Life of a Revolutionary*. London: Bookmarks, 2000.

Clouatre, Dallas L. "The Concept of Class in French Culture Prior to the Revolution," *Journal of the History of Ideas* 45, no. 2 (April 1984): 219–44.

Coates, Colin M. "The Rebellion of 1837–38 and the Other Bourgeois Revolutions in Quebec History," *International Journal of Canadian Studies* 20 (Fall 1999): 19–34.

Cobban, Alfred [1955]. "The Myth of the French Revolution." In *Aspects of the French Revolution*, 90–112. London: Paladin, 1971.

————. *The Social Interpretation of the French Revolution*. Cambridge: Cambridge University Press, 1964.

Cockburn, Henry [1856]. *Memorials of His Time*. Edinburgh: T. N. Foulis, 1909.

Cohen, Nick. "I Still Fight Oppression," *Observer* (London) (August 7, 2005).

Cohn, Norman [1957]. *The Pursuit of the Millennium: Revolutionary Millenarians and Mystical Anarchists of the Middle Ages*. Second edition, London: Paladin, 1970.

———— [1993]. *Cosmos, Chaos and the World to Come: The Ancient Roots of Apocalyptic Faith*. New Haven, CT: Yale University Press, 2001.

Cohn, Samuel K. *Lust for Liberty: The Politics of Social Revolt in Medieval Europe, 1200–1425*. Cambridge, MA: Harvard University Press, 2006.

Coleman, Donald C. *Industry in Tudor and Stuart England*. London: Macmillan, 1975.

Collier, Andrew. *Marx*. Oxford: Oneworld, 2004.

Comninel, George. C. *Rethinking the French Revolution: Marxism and the Revisionist Challenge*. London: Verso, 1987.

Commission of the C.C. of the C.P.S.U. (B.). [1938]. *History of the Communist Party of the Soviet Union (Bolsheviks): Short Course*. Moscow: Foreign Languages Publishing House, 1943.

Communist International [1920]. "Fourth Session, July 28." In *Second Congress of the Communist International: Minutes of the Proceedings*, vol. 1, 109–31. London: New Park, 1977.

"Congress Debate on Colonial Policy." In *Lenin's Struggle for a Revolutionary International. Documents: 1907–1916, the Preparatory Years*, edited by John Riddell, 9–15. New York: Pathfinder, 1984.

Congressional Globe, new series, 68 (March 6, 1862).

Corcoran, Paul E. "The Bourgeoisie and Other Villains," *Journal of the History of Ideas* 38, no. 3 (July 1977): 477–85.

Corish, Patrick. J. "The Cromwellian Conquest, 1649–53." In *A New History of Ireland*, vol. 3, *Early Modern Ireland, 1534–1691*, edited by T. W. Moody, F. X. Martin, and F. J. Byrne, 336–52. Oxford: Oxford University Press, 1976.

Court, Pieter de la [1662/9]. "The True Interest, and Political Maxims of the Republick of Holland and West Friesland." In *Commerce, Culture, and Liberty: Readings on Capitalism before Adam Smith*, edited by Henry C. Clark, 9–36. Indianapolis: Liberty Fund, 2003.

Coveney, Peter J. "An Early Modern European Crisis?" *Renaissance and Modern Studies* 26 (1982): 1–26.

Craig, Thomas [1603/1655]. *The Jus Feudale by Sir Thomas Craig of Riccarton with an Appendix Containing the Books of the Feus*, vol. 1. Edinburgh: W. Hodge, 1934.

Creighton, Donald G. *The Commercial Empire of the St. Lawrence, 1760–1850*. New Haven, CT: Yale University Press, 1937.

————. *The Road to Confederation: The Emergence of Canada, 1863–1867*. Toronto: Macmillan, 1964.

Cromwell, Oliver [1658]. "Speech XVII," January 16, 1658. In *Oliver Cromwell's Letters and Speeches: with Elucidations*, vol. 5, edited by Thomas Carlyle, 101–24. London: Chapman and Hall, 1872.

Crone, Patricia. *Pre-industrial Societies*. Oxford: Basil Blackwell, 1989.

Croot, Patricia and David Parker [1978]. "Agrarian Class Structure and the Development of

Capitalism: France and England Compared." In *The Brenner Debate: Agrarian Class Structure and Economic Development in Pre-Industrial Europe*, edited by T. H. Aston and C. H. E. Philpin, 79–90. Cambridge: Cambridge University Press, 1985.

Crossman, Richard H. S. "Towards a Philosophy of Socialism." In *New Fabian Essays*, ed. Richard S. H. Crossman, 1–32. London: Turnstile, 1952.

Crouzet, François. "Western Europe and Great Britain: 'Catching Up' in the First Half of the Nineteenth Century," in *Britain Ascendant: Comparative Studies in Franco-British History*, 341–84. Cambridge and Paris: Cambridge University Press and Editions de la Maison des Sciences de L'Homme, 1990.

Crow, Thomas. "The Tensions of Enlightenment: Goya." In *Nineteenth Century Art: A Critical History*, edited by Stephen E. Eisenman, 78–97. London: Thames and Hudson, 1994.

Cruz, Jesús. *Gentlemen, Bourgeois, and Revolutionaries: Political Change and Cultural Persistence among the Spanish Dominant Groups, 1750–1850*. Cambridge: Cambridge University Press, 1996.

Cuoco, Vincenzo [1801]. *Saggio storico sulla rivoluzione napoletana del 1799*, edited by Nino Cortese. Florence: Vallecchi, 1926.

Curtin, Peter. *The World and the West: The European Challenge and the Overseas Response in the Age of Empire*. Cambridge: Cambridge University Press, 2000.

Daalder, Hans. "Consociationalism, Center and Periphery in the Netherlands." In *Mobilization, Center-Periphery Structures and Nation-Building: A Volume in Commemoration of Stein Rokkan*, edited by Per Torsvick, 181–240. Bergen: Universitetsforlaget, 1981.

Dabat, Alejandro and Luis Lorenzano [1982]. *Argentina: The Malvinas and the End of Military Rule*. Expanded and revised edition, London: Verso, 1984.

Dadoo, Yusuf M. "Introduction." In *South African Communists Speak: Documents from the History of the South African Communist Party, 1915–1980*, edited by Brian Bunting, xv–xix. London: Inkululenko Publications, 1981.

Dalrymple, James [1681]. *The Institutions of the Laws of Scotland*. Edinburgh and Glasgow: Universities of Edinburgh and Glasgow, 1981.

———. *An Essay towards a General History of Feudal Property in Great Britain*. London: A. Millar, 1757.

Dalziel, Raewyn. "Southern Islands: New Zealand and Polynesia." In *The Nineteenth Century*, vol. 3 of *The Oxford History of the British Empire*, edited by Andrew Porter, 573–96. Oxford: University of Oxford Press, 1999.

Darwin, John. *After Tamerlane: The Global History of Empire since 1405*. London: Allen Lane, 2007.

Davenant, Charles. *Essays Upon: I. The Balance of Power. II. The Right of Making War, Peace and Alliances. III. Universal Monarchy: To which Is Added an Appendix Containing the Records Referr'd to in the Second Essay*. London: Knapton, 1701.

Davidson, Neil. *The Origins of Scottish Nationhood*. London: Pluto, 2000.

———. *Discovering the Scottish Revolution, 1692–1746*. London: Pluto, 2003.

———. "Class Consciousness and National Consciousness in the Scottish General Strike of 1820." In *New Approaches to Socialist History*, edited by Keith Flett and David Renton, 133–48. Cheltenham: New Clarion, 2003.

———. "The Scottish Path to Capitalist Agriculture 2: The Capitalist Offensive (1747–1815)," *Journal of Agrarian Change* 4, no. 4 (October 2004): 411–60.

———. "The Prophet, His Biographer and the Watchtower," *International Socialism*, second series, 104 (Autumn 2004): 95–118.

———. "Bourgeois Revolutions: on the Road to Salvation for All Mankind," *Socialist Review* 291 (December 2004): 23–5.

———. "The Scottish Path to Capitalist Agriculture 3: The Enlightenment as the Theory and Practice of Improvement," *Journal of Agrarian Change* 5, no. 1 (2005): 1–72.

———. "How Revolutionary Were the Bourgeois Revolutions?" *Historical Materialism* 13, no. 3 (2005): 3–38;

———. "How Revolutionary Were the Bourgeois Revolutions? Continued," *Historical Materialism* 13, no. 4 (2005): 3–54.

———. "From Uneven to Combined Development." In *100 Years of Permanent Revolution: Results and Prospects*, edited by Bill Dunn and Hugo Radice, 10–26. London: Pluto Press, 2006.

———. "China: Unevenness, Combination, Revolution?" In *100 Years of Permanent Revolution: Results and Prospects*, edited by Bill Dunn and Hugo Radice, 211–229. London: Pluto Press, 2006.

———. "Walter Benjamin and the Classical Marxist Tradition," in *International Socialism*, second series, 121 (Winter 2008/9): 157–72.

———. "Putting the Nation Back into 'the International,'" *Cambridge Review of International Affairs* 22, no. 1 (March 2009): 9–28.

———. "What Was Neoliberalism?" In *Neoliberal Scotland: Class and Society in a Stateless Nation*, edited by Neil Davidson, Patricia McCafferty, and David Miller, 1–89. Newcastle: Cambridge Scholars, 2010.

———. "Many Capitals, Many States: Contingency, Logic or Mediation?" In *Marxism and Global Politics: Contesting Global Capitalism*, edited by Alexander Anievas, 77–93. London: Routledge, 2010.

———. "Scotland: Birthplace of Passive Revolution?" *Capital and Class* 34, no. 3, special issue on *Approaching Passive Revolutions*, edited by Adam David Morton (October 2010): 343–59.

———. *Violating All the Laws of History: Combined Development, Nation-States, and Neoliberal Capitalism*. Leiden: Brill Academic Publications, forthcoming in 2013.

Davis, Mike. "'Fordism' in Crisis: A Review of Michael Aglietta's *Regulation et Crises: Le experience des Etats-Unis*," *Review* 2, no. 2 (1978): 207–69.

———. "The Political Economy of Late Imperial America." In *Prisoners of the American Dream: Politics and Economy in the History of the American Working Class*, 181–230. London: Verso, 1986.

———. *Late Victorian Holocausts: El Niño Famines and the Making of the Third World*. London: Verso, 2001.

———. "Sand, Fear and Money in Dubai." In *Evil Paradises: Dreamworlds of Neoliberalism*, ed. Mike Davis and Daniel Bertrand Monk, 48–68. London: Verso 2007.

Dawson, Andrew. "Northern Manufacturers and the Coming of the American Civil War." In *New Approaches to Socialist History*, edited by Keith Flett and David Renton, 105–16. Cheltenham: New Clarion Press, 2003.

Day, Richard B. and Daniel Gaido, "Introduction: The Historical Origin of the Expression 'Permanent Revolution.'" In *Witnesses to Permanent Revolution: The Documentary Record*, edited by Richard B. Day and Daniel Gaido, 1–58. Leiden: E. J. Brill, 2009.

De Leon, Daniel [1903]. *Two Pages from Roman History: Plebs Leaders and Labor Leaders and the Warning of the Gracchi*. Palo Alto: New York Labour News, 1988.

D'Houdetot, Elisabeth F. S. L. de B [1790]. D'Houdetot to Jefferson, September 3, 1790. In *Les amitiès Amèricaines de Madame d'Houdetot, d'après sa correspondance inèdite avec Benjamin Franklin et Thomas Jefferson*, édite by Gilbert Chinard. Paris: É. Champion, 1924.

Dennison, Tracy K. and A. W. Carus, "The Invention of the Russian Rural Commune: Haxthausen and the Evidence," *Historical Journal* 46, no. 3 (September 2003): 561–82.

Denyenko, Marina. "'Middle Class Backs Orange Revolution," BBC World Service (December 4, 2004), http://news.bbc.co.uk/1/hi/world/europe/4057839.stm.

Deutsch, Karl W. and Hermann Weilenmann, "The Swiss City Canton: A Political Invention," *Contemporary Studies in Society and History* 7 (1964/5): 393–408.

Deutscher, Isaac [1949]. *Stalin: A Political Biography*. Revised edition, Harmondsworth: Pen-

guin, 1966.
———— [1950]. "The Ex-Communist and His Conscience." In *Heretics and Renegades and Other Essays*, 9–22. London: Hamish Hamilton, 1955.
———— [1954]. *The Prophet Armed: Trotsky, 1879–1921*. London: Verso, 2003.
———— [1956]. "Russia in Transition." In *Ironies of History: Essays on Contemporary Communism*, 27–51. Berkeley, CA: Ramparts Press, 1971.
———— [1958]. "The Tragedy of the Polish Communist Party." In *Marxism in Our Time*, edited by Tamara Deutscher, 113–160. Berkeley, CA: Ramparts Press, 1971.
———— [1959]. *The Prophet Unarmed: Trotsky, 1921–1929*. London: Verso, 2003.
———— [1960]. *The Great Contest: Russia and the West*. London: Oxford University Press, 1960.
———— [1963]. *The Prophet Outcast: Trotsky, 1929–1940*. London: Verso, 2003.
————. *The Unfinished Revolution, 1917–1967*. Oxford: Oxford University Press, 1967.
————. "The Unfinished Revolution, 1917–1967," *New Left Review*, no. 43 (May/June 1967): 27–39.
———— [1967]. "Germany and Marxism." In *Marxism in Our Time*, edited by Tamara Deutscher, 167–80. Berkeley, CA: Ramparts Press, 1971.
————. "Marxism in Our Time." In *Marxism in Our Time*, edited by Tamara Deutscher, 15–30. Berkeley, CA: Ramparts Press, 1971.
Deutscher, Tamara. "Isaac Deutscher, 1907–1967." In Isaac Deutscher, *The Non-Jewish Jew and Other Essays*, edited by Tamara Deutscher, vii–x. London: Merlin Press, 1981.
Desmond, Adrian and James Moore, *Darwin*. Harmondsworth: Penguin, 1992.
Devine, Pat. *Democracy and Economic Planning*. Cambridge: Polity, 1988.
Devine, Thomas M. *Scotland's Empire, 1600–1815*. London: Allen Lane, 2003.
Diamond, Jared. *The Rise and Fall of the Third Chimpanzee*. New York: Radius, 1991.
————. *Guns, Germs and Steel: A Short History of Everybody for the Last 13,000 Years*. London: Vintage, 1998.
————. *Collapse: How Societies Choose to Fail or Survive*. Harmondsworth: Penguin, 2006.
Dimitroff, Georgi. [1935]. "The Fascist Offensive and the Tasks of the Communist International." In *The United Front: The Struggle against Fascism and War*, 9–93. London: Lawrence and Wishart, 1938.
Dockes, Pierre. *Medieval Slavery and Liberation*. London: Methuen, 1982.
Dobb, Maurice [1946]. *Studies in the Development of Capitalism*. Revised edition, London: Macmillan, 1963.
Douglas, Elisha P. *Rebels and Democrats: The Struggle for Equal Political Rights and Majority Rule during the American Revolution*. Chapel Hill: University of North Carolina Press, 1955.
Douglass, Frederick [1852], "The Meaning of July Fourth for the Negro." In *The Life and Writings of Frederick Douglass*, vol. 2, *Pre-Civil War Decade, 1850–1860*, 181–206, edited by Phillip S. Foner. New York: International Publishers, 1950.
———— [1857], "West India Emancipation." In *The Life and Writings of Frederick Douglass*, vol. 2, *Pre-Civil War Decade, Pre-Civil War Decade, 1850–1860*, 426–39, edited by Phillip S. Foner. New York: International Publishers, 1950.
———— [1860], "The Constitution of the United States: Is It Pro-Slavery or Anti-Slavery." In *The Life and Writings of Frederick Douglass*, vol. 2, *Pre-Civil War Decade, 1850–1860*, 467–480, edited by Phillip S. Foner. New York: International Publishers, 1950.
———— [1863], "Why Should a Colored Man Enlist?" In *The Life and Writings of Frederick Douglass*, vol. 3, *The Civil War, 1861–1865*, 340–44, edited by Phillip S. Foner. New York: International Publishers, 1952.
———— [1866], "The Future of the Colored Race." In *The Life and Writings of Frederick Douglass*, vol. 4, *Reconstruction and After*, 193–96, edited by Phillip S. Foner. New York: International Publishers, 1955.
Doyle, William [1980]. *Origins of the French Revolution*. Second edition, Oxford: Oxford Uni-

versity Press, 1988.

Draper, Hal [1963–4]. "The Myth of Lenin's 'Concept of the Party': Or What They Did to *What Is to Be Done?" Historical Materialism* 4 (Summer 1999): 187–214.

——— [1966]. "The Two Souls of Socialism." In *Socialism from Below*, edited E. Haberkern, 1–33. Atlantic Highlands, NJ: Humanities Press, 1992.

———. *Karl Marx's Theory of Revolution*, vol. 1, *State and Bureaucracy*, New York: Monthly Review Press, 1977.

———. *Karl Marx's Theory of Revolution*, vol. 2, *The Politics of Social Classes*, New York: Monthly Review Press, 1978.

———. *Karl Marx's Theory of Revolution*, vol. 3, *The "Dictatorship of the Proletariat."* New York: Monthly Review Press, 1986.

———. *The "Dictatorship of the Proletariat" from Marx to Lenin*. New York: Monthly Review Press, 1987.

Drayton, William. *The South Vindicated from the Treason and Fanaticism of the Northern Abolitionists*. Philadelphia: H. Manly, 1836.

Dryden, John [1681]. "Absalom and Achitophel: A Poem." In *The Poems and Fables of John Dryden*, edited by James Kinsley, 188–216. Oxford: Oxford University Press, 1970.

——— [1700]. "Prologue, Epilogue, Song and Secular Masque from *The Pilgrim*." In *The Poems and Fables of John Dryden*, edited by James Kinsley, 832–39. Oxford: Oxford University Press, 1970.

Duby, Georges. *The Early Growth of the European Economy: Warriors and Peasants from the Seventh to the Twelfth Century*. London: Weidenfeld and Nicolson, 1974.

——— [1978]. *The Three Orders: Feudal Society Imagined*. Chicago: Chicago University Press, 1980.

———[1987]. *France in the Middle Ages, 987–1460: From Hugh Capet to Joan of Arc*. Oxford: Oxford University Press, 1991.

Duchesne, Ricardo. "On *The Origins of Capitalism*," *Rethinking Marxism* 14, no. 3 (Fall 2002): 12937.

———. "Rodney Hilton and the Peasant Road to 'Capitalism' in England," *Journal of Peasant Studies* 30, no. 2 (January 2003): 129–45.

Duffy, Christopher. *The Military Experience in the Age of Reason*. London: Routledge, 1987.

Duggan, Christopher. *The Force of Destiny: A History of Italy since 1796*. London: Allen Lane, 2007.

Dumont, Paul. *Du socialisme ottoman à l'internationalisme anatolien*. Istanbul: les éditions Isis, 1997.

Dunayevskaya, Raya [1958]. *Marxism and Freedom: From 1776 until Today*. London: Pluto, 1971.

Dunn, John. "The Politics of Locke in England and America in the Eighteenth Century." In *John Locke: Problems and Perspectives. A Collection of New Essays*, edited by John W. Yolton, 45–80. Cambridge: Cambridge at the University Press, 1969.

Duplessis, Robert S. *Transitions to Capitalism in Early Modern Europe*. Cambridge: Cambridge University Press, 1997.

Dwyer, John. *The Age of the Passions: An Interpretation of Adam Smith and Scottish Enlightenment Culture*. East Linton: Tuckwell, 1998.

Dylan, Bob. *Chronicles: Volume 1*. New York, Simon and Schuster, 2004.

Eagleton, Terry. *Walter Benjamin or Towards a Revolutionary Criticism*. London: Verso, 1981.

———. *The Illusions of Postmodernism*. Cambridge, MA: Blackwell, 1994.

———. *Why Marx Was Right*. New Haven, CT: Yale University Press, 2011.

Economist. "The Trouble with Revolutions," *Economist* (July 8, 1989): 13–14.

Eisenstein, Hester. *Feminism Seduced: How Global Elites Use Women's Labor and Ideas to Exploit the World*. Boulder, CO: Paradigm Publishers, 2009.

Elbaum, Max, *Revolution in the Air: Sixties Radicals Turn to Lenin, Mao and Che*. New York: Verso, 2002.

Eley, Geoff. "The British Model and the German Road: Rethinking the Course of German History before 1914." In David Blackbourn and Geoff Eley, *The Peculiarities of German History: Bourgeois Society and Politics in Nineteenth-Century Germany*, 37–155. Oxford: Oxford University Press, 1984.

———. *Forging Democracy: the History of the Left in Europe, 1850–2000*, Oxford: Oxford University Press, 2002.

Elliot, Gregory. *Perry Anderson: The Merciless Laboratory of History*. Minneapolis: University of Minnesota, 1998.

Elliott, John H. [1963]. *Imperial Spain, 1469–1716*. Harmondsworth: Penguin, 1970.

——— [1990]. "A Non-Revolutionary Society: Castille in the 1640s." In *Spain, Europe and the Wider World, 1500–1800*, 74–91. New Haven, CT: Yale University Press, 2009.

Elton, Geoffrey R. "A High Road to Civil War?" In *From Renaissance to Counter-Reformation: Essays in Honor of Garrett Mattingly*, edited by Charles H. Carter, 325–47. New York: Random House, 1965.

Elvin, Mark. *The Pattern of Chinese History*. Stanford: Stanford University Press, 1973.

Enmale, Richard [Herbert Morais]. "Introduction." In Karl Marx and Frederick Engels, *The Civil War in the United States*, edited by Richard Enmale, i–xxv. New York: International Publishers, 1938.

Emerson, Roger L. "The Social Composition of Enlightened Scotland: The Select Society of Edinburgh, 1754–1764," *Studies on Voltaire and the Eighteenth Century* 114 (1973): 291–329.

Engels, Friedrich [1842]. "The Internal Crises." In *Collected Works*, vol. 2, 370–374. London: Lawrence and Wishart, 1975.

——— [1843]. "Outlines of a Critique of Political Economy." In *Collected Works*, vol. 3, 418–43. London: Lawrence and Wishart, 1975.

———[1844]. "The Condition of England: The Eighteenth Century." In *Collected Works*, vol 3, 469–88. London: Lawrence and Wishart, 1975.

——— [1845]. "Speeches in Elberfeld: February 15, 1845." In *Collected Works*, vol. 4, 256–64. London: Lawrence and Wishart, 1975.

——— [1845]. *The Condition of the Working Class in England: From Personal Observation and Authentic Sources*. In *Collected Works*, vol. 4, 295–583. London: Lawrence and Wishart, 1975.

——— [1845]. "The Festival of Nations in London." In *Collected Works*, vol. 6, 3–14. London: Lawrence and Wishart, 1976.

——— [1845]. "The State of Germany: Letter 1 to the Editor of the *Northern Star*." In *Collected Works*, vol. 6, 15–21. London: Lawrence and Wishart, 1976.

——— [1847]. "[The Constitutional Question in Germany]." In *Collected Works*, vol. 6, 75–91. London: Lawrence and Wishart, 1976.

——— [1847]. "Principles of Communism." In *Collected Works*, vol. 6, 341–57. London: Lawrence and Wishart, 1976.

——— [1847]. "The Civil War in Switzerland." In *Collected Works*, vol. 6, 367–74. London: Lawrence and Wishart, 1976.

——— [1848]. "Extraordinary Revelations—Abd-El-Kader—Guizot's Foreign Policy." In *Collected Works*, vol. 6, 469–72. London: Lawrence and Wishart, 1976.

——— [1849]. "The Magyar Struggle." In *The Revolutions of 1848, Political Writings*, vol. 1, edited by David Fernbach, 213–26. Harmondsworth: Penguin/New Left Review, 1973.

——— [1849]. "Democratic Pan-Slavism." In *The Revolutions of 1848, Political Writings*, vol. 1, edited by David Fernbach, 226–45. Harmondsworth: Penguin/New Left Review, 1973.

——— [1849–50]. "The Campaign for the German Imperial Constitution." In *Collected Works*, vol. 10, 147–239. London: Lawrence and Wishart, 1978.

——— [1850]. *The Peasant War in Germany*. In *Collected Works*, vol. 10, 397–482. London: Lawrence and Wishart, 1978.

——— [1856]. Engels to Marx, May 23, 1856. In Collected Works, vol. 40, 49–50. London:

Lawrence and Wishart, 1983.

——— [1862]. Engels to Marx, May 12, 1862. In *Collected Works*, vol. 41, 363–64. London: Lawrence and Wishart, 1995.

——— [1865], "The Prussian Military Question and the German Workers' Party [Extract]." In *The First International and After, Political Writings*, vol. 3, edited by David Fernbach, 121–46. Harmondsworth: Penguin/New Left Review, 1974.

——— [1865]. "Plan of Chapter Two, and Fragments for *The History of Ireland*." In *Collected Works*, vol. 21, 308–15. London: Lawrence and Wishart, 1985.

——— [1870]. "Preface [to the Second Edition of *The Peasant War in Germany*"]. In *Collected Works*, vol. 21, 93–100. London: Lawrence and Wishart, 1985.

——— [1870]. "[*The History of Ireland*]." In *Collected Works*, vol. 21, 145–87. London: Lawrence and Wishart, 1985.

——— [1874]. "Supplement to the Preface of 1870 for *The Peasant War in Germany*." In *Collected Works*, vol. 23, 626–31. London: Lawrence and Wishart, 1988.

——— [1876–78]. *Anti-Dühring: Herr Eugen Dühring's Revolution in Science*. In *Collected Works*, vol. 25, 5–309. London: Lawrence and Wishart, 1987.

——— [1878–82]. "[On the Early History of the Germans]." In *Collected Works*, vol. 26, 6–57. London: Lawrence and Wishart, 1990.

——— [1882]. Engels to Kautsky, February 7, 1882. In *Collected Works*, vol. 46, 191–95. London: Lawrence and Wishart, 1992.

——— [1882]. Engels to Kautsky, September 12, 1882. In *Collected Works*, vol. 46, 320–23. London: Lawrence and Wishart, 1992.

——— [1882] "Additions to the Text of *Anti-Dühring* Made by Engels in the Pamphlet *Socialism Utopian and Scientific*." In *Collected Works*, vol. 25, 630–42. London: Lawrence and Wishart, 1987.

——— [1884]. *The Origin of the Family, Private Property and the State: In the Light of the Researches of Lewis H. Morgan*. In *Collected Works*, vol. 26, 127–276. London: Lawrence and Wishart, 1990.

——— [1884]. Engels to Bebel, November 18, 1884. In *Collected Works*, vol. 47, 220–23. London: Lawrence and Wishart, 1993.

——— [1884]. "On the Peasant War." In *Collected Works*, vol. 26, 554–55. London: Lawrence and Wishart, 1990.

——— [1884]. "On the Decline of Feudalism and the Emergence of National States." In *Collected Works*, vol. 26, 556–65. London: Lawrence and Wishart, 1990.

——— [1884]. "The Peasant Question in France and Germany." In *Collected Works*, vol. 27, 481–502. London: Lawrence and Wishart, 1990.

——— [1885], "England in 1845 and in 1885." In *Collected Works*, vol. 26, 295–301. London: Lawrence and Wishart, 1990.

——— [1885]. "Preface to the Third German Edition of *The Eighteenth Brumaire of Louis Bonaparte* by Marx." In *Collected Works*, vol. 26, 302–3. London: Lawrence and Wishart, 1990.

——— [1886], *Ludwig Feuerbach and the End of Classical German Philosophy*. In *Collected Works*, vol. 26, 357–98. London: Lawrence and Wishart, 1990.

——— [1887]. "The Role of Force in History." In *Collected Works*, vol. 26, 453–510. London: Lawrence and Wishart, 1990.

——— [1888]. "Preface to the English Edition of 1888." In *The Revolutions of 1848*, vol. 1 of *Political Writings*, edited by David Fernbach, 62–66. Harmondsworth: Penguin/New Left Review, 1973.

——— [1889]. Engels to Kautsky, February 20, 1889. In *Collected Works*, vol. 48, 266–70. London: Lawrence and Wishart, 2001.

——— [1890]. Engels to Danielson, June 10, 1890, in *Collected Works*, vol. 48, 506–7. London: Lawrence and Wishart, 2001.

——— [1890]. Engels to Bloch, September 21, 1890. In *Collected Works*, vol. 49, 33–36. London: Lawrence and Wishart, 2001.

——— [1892]. "Introduction to the English Edition (1892) of *Socialism: Utopian and Scientific*." In *Collected Works*, vol. 27, 278–302. London: Lawrence and Wishart, 1990.

——— [1892]. Engels to Danielson, September 22, 1892. In *Collected Works*, vol. 49, 535–538. London: Lawrence and Wishart, 2001.

——— [1894]. "Afterword (1894) [to 'On Social Relations in Russia']." In *Collected Works*, vol. 27, 421–33. London: Lawrence and Wishart, 1990.

——— [1894]. Engels to Borgius, January 25, 1894. In *Collected Works*, vol. 50, 264–65. London: Lawrence and Wishart, 2005.

——— [1894]. "The Future Italian Revolution and the Socialist Party." In *Collected Works*, vol. 27, 437–40. London: Lawrence and Wishart, 1990.

——— [1894]. Engels to Turati, January 26, 1894. In *Collected Works*, vol. 50, 266–67. London: Lawrence and Wishart, 2005.

——— [1895]. "Introduction [to Karl Marx's *The Class Struggle in France 1848 To 1850*]." In *Collected Works*, vol. 27, 506–24. London: Lawrence and Wishart, 1990.

——— [1895]. Engels to Schmidt, March 12, 1895. In *Collected Works*, vol. 50, 564–65. London: Lawrence and Wishart, 2005.

Engerman, Stanley. "Slavery, Serfdom and Other Forms of Coerced Labor: Similarities and Differences." In *Serfdom and Slavery: Studies in Legal Bondage*, edited by Michael L. Bush, 18-41. London, Longman, 1996.

Ennew, Judith, Paul Q. Hirst, and Keith Tribe. "'Peasantry' as an Economic Category," *Journal of Peasant Studies* 4, no. 4 (July 1977): 295–322.

Epstein, Stephen R. "The Late Medieval Crisis as an 'Integration' Crisis." In *Early Modern Capitalism: Economic and Social Change in Europe, 1400–1800*, edited by Maarten Pak, 25–50. London: Routledge, 2001.

Evans, Richard J. "The Myth of Germany's Missing Revolution," *New Left Review* 1 , no. 149, (January/February 1985): 67–94.

———. *In Defence of History*. London: Granta, 1997.

———. *The Coming of the Third Reich*. London: Allen Lane, 2003.

———. *Cosmopolitan Islanders: British Historians and the European Continent*. Cambridge: Cambridge University Press, 2009.

Evans, Richard J., Peter Jones, Kevin Morgan, Mike Savage, Jim Sharpe, and Eileen Yeo. "History Today: Round-table Dialogue," *Socialist History* 14 (1999): 1–39.

Fanon, Frantz [1961]. *The Wretched of the Earth*. Harmondsworth: Penguin, 1967.

Ferguson, Adam [1767]. *An Essay on the History of Civil Society*, edited by Duncan Forbes. Edinburgh: Edinburgh University Press, 1966.

Ferguson, William. *Scotland's Relations with England: A Survey to 1707*. Edinburgh: John Donald, 1977.

Fernbach, David. "Introduction." In Karl Marx, *Surveys from Exile*, vol. 1 of *Political Writings*, 7–34. Harmondsworth: Penguin/New Left Review, 1973.

Ferraro, Joseph. *Freedom and Determination in History According to Marx and Engels*. New York: Monthly Review Press, 1992.

Fields, Barbara J. "Slavery, Race and Ideology in the United States of America," *New Left Review* 1, no. 181 (May/June 1990): 95–118.

Finley, Moses [1973]. *The Ancient Economy*. Second edition, Harmondsworth: Penguin, 1985.

——— [1980]. *Ancient Slavery and Modern Ideology*. Harmondsworth: Penguin, 1983.

——— [1983]. *Politics in the Ancient World*. Cambridge: Canto, 1991.

———. "Revolution in Antiquity." In *Revolution in History*, edited by Roy Porter and Milukas Teich, 47–60. Cambridge: Cambridge University Press, 1986.

Fitzgerald, Frank T. "Sociologies of Development." In *Neo-Marxist Theories of Development*, edited by Peter Limqueco and Bruce McFarlane, 12–28. London: Croom Helm, 1983.

Fleischacker, Samuel. "The Impact on America: Scottish Philosophy and the American Founding." In *The Cambridge Companion to the Scottish Enlightenment*, edited by Alexander Broadie, 316–37. Cambridge: Cambridge University Press, 2003.

Fletcher, Andrew [1689]. Fletcher to Russell, January 8, 1689, Scottish Record Office, Andrew Russell Papers, RH15/106/690, no. 7.

———— [1698]. "A Discourse of Government with Relation to Militias." In *Political Writings*, edited by John Robertson, 1–31. Cambridge: Cambridge University Press, 1997.

———— [1698]. "Two Discourses Concerning the Affairs of Scotland: Written in the Year 1698." In *Political Writings*, edited by John Robertson, 33–81. Cambridge: Cambridge University Press, 1997.

Fogel, Robert. *Without Consent or Contract: The Rise and Fall of American Slavery*. New York: W. W. Norton, 1989.

Foner, Eric. *Reconstruction: America's Unfinished Revolution, 1863–1877*. New York: Harper and Row, 1988.

———— [1990]. "The Russians Write a New History." In *Who Owns History? Rethinking the Past in a Changing World*, 75–87. New York: Hill and Wang, 2002.

Forgacs, David. "Gramsci and Marxism in Britain," *New Left Review* 1, no. 176 (July/August 1989): 70–88.

Foster, John Bellamy, Brett Clark, and Richard York. *Critique of Intelligent Design: Materialism versus Creationism from Antiquity to the Present*. New York: Monthly Review Press, 2008.

Foucault, Michel [1977]. "Truth and Power." In *Power/Knowledge: Selected Interviews and Other Writings, 1972–1977*, edited by Colin Gordon, 109–133. Brighton: Harvester, 1980.

Frank, Andre Gunder [1967]. *Sociology of Development and Underdevelopment of Sociology*. London: Pluto Press, 1971.

————. *Capitalism and Underdevelopment in Latin America*. Harmondsworth: Penguin, 1971.

————. *Lumpenbourgeoisie—Lumpendevelopment*. New York: Monthly Review Press, 1972.

————. "Dependence Is Dead: Long Live Dependence and the Class Struggle: A Reply to Critics," *Latin American Perspectives* 1, no. 1 (Spring 1974): 87–106.

————. *World Accumulation, 1492–1789*. New York: Monthly Review Press, 1978.

————. "The Modern World System Revisited: Rereading Braudel and Wallerstein." In *Civilization and World Systems: Studying World Historic Change*, edited by Stephen K. Sanderson, 163–94. Walnut Creek: AltaMira Press, 1995.

————. *ReOrient: Global Economy in the Asian Age*. Berkeley and Los Angeles: University of California, 1998.

Frankel, Harry [Harry Braverman]. "Class Forces in the American Revolution," *Fourth International* 6, no. 3 (March 1946): 89–93.

Fraser, Ronald. *Blood of Spain: The Experience of Civil War, 1936–1939*. London: Allen Lane, 1979.

————. *Napoleon's Cursed War: Popular Resistance in the Spanish Peninsular War, 1808–1814*. London: Verso, 2008.

Freeman, Joseph. *An American Testament: A Narrative of Rebels and Romantics*. London: Victor Gollancz, 1938.

Friedman, Thomas L. "It's No Vietnam," *New York Times*, October 30, 2003.

Friedrichs, Christopher R. "The War and German Society." In *The Thirty Years' War*, ed. Geoffrey Parker, 208–15. London: Routledge, 1984.

Fulbrook, Mary. "The English Revolution and the Revisionist Revolt," *Social History* 7, no. 3 (October 1982): 249–64.

Furet, François [1978]. "The French Revolution Is Over." In *Interpreting the French Revolution*, 1–79. Cambridge: Cambridge University Press, 1981.

———— [1978]. "The Revolutionary Catechism." In *Interpreting the French Revolution*, 81–131.

Cambridge: Cambridge University Press, 1981.

———. "Terror." In *The French Revolution in Social and Political Perspective*, edited by Peter Jones, 450–65. London: Arnold, 1996.

Furet, François and David Richet [1965]. *La révolution française*. Revised edition, Paris: Gallimard, 1970.

Gall, Lothar. *Bismarck: The White Revolutionary*, vol. 1, *1851–1871*. London: Allen and Unwin, 1986.

Gamble, Andrew. *An Introduction to Modern Social and Political Thought*. Houndmills: Macmillan, 1981.

———. *Hayek: The Iron Cage of Liberty*. Boulder, CO: Westview Press, 1996.

García Linera, Álvaro. "State Crisis, Popular Power," *New Left Review* 2, no. 37 (January/February 2006): 73–85.

———. "The MAS Is of the Center-Left," *International Viewpoint* 373 (December 2005), http://www.internationalviewpoint.org/spip.php?article938.

Gardiner, Samuel R. [1888]. *History of the Great Civil War*, vol. 1, *1642–44*. London and New York: Windrush Press in association with the Phoenix Press, 2002.

Garfield, James Abram. *Garfield's Words: Suggestive Passages from the Public and Private Writings of James Abram Garfield*, edited by William Ralston Balch. London: Sampson Low, Marston, Searle and Rivington, 1881.

Garman, Douglas. "A Reply to P. F.," *Labour Monthly*, 22, no. 12 (December 1940): 651–53.

Gatrell, Peter. *Government, Industry and Rearmament in Russia, 1900–1914*. Cambridge: Cambridge University Press, 1994.

Gelderen, Martin van. *The Political Thought of the Dutch Revolt, 1555–1590*. Cambridge: Cambridge University Press, 1992.

Gellner, Ernest. *Thought and Change*. Chicago: University of Chicago Press, 1964.

———. "Soviets against Wittfogel: Or, the Anthropological Preconditions of Mature Marxism." In *States in History*, ed. John A. Hall, 78–108. Oxford: Basil Blackwell, 1986.

——— [1988]. *Plough, Book and Sword: The Structure of Human History*. London: Paladin, 1991.

Genovese, Elizabeth Fox and Eugene D. Genovese, "The Political Crisis of Social History: Class Struggle as Subject and Object." In *Fruits of Merchant Capital: Slavery and Bourgeois Property in the Rise and Expansion of Capitalism*, 179–212. Oxford: Oxford University Press, 1983.

———, "On the Social History of the French Revolution: New Methods, Old Ideologies." In *Fruits of Merchant Capital: Slavery and Bourgeois Property in the Rise and Expansion of Capitalism*, 213–48. Oxford: Oxford University Press, 1983.

Genovese, Eugene D. |1968|. "Marxist Interpretations of the Slave South." In *In Red and Black: Marxian Explorations in Southern and Afro-American History*, 315–53. New York: Vintage, 1972.

Geras, Norman. "Between the Russian Revolutions." In *The Legacy of Rosa Luxemburg*, 43–109. London: New Left Books, 1976.

———. *Marx and Human Nature: Refutation of a Legend*. London: Verso, 1983.

Gernet, Jacques [1972]. *A History of Chinese Civilisation*. Second edition, Cambridge: Cambridge University Press, 1982.

Gerschenkron, Alexander. *Economic Backwardness in Historical Perspective*. Cambridge, MA: Harvard University Press, 1962.

Gerstenberger, Heide [1990]. *Impersonal Power: History and Theory of the Bourgeois State*. Leiden: E. J. Brill, 2007.

Gibbon, Edward [1776]. *The Decline and Fall of the Roman Empire*, vol. 1. London: Frederick Warne and Company, no date.

Giddens, Anthony. *The Class Structure of the Advanced Societies*. London: Hutchison University Library, 1973.

Gilly, Adolfo [1971]. *The Mexican Revolution*. Expanded and revised edition, London: Verso, 1983.

Ginsborg, Paul. "Gramsci and the Era of Bourgeois Revolution in Italy." In *Gramsci and Italy's Passive Revolution*, edited by John Davis, 31–36. London: Croom Helm, 1979.

———. *A History of Contemporary Italy: Society and Politics, 1943–1988*. Harmondsworth: Penguin, 1990.

Glucksmann, André [1977]. *The Master Thinkers*. Brighton: Harvester, 1980.

Göçmen, Dogan. *The Adam Smith Problem: Human Nature and Society in* The Theory of Moral Sentiments *and* The Wealth of Nations. London: I. B. Tauris, 2007.

Godelier, Maurice [1964/1968]. "The Concept of the 'Asiatic Mode of Production' and Marxist Models of Social Evolution." In *Relations of Production: Marxist Approaches to Economic Anthropology*, edited by David D. Seddon, 209–57. London: Frank Cass, 1978.

Goldmann, Lucien. *The Hidden God: A Study of Tragic Vision in the Pensees of Pascal and the Tragedies of Racine*. London: Routledge and Kegan Paul, 1964.

Goldstone, Jack A. "East and West in the Seventeenth Century: Political Crises in Stuart England, Ottoman Turkey, and Ming China," *Comparative Studies in Society and History* 30, no. 1 (January 1988): 103–42.

Goodwin, Jeff. *No Other Way Out: States and Revolutionary Movements, 1945–1991*. Cambridge: Cambridge University Press, 2001.

Goodwin, Peter. "'Razor Sharp Factional Minds'—the Fourth International debates Kampuchea," *International Socialism*, second series, 5 (Summer 1979): 106–14.

Goody, Jack. *Capitalism and Modernity: the Great Debate*. Cambridge: Polity, 2004.

———. *The Theft of History*. Cambridge: Cambridge University Press, 2006.

Gordon, Daniel [1999]. "On the Supposed Obsolescence of the French Enlightenment." In *Postmodernism and the Enlightenment: New Perspectives on Eighteenth-Century French Intellectual History*, edited by Daniel Gordon, 201–21. London: Routledge, 2001.

Gould, Stephen J. *The Individual in Darwin's World*, the Second Edinburgh Medal Address, edited by Ian Wall, Ian Rolfe, Simon Gage, Vivian Bone, and Helen Simms. Edinburgh: Edinburgh University Press, 1990.

Gouldner, Alvin W. *The Future of Intellectuals and the Rise of the New Class: A Frame of Reference, Theses, Conjectures, Arguments and an Historical Perspective on the Role of Intellectuals and Intelligentsia in the International Class Contest of the Modern Era*. New York: Continuum Books, 1979.

Gowan, Peter [1991]. "The Gulf War, Iraq and Western Liberalism." In *The Global Gamble: Washington's Faustian Bid for World Dominance*, 141–86. London: Verso, 1999.

Gramsci, Antonio [1917]. "The Revolution against 'Capital.'" In *Selections from the Political Writings (1910–1920)*, edited by Quintin Hoare, 34–37. London: Lawrence and Wishart, 1977.

——— [1917]. "The Return to Freedom . . ." In *Selections from the Political Writings (1910–1920)*, edited by Quintin Hoare, 69–72. London: Lawrence and Wishart, 1977.

——— [1922]. "Origins of the Mussolini Cabinet." In *Selections from the Political Writings (1921–1926)*, edited by Quintin Hoare, 129–31. London: Lawrence and Wishart, 1978.

——— [1923]. "[A Letter to Trotsky on Futurism]." In *Selections from Cultural Writings*, edited by David Forgacs and Geoffrey Nowell-Smith, 52–54. London: Lawrence and Wishart, 1985.

——— [1929]. Gramsci to Carlo, December 19, 1929, in *Letters from Prison*, vol. 1, ed. Frank Rosengarten, 297–300. New York: Columbia University Press, 1994.

——— [1932]. Gramsci to Tania, June 6, 1932. In *Prison Letters*, 221–23. London: Pluto, 1996.

——— [1927–34]. "The Intellectuals." In *Selections from the Prison Notebooks*, edited by Quintin Hoare and Geoffrey Nowell-Smith, 5–23. London: Lawrence and Wishart, 1971.

——— [1927–34]. "Notes on Italian History." In *Selections from the Prison Notebooks*, edited by Quintin Hoare and Geoffrey Nowell-Smith, 52–120. London: Lawrence and Wishart, 1971.

——— [1927–34]. "The Modern Prince." In *Selections from the Prison Notebooks*, edited by Quintin Hoare and Geoffrey Nowell-Smith, 124–205. London: Lawrence and Wishart, 1971.

——— [1927–34]. "State and Civil Society." In *Selections from the Prison Notebooks*, edited by Quintin Hoare and Geoffrey Nowell-Smith, 210–78. London: Lawrence and Wishart, 1971.

——— [1927–34]. "Americanism and Fordism." In *Selections from the Prison* Notebooks, edited by Quintin Hoare and Geoffrey Nowell-Smith, 279–318.

——— [1927–34]. "Problems of Marxism: Some Problems in the Study of the Philosophy of Praxis." In *Selections from the Prison Notebooks*, edited by Quintin Hoare and Geoffrey Nowell-Smith, 381–472. London: Lawrence and Wishart, 1971.

——— [1927–34]. "The Question of the Language and the Italian Intellectual Classes." In *Selections from the Cultural Writings*, edited by David Forgacs and Geoffrey Nowell-Smith, 167–71. London: Lawrence and Wishart, 1985.

——— [1927–34]. "The Renaissance." In *Selections from the Cultural Writings*, edited by David Forgacs and Geoffrey Nowell-Smith, 220–22. London: Lawrence and Wishart, 1985.

——— [1927–34]. "Passive Revolution and Planned Economy." In *Further Selections from the Prison Notebooks*, edited by David Boothman, 277. Minneapolis: University of Minnesota Press, 1995.

——— [1927–34]. "Reference Points for an Essay on B. Croce." In *Further Selections from the Prison Notebooks*, edited by David Boothman, 326–61. Minneapolis: University of Minnesota Press, 1995.

——— [1927–34]. "The Philosophy of Benedetto Croce." In *Further Selections from the Prison Notebooks*, edited by David Boothman, 362–475. Minneapolis: University of Minnesota Press, 1995.

———. *The Modern Prince and Other Writings*, edited by Louis Marks. London: International Publishers, 1957.

———. *The Open Marxism of Antonio Gramsci*, edited by Carl Marzani. New York: Cameron Associates, 1957.

———. *Prison Notebooks*, vol. 1, edited by Joseph A. Buttigieg. New York: Columbia University Press, 1992.

———. *Prison Notebooks*, vol. 2, edited by Joseph A. Buttigieg. New York: Columbia University Press, 1996.

———. *Prison Notebooks*, vol. 3, edited by Joseph A. Buttigieg. New York: Columbia University Press, 2007.

Graus, Frantisek. "From Resistance to Revolt: The Late Medieval Peasant Wars in the Context of Social Crisis," *Journal of Peasant Studies* 3, no. 1 (October 1975): 1–9.

Green, John R. *A Short History of the English People*. Revised edition, London: Macmillan and Company, 1888.

Green, Peter. "The First Sicilian Slave War," *Past and Present* 20 (November 1961): 10–29.

Greenberg, Clement [1939]. "Avant-Garde and Kitsch." In *The Collected Essays and Criticism*, vol. 1, *Perceptions and Judgments, 1939–1944*, edited by John O'Brian, 5–22. Chicago: University of Chicago Press, 1986.

——— [1940]. "Towards a Newer Loacoon." In *The Collected Essays and Criticism*, vol. 1, *Perceptions and Judgments, 1939–1944*, edited by John O'Brian, 22–38. Chicago: University of Chicago Press, 1986.

Greenfield, Liah. *The Spirit of Capitalism: Nationalism and Economic Growth*. Cambridge, MA: Harvard University Press, 2001.

Griffin, Roger. "Revolution from the Right: Fascism." In *Revolutions and the Revolutionary Tradition in the West, 1560–1991*, edited by David Parker, 185–201. London: Routledge, 2000.

Griffiths, Jay. *Pip Pip: A Sideways Look at Time*. London: Flamingo, 2000.

Grossmann, Henryk [1929]. *The Law of Accumulation and Breakdown of the Capitalist System: Bring Also a Theory of Crises*. London: Pluto Press, 1992.

Grossman, Henryk. "The Evolutionist Revolt against Classical Economics: II. In England— James Steuart, Richard Jones, Karl Marx," *Journal of Political Economy* 51, no. 6 (December 1943): 506–22.

Grotius, Hugh [1625]. *Of the Rights of War and Peace*, vol. 2. London: D. Brown, T. Ward and W. Meares, 1715.

Gruber, Helmut. *Soviet Russia Masters the Comintern: International Communism in the Era of Stalin's Ascendancy*. New York: Anchor Press/Doubleday, 1974.

Gruner, Shirley. "The Revolution of July 1830 and the Expression 'Bourgeoisie,'" *Historical Journal* 11, no. 3 (1968): 462–71.

Guérin, Daniel [1946]. *La lutte de classes sous la première république*, vol. 1. Revised edition, Paris: Galimard, 1968.

——— [1946]. *Class Struggle in the First French Republic: Bourgeois et Bras Nus, 1793–1795*. London: Pluto, 1977.

Guevara, Ernest "Che" [1960]. "On Sacrifice and Dedication." In *Venceremos! The Speeches and Writings of Ernesto Che Guevara*, edited by John Gerassi, 144–66. London: Panther, 1969.

Guizot, François P. G. [1823]. *Essais sur l'histoire de France*. Paris: printemps chez Bonaventure et Ducessais, 1857.

——— [1826]. "Preface." In *History of Charles the First and the English Revolution from the Accession of Charles the First to His Execution*, ix–xxii. London: David Bogue, 1846.

——— [1828–1830]. *General History of Civilisation in Europe from the Fall of the Roman Empire to the French Revolution*. Oxford and London: Beckwith, 1837.

——— [1828–1830]. "The History of Civilization in Europe." In *Historical Essays and Lectures*, edited by Stanley Mellon. Chicago: University of Chicago Press, 1972.

Guy, Jeff. "The Destruction and Reconstruction of Zulu Society." In *Industrialization and Social Change in South Africa: African Class Formation, Culture and Consciousness 1870–1930*, edited by Shula Marks and Richard Rathbone, 167–94. London: Longman, 1982.

Habermas, Jürgen [1962]. *The Structural Transformation of the Public Sphere: An Inquiry into a Category of Bourgeois Society*. London: Polity, 1989.

Habib, Irfan [1968]. "Potentialities of Capitalist Development in the Economy of Mughal India." In *Essays in Indian History: Towards a Marxist Perception*, 180–232. London: Anthem Press, 2002.

Hacker, Louis M. *The Triumph of American Capitalism: The Development of Forces in American History to the end of the Nineteenth Century*. New York: Columbia University Press, 1940.

———. "The Anticapitalist Bias of American Historians." In *Capitalism and the Historians*, edited by Frederick A. Hayek, 62–90. Chicago: University of Chicago Press, 1954.

Haldon, John. "The Feudalism Debate Once More: The Case of Byzantium," *Journal of Peasant Studies* 17, no. 1 (October 1989): 5–40.

———. *The State and the Tributary Mode of Production*. London: Verso, 1993.

Hall, John A. "States and Societies: The Miracle in Comparative Perspective." In *Europe and the Rise of Capitalism*, edited by Jean Baechler, John A. Hall, and Michael Mann, 20–38. Oxford: Basil Blackwell, 1988.

Hall, Stuart. "The Neoliberal Revolution," *Soundings* (Summer 2011): 9–27.

Hallas, Duncan. *Trotsky's Marxism*. London: Pluto, 1979.

———. "The Bourgeois Revolution," *Socialist Worker Review* 105 (January 1988): 17–20.

Halliday, Fred [1990]. "'The Sixth Great Power': Revolutions and the International System." In *Rethinking International Relations*. London: Macmillan, 1994.

Halliday, Fred. *Revolution and World Politics: The Rise and Fall of the Sixth Great Power*. London: Macmillan, 1999.

Halliday, Fred and Maxine Molyneux. *The Ethiopian Revolution*. London: Verso, 1981.

Halperin, Sandra. *In the Mirror of the Third World: Capitalist Development in Modern Europe*. Ithaca, NY: Cornell University Press, 1997.

Hamilton, Alexander [1787]. "The Federalist, No. 17." In Alexander Hamilton, John Jay, and James Madison, *The Federalist Papers*, 95–99. New York: Bantam Dell, 1982.

Hampson, Norman. "Review of *The Social Interpretation of the French Revolution*," *Irish Historical Studies* 14 (1964–5): 190–92.

Hardt, Michael and Antonio Negri. *Empire*. Cambridge, MA: Harvard University Press, 2000.

Harman, Chris [1967]. "How the Revolution Was Lost." In *Selected Writings*, 101–19. London: Bookmarks, 2010.

———. *Explaining the Crisis: A Marxist Reappraisal*. London: Bookmarks, 1984.

———. "From Feudalism to Capitalism," *International Socialism*, second series, 45 (Winter 1989–90): 35–87.

———. "The Storm Breaks," *International Socialism*, second series, 46 (Spring 1990): 3–93.

———. "Change at the First Millennium," *International Socialism*, second series, 62 (Spring 1994): 91–96.

——— [1994]. "The Prophet and the Proletariat." In *Selected Writings*, 301–61. London: Bookmarks, 2010.

Harrington, James [1656]. "The Commonwealth of Oceana." In *The Political Works of James Harrington*, edited by J. G. A. Pocock, 155–359. Cambridge: Cambridge University Press, 1977.

——— [1658], "The Prerogative of Popular Government: A Political Discourse in Two Books." In *The Political Works of James Harrington*, edited by J. G. A. Pocock, 389–566. Cambridge: Cambridge University Press, 1977.

Harris, Nigel. "India: Part One," *International Socialism*, first series, 17 (Summer 1964): 4–14.

———. "Marxism: Leninism–Stalinism–Maoism," *International Socialism*, first series, 26 (Autumn 1965): 9–18, 27–32.

———. *The Mandate of Heaven: Marx and Mao in Modern China*, London: Quartet, 1978.

———. *Of Bread and Guns: The World Economy in Crisis*. Harmondsworth: Penguin, 1983.

———. *The End of the Third World: Newly Industrializing Countries and the Decline of an Ideology*. Harmondsworth: Penguin, 1986.

———. *The Return of Cosmopolitan Capital: Globalization, the State and War*. London: I. B. Tauris, 2003.

Hartz, Louis. *The Liberal Tradition in America*. New York: Harcourt, Brace, 1955.

Harvey, David [1978]. "On Countering the Marxian Myth—Chicago Style." In *Spaces of Capital: Towards a Critical Geography*, 68–89. Edinburgh: Edinburgh University Press, 2001.

———. *Paris, Capital of Modernity*. New York: Routledge, 2003.

———. *A Brief History of Neoliberalism*. Oxford: Oxford University Press, 2005.

———. *The Enigma of Capital and the Crises of Capitalism*. London: Profile Books, 2010.

Hatto, Arthur. "'Revolution': An Enquiry into the Usefulness of an Historical Term," *Mind* 58, no. 232 (1949): 495–517.

Hayek, Frederick A. *The Road to Serfdom*, London: George Routledge and Sons, 1944.

———. "History and Politics." In *Capitalism and the Historians*, edited by Frederick A. Hayek, 3–29. Chicago: University of Chicago Press, 1954.

———. *The Constitution of Liberty*. London: Routledge and Kegan Paul, 1960.

———. *The Fatal Conceit: The Errors of Socialism*, vol. 1 of *Collected Works*, edited by W. W. Bartley. London: Routledge 1988.

Haynes, Michael. *Nikolai Bukharin and the Transition from Capitalism to Socialism*. London: Croom Helm, 1985.

Haynes, Michael. "Columbus, the Americas and the Rise of Capitalism," *International Socialism*, second series, 57 (Winter 1992–93): 55–100.

————. *Russia: Class and Power, 1917–2000*. London: Bookmarks, 2002.

Hegel, G. W. F. [1807]. "Preface.," In *The Phenomenology of Mind*, vol. 1. London: George Allen and Unwin, 1910.

———— [1821]. "Preface." In *The Philosophy of Right*, 1–36. Oxford: Oxford University Press, 1953.

———— [1830–1831]. *The Philosophy of History*. New York: Dover Publications, 1956.

Heller, Henry. *The Conquest of Poverty: The Calvinist Revolt in Sixteenth-Century France*, Leiden: E. J. Brill, 1986.

————. *Labor, Science and Technology in France, 1500–1620*. Cambridge: Cambridge University Press, 1996.

————. *The Bourgeois Revolution in France, 1789–1815*. New York: Berghahn Books, 2006.

————. "Marx, the French Revolution, and the Specter of the Bourgeoisie," *Science and Society* 74, no. 2 (April 2010): 184–214.

Herzen, Alexander [1864]. "To an Opponent: Letter 1." In *Selected Philosophical Works*, 546–50. Moscow: Foreign Languages Publishing House, 1956.

———— [1869]. "To an Old Comrade: Letter 1." In *Selected Philosophical Works*, 576–82. Moscow: Foreign languages Publishing House, 1956.

Hexter, J. H. [1948/50]. "The Myth of the Middle Class in Tudor England." In *Reappraisals in History*, 71–116. London: Longmans, Green and Company, 1961.

———— [1958]. "Storm over the Gentry." In *Reappraisals in History*, 117–62. London: Longmans, Green and Company, 1961.

————. "Power Struggle, Parliament and Liberty in Early Stuart England," *Journal of Modern History* 50, no. 1 (March 1978): 1–50.

Higonnet, Patrice. "Terror, Trauma and the 'Young Marx' Explanation of Jacobin Politics," *Past and Present* 191 (May 2006): 121–64.

Hilferding, Rudolph [1910]. *Finance Capital: A Study of the Latest Phase of Capitalist Development*, edited by Tim Bottomore. London: Routledge and Kegan Paul, 1981.

Hill, Christopher [1940]. "The English Revolution." In *The English Revolution 1640: Three Essays*, edited by Christopher Hill, 9–82. London: Lawrence and Wishart, 1949.

————. "The English Civil War Interpreted by Marx and Engels," *Science and Society* 12, no. 1 (Winter 1948): 130–56.

———— [1954]. "The Norman Yoke." In *Puritanism and Revolution: Studies in the Interpretation of the English Revolution of the Seventeenth Century*, 3–31. London: Secker and Warburg, 1958.

———— [1956]. "Recent Interpretations of the Civil War." In *Puritanism and Revolution: Studies in the Interpretation of the English Revolution of the Seventeenth Century*, 50–122. London: Secker and Warburg, 1958.

————. *Economic Problems of the Church from Archbishop Whitgift to the Long Parliament*. Oxford: Oxford University Press, 1956.

————. "Introduction." In *The Good Old Cause: The English Revolution of 1640–1660, Its Causes, Course and Consequences*, edited by Christopher Hill and Edmund Dell, 1–32. Second revised edition, London: Frank Cass, 1969.

————. "The Theory of Revolutions." In *Isaac Deutscher: The Man and His Work*, edited by David Horowitz, 115–31. London: Macdonald and Company, 1971.

———— [1972]. *The World Turned Upside Down: Radical Ideas in the English Revolution*. Harmondsworth: Penguin, 1975.

————. *Change and Continuity in Seventeenth-Century England*, London: Weidenfeld and Nicolson, 1974.

———— [1976]. "A Bourgeois Revolution?" In *Three English Revolutions: 1640, 1688, 1776*, edited by J. G. A. Pocock, 109–39. Princeton, NJ: Princeton University Press, 1980.

————. "Parliament and People in Seventeenth-Century England," *Past and Present* 92 (August 1981): 100–124.

———— [1984]. *The Experience of Defeat: Milton and Some Contemporaries*. London: Bookmarks, 1994.

————. "The Bourgeois Revolution in Soviet Scholarship,'" *New Left Review* 1, no. 155 (January–February, 1986): 107–13.

———— [1986]. "The Word 'Revolution.'" In *A Nation of Change and Novelty*, 100–120. Revised edition, London: Bookmarks, 1993.

———— [1988]. "The Place of the Seventeenth-Century Revolution in English History." In *A Nation of Change and Novelty*, 19–37. Revised edition, London: Bookmarks, 1993.

————. "Foreword." In Harvey J. Kaye, *The Education of Desire: Marxists and the Writing of History*. London: Routledge, 1992.

Hill, Lisa. "Adam Smith, Adam Ferguson and Karl Marx on the Division of Labour," *Journal of Classical Sociology* 7, no. 3 (2007): 339–66.

Hilton, Rodney H. [1949]. "Peasant Movements in England before 1381." In *Class Conflict and the Crisis of Feudalism: Essays in Medieval Social History*, 49–65. Revised second edition, London: Verso, 1990.

———— [1951]. "Was There a General Crisis of Feudalism?" In *Class Conflict and the Crisis of Feudalism: Essays in Medieval Social History*, 166–72. Revised second edition, London: Verso, 1990.

————. *Bond Men Made Free: Medieval Peasant Movements and the English Rising of 1381*. London: Methuen, 1973.

———— [1984]. "Feudalism in Europe: Problems for Historical Materialists." In *Class Conflict and the Crisis of Feudalism: Essays in Medieval Social History*, 1–11. Revised second edition, London: Verso, 1990.

Hipkin, Stephen. "Property, Economic Interest and the Configuration of Rural Conflict in Sixteenth and Seventeenth-Century England," *Socialist History* 23 (2003): 67–88.

Hirik, Serhiy. "'The Permanent Revolution' and 'Asian Renaissance': Parallels between the Political Conceptions of Leon Trotsky and Mykola Khvylovy," *Debatte: Journal of Contemporary Central and Eastern Europe* 17, no. 2 (August 2009): 181–91.

Hirschman, Albert O. [1977]. *The Passions and the Interests: Political Arguments for Capitalism before Its Triumph*. Twentieth anniversary edition, Princeton, NJ: Princeton University Press, 1997.

Hirst, Paul Q. [1975]. "The Uniqueness of the West—Perry Anderson's Analysis of Absolutism and Its Problems." *Marxism and Historical Writing*. London: Routledge and Kegan Paul, 1985.

Hitchens, Christopher. *Regime Change*. Harmondsworth: Penguin, 2003.

———— [2003]. "A Liberating Experience." In *Love, Poverty and War: Journalism and Essays*, 463–75. London: Atlantic Books, 2005.

———— [2004]. "The Old Man." In *Love, Poverty and War: Journalism and Essays*, 43–53. London: Atlantic Books, 2005.

Hobbes, Thomas [1651]. *Leviathan: Or the Matter, Form, and Power of a Commonwealth Ecclesiastical and Civil*, edited by C. B. MacPherson. Harmondsworth: Penguin, 1968.

———— [1668]. *Behemoth: Or, the Long Parliament*, edited by Ferdinand Tönnies. London: Simpkin, Marshall, 1889.

Hobsbawm, Eric J. [1954]. "The Crisis of the Seventeenth Century." In *Crisis in Europe, 1560–1660: Essays from Past and Present*, edited by Trevor Aston, 5–58. London: Routledge and Kegan Paul, 1965.

———— [1959]. *Primitive Rebels: Studies in Archaic Forms of Social Movement in the 19th and 20th Centuries*. Manchester: Manchester University Press, 1971.

———— [1962]. *The Age of Revolution: Europe, 1789–1848*. London: Weidenfeld and Nicolson, 1995.

————. "Introduction." In Karl Marx, *Pre-Capitalist Economic Formations*, 9–65. New York:

International Publishers, 1965.

————. 1969, *Industry and Empire*, Harmondsworth: Penguin.

———— [1975]. *The Age of Capital, 1848–1875*. London: Weidenfeld and Nicolson, 1995.

————. "The Historians Group of the Communist Party." In *Rebels and Their Causes: Essays in Honor of A. L. Morton*, edited by Maurice Cornforth, 21–47. London: Lawrence and Wishart, 1978.

————. [1982]. "Marx, Engels and Politics." In *How to Change the World: Tales of Marx and Marxism*, 48–88. London: Little, Brown, 2011.

———— [1982]. "The Fortunes of Marx's and Engels' Writings." In *How to Change the World: Tales of Marx and Marxism*, 176–96. London: Little, Brown, 2011.

————. "Revolution." In *Revolution in History*, edited by Roy Porter and Milukas Teich, 5–46. Cambridge: Cambridge University Press, 1986.

————. [1987]. *The Age of Empire, 1875–1914*. London: Weidenfeld and Nicolson, 1995.

————. *Echoes of the Marseillaise: Two Centuries Look Back on the French Revolution*. London: Verso, 1990.

———— [1994]. "Identity History Is Not Enough." In *On History*, 266–77. London: Weidenfeld and Nicolson, 1997.

————. *Interesting Times: A Twentieth-Century Life*. London: Allen Lane, 2002.

Hobson, John M. *The Eastern Origins of Western Civilization*. New York: Cambridge University Press, 2004.

Hoffman, Phillip. *Growth in a Traditional Society: The French Countryside, 1450–1815*, Princeton, NJ: Princeton University Press, 1996.

Hofmann, Werner. *Ideengeschichte der Sozialen Bewegung des 19. und 20. Jahrhunderts*. Berlin: Walter de Gruyter, 1968.

Hofstadter, Richard. *The American Political Tradition and the Men Who Made It*. New York: Alfred A. Koopf. 1948.

Holstun, James. *Ehud's Dagger: Class Struggle in the English Revolution*. London: Verso, 2000.

————. "Communism, George Hill and the *Mir*: Was Marx a Nineteenth-century Winstanleyan?" In *Winstanley and the Diggers, 1649–1999*, edited by Andrew Bradstock, 121–48. London: Frank Cass, 2000.

————. "Utopia Pre-empted : Kett's Rebellion, Commoning, and the Hysterical Sublime," *Historical Materialism* 16, no. 3 (2008): 3–53.

Hont, Istvan. "The Language of Sociability and Commerce: Samuel Pufendorf and the Theoretical Foundations of the 'Four Stages Theory.'" In *The Language of Political Theory in Early Modern Europe*, edited by Anthony Pagden, 253–76. Cambridge: Cambridge University Press, 1987.

Hoodbhoy, Pervez A. *Islam and Science: Religious Orthodoxy and the Battle for Rationality*. London: Zed Books, 1991.

Hook, Andrew. "Scott and America." In *From Goosecreek to Gandercleugh: Studies in Scottish-American Literary and Cultural History*, 94–115. East Linton, Scotland: Tuckwell Press, 1999.

Hook, Andrew. "The South, Scotland, and William Faulkner." In *From Goosecreek to Gandercleugh: Studies in Scottish-American Literary and Cultural History*, 193–212. East Linton, Scotland: Tuckwell Press, 1999.

Hook, Sydney. *Towards the Understanding of Karl Marx: a Revolutionary Interpretation*. New York: John Day, 1933.

Hoppit, Julian. *A Land of Liberty? England, 1689–1727*. Oxford: Clarendon Press, 2000.

Horkheimer, Max [1941]. "The End of Reason." In *The Essential Frankfurt School Reader*, edited by Anthony Arato and Eike Gebhardt, 26–48. Oxford: Basil Blackwell, 1978.

Horne, Donald. *The Great Museum: The Re-presentation of History*. London: Pluto Press, 1984.

Hoston, Germaine. "Conceptualizing Bourgeois Revolution: The Prewar Japanese Left and the Meiji Restoration," *Comparative Studies in Society and History* 33, no. 3 (July 1991): 539–87.

Hotman, François [1567–72]. *Francogallia*, edited by Ralph E. Geisey. Cambridge: Cambridge University Press, 1972.

Howe, Daniel Walker. "Why the Scottish Enlightenment Was Useful to the Framers of the American Constitution," *Comparative Studies in Society and History* 31 (1989): 572–87.

Hoyle, Richard. "Tenure and the Land Market in Early Modern England: Or, a Late Contribution to the Brenner Debate," *Economic History Review*, second series, vol. 43, no. 1 (January 1990): 1–20.

Hughes, H. Stuart [1958]. *Consciousness and Society: The Reorientation of European Social Thought, 1890–1930*. London: Paladin, 1974.

Hume, David [1739]. *A Treatise of Human Nature: Being an Attempt to Introduce the Experimental Method of Reasoning into Moral Subjects*, Book 1, *Of the Understanding*, edited by Donald G. C Macnabb. London: Fontana, 1962.

——— [1739–40]. *A Treatise of Human Nature: Being an Attempt to Introduce the Experimental Method of Reasoning into Moral Subjects*, Book 2, *Of the Passions* and Book 3, *Of Morals*, edited by Pall S. Ardal. London: Fontana, 1972.

——— [1741]. "Whether the British Government Inclines More to Absolute Monarchy or to a Republic." In *Political Essays*, edited by Knud Haakonsen, 28–32. Cambridge: Cambridge University Press, 1994.

——— [1752]. "Of Refinement of the Arts." In *Political Essays*, edited by Knud Haakonsen, 105–14. Cambridge: Cambridge University Press, 1994.

——— [1752]. "Of Interest." In *Political Essays*, edited by Knud Haakonsen, 126–35. Cambridge, Cambridge University Press, 1994.

——— [1754–1762]. *The History of England from the Invasions of Julius Caesar to the Revolution of 1688*. 6 volumes, London: T. Cadell, 1778.

Ignatieff, Michael. *Isaiah Berlin: A Life*. London: Chatto and Windus, 1998.

Israel, Jonathan I. *The Dutch Republic: Its Rise, Greatness, and Fall, 1477–1806*. Oxford: Clarendon Press, 1998.

———. *Radical Enlightenment: Philosophy and the Making of Modernity, 1650–1750*. Oxford: Oxford University Press, 2001.

———. *Enlightenment Contested: Philosophy, Modernity, and the Emancipation of Man, 1670–1752*. Oxford: Oxford University Press, 2006.

———. *A Revolution of the Mind: Radical Enlightenment and the Intellectual Origins of Modern Democracy*. Princeton, NJ: Princeton University Press, 2010.

———. *Democratic Enlightenment: Philosophy, Revolution, and Human Rights, 1750–1790*. Oxford: Oxford University Press, 2010.

Itoh, Makoto. *Value and Crisis: Essays in Marxian Economics in Japan*. London: Pluto Press, 1980.

Jackson, T. A. *Solo Trumpet: Some Memories of Socialist Agitation and Propaganda*. London: Lawrence and Wishart, 1953.

Jago, Charles. "The 'Crisis of the Aristocracy' in Seventeenth-Century Castile," *Past and Present* 84 (August 1979): 60–90.

James, C. L. R. [1938]. *The Black Jacobins: Toussaint L'Overture and the San Domingo Revolution*. New edition, London: Alison and Busby, 1980.

James, Margaret [1940]. "Contemporary Materialist Interpretations of Society in the English Revolution." In *The English Revolution 1640: Three Essays*, edited by Christopher Hill, 83–100. London: Lawrence and Wishart, 1649.

Jameson, Fredric [1984]. 'The Cultural Logic of Late Capitalism,' in *Postmodernism, or, the Cultural Logic of Late Capitalism*, 1–54. London: Verso, 1991.

———. "Postmodernism and the Market." In *Postmodernism, or, the Cultural Logic of Late Capitalism*, 260–78. London: Verso, 1991.

Jardin, André. *Tocqueville: A Biography*. New York: Farrar, Straus, Giroux, 1988.

Jardine, Lisa. *Going Dutch: How England Plundered Holland's Glory*. London: HarperCollins, 2008.

Jaurès, Jean [1901]. "General Introduction to *The Socialist History of the French Revolution*." In *The Varieties of History: from Voltaire to the Present*, edited by Fritz Stern, 164–69. Second edition, London: Macmillan, 1970.

Jefferson, Thomas [1785]. Jefferson to Jay, August 23, 1785. In *Political Writings*, edited by Joyce Appleby and Terence Ball. Cambridge: Cambridge University Texts, 1999.

Jefferson, Thomas et al. [1776]. "The Unanimous Declaration of the Thirteen United States of America, July 4, 1776." In *Revolution from 1789 to 1906*, edited by Raymond Postgate, 4. London: Grant Richards, 1920.

Jenkins, Keith [1991]. *Re-thinking History*. London: Routledge, 2003.

Jolly, William. *The Life of John Duncan, Scotch Weaver and Botanist with Sketches of His Friends and Notices of the Times*. Second edition, London: Kegan Paul, Trench, 1883.

Jones, Colin [1990]. "Bourgeois Revolution Revivified: 1789 and Social Change." In *The French Revolution: Recent Debates and New Controversies*, edited by Gary Kates, 87–112. Second edition, London: Routledge, 2006.

Jones, Gareth Stedman. "The Specificity of US Imperialism," *New Left Review* 1, no. 60 (March–April 1970): 59–86.

———. "Society and Politics at the Beginning of the World Economy," *Cambridge Journal of Economics* 1 (1977): 77–92.

Jones, James R. *The Anglo-Dutch Wars of the Seventeenth Century*. London: Longman, 1996.

Jones, John [1651]. Jones to Stane, November 19, 1651, in "Inedited Letters of Cromwell, Colonel Jones, Bradshaw and Other Regicides," edited by Joseph Mayer, *Transactions of the Historical Society of Lancashire and Cheshire*, new series, vol. 13 (1861): 177–300.

Johnson, Richard. "Barrington Moore, Perry Anderson and English Social Development," *Working Papers in Cultural Studies* 9 (Spring 1976): 7–28.

Johnson, R. W. "False Start in South Africa," *New Left Review* 2, no. 58 (July/August 2009): 61–74.

Jones, P. J. "Communes and Despots: the City-State in Late-Medieval Italy," *Transactions of the Royal Historical Society*, fifth series, 15 (1964): 71–96.

Joseph, Keith. "Is Beckerman Among the Sociologists?" *New Statesman*, 4 April 4, 1975, 501–2.

Kamen, Henry [1971]. *European Society, 1500–1700*. London: Hutchison, 1984.

Kamanev, Lev [1934]. "Preface to Machiavelli," *New Left Review* 1, no. 15 (May/June 1962): 390–42.

Kames, Lord (Henry Home) [1746]. *Essays upon Several Subjects Concerning British Antiquities*. Second edition, London: printed for M. Cooper, 1749.

———. *Historical Law Tracts*, vol. 1. Edinburgh: A. Millar, A. Kincaid, and J. Bell, 1758.

——— [1776]. "Preface," in *The Gentleman Farmer: Being an Attempt to Improve Agriculture by Subjecting It to the Test of Rational Principles*, i–xxxii. Sixth edition, Edinburgh: Bell and Bradfute, 1815.

Kates, Gary [1998]. "Introduction." In *The French Revolution: Recent Debates and New Controversies*, edited by Gary Kates, 1–14. Second edition, London: Routledge, 2006.

Katz, Claudio J. *From Feudalism to Capitalism: Marxian Theories of Class Struggle and Social Change*. New York: Greenwood Press, 1989.

Kautsky, Karl [1895]. *Vorläufer der neueren Sozialismus*, Erster band, *Der Kommunismus in der Deutschen Reformation*. Berlin: J. H. W. Dietz, 1923.

——— [1888]. *Thomas More and His Utopia*. London: A. C. Black, 1927.

——— [1889]. "The *Sans-Culottes* of the French Revolution." In *Witnesses to Permanent Revolution: The Documentary Record*, edited by Richard B. Day and Daniel Gaido, 537–42. Leiden: E. J. Brill, 2009.

——— [1899]. *The Agrarian Question*. 2 volumes, London: Zwan, 1988.

——— [1902]. "The Slavs and Revolution." In *Witnesses to Permanent Revolution: The Documentary Record*, edited by Richard B. Day and Daniel Gaido, 56–65. Leiden: E. J. Brill, 2009.

——— [1903/1906]. "To What Extent Is the *Communist Manifesto* Obsolete?" In *Witnesses to Permanent Revolution: The Documentary Record*, edited by Richard B. Day and Daniel Gaido, 169–86. Leiden: E. J. Brill, 2009.

——— [1904]. "Revolutionary Questions." In *Witnesses to Permanent Revolution: The Documentary Record*, edited by Richard B. Day and Daniel Gaido, 187–249. Leiden: E. J. Brill, 2009.

——— [1905]. "Old and New Revolution." In *Witnesses to Permanent Revolution: The Documentary Record*, edited by Richard B. Day and Daniel Gaido, 529–36. Leiden: E. J. Brill, 2009.

——— [1906]. "The Driving Forces of the Russian Revolution and Its Prospects." In *Witnesses to Permanent Revolution: The Documentary Record*, edited by Richard B. Day and Daniel Gaido, 586–607. Leiden: E. J. Brill, 2009.

——— [1906]. "The American Worker." In *Witnesses to Permanent Revolution: The Documentary Record*, edited by Richard B. Day and Daniel Gaido, 609–61. Leiden: E. J. Brill, 2009.

——— [1908]. *Foundations of Christianity: A Study of Christian Origins*. London: Orbach and Chambers, no date of publication.

———. [1918]. "Dictatorship and Democracy" [extracted from *The Dictatorship of the Proletariat*]. In *Selected Political Writings*, edited by Patrick Goode, 97–125. London: Macmillan, 1983.

———. *Terrorism and Communism: A Contribution to the Natural History of Revolution*. London: National Labour Press, 1920.

——— [1927]. *The Materialist Conception of History*, edited by John H. Kautsky. New Haven, CT: Yale University Press, 1978.

———. *Bolshevism at a Deadlock*. London: Allen and Unwin, 1931.

Kermode, Jenny. *Medieval Merchants: York, Beverley and Hull in the Later Middle Ages*. Cambridge: Cambridge University Press, 1998.

Kelly, Brian. "Materialism and the Persistence of Race in the Jim Crow South," *Historical Materialism* 12, no. 2 (2004): 3–19.

Kershaw, Ian. *Hitler, 1889–1936: Hubris*. London: Allen Lane, 1998.

Keynes, John Maynard [1931]. "A Pure Theory of Money: A Reply to Dr Hayek." In *Collected Works*, vol. 13. Part 1, *The General Theory and After: Preparation*, edited by Donald E. Moggridge, 243–56. London: Macmillan, 1972.

Khaldun, Ibn el. *The Muqaddimah: An Introduction to History*, edited by N. J. Dawood. London: Routledge and Kegan Paul, 1967.

Kiernan, Victor G. [1947/8]. "Theses for Discussion on Absolutism no. 2: The Tudor State in English History." In *Ideology, Absolutism and the English Revolution: Debates of the British Communist Historians, 1940–1956*, edited by David Parker, 91–100. London: Lawrence and Wishart, 2008.

———. [1948]. "Postscript (Absolutism)." In *Ideology, Absolutism and the English Revolution: Debates of the British Communist Historians, 1940–1956*, edited by David Parker, 137–42. London: Lawrence and Wishart, 2008.

———. "Revolution and Reaction, 1789–1848," *New Left Review* 1, no. 19 (March/April 1963): 69–78.

———. *State and Society in Europe, 1550–1650*. Oxford: Basil Blackwell, 1980.

Kidron, Michael. "Imperialism: Highest Stage but One," *International Socialism*, first series, 9 (Summer 1962): 15–21.

——— [1968]. *Western Capitalism since the War*. Revised edition, Harmondsworth: Penguin, 1970.

Knight, Alan. "The Mexican Revolution: Bourgeois? Nationalist? Or Just a 'Great Rebellion'? *Bulletin of Latin American Research* 4, no. 2 (1985): 1–37.

King James VI and I [1599]. "Basilicon Doron." In *Political Writings*, edited by Johann P. Sommerville, 1–61. Cambridge: Cambridge University Press, 1994.

King, Richard H. "Hannah Arendt and the Concept of Revolution in the 1960s," *New For-*

mations 71 (Spring 2011): 30–46.

Kingsnorth, Paul. *One No, Many Yeses: A Journey to the Heart of the Global Resistance Movement.* London: Free Press, 2003.

Kissinger, Henry A. *A World Restored: Metternich, Castlereagh and the Problems of Peace 1812–1822.* Boston: Houghton Mifflin, 1957.

Kitsikopoulos, Harry. "Technological Change in Medieval England: A Critique of the Neo-Malthusian Argument," *Proceedings of the American Philosophical Society* 144, no. 4 (December 2000): 397–449.

Klassen, John. "The Disadvantaged and the Hussite Revolution," *International Review of Social History* 35 (1990): 249–72.

Klooster, Wim. *Revolutions in the Atlantic World: A Comparative History.* New York: New York University Press, 2009.

Klugman, Jack [1977]. "Introduction: Crisis in the Thirties: A View from the Left." In *Culture and Crisis in Britain in the Thirties,* edited by Jon Clark, Margot Heinemann, David Margolies, and Carole Snee, 13–36. London: Lawrence and Wishart, 1979.

Koebner, Richard. "Adam Smith and the Industrial Revolution," *Economic History Review,* second series, vol. 11, no. 3 (April 1959): 381–91.

Koenigsberger, Hans G. "Republics and Courts in Italian and European Culture in the Sixteenth and Seventeenth Centuries," *Past and Present* 83 (May 1979): 32–56.

Koenker, Diane and William Rosenberg, *Strikes and Revolution in Russia, 1917.* Princeton, NJ: Princeton University Press, 1989.

Kolchin, Peter. *American Slavery, 1619–1877.* Harmondsworth: Penguin, 1993.

Kouvelakis, Stathis. *Philosophy and Revolution: from Kant to Marx.* London: Verso, 2003.

Krasso, Nicolas. "Trotsky's Marxism," *New Left Review* 1, no. 44 (July–August 1967): 64–86.

Kreidte, Peter. *Peasants, Landlords and Merchant Capitalists: Europe and the World Economy, 1500–1800,* Leamington Spa: Berg Publishers, 1983.

Kristol, Irving. *The American Revolution as a Successful Revolution.* Washington, DC: American Institute for Public Policy Research, 1973.

Kula, Witfold [1962]. *An Economic Theory of the Feudal System: Towards a Model of the Polish Economy, 1500–1800,* London: New Left Books, 1976.

Kulikoff, Allen. "Was the American Revolution a Bourgeois Revolution?" In *Transforming Hand of Revolution: Reconsidering the American Revolution as a Social Movement,* edited by Ronald Hoffman and Peter J. Albert, 59–89. Charlottesville: University of Virginia Press, 1996.

Kurlantzick, Joshua. "The Bourgeois Revolution: How the Middle Class Declared War on Democracy," *Foreign Policy* (April 2009), http://www.foreignpolicy.com/articles/2009/04/27/the_bourgeois_revolution.

Labriola, Antonio [1896]. "Historical Materialism." In *Essays on the Materialist Conception of History,* 95–246. Chicago: Charles H. Kerr, 1908.

Laclau, Ernesto [1971]. "Feudalism and Capitalism in Latin America." In *Politics and Ideology in Marxist Theory: Capitalism—Fascism—Populism.* London: Verso, 1977.

Ladendorf, Otto. *Historisches Schlagwörterbuch: Ein Versuch.* Strassburg and Berlin: Trübner, 1906.

Lafargue, Paul [1890]. Extract from "Recollections of Marx." In *Marx/Engels on Literature and Art,* edited by Lee Baxandall and Stefan Morawski, 152–53. New York: International General, 1974.

Lakatos, Imre. "Falsification and the Methodology of Scientific Research Programmes." In *Criticism and the Growth of Knowledge,* edited by Imre Lakatos and Alan Musgrave, 91–196. Cambridge: Cambridge at the University Press, 1970.

Lampedusa, Guiseppe Tomasi di [1958]. *The Leopard.* Glasgow: Fontana, 1963.

Larner, John. *Italy in the Age of Dante and Petrarch, 1216–1380.* London: Longman, 1980.

Larsson, Reidar. *Theories of Revolution: From Marx to the First Russian Revolution*. Stockholm: Almquist and Wiksell, 1970.

Laslett, Peter. "The English Revolution and Locke's 'Two Treatises of Government,'" *Cambridge Historical Journal* 12, no. 1 (January 1956): 40–55.

———— [1965]. *The World We Have Lost: England before the Industrial Age*. Second edition, London: Methuen, 1971.

————. "Introduction." In John Locke, *Two Treatises of Civil Government*, edited by Peter Laslett, 3–126. Cambridge: Cambridge University Press, 1988.

Lefebvre, Georges [1927]. *The Thermidorians*. London: Routledge and Keegan Paul, 1965.

———— [1939]. *The Coming of the French Revolution*. Princeton, NJ: Princeton University Press, 1947.

———— [1957]. *The French Revolution: From 1793 to 1799*. London: Routledge and Kegan Paul, 1964.

Leff, Gordon [1967]. *Heresy in the Later Middle Ages: The Relation of Heterodoxy to Dissent, c. 1250–c. 1450*. Manchester: Manchester University Press, 1999.

Lehmann, William C. *John Millar of Glasgow, 1735–1801: His Life and Thought and His Contributions to Sociological Analysis*. Glasgow: Cambridge at the University Press, 1960.

Lenin, Vladimir I. [1895]. "The Economic Content of Narodism and the Criticism of It in Mr. Struve's Book (*The Reflection of Marxism in Bourgeois Literature*)." In *Collected Works*, vol. 1, *1893–1894*, 333–507. Moscow: Foreign Languages Publishing House, 1960.

———— [1899]. *The Development of Capitalism in Russia: The Process of the Formation of Home Market for Large Scale Industry*. In *Collected Works*, vol. 3, *1899*, 23–607. Moscow: Foreign Languages Publishing House, 1960.

———— [1899]. "What Is to Be Done? Burning Questions of Our Movement." In *Collected Works*, vol. 5, *May 1901–February 1902*, 347–529. Moscow: Foreign Languages Publishing House, 1961.

———— [1905]. "The Fall of Port Arthur." In *Collected Works*, vol. 8, January–July 1905, 47–55. Moscow: Foreign Languages Publishing House, 1962.

———— [1905]. "Two Tactics of Social-Democracy in the Democratic Revolution." In *Collected Works*, vol. 9, *June–November 1905*, 15–140. Moscow: Foreign Languages Publishing House, 1962.

———— [1905]. "Social Democracy's Attitude towards the Peasant Movement." In *Collected Works*, vol. 9, *June–December 1905*, 230–39. Moscow: Foreign Languages Publishing House, 1962.

———— [1905]. "Lessons of the Moscow Events." In *Collected Works*, vol. 9, *June–November 1905*, 376–87. Moscow: Foreign Languages Publishing House, 1962.

———— [1905]. "The Socialist Party and Non-Party Revolutionism." In *Collected Works*, vol. 10, *November 1905–June 1906*, 75–82. Moscow: Foreign Languages Publishing House, 1962.

———— [1906]. "Preface to the Russian Translation of K. Kautsky's pamphlet *The Driving Forces and Prospects of the Russian Revolution*," in *Collected Works* vol. 11, *June 1906–January 1907*, 408–13. Moscow: Foreign Languages Publishing House, 1962.

———— [1907]. "The Agrarian Question and the Forces of the Revolution." In *Collected Works*, vol. 12, *January–June 1907*, 333–36. Moscow: Foreign Languages Publishing House, 1962.

———— [1907]. "Notes of a Publicist." In *Collected Works*, vol. 13, *June 1907–April 1908*, 62–74. Moscow: Foreign Languages Publishing House, 1962.

———— [1907]. "The Agrarian Programme of Social-Democracy in the First Russian Revolution, 1905–1907." In *Collected Works*, vol. 13, *June 1907–April 1908*, 217–431. Moscow: Foreign Languages Publishing House, 1962.

———— [1908]. "The Assessment of the Russian Revolution." In *Collected Works*, vol. 15, *March 1908–August 1909*, 50–62. Moscow: Foreign Languages Publishing House, 1963.

———— [1909]. "The Aim of the Proletarian Struggle in Our Revolution." In *Collected Works*, vol. 15, *March 1908–August 1909*, 360–79. Moscow: Foreign Languages Publishing House, 1963.

——— [1910]. "Notes of a Publicist." In *Collected Works*, vol. 16, *September 1909–December 1910*, 195–259. Moscow: Foreign Languages Publishing House, 1963.

——— [1911]. "The 'Peasant Reform' and the Proletarian-Peasant Revolution." In *Collected Works*, vol 17, *December 1910–April 1912*, 119–28. Moscow: Foreign Languages Publishing House, 1963.

——— [1911]. "A Conversation between a Legalist and an Opponent of Liquidationism." In *Collected Works*, vol. 17, *December 1910–April 1912*, 179–88. Moscow: Foreign Languages Publishing House, 1963.

——— [1911]. "Reformism in the Russian Social-Democratic Movement," In *Collected Works*, vol. 17, *December 1910–April 1912*, 229–41. Moscow: Foreign Languages Publishing House, 1963.

——— [1912]. "Democracy and Narodism in China." In *Collected Works*, vol. 18, *April 1912–March 1913*, 163–69. Moscow: Foreign Languages Publishing House, 1963.

——— [1913]. "The Historical Destiny of the Doctrine of Karl Marx." In *Collected Works*, vol. 18, *April 1912–March 1913*, 582–85. Moscow: Foreign Languages Publishing House, 1964.

——— [1913]. "The Three Sources and Three Component Parts of Marxism." In *Collected Works*, vol. 19, *March–December 1913*, 21–28. Moscow: Foreign Languages Publishing House, 1963.

——— [1913]. "Backward Europe and Advanced Asia." In *Collected Works*, vol. 19, *March–December 1913*, 99–100. Moscow: Foreign Languages Publishing House, 1963.

——— [1914]. "The Right of Nations to Self-Determination." In *Collected Works*, vol. 20, *December 1913–August 1914*, 393–454. Moscow: Foreign Languages Publishing House, 1964.

——— [1914–16]. "Conspectus of Hegel's book, *The Science of Logic*." In *Collected Works*, vol. 38, *Philosophical Notebooks*, 85–237. Moscow: Foreign Languages Publishing House, 1960.

——— [1914–16]. "Conspectus of Hegel's book, *Lectures on the History of Philosophy*." In *Collected Works*, vol. 38, *Philosophical Notebooks*, 243–302. Moscow: Foreign Languages Publishing House, 1960.

——— [1914]. "The War and Russian Social-Democracy." In *Collected Works*, vol. 21, *August 1914–December 1915*, 25–34. Moscow: Foreign Languages Publishing House, 1964.

——— [1915]. "The Collapse of the Second International." In *Collected Works*, vol. 21, *August 1914–December 1915*, 205–59. Moscow: Foreign Languages Publishing House, 1964.

——— [1915]. "On the Slogan for a United States of Europe." In *Collected Works*, vol. 21, *August 1914–December 1915*, 339–43. Moscow: Foreign Languages Publishing House, 1964.

——— [1915]. "New Data on the Laws Governing the Development of Capitalism in Agriculture, Part One: Capitalism and Agriculture in the United States of America," in *Collected Works*, vol. 22, *December 1915–July 1916*, 13–102. Moscow: Foreign Languages Publishing House. 1964.

——— [1916]. "Imperialism, the Highest Stage of Capitalism: A Popular Outline." In *Collected Works*, vol. 22, *December 1915–July 1916*, 185–304. Moscow: Foreign Languages Publishing House, 1964.

——— [1916]. "The Discussion on Self-determination Summed-Up." In *Collected Works*, vol. 22, *December 1915–July 1916*, 320–60. Moscow: Foreign Languages Publishing House, 1964.

——— [1917]. "Farewell Letter to Swiss Workers." In *Collected Works*, vol. 23, *August 1916–March 1917*, 367–73. Moscow: Foreign Languages Publishing House, 1964.

——— [1917]. "The Tasks of the Proletariat in the Present Revolution." In *Collected Works*, vol. 24, *April–June 1917*, 19–26. Moscow: Foreign Languages Publishing House, 1964.

——— [1917]. "The Dual Power." In *Collected Works*, vol. 24, *April–June 1917*, 38–41. Moscow: Foreign Languages Publishing House, 1964.

———— [1917]. "Letters on Tactics." In *Collected Works*, vol. 24, *April–June 1917*, 42–54. Moscow: Foreign Languages Publishing House, 1964.

———— [1917]. "The Tasks of the Proletariat in Our Revolution," in *Collected Works*, vol 24, *April–June 1917*, 55–91, Moscow: Foreign Languages Publishing House, 1964.

———— [1917]. "The State and Revolution: The Marxist Theory of the State and the Tasks of the Proletariat in the Revolution." In *Collected Works*, vol. 25, *June–September 1917*, 385–497. Moscow: Foreign Languages Publishing House, 1964.

———— [1918]. "Report on the Activities of the Council of People's Commissars, January 11 (24)." In *Collected Works*, vol. 26, *September 1917–February 1918*, 455–72. Moscow: Foreign Languages Publishing House, 1964.

—— — [1918]. "'Left Wing' Childishness and the Petty Bourgeois Mentality." In *Collected Works*, vol. 27, *February–July 1918*, 323–54. Moscow: Foreign Languages Publishing House, 1965.

———— [1918]. "Report on Foreign Policy Delivered at a Joint Meeting of the All-Russia Central Executive Committee and the Moscow Soviet: May 14, 1918." In *Collected Works*, vol. 27, *February–July 1918*, 365–81. Moscow: Foreign Languages Publishing House, 1965.

———— [1919]. "The State." In *Collected Works*, vol. 29, *March–August 1919*, 470–88. Moscow: Foreign Languages Publishing House, 1965.

———— [1920]. "'Left-Wing' Communism—an Infantile Disorder." In *Collected Works*, vol. 31, *April–December 1920*, 17–117. Moscow: Foreign Languages Publishing House, 1966.

———— [1920]. "The Trade Unions, the Present Situation and Trotsky's Mistakes." In *Collected Works*, vol. 32, *December 1920–August 1921*, 19-42. Moscow: Foreign Languages Publishing House, 1965.

———— [192]. "The Party Crisis." In *Collected Works*, vol. 32, *December 1920–August 1921*, 43-53. Moscow: Foreign Languages Publishing House, 1965.

———— [1921]. "Fourth Anniversary of the October Revolution." In *Collected Works*, vol. 33, *August 1921–March 1923*, 51–59. Moscow: Foreign Languages Publishing House, 1966.

———— [1923]. "On Co-operation." In *Collected Works*, vol. 33, *August 1921–March 1923*, 467–75. Moscow: Foreign Languages Publishing House, 1966.

———— [1923]. "Our Revolution (Apropos of N. Sukhanov's Notes)." In *Collected Works*, vol. 33, *August 1921–March 1923*, 476–80. Moscow: Foreign Languages Publishing House, 1966.

Lenman, Bruce J. *Britain's Colonial Wars, 1688–1783*. Harlow: Longman, 2001.

Lepore, Jill. *The Whites of Their Eyes: The Tea Party's Revolution and the Battle over American History*. Princeton, NJ: Princeton University Press, 2010.

Leslie, Esther. *Walter Benjamin: Overpowering Conformism*. London: Pluto, 2000.

————. *Walter Benjamin*. London: Reaktion, 2007.

Lewin, Moshe [1978]. "Society, State, and Ideology during the First Five-Year Plan." In *The Making of the Soviet System: Essays in the Social History of Interwar Russia*. New York: Pantheon Books, 1985.

Lewis, Tom. "Structures and Agents: The Concept of 'Bourgeois Revolution' in Spain," *Arizona Journal of Hispanic Cultural Studies* 3 (1999): 7–16.

Leys, Colin. *Market-Driven Politics: Neoliberal Democracy and the Public Interest*. London: Verso, 2001.

Lih, Lars T. *Lenin Rediscovered: What Is to Be Done? in Context*. Leiden: Brill Academic Publishing, 2005.

————. "'Our Position Is in the Highest Degree Tragic': Bolshevik 'Euphoria' in 1920," in *History and Revolution: Refuting Revisionism*, edited by Michael J. Haynes and Jim Wolfreys, 118–37. London: Verso, 2007.

Linden, Marcel van der. "Marx and Engels, Dutch Marxism and the 'Model Capitalist Nation of the Seventeenth Century,'" *Science and Society* 61, no. 2 (Summer 1997): 161–92.

————. *Western Marxism and the Soviet Union: A Survey of Critical Theories and Debates since 1917*. Leiden: E. J. Brill, 2007.

Linebaugh, Peter. "Review of *The Making of New World Slavery*," *Historical Materialism* 1 (Autumn 1997): 185–95.

Linebaugh, Peter and Marcus Rediker. *The Many-Headed Hydra: The Hidden History of the Revolutionary Atlantic*. London: Verso, 2000.

Lipset, Seymour Martin and Gary Marks. *It Didn't Happen Here: Why Socialism Failed in the United States*. New York: W. W. Horton, 2000.

List, Frederick [1840]. *The National System of Political Economy*. New edition, London: Longman, Green and Company, 1904.

Livesey, James. *Making Democracy in the French Revolution*. Cambridge, MA: Harvard University Press, 2001.

Lochhead, Robert. *The Bourgeois Revolutions*. International Institute for Research and Education, Notebooks for Research and Study, no. 11/12 (1989).

Lockhart, John G. [1836]. *The Life of Sir Walter Scott, Bart., 1771–1832*. New popular edition, London: Adam and Charles Black, 1893.

Lockwood, David. "Historical Materialism and the State," *Critique* 34, no. 2 (August 2006): 163–78.

Locke, John [1669]. "The Fundamental Constitutions of Carolina." In *Political Writings*, edited by David Wooton, 210–31. Harmondsworth: Penguin, 1993.

———— [1679–1683, 1689]. "An Essay Concerning the True Original, Extent, and End of Civil Government." In *Two Treatises of Civil Government*, edited by Peter Laslett, 265–428. Cambridge: Cambridge University Press, 1988.

———— [1689]. Locke to Clarke, February 8, 1689. In *The Correspondence of John Locke*, vol. 3, edited by Esmond S. de Beer Oxford: Oxford University Press, 1978.

———— [1690]. "John Locke on the Glorious Revolution: A Rediscovered Document," edited by J. Farr and C. Roberts, *Historical Journal* 28, no. 2 (June 1985): 385–98.

Losurdo, Domenico [2006]. *Liberalism: A Counter-history*. London: Verso, 2011.

Love, Joseph L. "Raúl Prebish and the Origins of the Doctrine of Unequal Exchange," *Latin American Research Review* 15, no. 3 (1980): 47–72.

Lowe, Lisa. *Immigrant Acts: On Asian American Cultural Politics*. Durham, NC: Duke University Press, 1996.

Löwith, Karl [1960]. *Max Weber and Karl Marx*, edited by Tom Bottomore and William Outhwaite. London: George Allen and Unwin, 1982.

Löwy, Michael [1970]. *The Theory of Revolution in the Young Marx*. Leiden: E. J. Brill, 2003.

————. "From the Great Logic of Hegel to the Finland Station," *Critique* 6 (Spring 1976): 5–15.

————. *Georg Lukács—from Romanticism to Bolshevism*. London: New Left Books, 1979.

————. *The Politics of Combined and Uneven Development: The Theory of Permanent Revolution*. London: Verso, 1981.

————. "'The Poetry of the Past': Marx and the French Revolution," *New Left Review* 1, no. 177 (September/October 1989): 111–24.

————. *Fire Alarm: On Reading Walter Benjamin's "On the Concept of History."* London: Verso, 2005.

Lublinskaya, A. D. [1965]. *French Absolutism: The Crucial Phase, 1620–1629*. New York, Cambridge University Press, 1968.

Lucas, Colin. "Nobles, Bourgeois and the Origins of the French Revolution," *Past and Present* 60 (August 1973): 84–126.

Ludtke, Alf. "The Role of State Violence in the Transition to Industrial Capitalism: The Example of Prussia from 1815 to 1848," *Social History* 4, no. 2 (May 1979): 175–221.

Lukács, Georg [1923]. "What Is Orthodox Marxism?" In *History and Class Consciousness: Studies in Marxist Dialectics*, 1–26. London: Merlin, 1971.

——— [1923]. "The Marxism of Rosa Luxemburg." In *History and Class Consciousness: Studies in Marxist Dialectics*, 27–45. London: Merlin, 1971.

——— [1923]. "Class Consciousness." In *History and Class Consciousness: Studies in Marxist Dialectics*, 46–82. London: Merlin, 1971.

——— [1923]. "Reification and the Consciousness of the Proletariat." In *History and Class Consciousness: Studies in Marxist Dialectics*, 83–222. London: Merlin, 1971.

——— [1923]. "The Changing Function of Historical Materialism." In *History and Class Consciousness: Studies in Marxist Dialectics*, 223–55. London: Merlin, 1971.

——— [1923]. "Legality and Illegality." In *History and Class Consciousness: Studies in Marxist Dialectics*, 256–71. London: Merlin, 1971.

——— [1923]. "Critical Observations on Rosa Luxemburg's 'Critique of the Russian Revolution.'" In *History and Class Consciousness: Studies in Marxist Dialectics*, 272–94. London: Merlin, 1971.

——— [1923]. "Towards a Methodology of the Problem of Organisation." In *History and Class Consciousness: Studies in Marxist Dialectics*, 295–342. London: Merlin, 1971.

——— [1924]. *Lenin: A Study in the Unity of His Thought*, London: New Left Books, 1970.

——— [1925–6]. "Tailism and the Dialectic." In *A Defence of* History and Class Consciousness, 45–149. London: Verso, 2000.

——— [1928]. "Blum Theses (Extracts)." In *Tactics and Ethics: Political Writings, 1919–1929*, edited by Rodney Livingstone, 227–53. London: New Left Books, 1972.

——— [1934]. "Hölderlin's Hyperion." In *Goethe and His Age*, 136–56. London: Merlin, 1968.

——— [1938]. *The Young Hegel. Studies in the Relationship between Dialectics and Economics*, London: Merlin, 1975.

——— [1952]. *The Destruction of Reason*. London: Merlin, 1980.

——— [1967]. "Preface to the New Edition (1967)." In *History and Class Consciousness: Studies in Marxist Dialectics*, ix–xlvii. London: Merlin, 1971.

——— [1967]. *Conversations with Lukács*, edited by Theo Pinkus. London: Merlin Press, 1974.

——— [1968]. "On His Life and Work," *New Left Review* 1, no. 68 (July–August 1971): 49–58.

Luraghi, Raimondo. "The Civil War and the Modernization of American Society: Social Structure and Industrial Revolution in the Old South Before and During the War," *Civil War History* 18 (September 1972): 230–50.

Luther, Martin [1517–46]. *Conversations with Luther: Selections from the Recently Published Sources of the Table Talk*, edited by Preserved Smith and Herbert Percival Gallinger. New Canaan, CT: Keats Publishing, 1979.

Luttwak, Edward. *Turbo-capitalism: Winners and Losers in the Global Economy*. London: Weidenfeld and Nicolson, 1998.

Luxemburg, Rosa [1896]. "Social Democracy and the National Struggles in Turkey," *Revolutionary History* 8, no. 3, *The Balkan Socialist Tradition and the Balkan Federation, 1871–1915* (2003): 37–46.

——— [1905]. "The Russian Revolution." In *Witnesses to Permanent Revolution: The Documentary Record*, edited by Richard B. Day and Daniel Gaido, 521–28. Leiden: E. J. Brill, 2009.

——— [1908–9]. "The National Question and Autonomy." In *The National Question: Selected Writings*, edited by Howard B. Davis, 101–287. New York: Monthly Review Press, 1976.

——— [1913]. *The Accumulation of Capital*. London: Routledge and Kegan Paul, 1963.

Lynch, John. *The Spanish American Revolutions, 1808–1826*. London: Weidenfeld and Nicolson, 1973.

Lyotard, Jean-François [1979]. *The Postmodern Condition: A Report on Knowledge*. Manchester: Manchester University Press, 1984.

Macaulay, Thomas B. [1830]. *Napoleon and the Restoration of the Bourbons*, edited by Joseph Hamburger. London: Longmans, 1977.

——— [1831]. "Parliamentary Reform: A Speech Delivered in the House of Commons on

March 2, 1831." In *Speeches on Politics and Literature by Lord Macaulay*, 1–14. London: J. M. Dent and Sons, 1909.

——— [1842]. "The People's Charter: A Speech Delivered in the House of Commons on May 3, 1842." In *Speeches on Politics and Literature by Lord Macaulay*, 189–199 London: J. M. Dent and Sons, 1909.

———. *The History of England from the Accession of James II*, vols 1–2. London: Longman, Brown, Green and Longmans, 1849.

Macfarlane, Alan. *The Origins of English Individualism: The Family, Property and Social Transition*. Oxford: Blackwell, 1978.

———. "Socio-economic Revolution in England and the Origin of the Modern World." In *Revolution in History*, edited by Roy Porter and Mikulas Teich, 145–66. Cambridge: Cambridge University Press, 1986.

Machiavelli, Niccolo [1513–14]. *The Prince*. Harmondsworth: Penguin, 1975.

——— [1513–19]. *The Discourses*. Harmondsworth: Penguin, 1983.

MacIntyre, Alasdair. *Marxism: An Interpretation*. London: Student Christian Movement Press, 1953.

——— [1958–59]. "Notes from the Moral Wilderness." In *Alasdair MacIntyre's Engagement with Marxism: Selected Writings, 1953–1974*, edited by Paul Blackledge and Neil Davidson, 45–68. Leiden: E. J. Brill, 2008.

——— [1959]. "Hume on 'Is' and 'Ought.'" In *Against the Self-Images of the Age: Essays on Ideology and Philosophy*, 109–124. London: Duckworth, 1971.

——— [1960]. "Breaking the Chains of Reason." In *Alasdair MacIntyre's Engagement with Marxism: Selected Writings, 1953–1974*, edited by Paul Blackledge and Neil Davidson, 135–66. Leiden: E. J. Brill, 2008.

——— [1963]. "Trotsky in Exile." In *Alasdair MacIntyre's Engagement with Marxism: Selected Writings, 1953–1974*, edited by Paul Blackledge and Neil Davidson, 267–76. Leiden: E. J. Brill, 2008.

——— [1964]. "Pascal and Marx: On Lucien Goldmann's *Hidden God*." In *Alasdair MacIntyre's Engagement with Marxism: Selected Writings, 1953–1974*, edited by Paul Blackledge and Neil Davidson, 305–316. Leiden: E. J. Brill, 2008.

——— [1965]. "Marxist Mask and Romantic Face: Lukács on Thomas Mann." In *Alasdair MacIntyre's Engagement with Marxism: Selected Writings, 1953–1974*, edited by Paul Blackledge and Neil Davidson, 317–27. Leiden: E. J. Brill, 2008.

———. *A Short History of Ethics* London: Routledge and Kegan Paul, 1967.

——— [1968]. "How to Write about Lenin—and How Not To." In *Alasdair MacIntyre's Engagement with Marxism: Selected Writings, 1953–1974*, edited by Paul Blackledge and Neil Davidson, 355–67. Leiden: E. J. Brill, 2008.

——— [1968]. "Marxism of the Will." In *Alasdair MacIntyre's Engagement with Marxism: Selected Writings, 1953–1974*, edited by Paul Blackledge and Neil Davidson, 373–79. Leiden: E. J. Brill, 2008.

——— [1953/1968]. *Marxism and Christianity*. Harmondsworth: Penguin, 1971.

———. *Marcuse: An Exposition and a Polemic*. London: Fontana, 1970.

———. "The End of Ideology and the End of the End of Ideology." In *Against the Self-Images of the Age: Essays on Ideology and Philosophy*, 3–11. London: Duckworth, 1971.

MacIntyre, Stuart. *A Proletarian Science: Marxism in Britain, 1917–1933*. London: Lawrence and Wishart, 1980.

Mackintosh, James [1791]. *Vindiciae Gallicae: Defence of the French Revolution and Its English Admirers Against the Accusations of the Right Honorable Edmund Burke including Some Strictures on the Late Production of Monsieur de Calonne*. Fourth edition, with additions, London: G. G. J. and J. Robinson, 1792.

MacLachlan, Alastair. *The Rise and Fall of Revolutionary England: An Essay on the Fabrication of Seventeenth-Century History*. Houndmills: Macmillan, 1996.

Maclean, John [1923]. "All Hail, the Scottish Workers' Republic!" In *In the Rapids of Revolution*, edited by Nan Milton, London: Croom Helm, 1978.

MacLeod, Ken. *The Restoration Game*. London: Orbit, 2010.

MacPherson, C. B. [1962]. *The Political Theory of Possessive Individualism: Hobbes to Locke*. Oxford: Oxford University Press, 1964.

———. "Introduction." In Thomas Hobbes, *Leviathan*, edited by C. B. MacPherson. Harmondsworth: Penguin, 1968.

———. *Burke*. Oxford: Oxford University Press, 1981.

Maddison, Angus. "Economic Policy and Performance in Europe, 1913–1970." In *The Fontana Economic History of Europe*, vol. 6, *The Twentieth Century*, Part Two, edited by Carlo M. Cipolla, 442–508. Glasgow: Fontana Books, 1976.

———. *Phases of Capitalist Development*. Oxford: Oxford University Press, 1982.

Madison, James [1787]. "The Federalist, No.10." In Alexander Hamilton, John Jay, and James Madison, *The Federalist Papers*, 50–58. New York: Bantam Dell, 1982.

——— [1787]. "The Federalist, No. 14." In Alexander Hamilton, John Jay, and James Madison, *The Federalist Papers*, 74–80. New York: Bantam Dell, 1982.

——— [1788]. "The Federalist, No. 52." In Alexander Hamilton, John Jay, and James Madison, *The Federalist Papers*, 320–25. New York: Bantam Dell, 1982.

——— [1788]. "The Federalist, No. 54." In Alexander Hamilton, John Jay, and James Madison, *The Federalist Papers*, 331–36. New York: Bantam Dell, 1982.

Maier, Pauline. *American Scripture: Making the Declaration of Independence*. New York: Alfred A. Knopf, 1998.

Maitan, Livio [1969]. *Party, Army and Masses in China: A Marxist Interpretation of the Cultural Revolution*. London: New Left Books, 1976.

Makey, Walter. *The Church of the Covenant, 1637–1651*. Edinburgh: John Donald, 1979.

Malherbe, Michel. "The Impact on Europe." In *The Cambridge Companion to the Scottish Enlightenment*, edited by Alexander Broadie, 298–315. Cambridge: Cambridge University Press, 2003.

Malia, Martin. *History's Locomotives: Revolutions and the Making of the Modern World*, edited by Terence Emmons. New Haven, CT: Yale University Press, 2006.

Mandel, Bernard [1955]. *Labour Free and Slave: Workingmen and the Anti-slavery Movement in the United States*. Urbana and Chicago: University of Illinois, 2007.

Mandel, Ernest. *The Formation of the Economic Thought of Karl Marx*, New York: Monthly Review Press, 1971.

——— [1969]. "The Inconsistencies of State Capitalism." In *Readings on "State Capitalism,"* 7–26. London: International Marxist Group Publications, 1973.

———. *Late Capitalism*. London: New Left Books, 1975.

———. *Revolutionary Marxism Today*, edited by Jon Rothschild. London: New Left Books, 1979.

———. *Trotsky as Alternative*. London: Verso, 1995.

Mann, Michael. *The Sources of Social Power*, vol. 1, *A History of Power from the Beginning to 1760 AD*. Cambridge: Cambridge University Press, 1986.

———. "Ruling Class Strategies and Citizenship." In *States, Wars and Capitalism: Studies in Political Sociology*, 188–210. Oxford: Oxford University Press, 1988.

———. *The Sources of Social Power*, vol. 2, *The Rise of Classes and Nation-States, 1760–1914*. Cambridge: Cambridge University Press, 1993.

Manning, Brian [1976]. *The English People and the English Revolution, 1640–1649*. Second edition, London: Bookmarks, 1991.

———. *1649: The Crisis of the English Revolution*. London: Bookmarks, 1992.

———. "The English Revolution and the Transition from Feudalism to Capitalism," *International Socialism*, second series, 63 (Summer 1994): 75–87.

————. "The English Revolution: The Decline and Fall of Revisionism," *Socialist History* 14 (1999): 40–53.

Mao Tse-tung [1935]. "On Tactics against Japanese Imperialism." In *Selected Works*, vol. 1, 153–74. London: Lawrence and Wishart, 1954.

———— [1937]. "Strive to Win over Millions upon Millions of the Masses to the Anti-Japanese National United Front." In *Selected Works*, vol. 1, 273–81. London: Lawrence and Wishart, 1954.

———— [1939]. "The Chinese Revolution and the Chinese Communist Party." In *Selected Works*, vol. 3, 72–101. London: Lawrence and Wishart, 1954.

Maravall, José Antonio. *La Cultura del Barroco: Análisis de una Estructura Histórica*. Barcelona: Ariel, 1975.

Marcuse, Herbert [1964]. "Industrialization and Capitalism in Max Weber." In *Negations: Essays in Critical Theory*, 201–26. Harmondsworth: Penguin, 1972.

Margerison, Kenneth. "P.-L. Roederer: The Industrial Capitalist as Revolutionary," *Eighteenth Century Studies* 11, no. 2 (Summer 1978): 473–88.

Marshall, Gordon. *Presbyteries and Profits: Calvinism and the Development of Capitalism in Scotland, 1560–1707*. Oxford: Clarendon Press, 1980.

[Marten, Hugh, Richard Overton and William Walwyn] [1646]. "A Remonstrance of Many Thousand Citizens, and Other Free-Born People of England to Their Own House of Commons." In *Leveller Manifestoes of the Puritan Revolution*, edited by D. M. Wolfe., 113–30. New York: Thomas Nelson and Sons, 1944.

Martin, Ged. *Britain and the Origins of Canadian Confederation, 1837–67*. Houndmills: Macmillan, 1995.

Marwick, Arthur. *The Sixties: Cultural Revolution in Britain, France, Italy, and the United States, c. 1958–c. 1974*. Oxford: Oxford University Press.

Marx, Eleanor [1895]. "Recollections of Mohr." In *Marx/Engels on Literature and Art*, edited by Lee Baxandall and Stefan Morawski, 149–50. New York: International General, 1974.

Marx, Karl [1843]. "Critique of Hegel's Doctrine of the State." In *Early Writings*, 58–198. Harmondsworth: Penguin Books, 1975.

———— [1843]. "On the Jewish Question." In *Early Writings*, 212–41. Harmondsworth: Penguin Books, 1975.

———— [1843–4]. "Critique of Hegel's Philosophy of Right. Introduction." In *Early Writings*, 233–57. Harmondsworth: Penguin Books, 1975.

———— [1844]. "Economic and Philosophical Manuscripts." In *Early Writings*, 279–400. Harmondsworth: Penguin Books, 1975.

———— [1844]. "Critical Notes on 'The King of Prussia and Social Reform. By a Prussian.'" In *Early Writings*, 402–20. Harmondsworth: Penguin Books, 1975.

———— [1847]. *The Poverty of Philosophy: Answer to the* Philosophy of Poverty *by M. Proudhon*. In *Collected Works*, vol. 6, 105–212. London: Lawrence and Wishart, 1976.

———— [1847]. "Moralizing Criticism and Critical Morality: A Contribution to German Cultural History *Contra* Karl Heinzen." In *Collected Works*, vol. 6, 312–40. London: Lawrence and Wishart, 1976.

———— [1848]. "Die Bourgeoisie und die Kontrerevolution," in *Werke*, Band 6, S, 102–24. Berlin: Dietz Verlag, 1959.

———— [1848]. "The Bourgeoisie and the Counter-Revolution." In *The Revolutions of 1848*, vol. 1 of *Political Writings*, edited by David Fernbach, 186–212. Harmondsworth: Penguin/New Left Review, 1973.

———— [1848]. "The Paris *Reforme* on the Situation in France." In *Collected Works*, vol. 7, 493–95. London: Lawrence and Wishart, 1977.

———— [1848]. "Counter-Revolution in Berlin." In *Collected Works*, vol. 8, 14–19. London: Lawrence and Wishart, 1977.

—— [1849]. "The Trial of the Rhenish District Committee of Democrats. Speech by Karl Marx in his Own Defence." In *The Revolutions of 1848*, vol. 1 of *Political Writings*, edited by David Fernbach, 245–64. Harmondsworth: Penguin/New Left Review, 1973.

—— [1847/9], "Wage Labour and Capital." In *Collected Works*, vol. 9, London: Lawrence and Wishart, 1977.

—— [1850]. "Address of the Central Committee to the Communist League (March 1850)." In *The Revolutions of 1848*, vol. 1 of *Political Writings*, edited by David Fernbach, 319–30. Harmondsworth: Penguin/New Left Review, 1973.

—— [1850]. "The Class Struggles in France: 1848 to 1850." In *Surveys from Exile*, vol. 2 of *Political Writings*, edited by David Fernbach, 35–142. Harmondsworth: Penguin/New Left Review, 1973.

—— [1850]. "Review of Guizot's Book on the English Revolution." In *Surveys from Exile*, vol. 2 of *Political Writings*, edited by David Fernbach, 250–55. Harmondsworth: Penguin/New Left Review, 1973.

—— [1852]. "The Eighteenth Brumaire of Louis Bonaparte." In *Surveys from Exile*, vol. 2 of *Political Writings*, edited by David Fernbach, 143–249. Harmondsworth: Penguin/New Left Review, 1973.

—— [1852]. Marx to Weydemeyer, March 5, 1852. In *Collected Works*, vol, 39. London: Lawrence and Wishart, 1983.

—— [1853]. "The British Rule in India." In *Surveys from Exile*, vol. 2 of *Political Writings*, edited by David Fernbach, 301–7. Harmondsworth: Penguin/New Left Review, 1973.

—— [1853]. "The East India Company Its History and Revolt." In *Surveys from Exile*, vol. 2 of *Political Writings*, edited by David Fernbach, 307–16. Harmondsworth: Penguin/New Left Review, 1973.

—— [1953]. "The Future Results of the British Rule in India." In *Surveys from Exile*, vol. 2 of *Political Writings*, edited by David Fernbach, 319–25. Harmondsworth: Penguin/New Left Review, 1973.

—— [1854]. Marx to Frederick Engels, July 27, 1854. In *Collected Works*, vol. 39, 472–76. London: Lawrence and Wishart, 1983.

—— [1855]. "Ireland's Revenge." In *Collected Works*, vol. 14, 78–80. London: Lawrence and Wishart, 1980.

—— [1855]. "Another British Revelation." In *Collected Works*, vol. 14, 513–18. London: Lawrence and Wishart, 1980.

—— [1856]. "Speech at the Anniversary of the *People's Paper*." In *Surveys From Exile*, vol. 2 of *Political Writings*, edited by David Fernbach, 299–300. Harmondsworth: Penguin/New Left Review, 1973.

—— [1856]. Marx to Engels, April 16, 1856. In *Collected Works*, vol. 40, 37–41. London: Lawrence and Wishart, 1983.

—— [1857–58]. *Grundrisse: Foundations of the Critique of Political Economy (Rough Draft)*. Harmondsworth: Penguin/New Left Review, 1973.

—— [1858]. Marx to Engels, October 8, 1858. In *Collected Works*, vol. 40. Lawrence and Wishart, 1983.

—— [1859]. "Preface to *A Contribution to the Critique of Political Economy*." In *Early Writings*, 424–28. Harmondsworth: Penguin/New Left Review, 1975.

—— [1859]. *A Contribution to the Critique of Political Economy*. In *Collected Works*, vol. 29, 257–40. London: Lawrence and Wishart, 1987.

—— [1859]. "Erfurtery in the Year 1859." In *Collected Works*, vol. 16, 404–6. London: Lawrence and Wishart, 1980.

—— [1861]. Marx to Lassalle, January 16, 1861. In *Collected Works*, vol. 41. London: Lawrence and Wishart, 1995.

—— [1861]. Marx to Lion Phillips, May 6, 1861. In *Collected Works*, vol. 41. London:

Lawrence and Wishart, 1995.

———— [1861]. "The Civil War in the United States." In *Surveys from Exile*, vol. 2 of *Political Writings*, edited by David Fernbach, 344–53. Harmondsworth: Penguin/New Left Review, 1973.

———— [1862]. "Chinese Affairs." In *Collected Works*, vol. 19, 216–18. London: Lawrence and Wishart, 1984.

———— [1862]. "Comments on the North American Events." In *Collected Works*, vol. 19, 248–51. London: Lawrence and Wishart, 1984.

———— [1862–3]. *Theories of Surplus Value*, part 1, edited by S. Ryazanskaya. Moscow: Progress Publishers, 1963.

———— [1862–3]. *Theories of Surplus Value*, part 2, edited by S. Ryazanskaya. Moscow: Progress Publishers, 1969.

———— [1862–3]. *Theories of Surplus Value*, part 3, edited by S. Ryazanskaya. Moscow: Progress Publishers, 1971.

———— [1864]. "To Abraham Lincoln, President of the United States of America." In *Collected Works*, vol. 20, 19–21. London: Lawrence and Wishart, 1995.

———— [1867]. *Capital: A Critique of Political Economy*, vol. 1, Harmondsworth: Penguin/New Left Review, 1976.

———— [1870]. "The General Council to the Federal Council of Romance Switzerland." In *Collected Works*, vol. 21, 84–91. London: Lawrence and Wishart, 1985.

———— [1870]. Marx to Meyer and Vogt, April 9, 1870. In *The First International and After*, vol. 3 of *Political Writings*, edited by David Fernbach, 187–234. Harmondsworth: Penguin/New Left Review, 1974.

———— [1871]. "The Civil War in France: Address of the General Council." In *The First International and After*, vol. 3 of *Political Writings*, edited by David Fernbach, 187–234. Harmondsworth: Penguin/New Left Review, 1974.

———— [1871]. "First Draft of 'The Civil War in France' [Extract]." In *The First International and After*, vol. 3 of *Political Writings*, edited by David Fernbach, 236–68. Harmondsworth: Penguin/New Left Review, 1974.

———— [1875]. "Critique of the Gotha Programme." In *The First International and After*, vol. 3 of *Political Writings*, edited by David Fernbach, 339–59. Harmondsworth: Penguin/New Left Review, 1974.

———— [1877]. "[Letter to *Otechesivenniye Zapiski*]," in *Collected Works*, vol. 24, 196–201. London: Lawrence and Wishart, 1989.

———— [1881]. "[Third Draft]," "[Drafts of the Letter to Vera Zasulich]." In *Collected Works*, vol. 24, 360–63. London: Lawrence and Wishart, 1989.

———— [1881]. Marx to Nieuwenhuis, February 22, 1881, in *Collected Works*, vol. 46, 65–66. London: Lawrence and Wishart, 1992.

———— [1881]. Marx to Zasulich, March 8, 1881. In *Collected Works*, vol. 46, 71. London: Lawrence and Wishart, 1992.

———— [1894]. *Capital: A Critique of Political Economy*, vol. 3. Harmondsworth: Penguin/New Left Review, 1981.

Marx, Karl and Frederick Engels [1844]. *The Holy Family or Critique of Critical Criticism: Against Bruno Bauer and Company*. In *Collected Works*, vol. 4, 5–212. London: Lawrence and Wishart, 1975.

————. [1845–46]. *The German Ideology: Critique of Modern German Philosophy According to Its Representatives Feuerbach, B. Bauer and Stirner, and of German Socialism According to Its Various Prophets*. In *Collected Works*, vol. 5, 19–539. London: Lawrence and Wishart, 1975.

———— [1848]. "The Manifesto of the Communist Party." In *The Revolutions of 1848*, vol. 1 of *Political Writings*, edited by David Fernbach, 67–98. Harmondsworth: Penguin/New

Left Review, 1973.

———— [1882]. "Preface to the Second Russian Edition of 'The Manifesto of the Communist Party,'" in *Collected Works*, vol. 24, 425–26. London: Lawrence and Wishart, 1989.

Maza, Sarah. "Luxury, Morality, and Social Change: Why There Was No Middle-Class Consciousness in Prerevolutionary France," *Journal of Modern History* 69, no. 2 (June 1997): 199–229.

————. *The Myth of the French Bourgeoisie: An Essay on the Social Imaginary, 1750–1850.* Cambridge, MA: Harvard University Press, 2003.

Mazzini, Giuseppe [1835]. "Thoughts on the French Revolution of 1789." In *The Duty of Man and Other Essays by Joseph Mazzini*, 251–80. New York: Dutton, 1912.

Mayer, Arno. *The Persistence of the Old Regime: Europe to the Great War*, London: Croom Helm, 1981.

————. *Why Did the Heavens Not Darken? The "Final Solution" in History*, London: Verso, 1990.

McDaniel, Tim. *Autocracy, Capitalism, and Revolution in Russia*. Berkeley and Los Angeles: University of California Press, 1988.

McDonald, Forrest. *Alexander Hamilton: A Biography*. New York: W. W. Norton, 1979.

McLennan, David [1973]. *Karl Marx: His Life and Thought*. London: Grenada, 1976.

McLynn, Frank J. *The Jacobites*. London: Routledge and Kegan Paul, 1985.

————. *1759: The Year Britain Became Master of the World*. London: BCA, 2004.

McNally, David. *Political Economy and the Rise of Capitalism*. Berkeley and Los Angeles: University of California Press, 1988.

————. "Locke, Levellers and Liberty: Property and Democracy in the Thought of the First Whigs," *History of Political Thought* 10, no. 1 (Spring 1989): 17–40.

McPherson, James [1964]. *The Struggle for Equality: Abolitionist and the Negro in the Civil War and Reconstruction*. Princeton, NJ: Princeton University Press, 1995.

McPherson, James M. [1982]. "The Second American Revolution." In *Abraham Lincoln and the Second American Revolution*, 3–22. New York: Oxford University Press, 1991.

————. *Battle Cry of Freedom: The Civil War Era*. New York: Oxford University, 1988.

————. *For Cause and Comrades*. New York: Oxford University, 1997.

Medway, Lewis [William Paterson]. *An Inquiry into the Reasonableness and Consequences of a Union with Scotland . . . as Communicated to Lawrence Phillips, Esquire; Near York*. London, printed by Benjamin Bragg, 1706.

Meek, Ronald L. [1954]. "The Scottish Contribution to Marxist Sociology." In *Economics and Ideology and Other Essays: Studies in the Development of Economic Thought*, 34–50. London: Chapman and Hall, 1967.

———— [1956]. *Studies in the Labour Theory of Value*. Second edition, London: Lawrence and Wishart, 1973.

———— [1958]. "The Rehabilitation of Sir James Steuart." In *Economics and Ideology and Other Essays: Studies in the Development of Economic Thought*, 3–17. London: Chapman and Hall, 1967.

———— [1971]. "Smith, Turgot and the 'Four Stages' Theory." In *Smith, Marx, and After*, 18–32. London: Chapman and Hall, 1977,

————. "Introduction." In *Turgot on Progress, Sociology and Economics*, 1–33. Cambridge: Cambridge University Press, 1973.

————. *Social Science and the Ignoble Savage*. Cambridge: Cambridge University Press, 1976.

Mehring, Franz [1897]. "Conditions in Germany." In *Absolutism and Revolution in Germany, 1525–1848*, 149–84. London: New Park, 1975.

———— [1897]. "The German Reformation and Its Consequences." In *Absolutism and Revolution in Germany, 1525–1848*, 1–32. London: New Park, 1975.

Mellon, Stanley. *The Political Uses of History: A Study of Historians in the French Restoration*. Stanford: Stanford University Press, 1958.

Merleau-Ponty, Maurice [1955]. *Adventures of the Dialectic*. London: Heinemann Educational Books, 1974.

Merrill, Michael. "The Anticapitalist Origins of the United States," *Review* 13, no. 4 (Fall 1990): 465–97.

Merrington, John. "Town and Country in the Transition to Capitalism." In *The Transition from Feudalism to Capitalism*, edited by Rodney H. Hilton, 170–195. London: New Left Books, 1976.

Michels, Robert [1911]. *Political Parties: A Sociological Study of the Emergence of Leadership, the Psychology of Power, and the Oligarchic Tendencies of Organization*. New York: Dover Publications, 1959.

Mielants, Eric H. *The Origins of Capitalism and the "Rise of the West."* Philadelphia: Temple University Press.

Miéville, China. *Between Two Rights: A Marxist Theory of International Law*. Leiden: E. J. Brill, 2005.

Mignet, François Auguste Marie [1824]. *History of the French Revolution from 1789 to 1814*. London: George Bell and Sons, 1907.

Mikhailova, Julia. "Soviet Japanese Studies on the Problem of the Meiji Ishin and Development of Capitalism in Japan." In *War, Revolution and Japan*, edited by Ian Neary, 33–38. Folkestone: Curzon Press, 1993.

Miliband, Ralph. "Barnave: A Case of Bourgeois Class Consciousness." In *Aspects of History and Class Consciousness*, edited by Istvan Meszaros, 22–48. London: Routledge and Kegan Paul, 1971.

——— [1075]. "Political Power and Historical Materialism." In *Class Power and State Power*, 50–62. London: Verso, 1983.

Millar, John [1771]. *The Origin of the Distinction of Ranks: Or, an Inquiry into the Circumstances which Give Rise to Influence and Authority in the Different Members of Society*. Fourth edition, Edinburgh: William Blackwood, 1806.

——— [1787]. *An Historical View of English Government: From the Settlement of the Saxons in Britain to the Revolution in 1688; to which are Subjoined some Dissertations Connected with the History of Government from the Revolution to the Present Time*, edited by J. Craig and J. Milne. Third edition, London: J. Mawman, 1803.

Milne, Seumas. *The Enemy Within: MI5, Maxwell and the Scargill Affair*. London: Verso, 1994.

Milner, Clyde A. "National Initiatives." In *The Oxford Book of the American West*, edited by Clyde A. Milner, Carol A. O'Connor and Martha A. Sandweiss, 155–93. New York: Oxford University Press, 1994.

Milonakis, Dimitris and Ben Fine. *From Political Economy to Economics: Method, the Social and the Historical in the Evolution of Economic Theory*. London: Routledge, 2009.

"Minutes 10/11 January 1948: Discussion on Absolutism (cont)." In *Ideology, Absolutism and the English Revolution: Debates of the British Communist Historians, 1940–1956*, edited by David Parker, 127–37. London: Lawrence and Wishart, 2008.

Mollat, Michael and Phillipe Wolff. *The Popular Revolutions of the Middle Ages*. London: George Allen and Unwin, 1973.

Molyneux, John. *Leon Trotsky's Theory of Revolution*. Brighton: Harvester, 1981.

Mommsen, Theodore [1854]. *The History of Rome*, vol. 1. London: Richard Bentley and Son, 1877.

Montesquieu, Charles-Louis de Secondat [1748]. *The Spirit of the Laws*. Kitchener, Ontario: Batoche Books, 2001.

Mooers, Colin. *The Making of Bourgeois Europe: Absolutism, Revolution and the Rise of Capitalism in England, France and Germany*. London: Verso, 1991.

Moore, Barrington [1966]. *The Social Origins of Dictatorship and Democracy: Lord and Peasant in the Making of the Modern World*. Harmondsworth: Penguin, 1973.

Moore, James and Michael Silverthorne. "Gershom Carmichael and the Natural Jurisprudence

Tradition in Eighteenth-Century Scotland." In *Wealth and Virtue: The Shaping of Political Economy in the Scottish Enlightenment*, edited by Istvan Hont and Michael Ignatieff, 73–87. Cambridge: Cambridge University Press, 1983.

Morrill, John S. *The Revolt of the Provinces: Conservatives and Radicals in the English Civil War, 1630–1650*. London: Longman, 1976.

Morris, William. "'A Dream of John Ball." In *A Dream of John Ball* and *A King's Lesson*, London: Reeves and Turner, 1888.

Morrison, John. "Parish of Canisbay (County of Caithness)." In *The Statistical Account of Scotland*, vol. 8, edited by John Sinclair, 142–69. Edinburgh: published for W. Creech, 1792.

Morton, Adam David. *Unravelling Gramsci: Hegemony and Passive Revolution in the Global Economy*. London: Pluto, 2007.

———. "Disputing the Geopolitics of Global Capitalism," *Cambridge Review of International Affairs* 20, no. 4 (2007): 599–617.

Mukersic, John. "Parish of West Calder (County of Midlothian)." In *The Statistical Account of Scotland* 18, edited by John Sinclair, 190–98. Edinburgh: published for W. Creech, 1794.

Mukherjee, S. N. "The Idea of Feudalism: From the *Philosophes* to Karl Marx." In *Feudalism: Comparative Studies*, edited by Edmund Leach, S. N. Mukherjee, and John Ward, *Sydney Studies in Society and Culture* 2 (1985): 25–39.

Murrin, John M. "The Great Inversion, or Court versus Country: A Comparison of the Revolution Settlements in England (1688–1721) and America (1776–1816)." In *Three British Revolution: 1641, 1688, 1776*, edited by J. G. A. Pocock, 368–453. Cambridge: Cambridge University Press, 1980.

———. "A Roof without Walls: The Dilemma of American National Identity.," In *Beyond Confederation: Origins of the Constitution and American National Identity*, edited by Richard Beeman, Stephen Botein and Edward C. Carter II, 333–48. Chapel Hill: University of North Carolina Press, 1987.

Musgrove, Peter. *The Early Modern European Economy*, Houndmills: Macmillan, 1999.

Nairn, Tom. "La nemesi borghese," *Il Contemporaneo* 6, nos. 63–64 (1963): 120–41.

———. "The Twilight of the British State," *New Left Review* 1, no. 101–2 (February–April 1977): 3–61.

———. *The Enchanted Glass: Britain and Its Monarchy*, Second edition, London: Vintage, 1994.

Nash, Gary B. *The Unknown American Revolution: The Unruly Birth of Democracy and the Struggle to Create America*. London: Jonathan Cape, 2006.

Nauert, Charles G. *Humanism and the Culture of Renaissance Europe*. Cambridge: Cambridge University Press, 1995.

Neale, R. S. "'The Bourgeoisie, Historically, Has Played a Most Revolutionary Part.'" In *Feudalism, Capitalism and Beyond*, edited by Eugene Kamenka and R. S. Neale, 84–102. London: Edward Arnold, 1975.

Needham, Joseph. *History Is on Our Side: A Contribution to Political Religion and Scientific Faith*. London: Allen and Unwin, 1946.

——— [1956]. *The Shorter Science and Civilisation in China*, vol. 1, abridged by Colin A. Ronan. Cambridge: Cambridge University Press, 1978.

Neocleous, Mark. *Administering Civil Society: Towards a Theory of State Power*. Houndmills: Macmillan, 1996.

Nesbitt, Nick. *Universal Emancipation: The Haitian Revolution and the Radical Enlightenment*. Charlottesville; University of Virginia, 2008.

Newitt, Malyn D. D. "Plunder and the Rewards of Office in the Portuguese Empire." In *The Military Revolution and the State, 1500–1800*, edited by Michael Duffy, 10–28. Exeter: University of Exeter Press, 1980.

Nicolaievsky, Boris and Otto Maenchen-Helfen [1933]. *Karl Marx: Man and Fighter*. Harmondsworth: Penguin, 1976.

Nimni, Ephraim. "Marx, Engels and the National Question," *Science and Society* 53, no. 3 (Autumn 1990): 297–326.

Nimtz, August H. *Marx and Engels: Their Contribution to the Democratic Breakthrough*. Albany: State University of New York, 2000.

Nischan, Bodo. "Confessionalism and Absolutism: The Case of Brandenburg." In *Calvinism in Europe, 1540–1620*, edited by Andrew Pettigree, Alastair Duke, and Gillian Lewis, 181–204. Cambridge: Cambridge University Press, 1994.

Noble, Andrew. "Version of Scottish Pastoral: the Literati and the Tradition, 1780–1830." In *Order in Space and Society: Architectural Form and Its Context in the Scottish Enlightenment*, edited by T.A. Markus, 263–310. Edinburgh: Mainstream, 1982.

Novack, George. "Introduction." In *America's Revolutionary Heritage*, edited by George Novak, 9–20. New York: Pathfinder, 1976.

Novick, Peter. *That Noble Dream: The "Objectivity Question" and the American Historical Profession*, Cambridge: Cambridge University Press, 1988.

Nygaard, Bertel. "Constructing Marxism: Karl Kautsky and the French Revolution," *History of European Ideas* 35, no. 4 (December 2009): 450–64.

Oakley, Francis. "On the Road from Constance to 1688: The Political Thought of John Major and George Buchanan," *Journal of British Studies* 1, no. 2 (May 1962): 1–31.

Oakeshott, Michael [1946]. "Introduction to *Leviathan*." In *Rationalism in Politics and Other Essays*, 221–94. New and expanded edition, Indianapolis: Liberty Fund, 1991.

——— [1961]. "The Masses in Representative Democracy." In *Rationalism in Politics and Other Essays*, 363–83. New and expanded edition, Indianapolis: Liberty Fund, 1991.

O'Brien, Bronterre [1837]. "A View of Social Development." In *From Cobbett to the Chartists: Nineteenth Century*, vol. 1, *1815–1848*, edited by Max Morris, 161–62. London: Lawrence and Wishart, 1948.

O'Brien, Patrick K. "The Impact of the Revolutionary and Napoleonic wars, 1793–1815, on the Long-run Growth of the British Economy," *Review* 12 (1989): 335–95.

Ogilvie, Sheilagh C. "Social Institutions and Proto-Industrialisation.," In *European Proto-Industrialization*, edited by Sheilagh C. Ogilvie and Markus Cerman, 23–37. Cambridge: Cambridge University Press, 1996.

[Ogilvie, William]. *An Essay on the Right of Property in Land, with Respect to Its Foundation in the Laws of Nature; Its Present Establishment by the Municipal Laws of Europe; and the Regulation by Which It Might be Rendered More Beneficial to the Lower Ranks of Mankind*. London: J. Walter, 1782.

Ohlmeyer, Jane. "The Civil Wars in Ireland." In *The Civil Wars: A Military History of England, Scotland and Ireland, 1638–1660*, edited by John Kenyon and Jane Ohlmeyer, 73–102. Oxford: Oxford University Press, 1998.

Ollman, Bertell [1979]. "Marxism and Political Science: Prolegomenon to a Debate on Marx's Method." In *Dance of the Dialectic: Steps in Marx's Method*, 135–54. Urbana: University of Illinois Press, 2003.

——— [2001]. "Why Does the Emperor Need the Yakuza? Prolegomenon to a Marxist Theory of the Japanese State." In *Dance of the Dialectic: Steps Marx's Method*, 193–216. Urbana: University of Illinois, 2003.

O'Rourke, Kevin H. "The Worldwide Economic Impact of the French Revolutionary and Napoleonic Wars, 1793–1815," *Journal of Global History* 1 (2006): 123–49.

Orwell, George [1942]. "Looking Back on the Spanish War." In *The Collected Essays, Journalism and Letters*, vol. 2, *My Country Right or Left, 1940–1943*, edited by Sonia Orwell and Ian Angus, 286–306. Harmondsworth: Penguin, 1970.

——— [1945]. "Catastrophic Gradualism." In *The Collected Essays, Journalism and Letters*, vol. 4, *In Front of Your Nose, 1945–1950*, edited by Sonia Orwell and Ian Angus, 33–37. Harmondsworth: Penguin, 1970.

——— [1949]. *Nineteen Eighty-Four: A Novel.* Harmondsworth: Penguin, 1954.

Ossowski, Stanislaw [1957]. *Class Structure in the Social Consciousness.* London: Routledge and Kegan Paul, 1963.

Outhwaite, R. B. "Progress and Backwardness in English Agriculture, 1500–1650," *Economic History Review*, second series, vol. 39, no. 1 (February 1986): 1–18.

Outram, Dorinda. *The Enlightenment.* Cambridge: Cambridge University Press, 1995.

Overton, Mark, *Agricultural Revolution in England: The Transformation of Agrarian Economy, 1500–1800.* Cambridge: Cambridge University Press, 1996.

Paine, Thomas [1776]. *Common Sense*, edited by Isaac Kramnick. Harmondsworth: Penguin, 1976.

——— [1790]. Paine to Burke, January 17, 1790. In *The Correspondence of Edmund* Burke, vol. 6, edited by Alfred Cobban and Robert A. Smith. Cambridge: Cambridge University Press, 1967.

——— [1791–2]. *Rights of Man: Being an Answer to Mister Burke's Attack on the French Revolution*, edited by Henry Collins. Harmondsworth: Penguin, 1969.

——— [1803/5]. "To the Citizens of the United States and Particularly the Leaders of the Federal Faction. Letter 8." In *The Complete Writings of Thomas Paine*, vol. 2, edited by Phillip S. Foner. New York: Citadel Press, 1969.

Palmer, Bryan D. *Descent into Discourse: The Reification of Language and the Writing of Social History.* Philadelphia: Temple University Press, 1990.

Panitch, Leo. *Renewing Socialism: Democracy, Strategy, and Imagination.* Boulder, CO: Westview Press, 2001.

Parker, David. *Class and State in Ancien Regime France: The Road to Modernity?* London: Routledge, 1996.

———. "Introduction." In *Ideology, Absolutism and the English Revolution: Debates of the British Communist Historians, 1940–1956*, edited by David Parker, 9–71. London: Lawrence and Wishart, 2008.

Parker, Geoffrey. *The Military Revolution: Military Innovation and the Rise of the West, 1500–1800.* Cambridge: Cambridge University Press, 1988.

Parvus [Alexander Helphand] [1905]. "What Was Accomplished on the 9th of January." In *Witnesses to Permanent Revolution: The Documentary Record*, edited by Richard B. Day and Daniel Gaido, 262–72. Leiden: E. J. Brill, 2009.

Pascal, Gabriel [1647]. "Preface to the Treatise on the Vacuum." In *Scientific Treatises.* Chicago: Chicago University Press, 1952.

——— [1657–62]. *Pensees.* Harmondsworth: Penguin, 1966.

Pascal, Roy. "Property and Society: The Scottish Historical School of the Eighteenth Century," *Modern Quarterly* (March 1938): 167–79.

Patterson, Thomas C. *The Inca Empire.* Providence: Berg, 1991.

———. *Inventing Western Civilisation.* New York: Monthly Review Press, 1997.

Paulin, Tom. "Introduction." In *The Faber Book of Political Verse*, 15–52. London: Faber and Faber, 1986.

Peck, Jamie. *Constructions of Neoliberal Reason.* Oxford: Oxford University Press, 2010.

Pellicani, Luciano. "Weber and the Myth of Calvinism," *Telos* 75 (Spring 1988): 57–85.

Peng Shu-tse [1974]. "Introduction." In Leon D. Trotsky, *Leon Trotsky on China*, edited by Les Evans and Russell Block, 31–97. New York: Monad Press, 1976.

Perelman, Michael. *The Invention of Capitalism: Classical Political Economy and the Secret History of Primitive Accumulation.* Durham, NC: Duke University Press, 2000.

Perkin, Harold. "The Social Causes of the Industrial Revolution," *Transactions of the Royal Historical Society*, Fifth Series, 18 (1968): 123–43.

Pilbeam. Pamela M. *The Middle Classes in Europe, 1789–1914: France, Germany, Italy and Russia.* London: Macmillan, 1990.

Pinder, John. "Europe in the World Economy, 1920–1970." In *The Fontana Economic History of Europe, Contemporary Economies*, Part 1, 323–375. Glasgow: Fontana, 1976.

Pinkus, Steve. *1688: The First Modern Revolution*. New Haven, CT: Yale University Press, 2009.

P.F. [Jurgen Kuczynski]. "England's Revolution," *Labour Monthly* 22, no. 11 (November 1940): 558–59.

———. "A Rejoinder," *Labour Monthly* 22, no. 12 (December 1940): 653–55.

Plekhanov, Georgy V. [1883]. "Socialism and the Political Struggle." In *Selected Philosophical Works*, vol. 1, 57–121. Moscow: Foreign Languages Publishing House, 1961.

——— [1884]. "Our Differences." In *Selected Philosophical Works*, vol. 1, 122–399. Moscow: Foreign Languages Publishing House, 1961.

——— [1889]. "Speech at the International Worker's Socialist Congress in Paris (July, 14–21, 1889): Second Version." In *Selected Philosophical Works*, vol. 1, 451–54. Moscow: Foreign Languages Publishing House, 1961.

——— [1890–1]. "How the Bourgeoisie Remembers Its Own Revolution." In *The Bourgeois Revolution: The Political Birth of Capitalism*. New York: New York Labor News, 1968.

——— [1895]. "The Development of the Monist View of History." In *Selected Philosophical Works*, vol. 1, 542–782. Moscow: Foreign Languages Publishing House, 1961.

——— [1903]. "'Orthodox' Pedantry." In *Witnesses to Permanent Revolution: The Documentary Record*, edited by Richard B. Day and Daniel Gaido, 133–67. Leiden: E. J. Brill, 2009.

Plyushch, Leonid. "Forward Together or Down Together.'" In *Power and Opposition in Revolutionary Societies*, edited by *Il Manifesto*, 37–46. London: Ink Links, 1979.

Pocock, J. G. A. "Virtue and Commerce in the Eighteenth Century," *Journal of Interdisciplinary History* 1, no. 3 (Summer 1972): 119–34.

——— [1975]. *The Machiavellian Moment: Florentine Political Thought and the Atlantic Republican Tradition*. Princeton, NJ: Princeton University Press, 2003.

———. "Historical Introduction." In *The Political Works of James Harrington*, edited by J. G. A. Pocock, 1–152. Cambridge: Cambridge University Press, 1977.

———. "1776: the Revolution against Parliament." In *Three British Revolution: 1641, 1688, 1776*, edited by J. G. A. Pocock, 265–88. Cambridge: Cambridge University Press, 1980.

———. "Edmund Burke and the Redefinition of Enthusiasm: The Context as Counter-Revolution," in *The French Revolution and the Creation of Modern Political Culture*, vol. 3, *The Transformation of Political Culture, 1789–1848*, edited by François Furet and Mina Ozouf, 19–43. Oxford: Pergammon Press, 1989.

Pointon, Marcia. *Naked Authority: The Body in Western Painting, 1830–1908*. Cambridge: Cambridge University Press, 1990.

Polanyi, Karl [1944]. *The Great Transformation*. Boston: Harper Torchbooks, 1957.

Polisensky, Josef V [1970]. *The Thirty Years' War*. London: New English Library, 1974.

"Political Education" [1582]. In *The Dutch Revolt*, edited by Martin van Gelderen, 165–226. Cambridge: Cambridge University Press, 1993.

Poly, Jean-Pierre and Eric Bournazel [1984]. *The Feudal Transformation: 900–1200*. New York: Holmes and Meier, 1991.

Polybius, *The Rise of the Roman Empire*. Harmondsworth: Penguin Books, 1979.

Pomeranz, Kenneth. *The Great Divergence: China, Europe and the Making of the Modern World Economy*. Princeton, NJ: Princeton University Press, 2000.

Popper, Karl. *The Poverty of Historicism*. London: Routledge and Kegan Paul, 1957.

Porter, Bernard. *Empire and Superempire: Britain, America and the World*. New Haven, CT: Yale University Press, 2006.

Porter, Roy. *Enlightenment: Britain and the Creation of the Modern World*, London: Allen Lane, 2000.

Post, Charles [1995]. "The Agrarian Origins of US-capitalism: The Transformation of the Northern Countryside before the Civil War." In *The American Road to Capitalism: Studies in Class-Structure, Economic Development and Political Conflict, 1620–1877*, 37–102.

Leiden: E. J. Brill, 2011.
———. "Comments on the Brenner-Wood Exchange on the Low Countries," *Journal of Agrarian Change* 2, no. 1 (January 2002): 88–95.
——— [2009]. "Agrarian Class-Structure and Economic Development in Colonial-British North America: The Place of the American Revolution in the Origins of US-Capitalism." In *The American Road to Capitalism: Studies in Class-Structure, Economic Development and Political Conflict, 1620–1877*, 155–93. Leiden: E. J. Brill, 2011.
———. "Exploring Working-Class Consciousness: A Critique of the Theory of the 'Labor-Aristocracy,'" *Historical Materialism* 18, no. 4 (2010): 3–38.
———. "Introduction" In *The American Road to Capitalism: Studies in Class-Structure, Economic Development and Political Conflict, 1620–1877*, 1–5. Leiden: E. J. Brill, 2011.
———. "Social Property Relations, Class Conflict and the Origins of the US Civil War: Toward a New Social Interpretation." In *The American Road to Capitalism: Studies in Class-Structure, Economic Development and Political Conflict, 1620–1877*, 195–251. Leiden: E. J. Brill, 2011.
Postan, Michael M. [1972]. *The Medieval Economy and Society*. Harmondsworth: Penguin, 1975.
Poulantzas, Nicos [1968]. *Political Power and Social Classes*. London: New Left Books, 1973.
Pozo, Gonzalo. "Reassessing the Permanent Arms Economy," *International Socialism*, second series, 127 (Summer 2010): 111–42.
Preobrazhensky, Evgeny A. [1924/1926]. *The New Economics*. Oxford: Clarendon Press, 1965.
Prinz, Arthur M. "Background and Alternative Motive of Marx's 'Preface' of 1859," *Journal of the History of Ideas* 30, no. 3 (July–September 1969): 437–51.
Prynne, William. *The Soveraigne Power of Parliaments and Kingdoms*. London: 1643.
Przeworski, Adam. *Capitalism and Social Democracy*. Cambridge: Cambridge University Press, 1985.
Pufendorf, Samuel [1673]. *On the Duty of Man and Citizen According to Natural Law*, edited by James Tully. Cambridge: Cambridge University Press, 1991.
Puritanism and Liberty: Being the Army Debates (1647–49) from the Clarke Manuscripts with Supplementary Documents [1647–1649], edited by A. S. P. Woodhouse, London: J. M. Dent and Sons, 1986.
Rabb, Theodore K. "Revisionism Revised: The Role of the Commons," *Past and Present* 92 (August 1981): 55–78.
Rakovsky, Christian [1928]. "The 'Professional Dangers' of Power." In *Selected Writings on the Opposition in the USSR, 1929–30*, edited by Gus Fagan, 124–36. London: Allison and Busby, 1980.
Radek, Karl [1922]. "The Paths of the Russian Revolution." In *In Defence of the Russian Revolution: A Selection of Bolshevik Writings, 1917–1923*, edited by Al Richardson, 35–75. London: Porcupine Press, 1995.
Ransom, Richard and Richard Sutch. "Capitalists without Capital: The Burden of Slavery and the Impact of Emancipation," *Agricultural History* 62, no. 3 (1988): 133–60.
Raphael, Ray. *The American Revolution: A People's History*. London: Profile Books, 2001.
Rediker, Marcus. *Between the Devil and the Deep Blue Sea: Merchant Seaman, Pirates and the Anglo-American Maritime World, 1700–1750*. Cambridge: Cambridge University Press, 1987.
——— [1973]. *Villains of All Nations: Atlantic Pirates in the Golden Age*. London: Verso, 2004.
Redpath, James. *The Roving Editor, or, Talks with Slaves in the Southern States*. New York: A.B. Burdick, 1859.
Reed, John [1919]. *Ten Days That Shook the World*. Harmondsworth: Penguin, 1977.
Rees, John. *The Algebra of Revolution: The Dialectic and the Classical Marxist Tradition*. London: Macmillan, 1998.
———. "The Democratic Revolution and the Socialist Revolution," *International Socialism*, second series, 83 (Summer 1999): 3–84.

————. *Imperialism and Resistance*. London: Routledge, 2006.

Reiber, Alfred. *Merchants and Entrepreneurs in Imperial Russia*. Chapel Hill: University of North Carolina Press, 1982.

Reiman, Michael [1979]. *The Birth of Stalinism: The USSR on the Eve of the "Second Revolution."* London: I. B. Tauris, 1987.

Renton, David. *Classical Marxism: Socialist Theory and the Second International*. Cheltenham: New Clarion Press, 2002.

Ricardo, David [1817]. *The Works and Correspondence of David Ricardo*, vol. 1, *On the Principles of Political Economy and Taxation*, edited by Piero Sraffa with the collaboration of Maurice H. Dobb. Cambridge: University of Cambridge Press for the Royal Economic Society, 1951.

Ridpath, George [1751–61]. *Diary of George Ridpath: Minister of Stichel, 1755–1761*, edited by James B. Paul. Edinburgh: Scottish History Society, 1922.

Rigby, Stephen H. *Marxism and History: A Critical Introduction*. Second edition, Manchester: Manchester University Press, 1998.

Riley, Dylan J. and Manali Desai. "The Passive Revolutionary Route to the Modern World: Italy and India in Comparative Perspective," *Comparative Studies in Society and History* 49, no. 4 (2007): 815–417.

Ritzer, George [1993]. *The McDonaldization of Society: An Investigation into the Changing Character of Social Life*. Revised edition, Thousand Oaks, CA: Pine Forge Press, 1996.

Robertson, John. "The Enlightenment above National Context: Political Economy in Eighteenth-Century Scotland and Naples," *Historical Journal* 40, no. 3 (July 1997): 667–97.

————. *The Case for Enlightenment: Scotland and Naples, 1680–1760*. Cambridge: Cambridge University Press, 2005.

Robertson, William [1777]. *The History of America*. Sixth edition, 3 volumes. Edinburgh: J. Balfour, 1792.

Robespierre, Maximilien [1792]. "Sur la guerre." In *Œuvres Complètes*, tome 8, *Discours*, troisième partie, (*octobre 1791–septembre 1792*), s.d. Mark Bouloiseau, George Lefebvre and Albert Soboul, 74–98. Ivry: Société des études Robespierristes/Phénix Éditions, 2000.

———— [1792]. "Extracts from 'Answer to Louvet's Accusation.'" In *Virtue and Terror*, 39–48. London: Verso, 2007.

Robin, Corey [2008]. "The First Counter-revolutionary." In *The Reactionary Mind: Conservatism from Edmund Burke to Sarah Palin*, 61–75. New York: Oxford University Press, 2011.

Rodinson, Maxime [1966]. *Islam and Capitalism*. Harmondsworth: Penguin, 1977.

Roederer, Pierre-Louis [1799]. "The Impact of the Philosophical Ideas of the Revolution." In *The Spirit of the Revolution of 1789 and Other Writings of the Revolutionary Epoch*, edited by Murray G. Forsyth, 90–100. Aldershot: Scolar, 1989.

———— [1815]. "The Spirit of the Revolution of 1789." In *The Spirit of the Revolution of 1789 and Other Writings of the Revolutionary Epoch*, edited by Murray G. Forsyth, 1–69. Aldershot: Scolar, 1989.

Rousseau, Jean-Jacques [1752]. "Preface to *Narcissus, or the Lover of Himself*." In *Collected Writings*, vol. 2, Hanover, NH: University Press of New England, 1992.

———— [1755]. *A Discourse on Inequality*. Harmondsworth: Penguin, 1984.

Rosdolsky, Roman [1948]. *Engels and the "Non-Historic Peoples": The National Question in the Revolution of 1848*, ed. John-Paul Himka, 16–189. *Critique* 18/19, Special Issue (1986), 129.

———— [1968]. *The Making of Marx's Capital*. London: Pluto Press, 1977.

Rosemont, Franklin. "Karl Marx and the Iroquois," *Arsenal/Surrealist Subversion* 4 (1989): 201–13.

Rosenberg, Justin. "Isaac Deutscher and the Lost History of International Relations," *New Left Review* 1, no. 215 (January–February 1996): 3–15.

Rostow, Walter W. *The Stages of Economic Growth: A Non-Communist Manifesto*. Cambridge: Cambridge University Press, 1960.

Rothschild, Emma. *Economic Sentiments: Adam Smith, Condorcet, and the Enlightenment.* Cambridge, MA: Harvard University Press, 2001

Roxborough, Ian. *Theories of Underdevelopment.* London: Macmillan, 1979.

Roy, Manabendra N. [1920]. "An Indian Communist Manifesto." In *Selected Works of M. N. Roy*, vol. 1, *1917–1922*, edited by Sibnarayan Ray, 161–64. New Delhi: Oxford India Publications, 1982.

——— [1920]. "Beware the Nationalist Bourgeoisie; Support the Class Struggle." In Helmut Gruber, *Soviet Russia Masters the Comintern: International Communism in the Era of Stalin's Ascendancy*, 316–19. New York: Anchor Press/Doubleday, 1974.

Roy, Oliver. *Islam and Resistance in Afghanistan.* Cambridge: Cambridge University Press, 1986.

Royer-Collard, Pierre P. *Opinion sur le project de loi relative à la répression dit délits de presse.* Paris: no publisher identified, 1822.

Rubel, Maximilien. "Fragments sociologiques dans les inédits de Marx," *Cahiers internationaux de Sociologie* 22 (January–June 1957): 128–46.

Rubin, Isaak I. [1929]. *A History of Economic Thought*, edited by Donald Fitzer. London: Ink Links 1979.

Rudé, George. *Interpretations of the French Revolution*, Historical Association pamphlet 47. London: Routledge and Kegan Paul, 1961.

Rudra, Ashok. "Pre-Capitalist Modes of Production in Non-European Societies," *Journal of Peasant Studies* 15, no. 3 (April 1988): 373–94.

Runciman, Steven [1951]. *A History of the Crusades*, vol. 1, *The First Crusade and the Foundation of the Kingdom of Jerusalem.* Harmondsworth: Penguin, 1965.

Runkle, Gerald. "Karl Marx and the American Civil War," *Comparative Studies in Society and History* 6 (1963–1964): 117–41.

Rush, Benjamin [1777]. "Observations on the Government of Pennsylvania: Letter III." In *Selected Writings of Benjamin Rush*, edited by Dagobert D. Runes, 54–86. New York: Philosophical Library, 1947.

Rühle, Otto [1924]. *From the Bourgeois Revolution to the Socialist Revolution.* Glasgow and London: Revolutionary Perspectives and Socialist Reproduction, 1974.

Russell, Conrad. "Perspectives in Parliamentary History, 1604–1629," *History* 61, no. 201 (1976): 1–27.

———. "The Bourgeois Revolution: A Mirage?" *History Today* 40, no. 9 (September 1990): 7–9.

Ryazanov, David [1924]. "Iskra and the Tasks of Russian Social Democrats." In *Witnesses to Permanent Revolution: The Documentary Record*, edited by Richard B. Day and Daniel Gaido, 67–134. E. J. Brill: Leiden, 2009.

Said, Edward W [1978]. *Orientalism.* Harmondsworth: Penguin, 1985.

Saint-Simon, Henri [1818]. "On the Political History of Industry." In *Selected Writings on Science, Industry and Social Organisation*, edited by Keith Taylor, 174–80. London: Croom Helm, 1975.

——— [1820]. "Consideration on Measures to be taken to End the Revolution." In *Selected Writings on Science, Industry and Social Organisation*, edited by Keith Taylor, 211–16. London: Croom Helm, 1975.

——— [1820]. "Letters on the Bourbons." In *Selected Writings on Science, Industry and Social Organisation*, edited by Keith Taylor, 219–22. London: Croom Helm, 1975.

——— [1821]. "[From Feudalism to Industrialism: The Role of the Lawyers and Metaphysicians]." In *Selected Writings on Science, Industry and Social Organisation*, edited by Keith Taylor, 227–28. London: Croom Helm, 1975.

——— [1823]. "[On the Intermediate (Bourgeois) Class]." In *Selected Writings on Science, Industry and Social Organisation*, edited by Keith Taylor, 250–52. London: Croom Helm, 1975.

Saint-Simon, Henri and Jacques N. Augustin Thierry [1814]. "The Reorganization of the European Community or the Necessity and the Means of Uniting the Peoples of Europe in a Single Body Politic While Preserving for Each their National Independence." In *Henri Compte de Saint-Simon, 1760–1825: Selected Writings*, edited by F. M. H. Markham, 28–68. London: Hyperion Press, 1952.

Salmon, J. H. M. "The Paris Sixteen, 1584–94: The Social Analysis of a Revolutionary Movement," *Journal of Modern History* 44, no. 4 (December 1972): 540–76.

Salter, John. "Adam Smith on Feudalism, Commerce and Slavery," *History of Political Thought* 13, no. 2 (April 1992): 219–41.

Salvadori, Massimo L. [1976]. *Karl Kautsky and the Socialist Revolution, 1880–1938*. London: Verso, 1990.

Samuel, Raphael. "British Marxist Historians I," *New Left Review* 1, no. 120 (March–April 1980): 21–96.

Sapir, Boris. "The Conception of the Bourgeois Revolution." In *The Mensheviks: From the Revolution of 1917 to the Second World War*, edited Leopold H. Haimson, 366–88. Chicago: University of Chicago Press, 1974.

Sassoon, Donald. *One Hundred Years of Socialism: The West European Left in the Twentieth Century*. London: Fontana, 1997.

Saville, John. *The Consolidation of the Capitalist State, 1800–1850*. London: Pluto, 1994.

Sawer, Marion. "The Soviet Discussion of the Asiatic Mode of Production," *Survey* 24, no. 3 (Summer 1979): 108–27.

Sayer, Derek. *Marx's Method: Ideology, Science and Critique in* Capital. Brighton: Harvester, 1979.

Schama, Simon [1977]. *Patriots and Liberators: Revolution in the Netherlands, 1780–1813*. Second edition, London: Fontana, 1992.

———. *Citizens: A Chronicle of the French Revolution*. Harmondsworth, Penguin, 1989.

Schmitt, Carl [1932]. "The Concept of the Political." In *The Concept of the Political*, 19–79. Expanded edition, Chicago: University of Chicago Press, 2007.

Schneiderman, Jeremiah. *Sergei Zubatov and Revolutionary Marxism: The Struggle for the Working Class in Tsarist Russia*. Ithaca, NY: Cornel University Press, 1976.

Schoenberger, Erica. "The Origins of the Market Economy: State Power, Territorial Control, and Modes of War Fighting," *Comparative Studies in Society and History* 50, no. 3 (2008): 663–91.

Schram, Stuart R. *The Political Thought of Mao Tse-tung*. Enlarged and revised edition, Harmondsworth: Penguin, 1969.

Schumpeter, Joseph A. [1919]. "The Sociology of Imperialisms." In *Imperialism and Social Classes*, edited by Paul M. Sweezy, 3–98. Oxford: Blackwell, 1951.

Scots Independent, vol. 3, no. 10 (June 1938).

Scott, Walter [1816]. *Old Mortality*, edited by Angus Calder. Harmondsworth: Penguin, 1975.

——— [1824]. *Redgauntlet*, edited by G. A. M. Wood and David Howitt. Harmondsworth: Penguin, 2000.

——— [1829]. *Anne of Geierstein: Or, the Maiden of the Mist*, edited by J. H. Alexander. Edinburgh: Edinburgh University Press, 2000.

Scurr, Ruth. "Pierre-Louis Roederer and the Debate on Forms of Government in Revolutionary France," *Political Studies* 52, no. 2 (June 2004): 251–68.

———. "Inequality and Political Stability from the Ancien Regime to Revolution: The Reception of Adam Smith's Theory of Moral Sentiments in France," *History of European Ideas* 35, no. 4 (December 2009): 441–49.

Schurz, Carl [1865]. "Report on the Condition of the South." In *Speeches, Correspondence, and Political Papers* Volume 1, *October 20, 1852 to November 26, 1870*, edited by Frederic Bancroft, New York: G. P. Putnam's Sons, 1913.

Sedgwick, Peter [1963/1977]. "Introduction." In Victor Serge, *Memoirs of a Revolutionary, 1901–1941*, edited by Peter Sedgwick, ix–xxiv. Oxford: Oxford University Press, 1978.

Selwyn, Ben. "Trotsky, Gerschenkron and the Political Economy of Late Development," *Economy and Society* 40, no. 3 (July 2011): 121–50.

Semo, Enrique. *Historia Mexicana: Economía y Lucha de Clases*. México DF: Serie Popular Era, 1978.

———. "Reflexiones sobre la Revolución Mexicana." In Adolfo Gilly, Arnaldo Córdova, Armando Bartra, Manuel Aguilar Mora, and Enrique Semo, 135–50. *Interpretaciones de la Revolución Mexicana*. Mexico City: Nueva Imagen, 1979.

Serge, Victor [1931]. *The Birth of Our Power*. London: Writers and Readers, 1977.

——— [1936–38]. *Midnight in the Century*. London: Writers and Readers, 1982.

——— [1942–43]. *Memoirs of a Revolutionary, 1901–1941*, edited by Peter Sedgwick. Oxford: Oxford University Press, 1978.

Sewell, William, *A Rhetoric of Bourgeois Revolution: The Abbe Sieyès and* What Is the Third Estate? Durham, NC: Duke University Press, 1994.

Shachtman, Max [1933]. "Communism and the Negro." In *Race and Revolution*, edited by Christopher Phelps, 1–102. London: Verso, 2003.

——— [1949]. "Isaac Deutscher's Stalin." In *The Bureaucratic Revolution: The Rise of the Stalinist State*. New York: Donald Press, 1962.

Shafer, Boyd C. "Bourgeois Nationalism in the Pamphlets on the Eve of the French Revolution," *Journal of Modern History* 10, no. 1 (March 1938): 31–50.

Shaftesbury, Lord (Anthony Ashley Cooper) [1705]. Shaftesbury to Le Clerc, March 6, 1705. In *The Life, Unpublished Letters and Philosophical Regimen of Anthony, Earl of Shaftesbury* edited by Benjamin Rand. London: Swan Sonnenschein, 1900.

Shanin, Teodor. "Late Marx: Gods and Craftsmen." In *Late Marx and the Russian Road: A Case Presented by Teodor Shanin*, 3–39. London: Routledge and Kegan Paul, 1983.

———. *Russia, 1905–07: Revolution as a Moment of Truth*, vol. 2 of *The Roots of Otherness: Russia's Turn of the Century*. Houndmills: Macmillan, 1986.

Shillory, Ben-Ami. "The Meiji Restoration: Japan's Attempt to Inherit China." In *War, Revolution and Japan*, edited by Ian Neary, Folkestone: Curzon Press, 1993.

Shklar, Judith N. "Ideology Hunting: The Case of James Harrington," *American Political Science Review* 53, no. 3 (September 1959): 662–92.

Siedentop, Larry. *Tocqueville*. Oxford: Oxford University Press, 1994.

Siegel, Paul M. *The Meek and the Militant: Religion and Power across the World*. London: Zed, 1986.

Silver, Beverley. *Forces of Labour: Workers' Movements and Globalisation since 1870*. Cambridge: Cambridge University Press, 2003.

Simms, Brendan. *Three Victories and a Defeat: The Rise and Fall of the First British Empire, 1714–1783*. Harmondsworth: Penguin, 2008.

Sixteenth and Seventeenth Century Section of the Historians Group of the Communist Party [1948]. "State and Revolution in Tudor and Stuart England." In *Ideology, Absolutism and the English Revolution: Debates of the British Communist Historians, 1940–1956*, edited by David Parker, 143–51. London: Lawrence and Wishart, 2008.

Skidelsky, William. "Empire State of Mind," *Observer* London, February 20, 2011.

Skinner, Quentin. *The Foundations of Modern Political Thought*, vol. 1, *The Renaissance*. Cambridge: Cambridge University Press, 1978,

———. *The Foundations of Modern Political Thought*, vol. 2, *The Age of Reformation*. Cambridge: Cambridge University Press, 1978,

———. "The Origins of the Calvinist Theory of Revolution." In *After the Reformation: Essays in Honor of J. H. Hexter*, edited by Barbara C. Malament, 309–30. Manchester, Manchester University Press, 1980.

Skocpol, Theda. *States and Social Revolutions: A Comparative Analysis of France, Russia and China*. Cambridge: Cambridge University Press, 1979.

Slovo, Joe. "South Africa—No Middle Road." In Basil Davidson, Joe Slovo, and Anthony R. Wilkinson, *Southern Africa: The New Politics of Revolution*, 103–210. Harmondsworth: Penguin, 1976.

Smith, Adam [1762–63, 1766]. *Lectures on Jurisprudence*, edited by Ronald L. Meek, David D. Raphael, and Peter G. Stein, Oxford: Oxford University Press, 1978.

———— [1776]. *An Inquiry into the Nature and Causes of the Wealth of Nations*, edited by Edwin Cannan. Chicago: University of Chicago Press, 1976.

———— [1779]. Smith to Carlisle, November 8, 1779. In *The Correspondence of Adam Smith*, edited by Ernest C. Mossner and I. S. Ross. Oxford: Oxford University Press, 1977.

Smith, Neil [1984]. *Uneven Development: Nature, Capital and the Production of Space*. London: Blackwell 1990.

Smith, Sydney. "Preface" [1839]. In *The Works of the Reverend Sydney Smith*, vol. 1, iii–vi. London: Longman, Brown, Green and Longmans, 1851.

Smout, T. C. "The Culture of Migration: Scots as Europeans, 1500–1800," *History Workshop Journal* 40 (Autumn 1995): 108–17.

Snow, Vernon F. "The Concept of Revolution in Seventeenth-Century England," *Historical Journal* 2 (1962): 167–90.

Soboul, Albert [1954]. "Class and Class Struggle during the Revolution." In *Understanding the French Revolution*. London: Merlin Press, 1988. Soboul, Albert [1958]. *The Parisian Sans-Culottes and the French Revolution, 1793–4*. Oxford: Clarendon Press, 1964.

———— [1962]. *The French Revolution, 1787–1799: From the Storming of the Bastille to Napoleon*, London: Unwin Hyman, 1989.

———— [1965]. *A Short History of the French Revolution, 1789–1799*. Berkeley and Los Angeles: University of California Press, 1977.

Sombart, Werner [1913]. *The Quintessence of Capitalism: A Study of the History and Psychology of the Modern Business Man*. New York: Fetig, 1967.

Spadafora, David. *The Idea of Progress in Eighteenth Century Britain*. New Haven, CT: Yale University Press, 1990.

Spelman, Henry [1639]. "The Original Growth, Propagation and Condition of Feuds and Tenures by Knight-Service in England." In *The English Works of Sir Henry Spelman, Published in his Life-Time; Together with his Posthumous Works Relating to the Laws and Antiquities of England*, part 2, 1–46. Second edition, London: D. Browne Senior and Junior, W. Mears, F. Clay and Fletcher Gyles, 1727.

Spencer, Herbert [1860]. "The Social Organism." In *The Man versus the State: With Four Essays on Politics and Society*, edited by Donald MacRae, 195–233. Harmondsworth: Penguin, 1969.

Spinoza, Baruch [1670]. *Tractatus Theologicus-Politicus*. Leiden: E. J. Brill, 1989.

Spufford, Peter. *Power and Profit: The Merchant in Medieval Europe*. London: Thames and Hudson, 2002.

Staël, Anne Louise Germaine de. *Considerations on the Principal Events of the French Revolution*, edited by Achille L. V. Broglie and Auguste L. Holstein-Stael. New York: James Eastburn, 1818.

Stalin, Joseph V. [1913]. "Marxism and the National Question." In *Works*, vol. 2, *1907–1913*, 300–81. Moscow: Foreign Languages Publishing House, 1953.

———— [1924]. "The Foundations of Leninism." In *Works*, vol. 6, *1924*, 71–196. Moscow: Foreign Languages Publishing House, 1953.

———— [1924]. "The October Revolution and the Tactics of the Russian Communists." In *Works*, vol. 6, *1924*, 374–420. Moscow: Foreign Languages Publishing House, 1953.

———— [1925]. "The Results of the Work of the Fourteenth Conference of the R. C. P. (B.)." In *Works*, vol. 7, 1925, 90–134. Moscow: Foreign Languages Publishing House, 1954.

———— [1925]. "A Letter to Comrade Yermakovsky." In *Works*, vol. 7, 1925, 237–39. Moscow: Foreign Languages Publishing House, 1954.

———— [1926]. "Concerning Questions of Leninism." In *Works*, vol. 8, *January–November 1926*, 13–96. Moscow: Foreign Languages Publishing House, 1954.

———— [1927]. "The Revolution in China and the Tasks of the Comintern." In *Works*, vol. 9, *December 1926–July 1927*, 288–318. Moscow: Foreign Languages Publishing House, 1954.

———— [1927]. "The International Situation and the Defence of the USSR." In *Works*, vol. 10, *August–September 1927*, 3–62. Moscow: Foreign Languages Publishing House, 1954.

———— [1931]. "The Tasks of Business Executives: Speech Delivered at the First All-Union Conference of Leading Personnel of Socialist Industry, February 4, 1931." In *Works*, vol. 13, *July 1930–January 1934*, 31–44. Moscow: Foreign Languages Publishing House, 1955.

———— [1931]. "Reply to Oekhnovich and Aristov," in *Works*, vol. 13, *July 1930–January 1934*, 128–34. Moscow: Foreign Languages Publishing House, 1955.

———— [1933]. "The Results of the First Five-Year Plan: Report Delivered on January 7, 1933." In *Works*, vol. 13, *July 1930–January 1934*, 163–219. Moscow: Foreign Languages Publishing House, 1955.

———— [1937]. "Report and Speech in Reply to Debate at the Plenum of the Central Committee of the C. P. S. U. (March 3–5, 1937): Defects in Party Work and Measures for Liquidating Trotskyites and Other Double Dealers." In *Works*, vol. 14, *1934–1940*, 241–273. Moscow: Foreign Languages Publishing House, 1955.

Ste. Croix, Geoffrey de. *The Class Struggle in the Ancient Greek World: From the Archaic Age to the Arab Conquests*. London: Duckworth, 1981.

Stern, Robert. *Changing India: Bourgeois Revolution in the Subcontinent*. Second edition, Cambridge: Cambridge University Press, 2003.

Stern, Steve J. *Peru's Indian Peoples and the Challenge of Spanish Conquest: Huamanga to 1640*. Madison: University of Wisconsin Press, 1982.

Steuart, James [1767]. *An Inquiry into the Principles of Political Economy: Being an Essay on the Science of Domestic Policy in Free Nations in Which Are Particularly Considered, Population, Agriculture, Trade, Industry, Money, Coin, Interest, Circulation, Banks, Exchange, Public Credit, and Taxes*, vol. 1, edited by Andrew S. Skinner. Edinburgh: Oliver and Boyd for the Scottish Economic Society, 1966.

Stewart, David. *Sketches of the Character, Institutions and Customs of the Highlanders of Scotland: With Details of the Military Service of the Highland Regiments*. New edition, Inverness: A and W. Mackenzie, 1885.

Stewart, Dugald [1792]. *Elements of the Philosophy of the Human Mind*. In *Collected Works*, vol. 2, edited by W. Hamilton. Edinburgh: Thomas Constable, 1854.

Stone, Lawrence [1970/1972]. "The Causes of the English Revolution." In *The Causes of the English Revolution, 1529–1642*, 47–164. London: Routledge and Kegan Paul, 1972.

Stone, Norman [1975]. *The Eastern Front, 1914–1917*. Harmondsworth: Penguin, 1998.

————. *Europe Transformed, 1878–1919*. London: Fontana, 1983.

————. "Owning Up to a Revolution," *Sunday Times*, March 6, 1988.

Strawson, John. "Culture and Imperialism," *Socialist History* 14 (1999): 68–70.

Stonor Saunders, Frances. *Who Paid the Piper? The CIA and the Cultural Cold War*. London: Granta, 1999.

Struve, Peter B. [1898]. "Manifesto of the Russian Social Democratic Party (March 1898)." In *Marxism in Russia: Key Documents, 1879–1906*, edited by Neil Harding, 223–24. Cambridge: Cambridge University Press, 1983.

Stubbe, Henry. *A Letter to an Officer of the Army Concerning a Select Senate Mentioned by Them in Their Proposals to the Late Parliament: The Necessity and Prudentialness of Such a Senate is Here Asserted by Reason and History: Whereunto Are Added Sundry Positions About Government, and an Essay Towards an Secure Settlement*. London: Printed for T.B., 1659.

British Library E.1001 (9).

Sukhanov, Nikolai N [1922]. *The Russian Revolution 1917: A Personal Record*, edited by Joel Carmichael. Princeton, NJ: Princeton University Press, 1984.

Sutherland, Donald M. G. *France, 1789–1815: Revolution and Counter-Revolution*. London: Fontana, 1985.

Sweezy, Paul M. [1950]. "A Critique." In *The Transition from Feudalism to Capitalism*, edited by Rodney H. Hilton, 33–56. London: New Left Books, 1976.

—— [1953]. "A Rejoinder." In *The Transition from Feudalism to Capitalism*, edited by Rodney H. Hilton, 102–8. London: New Left Books, 1976.

Tacitus [AD 98]. "Agricola." In *The Agricola and the Germania*, 51–99. Harmondsworth: Penguin, 1970.

Takahashi, Kohachiro [1952]. "A Contribution to the Discussion." In *The Transition from Feudalism to Capitalism*, edited by Rodney H. Hilton. London: New Left Books, 1976.

Talmon, Jacob L. [1952]. *The Origins of Totalitarian Democracy*. London: Mercury Books, 1961.

Tapia, Luis. "Constitution and Constitutional Reform in Bolivia." In *Unresolved Tensions: Bolivia Past and Present*, edited by John Crabtree and Lawrence Whitehead, 160–76. Pittsburgh: University of Pittsburg, 2008.

Tawney, R. H. [1922/1926]. "Preface to the 1937 Edition." In *Religion and the Rise of Capitalism*, vi–xiii. Harmondsworth: Penguin, 1961.

——. "Introduction." In Thomas Wilson [1572], *A Discourse upon Usury by Way of Dialogue and Orations, for the Better Variety and More Delight of All Those That Shall Read This Treatise*. I–viii. New York: Harcourt Brace, 1925.

——. "The Rise of the Gentry, 1558–1640," *Economic History Review*, vol. 11 (1941): 1–38.

——. "Harrington's Interpretation of His Age," *Proceedings of the British Academy* 27 (1941): 199–223.

Taylor, George V. "Types of Capitalism in Eighteenth-century France," *English Historical Review* 79 (1964): 478–97.

——. "Noncapitalist Wealth and the Origins of the French Revolution," *American Historical Revue* 72, no. 2 (January 1967): 469–96.

Tchakerian, Viken. "Productivity, Extent of Markets, and Manufacturing in the Late Antebellum South and Midwest," *Journal of Economic History* 54, no. 3 (1994): 497–525.

Teeple, Gary. *Globalization and the Decline of Social Reform*, Second edition, Toronto: Prometheus, 2000.

Teich, Mikulas. "Afterword." In *The Enlightenment in National Context*, edited by Roy Porter and Mikulas Teich, 215–217. Cambridge: Cambridge University Press, 1981.

Teichgraeber, Richard F. "'Less Abused Than I Had Reason to Expect': The Reception of the Wealth of Nations in Britain, 1776–1790," *Historical Journal* 30, no. 2 (June 1987): 337–66.

Terrill, Ross. *R. H. Tawney and His Times: Socialism as Fellowship*. Cambridge, MA: Harvard University Press, 1973.

Teschke, Benno. *The Myth of 1648: Class, Geopolitics and the Making of Modern International Relations*, London: Verso, 2003.

——. "Bourgeois Revolution, State Formation and the Absence of the International," *Historical Materialism* 13, no. 2 (2005): 3–26.

Thackeray, William Makepeace [1853–55]. *The Newcomes: Memoirs of a Most Respectable Family*, ed. David Pardoe. Harmondsworth: Penguin, 1996.

Thatcher, Margaret. *The Downing Street Years*. London: HarperCollins, 1993.

Therborn, Goran. *Science, Class and Society: On the Formation of Sociology and Historical Materialism*. London: New Left Books, 1976.

——. "The Rule of Capital and the Rise of Democracy," *New Left Review* 1, no. 103 (May–June 1977): 3–42.

————. *European Modernity and Beyond: The Trajectory of European Societies, 1945–2000*. London: Sage Publications, 1995.

Thomas, Peter D. *The Gramscian Moment: Philosophy, Hegemony and Marxism*. Leiden: E. J. Brill, 2009.

Thompson, Edward P. [1963]. *The Making of the English Working Class*. Second edition, Harmondsworth: Penguin, 1980.

————. "The Peculiarities of the English." In *The Socialist Register*. Edited by Ralph Miliband and John Saville, 311–62. London: Merlin Press, 1965.

————. "The Poverty of Theory or an Orrery of Errors." In *The Poverty of Theory and Other Essays*, London: Merlin, 1978.

————. "The Patricians and the Plebs." In *Customs in Common*, 16–96. London: Merlin, 1991.

————. "The Moral Economy Reviewed." In *Customs in Common*, 259–351. London: Merlin, 1991.

Thompson, Willie. "Tom Nairn and the Crisis of the British State," *Contemporary Record* 6, no. 2 (Autumn 1992): 306–25.

Tibebu, Tishale. "On the Question of Feudalism, Absolutism, and the Bourgeois Revolution," *Review* 13, no. 1 (Winter 1990): 49–152.

Tocqueville, Alexis de [1850]. *Recollections*, edited by J. P. Mayer. London: Harvill Press, 1848.

———— [1856]. *The Ancien Regime and the French Revolution*. London: Fontana, 1966.

Togliatti, Palmiro [1936]. "Sulle particularita della rivoluzione Spagnola." In *Sul movimento operario internazionale*. Roma: Riuniti, 1964.

Torr, Dona. *Tom Mann and His Times*, vol. 1 *(1856–1890)*. London: Lawrence and Wishart, 1956.

Torrance, John. "Reproduction and Development: A Case for a 'Darwinian' Mechanism in Marx's Theory of History," *Political Studies* 33, no. 3 (1985): 382–98.

Torras, Jaime. "Class Struggle in Catalonia: A Note on Brenner," *Review* 4, no. 2 (Fall 1980): 253–65.

Torras, Jaume. "Peasant Counter-Revolution?" *Journal of Peasant Studies* 5, no. 1 (October 1977): 66–78.

Townsend, Sally and Paul Webster, "What Does Marx Mean to You?" *Marxism Today* (March 1983): 27–33.

Treblicock, Clive. *The Industrialization of the Continental Powers*. Harlow: Longman, 1981.

Trevor-Roper, Hugh R. "The Gentry, 1540–1640," *Economic History Review*, Supplement 1 (April 1953).

———— [1955]. "The Social Causes of the Great Rebellion." In *Historical Essays*, 195–205. London: Macmillan, 1957.

———— [1955]. "Karl Marx and the Study of History," In *Historical Essays*, 285–98. London: Macmillan, 1957.

———— [1959]. "The General Crisis of the Seventeenth Century." In *Crisis in Europe, 1560–1660: Essays from Past and Present*, edited by Trevor Aston, 59–95. London: Routledge and Kegan Paul, 1965.

———— [1961/1963]. "Religion, the Reformation and Social Change." In *Religion, the Reformation and Social Change and Other Essays*, 1–45. London: Macmillan, 1967.

———— [1963]. "Scotland and the Puritan Revolution." In *Religion, the Reformation and Social Change and Other Essays*, 392–444. London: Macmillan, 1967.

————. "The Religious Origins of the Enlightenment." In *Religion, the Reformation and Social Change and Other Essays*, London: Macmillan, 1967.

Tribe, Keith. *Genealogies of Capitalism*. London: Macmillan, 1981.

Trimberger, Ellen Kay. *Revolution from Above: Military Bureaucrats and Development in Japan, Turkey, Egypt and Peru*. New Brunswick, NJ: Transaction Books, 1978.

Trotsky, Leon D. [1904]. *Our Political Tasks*. London: New Park, no publication date.

———— [1905]. "Up to the Ninth of January," In *Witnesses to Permanent Revolution: The*

Documentary Record, edited by Richard B. Day and Daniel Gaido, 273–332. Leiden: E. J. Brill, 2009.

——— [1905]. "Introduction to *Ferdinand Lassalle's Speech to the Jury*." In *Witnesses to Permanent Revolution: The Documentary Record*, edited by Richard B. Day and Daniel Gaido, 409–46. Leiden: E. J. Brill, 2009.

——— [1905]. "Social Democracy and Revolution." In *Witnesses to Permanent Revolution: The Documentary Record*, edited by Richard B. Day and Daniel Gaido, 447–55. Leiden: E. J. Brill, 2009.

——— [1906]. *Results and Prospects*. In *The Permanent Revolution* and *Results and Prospects*, 35–122. Third edition, New York: Pathfinder, 1969.

——— [1908–1909/1922]. *1905*. Harmondsworth: Penguin, 1972.

——— [1908]. "The Turkish Revolution and the Tasks of the Proletariat." In *The Balkan Wars, 1912–1913*, edited by George Weissman and Duncan Williams, 3–7. New York: Monad Press, 1980.

——— [1909]. "The New Turkey." In *The Balkan Wars, 1912–1913*, edited by George Weissman and Duncan Williams, 9–15. New York: Monad Press, 1980.

——— [1912]. "In a Backward Country." In *The Balkan Wars, 1912–1913*, edited by George Weissman and Duncan Williams, 47–51. New York: Monad Press, 1980.

——— [1913]. "Stojan Novakovic." In *The Balkan Wars, 1912–1913*, edited by George Weissman and Duncan Williams, 82–89. New York: Monad Press, 1980.

——— [1919]. "Preface to the Re-Issue of This Work [*Results and Prospects*] Published in Moscow in 1919." In *The Permanent Revolution* and *Results and Prospects*, 27–35. Third edition, New York: Pathfinder, 1969.

——— [1919]. "Karl Kautsky." In *Portraits, Personal and Political*, ed. George Breitman and George Saunders, 65–69. New York: Pathfinder, 1977.

——— [1919]. Trotsky to the Central Committee of the Russian Communist Party, August 5, 1919. In *The Trotsky Papers, 1917–1922*, vol. 1, *1917–1919*, edited by Jan M. Meijer, 621–27. The Hague: Mouton, 1964.

——— [1920]. *Terrorism and Communism: A Reply to Karl Kautsky*. London: New Park, 1975.

——— [June 23, 1921]. "Report on the World Economic Crisis and the Tasks of the Communist International." In *The First Five Years of the Communist International*, vol. 1, 226–78. London: New Park, 1974.

——— [1921]. "Flood Tide." In *The First Five Years of the Communist International*, vol. 2, 74–84. London: New Park, 1974.

——— [1920]. Trotsky to the People's Commissariat of Foreign Affairs, June 4, 1920. In *The Trotsky Papers, 1917–1922*, vol. 2, *1920–1922*, edited by Jan M. Meijer, 208–11. The Hague: Mouton, 1971.

——— [1921]. "Trotsky's Letter to Ispart," August 25, 1921, *Revolutionary History* 9, no. 1, *The Russian Revolution of 1905: Change through Struggle* (2005): 117–19.

——— [1921]. Trotsky to Ol'minskij, December 6, 1921. In *The Trotsky Papers, 1917–1922*, vol. 2, *1920–1922*, edited by Jan M. Meijer, 642–45. The Hague: Mouton, 1971.

——— [1922]. "Attention to Theory!" In *Problems of Everyday Life: Creating the Foundations for a New Society in Revolutionary Russia*, 250–63. New York: Pathfinder, 1973.

——— [1922]. "Report to the Fourth World Congress." In *The First Five Years of the Communist International*, vol. 2, 304-333. London: New Park, 1974.

——— [1923]. "Can a Counter-Revolution or a Revolution Be Made on Schedule?" In *The First Five Years of the Communist International*, vol 2, 347–53. London: New Park, 1974.

——— [1923]. "The New Course.," In *The Challenge of the Left Opposition (1923–25)*, edited by Naomi Allen, 64–144. New York: Pathfinder, 1975.

——— [1923]. "The Lessons of October." In *The Challenge of the Left Opposition (1923–25)*, edited by Naomi Allen, 199–258. New York: Pathfinder, 1975.

———— [1924]. "Prospects and Tasks for the East." In *Leon Trotsky Speaks*, 198–208. New York: Pathfinder, 1972.

———— [1925]. "Letter to the Plenum of the Central Committee." In *The Challenge of the Left Opposition (1923–25)*, edited by Naomi Allen, 304–8. New York: Pathfinder, 1980.

———— [1925]. "Where Is Britain Going?" In *Collected Writings and Speeches on Britain*, vol. 2, edited by R. Chappell and Alan Clinton, 1–123. London: New Park, 1974.

———— [1926]. "Radio, Science, Technology and Society." In *Problems of Everyday Life: Creating the Foundations for a New Society in Revolutionary Russia*, 250–63. New York: Pathfinder, 1973.

———— [1926]. "Speech to the Seventh (Enlarged) Plenum of the ECCI." In *The Challenge of the Left Opposition (1926–27)*, edited by Naomi Allen and George Saunders, 258–64. New York: Pathfinder, 1980.

———— [1927]. "Class Relations in the Chinese Revolution." In *Leon Trotsky on China*, edited by Les Evans and Russell Block, 136–48. New York: Monad, 1976.

———— [1927]. "On the Slogan of Soviets in China." In *Leon Trotsky on China*, edited by Les Evans and Russell Block, 149–56. New York: Monad, 1976.

————[1927]. "The Chinese Revolution and the Theses of Comrade Stalin." In *Leon Trotsky on China*, edited by Les Evans and Russell Block, 158–98. New York: Monad, 1976.

———— [1927]. "Thermidor." In *The Challenge of the Left Opposition (1926–27)*, edited by Naomi Allen and George Saunders, 173–89. New York: Pathfinder, 1980.

———— [1927]. "New Opportunities for the Chinese Revolution, New Tasks, and New Mistakes." In *Leon Trotsky on China*, edited by Les Evans and Russell Block, 256–69. New York: Monad, 1976.

———— [1928]. "Marxism and the Relation between Proletarian and Peasant Revolution." In *The Challenge of the Left Opposition (1928–29)*, edited by Naomi Allen and George Saunders, 347–51. New York: Pathfinder, 1981.

———— [1928]. "The Draft Programme of the Communist International—a Critique of Fundamentals." In *The Third International after Lenin*, 1–175. London: New Park, 1974.

———— [1928]. "Summary and Perspectives of the Chinese Revolution: Its Lessons for the Countries of the Orient and for the Whole of the Comintern." In *Leon Trotsky on China*, edited by Les Evans and Russell Block, 291–341. New York: Monad, 1976.

———— [1929]. *The Permanent Revolution*. In *The Permanent Revolution* and *Results and Prospects*, 158–281. Third edition, New York: Pathfinder, 1969.

———— [1929]. "Introduction to the First (Russian) Edition (Published in Berlin)." In *The Permanent Revolution* and *Results and Prospects*, 125–43. Third edition, New York: Pathfinder, 1969.

———— [1930]. "Introduction to the German Edition." In *The Permanent Revolution* and *Results and Prospects*, 144–57. Third edition, New York: Pathfinder, 1969.

———— [1930]. *My Life: An Attempt at an Autobiography*. Harmondsworth: Penguin, 1975.

———— [1930–32]. *The History of the Russian Revolution*. London: Pluto, 1977.

———— [1931]. "The Revolution in Spain." In *The Spanish Revolution (1931–1939)*, edited by Naomi Allen and George Breitman, 67–88. New York: Pathfinder, 1973.

———— [1931]. "The Spanish Revolution and the Dangers Threatening It." In *The Spanish Revolution (1931–39)*, ed. Naomi Allen and George Breitman, 111–34. New York: Pathfinder, 1973.

———— [1932]. "What Next? Vital Questions for the German Proletariat." In *The Struggle against Fascism in Germany*, 110–244. Harmondsworth: Penguin, 1975.

———— [1932]. "In Defence of the Russian Revolution." In *Leon Trotsky Speaks*, 244–69. New York: Pathfinder, 1972.

———— [1932]. "Peasant War in China and the Proletariat." In *Leon Trotsky on China*, edited by Les Evans and Russell Block, 522–31. New York: Monad, 1976.

———— [1933]. "The Negro Question in America." In *Leon Trotsky on Black Nationalism and Self Determination*, edited by George Breitman, 20–31. New York: Pathfinder, 1978.

———— [1933]. "Uneven and Combined Development and the Role of American Imperialism: Minutes of a Discussion," *Writings of Leon Trotsky [1932–33]*, ed. George Breitman and Sarah Lovell, 116–20. New York: Pathfinder, 1972.

———— [1933]. "Japan Heads for Disaster." In *Writings of Leon Trotsky [1932–33]*, edited by George Breitman and Sarah Lovell, 287–94. New York: Pathfinder, 1972.

———— [1933]. "What Is National Socialism?" In *The Struggle against Fascism in Germany*, 406–15. Harmondsworth: Penguin, 1975.

———— [1933]. "After Talks with Fritz Sternberg." In *Writings of Leon Trotsky Supplement (1929–33)*, edited by George Breitman, 289–91. New York: Pathfinder, 1979.

———— [1933–5]. "The Notebooks in Translation." In *Trotsky's Notebooks, 1933–1935: Writings on Lenin, Dialectics, and Evolutionism*, 75–116. New York: Columbia University Press, 1986.

———— [1935]. "The Worker's State, Thermidor and Bonapartism." In *Writing of Leon Trotsky [1934–35]*, edited by George Breitman and Bev Scott, 166–84. New York: Pathfinder, 1971.

————[1935]. "Once Again, Whither France?" In *Whither France?* 49–117. New York: Merit, 1968.

————[1935]. "The Italo-Ethiopian Conflict." In *Writings of Leon Trotsky [1935–36]*, ed. Naomi Allen and George Breitman, 41. New York: Pathfinder, 1970.

————[1935]. *Trotsky's Diary in Exile 1935*. London: Faber and Faber, 1958.

————[1936]. *"France at the Turning Point"* In *Whither France?* 119–39. New York: Merit, 1968.

————. *The Revolution Betrayed: What Is the Soviet Union and Where Is It Going?* New York: Pathfinder, 1937.

————. [1937]. "Ninety Years of the Communist Manifesto." In *Writings of Leon Trotsky [1937–38]*, ed. Naomi Allen and George Breitman, 18–27. Second edition, New York: Pathfinder, 1976.

———— [1937]. "Not a Worker's State and Not a Bourgeois State?" In *Writings of Leon Trotsky [1937–38]*, edited by Naomi Allen and George Breitman, 60–71. Second edition, New York: Pathfinder, 1976.

———— [1937]. "The Lessons of Spain: The Last Warning." In *The Spanish Revolution (1931–1939)*, edited by Naomi Allen and George Breitman, 306–26. New York: Pathfinder, 1973.

————[1938]. "Revolution and War in China." In *Leon Trotsky on China*, edited by Les Evans and Russell Block, 578–91. New York: Monad, 1976.

————[1938]. "The Death Agony of Capitalism and the Tasks of the Fourth International," in *The Transitional Program for Socialist Revolution*, edited by George Breitman and Fred Stanton, 111–52. New York: Pathfinder, 1973.

———— [1938]. "A Fresh Lesson: After the Imperialist 'Peace' at Munich." In *Writings of Leon Trotsky [1938–39]*, edited by Naomi Allen and George Breitman, 52–78. Second edition, New York: Pathfinder, 1974.

———— [1939], "Three Conceptions of the Russian Revolution." In *Writings of Leon Trotsky [1939–40]*, edited by Naomi Allen and George Breitman, 55–73. Second edition, New York: Pathfinder, 1973.

————[1939]. "The USSR in War." In *In Defence of Marxism (Against the Petty Bourgeois Opposition)*, 3–26. London: New Park, 1966.

————[1940]. "A Serious Work on Russian Revolutionary History." In *Writings of Leon Trotsky Supplement (1934–40)*, edited by George Breitman, 857–59. New York: Pathfinder, 1979.

————. "Karl Marx." In *Leon Trotsky Presents the Living Thoughts of Karl Marx*, 1–45. London: Cassell, 1940.

————. [1940]. "Trade Unions in the Epoch of Imperialist Decay," *Fourth International* 2, no. 2 (February 1941): 40–43.

————[1940]. *Stalin: An Appraisal of the Man and His Influence*, edited by Charles Malamuth. London: Hollis and Carter, 1947.

————[1940]. "Fragments from the First Seven Months of the War," in *Writings of Leon Trotsky: Supplement (1934–40)*, edited by George Breitman, 872–79. New York: Pathfinder Press, 1979.

Turgot, Anne-Robert [1750]. "A Philosophical Review of the Successive Advances of the Human Mind." In *Turgot on Progress, Sociology and Economics*, 41–59. Cambridge: Cambridge University Press, 1973.

————[1759–66]. "Reflections on the Formation and Distribution of Wealth." In *Turgot on Progress, Sociology and Economics*, 119–82. Cambridge: Cambridge University Press, 1973.

————. Turley, David. "Slave Emancipations in Modern History." In *Serfdom and Slavery: Studies in Legal Bondage*, edited by Michael Bush, 181–96. London: Longman, 1996.

Twain, Mark [1883]. *Life on the Mississippi.* Teddington: Echo Press, 2006.

Unger, Richard W. *The Ship in the Medieval Economy, 600–1600.* London and Montreal: Croom Helm and McGill Queen's University Press, 1980.

Vacca, Giuseppe. *Togliatti sconosciuto.* Rome: L'Unita editrice, 1994.

Vanaik, Achin. "Subcontinental Strategies," *New Left Review* 2, no. 70 (July/August 2011): 101–14.

Vance, T. N. "After Korea—What? An Economic Interpretation of US Perspectives," *New International* 16, no. 6 (November–December 1950): 325–33.

————[1951]. "The Permanent War Economy." In *The Permanent War Economy*, edited by Hal Draper, 5–62. Berkeley, CA: Independent Socialist Press, 1970.

Vasilyeva, Tatyana. "Preface." In Karl Marx and Frederick Engels, *Collected Works*, vol. 7, xv–xxi. London: Lawrence and Wishart, 1977.

Veblen, Thorstein [1915]. *Imperial Germany and the Industrial Revolution.* Ann Arbor: University of Michigan Press, 1966.

Veitch, John. "Memoir of Dugald Stewart." In Dugald Stewart, *Collected Works*, vol. 10, edited by W. Hamilton, i–clxxvii. Edinburgh: Thomas Constable and Co, 1854.

Venturi, Franco. *Utopia and Reform in the Enlightenment.* Cambridge: Cambridge University Press, 1971.

Verthoff, Rowland and John M. Murrin. "Feudalism, Communalism, and the Yeoman Freeholder: The American Revolution Considered as a Social Accident." In *Essays on the American Revolution*, edited by Stephen G. Kurtz and James H. Hutson, 256–88. Chapel Hill and New York: University of North Carolina Press and W. W. Norton and Company, 1973.

Vilar, Pierre [1956]. "The Age of Don Quixote," *New Left Review* 1, no. 68 (July–August 1971): 59–71.

Viliesis, Danga. "Der unbekannte Beitrag Adam Ferguson's zum materialistischen Geschichtsverstandnis von Karl Marx," *Beitrage zur Marx-Engels-Forschung. Neue Folge 2008: Quellen– und Kapital-interpretation; Manifest-Rezeption; Erinnerungen* (2009): 7–60.

Volkogonov, Dimitri. *Trotsky: The Eternal Revolutionary.* New York: HarperCollins, 1996.

Voltaire [1768]. Voltaire to D'Alembert, September 2, 1768. In *Oeuvres Complètes*, vol. 46. Paris: Bernier Frères, 1880.

Vries, Jan de. "The Transition to Capitalism in a Land without Feudalism." In *Peasants into Farmers? The Transformation of Rural Economy and Society in the Low Countries (Middle Ages–19th Century) in Light of the Brenner Debate*, edited by Peter Hoppenbrouwers and Jan Luiten van Zanden, 67–84. Turnhout, Belgium: Brepols, 2001.

Wade, John. *History of the Middle and Working Classes with a Popular Exposition of the Economical and Political Principles Which Have Influenced the Past and Present Condition of the Industrious Orders, also an Appendix of Prices, Rates of Wages, Population, Poor-Rates, Mortality, Marriages, Crimes, Education, Occupations, and Other Statistical Information, Illustrative of the Former and Present State of the Agricultural, Commercial, and Manufacturing Classes.* London: Effingham Wilson, 1833.

Wald, Alan M. *The New York Intellectuals: The Rise and Decline of the Anti-Stalinist Left from the 1930s to the 1980s*. Chapel Hill: University of North Carolina Press, 1987.

Wallerstein, Immanuel. *The Modern World-System I: Capitalist Agriculture and the Origins of the European World-Economy in the Sixteenth Century*. New York: Academic Press, 1974.

———. "The Rise and Future Demise of the World Capitalist System: Concepts for Competitive Analysis," *Comparative Studies in Society and History* 16 (1974): 387–415.

———. "From Feudalism to Capitalism: Transition or Transitions?" *Social Forces* 55, no. 2 (December 1976): 273–83.

———. *The Modern World System II: Mercantilism and the Consolidation of the European World-Economy, 1600–1750*. New York: Academic Press, 1980.

———. *Historical Capitalism*. London: Verso, 1983.

———. *The Modern World-System III: The Second Era of Great Expansion of the Capitalist World-Economy, 1730–1840s*. New York: Academic Press, 1989.

———. "Eurocentrism and Its Avatars: The Dilemmas of Social Science," *New Left Review* 1, no. 226 (November/December 1997): 83–107.

Waswo, Ann. *Japanese Landlords: The Decline of a Rural Elite*, Berkeley and Los Angeles: University of California Press, 1977.

Waszek, Norbert. "The Division of Labour: From the Scottish Enlightenment to Hegel," *Owl of Minerva* 15, no.1 (Fall 1983): 51–75.

———. *The Scottish Enlightenment and Hegel's Account of "Civil Society."* Dordrecht: Kluwer, 1988.

Watts, Michael. "Black Acts," *New Left Review* 2, no. 9 (May/June 2001): 125–39.

Weber, Eugene. "Revolution? Counter-revolution? What Revolution?" In *Fascism, a Reader's Guide: Analyses, Interpretation, Bibliography*, edited by Thomas Laqueur, 435–68. Harmondsworth: Penguin, 1976.

Weber, Max [1904–5]. *The Protestant Ethic and the Spirit of Capitalism*. London: George Allen and Unwin, 1976.

——— [1908]. *The Agrarian Sociology of Ancient Civilizations*. London: Verso, 1998.

——— [1917]. "Suffrage and Democracy in Germany." In *Political Writings*, edited by Peter Lassman and Ronald Speirs, 80–129. Cambridge: Cambridge University Press, 1994.

———[1917/8]. "Parliament and Democracy in Germany under a New Political Order." In *Political Writings*, edited by Peter Lassman and Ronald Speirs, 130–269. Cambridge: Cambridge University Press, 1994.

———[1919–20]. *General Economic History*. London: Collier-Macmillan, 1961.

———[1921]. *Economy and Society: An Outline of Interpretative Sociology*, vol. 1, edited by Guenther Roth and Claus Wittich. Berkeley and Los Angeles: University of California Press, 1978.

Webber, Jeffery R. "Rebellion to Reform in Bolivia. Part II: Revolutionary Epoch, Combined Liberation and the December 2005 Elections," *Historical Materialism* 16, no. 3 (2008): 55–76.

———. *From Rebellion to Reform in Bolivia: Class Struggle, Indigenous Liberation, and the Politics of Evo Morales*. Chicago: Haymarket, 2011.

Webster, Alison. "J. Barnave: Philosopher of Revolution," *History of European Ideas* 17, no. 1 (1993): 53–71.

[Wedderburn, Andrew]. "Preface," *Edinburgh Review* 1 (1755): i–ii.

[Wedderburn, Robert]. [1549]. *The Complaynt of Scotland wyth ane Exortatione to the Three Estaits to Be Vigilante in the Deffens of their Public Veil*. 1549. With an appendix of contemporary English tracts, re-edited from the originals by J. A. H. Murray. London: Scottish Text Society, 1822.

Wedgewood, Josiah [1766]. Wedgewood to Bentley, October 1, 1766. In *The Selected Letters of Josiah Wedgewood*, edited by Ann Finer and George S. Wedgewood. London: Cory, Adams and McKay, 1965.

Weil, Boris. "Marx and Lenin Read in the Camps." In *Power and Opposition in Revolutionary Societies*, edited by *Il Manifesto*, 90–98. London: Ink Links, 1979.

Wheen, Francis. *Karl Marx*. London: Fourth Estate, 1999.

Whitelaw, W. Menzies. "Reconstructing the Quebec Conference," *Canadian Historical Review* 19, no. 2 (June 1938): 123–37.

Whittle, Jane. *The Development of Agrarian Capitalism: Land and Labour in Norfolk, 1450–1550*. Oxford: Clarendon Press, 2000.

Wickham, Chris [1984]. "The Other Transition: From the Ancient World to Feudalism." In *Land and Power: Studies in Italian and European Social History, 400–1200*, 7–42. London: British School at Rome, 1994.

——— [1985]. "The Uniqueness of the East." In *Land and Power: Studies in Italian and European Social History, 400–1200*, 43–75. London: British School at Rome, 1994.

———. "Historical Materialism, Historical Sociology," *New Left Review* 1, no. 171 (September/October 1988): 63–78.

———. *Framing the Early Middle Ages, Europe and the Mediterranean, 400–800*. Oxford: Oxford University Press, 2005.

———. "Productive Forces and the Economic Logic of the Feudal Mode of Production," *Historical Materialism* 16, no. 2 (2008): 3–22.

Widgery, David. *The Left in Britain, 1956–1968*. Harmondsworth: Penguin, 1976.

———. "Ten Years for Pandora," *Socialist Review* 2 (May 1978): 8–11.

Williams, Gwyn A. "The Concept of 'Egomania' in the Thought of Antonio Gramsci: Some Notes on Interpretation," *Journal of the History of Ideas* 21, no. 4 (October–December 1960): 586–99.

———. "The Making and Unmaking of Antonio Gramsci," *New Edinburgh Review* 27, Special Gramsci issue 3 (1975): 7–15.

———. *Goya and the Impossible Revolution*. London: Allen Lane, 1976.

Williams, Nigel. *Witchcraft*. London: Faber and Faber, 1987.

Williams, Raymond. "Capitalism." In *Keywords*, 42–44. Glasgow: Fontana, 1976.

Wills, Garry. *Inventing America: Jefferson's Declaration of Independence*. New York: Doubleday, 1978.

Wilson, Peter H. *Europe's Tragedy: a History of the Thirty Years War*. London: Allen Lane, 2009.

Winch, Donald. "Adam Smith's 'Enduring Particular Result': A Political and Cosmopolitan Perspective." In *Wealth and Virtue: The Shaping of Political Economy in the Scottish Enlightenment*, edited by Istvan Hont and Michael Ignatieff, 253–69. Cambridge: Cambridge University Press, 1983.

Winn, James Anderson. *John Dryden and His World*. New Haven, CT: Yale University Press, 1987.

Winstanley, Gerrard [1651]. "The Law of Freedom in a Platform: Or, True Magistracy Restored." In *The Law of Freedom and Other Writings*, edited by Christopher Hill, 273–89. Harmondsworth: Penguin, 1973.

Wohlforth, Tim [1963]. "The Theory of Structural Assimilation." In *"Communists" against Revolution: Two Essays on Post-war Stalinism*, 1–91. London, Folrose Books, 1978.

Wolf, Eric R. [1969]. *Peasant Wars of the Twentieth Century*. London: Faber and Faber, 1973.

———. *Europe and the Peoples without History*. Berkeley and Los Angeles: University of California Press, 1982.

Wolin, Sheldon S. *Tocqueville between Two Worlds: The Making of a Political and Theoretical Life*, Princeton, NJ: Princeton University Press, 2001.

Wood, Ellen Meiksins. "The Separation of the Economic and Political in Capitalism," *New Left Review* 1, no. 127 (May/June 1981): 66–95.

———. "Marxism and the Course of History," *New Left Review* 1, no. 147 (September–October 1984): 95–108.

———. *The Retreat from Class: A New "True" Socialism.* London: Verso, 1986.

———. *The Pristine Culture of Capitalism: An Essay on Old Regimes and Modern States*, London:

Verso, 1991.

———. "Capitalism, Merchants and Bourgeois Revolution: Reflections on the Brenner Debate and Its Sequel," *International Review of Social History* 41, no. 2 (August 1996): 209–32.

———. "Horizontal Relations: A Note on Brenner's Heresy," *Historical Materialism* 4 (Summer 1999): 171–79.

———[1999]. *The Origin of Capitalism: A Longer View.* London: Verso, 2002.

———. "The Question of Market Dependence," *Journal of Agrarian Change* 2, no. 1 (January 2002): 50–87.

———. *Citizens to Lords: A Social History of Western Political Thought from Antiquity to the Middle Ages.* London: Verso, 2008.

Wood, Ellen Meiksins and Neal Wood. *A Trumpet of Sedition: Political Theory and the Rise of Capitalism, 1509–1688.* London: Pluto Press, 1997.

Wood, Neal. *John Locke and Agrarian Capitalism.* Berkeley and Los Angeles: University of California Press, 1984.

Wood, Gordon S. *The Radicalism of the American Revolution.* New York: Vintage, 1992.

———. "No Thanks for the Memories," *New York Review of Books,* January 13, 2011.

Wood, Paul. "Marxism and Modernism: An Exchange between Alex Callinicos and Paul Wood," *Oxford Art Journal* 15, no. 2 (1992): 12025.

———. "The Avant-Garde from the July Monarchy to the Second Empire." In *The Challenge of the Avant-Garde,* edited by Paul Wood, 35–55. New Haven, CT: Yale University Press, 1999.

Woodward, Donald, "Wage Rates and Living Standards in Pre-Industrial England," *Past and Present* 91, (May 1981): 28–46.

Woolf, Stuart. "The Construction of a European World-View in the Revolutionary-Napoleonic Years," *Past and Present* 137 (November 1992): 72–101.

Worden, Blair. *The English Civil Wars.* London: Weidenfeld and Nicolson, 2009.

Wordie, J. R. "The Chronology of English Enclosure, 1500–1914," *Economic History Review,* second series, vol. 36, no. 4 (November, 1983): 483–505.

Wordsworth, William [1797–1850]. *The Prelude or; Growth of a Poet's Mind: An Autobiographical Poem.* London: Edward Moxon, 1850.

Wright, Eric Olin [1974]. "Bureaucracy and the State," in *Class, Crisis and the State,* 181–225. London: Verso, 1979.

———. "Gidden's Critique of Marx," *New Left Review* 1, no. 138 (March–April 1983): 11–35.

———. "Exploitation, Identity, and Class Structure: A Reply to My Critics." In *The Debate on Classes,* 191–211. Verso: London, 1989.

Wright, Eric Olin, Andrew Levine, and Elliot Sober. *Reconstructing Marxism: Essays on Explanation and the Theory of History.* London: Verso, 1992.

Wright, Gavin. "Capitalism and Slavery on the Islands: A Lesson from the Mainland," *Journal of Interdisciplinary History* 17, no. 4 (1987): 851–70.

Young, Alfred F. "American Historians Confront 'the Transforming Hand of Revolution.'" In *The Transforming Hand of Revolution: Reconsidering the American Revolution as a Social Movement,* edited by Ronald Hoffman and Peter J. Albert, 346–492. Charlottesville: University of Virginia Press, 1996.

Young, Arthur. *Travels during the Years 1787, 1788 and 1789. Undertaken More Particularly with a View to Ascertaining the Cultivation of Wealth, Resources and National Prosperity of the Kingdom of France.* Bury St. Edmunds: printed by J. Rackham, 1792.

Young, James D. *The Rousing of the Scottish Working Class.* London: Croom Helm, 1979.

Young, Robert J. C. *White Mythologies: History Writing and the West.* London: Routledge, 1990.

Youngson, A. J. *The Making of Classical Edinburgh, 1750–1840.* Edinburgh: Edinburgh at the University Press, 1966.

Zagorin, Perez [1954]. *A History of Political Thought in the English Revolution.* Bristol: Theommes Press, 1997.

————. *Rebels and Rulers, 1500–1660,* vol. 1, *Society, States and Early Modern Revolutions: Agrarian and Urban Rebellions.* Cambridge: Cambridge University Press, 1982.

Zapperi, Roberto. *Per la critica del concetto di rivoluzione borghese.* Bari: De Donato, 1974.

Zheng Chaolin [1941]. "On the Nature of Revolution," *Revolutionary History* 2, no. 4 (Spring 1990): 28–31.

Zinn, Howard. *A People's History of the United States.* Harlow: Longman, 1980.

Zinoviev, Gregory [1916]. "The Social Roots of Reformism." In *Lenin's Struggle for a Revolutionary International. Documents: 1907–1916, the Preparatory Years,* edited by John Riddell, 475–96. New York: Pathfinder, 1984.

Žižek, Slavoj. "Afterword: Lenin's Choice." In Vladimir I. Lenin, *Revolution at the Gates: A Selection of Writings from February to October 1917,* edited by Slavoj Žižek, 167–336. London: Verso, 2002.

Index

About Haymarket Books

Haymarket Books is a nonprofit, progressive book distributor and publisher, a project of the Center for Economic Research and Social Change. We believe that activists need to take ideas, history, and politics into the many struggles for social justice today. Learning the lessons of past victories, as well as defeats, can arm a new generation of fighters for a better world. As Karl Marx said, "The philosophers have merely interpreted the world; the point however is to change it."

We take inspiration and courage from our namesakes, the Haymarket Martyrs, who gave their lives fighting for a better world. Their 1886 struggle for the eight-hour day reminds workers around the world that ordinary people can organize and struggle for their own liberation.

For more information and to shop our complete catalog of titles, visit us online at www.haymarketbooks.org.

Also from Haymarket Books

American Road to Capitalism
Studies in Class-Structure, Economic Development and Political Conflict, 1620–1877, Charles Post

The Comintern
Duncan Hallas

The German Revolution, 1917–1923
Pierre Broué

History of the Russian Revolution
Leon Trotsky

Lenin's Political Thought
Theory and Practice in the Democratic and Socialist Revolutions, Neil Harding

On Changing the World
Essays in Marxist Political Philosophy, from Karl Marx to Walter Benjamin, Michael Löwy

The Paris Commune
A Revolution in Democracy, Donny Gluckstein

The Politics of Combined and Uneven Development
The Theory of Permanent Revolution, Michael Löwy

Theory as History
Essays on Modes of Production and Exploitation, Jarius Banaji

ABOUT THE AUTHOR

© Cathy Watkins

Neil Davidson teaches sociology at the University of Strathclyde and is the author of *The Origins of Scottish Nationhood* and *Discovering the Scottish Revolution* for which he was given the Isaac and Tamara Deutscher Memorial Prize and the Andrew Fletcher of Saltoun Award. Davidson also sits on the editorial board of the journal *International Socialism*.